An Introduction to
Community & Public Health

NINTH EDITION

James F. McKenzie, PhD, MPH, MCHES
Professor Emeritus
Ball State University

Robert R. Pinger, PhD
Professor Emeritus
Ball State University

Denise M. Seabert, PhD, MCHES
Professor and Associate Dean
Ball State University

JONES & BARTLETT
L E A R N I N G

World Headquarters
Jones & Bartlett Learning
5 Wall Street
Burlington, MA 01803
978-443-5000
info@jblearning.com
www.jblearning.com

Jones & Bartlett Learning books and products are available through most bookstores and online booksellers. To contact Jones & Bartlett Learning directly, call 800-832-0034, fax 978-443-8000, or visit our website, www.jblearning.com.

Substantial discounts on bulk quantities of Jones & Bartlett Learning publications are available to corporations, professional associations, and other qualified organizations. For details and specific discount information, contact the special sales department at Jones & Bartlett Learning via the above contact information or send an email to specialsales@jblearning.com.

10849-1

Production Credits

VP, Executive Publisher: David D. Cella
Publisher: Cathy L. Esperti
Editorial Assistant: Carter McAlister
Director of Production: Jenny L. Corriveau
Associate Production Editor: Alex Schab
Director of Marketing: Andrea DeFronzo
VP, Manufacturing and Inventory Control: Therese Connell

Composition: Integra Software Services Pvt. Ltd.
Cover Design: Kristin E. Parker
Rights & Media Specialist: Jamey O'Quinn
Media Development Editor: Troy Liston
Printing and Binding: LSC Communications
Cover Printing: LSC Communications

Library of Congress Cataloging-in-Publication Data
Names: McKenzie, James F., 1948- author. | Pinger, R. R., author. | Seabert, Denise M., author.
Title: An introduction to community & public health / James F. McKenzie, Robert R. Pinger, Denise M. Seabert.
Other titles: Introduction to community and public health
Description: Ninth edition. | Burlington, Massachusetts : Jones & Bartlett Learning, [2017] | Includes bibliographical references and index.
Identifiers: LCCN 2016037285 | ISBN 9781284108415
Subjects: | MESH: Community Health Services | Delivery of Health Care | Public Health Practice | Epidemiologic Factors | United States
Classification: LCC RA445 | NLM WA 546 AA1 | DDC 362.1–dc23
LC record available at https://lccn.loc.gov/2016037285

6048

Printed in the United States of America
20 19 18   10 9 8 7 6 5 4

CONTENTS

Disparate populations + Community + Public Health changed

WK

15

PREFACE

As its title suggests, *An Introduction to Community & Public Health* was written to introduce students to community and public health. Our textbook combines the power of today's electronic technology, via the Internet, with a traditional textbook presentation. We believe that your students will find *An Introduction to Community & Public Health* easy to read, understand, and use. If they read the chapters carefully, respond to the chapter scenarios, and make an honest effort to answer the review questions and to complete some of the activities, we are confident that your students will gain a comprehensive introduction to the realm of community and public health. *An Introduction to Community & Public Health* incorporates a variety of pedagogical elements that assist and encourage students to understand complex community health issues. Each chapter of the book includes

- Chapter objectives
- Scenario
- Introduction
- Marginal definitions of key terms presented in boldface type
- Chapter summary
- Scenario analysis and response
- Review questions
- Activities
- References

Carefully selected figures, tables, boxes, and photos illustrate and clarify the concepts presented in the text. Select content in each chapter refers to the *Healthy People 2020* goals and objectives.

COMMUNITY AND PUBLIC HEALTH NAVIGATE 2 ADVANTAGE ACCESS

Introduction to Community & Public Health, Ninth Edition includes learning tools for students and teaching tools for instructors to further explore the chapter's content.

WHAT IS NEW TO THIS EDITION?

Although the format of this edition is similar to previous editions, much has changed. First, the content and statistics throughout the book have been reviewed and updated with the latest information. New tables, figures, boxes, and photographs have been added. Second, where possible, we have made change requested by the reviewers of the previous edition.

Here are the chapter-specific changes made to this edition:

- The major change to **Chapter 1** was a shortening of the history section of the chapter and placing more of the

information in table format. In addition, new information was added regarding influences on the health of a community, including the built environment, public health preparedness, the Affordable Care Act, opioid pain reliever abuse, and the impact of conflict on the health of people around the world.

- In **Chapter 2**, new information has been included on the World Health Organization (WHO)'s new sustainable development goals, changes to the organization of the U.S. Department of Health and Human Services, the work of the Centers for Disease Control and Prevention (CDC), and an introduction to the Whole School, Whole Community, Whole Child (WSCC) model.
- **Chapter 3** includes an updated list of notable epidemics in the United States, expanded information on avian influenza that includes H7N9, a simplified section on rates, and a simplified analytic study section that now only includes a basic overview of observational and experimental studies.
- **Chapter 4** has been retitled "Communicable and Noncommunicable Diseases: Prevention and Control of Diseases and Health Conditions." Chapter 4 now includes an example of information that may be needed to prevent the transmission of a disease (measles) using the new edition of the American Public Health Association (APHA)'s *Control of Communicable Diseases Manual*, information about how the communicable disease model (the epidemiology triangle) can be adapted for noncommunicable diseases, and new information on active and passive immunity.
- **Chapter 5** includes expanded discussions on evidence-based practice, the socio-ecological perspective, and CDC's *Framework for Program Evaluation*. The chapter also includes two new boxes—one on the increased emphasis on needs assessment and the other on sources of evidence.
- The school health education chapter—**Chapter 6**—includes a new scenario, an introduction to the *Framework for the 21st Century School Nursing Practice*, a detailed discussion on the Whole School, Whole Community, Whole Child (WSCC) model, and core competencies for school-based health centers (SBHCs).
- **Chapter 7**, in addition to being updated throughout, includes new information about the impact of the Affordable Care Act on family planning, and preconception health care and counseling, which are relatively new foci for pregnancy health; information was also added on barriers to prenatal care and the importance of nutrition and vitamin supplementation during pregnancy. A brief review was included on the recent outbreak of measles at Disneyland in California, and a discussion was added about

vaccine safety and nonvaccination due to religious and philosophical exceptions, which affect vulnerable populations.

- **Chapter 8** has been updated with the most recently available data regarding the health of adolescents, young adults, and adults. New information has been added on the leading cause of death and the impact of the Family Smoking Prevention and Control Act on the authority of the U.S. Food and Drug Administration to regulate the manufacturing, distribution, sale, labeling, advertising, and promotion of tobacco products to protect public health.

- The title of **Chapter 9**, along with other terminology in the chapter, has been changed from "Elders" to "Older Adults" to better describe those who are aged 65 years and older. In addition, information on the demography of aging in the United States has been streamlined, more connections have been made between older adults and community health programming and services, and the information on impairments and chronic conditions has been expanded.

- **Chapter 10** has been revised and updated to include new data in 16 tables and figures presented in the chapter. In addition, a new section has been included on the "Social Determinants of Health and Racial and Ethnic Disparities in Health" and the section on "Equity in Minority Health" has been expanded.

- The revision of **Chapter 11** includes new information on the relationship of mental health to general health, outpatient commitment—a practice designed to reduce risk of self-harm and protect the public, new law enforcement policies regarding how to handle people with mental health crises, a summary of supported employment services as a component of psychiatric rehabilitation, and details on the integrative medical–mental health approach to care.

- **Chapter 12** features a new scenario and new sections have been added on electronic or e-cigarettes, abuse of opioid pain relievers, and the move by some states to legalize the use of marijuana for medical or recreational use.

- **Chapter 13**, which combines the structure and function of health care delivery in the United States, includes new data throughout. In addition, new information has been added on Federally Qualified Health Centers, the National Quality Strategy, accountable care organizations, patient-centered medical homes, pay-for-performance (P4P), and comparison of select health systems throughout the world. Information about the changes to the Affordable Care Act since its inception in 2010 includes the three challenges to the law that reached the U.S. Supreme Court.

- **Chapter 14** has been thoroughly revised and updated. New information has been included about mold as an indoor pollutant, runoff and lead as water pollutants, complex disasters, the Zika virus, and emergency preparedness and response. In addition, a new box on the Flint, Michigan drinking water crisis has been included.

- A new scenario has been created for **Chapter 15**. In addition, the discussion on "Community Approaches to the Prevention of Unintentional Injuries" has been expanded. The discussion of firearms on college campuses has been updated and a new definition of intimate partner violence is introduced.

- **Chapter 16** has been updated with the most recently available nonfatal and fatal workplace injury statistics from the Bureau of Labor Statistics. The section on agricultural safety and health, particularly as it relates to families and children, has been updated and expanded. Regarding workplace-acquired respiratory disorders, the alarming increase in cases of progressive massive fibrosis, a lethal form of coal workers' pneumoconiosis occurring in certain coal mining regions, is discussed. The worksite health promotion discussion has been expanded to include descriptions of worksite health and wellness promotion programs, work–life balance approaches, and the CDC's Total Worker Health policies, programs, and practices.

HOW TO USE THIS BOOK

Chapter Objectives

The chapter objectives identify the knowledge and competencies that students need to master as they read and study the chapter material, answer the end-of-chapter review questions, and complete the activities. To use the objectives effectively, students should review them before and after reading the chapters. This will help students focus on the major knowledge points in each chapter and facilitate answering the questions and completing the activities at the end of each chapter.

Chapter Objectives

After studying this chapter, you should be able to:

1. Explain the concept of diversity as it describes the American people.
2. Discuss the impact of a more diverse population in the United States as it relates to community and public health efforts.
3. Summarize the importance of the 1985 landmark report, *The Secretary's Task Force Report on Black and Minority Health*.
4. List the racial and ethnic categories currently used by the U.S. government in statistical activities and program administration reporting.
5. State some limitations related to collecting racial and ethnic health data.
6. Discuss selected sociodemographic characteristics of minority groups in the United States.
7. List and describe the six priority areas of the Race and Health Initiative.
8. Explain the role socioeconomic status plays in health disparities among racial and ethnic minority groups.
9. Define cultural and linguistic competence and the importance of each related to minority community and public health.

Scenarios

Short scenarios are presented at the beginning of each chapter. The purpose of these scenarios is to bridge the gap between your students' personal experiences and ideas discussed within the chapter. The chapter content will enable your students to propose solutions to the community or public health problem posed in the scenario.

Scenario

Joan is 18 years old and a recent high school graduate. She lives in a small town of about 2,700 people. Most of the town's residents rely on a larger city nearby for shopping, recreation, and health care. Joan had dated Dave the past 2 years, but there was never any talk of marriage. Just before graduation she learned that she was pregnant. At Thanksgiving, just as she was completing her seventh month of pregnancy, she went into premature labor. An ambulance rushed her to the emergency room of the hospital in the nearby city for what became the premature birth of her baby. While Joan was in recovery, doctors determined that her baby was not only premature, it also appeared to have other "developmental abnormalities." When asked whether she had received any prenatal care, Joan replied, "No, I couldn't afford it; besides, I didn't know where to go to get help."

Introduction

Each chapter begins with a brief introduction that informs the reader of the topics to be presented and explains how these topics relate to others in the book.

Introduction

Creating a health profile of Americans requires a clear understanding of the health-related problems and opportunities of all Americans. Elsewhere in the text we discussed the role of descriptive epidemiology in understanding the health of populations. In describing the personal characteristics of a population, age is the first and perhaps the most important population characteristic to consider when describing the occurrence of disease, injury, and/or death in a population. Because health and age are related, community and public health professionals look at rates for specific age groups when comparing the amount of disease between populations. When they analyze data by age, they use groups that are narrow enough to detect any age-related patterns, which may be present as a result of either the natural life cycle or behavioral patterns. Viewing age-group profiles in this manner enables community and public health workers to identify risk factors for specific age groups within the population and to develop interventions aimed at reducing these risk factors. Health promotion and disease prevention programs that are successful in reducing exposure to such risk factors within specific age groups can improve the health status of the entire population.

Marginal Definitions

Understanding the key terms helps drive stronger comprehension of the core knowledge and competencies contained within the chapter. These terms are presented in **boldface** type in the text and defined in the margin. Before reading each chapter, we suggest that students review the chapter's key terms in preparation for encountering them in the text. The boldfaced terms also appear in the glossary at the end of the book.

Fetal alcohol syndrome (FAS) a group of abnormalities that may include growth retardation, abnormal appearance of face and head, and deficits of central nervous system function, including mental retardation, in babies born to mothers who have consumed heavy amounts of alcohol during their pregnancies

Chapter Summary

At the end of each chapter are several bulleted points that review the major concepts contained in each chapter. These provide a great way to review knowledge and comprehension of the material.

Chapter Summary

- Adolescence and young adulthood (10–24 years old) and adulthood (25–64 years old) are the most productive periods of people's lives. Although most people enjoy good health during these years, there is substantial room for improvement.
- The overall health status of these age groups could be improved by reducing the prevalence of high-risk behaviors (e.g., cigarette smoking, excessive alcohol consumption, and physical inactivity), increasing participation in health screenings, institutionalizing preventive health care, and making environments more health-enhancing in our society.
- Approximately 75% of adolescent and young adult mortality can be attributed to motor vehicle crashes, other unintentional injuries, homicide and legal intervention, and suicide.
- Adolescents and young adults remain at considerable risk for STD morbidity.
- College students are at considerable risk for STDs due to unprotected sexual activity and the use of alcohol and other drugs.
- Mortality rates for older adults (45–64 years old) have declined in recent years, but cancer is still the overall leading cause of death, followed by cardiovascular disease.
- Reductions in deaths from cardiovascular diseases in adults have been substantial, but health problems resulting from unhealthy behaviors—such as smoking, poor diet, and physical inactivity—can be reduced further if environments are created to help support healthy behaviors (e.g., increased access to fruits and vegetables, the creation of more walkable communities, etc.)
- No matter how the health of adolescents and young adults and adults in the United States is broken down and described, it can be summarized by saying that the health of Americans in these age groups has come a long way in the past 50 years, but there is still room for improvement.

Scenario: Analysis and Response

Following the chapter summary, students are provided with an opportunity to respond to the scenario presented earlier in the chapter. The content presented in the chapter will help the students to formulate their responses or solutions.

Scenario: Analysis and Response

1. What are the primary reasons that Annie stated Dayna might have developed diabetes?
2. Comment on the attitudes of Annie and Connor about Dayna's recent diabetes diagnosis. Do you agree with Connor that the only way for Dayna to be healthy is to move away from the neighborhood where she lives? Why or why not?
3. If you were a community health worker in this urban community that has limited places where residents can purchase healthy food and safely exercise outside, what could you do to help adolescents like Dayna?
4. Do high schools have an obligation to develop prevention programs, including offering physical activity

opportunities at school, to keep students healthy? Why or why not?

5. Say you were friends with Annie. She got so concerned with Dayna's health problem that she wanted to take action, especially to figure out how to help the local corner store that Dayna visits every day offer healthy foods for her. She thought that maybe she would do an online search to see if there are any corner stores that offer healthy foods and how they do it. You told her that you would help her see if there is anything on the Internet. Go online and use a search engine (e.g., Google, Bing) and enter "healthy corner stores." What did you find that might be of help to Annie?

Review Questions

Review questions at the end of each chapter provide students with feedback regarding their mastery of the chapter's content. The questions reinforce the chapter objectives and key terms.

Review Questions

1. Why is it important for community and public health workers to be aware of the significant health problems of the various age groups in the United States?
2. What ages are included in the following two age groups: adolescents and young adults and adults? What are the ages of the two subgroups of adults?
3. Why are the number of adolescents and young adults, living arrangements, and employment status such key demographic characteristics of young people in regard to community health? Briefly summarize the data available on these characteristics.
4. What are the leading causes of death for adolescents and young adults, and for adults?
5. What are the Youth Risk Behavior Surveillance System (YRBSS) and the Behavioral Risk Factor Surveillance System (BRFSS), and what type of data do they generate?
6. What are the behaviors that put each of these cohorts—adolescents, college students, and adults—at greatest risk, and how does a person's environment impact these behaviors?
7. How would you summarize the health profile of the two cohorts (adolescents and young adults and adults) presented in this chapter?

Activities

The activities at the end of each chapter provide an opportunity for students to apply new knowledge in a meaningful way. The activities, which are presented in a variety of formats, should appeal to the varying learning styles of students.

Activities

1. Obtain a copy of the most recent results of the Youth Risk Behavior Surveillance System (YRBSS) and the Behavioral Risk Factor Surveillance System (BRFSS) for your state. Review the data presented, and then prepare a two-page summary on the "Health Behavior Profile of the Adolescents, Young Adults, and Adults" of your state.

2. Obtain data presenting the 10 leading causes of death according to age and race for the age groups presented in this chapter. Review the data, and prepare a summary paper discussing conclusions that can be drawn about race, the leading causes of death, and age.

3. Interview a small group (about 10) of adults (aged 45–64) about their present health status. Ask them questions about their health behavior and health problems. Then, summarize the data you collect in writing and compare it to the information in this chapter on this age group. How are the data similar? How do they differ?

4. Pick either adolescents and young adults or adults, and write a two-page paper that presents ideas on how the health profile of that age group can be improved in your state.

STUDENT AND INSTRUCTOR RESOURCES

Each new book comes complete with a dynamic technology solution. Navigate 2 Advantage Access provides an interactive eBook, student activities and assessments, knowledge checks, learning analytics reporting tools, and more.

Instructor Resources

- Test Bank
- Slides in PowerPoint format
- Instructor's Manual

Navigate also provides a dashboard that reports actionable assessment data.

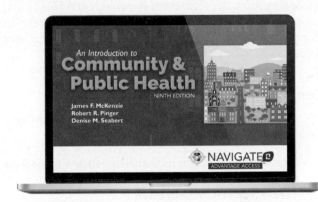

ACKNOWLEDGMENTS

A project of this nature could not be completed without the assistance and understanding of many individuals.

Special Thank You

A special thank you to our families for their love, support, encouragement, and tolerance of all the time that writing takes away from family activities.

We would also like to thank Dale B. Hahn, PhD, Professor Emeritus, Department of Physiology and Health Science, Ball State University, for encouraging us to take on this project over 25 years ago, and our students who have helped us to improve the book over the years.

Contributors

We would like to thank those individuals who have brought their expertise to the writing team:

Chapter 2 Organizations that Help Shape Community and Public Health
Teresa T. Kern, MSEd, PhD
Assistant Professor, Department of Public Health Sciences
Penn State–Hershey

Chapter 3 Epidemiology: The Study of Disease, Injury, and Death in the Community and Chapter 4 Communicable and Noncommunicable Diseases: Prevention and Control of Diseases and Health Conditions
Jennifer L. Collins, MPH
Epidemiologist
Cincinnati Children's Hospital Medical Center

Chapter 7 Maternal, Infant, and Child Health **Note:** *The work completed by Dr. Bicking Kinsey represents her views and does not necessarily represent the official position of the Centers for Disease Control and Prevention or the U.S. government.*
Cara Bicking Kinsey, PhD, MPH, RNC
Epidemic Intelligence Officer
Centers for Disease Control and Prevention

Chapter 9 Older Adults
Charity Bishop, MA, CHES Lecturer
Richard M. Fairbanks School of Public Health
Indiana University

Chapter 10 Community and Public Health and Racial/Ethnic Populations
Miguel A. Perez, PhD, MCHES
Professor and Internship Coordinator
Department of Public Health
Fresno State University

Chapter 11 Community Mental Health
David V. Perkins, PhD
Professor
Department of Psychological Sciences
Ball State University

Chapter 12 Alcohol, Tobacco, and Other Drugs: A Community Concern
Farah Kauffman, MPH
Instructor
Department of Public Health Sciences
Penn State–Hershey

Chapter 14 Community and Public Health and the Environment
Jamie H. Wright, MHS, MS, CHMM
Emergency Management Specialist
Consolidated Nuclear Security, LLC

Their expertise is both welcomed and appreciated.

We also acknowledge Ms. Jenni Flanagan, Wellness Coordinator at Working Well, Ball State University, for her advice and expertise on worksite wellness and work-life balance programming.

Reviewers

We would like to express our appreciation to those professionals who took the time and effort to review and provide feedback for this edition. They include:

- Allan Weiss, George Mason University
- Ari Fisher, Louisiana State University
- Erin Reynolds, University of Southern Indiana
- Hans Schmalzried, Bowling Green State University
- Joni Roberts, University of Mississippi Medical Center
- Ken Watkins, University of South Carolina
- Kenneth Campbell, City Colleges of Chicago
- Kerry J. Redican, Virginia Tech
- Kevin Breen, Rutgers University
- Miryha Runnerstrom, University of California Irvine
- Nikki Keene Woods, Wichita State University
- Tara Underwood, Columbus State University
- Todd M. Sabato, University of North Dakota
- Yvonne Barry, John Tyler Community College

Jones & Bartlett Learning Team

We would like to thank all of the employees of Jones & Bartlett Learning. Their hard work, support, guidance, and confidence in us have been most helpful in creating this and all previous editions of this text. Specifically, we would like to thank: Cathy Esperti, Publisher; Carter McAlister, Editorial Assistant; Alex Schab, Associate Production Editor; Jamey O'Quinn, Rights & Media Specialist; Troy Liston, Media Development Editor; and Andrea DeFronzo, Director of Marketing.

Foundations of Community and Public Health

CHAPTER 1

Community and Public Health: Yesterday, Today, and Tomorrow

Chapter Outline

Chapter Objectives

After studying this chapter, you will be able to:

1. Define the terms *health, community, community health, population health, public health, public health system,* and *global health.*

2. Briefly describe the five major determinants of health.

3. Explain the difference between personal and community health activities.

4. List and discuss the factors that influence a community's health.

5. Briefly relate the history of community and public health, including the recent U.S. history of community and public health in the twentieth and early twenty-first centuries.

6. Provide a brief overview of the current health status of Americans.

7. Describe the purpose of the *Healthy People 2020* goals and objectives as they apply to the planning process of the health of Americans.

8. Summarize the major community and public health problems facing the United States and the world today.

Scenario

Amy and Eric are a young working couple who are easing into a comfortable lifestyle. They have good-paying jobs, drive nice cars, have two healthy preschool children, and, after living in an apartment for several years, are now buying a home in a good neighborhood. When Amy picked her children up from day care earlier in the day she was told that another parent had reported that his child was diagnosed with hepatitis. This news frightened Amy and made her begin to question the quality of the day care center. Amy told Eric of this situation when he got home. As the couple discussed whether or not they should take their children to day care as usual the following day, they discovered that they had many unanswered questions. How serious is hepatitis? What is the likelihood that their children will be at serious risk for getting the disease? What steps are being taken to control the outbreak? Is any state or local agency responsible for standardizing health practices at private day care centers in the community? Does the city, county, or state carry out any type of inspection when they license these facilities? And, if the children do not attend day care, which parent will stay home with them?

Introduction

Since 1900, tremendous progress had been made in the health and life expectancy of those in the United States (see **Box 1.1**) and of many people of the world since 1900. Infant mortality dropped, many of the infectious diseases have been brought under control, and better family planning became available. However, much still needs to be done to improve health especially when it comes to health disparities found in certain ethnic and racial groups. Individual health behaviors, such as the use of tobacco, poor diet, and physical inactivity, have given rise to an unacceptable number of cases of illness and death from noninfectious diseases such as cancer, diabetes, and heart disease. Continued use of an outdated infrastructure, such as the old water pipes in Flint, Michigan, has exposed many to unnecessary health risks. New and emerging infectious diseases, such as Zika virus disease and those caused by superbugs (i.e., drug-resistant pathogens), are stretching resources available to control them. And events stemming from natural disasters such as floods, tornadoes, and hurricanes; human-made disasters such as the Gulf oil spill; and terrorism, such as the 2013 bombings at the Boston Marathon have caused us to refocus our priorities. All of these events have severely disrupted Americans' sense of security[1] and sense of safety in the environment. In addition, many of these events revealed the vulnerability of the United States' and the world's ability to respond to such circumstances and highlighted the need for improvement in emergency response preparedness and infrastructure of the public health system.

Even with all that has happened in recent years in the United States and around the world, the achievement of good health remains a worldwide goal of the twenty-first century. Governments, private organizations, and individuals throughout the world are working to improve health. Although individual actions to improve one's own personal health certainly contribute to the overall health of the community, organized community actions are often necessary when health problems exceed the resources of any one individual. When such actions are not taken, the health of the entire community is at risk.

This chapter introduces the concepts and principles of community and public health, explains how community and public health differ from personal health, and provides a brief history of community and public health. Some of the key health problems facing Americans are also described, and an outlook for the twenty-first century is provided.

Definitions

The word health means different things to different people. Similarly, there are other words that can be defined in various ways. Some basic terms we will use in this book are defined in the following paragraphs.

As the twentieth century came to a close, the overall health status and life expectancy in the United States were at all-time highs. Between 1900 and 2000 life expectancy at birth of U.S. residents increased by 62% from 47.3 years to 76.8 years;[2] 25 of these years have been attributed to advances in public health.[3] U.S. life expectancy is now at 78.8 years.[2] Many public health achievements can be linked to this gain in life expectancy, however. The Centers for Disease Control and Prevention (CDC), the U.S. government agency charged with protecting the public health of the nation, singled out "Ten Great Public Health Achievements" in the United States between 1900 and 1999. Here is the list[4]:

1. *Vaccination*
2. *Motor vehicle safety*
3. *Safer workplaces*
4. *Control of infectious diseases*
5. *Decline of deaths from coronary heart disease and stroke*
6. *Safer and healthier foods*
7. *Healthier mothers and babies*
8. *Family planning*
9. *Fluoridation of drinking water*
10. *Recognition of tobacco use as a health hazard*

At the conclusion of 2010, public health scientists at CDC were asked to nominate noteworthy public health achievements that occurred in the United States during 2001–2010. Below, in no specific order, are the ones selected from the nominations.[5]

- *Vaccine-Preventable Deaths.* Over the 10-year period there was a substantial decline in cases, hospitalizations, deaths, and health care costs associated with vaccine-preventable diseases.
- *Prevention and Control of Infectious Diseases.* Improvements in public health infrastructure along with innovative and targeted prevention efforts yielded significant progress in controlling infectious diseases (e.g., tuberculosis cases).

- *Tobacco Control.* Tobacco still remains the single largest preventable cause of death and disease in the United States but the adult smoking prevalence dropped to 16.8% in 2014[6] and approximately half of the states have comprehensive smoke-free laws.
- *Maternal and Infant Health.* During the 10-year period there were significant reductions in the number of infants born with neural tube defects and an expansion of screening of newborns for metabolic and other heritable disorders.
- *Motor Vehicle Safety.* There were significant reductions in motor vehicle deaths and injuries, as well as pedestrian and bicyclist deaths. All attributed to safer vehicles, roads, and safer road use.
- *Cardiovascular Disease Prevention.* Death rates for both stroke and coronary heart disease continue to trend down. Most can be attributed to reduction in the prevalence of risk factors, and improved treatments, medications, and quality of care.
- *Occupational Safety.* Much progress was made in improving working conditions and reducing the risk for workplace-associated injuries over the 10 years.
- *Cancer Prevention.* A number of death rates due to various cancers dropped during the 10 years and much of the progress can be attributed to the implementation of the evidence-based screening recommendations.
- *Childhood Lead Poisoning Prevention.* There was a steep decline in the percentage of children ages 1–5 years with blood levels $\geq$ 10 micrograms/dL. Much of the progress can be traced to the 23 states in 2010 that had comprehensive lead poisoning prevention laws. As of 2016, experts now use a reference level of 5 micrograms/dL to identify children with high blood lead levels.[7]
- *Public Health Preparedness and Response.* Following the terrorists' attacks of 2001 on the United States great effort was put into both expanding and improving the capacity of the public health system to respond to public health threats.

Data from: Centers for Disease Control and Prevention (1999). "Ten Great Public Health Achievements—United States, 1900–1999." *Morbidity and Mortality Weekly Report, 48*(12): 241-243; and U.S. Department of Health and Human Services, Centers for Disease Control and Prevention (2011). "Ten Great Public Health Achievements—United States, 2001-2010." *Morbidity and Mortality Weekly Report*, 60(19): 619-623.

Health

Health a dynamic state or condition of the human organism that is multidimensional in nature, a resource for living, and results from a person's interactions with and adaptations to his or her environment; therefore, it can exist in varying degrees and is specific to each individual and his or her situation

The word *health* is derived from *hal*, which means "hale, sound, whole." When it comes to the health of people, the word health has been defined in a number of different ways—often in its social context, as when a parent describes the health of a child or when an avid fan defines the health of a professional athlete. The most widely quoted definition of health was the one created by the World Health Organization (WHO) in 1946, which states "health is a state of complete physical, mental, and social well-being and not merely the absence of disease and infirmity."[8] Further, the WHO has indicated that "health is a resource for everyday life, not the object of living, and is a positive concept emphasizing social and personal resources as well as physical capabilities."[8] Others have stated that health cannot be defined as a state because it is ever changing. Therefore, we have chosen to define **health** as a dynamic state or condition of the human organism that is multidimensional (i.e., physical, emotional, social, intellectual, spiritual, and occupational) in nature, a resource for living, and results from a person's interactions with and adaptations to his or her environment. Therefore, it can exist in varying degrees and is specific to each individual and his or her situation. "A person can have a disease or injury and still be healthy or at least feel well. There are many examples, but certainly Olympic wheelchair racers fit into this category."[9]

A person's health status is dynamic in part because of the many different factors that determine one's health. It is widely accepted that health status is determined by the interaction of five domains: gestational endowments (i.e., genetic makeup), social circumstances (e.g., education, employment, income, poverty, housing, crime, and social cohesion), environmental conditions where people live and work (e.g., toxic agents, microbial agents, and structural hazards), behavioral choices (e.g., diet, physical activity, substance use and abuse), and the availability of quality medical care.[10] "Ultimately, the health fate of each of us is determined by factors acting not mostly in isolation but by our experience where domains interconnect. Whether a gene is expressed can be determined by environmental exposures or behavioral patterns. The nature and consequences of behavioral choices are affected by social circumstances. Our genetic predispositions affect the health care we need, and our social circumstances affect the health care we receive"[11] (see **Figure 1.1**).

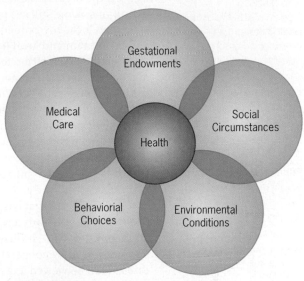

FIGURE 1.1   Interconnections of the determinants of health.

Community

Traditionally, a community has been thought of as a geographic area with specific boundaries—for example, a neighborhood, city, county, or state. However, in the context of community and public health, a **community** is "a collective body of individuals identified by common characteristics such as geography, interests, experiences, concerns, or values."[12] Communities are characterized by the following elements: (1) membership—a sense of identity and belonging; (2) common symbol systems—similar language, rituals, and ceremonies; (3) shared values and norms; (4) mutual influence—community members have influence and are influenced by each other; (5) shared needs and commitment to meeting them; and (6) shared emotional connection—members share common history, experiences, and mutual support.[13] Examples of communities include the people of the city of Columbus (location), the Asian community of San Francisco (race), the Hispanic community of Miami (ethnicity), seniors in the church (age), the business or the banking communities (occupation), the homeless of Indiana (specific problem), those on welfare in Ohio (particular outcome), local union members (common bond), or those who are members of an electronic social network (cyber). A community may be as small as the group of people who live on a residence hall floor at a university or as large as all of the individuals who make up a nation. "A healthy community is a place where people provide leadership in assessing their own resources and needs, where public health and social infrastructure and policies support health, and where essential public health services, including quality health care, are available."[14]

Public, Community, Population, and Global Health

Prior to defining the four terms public health, community health, population health, and global health, it is important to note that often the terms are used interchangeably by both laypeople and professionals who work in the various health fields. When the terms are used interchangeably, most people are referring to the collective health of those in society and the actions or activities taken to obtain and maintain that health. The definitions provided here for the four terms more precisely define the group of people in question and the origin of the actions or activities.

Community a collective body of individuals identified by common characteristics such as geography, interests, experiences, concerns, or values

Public health actions that society takes collectively to ensure that the conditions in which people can be healthy

Public health system the organizational mechanism of those activities undertaken within the formal structure of government and the associated efforts of private and voluntary organizations and individuals

Community health the health status of a defined group of people and the actions and conditions to promote, protect, and preserve their health

Population health "the health outcomes of a group of individuals, including the distribution of such outcomes within the group."[16]

Global health describes health problems, issues, and concerns that transcend national boundaries, may be influenced by circumstances or experiences in other countries, and are best addressed by cooperative actions and solutions

Of the four terms, public health is the most inclusive. The Institute of Medicine (IOM) defined **public health** in 1988 in its landmark report *The Future of Public Health* as "what we as a society do collectively to assure the conditions in which people can be healthy."[15] The **public health system**, which has been defined as "activities undertaken within the formal structure of government and the associated efforts of private and voluntary organizations and individuals,"[15] is the organizational mechanism for providing such conditions. Even with these formal definitions, some still see public health activities as only those efforts that originate in federal, state, and local governmental public health agencies such as the Centers for Disease Control and Prevention and local (i.e., city and county) health departments.

Community health refers to the health status of a defined group of people and the actions and conditions to promote, protect, and preserve their health. For example, the health status of the people of Elizabethtown, Pennsylvania, and the private and public actions taken to promote, protect, and preserve the health of these people would constitute community health.

The term population health is similar to community health. Although the term has been around for a number of years, it is appearing more commonly in the literature today. As such it has been defined in several different ways. The most common definition used for **population health** is "the health outcomes of a group of individuals, including the distribution of such outcomes within the group."[16]

Another term that has been used increasingly more in recent years is global health. **Global health** is a term that describes "health problems, issues, and concerns that transcend national boundaries, may be influenced by circumstances or experiences in other countries, and are best addressed by cooperative actions and solutions."[17] Therefore, an issue such as Zika virus disease can be viewed as a global health issue. Much of the rise in concern about global health problems comes from the speed of international travel and how easy it is for people who may be infected with a disease to cross borders into another country.

Personal Health Activities versus Community and Public Health Activities

To further clarify the definitions presented in this chapter, it is important to distinguish between the terms personal health activities and community and public health activities.

Personal Health Activities

Personal health activities are individual actions and decision-making that affect the health of an individual or his or her immediate family members or friends. These activities may be preventive or curative in nature but seldom directly affect the behavior of others. Choosing to eat wisely, to regularly wear a safety belt, and to visit the physician are all examples of personal health activities.

Community and Public Health Activities

Community and public health activities are activities that are aimed at protecting or improving the health of a population or community. Maintenance of accurate birth and death records, protection of the food and water supply, and participating in fund drives for voluntary health organizations such as the American Lung Association are examples of community health activities.

FIGURE 1.2 Factors that affect the health of the community.

Factors That Affect the Health of a Community

Many factors affect the health of a community. As a result, the health status of each community is different. These factors may be physical, social, and/or cultural. They also include the ability of the community to organize and work together as a whole as well as the individual behaviors of those in the community (see **Figure 1.2**).

Physical Factors

Physical factors include the influences of geography, the environment, community size, and industrial development.

Geography

A community's health problems can be directly influenced by its altitude, latitude, and climate. In tropical countries where warm, humid temperatures and rain prevail throughout the year, parasitic and infectious diseases are a leading community health problem (see **Figure 1.3**). In many tropical countries, survival from these diseases is made more difficult because poor soil conditions result in inadequate food production and malnutrition. In temperate climates with fewer parasitic and infectious diseases and a more than adequate food supply, obesity and heart disease are important community and public health problems.

FIGURE 1.3   In tropical countries, parasitic and infectious diseases are leading community health problems.

Courtesy of Lian Bruno.

Environment

The quality of our natural environment is directly related to the quality of our stewardship of it. Many experts believe that if we continue to allow uncontrolled population growth and continue to deplete nonrenewable natural resources, succeeding generations will inhabit communities that are less desirable than ours. Many feel that we must accept responsibility for this stewardship and drastically reduce the rate at which we foul the soil, water, and air.

When speaking about the environment we must also consider the impact the built environment has on community and public health. The term **built environment** refers to "the design, construction, management, and land use of human-made surroundings as an interrelated whole, as well as their relationship to human activities over time."[18] It includes but is not limited to: transportation systems (e.g., mass transit); urban design features (e.g., bike paths, sidewalks, adequate lighting); parks and recreational facilities; land use (e.g., community gardens, location of schools, trail development); building with health-enhancing features (e.g., green roofs, stairs); road systems; and housing free from environmental hazards.[18, 19, 20] The built environment can be structured to give people more or fewer opportunities to behave in health enhancing ways.

Community Size

The larger the community, the greater its range of health problems and the greater its number of health resources. For example, larger communities have more health professionals and better health facilities than smaller communities. These resources are often needed because communicable diseases can spread more quickly and environmental problems are often more severe in densely populated areas. For example, the amount of trash generated by the approximately 8.5 million people in New York City is many times greater than that generated by the entire state of Wyoming, with its population of 584,153.

It is important to note that a community's size can have both a positive and negative impact on that community's health. The ability of a community to effectively plan, organize, and utilize its resources can determine whether its size can be used to good advantage.

Industrial Development

Industrial development, like size, can have either positive or negative effects on the health status of a community. Industrial development provides a community with added resources for community health programs, but it may bring with it environmental pollution and occupational injuries and illnesses. Communities that experience rapid industrial development must eventually regulate (e.g., laws and ordinances) the way in which industries (1) obtain raw materials, (2) discharge by-products, (3) dispose of wastes, (4) treat and protect their employees, and (5) clean up environmental accidents. Unfortunately, many of these laws are usually passed only after these communities have suffered significant reductions in the quality of their life and health.

Social and Cultural Factors

Social factors are those that arise from the interaction of individuals or groups within the community. For example, people who live in urban communities, where life is fast paced, experience higher rates of stress-related illnesses than those who live in rural communities, where life is more leisurely. On the other hand, those in rural areas may not have access to the same quality

Built environment "the design, construction, management, and land use of human-made surroundings as an interrelated whole, as well as their relationship to human activities over time."[18]

or selection of health care (i.e., hospitals or medical specialists) that is available to those who live in urban communities.

Cultural factors arise from guidelines (both explicit and implicit) that individuals "inherit" from being a part of a particular society. Some of the factors that contribute to culture are discussed in the following sections.

Beliefs, Traditions, and Prejudices

The beliefs, traditions, and prejudices of community members can affect the health of the community. The beliefs of those in a community about such specific health behaviors as exercise and smoking can influence policy makers on whether or not they will spend money on bike lanes on the roads and recreational bike trails and work toward no-smoking ordinances. The traditions of specific ethnic groups can influence the types of food, restaurants, retail outlets, and services available in a community. Prejudices of one specific ethnic or racial group against another can result in acts of violence and crime. Racial and ethnic disparities will continue to put certain groups, such as black Americans or certain religious groups, at greater risk.

Economy

Both national and local economies can affect the health of a community through reductions in health and social services. An economic downturn means lower tax revenues (fewer tax dollars) and fewer contributions to charitable groups. Such actions will result in fewer dollars being available for programs such as welfare, food stamps, community health care, and other community services. This occurs because revenue shortfalls cause agencies to experience budget cuts. With fewer dollars, these agencies often must alter their eligibility guidelines, thereby restricting aid to only individuals with the greatest need. Obviously, many people who had been eligible for assistance before the economic downturn become ineligible.

Employers usually find it increasingly difficult to provide health benefits for their employees as their income drops. Those who are unemployed and underemployed face poverty and deteriorating health. Thus, the cumulative effect of an economic downturn significantly affects the health of the community.

Politics

Those who happen to be in political office can improve or jeopardize the health of their community by the decisions (i.e., laws and ordinances) they make. In the most general terms, the argument is over greater or lesser governmental participation in health issues. For example, there has been a longstanding discussion in the United States on the extent to which the government should involve itself in health care. Historically, Democrats have been in favor of such action while Republicans have been against it. State and local politicians also influence the health of their communities each time they vote on health-related measures brought before them, such as increasing the minimum legal sales age (MLSA) for tobacco products to 21 years.

Religion

A number of religions have taken a position on health care and health behaviors. For example, some religious communities limit the type of medical treatment their members may receive. Some do not permit immunizations; others do not permit their members to be treated by physicians. Still others prohibit certain foods. For example, kosher dietary regulations permit Jews to eat the meat only of animals that chew cud and have cloven hooves and the flesh only of fish that have both gills and scales, while still others, like the Native American Church of the Morning Star, use peyote, a hallucinogen, as a sacrament.

Some religious communities actively address moral and ethical issues such as abortion, premarital intercourse, and homosexuality. Still other religions teach health-promoting codes of living to their members. Obviously, religion can affect a community's health positively or negatively (see **Figure 1.4**).

Social Norms

The influence of social norms on community and public health can be positive or negative and can change over time. Cigarette smoking is a good example. During the 1940s, 1950s, and 1960s, it was socially acceptable to smoke in most settings. As a matter of fact, in 1965, 51.2% of American men and 33.7% of American women smoked. Thus, in 1965 it was socially acceptable to be a smoker, especially if you were male. Now, in the second decade of the twenty-first century, those percentages have dropped to 18.8% (for males) and 14.8% (for females),[6] and in most public places it has become socially unacceptable to smoke. The lawsuits against tobacco companies by both the state attorneys general and private citizens provide further evidence that smoking has fallen from social acceptability. Because of this change in the social norm, there is less secondhand smoke in many public places, and in turn the health of the community has improved.

Unlike smoking, alcohol consumption represents a continuing negative social norm in America, especially on college campuses. The normal expectation seems to be that drinking is fun (and almost everyone wants to have fun). Despite the fact that most college students are too young to drink legally, approximately 59.5% of college students drink.[21] In the same survey, when college students were asked what percentage of other college students consumed alcohol the mean response was 92.1%.[21] It seems fairly obvious that the American alcoholic-beverage industry has influenced our social norms.

Socioeconomic Status

Differences in socioeconomic status (SES), whether "defined by education, employment, or income, both individual- and community-level socioeconomic status have independent effects on health."[22] There is a strong correlation between SES and health status—individuals in lower SES groups, regardless of other characteristics, have poorer health status. This correlation applies both across racial groups and within racial groups.[23]

Community Organizing

The way in which a community is able to organize its resources directly influences its ability to intervene and solve problems, including health problems. **Community organizing** is "the process by which community groups are helped to identify common problems or change targets, mobilize resources, and develop and implement strategies for reaching their collective goals."[24] It is not a science but an art of building consensus within a democratic process.[25] If a community can organize its resources effectively into a unified force, it "is likely to produce benefits in the form of increased effectiveness and productivity by reducing duplication of efforts and avoiding the imposition of solutions that are not congruent with the local culture and needs."[14] For example, many communities in the United States have faced community-wide drug problems. Some have been able to organize their resources to reduce or resolve these problems, whereas others have not.

Individual Behavior

The behavior of the individual community members contributes to the health of the entire community. It takes the concerted effort of many—if not most—of the individuals in a community to make a program work. For example, if each individual consciously recycles his or her trash each week, community recycling will be successful. Likewise, if each occupant would wear a safety belt, there could be a significant reduction in the number of facial injuries and deaths from car crashes for the entire community. In another example, the more individuals who become immunized against a specific communicable disease, the slower the disease will spread and the fewer people will be exposed. This concept is known as **herd immunity**.

A History of Community and Public Health

The history of community and public health is almost as long as the history of civilization. This summary provides an account of some of the accomplishments and failures in community and public health. It is hoped that knowledge of the past will enable us to better prepare for future challenges to our community's health.

Community organizing the process by which community groups are helped to identify common problems or change targets, mobilize resources, and develop and implement strategies for reaching their collective goals

Herd immunity the resistance of a population to the spread of an infectious agent based on the immunity of a high proportion of individuals

Spiritual era of public health a time during the Middle Ages when the causation of communicable disease was linked to spiritual forces

Earliest Civilizations

In all likelihood, the earliest community health practices went unrecorded. Perhaps these practices involved taboos against defecation within the tribal communal area or near the source of drinking water. Perhaps they involved rites associated with burial of the dead. Certainly, the use of herbs for the prevention and curing of diseases and communal assistance with childbirth are practices that predate archeological records.

Excavations at sites of some of the earliest known civilizations, dating from about 2000 B.C.E., have uncovered archeological evidence of community health activities (see **Figure 1.5**). A combination of additional archeological findings and written history provides much more evidence of community and public health activities through the seventeenth century. **Box 1.2** provides a timeline and some of the highlights of that history for the Ancient Societies (before 500 B.C.E.), the Classical Cultures (500 B.C.E.–500 C.E.), the Middle Ages (500–1500 C.E.), and the period of Renaissance and Exploration (1500–1700 C.E.).

BOX 1.2   Timeline and Highlights of Community and Public Health Prior to 1700 C.E.

A. Early Civilizations
  1. Ancient Societies (before 500 B.C.E.)
     a. Prior to 2000 B.C.E.: Archeological findings provide evidence of sewage disposal and written medical prescriptions.
     b. Circa 1900 B.C.E.: Perhaps the earliest written record of public health was the Code of Hammurabi; included laws for physicians and health practices.[26]
     c. Circa 1500 B.C.E.: Bible's Book of Leviticus written; includes guidelines for personal cleanliness and sanitation.[26]
  2. Classical Cultures (500 B.C.E.–500 C.E.)
     a. Fifth and sixth centuries B.C.E.: Evidence that Greek men participated in games of strength and skill and swam in public facilities.[27]
     b. Greeks were involved in practice of community sanitation; involved in obtaining water from sources far away and not just local wells.[28]
     c. Romans were community minded; improved on community sanitation of Greeks; built aqueducts to transport water from miles away; built sewer systems; created regulation for building construction, refuse removal, and street cleaning and repair;[27] created hospitals as infirmaries for slaves.[29]
     d. Christians created hospitals as benevolent charitable organizations.[29]
     e. 476 C.E.: Roman Empire fell and most public health activities ceased.
B. Middle Ages (500–1500 C.E.)
  1. 500–1000 C.E. (Dark Ages): Growing revulsion for Roman materialism and a growth of spirituality; health problems were considered to have both spiritual causes and spiritual solutions,[29] a time referred to as the **spiritual era of public health**.

  2. Failure to take into account the role of the physical and biological environment in the causation of communicable diseases resulted in many unrelenting epidemics in which millions suffered and died.
     a. Deadliest epidemics were from plague ("Black Death"); occurred in 543 C.E. and 1348 C.E. (this one killed 25 million; half of population of London lost and in some parts of France only 1 in 10 survived).[26]
     b. 1200 C.E.: More than 19,000 leper houses.
     c. Other epidemics of period: Smallpox, diphtheria, measles, influenza, tuberculosis, anthrax, and trachoma.
     d. 1492 C.E.: Syphilis epidemic was last epidemic of the period.
C. Renaissance and Exploration (1500–1700 C.E.)
  1. Rebirth of thinking about the nature of world and humankind.
  2. Belief that disease was caused by environmental, not spiritual, factors; for example, the term *malaria*, meaning *bad air*, is a direct reference to humid or swampy air.
  3. Observation of ill led to more accurate descriptions of symptoms and outcomes of diseases; observations led to first recognition of whooping cough, typhus, scarlet fever, and malaria as distinct and separate diseases.[28]
  4. 1662: John Graunt published the *Observations on the Bills of Mortality*, which was the beginning of vital statistics.
  5. Epidemics (e.g., smallpox, malaria, and plague) still rampant; plague epidemic killed 68,596 (15% of the population) in London in 1665.
  6. Explorers, conquerors, and merchants and their crews spread disease to colonists and indigenous people throughout the New World.

The Eighteenth Century

The eighteenth century was characterized by industrial growth. Despite the beginnings of recognition of the nature of disease, living conditions were hardly conducive to good health. Cities were overcrowded, and water supplies were inadequate and often unsanitary. Streets were usually unpaved, filthy, and heaped with trash and garbage. Many homes had unsanitary dirt floors.

Workplaces were unsafe and unhealthy. A substantial portion of the workforce was made up of the poor, which included children, who were forced to work long hours as indentured servants. Many of these jobs were unsafe or involved working in unhealthy environments, such as textile factories and coal mines (see **Box 1.3**).

The Nineteenth Century

Epidemics continued to be a problem in the nineteenth century, with outbreaks in major cities in both Europe and America. In 1854, another cholera epidemic struck London. Dr. John Snow studied the epidemic and hypothesized that the disease was being caused by the drinking water from the Broad Street pump. He obtained permission to remove the pump handle, and the epidemic was abated (see **Figure 1.6**). Snow's action was remarkable because it predated the discovery that microorganisms can cause disease. The predominant theory of contagious disease at the time was the "miasmas theory," which postulated vapors, or miasmas, were the source of many diseases. The miasmas theory remained popular throughout much of the nineteenth century.

In the United States in 1850, Lemuel Shattuck drew up a health report for the Commonwealth of Massachusetts that outlined the public health needs for the state. It included recommendations for the establishment of boards of health, the collection of vital statistics, the implementation of sanitary measures, and research on diseases. Shattuck also recommended health education and controlling exposure to alcohol, smoke, adulterated food, and nostrums (quack medicines).[26] Although some of his recommendations took years to implement (the Massachusetts Board of Health was not founded until 1869), the significance of Shattuck's report is such that 1850 is a key date in American public health; it marks the beginning of the **modern era of public health**.

Real progress in the understanding of the causes of many communicable diseases occurred during the last third of the nineteenth century. One of the obstacles to progress was the theory of spontaneous generation, the idea that living organisms could arise from inorganic or nonliving matter. Akin to this idea was the thought that one type of contagious microbe could change into another type of organism.

In 1862, Louis Pasteur of France proposed his germ theory of disease. Throughout the 1860s and 1870s, he and others carried out experiments and made observations that supported this

Modern era of public health the era of public health that began in 1850 and continues today

FIGURE 1.5 Archeological findings reveal community and public health practices of the past.

© Styve Reineck/ShutterStock, Inc.

BOX 1.3   Timeline and Highlights of Community and Public Health from 1700 to 1848

A. Eighteenth Century (1700s)
 1. 1790: First U.S. census.
 2. 1793: Yellow fever epidemic in Philadelphia.[30]
 3. 1796: Dr. Edward Jenner successfully demonstrated smallpox vaccination.
 4. 1798: Marine Hospital Service (forerunner to U.S. Public Health Service) was formed.

 5. By 1799: Several of America's largest cities, including Boston, Philadelphia, New York, and Baltimore, had municipal boards of health.

B. First Half of the Nineteenth Century (1800–1848)
 1. U.S. government's approach to health was *laissez faire* (i.e., noninterference).
 2. 1813: First visiting nurse in United States.

Bacteriological period of public health the period of 1875–1900, during which the causes of many bacterial diseases were discovered

theory and disproved spontaneous generation. Pasteur is generally given credit for providing the deathblow to the theory of spontaneous generation.

It was the German scientist Robert Koch who developed the criteria and procedures necessary to establish that a particular microbe, and no other, causes a particular disease. His first demonstration, with the anthrax bacillus, was in 1876. Between 1877 and the end of the century, the identity of numerous bacterial disease agents was established, including those that caused gonorrhea, typhoid fever, leprosy, tuberculosis, cholera, diphtheria, tetanus, pneumonia, plague, and dysentery. This period (1875–1900) has come to be known as the **bacteriological period of public health**.

Although most scientific discoveries in the late nineteenth century were made in Europe, significant public health achievements were occurring in America as well. The first law prohibiting the adulteration of milk was passed in 1856, the first sanitary survey was carried out in New York City in 1864, and the American Public Health Association was founded in 1872. The Marine Hospital Service gained new powers of inspection and investigation under the Port Quarantine Act of 1878.[26] In 1890, the pasteurization of milk was introduced, and in 1891 meat inspection began. It was also during this time that nurses were first hired by industries (in 1895) and schools (in 1899). Also in 1895, septic tanks were introduced for sewage treatment. In 1900, Major Walter Reed of the U.S. Army announced that mosquitoes transmitted yellow fever (see **Box 1.4**).

FIGURE 1.6 In London, England, in 1854, John Snow helped interrupt a cholera epidemic by having the handle removed from this pump, located on Broad Street.

© Robert Pinger.

The Twentieth Century

As the twentieth century began, life expectancy was still less than 50 years.[2] The leading causes of death were communicable diseases—influenza, pneumonia, tuberculosis, and infections of the gastrointestinal tract. Other communicable diseases, such as typhoid fever, malaria, and diphtheria, also killed many people.

There were other health problems as well. Thousands of children were afflicted with conditions characterized by noninfectious diarrhea or by bone deformity. Although the symptoms of pellagra and rickets were known and described, the causes of these ailments remained a mystery at the turn of the century. Discovery that these conditions resulted from vitamin deficiencies was slow because some scientists were searching for bacterial causes.

Vitamin deficiency diseases and one of their contributing conditions, poor dental health, were extremely common in the slum districts of both European and American cities. The unavailability of adequate prenatal and postnatal care meant that deaths associated with pregnancy and childbirth were also high.

Health Resources Development Period (1900–1960)

Much growth and development took place during the 60-year period from 1900 to 1960. Because of the growth of health care facilities and providers, this period of time is referred to as the

---

BOX 1.4   Timeline and Highlights of Community and Public Health for the Second Half of Nineteenth Century (1848–1900)

1. 1849,1854: London cholera epidemics.
2. 1850: Modern era of public health begins.
3. 1850: Shattuck's report was published.
4. 1854: Snow had pump handle removed from Broad Street pump.
5. 1863: Pasteur proposed germ theory.
6. 1872: American Public Health Association founded.
7. 1875–1900: Bacteriological period of public health.
8. 1876: Koch established relationship between a particular microbe and a particular disease.
9. 1900: Reed announced that yellow fever was transmitted by mosquitos.

health resources development period. This period can be further divided into the reform phase (1900–1920), the 1920s, the Great Depression and World War II, and the postwar years.

The Reform Phase (1900–1920)

During the first 20 years of the twentieth century (i.e., the **reform phase of public health**), there was a growing concern about the many social problems in America. The remarkable discoveries in microbiology made in the previous years had not dramatically improved the health of the average citizen. By 1910, the urban population had grown to 45% of the total population (up from 19% in 1860). Much of the growth was the result of immigrants who came to America for the jobs created by new industries (see **Figure 1.7**). Northern cities were also swelling from the northward migration of black Americans from the southern states. Many of these workers had to accept poorly paying jobs involving hard labor. There was also a deepening chasm between the upper and lower classes, and social critics began to clamor for reform.

In 1906 the plight of the immigrants working in the meat packing industry was graphically depicted by Upton Sinclair in his book *The Jungle*. Sinclair's goal was to draw attention to unsafe working conditions. What he achieved was greater governmental regulation of the food industry through the passage of the Pure Food and Drugs Act of 1906.

The reform movement was broad, involving both social and moral as well as health issues. In 1909 it was noted that "[i]ll health is perhaps the most constant of the attendants of poverty."[31] The reform movement finally took hold when it became evident to the majority that neither the discoveries of the causes of many communicable diseases nor the continuing advancement of

Health resources development period the years of 1900–1960, a time of great growth in health care facilities and providers

Reform phase of public health the years of 1900–1920, characterized by social movements to improve health conditions in cities and in the workplace

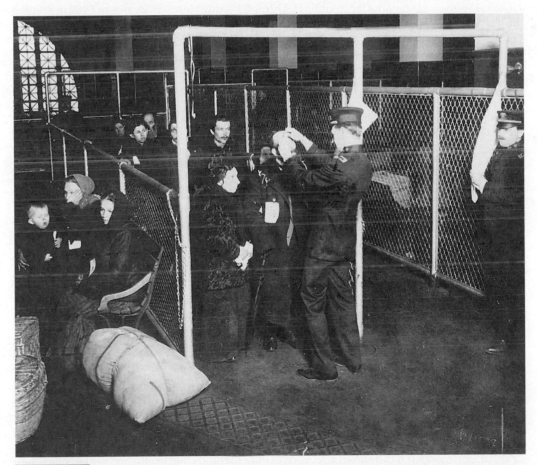

FIGURE 1.7   Ellis Island immigration between 1860 and 1910 resulted in dramatic increases in urban population in America.

Courtesy of Library of Congress, Prints & Photographs Division [reproduction number LC-USZ62-7386].

industrial production could overcome continuing disease and poverty. Even by 1917, the United States ranked fourteenth of 16 "progressive" nations in maternal death rate.[31]

Although the relationship between occupation and disease had been pointed out 200 years earlier in Europe, occupational health in America in 1900 was an unknown quantity. However, in 1910 the first International Congress on Occupational Diseases was held in Chicago.[32] That same year, the state of New York passed a tentative Workman's Compensation Act, and over the next 10 years most other states passed similar laws. Also in 1910, the U.S. Bureau of Mines was created and the first clinic for occupational diseases was established in New York at Cornell Medical College.[31] By 1910, the movement for healthier conditions in the workplace was well established.

This period also saw the birth of the first national-level volunteer health agencies. The first of these agencies was the National Association for the Study and Prevention of Tuberculosis (TB), which was formed in 1902. It arose from the first local voluntary health agency, the Pennsylvania Society for the Prevention of Tuberculosis, organized in 1892.[33] The American Cancer Society, Inc. was founded in 1913. That same year, the Rockefeller Foundation was established in New York. This philanthropic foundation has funded a great many public health projects, including work on hookworm and pellagra, and the development of a vaccine against yellow fever.

Another movement that began about this time was that of public health nursing. The first school nursing program was begun in New York City in 1902. In 1918, the first School of Public Health was established at Johns Hopkins University in Baltimore. This was followed by establishment of the Harvard School of Public Health in 1923. Also in 1918 was the birth of school health instruction as we know it today.

These advances were matched with similar advances by governmental bodies. The Marine Hospital Service was renamed the Public Health and Marine Hospital Service in 1902 in keeping with its growing responsibilities. In 1912, it became the U.S. Public Health Service.[26]

By 1900, 38 states had state health departments. The rest followed during the first decades of the twentieth century. The first two local (county) health departments were established in 1911, one in Guilford County, North Carolina, and the other in Yakima County, Washington.

The 1920s

In comparison with the preceding period, the 1920s represented a decade of slow growth in public health, except for a few health projects funded by the Rockefeller and Millbank Foundations. Prohibition resulted in a decline in the number of alcoholics and alcohol-related deaths. Although the number of county health departments had risen to 467 by 1929, 77% of the rural population still lived in areas with no health services.[33] However, it was during this period in 1922 that the first professional preparation program for health education specialists was begun at Columbia University by Thomas D. Wood, MD, whom many consider the father of health education. The life expectancy in 1930 had risen to 59.7 years.

The Great Depression and World War II

Until the Great Depression (1929–1935), individuals and families in need of social and medical services were dependent on friends and relatives, private charities, voluntary agencies, community chests, and churches. By 1933, after 3 years of economic depression, it became evident that private resources could never meet the needs of all the people who needed assistance. The drop in tax revenues during the Depression also reduced health department budgets and caused a virtual halt in the formation of new local health departments.[33]

Beginning in 1933, President Franklin D. Roosevelt created numerous agencies and programs for public works as part of his New Deal. Much of the money was used for public health, including the control of malaria, the building of hospitals and laboratories, and the construction of municipal water and sewer systems.

The Social Security Act of 1935 marked the beginning of the government's major involvement in social issues, including health. This legislation provided substantial support for state health departments and their programs, such as maternal and child health and sanitary facilities. As progress against the communicable diseases became visible, some turned their attention toward other health problems, such as cancer. The National Cancer Institute was formed in 1937.

America's involvement in World War II resulted in severe restrictions on resources available for public health programs. Immediately following the conclusion of the war, however, many of the medical discoveries made during wartime made their way into civilian practice. Two examples are the antibiotic penicillin, used for treating pneumonia, rheumatic fever, syphilis, and strep throat, and the insecticide DDT, used for killing insects that transmit diseases.

During World War II, the Communicable Disease Center was established in Atlanta, Georgia. Now called the Centers for Disease Control and Prevention (CDC), it has become the premier epidemiological center of the world.

The Postwar Years

Following the end of World War II, there was still concern about medical care and the adequacy of the facilities in which that care could be administered. In 1946, the U.S. Congress passed the National Hospital Survey and Construction Act (the Hill-Burton Act). The goal of the legislation was to improve the distribution of medical care and to enhance the quality of hospitals. From 1946 through the 1960s, hospital construction occurred at a rapid rate with relatively little thought given to planning. Likewise, attempts to set national health priorities or to establish a national health agenda were virtually nonexistent.

The two major health events in the 1950s were the development of a vaccine to prevent polio and President Eisenhower's heart attack. The latter event helped America to focus on its number one killer, heart disease. When the president's physician suggested exercise, some Americans heeded his advice and began to exercise on a regular basis.

Period of Social Engineering (1960–1973)

The 1960s marked the beginning of a period when the federal government once again became active in health matters. The primary reason for this involvement was the growing realization that many Americans were still not reaping any of the benefits of 60 years of medical advances. These Americans, most of whom were poor or elderly, either lived in underserved areas or simply could not afford to purchase medical services.

In 1965, Congress passed the Medicare and Medicaid bills (amendments to the Social Security Act of 1935). **Medicare** assists in the payment of medical bills for older adults and certain people with disabilities, and **Medicaid** assists in the payment of medical bills for the poor. These pieces of legislation helped provide medical care for millions who would not otherwise have received it; this legislation also improved standards in health care facilities. Unfortunately, the influx of federal dollars accelerated the rate of increase in the cost of health care for everyone. As a result, the 1970s, 1980s, and the 1990s saw repeated attempts and failures to bring the growing costs of health care under control (see **Box 1.5**).

Medicare government health insurance for older adults and those with certain disabilities

Medicaid government health insurance for the poor

BOX 1.5   Timeline and Highlights of Community and Public Health for the Health Resources Development Period (1900–1960)

A. The Reform Phase (1900–1920)
1. 1902: First national-level voluntary health agency created.
2. 1906: Sinclair's *The Jungle* published.
3. 1910: First International Congress on Diseases of Occupation.
4. 1910: 45% of U.S. population was in the cities.
5. 1911: First local health department established.
6. 1913: American Cancer Society founded.
7. 1917: United States ranked 14th of 16 in maternal death rate.
8. 1918: Birth of school health instruction.
9. 1918: First school of public health established in United States.

B. 1920s
1. 1922: Wood created first professional preparation program for health education specialists.

2. 1930: Life expectancy in the United States was 59.7 years.

C. The Great Depression and World War II
1. 1933: New Deal; included unsuccessful attempt at national health care program.
2. 1935: Social Security Act passed.
3. 1937: National Cancer Institute formed.

D. Postwar Years
1. 1946: National Hospital Survey and Construction (Hill-Burton) Act passed.
2. 1952: Development of polio vaccine.
3. 1955: Eisenhower's heart attack.

E. Period of Social Engineering (1960–1973)
1. 1965: Medicare and Medicaid bills passed.

Healthy People 2020 the fourth set of health goals and objectives for the U.S that defines the nation's health agenda and guides its health policy

Period of Health Promotion (1974–Present)

By the mid-1970s, it had become apparent that the greatest potential for saving lives and reducing health care costs in America was to be achieved through means other than health care.

Most scholars, policymakers, and practitioners in health promotion would pick 1974 as the turning point that marks the beginning of health promotion as a significant component of national health policy in the twentieth century. That year Canada published its landmark policy statement, *A New Perspective on the Health of Canadians.*[34] In [1976] the United States Congress passed PL 94-317, the Health Information and Health Promotion Act, which created the Office of Health Information and Health Promotion, later renamed the Office of Disease Prevention and Health Promotion.[35]

In the late 1970s, the Centers for Disease Control conducted a study that examined premature deaths (defined then as deaths prior to age 65, but now as deaths prior to age 75) in the United States in 1977. That study revealed that approximately 48% of all premature deaths could be traced to one's lifestyle or health behavior—choices that people make. Lifestyles characterized by a lack of exercise, unhealthy diets, smoking, uncontrolled hypertension, and the inability to control stress were found to be contributing factors to premature mortality.[36] This led the way for the U.S. government's publication *Healthy People: The Surgeon General's Report on Health Promotion and Disease Prevention.*[37] "This document brought together much of what was known about the relationship of personal behavior and health status. The document also presented a 'personal responsibility' model that provided Americans with the prescription for reducing their health risks and increasing their chances for good health."[38]

Healthy People was then followed by the release of the first set of health goals and objectives for the nation, called *Promoting Health/Preventing Disease: Objectives for the Nation.*[39] *Healthy People 2020* is the fourth edition of these goals and objectives. Since their inception, these *Healthy People* documents have defined the nation's health agenda and guided its health policy since their inception (see **Box 1.6**).

All four editions of the *Healthy People* documents include several overarching goals and many supporting objectives for the nation's health. The goals provide a general focus and direction, while the objectives are used to measure progress within a specified period of time. Formal reviews (i.e., measured progress) of these objectives are conducted both at midcourse (i.e., halfway through the 10-year period) and again at the end of 10 years. The midcourse review provides an opportunity to update the document based on the events of the first half of the decade for which the objectives are written.

Healthy People 2020 was released in December 2010, and includes a vision statement, a mission statement, four overarching goals (see **Table 1.1**), and almost 1,200 science-based objectives spread over 42 different topic areas (see **Table 1.2**).[40] On the Healthy People.gov website each topic has its own Web page. At a minimum each page contains a concise goal statement, a brief overview of the topic that provides the background and context for the topic, a statement about the importance of the topic backed up by appropriate evidence, and references.

BOX 1.6   **Timeline and Highlights of Community and Public Health for the Period of Health Promotion (1974–Present)**

A. Late Twentieth Century
1. 1974: Nixon's unsuccessful attempt at national health care program.
2. 1974: *A New Perspective on the Health of Canadians* published.
3. 1976: Health Information and Health Promotion Act passed.
4. 1979: *Healthy People* published.
5. 1980: *Promoting Health/Preventing Disease: Objectives of the Nation* published.

6. 1990: *Healthy People 2000* published.
7. 1997: Clinton's unsuccessful attempt at a national health care program.

B. Early Twenty-First Century
1. 2000: *Healthy People 2010* published.
2. 2010: Affordable Care Act becomes law.
3. 2010: *Healthy People 2020* published.

TABLE 1.1 *Healthy People 2020* Vision, Mission, and Goals

Vision

A society in which all people live long, healthy lives.

Mission

Healthy People 2020 strives to:
- Identify nationwide health improvement priorities.
- Increase public awareness and understanding of the determinants of health, disease, and disability and the opportunities for progress.
- Provide measurable objectives and goals that are applicable at the national, state, and local levels.
- Engage multiple sectors to take actions to strengthen policies and improve practices that are driven by the best available evidence and knowledge.
- Identify critical research, evaluation, and data collection needs.

Overarching Goals

- Attain high-quality, longer lives free of preventable disease, disability, injury, and premature death.
- Achieve health equity, eliminate disparities, and improve the health of all groups.
- Create social and physical environments that promote good health for all.
- Promote quality of life, healthy development, and healthy behaviors across all life stages.

Data from: U.S. Department of Health and Human Services (2016). *About Healthy People.* Available at https://www.healthypeople.gov/2020/About-Healthy-People.

TABLE 1.2 *Healthy People 2020* Topic Areas

1. Access to Health Services	22. HIV
2. Adolescent Health	23. Immunization and Infectious Diseases
3. Arthritis, Osteoporosis, and Chronic Back Conditions	24. Injury and Violence Prevention
4. Blood Disorders and Blood Safety	25. Lesbian, Gay, Bisexual, and Transgender Health
5. Cancer	26. Maternal, Infant, and Child Health
6. Chronic Kidney Disease	27. Medical Product Safety
7. Dementias, Including Alzheimer's Disease	28. Mental Health and Mental Disorders
8. Diabetes	29. Nutrition and Weight Status
9. Disability and Health	30. Occupational Safety and Health
10. Early and Middle Childhood	31. Older Adults
11. Educational and Community-Based Programs	32. Oral Health
12. Environmental Health	33. Physical Activity
13. Family Planning	34. Preparedness
14. Food Safety	35. Public Health Infrastructure
15. Genomics	36. Respiratory Diseases
16. Global Health	37. Sexually Transmitted Diseases
17. Health Communication and Health Information Technology	38. Sleep Health
18. Health-Related Quality of Life and Well-Being	39. Social Determinants of Health
19. Health care-Associated Infections	40. Substance Abuse
20. Hearing and Other Sensory or Communication Disorders	41. Tobacco Use
21. Heart Disease and Stroke	42. Vision

Data from U.S. Department of Health and Human Services (2016). 2020 *Topics and Objectives – Objectives A–Z.* Available at https://www.healthypeople.gov/2020/topics-objectives.

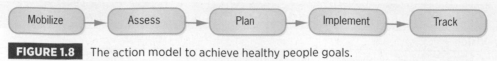

FIGURE 1.8 The action model to achieve healthy people goals.

Data from: U.S. Department of Health and Human Services (2016). *Program Planning*. Available at https://www.healthypeople.gov/2020/tools-and-resources/Program-Planning.

The developers of *Healthy People 2020* think that the best way to implement the national objectives is with the framework referred to as MAP-IT (see **Figure 1.8**). MAP-IT stands for Mobilize, Assess, Plan, Implement, and Track. The Mobilize step of MAP-IT deals with bringing interested parties together within communities to deal with health issues. The second step, Assess, is used to find out who is affected by the health problem and examine what resources are available to deal with the problem. In the Plan step, goals and objectives are created and an intervention is planned that has the best chances of dealing with the health problem. The Implement step deals with putting the intervention into action. And the final step, Track, deals with evaluating the impact of the intervention on the health problem.[40]

In addition to the *Healthy People* initiative, the United States also has its National Prevention Strategy, which was released in 2011. The Affordable Care Act (ACA) "created the National Prevention Council (NPC) and called for the development of the National Prevention Strategy to realize the benefits of prevention for all Americans' health. The National Prevention Strategy is critical to the prevention focus of the Affordable Care Act and builds on the law's efforts to lower health care costs, improve the quality of care, and provide coverage options for the uninsured."[41]

The NPC provides leadership for the Strategy and is comprised of representatives from 20 federal departments, agencies, and offices and is chaired by the U.S. Surgeon General. Although the NPC "provides coordination and leadership at the federal level and identifies ways that agencies can work individually, as well as together, to improve our nation's health,"[41] public and private partners have provided much input in creating the National Prevention Strategy. Such input has been provided by the Advisory Group on Prevention, Health Promotion, and Integrative and Public Health referred to as the Prevention Advisory Group. This group was also created by the ACA and is comprised of 21 nonfederal members appointed by the President.[41]

The goal of the Strategy is to "increase the number of Americans who are healthy at every stage of life."[41] At the foundation of the Strategy are four Strategic Directions that include Healthy and Safe Community Environments, Clinical and Community Preventive Services, Empowered People, and Elimination of Health Disparities (see **Figure 1.9**). "Each Strategy Direction can stand alone and can guide actions that will demonstrably improve health. Together, the Strategic Directions create the web needed to fully support Americans in leading longer and healthier lives."[41] The Strategy also has seven targeted Priorities (Tobacco-Free Living, Preventing Drug Abuse and Excessive Alcohol Use, Healthy Eating, Active Living, Injury and Violence Free Living, Reproductive and Sexual Health, and Mental and Emotional Well-Being). The "Priorities are designed to improve health and wellness for the entire U.S. population, including those groups disproportionately affected by disease and injury."[41] "Preference has been given to efforts that will have the greatest impact on the largest number of people and can be sustained over time."[41]

The Strategy includes: key facts and documents, a list of recommended policies, programs, and system approaches to address each of the Strategic Directions and Priorities, and actions for both the federal government and for the partners. The actions for the partners are specific to type of partners which include: (1) state, tribal, local, and territorial governments, (2) employers, (3) health care organizations, insurers, and clinicians, (4) educational organizations, (5) community groups, and (6) faith-based organizations. Also, within each of the Strategic Directions and Priorities are key indicators that will be used to measure the progress toward the overarching goal based on 10-year targets. In addition to measuring progress in prevention, the indicators "will be used to plan and implement future prevention efforts. Key indicators will be reported for the overall population and by subgroups as data become available. Indicators and 10-year

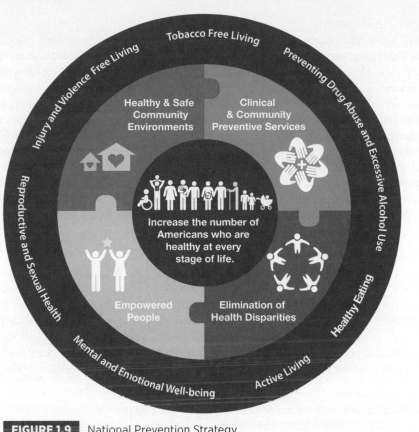

FIGURE 1.9 National Prevention Strategy.

Reproduced from: National Prevention Council, U.S. Department of Health and Human Services, Office of the Surgeon General (2011). *National Prevention Strategy*. Available at http://www.surgeongeneral.gov/priorities/prevention/strategy/index.html.

targets are drawn from existing measurement efforts, especially *Healthy People 2020*. As data sources and metrics are developed or enhanced, National Prevention Strategy's key indicators and targets will be updated."[41]

The Twenty-First Century

Now in the second decade of the twenty-first century the need to improve community and public health continues. Below we have outlined some of the major problems still facing the United States and the world.

U.S. Community and Public Health in the Twenty-First Century

With a little more than one-sixth of the twenty-first century behind us, it is widely agreed that although decisions about health are an individual's responsibility to a significant degree, society has an obligation to provide an environment in which the achievement of good health is possible and encouraged. Furthermore, many recognize that certain segments of our population whose disease and death rates exceed the general population may require additional resources, including education, to achieve good health.

The American people face a number of serious public health problems. These problems include the continuing rise in health care costs, growing environmental concerns, the ever-present lifestyle diseases, emerging and reemerging communicable diseases, serious substance abuse problems, and disasters, both natural and human-made. In the paragraphs that follow, we have elaborated on each of these problems briefly because they seem to represent a significant portion of the community and public health agenda for the years ahead.

Health care Delivery

In 2010, significant changes were made to the U.S. health care system with the passage of the Patient Protection and Affordable Care Act (PPACA; Public Law 111-148) and the Health Care and Education Reconciliation Act of 2010 (HCERA; Public Law 111-152). These two acts were consolidated shortly thereafter with other approved legislation and are now referred to as the *Affordable Care Act* (or ACA, nicknamed ObamaCare). Though the law has many components, the primary focus was to increase the number of Americans with health insurance. The ACA does this, but by providing health insurance to millions of Americans who did not have it before, the costs will also go up, which will continue to make U.S. health care the most expensive in the world. In 2016, health expenditures were projected to be just over $3.35 trillion, consume 18.1% of the gross domestic product (GDP), and were expected to reach $5.63 trillion and 20.1% of the GDP by 2025.[42] The United States spends more per capita annually on health care (estimated at $10,345 in 2016)[42] than any other nation. The cost of health care is an issue that still needs to be addressed.

Environmental Problems

Millions of Americans live in communities where the air is unsafe to breathe, the water is unsafe to drink, or solid waste is disposed of improperly. With a few minor exceptions, the rate at which we pollute our environment continues to increase. Many Americans still believe that our natural resources are unlimited and that their individual contributions to the overall pollution are insignificant. In actuality, we must improve on our efforts in resource preservation and energy conservation if our children are to enjoy an environment as clean as ours. These environmental problems are compounded by the fact that the world population continues to grow; it is now more than 7.3 billion people and expected to reach 8 billion by the year 2025.[43]

Lifestyle Diseases

The leading causes of death in the United States today are not the communicable diseases that were so feared 100 years ago but chronic illnesses. The four leading causes of death in the second decade of the twenty-first century are heart disease, cancer, chronic lower respiratory diseases, and unintentional injuries.[44] Although it is true that everyone has to die from some cause sometime, too many Americans die prematurely. Seven out of every 10 deaths among Americans each year are from chronic diseases, while heart disease, cancer, and stroke account for approximately 50% of deaths annually.[45] In addition, more than 86% of all health care spending in the United States is on people with chronic conditions.[45] Chronic diseases are not only the most common, deadly, and costly conditions, they are also the most preventable of all health problems in the United States.[45] They are the most preventable because four modifiable risk behaviors—lack of exercise or physical activity, poor nutrition, tobacco use, and excessive alcohol use—are responsible for much of the illness, suffering, and early death related to chronic diseases.[45] In fact, one study estimates that all causes of mortality could be cut by 55% by never smoking, engaging in regular physical activity, eating a healthy diet, and avoiding being overweight.[46] (See **Table 1.3.**)

Communicable Diseases

Although communicable (infectious) diseases no longer constitute the leading causes of death in the United States, they remain a concern for several reasons. First, they are the primary reason for days missed at school or at work. The success in reducing the life-threatening nature of these diseases has made many Americans complacent about obtaining vaccinations or taking other precautions against contracting these diseases. With the exception of smallpox, none of these diseases has been eradicated, although several should have been, such as measles.

Second, as new communicable diseases continue to appear, old ones such as tuberculosis reemerge, sometimes in drug-resistant forms (i.e., caused by superbugs), demonstrating that communicable diseases still represent a serious community health problem in America. Legionnaires' disease, toxic shock syndrome, Lyme disease, acquired immunodeficiency syndrome (AIDS), severe acute respiratory syndrome (SARS), and Zika virus disease are diseases that were unknown only 60 years ago. The first cases of AIDS were reported in June 1981.[47] By August 1989, 100,000 cases had been reported,[48] and it took only an additional two years to report the second 100,000 cases.[49] By 2015, more than 1.2 million cases of the disease had

TABLE 1.3   Comparison of Most Common Causes of Death and Actual Causes of Death

Most Common Causes of Death, United States, 2013	Actual Causes of Death, United States, 2000
1. Heart disease	1. Tobacco
2. Cancer	2. Poor diet and physical inactivity
3. Chronic lower respiratory diseases	3. Alcohol consumption
4. Unintentional injuries	4. Microbial agents
5. Stroke	5. Toxic agents
6. Alzheimer's disease	6. Motor vehicles
7. Diabetes	7. Firearms
8. Influenza and pneumonia	8. Sexual behavior
9. Nephritis, nephrotic syndrome, and nephrosis	9. Illicit drug use
10. Intentional self-harm (suicide)	

Data from National Center for Health Statistics (2016). *Deaths and Mortality*. Available at http://www.cdc.gov/nchs/fastats /deaths.htm; Mokdad, A. H., J. S. Marks, D. F. Stroup, and J. L. Gerberding (2004). "Actual Causes of Death, in the United States, 2000." *Journal of the American Medical Association*, 291(10): 1238–1245; and Mokdad, A. H., J. S. Marks, D. F. Stroup, and J. L. Gerberding (2005). "Correction: Actual Causes of Death, in the United States, 2000." *Journal of the American Medical Association*, 293(3): 293–294.

Bioterrorism the threatened or intentional release of biological agents for the purpose of influencing the conduct of government or intimidating or coercing a civilian population to further political or social objectives

been reported to the CDC[50] (see **Figure 1.10**). The total number of cases continues to grow with close to 50,000 new HIV cases being diagnosed each year.[50] Also, diseases that were once only found in animals are now crossing over to human populations and causing much concern and action. Included in this group of diseases are avian flu, *Escherichia coli* O157:H7, hantavirus, mad cow disease, and SARS.

Third, and maybe the most disturbing, is the use of communicable diseases for bioterrorism. **Bioterrorism** involves "the threatened or intentional release of biological agents (virus, bacteria, or their toxins) for the purpose of influencing the conduct of government or intimidating or coercing a civilian population to further political or social objectives. These agents can be released by way of the air (as aerosols) food, water or insects."[9] Concern in the United States over bioterrorism was heightened after September 11, 2001 (9/11) and the subsequent intentional distribution of *Bacillus anthracis* spores through the U.S. postal system (the anthrax mailings).

> Since then, a heightened awareness of potential threats posed by chemical and biological weapons and low-grade nuclear materials have prompted public officials nationwide to review and revamp the [public health] system. Large-scale bioterrorism has not yet occurred, but global unrest amid the rise of extremism makes it a real possibility in the future.[51]

Alcohol and Other Drug Abuse

Drug abuse and addiction due to the use of tobacco, alcohol, and illegal drugs have a number of negative effects on individuals and society including but not limited to failure in school, child abuse, disintegration of the family, domestic violence, loss of employment, violent crimes, and even death. Estimates of the total overall costs of substance abuse in the United States, including lost productivity, and health and crime-related costs, exceed $700 billion annually.[52] Federal, state, and local governments as well as private agencies attempt to address the

FIGURE 1.10   AIDS is one of the most feared communicable diseases today.

© coka/ShutterStock, Inc.

Health disparities the difference in health among different populations

supply and demand problems associated with the abuse of alcohol and other drugs, but a significant challenge remains for America. A recent example of this challenge has been the response to opioid pain reliever overdose. "In 2014, more than 18,000 people died from an opioid pain reliever overdose, or nearly 50 people per day, and over 10,000 died from heroin-related overdoses, a rate that has more than quadrupled since 2002."[53] In response two major steps have been taken. The first was the U.S. Food and Drug Administration (FDA)'s approval of intranasal naloxone—a nasal spray formulation of the medication designed to rapidly reverse opioid overdose—which provides family members, caregivers, and first responders with an alternative to injectable naloxone for use during a suspected opioid overdose.[54] The second was the development by the CDC of guidelines for prescribing opioids for chronic pain that provide "recommendations for the prescribing of opioid pain medication for patients 18 and older in primary care settings."[55]

Health Disparities

It has long been "recognized that some individuals lead longer and healthier lives than others, and that often these differences are closely associated with social characteristics such as race, ethnicity, gender, location, and socioeconomic status."[56] These gaps between groups have been referred to as health disparities (also call health inequalities in some countries). More formally, **health disparities** have been defined as the difference in health among different populations. Health disparities are a problem in the United States in that many minority groups' health status, on many different measures, is not as good as the white population. Efforts have been put forth to eliminate the disparities, as evidenced by one of the *Healthy People 2020* overarching goals to "achieve health equity, eliminate disparities, and improve the health for all groups."[40] Many experts think these differences have been caused by two health inequities—lack of access to health care, and/or when health care is received the quality has not been as good for those in minority groups. Whatever the reason, health disparities continue to be a problem and much more needs to be done.

Disasters

Disasters can be classified into two primary categories—natural (or conventional) and human-made (or technological disasters).[1] Whereas natural disasters are the result of the combination of the forces of nature (e.g., hurricane, flood, blizzard, tornado, earthquake, landslide) and human activities,[57] human-made disasters result from either unintentional (e.g., spill of a toxic substance into the environment) or intentional (e.g., bioterrorism) human activities, often associated with the use or misuse of technology. Both types of disasters have the potential to cause injury, death, disease, and damage to property on a large scale.[1] In recent years, the United States has felt the large-scale impact of both types of disasters via wildfires, the BP Gulf oil spill, Hurricanes Katrina and Rita, severe flooding, and the bombings in Paris, Brussels, and at the 2013 Boston Marathon (see **Figure 1.11**). All of these events showed us that the preparation for such disasters was not adequate and that each type of disaster required different resources and a different response.

Even though the causes of the two categories of disasters are different, preparedness for them has many common elements. It has been noted that preparedness for natural disasters is the foundation for preparedness for human-made disasters.[58] That is, in preparing for natural disasters, the basic components of an adequate disaster response system have been defined, and the steps necessary to build disaster preparedness capacity have been established.[58] What needs to be added are specific steps to deal with the peculiarity of the human-made disasters. An example of this would be the need for decontamination following exposure to a biological agent.

Even given the devastating consequences of natural disasters, such as hurricanes, flooding, or the forest fires that consume many thousands of acres of woodlands each year, it has been the intentional human-made disasters—specifically terrorism—that have occupied much of our attention in recent years.

FIGURE 1.11   Terrorism has become a concern throughout the world.
© FRANCK FIFE / Getty Images.

Mention was made earlier of the use of a communicable disease as part of terrorism. In fact a number of agents could be used as part of terrorism. Since the anthrax mailings, community and public health professionals have focused on the possibility that future terrorism could include chemical, biological, radiological, and/or nuclear (CBRN) agents, resulting in mass numbers of casualties. Such concern led to an evaluation of community and public health emergency preparedness and response. "Determining the level of state and local health departments' emergency preparedness and response capacities is crucial because public health officials are among those, along with firefighters, emergency medical personnel, and local law enforcement personnel, who serve on 'rapid response' teams when large-scale emergency situations arise."[14] Results of that evaluation showed that the public health infrastructure was not where it should be to handle large-scale emergencies, as well as a number of more common public health concerns.

> The . . . public health infrastructure has suffered from political neglect and from the pressure of political agendas and public opinion that frequently override empirical evidence. Under the glare of a national crisis, policy makers and the public became aware of vulnerable and outdated health information systems and technologies, an insufficient and inadequately trained public health workforce, antiquated laboratory capacity, a lack of real-time surveillance and epidemiological systems, ineffective and fragmented communications networks, incomplete domestic preparedness and emergency response capabilities, and communities without access to essential public health services.[14]

Based on the results of several different evaluations that exposed many weaknesses in emergency preparedness in general and in the public health infrastructure more specifically, investment in public health preparedness has increased since 9/11. Those federal departments that have been responsible for most of the effort have been the U.S. Departments of Homeland Security (DHS) and Health and Human Services (HHS). The DHS has the responsibility of protecting America, whereas the HHS has taken the leadership for public health and medical preparedness. **Public health preparedness** has been defined as "the ability of the *public health system, community*, and *individuals* to prevent, protect against, quickly respond to, and recover from health emergencies, particularly those in which scale, timing, or unpredictability threatens to overwhelm routine capabilities";[59] **Medical preparedness** has been defined as "the ability of the *health care system* to prevent, protect against, quickly respond to, and recover from health emergencies, particularly those whose scale, timing, or unpredictability threatens to overwhelm routine capabilities."[59] Information about emergency preparedness and response can be found on the websites of all HHS agencies; however, those that have been most visible have been the Centers for Disease Control and Prevention (CDC), the Health Resources and Services Administration (HRSA), and the Agency for Health care Research and Quality (AHRQ).

After 9/11, the federal government, through a variety of funding sources and programs, has worked to strengthen homeland security, emergency preparedness, and response at all levels. The funding was used to create or enhance the various components needed in disaster situations (i.e., communication, coordination, and the workforce). The funding also had to be used to bring much of the public health system up to date (e.g., laboratories, personnel, and surveillance) after many years of neglect. However, in part because of the lull in the economy, there has been a decrease in public health preparedness funding the past few years,[60] which has started to erode a decade's worth of progress.[56]

Though the United States is better prepared than prior to 9/11, much still needs to be done. In December 2012, the Trust for America's Health (TFAH), a nonprofit, nonpartisan organization, and the Robert Wood Johnson Foundation released their tenth report on the state of public health preparedness in the United States.[61] The authors of the report noted "that while there has been significant progress toward improving public health preparedness over the past 10 years, particularly in core capabilities, there continue to be persistent gaps in the country's ability to respond to health emergencies, ranging from bioterrorist threats to serious disease outbreaks to extreme weather events."[61] Central to the report is a scorecard that rates

Public health preparedness the ability of the public health system, community, and individuals to prevent, protect against, quickly respond to, and recover from health emergencies, particularly those in which scale, timing, or unpredictability threatens to overwhelm routine capabilities

Medical preparedness the ability of the health care system to prevent, protect against, quickly respond to, and recover from health emergencies, particularly those whose scale, timing, or unpredictability threatens to overwhelm routine capabilities

all 50 states and the Washington, D.C. based on 10 key indicators to assess health emergency preparedness capabilities.

In the most recent report, scores ranged from three (in Kansas and Montana) to eight (in Maryland, Mississippi, North Carolina, Vermont, and Wisconsin). Thirty-five states scored six or lower. Data from the report showed that 29 states cut public health funding from fiscal years 2010–2011 to 2011–2012. Only two states met the national goal for vaccinating 90% of young children (i.e., 19 to 36 months old) against pertussis (whooping cough). Thirty-five states and Washington, D.C., do not have complete climate change adaption plans that include dealing with extreme weather events. Twenty states do not mandate licensed child care facilities to have a multi-hazard written evacuation plan. Thirteen state public health laboratories report they do not have sufficient capacity to work 5 12-hour days for 6 to 8 weeks in response to an infectious disease outbreak.[61] Obviously, there is still much work to be done.

World Community and Public Health in the Twenty-First Century

Like the United States, much progress has been made in the health of the people throughout the world in recent years. Life expectancy has increased by 6 years globally since 1990,[62] due primarily to (1) social and economic development, (2) the wider provision of safe water and sanitation facilities, and (3) the expansion of national health services. And, like in the United States a number of public health achievements took place in the first 10 years of the twenty-first century (see **Box 1.7**). However, all people of the world do not share in this increased life expectancy and better health. "There is still a major rich–poor divide: people in high-income countries continue to have a much better chance of living longer than people in low-income countries."[63]

In the paragraphs below we have identified some of the community and public health issues that the peoples of the world will be facing in years ahead.

Communicable Diseases

Even though information presented in Box 1.7 suggests that there have been a number of achievements with regard to communicable diseases throughout the world between 2001 and 2010, the burden of communicable diseases worldwide is still great. It is most vivid when looking at mortality. The leading causes of death in the world do not look much different than the leading causes of death in the United States. In fact, heart disease and cerebrovascular disease are the number one and two killers worldwide. However, when the leading causes of death are broken down by the wealth of the countries big differences appear. Five of the 10 leading causes of death are infectious diseases (e.g., lower respiratory infections, HIV/AIDS, diarrhoeal disease, malaria, and tuberculosis) in low- and middle-income countries, while nine of the 10 leading causes are noncommunicable diseases in high-income countries.[67] Similar trends appear when life expectancy is compared with the wealth of the countries. "A boy born in 2012 in a high-income country can expect to live to 75.8 years—more than 15 years longer than a boy born in a low-income country (60.2 years). For girls, the difference is even more marked; a gap of 18.9 years separates life expectancy in high-income (82.0 years) and low-income countries (63.1 years)."[62]

Poor Sanitation and Unsafe Drinking Water

Closely related to the problem of communicable diseases and related death are unsafe drinking water and poor sanitation. Worldwide, one out of every five deaths in children under the age of 5 years is due to a water-related disease.[68] Further, approximately 80% of all illnesses in developing countries are linked to poor water quality and unsanitary conditions.[68] For those individuals who grew up in a high-income country the thought of not having clean water and sanitary conditions is hard to understand. Yet, worldwide one in nine people, almost 900 million people,[69] do not have access to safe and clean drinking water, with over a third of those people living in sub-Saharan Africa.[68] In addition, an estimated 2.5 million people (more than 35% of the world's population) lack basic sanitation.[69] Access to safe drinking water, adequate sanitation, and proper hygiene education are essential to reducing illness and death, which in turn leads to improved health, poverty reduction, and socioeconomic development.[70]Access to safe drinking water, sanitation, and hygiene (WASH) are basic human rights.

BOX 1.7   Ten Great Public Health Achievements—Worldwide 2001–2010

At the conclusion of 2010, experts in global public health were asked to nominate noteworthy public health achievements that occurred outside of the United States during 2001–2010. From them, 10 were selected. Below, in no specific order, are the ones selected from the nominations.[64]

- *Reductions in Child Mortality.* Currently, an estimated 8.1 million children die each year before reaching their fifth birthday, a decrease of approximately 2 million between 2001–2010. Almost all (~99%) childhood deaths occur in low-income and middle-income countries, with 49% occurring in sub-Saharan Africa and 33% in southern Asia.
- *Vaccine-Preventable Deaths.* Over the 10-year period an estimated 2.5 million deaths were prevented each year among children less than 5 years of age through the use of measles, polio, and diphtheria-tetanus-pertussis vaccines.
- *Access to Safe Water and Sanitation.* Diarrhea, most of which is related to inadequate water, sanitation, and hygiene (WASH), kills 1.5 million children younger than 5 years of age annually. The proportion of the world's population with access to improved drinking water sources increased from 83% to 87% (covering an additional 800 million persons), and the proportion with access to improved sanitation increased from 58% to 61% (covering an additional 570 million persons).
- *Malaria Prevention and Control.* Malaria is the fifth leading cause of death from infectious disease worldwide and the second leading cause in Africa. Increased coverage with insecticide-treated bednets, indoor residual spraying, rapid diagnosis and prompt treatment with artemisinin combination therapy, and intermittent preventive treatment during pregnancy resulted a 21% decrease in estimated global malaria deaths between 2000 and 2009.
- *Prevention and Control of HIV/AIDS.* The HIV epidemic continues to be a global health challenge with 35.0 million people living with HIV at the end of 2013.[65] However, a number of public health interventions including provider-initiated HIV testing and counseling, prevention of mother-to-child HIV transmission, expanded availability and use of condoms and sterile injection equipment,

improved blood safety, and antiretroviral therapy (ART) have helped to reduce the number of new infections.
- *Tuberculosis Control.* Due in large part to the World Health Organization's (WHO) directly observed therapy, short-course (DOTS) strategy for TB control, focusing on finding and successfully treating TB cases with standardized regimens and rigorous treatment, and program monitoring during the decade, case detection and treatment success rates each have risen nearly 20%, with incidence and prevalence declining in every region.
- *Control of Neglected Tropical Diseases.* Neglected tropical diseases affect approximately one billion persons worldwide. Three of these diseases have been targeted for elimination or eradication: dracunculiasis (Guinea worm disease), onchocerciasis (river blindness) in the Americas, and lymphatic filariasis. Those programs targeting dracunculiasis and onchocerciasis in the Americas are on the verge of success, while the lymphatic filariasis programs are making progress.
- *Tobacco Control.* The global tobacco epidemic kills approximately six million people each year.[66] However, during the decade 168 countries adopted WHO's first global health treaty aimed at tobacco, 163 countries tracked tobacco use via surveys, and the total global population covered by smoke-free laws increased.
- *Increased Awareness and Response for Improving Global Road Safety.* Approximately 1.3 million persons die on the world's roads each year (3,000 every day), and this number is projected to double by 2030. Though the number of road deaths did not slow down during the past 10 years, a significant global effort was made to create a plan to reduce the forecasted growth in road fatalities.
- *Improved Preparedness and Response to Global Health Threats.* During the 10-year period of time, the public health community has improved preparedness for and detection of pandemic threats and is now responding more effectively than before. This is due in part to modernization of the international legal framework, better diseases surveillance techniques, better public health networking, and better global disease detection systems.

Hunger

Hunger can be defined in several different ways but the definition that applies here is the severe lack of food.[71] World hunger is not a problem of the amount of food but rather the maldistribution of the available food. Too many people are too poor to buy the available food, but lack the land and resources to grow it themselves,[72] or live in a climate that is not conducive to food production. Despite a 27% reduction in hunger worldwide since 2000[73] and an 11% decline in malnourished children in developing countries since 1990,[74] an estimated 795 million people, or about one in nine people in the world, are suffering from chronic undernourishment. Almost all these hungry people, 780 million, live in developing countries.[73] Furthermore, "malnutrition remains the underlying cause of death in an estimated 35% of all deaths among children under 5 years of age."[74]

Migration and Health

Recent political events in the Middle East and North Africa have ignited a dramatic increase in migration and the number of displaced people. By the end of 2013, 51.2 million individuals were displaced worldwide as a result of persecution, conflict, generalized violence, or human rights violations. Of this number, 16.7 million were refugees, 33 million were internally displaced persons (IDPs), and close to 1.2 million were asylum seekers.[75] Millions of people have lost everything.

The surge of refugees and migrants creates challenges that require adequate preparedness, rapid humanitarian responses, and increased technical assistance.[76] "It also causes unexpected pressure on health systems, especially at the local level where influx is first managed. Responding quickly and efficiently to the arrival of large groups of people in a country can be complex, resource-intensive, and challenging, especially when host countries are affected by economic crisis or are not fully prepared and local systems are not adequately supported."[76] Consider how difficult it is sometimes to get the appropriate health care in a resource-rich country like the United States, then consider how difficult it might be to receive appropriate health care in a new country where you are not familiar with the structure of the health care system, where you do not speak the language, where you lack transportation, and where you lack resources to pay for the services. What makes this situation even worse is that many of the refugees and migrants are in countries that lack enough resources for their own residents and are therefore overwhelmed by the influx of people.

Chapter Summary

- A number of key terms are associated with the study of community and public health, including health, community, community health, population health, public health, public health system, and global health.

- The four factors that affect the health of a community are physical (e.g., community size), social and cultural (e.g., religion), community organization, and individual behaviors (e.g., exercise and diet).

- It is important to be familiar with and understand the history of community health to be able to deal with the present and future community and public health issues.

- The earliest community and public health practices went unrecorded; however, archeological findings of ancient societies (before 500 B.C.E.) show evidence of concern for community and public health. There is evidence during the time of the classical cultures (500 B.C.E.–500 C.E.) that people were interested in physical strength, medicine, and sanitation.

- The belief of many living during the Middle Ages (500–1500 C.E.) was that health and disease were associated with spirituality. Many epidemics were seen during this period.

- During the Renaissance period (1500–1700 C.E.), there was a growing belief that disease was caused by the environment, not spiritual factors.

- The eighteenth century was characterized by industrial growth. Science was being used more in medicine and it was during this century that the first vaccine was discovered.

- The nineteenth century ushered in the modern era of public health. The germ theory was introduced during this time, and the last fourth of the century is known as the bacteriological period of public health.

- The twentieth century can be divided into several periods. The health resources development period (1900–1960) was a time when many public and private resources were used to improve health. The period of social engineering (1960–1973) saw the U.S. government's involvement in health insurance through Medicare and Medicaid. The health promotion period began in 1974 and continues today.

- *Healthy People 2020* and the National Prevention Strategy are important components of the community and public health agenda in the United States.

- In the second decade of twenty-first century great concern still exists in the United States for health care, the environment, diseases caused by an impoverished lifestyle, the spread of communicable diseases (such as AIDS, Legionnaires' disease, toxic shock syndrome, and Lyme disease), the harm caused by alcohol and other drug abuse, and terrorism.

- Although the health of the world population is improving, communicable diseases, poor sanitation and unsafe drinking water, hunger, and migration are burdens for many and impact the people who are poor much more than those who are not poor.

Scenario: Analysis and Response

The Internet has many sources of information that could help Amy and Eric with the decisions that they will have to make about the continued use of the day care center for their children. Use a search engine (e.g., Google, Bing) and enter (a) hepatitis and (b) hepatitis and day care centers. Print out the information that you find and use it in answering the following questions.

1. Based on the information you found on the Internet, if you were Amy or Eric would you take your children to the day care center the next day? Why or why not?

2. Do you believe the hepatitis problem in day care centers is a personal health concern or a community health concern? Why?

3. Which of the factors noted in this chapter that affect the health of a community play a part in the hepatitis problem faced by Amy and Eric?

4. Why does the hepatitis problem remind us of the health problems faced by people in this country prior to 1900?

5. Under which of the focus areas in the *Healthy People 2020* would hepatitis fall? Why?

Review Questions

1. How did the WHO define health in 1946? How has that definition been modified?

2. What is public health?

3. What are the differences among community health, population health, and global health?

4. What are the five major domains that determine a person's health?

5. What is the difference between personal health activities and community and public health activities?

6. Define the term *community*.

7. What are four major factors that affect the health of a community? Provide an example of each.

8. Identify some of the major events of community and public health in each of the following periods of time:

   Early civilizations (prior to 500 C.E.)

   Middle Ages (500–1500 C.E.)

   Renaissance and Exploration (1500–1700 C.E.)

   The eighteenth century

   The nineteenth century

9. Provide a brief explanation of the origins from which the following twentieth-century periods get their names:

   Health resources development period

   Period of social engineering

   Period of health promotion

10. What significance do the *Healthy People* documents have in community and public health development in recent years?

11. What significance do you think *Healthy People 2020* will have in the years ahead?

12. What is the National Prevention Strategy and who is responsible for it?

13. What are the major community and public health problems facing the United States and the World in the twenty-first century?

Activities

1. Write your own definition for health.

2. In a two-page paper, explain how the five major determinants of health could interact to cause a disease such as cancer.

3. In a one-page paper, explain why heart disease can be both a personal health problem and a community and public health problem.

4. Select a community and public health problem that exists in your hometown; then, using the factors that affect the health of a community noted in this chapter, analyze and discuss in a two-page paper at least three factors that contribute to the problem in your hometown.

5. Select one of the following individuals (all have been identified in this chapter). Using the Internet find three reliable websites that provide information on the individual, and then write a two-page paper on the person's contribution to community and public health.

Edward Jenner

John Snow

Lemuel Shattuck

Louis Pasteur

Robert Koch

Walter Reed

6. Review the *Healthy People 2020* website. Then, set up a time to talk with an administrator in your hometown health department. Find out which of the objectives the health department has been working on as priorities. Summarize in a paper what the objectives are, what the health department is doing about them, and what it hopes to accomplish by the year 2020.

References

1. Schneider, M.-J. (2017). *Introduction to Public Health*, 5th ed. Burlington, MA: Jones and Bartlett Learning.

2. National Center for Health Statistics. (2016). *Health, United States, 2015: With Special Feature on Racial and Ethnic Health Disparities.* Hyattsville, MD: CDC, National Center for Health Statistics. Available at http://www.cdc.gov/nchs/data/hus/hus15.pdf

3. Bunker, J. P., H. S. Frazier, and F. Mosteller (1994). "Improving Health: Measuring Effects of Medical Care." *Milbank Quarterly*, 72: 225–258.

4. Centers for Disease Control and Prevention (1999). "Ten Great Public Health Achievements—United States, 1900–1999." *Morbidity and Mortality Weekly Report*, 48(12): 241–243.

5. U.S. Department of Health and Human Services, Centers for Disease Control and Prevention (2011). "Ten Great Public Health Achievements—United States, 2001–2010." *Morbidity and Mortality Weekly Report*, 60(19): 619–623. Available at http://www.cdc.gov/mmwr/preview/mmwrhtml/mm6019a5.htm?s_cid=mm6019a5_w.

6. U.S. Department of Health and Human Services, Centers for Disease Control and Prevention (2015). "Current Cigarette Smoking Among Adults — United States, 2005–2014." *Morbidity and Mortality Weekly Report*, 64(44): 1233–1240. Available at http://www.cdc.gov/mmwr/pdf/wk/mm6444.pdf#page=1.

7. Centers for Disease Control and Prevention. (2016). Lead: What Do Parents Need to Know to Protect Their Children? Available at http://www.cdc.gov/nceh/lead/acclpp/blood_lead_levels.htm.

8. World Health Organization (2016). Glossary of Globalization, Trade, and Health Terms. Geneva, Switzerland: Author. Available at http://www.who.int/trade/glossary/story046/en/.

9. Turnock, B. J. (2016). *Public Health: What It Is and How It Works*, 6th ed. Burlington, MA: Jones & Bartlett Learning.

10. World Health Organization (2016). The Determinants of Health. Available at http://www.who.int/hia/evidence/doh/en/.

11. McGinnis, J. M., P. Williams-Russo, and J. R. Knickman (2002). "The Case for More Active Policy Attention to Health Promotion." *Health Affairs*, 21(2): 78–93.

12. Joint Committee on Health Education and Promotion Terminology. (2012). *Report of the 2011 Joint Committee on Health Education and Promotion Terminology*. Reston, VA: American Association of Health Education.

13. Israel, B. A., B. Checkoway, A. Schulz, and M. Zimmerman (1994). "Health Education and Community Empowerment: Conceptualizing and Measuring Perceptions of Individual, Organizational, and Community Control." *Health Education Quarterly*, 21(2): 149–170.

14. Institute of Medicine (2003). *The Future of the Public's Health in the 21st Century*. Washington, DC: National Academies Press.

15. Institute of Medicine (1988). *The Future of Public Health*. Washington, DC: National Academies Press.

16. Kindig, D., and G. Stoddart (2003). "What Is Population Health?" *American Journal of Public Health*, 93(3): 380–383.

17. Institute of Medicine (1997). *America's Vital Interest in Global Health: Protecting Our People, Enhancing Our Economy, and Advancing Our International Interests*. Washington, DC: National Academies Press. Available at http://books.nap.edu/openbook.php?record_id=5717&page=R1.

18. Coupland, K., S. Rikhy, K. Hill, and D. McNeil (2011). *State of Evidence: The Built Environment and Health 2011–2015*. Alberta, Canada: Public Health Innovation and Decision Support, Population, & Public Health, Alberta Health Services.

19. Davidson, A. (2015). *Social Determinants of Health: A Comparative Approach*. Ontario, Canada: Oxford University Press.

20. Institute of Medicine (IOM). (2005). *Does the Built Environment Influence Physical Activity? Examining the Evidence*. Washington, DC: National Academies Press.

21. American College Health Association (2015). *American College Health Association—National College Health Assessment II (ACHA-NCHA II) Fall 2015: Reference Group Executive Summary*. Available at http://www.acha-ncha.org/docs/NCHA-II%20FALL%202015%20REFERENCE%20GROUP%20EXECUTIVE%20SUMMARY.pdf.

22. Shi, L., and D. A. Singh (2017). *Essentials of the US Health Care System*, 4th ed. Burlington, MA: Jones and Bartlett Learning.

23. Issel, L. M. (2014). *Health Program Planning and Evaluation: A Practical Systematic Approach for Community Health*, 3rd ed. Burlington, MA: Jones and Bartlett Learning.

24. Minkler, M., and N. Wallerstein (2012). "Improving Health through Community Organization and Community Building: Perspectives from Health Education and Social Work." In M. Minkler, ed., *Community Organizing and Community Building for Health and Welfare*, 3rd ed. New Brunswick, NJ: Rutgers University Press, 37–58.

25. Ross, M. G. (1967). *Community Organization: Theory, Principles, and Practice*. New York: Harper & Row.

26. Pickett, G., and J. J. Hanlon (1990). *Public Health: Administration and Practice*, 9th ed. St. Louis: Times Mirror/Mosby.

27. Legon, R. P. (1986). "Ancient Greece." *World Book Encyclopedia*. Chicago: World Book.

28. Rosen, G. (1958). *A History of Public Health*. New York: MD Publications.

29. Burton, L. E., H. H. Smith, and A. W. Nichols (1980). *Public Health and Community Medicine*, 3rd ed. Baltimore: Williams & Wilkins.

30. Woodruff, A. W. (1977). "Benjamin Rush, His Work on Yellow Fever and His British Connections." *American Journal of Tropical Medicine and Hygiene*, 26(5): 1055–1059.

31. Rosen, G. (1975). *Preventive Medicine in the United States, 1900–1975*. New York: Science History Publications.

32. Smillie, W. G. (1955). *Public Health: Its Promise for the Future*. New York: Macmillan.

33. Duffy, J. (1990). *The Sanitarians: A History of American Public Health*. Chicago: University of Illinois Press.

34. Lalonde, M. (1974). *A New Perspective on the Health of Canadians: A Working Document*. Ottawa, Canada: Minister of Health.

35. Green, L. W. (1999). "Health Education's Contributions to the Twentieth Century: A Glimpse through Health Promotion's Rearview Mirror." In J. E. Fielding, L. B. Lave, and B. Starfield, eds., *Annual Review of Public Health*. Palo Alto, CA: Annual Reviews, 67–88.

36. U.S. Department of Health and Human Services, Public Health Service (1980). *Ten Leading Causes of Death in the United States, 1977*. Washington, DC: U.S. Government Printing Office.

37. U.S. Department of Health, Education, and Welfare (1979). *Healthy People: The Surgeon General's Report on Health Promotion and Disease Prevention* (DHEW pub. no. 79-55071). Washington, DC: U.S. Government Printing Office.

38. McKenzie, J. F., B. L. Neiger, and R. Thackeray (2017). *Planning, Implementing, and Evaluating Health Promotion Programs: A Primer*, 7th ed. Upper Saddle River, NJ: Pearson.

39. U.S. Department of Health and Human Services (1980). *Promoting Health/Preventing Disease: Objectives for the Nation*. Washington, DC: U.S. Government Printing Office.

40. U.S. Department of Health and Human Services (2016). *Healthy People.gov*. Available at https://www.healthypeople.gov/.

41. U.S. Department of Health and Human Services, Office of the Surgeon General (2011). *National Prevention Strategy*. Available at http://www.surgeongeneral.gov/priorities/prevention/strategy/index.html.

42. Keehan, S. P. et al. (2016). "National Health Expenditure Projections, 2015–25: Economy, Prices, and Aging Expected to Shape Spending and Enrollment." Health Affairs, 35(7): online. Available at http://content.healthaffairs.org/content/early/2016/07/15/hlthaff.2016.0459.full?sid=0f04d9b8-fb59-4a91-h8h4-7de5beb50538.

43. U.S. Census Bureau (2015). *World Population: Total Midyear Population for the World: 1950–2050*. Available at http://www.census.gov/population/international/data/worldpop/table_population.php.

44. National Center for Health Statistics (2015). *Mortality in the United States, 2014*. Available at: http://www.cdc.gov/nchs/data/databriefs/db229.htm.

45. Centers for Disease Control and Prevention (CDC). (2015). *Chronic Disease Overview*. Available at: http://www.cdc.gov/chronicdisease/overview/index.htm.

46. van Dam, R. M., T. Li, D. Spiegelman, O. H. Franco, and F. B. Hu (2008). "Combined Impact of Lifestyle Factors on Mortality: Prospective Cohort Study of U.S. Women." *British Medical Journal*, 337, a1440.

47. Centers for Disease Control (1981). "Pneumocystis Pneumonia—Los Angeles." *Morbidity and Mortality Weekly Report*, 30: 250–252.

48. Centers for Disease Control (1989). "First 100,000 Cases of Acquired Immunodeficiency Syndrome—United States." *Morbidity and Mortality Weekly Report*, 38: 561–563.

49. Centers for Disease Control (1992). "The Second 100,000 Cases of Acquired Immunodeficiency Syndrome—United States, June 1981–December 1991." *Morbidity and Mortality Weekly Report*, 42(2): 28–29.

50. Centers for Disease Control and Prevention (2015). *HIV in the United States: At a Glance*. Available at http://www.cdc.gov/hiv/statistics/overview/ataglance.html.

51. Shi, L., and D. A. Singh (2013). *Essentials of the US Health Care System*, 3rd ed. Burlington, MA: Jones and Bartlett Learning.

52. National Institute on Drug Abuse (2015). *Trends & Statistics: Costs of Substance Abuse*. Available at https://www.drugabuse.gov/related-topics/trends-statistics.

53. National Institute on Drug Abuse (2015). *Naloxone Prescriptions from Pharmacies Increased Ten-Fold*. Available at https://www.drugabuse.gov/news-events/news-releases/2016/02/naloxone-prescriptions-pharmacies-increased-ten-fold.

54. National Institute on Drug Abuse (2015). *FDA Approves Naloxone Nasal Spray to Reverse Opioid Overdose*. Available at https://www.drugabuse.gov/news-events/news-releases/2015/11/fda-approves-naloxone-nasal-spray-to-reverse-opioid-overdose.

55. Centers for Disease Control and Prevention (2016). *CDC Guideline for Prescribing Opioids for Chronic Pain*. Available at http://www.cdc.gov/drugoverdose/prescribing/guideline.html.

56. King, N. B. (2014). "Health Inequalities and Health Inequities." In E. E. Morrison and B. Furlong, eds., *Health Care Ethics: Critical Issues for the 21st Century*. Burlington, MA: Jones and Bartlett Learning, 301–316.

57. Federal Emergency Management Agency (2014). "Are You Ready? An In-Depth Guide to Citizen Preparedness." Available at https://www.ready.gov/are-you-ready-guide.

58. Agency for Health Care Research and Quality (2004). *Bioterrorism and Health System Preparedness* (Issue Brief no. 2). Available at http://archive.ahrq.gov/news/ulp/btbriefs/btbrief2.pdf.

59. Centers for Disease Control and Prevention (2014). *The Community Guide: Emergency Preparedness and Response*. Available at http://www.thecommunityguide.org/emergencypreparedness/index.html.

60. Katz, R. (2013). *Essentials of Public Health Preparedness*. Burlington, MA: Jones & Bartlett Learning.

61. Trust for America's Health and the Robert Wood Johnson Foundation (2012). *Ready or Not?: Protecting the Public's Health from Disease, Disasters, and Bioterrrorism*. Available at http://healthyamericans.org/report/101/.

62. World Health Organization (2014). *World Health Statistics 2014: A Wealth of Information on Global Public Health*. Available at http://www.who.int/gho/publications/world_health_statistics/2014/en/.

63. World Health Organization (2016). *World Health Statistics 2014: Large Gains in Life Expectancy*. Available at http://www.who.int/mediacentre/news/releases/2014/world-health-statistics-2014/en/.

64. U.S. Department of Health and Human Services, Centers for Disease Control and Prevention (2011). "Ten Great Public Health Achievements — Worldwide, 2001–2010." *Morbidity and Mortality Weekly Report*, 60(24): 814–818. Available at http://www.cdc.gov/mmwr/preview/mmwrhtml/mm6024a4.htm.

65. World Health Organization (2016). *Global Health Observatory (GHO) Data: HIV/AIDS*. Available at http://www.who.int/gho/hiv/en/.

66. World Health Organization (2016). *Tobacco-Free Initiative (TFI): Tobacco Control Economics*. Available at http://www.who.int/tobacco/economics/en/.

67. World Health Organization (2014). *The Top 10 Causes of Death*. Available at http://www.who.int/mediacentre/factsheets/fs310/en/.

68. The Water Project (2014). *Facts About Water: Statistics of the Water Crisis*. Available at https://thewaterproject.org/water_stats.

69. Centers for Disease Control and Prevention (2015). *Sanitation & Hygiene*. Available at http://www.cdc.gov/healthywater/global/sanitation/index.html.

70. Centers for Disease Control and Prevention (2015). *Global Water, Sanitation & Hygiene (WASH)*. Available at http://www.cdc.gov/healthywater/global/sanitation/index.html.

71. "Hunger." (n.d.). *Merriam-Webster Dictionary*. Available at http://www.merriam-webster.com/dictionary/hunger.

72. United Nations (2006). *Opportunities and Risks: Food Security.* Available at http://www.unep.org/dewa/Africa/publications/AEO-2/content/157.htm.

73. International Food Policy Research Institute (2015). *Global Hunger Index 2015 Fact Sheet.* Available at http://www.ifpri.org/news-release/global-hunger-index-2015-fact-sheet.

74. World Health Organization (2014). *Twelfth General Programme of Work: Not Merely the Absence of Disease.* Available at http://www.who.int/about/resources_planning/twelfth-gpw/en/.

75. United Nations High Commission for Refugees (UNHCR) (2014). *UNHCR: Global Trends 2013.* Available at http://www.scribd.com/doc/230536635/UNHCR-Global-Trends-Report-2014#scribd.

76. World Health Organization, Regional Office for Europe (2014). *Stepping Up Action on Refugee and Migrant Health.* Available at http://www.euro.who.int/—data/assets/pdf_file/0008/298196/Stepping-up-action-on-refugee-migrant-health.pdf.

CHAPTER 2

Organizations that Help Shape Community and Public Health

Chapter Outline

Chapter Objectives

After studying this chapter, you will be able to:

1. Summarize the need for organizing to improve community and public health.

2. Explain what a governmental health organization is and give an example of one at each of the following levels—international, national, state, and local.

3. Discuss the role the World Health Organization (WHO) plays in community and public health.

4. Briefly describe the structure and function of the United States Department of Health and Human Services (HHS).

5. State the three core functions of public health.

6. List the 10 essential public health services.

7. Describe the relationship between a state and local health department.

8. Explain what is meant by the term Whole School, Whole Community, Whole Child (WSCC).

9. Define the term quasi-governmental and explain why some health organizations are classified under this term.

10. List the four primary activities of most voluntary health organizations.

11. Explain the purpose of a professional health organization/association.

12. Demonstrate how philanthropic foundations contribute to community and public health.

13. Discuss the role that service, social, and religious organizations play in community and public health.

14. Identify the major reason why corporations are involved in community and public health and describe some corporate activities that contribute to community and public health.

Scenario

Mary is a hardworking senior at the local university. She is majoring in physical education and looking forward to teaching elementary physical education after graduation. Mary has always been involved in team sports and has been a lifeguard at the local swimming pool for the past 4 years. Mary has a fair complexion with honey-blonde hair and blue eyes. She has always tanned easily, so has not bothered very much with sunscreens. For the past few weeks, Mary has noticed a red, scaly, sharply outlined patch of skin on her forehead. She has put creams and ointments on it, but it will not go away and may be getting larger. Her roommate, Clare, suggests that she should make an appointment with the campus health services office. Mary lets it go another week and then decides to see the doctor.

After looking at the patch of skin, the doctor refers Mary to a specialist, Dr. Rice, who is a dermatologist. The dermatologist suggests a biopsy be taken of the lesion to test for skin cancer. The specialist tells Mary that if it is cancer, it is probably still in its early stages and so the prognosis is good.

A potential diagnosis of cancer often raises a lot of questions and concerns. Are there any resources in the community to which Mary can turn for help?

Introduction

The history of community and public health dates to antiquity. For much of that history, community and public health issues were addressed only on an emergency basis. For example, if a community faced a drought or an epidemic, a town meeting would be called to deal with the problem. It has been only in the last 100 years or so that communities have taken explicit actions to deal aggressively with health issues on a continual basis.

Today's communities differ from those of the past in several important ways. Although individuals are better educated, more mobile, and more independent than in the past, communities are less autonomous and are more dependent on state and federal funding for support. Contemporary communities are too large and complex to respond effectively to sudden health emergencies or to make long-term improvements in community and public health without community organization and careful planning. Better community organizing and careful long-term planning are essential to ensure that a community makes the best use of its resources for health, both in times of emergency and over the long run.

The ability of today's communities to respond effectively to their own problems is hindered by the following characteristics: (1) highly developed and centralized resources in our national institutions and organizations; (2) continuing concentration of wealth and population in the largest metropolitan areas; (3) rapid movement of information, resources, and people made possible by advanced communication and transportation technologies that eliminate the need for local offices where resources were once housed; (4) the globalization of health; (5) limited horizontal relationships between/among organizations; and (6) a system of **top-down funding** (an approach where money is transmitted from either the federal or state government to the local level) for many community programs.[1]

In this chapter, we discuss organizations that help to shape a community's ability to respond effectively to health-related issues by protecting and promoting the health of the community and its members. These community organizations can be classified as governmental, quasi-governmental, and nongovernmental—according to their sources of funding, responsibilities, and organizational structure.

Top-down funding a method of funding in which funds are transmitted from federal or state government to the local level

Governmental health agencies health agencies that are part of the governmental structure (federal, state, or local) and that are funded primarily by tax dollars

Governmental Health Agencies

Governmental health agencies are part of the governmental structure (federal, state, tribal and/or territorial, or local). They are funded primarily by tax dollars and managed by government officials. Each governmental health agency is designated as having authority over some geographic area. Such agencies exist at the four governmental levels—international, national, state, and local.

International Health Agencies

The most widely recognized international governmental health organization today is the **World Health Organization (WHO)** (see **Figure 2.1**). Its headquarters is located in Geneva, Switzerland, and there are six regional offices around the world. The names, acronyms, and cities and countries of location for WHO regional offices are as follows: Africa (AFRO), Brazzaville, Congo; Americas (PAHO), Washington, D.C., United States; Eastern Mediterranean (EMRO), Cairo, Egypt; Europe (EURO), Copenhagen, Denmark; Southeast Asia (SEARO), New Delhi, India; and Western Pacific (WPRO), Manila, Philippines.[2]

Although the WHO is now the largest international health organization, it is not the oldest. Among the organizations (listed with their founding dates) that predate WHO are the following:

* International D'Hygiène Publique (1907); absorbed by the WHO
* Health Organization of the League of Nations (1919); dissolved when the WHO was created
* United Nations Relief and Rehabilitation Administration (1943); dissolved in 1946—its work is carried out today by the Office of the United Nations High Commissioner for Refugees (UNHCR) (1950)
* United Nations Children's Fund (UNICEF) (1946); formerly known as the United Nations International Children's Emergency Fund
* Pan American Health Organization (PAHO) (1902); still an independent organization but is integrated with WHO in a regional office

Because the WHO is the largest and most visible international health agency, it is discussed at greater length in the following sections.

World Health Organization (WHO) the most widely recognized international governmental health organization

FIGURE 2.1   China's Margaret Chan, Director General of the World Health Organization, speaks during an end-of-year press conference at the World Health Organization (WHO) headquarters in Geneva, Switzerland.
© Laurent Gillieron/Keystone/AP Images.

History of the World Health Organization

Planning for the WHO began when a charter of the United Nations was adopted at an international meeting in 1945. Contained in the charter was an article calling for the establishment of a health agency with wide powers. In 1946, at the International Health Conference, representatives from all of the countries in the United Nations succeeded in creating and ratifying the constitution of the WHO. However, it was not until April 7, 1948 that the constitution went into force and the organization officially began its work. In recognition of this beginning, April 7 is commemorated each year as World Health Day.[2] The sixtieth anniversary of the WHO was celebrated in 2008.

Organization of the World Health Organization

"WHO is a United Nations specialized agency concentrating exclusively on health by providing technical cooperation, carrying out programmes to control and eradicate disease and striving to improve the quality of human life."[3] Membership in the WHO is open to any nation that has ratified the WHO constitution and receives a majority vote of the World Health Assembly. At the beginning of 2016, 194 countries were members. The World Health Assembly comprises the delegates of the member nations. This assembly, which meets in general sessions annually and in special sessions when necessary, has the primary tasks of approving the WHO program and the budget for the following biennium and deciding major policy questions.[2]

The WHO is administered by a staff that includes an appointed director–general, deputy director–general, seven assistant directors–general, and six regional directors. Great care is taken to ensure political balance in staffing WHO positions, particularly at the higher levels of administration. "More than 7,000 people from more than 150 countries work for the Organization in over 150 WHO country offices, 6 regional offices, at the Global Service Centre in Malaysia and at the headquarters in Geneva, Switzerland."[2]

Purpose and Work of the World Health Organization

The primary objective of the WHO "shall be the attainment by all peoples of the highest possible level of health."[4] To achieve this objective, the WHO has 6 core functions that describe the nature of its work. They are:[5]

- Providing leadership on matters critical to health and engaging in partnerships where joint action is needed
- Shaping the research agenda and stimulating the generation, translation, and dissemination of valuable knowledge
- Setting norms and standards, and promoting and monitoring their implementation;
- articulating ethical and evidence-based policy options
- Providing technical support, catalyzing change, and building sustainable institutional capacity
- Monitoring the health situation and assessing health trends

The work of the WHO is financed by its member states with assessed and voluntary contributions. Each member state is assessed according to its ability to pay; the wealthiest countries contribute the most. Voluntary contributions also come from the member states and account for more than three quarters of the budget financing.[2]

Although the WHO has sponsored and continues to sponsor many worthwhile programs, an especially noteworthy one was the work of the WHO in helping to eradicate smallpox. At one time, smallpox was the world's most feared disease until it was eradicated by a collaborative global vaccination program led by WHO.[2] The year 2015 marked the thirty-fifth anniversary of this eradication. In 1967, smallpox was active in 31 countries. During that year, 10 million to 15 million people contracted the disease, and of those, approximately 2 million died. Many millions of others were permanently disfigured or blinded. The last known natural case of smallpox was diagnosed on October 26, 1977, in Somalia.[2] In 1978, a laboratory accident in Birmingham, England resulted in one death and a limited outbreak of the acute disease. In 1979, the World Health Assembly declared the global eradication of this disease. Using the smallpox mortality figures from 1967, it can be estimated that more than 60 million lives have been saved since the eradication.

More recently, the WHO has led the efforts to contain the outbreaks of Ebola. Since July 2014 unparalleled progress has been made in establishing systems and tools that allow for rapid and effective response. Thanks to the diligence and dedication of tens of thousands of responders, scientists, researchers, developers, volunteers, and manufacturers, there are now six rapid diagnostic tools that can detect the Ebola virus in a matter of hours, 24 worldwide testing laboratories, an Ebola vaccine, registered foreign medical teams, and thousands of trained responders who can rapidly deploy to outbreaks.[6]

The work of WHO is outlined in its "general programme of work." This document, which is a requirement of the WHO constitution, "provides a vision and is used to guide the work of the organization during a pre-determined period of time."[4] At the time this book was revised the WHO was working under the *Twelfth General Programme of Work*,[5] which covers the six years from 2014 to 2019. The categories of work covered in this document include communicable diseases, noncommunicable diseases, health throughout the life cycle, health systems, preparedness, surveillance, and response; and, corporate services and enabling functions.

In addition to the program of work, much of the recent work of WHO is outlined in the United Nations Millennium Declaration, which was adopted at the Millennium Summit in 2003.[7] The declaration set out principles and values in seven areas (peace, security, and disarmament; development and poverty eradication; protecting our common environment; human rights, democracy, and good governance; protecting the vulnerable; meeting special needs of Africa; and strengthening the United Nations) that should govern international relations in the twenty-first century.[7] Following the summit, the *Road Map* was prepared, which established goals and targets to be reached by 2015 in each of the seven areas.[8] The resulting eight goals in the area of development and poverty eradication were referred to as the Millennium Development Goals (MDGs). More specifically, the MDGs were aimed at reducing poverty and hunger,

TABLE 2.1 Selected Achievements Found in the Millennium Development Goals

- "Extreme poverty has declined significantly over the last two decades. In 1990, nearly half of the population in the developing world lived on less than $1.25 a day; that proportion dropped to 14 percent in 2015."
- "The primary school net enrollment rate in the developing regions has reached 91 percent in 2015, up from 83 percent in 2000."
- "Many more girls are now in school compared to 15 years ago. The developing regions as a whole have achieved the target to eliminate gender disparity in primary, secondary, and tertiary education."
- "The global under-five mortality rate has declined by more than half, dropping from 90 to 43 deaths per 1,000 live births between 1990 and 2015."
- "Since 1990, the maternal mortality ratio has declined by 45 percent worldwide, and most of the reduction has occurred since 2000."
- "New HIV infections fell by approximately 40 percent between 2000 and 2013, from an estimated 3.5 million cases to 2.1 million."
- "Ozone-depleting substances have been virtually eliminated since 1990, and the ozone layer is expected to recover by the middle of this century."
- "Official development assistance from developed countries increased by 66 percent in real terms between 2000 and 2014, reaching $135.2 billion."

Data from: United Nations (2015). *The Millennium Development Goals Report: 2015*. New York: Author. Available at http://www.un.org/millenniumgoals/2015_MDG_Report/pdf/MDG%202015%20rev%20%28July%201%29.pdf.

Sustainable Development Goals (SDGs) goals created by the WHO to build on the work accomplished via the Millennium Development Goals (MDGs).

tackling ill health, gender inequality, lack of education, lack of access to improved drinking water, and environmental degradation. Much success was made with the MDGs. Unified efforts have produced data that prove the MDGs have saved millions of lives and improved conditions from targeted interventions, sound strategies, and adequate resources. The momentum must continue because uneven achievements and shortfalls continue to exist; therefore, the work must continue into the new development era[9](see **Table 2.1**). As noted above, the MDGs were not exclusively aimed at health, but there were interactive processes between health and economic development that create a crucial link. That is, better health is "a prerequisite and major contributor to economic growth and social cohesion. Conversely, improvement in people's access to health technology is a good indicator of the success of other development processes."[10]

Strategies for achieving large-scale and rapid progress toward meeting the MDGs involved strong government leadership and policies and strategies that meet the needs of the poor, combined with sufficient funding and technical support from the international community.[9]

The work behind the MDGs has proven to be effective in monitoring development through measurable data to track interventions, performance, and accountability. Although much progress has been made, there is still much more work to be done. Moving forward, challenges will be addressed through a new universal and transformative post-2015 development agenda of MDGs supported by a set of 17 goals referred to as the **Sustainable Development Goals** (SDGs). SDGs were established to be interconnected and concentrated towards eradicating poverty, addressing climate change, and increasing economic growth. The goals were developed by world leaders in September 2015 to build on the MDGs and improve the lives of people through a global, unified effort.[11] SDGs are not considered legally binding; however, they do seek improved availability, quality, and timeliness of data, national level analyses, and global level outcome.[11] **Table 2.2** provides a listing of the 17 SDGs.

National Health Agencies

Each national government has a department or agency that has the primary responsibility for the protection of the health and welfare of its citizens. These national health agencies meet their responsibilities through the development of health policies, the enforcement of health regulations, the provision of health services and programs, the funding of research, and the support of their respective state and local health agencies.

TABLE 2.2	Seventeen Sustainable Development Goals
Goal 1	End poverty in all its forms everywhere.
Goal 2	End hunger, achieve food security and improved nutrition, and promote sustainable agriculture.
Goal 3	Ensure healthy lives and promote well-being for all at all ages.
Goal 4	Ensure inclusive and equitable quality education and promote lifelong learning opportunities for all.
Goal 5	Achieve gender equality and empower all women and girls.
Goal 6	Ensure availability and sustainable management of water and sanitation for all.
Goal 7	Ensure access to affordable, reliable, sustainable, and modern energy for all.
Goal 8	Promote sustained, inclusive, and sustainable economic growth; full and productive employment; and decent work for all.
Goal 9	Build resilient infrastructure, promote inclusive and sustainable industrialization, and foster innovation.
Goal 10	Reduce inequality within and among countries.
Goal 11	Make cities and human settlements inclusive, safe, resilient, and sustainable.
Goal 12	Ensure sustainable consumption and production patterns.
Goal 13	Take urgent action to combat climate change and its impacts.
Goal 14	Conserve and sustainably use the oceans, seas, and marine resources for sustainable development.
Goal 15	Protect, restore, and promote sustainable use of terrestrial ecosystems, sustainably manage forests, combat desertification, and halt and reverse land degradation and halt biodiversity loss.
Goal 16	Promote peaceful and inclusive societies for sustainable development, provide access to justice for all, and build effective, accountable, and inclusive institutions at all levels.
Goal 17	Strengthen the means of implementation and revitalize the global partnership for sustainable development.

Data from: United Nations (2016). *Sustainable Development Goals: 17 Goals to Transform Our World.* Available at http://www.un.org/sustainabledevelopment/

In the United States, the primary national health agency is the Department of Health and Human Services (HHS). HHS "is the United States government's principal agency for protecting the health of all Americans and providing essential human services, especially for those who are least able to help themselves."[12] It is important to note, however, that other federal agencies also contribute to the betterment of our nation's health. For example, the Department of Agriculture inspects meat and dairy products and coordinates the Special Supplemental Nutrition Program for Women, Infants, and Children, better known as the WIC food assistance program; the Environmental Protection Agency (EPA) regulates hazardous wastes; the Department of Labor houses the Occupational Safety and Health Administration (OSHA), which is concerned with safety and health in the workplace; the Department of Commerce, which includes the Bureau of the Census, collects much of the national data that drive our nation's health programs; and the Department of Homeland Security (DHS) deals with all aspects of terrorism within the United States. A detailed description of the Department of Health and Human Services follows.

Department of Health and Human Services

The HHS is headed by the Secretary of Health and Human Services, who is appointed by the president and is a member of his or her cabinet. The Department of Health and Human Services was formed in 1980 (during the administration of President Jimmy Carter), when the Department of Health, Education, and Welfare (HEW) was divided into two new departments, HHS and the Department of Education. HHS is the department most involved with the nation's human concerns. In one way or another it touches the lives of more Americans than any other federal agency. It is literally a department of people serving people, from newborn infants to persons requiring health services to our most elderly citizens. With an annual budget in excess of approximately $1.150 trillion (representing about 25% of the federal budget), HHS is the largest department in the federal government.[12,13]

The fiscal year 2010 overview document of the United States government budget indicated that the approved HHS budget established a reserve fund of more than $630 billion, over a 10-year period, to fund health care system reform. According to the HHS budget document, "the reserve is funded half by new revenue and half by savings proposals that promote efficiency and accountability, align incentives toward quality, and encourage shared responsibility. In addition, the Budget calls for an effort beyond this down payment, to put the Nation on a path to health insurance coverage for all Americans."[14] To date, some significant legislation has been passed that works toward fundamental health care reform, such as the American Recovery and Reinvestment Act (ARRA) of 2009, which includes $22 billion for health information technology, subsidies for those who are recently unemployed to maintain health insurance, and $1 billion for continued effectiveness research in health.[13] Moreover, in March 2010, a sweeping bill to overhaul the American medical system, put forth by President Barack Obama, was passed by a historic vote of 219 votes to 212. The new health care reform law provided a series of duties and responsibilities for the HHS. Among these were (1) the implementation of new provisions to assist families and small business owners in getting information to make the best choices for insurance coverage, in a new transparent, competitive insurance marketplace; (2) working with states and additional partners to strengthen public programs, such as the Children's Health Insurance Program (CHIP), Medicare, and Medicaid; (3) coordinating efforts with other departments to design and implement "a prevention and health promotion strategy" to promote prevention, wellness, and public health; (4) taking action to strengthen and support the primary care workforce; (5) taking on the new and improved authority to establish a transparent health care system to oversee that every dollar authorized to be spent in the act is done so in a wise and transparent manner; (6) the implementation of new provisions to decrease the costs of medications; (7) taking on authority to establish the Community Living Assistance Services and Supports Act (CLASS Act), which is a voluntary, self-funded long-term care insurance option; and (8) the implementation of the Indian Health Care Improvement Act (IHCIA), which was reauthorized in the new health care law and provides modernized and improved health care services to Alaska Natives and American Indians.[14] This revolutionary commitment has advanced access, quality, and affordability in the nation's health care system to historic levels by providing more than 90% of American with health care coverage through the Affordable Care Act.[14]

Since its formation, HHS has undergone several reorganizations. Some of the more recent changes have been the addition of the Center for Faith-Based and Community Initiatives and an Assistant Secretary for Public Health Emergency Preparedness. Currently, the HHS is organized into 11 operating agencies (see **Figure 2.2**) whose heads report directly to the Secretary. In addition, the HHS has 10 regional offices (see **Table 2.3**). These offices serve as representatives of the Secretary of HHS in direct, official dealings with the state and local governmental organizations. Eight of the 11 operating divisions of HHS (AHRQ, ATSDR, CDC, FDA, HRSA, IHS, NIH, and SAMSHA—see their descriptions below), along with Office of Global Affairs (OGA), the Office of Public Health and Science (OPHS), and the Office of the Assistant Secretary for Preparedness and Response (ASPR), now constitute the Public Health Service (PHS). Another three operating divisions (CMS, ACF, and ACL) comprise the human services operating divisions.

Administration for Community Living (ACL)

The ACL, which was established in 2012, is the division of the HHS that integrates efforts of the Administration on Aging (AoA), the Administration on Disabilities (AoD), the National Institute on Disability, Independent Living, and Rehabilitation Research (NIDILRR), the Center for Integrated Programs (CIP), the Center for Management and Budget (CMB), and the Center for Policy and Evaluation (CPE).[15] The ACL serves as the federal agency responsible for increasing access to community supports, while focusing attention and resources on the unique needs of older Americans and people with disabilities across the lifespan.

Administration for Children and Families (ACF)

The ACF is composed of a number of smaller agencies and is responsible for providing direction and leadership for all federal programs to ensure children and families are resilient and

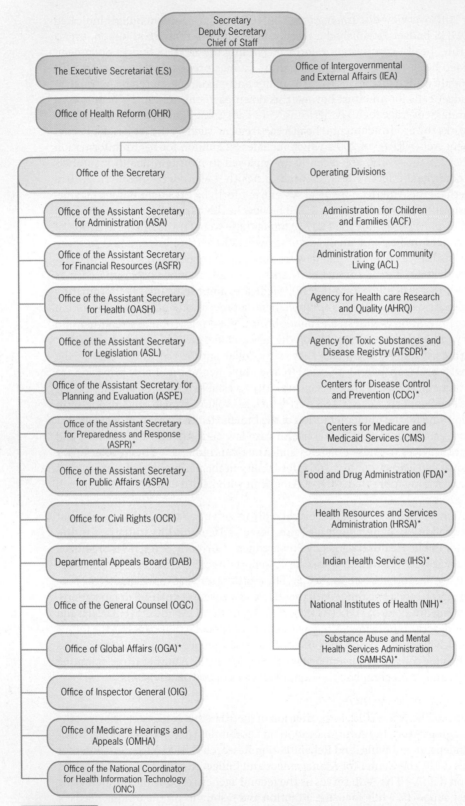

FIGURE 2.2   Organizational chart for the U.S. Department of Health and Human Services (HHS).

*Designates a component of the U.S. Public Health Service

Data from: U.S. Department of Health and Human Services (2016). U.S. Department of Health and Human Services Organizational Chart. Available at http://www.hhs.gov/about/agencies/orgchart/index.html.

TABLE 2.3 Regional Offices of the U.S. Department of Health and Human Services

Region/Areas Served	Office Address	Telephone Number
Region 1: CT, MA, ME, NH, RI, VT	John F. Kennedy Bldg. Government Center Boston, MA 02203	(617) 565-1500
Region 2: NJ, NY, Puerto Rico, Virgin Islands	Jacob K. Javits Federal Bldg. 26 Federal Plaza, Suite 3835 New York, NY 10278	(212) 264-4600
Region 3: DE, MD, PA, VA, WV, DC	Public Ledger Building 150 S. Independence Mall West Suite 436 Philadelphia, PA 19106	(215) 861-4633
Region 4: AL, FL, GA, KY, MS, NC, SC, TN	Atlanta Federal Center 61 Forsyth Street, SW Atlanta, GA 30303	(404) 562-7888
Region 5: IL, IN, MI, MN, OH, WI	233 N. Michigan Avenue, Suite 1300 Chicago, IL 60601	(312) 353-5160
Region 6: AR, LA, NM, OK, TX	1301 Young Street, Suite 1124 Dallas, TX 75202	(214) 767-3301
Region 7: IA, KS, MO, NE	Bolling Federal Building 601 East 12th Street, Room S1801 Kansas City, MO 64106	(816) 426-2821
Region 8: CO, MT, ND, SD, UT, WY	Bryon G. Rogers Federal Office Building 999 18th Street, Suite 400 Denver, CO 80202	(303) 844-3372
Region 9: AZ, CA, HI, NV, American Samoa, Guam, Commonwealth of the Northern Mariana Islands, Federated States of Micronesia, Republic of the Marshall Islands, Republic of Palau	Federal Office Building 50 United Nations Plaza 90 Seventh Street, Suite 5-100 San Francisco, CA 94103	(415) 437-8500
Region 10: AK, ID, OR, WA	701 Fifth Avenue, Suite 1600 MS-01 Seattle, WA 98121	(206) 615-2010

Data from: U.S. Department of Health and Human Services. *HHS Region Map.* Available at http://www.hhs.gov/about/agencies/iea/regional-offices/index.html.

economically secure. One of the better-known programs originating from this division is Head Start, which serves nearly one million preschool children. Other programs are aimed at family assistance, refugee resettlement, and child support enforcement. In 2015, Head Start celebrated 50 years of service in school readiness of young children from low-income families.

Agency for Health Care Research and Quality (AHRQ)

Prior to 1999, this division of the HHS was called the Agency for Health Care Policy and Research, but its name was changed as part of the Health Care Research and Quality Act of 1999. AHRQ is "the Nation's lead federal agency for research on health care quality, costs, outcomes, and patient safety."[16] AHRQ sponsors and conducts research that provides evidence-based information on health care outcomes; quality; and cost, use, and access. The information helps health

Superfund legislation
legislation enacted to deal with the cleanup of hazardous substances in the environment

care decision makers—patients and clinicians, health system leaders, and policy makers—make more informed decisions and improve the quality of health care services.

Agency for Toxic Substances and Disease Registry (ATSDR)

This agency was created by the **Superfund legislation** (Comprehensive Environmental Response, Compensation, and Liability Act) in 1980. This legislation was enacted to deal with the cleanup of hazardous substances in the environment. ATSDR's mission is to "serve the public through responsive public health actions to promote healthy and safe environments and prevent harmful exposures."[17]

To carry out its mission and to serve the needs of the American public, ATSDR evaluates information on hazardous substances released into the environment in order to assess the impact on public health; conducts and sponsors studies and other research related to hazardous substances and adverse human health effects; establishes and maintains registries of human exposure (for long-term follow-up) and complete listings of areas closed to the public or otherwise restricted in use due to contamination; summarizes and makes data available on the effects of hazardous substances; and provides consultations and training to ensure adequate response to public health emergencies. Although ATSDR has been responding to chemical emergencies in local communities across the country for the last 35 + years, like many of the other federal health agencies its work has taken on new meaning since 9/11. For example, some of the projects the agency's staff worked on or continue to work on include sampling dust in New York City residences after 9/11; working with New York health agencies to create a registry of people who lived or worked near the World Trade Center (WTC) on 9/11 to collect health information on those most heavily exposed to smoke, dust, and debris from the collapse of the WTC; conducting environmental sampling at anthrax-contaminated buildings; and disseminating critical information to agencies and organizations with a role in terrorism preparedness and response.[18]

Centers for Disease Control and Prevention (CDC)

The CDC, located in Atlanta, Georgia (see **Figure 2.3**), "is the nation's leading health agency, dedicated to saving lives and protecting the health of Americans."[19] "The CDC serves as the national focus for developing and applying disease prevention and control, environmental health, and health promotion and education activities designed to improve the health of the people of the United States."[20] Once known solely for its work to control communicable diseases, the CDC now also maintains records, analyzes disease trends, and publishes epidemiological reports on all types of diseases, including those that result from lifestyle, occupational, and environmental causes. Beyond its own specific responsibilities, the CDC also supports state and local health departments and cooperates with similar national health agencies from other WHO member nations.

Currently, the CDC uses the tagline of "CDC 24/7" as a summary statement for its current role, which includes:

FIGURE 2.3 The Centers for Disease Control and Prevention (CDC) in Atlanta, Georgia is one of the major operating components of the Department of Health and Human Services (HHS).
Courtesy of James Gathany/CDC.

- "Detecting and responding to new and emerging health threats
- Tackling the biggest health problems causing death and disability for Americans
- Putting science and advanced technology into action to prevent disease
- Promoting healthy and safe behaviors, communities, and environment
- Developing leaders and training the public health workforce, including disease detectives
- Taking the health pulse of our nation."[21]

To carry out its work the CDC is organized into Centers, Institutes, and Offices (CIOs). The CIOs "allow the agency to be more responsive and effective when dealing with public health concerns. Each group implements the CDC's response in their areas of expertise, while also providing intra-agency support and resource-sharing for cross-cutting issues and specific health threats."[22] **Figure 2.4** shows how the CIOs are organized in the CDC.

Like other public health agencies, the CDC's most important achievements are the outbreaks that do not happen, the communicable diseases that are stopped before spreading, and the lives saved from preventable chronic diseases and injuries.[23] Some of the most recent visible work of the CDC has included the Ebola outbreak in 2014 and the Zika outbreak in 2015–16. When West Africa experienced the largest Ebola outbreak in history, the CDC was there to help. "In response to the outbreak, CDC activated its Emergency Operations Center to coordinate technical assistance and control activities with other U.S. government agencies, the World Health Organization, and other domestic and international partners. CDC also deployed teams of public health experts to West Africa".[24]

While the Ebola outbreak was half a world away, the Zika virus was much closer in South America with the potential to move northward into the United States. In an effort to assist in controlling the outbreak, personnel from the CDC and the Pan American Health Organization worked with public health experts in Brazil and other affected countries to investigate the link between the Zika virus infection and Group B streptococcus (GBS), microcephaly, and other pregnancy outcomes. The CDC also worked with officials in the Puerto Rico Department of Health to learn more about the spectrum of birth outcomes and developmental concerns among infants and children born to women with Zika virus during pregnancy. Back home, the CDC's work included the development of a registry to learn more about pregnant women in the United States with confirmed Zika virus infection and their infants."[25]

Food and Drug Administration (FDA)

The FDA touches the lives of virtually every American every day. It "is charged with protecting the public health by ensuring the safety, efficacy, and security of human and veterinary drugs, biological products, and medical devices; ensuring the safety of foods, cosmetics, and radiation-emitting products; and regulating tobacco products.

Specifically, FDA is responsible for advancing the public health by:

- Helping to speed innovations that make medicines and foods safer and more effective
- Providing the public with the accurate, science-based information they need to use medicines and foods to improve their health
- Regulating the manufacture, marketing, and distribution of tobacco products to protect the public and reduce tobacco use by minors
- Addressing the nation's counterterrorism capability and ensuring the security of the supply of foods and medical products."[26]

Much of this work revolves around regulatory activities and the setting of health and safety standards as spelled out in the Federal Food, Drug, and Cosmetic Act and other related laws. However, because of the complex nature of its standards and the agency's limited resources, enforcement of many FDA regulations is left to other federal agencies and to state and local agencies. For example, the Department of Agriculture is responsible for the inspection of many foods, such as meat and dairy products. Restaurants, supermarkets, and other food outlets are inspected by state and local public health agencies.

Centers for Medicare and Medicaid Services (CMS)

Established as the Health Care Financing Administration (HCFA) in 1977, the CMS is responsible for overseeing the Medicare program (health care for the elderly and the disabled), the federal portion of the Medicaid program (health care for low-income individuals), and the related quality assurance activities. Both Medicare and Medicaid were created in 1965 to ensure that the special groups covered by these programs would not be deprived of health care because of cost. Currently, about 124 million Americans are covered by these programs.[27] In 1997, the State

DEPARTMENT OF HEALTH AND HUMAN SERVICES CENTERS FOR DISEASE CONTROL AND PREVENTION (CDC)

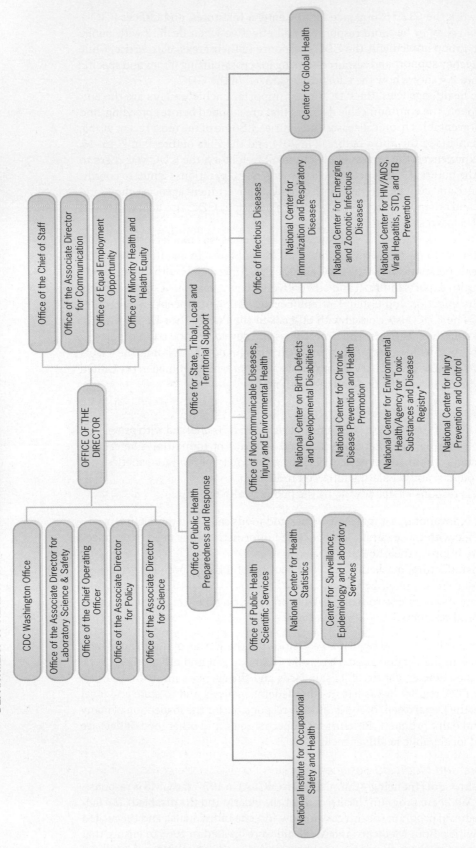

FIGURE 2.4   Organizational chart of the Centers for Disease Control and Prevention.

*ATSDR is an OPDIV within DHHS but is managed by a common director's office.

Data from: Centers for Disease Control and Prevention (2015). Management Analysis and Services Office. Available at http://www.cdc.gov/maso/mab_Charts.htm.

Children's Health Insurance Program (SCHIP), now known as the Children's Health Insurance Program (CHIP), also became the responsibility of the CMS. Medicare, Medicaid, and CHIP are discussed in greater detail elsewhere in the text.

Health Resources and Services Administration (HRSA)

The HRSA is the principal primary health care service agency of the federal government that provides access to essential health care services for people who are low income, uninsured, or who live in rural areas or urban neighborhoods where health care is scarce.[12] It "is the primary federal agency for improving access to health care services for people who are underinsured, isolated, or medically vulnerable."[28] The cited mission of HRSA is "to improve health and achieve health equity through access to quality services, a skilled health workforce, and innovative programs."[28] HRSA "maintains the National Health Service Corps and helps build the health care workforce through training and education programs."[12] The agency "administers a variety of programs to improve the health of mothers and children and serves people living with HIV/AIDS through the Ryan White CARE Act programs."[12] HRSA is also responsible for overseeing the nation's organ transplantation system.[12]

Indian Health Service (IHS)

The IHS "is responsible for providing federal health services to American Indians and Alaska Natives."[29] Currently, it "provides a comprehensive health service delivery system for approximately 1.9 million American Indians and Alaska Natives who belong to 567 federally recognized tribes in 35 states."[29] "The provision of health services to members of federally recognized tribes grew out of the special government-to-government relationship between the federal government and Indian tribes. This relationship, established in 1787, is based on Article I, Section 8 of the Constitution, and has been given form and substance by numerous treaties, laws, Supreme Court decisions, and Executive Orders. The IHS is the principal federal health care provider and health advocate for Indian people."[29] The mission of the IHS is "to raise the physical, mental, social, and spiritual health of American Indians and Alaska Natives to the highest level,"[29] while its goal is "to assure that comprehensive, culturally acceptable personal and public health services are available and accessible to American Indian and Alaska Native people."[29]

Though health services have been provided sporadically by the United States government since the early nineteenth century, it was not until 1989 that the IHS was elevated to an agency level; prior to that time it was a division in HRSA.

National Institutes of Health (NIH)

Begun as a one-room Laboratory of Hygiene in 1887, the NIH today is one of the world's foremost medical research centers, and the federal focal point for medical research in the United States.[30] The mission of the NIH "is to seek fundamental knowledge about the nature and behavior of living systems and the application of that knowledge to enhance health, lengthen life, and reduce the burdens of illness and disability."[30] Although a significant amount of research is carried out by NIH scientists at NIH laboratories in Bethesda and elsewhere, a much larger portion of this research is conducted by scientists at public and private universities and other research institutions. These scientists receive NIH funding for their research proposals through a competitive, peer-review grant application process. Through this process of proposal review by qualified scientists, NIH seeks to ensure that federal research monies are spent on the best-conceived research projects. **Table 2.4** presents a listing of all the institutes and centers located in NIH.

Substance Abuse and Mental Health Services Administration (SAMHSA)

The SAMHSA was established in 1992 as the primary federal agency responsible for ensuring that up-to-date information and state-of-the-art practice are effectively used for the prevention and treatment of addictive and mental disorders. "SAMHSA's mission is to reduce the impact of substance abuse and mental illness on American's communities."[31] Within SAMHSA, there are four centers—the Center for Substance Abuse Treatment (CSAT), the Center for Substance Abuse Prevention (CSAP), and the Center for Mental Health Services (CMHS), and the Center for Behavioral Health Statistics and Quality (CBHSQ), formerly known as the Office of Applied Studies.[31] Each of these centers has its own mission that contributes to the overall mission of SAMHSA.

Core functions of public health assessment, policy development, and assurance

TABLE 2.4 Units within the National Institutes of Health (NIH)	
National Cancer Institute (NCI)	National Institute of Environmental Health Sciences (NIEHS)
National Eye Institute (NEI)	National Institute of General Medical Sciences (NIGMS)
National Heart, Lung, and Blood Institute (NHLBI)	National Institute of Mental Health (NIMH)
National Human Genome Research Institute (NHGRI)	National Institute on Minority Health and Health Disparities (NIMHD)
National Institute on Aging (NIA)	National Institute of Neurological Disorders and Stroke (NINDS)
National Institute on Alcohol Abuse and Alcoholism (NIAAA)	National Institute of Nursing Research (NINR)
National Institute of Allergy and Infectious Diseases (NIAID)	National Library of Medicine (NLM)
National Institute of Arthritis and Musculoskeletal and Skin Diseases (NIAMS)	NIH Clinical Center (CC)
National Institute of Biomedical Imaging and Bioengineering (NIBIB)	Center for Information Technology (CIT)
Eunice Kennedy Shriver National Institute of Child Health and Human Development (NICHD)	National Center for Complementary and Integrative Health (NCCIH)
National Institute on Deafness and Other Communication Disorders (NIDCD)	Fogarty International Center (FIC)
National Institute of Dental and Craniofacial Research (NIDCR)	Center for Scientific Review (CSR)
National Institute of Diabetes and Digestive and Kidney Diseases (NIDDK)	National Center for Advancing Translational Sciences (NCATS)
National Institute on Drug Abuse (NIDA)	

Data from: National Institutes of Health (2016). *Institutes, Centers, and Offices.* Available at http://www.nih.gov/institutes-nih/list-nih-institutes-centers-offices.

FIGURE 2.5 Each of the 50 states has its own health department.

© James F. McKenzie.

State Health Agencies

All 50 states have their own state health departments (see **Figure 2.5**). Although the names of these departments may vary from state to state (e.g., Ohio Department of Health, Indiana State Department of Health), their purposes remain the same: to promote, protect, and maintain the health and welfare of their citizens. These purposes are represented in the **core functions of public health**, which include assessment of information on the health of the community, comprehensive public health policy development, and assurance that public health services are provided to the community.[32] These core functions have been defined further with the following 10 essential public health services.[33]

1. Monitor health status to identify community health problems.
2. Diagnose and investigate health problems and health hazards in the community.
3. Inform, educate, and empower people about health issues.
4. Mobilize community partnerships to identify and solve health problems.
5. Develop policies and plans that support individual and community health efforts.
6. Enforce laws and regulations that protect health and ensure safety.

7. Link people to needed personal health services and assure the provision of health care when otherwise unavailable.

8. Ensure a competent public health and personal health care workforce.

9. Evaluate effectiveness, accessibility, and quality of personal and population-based health services.

10. Research for new insights and innovative solutions to health problems (see **Figure 2.6**).

The head of the state health department is usually a medical doctor, appointed by the governor, who may carry the title of director, commissioner, or secretary. However, because of the political nature of the appointment, this individual may or may not have extensive experience in community or public health. Unfortunately, political influence sometimes reaches below the level of commissioner to the assistant commissioners and division chiefs; it is the commissioner, assistant commissioners, and division chiefs who set policy and provide direction for the state health department. Middle- and lower-level employees are usually hired through a merit system and may or may not be able to influence health department policy. These employees, who carry out the routine work of the state health department, are usually professionally trained health specialists such as microbiologists, engineers, sanitarians, epidemiologists, nurses, and health education specialists.

Most state health departments are organized into divisions or bureaus that provide certain standard services. Typical divisions include Administration, Communicable Disease Prevention and Control, Chronic Disease Prevention and Control, Vital and Health Statistics, Environmental Health, Health Education or Promotion, Health Services, Maternal and Child Health, Mental Health, Occupational and Industrial Health, Dental Health, Laboratory Services, Public Health Nursing, Veterinary Public Health, and most recently, a division of Public Health Preparedness to deal with bioterrorism issues.

In promoting, protecting, and maintaining the health and welfare of their citizens, state health departments play many different roles. They can establish and promulgate health regulations that have the force and effect of law throughout the state. The state health departments also provide an essential link between federal and local (city and county) public health agencies. As such, they serve as conduits for federal funds aimed at local health problems. Federal funds come to the states as block grants. Funds earmarked for particular health projects are distributed to local health departments by their respective state health departments in accordance with previously agreed upon priorities. State health departments may also link local needs with federal expertise. For example, epidemiologists from the CDC are sometimes made available to investigate local disease outbreaks at the request of the state health department. State health departments usually must approve appointments of local health officers and can also remove any local health officers who neglect their duties.

The resources and expertise of the state health department are also at the disposal of local health departments. One particular area where the state health departments can be helpful is laboratory services; many modern diagnostic tests are simply too expensive for local health departments. Another area is environmental health. Water and air pollution problems usually extend beyond local jurisdictions, and their detection and measurement often require equipment too expensive for local governments to afford. This equipment and expertise are often provided by the state health department.

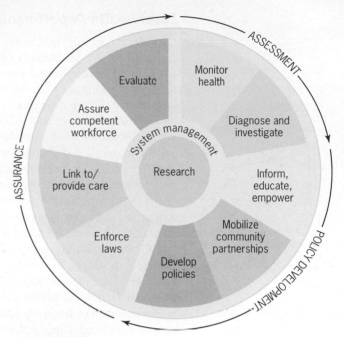

FIGURE 2.6   Core functions of public health and the 10 essential services.

Reproduced from: Centers for Disease Control and Prevention (2014). *The Public Health System and the 10 Essential Public Health Services.* Available at http://www.cdc.gov/nphpsp/essentialservices.html.

Local Health Departments

Local-level governmental health organizations, referred to as local health departments (LHDs), are usually the responsibility of the city or county governments. In large metropolitan areas, community health needs are usually best served by a city health department. In smaller cities with populations of up to 50,000, people often come under the jurisdiction of a county health department. There are most of the population is concentrated in a single city, a LHD may have jurisdiction over both city and county residents. In sparsely populated rural areas, it is not uncommon to find more than one county served by a single health department. There are approximately 2,800 agencies or units that met the Profile definition of an LHD. However, for the 2013 Profile Study 2,532 LHDs were included in the study population; of that number, 61% were located in nonmetropolitan areas and 49% were in metropolitan areas.[34]

It is through LHDs that health services are provided to the people of the community. A great many of these services are mandated by state laws, which also set standards for health and safety. Examples of mandated local health services include the inspection of restaurants, public buildings, and public transportation systems; the detection and reporting of certain diseases; and the collection of vital statistics such as births and deaths. Other programs such as safety belt programs and immunization clinics may be locally planned and implemented. In this regard, local health jurisdictions are permitted (unless preemptive legislation is in place) to enact ordinances that are stricter than those of the state, but these jurisdictions cannot enact codes that fall below state standards. It is at this level of governmental health agencies that sanitarians implement the environmental health programs, nurses and physicians offer the clinical services, and health education specialists present health education and promotion programs.

Organization of Local Health Departments

Each LHD is headed by a health officer/administrator/commissioner (see **Figure 2.7**). In most states, there are laws that prescribe who can hold such a position. Those often noted are physicians, dentists, veterinarians, or individuals with a master's or doctoral degree in public health. If the health officer is not a physician, then a physician is usually hired on a consulting basis to advise as needed. Usually, this health officer is appointed by a board of health, the members of which are themselves appointed by officials in the city or county government or, in some situations, elected by the general public. The health officer and administrative assistants may recommend which programs will be offered by the LHDs. However, they may need final approval from a board of health. Although it is desirable that those serving on the local board of health have some knowledge of community health programs, most states have no such requirement. Often, politics plays a role in deciding the makeup of the local board of health.

The local health officer, like the state health commissioner, has far-reaching powers, including the power to arrest someone who refuses to undergo treatment for a communicable disease (tuberculosis, for example) and who thereby continues to spread disease in the community. The local health officer has the power to close a restaurant on the spot if it has serious health law violations or to impound a shipment of food if it is contaminated. Because many local health

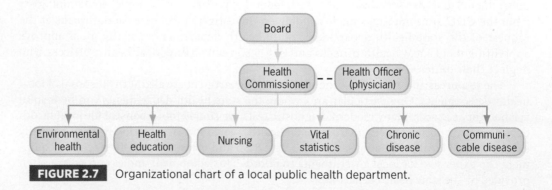

FIGURE 2.7   Organizational chart of a local public health department.

departments cannot afford to employ a full-time physician, the health officer is usually hired on a part-time basis. In such cases, the day-to-day activities of the LHD are carried out by an administrator trained in public health. The administrator is also hired by the board of health based upon qualifications and the recommendation of the health officer.

Local sources provide the greatest percentage of LHD revenues, followed by state funds and federal pass-through funds. A limited number of LHD services are provided on a fee-for-service basis. For example, there is usually a fee charged for birth and death certificates issued by the LHD. Also, in some communities, minimal fees are charged to offset the cost of providing immunizations, lab work, or inspections. Seldom do these fees cover the actual cost of the services provided. Therefore, income from service fees usually makes up a very small portion of any LHD budget. And, it is not unusual to find that many LHDs use a **sliding scale** to determine the fee for a service.

Whole School, Whole Community, Whole Child (WSCC) Model

Few people think of public schools as governmental health agencies. Consider, however, that schools are funded by tax dollars, are under the supervision of an elected school board, and include as a part of their mission the improvement of the health of those in the school community. Because school attendance is required throughout the United States, the potential for school health programs to make a significant contribution to community and public health is enormous, especially when it comes to "promoting the health and safety of young people and helping them establish lifelong healthy behavior patterns."[35] In fact, it has been stated that schools "could do more perhaps than any other single agency in society to help young people, and the adults they will become, to live healthier, longer, more satisfying, and more productive lives."[36]

Current thinking is that schools, along with government agencies, community organizations, and other community members, can be a part of a collaborative and comprehensive approach to have a positive impact on the health outcomes of young people.[35] To create such a program the CDC and the ASCD (previously known as the Association for Supervision and Curriculum Develop) developed the Whole School, Whole Community, Whole Child (WSCC) model. "The focus of the WSCC model is an ecological approach that is directed at the whole school, with the school in turn drawing its resources and influences from the whole community and serving to address the needs of the whole child."[37] The WSCC model expands on the eight elements of CDC's coordinated school health (CSH) approach and is combined with the tenets of the whole child approach.[34] The eight elements of CSH include: health education (i.e., a carefully planned health curriculum); nutritional environment and services; employee wellness; health services; counseling, psychological, and social services; physical education; healthy and safe school environment; and family/community involvement. The expansion of these eight elements to form the WSCC model takes place with the last two elements into four distinct components—social and emotional climate, physical environment, community involvement, and family engagement. This expansion "meets the need for greater emphasis on both the psychosocial and physical environment as well as the ever-increasing and growing roles that community agencies and families must play. This new model also addresses the need to engage students as active participants in their learning and health."[35] If communities were willing to work with the public health and education sectors, the contribution of Whole School, Whole Community, Whole Child model programs to community and public health could be almost unlimited.

Quasi-Governmental Health Organizations

The **quasi-governmental health organizations**—organizations that have some official health responsibilities but operate, in part, like voluntary health organizations—make important contributions to community health. Although they derive some of their funding and

Sliding scale the scale used to determine the fee for services based on ability to pay

Quasi-governmental health organizations organizations that have some responsibilities assigned by the government but operate more like voluntary agencies

legitimacy from governments, and carry out tasks that may be normally thought of as government work, they operate independently of government supervision. In some cases, they also receive financial support from private sources. Examples of quasi-governmental agencies are the American Red Cross (ARC), the National Science Foundation, and the National Academy of Sciences.

The American Red Cross

The ARC, founded in 1881 by Clara Barton[38] (see **Figure 2.8**), is a prime example of an organization that has quasi-governmental status. Although it has certain "official" responsibilities placed on it by the federal government, it is funded by voluntary contributions. "Official" duties of the ARC include (1) providing relief to victims of natural disasters such as floods, tornadoes, hurricanes, and fires (Disaster Services) and (2) serving as the liaison between members of the active armed forces and their families during emergencies (Services to the Armed Forces and Veterans). In this latter capacity, the ARC can assist active-duty members of the armed services in contacting their families in case of an emergency, or vice versa.

In addition to these "official" duties, the ARC also engages in many nongovernmental services. These include blood drives, safety services (including water safety, first aid, CPR, and HIV/AIDS instruction), nursing and health services, youth services, community volunteer services, and international services.

The ARC was granted a charter by Congress in 1900, and the ARC and the federal government have had a special relationship ever since. The president of the United States is the honorary chairman of the ARC.[38] The U.S. Attorney General and Secretary of the Treasury are honorary counselor and treasurer, respectively.

The Red Cross idea was not begun in the United States. It was begun in 1863 by five Swiss men in Geneva, Switzerland, who were concerned with the treatment provided to the wounded during times of war.[39] The group, which was called the International Committee for the Relief to the Wounded, was led by Henry Dunant (1828–1910 C.E.).[39] With the assistance of the Swiss government, the International Committee brought together delegates from 16 nations in 1864 to the Geneva Convention for the Amelioration of the Condition of the Wounded in Armies in the Field (now known as the first Geneva Convention) to sign the Geneva Treaty.[39]

The efforts of Henry Dunant and the rest of the International Committee led to the eventual establishment of the International Committee of the Red Cross (ICRC). The ICRC, which is still headquartered in Geneva and governed by the Swiss, continues to work today during times of disaster and international conflict. It is the organization that visits prisoners of war to ensure they are being treated humanely.[39]

Today, the international movement of the Red Cross comprises the Geneva-based ICRC, the International Federation of Red Cross and Red Crescent Societies (the red crescent emblem is used in Moslem countries), and the over 190 National Red Cross and Red Crescent Societies.[39] There are a number of other countries that believe in the principles of the Red Cross Movement but have not officially joined because the emblems used by the movement are offensive. Thus, the ICRC created a third emblem that meets all the criteria for use as a protective device and at the same time is free of any national, political, or religious connotations. The design is composed of a red frame in the shape of a square on the edge of a white background. The name chosen for this distinctive emblem was "red crystal," to signify purity[40] (see **Figure 2.9**).

Other Quasi-Governmental Organizations

Two other examples of quasi-governmental organizations in the United States are the National Science Foundation (NSF) and the National Academy of Sciences (NAS). The purpose of NSF is the funding and promotion of scientific research and the development of individual scientists. NSF receives and disperses federal funds but operates independently of governmental supervision. Chartered by Congress in 1863, NAS acts as an advisor to the government on the question of science and technology. Included in its membership are some of America's most renowned scientists. Although neither of these agencies exists specifically to address health problems, both organizations fund projects, publish reports, and take public stands on health-related issues.

Voluntary health agencies
nonprofit organizations created by concerned citizens to deal with a health need not met by governmental health agencies

Nongovernmental Health Agencies

Nongovernmental health agencies are funded by private donations or, in some cases, by membership dues. There are thousands of these organizations that all have one thing in common: They arose because there was an unmet need. For the most part, the agencies operate free from governmental interference as long as they meet Internal Revenue Service guidelines with regard to their specific tax status. In the following sections, we discuss the types of nongovernmental health agencies—voluntary, professional, philanthropic, service, social, religious, and corporate.

Voluntary Health Agencies

Voluntary health agencies are an American creation. Each of these agencies was created by one or more concerned citizens who thought that a specific health need was not being met by existing governmental agencies. In a sense, these new voluntary agencies arose by themselves, in much the same way as a "volunteer" tomato plant arises in a vegetable garden. New voluntary agencies continue to be born each year. Examples of recent additions to the perhaps 100,000 agencies already in existence are the Alzheimer's Association and the First Candle (formerly SIDS Alliance). A discussion of the commonalities of voluntary health agencies follows.

Organization of Voluntary Health Agencies

Most voluntary agencies exist at three levels—national, state, and local. At the national level, policies that guide the agency are formulated. A significant portion of the money raised locally is forwarded to the national office, where it is allocated according to the agency's budget. Much of the money is designated for research. By funding research, the agencies hope to discover the cause of and cure for a particular disease or health problem. There have been some major successes. The March of Dimes, for example, helped to eliminate polio as a major disease problem in the United States through its funding of immunization research.

There is not always a consensus of opinion about budget decisions made at the national level; some believe that less should be spent for research and more for treating those afflicted with the disease. Another common internal disagreement concerns how much of the funds raised at the local level should be sent to the national headquarters instead of being retained for local use. Those outside the agency sometimes complain that when an agency achieves success, as the March of Dimes did in its fight against polio, it should dissolve. This does not usually occur; instead, successful agencies often find a new health concern. The March of Dimes now fights birth defects; and when tuberculosis was under control, the Tuberculosis Society changed its name to the American Lung Association to fight all lung diseases.

The state-level offices of voluntary agencies are analogous to the state departments of health in the way that they link the national headquarters with local offices. The primary work at this level is to coordinate local efforts and to ensure that policies developed at the national headquarters are carried out. The state-level office may also provide training services for employees and volunteers of local-level offices and are usually available as consultants and problem solvers.

In recent years, some voluntary agencies have been merging several state offices into one to help reduce overhead expenses.

The local-level office of each voluntary agency is usually managed by a paid staff worker who has been hired either by the state-level office or by a local board of directors. Members of the local board of directors usually serve in that capacity on a voluntary basis. Working under the manager of each agency are local volunteers, who are the backbone of voluntary agencies. It has been said that the local level is where the "rubber meets the road." In other words, this is where most of the money is raised, most of the education takes place, and most of the service is rendered. Volunteers are of two types, professional and lay. Professional volunteers have had training in a medical profession, while lay volunteers have had no medical training. The paid employees help facilitate the work of the volunteers with expertise, training, and other resources.

Purpose of Voluntary Health Agencies

Voluntary agencies share four basic objectives: (1) to raise money to fund their programs, with the majority of the money going to fund research, (2) to provide education both to professionals and to the public, (3) to provide service to those individuals and families that are afflicted with the disease or health problem, and (4) to advocate for beneficial policies, laws, and regulations that affect the work of the agency and in turn the people they are trying to help.

Fundraising is a primary activity of many voluntary agencies. Whereas in the past this was accomplished primarily by door-to-door solicitations, today mass-mailing, emailing, and telephone solicitation are more common. In addition, most agencies sponsor special events such as golf outings, dances, or dinners. One type of special event that is very popular today is the "a-thon" (see **Figure 2.10**). The term "a-thon" is derived from the name of the ancient Greek city Marathon and usually signified some kind of "endurance" event. Examples include bike-a-thons, rock-a-thons, telethons, skate-a-thons, and dance-a-thons. These money-making "a-thons" seem to be limited in scope only by the creativity of those planning them. In addition, some of these agencies have become United Way agencies and receive some funds derived from the annual United Way campaign, which conducts fundraising efforts at worksites. The three largest voluntary agencies in the United States today (in terms of dollars raised) are the American Cancer Society (see **Box 2.1**), the American Heart Association, and the American Lung Association.

Over the years, the number of voluntary agencies formed to help meet special health needs has continually increased. Because of the growth in the number of new agencies, several consumer "watchdog" groups have taken a closer look into the practices of the agencies. A major concern of these consumer groups has been the amount of money that the voluntary agencies spend on the cause (e.g., cancer, heart disease, AIDS) and how much they spend on fundraising and overhead (e.g., salaries, office furniture, leasing of office space). Well-run agencies will spend less than 15% of what they raise on fundraising. Some of the not-so-well-run agencies spend as much as 80% to 90% of money raised on fundraising. All consumers should ask agencies how they spend their money prior to contributing.

Professional Health Organizations/Associations

Professional health organizations and associations are made up of health professionals who have completed specialized education and training programs and have met the standards of registration, certification, and/or licensure for their respective fields. Their mission is to promote high standards of professional practice for their specific profession, thereby improving the health of society by improving the people in the profession. Professional organizations are funded primarily by membership

FIGURE 2.10   Most voluntary health agencies hold special events to raise money for their causes.

© Suzanne Tucker/ShutterStock, Inc.

BOX 2.1   A Closer Look at One Voluntary Health Agency: The American Cancer Society

The American Cancer Society (ACS) was founded in 1913 by 10 physicians and 5 laymen.[41] At that time, it was known as the American Society for the Control of Cancer. Today, with offices throughout the country and approximately 2.5 million volunteers, ACS is the largest voluntary health organization.[42] Despite success, its mission has remained constant since its founding. It is "dedicated to eliminating cancer as a major health problem by preventing cancer, saving lives, and diminishing suffering from cancer, through research, education, advocacy and service."[43]

The mission of the ACS includes both short- and long-term goals. Its short-term goals are to save lives and diminish suffering. This is accomplished through education, advocacy, and service. Its long-term goal, the elimination of cancer, is being approached through the society's support of cancer research.

The American Cancer Society's educational programs are targeted at two different groups—the general public and the health professionals who treat cancer patients. The public education program promotes the following skills and concepts to people of all ages: (1) taking the necessary steps to prevent cancer, (2) knowing the seven warning signals, (3) understanding the value of regular checkups, and (4) coping with cancer. The society accomplishes this by offering free public education programs, supported by up-to-date literature and audiovisual materials, whenever and wherever they may be requested. These programs may be presented in homes, worksites, churches, clubs, organizations, and schools. A few of their better-known programs include Circle of Life, I Can Cope, and Reach to Recovery.[44] From time to time, the ACS also prepares public service messages for broadcasting or televising.

The Society's professional education program is aimed at the professionals who work with oncology patients. The objective of this program is to motivate physicians and other health care professionals to maintain and improve their knowledge of cancer prevention, detection, diagnosis, treatment, and palliative care. Such education is provided through professional publications, up-to-date audiovisual materials, conferences, and grants that fund specialized education experiences.

The ACS offers patient service and rehabilitation programs that ease the impact of cancer on those affected. The services offered include information and referral to appropriate professionals, home care supplies and equipment for the comfort of patients, transportation of patients to maintain their medical and continuing care programs, and specialized education programs for cancer patients to help them cope and feel better about themselves. There are also rehabilitation programs that provide social support for all cancer patients and specific programs for those who have had a mastectomy, laryngectomy, or ostomy.

The ACS is the largest source of private, not-for-profit cancer research funds in the United States, second only to the federal government in total dollars spent. Since 1946, when the ACS first started awarding grants, it has invested about $4.0 billion in cancer research. The research program consists of three components: extramural grants, intramural epidemiology and surveillance research, and the intramural behavioral research center.[45] The most recent addition to the work of the ACS is in the area of advocacy. Specifically, the ACS works to (1) support cancer research and programs to prevent, detect, and treat cancer; (2) expand access to quality cancer care, prevention, and awareness; (3) reduce cancer disparities in minority and medically underserved populations; and (4) reduce and prevent suffering from tobacco-related illnesses.

All ACS programs—education, service, research, and advocacy—are planned primarily by the society's volunteers. However, the society does employ staff members to carry out the day-to-day operations and to help advise and support the work of the volunteers. This arrangement of volunteers and staff working together has created a very strong voluntary health agency.

dues. Examples of such organizations are the American Medical Association, the American Dental Association, the American Nursing Association, the American Public Health Association, and the Society for Public Health Education, Inc.

Although each professional organization is unique, most provide similar services to their members. These services include the certification of continuing education programs for professional renewal, the hosting of annual conventions where members share research results and interact with colleagues, and the publication of professional journals and other reports. Some examples of journals published by professional health associations are the *Journal of the American Medical Association* (*JAMA*), the *American Journal of Public Health*, and *Health Promotion Practice*.

Like voluntary health agencies, another important activity of some professional organizations is advocating on issues important to their membership. The American Medical Association, for example, has a powerful lobby nationally and in some state legislatures. Their purpose is to affect legislation in such a way as to benefit their membership and their profession. Many professional health organizations provide the opportunity for benefits, including group

Philanthropic foundation
an endowed institution that donates money for the good of humankind

insurance and discount travel rates. There are hundreds of professional health organizations in the United States, and it would be difficult to describe them all here.

Philanthropic Foundations

Philanthropic foundations have made and continue to make significant contributions to community and public health in the United States and throughout the world. These foundations support community health by funding programs and research on the prevention, control, and treatment of many diseases. Foundation directors, sometimes in consultation with a review committee, determine the types of programs that will be funded. Some foundations fund an array of health projects, whereas others have a much narrower scope of interests. Some foundations, such as the Bill and Melinda Gates Foundation, fund global health projects, whereas others restrict their funding to domestic projects. The geographical scope of domestic foundations can be national, state, or local. Local foundations may restrict their funding to projects that only benefit local citizens.

The activities of these foundations differ from those of the voluntary health agencies in two important ways. First, foundations have money to give away, and therefore no effort is spent on fundraising. Second, foundations can afford to fund long-term or innovative research projects, which might be too risky or expensive for voluntary or even government-funded agencies. The development of a vaccine for yellow fever by a scientist funded by the Rockefeller Foundation is an example of one such long-range project.

Some of the larger foundations, in addition to the Bill and Melinda Gates Foundation, that have made significant commitments to community health are the Commonwealth Fund, which has contributed to community health in rural communities, improved hospital facilities, and tried to strengthen mental health services; the Ford Foundation, which has contributed greatly to family-planning and youth sexuality efforts throughout the world; the Robert Wood Johnson Foundation, which has worked to improve the culture of health and policies dealing with health-related systems; the Henry J. Kaiser Family Foundation, which has supported the health care reform and community health promotion; the W. K. Kellogg Foundation, which has funded many diverse health programs that address human issues and provide a practical solution; and the Milbank Memorial Fund, which has primarily funded projects dealing with the integration of people with disabilities into all aspects of life.

Service, Social, and Religious Organizations

Service, social, and religious organizations have also played a part in community and public health over the years (see **Figure 2.11**). Examples of service and social groups involved in community health are the Jaycees, Kiwanis Club, Fraternal Order of Police, Rotary Club, Elks, Lions, Moose, Shriners, American Legion, and Veterans of Foreign Wars. Members of these groups enjoy social interactions with people of similar interests in addition to fulfilling the groups' primary reason for existence—service to others in their communities. Although health may not be the specific focus of their mission, several of these groups make important contributions in that direction by raising money and funding health-related programs. Sometimes, their contributions are substantial. Examples of such programs include the Shriners' children's hospitals and burn centers; the Lions' contributions to pilot (lead) dog programs and other services for those who are visually impaired, such as the provision of eyeglasses for school-aged children unable to afford them; and the Lions' contributions to social and emotional learning of PreK–12 children via the educational program named "Lions Quest."[46]

FIGURE 2.11 Community service groups contribute needed resources for the improvement of the health of the community.

© James F. McKenzie

The contributions of religious groups to community and public health have also been substantial. Such groups also have been effective avenues for promoting health programs because (1) they have had a history of volunteerism and preexisting reinforcement contingencies for volunteerism, (2) they can influence entire families, and (3) they have accessible meeting room facilities.[47] One way in which these groups contribute is through donations of money for missions for the less fortunate. Examples of religious organizations that solicit donations from their members include the Protestants' One Great Hour of Sharing, the Catholics' Relief Fund, and the United Jewish Appeal. Other types of involvement in community health by religious groups include (1) the donation of space for voluntary health programs such as blood donations, Alcoholics Anonymous, and other support groups; (2) the sponsorship of food banks and shelters for the hungry, poor, and homeless; (3) the sharing of the doctrine of good personal health behavior; and (4) allowing community and public health professionals to deliver their programs through the congregations. This latter contribution has been especially useful in black American communities because of the importance of churches in the culture of this group of people.

In addition, it should be noted that some religious groups have hindered the work of community and public health workers. Almost every community in the country can provide an example where a religious organization has protested the offering of a school district's sex education program, picketed a public health clinic for providing reproductive information or services to women, or has spoken out against homosexuality.

Corporate Involvement in Community and Public Health

From the way it treats the environment by its use of natural resources and the discharge of wastes, to the safety of the work environment, to the products and services it produces and provides, to the provision of health care benefits for its employees, corporate America is very much involved in community and public health. Though each of these aspects of community and public health is important to the overall health of a community, because of the concern for the "bottom line" in corporate America, it is the provision of health care benefits that often receives the most attention. In fact, many corporations today find that their single largest annual expenditure behind salaries and wages is for employee health care benefits. Consider, for example, the cost of manufacturing a new car. The cost of health benefits for those who build the car now exceeds the cost of the raw materials for the car itself.

In an effort to keep a healthy workforce and reduce the amount paid for health care benefits, many companies support health-related programs both at and away from the worksite. Worksite programs aimed at trimming employee medical bills have been expanded beyond the traditional safety awareness programs and first aid services to include such programs as substance abuse counseling, nutrition education, smoking cessation, stress management, physical fitness, and disease management. Many companies also are implementing health promotion policies and enforcing state and local laws that prohibit (or severely restrict) smoking on company grounds or that mandate the use of safety belts at all times in all company-owned vehicles.

Chapter Summary

- Contemporary society is too complex to respond effectively to community and public health problems on either an emergency or a long-term basis. This fact necessitates organizations and planning for health in our communities.

- The different types of organizations that contribute to the promotion, protection, and maintenance of health in a community can be classified into three groups according to their sources of funding and organizational structure—governmental, quasi-governmental, and nongovernmental.

- Governmental health agencies exist at the local, state, federal, and international levels and are funded primarily by tax dollars.

- WHO is the largest and most visible governmental health agency on the international level.

- The Department of Health and Human Services (HHS) is the U.S. government's principal agency for the protection of the health of all Americans and for providing essential human services, especially for those who are least able to help themselves.

- The Whole School, Whole Community, Whole Child (WSCC) model expands on the coordinated school health model and incorporates an ecological approach directed at the whole school, with the school drawing its resources and influences from the whole community to address the needs of the whole child.

- The core functions of public health include the assessment of information on the health of the community, comprehensive public health policy development, and assurance that public health services are provided to the community. Ten essential services are used to meet these core functions.

- Quasi-governmental agencies, such as the American Red Cross, share attributes with both governmental and nongovernmental agencies.

- Nongovernmental organizations include voluntary and professional associations, philanthropic foundations, and service, social, and religious groups.

- Corporate America has also become more involved in community and public health, both at the worksite and within the community.

Scenario: Analysis and Response

After having read this chapter, please respond to the following questions in reference to the scenario at the beginning of the chapter.

1. What type of health agency do you think will be of most help to Mary?

2. If this scenario were to happen to someone in your community, what recommendations would you give to him or her on seeking help from health agencies?

3. The Internet has many sources of information that could help Mary. Use a search engine (e.g., Google, Bing, Yahoo) and enter the word "cancer." Find the website of one governmental health agency at the national level and one voluntary health agency that might be able to help her. Explain how these agencies could be of help.

4. If Mary did not have Internet access, how would you suggest she find out about local health agencies in her area that could help her?

Review Questions

1. What characteristics of modern society necessitate planning and organization for community and public health?

2. What is a governmental health agency?

3. What is the World Health Organization (WHO), and what does it do?

4. Which federal department in the United States is the government's principal agency for protecting the health of all Americans and for providing essential human services, especially to those who are least able to help themselves? What major services does this department provide?

5. What are the three core functions of public health?

6. What are the 10 essential public health services?

7. How do state and local health departments interface?

8. Briefly explain the Whole School, Whole Community, Whole Child model? What are the major components of it?

9. What is meant by the term quasi-governmental agency? Name one such agency.

10. Describe the characteristics of a nongovernmental health agency.

11. What are the major differences between a governmental health organization and a voluntary health agency?

12. What does a health professional gain from being a member of a professional health organization?

13. How do philanthropic foundations contribute to community health? List three well-known foundations.

14. How do service, social, and religious groups contribute to the health of the community?

15. Why has corporate America become involved in community and public health?

Activities

1. Using the Internet, identify 15 health-related organizations that service your community. Divide your list by the three major types of health organizations noted in this chapter.

2. Make an appointment to interview someone at one of the organizations identified in Activity 1. During your visit, find answers to the following questions:

   a. How did the organization begin?

   b. What is its mission?

   c. How is it funded?

   d. How many people (employees and volunteers) work for the organization, and what type of education/training do they have?

   e. What types of programs/services does the organization provide?

3. Obtain organizational charts from the U.S. Department of Health and Human Services (see Figure 2.2), your state department of health, and your local health department. Compare and contrast these charts, and describe their similarities and differences.

4. Call a local voluntary health organization in your community and ask if you could volunteer to work 10 to 15 hours during this academic term. Then, volunteer those hours and keep a journal of your experience.

References

1. Green, L. W. (1990). "The Revival of Community and the Public Obligation of Academic Health Centers." In R. E. Bulger and S. J. Reiser, eds., *Integrity in Institutions: Humane Environments for Teaching, Inquiry and Health.* Iowa City: University of Iowa Press, 165–180.

2. World Health Organization (2016). *World Health Organization.* Geneva, Switzerland: Author. Available at http://www.who.int/about/en/.

3. World Health Organization (1946). *World Health Organization.* Available at http://www.who.int/trade/glossary/story096/en/.

4. World Health Organization (1946). *Constitution of the World Health Organization.* Available at http://apps.who.int/gb/bd/PDF/bd47/EN/constitution-en.pdf?ua-1.

5. World Health Organization (2014). *Twelfth General Programme of Work 2014–2019.* Available at http://apps.who.int/iris/bitstream/10665/112792/1/GPW_2014-2019_eng.pdf?ua=1.

6. World Health Organization (2016). *Ebola Response in Action.* Available at http://apps.who.int/ebola/our-work/achievements.

7. United Nations (2000). *United Nations Millennium Declaration.* New York: Author. Available at http://www.un.org/millennium/declaration/ares552e.htm.

8. United Nations (2002). *Road Map Towards the Implementation of the United Nations Millennium Declaration.* New York: Author. Available at http://www.un.org/millenniumgoals/sgreport2001.pdf?OpenElement.

9. United Nations (2015). *The Millennium Development Goals Report: 2015.* New York: Author. Available at http://www.un.org/millenniumgoals/2015_MDG_Report/pdf/MDG%202015%20rev%20%28July%201%29.pdf.

10. World Health Organization (2015). *Millennium Development Goals (MDGs): Fact Sheet.* Available at http://www.who.int/mediacentre/factsheets/fs290/en/.

11. United Nations (2016) *Sustainable Development Goals: 17 Goals to Transform Our World.* Available at http://www.un.org/sustainabledevelopment/.

12. U.S. Department of Health and Human Services (2016). *United States Department of Health and Human Services.* Washington, DC: Author. Available at http://www.hhs.gov/about/index.html.

13. Government Printing Office Access (2016). *Budget of the United States Government: Browse Fiscal Year 2017.* Washington, DC: Author. Available at http://www.gpo.gov/fdsys/browse/collection GPO.action?collectionCode=BUDGET.

14. U.S. Department of Health and Human Services (2016) *Health Reform and the Department of Human Services.* Washington, DC: Author. Available at http://www.healthreform.gov/health_reform_and_hhs.html.

15. U.S. Department of Health and Human Services (2016). *Administration for Community Living.* Available at http://www.acl.gov/About_ACL/Index.aspx.

16. Agency for Health care Research and Quality (2016). *What Is AHRQ?* Rockville, MD: Author. Available at http://archive.ahrq.gov/about/whatis.htm.

17. Agency for Toxic Substances and Disease Registry (2016). *Agency for Toxic Substances and Disease Registry.* Available at http://www.atsdr.cdc.gov/.

18. Falk, H. (2003) "A Message from Dr. Henry Falk, ATSDR Assistant Administrator." *Public Health and the Environment,* 2(1/2): 1.

19. Centers for Disease Control and Prevention (n.d.). *Fast Facts About CDC.* Atlanta, GA: Author. Available at http://www.cdc.gov/about/pdf/facts/cdcfastfacts/cdcfastfacts.pdf.

20. Centers for Disease Control and Prevention (2013). *Centers for Disease Control and Prevention.* Available at http://www.cdc.gov/maso/pdf/cdcmiss.pdf.

21. Centers for Disease Control and Prevention (2013). *Mission, Role, and Pledge.* Available at http://www.cdc.gov/about/organization/mission.htm.

22. Centers for Disease Control and Prevention (2016). *Centers for Disease Control and Prevention.* Available at http://www.cdc.gov/.

23. Centers for Disease Control and Prevention (2016). *Press Materials.* Available at http://www.cdc.gov/media/pressmaterials.html.

24. Centers for Disease Control and Prevention. (2016). *2014 Ebola Outbreak in West Africa.* Available at http://www.cdc.gov/vhf/ebola/outbreaks/2014-west-africa/index.html#overview.

25. Centers for Disease Control and Prevention. (2016). *Zika Virus.* Available at http://www.cdc.gov/media/dpk/2016/dpk-zika-virus.html.

26. U.S. Food and Drug Administration (2015). *FDA Strategic Priorities 2011–2018.* Available at http://www.fda.gov/aboutfda/reports manualsforms/reports/ucm227527.htm.

27. U.S. Department of Health and Human Services, Centers for Medicare & Medicaid Services (2016). *CMS Fast Facts*. Available at https://www.cms.gov/fastfacts/.

28. Health Resources and Services Administration (2016). *About HRSA*. Available at http://www.hrsa.gov/about/index.html.

29. Indian Health Service (2015). *Indian Health Service Introduction*. Rockville, MD: Author. Available at http://www.ihs.gov/aboutihs/.

30. National Institutes for Health (2015). *Questions and Answers about NIH*. Bethesda, MD: Author. Available at http://www.nih.gov/about /mission.htm.

31. Substance Abuse and Mental Health Services Administration (2014). *SAMSHA: Who Are We?* Rockville, MD: Author. Available at http://beta.samhsa.gov/about-us/who-we-are.

32. National Academy of Sciences, Institute of Medicine (1988). *The Future of Public Health*. Washington, DC: National Academies Press.

33. Center for Disease Control and Prevention (2014). *National Public Health Performance Standards: The Public Health System and the 10 Essential Public Health Services*. Available at http://www.cdc.gov /nphpsp/essentialservices.html.

34. National Association of County and City Health Officials (2015). *2013 National Profile of Local Health Departments*. Washington, DC: Author. Available at http://nacchoprofilestudy.org/.

35. Centers for Disease Control and Prevention (2015). *Healthy Schools: Whole School, Whole Community, Whole Child (WSCC)*. Atlanta, GA: Author. Available at http://www.cdc.gov/healthyschools/wscc /index.htm.

36. Allensworth, D. D., and L. J. Kolbe (1987). "The Comprehensive School Health Program: Exploring an Expanded Concept." *Journal of School Health*, 57(10): 409–412.

37. ASCD (2016). *Whole School, Whole Community, Whole Child (WSCC)*. Available at http://www.ascd.org/programs/learning-and-health/wscc-model.aspx.

38. American Red Cross (2016). *Red Cross History*. Washington, DC: Author. Available at http://www.redcross.org/.

39. International Committee of the Red Cross (2016). *History*. Geneva, Switzerland: Author. Available at https://www.icrc.org/en /who-we-are/history.

40. International Committee of the Red Cross (2005). *An Additional Emblem– the Red Crystal Alongside the Red Cross and Red Crescent*. Available at https://www.icrc.org/eng/resources/documents /press-briefing/emblem-press-briefing-081205.htm.

41. American Cancer Society (2016). *Our History*. Atlanta, GA: Author. Available at http://www.cancer.org/aboutus/whoweare /our-history.

42. American Cancer Society (2016). *Facts about the American Cancer Society*. Available at http://www.cancer.org/aboutus/whoweare /acs-fact-sheet.

43. American Cancer Society (2015). *ACS Mission Statements*. Available at http://www.cancer.org/aboutus/whoweare/our-history.

44. American Cancer Society (2016). *American Cancer Society*. Available at http://www.cancer.org/index.

45. American Cancer Society (2016). *Current Funded Cancer Research*. Available at http://www.cancer.org/index.

46. Lions Clubs International (2015). *Lions Quest*. Oak Brook, IL: Author. Available at https://www.lions-quest.org/.

47. Lasater, T. M., B. L. Wells, R. A. Carleton, and J. P. Elder (1986). "The Role of Churches in Disease Prevention Research Studies." *Public Health Report*, 101(2): 123–131.

CHAPTER 3

Epidemiology: The Study of Disease, Injury, and Death in the Community

Chapter Objectives

After studying this chapter, you will be able to:

1. Define the terms *epidemic, endemic, pandemic, epidemiology,* and *epidemiologist,* and explain their importance in community and public health.

2. List some diseases that caused epidemics in the past and some that are causing epidemics today.

3. Discuss how the practice of epidemiology has changed since the days of Benjamin Rush and John Snow.

4. Explain why rates are important in epidemiology and list some of the commonly used rates.

5. Define incidence and prevalence rates and provide examples of each.

6. Discuss the importance of disease reporting to a community's health and describe the reporting process.

7. Summarize the following standardized measurements of health status—life expectancy, years of potential life lost (YPLL), disability-adjusted life years (DALYs), and health-adjusted life expectancy (HALE).

8. Identify sources of secondary data used by epidemiologists, community health workers, and health officials and list the types of data available from each source.

9. Describe the two main types of epidemiological studies.

10. List the criteria used to evaluate whether or not a risk factor causes a disease.

Scenario

John thought about this afternoon's picnic. Everyone had a great time. For a while it had seemed almost too warm, but plenty of cold drinks were available, and by late afternoon it had become quite pleasant. The games were fun, too...Frisbee, soccer, softball, and volleyball. Then, there was the picnic itself—turkey, potato salad, bread and butter, milk, and dessert—served about noon.

It was now 8 P.M. the next night, and instead of studying as he had planned, John was lying on his bed with a bad stomachache. He was experiencing severe diarrhea and had made several hurried trips to the bathroom in the last half-hour.

John received a message from his roommate Michael. He had gone to his girlfriend's house after the picnic to work on a class project with her. He and Caroline were both sick with stomach cramps and diarrhea, and Michael was wondering if John was sick, too. John began to think about what a coincidence it was that all three of them were sick with the same symptoms at about the same time. Could they have become ill from food they ate at the picnic? There were about 50 people at the picnic; how many others might also be sick? Was it the heat? Was it the food? Was this an epidemic? A half-hour later, John messaged Michael to tell him that he had decided to go to the campus health center.

Elsewhere...

This had turned out to be an interesting volunteer experience. As a requirement for her community health class, Kim had agreed to volunteer at the local health department. The spring semester was almost over now, and she was writing a final report of her activities. During the term, she had spent her Friday afternoons accompanying a sanitarian on his inspections of restaurants and retail food stores. She also had helped him complete his reports on substandard housing and malfunctioning septic tanks.

Dr. Turner, the health officer, had given Kim permission to use one of the department's computers for preparing her final report. Because it was late Sunday evening, she was alone in the health department office when the telephone rang. She briefly considered not answering it but finally picked up the receiver. It was Dr. Lee from the University Health Center. He said he was calling in the hope that someone might be there because he needed to reach Dr. Turner immediately. He said that he had admitted six students to the infirmary with severe stomach cramps, vomiting, and diarrhea. The students had been at a picnic the previous day, and he thought they could have a foodborne illness. He called to ask Dr. Turner to investigate this outbreak and asked Kim to try to reach him as soon as possible.

Introduction

When you become ill and visit a doctor, the first thing the physician does is take measurements and collect information. The measurements include your temperature, heart rate, and blood pressure. The information includes time of onset of your illness, where you have traveled, and what you might have eaten. Next, you may be given a physical examination and asked to provide a specimen such as urine or blood for laboratory examination. The information gathered helps the physician understand the nature of your illness and prescribe an appropriate treatment.

While a primary care physician is concerned with the health of an individual patient, an epidemiologist is concerned with the health of a population. Monitoring health at a population level is important to determine when unexpected or unacceptable levels of health events occur, such as illness, injury, or death. When this happens, epidemiologists seek to collect information about the health status of the community. First, epidemiologists want to know how many people are sick. Second, they want to know who is sick—the old? the young? males? females? rich? poor? They also want to know when the people became sick, and finally, where the sick people live or have traveled. In summary, epidemiologists want to know what it is that the sick people have in common. For this reason, epidemiology is sometimes referred to as population medicine. Although epidemiology was originally applied to infectious diseases, its application has expanded to other areas including, but not limited to, chronic diseases (e.g., diabetes and cancer), reproductive health issues (e.g., infertility and preterm birth), environmental health concerns (e.g., pollution), occupational health hazards (e.g., asbestos exposure), and understanding health disparities in disease risk and outcomes.

Epidemiology is one of the community health activities "aimed at protecting or improving the health of a population or community." Information gathered from epidemiological studies assists community decision makers to make the best use of the community's resources. Data gathered at local, state, and national levels can be used not only to prevent disease outbreaks or control those that are in progress, but also to assess whether an ongoing disease prevention program is effective.

Definition of Epidemiology

Before we discuss the types of questions an epidemiologist asks, we need to define the term epidemiology. **Epidemiology** is "the study of the distribution and determinants of health-related states or events in specified populations, and the application of this study to control health problems."[1] The term *epidemiology* is derived from Greek words that can be translated into the phrase "the study of that which is upon the people." The goal of epidemiology is to limit undesirable health events in a community. For example, illness can be limited by identifying the food that is making people sick or determining modifiable risk factors for heart disease. This is accomplished by describing the distribution and determinants of health events to validate new approaches to prevention, control, and treatment. Through these practices, epidemiologists contribute to our knowledge of how diseases begin and spread through populations, and how they can be prevented, controlled, and treated.

The question might be asked, how many cases are required before a disease outbreak is considered an epidemic—10 cases? 100 cases? 1,000 cases? The answer is that it depends on the disease and the population, but any unexpectedly large number of cases of an illness, specific health-related behavior, or other health-related event in a particular population at a particular time and place can be considered an **epidemic**. Some recent epidemics in the United States are presented in **Table 3.1**.

The question might be asked: What are diseases called that occur regularly in a population but are not epidemic? These diseases are referred to as **endemic diseases**. Whether a disease is epidemic or endemic depends on the disease and the population. Heart disease is endemic in America, while in many regions of equatorial Africa, malaria is endemic.

An **epidemiologist** is "an investigator who studies the occurrence of disease or other health-related conditions or events in defined populations."[1] Some epidemics begin as outbreaks of disease in animals, known as epizootics, and then spread to human populations. Examples are bubonic plague that first affects rodents and West Nile fever virus that first affects birds. Occasionally, an epidemic will spread over a wide area, perhaps even across an entire continent or around the world. Such a widespread epidemic is termed a **pandemic**. The influenza

Epidemiology the study of the distribution and determinants of health-related states or events in specified populations, and the application of this study to control health problems

Epidemic an unexpectedly large number of cases of an illness, specific health-related behavior, or other health-related event in a particular population

Endemic disease a disease that occurs regularly in a population as a matter of course

Epidemiologist one who practices epidemiology

Pandemic an outbreak of disease over a wide geographical area such as a continent or multiple continents

TABLE 3.1 Notable Epidemics in the United States

Disease	Cases In Previous Years	Epidemic Period	Number of Cases
St. Louis encephalitis	5–72	1975	1,815[5]
Legionnaires' disease	Unknown	1976	235[6]
Toxic shock syndrome	11–272	1980	877[7]
HIV/AIDS	Unknown (before 1975)	1981–2012	1,115,215 diagnosed with Stage 3 AIDS,[8] 652,409 deaths[9]
West Nile virus	Unknown in United States	1999–2014	41,762[10]
Mumps	231–338	2006	6,584[11]
Mumps	231–800	2009–2010	Approximately 3,000[11,12]
2009 (H1N1)	This strain was previously unknown in the United States	April 2009–April 2010	An estimated 60.8 million cases and 12,469 deaths[13]
Pertussis	7,580–27,550	2012	48,277[11]

FIGURE 3.1   More than 25 million people died during the influenza pandemic of 1918-1919.

Courtesy of The National Archives.

pandemic of 1918 is an example (see **Figure 3.1**). This disease spread in Europe, Asia, and North America simultaneously.[2] An estimated 25 million people died over several years as a result of this pandemic. The spread of 2009 H1N1 influenza, which disproportionately affected young people, also reached pandemic status. The pandemic potential of avian influenza is also a concern (see **Box 3.1**). The current outbreak of acquired immunodeficiency syndrome (AIDS) is another example of a pandemic. During 2014, an estimated 1.2 million people died of AIDS worldwide, and about 36.9 million people were living with HIV (human immunodeficiency virus).[3] The number of new HIV infections has declined 35% since 2000.[4]

History of Epidemiology

If one searches diligently, it is possible to trace the roots of epidemiological thinking back to the "Father of Medicine," Hippocrates, who as early as 300 B.C.E. suggested a relationship between the occurrence of disease and the physical environment.[14] For example, cases of a disease fitting the description of malaria were found to occur in the vicinity of marshes and swamps.

With the fall of the classical civilizations of Greece and Rome and the return in Europe to a belief in spiritual causes of disease, few advances were made in the field of epidemiology. As a result, epidemics continued to occur. There were three waves of plague—one in 542 to 543, one in 1348 to 1349, and another in 1664 to 1665.[15] There were also epidemics of leprosy, smallpox, malaria, and, later, syphilis and yellow fever.

Epidemics occurred in the New World as well. One such epidemic of yellow fever struck Philadelphia in 1793, causing the death of 4,044 people. Yellow fever was epidemic again in Philadelphia in 1797, 1798, and in 1803.[16] Dr. Benjamin Rush, a prominent Philadelphia physician and signatory of the Declaration of Independence, was able to trace the cases of yellow fever to the docks where ships arrived from tropical ports. However, his conclusion that the disease was caused by vapors arising from decaying coffee beans in port warehouses was incorrect. He could not have known that yellow fever is caused by a virus and is carried by the yellow fever mosquito, *Aedes aegypti*. These facts were discovered by Major Walter Reed of the U.S. Army and his associates a century later.

In 1849, some 50 years after the yellow fever outbreaks in Philadelphia, cholera became epidemic in London. A prominent physician, John Snow, investigated the outbreak by interviewing numerous victims and their families. He concluded that the source of the epidemic was probably water drawn from a particular communal well located on Broad Street. Snow

BOX 3.1   Avian Influenza: The Next Pandemic?

The influenza virus evolves rapidly, which is why a new vaccine must be developed each year to protect the public against the strains of the virus that are circulating at the time. In some cases, strains that are normally only seen in animals, particularly pigs and birds, can evolve to infect and spread among humans as well. In 1997, Hong Kong reported the first documented cases where humans were directly infected with an avian influenza virus from birds.

The avian flu virus strain that infected people directly has been identified as the virulent H5N1 strain. Avian and human immunity to this strain is very low, so that most birds and people who become infected become very ill and many die. In December 2003, 19,000 of 25,000 chickens died on a farm in the Republic of Korea, and over the next several weeks more than a million chickens and ducks died. The virus next turned up in Vietnam and then Thailand, where human cases were reported. In these two countries there were 19 deaths among the 25 human cases in 2004. According to the World Health Organization (WHO), human H5N1 cases have been reported primarily in African and Asian countries with a single case occurring in Canada after travel to China. Since the first human case in 2003 through December 2015, 844 laboratory-confirmed cases and 449 deaths were reported.

H/N9 is another strain of avian influenza that has been transmitted to humans. The first human case was identified in China in 2013, and most cases have been the result of exposure to infected poultry or contaminated environments rather than human-to-human transmission. In total there have been 683 laboratory-confirmed cases and 275 deaths attributed to H7N9.

Other strains have caused clusters of human diseases as well, and the public health agencies, including the WHO and the Centers for Disease Control and Prevention (CDC), closely monitor all influenza activity due to the potential spread throughout human populations. This potential is high for avian influenza viruses for the following reasons:

- They can be especially virulent.
- They are spread by migratory birds.
- They can be transmitted from birds to mammals and in some limited circumstances to humans.
- They continue to evolve, which means (1) there is little to no immunity among humans from previous exposure to influenza, and (2) developing a vaccine is challenging due to the virus changing.

The best source of information about avian influenza is the CDC website (http://www.cdc.gov/flu/avianflu/index.htm). It provides an overview of the current situation, the virus in birds and humans, transmission from birds to humans, past outbreaks, prevention and treatment, and an inventory of genetic changes in the avian flu virus.

Another useful site is the World Health Organization's website (http://www.who.int/influenza/human_animal_interface/en/), which provides disease outbreak news, a timeline of events, epidemiology, information for laboratories and vaccine development, documents to aid in the assessment of public health risk, and ongoing projects related to the avian flu.

Data from: Centers for Disease Control and Prevention, *Information on Avian Influenza*. Available at http://www.cdc.gov/flu/avianflu/index.htm; World Health Organization. *Avian Influenza at the Human-Animal Interface (HAI)*. Available at http://www.who.int/influenza/human_animal_interface/en/.

extinguished the epidemic in 1854 when he removed the pump handle from the Broad Street pump, thus forcing people to obtain their water elsewhere.[17]

John Snow's quashing of the London cholera epidemic in 1854 is a classic example of how epidemiological methods can be used to limit disease and deaths. His achievement was even more remarkable because it occurred 30 years before Louis Pasteur proposed his "germ theory of disease." It was not until 1883 that Robert Koch discovered the organism that causes cholera, *Vibrio cholerae*.

From its early use for the description and investigation of communicable diseases, epidemiology has developed into a sophisticated field of science. John Snow's method of going door to door to collect information is known as shoe leather epidemiology. While face-to-face interviewing is still used to collect data, epidemiologists also use other available methods, such as telephones and surveys to collect information. Modern epidemiologists may also use advanced statistical methods and powerful software to describe associations and patterns in the data. Epidemiological methods are used to evaluate everything from the effectiveness of vaccines to the possible causes of occupational illnesses and unintentional injury deaths.

Knowledge of epidemiology is important to the community health worker who wishes to establish the presence of a set of needs or conditions for a particular health service or program or to justify a request for funding. Likewise, epidemiological methods are used to evaluate the effectiveness of programs already in existence and to plan to meet anticipated needs for facilities and personnel.

Cases people afflicted with a disease

Rate the number of events that occur in a given population in a given period of time

Natality (birth) rate the number of live births divided by the total population

Morbidity rate the number of people who are sick divided by the total population at risk

Mortality (fatality) rate the number of deaths in a population divided by the total population

Population at risk those in the population who are susceptible to a particular disease or condition

Incidence rate the number of new health-related events or cases of a disease divided by the total number in the population at risk

Acute disease a disease that lasts 3 months or less

Attack rate an incidence rate calculated for a particular population for a single disease outbreak and expressed as a percentage

The Importance of Rates

Epidemiologists are concerned with numbers. Of prime importance is the number of health-related events, the number of **cases** (people who are sick), and, of course, the number of deaths. These numbers alone, however, are not enough to provide a description of the extent of the disease in a community. Epidemiologists must also know the total number in the susceptible population so that rates can be calculated. A **rate** is the number of events (births, cases of disease, or deaths) in a given population over a given period or at a given point in time. Three general categories of rates are **natality (birth) rates**, **morbidity** (sickness) **rates**, and **mortality** or **fatality (death) rates**.

Why are rates important? Why not simply enumerate the sick or dead? The answer is that rates enable one to compare health events that occur at different times or in different places. For example, by using rates it is possible to determine whether there are more cases of gonorrhea per capita this year than there were last year or whether there are more homicides per capita in City A than in City B. To do this, the population at risk must be considered.

For example, suppose you wish to compare deaths among young children of different races. In 2012, there were 2,958 deaths among white children aged 1–4 years and 1,021 deaths among black children in the same age group. Without calculating rates, one might assume that deaths were more common among young white children. However, if you knew the population at risk, you could calculate the death rate, the number of deaths divided by the population at risk, for each race[18] (see **Table 3.2**). These rates have greater meaning because they are based on the **population at risk**, those who are susceptible to disease or death from a particular cause. In this case, the death rate is actually higher among black children aged 1-4 years, thus deaths are actually more common among young black children.

Incidence, Prevalence, and Attack Rates

Two important types of morbidity rates are incidence rates and prevalence rates. An **incidence rate** is defined as the number of new health-related events or cases of a disease in a population exposed to that risk in a given time period divided by the total population at risk—the number of new cases of influenza in a community over a week's time divided by the number of people in the community who were susceptible, for example. Those who became ill with influenza during the previous week and remain ill during the week in question are not counted in an incidence rate. Incidence rates are important in the study of **acute diseases**, diseases in which the peak severity of symptoms occurs and subsides within days or weeks. These diseases usually move quickly through a population. Examples of acute diseases are the common cold, influenza, chickenpox, measles, and mumps.

An **attack rate** is a special incidence rate calculated for a particular population for a single disease outbreak and expressed as a percentage (see **Table 3.3**). For example, suppose a number of people who traveled on the same airline flight developed a similar illness, and epidemiologists suspected that the cause of this illness was associated with the flight itself. An attack rate could be calculated for the passengers on that flight to express the percentage who became ill. Furthermore, attack rates could be calculated for various subpopulations, such as those seated at various locations in the plane, those who selected specific entrees from the menu, those of particular age

TABLE 3.2 Deaths and Death Rates for Children Aged 1–4 Years, by Race, 2012

	White	Black
Number of deaths	2,958	1,021
Number at risk (population)	12,043,507	2,734,701
Death rate (per 100,000 population)	24.6	37.3

Data from: Murphy, S.L., Kochanek, K.D., Xu, J., and Heron, M. (2015). "Deaths: Final Data for 2012." *National Vital Statistics Reports*, 63(9). Hyattsville, MD: National Center for Health Statistics. Available at http://www.cdc.gov/nchs/data/nvsr63/nvsr63_09.pdf.

TABLE 3.3 Incidence Rates, Prevalence Rates, and Attack Rates

Name of Rate	Definition of Rate
Incidence rate =	$\dfrac{\text{Number of new health-related events or cases of a disease}}{\text{Number of people exposed to risk during this period}}$
Attack rate* =	$\dfrac{\text{The cumulative incidence of infection in a group observed during an epidemic}}{\text{Number of people exposed}} \times 100$
Prevalence rate =	$\dfrac{\text{Total number of all individuals who have an attribute or disease at a time}}{\text{Population at risk of having the attribute or disease at this point or period of time}}$

*Attack rates are usually given as a percentage.

Prevalence rate the number of new and old cases of a disease in a population in a given period of time, divided by the total number in that population

Chronic disease a disease or health condition that lasts longer than 3 months

Crude rate a rate in which the denominator includes the total population

Age-adjusted rate a rate used to make comparisons across groups and over time when groups differ in age structure

groups, or those who boarded the flight at specific stops. Differences in attack rates for different subpopulations might indicate to the epidemiologists the source or cause of the illness.

Prevalence rates are calculated by dividing all current cases of a disease (old and new) by the total population. Prevalence rates are useful for the study of **chronic disease**, diseases that usually last 3 months or longer. In these cases, it is more important to know how many people are currently suffering from a chronic disease—such as arthritis, heart disease, cancer, or diabetes—than it is to know when they became afflicted. Furthermore, with many chronic diseases, it is difficult or impossible to determine the date of onset of disease. Because a preponderance of health services and facilities are used for the treatment of persons with chronic diseases and conditions, prevalence rates are more useful than incidence rates for the planning of public health programs, personnel needs, and facilities.

Interpretation of Rates

Incidence and prevalence rates can be expressed in two forms—crude and adjusted. **Crude rates** are those in which the denominator includes the total population. Crude rates are relatively easy to obtain and are useful when comparing similar populations. However, crude rates can be misleading when populations differ in age structure or by some other attribute. For example, crude birth rates are normally higher in younger populations, which have a higher proportion of people of reproductive age, than in populations with more elderly people. Conversely, crude death rates are normally higher in older populations. This makes it difficult to use crude rates to compare the risk of death in different populations, such as those of the states of Florida and Alaska. To show what the level of mortality would be if the age composition of different populations were the same, epidemiologists use **age-adjusted rates**. For example, in 2013 because of its larger senior population, Florida had a higher crude death rate (926.3 per 100,000) compared with Alaska's (543.7 per 100,000), where the population is younger. However, when these death rates are adjusted for differences in the age structures of the populations of these two states, one can see that the death rate in Florida (663.4 per 100,000) compares favorably with the death rate in Alaska (724.4 per 100,000; see **Table 3.4**).[19]

TABLE 3.4 Crude and Age-Adjusted Mortality Rates for Alaska and Florida, 2012

State	Number of Deaths	Crude Death Rate*	Age-Adjusted Death Rate*
Alaska	3,997	543.7	724.4
Florida	181,112	926.3	663.4

*Deaths per 100,000 population.

Data from: Centers for Disease Control and Prevention (2015). "Deaths: Preliminary Data for 2013." *National Vital Statistics Reports*, 64(2). Hyattsville, MD: National Center for Health Statistics. Available at http://www.cdc.gov/nchs/data/nvsr/nvsr64/nvsr64_02.pdf.

Notifiable diseases diseases for which health officials request or require reporting for public health reasons

National Electronic Telecommunications System (NETS) the electronic reporting system used by state health departments and the CDC

There are many types of rates including those that focus on a particular population or condition. Details about these and methods for calculating various rates can be found in standard epidemiology textbooks.

Reporting of Births, Deaths, and Diseases

It is important to epidemiologists that births, deaths, and cases of diseases be recorded promptly and accurately. Physicians, clinics, and hospitals are required by law to report all births and deaths as well as all cases of certain **notifiable diseases** to their local health departments. Notifiable diseases are infectious diseases that can become epidemic and for which health officials maintain weekly records. The Centers for Disease Control and Prevention (CDC) issues a list of notifiable diseases for which it requests reports from each state health department. This list is revised periodically. In 2016, more than 80 diseases were designated as notifiable at the national level (see **Table 3.5**).[20] The reporting requirements vary for each condition listed. For example, some conditions require immediate/urgent reporting (e.g., anthrax), while others require only annual reporting (e.g., cancer). Further, the requirements also specify which types of cases must be reported for each disease. The CDC website has more information about the national reporting requirements for each condition.[20] Individual states may require the reporting of additional diseases that are of local public health concern. Local health departments are required by their respective state health departments to summarize all records of births (see **Figure 3.2**), deaths, and notifiable diseases and to report them. State health departments summarize these reports and relay them to the CDC through the **National Electronic Telecommunications System (NETS)**. The reporting scheme for notifiable disease is shown in **Figure 3.3**.

The CDC summarizes state and territorial data and uses it to plan epidemiological research, detect outbreaks, conduct investigations, and issue reports. One series of reports, published weekly by the CDC, is called the *Morbidity and Mortality Weekly Report (MMWR). MMWR*s are available to the public at the CDC website (www.cdc.gov/mmwr). Paper copies can usually be found in the government documents areas of certain larger libraries.

Unfortunately, the information reported is not always as good as it could be. Clinics and laboratories may not report each and every case of less severe illnesses, may be unfamiliar with the requirements for reporting, or may be understaffed or simply too busy to keep up with reporting. In other cases, patients recover—with or without treatment—before a diagnosis is confirmed and some may never even seek care. Also, changes in local and state government administration or other key personnel often interfere with the timely reporting of disease data. Both the accuracy and completeness of disease reporting also depend on the type of disease.[21]

TABLE 3.5 Nationally Notifiable Conditions, 2016	
Anaplasmosis	Malaria
Anthrax	Measles
Arboviral disease[a]	Meningococcal disease (*Neisseria meningitides*)
Babesiosis	Mumps
Botulism	Novel influenza A virus infection, initial detections
Brucellosis	Paralytic poliomyelitis
Campylobacteriosis	Pertussis

(Continues)

Cancer[b]	Pesticide-related illness, acute
Chancroid	Plague
Chlamydia trachomatis infections	Poliovirus infection, nonparalytic
Coccidioidomycosis	Psittacosis
Cryptosporidiosis	Q fever (acute and chronic)
Cyclosporiasis	Rabies in a human or animal
Dengue virus infections[c]	Rickettsiosis, spotted fever
Diphtheria	Rubella
Ehrlichiosis	Rubella, congenital syndrome
Escherichia coli, Shiga toxin-producing (STEC)	Salmonellosis
Foodborne disease outbreaks[d]	SARS-associated coronavirus
Giardiasis	Shigellosis
Gonorrhea	Silicosis
Haemophilus influenzae, invasive disease	Smallpox
Hansen's disease	*Staphylococcus aureus* infection (Vancomycin-intermediate or Vancomycin-resistant)
Hantavirus pulmonary syndrome	Streptococcal toxic-shock syndrome (STSS)
Hemolytic uremic syndrome, post diarrheal	*Streptococcus pneumoniae*, invasive disease (IPD)
Hepatitis A, acute	Syphilis
Hepatitis B, acute	Tetanus
Hepatitis B, chronic	Toxic-shock syndrome (non-Strep)
Hepatitis B virus, perinatal infection	Trichinellosis (Trichinosis)
Hepatitis C, acute	Tuberculosis
Hepatitis C, chronic	Tularemia
HIV infection	Typhoid fever
Influenza-associated mortality, pediatric	Varicella
Lead, exposure screening test result[e]	*Vibrio cholerae* infection (cholera)
Legionellosis	Vibriosis
Leptospirosis	Viral hemorrhagic fevers[f]
Listeriosis	Waterborne disease outbreaks
Lyme disease	Yellow fever

Note. Approved by the Council of State and Territorial Epidemiologists (CSTE) June 2015, implemented January 2016.
[a]Arboviral diseases: California serogroup virus disease, Eastern equine encephalitis virus disease (EEE), Powassan virus disease, St. Louis encephalitis virus disease (SLE), Western equine encephalitis virus disease (WEE), West Nile virus disease (WNV).
[b]Notification for all confirmed cases of cancers should be made at least annually.
[c]Dengue virus infections include dengue and severe dengue.
[d]Outbreaks are defined by state and local health departments, all situations deemed by a local or state health department to be an outbreak are notifiable.
[e]Notification for lead exposure screening results should be submitted quarterly for children and twice a year for adults.
[f]Viral hemorrhagic fever diseases: Ebola, Marburg, Lassa, Lujo, new world Arenavirus (Guanarito, Machupo, Junin, and Sabia viruses), or Crimean-Congo.

Modified from: Centers for Disease Control and Prevention (2016). *Protocol for Public Health Agencies to Notify CDC about the Occurrence of National Notifiable Conditions, 2016.* Available at http://www.cdc.gov/nndss/document/NNC-2016-Notification-Requirements-By-Condition.pdf.

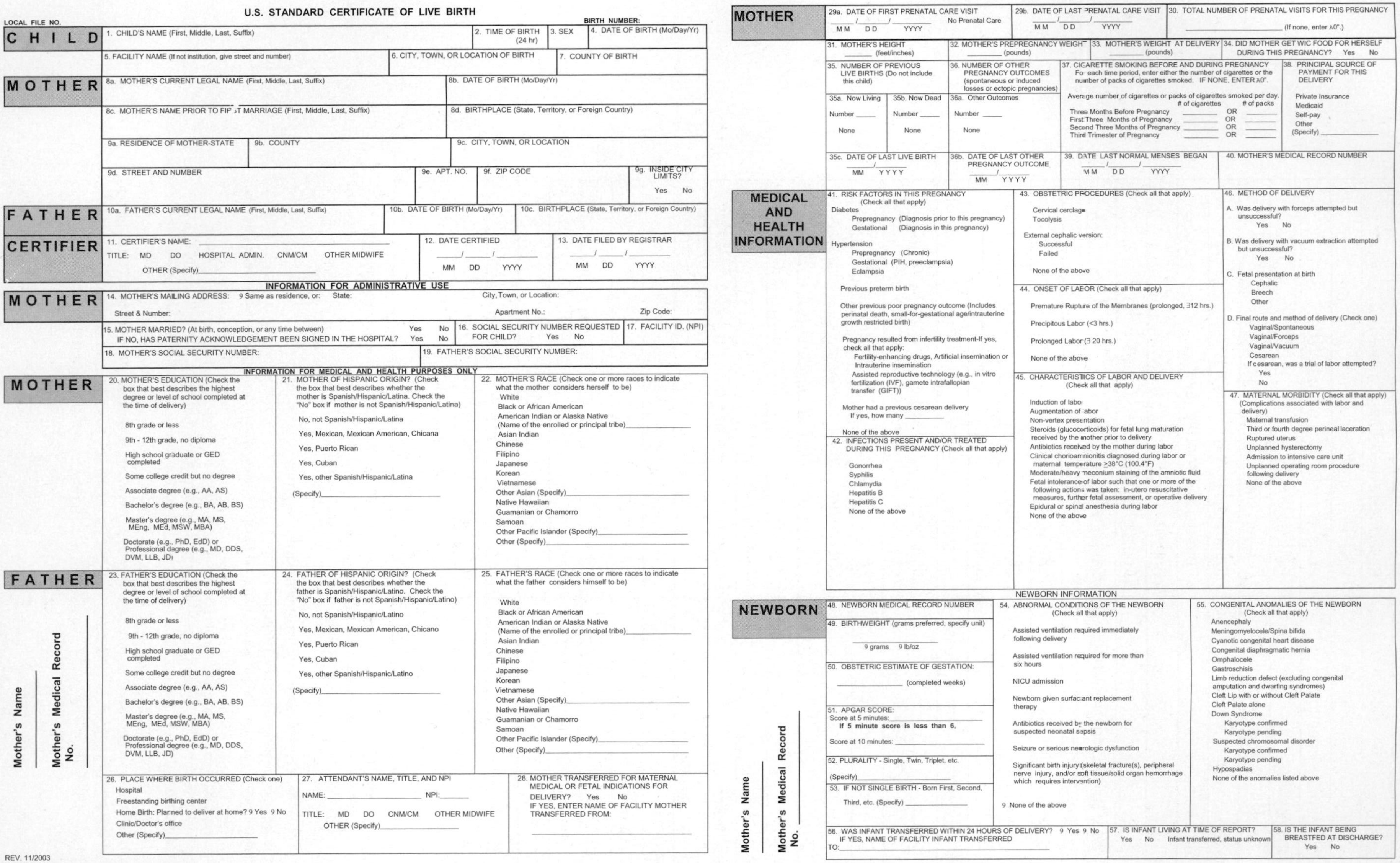

U.S. STANDARD CERTIFICATE OF LIVE BIRTH

LOCAL FILE NO. BIRTH NUMBER:

CHILD
1. CHILD'S NAME (First, Middle, Last, Suffix)
2. TIME OF BIRTH (24 hr)
3. SEX
4. DATE OF BIRTH (Mo/Day/Yr)
5. FACILITY NAME (If not institution, give street and number)
6. CITY, TOWN, OR LOCATION OF BIRTH
7. COUNTY OF BIRTH

MOTHER
8a. MOTHER'S CURRENT LEGAL NAME (First, Middle, Last, Suffix)
8b. DATE OF BIRTH (Mo/Day/Yr)
8c. MOTHER'S NAME PRIOR TO FIRST MARRIAGE (First, Middle, Last, Suffix)
8d. BIRTHPLACE (State, Territory, or Foreign Country)
9a. RESIDENCE OF MOTHER-STATE
9b. COUNTY
9c. CITY, TOWN, OR LOCATION
9d. STREET AND NUMBER
9e. APT. NO.
9f. ZIP CODE
9g. INSIDE CITY LIMITS? Yes No

FATHER
10a. FATHER'S CURRENT LEGAL NAME (First, Middle, Last, Suffix)
10b. DATE OF BIRTH (Mo/Day/Yr)
10c. BIRTHPLACE (State, Territory, or Foreign Country)

CERTIFIER
11. CERTIFIER'S NAME: ____
TITLE: MD DO HOSPITAL ADMIN. CNM/CM OTHER MIDWIFE
OTHER (Specify)____
12. DATE CERTIFIED ___/___/___ MM DD YYYY
13. DATE FILED BY REGISTRAR ___/___/___ MM DD YYYY

INFORMATION FOR ADMINISTRATIVE USE

MOTHER
14. MOTHER'S MAILING ADDRESS: 9 Same as residence, or: State: City, Town, or Location:
Street & Number: Apartment No.: Zip Code:
15. MOTHER MARRIED? (At birth, conception, or any time between) Yes No
IF NO, HAS PATERNITY ACKNOWLEDGEMENT BEEN SIGNED IN THE HOSPITAL? Yes No
16. SOCIAL SECURITY NUMBER REQUESTED FOR CHILD? Yes No
17. FACILITY ID. (NPI)
18. MOTHER'S SOCIAL SECURITY NUMBER:
19. FATHER'S SOCIAL SECURITY NUMBER:

INFORMATION FOR MEDICAL AND HEALTH PURPOSES ONLY

MOTHER
20. MOTHER'S EDUCATION (Check the box that best describes the highest degree or level of school completed at the time of delivery)
8th grade or less
9th - 12th grade, no diploma
High school graduate or GED completed
Some college credit but no degree
Associate degree (e.g., AA, AS)
Bachelor's degree (e.g., BA, AB, BS)
Master's degree (e.g., MA, MS, MEng, MEd, MSW, MBA)
Doctorate (e.g., PhD, EdD) or Professional degree (e.g., MD, DDS, DVM, LLB, JD)

21. MOTHER OF HISPANIC ORIGIN? (Check the box that best describes whether the mother is Spanish/Hispanic/Latina. Check the "No" box if mother is not Spanish/Hispanic/Latina)
No, not Spanish/Hispanic/Latina
Yes, Mexican, Mexican American, Chicana
Yes, Puerto Rican
Yes, Cuban
Yes, other Spanish/Hispanic/Latina
(Specify)____

22. MOTHER'S RACE (Check one or more races to indicate what the mother considers herself to be)
White
Black or African American
American Indian or Alaska Native (Name of the enrolled or principal tribe)____
Asian Indian
Chinese
Filipino
Japanese
Korean
Vietnamese
Other Asian (Specify)____
Native Hawaiian
Guamanian or Chamorro
Samoan
Other Pacific Islander (Specify)____
Other (Specify)____

FATHER
23. FATHER'S EDUCATION (Check the box that best describes the highest degree or level of school completed at the time of delivery)
8th grade or less
9th - 12th grade, no diploma
High school graduate or GED completed
Some college credit but no degree
Associate degree (e.g., AA, AS)
Bachelor's degree (e.g., BA, AB, BS)
Master's degree (e.g., MA, MS, MEng, MEd, MSW, MBA)
Doctorate (e.g., PhD, EdD) or Professional degree (e.g., MD, DDS, DVM, LLB, JD)

24. FATHER OF HISPANIC ORIGIN? (Check the box that best describes whether the father is Spanish/Hispanic/Latino. Check the "No" box if father is not Spanish/Hispanic/Latino)
No, not Spanish/Hispanic/Latino
Yes, Mexican, Mexican American, Chicano
Yes, Puerto Rican
Yes, Cuban
Yes, other Spanish/Hispanic/Latino
(Specify)____

25. FATHER'S RACE (Check one or more races to indicate what the father considers himself to be)
White
Black or African American
American Indian or Alaska Native (Name of the enrolled or principal tribe)____
Asian Indian
Chinese
Filipino
Japanese
Korean
Vietnamese
Other Asian (Specify)____
Native Hawaiian
Guamanian or Chamorro
Samoan
Other Pacific Islander (Specify)____
Other (Specify)____

Mother's Name ____
Mother's Medical Record No. ____

26. PLACE WHERE BIRTH OCCURRED (Check one)
Hospital
Freestanding birthing center
Home Birth: Planned to deliver at home? 9 Yes 9 No
Clinic/Doctor's office
Other (Specify)____

27. ATTENDANT'S NAME, TITLE, AND NPI
NAME: ____ NPI: ____
TITLE: MD DO CNM/CM OTHER MIDWIFE
OTHER (Specify)____

28. MOTHER TRANSFERRED FOR MATERNAL MEDICAL OR FETAL INDICATIONS FOR DELIVERY? Yes No
IF YES, ENTER NAME OF FACILITY MOTHER TRANSFERRED FROM:

REV. 11/2003

MOTHER
29a. DATE OF FIRST PRENATAL CARE VISIT ___/___/___ MM DD YYYY No Prenatal Care
29b. DATE OF LAST PRENATAL CARE VISIT ___/___/___ MM DD YYYY
30. TOTAL NUMBER OF PRENATAL VISITS FOR THIS PREGNANCY ____ (If none, enter A0".)
31. MOTHER'S HEIGHT ____ (feet/inches)
32. MOTHER'S PREPREGNANCY WEIGHT ____ (pounds)
33. MOTHER'S WEIGHT AT DELIVERY ____ (pounds)
34. DID MOTHER GET WIC FOOD FOR HERSELF DURING THIS PREGNANCY? Yes No
35. NUMBER OF PREVIOUS LIVE BIRTHS (Do not include this child)
35a. Now Living Number ____ None
35b. Now Dead Number ____ None
35c. DATE OF LAST LIVE BIRTH ___/___ MM YYYY
36. NUMBER OF OTHER PREGNANCY OUTCOMES (spontaneous or induced losses or ectopic pregnancies)
36a. Other Outcomes Number ____ None
36b. DATE OF LAST OTHER PREGNANCY OUTCOME ___/___ MM YYYY
37. CIGARETTE SMOKING BEFORE AND DURING PREGNANCY
For each time period, enter either the number of cigarettes or the number of packs of cigarettes smoked. IF NONE, ENTER A0".
Average number of cigarettes or packs of cigarettes smoked per day.

	# of cigarettes		# of packs
Three Months Before Pregnancy	____	OR	____
First Three Months of Pregnancy	____	OR	____
Second Three Months of Pregnancy	____	OR	____
Third Trimester of Pregnancy	____	OR	____

38. PRINCIPAL SOURCE OF PAYMENT FOR THIS DELIVERY
Private Insurance
Medicaid
Self-pay
Other (Specify)____
39. DATE LAST NORMAL MENSES BEGAN ___/___/___ MM DD YYYY
40. MOTHER'S MEDICAL RECORD NUMBER

MEDICAL AND HEALTH INFORMATION
41. RISK FACTORS IN THIS PREGNANCY (Check all that apply)
Diabetes
Prepregnancy (Diagnosis prior to this pregnancy)
Gestational (Diagnosis in this pregnancy)
Hypertension
Prepregnancy (Chronic)
Gestational (PIH, preeclampsia)
Eclampsia
Previous preterm birth
Other previous poor pregnancy outcome (Includes perinatal death, small-for-gestational age/intrauterine growth restricted birth)
Pregnancy resulted from infertility treatment-If yes, check all that apply:
Fertility-enhancing drugs, Artificial insemination or Intrauterine insemination
Assisted reproductive technology (e.g., in vitro fertilization (IVF), gamete intrafallopian transfer (GIFT))
Mother had a previous cesarean delivery
If yes, how many ____
None of the above

42. INFECTIONS PRESENT AND/OR TREATED DURING THIS PREGNANCY (Check all that apply)
Gonorrhea
Syphilis
Chlamydia
Hepatitis B
Hepatitis C
None of the above

43. OBSTETRIC PROCEDURES (Check all that apply)
Cervical cerclage
Tocolysis
External cephalic version:
Successful
Failed
None of the above

44. ONSET OF LABOR (Check all that apply)
Premature Rupture of the Membranes (prolonged, ≥12 hrs.)
Precipitous Labor (<3 hrs.)
Prolonged Labor (≥20 hrs.)
None of the above

45. CHARACTERISTICS OF LABOR AND DELIVERY (Check all that apply)
Induction of labor
Augmentation of labor
Non-vertex presentation
Steroids (glucocorticoids) for fetal lung maturation received by the mother prior to delivery
Antibiotics received by the mother during labor
Clinical chorioamnionitis diagnosed during labor or maternal temperature ≥38°C (100.4°F)
Moderate/heavy meconium staining of the amniotic fluid
Fetal intolerance of labor such that one or more of the following actions was taken: in-utero resuscitative measures, further fetal assessment, or operative delivery
Epidural or spinal anesthesia during labor
None of the above

46. METHOD OF DELIVERY
A. Was delivery with forceps attempted but unsuccessful? Yes No
B. Was delivery with vacuum extraction attempted but unsuccessful? Yes No
C. Fetal presentation at birth
Cephalic
Breech
Other
D. Final route and method of delivery (Check one)
Vaginal/Spontaneous
Vaginal/Forceps
Vaginal/Vacuum
Cesarean
If cesarean, was a trial of labor attempted?
Yes
No

47. MATERNAL MORBIDITY (Check all that apply) (Complications associated with labor and delivery)
Maternal transfusion
Third or fourth degree perineal laceration
Ruptured uterus
Unplanned hysterectomy
Admission to intensive care unit
Unplanned operating room procedure following delivery
None of the above

NEWBORN INFORMATION

NEWBORN
48. NEWBORN MEDICAL RECORD NUMBER
49. BIRTHWEIGHT (grams preferred, specify unit) ____ 9 grams 9 lb/oz
50. OBSTETRIC ESTIMATE OF GESTATION: ____ (completed weeks)
51. APGAR SCORE:
Score at 5 minutes: ____
If 5 minute score is less than 6,
Score at 10 minutes: ____
52. PLURALITY - Single, Twin, Triplet, etc. (Specify)____
53. IF NOT SINGLE BIRTH - Born First, Second, Third, etc. (Specify)____

54. ABNORMAL CONDITIONS OF THE NEWBORN (Check all that apply)
Assisted ventilation required immediately following delivery
Assisted ventilation required for more than six hours
NICU admission
Newborn given surfactant replacement therapy
Antibiotics received by the newborn for suspected neonatal sepsis
Seizure or serious neurologic dysfunction
Significant birth injury (skeletal fracture(s), peripheral nerve injury, and/or soft tissue/solid organ hemorrhage which requires intervention)
9 None of the above

55. CONGENITAL ANOMALIES OF THE NEWBORN (Check all that apply)
Anencephaly
Meningomyelocele/Spina bifida
Cyanotic congenital heart disease
Congenital diaphragmatic hernia
Omphalocele
Gastroschisis
Limb reduction defect (excluding congenital amputation and dwarfing syndromes)
Cleft Lip with or without Cleft Palate
Cleft Palate alone
Down Syndrome
Karyotype confirmed
Karyotype pending
Suspected chromosomal disorder
Karyotype confirmed
Karyotype pending
Hypospadias
None of the anomalies listed above

Mother's Name ____
Mother's Medical Record No. ____

56. WAS INFANT TRANSFERRED WITHIN 24 HOURS OF DELIVERY? 9 Yes 9 No
IF YES, NAME OF FACILITY INFANT TRANSFERRED TO: ____
57. IS INFANT LIVING AT TIME OF REPORT? Yes No Infant transferred, status unknown
58. IS THE INFANT BEING BREASTFED AT DISCHARGE? Yes No

FIGURE 3.2 Birth certificates are issued by local health departments that have jurisdiction where the birth occurred.

Reproduced from: Centers for Disease Control and Prevention (2003). *U.S. Standard Certificate of Live Birth*. Available at http://www.cdc.gov/nchs/data/dvs/birth11-03final-acc.pdf.

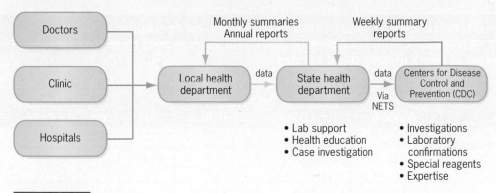

FIGURE 3.3   Scheme for the reporting of notifiable diseases.

For example, reporting may be more complete for diseases that are rare and life threatening or those that pose a larger public health threat or burden. Therefore, morbidity data—although useful for reflecting disease trends—cannot always be considered to be precise counts of the actual number of cases of diseases.

Standardized Measurements of Health Status of Populations

It is often difficult to precisely measure the level of wellness or, for that matter, ill health. On the other hand, death can be clearly defined. For this reason, mortality statistics, particularly infant mortality, continue to be the single most reliable indicator of a population's health status. Although mortality statistics do not completely describe the health status of a population, they can be used to calculate other useful measurements; two of these are life expectancy and years of potential life lost. Finally, there are measurements of ill health that, although less precise than mortality, can nonetheless be meaningful. Such measurements are disability-adjusted life years and health-adjusted life expectancy.

Mortality Statistics

In 2013, 2,596,993 deaths were registered in the United States. The crude mortality rate was 821.5 per 100,000. The age-adjusted death rate, which eliminates the effects of the aging population, was 731.9 deaths per 100,000 U.S. standard population. This was a record low.[19] Age-adjusted death rates show what the level of mortality would be if no changes occurred in the age makeup of the population from year to year. Thus, they are a better indicator than are unadjusted (crude) death rates for examining changes in the risk of death over a period of time when the age distribution of the population is changing. Death rates and age-adjusted death rates for the 15 leading causes of death in the United States in 2013 are presented in (see **Table 3.6**).[19]

Naturally, morbidity and mortality rates vary greatly depending on age, sex, race, and ethnicity. For example, whereas heart disease is the leading cause of death for the general population and especially for older adults (those who have reached 65 years of age), cancer is the leading cause of death for the 45- to 64-year-old age group, and unintentional injuries are the leading cause of death for all age groups between 1 and 44 years.[17]

There has been a shift in the leading causes of death since the beginning of the twentieth century. When the century began, communicable diseases such as pneumonia, tuberculosis, and gastrointestinal infections were the leading causes of death.[22] However, a century of progress in public health practice and in biomedical research resulted in a significant reduction in the proportion of deaths from communicable diseases so that the four leading causes of death today are noncommunicable diseases (see **Table 3.7**). In 2013, the five leading causes of death in the United States—heart disease, cancer, chronic lower respiratory disease, unintentional injuries (accidents and adverse effects), and stroke—accounted for about 62% of all deaths (see Table 3.7).[19] In 2012, the five leading causes of death worldwide were heart

TABLE 3.6   Number of Deaths, Percentage of Total Deaths, Death Rates, and Age-Adjusted Death Rates for 2013, Percentage Change in Age-Adjusted Death Rates in 2013 from 2012 for the 15 Leading Causes of Death in 2013: United States

Rank[a]	Cause of Death (Based on ICD-10)	Number	Percent of Total Deaths	Crude Death Rate	Age-Adjusted Death Rate		
					2013	2012	Percent Change
...	All causes	2,596,993	100.0	821.5	731.9	732.8	-0.1
1	Diseases of heart (I00-I09, I11, I13, I20-I51)	611,105	23.5	193.3	169.8	170.5	-0.4
2	Malignant neoplasms (C00-C97)	584,881	22.5	185.0	163.2	166.5	-2.0
3	Chronic lower respiratory diseases (J40-J47)	149,205	5.7	47.2	42.1	41.5	1.4
4	Accidents (unintentional injuries) (V01-X59, Y85-Y86)	130,557	5.0	41.3	39.4	39.1	0.8
5	Cerebrovascular diseases (I60-I69)	128,978	5.0	40.8	36.2	36.9	-1.9
6	Alzheimer's disease (G30)	84,776	3.3	26.8	23.5	23.8	-1.2
7	Diabetes mellitus (E10-E14)	75,578	2.9	23.9	21.2	21.2	0.0
8	Influenza and pneumonia (J09-J18)	56,979	2.2	18.0	15.9	14.4	10.4
9	Nephritis, nephrotic syndrome and nephrosis (N00-N07, N17-N19, N25-N27)	47,112	1.8	14.9	13.2	13.1	0.8
10	Intentional self-harm (suicide) (*U03, X60-X84, Y87.0)	41,149	1.6	13.0	12.6	12.6	0.0
11	Septicemia (A40-A41)	38,156	1.5	12.1	10.7	10.3	3.9
12	Chronic liver disease and cirrhosis (K70, K73-K74)	36,427	1.4	11.5	10.2	9.9	3.0
13	Essential hypertension and hypertensive renal disease (I10, I12, I15)	30,770	1.2	9.7	8.5	8.2	3.7
14	Parkinson's disease (G20-G21)	25,196	1.0	8.0	7.3	7.0	4.3
15	Pneumonitis due to solids and liquids (J69)	18,579	0.7	5.9	5.2	5.1	2.0
...	All other causes (Residual)	537,554	20.7	170.0	...	...	...

[a]Rank based on number of deaths.

Data from: Centers for Disease Control and Prevention (2015). "Deaths: Preliminary Data for 2013." *National Vital Statistics Reports*, 64(2). Hyattsville, MD: National Center for Health Statistics. Available at http://www.cdc.gov/nchs/data/nvsr/nvsr64/nvsr64_02.pdf; Centers for Disease Control and Prevention (2014). "Deaths, Percent of Total Deaths, and Death Rates for the 15 Leading Causes of Death: United States and Each State, 2013." *National Vital Statistics System Mortality Tables*. Hyattsville, MD: National Center for Health Statistics. Available at http://www.cdc.gov/nchs/data/dvs/LCWK9_2013.pdf.

disease, stroke, chronic obstructive pulmonary disease, lower respiratory infections, and tracheal, bronchus, and lung cancers.[23]

This domination of annual mortality statistics by noncommunicable diseases masks the importance of communicable diseases as causes of deaths in certain age groups. For example,

TABLE 3.7   Leading Causes of Death in the United States: 1900, 1940, 2013

1900	
1.	Pneumonia, influenza
2.	Tuberculosis
3.	Diarrhea
4.	Diseases of the heart
5.	Cerebrovascular diseases (stroke)
6.	Nephritis
7.	Unintentional injuries (accidents)
8.	Malignant neoplasms (cancers)
9.	Senility
10.	Diphtheria
1940	
1.	Diseases of the heart
2.	Malignant neoplasms (cancers)
3.	Cerebrovascular diseases (stroke)
4.	Nephritis
5.	Pneumonia, influenza
6.	Unintentional injuries (non-motor vehicle)
7.	Tuberculosis
8.	Diabetes mellitus
9.	Unintentional injuries (motor vehicle)
10.	Premature birth
2013	
1.	Diseases of the heart
2.	Malignant neoplasms (cancers)
3.	Chronic lower respiratory diseases
4.	Accidents (unintentional injuries)
5.	Cerebrovascular diseases (stroke)
6.	Alzheimer's disease
7.	Diabetes mellitus
8.	Influenza and pneumonia
9.	Nephritis, nephrotic syndrome, and nephrosis (kidney diseases)
10.	Intentional self-harm (suicide)

Adapted from: Centers for Disease Control and Prevention (2015). "Deaths: Preliminary Data for 2013." *National Vital Statistics Reports*, 64(2). Hyattsville, MD: National Center for Health Statistics. Available at http://www.cdc.gov/nchs/data/nvsr/nvsr64/nvsr64_02.pdf; Centers for Disease Control and Prevention, National Center for Health Statistics (1998). "Leading Causes of Death, 1900–1998." Available at http://www.cdc.gov/nchs/data/dvs/lead1900_98.pdf.

pneumonia and influenza account for a larger portion of deaths among young children and older adults compared with other age groups. Thus, it is important to remember that viewing the leading causes of death for the entire population does not provide a clear picture of the health for any one segment of the population.

TABLE 3.8 Life Expectancy at Birth, at 65 Years of Age, and at 75 Years of Age According to Sex: In the United States, During the Selected Years 1900–2013

Year	At Birth			At 65 Years			At 75 Years		
	Both Sexes	Male	Female	Both Sexes	Male	Female	Both Sexes	Male	Female
1900	47.3	46.3	48.3	11.9	11.5	12.2	*	*	*
1950	68.2	65.6	71.1	13.9	12.8	15.0	*	*	*
1960	69.7	66.6	73.1	14.3	12.8	15.8	*	*	*
1970	70.8	67.1	74.7	15.2	13.1	17.0	*	*	*
1980	73.7	70.7	77.4	16.4	14.1	18.3	10.4	8.8	11.5
1990	75.4	71.8	78.8	17.2	15.1	18.9	10.9	9.4	12.0
2000	76.8	74.1	79.3	17.6	16.0	19.0	11.0	9.8	11.8
2010	78.7	76.2	81.0	19.1	17.7	20.3	12.1	11.0	12.9
2013	78.8	76.4	81.2	19.3	17.9	20.5	12.2	11.2	12.9

*Data not available.

Data from: National Center for Health Statistics (2015). *Health, United States, 2014: With Special Feature on Adults Aged 55–64*. Available at http://www.cdc.gov/nchs/data/hus/hus14.pdf.

Life Expectancy

Life expectancy is another standard measurement used to compare the health status of various populations. Also based on mortality, **life expectancy** is defined as the average number of years a person from a specific cohort is projected to live from a given point in time. Whereas life insurance companies are interested in life expectancy at every age, health statisticians are usually concerned with life expectancy at birth, at the age of 65 years, and, more recently, at age 75. It must be remembered that life expectancy is an average for an entire cohort (usually of a single birth year) and is not necessarily a useful prediction for any one individual. Moreover, it certainly cannot describe the quality of one's life. However, the ever-increasing life expectancy for Americans suggests that as a country, we have managed to control some of those factors that contribute to early deaths.

Table 3.8 provides a summary of life expectancy figures for the United States from 1900 to 2013. The data presented indicate that the overall life expectancy at birth, at 65 years, and at 75 years has generally increased since 1900. Life expectancies at birth for both sexes rose from 47.3 years in 1900 to 78.8 years in 2013, when the life expectancy of a newborn baby girl was 81.2 years compared with a newborn baby boy—76.4 years.[24]

When compared with the life expectancy figures of other countries (see **Table 3.9**), the United States figures (approximately 79 years for both ages combined) roughly correspond with those of other countries with well-developed economies. The highest life expectancy figures are reported in Japan (84 years); while the lowest are reported from countries in Africa (51 years in the Central African Republic).[25]

Years of Potential Life Lost

Life expectancy the average number of years a person from a specific cohort is projected to live from a given point in time

Years of potential life lost (YPLL) the number of years lost when death occurs before the age of 65 or 75

Whereas standard mortality statistics, such as leading causes of death, provide one measure of the importance of various diseases, **years of potential life lost (YPLL)** provides another, different measure. YPLL is calculated by subtracting a person's age at death from a predefined, standard age. Each person may have a different life expectancy at any given time, so the age 75 years is often used in these calculations. For example, for a person who dies at age 59, the YPLL-75 is 16. Although age 75 is typically used for calculations, the standard age could be 65, 70, 80, or any other predefined age.

YPLL weights deaths such that the death of a very young person counts more than the death of a very old person. **Table 3.10** provides a summary of the age-adjusted YPLL before age 75 (YPLL-75)

TABLE 3.9   Life Expectancy at Birth for Selected Countries by Sex in 2013

	Male	Female
Central African Republic	50	52
Ethiopia	63	66
Malawi	58	61
India	65	68
Nicaragua	71	77
Ecuador	73	79
Congo	58	60
Thailand	71	79
Malaysia	72	76
South Africa	57	64
Brazil	72	79
Latvia	69	79
Republic of Korea	78	85
Greece	79	84
New Zealand	80	84
United Kingdom	79	83
United States	76	81
Sweden	80	84
Japan	80	87

Data from: World Health Organization (2015). *World Health Statistics: Part II Global Health Indicators.* Available at http://www.who.int/gho/publications/world_health_statistics/EN_WHS2015_Part2.pdf.

for the 10 leading causes of death in the United States for 1990 and 2013.[24] In examining this table, note that the number of YPLL-75 per 100,000 population was highest for malignant neoplasms (cancer) unintentional injuries. This is because unintentional injuries and malignant neoplasms (cancer) are more commonly causes of death for people who are young. These differences can also be seen in the two pie charts shown in **Figure 3.4**. Also, notice that the YPLL-75 per 100,000 population declined for most of the leading causes of death between 1990 and 2013.

YPLL from specific causes varies depending on the subpopulation under consideration. For example, the YPLL-75 per 100,000 population resulting from unintentional injuries is nearly two and a half times higher for men compared to women. The YPLL-75 per 100,000 for diseases of the heart for blacks is nearly twice that for whites, and for homicide, it is over six times greater.[24]

Disability-Adjusted Life Years

Mortality does not entirely express the burden of disease. For example, chronic depression and paralysis caused by polio are responsible for great loss of healthy life but are not reflected in mortality tables. Because of this, the World Health Organization (WHO) and the World Bank have developed a measure called the **disability-adjusted life years (DALYs)**.[26]

One DALY is one lost year of healthy life. Total DALYs for a given condition for a particular population can be calculated by estimating the total years of life lost and the total years of life lived with disability, and then by summing these totals. As an example, the DALYs incurred through firearm injuries in the United States could be calculated by adding the total of YPLL incurred from fatal firearm injuries to the total years of life lived with disabilities by survivors of firearm injuries. **Figure 3.5** illustrates the number of DALYs lost per 1,000 population in 2012 from six demographic regions of the world.[27]

Disability-adjusted life years (DALYs) a measure for the burden of disease that takes into account premature death and loss of healthy life resulting from disability

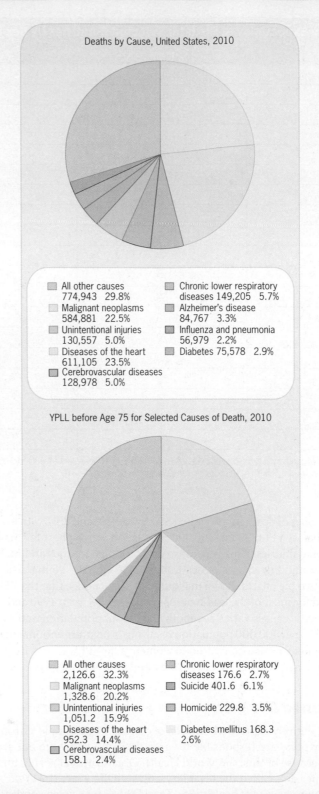

Deaths by Cause, United States, 2010

- All other causes 774,943 29.8%
- Malignant neoplasms 584,881 22.5%
- Unintentional injuries 130,557 5.0%
- Diseases of the heart 611,105 23.5%
- Cerebrovascular diseases 128,978 5.0%
- Chronic lower respiratory diseases 149,205 5.7%
- Alzheimer's disease 84,767 3.3%
- Influenza and pneumonia 56,979 2.2%
- Diabetes 75,578 2.9%

YPLL before Age 75 for Selected Causes of Death, 2010

- All other causes 2,126.6 32.3%
- Malignant neoplasms 1,328.6 20.2%
- Unintentional injuries 1,051.2 15.9%
- Diseases of the heart 952.3 14.4%
- Cerebrovascular diseases 158.1 2.4%
- Chronic lower respiratory diseases 176.6 2.7%
- Suicide 401.6 6.1%
- Homicide 229.8 3.5%
- Diabetes mellitus 168.3 2.6%

FIGURE 3.4   Deaths by cause in the United States, 2013, and the years of potential life lost before age 75 (YPLL-75) per 100,000 population for selected causes of death within the United States, 2013.

Data from: Centers for Disease Control and Prevention (2014). "Deaths, Percent of Total Deaths, and Death Rates for the 15 Leading Causes of Death: United States and Each State, 2013." *National Vital Statistics System Mortality Tables*. Hyattsville, MD: National Center for Health Statistics. Available at http://www.cdc.gov/nchs/data/dvs/LCWK9_2013.pdf.; National Center for Health Statistics (2015). *Health, United States, 2014: With Special Feature on Adults Aged 55–64*. Available at http://www.cdc.gov/nchs/data/hus/hus14.pdf.

TABLE 3.10 Age-Adjusted Years of Potential Life Lost Before 75 (YPLL-75) for the 10 Leading Causes of Death, United States, 1990 and 2013		
	YPLL per 100,000 Population	
Cause	1990	2013
Diseases of the heart	1,617.7	952.3
Malignant neoplasms (cancer)	2,003.8	1,328.6
Cerebrovascular diseases (stroke)	259.6	158.1
Chronic lower respiratory diseases	187.4	176.6
Unintentional injuries	1,162.1	1,051.2
Influenza and pneumonia	141.5	82.3
Diabetes mellitus	155.9	168.3
Human immunodeficiency virus infection (HIV/AIDS)	383.8	58.1
Suicide	393.1	401.8
Homicide	417.4	229.8

Data from: National Center for Health Statistics (2015). *Health, United States, 2014: With Special Feature on Adults Aged 55–64.* Available at http://www.cdc.gov/nchs/data/hus/hus14.pdf.

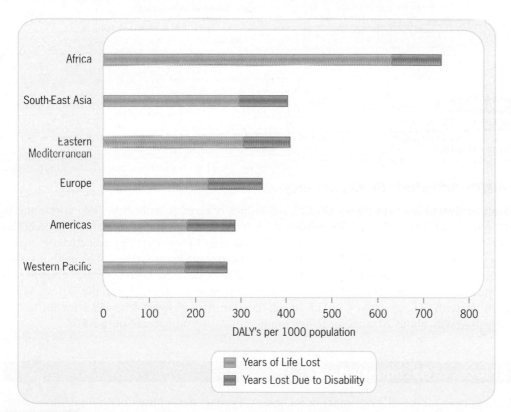

FIGURE 3.5   Burden of disease: years of life lost due to premature mortality (YLL) and years of life lived with a disability (YLD) per thousand by region, 2012. DALYs: disability-adjusted life years.

Data from: World Health Organization (2016). *Estimates for 2000–2012, Disease Burden.* Available at http://www.who.int/healthinfo/global_burden_disease/estimates/en/index2.html.

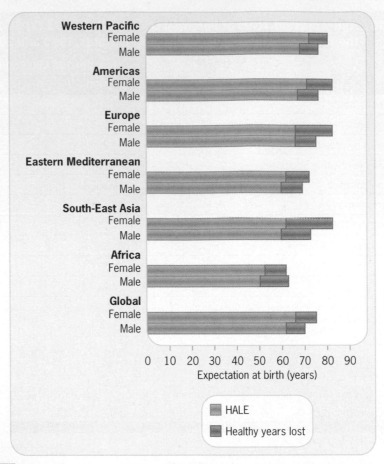

FIGURE 3.6   Life expectancy, health-adjusted life expectancy (HALE), and lost healthy years by region and sex, 2013.

Data from: World Health Organization. (2015). *Life Expectancy Data by WHO Region.* Available at http://apps.who.int/gho/data/view .main.690?lang=en.

Health-Adjusted Life Expectancy

Health-adjusted life expectancy (HALE), sometimes referred to as healthy life expectancy, is the number of years of healthy life expected, on average, in a given population or region of the world. The HALE indicator used by the WHO is similar to the disability-adjusted life expectancy (DALE) first reported in the original Global Burden of Disease study.[26] The methods used to calculate HALE are beyond the scope of this textbook, but have been described elsewhere.[28] Worldwide, HALE at birth in 2013 was 60 years, 8 years lower than overall life expectancy at birth. As with life expectancy, HALE in sub-Saharan Africa is very low—49 years for males, compared with about 70 years for females in high-income countries (**Figure 3.6**).[29]

Sources of Secondary Data

Data sources can be either primary or secondary. Primary data consist of original information collected first hand, whereas secondary data have been collected by someone else, possibly for another purpose. Because demographic and epidemiological data are used in the planning of public health programs and facilities, students of community health should be aware of the sources of these secondary data. Students can obtain secondary data for use in community health work from the following sources: the U.S. Census, *National Vital Statistics Reports, Morbidity and Mortality Weekly Reports,* the National Health Interview Survey, the National

Health-adjusted life expectancy (HALE) the number of years of healthy life expected, on average, in a given population

Health and Nutrition Examination Survey, the Behavioral Risk Factor Surveillance System, the Youth Risk Behavior Surveillance System, and the National Health Care Surveys. This is only a small selection of secondary data sources commonly used in community health; many more sources of secondary data exist on a variety of topics.

Each of these sources of national data has a specific value and usefulness to those in the public health field. Students interested in studying local health problems can obtain data from state and local health departments, hospitals, volunteer agencies, and disease registries. The study and analysis of these data provide a basis for planning appropriate health programs and facilities in your communities.

U.S. Census the enumeration of the population of the United States that is conducted every 10 years

Vital statistics statistical summaries of records of major life events such as births, deaths, marriages, divorces, and infant deaths

The U.S. Census

The **U.S. Census**, taken every 10 years, is an enumeration of the population living in the United States. George Washington ordered the first census in 1790 for the purpose of apportioning representation to the House of Representatives. Through the years, the census form has become much more complex than the one filled out more than 200 years earlier. Data are gathered about income, employment, family size, education, dwelling type, and many other social indicators. Copies of the U.S. Census results are available in most libraries and online at www.census.gov.

Census data are important to health workers because they are used for calculating disease and death rates and for program planning. The U.S. Census is carried out by the Bureau of the Census, located in the U.S. Department of Commerce.

Vital Statistics Reports

The National Center for Health Statistics (NCHS), one of the Centers for Disease Control and Prevention, provides the most up-to-date national vital statistics available. These statistics appear in the *National Vital Statistics Reports*, published by the NCHS in Hyattsville, Maryland. **Vital statistics** are statistical summaries of vital records, that is, records of major life events. Listed are births, deaths, marriages, and divorces. Detailed reports of data from the birth and death certificates are published in preliminary and final reports each year. The birth reports include data on a wide range of topics including maternal and infant characteristics as well as details about prenatal care and delivery. The death report includes data on death rates, life expectancy, leading causes of death, and infant mortality. In addition to these reports, four to six reports are published each year on special topics related to vital statistics. *National Vital Statistics Reports* are available at www.cdc.gov/nchs/.

Morbidity and Mortality Weekly Report

Reported cases of specified notifiable diseases are reported weekly in the *Morbidity and Mortality Weekly Report (MMWR)*, which lists morbidity and mortality data by state and region of the country. The report is prepared by the CDC based on reports from state health departments. This report is printed and distributed through an agreement with the Massachusetts Medical Society, publishers of the *New England Journal of Medicine*. Each weekly issue also contains several reports of outbreaks of disease, environmental hazards, unusual cases, or other public health problems. The *MMWR* and its annual summary reports are available on the website www.cdc.gov/mmwr.

National Health Surveys

Another source of secondary data is the national health surveys. These surveys are a result of the National Health Survey Act of 1956, which authorized a continuing survey of the amount, distribution, and effects of illness and disability in the United States. The intent of this Act is currently being fulfilled by three types of surveys: (1) health interviews of people; (2) clinical tests, measurements, and physical examinations of people; and (3) surveys of places where people receive medical care, such as hospitals, clinics, and doctors' offices. The following paragraphs describe these surveys. More information about these surveys and results is available at the National Center for Health Statistics website, www.cdc.gov/nchs.

National Health Interview Survey

In the National Health Interview Survey (NHIS), conducted by the National Center for Health Statistics (NCHS), people are asked numerous questions about their health. One of the questions asks respondents to describe their health status using one of five categories—excellent, very good, good, fair, or poor. Fewer than 1 in 8 of the adult respondents in 2014 described their health status as either fair or poor, while approximately 6 in 10 Americans believe they are in very good or excellent health. College graduates were more likely than persons who had not graduated from high school to describe their health as excellent or very good (75.2% and 40.1%, respectively). Persons with family incomes of $100,000 or more were also more likely than those with incomes of less than $35,000 to describe their health as excellent or very good (76.9% and 47.8%, respectively). There were also differences when comparing race, ethnicity, age, marital status, and place of residence.[30]

It is important to remember that these data were generated by self-reported responses to NHIS questions and not by actual examinations objectively generated in a clinic. As such, respondents may overreport good health habits or underreport bad ones. Such reporting is often dependent on the respondent's perceived social stigma or support for a response and the degree to which people's responses are confidential or anonymous. Furthermore, people have widely divergent views on what constitutes poor or good health. For example, many sedentary, cigarette-smoking, high-stress people see themselves as being in good health, while "health nuts" may feel their health is deteriorating when they miss a day of exercise. In general, the young assess their health better than the old do, males better than females, whites better than blacks, and those with large family incomes better than those with smaller ones. Other topics covered by the National Health Interview Survey include limitations and injuries, health care access and use, and health insurance coverage.

National Health and Nutrition Examination Survey

Another of the national health surveys is the National Health and Nutrition Examination Survey (NHANES). The purpose of the NHANES is to assess the health and nutritional status of the general U.S. population. Using a mobile examination center (see **Figure 3.7**), the data are collected through direct physical examinations, clinical and laboratory testing, and related procedures on a representative group of Americans. These examinations result in the most

FIGURE 3.7   A National Health and Nutrition Examination Survey (NHANES) mobile examination center.

Both: Courtesy of CDC.

authoritative source of standardized clinical, physical, and physiological data on the American people. Included in the data are the prevalence of specific conditions and diseases and data on blood pressure, serum cholesterol, body measurements, nutritional status and deficiencies, and exposure to environmental toxins.

The first series of these surveys, known as National Health Examination Surveys (NHES), were carried out during the 1960s. Beginning in the 1970s, nutrition was added as a new focus, and the surveys became known as the National Health and Nutrition Examination Survey (NHANES). Three cycles of the NHANES were conducted at periodic time intervals by the National Center for Health Statistics, the third ending in 1994. The survey became a continuous, rather than periodic, program in 1999. The program's focus changes on a variety of health and nutrition measurements to meet emerging needs.

Results of NHANES benefit people in the United States in important ways. Facts about the distribution of health problems and risk factors in the population give researchers important clues to the causes of disease. Information collected from the current survey is compared with information collected in previous surveys. This allows health planners to detect the extent various health problems and risk factors have changed in the U.S. population over time. By identifying the health care needs of the population, government agencies and private sector organizations can establish policies and plan research, education, and health promotion programs that help improve present health status and will prevent future health problems.[31]

Each year, the survey examines a nationally representative sample of about 5,000 persons, located in 15 counties across the country using mobile examination centers.

Behavioral Risk Factor Surveillance System

The Behavioral Risk Factor Surveillance System (BRFSS) is a state-based telephone survey of the civilian, non-institutionalized, adult population conducted by the Office of Surveillance, Epidemiology, and Laboratory Services at the CDC. This survey seeks to ascertain the prevalence of such high-risk behaviors as cigarette smoking, excessive alcohol consumption, and physical inactivity, and the lack of preventive health care such as screening for cancer. These results are published periodically as part of *MMWR's CDC Surveillance Summaries* and are available wherever copies of the *CDC MMWR* are found. Information is also available at www.cdc.gov/brfss.

Youth Risk Behavior Surveillance System

The national Youth Risk Behavior Survey (YRBS) monitors six categories of priority health-risk behaviors among youth and young adults, including behaviors that contribute to unintentional injuries and violence; tobacco use; alcohol and other drug use; sexual behaviors that contribute to unintended pregnancy and sexually transmitted infections (STIs), including human immunodeficiency virus (HIV) infection; unhealthy dietary behaviors; and physical inactivity. In addition, the national YRBS monitors the prevalence of obesity and asthma. The national YRBS is conducted every 2 years during the spring semester and provides data representative of 9th through 12th grade students in public and private schools in the United States.[32]

YRBS includes a national school-based survey conducted by the CDC, and state and local school-based surveys conducted by state and local education and health agencies. The YRBS is conducted by the CDC's Division of Adolescent and School Health. More information about YRBS is available at www.cdc.gov/healthyyouth/yrbs/.

National Health Care Surveys

The National Health Care Surveys (NHCS) comprise 11 different national surveys that gather information on the nation's health care system. The purpose of these surveys is to help health care providers, policy makers, and researchers answer questions about resources, care quality, and disparities in services for care provided in the United States. The surveys are delivered according to settings that include physician offices and community health centers, hospitals,

Descriptive study an epidemiological study that describes a disease with respect to person, place, and time

ambulatory surgery centers, long-term care facilities, hospice and home health, and prisons. Summaries of the results of these surveys are published by the National Center for Health Statistics and are available at http://www.cdc.gov/nchs/dhcs.htm.

Epidemiological Studies

Epidemiologists conduct investigations to better understand the how disease is distributed in the population and what determines who gets sick and who does not. These investigations may be descriptive or analytic (observational or experimental/interventional) in nature, depending on the objectives of the specific study.

Descriptive Studies

Descriptive studies seek to describe the extent of disease in regard to person, time, and place. These studies are designed to answer the questions who, when, and where. To answer the first question (who), epidemiologists first take a "head count" to determine how many cases of a disease have occurred. At this time, they also try to determine who is ill—children, older adults, men, women, or both. The data they gather should permit them to develop a summary of cases by age, sex, race, marital status, occupation, employer, and other relevant characteristics of the people involved. These data provide important information to identify disparities in health outcomes among different segments of the population.

To answer the second question (when), epidemiologists will characterize health events by time of occurrence. The time period of interest will vary and usually depends on the health condition in question. For example, data for the number of people with cancer may be summarized by year, whereas the onset of illness for an infectious disease may be reported by hour. Two ways of displaying time-related data are secular and seasonal curves. The secular display of a disease shows the distribution of cases over many years (e.g., cases of varicella for the period 1991 to 2013; see **Figure 3.8**). Secular graphs illustrate the long-term trend of

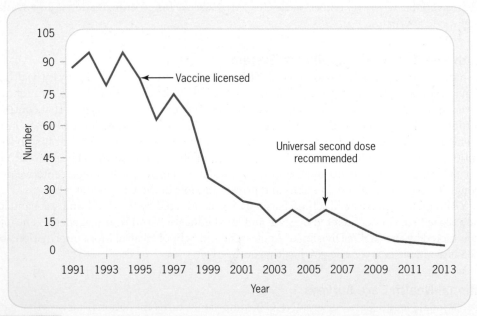

FIGURE 3.8 Varicella (chickenpox). Number* of reported cases—Illinois, Michigan, Texas, and West Virginia, 1991–2013.

*In thousands
Reproduced from: Centers for Disease Control and Prevention (2015). "Summary of Notifiable Infectious Diseases and Conditions—United States, 2013." *Morbidity and Mortality Weekly Report*, 62(53): 1–119. Available at http://www.cdc.gov/mmwr/preview/mmwrhtml/mm6253a1.htm.

a disease. A graph of the case data by season or month is usually prepared to show cyclical changes in the numbers of cases of a disease. Cases of influenza-like illness, for example, peak in the winter months (see **Figure 3.9**). Data for infectious diseases is often characterized using an **epidemic curve**, a graphic display of the cases of disease by the time or date of the onset of their symptoms.

Epidemic curves for single epidemics vary in appearance with each disease outbreak; however, two classic types exist. The first is the **common source epidemic curve** (see **Figure 3.10**). In a common source epidemic, each case can be traced to an exposure to the same source—spoiled food, for example. Because an epidemic curve shows cases of a disease by time or date of the onset of their symptoms, the epidemic curve for a single epidemic can be used to calculate the **incubation period**, the period of time between exposure to an infectious agent and the onset of symptoms. The incubation period, together with the symptoms, can often help epidemiologists determine the cause of the disease. A common source epidemic can be further categorized as **point source**, where exposure occurs at a single point in time, or as a **continuous source**, where exposure is continuous or intermittent. Identifying the source is especially important when exposure is continuous because individuals will continue to be exposed until transmission is interrupted. The cholera epidemic mentioned earlier in this chapter is a classic example of a continuous source epidemic. When John Snow determined that the common source was the Broad Street pump, he was able to remove the handle and stop the epidemic.

The second type of epidemic curve for an outbreak is a **propagated epidemic curve**. In this type of epidemic, primary cases appear first at the end of the incubation period following exposure to an infected source. Secondary cases arise after a second incubation period, and they represent exposure to the primary cases; tertiary cases appear even later as a result of exposure to secondary cases, and so on. Because new cases give rise to more new cases, this

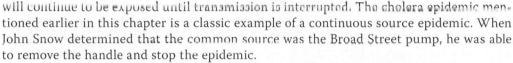

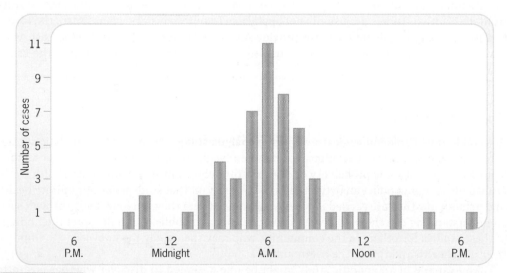

FIGURE 3.9   Peak influenza activity, by month— United States, 1982–83 through 2013–14 influenza seasons.

Reproduced from: Centers for Disease Control and Prevention (2014). *The Flu Season*. Available at http://www.cdc.gov/flu/about/season/flu-season.htm.

FIGURE 3.10   Point source epidemic curve: cases of gastroenteritis following ingestion of a common food source.

Reproduced from: Centers for Disease Control and Prevention.

Epidemic curve a graphic display of the cases of disease according to the time or date of onset of symptoms

Common source epidemic curve a graphic display of a disease where each case can be traced to a single source of exposure

Incubation period the period between exposure to a disease and the onset of symptoms

Point source epidemic a type of epidemic where all cases were exposed at the same point in time

Continuous source epidemic a type of epidemic where cases are exposed to a common source over time

Propagated epidemic curve an epidemic curve depicting a distribution of cases traceable to multiple sources of exposure

Analytic study an epidemiological study aimed at testing hypotheses

Risk factors factors that increase the probability of disease, injury, or death

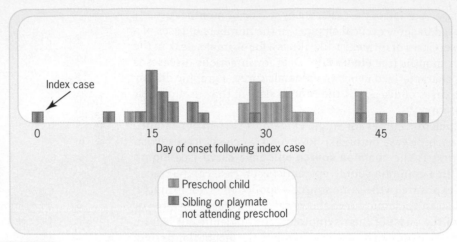

FIGURE 3.11   Propagated epidemic curve: cases of chickenpox during April through June.

Reproduced from: Centers for Disease Control and Prevention.

type of epidemic is termed a propagated epidemic. Epidemics of communicable diseases such as chickenpox follow this pattern (see **Figure 3.11**).

Finally, epidemiologists must determine where the outbreak occurred. To determine where the illnesses may have originated, the residential address and travel history, including restaurants, schools, shopping trips, and vacations, of each case are recorded. This information provides a geographic distribution of cases and helps to delineate the extent of the outbreak. By plotting cases on a map, along with natural features such as streams and human-made structures such as factories, it is sometimes possible to learn something about the source of the disease.

A descriptive study is usually the first epidemiological study carried out on a disease. Descriptive data provide valuable information to health care providers and administrators, enabling them to allocate resources efficiently and to plan effective prevention and education programs. Also, detectable patterns of cases may provide investigators with ideas that can lead to a hypothesis about the cause or source of the disease outbreak. This hypothesis can subsequently be tested in an analytic study.

As important and useful as they are, descriptive studies have some limitations. Results from descriptive studies are usually not applicable to outbreaks elsewhere. Also, the investigation of a single epidemic cannot provide information about disease trends. Last, with few exceptions, descriptive studies by themselves rarely identify with certainty the cause of an outbreak.

Analytic Studies

A second type of epidemiological study is the **analytic study**. The purpose of analytic studies is to test hypotheses about relationships between health problems and possible **risk factors**, factors that increase the probability of disease. Although front-line community health workers usually do not conduct analytic studies, it is important that students of community health understand how they are carried out and what kinds of data they generate. Only through such an understanding can those who work in community and public health interpret the findings of these studies for others in the community, who may then apply the knowledge to improve their own health and that of the community.

An example of an analytic study might be one designed to discover whether cigarette smoking (possible risk factor) is associated with lung cancer (health problem) or whether improperly prepared food (possible risk factor) is associated with an outbreak of salmonella (health problem). It is important to remember that the associations discovered through analytic epidemiological studies are not always cause-and-effect associations.

There are two types of analytic studies—observational and experimental (interventional). These differ in the role played by the investigator. In **observational studies** the investigator simply observes the natural course of events, taking note of who is exposed or unexposed and who has or has not developed the disease of interest. **Experimental studies** are carried out to identify the cause of a disease or to determine the effectiveness of a vaccine, therapeutic drug, surgical procedure, or behavioral or educational intervention. The central feature of experimental (interventional) studies is that the investigator can control the intervention or variable of interest. For example, groups of study participants could be followed after receiving different medications or being asked to adhere to different diets to see which interventions were most effective.

An example of just such an experiment was performed to see whether or not a vaccine could prevent severe rotavirus gastroenteritis.[33] Rotavirus is the most common cause of severe diarrheal disease among young people worldwide. Participants were assigned to vaccine or **placebo**. There were 31,673 children in the vaccine group and 31,552 children in the placebo group. Oral doses of either vaccine or placebo were administered to infants at 2 and 4 months of age. The severity of gastroenteritis was measured using the Vesikari scale, which ranges from zero to 20 with higher numbers indicating more severe illness. **Table 3.11** shows the number of children with one or more episodes per 1,000 infants per year at different Vesikari scores. The results of this study indicated that the vaccine was highly effective against rotavirus and significantly reduced the number of severe gastroenteritis cases. The vaccine tested in this trial was approved in 2008 and is one of two rotavirus vaccines recommended by the CDC. These studies were highly controlled and achieved under conditions that are as ideal as possible and may not reflect what would occur in a more natural setting. In summary, epidemiologists carefully plan studies to define outbreaks of disease, injury, and death in specific populations and develop hypotheses about the causes of these outbreaks. By designing and carrying out analytic and experimental studies, epidemiologists test these hypotheses. The results of hypothesis tests are assimilated across studies and provide evidence on which to base public health practice.

Determining Causation

Often, even after numerous epidemiologic studies have identified an association between exposure to a suspected risk factor (A) and the development of a specific disease (B), it may not be clear that A causes B in the same way we state that infection with the malaria parasite causes the disease malaria. For example, if researchers found an association between wearing a nicotine patch and abstaining from smoking, that is not quite the same as stating that wearing

Observational study an analytic, epidemiological study in which the investigator observes the natural course of events, noting exposed and unexposed subjects and disease development

Experimental (interventional) studies analytic studies in which the investigator allocates exposure or intervention and follows development of disease

Placebo a blank treatment

TABLE 3.11 Number of Subjects with One or More Episode of Severe Rotavirus Gastroenteritis per 1,000 Infants per Year by Vesikari Score*

Vesikari Score	Vaccine Group	Placebo Group
≥ 11	1.9	12.2
≥ 15	1.2	0.3
≥ 19	0	0.8

*During the time period from 2 weeks after the second dose to 1 year of age.

Data from: Ruiz-Palacios, G.M., I. Perez-Schael, F.R. Velezquez, H. Abate, et al., Human Rotavirus Vaccine Study Group (2006). "Safety and Efficacy of an Attenuated Vaccine against Severe Rotavirus Gastroenteritis." *New England Journal of Medicine*, 354(1): 11–22; *New England Journal of Medicine*, 325(5): 311–315.

the nicotine patch causes smoking abstention. In 1965, this problem was addressed by Austin Bradford Hill, who laid out criteria that should be considered when deciding whether an association might be one of causation.[34] As he developed these criteria, he often cited the behavior of cigarette smoking and the development of lung cancer as examples. With minor modifications, Hill's criteria are outlined here:

Strength. How strong is the association between the exposure and the disease? Are those exposed 3, 5, 10, or 100 times more likely to develop disease than those who are not exposed? How many times more likely are cigarette smokers to get lung cancer than nonsmokers? Also, is there a dose-response relationship? Is it the case that the greater the exposure to a particular risk factor results in a higher rate of disease or death? Are those who smoke more heavily, more likely to develop lung cancer than lighter smokers are?

Consistency. Has the association been reported in a variety of people exposed in a variety of settings? Are the results repeatable by other researchers?

Specificity. Is the disease or health problem associated with the exposure the only one? When someone becomes ill after exposure is it always, or almost always, the same disease? When cigarette smokers become ill, is it always, or almost always lung cancer?

Temporality. Does A (the exposure) always precede B (the disease)? Does the behavior of cigarette smoking precede the onset of lung cancer, or do those with lung cancer take up the habit of smoking for some reason?

Biological plausibility. Does the suspected causation make sense with what we know about biology, physiology, and other medical knowledge? Does it make sense, in light of what we know about biology and physiology, that cigarette smoking could produce lung cancer?

These criteria are guidelines rather than rules. They should be considered along with careful interpretation of epidemiologic studies and other evidence. Using these criteria together with analytic, epidemiological data, health researchers often can persuade legislatures and public officials to pass laws or alter public policies that promote health. In the next chapter, we examine how epidemiological studies can be used to prevent and control diseases and health problems in the community.

Chapter Summary

- Epidemiology is the study of the distribution and determinants of health-related states or events in specified populations, and the application of this study to control health problems.

- Rates of birth, death, injury, and disease are essential tools for epidemiologists.

- Incidence rates are a measurement of the number of new cases of disease, injury, or death in a population over a given period of time. Prevalence rates measure all cases. An attack rate is a special kind of incidence rate used for a single outbreak.

- Cases of certain diseases, called notifiable or reportable diseases, are reported by doctors, clinics, medical laboratories, and hospitals to local health agencies. These agencies then report them to state health agencies, who then forward the data to the CDC. These reports assist epidemiologists who study disease trends.

- The health status of a population or community can be measured in a number of different ways, including mortality statistics, life expectancy, years of potential life lost (YPLL), disability-adjusted life years (DALYs), and health-adjusted life expectancy (HALE).

- Epidemiologists also consult the data available from the U.S. Census, the vital statistics reports, the *Morbidity and Mortality Weekly Report*, and a variety of national health surveys.

- Epidemiologists conduct two general types of studies to learn about disease and injury in populations—descriptive studies and analytic studies.
- Descriptive studies describe the extent of outbreaks in regard to person, place, and time.
- Analytic studies test hypotheses regarding associations between diseases and risk factors.
- Analytic studies can be either observational or experimental.

- Criteria for judging whether an association identified in epidemiological studies represents a causal relationship include strength of association, consistency, specificity, temporal correctness, and biological plausibility.
- Epidemiological studies provide the data and information that enable public health officials and policy makers to make decisions and take actions to improve health.

Scenario: Analysis and Response

Assume that you were Kim and you were able to reach Dr. Turner, the local health officer. He then asked whether you would like to help in the investigation of the foodborne outbreak mentioned in the scenario. You agreed to help. So far, you have learned that on Sunday, May 28, 49 people were at a picnic where they had eaten, beginning about noon. People began to report their illnesses later that night. Dr. Turner developed a foodborne outbreak investigation worksheet, which you helped to complete by making numerous phone calls and house visits with the public health nurse. The histories of people attending the picnic appear in **Table 3.12**. Using **Table 3.13**, the Epidemic Curve Tally Sheet, you tally the cases by hour of onset of illness. Using the results of the tally, you establish the incubation period—the range of hours (after the meal) over which symptoms started. Next, you prepare a graph to illustrate the epidemic curve of the outbreak. Try to answer the following questions:

1. What is the incubation period?
2. Does the curve you prepared suggest a single- or multiple-exposure epidemic?
3. Based solely on the incubation period, can you make a guess as to the cause of the outbreak?

Unfortunately, by the time the investigation began, all the picnic food had been discarded, and no samples were available for laboratory testing. To determine which food at the picnic might have caused the outbreak, you need to calculate attack rates for people eating each food as well as for people not eating each food. Using **Table 3.14**, the Attack Rate Worksheet, calculate the attack rates for those who ate and did not eat each food served.

TABLE 3.12 Histories Obtained from Persons Eating Picnic Lunch								
Person No.	Bread	Butter	Turkey	Potato Salad	Milk	Jell-O	Ill*	Not Ill
1			X	X	X		7:30*	
2	X	X		X	X			X
3	X	X	X	X	X	X	8:00	
4			X		X	X		X
5			X	X	X		9:15	
6			X	X	X		7:40	
7	X	X		X	X			X
8	X	X	X	X	X	X	8:10	
9			X		X	X		X
10			X	X	X	X	10:15	
11	X			X		X		X
12	X	X	X	X	X	X	8:30	
13			X		X			X
14	X	X	X	X	X	X	9:30	

(Continues)

TABLE 3.12 Histories Obtained from Persons Eating Picnic Lunch (Continued)

Person No.	Bread	Butter	Turkey	Potato Salad	Milk	Jell-O	Ill*	Not Ill
15	X	X		X	X	X		X
16	X			X		X		X
17	X	X	X	X	X	X	8:35	
18			X		X			X
19	X	X	X	X	X	X	10:05	
20	X	X		X	X	X		X
21			X		X	X	9:15	
22	X	X		X	X	X		X
23	X	X			X	X	8:30	
24	X	X			X	X		X
25	X	X	X	X	X	X	12:30 A.M.	
26			X		X	X	9:20	
27	X	X		X	X	X		X
28	X	X	X		X	X	8:40	
29	X	X			X	X		X
30	X	X	X	X	X		12:15 A.M.	
31			X	X	X		7:30	
32	X	X		X	X			X
33	X	X	X	X	X	X	8:00	
34			X		X	X		X
35			X	X	X		10:30	
36			X	X	X		7:30	
37	X	X		X	X			X
38	X	X	X	X	X	X	8:05	
39			X		X	X		X
40			X	X	X	X	9:45	
41	X			X		X		X
42	X	X	X	X	X		8:30	
43			X		X			X
44	X	X	X	X	X	X	9:30	
45	X	X		X	X	X		X
46	X			X		X		X
47	X	X	X	X	X	X	8:30	
48			X		X	X		X
49	X	X	X	X	X	X	10:10	

*All times are P.M. unless otherwise indicated.

TABLE 3.13   Epidemic Curve Tally Sheet

Time of Onset	Tally	Number	Incubation Period
7:00–7:59			
8:00–8:59			
9:00–9:59			
10:00–10:59			
11:00–11:59			
12:00–12:59			

TABLE 3.14   Attack Rate Worksheet

	Persons Eating Food				Persons Not Eating Food			
Food	Total	Ill	Not Ill	Attack Rate	Total	Ill	Not Ill	Attack Rate
Bread								
Butter								
Turkey								
Potato salad								
Milk								
Jell-O								

1. Which food would you most suspect of causing the illness?

2. Based on this information, what might the causative agent have been?

3. How could the Internet be of assistance to health department officials in this situation?

Review Questions

1. What is an epidemic? A pandemic? Name some diseases that caused epidemics in the past. Name some diseases that are epidemic today.

2. Why are epidemiologists sometimes interested in epizootics?

3. What does the term *endemic disease* mean? Give examples of such diseases.

4. What is the difference between natality, morbidity, and mortality?

5. Why are rates important in community health?

6. What is the difference between crude and adjusted rates?

7. Why are prevalence rates more useful than incidence rates for measuring chronic diseases?

8. What is an infant mortality rate? Why is it such an important rate in community health?

9. What are notifiable diseases? Give some examples.

10. In general, contrast the leading causes of death in the United States in 1900 with those in 2013. Comment on the differences.

11. At what ages is life expectancy calculated? What does it tell us about a population? Which country has the longest life expectancy?

12. What are years of potential life lost (YPLL)? How does calculating YPLL change the way we think about the leading causes of death?

13. How would you define disability-adjusted life years (DALYs)? How would you define health-adjusted life expectancy (HALE)?

14. What is the U.S. Census? How often is it conducted? What types of data does it gather?

15. What kinds of data would you expect to find in the Centers for Disease Control and Prevention's *Morbidity and Mortality Weekly Report*?

16. List five important national health surveys that are valuable sources of data about the health and health care of our population.

17. What can be said about the reliability of self-reported health data?

18. What is the National Health and Nutrition Examination Survey? Why is it carried out?

19. In a descriptive epidemiological study, what types of information does the epidemiologist gather?

20. What is the purpose of an analytic study?

21. How do experimental studies differ from observational studies?

22. What are Hill's criteria for judging whether an association between a risk factor and a disease can be considered causal?

Activities

1. When you hear the word epidemic, what disease comes to your mind first? Ask this question of 10 people you know, allowing them time to think and give you an answer. Try to find people of different ages as you complete your informal poll. List their answers on paper. Are there any answers that surprise you? Does your list include both classic and contemporary epidemic diseases?

2. Look at the data in **Table 3.15**. What conclusion can you draw about the risk for acquiring tuberculosis for populations in each age group? Write down your answer. Now examine **Table 3.16**. Which age groups exhibit the highest disease rates? Explain why it is important to calculate rates to report disease outbreaks accurately.

3. There are 346 students at Hillside School. During March and April, 56 pupils were absent with chickenpox. What is the attack rate for chickenpox at Hillside School? The 56 pupils who were absent had 88 brothers and sisters at home. Of the 88 siblings, 19 developed chickenpox. What was the attack rate among these children? Of the 75 total cases of chickenpox, one child died. Calculate the case fatality rate for chickenpox in this epidemic.

4. Contact your state or local health department or visit their website. Ask for or determine the total number of birth and death certificates issued for the latest year for which complete data are available. Assuming no migration into or out of your state or county occurred, what is the natural rate of population increase (number of births minus number of deaths)? Try to obtain an estimate of the total population of the state or county for that same year. Calculate a crude birth rate and a crude death rate (number of births and deaths) per 1,000 population.

5. Using the data presented in Table 3.8, estimate (as best you can) the life expectancy of your siblings, parents, and grandparents at birth. If your grandparents are older than 65, determine what their life expectancies were when they turned 65. If you were to fulfill your life expectancy exactly, in what year can you expect to die?

6. Visit your campus library and locate the *American Journal of Epidemiology*. Examine several recent issues, taking note of the different types of articles as they appear in the table of contents. Select six articles and read the abstracts. On a piece of paper, list the titles of these articles. Were these descriptive, analytic, or experimental studies? After each title that you have listed, put either the letter D (descriptive), A (analytic), or E (experimental) to denote the type of study that you examined.

TABLE 3.15 Reported Tuberculosis Cases by Age Group, Low Socioeconomic Area, City of Dixon, 1960

Age Group in Years	Number of Cases	Age Group in Years	Number of Cases
0–4	7	35–44	6
5–14	7	45–54	9
15–24	6	55–64	8
25–34	10	65+	7

Data from: Centers for Disease Control and Prevention.

TABLE 3.16 Reported Tuberculosis Cases and Incidence Rates per 100,000, Low Socioeconomic Area, City of Dixon, 1960

Age Group in Years	Number of Cases	Population of Age Group	Rate*
1–4	7	8,638	81.0
5–14	7	13,098	53.4
15–24	6	10,247	58.5
25–34	10	8,680	115.2
35–44	6	7,528	79.7
45–54	9	6,736	133.6
55–64	8	4,534	176.4
65+	7	4,075	171.8
Total	60	63,536	94.4

*Example: 7 cases ÷ 8,638 population × 100,000 = 81.0.

Data from: Centers for Disease Control and Prevention.

References

1. Last, J. M., ed. (2001). *A Dictionary of Epidemiology*. New York: Oxford University Press.
2. Taubenberer, J. K. and D. M. Morens (2006). "1918 Influenza: The Mother of All Pandemics." *Emerging Infectious Diseases*, 12(1): 15–22.
3. World Health Organization HIV/AIDS Department (2015). *Global Summary of the AIDS Epidemic, 2014*. Available at http://www.who.int/hiv/data/epi_core_july2015.png?ua=1.
4. Joint United Nations Programme on HIV/AIDS (UNAIDS) (n.d.). *Fact Sheet 2015*. Available at http://www.unaids.org/en/resources/campaigns/HowAIDSchangedeverything/factsheet.
5. Monath, T. P. (1980). *St. Louis Encephalitis*. Washington, DC: American Public Health Association.
6. Centers for Disease Control and Prevention (2003). "Summary of Notifiable Diseases—United States, 2001." *Morbidity and Mortality Weekly Report*, 50(53): 1–108.
7. Centers for Disease Control and Prevention (1981). "Toxic Shock Syndrome—United States, 1970–1980." *Morbidity and Mortality Weekly Report*, 30(3): 25–33.
8. Centers for Disease Control and Prevention (2014). "HIV/AIDS Surveillance Report: Diagnoses of HIV Infection in the United States and Dependent Areas, 2012." *HIV Surveillance Report, 24*. Available at http://www.cdc.gov/hiv/pdf/statistics_2012_HIV_Surveillance_Report_vol_24.pdf.
9. Centers for Disease Control and Prevention (2015). "HIV/AIDS Surveillance Report: Diagnoses of HIV Infection in the United States and Dependent Areas, 2013." *HIV Surveillance Report, 25*. Available at http://www.cdc.gov/hiv/pdf/library/reports/surveillance/cdc-hiv-surveillance-report-vol-25.pdf.
10. Centers for Disease Control and Prevention (2015). *West Nile Virus Disease Cases and Deaths Reported to CDC by Year and Clinical Presentation, 1999–2014*. Available at http://www.cdc.gov/westnile/resources/pdfs/data/1-wnv-disease-cases-by-year_1999 2014_06042015.pdf.
11. Centers for Disease Control and Prevention (2014). "Summary of Notifiable Diseases—United States, 2012." *Morbidity and Mortality Weekly Report*, 61(53): 1–121.
12. Centers for Disease Control and Prevention (2016). *Mumps Cases and Outbreaks*. Available at http://www.cdc.gov/mumps/outbreak.html.
13. Shrestha, S. S., Swerdlow, D. L., Brose, R. H., Prabhu, V. S., et al. (2011). "Estimating the Burden of 2009 Pandemic Influenza A (H1N1) in the United States (April 2009–April 2010)." *Clinical Infectious Diseases*, Suppl 1: S75–82.
14. Markellis, V. C. (December 1985–January 1986). "Epidemiology: Cornerstone for Health Education." *Health Education, 15–17*.
15. Gale, A. H. (1959). *Epidemiologic Disease*. London, England: Pelican Books, 25.
16. Woodruff, A. W. (1977). "Benjamin Rush, His Work on Yellow Fever and His British Connections." *American Journal of Tropical Medicine and Hygiene*, 26(5): 1055–1059.
17. Johnson, S. R. (2006). *The Ghost Map: The Story of London's Most Terrifying Epidemic—and How It Changed Science, Cities, and the Modern World*. New York: Riverhead Books.
18. Murphy, S. L., Kochanek, K. D., Xu, J. and M. Heron (2015). "Deaths: Final Data for 2012." *National Vital Statistics Reports*, 63(9). Hyattsville, MD. National Center for Health Statistics. Available at http://www.cdc.gov/nchs/data/nvsr/nvsr63/nvsr63_09.pdf.
19. Centers for Disease Control and Prevention (2015). "Deaths: Preliminary Data for 2013." *National Vital Statistics Reports*, 64(2). Hyattsville, MD: National Center for Health Statistics. Available at http://www.cdc.gov/nchs/data/nvsr/nvsr64/nvsr64_02.pdf.
20. Centers for Disease Control and Prevention (2015). *Protocol for Public Health Agencies to Notify CDC about the Occurrence of National Notifiable Conditions, 2016*. Available at http://www.cdc.gov/nndss/document/NNC-2016-Notification-Requirements-By-Condition.pdf
21. Doyle, T. J., Glynn, M. K., and S. L. Groseclose (2002). "Completeness of Notifiable Infectious Disease Reporting in the United States: An Analytical Literature Review." *American Journal of Epidemiology*, 155(9): 866–874.
22. Centers for Disease Control and Prevention, National Center for Health Statistics (1998). *Leading Causes of Death, 1900–1998*. Available at http://www.cdc.gov/nchs/data/dvs/lead1900_98.pdf.

23. World Health Organization (2014). *The Top 10 Causes of Death.* Available at http://www.who.int/mediacentre/factsheets/fs310/en/.

24. National Center for Health Statistics (2015). *Health, United States, 2014: With Special Feature on Adults Aged 55–64.* Available at http://www.cdc.gov/nchs/data/hus/hus14.pdf.

25. World Health Organization (2015). *World Health Statistics: Part II Global Health Indicators.* Available at http://www.who.int/gho/publications/world_health_statistics/EN_WHS2015_Part2.pdf.

26. Murray, D. J. L. and A. D. Lopez, eds. (1996). *The Global Burden of Disease: A Comprehensive Assessment of Mortality and Disability from Diseases, injuries and Risk Factors in 1990 and Projected to 2020. Global Burden of Disease and Injury, Vol. 1.* Cambridge, MA: Harvard School of Public Health on behalf of WHO.

27. World Health Organization (2008). "The Global Burden of Disease: 2004 Update." Available at http://www.who.int/healthinfo/global_burden_disease/GBD_report_2004update_full.pdf.

28. Mathers, C. C., R. Sdana, J. A. Salomon, C. J. L. Murray, and A. D. Lopez (2000). "Estimates of DALE for 191 Countries: Methods and Results." *Global Programme on Evidence for Health Policy Working Paper No. 16.* Geneva, Switzerland: World Health Organization. Available at http://www.who.int/healthinfo/paper16.pdf.

29. World Health Organization (2015). *Life Expectancy Data by WHO Region.* Available at http://apps.who.int/gho/data/view.main.690?lang=en.

30. National Center for Health Statistics (2015). *Summary Health Statistics: National Health Interview Survey, 2014.* Available at http://ftp.cdc.gov/pub/Health_Statistics/NCHS/NHIS/SHS/2014_SHS_Table_A-11.pdf.

31. Centers for Disease Control and Prevention (2015). *National Health and Nutrition Examination Survey: About the National Health and Nutrition Examination Survey.* Available at http://www.cdc.gov/nchs/nhanes/about_nhanes.htm.

32. Centers for Disease Control and Prevention (2015). *Youth Risk Behavior Surveillance System (YRBSS).* Available at http://www.cdc.gov/healthyyouth/data/yrbs/index.htm.

33. Ruiz-Palacios, G. M., Pérez-Schael, I., Velázquez, F. R., H. Abate, et al.; Human Rotavirus Vaccine Study Group (2006). "Safety and Efficacy of an Attenuated Vaccine against Severe Rotavirus Gastroenteritis." *New England Journal of Medicine*, 354(1): 11–22.

34. Hill, A. B. (1965). "The Environment and Disease: Association or Causation?" *Proceeding of the Royal Society of Medicine*, 58: 295–300.

CHAPTER 4

Communicable and Noncommunicable Diseases: Prevention and Control of Diseases and Health Conditions

Chapter Objectives

After studying this chapter, you will be able to:

1. Discuss the differences between communicable (infectious) and noncommunicable (noninfectious) diseases and between acute and chronic diseases and provide examples of each.

2. Describe and explain communicable and multicausation disease models.

3. Explain how communicable diseases are transmitted in a community using the "chain of infection" model and use a specific communicable disease to illustrate your explanation.

4. Identify why noncommunicable diseases are a community and public health concern and provide some examples of important noncommunicable diseases.

5. Compare and contrast between primary, secondary, and tertiary prevention of disease and provide examples of each.
6. State and describe the various criteria that communities might use to prioritize their health problems in preparation for the allocation of prevention and control resources.
7. List and discuss important measures for preventing and controlling the

spread of communicable diseases in a community.
8. List and discuss approaches to noncommunicable disease control in the community.
9. Define and explain the purpose and importance of health screenings.
10. Outline a chronic, noncommunicable disease control program that includes primary, secondary, and tertiary disease prevention components.

Scenario

Adam had always been an active and athletic person. He lettered in three sports in high school and played varsity tennis in college. Following graduation last May, he was lucky enough to land a job with one of the Fortune 500 companies in nearby Indianapolis. He shares an apartment with Brandon, a business colleague, and both work long hours in the hope that hard work will mean success and advancement. Neither seems to find time to exercise regularly, and both rely increasingly on fast-food restaurants. Adam's weight is now 12 pounds above his weight at graduation.

Adam is beginning to wonder whether he is compromising his health for financial success. When he first came to the company, he took the stairs between floors two at a time and was never winded, even after climbing several flights. Now he becomes tired after two flights. Adam also recently participated in a free serum cholesterol screening, and his cholesterol level was 259 mg/dL. Adam decided it was time to have a complete physical examination.

Introduction

Elsewhere in the text we discussed the measurement and reporting of disease and the use of incidence and prevalence to describe disease occurrence. We also explained how epidemiologists describe disease outbreaks by person, place, and time and how they search for associations through analytic and experimental studies.

In this chapter, we extend our discussion of epidemiology. We begin by describing the different ways to classify diseases and other health conditions. Then, we explain models of communicable and noncommunicable diseases, which are conceptual frameworks used by epidemiologists to develop prevention and control strategies.

We also discuss criteria used by communities to prioritize their health problems and allocate health resources. Finally, we discuss some approaches to disease prevention and control; introduce the concepts of primary, secondary, and tertiary prevention; and provide examples of their application to a communicable and noncommunicable disease.

Classification of Diseases and Health Problems

Diseases and health problems can be classified in several meaningful ways. The public often classifies diseases by organ or organ system, such as kidney disease, heart disease, respiratory infection, and so on. Another method of classification is by causative agent—viral disease, chemical poisoning, physical injury, and so forth. In this scheme, causative agents may be biological, chemical, or physical. Biological agents include viruses, rickettsiae, bacteria, protozoa, fungi, and metazoa (multicellular organisms). Chemical agents include drugs, pesticides, industrial chemicals, food additives, air pollutants, and cigarette smoke. Physical agents that can cause injury or disease include various forms of energy such as heat, ultraviolet light, radiation, noise vibrations,

TABLE 4.1 Causative Agents for Diseases and Injuries

Biological Agents	Chemical Agents	Physical Agents
Viruses	Pesticides	Heat
Rickettsiae	Food additives	Light
Bacteria	Pharmacologics	Radiation
Fungi	Industrial chemicals	Noise
Protozoa	Air pollutants	Vibration
Metazoa	Cigarette smoke	Speeding objects

Communicable (infectious) disease an illness caused by some specific biological agent or its toxic products that can be transmitted from an infected person, animal, or inanimate reservoir to a susceptible host

Noncommunicable (noninfectious) disease d disease that cannot be transmitted from infected host to susceptible host

and speeding or falling objects (see **Table 4.1**). In community health, diseases are usually classified as acute or chronic, and as communicable (infectious) or noncommunicable (noninfectious).

Communicable versus Noncommunicable Diseases

Communicable (infectious) diseases are those diseases for which biological agents or their products are the cause and that are transmissible from one individual to another. The disease process begins when the agent is able to enter and grow or reproduce within the body of the host. The establishment of a communicable disease agent in a host organism is called an *infection*.

Noncommunicable (noninfectious) diseases or illnesses are those that cannot be transmitted from one person to another. Delineating the causes of noncommunicable diseases is often more difficult because several, or even many, factors may contribute to the development of a given noncommunicable health condition. These contributing factors may be genetic, environmental, or behavioral in nature. For this reason, many noncommunicable health conditions are called multicausation diseases; an example of such is heart disease. Genetics, environmental factors such as stress, and behavioral choices such as poor diet and lack of exercise can all contribute to heart disease.

Acute versus Chronic Diseases and Illnesses

In the acute/chronic classification scheme, diseases are classified by their duration of symptoms. Acute diseases are diseases in which the peak severity of symptoms occurs and subsides within 3 months (usually sooner) and the recovery of those who survive is usually complete. Examples of acute communicable diseases include the common cold, influenza (flu), chickenpox, measles, mumps, Rocky Mountain spotted fever, and plague. Examples of acute noncommunicable illnesses are appendicitis, injuries from motor vehicle crashes, acute alcohol intoxication or drug overdose, and sprained ankles (see **Table 4.2**).

TABLE 4.2 Classification of Diseases

Types of Diseases	Examples
Acute diseases	
Communicable	Common cold, pneumonia, mumps, measles, pertussis, typhoid fever, cholera
Noncommunicable	Appendicitis, poisoning, injury (due to motor vehicle crash, fire, gunshot, etc.)
Chronic diseases	
Communicable	AIDS, Lyme disease, tuberculosis, syphilis, rheumatic fever following streptococcal infections, hepatitis B
Noncommunicable	Diabetes, coronary heart disease, osteoarthritis, cirrhosis of the liver due to alcoholism

Chronic diseases or conditions are those in which symptoms continue longer than 3 months and, in some cases, for the remainder of one's life (see **Figure 4.1**). Recovery is slow and sometimes incomplete. These diseases can be either communicable or noncommunicable. Examples of chronic communicable diseases are AIDS, tuberculosis, herpes virus infections, syphilis, and Lyme disease. Chronic noncommunicable illnesses include hypertension, hypercholesterolemia, coronary heart disease, diabetes, and many types of arthritis and cancer.

Communicable Diseases

Whereas **infectivity** refers to the ability of a biological agent to enter and grow in a host, the term **pathogenicity** refers to an infectious disease agent's ability to produce disease. Selected pathogenic agents and the diseases they cause are listed in **Table 4.3**. Under certain conditions, pathogenic biological agents can be transmitted from an infected individual in the community to an uninfected, susceptible one. Communicable disease agents may be further classified according to the manner in which they are transmitted.

The elements of a simplified **communicable disease model**—agent, host, and environment—are presented in **Figure 4.2**. These three factors are the minimal requirements for the occurrence and spread of communicable diseases in a population. In this model, the **agent** is the element that must be present for disease to occur. For example, the influenza virus must be present for a person to become ill with flu.

The **host** is any susceptible organism—a single-celled organism, a plant, an animal, or a human—invaded by an infectious agent. The environment includes all other factors—physical, biological, or social—that inhibit or promote disease transmission. Communicable disease transmission occurs when a susceptible host and a pathogenic agent exist in an environment conducive to disease transmission.

FIGURE 4.1 Arthritis is a noninfectious chronic condition that can persist for one's entire life.
Photograph by the U.S. Census Bureau, Public Information Office (PIO).

Infectivity the ability of a biological agent to enter and grow in the host

Pathogenicity the capability of a communicable disease agent to cause disease in a susceptible host

Communicable disease model the minimal requirements for the occurrence and spread of communicable diseases in a population—agent, host, and environment

Agent (pathogenic agent) the cause of the disease or health problem

Host a person or other living organism that affords subsistence or lodgment to a communicable agent under natural conditions

TABLE 4.3 Biological Agents of Disease		
Type of Agent	**Name of Agent**	**Disease**
Viruses	Varicella virus	Chickenpox
	Human immunodeficiency virus (HIV)	Acquired immune deficiency syndrome (AIDS)
	Rubella virus	German measles
Rickettsiae	*Rickettsia rickettsii*	Rocky Mountain spotted fever
Bacteria	*Vibrio cholerae*	Cholera
	Clostridium tetani	Tetanus
	Yersinia pestis	Plague
	Borrelia burgdorferi	Lyme disease
Protozoa	*Entamoeba histolytica*	Amebic dysentery
	Plasmodium falciparum	Malaria
	Trypanosoma gambiense	African sleeping sickness
Fungi and yeasts	*Tinea cruris*	Jock itch
	Tinea pedis	Athlete's foot
Nematoda (worms)	*Wuchereria bancrofti*	Filariasis (elephantiasis)
	Onchocerca volvulus	Onchocerciasis (river blindness)

Chain of Infection

Communicable disease transmission is a complicated but well-studied process that is best understood through a conceptual model known as the **chain of infection** (see **Figure 4.3**). Using the chain of infection model, one can visualize the step-by-step process by which communicable diseases spread from an infected person to an uninfected person in the community. The pathogenic (disease-producing) agent leaves its reservoir (infected host) via a portal of exit. Transmission occurs in either a direct or indirect manner, and the pathogenic agent enters a susceptible host through a portal of entry to establish infection. For example, let us follow the common cold through the chain of infection. The agent (the cold virus) leaves its reservoir (the throat of an infected person), perhaps when the host sneezes. The portals of exit are the nose and mouth. Transmission may be direct if saliva droplets enter the respiratory tract of a susceptible host at close range (someone standing nearby breathes in the droplets), or it may be indirect if droplets dry and become airborne. The portal of entry could be the nose or mouth of a susceptible host. The agent enters, and a new infection is established.

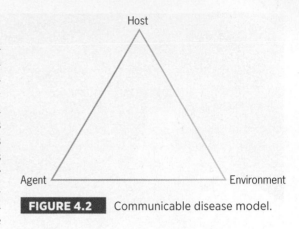

FIGURE 4.2   Communicable disease model.

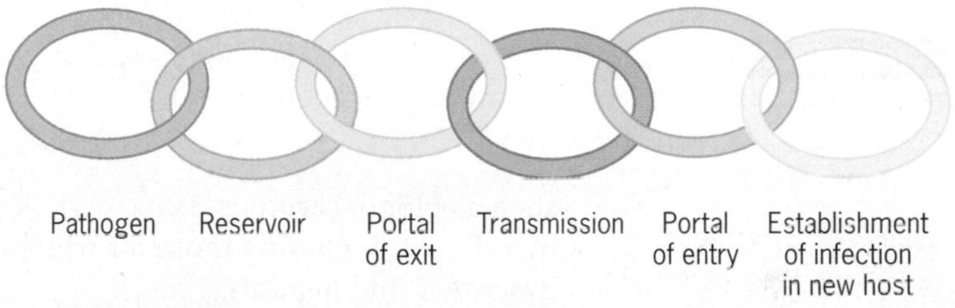

Pathogen   Reservoir   Portal of exit   Transmission   Portal of entry   Establishment of infection in new host

FIGURE 4.3   Chain of infection.

There are many variations in the chain of infection, depending on the disease agent, environmental conditions, infectivity, and host susceptibility. For example, the reservoir for a disease may be a **case**—a person who has the disease—or a **carrier**—one who is well but infected and is capable of serving as a source of infection. A carrier could be someone who is incubating the disease, such as a person who is HIV positive but has no signs of AIDS, or someone who has recovered from the disease (is asymptomatic) but still infectious, as is sometimes the case in typhoid fever. For some diseases, the reservoir is not humans but animals. Diseases for which the reservoir resides in animal populations are called **zoonosis**. Plague, rabies, Rocky Mountain spotted fever, and Lyme disease are zoonoses. Diseases for which humans are the only known reservoir, like measles, are known as **anthroponoses**.

Portals of exit (see **Figure 4.4**) and entry vary from disease to disease. Natural portals of exit and examples of diseases that use them are the respiratory tract (cold, influenza, measles, tuberculosis, and whooping cough), urogenital tract (gonorrhea, syphilis, herpes, and AIDS), digestive tract (amebic dysentery, shigellosis, polio, typhoid fever, and cholera), and skin (ringworm and jock itch). The skin is actually a good barrier to infection, but it can be bypassed by a hypodermic needle or when there is an open wound. Blood-sucking insects and ticks make their own portals of entry with mouth parts that penetrate the skin. Finally, many pathogenic agents can cross the placenta from mother to fetus (for example, rubella virus, syphilis spirochetes, and hepatitis B virus).

Modes of Transmission

As noted in the previous paragraphs, communicable disease transmission may be direct or indirect. **Direct transmission** implies the immediate transfer of the disease agent between the infected and the susceptible individuals by direct contact "such as touching, biting, kissing, sexual intercourse, or by direct projection (droplet spread) of droplet spray onto the conjunctiva or onto the mucous membranes of the eye, nose or mouth during sneezing, coughing, spitting, singing or talking (usually limited to a distance of one meter or less)."[1] Examples of diseases for which transmission is usually direct are AIDS, syphilis, gonorrhea, rabies, and the common cold.

Indirect transmission may be one of three types—airborne, vehicleborne, or vectorborne. Airborne transmission is the dissemination of microbial aerosols to a suitable portal of entry,

Chain of infection a model to conceptualize the transmission of a communicable disease from its source to a susceptible host

Case a person who is sick with a disease

Carrier a person or animal that harbors a specific communicable agent in the absence of discernible clinical disease and serves as a potential source of infection to others

Zoonosis a communicable disease transmissible under natural conditions from vertebrate animals to humans

Anthroponosis a disease that infects only humans

Direct transmission the immediate transfer of an infectious agent by direct contact between infected and susceptible individuals

Indirect transmission communicable disease transmission involving an intermediate step

FIGURE 4.4   Portal of exit: The causative agents for many respiratory diseases leave their host via the mouth and nose.

© Custom Medical Stock Photo.

Vehicle an inanimate material or object that can serve as a source of infection

Vector a living organism, usually an arthropod (e.g., mosquito, tick, louse, or flea), that can transmit a communicable agent to susceptible hosts

usually the respiratory tract. Microbial aerosols are suspensions of dust or droplet nuclei made up wholly or in part of microorganisms. In contrast to droplets, which spread no more than several feet, airborne particles may remain suspended and infective for long periods of time. Tuberculosis, influenza, histoplasmosis, legionellosis, and measles (see **Box 4.1**) are examples of airborne diseases.

In vehicleborne transmission, contaminated materials or objects (fomites) serve as **vehicles**—nonliving objects by which communicable agents are transferred to a susceptible host. The agent may or may not have multiplied or developed on the vehicle. Examples of vehicles include toys, handkerchiefs, soiled clothes, bedding, food service utensils, and surgical instruments. Also considered vehicles are water, milk, food, or biological products such as blood, serum, plasma, organs, and tissues. Almost any disease can be transmitted by vehicles, including those for which the primary mode of transmission is direct, such as dysentery and hepatitis.

Vectorborne transmission is the transfer of disease by a living organism such as a mosquito, fly, or tick. Transmission may be mechanical, via the contaminated mouth parts or feet of the **vector**, or biological, which involves multiplication or developmental changes of the agent in the vector before transmission occurs. In mechanical transmission, multiplication and development of the disease organism usually do not occur. For example, organisms that

---

BOX 4.1   Preventing Transmission of Communicable Diseases

Interrupting the spread of disease requires information about the symptoms, what causes the disease, how it's diagnosed, the reservoir, the incubation period, how it's transmitted, who may be at risk, prevention measures, and how to manage an ill patient and his or her surroundings.[1]

For example, to understand the spread of measles, we would want to know the following:

- **Symptoms:** Measles is a very contagious disease, and symptoms include fever, conjunctivitis (red, watery eyes), cough, white spots on the insides of the cheeks, runny nose, and rash beginning on the face but spreading down the neck, truck, arms, legs, and feet.
- **Causative Agent:** Measles virus.
- **Diagnosis:** Diagnosis is based on symptoms, laboratory testing, and history of contact with infected persons.
- **Occurrence:** Measles was very common prior to the availability of a vaccine. Since a vaccine has been available, the incidence of measles has dropped dramatically and is now seen among individuals with incomplete or no vaccination to measles.
- **Reservoir:** Humans.

- **Incubation Period:** An average of 14 days passes from the time a patient is exposed to the virus to the onset of the rash (range: 7 to 21 days).
- **Transmission:** Airborne through droplet spread or direct transmission through contact with nose or throat secretions from an infected individual.
- **Risk Groups:** Individuals who have not had the disease, are unvaccinated, or did not receive both doses of the vaccine are at risk of acquiring measles.
- **Prevention:** Prevention measures primarily include steps to ensure susceptible individuals receive all recommended vaccinations.
- **Management of Patient:** Individuals with measles may be isolated from others (e.g., children kept out of school) while ill or during particularly infectious periods of the illness to prevent spread to others. There is no treatment for measles, but complications can be managed.
- **Management of Contacts and the Immediate Environment:** Exposed individuals may be given vaccinations (if unvaccinated) or medications to prevent infection after exposure. Health professionals should conduct investigations to identify contacts and ensure these measures are taken to prevent spread.

Data from: Heymann, D.L. (2014). *Control of Communicable Diseases Manual*, 20th ed. Washington, DC: American Public Health Association.

cause dysentery, polio, cholera, and typhoid fever have been isolated from insects such as cockroaches and houseflies and could presumably be deposited on food prepared for human consumption.

In biological transmission, multiplication and/or developmental changes of the disease agent occur in the vector before transmission occurs. Biological transmission is much more important than mechanical transmission in terms of its impact on community health. Examples of biological vectors include mosquitoes, fleas, lice, ticks, flies, and other insects. Mosquitoes are by far the most important vectors of human disease. They transmit the viruses that cause yellow fever, dengue fever, West Nile fever, and more than 200 other viruses, including Zika virus. They also transmit malaria, which infects 100 million people in the world each year (mostly in tropical areas), killing at least 1 million of them. Ticks, another important vector, transmit Rocky Mountain spotted fever, relapsing fever, and Lyme disease (see **Figure 4.5**). Other insect vectors (and the diseases they transmit) are flies (African sleeping sickness, onchocerciasis, loiasis, and leishmaniasis), fleas (plague and murine typhus), lice (epidemic typhus and trench fever), and kissing bugs (Chagas' disease).

FIGURE 4.5   A female blacklegged tick, *Ixodes scapularis*, a vector of Lyme disease.
Courtesy of Scott Bauer/United States Department of Agriculture (USDA).

Noncommunicable Diseases

Although communicable diseases remain an important concern for communities, certain non-communicable diseases, such as heart disease, stroke, and cancer, now rank high among the nation's leading causes of death. Although these diseases are not infectious, they nonetheless can occur in epidemic proportions. Furthermore, the chronic nature of many of these diseases means that they can deplete a community's resources quite rapidly.

The model showing agent, host, and environment is specific to communicable diseases but can be adapted for noncommunicable diseases where *agent* is the population and their characteristics, *host* are the factors that may cause disease, and *environment* is the physical environment, behaviors, cultural factors, physiology, and other external factors that impact disease.[2] Because the **etiologies** (causes) of many of the noncommunicable diseases, such as coronary heart disease, are very complex, they are often illustrated using a **multicausation disease model** (see **Figure 4.6**). In this model, the human host is pictured in the center of the environment in which he or she lives. Within the host, there exists a unique genetic endowment that is inalterable. The host exists in a complex environment that includes exposures to a multitude of risk factors that can contribute to the disease process. These environmental risk factors may be physical, chemical, biological, or social in nature.

Physical factors include the latitude, climate, and physical geography of where one lives. The major health risks in the tropics—communicable and parasitic diseases—are different from those in temperate regions with cold winters—difficulty in finding food and remaining warm. Chemical factors include not only natural chemical hazards of polluted water and air but also the added pollutants of our modern, industrial society. Biological hazards include communicable disease agents such as pathogenic viruses, bacteria, and fungi. Social factors include one's occupation, recreational activities, and living arrangements. Poor choices in life can increase the number and severity of one's risk factors and be detrimental to one's health.

Diseases of the Heart and Blood Vessels

Diseases of the heart and blood vessels, cardiovascular diseases (CVDs), are a leading cause of death in the United States. **Coronary heart disease (CHD)** is the number one killer of Americans. In 2013 alone, 611,105 people died of heart disease in the United States, accounting for nearly one in four deaths that year.[3] It is estimated that more than 85 million adults in the United States were living with CVD in 2012.[4]

Etiology the cause of a disease

Multicausation disease model a visual representation of the host together with various internal and external factors that promote and protect against disease

Coronary heart disease (CHD) a chronic disease characterized by damage to the coronary arteries in the heart

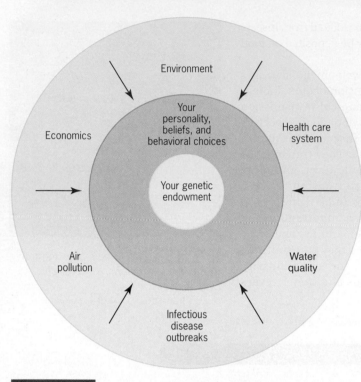

FIGURE 4.6 Multicausation disease model.

The American Heart Association lists nine types of CVDs: CHD, stroke, high blood pressure, arrhythmias, diseases of the arteries, congestive heart failure, valvular heart disease, rheumatic fever/rheumatic heart disease, and congenital heart defects.[4] CHD causes nearly half of all cardiovascular disease deaths. Sometimes called coronary artery disease, CHD is characterized by damage to the coronary arteries, the blood vessels that carry oxygen-rich blood to the heart muscle. Damage to the coronary arteries usually evolves from the condition known as atherosclerosis, a narrowing of the blood vessels. This narrowing usually results from the buildup of fatty deposits on the inner walls of arteries. When blood flow to the heart muscle is severely reduced or interrupted, a heart attack can occur. If heart damage is severe, the heart may stop beating—a condition known as cardiac arrest.

Heart disease became the leading cause of death in 1921, and stroke was the third leading cause of death beginning in 1938. However, the age-adjusted death rates from cardiovascular disease declined dramatically during the twentieth century, representing a significant public health achievement of that time.[5] Further reductions in cardiovascular disease were also noted as an important public health achievement in the first decade of the twenty-first century (see **Box 4.2**). Numerous risk factors for coronary artery disease have been identified. Whereas some of these risk factors cannot be altered by changes in lifestyle or behavior, others can. Factors that cannot be altered include one's age, sex, race, and the genetic tendency toward developing the disease. Factors that can be modified include cigarette smoking, high blood pressure, high blood cholesterol, physical inactivity, obesity, diabetes, and stress.

Cerebrovascular disease (stroke) is the fifth leading cause of death in the United States. Strokes killed 128,978 people in 2013.[3] During a stroke, or cerebrovascular accident, the blood supply to the brain is interrupted. The risk factors for developing cerebrovascular disease are similar to those for CHD and include hereditary, behavioral, and environmental factors. Hypertension and cigarette smoking are especially important risk factors for cerebrovascular disease.

Cerebrovascular disease (stroke) a chronic disease characterized by damage to blood vessels of the brain resulting in disruption of circulation to the brain

---

BOX 4.2   Ten Great Public Health Achievements, 2001–2010: Decline in Deaths from Coronary Heart Disease and Stroke

You Gotta Have Heart

The decline in cardiovascular disease death rates that began in the twentieth century continued from 2001 to 2010, making the list of important public health achievements. Age-adjusted death rates for coronary heart disease declined from 195 to 126 per 100,000 population from 2001 to 2010. During the same time period, age-adjusted death rates for stroke declined from 61.6 to 42.2 per 100,000 population. This reduction resulted in

stroke moving from third to fourth as a leading cause of death.

Advances in Prevention, Treatment, and Quality of Care

Prevention efforts resulting in lower prevalence of risk factors, such as hypertension, high cholesterol, smoking, and improvements in treatment, medications, and care have contributed to declines in CVD.

Data from: Centers for Disease Control and Prevention (2011). "Ten Great Public Health Achievements—United States, 2001-2010." *Morbidity and Mortality Weekly Report*, 60(19): 619–623. Available at http://www.cdc.gov/mmwr/preview/mmwrhtml/mm6019a5.htm.

Malignant Neoplasms (Cancer)

A total of 584,881 people died from malignant neoplasms (cancer) in 2013, making it the second leading cause of death in the United States.[3] **Malignant neoplasms** occur when cells lose control over their growth and division. Normal cells are inhibited from continual growth and division by virtue of their contact with adjacent cells. Malignant (cancerous) cells are not so inhibited; they continue to grow and divide, eventually piling up in a "new growth," a neoplasm or tumor. Early-stage tumors, sometimes called in situ cancers, are more treatable than are later-stage cancers because they are confined to the location where they started and have not spread to other parts of the body. As tumor growth continues, parts of the neoplasm can break off and be carried to distant parts of the body, where they can lodge and continue to grow. When this occurs, the cancer is said to have **metastasized**. When malignant neoplasms have spread beyond the original cell layer where they developed, the cancer is said to be invasive.[6] The more the malignancy spreads, the more difficult it is to treat and the lower the survival rates. For more information on the staging of cancer, see **Box 4.3**.

Common cancer sites in order of frequency of reported cases and deaths for both men and women are shown in **Figure 4.7**. Cancer sites with the highest number of reported cases are the prostate gland (men) and breast (women), but cancer frequently occurs in other sites, including the lung, colon and rectum, pancreas, uterus, ovaries, mouth, bladder, and skin. Lung cancer is the leading cause of cancer deaths in both sexes. An estimated 221,200 new cases of lung cancer and an estimated 158,040 lung cancer deaths were expected to occur in 2015 alone. Cigarette smoking is the most important risk factor for developing lung cancer. Alcohol contributes to cancers of the breast, colon and rectum, liver, oral cavity and pharynx, and pancreas; tobacco is a modifiable risk factor for cancers of the colon and rectum, kidney, lung and bronchus, oral cavity and pharynx, ovaries, urinary bladder, and pancreas.[6]

It is estimated that 3.5 million new cases of basal cell or squamous cell skin cancer were diagnosed among 2.2 million people in the United States in 2006.[6] Almost all of these cases are attributable to exposure to the sun, and yet many people continue to sunbathe or use tanning salons, believing that a tanned body is a healthy one. The number of cases of nonmelanoma skin cancer is expected to rise as long as the ozone layer in the atmosphere continues to be eroded. This is one example of how environmental policy affects public health.

Other Noncommunicable Disease Problems

Other noncommunicable diseases of major concern are (1) chronic obstructive pulmonary disease and allied conditions (the third leading cause of death), (2) diabetes mellitus (the seventh leading cause of death), and (3) chronic liver disease and cirrhosis (the twelfth leading cause of death).[3] Each of these chronic noncommunicable diseases and those listed in **Table 4.4** place a burden not only on the afflicted individuals and their families but on the community's health resources as well.

> **Malignant neoplasm** uncontrolled new tissue growth resulting from cells that have lost control over their growth and division
>
> **Metastasis** the spread of cancer cells to distant parts of the body by the circulatory or lymphatic system

---

BOX 4.3 How Is Cancer Staged?

According to the American Cancer Society, "staging describes the extent or spread of the disease." A number of different staging systems exist. One of the most popular is the TNM staging system, which assesses tumors in three ways: the extent of the primary tumor (T), absence or presence of regional lymph node involvement (N), and absence or presence of distant metastases (M). Once the T, N, and M are determined, a stage of I, II, III, or IV is assigned, with stage I being early stage and stage IV being advanced.

A different system of summary staging (in situ, local, regional, and distant) is used for descriptive and statistical analysis of tumor registry data. If cancer cells are present only in the layer of cells where they developed and have not spread, the stage is in situ. If the cancer has spread beyond the original layer of tissue, the cancer is invasive.

Data from: American Cancer Society (2015). *Cancer Facts and Figures 2015*. Available at http://www.cancer.org/acs/groups/content/@editorial/documents/document/acspc-044552.pdf.

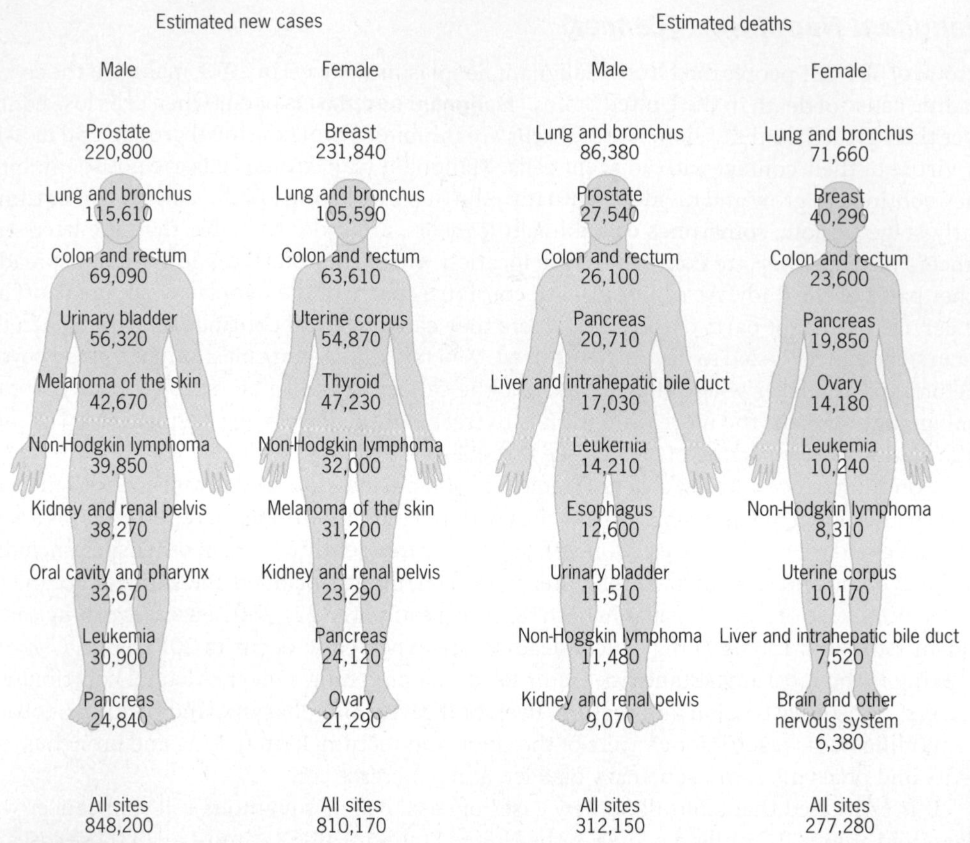

Estimated new cases

Estimated deaths

Male	Female	Male	Female
Prostate 220,800	Breast 231,840	Lung and bronchus 86,380	Lung and bronchus 71,660
Lung and bronchus 115,610	Lung and bronchus 105,590	Prostate 27,540	Breast 40,290
Colon and rectum 69,090	Colon and rectum 63,610	Colon and rectum 26,100	Colon and rectum 23,600
Urinary bladder 56,320	Uterine corpus 54,870	Pancreas 20,710	Pancreas 19,850
Melanoma of the skin 42,670	Thyroid 47,230	Liver and intrahepatic bile duct 17,030	Ovary 14,180
Non-Hodgkin lymphoma 39,850	Non-Hodgkin lymphoma 32,000	Leukemia 14,210	Leukemia 10,240
Kidney and renal pelvis 38,270	Melanoma of the skin 31,200	Esophagus 12,600	Non-Hodgkin lymphoma 8,310
Oral cavity and pharynx 32,670	Kidney and renal pelvis 23,290	Urinary bladder 11,510	Uterine corpus 10,170
Leukemia 30,900	Pancreas 24,120	Non-Hodgkin lymphoma 11,480	Liver and intrahepatic bile duct 7,520
Pancreas 24,840	Ovary 21,290	Kidney and renal pelvis 9,070	Brain and other nervous system 6,380
All sites 848,200	All sites 810,170	All sites 312,150	All sites 277,280

FIGURE 4.7   Leading sites of new cancer cases* and deaths—United States, 2015 estimates.

* Excludes basal and squamous cell skin cancer and in situ carcinomas except urinary bladder.

Reproduced from: American Cancer Society (2015). *Cancer Facts and Figures 2015.* Available at http://www.cancer.org/acs/groups/content /@editorial/documents/document/acspc-044552.pdf.

TABLE 4.4 Some Noncommunicable Health Conditions That Affect Americans		
Allergic disorders	Endogenous depression	Multiple sclerosis
Alzheimer's disease	Epilepsy	Osteoporosis
Arthritis	Fibrocystic breast condition	Premenstrual syndrome
Cerebral palsy	Lower back pain	Sickle cell trait and sickle cell disease

Prioritizing Prevention and Control Efforts

Communities are confronted with a multitude of health problems—communicable and non-communicable diseases, unintentional injuries, violence, substance abuse problems, and so on. How can health officials make logical and responsible choices about the allocation of community resources to prevent or control these problems? Which problems are indeed the most urgent? Which problems will benefit the most from a timely intervention? Many criteria can be used to judge the importance of a particular disease to a community. Among these are (1) the number of people who die from a disease, (2) the number of years of potential life lost attributable to a particular cause, and (3) the economic costs associated with a particular disease or health condition. Communities may collect primary data or use secondary sources to inform prioritization of community health issues. Other useful sources of secondary data include Kaiser State Health Facts (www.statehealthfacts.org), Kids Count (datacenter.kidscount.org), and County Health Rankings (www.countyhealthrankings.org). Each of these sources provide data on numerous health, social, economic, and environmental factors. These tools also allow comparison of geographic areas, which is useful if a community wants to show how they compare with either other communities, the state, or the nation.

Leading Causes of Death

The National Center for Health Statistics (NCHS) regularly publishes a list of the leading causes of death. For more than 80 years, the leading cause of death in America has been heart disease. Nearly one in every four deaths can be attributed to diseases of the heart. Cancers (malignant neoplasms) represent the second leading killer. Chronic lower respiratory disease ranks third, unintentional injuries rank fourth, and cerebrovascular disease (stroke) ranks fifth.[3]

One might prioritize expenditures of health care resources solely on the basis of the number of deaths, but in doing so one would spend about two-thirds of the entire health budget on the four leading health problems alone. Very little or perhaps none of the resources would be available for infant and childhood nutrition programs, for example, which have been shown to prevent more serious health care problems in later life. Nor would there be any funds available for the treatment of those with debilitating, but usually nonfatal, diseases such as chronic arthritis or mental illness.

Years of Potential Life Lost

Another approach to prioritizing a community's health care problems is by using the years of potential life lost (YPLL) statistic. Using this approach, diseases that kill people of all ages become as important as those that kill primarily older adults. Recall, for example, that malignant neoplasms (cancers) are the leading cause of age-adjusted YPLL before age 75 (YPLL-75) in the United States and account for 20% of all YPLL-75 compared with CVD, which accounts for only about 14.4%. Unintentional injuries are the second leading cause of YPLL-75, accounting for 15.9% of the total YPLL.[7]

Economic Cost to Society

Still another way to evaluate the impact of a particular disease or health problem is to estimate the economic cost to the country or community. Economic cost data are hard to come by, and sometimes even experts cannot agree on the estimates obtained. An example of such an estimate is the cost to our federal, state, and local governments' spending resulting from the use and abuse of alcohol and other drugs, a whopping $467.7 billion annually, more than $1 billion per day. This figure amounts to 11% of the $3.3 trillion in spending.[8]

Prevention, Intervention, Control, and Eradication of Diseases

The goals of epidemiology are to prevent, control, and in rare cases, to eradicate diseases and injuries. **Prevention** implies the planning for and taking of action to prevent or forestall the occurrence of an undesirable event, and is therefore more desirable than **intervention**, the taking of action during an event. For example, immunizing to prevent a disease is preferable to taking an antibiotic to cure one.

Control is a general term for the containment of a disease and can include both prevention and intervention measures. The term control is often used to mean the limiting of transmission of a communicable disease in a population. **Eradication** is the uprooting or total elimination of a disease from the human population. It is an elusive goal, one that is only rarely achieved in public health. Smallpox is the only communicable disease that has been eradicated (see **Box 4.4**). Several characteristics of smallpox made eradication possible: Humans are the only reservoir, the disease is visible shortly after infection so individuals can

Prevention the planning for and taking of action to forestall the onset of a disease or other health problem

Intervention efforts to control a disease in progress

Eradication the complete elimination or uprooting of a disease (e.g., smallpox eradication)

BOX 4.4 Community Health in Your World: Smallpox Eradication

October 2015 marked 38 years since the last naturally acquired case of smallpox in the world. This last case occurred in Somalia in October 1977.[1] Although two cases of smallpox were reported in the United Kingdom in 1978, these were associated with a research laboratory and did not represent a natural recurrence.

Smallpox is caused by the variola virus. In its severest form, it is a disfiguring and deadly disease. Manifestations of the disease include fever, headache, malaise, and prostration. A rash appears and covers the body, and there is bleeding into the skin, mucous linings, and genital tract.

The circulatory system is also severely affected. Between 15% and 40% of cases die, usually within 2 weeks. Survivors are terribly scarred for life and are sometimes blinded.

Mass vaccinations and case-finding measures by the World Health Organization (WHO), with financial support from the United States, led to the eradication of smallpox from the world. Why was it possible to eradicate smallpox? Why have we been unable to eradicate any other diseases since 1977? Do you think we will ever be able to do so? If so, what disease will be eliminated next?

---

be identified before infecting a large number of other people, and infection results in lifelong immunity. After intense identification and vaccination efforts, the last case of naturally occurring human smallpox was in 1977.

Levels of Prevention

There are three levels of application of preventive measures in disease control—primary, secondary, and tertiary. The purpose of **primary prevention** is to forestall the onset of illness or injury during the prepathogenesis period (before the disease process begins). Examples of primary prevention include health education and health promotion programs, safe-housing projects, and character-building and personality development programs. Other examples are the use of immunizations against specific diseases, the practice of personal hygiene such as hand washing, the use of rubber gloves, and the chlorination of the community's water supply. These are illustrated in **Figure 4.8**.

Unfortunately, disease or injury cannot always be avoided. Chronic diseases in particular sometimes cause considerable disability before they are detected and treated. In these cases, prompt intervention can prevent death or limit disability. **Secondary prevention** is the early diagnosis and prompt treatment of diseases before the disease becomes advanced and disability becomes severe.

One of the most important secondary prevention measures is health screenings. The goal of these screenings is not to prevent the onset of disease but rather to detect its presence during early pathogenesis, thus permitting early intervention (treatment) and limiting disability. It is important to note that the purpose of a health screening is not to diagnose disease. Instead, the purpose is to economically and efficiently sort those who are probably healthy from those who could possibly be positive for a disease (see **Figure 4.9**). Those who screen positively can then be referred for more specific diagnostic procedures. Screenings for diabetes and high blood pressure are popular examples of health screenings, as are Pap smears and testicular self-examination.

The goal of **tertiary prevention** is to retrain, re-educate, and rehabilitate the patient who has already incurred a disability. Tertiary preventive measures include those that are applied after significant pathogenesis has occurred. Therapy for a heart patient is an example of tertiary prevention.

Prevention of Communicable Diseases

Prevention and control efforts for communicable diseases include primary, secondary, and tertiary approaches. Successful application of these approaches, particularly primary

Primary prevention preventive measures that forestall the onset of illness or injury during the prepathogenesis period

Secondary prevention preventive measures that lead to an early diagnosis and prompt treatment of a disease or injury to limit disability and prevent more severe pathogenesis

Tertiary prevention measures aimed at rehabilitation following significant pathogenesis

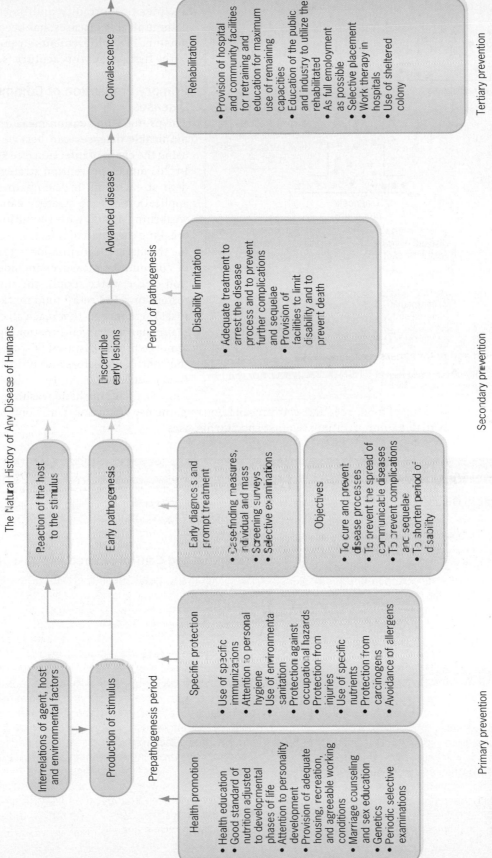

FIGURE 4.8 Applications of levels of prevention.

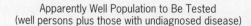

Apparently Well Population to Be Tested
(well persons plus those with undiagnosed disease)

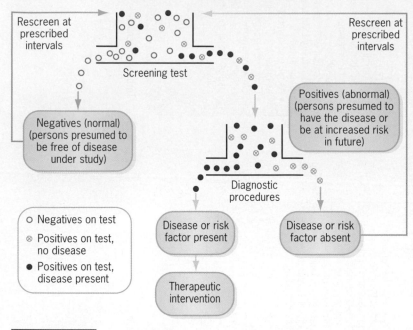

FIGURE 4.9   Flow diagram for a mass screening test.

Reproduced From: *Mausner, J. S. and S. Kramer (1985). Mausner and Bahn Epidemiology—An Introductory Text,*
2nd ed. Philadelphia, PA: W. B. Saunders Company, p. 216

prevention, resulting in unprecedented declines in morbidity and mortality from communicable diseases, has been one of the outstanding achievements in public health in the first part of this century (see **Box 4.5**).

Primary Prevention of Communicable Diseases

The primary prevention measures for communicable diseases can best be visualized using the chain of infection (see **Figure 4.10**). In this model, prevention strategies are evident at each link in the chain. Successful application of each strategy can be seen as weakening a link, with the ultimate goal of breaking the chain of infection, or interrupting the disease transmission cycle. Examples of community measures include chlorination of the water supply, the inspection of restaurants and retail food markets, immunization programs that reach all citizens, the maintenance of a well-functioning sewer system, the proper disposal of solid waste, and the control of vectors and rodents. To these can be added personal efforts at primary prevention, including hand washing, the proper cooking of food, adequate clothing and housing, the use of condoms, and obtaining all the available immunizations against specific diseases.

BOX 4.5   Ten Great Public Health Achievements, 2001–2010: Control of Infectious Diseases

Vaccine-Preventable Diseases

Vaccines are used to prevent infections, hospitalizations, and deaths caused by diseases that threatened our parents, grandparents, and great-grandparents during the twentieth century. From 2001 to 2010, many new vaccines were introduced including rotavirus, quadrivalent meningococcal conjugate, herpes zoster, pneumococcal conjugate, and human papillomavirus. Some vaccines were previously available only for children, but now adults and adolescents can get vaccines for tetanus, diphtheria, and pertussis. The availability of vaccines has a significant impact on the burden of disease. For example, it is estimated that if all children were vaccinated according to the Center for Disease Control and Prevention (CDC)'s recommended schedule, 42,000 deaths and 20 million cases of disease would be prevented.

Advancements made to older vaccines, such as hepatitis A, hepatitis B, and varicella, and the introduction of two new vaccines in particular, the pneumococcal conjugate vaccine and the rotavirus vaccine, have had major impacts on reducing hospitalizations and deaths from these diseases. Although vaccines have the power to substantially reduce the incidence of disease and potentially

even eradicate diseases, public health officials are still challenged with encouraging vaccination despite misconceptions and other barriers.

Prevention and Control of Infectious Diseases

Improvements in public health infrastructure, innovative and targeted prevention efforts, and advances in laboratory techniques and technology resulted in significant advancements in the prevention and control of infectious diseases from 2001 to 2010. For example, the number of reported U.S. tuberculosis cases and bloodstream infections associated with central lines decreased significantly during the first decade of this century. New laboratory capabilities and enhanced disease surveillance have resulted in more timely identification of the source of disease outbreaks. This information can then be used to implement control measures and prevent further spread of disease. Expanding the age range for HIV screening recommendations and screening blood donors for West Nile Virus has resulted in earlier identification and treatment of HIV and made blood transfusions safer than ever. In 2004, the CDC officially declared the United States free from canine rabies, a disease that can be deadly for humans. Although other animals may be

(Continues)

BOX 4.5   Ten Great Public Health Achievements, 2001–2010: Control of Infectious Diseases (Continued)

infected, elimination of canine rabies is an important step in prevention of human exposure to this disease.

Public Health Preparedness and Response

Local, state, and national public health agencies are all involved in preparedness and response efforts. Planning is the best way to minimize the potential impact of a public health threat. Preparedness activities may include making sure detection systems are in place, figuring how different organizations will work together, attending trainings, setting up processes, purchasing supplies and equipment, and having mock emergencies to see how the plan works.

The need for preparedness really became evident after the events of September 11, 2001, and has since become a priority for public health agencies. Bioterrorism threats

and severe disease outbreaks are especially concerning for public health because of the potential impact they could have. One of the achievements of the first decade of the century was that laboratories improved their capacity to identify and report on potentially harmful agents, such as bioterrorism agents or *E-coli* O157:H7. This allows officials to respond more quickly and reduce the impact of these agents.

Preparedness efforts were put to the test during the 2009 H1N1 influenza pandemic when agencies had to respond to a public health emergency in a coordinated and timely manner. Planning ahead was key in preventing cases, hospitalizations, and deaths. Public health agencies can also use what they learned from the pandemic to plan for future public health threats.

Data from: Centers for Disease Control and Prevention (2011). "Ten Great Public Health Achievements—United States, 2001–2010." *Morbidity and Mortality Weekly Report*, 60(19): 619–623. Available at http://www.cdc.gov/mmwr/preview/mmwrhtml/mm6019a5.htm.

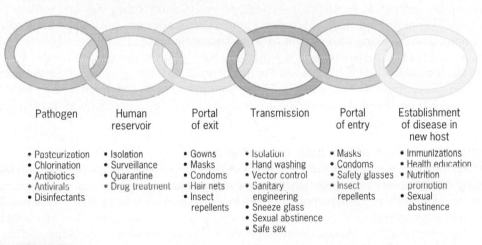

Pathogen	Human reservoir	Portal of exit	Transmission	Portal of entry	Establishment of disease in new host
• Pasteurization • Chlorination • Antibiotics • Antivirals • Disinfectants	• Isolation • Surveillance • Quarantine • Drug treatment	• Gowns • Masks • Condoms • Hair nets • Insect repellents	• Isolation • Hand washing • Vector control • Sanitary engineering • Sneeze glass • Sexual abstinence • Safe sex	• Masks • Condoms • Safety glasses • Insect repellents	• Immunizations • Health education • Nutrition promotion • Sexual abstinence

FIGURE 4.10   Chain of infection model showing disease prevention and control strategies.

Immunity can be developed actively or passively. **Active immunity** happens when a person is exposed to an organism that causes disease, and their body develops antibodies that know how to fight off that disease. A person can be exposed to a disease-causing organism through an infection or through a vaccine (see **Figure 4.11**). **Passive immunity** is where a person receives the antibodies rather than their body making them. For example, newborn babies receive antibodies from their mothers, which helps their immune systems fight off infections early in life. It is difficult to overstate the importance of vaccines or immunizations to community and public health. Vaccines prevent disease and save lives. They prevent disease in those who receive them and also protect those who come into contact with them. Many serious infectious diseases that were common as recently as the middle of the last century are rare now, including polio, measles, diphtheria, pertussis (whooping cough), rubella (German measles), mumps, tetanus, and *Haemophilus influenzae* type b (Hib).[9] Vaccines help the body fight off these diseases and help protect those members of the community who are unable to be vaccinated, namely, infants, those with certain diseases, such as childhood leukemia, and those unable to respond to an immunization. The Advisory Committee on Immunization Practices (ACIP), a group of medical and public health experts, issues recommendations for immunizations for

Active immunity occurs when exposure to a disease-causing organism prompts the immune system to develop antibodies against that disease

Passive immunity occurs when a person receives antibodies against a disease rather than their immune system producing them

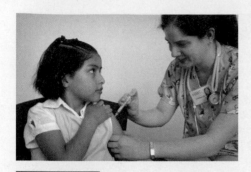

FIGURE 4.11   Child receiving a vaccination.
Courtesy of CDC

children, for teens and college students, and for adults. These recommendations include immunizations for about 15 different disease agents and often indicate the need for a series of doses to acquire adequate protection. The current recommendations can be accessed through the website http://www .cdc.gov/vaccines/acip/.[9]

Secondary Prevention of Communicable Diseases

Secondary preventive measures against communicable diseases for the individual involve either (1) self-diagnosis and self-treatment with nonprescription medications or home remedies, or (2) diagnosis and treatment with an antibiotic prescribed by a physician. Secondary preventive measures undertaken by the community against infectious diseases are usually aimed at controlling or limiting the extent of an epidemic. Examples include carefully maintaining records of cases and complying with the regulations requiring the reporting of notifiable diseases and investigating cases and contacts—those who may have become infected through close contact with known cases.

Occasionally, secondary disease control measures may include isolation and quarantine. These two practices are quite different from one another and are often confused. **Isolation** is the separation, for the period of communicability, of infected persons or animals from others so as to prevent the direct or indirect transmission of the communicable agent to a susceptible person. In health care settings, providers and visitors may be instructed to use isolation precautions, such as wearing a gown, gloves, and/or a mask (depending on the situation), when working with certain patients. **Quarantine** is the limitation of the freedom of movement of well persons or animals that have been exposed to a communicable disease until the incubation period has passed. Further control measures may include **disinfection**, the killing of communicable agents outside of the host, and mass treatment with antibiotics. Finally, public health education and health promotion should be used as both primary and secondary preventive measures.

Tertiary Prevention of Communicable Diseases

Tertiary preventive measures for the control of communicable diseases for the individual include convalescence from infection, recovery to full health, and return to normal activity. In some cases, such as paralytic poliomyelitis, return to normal activity may not be possible even after extensive physical therapy. At the community level, tertiary preventive measures are aimed at preventing the recurrence of an epidemic. The proper removal, embalming, and burial of the dead is an example. Tertiary prevention may involve the reapplication of primary and secondary measures in such a way as to prevent further cases. For example, in some countries, such as the Republic of Korea, people with colds or flu wear gauze masks in public to reduce the spread of disease.

Application of Prevention Measures in the Control of a Communicable Disease: HIV Infection and AIDS

Acquired immune deficiency syndrome (AIDS) is the late stage of an infection with the human immunodeficiency virus (HIV). HIV destroys specific blood cells (CD4+ T cells) that are crucial in fighting diseases. People can become infected when they come into contact with the virus through unprotected sexual activity, intravenous drug use, or exposure to the blood of an infected person. "Within a few weeks of being infected with HIV, some people develop flu-like symptoms that last for a week or two, but others have no symptoms at all. People living with HIV may appear and feel healthy for several years. However, even if they feel healthy, HIV is still affecting their bodies."[10]

The late stage of HIV infection is AIDS. People with AIDS have a difficult time fighting other communicable diseases and certain cancers. In the past, it took only a few years for someone infected to develop AIDS. Now, with the development of advanced medications, people can live much longer, perhaps even decades, after acquiring an HIV infection.[10]

Isolation the separation of infected persons from those who are susceptible

Quarantine limitation of freedom of movement of those who have been exposed to a disease and may be incubating it

Disinfection the killing of communicable disease agents outside the host, on countertops, for example

Despite advances in the diagnosis and treatment, HIV infections and AIDS are still epidemic in the United States and in the world.

HIV is responsible for a pandemic of unprecedented size. The WHO estimated that 36.9 million people were living with HIV/AIDS worldwide at the end of 2014. In the same year, 2 million people were newly infected with HIV and 1.2 million people died of HIV-related causes.[11] From the beginning of the epidemic through 2014, approximately 34 million people had died from AIDS-related causes.[12] The reservoir for HIV is the infected human population; there are no known animal or insect reservoirs. Referring to the chain of infection, HIV normally leaves its infected host (reservoir) during sexual activity. The portal of exit is the urogenital tract. Transmission is direct and occurs when reproductive fluids or blood are exchanged with the susceptible host. In the case of injection drug users, however, transmission is indirect, by contaminated needles (vehicle). The portal of entry is usually either genital, oral, or anal in direct (sexual) transmission or transdermal in the case of injection drug users or blood transfusion recipients. Transmission can also occur during medical procedures if there is an accidental needlestick or some other type of contamination with blood or other potentially infectious material.

A closer examination of the chain of infection reveals that prevention or control measures can be identified for each link. The pathogen in the diseased host can be held in check by the appropriate drug. Outside the host, measures such as sterilizing needles and other possible vehicles readily kill the virus and reduce the likelihood of transmission by contamination. The infected host (reservoir) can be identified through blood tests and educated to take precautions against the careless transmission of live virus through unsafe sex and needle sharing. Condoms can be used to reduce the likelihood of transmission through portals of exit (and entry). One set of *Healthy People 2020* objectives focuses on reducing the rate of HIV transmission and, thus, the number of new cases of AIDS. One way to do this is to increase condom use, particularly among high risk populations. Another way is to increase the number of persons living with HIV who know their level of antibodies to HIV (their serostatus). Finally, one objective aims to increase the proportion of adolescents and adults who have been tested for HIV in the past 12 months (see **Box 4.6**).

BOX 4.6   *Healthy People 2020* Objectives

Objectives HIV-2, HIV-3, HIV-13, HIV-14.1, HIV-18   Reduce new HIV infections, increase HIV testing and prevent risk, increase access to care and improve outcomes.

Target setting method: Consistent with the National HIV/AIDS Strategy; or 10% improvement

Data sources: National HIV Behavioral Surveillance System (NHBS), CDC/NCHHSTP

Targets and baselines:

Objective	Baseline	Status	2020 Target
HIV-2 Reduce the number of new HIV infections among adolescents and adults.	New infections among persons age 13 and older		
	48,600[a]	47,500[d]	36,450
HIV-3 Reduce the rate of HIV transmission among adolescents and adults.	New infections per 100 persons living with HIV		
	4.6[a]	4.2[d]	3.5
HIV-13 Increase the proportion of persons living with HIV who know their serostatus.	Persons 13 years and older living with HIV who are aware of their HIV infection		
	80.9%[a]	87.2%[f]	90.0%

(Continues)

BOX 4.6   *Healthy People 2020* Objectives (Continued)

Objective	Baseline	Status	2020 Target
HIV-14.1 Increase the proportion of adolescents and adults who have ever been tested for HIV.	Persons 15–44 years of age reporting that they have ever been tested for HIV		
	66.9%[c]	69.9%[g]	73.6%
HIV-18 Reduce the proportion of men who have sex with men (MSM) who reported unprotected anal intercourse with a partner of discordant or unknown status during their last sexual encounter.	MSM reporting unprotected anal intercourse with a partner having unknown or discordant status		
	13.7%[b]	13.7%[e]	10.3%

[a]In 2006.
[b]2008.
[c]2006–2010.
[d]2010.
[e]2011.
[f]2012.
[g]2011–2013.

For Further Thought

Reducing the rate of HIV transmission is the best way to decrease both the number of persons living with HIV infection and the number of new AIDS cases. Reducing the number of new AIDS cases decreases the number of deaths from AIDS. Can you think of ways to prevent the transmission of HIV in your community?

Data from: U.S. Department of Health and Human Services, Office of Disease Prevention and Health Promotion (2010). *Healthy People 2020.* Available at http://www.healthypeople.gov/2020/default.aspx.

Bloodborne pathogens disease agents, such as HIV, that are transmissible in blood and other body fluids

Bloodborne Pathogens Standard a set of regulations promulgated by OSHA that sets forth the responsibilities of employers and employees with regard to precautions to be taken concerning bloodborne pathogens in the workplace

For injection drug users, abstinence from such drug use would preclude transmission by needles and syringes. A more realistic approach to reducing the transmission of HIV/AIDS in this population is a syringe (and needle) exchange policy. Since 1988, Congress has banned the use of federal funding of needle exchange programs. In the interim, a number of research papers have provided evidence supporting the idea that syringe/needle exchange programs reduce the spread of HIV/AIDS, hepatitis, and other bloodborne diseases without increasing use. As of May 2015, 228 syringe exchange programs were operating in 35 states, the District of Columbia, Puerto Rico, and the Indian Nations (see **Figure 4.12**).[13] The ban on federal funding for needle exchange programs was lifted in 2009 but reinstated in late 2011 in what many saw as a step backward in the fight against HIV/AIDS.[14] In early 2016, the U.S. Congress enabled the use of federal funds for exchange programs, although not for the needles themselves.

For those working in the health professions, the risk of acquiring an HIV infection in the workplace is of particular concern. The Occupational Safety and Health Administration (OSHA) estimates that 5.6 million workers in the health care industry and related occupations are at risk of occupational exposure to **bloodborne pathogens**, including HIV, hepatitis B virus (HBV), hepatitis C virus (HCV), and others.[15] In 1991, OSHA, recognizing that workers in the health care industry were at risk of occupational exposure to bloodborne pathogens, issued the **Bloodborne Pathogens Standard**.

In November 2000, Congress, acknowledging the estimates of 600,000 to 800,000 needlestick and other percutaneous injuries occurring among health care workers annually, passed the Needlestick Safety and Prevention Act.[16] In 2001, in response to the Needlestick Safety and Prevention Act, OSHA revised its Bloodborne Pathogens Standard. This revised standard, currently in effect, added requirements for employers to select safer needle devices when available, seek employee input on choosing those devices, and to maintain a log of injuries from contaminated sharps.[17] The goal of all of these regulations and standards is to reduce the number of HIV/AIDS cases, as well as cases of other bloodborne diseases, resulting from workplace exposure.

Prevention of Noncommunicable Diseases

Both the individual and the community can contribute substantially to the prevention and control of multicausation diseases. The community can provide a pro-health environment—physical, economic, and social—in which it becomes easier for individuals to achieve a high level of health.

Primary Prevention of Noncommunicable Diseases

Primary preventive measures for noncommunicable diseases include adequate food and energy supplies; good opportunities for education, employment, and housing; and efficient community services. Beyond this foundation, a community should provide health promotion and health education programs, health and medical services, and protection from environmental and occupational hazards.

Individuals can practice primary prevention by obtaining an education that includes a knowledge about health and disease and the history of disease of others in one's family. In particular, the individual should take responsibility for eating properly, exercising adequately, maintaining appropriate weight, limiting alcohol use, and avoiding drugs. Individuals can also protect themselves from injury by adopting behaviors that reduce their risk of injuries. These behaviors include driving safely and wearing a safety belt at all times while traveling in a vehicle. Examples of primary prevention also include avoiding overexposure to the sun and limiting one's environmental pollutants that might cause cancer.

Secondary Prevention of Noncommunicable Diseases

Secondary preventive measures the community can take include the provision of mass screenings for chronic diseases (see **Figure 4.13**), case-finding measures, and the provision of adequate health personnel, equipment, and facilities for the community. Secondary prevention responsibilities of individual citizens include personal screenings such as self-examination of skin for abnormal moles and testes for lumps that could be cancerous, the Hemoccult test (for colorectal cancer), and medical screenings such as the Pap test (for cervical cancer), the PSA test (for prostate cancer), mammography (for breast cancer), and screenings for diabetes, glaucoma, or hypertension. Participating in such health screenings and having regular medical and dental checkups represent only the first step in the secondary prevention of noncommunicable diseases. This must be followed by the pursuit of definitive diagnosis and prompt treatment of any diseases detected.

FIGURE 4.12   Distribution of clean needles and destruction of contaminated needles reduces the transmission of bloodborne pathogens such as human immunodeficiency virus (HIV).

© Gustau Nacarino/Thomson Reuters.

FIGURE 4.13   Mammography, used for screening and early detection of breast cancer, is an example of secondary prevention.

© Photodisc.

Tertiary Prevention of Noncommunicable Diseases

Tertiary preventive measures for a community include adequate emergency medical personnel, services, and facilities to meet the needs of those citizens for whom primary and secondary preventive measures were unsuccessful. Examples include ambulance services, hospitals, physicians and surgeons, nurses, and other allied health professionals. Health care in the United States focuses mostly on tertiary prevention, and many experts feel that America should reallocate resources from tertiary prevention to primary and secondary preventive measures.

Tertiary prevention for the individual often requires significant behavioral or lifestyle changes. Examples include strict adherence to prescribed medications, exercise programs, and diet. For example, a heart attack patient could receive nutrition education and counseling and be encouraged to participate in a supervised exercise program, thus maximizing the use of remaining capabilities. This could lead to a resumption of employment and the prevention of a second heart attack. For certain types of noncommunicable health problems, such as those involving substance abuse, regular attendance at support group meetings, or counseling sessions may constitute an important part of a tertiary prevention program.

Application of Preventive Measures in the Control of a Noncommunicable Disease: CHD

One set of *Healthy People 2020* objectives aims at reducing risk factors and deaths from cardiovascular diseases including coronary heart disease (see **Box 4.7**). Many factors contribute to one's risk of developing this disease. Both the community and the individual can contribute to the prevention of CHD.

The Community's Role

The community must recognize the importance of preventing chronic disease; intervention following a crisis, such as a heart attack, is the least effective and most expensive way to provide help to a CHD patient. While individual behavioral changes hold the best prospects for reducing the prevalence of heart disease in this country, communities can provide a supporting environment for these behavioral changes. For example, the community can support restricting smoking areas and can provide a clear message to youth that smoking is damaging to health. Communities also can provide adequate opportunity for health screening for risk factors such as hypertension and serum cholesterol levels. In particular, schools can permit the administration of Youth Risk Behavior Surveillance System surveys and utilize these occasions as opportunities to teach students about the importance of healthy behavioral choices. Communities also can promote and assist in the development of areas for recreation and exercise, such as safe paths for jogging or cycling and lighted sidewalks for walking. Exercise reduces obesity and increases the high-density lipoproteins (HDLs) in the blood, thereby lowering risk for a heart attack. Finally, access to nutritious foods is critical, including providing healthy menus in schools and ensuring that communities have access to grocery stores with nutritious and affordable food selections.

BOX 4.7   *Healthy People 2020*: **Objectives**

Objectives HDS-2, HDS-3   Reduce the heart disease and stroke death rates.
Target setting method: Projection/trend analysis
Data source: National Vital Statistics System—Mortality (NVSS—M), CDC, NCHS
Targets and baselines:

Objective	2007 Baseline	2013 Status	2020 Target
HDS-2 Reduce coronary heart disease deaths.	Coronary heart disease deaths per 100,000 population		
	129.2	102.6	103.4
HDS-3 Reduce stroke deaths.	Stroke deaths per 100,000 population		
	43.5	36.2	34.8

Objective HDS-4   Increase the proportion of adults who have had their blood pressure measured.
Target setting method: 2% improvement
Data source: National Health Interview Survey (NHIS), CDC, NCHS
Targets and baselines:

Objective	2008 Baseline	2014 Status	2020 Target
HDS-4 Increase the proportion of adults who have had their blood pressure measured within the preceding 2 years and can state whether it is normal or high.	90.6%	91.8%	92.6%

Objectives HDS-5.1, 5.2   Reduce the proportion of persons in the population with hypertension.
Target setting method: 10% improvement
Data source: NHANES, CDC, NCHS
Targets and baselines:

Objective	2005–2008 Baseline	2009–2012 Status	2020 Target
HDS-5.1 Reduce the proportion of adults with hypertension.	Adults 18 years and older with high blood pressure		
	29.9%	29.0%	26.9%
HDS-5.2 Reduce the proportion of children and adolescents with hypertension.	Children and adolescents aged 8–17 years with blood pressure		
	3.5%	2.4%	3.2%

Objective HDS-6   Increase the proportion of adults who have had their blood cholesterol checked within the preceding 5 years.
Target setting method: 10% improvement
Data source: NHIS, CDC, NCHS
Targets and baselines:

Objective	2008 Baseline	2014 Status	2020 Target
HDS-6 Increase the proportion of adults who have had their cholesterol checked within the preceding 5 years.	Adults 18 years and older who had their blood cholesterol checked		
	74.6%	85.5%	82.1%

(Continues)

BOX 4.7 *Healthy People 2020:* **Objectives (Continued)**

Objective HDS-7   Reduce the proportion of adults with high total blood cholesterol levels.
Target setting method: 10% improvement
Data source: NHANES, CDC, NCHS
Targets and baselines:

Objective	2005–2008 Baseline	2009–2012 Status	2020 Target
HDS-7 Reduce the proportion of adults with high total blood cholesterol levels.	Percent of adults 20 years and older with total blood cholesterol levels of 240 mg/dL or greater		
	15%	12.9%	13.5%

Objective HDS-8   Reduce the mean total blood cholesterol levels among adults.
Target setting method: 10% improvement
Data source: NHANES, CDC, NCHS
Targets and baselines:

Objective	2005–2008 Baseline	2009–2012 Status	2020 Target
HDS-8 Reduce the mean total blood cholesterol levels among adults.	Mean total blood cholesterol level for adults 20 years and older		
	197.7 mg/dL	195.3 mg/dL	177.9 mg/dL

For Further Thought

Cardiovascular diseases are the leading causes of deaths in the United States. While significant progress has been made in lowering the death from heart attack and stroke, further progress is certainly achievable. Important contributing factors are high blood pressure, high blood cholesterol, and obesity.

What can individuals and communities do to reduce obesity, lower the average blood pressure, and lower the mean level of cholesterol in the blood? Have you noticed efforts in your community to provide blood pressure screenings and cholesterol testing? If so, what agencies are offering these services?

Data from: U.S. Department of Health and Human Services, Office of Disease Prevention and Health Promotion (2010). *Healthy People 2020*. Available at http://www.healthypeople.gov/2020/default.aspx.

The Individual's Role

In addition to community-level factors, each individual also has responsibility for his or her health. For example, each individual can increase his or her resistance to CHD by knowing the difference between the types of risk factors and by adopting behaviors that prevent or postpone the onset of CHD.

Each person is endowed with a unique genetic code. An individual's innate resistance or susceptibility to heart disease is encoded in the genes. **Unmodifiable risk factors** for CHD include one's race, gender, personality type, age, and basic metabolic rate. Also inherited is one's baseline serum cholesterol level. That is, children whose parents had high serum cholesterol levels are at risk for those same higher levels, independent of their diet.

Modifiable risk factors for CHD include environmental and behavioral factors over which an individual has some control. Modifiable risk factors that would increase the likelihood of CHD include smoking, a diet too rich in fats, lack of exercise, obesity, uncontrolled hypertension, and too much stress. Although none of these factors alone is likely to cause a premature heart attack, each can contribute to the likelihood of CHD.

Unmodifiable risk factor
Factor contributing to the development of a noncommunicable disease that cannot be altered by modifying one's behavior or environment.

Modifiable risk factor
Contributor of a noncommunicable disease that can be altered by modifying one's behavior or environment.

Chapter Summary

- Diseases can be classified as communicable (infectious) or noncommunicable (noninfectious), and acute or chronic.
- Acute diseases last for less than 3 months, whereas chronic diseases continue longer than 3 months.
- Communicable diseases are caused by biological agents and are transmissible from a source of infection to a susceptible host.
- The process of communicable disease transmission is best understood by the chain of infection model, in which the interruption of disease transmission can be visualized as the breaking of one or more links in the chain.
- Noncommunicable diseases are often the result of multiple risk factors that can be genetic, behavioral, and environmental in origin.
- Several of the noncommunicable diseases rank among the leading causes of death in United States.

- There are three levels of disease prevention—primary, secondary, and tertiary.
- Primary prevention includes measures that forestall the onset of disease or injury, while secondary prevention encompasses efforts aimed at early detection and intervention to limit disease and disability. Tertiary prevention includes measures aimed at re-education and rehabilitation after significant pathogenesis has occurred.
- Both the spread of communicable diseases and the prevalence of noncommunicable diseases can best be reduced by the appropriate application of primary, secondary, and tertiary preventive measures by the community and the individual.
- The prevention and control of noncommunicable diseases require both individual and community efforts.

Scenario: Analysis and Response

1. If Adam's roommate, Brandon, were to begin to show signs of the flu, what could Adam do to lessen his chances of becoming infected himself? (*Hint:* Think about the chain of infection.)
2. As an accountant, Adam spends most of his day behind a desk. To identify primary, secondary, and tertiary preventive measures Adam should take to reduce his risk for heart disease, visit one governmental and one nongovernmental website and find some information about prevention of heart disease. For each preventive measure you list, indicate whether it is primary, secondary, or tertiary prevention.
3. In what other health screenings should Adam and Brandon participate? Are there any health screenings available on the Internet?
4. What kinds of thoughts, behaviors, and conditions prevent people from participating in health screenings?

Review Questions

1. What are some of the ways in which diseases and health problems are classified in community health?
2. Contrast the terms acute disease and chronic disease. Provide three examples of each type of disease.
3. Contrast the terms communicable disease and noncommunicable disease. Provide three examples of each type of disease.
4. What is the difference between a communicable agent and a pathogenic agent?
5. What are the components of a simplified communicable disease model?
6. List some examples of environmental factors that can influence the occurrence and spread of disease.
7. Draw and explain the model for multicausation diseases.
8. What is the difference between prevention and intervention?
9. Explain the difference between primary, secondary, and tertiary prevention and provide an example of each.
10. What is the chain of infection model of disease transmission? Draw the model and label its parts.

11. Again referring to the chain of infection, indicate how prevention and control strategies could be implemented to interrupt the transmission of gonorrhea. Are most of these strategies primary, secondary, or tertiary prevention measures?

12. Define the following terms—*case, carrier, vector, vehicle.*

13. List five examples each of vectorborne diseases and nonvectorborne diseases.

14. Explain the difference between the public health practices of isolation and quarantine.

15. Explain the importance of vaccinations or immunizations in preventing diseases in the community.

16. Apply the principles of prevention and the examples given in this chapter to outline a prevention strategy for breast cancer that includes primary, secondary, and tertiary prevention components.

Activities

1. Look at your state health department's website to see if you can find out which communicable (infectious) disease problems are reported most frequently in your state. Which are the rarest? Is Lyme disease reportable?

2. List some of the infections you have had. How were these infections transmitted to you—directly, by vehicle, or by vector? Talk to an elderly person about diseases they can recall from their youth and how these diseases affected them and their families. Take notes on the response, and hand them in or share them orally in class.

3. Look up the disease bubonic plague on the Internet. After reading about the disease, see if you can complete a chain of infection model for plague. Identify the causative agent, the vector, the reservoir, and the mode of transmission. What types of prevention and control strategies were used in the past to stop the spread of this disease? What could be done differently today if there were an epidemic of plague?

4. Think about motor vehicle crashes. List some primary, secondary, and tertiary preventive measures that the community and you can take to reduce the number and seriousness of injuries caused by auto accidents.

References

1. Heymann, D. L., ed. (2014). *Control of Communicable Diseases Manual*, 20th ed. Washington, DC: American Public Health Association.

2. Merrill, R.M. (2012). *Introduction to Epidemiology*, 6th ed. Burlington, MA: Jones & Bartlett Learning, 13–14.

3. Centers for Disease Control and Prevention (2014). "Deaths, Percent of Total Deaths, and Death Rates for the 15 Leading Causes of Death: United States and Each State, 2013." *National Vital Statistics System Mortality Tables.* Hyattsville, MD: National Center for Health Statistics. Available at http://www.cdc.gov/nchs/data/dvs/LCWK9_2013.pdf.

4. American Heart Association (2015). *Heart Disease and Stroke Statistics—2015 Update: A Report of the American Heart Association.* Dallas, TX: Author. Available at http://circ.ahajournals.org/content/early/2014/12/18/CIR.0000000000000152.

5. Centers for Disease Control and Prevention (1999). "Ten Great Public Health Achievements—United States, 1900–1999." *Morbidity and Mortality Weekly Report 48*(12): 241–242. Available at www.cdc.gov/mmwr/PDF/wk/mm4812.pdf.

6. American Cancer Society (2015). *Cancer Facts and Figures—2015.* Atlanta, GA: Author. Available at http://www.cancer.org/acs/groups/content/@editorial/documents/document/acspc-044552.pdf.

7. National Center for Health Statistics (2015). *Health, United States, 2014, With Special Feature on Adults Aged 55–64.* Available at http://www.cdc.gov/nchs/data/hus/hus14.pdf.

8. National Center on Addiction and Substance Abuse at Columbia University (2009). *Shoveling Up II: The Impact of Substance Abuse on Federal, State and Local Budgets.* Available at http://www.centeronaddiction.org/addiction-research/reports/shoveling-ii-impact-substance-abuse-federal-state-and-local-budgets.

9. Centers for Disease Control and Prevention (2013). *Vaccines and Immunizations.* Atlanta, GA: Author. Available at http://www.cdc.gov/vaccines/.

10. Centers for Disease Control and Prevention (2015). *HIV Basics.* Available at http://www.cdc.gov/hiv/basics/index.html.

11. World Health Organization (2015). *HIV/AIDS.* Geneva, Switzerland: Author. Available at http://www.who.int/features/qa/71/en/.

12. World Health Organization (n.d.). *10 Facts on HIV/AIDS.* Available at http://www.who.int/features/factfiles/hiv/facts/en/index3.html.

13. North American Syringe Exchange Network (2016). *The Facts.* Available at https://nasen.org/.

14. Harm Reduction International (2011). *U.S. Reinstates Federal Funding Ban for Needle and Syringe Exchange Programmes*. Available at http://www.ihra.net/contents/1154.

15. Occupational Safety and Health Administration (2009). *Bloodborne Pathogens and Needlestick Prevention: Hazard Recognition*. Washington, DC: U.S. Department of Labor. Available at http://www.osha.gov/SLTC/bloodbornepathogens/index.html.

16. U.S. Congress (2000, October 3). "An Act to Require Changes in the Bloodborne Pathogens Standard in Effect under the Occupational Safety and Health Act of 1970." *Congressional Record*, 146.

17. United States Department of Labor (2001). *Revision to OSHA's Bloodborne Pathogens Standard: Technical Background and Summary*. Available at https://www.osha.gov/needlesticks/ncedlefact.html.

CHAPTER 5

Community Organizing/ Building and Health Promotion Programming

Chapter Objectives

After studying this chapter, you will be able to:

1. Explain the terms *evidence, evidence-based practice*, and *socio-ecological perspective*.
2. Define community organizing, community capacity, community participation, and empowered community.
3. Identify the assumptions that underlie the process of community organization.
4. Briefly explain the differences among planning and policy practice,

community capacity development, and social advocacy strategies to community organization.
5. Illustrate the difference between needs-based and strengths-based community organizing models.
6. List the steps for a generalized model for community organizing/building.
7. Explain what community building means.
8. Describe the difference between health education and health promotion.

9. State and summarize the steps involved in creating a health promotion program.

10. Define the term *needs assessment*.

11. Briefly explain the six steps used in assessing needs.

12. Discuss the difference between goals and objectives.

13. List the different types of intervention strategies.

14. Demonstrate the differences among best practices, best experiences, and best processes.

15. Explain the purposes of pilot testing in program development.

16. State the difference between formative and summative evaluation.

Scenario

It was becoming obvious to many that the suburb of Kenzington now had a drug problem, but few wanted to admit it. The community's residents liked their quiet neighborhoods, and most never thought that drugs would be a problem. In fact, the problem really sneaked up on everyone. The town had only one bar, and although occasionally someone drank too much, the bar's patrons usually controlled their drinking and didn't bother anyone. Occasionally, two or three high school seniors would be caught drinking beer given to them by their older friends. Yet these isolated incidents gave no indication of Kenzington's impending drug problem.

Within the past year, the climate of the town had changed considerably. Incidents of teenagers being arrested for possession of alcohol or even other drugs, such as marijuana and heroin, were being reported more regularly. There seemed to be more reports of burglaries, too. There had even been a robbery and two assaults reported within the last month. The population of young adults in the community seemed to be increasing, and many of these seemed to be driving impressive cars, using the hottest new digital devices, and wearing the latest clothes. All of these signs were obvious to a group of concerned citizens in Kenzington and suggested the possibility of a drug problem. So the concerned citizens decided to take their concern to the city council.

Introduction

To deal with the health issues that face many communities, community and public health professionals must possess specific knowledge and skills. They need to be able to identify problems, develop a plan to attack each problem, gather the resources necessary to carry out that plan, implement that plan, and then evaluate the results to determine the degree of progress that has been achieved. Elsewhere in the text, we described epidemiological methods as essential tools of the community and public health professional. In this chapter, we present two other important tools that each successful community and public health worker must master: the skills to organize/build a community and to plan a health promotion program.

Inherent in the community organizing/building and health promotion programming processes is behavior change. That is, for community organizing/building and health promotion programming efforts to be successful people must change their behavior. Some of the behaviors that need to change as part of these processes are health related and others are not. To be able to better understand the behavior change associated with community organizing/building and health promotion programming, we need to introduce two important concepts. The first is evidence-based practice and the second is the socio-ecological approach.

To understand evidence-based practice one first needs to be clear on the meaning of evidence. **Evidence** is the body of data that can be used to make decisions. When community and public health workers systematically find, appraise, and use evidence as the basis for decision making related to community organizing/building and health promotion programming, it is referred to as **evidence-based practice**.[1] Evidence comes in many different forms ranging from objective evidence, derived from science (e.g., systematic reviews of science-based research), to subjective evidence that can come from personal experiences and observations. Because

Evidence the body of data that can be used to make decisions

Evidence-based practice systematically finding, appraising, and using evidence as the basis for decision making

Socio-ecological approach (ecological perspective) Individuals influence and are influenced by their families, social networks, the organizations in which they participate (workplaces, schools, religious organizations), the communities of which they are a part, and the society in which they live

objective evidence comes from the scientific process, it is usually seen as a higher quality of evidence.[2] Community and public health workers should strive to use the best evidence possible, but also understand that scientific evidence associated some health problems may not be available or even exist and thus are faced with using the best evidence available.[3]

The underlying foundation of the **socio-ecological approach** (sometimes referred to as the **ecological perspective**) is that behavior has multiple levels of influence. That is, "[i]ndividuals influence and are influenced by their families, social networks, the organizations in which they participate (workplaces, schools, religious organizations), the communities of which they are a part, and the society in which they live."[4] In other words, the health behavior of individuals is shaped in part by the social context in which they live. Scholars who study and write about the levels of influence have used various labels to describe them. For many years, the commonly used labels for the levels included intrapersonal, interpersonal, institutional or organizational, community, and public policy.[5] More recently, two additional levels—physical environment and culture—have been added.[6]

An application of the socio-ecological approach can be seen in the efforts that have been put forth to encourage adults in the United States to exercise regularly. At the intrapersonal (or individual) level, most adults know that regular exercise is good for them, but many have found it difficult to start and maintain such a program. At the interpersonal level adults are often encouraged by people close to them, such as their physician and/or family and friends, to start an exercise program. After such encouragement some may attempt to get active on their own, while others may join a formal exercise group at a fitness facility. At the institutional (or organizational) level, a number of employers have developed worksite health promotion programs that include incentives (e.g., extra pay, reduced health care premiums, fitness facility memberships) to encourage their employees to engage in regular exercise to get healthier and reduce health care costs. At the community level, some towns, cities, and counties have passed ordinances to include bicycle lanes on the roads in order to make it easier to exercise. At the public policy level, many states and the U.S. government have spent lots of dollars on public service announcements (PSAs) and other forms of media advertising to encourage regular exercise. At the physical environment level, a number of communities have built new structures such as walking paths to make it more convenient to exercise. And, at the culture level a focus has been placed on getting and reinforcing regular exercise as the cultural norm. As can be seen by these examples, a central conclusion of the socio-ecological approach is that it takes multi-level interventions to achieve substantial changes in health behavior.[7]

As you read the rest of this chapter, consider the impact that evidence-based practice and the socio-ecological approach have on both community/organizing and health promotion programming.

Community Organizing/Building

Community and public health problems can range from small and simple to large and complex. Small, simple problems that are local and involve few people can often be solved with the effort of a small group of people and a minimal amount of organization. Large, complex problems that involve whole communities require significant skills and resources for their solution. For these larger problems, a considerable effort must be expended to organize the citizens of the community to work together to implement a lasting solution to their problem. For example, a trained smoking cessation facilitator could help a single person or a small group of people to stop smoking. But to reduce the smoking rates community wide, community collaboration is needed. The same smoking cessation facilitators are needed to work with individuals, but others are also needed. Schools are needed to provide appropriate tobacco education programs to youth, organizations (e.g., worksites) and institutions (e.g., religious communities) are needed to create smoking policies, government agencies are needed to enforce the laws associated with the sale of tobacco, and cities, counties, and states are needed to create clean indoor air ordinances or laws. This more comprehensive approach to reducing smoking rates needs to bring together, in an organized and coordinated effort, the people and groups interested in the issue and the resources necessary for change. In other words, a community organization effort is needed.

TABLE 5.1   Terms Associated with Community Organizing/Building

Community capacity	"Community characteristics affecting its ability to identify, mobilize, and address problems"[8]
Empowerment	"Social action process for people to gain mastery over their lives and the lives of their communities"[8]
Grassroots participation	"Bottom-up efforts of people taking collective actions on their own behalf, and they involve the use of a sophisticated blend of confrontation and cooperation in order to achieve their ends"[10]
Macro practice	The methods of professional change that deal with issues beyond the individual, family, and small group level
Participation and relevance	"Community organizing should 'start where the people are' and engage community members as equals"[8]
Social capital	"Processes and conditions among people and organizations that lead to their accomplishing a goal of mutual social benefit, usually characterized by interrelated constructs of trust, cooperation, civic engagement, and reciprocity, reinforced by networking"[11]

"The term community organization was coined by American social workers in the late 1880s to describe their efforts to coordinate services for newly arrived immigrants and the poor."[8] More recently, community organization has been used by a variety of professionals, including community and public health workers, and refers to various methods of interventions to deal with social problems. More formally, **community organizing** has been defined as "the process by which community groups are helped to identify common problems or change targets, mobilize resources, and develop and implement strategies for reaching their collective goals."[8] Community organizing is not a science but an art of consensus building within a democratic process.[9] (See **Table 5.1** for terms associated with community organizing/building.)

> **Community organizing**
> a process by which community groups are helped to identify common problems or change targets, mobilize resources, and develop and implement strategies for reaching their collective goals

Need for Organizing Communities

In recent years, the need to organize communities seems to have increased. Advances in electronics (e.g., handheld digital devices) and communications (e.g., multifunction cell phones and the Internet), household upgrades (e.g., energy efficiency), and increased mobility (i.e., frequency of moving and ease of worldwide travel) have resulted in a loss of a sense of community. Individuals are much more independent than ever before. The days when people knew everyone on their block are past. Today, it is not uncommon for people to never meet their neighbors (see **Figure 5.1**). In other cases, people see or talk to their neighbors only a few times each year. Because of these changes in community social structure, it now takes specific skills to organize a community to act together for the collective good. Note that the usefulness of community organizing skills extends beyond community health.

Assumptions of Community Organizing

According to Ross,[9] those who organize communities do so while making certain assumptions. The assumptions Ross outlines can be summarized as follows:

1. Communities of people can develop the capacity to deal with their own problems.
2. People want to change and can change.
3. People should participate in making, adjusting, or controlling the major changes taking place within their communities.
4. Changes in community living that are self-imposed or self-developed have a meaning and permanence that imposed changes do not have.
5. A "holistic approach" can successfully address problems with which a "fragmented approach" cannot cope.

FIGURE 5.1   In today's complex communities, it is not uncommon for people never to meet their neighbors.

© Hal_P/ShutterStock, Inc.

6. Democracy requires cooperative participation and action in the affairs of the community, and people must learn the skills that make this possible.

7. Frequently, communities of people need help in organizing to deal with their needs, just as many individuals require help in coping with their individual problems.

Community Organizing Methods

There is no single, preferred method for organizing a community. In fact, a careful review reveals that several different approaches have been successful, which led Rothman and Tropman to state, "We would speak of community organization methods rather than the community organization method."[12]

The early approaches to community organization used by social workers emphasized the use of consensus and cooperation to deal with community problems.[13] However, Rothman created an original typology of three primary methods of community organization: locality development, social planning, and social action.[14] More recently, the strategies have been renamed *planning and policy practice, community capacity development*, and *social advocacy*.[12] At the heart of the *planning and policy practice* strategy are data. By using data, community and public health workers generate persuasive rationales that lead toward proposing and enacting particular solutions.[15]

The *community capacity development* strategy is based on empowering those impacted by a problem with knowledge and skills to understand the problem and then work cooperatively together to deal with the problem. Group consensus and social solidarity are important components of this strategy.[15] The third strategy, *social advocacy*, is used to address a problem through the application of pressure, including confrontation, on those who have created the problem or stand as a barrier to a solution to the problem. This strategy creates conflict.[15]

Although each of these strategies has unique components, each strategy can be combined with the others to deal with a community problem. In fact, Rothman has offered a 3 × 3 matrix to help explain the combinations.[15] Whatever strategy is used, they all revolve around a common theme: The work and resources of many have a much better chance of solving a problem than the work and resources of a few.

Minkler and Wallerstein have done a nice job of summarizing the models, old and new, by presenting a typology that incorporates both needs- and strengths-based approaches (see **Figure 5.2**).[8] Their typology is divided into four quadrants, with strengths-based and needs-based on the vertical axis and consensus and conflict on the horizontal axis. Though this typology separates and categorizes the various methods of community organizing and building, Minkler and Wallerstein point out that when they

> … look at primary strategies, we see that the consensus approaches, whether needs based or strengths based, primarily use collaboration strategies, whereas conflict approaches use advocacy strategies and ally building to support advocacy efforts. Several concepts span these two strengths-based approaches, such as community competence, leadership development, and multiple perspectives on gaining power. Again, as with the Rothman model, many organizing efforts use a combination of these strategies at different times throughout the life of an organizing campaign and community building process.[8]

No matter what community organizing/building approach is used, they all incorporate some fundamental principles. These include "strengths-based approaches; the principle of relevance,

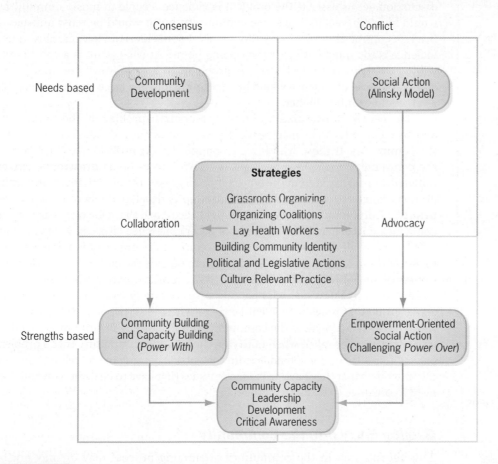

FIGURE 5.2   Community organization and community building typology.

Source: Minkler, M., and N. Wallerstein (2012). "Improving Health through Community Organization and Community Building: Perspectives from Health Education and Social Work." In M. Minkler, ed., *Community Organizing and Community Building for Health and Welfare*, 3rd ed. New Brunswick, NJ: Rutgers University Press, 43. Reprinted with permission.

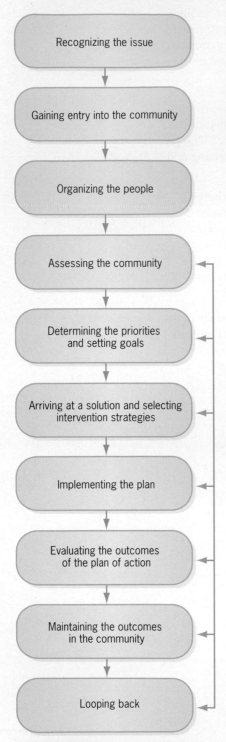

FIGURE 5.3 A summary of steps in community organizing and building.

Reproduced from Minkler, Meredith and Nina Wallerstein. "Figure 3.1: Community Organization and Community-Building Typology" in *Community-Organizing and Community Building for Health and Welfare.* Copyright © 2012 by Meredith Minkler. Reprinted by permission of Rutgers University Press.

or starting where the people are; the principle of participatory issue selection and choice of actions; and the importance of creating environments in which individuals and communities can become empowered as they increase their community capacity or problem-solving ability."[8]

The Process of Community Organizing/Building

It is beyond the scope of this textbook to explain all the approaches to community organizing/building in detail. Instead, we will present a generic approach (see **Figure 5.3**) created by McKenzie, Neiger, and Thackeray that draws upon many of these other approaches.[2] The 10 steps of this generic approach are briefly reviewed in the sections that follow.

Recognizing the Issue

The process of community organizing/building begins when someone recognizes that a problem exists in a community and decides to do something about it. This person (or persons) is referred to as the initial organizer. This individual may not be the primary organizer throughout the community organizing/building process. He or she is the one who gets things started. For the purposes of this discussion, let us assume the problem is violence. People in most communities would like to have a violence-free community, but it would be most unusual to live in a community that was without at least some level of violence. How much violence is too much? What is the tipping point? At what point is a community willing to organize to deal with the problem? In a small-town community, an acceptable level of violence would be very low, while in a large city, an acceptable level would be much higher.

The people, or organizers, who first recognize a problem in the community and decide to act, can be members of the community or individuals from outside the community. If those who initiate community organization are members of the community, then the movement is referred to as being **grassroots**, citizen initiated, or organized from the bottom up. "In grassroots organizing, community groups are built from scratch, and leadership is developed where none existed before."[16] Community members who might recognize that violence is a problem could include teachers, police officers, or other concerned citizens. When individuals from outside the community initiate community organization, it is referred to as *top-down organization*. Individuals from outside the community who might initiate organization could include a judge who presides over cases involving violence, a state social worker who handles cases of family violence, or a politically active group that is against violent behavior wherever it happens. In cases where the person who recognizes the community problem is not a community member, great care must be taken when notifying those in the community that a problem exists. "It is difficult for someone from the outside coming in and telling community members that they have problems or issues that have to be dealt with and they need to organize to take care of them."[2]

Gaining Entry into the Community

This second step in the community organizing process may or may not be needed, depending on whether the issue in step 1 was identified by someone from within the community or outside. If the issue is identified by someone outside the community, this step becomes a critical step in the process.[2] Gaining entry may seem like a relatively easy matter, but an error by organizers at this step could ruin the chances of successfully organizing the community. This may be the most crucial step in the whole process.

Braithwaite and colleagues have stressed the importance of tactfully negotiating entry into a community with the individuals who control, both formally and informally, the "political climate" of the community.[17] These people are referred to as the **gatekeepers**. Thus the term indicates that you must pass through this "gate" to get to your priority population.[18] These "power brokers" know their community, how it functions, and how to accomplish tasks within it. Long-time residents are usually able to identify the gatekeepers of their community. A gate-keeper can be a representative of an intermediary organization—such as a church or school—that has direct contact with your priority population.[18] Examples include politicians, leaders of activist groups, business and education leaders, and clergy, to name a few.

Organizers must approach such figures on the gatekeepers' own terms and play the gate-keepers' ball game. However, before approaching these important individuals, organizers must study the community well. They must be culturally sensitive and work toward cultural compe-tence. That is, they must be aware of the cultural differences within a community and effectively work with the cultural context of the community. Tervalon and Garcia have stated the need for cultural humility—openness to others' culture.[19] Organizers need to know where the power lies, the community power dynamics, what type of politics must be used to solve a problem, and whether the particular problem they wish to solve has ever been dealt with before in the community.[10] In the violence example, organizers need to know (1) who is causing the violence and why, (2) how the problem has been addressed in the past, (3) who supports and who opposes the idea of addressing the problem, and (4) who could provide more insight into the problem. This is a critical step in the community organization process because failure to study the com-munity carefully in the beginning may lead to a delay in organizing it later, a subsequent waste of time and resources, and possibly the inability to organize at all.

Once the organizers have a good understanding of the community, they are then ready to approach the gatekeepers. In keeping with the violence example, the gatekeepers would probably include the police department, elected officials, school board members, social service person-nel, members of the judicial system, and possibly some of those who are creating the violence.

When the top-down approach is being used, organizers might find it advantageous to enter the community through a well-respected organization or institution that is already established in the community, such as a religious organization, a service group, or another successful local group. If those who make up such an organization/institution can be convinced that the problem exists and needs to be solved, it can help smooth the way for gaining entry and achieving the remaining steps in the process.

Organizing the People

Obtaining the support of community members to deal with the problem is the next step in the process. It is best to begin by organizing those who are already interested in seeing that the problem is solved. This core group of community members, sometimes referred to as "executive participants,"[20] will become the backbone of the workforce and will end up doing the majority of the work. For our example of community violence, the core group could include law enforce-ment personnel, former victims of violence and their families (or victims' support groups), parent–teacher organizations, and public health officials. It is also important to recruit people from the subpopulation who are most directly affected by the problem. For example, if most of the violence in a community is directed toward teenagers, teenagers need to be included in the core group. If elderly persons are affected, they need to be included.

"From among the core group, a leader or coordinator must be identified. If at all possible, the leader should be someone with leadership skills, good knowledge of the concern and the community, and most of all, someone from within the community. One of the early tasks of the leader will be to help build group cohesion."[2]

Grassroots a process that begins with those who are affected by the problem/concern

Gatekeepers those who control, both formally and informally, the political climate of the community

Task force a temporary group that is brought together for dealing with a specific problem

Coalition formal alliance of organizations that come together to work for a common goal

Although the formation of the core group is essential, this group is usually not large enough to do all the work itself. Therefore, one of the core group's tasks is to recruit more members of the community to the cause. This step can take place via a networking process, which is when organizers make personal contacts with others who might be interested. Or, the organizers can call an organizing meeting at a local school, community center, or religious organization. By broadening the constituency, the core group can spread out the workload and generate additional resources to deal with the problem. However, recruiting additional workers can often be difficult. Over the last 30 years, the number of people in many communities interested in volunteering their time has decreased. Today, if you ask someone to volunteer, you may hear the reply, "I'm already too busy." There are two primary reasons for this response. First, there are many families in which both husband and wife work outside the home. And second, there are more single-parent households.

Therefore, when organizers are expanding their constituencies, they should be sure to (1) identify people who are affected by the problem that they are trying to solve, (2) provide "perks" for or otherwise reward volunteers, (3) keep volunteer time short, (4) match volunteer assignments with the abilities and expertise of the volunteers, and (5) consider providing appropriate training to make sure volunteers are comfortable with their tasks. For example, if the organizers need someone to talk with law enforcement groups, it would probably be a good idea to solicit the help of someone who feels comfortable around such groups and who is respected by them, such as another law enforcement person.

When the core group has been expanded to include these other volunteers, the larger group is sometimes referred to as a task force. A **task force** has been defined as "a self-contained group of 'doers' that is not ongoing. It is convened for a narrow purpose over a defined timeframe at the request of another body or committee."[21] There may even be an occasion where a coalition is formed. A **coalition** is "a formal alliance of organizations that come together to work for a common goal"[16]—often, to compensate for deficits in power, resources, and expertise. A larger group with more resources, people, and energy has a greater chance of solving a community problem than a smaller, less powerful group (see **Figure 5.4**). "Building and maintaining effective coalitions have increasingly been recognized as vital components of much effective community organizing and community building."[22]

FIGURE 5.4   Coalition building is often an important step in successful community organization.

© Jack Hollingsworth/Photodisc/Getty Images.

Assessing the Community

Earlier in this chapter we noted that there are a number of strategies that have been used for community organizing. Many of those strategies operate from the point of view that there is a deficiency (or a need) in the community and, if that deficiency can be dealt with, the community problem can be solved. In contrast to these strategies is community building. **Community building** is "an orientation to practice focused on community, rather than a strategic framework or approach, and on building capacities, not fixing problems."[20] Thus, one of the major differences between community organizing and the newer ideas of community building is the type of assessment that is used to determine where to focus the community's efforts. In the community organizing approach, the assessment is focused on the needs of the community, while in community building, the assessment focuses on the assets and capabilities of the community. It is assumed that a clearer picture of the community will be revealed and a stronger base will be developed for change if the assessment includes the identification of both needs and assets/capacities and involves those who live in the community. It is from these capacities and assets that communities are built.[23]

To determine the needs and assets/capacities of a community, an assessment must be completed. There are two reasons for completing an effective and comprehensive assessment: Information is needed for change, and it is also needed for empowerment.[24] This could include a traditional needs assessment and/or a newer technique called mapping community capacity.

Community building an orientation to practice focused on community, rather than a strategic framework or approach, and on building capacities, not fixing problems

A *needs assessment* is a process by which data about the issues of concern are collected and analyzed. From the analyzed data, concerns or problems emerge and are prioritized so that strategies can be created to tackle them.

Traditional forms of data collection for needs assessments have included techniques such as completing written questionnaires or interviewing people in the community. Because of the importance of getting participation from community members and "starting where the people are,"[25] some organizers have used participatory data collection processes. Such processes get those from whom the data are to be collected to help with data collection. Photovoice[26,27] and videovoice are two newer techniques that have been used to do this. With these techniques community members are provided with cameras and skills training, and then they use the cameras to convey their own images of community problems and strengths.[28] After the images have been collected, participants work together to select the images that best capture their collective thoughts and feelings and use them to tell their stories and to stimulate change through community organizing and building (*Note:* Needs assessment is discussed in greater length in the second half of this chapter, with regard to program planning.)

Mapping community capacity, on the other hand, is a process of identifying community assets, not concerns or problems. It is a process by which organizers literally use a map to identify the different assets of a community. McKnight and Kretzmann[23] have categorized assets and capacities into three different groups based on their availability to the community and refer to them as building blocks. Primary building blocks are the most accessible assets and capacities. They are located in the neighborhood and are controlled by those who live in the neighborhood. Primary building blocks can be organized into the assets and capacities of individuals (e.g., skills, talents, and incomes) and those of organizations or associations (e.g., faith-based and citizen organizations). The next most accessible building blocks are secondary building blocks. Secondary building blocks are assets located in the neighborhood but largely controlled by people outside (e.g., social service agencies, schools, hospitals, and housing structures). The least accessible assets are referred to as potential building blocks. Potential building blocks are resources originating outside the neighborhood and controlled by people outside (e.g., welfare expenditures and public information). By knowing the needs, assets, and capacities of the community, organizers can work to identify the true concerns or problems of the community and use the assets of the community as a foundation for dealing with the concerns or problems.

> **Mapping community capacity** a process of identifying community assets

Determining the Priorities and Setting Goals

An analysis of the community assessment data should result in the identification of the problems to be addressed. However, more often than not, the resources needed to solve all identified problems are not available. Therefore, the problems that have been identified must be prioritized. This prioritization is best achieved through general agreement or consensus of those who have been organized so that "ownership" can take hold. It is critical that all those working with the process feel that they "own" the problem and want to see it solved. Without this sense of ownership, they will be unwilling to give of their time and energy to solve it. For example, if a few highly vocal participants intimidate people into voting for certain activities to be the top priorities before a consensus is actually reached, it is unlikely that those who disagreed on this assignment of priorities will work enthusiastically to help solve the problem. They may even drop out of the process because they feel they have no ownership in the decision-making process.

Miller[29] has identified five criteria that community organizers need to consider when selecting a priority issue or problem. The issue or problem (1) must be winnable, ensuring that working on it does not simply reinforce fatalistic attitudes and beliefs that things cannot be improved; (2) must be simple and specific, so that any member of the organizing group can explain it clearly in a sentence or two; (3) must unite members of the organizing group and must involve them in a meaningful way in achieving resolution of the issue or problem; (4) should affect many people and build up the community; and (5) should be a part of a larger plan or strategy to enhance the community.

Once the problems have been prioritized, goals—the hoped for results—need to be identified and written to serve as guides for problem solving. The practice of consensus building should again be employed during the setting of goals. These goals, which will become the foundation for all the work that follows, can be thought of as the "hoped-for end result." In other words, once community action has occurred, what will have changed? In the community where violence is a problem, the goal may be to reduce the number of violent crimes or eliminate them altogether. Sometimes at this point in the process, some members of the larger group drop out because they do not see their priorities or goals included on consensus lists. Unable to feel ownership, they are unwilling to expend their resources on this process. Because there is strength in numbers, efforts should be made to keep them in. One strategy for doing so is to keep the goal list as long as possible.

Arriving at a Solution and Selecting Intervention Strategies

There are alternative solutions for every community problem. The group should examine the alternatives in terms of probable outcomes, acceptability to the community, probable long- and short-term effects on the community, and the cost of resources to solve the problem.[30] A solution involves selecting one or more intervention strategies (see **Table 5.2**). Each type of intervention strategy has advantages and disadvantages. The group must try to agree on the best strategy and then select the most advantageous intervention activity or activities. Again, the group must work toward consensus through compromise. If the educators in the group were asked to provide a recommended strategy, they might suggest offering more preventive-education programs; law enforcement personnel might recommend more enforceable laws; judges might want more space in the jails and prisons. The protectionism of the subgroups within the larger group is often referred to as *turfism*. It is not uncommon to have turf struggles when trying to build consensus.

TABLE 5.2   Intervention Strategies and Example Activities
1. *Health communication strategies:* Mass media, social media, billboards, booklets, bulletin boards, flyers, direct mail, newsletters, pamphlets, posters, and video and audio materials
2. *Health education strategies:* Educational methods (such as lecture, discussion, and group work) as well as audiovisual materials, computerized instruction, laboratory exercises, and written materials (books and periodicals)
3. *Health policy/enforcement strategies:* Executive orders, laws, ordinances, judicial decisions, policies, position statements, regulations, and formal and informal rules
4. *Environmental change strategies:* Those that are designed to change the structure of services, systems of care, or the built environment to improve health promotion services, such as removing physical or financial barriers to access, safety belts and air bags in cars, speed bumps in parking lots, or environmental cues such as *No Smoking* signs
5. *Health-related community services:* The use of health risk appraisals (HRAs), clinical screenings for health problems (e.g., hypertension), and immunization clinics
6. Other strategies: • *Behavior modification activities:* Modifying behavior to stop smoking, start to exercise, manage stress, and regulate diet • *Community advocacy activities:* Mass mobilization, social action, community planning, community service development, community education, and community advocacy (such as a letter-writing campaign) • *Organizational culture activities:* Activities that work to change norms and traditions within an organization • *Incentives and disincentives:* Items that can either encourage or discourage people to behave a certain way, which may include money and other material items or fines • *Social intervention activities:* Support groups, social activities, and social networks • *Technology-delivered activities:* Educating or informing people by using technology (e.g., social media, computers, and cell phones)

Data from McKenzie, J. F., B. L. Neiger, and R. Thackeray (2017). *Planning, Implementing, and Evaluating Health Promotion Programs: A Primer*, 7th ed. Boston: Pearson Education, Inc., 194–225.

The Final Steps in the Community Organizing/Building Process: Implementing, Evaluating, Maintaining, and Looping Back

The last four steps in this generalized approach to organizing/building a community include implementing the intervention strategy and activities that were selected in the previous step, evaluating the outcomes of the plans of action, maintaining the outcomes over time, and if necessary, going back to a previous step in the process—"looping back"—to modify or restructure the work plan to organize the community.

Implementation of the intervention strategy includes identifying and collecting the necessary resources for implementation and creating the appropriate time line for implementation. Often the resources can be found within a community, and thus horizontal relationships, the interaction of local units with one another, are needed. Other times the resources must be obtained from units located outside the community; in this case, vertical relationships, those where local units interact with extracommunity systems, are needed. An example of this latter relationship is the interaction between a local nonprofit organization and a state agency with which it has contact.

Evaluation of the process often involves comparing the long-term health and social outcomes of the process to the goals that were set in an earlier step. Some scholars[8] have indicated that such traditional evaluations of community organizing efforts are not easy to carry out and have some limitations. There are times when evaluations are not well planned or funded. As such they may fail to capture the shorter term, system-level effects with which community organizing is heavily concerned, such as improvements in organizational collaboration, community involvement, capacity, and healthier public policies or environments.

Maintaining or sustaining the outcomes may be one of the most difficult steps in the entire process. It is at this point that organizers need to seriously consider the need for a long-term capacity for problem solving. Finally, through the steps of implementation, evaluation, and maintenance of the outcomes, organizers may see the need to "loop back" to a previous step in the process to rethink or rework before proceeding onward in their plan.

A Special Note about Community Organizing/Building

Before we leave the processes of community organizing/building, it should be noted that no matter what approach or strategy is used in organizing/building a community, not all problems can be solved. In other cases, repeated attempts may be necessary before a solution is reached. In addition, it is important to remember that if a problem exists in a community, there are probably some people who benefit from its existence and who may work toward preventing a successful solution to the problem. Whether or not the problem is solved, the final decision facing the organized group is whether to disband the group or to reorganize in order to take on a new problem or attack the first problem from a different direction.

Health Promotion Programming

Elsewhere in the text we discuss how communities describe, analyze, and intervene to solve existing health problems such as disease outbreaks or other community problems. However, the 1979 U.S. Surgeon General's report on health promotion and disease prevention, *Healthy People* (see **Figure 5.5**), charted a new course for community and public health—away from curing diseases and toward preventing diseases and promoting health. Health promotion programming has now become an important tool of community and public health professionals. The second half of this chapter presents the process of health promotion programming.

Basic Understanding of Program Planning

Prior to discussing the process of program planning, two relationships must be presented. These are the relationships between health education and health promotion, and program planning and community organizing/building.

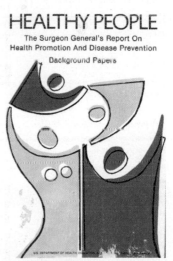

HEALTHY PEOPLE
The Surgeon General's Report On Health Promotion And Disease Prevention
Background Papers

FIGURE 5.5 *Healthy People*, the 1979 U.S. Surgeon General's report on health promotion and disease prevention, charted a new course for community health.

Courtesy of U.S. Surgeon General's Office.

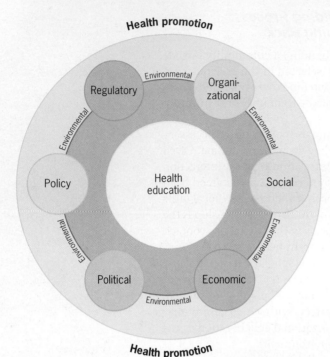

Health promotion

Environmental — Regulatory — Organizational

Environmental — Policy — Health education — Social

Environmental — Political — Economic

Environmental

Health promotion

FIGURE 5.6   The relationship of health education and health promotion.

Reproduced from: McKenzie, James F.; Neiger, Brad L.; Thackeray, Rosemary, *Planning, Implementing, & Evaluating Health Promotion Programs: A Primer*, 7th Ed., © 2017. Reprinted by permission of Pearson Education, Inc., New York, New York.

Health education and health promotion are terms that are sometimes used interchangeably. This is incorrect because health education is only a part of health promotion. The Joint Committee on Health Education and Promotion Terminology defined the process of **health education** as "any combination of planned learning experiences using evidence-based practices and/or sound theories that provide the opportunity to acquire knowledge, attitudes, and skills needed to adopt and maintain health behaviors."[31] The committee defined **health promotion** as "any planned combination of educational, political, environmental, regulatory, or organizational mechanisms that support actions and conditions of living conducive to the health of individuals, groups, and communities."[31] From these definitions, it is obvious that the terms are not the same and that health promotion is a much more encompassing term than health education. **Figure 5.6** provides a graphic representation of the relationship between the terms.

The first half of this chapter described the process of community organizing/building—the process by which individuals, groups, and organizations engage in planned action to influence social problems. Program planning may or may not be associated with community organizing/building. **Program planning** is a process in which an intervention is planned to help meet the needs of a specific group of people. It may take a community organizing/building effort to be able to plan such an intervention. The antiviolence campaign used earlier in the chapter is such an example, where many resources of the community were brought together to create interventions (programs) to deal with the violence problem. However, program planning need not be connected to community organizing/building. For example, a community organizing/building effort is not needed before a company offers a smoking cessation program for its employees or a religious organization offers a stress management class for its members. In such cases, only the steps of the program planning process need to be carried out. These steps are described in the following section.

Creating a Health Promotion Program

Health education any combination of planned learning experiences using evidence-based practices and/or sound theories that provide the opportunity to acquire knowledge, attitudes, and skills needed to adopt and maintain health behaviors

Health promotion any planned combination of educational, political, environmental, regulatory, or organizational mechanisms that support actions and conditions of living conducive to the health of individuals, groups, and communities

Program planning a process by which an intervention is planned to help meet the needs of a priority population

The process of developing a health promotion program, like the process of community organizing/building, involves a series of steps. Success depends on many factors, including the assistance of a professional experienced in program planning.

Experienced program planners use models to guide their work. Planning models are the means by which structure and organization are given to the planning process. Many different planning models exist, some of which are used more often than others. Some of the more frequently used models include the PRECEDE/PROCEED model,[32] Mobilizing Action through Planning and Partnerships (MAPP),[33] Intervention Mapping,[34] and the more recently developed consumer-based planning models that are based on health communication and social marketing such as CDCynergy[35] and Social Marketing Assessment and Response Tool (SMART).[36] Each of these planning models has its strengths and weaknesses, and each has distinctive components that make it unique. In addition, each of the models has been used to plan health promotion programs in a variety of settings, with many successes.

It is not absolutely necessary that the student studying community and public health for the first time have a thorough understanding of the models mentioned here, but it is important to know the basic steps in the planning process. Therefore, we present the Generalized Model[2] that draws on the major components of these other models. The steps of this generalized model are presented in **Figure 5.7** and explained in the following paragraphs.

Prior to undertaking the first step in the Generalized Model it is important to do some preplanning.[2] Preplanning is a quasi-step that allows program planners to gather answers to key questions, which will help to them understand the community and engage the **priority population (audience)**, those whom the health promotion program is intended to serve. Understanding the community means finding out as much as possible about the priority population and the environment in which it exists. Engaging the priority population means getting those in the population involved in the early stages of the health promotion program planning process. If the priority population was composed of the employees of a corporation, the planners would want to read all the material they could find about the company, spend time talking with various individuals and subgroups in the company (e.g., new employees, employees who had been with the company for a long time, management, clerical staff, labor representatives) to find out what they wanted from a health promotion program, and review old documents of the company (e.g., health insurance records, labor agreements, written history of the company). Also, the planners should consider forming a program planning committee with representation from the various subgroups of the workforce (e.g., management, labor, and clerical staff). The planning committee can help ensure that all segments of the priority population will be engaged in the planning process.

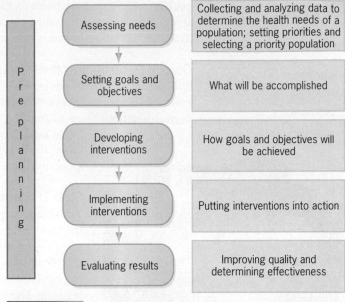

FIGURE 5.7   The Generalized Model.

Source: Mckenzie, James F.; Neiger, Brad L.; Thackeray, Rosemary, *Planning, Implementing, & Evaluating Health Promotion Programs: A Primer*, 7th Ed., © 2017. Reprinted by Permission of Pearson Education, Inc., New York, New York.

Assessing the Needs of the Priority Population

To create a useful and effective program for the priority population, planners, with the assistance of the planning committee, must determine the needs and wants of the priority population. This procedural step is referred to as a needs assessment. A **needs assessment** is "the process of identifying, analyzing, and prioritizing the needs of a priority population. Other terms that have been used to describe the process of determining needs include *community analysis, community diagnosis,* and *community assessment*"[32] (see **Box 5.1**). A needs assessment may be the most important part of the planning process in that it not only identifies and prioritizes health

Priority population (audience) those whom a program is intended to serve

Needs assessment the process of identifying, analyzing, and prioritizing the needs of a priority population

---

BOX 5.1   Increased Emphasis on Needs Assessment

Although a needs assessment has long been an important part of program planning, two recent actions have made the needs assessment process more visible to the public. The first dealt with the establishment of the Public Health Accreditation Board (PHAB) in 2007 to develop an accreditation process for health departments operated by tribes, states, local jurisdictions, and territories.[40] In 2011 the PHAB released the *Accreditation Standards and Measures*. The standards and measures, spread over 12 domains, outline what a health department must meet in order to be accredited. Domain 1 is "Conduct and Disseminate Assessments Focused on Population Health Status and Public Health Issues Facing the Community."[41]

The second action was the passing of the Patient Protection and Affordable Care Act (generally referred to as the Affordable Care Act, or ACA) that added section 501(r) to the Internal Revenue Code. Under this section of the code, 501(c)(3) organizations that operate one or more hospitals (i.e., nonprofit hospitals) must meet four general requirements in order to maintain their tax-exempt status. One of those four requirements is to conduct, at least once every 3 years, a community health needs assessment (CHNA) and to adopt an implementation strategy for addressing the identified needs.[42] In addition, the Internal Revenue Service guidelines require that the 501(c)(3) organizations partner with a public health agency in conducting the CHNA.

Primary data original data collected by the planners

Secondary data those that have been collected by someone else and are available for use by the planners

problems but it also establishes a baseline for evaluating program impact.[37] For those interested in a detailed explanation of the process of conducting a needs assessment, extensive accounts are available.[38,39] The following is a six-step approach that can be used to conduct a needs assessment.[2]

Step 1: Determining the Purpose and Scope of the Needs Assessment

The first step in the needs assessment process is to determine the purpose and the scope of the needs assessment. That is: What is the goal of the needs assessment? What does the planning committee hope to gain from the needs assessment? How extensive will the assessment be? What kind of resources will be available to conduct the needs assessment? Once these questions are answered, the planners are ready to begin gathering data.

Step 2: Gathering Data

The second step in the process is gathering the data that will help to identify the true needs of the priority population. Such data are categorized into two groups—primary and secondary. **Primary data** are those that are collected specifically for use in this process. An example is having those in the priority population complete a needs assessment questionnaire about their health behavior. The completion of the questionnaire may be in a traditional paper–pencil format, as an online survey, or via face-to-face or telephone interviews (see **Figure 5.8**). **Secondary data** are data that have already been collected for some other purpose, such as health insurance claims records or Behavioral Risk Factor Surveillance System (BRFSS) data. Using both primary and secondary data usually presents the clearest picture of the priority population's needs.

FIGURE 5.8 A telephone survey is a common form of data collection for a health needs assessment.

© iStockphoto/Thinkstock.

Step 3: Analyzing the Data

Collected data can be analyzed in one of two ways—formally or informally. Formal analysis consists of some type of statistical analysis, assuming that the appropriate statistical criteria have been met to collect the data. However, a more common means of analysis is an informal technique referred to as "eyeballing the data." With this technique, program planners look for the obvious differences between the health status or conditions of the priority population and the health behaviors, and programs and services available to close the gap between what is and what ought to be. Regardless of the method used, data analysis should yield a list of the problems that exist, with a description of the nature and extent of each.

The final part of the needs assessment process is prioritizing the list of problems. Prioritization must take place because, although all needs are important, seldom are there enough resources (personnel, money, and time) available to deal with all the problems identified. When prioritizing, planners should consider (1) the importance of the need,[32] (2) how changeable[32] the need is, and (3) whether adequate resources are available to address the problem.

Step 4: Identifying the Risk Factors Linked to the Health Problem

In this step of the process, planners need to identify and prioritize the risk factors that are associated with the health problem. "That is, what genetic, behavioral, and environmental risk factors are associated with the health problem?"[2] Thus, if the prioritized health problem identified in step 3 is heart disease, planners must analyze the genetic, behavioral, and environmental conditions of the priority population for known risk factors of heart disease. For example, higher than expected obesity and smoking behavior may be present in the priority population in addition to a community that lacks recreational facilities and areas for exercise. Once these risk factors are identified, they also need to be prioritized using the same three criteria noted in step 3.

Step 5: Identifying the Program Focus

With risk factors identified and prioritized, planners need to identify those predisposing, enabling, and reinforcing factors that seem to have a direct impact on the targeted risk factors. In the heart disease example, those in the priority population may not (1) have the knowledge and skills to begin an exercise program (predisposing factors), (2) have access to recreational facilities (enabling factor), or (3) have people around them who value the benefits of exercise (reinforcing factor). Once the predisposing, enabling, and reinforcing factors have been identified, like in steps 2 and 3, they too need to be prioritized. The resulting prioritized list provides the program focus.

Step 6: Validating the Prioritized Need

The final step in this process is to double-check or to confirm that the identified need and resulting program focus indeed need to be addressed in the priority population. For example, a limited amount of data may indicate the primary need of the priority group to be one thing—knowledge about heart disease, for example. However, more extensive data or more comprehensive networking may identify another problem such as lack of free or inexpensive recreational facilities. Before step 6 is completed, planners must make sure they have indeed identified a true need. In short, all work should be double-checked.

At the conclusion of a needs assessment, planners should be able to answer the following questions:

1. Who is the priority population?[39]
2. What are the needs of the priority population?[39]
3. Which subgroups within the priority population have the greatest need?[39]
4. Where are the subgroups located geographically?[39]
5. What is currently being done to resolve identified needs?[39]
6. How well have the identified needs been addressed in the past?[39]
7. What is the capacity of the community to deal with the needs?
8. What are the assets in a community on which a program can be built?

Setting Appropriate Goals and Objectives

Once the problem has been well defined and the needs prioritized, the planners can set goals and develop objectives for the program. The goals and objectives should be thought of as the foundation of the program and for the evaluation. The remaining portions of the programming process—intervention development, implementation, and evaluation—will be designed to achieve the goals by meeting the objectives.

The words goals and objectives are often used interchangeably, but there is really a significant difference between the two. "A goal is a future event toward which a committed endeavor is directed; objectives are the steps taken in pursuit of a goal."[43] "In comparison to objectives, goals are expectations that: provide overall direction for the program, are more general in nature, do not have a specific deadline, usually take longer to complete, and are often not measured in exact terms."[7] Goals are easy to write and include two basic components—who will be affected and what will change because of the program. Here are some examples of program goals:

1. To help employees learn how to manage their stress
2. To reduce the number of teenage pregnancies in the community
3. To help cardiac patients and their families deal with the lifestyle changes that occur after a heart attack

Objectives are more precise and, as noted earlier, can be considered the steps to achieve the program goals. Because some program goals are more complex than others, the number and type of objectives will vary from program to program. For example, the process of getting a group of people to exercise is a more complex activity than trying to get people to identify their risk factors for heart disease. The more complex a program, the greater the number of objectives needed. To deal with these different types of programs, McKenzie and colleagues[2] adapted a hierarchy of program objectives first developed by Deeds[44] and later updated by Cleary and Neiger.[45] **Table 5.3** presents the hierarchy and an example of an objective at each of the levels within the hierarchy.

TABLE 5.3   Hierarchy of Objectives and Examples of Each

Type of Objective	Program Outcomes	Possible Evaluation Measures	Type of Evaluation	Example Objective
Process objectives	Activities presented and tasks completed	Number of sessions held, exposure, attendance, participation, staff performance, appropriate materials, adequacy of resources, tasks on schedule	Process (form of formative)	During the next 6 months, a breast cancer brochure will be distributed to all female customers over the age of 18 at the Ross grocery store.
Impact objectives				
Learning objectives	Change in awareness, knowledge, attitudes, and skills	Increase in awareness, knowledge, attitudes, and skill development/ acquisition	Impact (form of summative)	When asked in class, 50% of the students will be able to list the four principles of cardiovascular conditioning.
Behavioral objectives	Change in behavior	Current behavior modified or discontinued, or new behavior adopted	Impact (form of summative)	During a telephone interview, 35% of the residents will report having had their blood cholesterol checked in the last 6 months.
Environmental objectives	Change in the environment	Measures associated with economic, service, physical, social, psychological, or political environments, e.g., protection added to, or hazards or barriers removed from, the environment	Impact (form of summative)	By the end of the year, all senior citizens who requested transportation to the congregate meals will have received it.
Outcome objectives	Change in quality of life (QOL), health status, or risk, and social benefits	QOL measures, morbidity data, mortality data, measures of risk (e.g., HRA)	Outcome (form of summative)	By the year 2020, infant mortality rates will be reduced to no more than 7 per 1,000 in Franklin County.

Data from: Deeds, S. G. (1992). *The Health Education Specialist: Self-Study for Professional Competence*. Los Alamitos, CA: Loose Cannon Publications; Cleary, M. J., and B. L. Neiger (1998). *The Certified Health Education Specialist: A Self-Study Guide for Professional Competence*, 3rd ed. Allentown, PA: National Commission for Health Education Credentialing; and McKenzie, J. F., B. L. Neiger, and R. Thackeray (2017). *Planning, Implementing, and Evaluating Health Promotion Programs: A Primer*, 7th ed. Boston: Pearson Education, Inc.

From the examples presented in Table 5.3, it should be obvious that the hierarchy goes from less complex to more complex levels. Thus, it takes less time and fewer resources to increase awareness in the priority population than to improve its health status. Close examination of the example objectives reveals that the objectives are written in specific terms. They are composed of four parts (who, what, when, and how much) and outline changes that should result from the implementation of the program.[2] Objectives that include these four parts are referred to as **SMART objectives**. SMART stands for specific, measurable, achievable, realistic, and time-phased.[35] Every objective written for a program should be SMART!

One final note about objectives: Elsewhere in the text *Healthy People 2020*, the national health goals and objectives of the nation, was discussed. Selected objectives from this publication are presented in boxes throughout this text (see **Box 5.2**). These goals and objectives provide

SMART objectives those that are specific, measurable, achievable, realistic, and time-phased

---

BOX 5.2   *Healthy People 2020*: Objectives

Educational and Community-Based Programs

Goal: Increase the quality, availability, and effectiveness of educational and community-based programs designed to prevent disease and injury, improve health, and enhance quality of life.

Objective: ECBP-10 Increase the number of community-based organizations (including local health departments, tribal health services, nongovernmental organizations, and state agencies) providing population-based primary prevention services in the following areas:

ECBP 10.8 Nutrition

Target: 94.7%.

Baseline: 86.1% of community-based organizations (including local health departments, tribal health services, nongovernmental organizations, and state agencies) provided population-based primary prevention services in nutrition in 2008.

Target-setting method: 10% improvement.

Data source: National Profile of Local Health Departments (NACCHO Profile), National Association of County and City Health Officials (NACCHO).

ECBP 10.9 Physical Activity

Target: 88.5%.

Baseline: 80.5% of community-based organizations (including local health departments, tribal health services, nongovernmental organizations, and state agencies) provided population-based primary prevention services in physical activity in 2008.

Target-setting method: 10% improvement.

Source: Data are from National Profile of Local Health Departments (NACCHO Profile), National Association of County and City Health Officials (NACCHO).

Note: Other areas covered by this objective include: 10.1 Injury, 10.2 Violence, 10.3 Mental Illness, 10.4 Tobacco Use, 10.5 Substance Abuse, 10.6 Unintended Pregnancy, and 10.7 Chronic Diseases Programs.

For Further Thought

If you had the opportunity to write one more objective to deal with the implementation of health promotion programs for use in *Healthy People 2020*, what would it be? What is your rationale for selecting such an objective?

Source: U.S. Department of Health and Human Services, Office of Disease Prevention and Health Promotion (2016). *Healthy People 2020*. Available at http://www.healthypeople.gov/2020/topics-objectives/topic/educational-and-community-based-programs.

---

a good model for developing goals and objectives for a new program. In fact, these goals and objectives can be adapted for use in most community and public health promotion programs.

Creating an Intervention That Considers the Peculiarities of the Setting

The next step in the program planning process is to design activities that will help the priority population meet the objectives and, in the process, achieve the program goals. These activities are collectively referred to as an **intervention**, or treatment. This intervention or treatment is the planned actions designed to prevent disease or injury or promote health in the priority population.

The number of activities in an intervention may be many or only a few. Although no minimum number has been established, it has been shown that multiple activities are often more effective than a single activity. For example, if the planners wanted to change the attitudes of community members toward a new landfill, they would have a greater chance of doing so by distributing pamphlets door to door, writing articles for the local newspaper, and speaking to local service groups, than by performing any one of these activities by itself. In other words, the size and amount of intervention are important in health promotion programming. Few people change an attitude or behavior based on a single exposure; instead, multiple exposures are generally needed to create change. It stands to reason that "hitting" the priority population from several angles or through multiple channels should increase the chances of making an impact.[2]

Two terms that relate to the size and amount of an intervention are *multiplicity* and *dose*. **Multiplicity** refers to the number of components or activities that make up the intervention, while **dose** refers to the number of program units delivered. Thus, if an intervention has two activities—say, an educational workshop and the release of a public service announcement via social networking sites—they define multiplicity, while the number of times each of the activities is presented defines the dose.[2]

Intervention an activity or activities designed to create change in people

Multiplicity the number of components or activities that make up the intervention

Dose the number of program units delivered as part of the intervention

Best practices
recommendations for interventions based on critical review of multiple research and evaluation studies that substantiate the efficacy of the intervention

Best experience intervention strategies used in prior or existing programs that have not gone through the critical research and evaluation studies and thus fall short of best practice criteria

Best processes original intervention strategies that the planners create based on their knowledge and skills of good planning processes including the involvement of those in the priority population and the use of theories and models

The actual creation of the intervention should begin by asking and answering a series of questions.[2] The first two are: What needs to change? and, Where is change needed? The answers to these questions come from the needs assessment and the resulting goals and objectives. The third question is: At what level of prevention (i.e., primary, secondary, or tertiary) will the program be aimed? The approach taken to a primary prevention need, that is, preventing a problem before it begins, would be different from a tertiary prevention need of managing a problem after it has existed for a while. The fourth question asks: At what level of influence will the intervention be focused? The various levels of influence (i.e., intrapersonal, interpersonal, institutional or organizational, community, public policy, physical environment, and culture) that were presented earlier in this chapter as part of the socio-ecological approach need to be considered. These levels provide the planners with a framework from which to think about how they will "attack" the needs of the priority population. For example, if the goal of a program is to reduce the prevalence of smoking in a community, the intervention could attack the problem by focusing the intervention on individuals through one-on-one counseling, via groups by offering smoking cessation classes, by trying to change policy by enacting a state law prohibiting smoking in public places, or by attacking the problem using more than one of these strategies.

The fifth question asks: Has an effective intervention strategy to deal with the focus of the problem already been created? "In other words, what does the evidence show about the effectiveness of various interventions to deal with the problem that the program is to address?"[2] Three sources of guidance for selecting intervention strategies—best practices, best experiences, and best processes.[32] **Best practices** refers to "recommendations for an intervention, based on critical review of multiple research and evaluation studies that substantiate the efficacy of the intervention in the populations and circumstances in which the studies were done, if not its effectiveness in other populations and situations where it might be implemented."[32] Examples of best practices related to health promotion programs are provided in *The Guide to Community Preventive Services: What Works to Promote Health,*[46] also know as *The Community Guide* (see **Box 5.3** for other sources of evidence).

When best practice recommendations are not available for use, planners need to look for information on best experiences. **Best experience** intervention strategies are those of prior or existing programs that have not gone through the critical research and evaluation studies and thus fall short of best practice criteria but nonetheless show promise in being effective. Best experiences can often be found by networking with others professionals and by reviewing the literature.

If neither best practices nor best experiences are available to planners, then the third source of guidance for selecting an intervention strategy is using best processes. **Best processes** intervention strategies are original interventions that the planners create based on their knowledge and skills of good planning processes including the involvement of those in the priority population and the theories and models used to change behaviors, such as Social Cognitive Theory[47] or the Transtheoretical Model of Change.[48]

BOX 5.3   Sources of Evidence

The Campbell Collaboration
    http://www.campbellcollaboration.org/
Centre for Reviews and Dissemination; University of York
    http://www.york.ac.uk/crd/
The Cochrane Collaboration
    http://www.cochrane.org
Canadian Task Force on Preventive Health Care
    http://www.canadiantaskforce.ca
Health Evidence, McMaster University, Canada
    http://healthevidence.org

National Cancer Institute, Research-tested Intervention Programs (RTIPs)
    http://rtips.cancer.gov/rtips/index/do
Substance Abuse and Mental Health Services, National Registry of Evidence-based Programs and Practices
    http://nrepp.samhsa.gov
U.S. Preventive Task Force
    http://www.ahrq.gov/professionals/clinicans-providers/guidelines-recommendations/uspstf

Once that it is known whether best practices, best experiences, or best processes will be used three more questions need to be asked. The sixth question asks: Is the intervention an appropriate fit for the priority population? In other words, does the planned intervention meet the specific characteristics of the priority population such as the educational level, developmental stages, or the specific cultural characteristics of the people being served?

The seventh question that needs to be asked is: Are the resources available to implement the intervention selected? Planners need to evaluate the amount of money, time, personnel, and/or space that is needed to carry out the various interventions and make a determination if such resources are available to implement the intervention.

The eighth, and final, question that needs to be asked is: Would it be better to use an intervention that consists of a single strategy or one that is made up of multiple strategies? A single strategy would probably be less expensive and time consuming, but multiple strategies would probably have a greater chance for change in the priority population.

Implementing the Intervention

The moment of truth is when the intervention is implemented. **Implementation** is the actual carrying out or putting into practice the activity or activities that make up the intervention. More formally, implementation has been defined as "the act of converting planning, goals, and objectives into action through administrative structure, management activities, policies, procedures, regulations, and organizational actions of new programs."[49]

To ensure a smooth-flowing implementation of the intervention, it is wise to pilot test it at least once and sometimes more. A **pilot test** is a trial run. It is when the intervention is presented to just a few individuals who are either from the intended priority population or from a very similar population. For example, if the intervention is being developed for fifth graders in a particular school, it might be pilot tested on fifth graders with similar educational backgrounds and demographic characteristics but from a different school.

The purpose of pilot testing an intervention is to determine whether there are any problems with it. Some of the more common problems that pop up are those dealing with the design or delivery of the intervention; however, any part of it could be flawed. For example, it could be determined during pilot testing that there is a lack of resources to carry out the intervention as planned or that those implementing the intervention need more training. When minor flaws are detected and corrected easily, the intervention is then ready for full implementation. However, if a major problem surfaces—one that requires much time and many resources to correct—it is recommended that the intervention be pilot tested again with the improvements in place before implementation.

An integral part of the piloting process is collecting feedback from those in the pilot group. By surveying the pilot group, planners can identify popular and unpopular aspects of the intervention, how the intervention might be changed or improved, and whether the program activities were effective. This information can be useful in fine-tuning this intervention or in developing future programs.

Once the intervention has been pilot tested and corrected as necessary, it is ready to be disseminated and implemented. If the planned program is being implemented with a large priority population and there is a lot at stake with the implementation, it is advisable that the intervention be implemented gradually rather than all at once. One way of doing so is by phasing in the intervention. **Phasing in** refers to a step-by-step implementation in which the intervention is introduced first to smaller groups instead of the entire priority population. Common criteria used for selecting participating groups for phasing in include participant ability, number of participants, program offerings, and program location.[2]

The following is an example of phasing in by location. Assume that a local health department wants to provide smoking cessation programs for all the smokers in the community (priority population). Instead of initiating one big intervention for all, planners could divide the priority population by residence location. Facilitators would begin implementation by offering the smoking cessation classes on the south side of town during the first month. During the second month, they would continue the classes on the south side and begin implementation on the west side of town. They would continue to implement this intervention until all sections of the town were included.

Implementation putting a planned intervention into action

Pilot test a trial run of an intervention

Phasing in implementation of an intervention with a series of small groups instead of the entire population

Evaluation determining the value or worth of an object of interest

Standard of acceptability a comparative mandate, value, norm, or group

Formative evaluation the evaluation that is conducted during the planning and implementing processes to improve or refine the program

Summative evaluation the evaluation that determines the effect of a program on the priority population

Impact evaluation the evaluation that focuses on immediate observable effects of a program

Outcome evaluation the evaluation that focuses on the end result of the program

Evaluating the Results

The final step in the generalized planning model is the evaluation. Although evaluation is the last step in this model, it really takes place in all steps of program planning. It is very important that planning for evaluation occur during the first stages of program development, not just at the end because the purpose of the evaluation is twofold—to improve the quality of programs and to measure their effectiveness.

Evaluation is the process in which planners determine the value or worth of the object of interest by comparing it against a **standard of acceptability**.[50] Common standards of acceptability include, but are not limited to, mandates (policies, statutes, and laws), values, norms, comparison/control groups, and the "how much" in an objective for the program.

Evaluation can be categorized further into summative and formative evaluation. **Formative evaluation** is done during the planning and implementing processes to improve or refine the program. Validating the needs assessment and pilot testing are both forms of formative evaluation. **Summative evaluation** begins with the development of goals and objectives and is conducted after implementation of the intervention to determine the program's effect on the priority population. Often, the summative evaluation is broken down into two categories—impact and outcome evaluation. **Impact evaluation** focuses on immediate observable effects of a program such as changes in awareness, knowledge, attitudes, skills, environmental surroundings, and behavior of those in the priority population, whereas **outcome evaluation** focuses on the end result of the program and is generally measured by improvements in morbidity, mortality, or vital measures of symptoms, signs, or physiologic indicators.[50]

Like other steps in the planning model, the evaluation step can be broken down into smaller steps. The Centers for Disease Control and Prevention[51] has developed a framework for program evaluation (see **Figure 5.9**) that includes these six steps: (1) engage stakeholders, (2) describe the program, (3) focus the evaluation design, (4) gather credible data, (5) justify conclusions, and (6) ensure use and share lessons learned. Prior to engaging in this six-step process it should be determined who will conduct the evaluation—an internal evaluator (one who already is involved in the program) or an external evaluator (one from outside the program).

Step 1: Engage Stakeholders

Stakeholders include (1) those involved in the creation and delivery of the program, (2) those in the priority population or affected by the program in some other way, and (3) those that will be the primary users of the evaluation results.[2] These individuals must be engaged to ensure that their perspectives are understood and that the evaluation results meet their expectations. If stakeholders are not engaged evaluation findings may be ignored, criticized, or resisted.[51]

Step 2: Describe the Program

A clear program description helps to clarify program components and the intended outcomes. Therefore, well-written goals and objectives and a well-conceived intervention are important steps in describing the program. A clear program description helps to focus the evaluation on the central and important questions to be answered.[52]

Step 3: Focus the Evaluation Design

This step of the evaluation process includes stating the purpose of the evaluation (i.e., improving the quality of the program or assessing its effects, or both) and formulating the questions to be answered by the evaluation. Once those things have been completed a specific evaluation design (i.e., qualitative or quantitative, or both) and the type of data analysis can be determined.

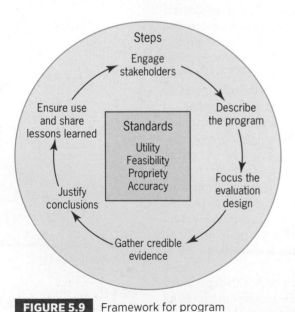

FIGURE 5.9 Framework for program evaluation.

Reproduced from: Centers for Disease Control and Prevention (1999). "Framework for Program Evaluation in Public Health." *Morbidity and Mortality Weekly Report*, 48(RR-11), 1–40.

Step 4: Gather Credible Data

Gathering credible data includes deciding what type of data needs to be collected, how to collect the data (e.g., with an online survey, from existing records, by observation), determining who will collect them, pilot testing the procedures, and performing the actual data collection. "Having credible evidence strengthens evaluation judgments and the recommendations that follow from them."[51]

Step 5: Justify Conclusions

Once the data are in hand, they must be analyzed and interpreted. This means that the evaluator will compare the collected data against the standards of acceptability to determine effectiveness, and ultimately, the value of the program.[2] In conducting this step, the evaluator must make every effort to increase objectivity and decrease subjectivity.[2] "When agencies, communities, and other stakeholders agree that the conclusions are justified, they will be more inclined to use the evaluation results for program improvement."[52]

Step 6: Ensure Use and Share Lessons Learned

After the data have been analyzed and interpreted the evaluation report should be written. Decisions must be made (if they have not been made already) regarding who should write the report, who should receive the report, in what form it should be distributed, and when it should be distributed. With the findings in hand, it then must be decided how they will be used. When time, resources, and effort are spent on an evaluation, it is important that the results be useful for reaching a constructive end. This is a time when a decision can be made to modify, continue, or discontinue the intervention based on the evaluation data.[2]

In addition to the six steps just presented, the framework for program evaluation also has four standards. The four standards of utility (i.e., needs of the stakeholders are met), feasibility (i.e., the evaluation is viable and pragmatic), propriety (i.e., the evaluation is ethical), and accuracy (i.e., the evaluation findings are correct) provide practical guidelines for an evaluator to follow when having to decide among evaluation options.[2,51] For example, these standards can help an evaluator avoid evaluations that may be accurate and feasible but not useful.[51]

Chapter Summary

- A knowledge of community organizing/building and program planning is essential for community and public health workers whose job it is to promote and protect the health of the community.

- When conducting community organizing/building and program planning processes, community and public health workers must keep in mind the concepts of the socio-ecological approach and evidence-based practice.

- Community organizing is a process by which community groups are helped to identify common problems or change targets, mobilize resources, and develop and implement strategies for reaching their collective goals.

- Community building is an orientation to practice focused on community, rather than a strategic framework or approach, and on building capacities, not fixing problems.

- The steps of the general model for community organizing/building include recognizing the issue, gaining entry into the community, organizing the people, assessing the community, determining the priorities and setting goals, arriving at a solution and selecting the intervention strategies, implementing the plan, evaluating the outcomes of the plan of action, maintaining the outcomes in the community, and, if necessary, looping back.

- Program planning is a process in which an intervention is planned to help meet the needs of a priority population.

- The steps in the program planning process include assessing the needs of the priority population, setting appropriate goals and objectives, creating an intervention that considers the peculiarities of the setting, implementing the intervention, and evaluating the results. In addition, the quasi-step of preplanning also must be addressed.

Scenario: Analysis and Response

The town of Kenzington sounds like a good candidate for a community organizing/building effort. Assume that Kenzington is the town in which you now live and you belong to the group that has taken the issue to the city council. Based on what you know about the problem in the scenario and what you know about your town, answer the following questions.

1. What is the real problem?

2. Who do you think the gatekeepers are in the community?

3. What groups of people in the community might be most interested in solving this problem?

4. What groups might have a vested interest in seeing the problem remain unsolved?

5. What interventions do you believe would be useful in dealing with the problem? What sources of evidence might you use to help with deciding on an intervention?

6. How would you evaluate your efforts to solve the problem?

7. What strategies might you recommend to make the solution lasting?

8. If you were to look for help on the Internet to deal with this problem, what keywords would you use to search the Web for help?

Review Questions

1. Briefly explain the concepts of the socio-ecological approach and evidence-based practice.

2. What is community organizing?

3. What are the assumptions (identified by Ross) under which organizers work when bringing a community together to solve a problem?

4. What is the difference between top-down and grassroots community organizing?

5. What does the term *gatekeepers* mean? Who would they be in your home community?

6. Identify the steps in the generalized approach to community organizing/building presented in this chapter.

7. What does community building mean?

8. What is a needs assessment? Why is it important in the health promotion programming process?

9. What are the five major steps and one quasi-step in program development?

10. What are the differences between goals and objectives?

11. What are intervention strategies? Provide five examples.

12. What are best practices, best experiences, and best processes? How are they different?

13. What does the term *pilot testing* mean? How is it useful when developing an intervention?

14. What is the difference between formative and summative evaluation? What are impact and outcome evaluation?

15. Name and briefly describe the six steps of the Centers for Disease Control and Prevention's framework for program evaluation.

Activities

1. From your knowledge of the community in which you live (or the use of the Internet), generate a list of 7 to 10 agencies that might be interested in creating a coalition to deal with community drug problems. Provide a one-sentence rationale for each why it might want to be involved.

2. Ask your instructor if he or she is aware of any community organizing/building efforts in a local community. If you are able to identify such an effort, make an appointment—either by yourself or with some of your classmates—to meet with the person who is leading the effort and ask the following questions:

- What is the problem the community faces?
- What is the goal of the group?
- What steps have been taken so far to organize/build the community, and what steps are yet to be taken?
- Who is active in the core group?
- Did the group conduct a community assessment?
- What intervention will be/has been used?
- Is it anticipated that the problem will be solved?

3. Using the socio-ecological approach explain how a local health department could create a childhood immunization program by intervening at a minimum of four levels of influence.

4. Using a nutrition education program for college students, write one program goal and an objective for each of the levels presented in Table 5.3.

5. Visit a voluntary health agency in your community, either by yourself or with classmates. Ask employees if you may review a written report of a recent program evaluation of one of their programs. Examine the report and compare its content to the six-step framework of evaluation of the Centers for Disease Control and Prevention's framework for program evaluation presented in this chapter. Then, in a two-page paper, briefly summarize your how the agency dealt with each of the steps.

References

1. Cottrell, R. R., and J. F. McKenzie (2011). *Health Promotion & Education Research: Using the Five-Chapter Thesis/Dissertation Model*, 2nd ed. Sudbury, MA: Jones and Bartlett Publishers.

2. McKenzie, J. F., B. L. Neiger, and R. Thackeray (2017). *Planning, Implementing, and Evaluating Health Promotion Programs: A Primer*, 7th ed. Boston: Pearson Education, Inc.

3. Muir Gray, J. A. (1997). *Evidence-Based Health care: How to Make Health Policy and Management Decisions*. Edinburgh, Scotland & New York, NY: Churchill Livingstone.

4. Institute of Medicine (2001). *Health and Behavior: The Interplay of Biological, Behavioral, and Societal Influences*. Washington, DC: National Academies Press.

5. McLeroy, K. R., D. Bibeau, A. Steckler, and K. Glanz (1988). "*An Ecological Perspective for Health Promotion Programs*." *Health Education Quarterly*, 15(4): 351–378.

6. Simons-Morton, B. G., K. R. McLeroy, and M. L. Wendel (2012). *Behavior Theory in Health Promotion Practice and Research*, Burlington, MA: Jones & Bartlett Learning.

7. Sallis, J. F., N. Owen, and E. B. Fisher (2008). "*Ecological Models of Health behavior*." In K. Glanz, B. K. Rimer, and K. Viswanath, eds., *Health Behavior and Health Education Practice: Theory, Research, and Practice*, 4th ed. San -Francisco: Jossey-Bass, 465–485.

8. Minkler, M., and N. Wallerstein (2012). "Improving Health through Community Organization and Community Building: Perspectives from Health Education and Social Work." In M. Minkler, ed., *Community Organizing and Community Building for Health and Welfare*, 3rd ed. New Brunswick, NJ: Rutgers University Press, 37–58.

9. Ross, M. G. (1967). *Community Organization: Theory, Principles, and Practice*. New York: Harper and Row, 86–92.

10. Perlman, J. (1978). "Grassroots Participation from Neighborhood to Nation." In S. Langton,*Citizen Participation in America*. Lexington, MA: Lexington Books, 65–79.

11. Last, J. M. (ed.) (2007). *A Dictionary of Public Health*. New York: Oxford University Press.

12. Rothman, J., and J. E. Tropman (1987). "Models of Community Organization and Macro Practice Perspectives: Their Mixing and Phasing." In F. M. Cox, J. L. Erlich, J. Rothman, and J. E. Tropman,*Strategies of Community Organization: Macro Practice*. Itasca, IL: Peacock Publishers, 3–26.

13. Garvin, C. D., and F. M. Cox (2001). "A History of Community Organizing Since the Civil War with Special Reference to Oppressed Communities." In J. Rothman, J. L. Erlich, and J. E. Tropman, *Strategies of Community Intervention*, 5th ed. Itasca, IL: Peacock Publishers, 65–100.

14. Rothman, J. (2001). "Approaches to Community Intervention." In J. Rothman, J. L. Erlich, and J. E. Tropman,*Strategies of Community Intervention*, 6th ed. Itasca, IL: Peacock Publishers.

15. Rothman, J. (2007). "Multi Modes of Intervention at the Macro Level." *Journal of Community Practice*, 15(4): 11–40.

16. Butterfoss, F. D. (2007). *Coalitions and Partnerships in Community Health*. San Francisco: Jossey-Bass.

17. Braithwaite, R. L., F. Murphy, N. Lythcott, and D. S. Blumenthal (1989). "Community Organization and Development for Health Promotion within an Urban Black Community: A Conceptual Model." *Health Education*, 20(5): 56–60.

18. Wright, P. A. (1994). *A Key Step in Developing Prevention Materials Is to Obtain Expert and Gatekeepers' Reviews* (Technical Assistance Bulletin).Bethesda, MD: Center for Substance Abuse Prevention (CASP) Communications Team, 1–6.

19. Tervalon, M., and J. Garcia (1998). "Cultural Humility versus Cultural Competence: A Critical Distinction in Defining Physician Training Outcomes in Multicultural Education." *Journal of Health Care for the Poor and Underserved*, 9(2): 117–125.

20. Brager, G., H. Specht, and J. L. Torczyner (1987). *Community Organizing*. New York: Columbia University Press, 55.

21. Butterfoss, F. D. (2013). *Ignite! Getting Your Community Coalition "Fired Up" for Change*. Bloomington, IN: AuthorHouse.

22. Minkler, M. (2012). "Introduction to Community Organizing and Community Building." In M. Minkler, ed., *Community Organizing and Community Building for Health and Welfare*, 3rd ed. New Brunswick, NJ: Rutgers University Press, 5–26.

23. McKnight, J. L., and J. P. Kretzmann (2012). "Mapping Community Capacity." In M. Minkler, *Community Organizing and Community Building for Health and Welfare*, 3rd ed. New Brunswick, NJ: Rutgers University Press, 171–186.

24. Hancock, T., and M. Minkler (2012). "Community Health Assessment or Healthy Community Assessment: Whose Community? Whose Health? Whose Assessment?" In M. Minkler, *Community Organizing and Community Building for Health and Welfare*, 3rd ed. New Brunswick, NJ: Rutgers University Press, 153–170.

25. Nyswander, D. B. (1956). "Education for Health: Some Principles and Their Application." *Health Education Monographs*, 14: 65–70.

26. Wang, C. C., and M. A. Burris (1994). "Empowerment through Photovoice: Portraits of Participation." *Health Education Quarterly*, 21(2): 171–186.

27. Wang, C. C., and M. A. Burris (1997). "Photovoice: Concept, Methodology, and Use for Participatory Needs Assessment." *Health Education and Behavior*, 24(3): 369–387.

28. Kramer, L., P. Schwartz, A. Cheadle, J. E. Borton, M. Wright, C. Chase, and C. Lindley (2010). "Promoting Policy and Environmental Change Using Photovoice in Kaiser Permanente Community Health Initiative." *Health Promotion Practice*, 11(3): 332–339.

29. Miller, M. (1986). "Turning Problems into Actionable Issues." Unpublished paper. San Francisco: Organize Training Center.

30. Archer, S. E., and R. P. Fleshman (1985). *Community Health Nursing*. Monterey, CA: Wadsworth Health Sciences.

31. Joint Committee on Health Education and Promotion Terminology (2012). "Report of the 2011 Joint Committee on Health Education and Promotion Terminology." Reston, VA: American Association of Health Education.

32. Green, L. W., and M. W. Kreuter (2005). *Health Program Planning: An Educational and Ecological Approach*, 4th ed. Boston: McGraw-Hill.

33. National Association of County and City Health Officials (2001). *Mobilizing for Action through Planning and Partnerships (MAPP)*. Washington, DC: Author.

34. Bartholomew, L. K., G. S. Parcel, G. Kok, N. H. Gottlieb, and M. E. Fernandez (2011). *Planning Health Promotion Programs: An Intervention Mapping Approach*, 3rd ed. San Francisco: Jossey-Bass.

35. Centers for Disease Control and Prevention, U.S. Department of Health and Human Services (2003). *CDCynergy 3.0: Your Guide to Effective Health Communication* [CD-ROM Version 3.0]. Atlanta: Author.

36. Neiger, B. L., and R. Thackeray (1998). "Social Marketing: Making Public Health Sense." Paper presented at the annual meeting of the Utah Public Health Association Provo, UT.

37. Grunbaum, J. A., P. Gingiss, P. Orpinas, L. S. Batey, and G. S. Parcel (1995). "A Comprehensive Approach to School Health Program Needs Assessment." *Journal of School Health*, 65(2),54–59.

38. Gilmore, G. D. (2012). *Needs and Capacity Assessment Strategies for Health Education and Health Promotion*, 4th ed. Burlington, MA: Jones & Bartlett Learning.

39. Peterson, D. J., and G. R. Alexander (2001). *Needs Assessment in Public Health: A Practical Guide for Students and Professionals*. New York: Kluwer Academic/Plenum Publishers.

40. Public Health Accreditation Board (2013). *Public Health Accreditation Background*. Alexandria, VA: Author. Available at http://www.phaboard.org/about-phab/public-health-accreditation-background/.

41. Public Health Accreditation Board (2013). *Standards and Measures: An Overview*. Alexandria, VA: Author. Available at http://www.phaboard.org/wp-content/uploads/StandardsOverview1.5_Brochure.pdf.

42. Centers for Disease Control and Prevention. (n.d.). Summary of the Internal Revenue Service's April 5, 2013 Notice of Proposed Rule Making on Community Health Needs Assessments for Charitable Hospitals. Atlanta, GA: Author. Available at from http://www.cdc.gov/phlp/docs/summary-irs-rule.pdf.

43. Ross, H. S., and P. R. Mico (1980). *Theory and Practice in Health Education*. Palo Alto, CA: Mayfield Press, 219.

44. Deeds, S. G. (1992). *The Health Education Specialist: Self-Study for Professional Competence*. Los Alamitos, CA: Loose Cannon Publications.

45. Cleary, M. J., and B. L. Neiger (1998). *The Certified Health Education Specialist: A Self-Study Guide for Professional Competence*, 3rd ed. Allentown, PA: National Commission for Health Education Credentialing.

46. Centers for Disease Control and Prevention (2016). *The Guide to Community Preventive Services—The Community Guide: What Works to Promote Health*. Atlanta, GA: Author. Available at http://www.thecommunityguide.org/.

47. Crosby, R. A., L. F. Salazar, and R. J. DiClemente (2013). *Social Cognitive Theory Applied to Health Behavior. In R. J. DiClemente, L. F. Salazar and R. A. Crosby, Health Behavior Theory in Public Health*. Burlington, MA: Jones and Bartlett Learning, 163–185.

48. DiClemente, R. J., C. A. Redding, R. A. Crosby, and L. F. Salazar (2013). "Stage Models for Health Promotion." In R. J. DiClemente, L. F. Salazar, and R. A. Crosby, *Health Behavior Theory in Public Health*. Burlington, MA: Jones & Bartlett Learning, 105–129.

49. Timmreck, T. C. (1997). *Health Services Cyclopedic Dictionary*, 3rd ed. Sudbury, MA: Jones & Bartlett Learning.

50. Green, L. W., and F. M. Lewis (1986). *Measurement and Evaluation in Health Education and Health Promotion*. Palo Alto, CA: Mayfield Press.

51. Centers for Disease Control and Prevention (1999). "Framework for Program Evaluation in Public Health." *Morbidity and Mortality Weekly Report*, 48(RR-11), 1–40.

52. Centers for Disease Control and Prevention (2011). *Introduction to Program Evaluation for Public Health Programs: A Self-Study Guide*. Atlanta, GA: Author. Available at http://www.cdc.gov/eval/guide.

CHAPTER 6

The School Health Program: A Component of Community and Public Health

Chapter Outline

Chapter Objectives

After studying this chapter, you will be able to:

1. Describe the Whole School, Whole Community, Whole Child model.
2. List the ideal members of a school health advisory council.
3. Illustrate why a school health program is important.
4. Summarize written school health policies and explain their importance to the school health program.

5. Discuss processes for developing and implementing school health policies.

6. State the 10 components of the Whole School, Whole Community, Whole Child model.

7. Describe the role of the school health coordinator.

8. Identify those services offered as part of school health services and explain why schools are logical places to offer such services.

9. Explain what is meant by a healthy school environment and discuss the two major environments.

10. Define school health education.

11. Identify the eight National Health Education Standards.

12. Demonstrate how a health education specialist could locate credible health education curricula.

13. Discuss and briefly explain four issues that are faced by school health advocates.

Scenario

Seldom does an elementary school teacher have a typical day. Each day seems to bring a variety of new experiences. Take, for example, the day Ms. Graff experienced last Wednesday. As students begin their morning work, many are eating their on-the-go breakfast they were able to access for free from the cafeteria. The school has learned that students perform better during their school day when they start it with a healthy breakfast. As more than 60% of students qualify for free or reduced breakfast and lunch, the school serves an important role in child nutrition.

Math class was disrupted when a student brought a gun to school. Police were called and students were locked into their classrooms in order to ensure that everyone was safe while police investigated the situation. While it was determined the gun was a BB gun, safety is the utmost importance at this school, so extreme precautions were taken and learning was disrupted.

After lunch, Ms. Graff began her writing lesson—students are practicing writing an essay with a beginning, middle, and end. She wasn't 10 minutes into her lesson when the school nurse stuck her head in the door and asked if Ms. Graff could send five students for their annual vision and hearing screenings. Reluctantly, Ms. Graff excused the students.

During the last half-hour of the school day, students were engaged in success time—focused instruction in preparation for standardized testing. Just before the last bell was to ring, Annie came up to Ms. Graff's desk and told her she was worried about her classmate, Joseph—he had not been in school the entire week and Annie had heard that his mom got a new job working nights.

There are a variety of issues that impact the success of students in Ms. Graff's class; there is not "typical day" in an elementary school that serves a population of high-risk students and families.

Introduction

The school health program is an important component of community and public health. Though the primary responsibility for the health of school-aged children lies with their parents/guardians, the schools have immeasurable potential for affecting the health of children, their families, and the health of the community. As former U.S. Surgeon General David Satcher stated, "The school setting is a great equalizer, providing all students and families—regardless of ethnicity, socioeconomic status or level of education—with the same access to good nutrition and physical activity. Because children also teach their parents, important lessons learned at school can help the entire family,"[1] thus improving the health of the entire community. Full-service community schools provide a good example of the link between school health and community health. These schools, using an integrated approach, offer a variety of educational, counseling, social, and health services to families in one location, resulting in improved educational outcomes. Such schools focus on the well-being of the child and family, and some of their services are available on a 24-hour basis. These school buildings serve as neighborhood hubs and institutions that are safe, attentive, and comfortable.[2,3]

In this chapter, we describe the Whole School, Whole Community, Whole Child (WSCC) model, explain who is involved in school health programs, explore the reasons why school health is important, discuss the components of the Whole School, Whole Community, Whole Child model, and present some of the issues facing school health programs today.

Whole School, Whole Community, Whole Child: A Collaborative Approach to Learning and Health

The **Whole School, Whole Community, Whole Child (WSCC)** model focuses on addressing the educational and health needs of children within the context of the school setting, which is a critical component of the local community. As a result, community strengths can boost the role of the school in addressing child health and learning needs, but also can be a reflection of areas of need in the community.[4] "Each child, in each school, in each of our communities deserves to be healthy, safe, engaged, supported, and challenged. That's what a whole child approach to learning, teaching, and community engagement really is about."[4] This model provides a shared framework and approach for schools and the community to work together to provide a systematic, integrated, and collaborative approach to health and learning[5] (see **Figure 6.1**).

WHOLE SCHOOL, WHOLE **COMMUNITY,** WHOLE CHILD
A collaborative approach to learning and health

FIGURE 6.1   Whole School, Whole Community, Whole Child model: A collaborative approach to learning and health.

Courtesy of ASCD. (2016).

The School Health Advisory Council

For WSCC efforts to be effective, a great deal of time and effort must be expended by individuals in schools with an investment in the health of students. When these individuals work together to plan and implement a school health program, they are referred to as the **school health advisory council**, sometimes called a school wellness council. The primary role of this council is to provide coordination of the various components of WSCC to help students improve health and learning outcomes. An ideal council would include representation from each of the WSCC components and district administrators, parents, students, and community representatives involved in the health and well-being of students. For the successful implementation of the work of this group, a full-time or part-time school health coordinator is critical. The school health coordinator should have an educational background that includes training in school health and should "be able to plan, implement, and evaluate [WSCC efforts]; be familiar with existing community resources; and have connections to local, state, and national health and education organizations."[6,7] The school health coordinator helps maintain active school health advisory councils and facilitates health programming in the district. Most often the school health coordinator is a health education specialist or school nurse.

The School Nurse

The school nurse is one of several people who is positioned to provide leadership for WSCC efforts (see **Figure 6.2**). The nurse not only has medical knowledge, but should also have formal training in health education and an understanding of the health needs of all children pre-K through 12th grade. Some of the key responsibilities of the school nurse as a member of the school health team include the following:[8]

1. Developing individual health care plans (e.g., 504, individualized education programs [IEPs], integrated health programs [IHPs], emergency plans)
2. Providing infectious disease information (e.g., outbreak management, pertussis, methicillin-resistant *Staphylococcus aureus* [MRSA])
3. Providing care for medically fragile students (e.g., tracheostomy, catheters, tube feedings)
4. Conducting physical assessments
5. Utilizing technology to support management of records and assessment intake (e.g., iPads, tablets, apps)
6. Supporting efforts to decrease absenteeism

While school nurses are in a good position to provide leadership to the school health advisory council, many school districts do not have the resources to hire a full-time school nurse or the caseload is such that additional duties are not feasible. Contracting with an outside health agency such as a local health department or hospital for nursing services is one strategy used for securing nursing services within a school district. When this scenario occurs, the contracted nurse completes only the nursing tasks required by state law and does not tend to take on the leadership responsibilities for the school health advisory council. This task may then be fulfilled by a school health education specialist. In fact, the health educator may even be responsible when a full-time nurse is present.

FIGURE 6.2 The school nurse is in a good position to guide the school health efforts.
© ZouZou/ShutterStock, Inc.

The Teacher's Role

Though the school nurse might provide the leadership for WSSC, classroom teachers carry a heavy responsibility in seeing that the program works

TABLE 6.1 **Health Education Standards for School Health Educators**
Standard I: Demonstrate the knowledge and skills of a health literate educator.
Standard II: Assess needs to determine priorities for school health education.
Standard III: Plan effective comprehensive school health education curricula and programs.
Standard IV: Implement health education instruction.
Standard V: Assess student learning.
Standard VI: Plan and coordinate a school health education program.
Standard VII: Serve as a resource person in health education.
Standard VIII: Communicate and advocate for health and school health education.

Source: American Association for Health Education (2008). *2008 NCATE Health Education Teacher Preparation Standards.* Available at http://www.shapeamerica.org/accreditation/upload/ncate-2008-standards.pdf. Accessed April 16, 2016.

(see **Figure 6.3**). On the average school day, teachers spend more waking hours with school-aged children than do the parents of many children. A teacher may spend 6 to 8 hours a day with any given child, while the parents spend an hour with that child before school and maybe 4 to 5 hours with the child after school and before bedtime. Teachers are also in a position to make observations on the "normal and abnormal" behaviors and conditions of children because they are able to compare the students in their classroom each day. Furthermore, many health teachers are receiving leadership training regarding WSCC in their undergraduate or postgraduate coursework, thus making them ideal individuals to lead the coordination. **Table 6.1** presents a suggested list of competencies for teachers who expect to be involved in school health education and WSCC leadership.

FIGURE 6.3 The classroom teacher's participation is essential for a successful school health program.
© auremar/ShutterStock, Inc.

The Need for School Health

The primary role of schools is to educate. However, an unhealthy child has a difficult time learning. Consider, for example, a student who arrives at school without having breakfast, with poor hygiene, and without adequate sleep. This student will be unable to concentrate on schoolwork and may distract others. As a reader, you know how difficult it is to study for a test or even to read this textbook when you do not feel well or are depressed or hungry (see **Box 6.1**).

"Health and success in school are interrelated. Schools cannot achieve their primary mission of education if students and staff are not healthy and fit physically, mentally, and socially."[9] More specifically, "educational progress will be profoundly limited if students are not *motivated and able to learn.* Health-related problems play a major role in limiting the motivation and ability to learn of (minority) youth. The interventions to address those problems can improve educational as well as health outcomes."[10] The WSCC model provides the integration of education and health.

The importance of the school health program is also evident by its inclusion in the national health objectives for the year 2020. Of all the objectives listed in the publication *Healthy People 2020: Understanding and Improving Health*, a significant number can either be directly attained by schools or their attainment can be influenced in important ways by schools (see **Box 6.2**).

Nevertheless, WSCC is not a cure-all. There are no quick and easy solutions to improving the overall health of a community. However, WSCC provides a strong base on which to build.

BOX 6.1   It Is Harder to Learn If You Are Not Healthy! A Look at the Impact of Childhood Obesity

It stands to reason that if children are not healthy, it is harder for them to concentrate and in turn to have a meaningful learning experience. One such example that is significantly affecting students and schools is the obesity epidemic. Childhood obesity has more than doubled in children and quadrupled in adolescents in the past 30 years, with the prevalence affecting nearly 20% of children and adolescents. Experts have determined that body mass index (BMI) is the most practical tool available to define obesity and screen for it.

Childhood obesity is often accompanied by numerous other health conditions, such as increased rates of type 2 diabetes, cardiovascular problems, sleep apnea, and bone and joint problems. The reasons for the obesity epidemic are varied but are slowly becoming understood. Many environments make it difficult for children to make healthy food choices and get enough physical activity. Advertising of less healthy foods, limited access to healthy affordable foods, availability of high-energy-dense food and sugar-sweetened beverages, and increasing portion sizes have been shown to contribute to the challenges youth experience to healthy eating. A lack of safe places to play or be active makes it difficult or unsafe to be physically active. Half of the children in the United States do not have a park, community center, or sidewalk in their neighborhood.

Researchers are now reporting some of the social, psychological, and educational consequences of obesity. A review of the literature determined that overweight and obese children are more likely to have low self-esteem, higher rates of anxiety disorders, and depression. Severely obese kids report many more missed days of school than the general student population. What is yet to be understood is why these kids miss more school—are they embarrassed to participate in physical activity? Are health conditions keeping them from school? Are they experiencing bullying or teasing? Although there is no known reason, the consequences are significant.

One way schools are addressing concerns about overweight children is by establishing policies related to improved nutritional offerings in the cafeteria, school parties and events, and vending machines, as well as increasing nutrition education and physical activity. The Child Nutrition and WIC Reauthorization Act of 2004 (Public Law 108-265) required all schools participating in the federally funded school feeding programs to establish a local wellness policy by the first day of the 2006–2007 school year. This law helped many districts begin the process of improving the school environment, not just to improve the obesity problem, but to make school a healthier place for all. With the passage of the 2010 Healthy Hunger-Free Kids Act (Public Law 111-296), greater emphasis has been placed on implementation, evaluation, and public reporting of local school wellness policies.

The issue of obesity has been a priority in the White House with First Lady Michelle Obama's "Let's Move!" campaign. The Let's Move! initiative has been dedicated to "solving the problem of obesity within a generation, so that children born today will grow up healthier and able to pursue their dreams." The campaign includes a comprehensive approach that will provide schools, families, and communities simple tools to help kids be more active, eat better, and get healthy. As part of this campaign, chefs across the country have gotten involved in the fight against obesity by adopting a school in their community and working with teachers, parents, school nutritionists, and administrators to help educate kids about food and nutrition. Further, President Obama has established the first ever Task Force on Childhood Obesity to develop and implement an interagency plan to reduce the childhood obesity rate to just 5% by 2030, the same rate before childhood obesity first began to rise in the late 1970s.

Most recently, in June 2013, the federal government announced its "Smart Snacks in Schools" nutrition standards for competitive foods. Competitive foods are those foods that are not part of the regular school meal programs. The standards set limits for calories, fat, sugar, and sodium. High-calorie sports drinks and candy bars are some of the items that will be removed from school vending machines and cafeteria lines as a result of these new standards. Many policies and programs have been successfully implemented over the years to address childhood obesity. What are you doing in the fight against obesity? The time to take action is now!

Data from: Taras, H., and W. Potts-Datema (2005). "Obesity and Student Performance at School." *Journal of School Health*, 75(8): 291–295; Centers for Disease Control and Prevention (2015). *Childhood Obesity Facts*. Available at http://www.cdc.gov/healthyschools/obesity/facts.htm; Centers for Disease Control and Prevention (2015). *Childhood Obesity Causes & Consequences*. Available at http://www.cdc.gov/obesity/childhood/causes.html; and The White House (2016). "Let's Move." Available at http://www.letsmove.gov/.

Foundations of the School Health Program

The true foundations of any school health program are (1) a school administration that supports such an effort; (2) a well-organized school health advisory council that is genuinely interested in providing a coordinated program for the students, families, and staff; and (3) written school health policies. A highly supportive administration is a must for quality WSCC. In almost all

BOX 6.2   *Healthy People 2020*

Educational and Community-Based Programs

Goal: Increase the quality, availability, and effectiveness of educational and community-based programs designed to prevent disease and injury, improve health, and enhance quality of life.

Objective: ECBP-2. Increase the proportion of elementary, middle, and senior high schools that provide comprehensive school health education to prevent health problems in the following areas: unintentional injury; violence; suicide; tobacco use and addiction; alcohol or other drug use; unintended pregnancy, HIV/AIDS, and STD infection; unhealthy dietary patterns; and inadequate physical activity.

ECBP 2.2 Unintentional Injury

Target: 89.9%.

Baseline: 81.7% of elementary, middle, and senior high schools provided comprehensive school health education to prevent unintentional injury in 2006.

Target-setting method: 10% improvement.

Data source: School Health Policies and Programs Study (SHPPS), CDC, National Center for Chronic Disease Prevention and Health Promotion (NCCDPHP).

ECBP 2.6 Alcohol and Other Drug Use

Target: 89.9%.

Baseline: 81.7% of elementary, middle, and senior high schools provided comprehensive school health education to prevent alcohol and other drug use in 2006.

Target-setting method: 10% improvement.

Data source: SHPPS, CDC, NCCDPHP.

ECBP 2.8 Unhealthy Dietary Patterns

Target: 92.7%.

Baseline: 84.3% of elementary, middle, and senior high schools provided comprehensive school health education to prevent unhealthy dietary patterns in 2006.

Target-setting method: 10% improvement.

Data source: SHPPS, CDC, NCCDPHP.

Note: Other areas covered by this objective include: 2.1 All Priority Areas, 2.3 Violence, 2.4 Suicide, 2.5 Tobacco Use and Addiction, 2.7 Unintended Pregnancy, HIV/AIDS, and STD Infection, and 2.9 Inadequate Physical Activity.

For Further Thought

Assuming money is available, why doesn't every school district in the nation initiate WSCC efforts?

Data from: U.S. Department of Health and Human Services, Office of Disease Prevention and Health Promotion (2016). *Healthy People 2020*. Available at https://www.healthypeople.gov/.

---

organizations—and schools are no different—the administration controls resources. Without leadership and support from top school administrators, it will be an ongoing struggle to provide a quality program. Furthermore, every effort should be made to employ personnel who are appropriately trained to carry out their responsibilities as members of the school health advisory council. For example, the National Association of School Nurses has taken the position that "every school-aged child deserves a school nurse who has a baccalaureate degree in nursing from an accredited college or university and is licensed as a registered nurse through the State Board of Nursing,"[11] yet many school nurses without college degrees and training in health education are asked to provide health education. Conversely, certified teachers who lack preparation in school health are required to teach health to secure a job.[12] Qualified personnel are a must.

School Health Policies

School health policies, which include "laws, mandates, regulations, standards, resolutions, and guidelines—provide a foundation for school district practices and procedures."[13] The written policy describes the nature of the program and the procedure for its implementation to those outside the program.[14] Well-written school health policies provide a sense of direction and a means of accountability and credibility, and strengthen the possibility that a school health program will become "an institutionalized part of the school culture."[15] They serve as an "important indicator of where school health is prioritized within the

School health policies
written statements that describe the nature and procedures of a school health program

overall education agenda."[10] Steps for creating local health-related policies include the following:[16,17]

1. Build a policy development team.
2. Assess the environment.
3. Draft the policy.
4. Adopt the policy.
5. Implement the policy.
6. Measure and evaluate.
7. Communicate the results.

Policy Development

The development of a set of written policies is not an easy task. This challenging and time-consuming task should be executed by the school health advisory council because the council includes those most knowledgeable about the school health program in addition to representing many different constituencies in the school community.

The policies should cover all facets of the school health program, such as storage and access to prescription medications, bullying, use of physical activity as punishment, foods permitted at school parties, in addition to policies associated with curriculum, health services, and maintaining a safe learning environment. Several professional associations that have an interest in school health programs have written policy statements relating to school health issues and provide guidance for providing current policy statements. A few such associations are the American Academy of Pediatrics (AAP) (information available at www.aap.org), the National Association of State Boards of Education (NASBE) (information available at http://nasbe.org), and the Association for Supervision and Curriculum Development (ASCD) (information available at www.ascd.org).

Once the policies have been written, it is important that they receive approval from key stakeholders. Although the school board is the final authority that adopts policies, approval from school administrators, school-based committees, parents, and other key stakeholders can aid in the implementation process.[17] The approval process provides credibility to the policies as well as legal protection for those who must implement the policies.[14]

Policy Implementation

The development of written policies is an important step in building a solid base for WSCC efforts. However, if the policies are never implemented, the school district will be no better off than before their development.

Implementation begins with the distribution of the policies to those who will be affected by them—faculty, staff, students, and parents. Some ideas for carrying out this process include (1) distributing the policies with a memorandum of explanation, (2) placing the policies in both faculty/staff and student handbooks, (3) presenting them at a gathering of the different groups (e.g., at staff or parent–teacher organization [PTO] meetings, or an open house), (4) holding a special meeting for the specific purpose of explaining the policies, and (5) placing them in the school district newsletter. News releases might even be considered if the policies include major changes. Each school district must decide the best way to disseminate its school health policies.

Policy Development Resources

Because of the requirements of the Child Nutrition and WIC Reauthorization Act of 2004 to implement a school wellness policy by districts,[18] numerous resources have become available to help schools develop policies. Action for Healthy Kids (AFHK) is one such organization that is advocating and providing support for "helping schools become healthier places so kids can live healthier lives"[19] by fighting childhood obesity, undernourishment, and physical inactivity. AFHK has created a partner network of more than 75 organizations, corporations, and government agencies concerned with the health and academic success of youth.[19] Sample wellness policies and a clearinghouse of related resources, including policy development guides, are available at the AFHK website (www.actionforhealthykids.org). Tools to assist schools in conducting needs assessments related to WSCC include the School Health Index, available free from the Centers for Disease Control and Prevention (CDC; http://www.cdc.gov/healthyschools/shi/index.htm) and the ASCD School Improvement Tool, available from ASCD (http://www.ascd.org/whole-child.aspx).

Monitoring the Status of School Health Policy in the United States

Because school health policy is an important foundation for WSCC, the Division of Adolescent Health at the CDC has periodically conducted a national survey to assess school health policies and practices at the state, district, school, and classroom levels. The survey, which is titled the School Health Policies and Practices Study (SHPPS) is used to do the following:[20]

- Describe characteristics of each component of school health at the state, district, school, and classroom levels.
- Describe the professional background of the personnel who deliver each component of the school health program.
- Describe collaboration among staff from each school health component and with staff from outside agencies and organizations.
- Describe how key policies and practices have changed over time.

Components of the Whole School, Whole Community, Whole Child Model

If implemented appropriately, a coordinated approach to child health and learning can have a significant positive impact on the overall health status of students, staff, and the community, which, in turn, can be linked to higher academic achievement for students. To do so, the 10 WSCC components need to be provided in a coordinated fashion. Because of the limitation of space, we discuss the importance of the administration and organization, and, provide an overview of three of the traditional components of the school health program—(1) school health services, (2) healthy school environment, and (3) health education—and provide a brief explanation of the remaining components.

Administration and Organization

Effective administration and organization of the school health program ensure that the people and activities that constitute the program work in a coordinated manner to meet the program's goals. Additionally, a dedicated coordinator is critical to maximizing existing resources and championing student health and wellness within the school, community, and district.[21] As previously noted, the responsibility for coordinating the program in each school district should be delegated to a properly trained and knowledgeable individual. Logical choices for this position of **school health coordinator** would be a trained school nurse or a health education specialist. Whereas nearly two-thirds of school districts in the United States employ school health coordinators, there are only a few states that require such a person.[20,22]

The following are responsibilities common to school health coordinators:[23,24]

- Ensuring that the instruction and services provided through various components of the school health program are mutually reinforcing and present consistent messages
- Facilitating collaboration among school health program personnel and between them and other school staff

School health coordinator
a trained professional at the state, district, or school level who is responsible for managing, coordinating, planning, implementing, and evaluating school health policies, programs, and resources

- Assisting the superintendent/school principal and other administrative staff with the integration, management, and supervision of the school health program
- Providing or arranging for necessary technical assistance
- Identifying necessary resources
- Facilitating collaboration between the district/school and other agencies and organizations in the community who have an interest in the health and well-being of children and their families
- Conducting evaluation activities that assess the implementation and results of the school health program, as well as assisting with reporting evaluation results

School Health Services

School health services "intervene with actual and potential health problems, including providing first aid, emergency care and assessment, and planning for management of chronic conditions."[5]

School health services also include wellness promotion, preventive services, and education; access and/or referrals to the medical home or private health care provider; support connecting school staff, students, families, community, and health care providers to promote the health care of students and a healthy and safe school environment; and remediation of detected health problems within the limits of state laws through referral and follow-up by the school nurse and teachers.[5] Originally, the intent of school health services was to supplement rather than to supplant the family's responsibility for meeting the health care needs of its children. However, because of the poorer health status of youth, the involvement of youth in high-risk behaviors (such as smoking, drinking, substance abuse, and unprotected sexual intercourse), and such barriers to health care as inadequate health insurance and lack of providers, there has been a broadening of the role of schools in providing health care.

Because school attendance is required throughout the United States, schools represent our best opportunity to reach many of those children in need of proper health care. More than 95% of all youths aged 5 to 17 years are enrolled in schools.[25] "The school's ability to reach children and youth slipping through the cracks of the health care system and at highest risk for poor health and potentially health-threatening behaviors is unmatched."[26] Some of the benefits of having school health services, and specifically a full-time nurse, include the following:[27]

- Students are less likely to visit the emergency room.
- Students are more likely to visit an appropriate health care provider if they have a medical referral from the school nurse.
- Students are less likely to miss school due to illness.
- The achievement gap that students with chronic health conditions face can be reduced.

Each school district is unique, from the demographics of its students to the availability of its health resources. The National Association of School Nurses has taken leadership in providing recommendations for evidence-based school nursing practice. The Framework for the 21st Century School Nursing Practice calls for student-centered nursing care focused on the key principles of care coordination, leadership, quality improvement, and community/public health with standards of practice as the foundation[28] (see **Figure 6.4**).

Expanded services are increasingly being offered through school-based, school-linked programs. School-based health centers (SBHCs) are exactly what the name implies, "the center of health in the schools they are based."[29] With an emphasis on prevention, early intervention, and risk reduction, students can "be treated for acute illnesses, such as flu, and chronic conditions, including asthma and diabetes. They can also be screened for dental, vision and hearing problems."[29] The idea of young people receiving more comprehensive health care within the context of the school setting is gaining momentum throughout the country and is discussed in greater detail later in this chapter.

Framework for 21st Century School Nursing Practice™

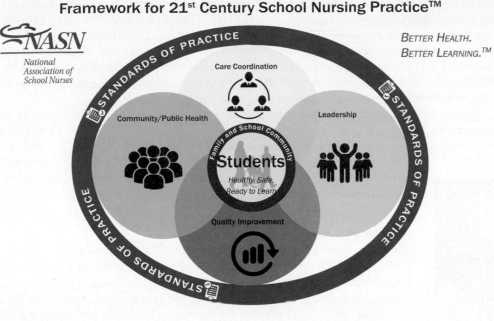

NASN's *Framework for 21st Century School Nursing Practice* (the *Framework*) provides structure and focus for the key principles and components of current day, evidence-based school nursing practice. It is aligned with the Whole School, Whole Community, Whole Child model that calls for a collaborative approach to learning and health (ASCD & CDC, 2014). Central to the *Framework* is student-centered nursing care that occurs within the context of the students' family and school community. Surrounding the students, family, and school community are the non-hierarchical, overlapping key principles of *Care Coordination, Leadership, Quality Improvement,* and *Community/ Public Health*. These principles are surrounded by the fifth principle, *Standards of Practice*, which is foundational for evidence-based, clinically competent, quality care. School nurses daily use the skills outlined in the practice components of each principle to help students be healthy, safe, and ready to learn.

Standards of Practice	Care Coordination	Leadership	Quality Improvement	Community/ Public Health
• Clinical Competence • Clinical Guidelines • Code of Ethics • Critical Thinking • Evidence-based Practice • NASN Position Statements • Nurse Practice Acts • Scope and Standards of Practice	• Case Management • Chronic Disease Management • Collaborative Communication • Direct Care • Education • Interdisciplinary Teams • Motivational Interviewing/ Counseling • Nursing Delegation • Student Care Plans • Student-centered Care • Student Self-empowerment • Transition Planning	• Advocacy • Change Agents • Education Reform • Funding and Reimbursement • Healthcare Reform • Lifelong Learner • Models of Practice • Technology • Policy Development and Implementation • Professionalism • Systems-level Leadership	• Continuous Quality Improvement • Documentation/Data Collection • Evaluation • Meaningful Health/ Academic Outcomes • Performance Appraisal • Research • Uniform Data Set	• Access to Care • Cultural Competency • Disease Prevention • Environmental Health • Health Education • Health Equity • Healthy People 2020 • Health Promotion • Outreach • Population-based Care • Risk Reduction • Screenings/Referral/ Follow-up • Social Determinants of Health • Surveillance

ASCD & CDC. (2014). *Whole school whole community whole child: A collaborative approach to learning and health*. Retrieved from http://www.ascd.org/ASCD/pdf/siteASCD/publications/wholechild/wscc-a-collaborative-approach.pdf

Rev. 10/26/15

FIGURE 6.4   Framework for 21st Century School Nursing Practice.

Source: National Association of School Nurses, 2015.

Healthy School Environment

The term *healthy school environment* designates the part of WSCC that provides for a safe—both physically and emotionally—learning environment (see **Figure 6.5**). If children are not placed in a safe environment, learning becomes difficult at best. The most

Healthy school environment the promotion, maintenance, and utilization of safe and wholesome surroundings in a school

comprehensive definition of **healthy school environment** was provided by the 1972–1973 Joint Committee on Health Education Terminology. They stated that providing a healthy school environment includes "the promotion, maintenance, and utilization of safe and wholesome surroundings, organization of day-by-day experiences and planned learning procedures to influence favorable emotional, physical and social health."[30] Within the WSCC model, the school environment includes the physical environment as well as the social and emotional school climate.[5]

By law, school districts are required to provide a safe school environment. However, the responsibility for maintaining this safe environment should rest with all who use it. Everyone, including those on the board of education, administrators, teachers, custodial staff, and students, must contribute to make a school a safer place through their daily actions. An unsafe school environment can exist only if those responsible for it and those who use it allow it to exist.

The Physical Environment

The physical environment encompasses the school building and its contents, the land on which the school is located, and the area surrounding it. A healthy school environment addresses the school's physical condition including ventilation, temperature, noise, and lighting; and protects occupants from physical threats such as crime, violence, traffic, and injuries; and biological and chemical agents in the air, water, and soil.[5] Each school district should have an appropriate protocol for dealing with and maintaining these aspects of the physical environment.[31]

The behavior of both the school personnel and students in the school environment also affects the safety of the environment. Each year a significant number of students throughout the country are injured on their way to, at, or on their way home from school. Some of these injuries occur from an unsafe physical plant that is in need of repair, but many occur from inappropriate behavior. Unsafe behavior that is observed too frequently in schools includes acts of violence between students and lack of proper supervision by school employees. However, most do not worry about a safe environment until they are faced with a problem. Every school building in the United States could become a safer environment if greater attention were given to prevention than to a cure.

FIGURE 6.5 The school should be a safe and healthy place to learn.
© Don Tremain/age fotostock.

The Psychosocial Environment

Although a safe physical environment is important, a safe social and emotional environment is equally important. This portion of the school environment "encompasses the attitudes, feelings, and values of students and staff."[32] Students who are fearful of responding to a teacher's question because the teacher might make fun of them if they answer incorrectly or students who avoid being in the halls during passing time because of fear of being bullied are not learning in a healthy psychosocial environment. For many, learning does not come easily, and anxiety-producing factors such as these can only make it more difficult.

The ways in which school personnel and students treat each other can also add much to the teaching/learning process (see **Figure 6.6**). All individuals within the school should be treated with respect. People should be polite and courteous to each other. This does not mean that high academic standards should be abandoned and that everyone should agree with all that others do, but students and teachers should not be afraid to express themselves in a cooperative, respectful way. For example, think back to your middle school and high school days. Think about the teachers you liked best. Did you like them

FIGURE 6.6 A healthy social environment, conducive to learning, is an important component of good school health.
© Digital Vision/Thinkstock.

because they were great teachers and knew their subject well? Or did you like them because of the way they treated and respected you? The psychosocial environment can have a significant impact on the school environment!

Implementing a school crisis plan can assist with addressing situations that affect both the physical and social environments. A clear, written plan that includes procedures for handling various emergencies (e.g., fire, tornado, death of a student or staff member, mass illness, terrorism, suicide attempt), communication procedures, staff training, practice drills, coordination with local public safety agencies, among other procedures, can help ensure, when threats occur, that safe practices are implemented.[20,31]

School Health Education

School health education provides students with "the knowledge and skills they need to become successful learners and healthy and productive adults."[33] If designed properly, school health education could be one of the most effective means to reduce serious health problems in the United States, including cardiovascular disease, cancer, motor vehicle crashes, homicide, and suicide.[34] Such a curriculum should focus on promoting the following priority health content:[33]

- Alcohol and other drugs
- Healthy eating
- Mental and emotional health
- Personal health and wellness
- Physical activity
- Safety
- Sexual health (abstinence and risk avoidance)
- Tobacco
- Violence prevention

School health education includes health education that takes place in the classroom as well as any other activities designed to positively influence the health knowledge and skills of students, parents, and school staff. For example, health education can take place when the school nurse gives a vision screening test to a student or when coaches talk with their teams about concussion safety.

For health education to be effective, it should be well conceived and carefully planned. The written plan for school health education is referred to as the health **curriculum**. The curriculum not only outlines the **scope** (what will be taught) and the **sequence** (when it will be taught) but also provides (1) learning objectives, (2) standards (see **Box 6.3**), (3) learning experiences leading to the adoption and maintenance of specific health-enhancing behaviors, (4) possible

School health education
the development, delivery, and evaluation of a planned curriculum, kindergarten through grade 12

Curriculum a written plan for instruction

Scope part of the curriculum that outlines what will be taught

Sequence part of the curriculum that states in what order the content will be taught

---

BOX 6.3   National Health Education Standards

1. Students will comprehend concepts related to health promotion and disease prevention to enhance health.
2. Students will analyze the influence of family, peers, culture, media, technology, and other factors on health behaviors.
3. Students will demonstrate the ability to access valid information and products and services to enhance health.
4. Students will demonstrate the ability to use interpersonal communication skills to enhance health and avoid or reduce health risks.
5. Students will demonstrate the ability to use decision-making skills to enhance health.
6. Students will demonstrate the ability to use goal setting to enhance health.
7. Students will demonstrate the ability to practice health-enhancing behaviors to avoid or reduce health risks.
8. Students will demonstrate the ability to advocate for personal, family, and community health.

Source: Reprinted with permission from the American Cancer Society. *National Health Education Standards: Achieving Excellence*, 2nd ed. (Atlanta, GA: Author), 8. Available at cancer.org/bookstore.

instructional resources, and (5) methods for assessment to determine the extent to which the objectives and standards are met. If health instruction is to be effective, the health curriculum should include lessons of appropriate scope and sequence for all grades from pre-K through 12th grade.

Results from CDC's School Health Policies and Practices Study (SHPPS) show that good school health instruction is not widespread. To enhance the state of health instruction in schools National Health Education Standards have been developed. The National Health Education Standards delineate the essential knowledge and skills that every student should know and be able to do following the completion of quality school health education. The standards are not a federal mandate or national curriculum, but rather provide a foundation for curriculum development, instructional delivery, and assessment of student knowledge and skills for students in grades pre-K through 12.[35] There are eight standards (see Box 6.3), and each standard has grade-level performance indicators set for grades pre-K–2, 3–5, 6–8, and 9–12. "The standards evolved from the health education profession's current thinking about what constitutes grade-appropriate and challenging content and performance expectations for students."[36]

Development of and Sources of Health Education Curricula

Each year, many school districts throughout the United States are faced with the task of developing a curriculum to guide health education. Such a task can be completed in one of several ways. First, a school district could obtain a prepackaged curriculum that has been developed by nationally recognized specialists. Some of these are prepared and sold by for-profit organizations, and others are available free of charge from nonprofit agencies (i.e., voluntary health agencies). A second means is to use the approved curriculum of either the state departments of education or health. A third method is to adopt a new health textbook series and consider the series as a district's curricular guide. And fourth, some districts may even develop their own in-house curriculum. Each of these approaches has its strengths and weaknesses, and school districts have to decide which approach best suits their particular situation.

Determining what is and what is not an effective curriculum can be a difficult process. Some very poor curricula, packaged in a slick way, can convince administrators that they have purchased a very fine product. Conversely, some educationally sound programs may not be well packaged. Fortunately, resources are available to help reduce the guesswork for those who must select curricula. See **Box 6.4** for a summary of characteristics of effective health education curricula, which can serve as a guide when evaluating and selecting materials.

BOX 6.4   Characteristics of Effective Health Education Curricula

- Focuses on clear health goals and related behavioral outcomes.
- Is research-based and theory-driven.
- Addresses individual values, attitudes, and beliefs.
- Addresses individual and group norms that support health-enhancing behaviors.
- Focuses on reinforcing protective factors and increasing perceptions of personal risk and harmfulness of engaging in specific unhealthy practices and behaviors.
- Addresses social pressures and influences.
- Builds personal competence, social competence, and self-efficacy by addressing skills.
- Provides functional health knowledge that is basic, accurate, and directly contributes to health-promoting decisions and behaviors.

- Uses strategies designed to personalize information and engage students.
- Provides age-appropriate and developmentally appropriate information, learning strategies, teaching methods, and materials.
- Incorporates learning strategies, teaching methods, and materials that are culturally inclusive.
- Provides adequate time for instruction and learning.
- Provides opportunities to reinforce skills and positive health behaviors.
- Provides opportunities to make positive connections with influential others.
- Includes teacher information and plans for professional development and training that enhances effectiveness of instruction and student learning.

Source: Centers for Disease Control and Prevention (2012). *Health Education Curriculum Analysis Tool*. Atlanta, GA: Author, 5–6.

A number of federal agencies have created processes for reviewing, approving, and recommending health education programs that are effective. The CDC maintains a list of registries sponsored by federal agencies that include programs effective in reducing youth risk behaviors.[37] Most of these registries allow curriculum developers to nominate their curricula for review. The review process typically involves peer review by three or more professionals with expertise in the specific area. Programs deemed worthy of recommendation based on the expert review process can be found on the various registries identified on the CDC website.[37] Additionally, the CDC has developed the Health Education Curriculum Analysis Tool (HECAT), a resource school districts, schools, and others involved in the curriculum process can use to conduct their own analysis of health curricula. The HECAT, which is based on the National Health Education Standards and CDC's *Characteristics of Effective Health Education Curriculum*, can help in the selection or development of appropriate and effective health education curricula and improve the delivery of health education.[33]

In addition to using programs described on the various registries or evaluating curriculum yourself, a number of other sources are available for obtaining health curricula. Some of them may be comprehensive (include a variety of topics and for every grade level, K–12), and others may be topic and/or grade-level specific. These other sources include the following:

- *State departments of education or health.* A number of states have either recommended or required a particular curriculum. Some states do not have comprehensive curricula but require instruction in some of the more controversial health topics, such as substance use and abuse and sexuality education.
- *Health agencies and associations.* Many of the voluntary health agencies (e.g., American Cancer Society, American Heart Association, and American Lung Association) and other health related organizations (e.g., National Dairy Council, Hazelden Foundation [cyberbullying], and Indiana Organ Procurement Organization) have developed curricula for grades K–12. Most of these are not comprehensive, but they are usually well done, supported by audiovisuals and handouts, and available either at very low or no cost.
- *Commercially produced curricula.* These curricula have been developed by private corporations for schools.

Counseling, Psychological, and Social Services

Counseling, psychological, and social services are services provided to support students' mental, behavioral, and social-emotional health. These services can include individual and group assessments, interventions, and referrals. Professionals such as certified school counselors, psychologists, and social workers provide these services.[5]

Physical Education and Physical Activity

The opportunity for students to be physically active throughout the school day is the goal of a comprehensive school physical activity program, which includes coordination of physical education, physical activity during school, physical activity before and after school, staff involvement, and family and community engagement.[5] Physical education serves as the academic subject and is characterized by a planned, sequential K–12 curriculum based on national standards for physical education. Emphasis is placed on physical fitness and skill development that lead to lifelong physical activity. Physical education should be taught by qualified teachers.[5]

Nutrition Environment and Services

The nutrition environment provides students with opportunities to learn about and practice healthy eating through available food choices, nutrition education, and messages about food. School nutrition services includes the cafeteria, vending machines, grab 'n' go kiosks, school stores, concession stands, classroom rewards and parties, school celebrations, and fundraisers. School nutrition services provide access to a variety of nutritious and appealing meals that accommodate the health and nutrition needs of all students in a school district.[5]

Community Involvement

Community groups, organizations, health clinics, and local businesses can be critical partners in improving health and learning for students, thus positively impacting families and the community. Sharing resources and volunteering to support student learning and health are some of the ways the community can strengthen schools and those schools serve. Reciprocally, schools, students, and their families can enhance the community through service-learning opportunities and by sharing school facilities with the community.[5]

Family Engagement

Family engagement efforts include families and school staff working together to support and improve the learning, development, and health of students.[29]

Employee Wellness

Schools, in addition to being a place of learning, are also worksites. Fostering school employees' physical and mental health results in positive role models and employees who are more productive and less likely to be absent.[5] "Employee wellness programs and healthy work environments can improve a district's bottom line by decreasing employee health insurance premiums, reducing employee turnover, and cutting costs of substitutes."[5]

Issues and Concerns Facing School Health

Like most other community and public health programs, the school health program is not without its issues and concerns. "In the 1940s, the three leading school discipline problems were talking, chewing gum, and making noise."[38] Today, many of the leading school discipline problems are related to health, such as bullying and other forms of violence, drug use, and the consequences of low self-esteem. In the remainder of this chapter, we summarize a few of the challenges that still lie ahead for those who work in school health.

Lack of Support for School Health Initiatives

"Schools offer the most systematic and efficient means available to improve the health of youth and enable young people to avoid health risks,"[39] yet, ironically, school health advocates have had limited success in getting coordinated school health or WSCC implemented in school districts across the country.

We have already pointed out that healthy children are better learners and that WSCC can contribute to the health of children. Coordinated school health efforts, like WSCC, "can provide a safe haven for teaching and learning by addressing the immediate needs of the whole child. In the long term, it can have a significant effect on youth development and academic achievement."[6]

Although many Americans support the idea that everyone is entitled to good health, we have not supported through legislation the notion that everyone is entitled to WSCC efforts in our schools. Obviously, getting legislation passed is a complicated process and is dependent on a number of different circumstances, including, but not limited to, economics, social action, and politics. Additionally, limited resources, lack of buy-in and investment, the inability of schools to demonstrate competence and effectiveness to stakeholders, lack of organizational capacity, leadership support, and continued emphasis on high-stakes testing have made it difficult for school districts to make WSCC efforts a priority.[40,41] This difficult task should not deter those who feel WSCC is vital. It is becoming clearer that many of the answers to current and future health problems lie with the resources found in the school—the one institution of society through which all of us must pass.

The need for coordinated school health efforts should be obvious to all. We have taken the liberty to rephrase a quote from a group of school health experts who say it best: Society should not be as concerned with what happens when we implement WSCC as about what is likely to happen if we do not.[42] Although garnering support for coordinated school health and WSCC has been an uphill battle, we are moving in the right direction. As mentioned earlier in the chapter, with the passing of the Child Nutrition and WIC Reauthorization Act of 2004,[18] school districts are required to institute local wellness policies promoting better nutrition, physical activity, and wellness. With the more recent passing of the Healthy, Hunger-Free Kids Act of 2010, school districts have greater accountability for implementation, evaluation, and public reporting related to local wellness policies.[43] Some states have taken this one step further by passing state legislation requiring districts to institute coordinated school health advisory councils.[44] Finally, "requiring schools to include health goals in their mandated school improvement plans . . . is perhaps the single most important policy that can be implemented, because it ensures that schools will be held accountable for their ongoing efforts and the success of their health policies and programs."[10]

School Health Curriculum Challenges

Controversy

The words sexual intercourse, suicide, substance use and abuse, sexually transmitted diseases, dating violence, contraception, death and dying, and even abstinence get attention. The very nature of the topics covered in a school health education curriculum today continues to create controversy in some districts and in different parts of the country. Yet, controversy is not new to school health education; it has followed health education ever since it first attempted to deal with the many issues that face youth (see **Figure 6.7**).

Controversy continues to be a challenge for health education for a number of reasons. Part of it deals with the pressure that has been applied to schools by conservative groups. These groups are interested in discouraging health instruction that includes values-clarification activities and open-ended decision-making processes.[45] Others believe that controversy exists because of the differences in family value systems and religious beliefs. Questions such as (1) Do students really need to learn in school how to use a condom? (2) Doesn't talk of suicide lead some students to think that it might be the best alternative for them? (3) Aren't chiropractors just health quacks? and (4) Why do students need to know about funeral preplanning in high school? create legitimate concerns, but they are also issues that today's adolescents face. Lack of awareness, knowledge, and skills is not an excuse for undesirable health behavior. If the students do not get this information at school, where will they get it? Studies have shown that the institutions of church and family have taught little about the controversial topics included in health curricula.

Improper Implementation

Improper implementation of the curriculum is another challenge to school health (see **Box 6.5**). Because health has not been considered a "core" subject in most school districts, it has received little attention and support. Additionally, the increased emphasis on standardized testing of the core subjects in recent years has further decreased the priority of health in the K–12 curriculum. In many school districts throughout the United States, the low priority given to health has meant that much of the instruction is provided by individuals other than health education specialists. These people are not incapable of teaching health, but they have not been educated to do so. Reliance on a textbook as the curriculum, lack of awareness/implementation

FIGURE 6.7   There are still many controversial issues that surround school health.

© Chitose Suzuki/AP Photos.

BOX 6.5 Barriers to Comprehensive School Health Education

Although the importance of school health education is being recognized more and more, there are several barriers to its implementation. Research by various authors has informed health education specialists of barriers to establishing effective health instruction. Those barriers include the following:

1. Lack of local administrative commitment
2. Lack of adequately prepared teachers
3. Lack of time in the school day/year
4. Lack of money/funds
5. Health education's lack of credibility as an academic subject
6. Lack of community/parental support for controversial topics

7. Policy constraints
8. Teacher priorities
9. Pressure to focus on subjects included in high-stakes tests
10. General lack of reinforcement by state and local education policymakers

The top three barriers tend to be seen as the most significant. Recommendations to address them include the following:

1. Inviting administrators to workshops and conferences dealing with current health issues
2. Conducting quality in-service programs
3. Advocacy to school administrators and professors of education

Sources: Bender, S. J., J. J. Neutens, S. Skonie-Hardin, and W. D. Sorochan (1997). *Teaching Health Science: Elementary and Middle School*, 4th ed. Burlington, MA: Jones & Bartlett Learning, 32; Butler, S. C. (1993). "Chief State School Officers Rank Barriers to Implementing Comprehensive School Health Education." *Journal of School Health*, 63(3): 130–132; Telljohann, S. K., C. W. Symons, B. Pateman, and D. Seabert (2015). *Health Education: Elementary and Middle School Applications*, 8th ed. New York: McGraw-Hill; Thackeray, R., B. L. Neiger, H. Bartle, S. C. Hill, and M. D. Barnes (2002). "Elementary School Teachers' Perspectives on Health Instruction: Implications for Health Education." *American Journal of Health Education*, 33(2): 77–82; and Sy, A., and K. Glanz (2008). "Factors Influencing Teachers' Implementation of an Innovative Tobacco Prevention Curriculum for Multiethnic Youth: Project SPLASH." *Journal of School Health*, 78(5): 264–273.

---

of state or national standards, an emphasis on content rather than skills, and limited, if any, coverage of topics that cause discomfort are some of the outcomes of improperly prepared teachers in the health classroom. The long-term result is young people do not learn the skills necessary to live a healthy lifestyle.

School districts can help reduce controversy and improve the quality of health instruction provided by (1) implementing age-appropriate curricula, (2) using effective teaching methods, (3) gaining parent/guardian approval of curricula and teaching methods, (4) developing a school policy that enables parents/guardians to review the curricula and to withdraw their children from lessons that go against family or religious beliefs, (5) implementing a school policy that provides for the handling of concern by parents/guardians,[46] and (6) making sure qualified and interested teachers teach health.

School-Based Health Centers

Earlier in the chapter, we mentioned that a number of school districts across the country have opened school-based or linked health centers (SLHC) to help meet the health needs of their students. In 1970, only one U.S. school had a SBHC/SLHC.[47] By 1984, that number had jumped to 31; by 1989 it had increased to 150.[48] Currently, there are more than 2,300 school-based health centers operating nationwide.[49] The majority (94%) of SBHCs are located on school property with a small number (3%) providing services through mobile units. Most (51%) of the SBHCs operating today are found in urban areas. Of the SBHCs currently operating, 23% are found in high schools, 9% in middle schools, and 15% in elementary schools. The other 53% are located in alternative, K–8, 6–12, or K–12 schools.[49]

Although there is no single model for SBHCs, this set of seven core competencies identify knowledge, expertise, policies, practices, and attributes and can be used to guide the delivery of health care in a school setting:[50]

- The SBHC assures students' access to health care and support services to help them thrive.
- The SBHC team and services are organized explicitly around relevant health issues that affect student well-being and academic success.

- The SBCH, although governed and administered separately from the school, integrates into the education and environment to support the school's mission of student success.
- The SBHC routinely evaluates its performance against accepted standards of quality to achieve optimal outcomes for students.
- The SBHC promotes a culture of health across the entire school community.
- The SBHC coordinates across relevant systems of care that share in the well-being of its patients.
- The SBHC employs sound management practices to ensure a sustainable business.

As mentioned earlier in the chapter, there are a number of sound reasons why health centers should be based in schools—the primary reason being the ability to reach, in a cost-effective manner, a large segment of the population that is otherwise without primary health care. "School-based health centers are the best model of health care in this country for at-risk populations . . . SBHCs increase access to health care, eliminate barriers and improve health outcomes for essentially every patient enrolled."[51] Yet, SBHCs have not experienced the level of implementation that might be expected of a program that could make such a positive impact on the health of young people. Early on, SBHCs were frequent targets of intense criticism at the local and national levels by political and religious groups.[52–54] Much of the controversy surrounding SBHCs centered around cultural wars and partisan politics.[55] The issue of cultural wars revolved around the views of conservatives versus liberals, and how and where people should receive their health care. Whereas some people who support SBHCs would want their child treated as quickly and effectively as possible for a health problem, others who oppose the centers can see nothing but the "image of a condom on a cafeteria tray."[55] The key to working through the "cultural wars" problem is compromise. That is, each area of the country is different and what are reasonable health services provided in an SBHC in one area are unacceptable in another. Thus, advocates of the centers say that the services provided by SBHCs are so badly needed that a single issue such as reproductive health care should not keep an SBHC from existing.[55]

Since their inception, funding for SBHCs has been an issue. Therefore, most of the SBHCs receive sponsorship from a variety of health system partnerships, including community health center or federally qualified health center (43%), hospital or medical center (19%), school system (12%), and private, nonprofit (10%), or local health department (8%). Currently 9 in 10 SBHCs seek reimbursement for services from public and private health insurers.[49]

Another one of the challenges facing SBHCs is the pressure for schools and school-related programs to be accountable for demonstrating their impact on improving the learning environment and academic outcomes.[56] Research studies have explored the link between SBHCs and health outcomes, resulting in positive findings. For example, there is a correlation between asthma and lower student attendance. For those students with asthma attending a school with an SBHC, there were fewer hospitalization days and school absences when compared with children at control schools without a SBHC.[57] In this current climate of accountability within the educational system, indirect links do not provide enough evidence that SBHCs positively affect academic outcomes. Research demonstrating the correlation between SBHCs and health and academic outcomes is needed for SBHCs to gain greater implementation.[56]

Violence in Schools

Over the years, schools have been viewed as safe havens for teaching and learning.[58] But in recent years there have been a number of high-profile incidents of violence in schools (e.g., Newtown, Connecticut; Columbine, Colorado) that have made the general public more aware of the violence in schools. "Any instance of crime or violence at school not only affects the individuals involved but also may disrupt the educational process and affect bystanders, the school itself, and the surrounding community."[58] The difference between violence in the schools today and years past is the means by which disagreements are settled. "Today the possibility that a disagreement among students will be settled with some type of weapon rather than an old-fashioned fist fight has significantly increased."[59] CDC Youth Risk Behavior data indicate that 1 of 14 U.S. high school students had missed at least 1 day of school in the preceding month because that student felt unsafe either being at school or going to and from school; 1 of 14 students had been threatened or injured with a weapon on school property during the preceding year; and more than 1 of nearly 13 students had been in a physical fight on school property.[60]

We know that males are involved in more violent acts than are females.[60] We also know that certain racial and ethnic groups participate and are victims of violence at school more often than other students are.[60] Yet, it is close to impossible to predict who will be next to commit a violent act in a school.

Another form of violence that has received significant attention recently is bullying. Bullying can be defined as "unwanted, aggressive behavior among school aged children that involves a real or perceived power imbalance."[61] Bullying can take many forms, such as physical (hitting); verbal (teasing or name calling); social (social exclusion or spreading rumors); and cyber (sending insulting messages or pictures by mobile phone or using the Internet).[61] Research indicates that approximately 20% of students are bullied with some frequency. Being bullied can affect academic achievement and self-esteem. Bullying can also affect bystanders by creating a climate of fear and disrespect in schools. Furthermore, bullying behavior can be a sign of other serious antisocial or violent behavior by those who bully their peers.[61]

With the technologic advances of late, concern has increased about the connection between electronic media and youth violence. Electronic aggression, which has been defined as "any kind of aggression perpetrated through technology—any type of harassment or bullying that occurs through email, a chat room, instant messaging, a website (including blogs), or text messaging,"[62] also called cyberbullying, is a growing phenomenon among youth. Between 7% and 15% of young people say they have been a victim of electronic aggression. Some evidence suggests that electronic aggression may peak around the end of middle school/beginning of high school.[62] Instant messaging appears to be the most common way electronic aggression is perpetrated, and it is most often experienced between a victim and perpetrator who know each other. Whether electronic aggression occurs at home or at school, it has implications for school. "Young people who were harassed online were more likely to get a detention or be suspended, to skip school, and to experience emotional distress than those who were not harassed."[62] This behavior also influences students' sense of safety at school.[62]

Like most other health problems, risk factors need to be identified and steps taken to reduce the risk of violent acts occurring in the schools. Many schools have taken steps to try to reduce the chances for violence, yet many more have stated that violence is not a problem at "our school." These are the schools that are most vulnerable to such a problem. The CDC makes the following recommendations for educators and educational policymakers for improving the school climate as it relates to violence, bullying, and electronic aggression:[62]

- *Explore current bullying prevention policies.* Determine if they need to be modified to reflect electronic aggression.
- *Work collaboratively to develop policies.* States, school districts, and boards of education must work in conjunction with other stakeholders to meet the needs of the state or district and those it serves. The CDC School Health Guidelines provide a general outline of steps to follow.[63]
- *Explore current programs to prevent bullying and youth violence.* A number of evidence-based programs exist.
- *Offer training on electronic aggression* for educators and administrators.
- *Talk to teens.* Provide opportunities for students to discuss their concerns.
- *Work with technology staff.* Ensure that all involved are aware and working on strategies for minimizing risk.

- *Create a positive school atmosphere.* Students who feel connected to their school are less likely to perpetrate any type of violence or aggression.
- *Have a plan in place* for what should happen if an incident is brought to the attention of school officials.

With the more recent phenomenon of electronic aggression, it becomes clear that violence is not a problem that will go away soon. While many school personnel do not believe it is a problem in their schools, life has shown us that it can happen anywhere. Violence is an issue that all schools need to face and something for which they need to plan to reduce the risks to school children and personnel. "We send our children out into the world every day to explore and learn, and we hope that they will approach a trusted adult if they encounter a challenge; now, we need to apply this message to the virtual world."[62]

Chapter Summary

- The potential impact of the Whole School, Whole Community, Whole Child (WSCC) effort on the health of children, their families, and the community is great because the school is the one institution through which we all must pass.
- To date, the full potential of school health has not been reached because of lack of support and interest.
- If implemented properly, WSCC can improve access to health services, educate students about pressing health issues, and provide a safe and healthy environment in which students can learn and grow.
- The foundations of the school health program include (1) a school administration that supports such an effort, (2) a well-organized school health advisory council that is genuinely interested in providing a coordinated program for the students, and (3) written school health policies.
- School health policies are critical for ensuring accountability, credibility, and the institutionalization of programs and efforts to make schools a healthy learning environment.

- The components of WSCC include (1) school health services; (2) a healthy school environment (physical and psychosocial); (3) school health education; (4) counseling, psychological, and social services; (5) physical education and physical activities; (6) nutrition services; (7) community engagement; (8) family involvement; and (9) employee wellness.
- The eight National Health Education Standards emphasize a skills-based curriculum focusing on the following: (1) core concepts; (2) analyzing influences; (3) accessing valid health information, products, and services; (4) demonstrating interpersonal communication skills; (5) utilizing decision-making skills; (6) utilizing goal-setting skills; (7) practicing health-enhancing behaviors; and (8) advocating for personal, family, and community health.
- A number of resources exist to assist health education specialists in locating and assessing available curricula.
- A number of issues face school health advocates, including a lack of support for WSCC efforts, health curriculum challenges, the implementation of school-based health centers, and violence in schools.

Scenario: Analysis and Response

Ms. Graff obviously had a very full day, which included several issues related to health and learning. Based on what you read in this chapter and other knowledge you have about school health, respond to the following questions:

1. Identify at least four health and learning concerns with which Ms. Graff had to deal.

2. For each of the concerns you identified in question 1, state how written policies may have helped or hindered Ms. Graff with her responsibilities.

3. How important do you think is the role of the classroom teacher in making school health initiatives like WSCC work? Why do you feel this way?

4. Say the school district in which Ms. Graff works was interested in opening up a school-based health center, but the superintendent needed more data to help "sell" the idea to the school board. Using a search engine on the Internet (e.g., Google, Firefox, Bing), enter "school-based health centers." Could you recommend some websites to the superintendent that would be useful?

Review Questions

1. Explain the Whole School, Whole Community, Whole Student model.
2. Which individuals (name by position) should be considered for inclusion on the school health advisory council?
3. Why are written school health policies needed?
4. Who should approve written school health policies?
5. What are the 10 components of WSCC?
6. Explain the Framework for the 21st Century School Nursing Practice developed by the National Association of School Nurses in terms of how it supports school health services and child health in schools.
7. Explain the importance of using a standards-based health curriculum.
8. How would a health education specialist go about locating credible health education curricula?
9. State four issues facing school health advocates and explain why they are issues.

Activities

1. Make arrangements to observe an elementary classroom in your town for a half day. While observing, keep a chart of all the activities that take place in the classroom that relate to health. Select one activity from your list and write a one-page paper describing the activity, why it was health related, how the teacher handled it, and what could have been done differently to improve the situation.

2. Visit a voluntary health agency in your community and ask the employees to describe the organization's philosophy on health education. Inquire if their health education materials are available for use in a school health program. Summarize your visit with a one-page reaction paper.

3. Make an appointment to interview either a school nurse or a school health coordinator. During your interview, ask the person to provide an overview of what his or her school offers in the way of WSCC efforts. Ask specifically about each of the components of WSCC and the issues of controversy presented in this chapter. Summarize your visit with a two-page written paper.

4. Make arrangements to interview a school administrator or school board member in a district where a school-based center exists. Ask the person to describe the process that the school district went through to start the center, what resistance the district met in doing so, and what the district would do differently if it had to implement it again or start another center.

References

1. Satcher, D. (2005). "Healthy and Ready to Learn." *Educational Leadership*, 63(1): 26–30.
2. Office of Planning, Evaluation and Policy Development (2010). *ESEA Blueprint for Reform*. Washington, DC: U.S. Department of Education.
3. Dryfoos, J. (2008). "Centers of Hope." *Educational Leadership*, 65(7): 38–43.
4. ASCD and Centers for Disease Control and Prevention (CDC) (2014). *Whole School, Whole Community, Whole Child: A Collaborative Approach to Learning and Health*. Alexandria, VA: Author.
5. Lewallen, T., H. Hunt, W. Potts-Datema, S. Zaza, and W. Giles. (2015). "The Whole School, Whole Community, Whole Child Model: A New Approach for Improving Educational Attainment and Healthy Development of Students." *Journal of School Health*, 85(11),729–739.
6. Fetro, J. V. (1998). "Implementing Coordinated School Health Programs in Local Schools." In E. Marx, S. F. Wooley, and D. Northrop, eds., *Health Is Academic: A Guide to Coordinated School Health Programs*. New York: Teachers College Press, 15–42.
7. Ottoson, J., G. Streib, J. Thomas, M. Rivera, and B. Stevenson (2004). "Evaluation of the National School Health Coordinator Leadership Institute." *Journal of School Health*, 74(5): 170–176.
8. National Association of School Nurses (2011). *Position Statement: Role of the School Nurse*. Available at http://www.nasn.org/portals /0/positions/2011psrole.pdf.
9. National Association of State Boards of Education (2000). *Fit, Healthy, and Ready to Learn: Part 1: Physical Activity, Healthy Eating, and Tobacco-Use Prevention*. Alexandria, VA: Author.
10. Basch, C. E. (2011). "Healthier Students Are Better Learners: High-Quality, Strategically Planned, and Effectively Coordinated

School Health Programs Must Be a Fundamental Mission of Schools to Help Close the Achievement Gap." *Journal of School Health*, 81(10): 650–662.

11. National Association of School Nurses (2016). *Position Statements, Resolution and Consensus Statements, and Joint Statements.* Available at http://www.nasn.org/portals/0/binder_papers _reports.pdf.

12. Centers for Disease Control and Prevention. (2015). *Results from the School Health Policies and Practices Study 2014.* U.S. Department of Health and Human Services. Available at http://www.cdc.gov /healthyyouth/data/shpps/results.htm.

13. Centers for Disease Control and Prevention (2016). *School Health Policy.* Available at http://www.cdc.gov/healthyyouth/about/policy .htm.

14. McKenzie, J. F. (1983). "Written Policies: Developing a Solid Foundation for a Comprehensive School Health Program." *Future Focus: Ohio Journal of Health, Physical Education, Recreation, and Dance*, 4(3): 9–11.

15. Grebow, P. M., B. Z. Greene, J. Harvey, and C. J. Head (2000). "Shaping Health Policies." *Educational Leadership*, 57(6): 63–66.

16. Bureau of Health and Nutrition Services and Child/Family/School Partnerships (2009). *Action Guide for School Nutrition and Physical Activity Policies.* Middletown, CT: Connecticut State Department of Education.

17. Action for Healthy Kids (2015). *Wellness Policy Tool.* Available at http://www.actionforhealthykids.org/tools-for-schools /revise-district-policy/wellness-policy-tool.

18. Food and Nutrition Service, U.S. Department of Agriculture (2004). *Child Nutrition and WIC Reauthorization Act of 2004.* Pub. L. No. 108-265, § 204 (2004). Available at http://www.fns.usda.gov/sites /default/files/108-265.pdf.

19. Action for Healthy Kids (2015). *About Us.* Available at http://www .actionforhealthykids.org/about-us.

20. Division of Adolescent and School Health, Centers for Disease Control and Prevention (2015). *School Health Policies and Practices Study.* Available at http://www.cdc.gov/healthyyouth/data/shpps /index.htm.

21. Murray, S., J. Hurley, and S. Ahmed. (2015). "Supporting the Whole Child Through Coordinated Policies, Processes, and Practices." *Journal of School Health*, 85(11): 795–801.

22. National Association of State Boards of Education (2016). *School Health Program Coordinators.* Available at http://www.nasbe.org/healthy _schools/hs/bytopics.php?topicid=6110&catExpand=acdnbtm_catF.

23. Connecticut State Department of Education (2007). *Guidelines for a Coordinated Approach to School Health.* Available at http://www .sde.ct.gov/sde/LIB/sde/PDF/deps/student/Guidelines_CSH.pdf.

24. American Academy of Pediatrics (2016). *Overarching Guidelines: Health and Safety Coordinator for School, For District.* Available at http://www.nationalguidelines.org/guideline .cfm?guideNum=0-04&pageRefresh=true.

25. U.S. Census Bureau (2015). *Digest of Education Statistics 2013.* Available at http://nces.ed.gov/pubs2015/2015011.pdf.

26. Schlitt, J. J. (June 1991). "Issue Brief—Bringing Health to School: Policy Implications for Southern States." Washington, DC: Southern Center on Adolescent Pregnancy Prevention and Southern Regional Project on Infant Mortality. Printed in *Journal of School Health*, 62(2): 60a–60h.

27. Rodriguez, E., D. Rivera, D. Perlroth, E. Becker, N. Wang, and M. Landau. (2013). "School Nurses' Role in Asthma Management, School Absenteeism, and Cost Savings: A Demonstration Project." *Journal of School Health*, 83(12): 842–850.

28. National Association of School Nurses. (2015). *Framework for 21st Century School Nursing Practice.* Available at http://www.nasn.org /Framework.

29. Health Resources and Services Administration, U.S. Department of Health and Human Services (2016). *School-Based Health Centers.* Available at http://www.hrsa.gov/ourstories/schoolhealthcenters/.

30. Joint Committee on Health Education Terminology (1974). "New Definitions: Report of the 1972–73 Joint Committee on Health Education Terminology." *Journal of School Health*, 44(1): 33–37.

31. Centers for Disease Control and Prevention (2014). *School Health Index: A Self-Assessment and Planning Guide.* Atlanta, GA: Author. Available at http://www.cdc.gov/healthyschools/shi/index.htm.

32. Henderson, A., and D. E. Rowe (1998). "A Healthy School Environment." In E. Marx, S. F. Wooley, and D. Northrop, eds., *Health Is Academic: A Guide to Coordinated School Health Programs.* New York: Teachers College Press, 96–115.

33. Centers for Disease Control and Prevention (2012). *Health Education Curriculum Assessment Tool.* Atlanta: Author. Available at http://www.cdc.gov/healthyyouth/HECAT/index.htm.

34. Institute of Medicine (1997). *Schools and Health: Our Nation's Investment.* Washington, DC: National Academies Press.

35. Joint Committee on National Health Education Standards (2007). *National Health Education Standards*, 2nd ed. Atlanta, GA: Author.

36. Joint Committee on National Health Education Standards (1995). *National Health Education Standards.* Atlanta, GA: American Cancer Society.

37. Division of Adolescent and School Health, Centers for Disease Control and Prevention (2012). *Adolescent and School Health: Registries of Programs Effective in Reducing Youth Risk Behaviors.* Available at http://www.cdc.gov/healthyyouth/AdolescentHealth/registries .htm.

38. U.S. Department of Health and Human Services, Office for Substance Abuse Prevention (1989). *Drug-Free Committees: Turning Awareness into Action* (DHHS pub. no. ADM 89–1562). Washington, DC: U.S. Government Printing Office.

39. U.S. Public Health Service. "Healthy People 2000: National Health Promotion and Disease Prevention Objectives and Health Schools." (1991). *Journal of School Health*, 61(7): 298–299.

40. Rosas, S., J. Case, and L. Tholstrup (2009). "A Retrospective Examination of the Relationship Between Implementation Quality of the Coordinated School Health Program Model and School-Level Academic Indicators Over Time." *Journal of School Health*, 79(3): 108–115.

41. Weiler, R., R. M. Pigg, and R. McDermott (2003). "Evaluation of the Florida Coordinated School Health Program Pilot Project." *Journal of School Health*, 73(1): 3–8.

42. Gold, R. S., G. S. Parcel, H. J. Walberg, R. V. Luepker, B. Portnoy, and E. J. Stone (1991). "Summary and Conclusions of the THTM Evaluation: The Expert Work Group Perspective." *Journal of School Health*, 61(1): 39–42.

43. U.S. Department of Agriculture Food and Nutrition Service, U.S. Department of Education, and DHHS Centers for Disease Control and Prevention (2016). *Local School Wellness Policy.* Available at http://www.fns.usda.gov/healthierschoolday /tools-schools#PolicyGuidance.

44. National Association of State Boards of Education (2016). *Coordinating or Advisory Councils.* Available at http://www.nasbe.org/healthy _schools/hs/bytopics.php?topicid=6100&catExpand=acdnbtm_catF.

45. Cleary, M. J. (1991). "School Health Education and a National Curriculum: One Disconcerting Scenario." *Journal of School Health*, 61(8): 355–358.

46. Centers for Disease Control and Prevention, Division of Adolescent and School Health (1997). "Is School Health Education Cost-Effective? An Exploratory Analysis of Selected Exemplary Components." As quoted in F. D. McKenzie and J. B. Richmond (1998). "Linking Health and Learning: An Overview of Coordinated School Health Programs." In E. Marx, S. F. Wooley, and D. Northrop, eds., *Health Is Academic: A*

Guide to Coordinated School Health Programs. New York: Teachers College Press, 1–14.

47. Council on Scientific Affairs, American Medical Association (1990). "Providing Medical Services through School-Based Health Programs." *Journal of School Health*, 60(3): 87–91.

48. Lear, J. G., L. L. Montgomery, J. J. Schlitt, and K. D. Rickett (1996). "Key Issues Affecting School-Based Health Centers and Medicaid." *Journal of School Health*, 66(3): 83–88.

49. School-Based Health Alliance. (2016). *2013–14 Census of School-Based Health Centers.* Available at http://www.sbh4all .org/school-health-care/national-census-of-school-based -health-centers/.

50. School-Based Health Alliance (2016). "Core Competencies." Available at http://www.sbh4all.org/resources/core-competencies/.

51. Ammerman, A. (2010). "School Based Health Care: Why It Is Common Sense." *SEEN Magazine.* Charlotte, NC: Knight Communications. Available at http://www.seenmagazine.us/Sections /ArticleDetail/tabid/79/ArticleID/582/smid/403/reftab/317 /Default.aspx.

52. Pacheco, M., W. Powell, C. Cole, N. Kalishman, R. Benon, and A. Kaufmann (1991). "School-Based Clinics: The Politics of Change." *Journal of School Health*, 61(2): 92–94.

53. Rienzo, B. A., and J. W. Button (1993). "The Politics of School-Based Clinics: A Community-Level Analysis." *Journal of School Health*, 63(6): 266–272.

54. The School-Based Adolescent Health Care Program (1993). *The Answer Is at School: Bringing Health Care to Our Students.* Washington, DC: Author.

55. Morone, J. A., E. H. Kilbreth, and K. M. Langwell (2001). "Back to School: A Health Care Strategy for Youth." *Health Affairs*, 20(1): 122–136.

56. Strolin-Goltzman, J. (2010). "The Relationship between School-Based Health Centers and the Learning Environment." *Journal of School Health*, 80(3): 153–159.

57. Webber, M., K. Carpiniello, T. Oruwariye, Y. Lo, W. Burton, and D. Appel. (2003). "Burden of Asthma in Inner-City Elementary School Children: Do School-Based Health Centers Make a Difference?" *Archives of Pediatrics and Adolescent Medicine*, 157: 125–129.

58. National Center for Education Statistics (2015). *Indicators of School Crime and Safety: 2014.* Available at https://nces.ed.gov/programs /crimeindicators/crimeindicators2014/.

59. Anspaugh, D. J., and G. Ezell (2001). *Teaching Today's Health*, 6th ed. Boston: Allyn and Bacon.

60. Centers for Disease Control and Prevention (2014). "Youth Risk Behavior Surveillance—United States, 2013." *MMWR Surveillance Summaries*, 63(SS-4).

61. U.S. Department of Health and Human Services (2016). stopbullying .gov. Available at http://www.stopbullying.gov/what-is-bullying /definition/index.html.

62. Hertz, M. F., and C. David-Ferdon (2008). *Electronic Media and Youth Violence: A CDC Issue Brief for Educators and Caregivers.* Atlanta, GA: Centers for Disease Control and Prevention.

63. Centers for Disease Control and Prevention (2001). "School Health Guidelines to Prevent Unintentional Injuries and Violence." *Morbidity and Mortality Weekly Report*, 50(RR-22): 1–75.

CHAPTER 7

Maternal, Infant, and Child Health

Chapter Objectives

After studying this chapter, you will be able to:

1. Summarize maternal, infant, and child health.

2. Explain the importance of maternal, infant, and child health as indicators of a society's health.

3. Discuss family planning and explain why it is important.

4. Identify consequences of teenage pregnancies.

5. Define legalized abortion and discuss *Roe v. Wade* and the pro-life and pro-choice movements.

6. Discuss maternal mortality rate.

7. Define preconception and prenatal care and the influence this has on pregnancy outcome.

8. Illustrate the major factors that contribute to infant health and mortality.

9. Explain the differences among infant mortality, neonatal mortality, and postneonatal mortality.

10. State the leading causes of childhood morbidity and mortality.

11. List the immunizations required for a 2-year-old child to be considered fully immunized.

12. Explain how health insurance and health care services affect childhood health.

13. Identify important governmental programs developed to improve maternal and child health.

14. Briefly describe what WIC programs are and who they serve.

15. Identify the major groups that are recognized as advocates for children.

Scenario

Joan is 18 years old and a recent high school graduate. She lives in a small town of about 2,700 people. Most of the town's residents rely on a larger city nearby for shopping, recreation, and health care. Joan had dated Dave the past 2 years, but there was never any talk of marriage. Just before graduation she learned that she was pregnant. At Thanksgiving, just as she was completing her seventh month of pregnancy, she went into premature labor. An ambulance rushed her to the emergency room of the hospital in the nearby city for what became the premature birth of her baby. While Joan was in recovery, doctors determined that her baby was not only premature, it also appeared to have other "developmental abnormalities." When asked whether she had received any prenatal care, Joan replied, "No, I couldn't afford it; besides, I didn't know where to go to get help."

Introduction

Creating a health profile of Americans requires a clear understanding of the health-related problems and opportunities of all Americans. Elsewhere in the text we discussed the role of descriptive epidemiology in understanding the health of populations. In describing the personal characteristics of a population, age is the first and perhaps the most important population characteristic to consider when describing the occurrence of disease, injury, and/or death in a population. Because health and age are related, community and public health professionals look at rates for specific age groups when comparing the amount of disease between populations. When they analyze data by age, they use groups that are narrow enough to detect any age-related patterns, which may be present as a result of either the natural life cycle or behavioral patterns. Viewing age-group profiles in this manner enables community and public health workers to identify risk factors for specific age groups within the population and to develop interventions aimed at reducing these risk factors. Health promotion and disease prevention programs that are successful in reducing exposure to such risk factors within specific age groups can improve the health status of the entire population.

In this chapter, we present a health profile of mothers, infants (those younger than 1 year), and children (ages 1–9 years). In the following two chapters, the health profiles will be presented for adolescents and young adults (10–24), adults (25–64), and older adults or seniors (65 and older). Various sources may group ages differently to describe and measure health status. In this book, we will consider children as those ages 1–9, which is consistent with how the World Health Organization and many public health professionals define the child age group.

Maternal, infant, and child health encompasses the health of women of childbearing age from pre-pregnancy through pregnancy, labor, delivery, and the postpartum period, and the health of the child prior to birth up to adolescence.[1] In this chapter, we define and discuss commonly used indicators for measuring maternal, infant, and child health; examine the risk factors associated with maternal, infant, and child morbidity and mortality; and review selected community programs aimed at improving the health of women of childbearing age, infants, and children in the United States.

Maternal, infant, and child health is important to a community for several reasons. First, maternal, infant, and child health statistics are regarded as important indicators of the effectiveness of the disease prevention and health promotion services in a community. It is known that unintended pregnancies, late or no prenatal care, poor maternal and child nutrition, maternal drug use, low immunization rates, poverty, limited education, and insufficient child care—combined with a lack of access to health care services in a community—are precursors to high rates of maternal, infant, and childhood morbidity and mortality. Second, we now know that many of the risk factors specified can be reduced or prevented with the early intervention of educational programs and preventive medical services for women, infants, and children. These early community efforts provide a positive environment that supports

Maternal, infant, and child health the health of women of childbearing age and that of the child up to adolescence

the physical and emotional needs of the family and reduces the need for more costly medical or social assistance to these same members of society later in their lives (see **Figure 7.1**).

During the past several decades, the United States has made important progress in reducing infant and maternal mortality. However, despite these declines in mortality rates, challenges remain. Possibly the most important concern is that infant and maternal mortality data for the United States are characterized by a continual and substantial disparity between mortality rates for white and black infants and mothers. The mortality rate among infants of non-Hispanic black mothers (11.1 per 1,000 live births) was over two times the rate among infants of non-Hispanic white mothers (5.06 per 1,000 live births) and infants of Hispanic mothers (5.00 per 1,000 live births) in 2013 (see **Figure 7.2**).[2] The pregnancy-related mortality ratio (a maternal death occurring within 1 year after the pregnancy ends, that was related to or aggravated by the pregnancy or its management) among black women (38.9 per 100,000 live births) was about three times the rate among white women (12.0 per 100,000 live births) during 2006 to 2010.[3] These disparities may not be directly attributable to race or ethnicity, although certain diseases do occur more often among individuals of certain races or ethnicities. Often race and ethnicity are proxy measures for other factors such as socioeconomic status that may actually be at the root of observed disparities. For example, research indicates that low income and limited education correlate very highly with poor health status.[4] The United States has a higher infant mortality rate than other industrialized nations; it ranked 26th in infant mortality in 2010 (see **Figure 7.3**).[5] These differences among industrialized nations mirror differences in the health status of women before and during pregnancy; availability of preventive care; and ease of access, quantity, and quality of medical care for pregnant women and their infants.

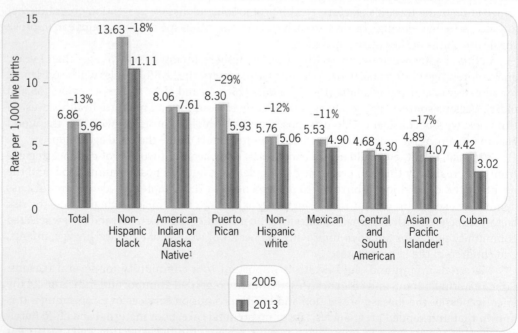

[1]Includes persons of Hispanic and non-Hispanic origin.

FIGURE 7.2 Infant mortality rates, by race and Hispanic origin of mother; United States, 2005 and 2013.

Source: Modified from: Mathews T.J., M.F. MacDorman, and M.E. Thoma. (2015). "Infant Mortality Statistics from the 2013 Period Linked Birth /Infant Death Data Set." *National Vital Statistics Reports*, 64(9). Hyattsville, MD: National Centers for Health Statistics. Available at http://www .cdc.gov/nchs/data/nvsr/nvsr64/nvsr64_09.pdf.

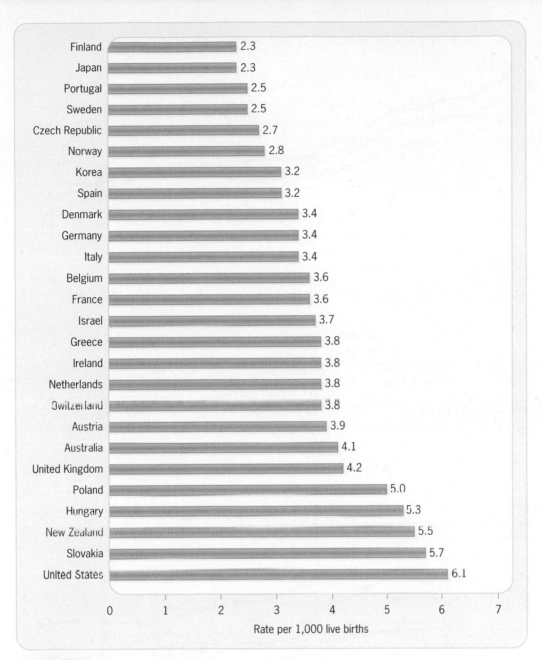

FIGURE 7.3   Comparison of national infant mortality rates, 2010.

Data from: Mathews T. J., M. F. MacDorman, A.G. Mohangoo, and J. Zeitlin (2014). "International Comparisons of Infant Mortality and Related Factors: United States and Europe, 2010" *National Vital Statistics Reports*, 63(5). Hyattsville, MD: National Centers for Health Statistics. Available at http://www.cdc.gov/nchs/data/nvsr/nvsr63/nvsr63_05.pdf.

Similar to the decline in infant and maternal mortality rates, the mortality rates of children and young adolescents (ages 1–14) have gone down significantly in the past couple of decades. The death rate declined from 64 to 26 per 100,000 population among 1- to 4-year-old children (see **Figure 7.4**) and 31 to 13 per 100,000 population among 5- to 14-year-olds between 1980 and 2013. Although the rates have declined over time, disparities between races and ethnicities persist (see **Figure 7.5**).[6]

Even with these improvements in child mortality rates, there is still much to be done to improve the health of American children. First, we must recognize that children today face other concerns that can put them at risk for poor health. These concerns have been referred to

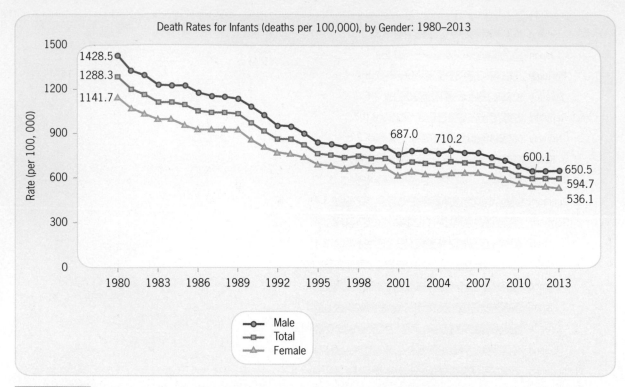

FIGURE 7.4 Death rates for Infants (deaths per 100,000): selected years, 1980–2013.

Data from: Child Trends DataBank (2015). "Infant, Child, and Teen Mortality." Available at http://www.childtrends.org/wp-content/uploads/2012/11/63_Child _Mortality.pdf.

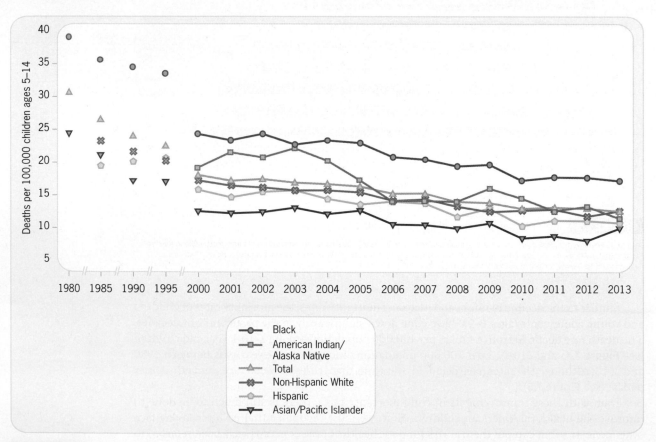

FIGURE 7.5 Death rates among children ages 5 to 14 by race and Hispanic origin: 1980–2013.

Data from: Child Trends DataBank (2015). "Infant, Child, and Teen -Mortality." Available at http://www.childtrends.org/wp-content/uploads/2012/11/63_Child_Mortality.pdf.

BOX 7.1   Each Day in America for All Children

2 mothers die in childbirth.

4 children are killed by abuse or neglect.

5 children or teens commit suicide.

7 children or teens are killed by guns.

24 children or teens die from accidents.

66 babies die before their first birthdays.

187 children are arrested for violent crimes.

408 children are arrested for drug crimes.

838 public school students are corporally punished.*

847 babies are born to teen mothers.

865 babies are born at low birth weight.

1,241 babies are born without health insurance.

1,392 babies are born into extreme poverty.

1,837 children are confirmed as abused or neglected.

2,723 babies are born into poverty.

2,857 high school students drop out.*

4,028 children are arrested.

4,408 babies are born to unmarried mothers.

16,244 public school students are suspended.*

*Based on 180 school days a year.

Reproduced from: Children's Defense Fund (2014). *The State of America's Children.* Available at http://www.childrensdefense.org/library/state-of
-americas-children/2014-soac.pdf?utm_source=2014-SOAC-PDF&utm_medium=link&utm_campaign=2014-SOAC. Accessed December 6, 2015.

---

as the "new morbidities" and include their family and social environments, behaviors, economic security, and education (see **Box 7.1**).[7] Second, we must be concerned about the difference in mortality rates between races. If the young are indeed the hope for the future, the United States must continue to work hard to ensure the health of each infant and child, regardless of race or socioeconomic status.

Whereas numerous factors affect the health of both infant and child, many reflect or are related to the health status of the mother and her immediate environment. One of the first steps to ensure healthy children is to ensure that pregnant women have access to prenatal care early in pregnancy and that they receive proper care throughout. There is nothing more dependent than a fetus in a mother's uterus relying on her to eat nutritiously and to avoid drugs or a newborn that is reliant on an adult to survive and develop into a healthy child. Therefore, we begin by looking at the health status of mothers and the family structure.

Family and Reproductive Health

The family is one of society's most treasured foundations. It represents a primary social group that influences and is influenced by other people and establishments. Moreover, families are the primary unit in which infants and children are nurtured and supported regarding their healthy development.[1] The U.S. Census Bureau defines a family as "a group of two people or more (one of whom is the householder) related by birth, marriage, or adoption and residing together; all such people (including related subfamily members) are considered as members of one family."[8] This definition does not include a variety of cultural styles and optional family structures that exist in our society today. Friedman broadens the definition of family to include "two or more persons who are joined together by bonds of sharing and emotional closeness and who identify themselves as being part of the family."[9] It is important to remember that the concept of family has changed over time, varies greatly depending on social and cultural norms and values, and may be conceptualized differently on an individual basis.

With delays in childbearing, increases in cohabitation, and changes in societal norms related to having children outside of marriage, the percentage of births to unmarried women has risen over the past several decades, although there was a decline between 2009 and 2013. In 2013, the percentage of births to unmarried women was 40.6%, or more than double the 18.4% of live births to unmarried women that occurred in 1980.[10] Historically, having children out of wedlock was associated with teen childbearing given that half of all women who had a baby out of wedlock were under 20 years of age. However, the distribution of unmarried childbearing has shifted with more births to older unmarried women.[11] Births to unmarried teenagers have dropped and births to unmarried women in their twenties and thirties have increased.[10,11]

Unmarried births also vary among other population subgroups. For example, in 2013, 35.8% of births to non-Hispanic white women were out of wedlock, whereas 71.0% of births to non-Hispanic black women were out of wedlock.[10] Unmarried women are more likely than married women to experience negative birth outcomes including low birth weight, preterm birth, small for gestational age, and fetal and infant death.[12,13] These associations are likely due to differences in social and financial support, as well as other factors that may differ between married and unmarried individuals. For example, a study using data from the National Survey of Family Growth (NSFG) found that unmarried women are more likely to smoke and to experience an unintended pregnancy compared with married women.[14] Married women were also more likely than those who were unmarried and non-cohabitating to initiate prenatal care during the first 4 months of pregnancy and were less likely to depend on government assistance to pay for prenatal care.[14]

It is important to keep in mind that within the marital status categories, women are still very heterogeneous. For example, "unmarried" includes both women who are single and those who are cohabitating with the father of their child. For the risk factors and pregnancy outcomes mentioned above, cohabitating women generally fall in between those who are married and those who are single but not cohabitating. For example, the odds of having a low birth weight baby are lowest for married women, higher for cohabitating women, and highest for single women who are not cohabitating.[12]

Teenage Births

Teenage childbearing represents a significant social and financial burden on both the family and the community. Teenage pregnancies are more likely to result in serious health consequences for these women and their babies compared to those who delay childbearing until their twenties. Teenage mothers are much less likely than women age 20 and older to receive early prenatal care and are more likely to smoke during pregnancy, have a preterm birth, and have a baby who has a low birth weight (see **Figure 7.6**).[15] As a consequence of these and other factors, babies born to teenagers are more likely to die during the first year of life than a baby born to a mother aged 20 years or older.[15] A teenage mother is at greater risk for many pregnancy complications including premature delivery and low birth weight.[15] Studies have also found that teen mothers are at an increased risk of intimate partner violence during pregnancy compared with older women.[16] Early and adequate prenatal care is critical for identifying and managing health and social issues early in the pregnancy to increase the likelihood of having a safe pregnancy and a healthy child.

Unfortunately, the adverse consequences related to teen pregnancy do not end when the child is born. Teenagers who become pregnant and have a child are more likely than their peers who are not mothers to (1) drop out of school, (2) not get married or to have a marriage end in divorce, (3) rely on public assistance, and (4) live in poverty.[17,18] It is difficult to determine the actual impact of teen pregnancy because the women who face educational, economic, and social hardships may be more likely to experience a teen pregnancy

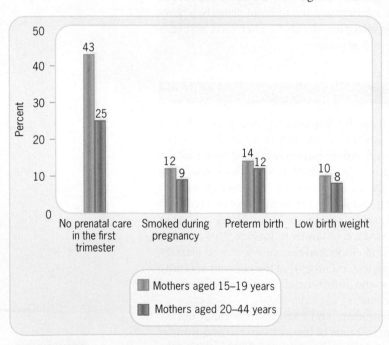

FIGURE 7.6 Selected characteristics by age of the mother—United States, 2010.

Note: Data for prenatal care and smoking are limited to those states using the 2003 revision of the U.S. birth certificate at the beginning of 2010. This includes 33 states plus the District of Columbia (76% of all births in the United States).

Data from: Kaye, K. (2012). *Why It Matters: Teen Childbearing and Infant Health.* The National Campaign to Prevent Teen and Unplanned Pregnancy. Available at http://www.thenationalcampaign.org/why-it-matters/pdf/Childbearing-Infant-Health.pdf.

in the first place. Although teen childbearing may not be the sole cause of these hardships, it does make it more difficult to overcome them. Children born to teenage mothers have an increased risk of being abused or neglected and of experiencing lower educational attainment. Sons of teen mothers are more likely to be imprisoned at some point, and daughters are more likely to become teenage mothers themselves when compared with children born to older mothers.[19] Teenage pregnancy and childbearing also have substantial economic consequences for society. In 2010, teenage childbearing cost taxpayers at least $9.4 billion in costs associated with health care, foster care, incarceration, and lost tax revenue.[20] The consequences of teen childbearing make it clear that teenage pregnancies are a significant community health concern in the United States.

Teen pregnancy and birth rates have declined steadily in recent years, in large part as a result of effective community and public health campaigns aimed at reducing teenage pregnancies. Between 1991 and 2013, the teenage birth rate in the United States declined by 57% to 26.5 births per 1,000 teenagers.[10] Despite the recently declining rates, roughly one in four teenage girls get pregnant at least once before they reach age 20, resulting in approximately 273,105 teen pregnancies per year.[10,21] In fact, the United States still leads the industrialized world in teen pregnancy and birth rates by a large margin.[22]

As stated in the introduction, the future of our nation depends on our children. The extent to which we actually believe this can be measured by the degree to which we plan, provide for, educate, and protect our children. Yet, every day in America, 4,408 babies are born to unmarried mothers; 2,723 are born into poverty; 1,837 are confirmed as abused or neglected; 1,241 are born without health insurance; 847 are born to teenage mothers; 865 are born at a low birth weight; and 66 die before their first birthdays.[7] The need to plan a pregnancy and thereby place children first in families and in communities must be reemphasized. Unwanted and unplanned childbearing has long been linked with adverse consequences for mothers, couples, and families as well as for the children themselves.[23]

The choice to become a parent is a critical decision that affects the individual and the community. People who become parents acquire the major responsibility for another human being. They must provide an environment conducive to child development—one that protects and promotes health. However, the broader community also contributes to this growth and development. This is best illustrated by an African proverb, "it takes an entire village to educate and raise a child."[24] Therefore, the community must also make provisions for a child's care, nurture, and socialization.

Family Planning

Family planning gives individuals and couples the ability to determine the number and spacing of their children. Deciding whether or not to become a parent is an important and consequential decision. Parenthood requires enormous amounts of time, energy, and financial commitment, but most notably it requires the willingness to take full responsibility for a child's growth and development. Planning a pregnancy is the first step to ensuring the best health for the mother and fetus during the pregnancy. Unfortunately, approximately one-half of pregnancies in the United States are unintended, and 43% of those end in abortion.[25] The United States has set a national goal of increasing the percentage of pregnancies that are intended to 56% by 2020.[23]

An unintended pregnancy is a pregnancy that at the time of conception is either mistimed (the woman did not want to be pregnant until later) or unwanted (the woman did not want to be pregnant at any time). Unintended pregnancy is associated with a range of behaviors that can adversely affect the health of mothers and their babies. These risky behaviors include delayed entry into prenatal care and the use of harmful substances such as tobacco or alcohol, likely due to failure to recognize the pregnancy as early as if it had been planned.[26] Planning for pregnancy affords opportunities to address health issues and to adopt healthy practices, such as taking folic acid, that will help to increase the likelihood of a healthy pregnancy and delivery. The rate of unintended births is highest among women ages

Family planning determining the preferred number and spacing of children and choosing the appropriate means to accomplish it

Title X a portion of the Public Health Service Act of 1970 that provides funds for family planning services for low-income people

Gag rule regulations that barred physicians and nurses in clinics receiving federal funds from counseling clients about abortions

18–24, unmarried women (particularly those who are cohabitating), low-income women, those with lower educational attainment, and minority women.[25]

The NSFG collects information to better understand unintended pregnancy. Using a 10-point scale, with 1 being "very unhappy to be pregnant" and 10 being "very happy to be pregnant," women were asked to report how they felt upon finding out they were pregnant. The average mean rating was 9.4 for intended pregnancies and 4.8 for unwanted pregnancies.[27] These indicators reemphasize the importance of community health education programs for family planning.

Family planning is critical for reducing unwanted pregnancies and their adverse consequences. **Family planning** is defined as the process of determining the preferred number and spacing of children in one's family and choosing the appropriate means to achieve this preference. Although many maternal, infant, and child morbidity and mortality outcomes cannot be completely prevented by effective family planning, the frequency of occurrence can be reduced. Thus, preconception education and good gynecological and maternal health care are required for effective family planning.[23] Given that nearly half of pregnancies are unintended, achieving and maintaining a good health status during the reproductive years is critical.

Preconception care focuses on the health of both men and women, even before they are considering having children. For women, this includes making healthy choices and working with a health care provider for education and early identification of any health issues. The goal is for a woman to be as healthy as possible before getting pregnant. For example, a woman may work with her health care provider to stop smoking, start taking folic acid, or achieve a healthy weight. Preconception health includes men too, as they need to maintain a healthy lifestyle and support healthy choices for their partner.

Community involvement in family planning programs has historically included both governmental and nongovernmental health organizations in the United States. The federal and state governments provide funding assistance through a myriad of family planning services, including Title X of the Public Health Service Act, Medicaid, state funds, the Maternal and Child Health Bureau, and Social Service block grants. Of these, Title X, or the Family Planning Act, is the only federal program dedicated solely to funding family planning and related reproductive health care services through the National Family Planning Program (Public Law 91-572).[28] **Title X** of the Public Health Service Act was signed into law by President Nixon in 1970 to provide family planning services to all who wanted, but could not afford them. For over four decades, Title X has been this nation's major program to reduce unintended pregnancy by providing contraceptive and other reproductive health care services, such as screening for sexually transmitted infections, to low-income women. Currently, it provides funding support to a network of 4,100 family planning centers nationwide. Every year approximately 4 million women receive health care services at family planning clinics funded by Title X. Those served are predominantly female, poor, uninsured, and have never had a child.[29]

Family planning services are provided through state, county, and local health departments, community centers, Planned Parenthood centers, and hospital-, school-, and faith-based organizations.[30] The administration of all Title X grants is through state health departments or regional agencies that subcontract with local agencies and clinics. In 2014, slightly more than half of the grantees were state and local health departments, and the rest were nonprofit agencies, independent service sites, and community health agencies.[29]

For clinics to receive funding under the Title X program, they must offer a broad range of acceptable family planning methods (e.g., oral contraceptives, condoms, sterilization, and abstinence); they must encourage family participation; they must give priority to low-income families, and they must not use abortion as a method of family planning.[31] In addition to family planning methods, clinics also provide a comprehensive group of other health services critical to their clients' sexual and reproductive health (see **Figure 7.7**).[32]

In 1981, family planning clinics that received federal funds were required to provide counseling on all options open to a pregnant woman, including abortion, as outlined in Title X. However, these facilities were not allowed to perform abortions. In 1984, the "**gag rule**" regulations

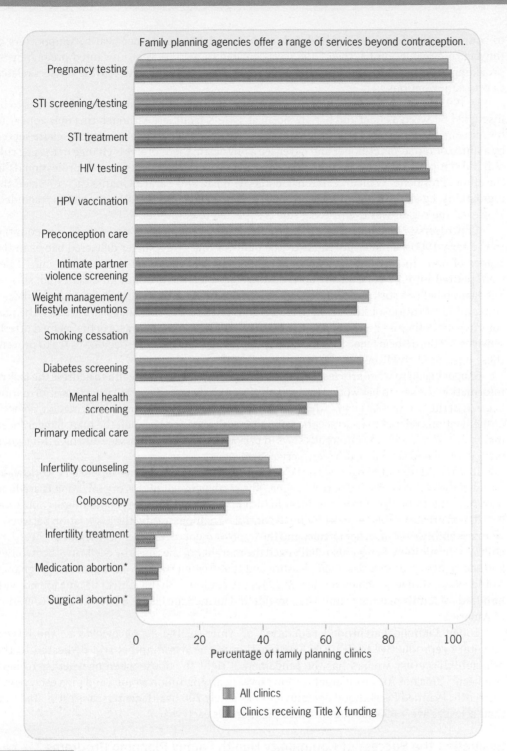

Family planning agencies offer a range of services beyond contraception.

FIGURE 7.7 A significant proportion of women rely on family planning clinics for their reproductive health care.

Data from: Frost J.J., et al. (2012). *Variation In Service Delivery Practices Among Clinics Providing Publicly Funded Family Planning Services in 2010.* New York: Guttmacher Institute. Available at www.guttmacher.org/pubs/clinic-survey-2010.pdf.

*Clinics receiving Title X funding that provide abortion services use private sources of funding to pay for these services.

were enacted. These regulations barred physicians and nurses in clinics receiving federal funds from counseling clients about abortions. Family planning providers challenged this legislation on the grounds that it denied women their right to information that was needed to make an informed decision. Many health care providers believed that the gag rule restricted their right to counsel a client even when childbirth could be detrimental to her health.[33] Supporters of the gag rule regulation felt that Title X was created to help prevent unwanted pregnancy by providing education and contraception services and was not intended to provide services related to pregnancy options.

In 1992, congressional action loosened the gag rule and allowed for abortion options to be discussed between a client and her physician at Title X facilities. Although this may appear to be a reasonable compromise, in reality most women who visit family planning clinics are served by a nurse or nurse-practitioner and never see a physician; therefore, this change in the gag rule still did not permit the free exchange of information between clients and all professionals in the clinic. Presidents William Clinton, George W. Bush, and Barack Obama each reversed the regulations regarding the gag rule set by their predecessor, and as of 2015, the rule is rescinded. However, the tug-of-war over the gag rule is expected to continue.[34]

Controversy regarding acceptable family planning methods is not new in our country. In the early 1900s, a maternity nurse by the name of Margaret Sanger delivered babies in the homes of poor, mostly immigrant women. She described her experiences by writing: "Tales were poured into my ears, a baby born dead, great relief, the death of an older child, sorrow but again relief of a sort . . . the story told a thousand times of death and abortion and children going into institutions. I shuddered with horror as I listened to the details and studied the reasons in back of them—destitution with excessive childbearing. The waste of life seemed utterly senseless."[35] So, disheartened by her inability to provide solutions, she decided to try to prevent these unwanted conditions in the first place.

Sanger began to write articles about sex education and women's health to address the lack of information she saw in her work. However, she faced challenges disseminating this information because of the "Comstock Laws," which made it a federal offense to provide information, devices, or medications related to contraception and unlawful abortion through the mail. Sanger faced many obstacles, including numerous stays in prison, to spread her message during a time when birth control and sexual health were very controversial.

In 1921, Margaret Sanger, with the help of funds from numerous supporters worldwide, founded the National Birth Control League. The establishment of this organization is credited with starting the birth control movement in the United States. The purpose of this organization was to win greater public support for birth control by demonstrating the association between a woman's ability to control her fertility and the improvement of both her health and the health of children. In addition, Sanger also challenged the morality of the times by declaring that women had the right to experience sexual pleasure and that freeing them from the fear of pregnancy would assist women in achieving this. In 1942, the National Birth Control League joined with hundreds of family planning clinics nationwide and formed the Planned Parenthood Federation of America.[36]

Today, Planned Parenthood Federation of America, Inc. has grown to be the largest voluntary reproductive health care organization in the world and is still dedicated to the principle that every woman has the fundamental right to choose when or whether to have children.[37] This not-for-profit organization serves nearly 5 million women and men each year.[38] Currently, Planned Parenthood operates approximately 700 health centers; it is estimated that their services avert >500,000 unintended pregnancies each year.[38]

Evaluating the Success of Community Health Family Planning Programs

The establishment of local family planning clinics, many of which receive funding through Title X, has resulted in an improvement in maternal and child health indicators for the communities served.[32] Many people in need of family planning services are uninsured and rely on family planning clinics that may provide contraception at minimal or no cost. Title X funding enables the support network of 4,100 clinics that provide comprehensive family planning services to approximately 4 million women each year, 91% of whom are low income, and a fifth of whom are adolescents.[29] By providing access to contraceptive materials, instructions on how to use contraception effectively, and counseling about reproductive health matters, community family planning clinics are able to show large reductions in unintended pregnancies, abortions, and births. Each year, publicly subsidized family planning services help prevent 1.7 million unplanned pregnancies, which would otherwise result in 831,000 unintended births and 572,000 abortions. Publicly funded family planning services are vital to enabling low-income women to avoid unintended pregnancy. In fact, the number of unintended pregnancies among poor women would be two times higher if publicly funded family planning services were not available.[39] From an economic perspective, each public health dollar spent to help women avoid unwanted pregnancies saves taxpayers $7.09 for every public dollar spent.[39]

The Affordable Care Act (ACA)'s expanded regulations required new private health plans written on or after August 1, 2012 to cover contraceptive counseling, services, and prescriptions at no out-of-pocket cost to patients. For many plans, this requirement took effect in January 2013.[40,41] Since that time, the changes have led to an estimated 48 million women having guaranteed access to free preventive women's health services, despite some inconsistencies in the implementation of the law.[40,41] However, despite the increase in health insurance coverage through the ACA, a 2014 study found that 36% of visits to Title X-funded clinics were by patients without insurance coverage, and many insured persons still depended upon these clinics to provide access to care.[42]

Abortion

One of the most important outcomes of community family planning programs is preventing abortions. Abortion has been legal throughout the United States since 1973 when the Supreme Court ruled in the **Roe v. Wade** case that women, in consultation with their physician, have a constitutionally protected right to have an abortion in the first trimester of pregnancy, free from government interference.[43] Since 1969, the Centers for Disease Control and Prevention (CDC) have been documenting the number and characteristics of women obtaining legal induced abortions to monitor unintended pregnancy and to assist with efforts to identify and reduce preventable causes of morbidity and mortality associated with abortions.[44] As a result of the *Roe v. Wade* decision, the number of women dying from illegal abortions has diminished sharply during the last three decades in the United States. However, doubters remain, largely among those whose main strategy for reducing abortion is to outlaw it. However, although it may seem paradoxical, the legal status of abortion appears to have relatively little connection to its overall pervasiveness.

The number, rate (number of abortions per 1,000 women 15–44 years of age), and ratio (number of abortions per 1,000 live births) of abortions declined gradually by 17%, 18%, and 14%, respectively between 2003 and 2012 (see **Figure 7.8**).[44] In 2012, 699,149 abortions were reported to the CDC by 49 reporting areas that provided data that year.[44] Women aged 20–29 make up the largest percentage of abortions (58.2%) and have the highest abortion rate compared with other age groups (**Figure 7.9**). A much higher percentage of abortions are to unmarried women (85.3%) compared to married women (14.7%).[44] Although the percentage of abortions to non-Hispanic white and non-Hispanic black women is similar (37.6% and 36.7%, respectively), non-Hispanic black women have the highest abortion rate (27.8 vs. 7.7 abortions per 1,000 non-Hispanic black women and non-Hispanic white women aged 15–44, respectively) and ratio (435 vs. 127 abortions per 1,000 live births for non-Hispanic black women and non-Hispanic white women, respectively).[44]

The fate of legalized abortion itself is as unclear as the right of a client to discuss abortion options in federally funded clinics. The Hyde Amendment of 1976 made it illegal to use federal funds to perform an abortion except in cases where the woman's life was in danger. The *Roe v. Wade* Supreme Court ruling made it unconstitutional for state laws to prohibit abortions. In effect, this decision concluded that an unborn child is not a person and therefore has no rights under the law. The decision of whether to have an abortion was left up to the woman until she was 12 weeks pregnant. After the twelfth week, an abortion was permissible only when the health of the mother was in question. In 1989, the Supreme Court appeared to reverse this decision. It ruled that the individual states could place restrictions on a woman's right to obtain an abortion. Some states now have a 24-hour waiting period after counseling before permitting an abortion.

Roe v. Wade a 1973 Supreme Court decision that made it unconstitutional for state laws to prohibit abortions in the first trimester for any reason and placed restrictions on the conditions under which states could regulate them in the second and third trimesters

Pro-life a medical/ethical position that holds that performing an abortion is an act of murder

Pro-choice a medical/ethical position that holds that women have a right to reproductive freedom

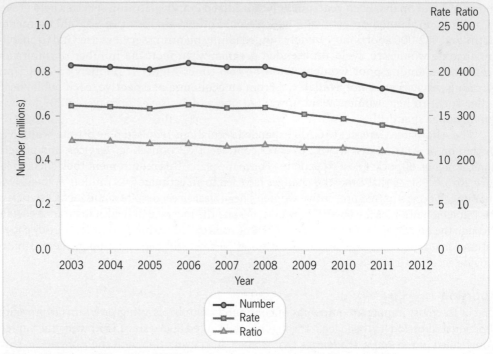

*Number of abortions per 1,000 women aged 15–44 years.
†Number of abortions per 1,000 live births.
§Data are for 47 reporting areas; excludes California, Louisiana, Maryland, New Hampshire, and West Virginia.

FIGURE 7.8   Number, rate, and ratio of abortions performed, by year in selected reporting areas—United States, 2003–2012.

Note: Rate is calculated as number of abortions per 1,000 women aged 15 to 44 years; ratio is calculated as number of abortions per 1,000 live births. Data are for 47 reporting areas (excludes California, Louisiana, Maryland, New Hampshire, and West Virginia).

Data from: Centers for Disease Control and Prevention (2015). "Abortion Surveillance—United States, 2012." *Morbidity and Mortality Weekly Report*, 64(10): 1–40.

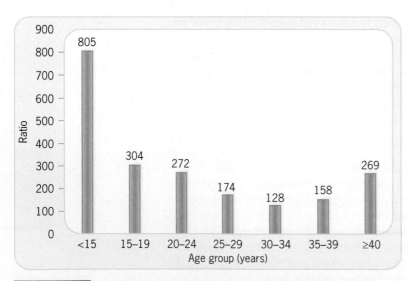

FIGURE 7.9   Abortion ratio, by age group in selected reporting areas—United States, 2012.

Note: Ratio is calculated as number of abortions per 1,000 live births. Data are for 45 areas (excludes California, District of Columbia, Florida, Maryland, New Hampshire, Vermont, and Wyoming).

Source: Modified from: Centers for Disease Control and Prevention (2015). "Abortion Surveillance—United States, 2012." *Morbidity and Mortality Weekly Report*, 64(10): 1–40.

The issue of abortion has become a hotly debated topic. Political appointments can be won or lost depending on a candidate's stance as "pro-life" or "pro-choice" on the abortion issue (see **Figure 7.10**).

Pro-life groups believe that life begins at conception and that an embryo is a person. Therefore, they conclude that performing an abortion is an act of murder. The **pro-choice** position is that women have a right to reproductive freedom. Pro-choice advocates think that the government should not be allowed to force a woman to carry to term and give birth to an unwanted child. Evidence shows that laws against abortion do not correspond with lower rates of abortion. In fact, the highest rates of abortion occur in countries where the practice is illegal, and the lowest rates are in countries where it is legal and access to contraception is high. This suggests that access to contraception and corresponding declines in unintended pregnancy are the most effective means to reducing abortions. In countries where abortion is illegal, women may resort to dangerous methods to terminate the pregnancy.[45] Unsafe abortions are a significant contributor to maternal death. There are also extenuating circumstances, such as rape or danger to the mother if she continues to carry the child, which make the issue less clear. There is no easy solution to the question of abortion, and determining when life begins can only be decided by each individual based on his or her own values and beliefs.

Maternal Health

Maternal health encompasses the health of women in the childbearing years, including those in the pre-pregnancy period, those who are pregnant, and those who are caring for young children (see **Figure 7.11**). The effect of pregnancy and childbirth on women is an important indicator of their health. Pregnancy and delivery can lead to serious health problems. Maternal mortality rates are the most severe measure of ill health for pregnant women.

The Tenth Revision of the *International Classification of Diseases* (ICD-10) defines a maternal death (maternal mortality) as "the death of a woman while pregnant or within 42 days of termination of pregnancy, irrespective of the duration and site of the pregnancy, from any cause related to or aggravated by the pregnancy or its management but not from accidental or incidental causes."[46] The maternal mortality rate is the number of mothers dying per 100,000 live births in a given year. Birth certificates can be used to determine the number of total live births, whereas the total number of pregnant women is unknown; therefore, the number of live births is used as the denominator even though maternal mortality includes women who died without having a live birth.

In the United States, the maternal mortality ratio has increased over time from 7.2 deaths per 100,000 live births in 1987 to 17.8 deaths per 100,000 live births in 2011. However, the reason for this increase is unclear and is likely due to changes in reporting.[47] Causes of maternal death vary greatly by geographic region, likely due to differences in medical care throughout pregnancy and delivery. Hemorrhage and hypertensive disorders (i.e., preeclampsia and eclampsia) account for the largest proportion of maternal deaths in developing countries.[48] In contrast, in the United States, deaths due to hemorrhage and hypertensive disorders have been declining as deaths due to complications related to cardiovascular disease and infection risk have been increasing. An increased number of pregnant women with chronic diseases such as hypertension and diabetes may be contributing to mortality in the United States (see **Figure 7.12**).[3,47]

Ninety-nine percent of maternal deaths occur in developing countries where the maternal mortality ratio is 239 deaths per 100,000 live births, compared with 12 per 100,000 live births in developed countries. Access to medical care is the primary reason for the difference in maternal mortality in developing countries.[49] Ensuring early initiation of prenatal care during maternity greatly contributes to reductions in perinatal illness, disability, and death for both the mother and the infant.[50] In addition, a number of underlying causes of high maternal morbidity and mortality rates include poverty, sociocultural factors, and limited education.

Preconception and Prenatal Health Care

Preconception and **prenatal health care** are essential for improving outcomes for mothers and infants. *Preconception care* is individualized care for both men and women that is designed to reduce maternal and fetal illness and mortality, increase the success of conception when pregnancy is desired, and to provide contraceptive education to prevent

FIGURE 7.10 Political appointments and elections can be won or lost on the issue of abortion.
© Joe Marquette/AP Photos.

FIGURE 7.11 Maternal health encompasses the health of women in the childbearing years.
© Monkey Business Images/Dreamstime.com.

Preconception health care medical care provided to a women of reproductive age to promote health prior to conception

Prenatal health care medical care provided to a pregnant woman from the time of conception until the birth process occurs

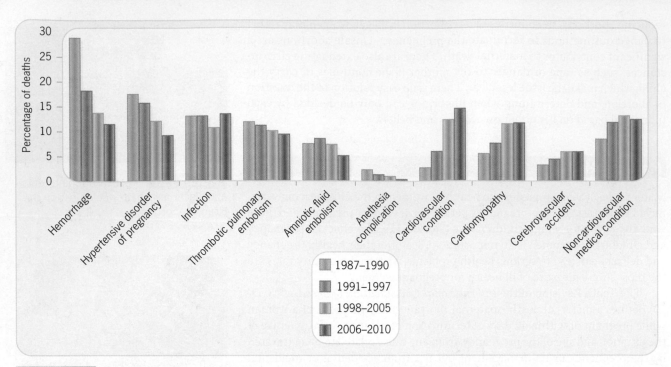

FIGURE 7.12   Cause-specific proportionate pregnancy-related mortality: United States, 1987–2010.

Reprinted from Creanga, A.A., C.J. Berg, C. Syverson, K. Seed, F.C. Bruce, and W.M. Callaghan (2015). Pregnancy-related mortality in the United States, 2006–2010. *Obstetrics and Gynecology*, 125(1), 5-12. doi: 10.1097/AOG.0000000000000564.

undesired pregnancy.[51] Often medical and behavioral risk factors that can lead to negative pregnancy outcomes can be identified and modified before conception.[52] Ideally, a woman will be obtaining preconception care prior to pregnancy and can transition into prenatal health care once her pregnancy begins. CDC encourages all women to develop a reproductive health plan and outlines steps that women can take to be ready for a healthy pregnancy (see **Box 7.2**).[53]

During prenatal visits, tests are performed on both the mother and fetus to assess any potential risks, to treat any maternal or fetal complications, and to monitor the growth and development of the fetus. In addition, counseling and guidance are provided regarding the various aspects of pregnancy, including weight gain, exercise, nutrition, and overall health. The woman and her provider will also discuss what to expect and options for the delivery.

BOX 7.2   Checklist for Preconception Health

1. Plan pregnancies.
2. Eat healthy foods.
3. Be active.
4. Take 400 micrograms (mcg) of folic acid daily.
5. Protect oneself from sexually transmitted infections (STIs).
6. Protect oneself from other infections.
7. Avoid harmful chemicals, metals, and other toxic substances around the home and in the workplace.
8. Make sure vaccinations are up to date.
9. Manage and reduce stress and get mentally healthy.
10. Stop smoking.
11. Stop using street drugs as well as prescription medicines that aren't yours.
12. Reduce alcohol intake before trying to get pregnant, and stop drinking while trying to get pregnant.
13. Stop partner violence.
14. Manage health conditions, such as asthma, diabetes, and overweight.
15. Learn about your family's health history.
16. Get regular checkups. See your doctor as needed for other problems.

Source: Centers for Disease Control and Prevention, National Center on Birth Defects and Developmental Disabilities. (n.d.). *Show Your Love: Steps to a Healthier Me and Baby-to-Be!* Available at http://www.cdc.gov/preconception/showyourlove/documents/Healthier_Baby_Me_Plan.pdf.

Nutrition counseling is especially critical early in pregnancy (and ideally would occur during preconception counseling), as many nutritional deficits can increase the risk for birth defects that develop in the first trimester. For example, pregnant women should have at least 400 micrograms of folic acid intake daily, which is often difficult to achieve through food sources alone, making prenatal vitamins an essential tool for prenatal nutritional health. Use of a multivitamin containing folic acid has been shown to reduce the risk of neural tube defects like spina bifida by two-thirds.[52,53]

Prenatal care is crucial to maternal and infant health. Women who receive early and continuous prenatal health care have better pregnancy outcomes than women who do not. A pregnant woman who receives no prenatal care is three times more likely to give birth to a **low birth weight infant** (one that weighs less than 5.5 pounds or 2,500 grams) as one who receives the appropriate care, and she is five times more likely to have her baby die in infancy.[54] Getting pregnant women into prenatal care early (during the first 3 months of pregnancy) is the main policy goal of most publicly funded programs designed to reduce the incidence of low birth weight and infant mortality in the United States. However, barriers to receiving prenatal care are complex and difficult to address. Barriers reported by women receiving late or no prenatal care included a lack of insurance coverage for visits; an inability to receive an appointment when desired; the mother being too busy, not having transportation, not knowing she was pregnant, and not wanting others to know she was pregnant.[55]

The percentage of women receiving prenatal care during the first trimester was 74.1% in 2012.[4] The target goal for 2020 is 77.9%.[23] Non-Hispanic black, non-Hispanic multiple race, Hispanic, American Indian/Alaska Native, and Native Hawaiian/Other Pacific Islander women were less likely to begin prenatal care in the first trimester in 2012.[4] Educational attainment is also associated with prenatal care—women with less than a high school education are the least likely to receive first trimester prenatal care (see **Figure 7.13**).[4]

> **Low birth weight infant**
> one that weighs less than 2,500 grams, or 5.5 pounds, at birth

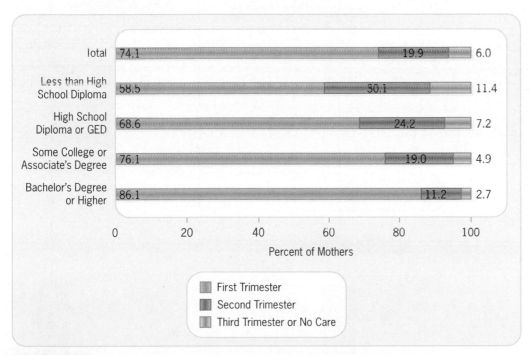

FIGURE 7.13   Timing of prenatal care initiation, by maternal education, 2012.

Note: Data are from the District of Columbia and 38 states that had implemented the 2003 revision of the U.S. birth certificate by the beginning of 2012. Percentages may not total to 100 due to rounding.

Data from: U.S. Department of Health and Human Services, Health Resources and Services Administration, Maternal and Child Health Bureau (2015). "Child Health USA 2014." Rockville, Maryland: U.S. Department of Health and Human Services. Available at http://mchb.hrsa.gov/chusa14/dl/chusa14.pdf.

Infant Health

An infant's health depends on many factors, which include the mother's health and her health behavior prior to and during pregnancy, genetic characteristics, level of prenatal care, the quality of her delivery, and the infant's environment after birth. The infant's environment includes not only the home and family environment, but also the availability of essential medical services such as a postnatal physical examination, regular visits to a physician, and the appropriate immunizations. The infant's health also depends on proper nutrition and other nurturing care in the home environment. Shortcomings in these areas can result in illness, developmental problems, and even the death of the child.

Infant Mortality

Infant death is an important measure of a nation's health because it is associated with a variety of factors, such as maternal health, quality of access to medical care, socioeconomic conditions, and public health practices.[23] An infant death (infant mortality) is the death of a child younger than 1 year (see **Figure 7.14**). The infant mortality rate is expressed as the number of deaths of children younger than 1 year per 1,000 live births.

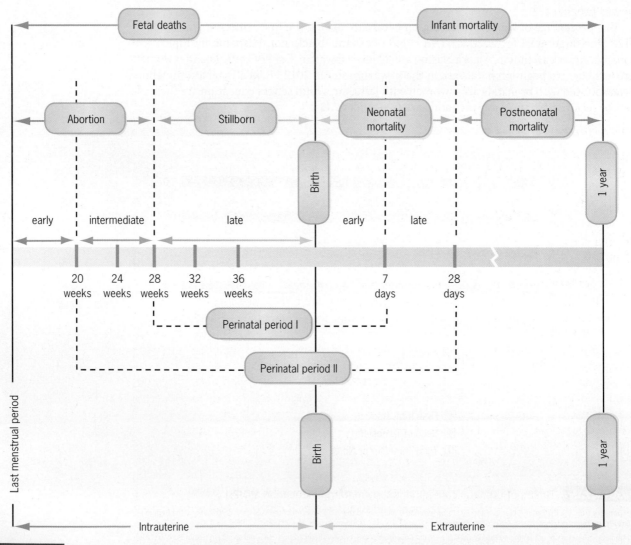

FIGURE 7.14   Important early-life mortality time periods.

The infant mortality rate has decreased substantially from the early 1900s.[4] Decreases in the infant mortality rate during this period have been attributed to economic growth, improved sanitation, advanced clinical care, improved access to health care, and better nutrition. Improvements made in the 1990s were attributed particularly to the availability of better treatment for respiratory distress syndrome and the recommendation that infants be placed on their backs when sleeping.[4] Between 2000 and 2005, there was a lack of improvement in infant mortality rates attributed to an increase in preterm births and obstetric interventions such as induction of labor and cesarean delivery. However, the rate has declined in more recent years (to 6.07 deaths per 1,000 live births in 2011) likely due to the decrease in early deliveries that were performed for non-medical reasons (see Figure 7.2).[4] The leading causes of infant death include congenital malformations, preterm birth/low birth weight, sudden infant death syndrome (SIDS), problems related to complications of pregnancy, and accidents.[56]

Infant deaths, or infant mortality, can be further divided into neonatal mortality and postneonatal mortality (see Figure 7.14). Neonatal mortality includes deaths that occur during the first 28 days after birth. Approximately two-thirds of all infant deaths take place during this period.[4] The most common causes of neonatal death are disorders related to short gestation (premature births) and low birth weight, congenital malformations, and complications of pregnancy.[56] Postneonatal mortality includes deaths that occur between 28 days and 365 days after birth. The most common causes of postneonatal deaths are SIDS, congenital malformations, and accidents.[56]

Disparities in infant mortality by racial and ethnicity are both great and persistent. In 2011, the infant mortality rate was highest for non-Hispanic Black mothers (11.45 per 1,000 live births). This is more than twice the rate for non-Hispanic White mothers. Both sudden unexplained infant death and increased rates of prematurity are thought to be the greatest contributor to these disparities in infant mortality in the United States.[4]

Improving Infant Health

In part because of medical research and public health and social services supported by both public and private organizations, infant mortality has declined considerably during the past couple of decades. However, there are many opportunities for decreasing infant deaths and improving infant health even further through reducing risk factors associated with these conditions.

Premature Births

The average length of gestation is 40 weeks, and premature (or preterm) babies are those born prior to 37 weeks of gestation. The preterm birth rate in the United States increased more than 20% between 1990 and 2006 but declined by 8% to 9.57% between 2007 and 2014.[11] Disorders related to short gestation and low birth weight are the leading causes of neonatal death in the United States.[56] Because premature babies usually have less developed organs than full-term babies, they are more likely to face serious multiple health problems following delivery. Premature babies often require neonatal intensive care, which utilizes specialized medical personnel and equipment. In the United States, preterm birth costs the health care system approximately $26 billion per year.[57] The majority of the expense is for medical care provided in infancy. Other factors that contribute to the economic burden are maternal care services, early intervention services, special education for preterm infants with learning difficulties, and lost labor productivity.[58] Although it is well established that babies born before 37 weeks have a higher risk of negative outcomes, development of key organs, such as the brain, lungs, and liver, actually occurs up until 39 weeks. In fact, the brain at 35 weeks only weighs two-thirds of what it will at 39 to 40 weeks. Infants born 39 weeks or later are less likely to have problems with vision and hearing, are more likely to gain adequate weight before delivery, and are more likely to be able to suck and swallow appropriately.[59] While labor occurs naturally for many women, some women decide with their doctors to have labor induced. This is where the doctor starts labor using medications or other methods, such as "breaking the woman's water." Inductions increase the risk of many problems including stronger, more painful contractions, infection, changes in the baby's heart rate, uterine rupture, and needing a cesarean section.[59] There has been a dramatic increase in labor inductions over the past two decades, with rates increasing from 9.6% in 1990 to 23.0% in 2013.[10,60] While inductions are sometimes done for medical reasons, there has been an increase in the number of inductions that are elective.[61] This means there is no medical reason for the induction, but it is done as a matter of convenience (e.g., scheduling the birth for a particular day and time) or preference (e.g., the woman is uncomfortable being pregnant or wants a certain doctor to perform the delivery). There are a lot of reasons a woman or her doctor could want an induction. Given the negative consequences associated with preterm and early term deliveries, an increase in elective inductions and elective cesarean section deliveries before 39 weeks gestation has resulted in a nationwide effort to reduce births before 39 weeks through provider and patient education and implementation of quality measures.[61]

Approximately half of all premature births have no known cause. Known major risk factors associated with preterm labor and birth include a woman's past history of preterm delivery, multiple fetuses, late or no prenatal care, cigarette smoking, drinking alcohol, using illegal drugs, exposure to domestic violence, lack of social support, low income, diabetes, anemia, high blood pressure, obesity, and being younger than 17 or older than 35 years of age.[58]

Therefore, although a number of causes of premature birth may have eluded researchers and are currently beyond our control, prenatal care and lifestyle changes can help women reduce their risk of having a premature delivery. Consequently, there is a lot that community health programs can do to assist a woman in reducing her risk of having a premature baby—specifically, educating parents about premature labor and what can be done to prevent it and expanding access to health care coverage so that more women can get prenatal care.

Low Birth Weight

In 2005, the average birth weight for infants born at 40 to 41 weeks gestation was 3,389 grams (approximately 7.5 pounds).[62] Low birth weight (LBW) infants are those that weigh less than 2,500 grams, or about 5.5 pounds. The fetal period is a critical time for development, and LBW infants have an increased risk of multiple medical problems and may require special care in a neonatal intensive care unit after delivery. These include health issues related to the development of the baby's respiratory, cardiovascular, and digestive systems. Interestingly, LBW has also been linked with problems later in life, such as high blood pressure, diabetes, and heart disease.[63]

The overall percentage of U.S. infants born at LBW has remained relatively stable (between 6.97% and 8.26%) in the last two decades (see **Figure 7.15**).[10] However, LBW must continue to be aggressively targeted, especially among non-Hispanic Black mothers, who have almost twice the rate of LBW babies.[10] Two factors generally recognized to govern infant birth weight are the duration of gestation (premature births) and intrauterine growth rate. Approximately two-thirds of LBW infants are born premature. Therefore, reduction in premature births holds the most potential for overall reduction in LBW. Intrauterine growth restriction (IUGR), or small for gestational age, is when a baby's weight is below the 10th percentile for his or her gestational age. Causes of IUGR include low maternal weight; poor nutrition during pregnancy; birth defects; use of drugs, cigarettes, or alcohol; maternal health problems; placental or umbilical cord abnormalities; and having multiples (i.e., twins, triplets, etc.).[64] Therefore, all pregnant women should (1) get early and regular prenatal care; (2) eat a balanced diet, including adequate amounts of folic acid; (3) gain the appropriate amount of weight based on Institute of Medicine (IOM) guidelines; and (4) avoid smoking and drinking alcohol.[65,66]

Cigarette Smoking

Research has shown that maternal cigarette smoking during pregnancy is one of the most common causes of infant morbidity and mortality in the United States, therefore making it an ideal target for intervention. Researchers estimate that smoking during pregnancy is linked to 5-8% of preterm deliveries and 5-7% of preterm-related deaths. Smoking during pregnancy is also linked to 23-34% of infant deaths related to sudden infant death syndrome.[67] Although the

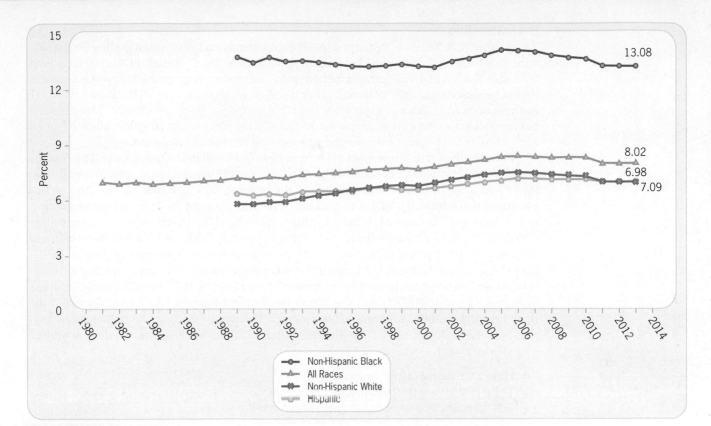

FIGURE 7.15 Percentage of infants born at low birth weight by race and Hispanic origin of the mother, 1981–2013.

Note: Persons of Hispanic origin may be of any race. "All races" includes races other than non-Hispanic white, non-Hispanic black, and Hispanic.

Data from: Martin J. A., B. E. Hamilton, M. J. K. Osterman, S. C. Curtin, and T. J. Mathews (2015). "Births: Final Data for 2013." *National Vital Statistics Reports*, 64(1). Hyattsville, MD: National Center for Health Statistics. Available at http://www.cdc.gov/nchs/data/nvsr/nvsr64/nvsr64_01.pdf.

percentage of women who smoked during pregnancy decreased significantly over time, from 13.2% in 2010 to 11.8% in 2006,[67] the United States is still far from reaching its goal of 98.6% of females abstaining from smoking cigarettes during pregnancy, or only 1.4% reporting smoking during pregnancy, by 2020.[23]

Alcohol and Other Drugs

Prenatal exposure to alcohol can cause a range of disorders, known as fetal alcohol spectrum disorders (FASDs). FASD refers to conditions such as **fetal alcohol syndrome (FAS)**, fetal alcohol effects (FAE), alcohol-related neurodevelopmental disorder (ARND), and alcohol-related birth defects (ARBD). No level of alcohol during pregnancy is known to be safe. Adverse effects are strongly associated with heavy consumption during the first few months of pregnancy, but alcohol at any time during pregnancy can be harmful.[68] Abstaining from alcohol altogether during pregnancy is highly recommended; however, data from the 2011 to 2013 Behavioral Risk Factor Surveillance System indicated that 10.2% of pregnant women used alcohol during the past 30 days.[69]

Other drug use can also result in a number of deleterious effects on the developing fetus, including impaired fetal growth, increased risk for preterm birth, birth defects, withdrawal symptoms, and learning or behavioral problems.[70] Because women who use illicit drugs during pregnancy are also more likely to engage in other risky behaviors, it is difficult to determine what specific effects various substances have on the developing fetus. Further, the impact of the drug(s) depends on when they were used during pregnancy and in what quantity. By understanding how the fetus develops throughout pregnancy, it is possible to determine how exposures at certain times may impact the fetus.

Fetal alcohol syndrome (FAS) a group of abnormalities that may include growth retardation, abnormal appearance of face and head, and deficits of central nervous system function, including mental retardation, in babies born to mothers who have consumed heavy amounts of alcohol during their pregnancies

Breastfeeding

The American Academy of Pediatrics (AAP) recommends exclusive breastfeeding for the first 6 months of life and continuing breastfeeding for the first year.[71] Breast milk is the ideal food for babies and has many advantages for both baby and mother. Breast milk contains substances that help babies resist infections and other diseases. As a result, breastfed babies have fewer ear infections and colds and experience less diarrhea and vomiting. In addition, breastfeeding has been shown to improve maternal health by reducing postpartum bleeding, allowing for an earlier return to pre-pregnancy weight, and reducing the risk of osteoporosis.[23]

Breastfeeding rates for women of all races have increased in the last decade. The *Healthy People 2020* objectives for breastfeeding are to increase the percentage of women ever breast-feeding to 82%, and those breastfeeding at 6 months to 60% (see **Box 7.3**). In 2012, it was estimated that nationally, 80% of infants have ever breastfed and 51.4% were breastfeeding at 6 months of age.[72] Breastfeeding rates are highest among children whose mothers are college educated (91.2% ever breastfed), among women 30 years and older (84.1% ever breastfed), and women who are married (87% ever breastfed).[72] Two voluntary community groups, the La Leche League and the Nursing Mother's Council, are good sources for breastfeeding information, advice, and support. In an effort to promote breastfeeding, the United Nations Children's Emergency Fund (UNICEF) and the World Health Organization (WHO) implemented the Baby Friendly Hospital Initiative. This program includes 10 steps at the organization level that have been shown to increase breastfeeding initiation, exclusivity, and continuation.[73] The steps include:

- Have a written breastfeeding policy.
- Train health care staff to implement the policy.
- Tell pregnant women about the benefits of breastfeeding.

BOX 7.3   *Healthy People 2020*: Objectives

Objective MICH-21: Increase the proportion of infants who are breastfed.

Target and baseline:

Objective	Increase in Infants Who Are Breastfeed	2006 Status	2020 Target
		Percent	
21.1	Ever breastfed*	74.0	81.9
21.2	At 6 months	43.5	60.6
21.3	At 1 year	22.7	34.1
21.5	Exclusively through 6 months**	14.1	25.5

Infants who are breastfed, by race/ethnicity of the mother and duration, 2006.[†]

* Reported that child was ever breastfed or fed human breast milk.

** Exclusive breastfeeding is defined as only human breast milk—no solids, water, or other liquids.

† Includes Hispanics.

Original Source of Data: Centers for Disease Control and Prevention, National Center for Health Statistics and National Center for Immunization and Respiratory Diseases (CDC/NCHS and CDC/NCIRP). (2015) *National Immunization Survey (NIS)*.

For Further Thought

An important public health goal is to increase the number of mothers who breastfeed. Human milk is acknowledged by the American Academy of Pediatrics as the most complete form of nutrition for infants, with a broad realm of benefits for infants' growth and development. What types of programs would you recommend to educate new mothers and their partners and to educate health care providers?

Data from: U.S. Department of Health and Human Services, Office of Disease Prevention and Health Promotion (2010). *Healthy People 2020*. Available at http://www.healthypeople.gov/2020/default.aspx. Accessed December 19, 2015.

- Help new mothers start breastfeeding within 1 hour of delivery.
- Show women how to breastfeed, even if they are not able to see their infant(s).
- Do not give infants any food or drink besides breast milk unless they need it for medical reasons.
- Allow the mothers and infants to stay in the same room during their entire time at the hospital.
- Encourage breastfeeding when the baby gives cues that he/she would like to.
- Do not give pacifiers or artificial nipples to infants who are breastfeeding.
- Help to establish breastfeeding support groups and tell mothers about these groups before they leave the hospital.

Sudden Infant Death Syndrome

Sudden infant death syndrome (SIDS) was listed as a cause of death for 1,679 infants in the United States in 2012. There were probably even more deaths caused by SIDS, but issues with correctly classifying infant causes of death result in underreporting.[56] SIDS is defined as the sudden unanticipated death of an infant in whom, after examination, there is no recognizable cause of death.[74] Because most cases of SIDS occur when a baby is sleeping in a crib, SIDS has been referred to as crib death. SIDS is the third leading cause of infant death. Moreover, after the first month of life, it is a leading cause of postneonatal mortality.[56] SIDS is just one type of sudden unexpected infant death (SUID), which also includes death due to unknown cause and accidental suffocation or strangulation in bed.[74]

There is currently no way of predicting which infants will die because of SIDS. However, research has shown that sleeping on the back all the time rather than the stomach or side greatly decreases the risk of SIDS.[75] In response to this research, the federal government initiated a national "Safe to Sleep" campaign, which began in 1994 as the "Back to Sleep" campaign, to educate parents and health professionals that placing babies on their backs to sleep can reduce the risk of SIDS. Since the dissemination of the recommendation, more infants have been put to bed on their backs, and the rate of SIDS has fallen by more than 50% (see **Figure 7.16**).[75]

> **Sudden infant death syndrome (SIDS)** sudden unanticipated death of an infant in whom, after examination, there is no recognized cause of death

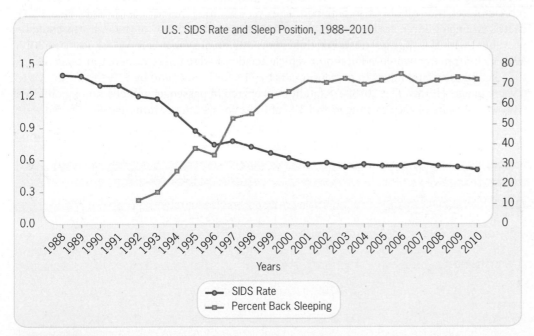

FIGURE 7.16   Rate of sudden infant death syndrome and sleep position: 1988–2010. Deaths are per 1,000 live births.

Data from: National Institutes of Health, Eunice Kennedy Shriver National Institute of Child Health and Human Development (NICHD), Safe to Sleep Public Education Campaign (2015). *About SIDS and Safe Infant Sleep*. Available at https://www.nichd.nih.gov/sts/about/Pages/default.aspx.

Child Health

Good health during the childhood years (ages 1–9) is essential to each child's optimal development and this country's future. Children are less likely to become productive members of society if they grow up in poverty, live in a violent environment, have poor or mediocre child care, or have no health insurance. Failure to provide timely and remedial care leads to unnecessary illness, disability, and death—events that are associated with much greater costs than the timely care itself. Vivid examples are the costs associated with late or no prenatal care given earlier in this chapter. For those who believe that access to basic care is a standard of justness and fairness in any socialized society, the United States lingers sadly behind many other nations in child health (see **Box 7.4**).[7]

In an effort to improve care, the AAP promotes the concept of a medical home, which is the provision of continuous, comprehensive, coordinated, family-oriented care. The physician not only addresses routine health issues and makes sure the child has his or her recommended immunizations, he or she also discusses growth and development, parenting, nutrition, safety, and psychosocial issues that may affect the child. The physician will also coordinate with other providers to ensure the well-being of each child. When possible, having the same provider means continuity of care and a centralized location for a comprehensive record of the child's well-being. The provider should also work to ensure that care is culturally appropriate. The medical home can be located in different types of locations, such as a physician's office or a health department, but this approach to care helps to provide effective and efficient care for children.[76]

Childhood Mortality

Childhood mortality rates are the most severe measure of health in children. The death of a child is an enormous tragedy for family and friends as well as a loss to the community. As mentioned in the introduction of this chapter, the mortality rates of children have generally declined over the past couple of decades (see Figures 7.4 and 7.5). Unintentional injuries are the leading cause of mortality in children (see **Figure 7.17**). In fact, unintentional injuries kill more children than all diseases combined. The overwhelming majority of unintentional injury deaths among children are the result of motor vehicle crashes. Many of these deaths could be prevented with the appropriate use of child restraints, such as seat belts or car seats. In 2013, 43% of children fatally injured in motor vehicle accidents were unrestrained. Car seats reduce the likelihood of fatal injury in passenger cars by 71% for infants and by 54% for children 1 to 4 years of age. However, in 2013, 278 fatalities occurred in passenger vehicles among children who were 4 years of age or younger, and 31% of those for whom restraint use was known were

---

BOX 7.4   How America Ranks Among Industrialized Countries in Investing in and Protecting Children

First in gross domestic product
First in number of billionaires
Second to worst in child poverty rates (just ahead of Romania)
Largest gap between the rich and the poor

First in military spending
First in military weapons exports
First in number of people incarcerated
Worst in protecting children against gun violence

30th in preschool enrollment rates
24th in reading scores for 15-year-olds
28th in science scores for 15-year-olds
36th in math scores for 15-year-olds

First in health expenditures
25th in low birth weight rates
26th in immunization rates
31st in infant mortality rates
Second to worst in teenage births (just ahead of Bulgaria)

Reproduced from: Children's Defense Fund (2014). *The State of America's Children*. Available at http://www.childrensdefense.org/library/state-of
-americas-children/2014-soac.pdf?utm_source=2014-SOAC-PDF&utm_medium=link&utm_campaign=2014-SOAC. Accessed December 20, 2015.

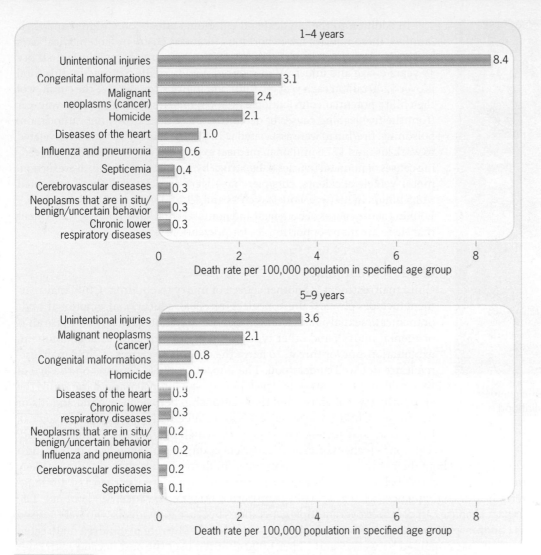

FIGURE 7.17   Leading causes of death in children aged 1 to 4 and 5 to 9; 2012.

Data from: XuHeron, M. (2012–2015). "Deaths: Preliminary Data for 2011 Leading Causes for 2012." National Vital Statistics Reports, 6164(610). Hyattsville, MD: *National Center for Health Statistics*. Available at http://www.cdc.gov/nchs/data/nvsr/nvsr61nvsr64/nvsr61nvsr64_0610.pdf.

not retrained in any manner.[77] Although all 50 states have primary child restraint laws that allow law enforcement officers to stop a driver if a child is not restrained, the provisions of these laws vary from state to state.

Childhood Morbidity

Although childhood for many children represents a time of relatively good overall health, it is a time when far too many suffer from acute illness, chronic disease, and disabilities. Childhood morbidity includes unintentional injuries, child maltreatment, and infectious diseases.

Unintentional Injuries

Unintentional injuries are the leading cause of death among children (see **Figure 7.18**).[56] The leading causes of injuries among children are drowning, falls, fires or burns, poisoning, suffocation, and injuries related to transportation (e.g., motor vehicle accidents). While unintentional injuries are an important concern for all children, the type of accidents varies based on the child's age. For example, toddlers are at especially high risk of drowning, whereas older children are most at risk of transportation-related injuries.[78]

FIGURE 7.18 Unintentional injuries are the leading cause of childhood morbidity and mortality.
© Kitti/ShutterStock, Inc.

In addition to the physical and emotional effects on children and their families, these injuries have enormous financial costs. In fact, medical care and societal costs total approximately $87 billion per year for injuries to those 19 years of age and under. With reduced quality of life factored in, this total is over $200 billion each year.[78] Childhood injuries can deprive the country of the child's potential contributions. In 2005, injuries to those 19 and younger from the five leading causes of death (motor vehicle, drowning, suffocation, poisoning, fire/burn) were associated with $11.9 billion in lifetime costs related to work loss and $77.6 million in medical expenses. Injuries from the five leading causes of nonfatal injuries (falls, struck by/against something, overexertion, motor vehicle accidents, cuts/piercings) were associated with an estimated $18.5 billion in lifetime work loss costs and $9.2 billion in medical expenses.[77] Looking at the causes of both fatal and nonfatal childhood injuries, it is evident that there are many opportunities for prevention.

Child Maltreatment

Child maltreatment is another source of injury to children. Child maltreatment includes physical abuse, neglect (physical, educational, emotional, and/or medical), sexual abuse, emotional abuse (psychological/verbal abuse and/or mental injury), and other types of maltreatment such as abandonment, exploitation, and/or threats to harm the child. The causes of child maltreatment are not well understood. The impact of abuse depends on the age of the child and their stage of development, the intensity and duration of the abuse, the type of abuse, and the relationship between the child and his or her abuser. Child abuse or neglect is associated with physical, psychological, behavioral, and societal consequences, which overlap and are intertwined.

The consequences of adverse experiences during childhood can impact individuals throughout their entire lifetime. For example, children who are abused are more likely to engage in high-risk behaviors as they mature, which in turn increases their risk for long-term health consequences such as sexually transmitted infections, cancer, and obesity. The impact of abuse can continue over multiple generations because individuals who were abused as children are more likely to victimize their own children.[79] The rate of children maltreated annually has remained between 9 and 13 per 1,000 children over the past decade, with rates decreasing to a low of 9.8 per 1,000 children in 2013.[80]

The oldest federal agency for children, the Children's Bureau (CB), located in the Administration for Children and Families, has worked to lead the public in taking a more informed and active part in child abuse prevention. The CB has been instrumental in defining the scope of the problem of child maltreatment and in promoting community responsibility for child protection. The CB believes that parents have a right to raise their children as long as they are willing to protect them. When parents cannot meet their children's needs and keep them from harm, the community has a responsibility to act on behalf of the child. If one suspects a child is being abused or neglected, it is important to call the proper authorities. Any action into the family life should be guided by federal and state laws. According to the CB, the community's responsibility for child protection is based on the following:[81]

- Communities should develop and implement programs to strengthen families and prevent the likelihood of child abuse and neglect.
- Child maltreatment is a community problem; no single agency or individual has the necessary knowledge, skills, resources, or societal mandate to provide the assistance to abused and neglected children and their families.
- Intervention must be sensitive to culture, values, religion, and other differences.
- Professionals must recognize that most parents do not intend to harm their children. Rather, abuse and neglect may be the result of a combination of psychological, social, situational, and societal factors.

- Service providers should recognize that many maltreating adults have the capacity to change their abusive/neglectful behavior, when given sufficient help and resources to do so.
- To help families protect their children and meet their basic needs, the community's response should be nonpunitive, noncritical, and conducted in the least intrusive manner possible.
- Growing up in their own family is optimal for children, as long as the children's safety can be assured.
- When parents cannot or will not meet their child's needs, removal from the home may be necessary. All efforts to develop a permanent plan for a child should be made as quickly as possible.[81]

Infectious Diseases

In the past, infectious diseases were the leading health concern for children in the United States, but increased public health action has resulted in a substantial reduction in both morbidity and mortality rates. Infectious disease control resulted from improvements in sanitation and hygiene and the implementation of universal vaccination programs. Because many vaccine-preventable diseases are more common and more deadly among infants and children, the CDC recommends vaccinating children against most vaccine-preventable diseases early in life. The 2016 recommended immunization schedule is shown in **Figure 7.19**.[82] Infectious diseases still account for many deaths among children worldwide, and pneumonia, an infectious disease, is the leading cause of death globally.[83]

The CDC keeps track of how many children receive key sets of vaccines like the diptheria, tetanus, and pertussis (DTP), polio, measles, mumps, and rubella (MMR), and *Haemophilus influenzae* type b (Hib) vaccines, collectively referred to as the 4:3:1:3 series, and the 4:3:1:3:3:1 series (those in the 4:3:1:3 series plus three doses of the hepatitis B vaccine and one dose of varicella vaccine; see **Figure 7.20**). The numbers in each series correspond with the number of doses recommended. Immunization rates are considered an important indicator of the adequacy of health care for children and of the level of protection a community values related to preventable infectious diseases. The proportion of children aged 19 months to 35 months receiving the combined 4:3:1:3 series increased from 69% in 1994 to 82% in 2013, and the proportion receiving the combined 4:3:1:3:3:1 series increased from 66% in 2002 to 78% in 2013 (see Figure 7.20).[84] There has been a lack of progress in the proportion of young children immunized in the past decade or so, and with approximately 20% of children missing key vaccinations, there is plenty of opportunity for improvement. In addition, the National Immunization Survey data showed considerable variation between states and urban areas and

Vaccine ↓ Age →	Birth	1 month	2 months	4 months	6 months	12 months	15 months	18 months	19–23 months	2–3 years	4–6 years
Hepatitis B	HepB	HepB				HepB					
Rotavirus			RV	RV	RV						
Diphtheria, Tetanus, Pertussis			DTaP	DTaP	DTaP		DTaP				DTaP
Haemophilus influenzae type b			Hib	Hib	Hib	Hib					
Pneumococcal			PCV	PCV	PCV	PCV					
Inactivated Poliovirus			IPV	IPV		IPV					IPV
Influenza						Influenza (yearly)					
Measles, Mumps, Rubella						MMR					MMR
Varicella						Varicella					Varicella
Hepatitis A						HepA (2 doses)					

Range of recommended ages for all children except certain high-risk groups

FIGURE 7.19   Recommended immunization schedule for persons aged 0 through 6 years—United States, 2016.

Data from: Centers for Disease Control and Prevention (2016). *Recommended Immunization Schedules for Persons Ages 0 Through 18 Years—United States, 2016.* Available at http://www.cdc.gov/vaccines/schedules/downloads/child/0-18yrs-child-combined-schedule.pdf.

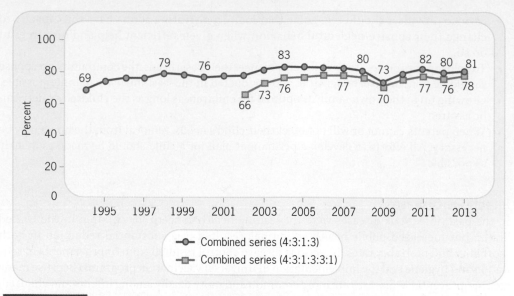

FIGURE 7.20   Percentage of children aged 19 to 35 months receiving the combined series vaccination (4:3:1:3) and the combined series vaccination (4:3:1:3:3:1), 1994–2013.

Reproduced from: Child Trends DataBank (2015). *Immunization.* Bethesda, MD: Author. Available at http://www.childtrends.org /?indicators=immunization.

by poverty level, indicating that all children are not equally vaccinated. The large number of unvaccinated children has been attributed to cost, lack of access to medical care, uneducated parents, concerns related to vaccine safety, and confusion around when to vaccinate children.

All children should be immunized beginning at birth and according to schedules available from the CDC for birth through age 6, 7 to 18 years of age, and adults 19 years of age and older.[82] By immunizing, the community safeguards its children against the potentially devastating effects of vaccine-preventable diseases. No child should ever have to endure the effects of these diseases simply because he or she was not vaccinated on time.

In 1989, a measles epidemic occurred in the United States, leading to approximately 55,000 reported cases of measles and hundreds of deaths. Even though many of the infected children had seen a health care provider, investigation of the outbreak revealed that more than half of them had not been immunized. In response to that epidemic, the Vaccines for Children (VFC) Program was created. The VFC Program provides vaccines to children whose families are not able to afford them to ensure that all children have a better chance of getting their recommended vaccinations on schedule. Eligible children are those who are Medicaid-eligible, uninsured, underinsured, or American Indian or Alaska Native.[85] It is estimated that among children born during 1994–2013, the era of the VFC, prevention of 322 million illnesses, 21 million hospitalizations, and 732,000 deaths can be attributed to vaccination over the course of a lifetime.[86]

Despite improvements in vaccination rates historically, and improved access to vaccines through the VFC Program and the ACA, fears about vaccine safety among parents continue to negatively impact vaccination. In December 2014, an outbreak of measles originated at a theme park in Orange County, California and 111 confirmed cases of measles occurred in the United States, Mexico, and Canada as a result. Many of the cases occurring in early 2015, including those in the theme park outbreak, were in unvaccinated persons who cited religious and philosophical reasons for not vaccinating (see **Figure 7.21**). A high proportion of cases also occurred in persons who were unable to receive the MMR vaccine, often because they were too young.[87] This outbreak highlights the widespread effects of having large numbers of children remain unvaccinated, reducing herd immunity and putting the health of infants and those who cannot be vaccinated at risk.

Fears about the safety of vaccines are largely a response to the now-debunked work of British doctor Andrew Wakefield, whose now-redacted study claimed that vaccines were linked

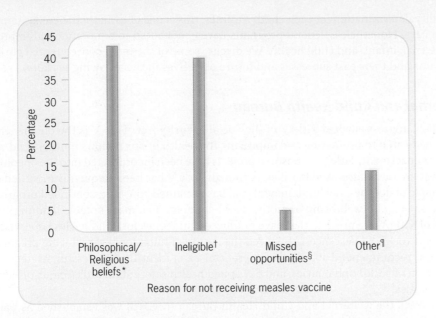

*Includes persons who were unvaccinated because of their own or a parent's beliefs.
†Includes persons ineligible for measles vaccination, generally those aged <12 months
and those with medical contraindications.
§Includes eligible children aged 16 months–4 years who had not been vaccinated and
international travelers aged 6–11 months who were unvaccinated.
¶Includes persons who were known to be unvaccinated and the reason was
unknown, and those who were born before 1957 and presumed to be immune.

FIGURE 7.21   Percentage of U.S. residents with measles who were unvaccinated (n = 68), by reason for not receiving measles vaccine—United States, January 4 to April 2, 2015.

Reproduced from: Clemmons, N. S., P. A. Gastanaduy, A. P. Fiebelkorn, S. B. Redd, and G. S. Wallace (2015). "Measles—United States, January 4–April 2, 2015." *Morbidity and Mortality Weekly Report*, 64(14). Available at http://www.cdc.gov/mmwr/pdf/wk/mm6414.pdf.

to the development of autism spectrum disorders. In the years since Dr. Wakefield's work was published, several large and rigorous studies by the IOM and the CDC have determined there is no link between autism and receipt of vaccines.[88] More stringent measures by the medical community are needed to ensure that all children are immunized. Opportunities to vaccinate are frequently missed by health care practitioners in primary care settings that do not routinely inquire about the immunization status of the child. Parents and health practitioners need to work together to ensure that youth are protected from communicable diseases; some states have started immunization registries to facilitate timely vaccination by notifying providers when a vaccination is due.[89]

Community Programs for Women, Infants, and Children

In the preceding pages, many problems associated with maternal, infant, and child health have been identified. Solutions for many of these problems have been proposed, and in many cases programs are already in place. Some of these programs are aimed at preventing or reducing the levels of maternal and infant morbidity and mortality, whereas others are aimed at the prevention or reduction of childhood morbidity and mortality.

The federal government has more than 35 health programs in 16 different agencies to serve the needs of our nation's children. The majority of these program help meet the needs of many children. However, others are **categorical programs**, meaning they are only available to people who can be categorized into a specific group based on disease, age, geography, financial need, or other variables. This means that too many children fall through the cracks and are not served. Some children require services from multiple programs, which complicates the

Categorical programs
programs available only to people who can be categorized into a group based on specific variables

eligibility determination for each child. At times, this can lead to an inefficient system of child health care. Nonetheless, federal programs have contributed to a monumental improvement in maternal, infant, and child health. We discuss some of the more consequential government programs and their past successes and future objectives in the following sections.

Maternal and Child Health Bureau

In 1935, Congress enacted Title V of the Social Security Act. Title V is the only federal legislation dedicated to promoting and improving the health of our nation's mothers and children. Since its enactment, Title V–sponsored projects have been incorporated into the ongoing health care system for children and families. Although Title V has been frequently modified over the last couple of decades, the fundamental goal has remained constant: continued progress in the health, safety, and well-being of mothers and children. The most notable landmark achievements of Title V are projects that have produced "guidelines for child health supervision from infancy through adolescence; influenced the nature of nutritional care during pregnancy and lactation; recommended standards for prenatal care; identified successful strategies for the prevention of childhood injuries; and developed health safety standards for out-of-home child care facilities."[90]

In 1990, the Maternal and Child Health Bureau (MCHB) was established as part of the Health Resources and Services Administration (HRSA) in the U.S. Department of Health and Human Services to administer Title V funding. This means the MCHB is charged with the responsibility for promoting and improving the health of our nation's mothers and children. MCHB's mission "is to provide leadership in partnership with key stakeholders, to improve the physical and mental health, safety and well-being of the maternal and child health (MCH) population, which includes all the nation's women, infants, children, adolescents, and their families, including fathers and children with special health care needs."[91] To fulfill its mission, the MCHB has maternal and child health programs that accomplish the following:[92]

- Ensure access to quality care, especially for those with low incomes or limited availability of care.
- Reduce infant mortality.
- Provide and ensure access to comprehensive prenatal and postnatal care, especially for low-income and at-risk women.
- An increase in health assessments and follow-up diagnostic and treatment services.
- Provide and ensure access to preventive and child care services as well as rehabilitative services for certain children.
- Implement family-centered, community-based systems of coordinated care for children with special health care needs.
- Provide assistance in applying for services to pregnant women with infants and children who are eligible for Medicaid.

The MCHB works on accomplishing its goals through the administration of four types of public health services: (1) infrastructure-building services, (2) population-based services, (3) enabling services, and (4) direct health care (gap-filling) services. MCHB uses the construct of a pyramid to provide a useful framework for understanding programmatic directions and resource allocation by the bureau and its partners (see **Figure 7.22**). MCHB continues to strive for a "society that recognizes and fully supports the important role that public health plays in promoting the health of the MCH population, including building, strengthening, and assuring MCH health services and infrastructure at all levels."[93]

Women, Infants, and Children (WIC) a special supplemental food program for women, infants, and children, sponsored by the USDA

Women, Infants, and Children Program

The **Women, Infants, and Children (WIC)** program is a clinic-based program designed to provide a variety of nutritional and health-related goods and services to pregnant, postpartum, and breastfeeding women, infants up to 1 year of age, and children under the age of 5. The WIC

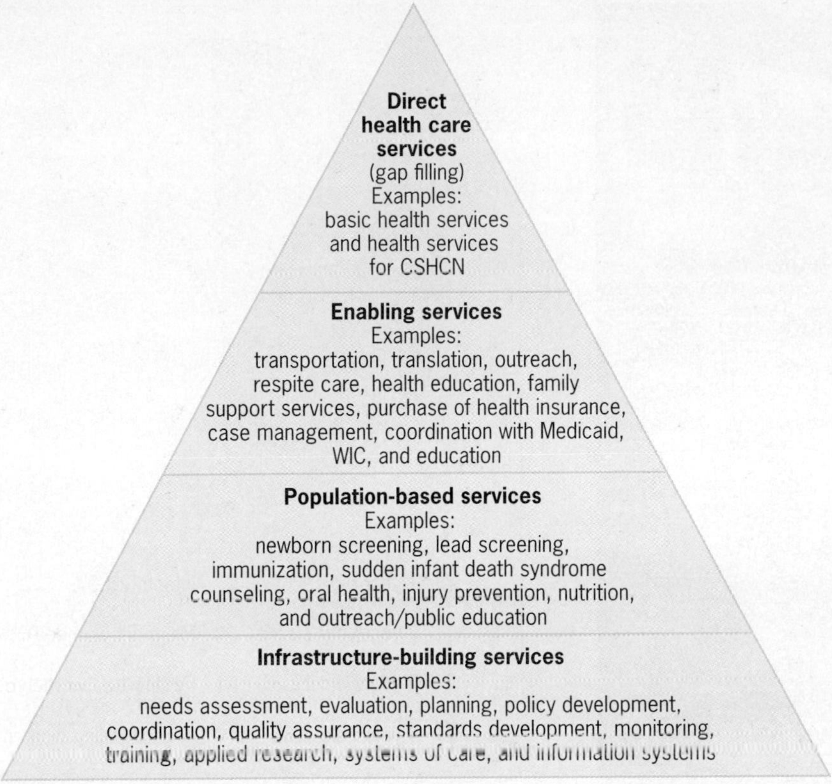

FIGURE 7.22   MCH pyramid of health services. The conceptual framework for the services of Title V Maternal and Child Health is envisioned as a pyramid with four tiers of services and levels of funding that provide comprehensive services for mothers and children.

Data from: U.S. Department of Health and Human Services, Health Resources and Services Administration, Maternal and Child Health (2003). *Maternal and Child Health Bureau Strategic Plan: FY 2003–2007.* Available at http://mchb.hrsa.gov/research/documents /mchbstratplan0307.pdf.

program began as a pilot in 1972 and received permanent federal funding in 1974, in response to growing evidence linking nutritional inadequacies to mental and physical health defects. Congress intended that WIC, unlike other food programs, would serve as "an adjunct to good health care, during critical times of growth and development, to prevent the occurrence of health problems."[94]

The U.S. Department of Agriculture (USDA) administers WIC. The USDA administers grants to the states, where the WIC programs are most often offered through local health departments or state health and welfare agencies (see **Figure 7.23**). Pregnant or postpartum women, infants, and children up to age 5 are eligible if they meet the following three criteria: (1) residency in the state in which they are applying, (2) income requirements (applicant must have a household income at or below 185% of the federal poverty income guidelines), (3) determination to be at "nutritional risk" by a health professional.[95]

Since WIC's inception as a national nutrition program, it has grown dramatically. In 1974, the average number of monthly WIC participants was 88,000; in 2014 that number was just over 9 million women, infants, and children. Among WIC participants, children make up one-half, infants one-quarter, and women one-quarter (see **Figure 7.24**).[96]

The WIC program has proven to be one of the most effective ways to improve the health of mothers, infants, and young children. Research indicates that participation in the WIC program during pregnancy provides women with a number of positive outcomes, some of which include birth to babies with higher birth weights, fewer fetal and infant deaths, and an increased rate of breastfeeding initiation.[97] In fact, rates of breastfeeding initiation among WIC participants has increased steadily with a rate of 41.5% in 1998 to a rate of 69.8% in 2014. However, rates

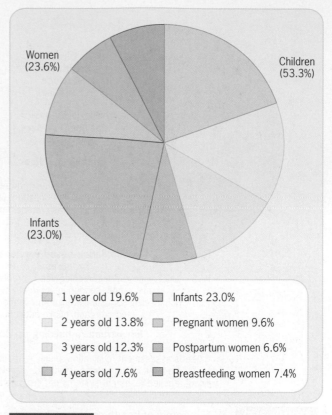

FIGURE 7.23 The WIC program has proven to be extremely effective in improving the health of woman, infants, and children in the United States.

© A. Ramey/PhotoEdit, Inc.

FIGURE 7.24 Distribution of individuals who participated in WIC.

Note: The percentage of children by age group is calculated from the total number of children by age group as a percentage of total WIC participation.

Data from: Thorn, B., C. Tadler, N. Huret, E. Ayo, and C. Trippe (2015). *WIC Participant and Program Characteristics Final Report*. Washington, DC: U.S. Department of Agriculture, Food and Nutrition Service, Office of Policy Support. Available at http://www.fns.usda.gov/sites/default/files/ops/WICPC2014.pdf.

continue to vary greatly across states (**Figure 7.25**).[96] The WIC program is also cost effective. USDA research has shown that for every dollar spent on WIC, the taxpayer saves $4 in future expenditures on Medicaid.[97] For this reason, the WIC program continues to receive strong bipartisan support in Congress.

Providing Health Insurance for Women, Infants, and Children

All children deserve to start life on the right track and to have access to comprehensive health services that provide preventive care when they are well and treatment when they are ill or injured. Health insurance provides access to critical preventive medical services as well as acute medical care in the case of illness or injury. When compared with children who are privately insured or have governmental insurance, children without health insurance are much more likely to have necessary care delayed or receive no care for health problems, putting them at greater risk for hospitalization.[98] Therefore, providing health insurance to low-income children is a critical health care safety net.

The government has two principal programs aimed at providing health care coverage to low-income children: the Medicaid program and the State Children's Health Insurance Program (formerly called SCHIP, now called CHIP). Medicaid, created in 1965, provides medical assistance for certain low-income individuals and families, mostly women and

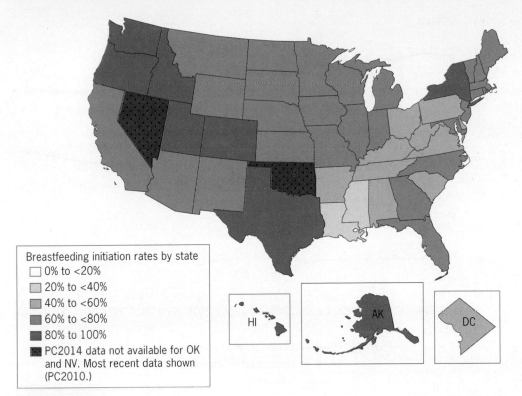

Breastfeeding initiation rates by state
☐ 0% to <20%
◻ 20% to <40%
◻ 40% to <60%
◼ 60% to <80%
◼ 80% to 100%
▨ PC2014 data not available for OK
    and NV. Most recent data shown
    (PC2010.)

FIGURE 7.25   Breastfeeding initiation rates by state for WIC infant participants, ages 6 to 13 months; April 2014.

Data from: Thorn, B., C. Tadler, N. Huret, E. Ayo, and C. Trippe (2015). *WIC Participant and Program Characteristics Final Report.* Washington, DC: U.S. Department of Agriculture, Food and Nutrition Service, Office of Policy Support. Available at http://www.fns.usda.gov /sites/default/files/ops/WICPC2014.pdf.

children. Medicaid is the single largest provider of health insurance for children in the United States, providing health coverage for over 33 million children.[99] A major reason that Medicaid is working well for American children is the multiphase program for preventive health called the Early and Periodic Screening, Diagnostic, and Treatment (EPSDT) for individuals younger than the age of 21. The Medicaid EPSDT provides children of low-income families with preventive health care screening and medically necessary diagnosis and treatment.[100]

Although the Medicaid program is a critical health care program for low-income children, being poor does not automatically qualify a child for Medicaid. Medicaid eligibility is determined by each state based on various age and income requirements. As a result, Medicaid coverage varies across the states and leaves a significant number of poor children uninsured. To broaden coverage to low-income children, Congress created CHIP under provisions in the Balanced Budget Act of 1997. Coverage eligibility for CHIP is also determined by the state, but as of 2015, all states had expanded CHIP coverage with an average income eligibility level for children of 241% of the federal poverty level.

Government-funded health insurance is an important source of coverage for children, and its significance has been growing. Government health insurance coverage for children increased from 23.3% of all children in 1999 to 42.6% in 2014. During the same time period, the percentage of children with private health insurance coverage decreased from 70% in 1999 to 61% in 2014 (see **Figure 7.26**).[101,102] The success in increasing the number of children with coverage is attributable not just to Medicaid but to the combined effects of Medicaid and CHIP. In 2014, approximately 6% of children younger than the age of 19 were uninsured, a sharp decrease that has been attributed to expansion of coverage under the Affordable Care Act.

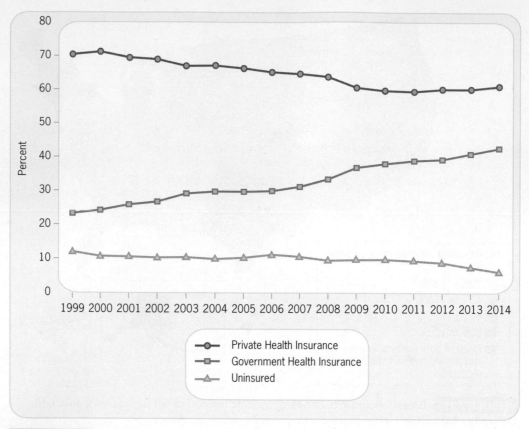

FIGURE 7.26   Percentage of children covered by health insurance, by type of insurance, 1999–2014.

Note: Government health insurance includes Medicaid, CHIP, and military health insurance. During 1999–2012, children were defined as individuals younger than age 18. During 2013–2014, children were defined as individuals younger than age 19.

Data from: DeNavas-Walt, C., B. D. Proctor, and J. C. Smith (2013). "Income, Poverty, and Health Insurance Coverage in the United States: 2012." *U.S. Census Bureau, Current Population Reports*, P60-243. Washington, DC: U.S. Government Printing Office. Available at http://www.census.gov/content/dam/Census/library/publications/2013/demo/p60-245.pdf; Smith, J. C., and C. Medalia (2015). "Health Insurance Coverage in the United States: 2014." *U.S. Census Bureau, Current Population Reports*, P60-253, Washington, DC: U.S. Government Printing Office. Available at http://www.census.gov/content/dam/Census/library/publications/2015/demo/p60-253.pdf.

Providing Child Care

Experiences during the first years of childhood significantly influence the health of a child. Research shows that early investments in the nurturing of children provide major advantages for families and society later. Whereas parents should accept the primary responsibility for raising their children, the government can assist families who need help making important investments. Two important investments into the health and welfare of America's children involve support for parenting during the first months of life and supporting the child's need for secure relationships with a small number of adults in safe settings as they develop during the first few years of life.

The **Family and Medical Leave Act (FMLA)** was signed into law in 1993 and provides job protection for individuals for medical- or family-related needs, including support for new parents. The FMLA grants 12 weeks of unpaid job-protected leave to men or women after the birth of a child, an adoption, or in the event of illness in the immediate family.[103] This legislation has provided employed parents with the time to nurture their children and develop their parenting skills. However, the FMLA only affects businesses with 50 or more employees. Those employees covered by the law include those who have worked 1,250 hours for an employer over a 12-month period (an average of 25 hours per week). This excludes about 40% of American employees who work in small businesses that do not fall under the law's guidelines. Also, employers covered

Family and Medical Leave Act (FMLA) federal law that provides up to a 12-week unpaid leave to men and women after the birth of a child, an adoption, or an event of illness in the immediate family

by the FMLA can exempt key salaried employees who are among their highest paid 10%, if they are needed to prevent "substantial and grievous" economic harm to the employer.[103] Some experts believe the law divides the people by class, helping those who can afford the 3 months without pay, and bypassing those who cannot. Experts have recommended a 6- to 12-month family care leave program with partial pay for at least 3 months. The United States is the only industrialized nation that has not enacted a paid infant-care leave.

Today more families are in need of child care than ever before. In 2011, 23.5% of preschool aged children attended a center-based setting like daycare and 11.2% were cared for in a home-based setting by someone other than a family member.[4] The greater need for professional child care has come about as women are increasingly working outside the home and as more children grow up in single-parent households. However, for many families, especially those with low and moderate incomes, high-quality, affordable child care is simply not available. The average cost of care for an infant ranges from $5,468 to $16,549 per year in a center-based setting and $4,560 to $10,727 per year in a family-based center with a wide range across states. The costs decrease as children get older; however, parents often pay for childcare for more than one child at a time.[104] These costs are beyond the reach of many working parents, half of whom earn $35,000 or less a year. The lack of high-quality child care prevents children from entering school ready to learn, hinders their success in school, and limits the ability of their parents to be productive workers.[104] Furthermore, after-school care is crucial because juvenile crime peaks between the hours of 3 P.M. and 7 P.M., and school-aged children may be at greater risk of engaging in activities that lead to problems such as violence and teen pregnancy.

In 1988, Congress passed the Family Support Act, which provided funding for child care assistance to welfare parents who are employed or participating in an approved training program. Unfortunately, states must match federal funds for this program, which makes meeting the needs of eligible participants difficult for some states.[105]

In 1990, Congress passed the Child Care and Development Block Grant Act (CCDBG), which provides child care subsidies for low-income children and funding to improve the quality of child care services through the Child Care and Development Fund (CCDF). With the creation of the CCDF, states were able to provide additional assistance to many more low-income families.[105] However, in 2012, of the 14.2 million children eligible for child care subsidies, only 15% received funding in an average month. Due in part to restrictions on income eligibility set by individual states, only one in five children who are eligible for child care assistance under federal law receive help.[106] This means that too many parents are unable to obtain necessary child care assistance.

Other Advocates for Children

Numerous groups advocate for children's health and welfare. Among them are the Children's Defense Fund, UNICEF, and the American Academy of Pediatrics.

Children's Defense Fund

Since 1973, the Children's Defense Fund (CDF) (www.childrensdefense.org) has been working to create a nation in which the network of family, community, private-sector, and government supports for children is so tightly intertwined that no child can slip through the cracks. The CDF is a private, nonprofit organization headquartered in Washington, DC, and it is dedicated to providing a voice for the children of America. It has never accepted government funds and supports its programs through donations from foundations, corporate grants, and individuals. The CDF focuses on the needs of poor, minority, and handicapped children and their families. The aim of the CDF is to educate the nation about the needs of children and to encourage preventive investment in children before they get sick or suffer. It provides information and technical assistance to state and local child advocates.

United Nations Children's Fund

Founded in 1946, the United Nations Children's Fund (UNICEF; www.unicefusa.org) is the only organization of the United Nations assigned exclusively to children. This organization works with other United Nations members, governments, and nongovernmental organizations to improve child conditions through community-based services in primary health care, basic education, and safe water and sanitation in more than 140 developing countries. UNICEF gathers data on the health of children throughout the world. UNICEF has assisted in mass vaccinations and has been involved in other international health efforts to protect children.

American Academy of Pediatrics

The American Academy of Pediatrics (AAP; www.aap.org) was founded in 1930 by 35 pediatricians who saw the need for an independent pediatric forum to address children's needs. When the Academy was established, the idea that children have special developmental and health needs was a new one. Preventive health practices now associated with child care, including immunizations and regular health exams, were only just beginning to change the custom of treating children as "miniature adults." The Academy is committed to the attainment of optimal physical, mental, and social health and well-being for all infants, children, adolescents, and young adults. The activities and efforts of the AAP include research, advocacy for children and youth, and public and professional education.

An example of a program that the AAP coordinates is the Healthy Child Care America (HCCA) program (www.healthychildcare.org). HCCA is partly funded by the Child Care Bureau (CCB), Office of Family Assistance (OFA), Administration for Children and Families (ACF), the Maternal and Child Health Bureau, HRSA, and the U.S. Department of Health and Human Services. The specific goals of the HCCA program are the following:

- To promote the healthy development and school readiness of children in early education and child care by strengthening partnerships between health and child care professionals
- To provide information and support necessary to strengthen children's access to health services
- To promote the cognitive, social, and physical development of children in early education and child care
- To provide technical assistance regarding health and safety for health professionals and the early childhood community
- To enhance the quality of early education and child care with health and safety resources
- To support the needs of health professionals interested in promoting healthy and safe early education and child care programs

Since the Healthy Child Care America program was launched in 1995, many communities around the country have been promoting collaborative partnerships between health and child care professionals to ensure that children receive the best and the highest quality care possible. By expanding and creating partnerships between families, child care providers, and government, the best care for millions of children continues to occur.

Chapter Summary

- Maternal, infant, and child health are important indicators of a community's overall health. Maternal health encompasses the health of women of childbearing age from pre-pregnancy through pregnancy, labor, and delivery, and in the postpartum period. Infant and child health refers to individuals through 9 years of age.

- Families are the primary unit in which infants and children are nurtured and supported regarding healthy development. Significant increases in births to unmarried women in the last two decades are among the many changes in American society that have affected family structure and the economic security of children. Teenage childbearing represents a significant social and financial burden on both the family and the community.

- The establishment of local family planning clinics with Title X funding has resulted in an improvement in maternal and child health indicators for the communities served.

- High-quality prenatal care is one of the fundamentals of a safe motherhood program. Ensuring early initiation of prenatal care during pregnancy greatly contributes to reductions in perinatal illness, disability, and death for the mother and the infant.

Scenario: Analysis and Response

- Good health during the childhood years (ages 1 to 9) is essential for each child's optimal development and the United States' future. The United States cannot hope for every child to become a productive member of society if children in this country are allowed to grow up with poor or mediocre child care, without health insurance, living in poverty, or living in a violent environment.

- The federal government has more than 35 health programs within 16 different agencies helping states to serve the needs of our nation's children. The majority of these programs are well respected and help to meet the needs of many children.

We have learned that a lack of prenatal care increases the risk of premature delivery and possible health problems for the infant.

1. If Joan had received prenatal care, how could it have helped in the normal development of the infant? How could the doctor have counseled Joan?

2. How could Joan have found out about opportunities for affordable prenatal care?

3. The cost of treating Joan's infant could run into the hundreds of thousands of dollars, and there is no guarantee that the child will survive. Do you think it would be more cost effective to ensure prenatal care to all women or to continue under the system that is in place now? How would you suggest the United States approach this problem?

4. What programs mentioned in this chapter could have helped Joan?

5. Visit the USDA website (www.usda.gov) and read about WIC. After reading about WIC, do you think this is something that could help Joan with the raising of her child? Why or why not?

Review Questions

1. What has been the trend in infant mortality rates in the United States in the last 15 years? What is the current rate? How does this rate compare with that of other industrial countries?

2. Why are preconception and prenatal care so important for mothers and infants? What types of services are included?

3. What are the consequences of teen pregnancy to the mother? To the infant? To the community?

4. What is included in family planning? Why is family planning important?

5. Discuss the pro-life and pro-choice positions on abortion.

6. Why was the *Roe v. Wade* court decision so important?

7. What are the leading causes of death in children ages 1 to 4 and ages 5 to 14 years?

8. Why are childhood immunizations so important?

9. What is the WIC program?

10. Why is health insurance important for women, infants, and children?

11. Name three groups that are advocates for the health of children and what they have done to show their support.

Activities

Write a two-page paper summarizing the results and/or information you gain from one of the following activities.

1. Survey 10 classmates and friends and ask them what leads to teen pregnancy. What prompts adolescents to

risk pregnancy when they have adequate knowledge of contraception? Ask if they know anyone who became pregnant as an adolescent. Are the reasons given the same as your own? Divide your list into categories of personal beliefs, barriers to action, and social pressure. For example, a comment that might fit under beliefs is, "they don't think they can get pregnant the first time"; under barriers, "they are too embarrassed to buy contraception"; and under social pressure, "all the messages in society promoting sex." Which of the three categories had the most responses? Does this surprise you? What implications does this have for programs trying to reduce the incidence of teen pregnancy?

2. Call your local health department and ask for information about the local WIC program. Ask permission to visit and talk to a representative about the program and clientele.

3. Visit, call, or get on the website of your state health department and obtain information concerning the number of childhood communicable diseases reported

in your state. What are your state laws concerning immunization of children? Does your state provide immunizations free of charge? What qualifications must a person meet to receive free immunizations?

4. Call a local obstetrician's office and ask if he or she accepts Medicaid reimbursement. What is the normal fee for prenatal care and delivery? If he or she does not take Medicaid, ask the obstetrician to whom he or she would refer a pregnant woman with no private insurance.

5. Create a record of your own (or a family member's) immunizations. Find out when and where you were immunized for each of the immunizations listed in Figure 7.20. Are there any immunizations that are still needed? When are you scheduled to get your next tetanus/toxoid immunization?

References

1. Pillitteri, A. (2013). *Maternal and Child Health Nursing: Care of the Childbearing and Childrearing Family*, 7th ed. Philadelphia: J. B. Lippincott.

2. Mathews T. J., M. F. MacDorman, and M. E. Thoma (2015). "Infant Mortality Statistics from the 2013 Period Linked Birth/Infant Death Data Set." *National Vital Statistics Reports*, 64(9). Hyattsville, MD: National Centers for Health Statistics. Available at http://www.cdc .gov/nchs/data/nvsr64/nvsr64_09.pdf.

3. Creanga, A. A., C. J. Berg, C. Syverson, K. Seed, F. C. Bruce, and W. M. Callaghan (2015). "Pregnancy-Related Mortality in the United States, 2006–2010." *Obstetrics and Gynecology*, 125(1),5–12. doi: 10.1097/AOG.0000000000000564.

4. U.S. Department of Health and Human Services, Health Resources and Services Administration, Maternal and Child Health Bureau (2015). *Child Health USA 2014*. Rockville, MD: U.S. Department of Health and Human Services. Available at http://mchb.hrsa.gov /chusa14/dl/chusa14.pdf.

5. Mathews T. J., M. F. MacDorman, A. G. Mohangoo, and J. Zeitlin (2014). "International Comparisons of Infant Mortality and Related Factors: United States and Europe, 2010." *National Vital Statistics Reports*, 63(5). Hyattsville, MD: National Centers for Health Statistics. Available at http://www.cdc.gov/nchs/data/nvsr63 /nvsr63_05.pdf.

6. Child Trends DataBank (2015). *Infant, Child, and Teen Mortality*. Available at http://www.childtrends.org/wp-content/uploads/2012/11/63 _Child_Mortality.pdf.

7. Children's Defense Fund (2014). *The State of America's Children*. Available at http://www.childrensdefense.org /library/state-of-americas-children/2014-soac.pdf?utm_source =2014-SOAC-PDF&utm_medium=link&utm_campaign =2014-SOAC.

8. United States Census Bureau (2015). *Current Population Survey (CPS)—Subject Definitions*. Available at http://www.census.gov/pro-grams-surveys/cps/technical-documentation/subject-definitions. html.

9. Friedman, M. (2003). *Family Nursing: Research, Theory and Practice*, 5th ed. Stamford, CT: Appleton & Lange.

10. Martin J. A., B. E. Hamilton, M. J. K. Osterman, S. C. Curtin, and T. J. Mathews (2015). "Births: Final Data for 2013." *National Vital Statistics Reports*, 64(1). Hyattsville, MD: National Center for Health

Statistics. Available at http://www.cdc.gov/nchs/data/nvsr/nvsr64 /nvsr64_01.pdf.

11. Hamilton, B. E., J. A. Martin, M.J.K. Osterman, and S.C. Curtin (2015). "Births: Preliminary Data for 2014." *National Vital Statistics Reports*, 64(6). Hyattsville, MD: National Center for Health Statistics. Available at http://www.cdc.gov/nchs/data/nvsr/nvsr64 /nvsr64_06.pdf.

12. Shah, P. S., J. Zao, S. Ali, and Knowledge Synthesis Group of Determinants of Preterm/LBW Births (2011). "Maternal Marital Status and Birth Outcomes: A Systematic Review and Meta-Analyses." *Maternal and Child Health Journal*, 15(7): 1097–1109.

13. Balayla, J., L. Azoulay, and H. A. Abenhaim (2011). "Maternal Marital Status and the Risk of Stillbirth and Infant Death: A Population-Based Cohort Study on 40 Million Births in the United States." *Women's Health Issues*, 21(5): 351–355.

14. Bird, S. T., A. Chandra, T. Bennett, and S. M. Harvey (2000). "Beyond Marital Status: Relationship Type and Duration and the Risk of Low Birth Weight." *Family Planning Perspectives*, 32(6): 281–287.

15. Kaye, K. (2012). *Why It Matters: Teen Childbearing and Infant Health*. The National Campaign to Prevent Teen and Unplanned Pregnancy. Available at http://www.thenational-campaign.org/why -it-matters/pdf/Childbearing-Infant-Health.pdf.

16. The National Campaign to Prevent Teen and Unplanned Pregnancy (2012). *Why It Matters: Teen Childbearing and Violence*. Available at http://www.thenationalcampaign.org/why-it-matters/pdf /violence.pdf.

17. The National Campaign to Prevent Teen and Unplanned Pregnancy (2012). *Why It Matters: Teen Childbearing, Education, and Economic Wellbeing*. Available at http://www.thenationalcampaign .org/why-it-matters/pdf/Childbearing-Education-Economic Wellbeing.pdf.

18. Stewart, A., and K. Kaye (2012). *Why It Matters: Teen Childbearing, Single Parenthood, and Father Involvement*. The National Campaign to Prevent Teen and Unplanned Pregnancy. Available at http://www .thenationalcampaign.org/why-it-matters/pdf/Childbearing-Single Parenthood-FatherInvolvement.pdf.

19. The National Campaign to Prevent Teen and Unplanned Pregnancy (2012). *Why It Matters: Teen Pregnancy and Overall Child Well-Being*. Available at http://www.thenationalcampaign.org/why-it -matters/pdf/child_well-being.pdf.

20. The National Campaign to Prevent Teen and Unplanned Pregnancy (2013). *Counting It Up: The Public Costs of Teen Childbearing: Key Data*. Available at http://thenationalcampaign.org/sites/default /files/resource-primary-download/counting-it-up-key-data-2013-update.pdf.

21. The National Campaign to Prevent Teen and Unplanned Pregnancy (2015). *Briefly: How Is the "Roughly 1 in 4" Statistic Calculated?* Available at http://thenationalcampaign.org/sites/default/files /resource-primary-download/briefly_1in4_jan2015_1.pdf.

22. Sedge, G., L. B. Finer, A. Bankole, M.A. Eilers, and S. Singh (2015). "Adolescent Pregnancy, Birth, and Abortion Rates Across Countries: Levels and Recent Trends." *Journal of Adolescent Health*, 56: 223–230. Available at http://www.jahonline.org/article /S1054-139X(14)00387-5/pdf.

23. U.S. Department of Health and Human Services, Office of Disease Prevention and Health Promotion (2010). *Healthy People 2020*. Washington, DC: U.S. Government Printing Office. Available at http://www.healthypeople.gov/2020/default.aspx.

24. Jackson, S. (1993). "Opening Session Comments: Laying the Groundwork for Working Together for the Future." *Journal of School Health*, 63(1): 11.

25. Finer, L. B., and M. R. Zolna (2011). "Unintended Pregnancy in the United States: Incidence and Disparities, 2006." *Contraception*, 84(5): 478–485.

26. Brown, S., and L. Eisenberg, eds. (1995). *"The Best Intentions: Unintended Pregnancy and the Well-Being of Children and Families."* Washington, DC: National Academies Press, 50–90.

27. Mosher, W. D., J. Jones, and J. C. Abma (2012). "Intended and Unintended Births in the United States: 1982–2010." *National Vital Statistics Reports*, 55. Available at http://www.cdc.gov/nchs/data /nhsr/nhsr055.pdf.

28. U.S. Department of Health and Human Services, Office of Population Affairs (2008). *Fact Sheet: Title X Family Planning Program*. Available at http://www.hhs.gov/opa/pdfs/title-x-family-planning -fact-sheet.pdf.

29. Fowler, C. I., J. Gable, J. Wang, and B. Lasater (2015). *Family Planning Annual Report: 2014 National Summary*. Available at http://www .hhs.gov/opa/pdfs/title-x-fpar-2014-national.pdf.

30. U.S. Department of Health and Human Services. Office of Population Affairs (n.d.). *Title X Family Planning*. Available at http://www .hhs.gov/opa/title-x-family-planning/.

31. U.S. Department of Health and Human Services, Office of Population Affairs (n.d.). *Title X Statutes and Regulations*. Available at http://www.hhs.gov/opa/title-x-family-planning/title-x-policies /statutes-and-regulations/.

32. Frost, J. J., et al. (2012). "Variation in Service Delivery Practices Among Clinics Providing Publicly Funded Family Planning Services in 2010." New York: Guttmacher Institute. Available at www .guttmacher.org/pubs/clinic-survey-2010.pdf.

33. U.S. Department of Health and Human Services, Office of Population Affairs (2000). *42 CFR Part 59, Standards of Compliance for Abortion-Related Services in Family Planning Services Projects*. Available at http://www.hhs.gov/opa/title-x-family-planning/title-x-policies /program-guidelines/final-rules-42-cfr-59.html.

34. Population Action International (n.d.). *Putting Politics Before Public Health: The Global Gag Rule*. Available at http://populationaction. org/topics/global-gag-rule/.

35. Hyde, J., and J. DeLamater (2003). *Understanding Human Sexuality*, 8th ed. Boston: McGraw-Hill.

36. Planned Parenthood Federation of America (2014). *History and Successes*. Available at http://www.plannedparenthood.org /about-us/who-we-are/history-and-successes.htm#Sanger.

37. Planned Parenthood Federation of America (2014). *Mission*. Available at https://www.plannedparenthood.org/about-us /who-we-are/mission.

38. Planned Parenthood Federation of America (2015). *By the Numbers*. Available at https://www.plannedparenthood.org/files/3314/3638/1447 /PP_Numbers.pdf?_ga=1.202746966.618222266.1470665358.

39. Frost, J. J., A. Sonfield, M. R. Zolna, and L. B. Finer (2014). "Return on Investment: A Fuller Assessment of the Benefits and Cost Savings of the US Publicly Funded Family Planning Program." *The Milbank Quarterly*, 92(4): 667–720. Available at http://www.guttmacher.org /pubs/journals/MQ-Frost_1468-0009.12080.pdf.

40. National Women's Law Center (2015). *State of Birth Control Coverage: Health Plan Violations of the Affordable Care Act*. Available at http://www.nwlc.org/sites/default/files/pdfs/stateofbirth control2015final.pdf.

41. Guttmacher Institute. (December 1, 2015). *State Policies in Brief: Insurance Coverage of Contraceptives*. Available at http://www .guttmacher.org/statecenter/spibs/spib_ICC.pdf.

42. Hasstedt, K., Y. Vierboom, and R. B. Gold (2015). "Still Needed: The Family Planning Safety Net Under Health Reform." *Guttmacher Policy Review*, 18(3): 56–61. Available at http://www.guttmacher .org/pubs/gpr/18/3/gpr1805615.pdf.

43. Cornell University Law School, Legal Information Institute (n. d.). *Roe v. Wade*. 410 U.S. 113 (1973). Available at http://www.law.cornell .edu/supct/html/historics/USSC_CR_0410_0113_ZS.html.

44. Centers for Disease Control and Prevention (2015). "Abortion Surveillance—United States, 2012." *Morbidity and Mortality Weekly Report*, 64(10): 1–40.

45. Alan Guttmacher Institute (n.d.). *Worldwide Abortion: Legality, Incidence and Safety*. Available at http://www.guttmacher.org /media/presskits/abortion-WW/index.html.

46. World Health Organization (2010). *International Statistical Classification of Diseases and Related Health Problems – 10th Revision*. Available at http://www.who.int/-classifications/icd/ICD10 Volume2_en_2010.pdf.

47. Centers for Disease Control and Prevention (2015). *Pregnancy Mortality Surveillance System*. Available at http://www.cdc.gov /reproductivehealth/MaternalInfantHealth/PMSS.html.

48. Khan, K. S., D. Wojdyla, L. Say, A. M. Gulmezoglu, and P. F. Van Look (2006). "WHO Analysis of Causes of Maternal Death: A Systematic Review." *Lancet*, 367(9516): 1066–1074.

49. World Health Organization (2015). *Maternal Mortality*. Available at http://www.who.int/mediacentre/factsheets/fs348/en/index.html.

50. U.S. Department of Health and Human Services, Health Resources and Services Administration (n.d.) *Prenatal – First Trimester Care Access*. Available at http://www.hrsa.gov/quality/toolbox/measures /prenatalfirsttrimester/.

51. American Academy of Family Physicians (2015). *Preconception Care* (Position Paper). Available from: http://www.aafp.org/about /policies/all/preconception-care.html.

52. Johnson, K., S. F. Posner, J. Biermann, MS[3], et al. (2006). "Recommendations to Improve Preconception Health and Health Care—United States." *Morbidity and Mortality Weekly Report*, 55(RR06): 1–23.

53. Centers for Disease Control and Prevention, National Center on Birth Defects and Developmental Disabilities (n.d.). *Show Your Love: Steps to a Healthier Me and Baby-to-Be!* Available at http://www .cdc.gov/preconception/showyourlove/documents/Healthier_Baby _Me_Plan.pdf.

54. Child Trends DataBank (2015). *Late or No Prenatal Care: Indicators on Children and Youth*. Available at http://www.childtrends.org /wp-content/uploads/2014/07/25_Prenatal_Care.pdf.

55. U.S. Department of Health and Human Services, Health Resources and Services Administration, Maternal and Child Health Bureau (2014). *Child Health USA 2013*. Rockville, MD: U.S. Department of Health and Human Services. Available at http://www.mchb.hrsa .gov/publications/pdfs/childhealth2013.pdf.

56. Heron, M. (2015). "Deaths: Leading Causes for 2012." *National Vital Statistics Reports*, 64(10). Hyattsville, MD: National Center

for Health Statistics. Available at http://www.cdc.gov/nchs/data/nvsr/nvsr64/nvsr64_10.pdf.

57. March of Dimes (2015). *The Impact of Premature Birth on Society*. Available at http://www.marchofdimes.org/mission/the-economic-and-societal-costs.aspx.

58. Behrman, R. E., and A. StithButer, eds. (2006). *Preterm Birth: Causes, Consequences, and Prevention*. Washington, DC: National Academies Press.

59. March of Dimes (2012). "Why at Least 39 Weeks Is Best for Your Baby." Available at http://www.marchofdimes.com/pregnancy/why-at-least-39-weeks-is-best-for-your-baby.aspx.

60. U.S. Census Bureau, Statistical Abstract of the United States (2012). *Births, Deaths, Marriages, and Divorces*. Available at http://www.census.gov/library/publications/2011/compendia/statab/131ed/births-deaths-marriages-divorces.html.

61. Main, E., B. Oshiro, B. Chagolla, D. Bingham, L. Dang-Kilduff, and L. Kowalewski (2010). *Elimination of Non-Medically Indicated (Elective) Deliveries Before 39 Weeks Gestational Age* (California Maternal Quality Care Collaborative Toolkit to Transform Maternity Care). Sacramento: California Department of Public Health; Maternal, Child and Adolescent Health Division. First edition published by March of Dimes. Contract #08-85012. Available at http://www.cdph.ca.gov/programs/mcah/Documents/MCAH-EliminationOfNon-Medically-IndicatedDeliveries.pdf.

62. Donahue, S. M., K. P. Kleinman, M. W. Gillman, and E. Okan (2010). "Trends in Birth Weight and Gestational Length Among Singleton Term Births in the United States: 1990–2005." *Obstetrics and Gynecology*, 115(2 Pt 1): 357–364.

63. March of Dimes (2012). *Low Birthweight*. Available at http://www.marchofdimes.com/baby/low-birthweight.aspx.

64. American Pregnancy Association (2007). *Intrauterine Growth Restriction (IUGR); Small for Gestational Age (SGA)*. Available at http://americanpregnancy.org/pregnancycomplications/iugr.htm.

65. Institute of Medicine (IOM) (2009). *Weight Gain During Pregnancy: Reexamining the Guidelines*. Washington, DC: The National Academies Press.

66. Chomitz, O. R., L. W. Cheung, and E. Lieberman (1995). "The Role of Lifestyle in Preventing Low Birthweight." *Future of Children*, 5(1): 162–175.

67. Tong, V. T., P. M. Dietz, B. Morrow, et al. (2013). "Trends in Smoking Before, During, and After Pregnancy—Pregnancy Risk Assessment Monitoring System, United States, 40 Sites, 2000–2010." *Morbidity and Mortality Weekly Report*, 62(SS06): 1–19. Available at http://www.cdc.gov/mmwr/preview/mmwrhtml/ss6206a1.htm#Tab3.

68. March of Dimes (2012). *Alcohol During Pregnancy*. Available at http://www.marchofdimes.com/pregnancy/alcohol-during-pregnancy.aspx.

69. Tan, C. H., C. H. Denny, N. E. Cheal, J. E. Sniezek, and D. Kanny (2015). "Alcohol Use and Binge Drinking Among Women of Childbearing Age—United States, 2011–2013." *Morbidity and Mortality Weekly Report*, 64(37): 1042–1046. Available at http://www.cdc.gov/mmwr/preview/mmwrhtml/mm6437a3.htm.

70. March of Dimes (2008). *Illicit Drug Use During Pregnancy*. Available at http://www.marchofdimes.com/pregnancy/illicit-drug-use-during-pregnancy.aspx.

71. American Academy of Pediatrics (2012). "Policy Statement: Breastfeeding and the Use of Human Milk." *Pediatrics*, 129(3): e827–e841. Available at http://pediatrics.aappublications.org/content/pediatrics/129/3/e827.full.pdf.

72. National Immunization Survey (2015). "Breastfeeding among U.S. Children Born 2002–2012." CDC National Immunization Surveys. Available at http://www.cdc.gov/breastfeeding/data/NIS_data/index.htm.

73. Baby-Friendly USA (2013). Available at http://www.babyfriendlyusa.org/about-us/baby-friendly-hospital-initiative/the-ten-steps.

74. Centers for Disease Control and Prevention (2015). *Sudden Unexpected Infant Death and Sudden Infant Death Syndrome*. Available at http://www.cdc.gov/sids/aboutsuidandsids.htm.

75. National Institutes of Health, Eunice Kennedy Shriver National Institute of Child Health and Human Development (NICHD), Safe to Sleep Public Education Campaign (2015). *About SIDS and Safe Infant Sleep*. Available at https://www.nichd.nih.gov/sts/about/Pages/default.aspx.

76. American Academy of Pediatrics (2002). "The Medical Home." *Pediatrics*, 110: 184.

77. U.S. Department of Transportation, National Highway Traffic Safety Administration (2015). *Traffic Safety Facts, 2013 Data*. Available at http://www-nrd.nhtsa.dot.gov/Pubs/812154.pdf.

78. Centers for Disease Control and Prevention, National Center for Injury Prevention and Control (2012). *National Action Plan for Child Injury Prevention*. Atlanta, GA: CDC, NCIPC. Available at http://www.cdc.gov/safechild/pdf/National_Action_Plan_for_Child_Injury_Prevention.pdf.

79. U.S. Department of Health and Human Services, Administration for Children and Families (2013). *Long-Term Consequences of Child Abuse and Neglect*. Available at https://www.childwelfare.gov/pubs/factsheets/long_term_consequences.pdf.

80. Federal Interagency Forum on Child and Family Statistics (2015). *America's Children: Key National Indicators of Well-Being, 2015*. Available at http://www.childstats.gov/pdf/ac2015/ac_15.pdf.

81. U.S. Department of Health and Human Services, Administration for Children and Families (2004). *Community Responsibility for Child Protection*. Available at http://nccanch.acf.hhs.gov/pubs/otherpubs/commresp.cfm.

82. Centers for Disease Control and Prevention (2016). *Recommended Immunization Schedules for Persons Ages 0 Through 18 Years—United States, 2016*. Available at http://www.cdc.gov/vaccines/schedules/downloads/child/0-18yrs-child-combined-schedule.pdf.

83. World Health Organization (2014). *Children: Reducing Mortality*. Available at http://www.who.int/mediacentre/factsheets/fs178/en/.

84. Child Trends DataBank (2015). *Immunization*. Available at http://www.childtrends.org/?indicators=immunization.

85. Centers for Disease Control and Prevention (2014). *Vaccines for Children Program: About VFC*. Available at http://www.cdc.gov/vaccines/programs/vfc/about/index.html.

86. Whitney, C. G., F. Zhou, J. Singleton, and A. Schuchat (2014). "Benefits from Immunization during the Vaccines for Children Program Era —United States, 1994–2013." *Morbidity and Mortality Weekly Report*, 63(16); 352–355. Available at http://www.cdc.gov/mmwr/preview/mmwrhtml/mm6316a4.htm.

87. Clemmons, N. S., P. A. Gastanaduy, A. P. Fiebelkorn, S. B. Redd, and G. S. Wallace (2015). "Measles—United States, January 4–April 2, 2015." *Morbidity and Mortality Weekly Report*, 64(14). Available at http://www.cdc.gov/mmwr/pdf/wk/mm6414.pdf.

88. Centers for Disease Control and Prevention (2015). *Vaccines Do Not Cause Autism*. Available at http://www.cdc.gov/vaccinesafety/concerns/autism.html.

89. Centers for Disease Control and Prevention (2013). *Immunization Information Systems: Frequently Asked Questions*. Available at http://www.cdc.gov/vaccines/programs/iis/resources-refs/faq.html.

90. U.S. Department of Health and Human Services, Health Resources and Services Administration, Maternal and Child Health Bureau (n.d.). *Maternal and Child Health Bureau Fact Sheet*. Available at http://www.hrsa.gov/about/pdf/mchb.pdf.

91. U.S. Department of Health and Human Services, Health Resources and Services Administration, Maternal and Child Health (n.d.). *About Us*. Available at http://mchb.hrsa.gov/about/index.html.

92. U.S. Department of Health and Human Services, Health Resources and Services Administration, Maternal and Child Health (n.d.). *Title V Maternal and Child Health Services Block Grant Program*.

Available at http://mchb.hrsa.gov/programs/titlevgrants/index. html.

93. U.S. Department of Health and Human Services, Health Resources and Services Administration, Maternal and Child Health (2003). *Maternal and Child Health Bureau Strategic Plan: FY 2003–2007.* Available at http://mchb.hrsa.gov/research/documents/mchbstrat plan0307.pdf.

94. U.S. Department of Agriculture, Food and Nutrition Service. "Special Supplemental Nutrition Program for Women, Infants, and Children." Title 7 *Code of Federal Regulations*, Pt. 246. 2013 ed.

95. U.S. Department of Agriculture, Food and Nutrition Service (2015). *WIC Eligibility Requirements.* Available at http://www.fns.usda.gov /wic/wic-eligibility-requirements.

96. Thorn, B., C. Tadler, N. Huret, E. Ayo, and C. Trippe (2015). *WIC Participant and Program Characteristics Final Report.* U.S. Department of Agriculture, Food and Nutrition Service, Office of Policy Support. Available at http://www.fns.usda.gov/sites/default/files /ops/WICPC2014.pdf.

97. National WIC Association (2013). *The Role of WIC in Public Health.* Available at https://s3.amazonaws.com/aws.upl/nwica.org/role_of _wic_public_health.pdf.

98. Institute of Medicine (2002). *Health Insurance Is a Family Matter.* Washington, DC: National Academies Press. Available at http://nap .edu/read/10503/chapter/1#ii.

99. American Academy of Pediatrics (n.d.). *Medicaid Matters for Children.* Available at https://www.aap.org/en-us/advocacy-and-policy /federal-advocacy/Pages/MedicaidMattersforChildren.aspx.

100. Centers for Medicare & Medicaid Services (n.d.). *Children's Health Insurance Program* Available at https://www.medicaid.gov/chip /chip-program-information.html

101. DeNavas-Walt, C., B. D. Proctor, and J. C. Smith (2013). "Income, Poverty, and Health Insurance Coverage in the United States: 2012." U.S. Census Bureau, *Current Population Reports*, P60-243. Washington, DC: U.S. Government Printing Office. Available at http ://www.census.gov/content/dam/Census/library/publications/2013 /demo/p60-245.pdf.

102. Smith, J. C. and C. Medalia (2015). "Health Insurance Coverage in the United States: 2014." U.S. Census Bureau, *Current Population Reports*, P60-253, Washington, DC: U.S. Government Printing Office. Available at http://www.census.gov/content/dam/Census /library/publications/2015/demo/p60-253.pdf.

103. Ruhm, C. J. (1997). "The Family and Medical Leave Act." *Journal of Economic Perspectives*, 3: 10–14.

104. Child Care Aware of America (2014). *Parents and the High Cost of Child Care: 2014 Report.* Available at http://www.naccrra.net /costofcare.

105. Cohen, A. J. (1996). "A Brief History of Federal Financing for Child Care in the United States." *The Future of Children*, 6(2). Available at http://futureofchildren.org/futureofchildren/publications /docs/06_02_01.pdf.

106. U.S. Department of Health and Human Services, Office of the Assistant Secretary for Planning and Evaluation (2015). *Estimates of Child Care Eligibility and Receipt for Fiscal Year 2012.* Available at https ://aspe.hhs.gov/sites/default/files/pdf/153591/ChildEligibility.pdf.

CHAPTER 8

Adolescents, Young Adults, and Adults

Chapter Outline

Chapter Objectives

After studying this chapter, you will be able to:

1. Explain why it is important for community health workers to be aware of the different health concerns of the various age groups in the United States.

2. Define by age the groups of adolescents, young adults, and adults.

3. Briefly describe key demographic characteristics of adolescents and young adults.

4. Summarize what the Youth Risk Behavior Surveillance System (YRBSS) and the Behavioral Risk Factor Surveillance System (BRFSS) are and what type of data they generate.

5. Provide a brief behavioral risk profile for adolescents, young adults (including college students), and adults.

6. Outline the health profiles for the various age groups—adolescents, young adults, and adults—listing the major causes of mortality, morbidity, and risk factors for each group.

7. Give examples of community health strategies for improving the health status of adolescents, young adults, and adults.

Scenario

Annie and Connor are about halfway through their sophomore year at a local high school in an urban area. This year, as chance would have it, they have similar class schedules and have ended up eating lunch together in the school cafeteria every day.

One day during lunch, Annie mentioned to Connor that her friend, Dayna, who is also a high school student, recently went to the doctor and was diagnosed with type 2 diabetes. Dayna was told that more and more kids her age are being diagnosed with this disease. Connor replied that he thought that only adults had that type of diabetes. Annie stated that she is concerned for Dayna because Dayna's doctor told her that she must start eating more fresh fruits and vegetables, drinking less sugary beverages, and exercising on a daily basis or else she will be at risk of developing serious health problems from having diabetes. Apparently, Dayna doesn't know where to buy fruits and vegetables because the corner store she visits every day before and after school only sells candy, soda, and alcohol, and she does not want to exercise outside because there has been a lot of violence in her neighborhood lately. Connor said that he thought Dayna might just have to move away from the neighborhood to be healthy.

Introduction

In this chapter, we present a profile of the health of Americans in two different groups—adolescents and young adults (10–24 years of age) and adults (25–64 years of age). Please note that different organizations and agencies use various age ranges to categorize adolescents and young adults. The age range of 10–19 years of age is used for adolescents in this book because it is used by leading health organizations, such as the World Health Organization.[1] Just like the age groups of Americans presented elsewhere in the text, each of these groups has its own set of health risks, problems, and assets to contribute to the solution of their health problems. Viewing these age group profiles enables public health workers to detect the causes of disease, injury, and death for specific priority populations and to propose interventions to reduce those causes. Effective interventions aimed at specific population age groups can reduce the risk factors that contribute to disease, injury, and death, and increase the protective factors that enhance the well-being for these groups as well as the entire population. We hope that you, the student, will become knowledgeable about the specific health problems and solutions to these problems of each age group and also become mindful of the subpopulations within these groups that are at special risk.

The years of life between the ages of 10 and 64 are some of the most productive, if not the most productive, of people's lives. Consider all that takes place during these years. Many people will complete their formal education, meet and commit to their lifelong partners, become parents and raise a family, find and develop their vocation, earn their greatest amount of wealth, actively engage in the development of their community, travel more than during any other time in their lives, become aunts or uncles and grandparents, become valued employees, serve as role models and mentors, and plan and save for retirement.[2] However, recent research shows that an increasing number of adolescents and young adults are delaying some of these life choices and taking longer to become independent, for a variety of reasons. It is also during this time that individuals typically enjoy some of the best health of their lives as well as have their current and future health and health behaviors shaped by their environment and life circumstances.

Adolescents and Young Adults

Adolescents and young adults are considered to be those people who fall into the 10-to-24-year-old age range. The individuals in this age group are considered very important by our society because they represent the future of our nation. This period of development of adolescence and young adulthood, often combined when reporting data about young people, can be further split into two subgroups. "Adolescence is generally regarded as the period of life from puberty to maturity."[3] This may not be an easy stage of life for individuals because it is a period of

Adolescents and young adults those people who fall into the 10-to-24-year-old age range

transition from childhood to adulthood. Adolescence "is a time when children psychologically move from areas of relative comfort and emotional security to places and situations that are far more complex and often much more challenging."[4] In addition to the psychological changes, this population of teenagers is also experiencing "hormonal changes, physical maturation, and frequently, opportunities to engage in risk behaviors."[3]

Young adults also face many physical, emotional, and educational changes. For example, many young adults complete their physical growth and maturity, and experience those situations and opportunities previously mentioned. Couple the demands of these personal changes with the demands of a fast-paced, ever-changing society and it is easy to see why this stage in life is considered one of the most difficult.[5] However, this stage of life can also be quite fulfilling. The combined period of adolescence and young adulthood is a critical one, in terms of health. It is during this period in one's life that many health-related beliefs, attitudes, and behaviors are adopted and challenged.[3,4,6] During this stage of life, young people have increased freedom and access to health-compromising substances and experiences—such as alcohol, tobacco, other drugs, and sexual risk taking—as well as opportunities for health-enhancing experiences such as regularly scheduled exercise, healthful diets, and opportunities to engage in behaviors and experiences that benefit their communities.[3,4,6] It is also during this stage that lifestyles are often established and shaped, resulting in long-term influences on health in later years of life. The concept that health status and environmental exposures in the early part of one's life will impact their adult health status is called the *life course approach* to understanding health and disease.[7] This is an important concept because it helps explain how every stage of a person's life impacts the individual's long-term health. Thus, those risk behaviors as well as protective factors in the adolescent and young adult years will have an influence on that person's well-being throughout his or her lifetime.

Demography

Several demographic variables affect the health of this age group, but the four variables that are most important to community health are the number of young people, their living arrangements, their employment status, and their access to health care. Please note that for some of the adolescent data in this chapter, especially for young adolescents (ages 10–14), information for children will also be included due to how the data were collected and reported. Mortality and morbidity information for young adolescents is discussed elsewhere in the text.

Number of Adolescents and Young Adults

According to the 2010 U.S. Census, 10-to-24-year olds made up over a fifth of the U.S. population.[8] As we look to the future, the proportion of adolescents and young adults in the general population will decrease, but the number of adolescents will continue to grow. The racial and ethnic makeup of adolescents will become increasingly diverse (see **Figure 8.1**). In 2014, approximately 54% of adolescents were non-Hispanic white.[9] It is estimated that by 2050, this percentage will drop to 40%.[9]

Living Arrangements

The percentage of children younger than the age of 18 living in a single-parent family has been on the rise ever since 1965. In fact, the percentage increased sharply in the 1970s and continued to rise slowly through the 1990s. The sharp rise in the 1970s can be attributed to the great increase in the divorce rate.[5] In 2012, more than a quarter of all children lived in single-parent families.[10] Additionally, black children (55%) and Hispanic children (31%) were more likely to live in a single-parent home than white children (21%). Regardless of race and ethnicity, children in a single-parent family are more likely to be living with their mother than their father.[10]

Family household statistics on single-parent families are only a snapshot of children's living status during a single year. Unfortunately, many children are affected over their lifetimes by growing up in single-parent families. Children living in single-parent families are more likely to experience economic disadvantages as well as negative impacts on their emotional, cognitive, and social well-being.[11]

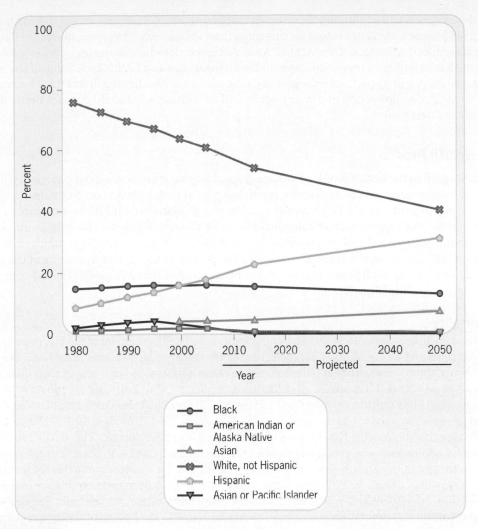

FIGURE 8.1   Race and Hispanic origin of adolescents 10–19 years of age: United States 1980–2050.

Data from: MacKay, A. P., and C. Duran (2007). *Adolescent Health in the United States.* Hyattsville, MD: National Center for Health Statistics, 9; U.S. Department of Health and Human Services (2016). *The Changing Face of America's Adolescent.* Available at http://www.hhs.gov/ash/oah /adolescent-health-topics/americas-adolescents/changing-face.html.

Employment Status and Health Care Access

Since the years of 1960 and the early 1980s, when there were significant increases in the participation of young women in the labor force, the proportion of all adolescents and young adults in the labor force has remained relatively constant. However, this age group is beginning to see some significant permanent changes in its labor-force participation, particularly 16-to-19-year-old males, mainly because of increased school attendance and enrollment in high school, college, and summer school over the past decade.[12] The youth labor force, composed of 16-to-24-year olds, makes up approximately 13% of the overall labor force.[13] However, when the unemployment rates of this age group are separated by race and ethnicity, differences appear. For example, regardless of sex, black adolescents and young adults are more likely to be unemployed than are whites.[14] White adolescents and young adults have the lowest proportion of unemployment.[14] These proportions, like so many others already discussed, are disproportionate by race/ethnicity.

These statistics historically have been important to community and public health because most health insurance, and thus access to health care, is connected to employment status. In 2013, 75% of young adults ages 18 to 25 had health insurance coverage, as compared to 92% of children ages 6 to 18.[15] Studies have shown that young adults have less access to health care and tend to use emergency rooms for care more than adolescents.[16] However, due to the Patient Protection and Affordable Care Act (ACA), as discussed elsewhere in the text, adolescents and young adults will have increased access to health insurance and health care. Some of the ways that the ACA will impact adolescents and young adults are highlighted in **Box 8.1**. The impact of the ACA on adolescents and young adults will be substantial, and this impact needs to be evaluated over time.

A Health Profile

With regard to the health profile of this age group, four major areas stand out—mortality, morbidity from specific infectious diseases, health behavior and lifestyle, and protective factors. The following information will be presented with the recognition that it is known and emphasized throughout this chapter that an individual's behavior and overall lifestyle are heavily impacted by factors both within and outside his or her control.[17] This is increasingly recognized by the community health workforce, and strategies to improve the health and well-being of the adolescent and young adult population are including approaches that will modify the environment to support healthy lifestyles.

Mortality

Although, on average, adolescents and young adults are a healthy segment of the U.S. population, adolescents and young adults suffer their share of life-threatening problems.[5] Due to the obesity epidemic, there is concern that today's youth may have a shorter life expectancy than their parents.[18] However, as it has been with most other age groups, the death rate for adolescents and young adults has significantly declined. Between 1950 and 2013, the death rate of adolescents and young adults ages 15–24 declined by nearly 50%, from 128.1 to 64.8 per 100,000.[15] Mortality data for early adolescents (10–13 years of age) showed a similar decline. This decline in death rates for adolescents and young adults, like that for children, can be attributed to advances in medicine and injury and disease prevention as well as behavior change among this age group.[9, 15]

Regardless of race or ethnicity, adolescent and young adult males have higher mortality rates than adolescent and young adult females.[15] Mortality rates for males and females were highest among blacks and American Indians/Alaska Natives. The lowest mortality rates of both men and women belong to Asian/Pacific Islanders.[15] The leading causes of death for young adolescents (who are reported in the 5–14 age group in national statistics) are unintentional injuries, malignant neoplasms (cancer), and suicide.[15] Much of the physical threat to older adolescents and young adults ages 15–24 stems from their behavior and their environment rather than from disease.[1,15] For young people overall, nearly three-fourths of all mortality can be attributed to three causes—unintentional injuries (mainly motor vehicle crashes; 41%), homicide (17%),

---

BOX 8.1   The ACA, Adolescents, and Young Adults

Some of the ways the ACA is affecting adolescents and young adults are...

- Increasing insurance coverage through allowing young adults to remain on their parents' plan through age 26 and other mechanisms.
- Prohibiting plans from imposing pre-existing condition exclusions (starting in 2010 for children and adolescents and in 2014 for adults).

- Establishing insurance marketplaces ("exchanges") where consumers can shop for, compare, and purchase insurance.
- Reducing premiums and cost-sharing in plans purchased in the marketplace, through subsidies and tax credits for many low-income individuals.
- Expanding Medicaid (required for children and adolescents; a state option for adults).
- Requiring coverage of certain preventive services without cost-sharing.

Data from: National Adolescent and Young Adult Health Information Center (2012). *The Affordable Care Act: Implications for Adolescents and Young Adults.* San Francisco: University of California. Available at http://nahic.ucsf.edu/resources/aca/.

and suicide (15%).[15] Mortality from unintentional injuries in this age group declined during the last half of the twentieth century. For example, since 1990, the mortality rates for deaths from motor vehicle–related injuries for 15-to-24-year olds has declined by almost 55%.[15] Even so, unintentional injury deaths remain the leading cause of death in adolescents and young adults ages 10 to 24 years, and alcohol is often a contributing factor for deaths caused by motor vehicle–related injuries.[9] (See **Figure 8.2** for death rates for 15-to-24-year olds).

Unlike other mortality data in this age group, white males have a higher rate of death in motor vehicles than do black males. Motor vehicle–related death rates of white and Native American males are the highest for this age group. The mortality rates for white and black women combined are lower than those for males of either race.[15] One of the most alarming mortality trends in this age group is the growing suicide rates, which have almost doubled over the past 50 years.[15] Suicide is the second leading cause of death in adolescents and young adults between the ages of 15 and 24. The suicide rate in Native American males is significantly higher than for other males, even though these rates have decreased by nearly one-third over the past 50 years. Although the number of completed suicides by adolescents and young adults is alarming, it represents only a fraction of all the suicides contemplated. Data from the 2013 Centers for Disease Control and Prevention's Youth Risk Behavior Surveillance System (YRBSS) indicate that approximately one in seven ninth to twelfth graders in the United States have thought seriously about attempting suicide (17.0%), while 8.0% have actually attempted suicide.[19]

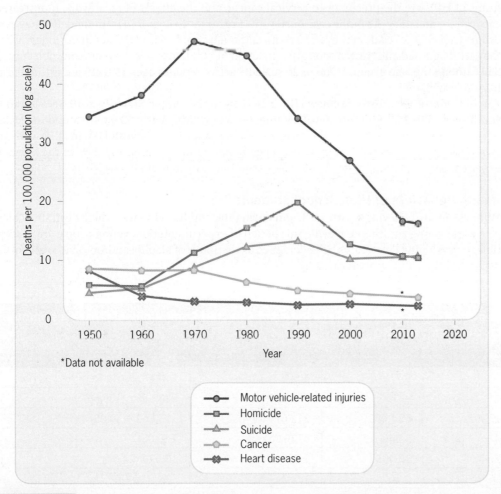

FIGURE 8.2   Death rates for leading causes of death for ages 15 to 24, 1950–2013.

Data from: National Center for Health Statistics. (2015). *Health, United States, 2014: With Special Feature on Adults Aged 55–64*. Hyattsville, MD: Author.

Homicide rates continue to be a significant concern among black males, as their rates are four times higher than Hispanic males and more than 10 times higher than other populations in this age group.[15] It is not race and gender, per se, that are risk factors for violent death, but rather socioeconomic status and environment. Differences in homicide rates between races are significantly reduced when socioeconomic factors are taken into account.

Morbidity

Although a higher proportion of adolescents and young adults survive to age 24 than ever before, this group still suffers significantly from a number of different communicable diseases. Due to medical advances and knowledge regarding immunizations, certain communicable diseases, such as the measles, have been significantly reduced or nearly eradicated. As shown in **Table 8.1**, change to the immunization schedule (number and frequency of vaccinations) has significantly reduced the number of measles cases.[20]

The other diseases that cause considerable morbidity in adolescents and young adults are sexually transmitted diseases (STDs), also known as sexually transmitted infections (STIs; see Table 8.1), with young people 15 to 24 years of age acquiring half of all new STDs. This population is at higher risk of acquiring STDs for a combination of behavioral, biological, and cultural reasons.[21] Whereas many STDs are completely curable with antibiotics, some viral infections, such as hepatitis, human immunodeficiency virus (HIV), or human papillomavirus (HPV), can be treated but never cured.[22] The effects of some STDs can last a lifetime. For example, some forms of HPV are the precursor to cervical cancer, and the effects of chlamydia, if untreated, can lead to infertility. As in the case of HIV, the precursor to acquired immunodeficiency syndrome (AIDS), the result may even be death, although people with HIV are living longer when they are diagnosed and treated soon after infection.[22, 23] Chlamydia is the most common curable STD among this age group.[24] One in 20 sexually active females ages 14 to 19 are estimated to have chlamydia.[25]

In terms of HIV, 26% of all new HIV infections in the United States in 2010 were found in youth ages 13 to 24.[26] Of these new HIV infections in youth, nearly 60% were found in blacks/African Americans.[26] However, the majority of youth ages 13 to 24 with HIV in 2010 were not aware they were infected.[26] "Estimates suggest that while representing 25% of the sexually experienced population, 15-to-24-year olds acquire nearly half of all new STDs."[21]

Health Behaviors of High School Students

Whereas many behavioral patterns begin during the childhood years, others begin in adolescence and young adulthood. During this period of experimentation, young people are susceptible to developing deleterious behaviors such as the abuse of alcohol and/or tobacco and other drugs, fighting, and weapon carrying.

TABLE 8.1   Number of Reported Cases (and Incidence Rates) of Selected Communicable Diseases among 15-to-24-Year Olds, 1981 to 2010

Disease and Age	1981#	1990#	2000	2010
AIDS	—	1,715	1,567 (4.16)	7,217 (16.75) (Reported as HIV)
Chlamydia	—	—	508,736 (1,349.42)	930,338 (2159.69)
Gonorrhea*	617,994	384,490	212,679 (564.13)	193,869 (450.05)
Measles	94	5,646	17 (0.05)	7 (0.02)
Syphilis*	12,965	16,408	1,338 (3.55)	10,629 (24.67)
Tuberculosis	2,198	1,867	1,623 (4.31)	1,220 (2.79)

Notes: # = rates not available; — = data not collected; * = civilian cases only, primary and secondary. Incidence rates per 100,000 population.

Data from: Centers for Disease Control and Prevention (various years). *Morbidity and Mortality Weekly Report: Annual Summaries*; "Summary of Notifiable Diseases—United States, 2000." *Morbidity and Mortality Weekly Report,* 49(53): 23; "Summary of Notifiable Diseases—United States, 2008." *Morbidity and Mortality Weekly Report,* 57(54): 32–33; and "Summary of Notifiable Diseases—United States, 2010." *Morbidity and Mortality Weekly Report,* 59(53): 39–40.

In 1990, the Centers for Disease Control and Prevention (CDC) initiated the Youth Risk Behavior Surveillance System (YRBSS) to better track selected health behaviors among young people. The YRBSS includes a national school-based survey, as well as state, territorial, tribal, and district surveys. In the spring of 1991, CDC conducted for the first time the national school-based Youth Risk Behavior Survey (YRBS). This survey continues to be conducted biennially during odd-numbered years among national probability samples of ninth- through twelfth-grade students from private and public schools. Results of the 2015 survey are included in the following sections. In 1990, CDC began offering to each state and to selected local education departments the YRBSS questionnaire and fiscal and technical assistance to conduct the Youth Risk Behavior Survey. During 2015, a representative sample from 39 states and 21 large urban school districts were surveyed.[19] In the time the YRBSS has been in operation, it has proved to be very helpful at both the state and local levels. A number of states and local communities have put into place programs and policies to reduce risk behaviors in youth. Continued support of YRBSS will help monitor and ensure the success of many public health and school health programs.

Behaviors That Contribute to Unintentional Injuries

Five different behaviors of high school students that relate to unintentional injuries are monitored as part of the YRBSS: seat belt use, bicycle helmet use, motorcycle helmet use, riding with a driver who has been drinking alcohol, and driving after drinking alcohol. Since 1991, the numbers of students engaging in these risk behaviors have declined. Yet in 2015 one-fifth of students nationwide had, in the 30 days preceding the survey, ridden with a driver who had been drinking alcohol and 10.0% had driven a vehicle after drinking alcohol.[19] In addition, 41.4% of students had texted or e-mailed while driving a vehicle on at least 1 day in the 30 days before the survey.[19]

Behaviors That Contribute to Violence

Behaviors that contribute to violence-related injuries of high school students include carrying a weapon (e.g., gun, knife, or club), engaging in a physical fight, engaging in dating violence, having been forced to have sexual intercourse, engaging in school-related violence including bullying, suicide ideation, and suicide attempts. Nationwide, one in five students (20.2%) had been bullied on school property in the past 12 months before the survey; whereas 14.8% of students reported being electronically bullied within the 12 months before the survey.[19] It is no wonder that many school districts around the country are taking steps to reduce violent behavior in school. Males are more likely than females are to get in a fight or carry a weapon. However, females are more likely than males to have been forced to have sexual intercourse and to report sadness, suicide ideation, and suicide attempts.[19]

Tobacco Use

The use of tobacco products represents one of the most widespread, high-risk health behaviors for this group. In 2015, approximately one-tenth of high school students (10.8.%) nationwide were current smokers—that is, smoked on at least 1 day in the past 30 days—which is a significant decrease from 1995, when 34.8% of students were current smokers. Similarly, a significant decrease has been seen among current frequent smokers—those who had smoked on 20 or more days in the past 30 days (2015, 3.4%; 1995, 16.1%).[19] Overall, white students (12.4%) were more likely to report current cigarette use than were Hispanic (9.2%) and black (6.5%) students.[19] The vast majority of people who become dependent on nicotine develop that dependency before the age of 18.[21] (See **Figure 8.3**.)

FIGURE 8.3   Each day, an estimated 2,100 young people who are occasional smokers progress to become daily smokers and more than 3,200 youth smoke their first cigarette.

© Faure et Blanchard/Getty Images.

Smokeless tobacco or spit tobacco, includes oral snuff, loose leaf chewing tobacco, plug chewing tobacco, and nasal snuff

In addition to cigarette smoking, the use of **smokeless tobacco** or spit tobacco (snuff and chewing tobacco) and cigars is a threat to the health of teenagers. In 2015, the overall prevalence of current smokeless tobacco use was 7.3% in high school students, which is a significant decrease from 1995 (11.4%). The number of students using cigars has significantly decreased since 1997 (22%), approximately one-tenth (10.3%) of students reported current cigar use.[19] Becoming a significant concern among high school students is the use of electronic vapor products (including e-cigarettes, e-cigars, e-pipes, vape pipes, vaping pens, e-hookahs, and hookah pens). Nationwide, in 2015, 24.1% of high school students reported current use of electronic vapor products, which is a significant increase from 1.5% in 2011.[19,21]

Because use of tobacco that begins during adolescence can lead to a lifetime of nicotine dependence and a variety of negative health consequences, the federal government has exerted considerable effort to keep tobacco out of the hands of adolescents. Many believed, and data from the YRBSS verified, that most adolescents have had easy access to tobacco products. With the recent invention of electronic cigarettes, or e-cigarettes, new challenges have been presented in our national tobacco prevention efforts.

The most sweeping changes related to the sale of cigarettes came in 1998 when 46 state attorneys general agreed to a settlement with tobacco companies. (Florida, Minnesota, Mississippi, and Texas were not included in the settlement because they had already settled individually with the tobacco companies.) The settlement called for the companies to make payments of $206 billion to the states over 25 years beginning in 2000 and to finance antismoking programs in exchange for the states dropping their health care lawsuits for smokers who were treated with Medicaid funds. In addition to paying the states, the tobacco companies agreed to spend $1.7 billion to study youth smoking and to finance antismoking advertising and accept restrictions on marketing practices that appeal to children, such as the use of cartoon characters (e.g., "Joe Camel").[22] While policy and prevention efforts have continued to positively affect the number of children who begin smoking, as can be observed by the 2009 passing of the Family Smoking Prevention and Tobacco Control Act, "which for the first time granted the U.S. Food and Drug Administration (FDA) the authority to regulate the manufacture, distribution, sale, labeling, advertising, and promotion of tobacco products to protect public health,"[23] states are spending only two cents of every dollar in tobacco revenue to fight tobacco use while tobacco companies are outspending prevention efforts 20 to 1 in the marketing of products.[22]

The invention of e-cigarettes has once again changed the challenges in prevention and cessation of tobacco use. As can be seen by **Figure 8.4**, e-cigarette advertising is significantly influencing e-cigarette use among youth. While states and other localities have worked to address tobacco-related issues through advocacy efforts and the establishment of policies, enormous challenges remain. An emerging strategy for addressing youth tobacco use is to increase the minimum legal sale age for tobacco to 21.[22]

Alcohol and Other Drugs

Although, for some, the first use of alcohol or other drugs begins during the childhood years, for most, experimentation with these substances occurs during the adolescent and young adult years. For example, nearly one-sixth (17.2%) of students surveyed for the YRBSS in 2015 indicated that they drank alcohol (more than a few sips) for the first time

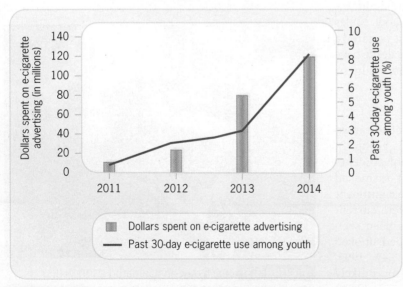

FIGURE 8.4 E-cigarette use among youth is rising as e-cigarette advertising grows.

Data from: Centers for Disease Control and Prevention (2016). *E-cigarette Ads and Youth Infographics.* Available at http://www.cdc.gov/vitalsigns/ecigarette-ads/infographic.html.

prior to 13 years of age.[19] One-third (32.8%) of all high school students reported drinking during the previous month and 17.7% engaged in episodic heavy drinking (five or more drinks of alcohol in a row).[19] Further, nearly 40% (38.6%) of high school students have tried marijuana with one-fifth reporting use within the past 30 days.[19]

Although 21.7% of all high school students have used marijuana during the preceding month, alcohol use and abuse continue to be major problems for adolescents, particularly among high school dropouts. As was reported earlier in this chapter, alcohol contributes significantly to motor vehicle crashes in this age group.[9] In addition to the use of marijuana, high school students are reporting the use of other illicit drugs. The 2015 YRBSS data indicated 5.2% of students had used some form of cocaine, 7.0% had used an inhalant, 5.0% had used ecstasy, 3.0% had used methamphetamines, and 3.5% had used steroids without a doctor's prescription.[19] A rising concern for adolescents and young adults is the misuse and abuse of prescription drugs. The 2015 YRBSS data indicated that one-sixth (16.8%) of students surveyed had taken prescription drugs (e.g., Oxycontin, Percocet, Vicodin, codeine, Adderall, Ritalin, or Xanax) without a doctor's prescription at least once.[19]

Sexual Behaviors That Contribute to Unintended Pregnancy and Sexually Transmitted Diseases

Adolescents in the United States continue to experience high rates of unintended pregnancies and STDs, including HIV infection.[24] YRBSS data from 2015 show that more than one-third (41.2%) of all high school students have engaged in sexual intercourse sometime in their lifetime. The prevalence of sexual intercourse ranged between 20.7% for ninth-grade girls to 59.0% for high school senior boys. Furthermore, it was more likely for black (48.5%) and Hispanic (42.5%) students to have ever engaged in sexual intercourse than for whites (39.9%).[19] **Table 8.2** shows the trends of selected sexual risk behaviors for high school students since 1995. These findings have important implications for the need for comprehensive sexual education prior to high school.

Although the teenage birth rate declined 9% from 2013 to 2014, teenage pregnancy remains a significant concern with more than 249,000 teen girls in the United States between the ages of 15 and 19 becoming pregnant each year.[26] Most of these pregnancies are unintended.[26] As was reported elsewhere in the text, teenage mothers are less likely than women age 20 and older to receive early prenatal care and are more likely to smoke during pregnancy, have a preterm birth, and have a baby who has a low birth weight.[26] In addition to the health risks associated with teenage pregnancies for both mother and child, there are educational, economic, and psychosocial risks to the mother and father as well.[27] Consequently, due to these negative health and psychosocial outcomes, the public health community must take steps to prevent pregnancy in the adolescent population.

TABLE 8.2   Percentage of High School Students Who Reported Selected Sexual Risk Behaviors, by Year—Youth Risk Behavior Survey, United States

Behavior	1995	2005	2015
Ever had sexual intercourse	53.1	46.8	41.2
Ever had sexual intercourse with four or more partners	17.8	14.3	11.5
Had sexual intercourse at least once during the 3 months preceding the survey	37.9	33.9	30.1
Used alcohol or drugs before last sexual intercourse	24.8	23.3	20.6
Did not use any method to prevent pregnancy (among students who were currently sexually active)	15.8	12.7	13.8
Used or partner used condom at last sexual intercourse	54.4	62.8	56.9

Data from: Centers for Disease Control and Prevention (2016). *Trends in Prevalence of Sexual Behaviors and HIV Testing, National YRBS: 1991–2015.* Available at http://www.cdc.gov/healthyyouth/data/yrbs/pdf/trends/2015_us_sexual_trend_yrbs.pdf.

Physical Activity and Sedentary Behaviors

Lack of physical activity by young people has increasingly become a concern. In 2015, nearly half (48.6%) of students had not been physically active for at least 60 minutes per day on 5 or more days during the 7 days prior to the YRBSS survey. Males (57.8%) were more likely than females (39.1%) to engage in sufficient physical activity. Nationally, 14.3% of students had not participated in 60 minutes of any kind of physical activity that increased their heart rate or made them breathe hard some of the time on at least 1 day during the 7 days preceding the survey.[19]

In contrast, 25% of students had watched television for at least 3 hours per day, and 42% of students had used the computer for something other than schoolwork for at least 3 hours per day.[19]

Overweight and Weight Control

Much like the concern for insufficient physical activity, the concern regarding students becoming overweight has received significant attention recently due to the negative health consequences associated with being overweight and obese, such as the potential to develop type 2 diabetes, as well as a variety of other health issues.[18] In 2015, approximately one-quarter of high school students were obese (13.9%) or overweight (16.8%),[19] while 31.5% described themselves as slightly or very overweight. Almost one-half of students were trying to lose weight (45.6%).

Health Behaviors of College Students

Two currently available data sources regarding the health behaviors of college students are the National College Health Assessment II (NCHA-II)[28] and Monitoring the Future.[29] The NCHA, first implemented in spring 2000, is a national, nonprofit research effort organized by the American College Health Association.[28] Monitoring the Future is conducted at the University of Michigan's Institute for Social Research and, since its inception in 1975, has been funded by the National Institute on Drug Abuse. Monitoring the Future specifically examines drug behaviors and related attitudes of a broad participant age range: eighth, tenth, and twelfth graders to adults through age 55,[29] whereas the NCHA examines a wide range of health behaviors in college students. These data sources, among others, can be helpful to those responsible for delivering health promotion education and services to many of the 20.6 million students enrolled in the nation's colleges and universities.[30]

Behaviors That Contribute to Unintentional Injuries

As mentioned throughout this chapter, the use of alcohol, both by the injured individual or a person with whom the individual is with at the time of injury, is a common cause of unintentional injuries among adolescents and young adults, especially college-aged students.[9,15] These injuries are often associated with the use of a motor vehicle at the time of the incident,[9] but this is not always the case. Unintentional injuries have been the leading cause of death for young adults throughout the past 50 years.[15]

Behaviors That Contribute to Violence

College campuses are communities just like small towns or neighborhoods in large cities. Thus, they have their share of violence. Knowing this, most colleges and universities have programs in place to address this issue. Though weapon carrying, fighting, and suicide ideation and attempts are important public health issues, sexual assault is particularly prevalent among college students. Although male college students do report sexual abuse/assault, female college students reported significantly more sexually abusive experiences in the past school year, all of which were without their consent. These included sexual touching (7.7%), verbal threats (15.1%), attempted penetration (3.4%), or sexual penetration (2.1%). Additionally, 10.9% of females and 6.1% of males reported being involved in an emotionally abusive relationship in the past school year.[28] Though not all the reasons for these sexual assaults are clear, alcohol is a contributing factor in many of these episodes.

Tobacco Use

Research indicates that the more education a person has, the less likely he or she is to use tobacco.[29] In 2015, the prevalence of daily smoking for college students was 5% versus 16% for age-mates not enrolled full time in college.[29] As shown in **Figure 8.5A**, the use of tobacco by college students had been steadily declining until the early 1990s, was inconsistent during the 1990s, and had an obvious decline again in the 2000s. The reason for the inconsistencies in prevalence over the past 20 years is unknown.[29] The new development of e-cigarettes has had an impact on tobacco use, particularly among males who are not enrolled in college, as shown in **Figure 8.5B**.[29]

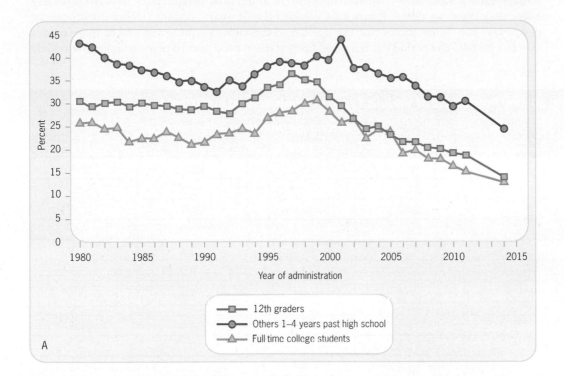

A

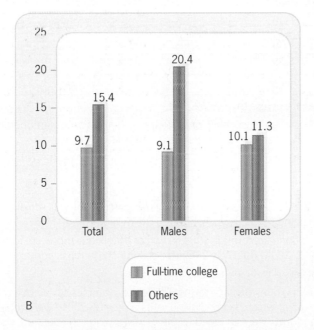

B

FIGURE 8.5   **A**. Cigarette use: trends in 30-day prevalence among college students versus others 1 to 4 years beyond high school. **B**. E-cigarette use: 30-day prevalence among male and female full-time college students and those 1 to 4 years beyond high school.

Data from: Johnston, L. D., P. M. O'Malley, J. G. Bachman, J. E. Schulenberg, and R.A. Meich (2015). *Monitoring the Future National Survey Results on Drug Use, 1975–2014. Vol II: College Students and Adults Ages 19–55.* Bethesda, MD: National Institute on Drug Abuse.

Alcohol and Other Drug Use

College and university campuses have long been thought of as places where alcohol and other drugs have been abused. **Table 8.3** shows that alcohol was the drug of choice on college campuses in 2014, with 63.1% of the students reporting that they had consumed alcohol in the previous 30 days. Table 8.3 also shows that illicit drug use continues to be an issue, but it is still considerably lower than it was in 1980.[29] **Figure 8.6A** presents the 34-year trend for alcohol use on college campuses. The figure shows that the number of individuals consuming one or more drinks over the past 30-day period has remained fairly stable for the past 10 years, with approximately

TABLE 8.3   Trends in 30-Day Prevalence of Various Types of Drugs among Full-Time College Students

| | Percentage Who Used in Past 30 Days | | | |
	1980	1990	2000	2014
Any illicit drug[a]	38.4	15.2	21.5	22.7
Any illicit drug other than marijuana	20.7	4.4	6.9	10.0
Marijuana	34.0	14.0	20.0	20.8
Inhalants[b]	1.5	1.0	0.9	0.3
Hallucinogens[c]	2.7	1.4	1.4	1.0
LSD	1.4	1.1	0.9	0.5
MDMA (ecstasy)[d]	NA	0.6	2.5	0.7
Cocaine	6.9	1.2	1.4	1.8
Heroin	0.3	0.0	0.2	*
Other narcotics[e,f]	1.8	0.5	1.7	1.2
Amphetamines, adj.[e,g]	NA	1.4	2.9	4.8
Barbiturates[e]	0.9	0.2	1.1	0.7
Tranquilizers[e,f]	2.0	0.5	2.0	1.7
Alcohol	81.8	74.5	67.4	63.1
Cigarettes	25.8	21.5	28.2	12.9

Notes: NA = data not available; * = a prevalence rate of less than 0.05%.

[a] "Any illicit drug" includes use of marijuana, hallucinogens, cocaine, or heroin, or other narcotics, amphetamines, sedatives (barbiturates), methaqualone (until 1990), or tranquilizers not under a doctor's orders.

[b] This drug was asked about in four of the five questionnaire forms in 1980–1989 and in three of the six forms in 1999–2005. Total *N* in 2005 (for college students) is 680.

[c] In 2001, the question text was changed on half the questionnaire forms. "Other psychedelics" was changed to "other hallucinogens," and "shrooms" was added to the list of examples. For tranquilizers, "Miltown" was replaced with "Xanax" in the list of examples. Beginning in 2002, the remaining forms were changed to the new wording.

[d] This drug was asked about in two of the five questionnaire forms in 1989, in two of the six questionnaire forms in 1990–2001, and in three of the six questionnaire forms in 2002–2005. Total *N* in 2005 (for college students) is approximately 680.

[e] Only drug use that was not under a doctor's orders is included here.

[f] In 2002 the question text was changed on half of the questionnaire forms. The list of examples of narcotics other than heroin was updated: Talwin, laudanum, and paregoric—all of which had negligible rates of use by 2001—were replaced by Vicodin, Oxycontin, and Percocet. In 2003, the remaining forms were changed to the new wording. The data are based on all forms in 2003 and beyond.

[g] Based on the data from the revised question, which attempts to exclude inappropriate reporting of nonprescription amphetamines.

Data from: Johnston, L. D., P. M. O'Malley, J. G. Bachman, J. E. Schulenberg, and R.A. Miech (2015). *Monitoring the Future National Survey Results on Drug Use, 1976–2014. Vol II: College Student and Adults Ages 19–55.* Bethesda, MD: National Institute on Drug Abuse.

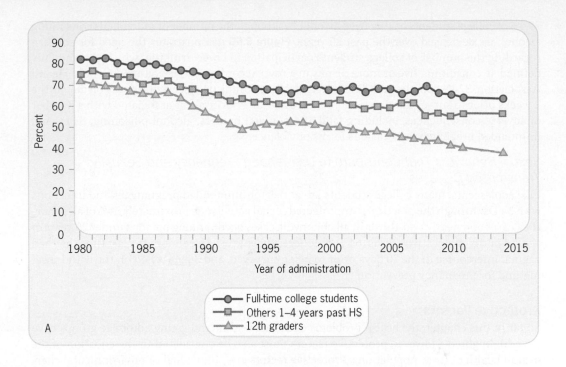

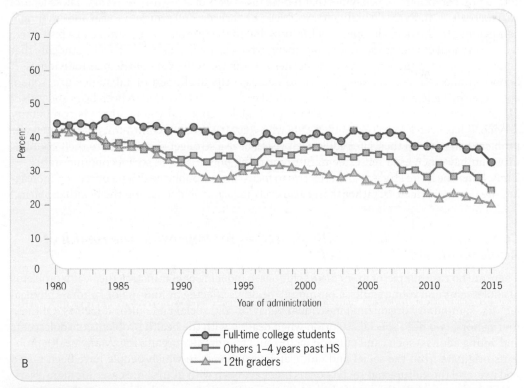

FIGURE 8.6   **A**. Alcohol: trends in 30-day prevalence among college students versus others 1 to 4 years beyond high school. **B**. Alcohol: trends in 2-week prevalence of five or more drinks in a row among college students versus others 1 to 4 years beyond high school.

Data from: Johnston, L. D., P. M. O'Malley, Bachman, J. G., J. E. Schulenberg, and R.A. Miech (2015). *Monitoring the Future National Survey Results on Drug Use, 1975–2014. Vol. II: College Students and Adults Ages 19–55*. Bethesda, MD: National Institute on Drug Abuse.

Protective factor factor that increases an individual's ability to avoid risks or hazards, and promotes social and emotional competence to thrive in all aspects of life

79.4% of college students having tried alcohol.[29] Although the number of individuals consuming alcohol has decreased over the past 25 years, **Figure 8.6B** demonstrates the need for concern regarding the number of college students participating in binge drinking, which is commonly defined as consuming five or more drinks in a row. According to the National College Health Association, 37.4% of males and 27.4% of females binge drank on at least one occasion during the 2 weeks prior to survey administration.[28] Excessive alcohol intake is associated with a number of adverse consequences, including fatal and nonfatal injuries, alcohol poisoning, STDs and unintended pregnancy, and various forms of violence.[31]

Sexual Behaviors That Contribute to Unintended Pregnancy and Sexually Transmitted Diseases

Like adolescents, many college students are at risk for unintended pregnancies and infections with STDs through the practice of unprotected sexual activity. Approximately 54% of all gonorrhea cases and nearly two-thirds of all chlamydia cases occur among persons under 25 years of age.[32] Approximately two-thirds (64%) of college students used a condom the last time they had vaginal intercourse in the 30 days prior to being surveyed, and 34.9% relied on the withdrawal method for pregnancy prevention.[28]

Protective Factors

So far in this chapter, the health problems of the adolescent and young adult age groups have been highlighted. However, protective factors must also be considered in the equation of the overall health of these populations. **Protective factors** are, "individual or environmental characteristics, conditions, or behaviors that reduce the effects of stressful life events. These factors also increase an individual's ability to avoid risks or hazards, and promote social and emotional competence to thrive in all aspects of life, now and in the future."[33] An example of a protective factor is school connectedness or engagement, which is defined as, "the belief by students that adults and peers in the school care about their learning as well as about them as individuals."[34] School connectedness has been shown to decrease the likelihood of substance use, school absenteeism, violence, unintentional injury, and early sexual initiation in both boys and girls.[34]

Another example of a protective factor for adolescents and young adults is community service. It has been shown that adolescents who volunteer in their community engage in fewer problem behaviors in their later adolescent years, have a stronger connection to their community, and have increased self-esteem, future earning potential, and socioeconomic status.[35,36] Thus, it may be more efficient and effective to focus limited public health resources on increasing the protective factors, rather than exclusively focusing on decreasing the health problem.

Community and Public Health Strategies for Improving the Health of Adolescents and Young Adults

There are no easy, simple, or immediate solutions to reducing or eliminating the health problems of adolescents and young adults. Community health is affected by four major factors—physical factors, community organizing, individual behavior, and social and cultural factors. Of these four factors, two need special attention when dealing with the health problems of adolescents and young adults—social and cultural factors and community organizing. Many health problems originate from the social and cultural environments in which people have been raised and live, and the culture and social norms that have been with us in some cases for many years.

Take, for example, the use of alcohol. It is safe to say that one of the biggest health problems facing adolescents and young adults in the United States today is the use of alcohol. Alcohol contributes to all the leading causes of mortality and morbidity in these age groups. If the norm of a community is to turn its back on adolescents consuming alcohol or young adults (of legal age) abusing alcohol, efforts need to be made to change the culture. However, in most communities, culture and social norms do not change quickly. Efforts to turn these health problems around will need to be community wide in nature and sustained over a long period of time. By "community wide," we mean the involvement of all the stakeholders in a community, not just those who are associated with health-related professions—in other words, a community organizing effort is needed. By "sustained over a long period," we mean institutionalizing the change in the culture. For examples of programs that have been effective in preventing or reducing substance abuse and other related high-risk behaviors in communities and schools, including college campus communities, visit the SAMHSA (Substance Abuse and Mental Health Services Administration) National Registry of Evidence-based Programs and Practices (NREPP) website at http://nrepp. samhsa.gov, which includes a searchable online registry of mental health and substance abuse interventions that have been reviewed and rated by independent reviewers.[37]

To change the culture as it relates to adolescents' use of alcohol, research has shown that alcohol prevention efforts need to be a part of a comprehensive school health education effort and should include components outside the classroom. Thus, prevention programs need to include components that focus on changing norms, interaction among peers, social skills training, and developmental and cultural appropriateness.[38–40] Although the adolescent and young adult age group encounters many health issues as described in this chapter, these individuals are typically the healthiest segments of the United States' population. The health challenges experienced by this age group need to be addressed at every level, especially the community level. The members of this age group also need to be involved in creating and implementing the solutions to these health challenges in order for these strategies to be effective.[41] These strategies should focus not only on decreasing the health problem, but also increasing the protective factor associated with that health problem.

Adults

The adult age group (those 25 to 64 years old) represents slightly more than half of the U.S. population.[8] The size of this segment of the overall population is expected to remain stable over the next couple of decades, but in proportion to the rest of the population this segment will become smaller. Therefore, provisions to deal with the health concerns of this age group will need to be maintained.

A Health Profile

The health profile of this age group of adults is characterized primarily by mortality from chronic diseases stemming from poor health behaviors impacted by health-detracting environments, and as previously mentioned, the health behaviors, events, and exposures experienced during the earlier years of life.[7]

Mortality

With life expectancy at birth between 75 and 80 years,[15] most Americans can expect to live beyond their 65th birthday. However, many do not. During the 1950s and 1960s, many of the leading causes of death in this age group resulted from preventable conditions associated with unhealthy behaviors and lifestyles. Since that time, the public health and medical communities have recognized how the environment, social, and cultural factors shape an individual's behavior.[42] As such, many adults have quit smoking, and more Americans than ever before are exercising regularly and eating healthier diets. These lifestyle improvements, along with successes in public health, such as an increased focus on the built environment (i.e. advocating for the need for more sidewalks versus more roads) and advances in medicine, have resulted in a significant decline in the death rate for adults.

In the past, leading causes of death for adults were reported only for the 25-to-64-year-old age group. More recently, the adult years have been subdivided into two groups: 25 to 44 years and 45 to 64 years, with some data being reported in 10-year age spans. In 2013, the death rate for all adults aged 25 to 34 years was 106.1 per 100,000, and for ages 35 to 44 years it was 172.0 per 100,000.[15] The leading causes of death for those in this age group in 2013 were unintentional injuries, malignant neoplasms (cancer), heart disease, and suicide.[15] The current leading causes of death were also at the top of the list for the 25-to-44 age group in 1980.[15] When these mortality data were broken down in 2013 by age, sex, and ethnicity, some differences appear. For 25-to-34-year olds, with the exception of HIV among blacks the six leading causes of death are the same, but differ in rank order by race and ethnic group. For 35-to-44-year olds, heart disease is the leading cause of death for blacks, whereas unintentional injuries is the leading cause of death for whites and Hispanics. In addition, diabetes is a leading cause of death for whites and blacks, and HIV is a leading cause of death for blacks but not for other racial groups (see **Table 8.4**).[43]

In 2013, the death rate for 45-to-54-year olds was 406.1 per 100,000, more than twice that of the 35-to-44 age group. The death rate for 55-to-64-year olds was 860.0 per 100,000, more than two times greater than the 45-to-54 age group.[15] The majority of these deaths were the result of noncommunicable health problems. They include cancer, heart disease, unintentional injuries, liver disease, chronic lower respiratory disease (which includes emphysema, asthma, and bronchitis), and diabetes. Though cancer and heart disease are the first and second causes of death for all three groups presented in **Table 8.5**, disparities among racial and ethnic groups exist.[1]

Cancer

Since 1983, the number one cause of death in the adult age group for those people ages 45 to 54 and 55 to 64 has been cancer (malignant neoplasms). Age-adjusted cancer death rates for both age groups have decreased since 1950 (175.1 and 390.7 per 100,000 in 1950 compared to 105.1 and 288.2 per 100,000 in 2013).[15] Four types of cancers account for these large numbers—prostate, lung, and colorectal for men; and breast, lung, and colorectal for women. The leading cause of cancer deaths and the most preventable type of cancer for both men and women is lung cancer.[44] This trend is expected to continue as large numbers of smokers continue to age. Of all lung cancer deaths, upward of 80% can be attributed to smoking.[44] Another leading cause of death resulting from cancer is colorectal cancer. Risk factors for this type of cancer include obesity, physical inactivity, a diet high in red or processed meats, smoking, and moderate to heavy alcohol consumption.[44]

Breast cancer is the other cancer of much concern. Until it was surpassed by lung cancer in the mid-1980s, it was the leading cause of cancer deaths in women. Although it is less deadly than is lung cancer, the number of cases of breast cancer is more than twice that of lung cancer in women.[44] Because of increased community awareness and the availability of diagnostic screening for breast cancer, survival rates are much higher than for lung cancer. However, breast cancer rates could be reduced even further if a higher percentage of women older than 39 years of age complied with the screening recommendations.[44]

TABLE 8.4   2013 Death Rates for Adults Ages 25–34 and 35–44 (Rate per 100,000 Population)

Cause	Non-Hispanic White		Non-Hispanic Black		Hispanic	
	25–34 (110.5)	35–44 (181.0)	25–34 (162.7)	35–44 (260.6)	25–34 (72.4)	35–44 (111.7)
Unintentional injuries	46.4	45.8	30.6	33.5	25.1	24.6
Cancer	8.3	29.3	11.1	36.3	8.3	20.8
Heart disease	7.1	25.3	16.8	53.2	4.3	12.7
Suicide	18.9	21.8	9.4	8.2	7.8	6.7
Homicide	3.7	3.4	42.4	23.5	8.3	5.3
Liver disease and cirrhosis	1.7	6.6	—	—	1.5	6.2
Diabetes mellitus	1.4	4.4	3.8	10.2	1.0	3.4
Stroke	0.9	3.1	2.5	9.3	1.2	3.9
HIV	—	—	6.8	13.0	1.2	2.5

Data from: Heron, M. (2016). "Deaths: Leading Causes for 2013." *National Vital Statistics Reports*, 65(2). Hyattsville, MD: National Center for Health Statistics.

TABLE 8.5   2013 Death Rates for Adults Ages 45–54 and 55–64 (Rate per 100,000 Population)

Cause	Non-Hispanic White		Non-Hispanic Black		Hispanic	
	45–54 (415.4)	55–64 (849.7)	45–54 (581.96)	55–64 (1301.1)	45–54 (269.6)	55–64 (610.7)
Cancer	110.0	292.1	131.9	396.8	67.7	190.1
Heart disease	80.4	177.7	139.0	320.4	43.1	118.5
Unintentional injuries	52.1	44.6	44.0	52.2	30.6	33.0
Liver disease and cirrhosis	21.1	30.5	13.5	28.5	23.1	38.4
Chronic lower respiratory disease	12.6	46.3	11.9	40.4	—	12.3
Diabetes mellitus	11.8	28.3	25.7	64.8	12.1	37.3
Stroke	9.9	24.2	26.7	63.5	11.4	26.5
Suicide	25.5	22.2	—	—	7.3	—
Septicemia	5.0	12.7	—	26.4	—	11.3
Influenza and pneumonia	5.0	11.5	—	—	—	9.9

Data from: Heron, M. (2016). "Deaths: Leading Causes for 2013." *National Vital Statistics Reports*, 65(2). Hyattsville, MD: National Center for Health Statistics.

Cardiovascular Diseases

Some of the greatest changes in cause-specific mortality rates in adults are those for the cardiovascular diseases. Age-adjusted mortality rates from diseases of the heart dropped from 588.8 per 100,000 in 1950 to 169.8 per 100,000 in 2013, while deaths from strokes dropped from 180.7 per 100,000 to 36.2 per 100,000 during the same period of time.[15] These statistics represent drops of about 71% and 80%, respectively. These changes are primarily the result of public health efforts, including changes to the environment, which have encouraged people to stop smoking, increase their physical activity, and eat more nutritionally. The reduction or postponement of deaths from heart disease has resulted in cancer becoming the leading cause of deaths in adults 45 to 64 years of age.

Health Behaviors

Many of the risk factors associated with the leading causes of morbidity and mortality in American adults are associated with health behaviors that are influenced by an individual's environment and other social determinants of health, such as income, access to food, and education.[45] Adults are in a position to take action, by modifying their health behaviors, to improve their health status. However, environmental support systems need to be in place to encourage these health behaviors or else it becomes increasingly difficult for these individuals to live a healthy lifestyle. We know that today, more than ever before, adults are watching what they eat, wearing their seat belts, controlling their blood pressure, and exercising with regularity. The prevalence of smoking among adults has declined, as has the incidence of drinking and driving. Although these are encouraging signs, still much more can be done.

As with the other age groups discussed in this chapter, the National Center for Health Statistics (NCHS) collects self-reported behavior risk data on adults. These data are collected via the Behavioral Risk Factor Surveillance System (BRFSS). One limitation of the data from this system is that they are collected, and usually reported, on all adults older than 18 years of age; the data are not broken down by the specific age groups (18–24, 25–44, and 45–64) discussed in this chapter. More detailed information about the health behaviors of adults in the United States is presented next.

Intensity cardiovascular workload measured by heart rate

Body mass index (BMI) the ratio of weight (in kilograms) to height (in meters, squared)

Risk Factors for Chronic Disease

The best single behavioral change Americans can make to reduce morbidity and mortality is to stop smoking. Cigarette smoking causes one out of five deaths in the United States each year.[46] It is an important risk factor for cancer, heart disease, and stroke. In 2014, nearly one-sixth (17%) of those aged 18 years and older smoked. This amounts to about 40 million Americans.[47] The proportion of Americans who smoke has dropped considerably since 1965, when 40% of all Americans smoked, but the consequences on individual health remains.[15] In general, smoking rates are higher among American Indians and Alaska Natives, people with fewer years of education, and those with lower incomes.[47]

Three other interrelated risk factors that contribute to disease and death in this age group are lack of exercise, poor nutrition, and drinking too much alcohol. Though American adults are exercising more than ever before, few are exercising on a regular basis. In 2011, more than half (52%) of U.S. adults did not meet recommendations for aerobic exercise or physical activity.[48] Although it was once thought that **intensity** had to be high for cardiovascular benefits from exercise to accrue, best practice recommendations encourage adults to engage in 2 hours and 30 minutes a week of moderate-intensity aerobic physical activity as well as engage in muscle-strengthening activities 2 or more days a week.[49]

Poor dietary habits are associated with an increased risk for Type 2 diabetes, hypertension, heart disease, certain cancers, and micronutrient deficiencies. In 2011, more than one-third (38%) of adults reported eating fruit less than once per day and nearly one-quarter (23%) ate vegetables less than once a day.[50]

The consequence of poor dietary habits and physical inactivity is obesity, in addition to the other chronic diseases mentioned above. More than one-third (34.9%) of U.S. adults are obese, with rates higher among middle-age adults, 40 to 59 years old (39.5%), compared to those younger (30.3%) and older (35.4%).[50] Obesity in the United States is truly an epidemic (see **Figure 8.7**.[50] **Body mass index (BMI)** is the primary way obesity is measured in the U.S. population, and in the adult population, a BMI of 30 or greater indicates an individual is obese.[50] The key to maintaining an appropriate weight throughout life is a combination of healthy eating and exercise. It is widely

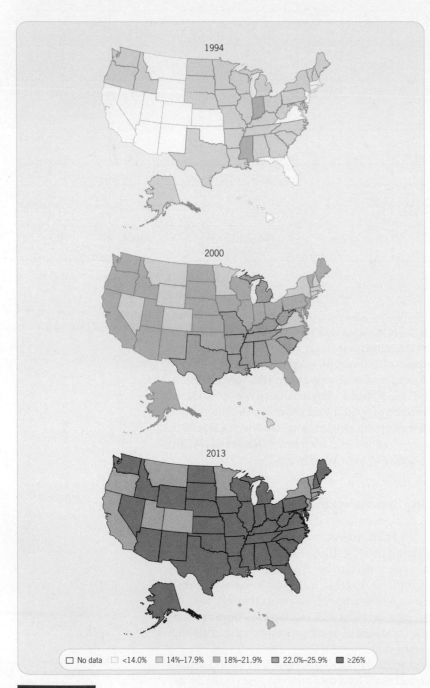

1994

2000

2013

| ☐ No data | ☐ <14.0% | 14%–17.9% | 18%–21.9% | 22.0%–25.9% | ≥26% |

FIGURE 8.7   Age-adjusted prevalence of obesity among U.S. adults: 1994, 2000, and 2013.

Note: Obesity is defined as a BMI >30, or about 30 pounds overweight for a 5-foot, 4-inch person.

Data from: Centers for Disease Control and Prevention, Division of Diabetes Translation. *National Diabetes Surveillance System.* Available at http://www.cdc.gov/diabetes/statistics.

recognized that a person's environment, including society and other life circumstances, impacts his or her ability to engage in these behaviors. Thus, increasingly, public health practitioners are implementing strategies to change policies, systems, and the environment to support healthier living for all individuals.[51]

As with other age groups, alcohol consumption often places adults at greater health risk. In 2014, nearly 57% of adult Americans reported consuming alcohol in the previous month, while nearly one-quarter (24.7%) of people ages 18 or older reported binge drinking in the past month.[52] Men are almost twice as likely as women to report binge drinking and heavy alcohol use.[53] Those who engage in binge drinking and heavy alcohol use are at greatest risk for developing a dependence on alcohol and for developing such alcohol-related health problems as cirrhosis, alcoholism, and alcohol psychosis.

One does not have to become dependent on alcohol to have a drinking problem. Alcohol contributes to society's problems in many other ways. As noted elsewhere in this text, alcohol increases the rates of homicide, suicide, family violence, and unintentional injuries such as those from motor vehicle crashes, boating incidents, and falls. The use of alcohol by pregnant women can cause fetal alcohol spectrum disorder, which can lead to several types of birth defects and disability.[54] Clearly, alcohol consumption adversely affects the health and well-being of Americans.

Awareness and Screening of Certain Medical Conditions

A number of regular, noninvasive or minimally invasive health screenings are recommended for adults to participate in, such as screenings for hypertension, diabetes, high blood cholesterol, and cancer.

There is no "ideal" blood pressure. Instead, the acceptable blood pressure falls within a range considered healthy, and an adult's (age 20 and over) blood pressure should be less than 120/80 mm Hg. **Hypertension** exists when systolic pressure is equal to or greater than 140 mm of mercury (Hg) and/or diastolic pressure is equal to or greater than 90 mm Hg for extended periods of time (more than one blood pressure reading). A hypertensive crisis exists when a person's systolic pressure is equal to or greater than 180 mm of mercury and/or diastolic pressure is equal to or greater than 110 mm of mercury.[55] Statistics show that hypertension is found in about one in three adults in the United States, and only about half of those individuals have their condition under control, making it a significant risk factor for cardiovascular disease in the United States.[56] Fortunately, once detected, hypertension is a risk factor that is highly modifiable (see **Figure 8.8**). The most desirable means of controlling hypertension is through a combination of diet modification, appropriate physical exercise, and weight management. In cases in which these measures prove ineffective, hypertension can usually still be controlled with medication. The keys to reducing morbidity and mortality resulting from hypertension are mass screenings that result in early detection of previously unidentified cases and their appropriate treatment.[55]

Diabetes results from failure of the pancreas to make or use a sufficient amount of insulin. Without insulin, food cannot be properly used by the body. Diabetes cannot be cured, but it can be controlled through a combination of diet, exercise, medications, and insulin injections. As reported earlier in the chapter, diabetes is one of the leading causes of death for adults, especially adults ages 45 to 64.[15] Members of specific racial and ethnic minority groups are particularly at risk for diabetes, with half of all Hispanic men and women and black women predicted to develop the disease.[57] However, many deaths resulting from diabetes could be postponed if diabetes was detected and treated appropriately. Approximately 29 million Americans, or 9.3% of the U.S. population, are estimated to have diagnosed or undiagnosed diabetes with nearly 1.7 million new cases diagnosed each year.[57] The percentage of adults with diagnosed diabetes has nearly quadrupled over the past 30 years (see **Figure 8.9**).[57]

Hypertension systolic pressure equal to or greater than 140 mm of mercury (Hg) and/or diastolic pressure equal to or greater than 90 mm Hg for extended periods of time

FIGURE 8.8   Hypertension is a highly modifiable risk factor.

© michaeljung/Shutterstock, Inc.

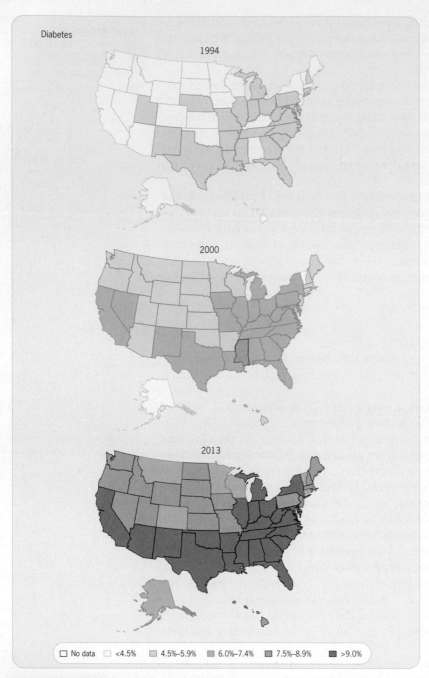

Diabetes

1994

2000

2013

| □ No data | □ <4.5% | □ 4.5%–5.9% | ■ 6.0%–7.4% | ■ 7.5%–8.9% | ■ >9.0% |

FIGURE 8.9   Age-adjusted prevalence of diagnosed diabetes among U.S. adults: 1994, 2000, 2013.

Data from: Centers for Disease Control and Prevention, Division of Diabetes Translation. National Diabetes Surveillance System. Available at http://www.cdc.gov/diabetes/statistics.

Cholesterol is a soft, fatlike substance that is necessary to build cell membranes. About 75% of cholesterol is produced by the liver and other cells in the body, with the other 25% coming from the foods we eat, specifically animal products. Elevated cholesterol levels in blood can put people at greater risk for heart disease and stroke. The higher the cholesterol level, the greater the risk.[58] A person's cholesterol level is affected by certain health conditions such as diabetes, lifestyle, age, and family history. While we cannot modify our age and family history, we can reduce our risk by engaging in healthy lifestyle behaviors.[58]

Dietary factors are associated with 4 of the 10 leading causes of death in this age group. Many dietary components are involved in the diet–health relationship, but chief among them is the disproportionate consumption of foods high in fat and added sugars, often at the expense of foods high in complex carbohydrates and dietary fiber. Limiting sugars, saturated fats, and sodium to the recommended dietary levels will go a long way in reducing a person's risk for diabetes, hypertension, heart disease, and stroke.[59] Based on several studies, blood cholesterol levels less than 200 mg/dL in middle-aged adults seem to indicate a relatively low risk of coronary heart disease. In contrast, people with a high total blood cholesterol have twice the risk for heart disease as people with ideal levels.[60] **Hypercholesterolemia** is the term used for high levels of cholesterol in the blood. Like diabetes, the key to controlling hypercholesterolemia is screening and treatment.[60]

The other prevalent medical condition in this age group that should be screened for on a regular basis is cancer. As noted earlier, malignant neoplasms are the leading cause of death in 45-to-64-year olds.[15] The American Cancer Society recommends a number of screenings for various age groups (see **Table 8.6**). However, many more adults in the United States could be getting screened. The earlier that cancer is detected, the greater the chance for successful treatment.

Community and Public Health Strategies for Improving the Health of Adults

Hypercholesterolemia high levels of cholesterol in the blood

As noted in the previous pages, adults in the United States face a number of health issues. Even so, for most individuals the years between 25 and 64 are some of the healthiest of their lifetime.

A key for keeping these people healthy is to understand that the health status of adults is often impacted by their current and previous health behaviors, as well as factors such as socioeconomic status—especially poverty and education level—along with previous influences on their health throughout their lives (i.e., exposure to violence as a child, childhood health status, etc.). Health behaviors are complex and heavily influenced by societal factors and an individual's local community. Consequently, it is important that community health workers understand that it is not enough to provide health education to adults about how to change behaviors that they have often exhibited for a significant part of their lifetime. Policy, systems, and environmental change strategies must also accompany health education strategies. For example, in order to reverse the obesity epidemic, we must change our physical and food environments.

TABLE 8.6   Summary of American Cancer Society Guidelines for the Early Detection of Cancer

Cancer Site	Population	Test or Procedure	Frequency
Breast	Women, age 40+	Mammography	Women ages 40–44 should have a choice to start annual breast cancer screenings. Women age 45 to 54, annual screenings. Women 55 and older, mammograms every 2 years.
Cervix	Women, ages 21–65	Pap test Pap test plus HPV test	Cervical cancer screening should begin at age 21. Women ages 21–29, Pap test every 3 years. Women ages 30–65, screening should be done every 5 years (Pap test alone every 3 years is acceptable). Women aged 65+ who have had regular cervical testing in the past 10 years with normal results should not be tested for cervical cancer.
Colorectal	Men and women, starting at age 50	Guaiac-based fecal occult blood test (gFOBT), **or** fecal immunochemical test (FIT), **or**	Annual, starting at age 50
		Stool DNA test	Every 3 years
		Flexible sigmoidoscopy (FSIG), **or**	Every 5 years, starting at age 50
		Double contrast barium enema (DCBE), **or**	Every 5 years
		Colonoscopy	Every 10 years
		CT colonography	Every 5 years
Endometrial	Women, at menopause	At the time of menopause, women at average risk should be informed about risks and symptoms of endometrial cancer and strongly encouraged to report any unexpected bleeding or spotting to their physicians.	
Lung	Current or former smokers ages 55–74 in good health with at least a 30 pack per year smoking history	Low-dose helical CT (LDCT) scan of the chest	

(Continues)

TABLE 8.6   (Continued)

Cancer Site	Population	Test or Procedure	Frequency
Prostate	Men, ages 50+	Prostate-specific antigen blood test (PSA) with or without a rectal exam	
Cancer-related checkup	Men and women, ages 20+	On the occasion of a periodic health examination, depending on age and gender, the cancer-related checkup should include examination for cancers of the thyroid, oral cavity, skin, lymph nodes, testes and ovaries, lymph.	

Data from: American Cancer Society (2015). *American Cancer Society Guidelines for Early Detection of Cancer.* Available at http://www.cancer.org/healthy /findcancerearly/cancerscreeningguidelines/american-cancer-society-guidelines-for-the-early-detection-of-cancer.

Specific federal guidelines have been developed in order to guide local communities in the effort to improve access to healthy foods and physical activity.[61] Learning from tobacco prevention and control efforts, we can guide communities in addressing other major health challenges. Tobacco control has required personal and community-level interventions—from screening and cessation efforts to smoking restrictions, media campaigns, and increasing the cost to purchase tobacco.[62] Thus, community health workers must recognize that the health of one person is not just an individual responsibility but also a community responsibility.

Chapter Summary

- Adolescence and young adulthood (10–24 years old) and adulthood (25–64 years old) are the most productive periods of people's lives. Although most people enjoy good health during these years, there is substantial room for improvement.

- The overall health status of these age groups could be improved by reducing the prevalence of high-risk behaviors (e.g., cigarette smoking, excessive alcohol consumption, and physical inactivity), increasing participation in health screenings, institutionalizing preventive health care, and making environments more health-enhancing in our society.

- Approximately 75% of adolescent and young adult mortality can be attributed to motor vehicle crashes, other unintentional injuries, homicide and legal intervention, and suicide.

- Adolescents and young adults remain at considerable risk for STD morbidity.

- College students are at considerable risk for STDs due to unprotected sexual activity and the use of alcohol and other drugs.

- Mortality rates for older adults (45–64 years old) have declined in recent years, but cancer is still the overall leading cause of death, followed by cardiovascular disease.

- Reductions in deaths from cardiovascular diseases in adults have been substantial, but health problems resulting from unhealthy behaviors—such as smoking, poor diet, and physical inactivity—can be reduced further if environments are created to help support healthy behaviors (e.g., increased access to fruits and vegetables, the creation of more walkable communities, etc.)

- No matter how the health of adolescents and young adults and adults in the United States is broken down and described, it can be summarized by saying that the health of Americans in these age groups has come a long way in the past 50 years, but there is still room for improvement.

Scenario: Analysis and Response

1. What are the primary reasons that Annie stated Dayna might have developed diabetes?

2. Comment on the attitudes of Annie and Connor about Dayna's recent diabetes diagnosis. Do you agree with Connor that the only way for Dayna to be healthy is to move away from the neighborhood where she lives? Why or why not?

3. If you were a community health worker in this urban community that has limited places where residents can purchase healthy food and safely exercise outside, what could you do to help adolescents like Dayna?

4. Do high schools have an obligation to develop prevention programs, including offering physical activity opportunities at school, to keep students healthy? Why or why not?

5. Say you were friends with Annie. She got so concerned with Dayna's health problem that she wanted to take action, especially to figure out how to help the local corner store that Dayna visits every day offer healthy foods for her. She thought that maybe she would do an online search to see if there are any corner stores that offer healthy foods and how they do it. You told her that you would help her see if there is anything on the Internet. Go online and use a search engine (e.g., Google, Bing) and enter "healthy corner stores." What did you find that might be of help to Annie?

Review Questions

1. Why is it important for community and public health workers to be aware of the significant health problems of the various age groups in the United States?

2. What ages are included in the following two age groups: adolescents and young adults and adults? What are the ages of the two subgroups of adults?

3. Why are the number of adolescents and young adults, living arrangements, and employment status such key demographic characteristics of young people in regard to community health? Briefly summarize the data available on these characteristics.

4. What are the leading causes of death for adolescents and young adults, and for adults?

5. What are the Youth Risk Behavior Surveillance System (YRBSS) and the Behavioral Risk Factor Surveillance System (BRFSS), and what type of data do they generate?

6. What are the behaviors that put each of these cohorts—adolescents, college students, and adults—at greatest risk, and how does a person's environment impact these behaviors?

7. How would you summarize the health profile of the two cohorts (adolescents and young adults and adults) presented in this chapter?

Activities

1. Obtain a copy of the most recent results of the Youth Risk Behavior Surveillance System (YRBSS) and the Behavioral Risk Factor Surveillance System (BRFSS) for your state. Review the data presented, and then prepare a two-page summary on the "Health Behavior Profile of the Adolescents, Young Adults, and Adults" of your state.

2. Obtain data presenting the 10 leading causes of death according to age and race for the age groups presented in this chapter. Review the data, and prepare a summary paper discussing conclusions that can be drawn about race, the leading causes of death, and age.

3. Interview a small group (about 10) of adults (aged 45–64) about their present health status. Ask them questions about their health behavior and health problems. Then, summarize the data you collect in writing and compare it to the information in this chapter on this age group. How are the data similar? How do they differ?

4. Pick either adolescents and young adults or adults, and write a two-page paper that presents ideas on how the health profile of that age group can be improved in your state.

References

1. World Health Organization (2016). *Adolescent Health*. Available at http://www.who.int/topics/adolescent_health/en/.

2. Berlin, G., F. F. Furstenberg, and M. C. Waters (2010). "Introducing the Issue. Transition to Adulthood." *The Future of Children*, 20(1): 3–18.

3. MacKay, A. P., L. A. Fingerhut, and C. R. Duran (2000). *Health, United States, 2000 with Adolescent Health Chartbook*. Hyattsville, MD: National Center for Health Statistics.

4. Seffrin, J. R. (1990). "The Comprehensive School Health Curriculum: Closing the Gap between State-of-the-Art and State-of-the-Practice." *Journal of School Health*, 60(4): 151–156.

5. Snyder, T., and L. Shafer (1996). *Youth Indicators, 1996* (NCES 96-027). Washington, DC: U.S. Department of Education, National Center for Education Statistics.

6. Valois, R. F., W. G. Thatcher. J. W. Drane, and B. M. Reininger (1997). "Comparison of Selected Health Risk Behaviors between Adolescents in Public and Private High Schools in South Carolina." *Journal of School Health*, 67(10): 434–440.

7. Power, C., D. Kuh, and S. Morton (2013). "From Developmental Origins of Adult Disease to Life Course Research on Adult Disease and Aging: Insights from Birth Cohort Studies." *Annual Review of Public Health*, 34: 7–28.

8. U.S. Census Bureau (2016). *Age and Sex Composition 2010: 2010 Census Brief*. Available at http://www.census.gov/prod/cen2010/briefs/c2010br-03.pdf.

9. U.S. Department of Health and Human Services (2016). *The Changing Face of America's Adolescent*. Available at http://www.hhs.gov/ash/oah/adolescent-health-topics/americas-adolescents/changing-face.html.

10. Vespa, J., J. M. Lewis, and R. M. Krieder (2013). *America's Families and Living Arrangements: 2012*. Available at http://www.census.gov/prod/2013pubs/p20-570.pdf.

11. Amato, P. R. (2005). "The Impact of Family Formation Change on the Cognitive, Social, and Emotional Well-Being of the Next Generation." *The Future of Children*, 15(2): 75–96.

12. Toossi, M. (2013, December). "Labor Force Projections to 2022: The Labor Force Participation Rate Continues to Fall." *Monthly Labor Review*. Available at http://www.bls.gov/opub/mlr/2013/article/labor-force-projections-to-2022-the-labor-force-participation-rate-continues-to-fall.htm.

13. Toossi, M. (2015, May). "Labor Force Projects to 2024: The Labor Force Is Growing, but Slowly." *Monthly Labor Review*. Available at http://www.bls.gov/opub/mlr/2015/article/labor-force-projections-to-2024-1.htm.

14. U.S. Bureau of Labor Statistics (2016). *Labor Force Statistics from the Current Population Survey*. Available at http://www.bls.gov/web/empsit/cpsee_e16.htm.

15. National Center for Health Statistics (2015). *Health, United States, 2014: With Special Feature on Adults Age 55–64*. Hyattsville, MD: Author.

16. Chua, K. P., M. A. Schuster, and J. M. McWilliams (2013). "Differences in Health Care Access and Utilization Between Adolescents and Young Adults With Asthma." *Pediatrics*, 131(5). doi: 10.1542/peds.2012-2881.

17. First International Conference on Health Promotion (1986). *The Ottawa Charter for Health Promotion*. Geneva, Switzerland: World Health Organization. Available at http://www.who.int/healthpromotion/conferences/previous/ottawa/en/.

18. Olshansky, S. J., D. J. Passaro, R. C. Hershow, J. Layden, B. A. Carnes, J. Brody, L. Hayflick, R. N. Butler, D. B. Allison, and D. S. Ludwig (2005). "A Potential Decline in Life Expectancy in the United States in the 21st Century." *The New England Journal of Medicine*, 352(11): 1138–1145.

19. Centers for Disease Control and Prevention (2016). "Youth Risk Behavior Surveillance—United States, 2015." *Morbidity and Mortality Weekly Report*, 65(6):1-180. Available at http://www.cdc.gov/healthyyouth/data/yrbs/results.htm.

20. Centers for Disease Control and Prevention (2013). "Prevention of Measles, Rubella, Congenital Rubella Syndrome, and Mumps, 2013." *Morbidity and Mortality Weekly Report*, 62(4): 2–25.

21. Centers for Disease Control and Prevention (2016). *Youth and Tobacco Use*. Available at http://www.cdc.gov/tobacco/data_statistics/fact_sheets/youth_data/tobacco_use/.

22. American Heart Association, American Cancer Society, Campaign for Tobacco-Free Kids, and American Lung Association (2015). *Broken Promises to Our Children: A State-by-State Look at the 1998 State Tobacco Settlement 17 Years Later*. Available at http://www.tobaccofreekids.org/content/what_we_do/state_local_issues/settlement/FY2016/Broken%20Promises%20to%20Our%20Children%2012.7.15.pdf.

23. Campaign for Tobacco-Free Kids. (2016). *FDA Authority over Tobacco*. Available at http://www.tobaccofreekids.org/what_we_do/federal_issues/fda/.

24. Centers for Disease Control and Prevention (2015). *Sexually Transmitted Disease Surveillance, 2014*. Atlanta, GA: U.S. Department of Health and Human Services.

25. Martin, J. A., B. E. Hamilton, and S. J. Ventura, et al. (2012). "Births: Final Data for 2010." *National Vital Statistics Reports*, 61(1). Hyattsville, MD: National Center for Health Statistics. Available at http://www.cdc.gov/nchs/data/nvsr/nvsr61/nvsr61_01.pdf.

26. The National Campaign to Prevent Teen and Unplanned Pregnancy (2016). *National and State Data*. Available at http://thenationalcampaign.org/data/landing.

27. The National Campaign to Prevent Teen and Unplanned Pregnancy (2016). *Costs and Consequences of Teen Pregnancy*. Available at https://thenationalcampaign.org/featured-topics/costs-and-consequences-teen-pregnancy.

28. American College Health Association (2016). *ACHA National College Health Assessment II: Reference Group Executive Summary Fall 2015*. Hanover, MD: Author.

29. Johnston, L. D., P. M. O'Malley, J. G. Bachman, J. E. Schulenberg, and R. A. Miech (2015). *Monitoring the Future National Survey Results on Drug Use, 1975–2015: Volume II, College Students and Adults Ages 19–55*. Ann Arbor: Institute for Social Research, The University of Michigan. Available at http://www.monitoringthefuture.org/pubs/monographs/mtf-vol2_2014.pdf.

30. U.S. Department of Education (2016). *Fast Facts*. Washington, DC: National Center for Education Statistics. Available at https://nces.ed.gov/fastfacts/display.asp?id=98.

31. Centers for Disease Control and Prevention (2015). *Fact Sheets – Binge Drinking*. Available at http://www.cdc.gov/alcohol/fact-sheets/binge-drinking.htm.

32. Centers for Disease Control and Prevention (2015). *CDC Fact Sheet: Reported STDs in the United States: 2014 National Data for Chlamydia, Gonorrhea, and Syphilis*. Available at http://www.cdc.gov/std/stats/.

33. Centers for Disease Control and Prevention (2015). *Protective Factors*. Available at http://www.cdc.gov/healthyyouth/protective/index.htm.

34. Centers for Disease Control and Prevention (2009). *School Connectedness: Strategies for Increasing Protective Factors Among Youth*. Atlanta, GA: U.S. Department of Health and Human Services.

35. Kuperminc, G. P., P. T. Holditch, and J. P. Allen (2001). "Volunteering and Community Service in Adolescence." *Adolescent Medicine*, 12(3): 445–457.

36. Opportunity Nation (2014). *Connecting Youth and Strengthening Communities: The Data Behind Civic Engagement and Economic*

Opportunity. Available at http://opportunitynation.org/app/uploads/2014/09/Opportunity-Nation-Civic-Engagement-Report-2014.pdf.

37. Substance Abuse and Mental Health Services Administration (2016). *SAMHSA National Registry of Evidence-based Programs and Practices*. Available at http://www.nrepp.samhsa.gov/.

38. Dusenbury, L., and M. Falco (1995). "Eleven Components of Effective Drug Abuse Prevention Curricula." *Journal of School Health*, 65: 420–425.

39. Joint Committee on National Health Education Standards (2007). *National Health Education Standards*, 2nd ed. Atlanta: American Cancer Society.

40. Centers for Disease Control and Prevention (2012). *Health Education Curriculum Analysis Tool (HECAT)*. Atlanta, GA: Author. Available at http://www.cdc.gov/healthyyouth/HECAT/index.htm.

41. Minkler, M., and N. Wallerstein (eds.) (2003). *Community-Based Participatory Research for Health*. San Francisco: Jossey-Bass Publishers.

42. Centers for Disease Control and Prevention (2015). *NCHHSTP Social Determinants of Health*. Available at http://www.cdc.gov/nchhstp/socialdeterminants/index.html.

43. Heron, M. (2016). "Deaths: Leading Causes for 2013." *National Vital Statistics Reports*. 65(2): 1–94. Available at http://www.cdc.gov/nchs/data/nvsr/nvsr65/nvsr65_02.pdf.

44. American Cancer Society (2016). *Cancer Facts and Figures, 2016*. Available at http://www.cancer.org/research/cancerfactsstatistics/cancerfactsfigures2016/index.

45. Office of Disease Prevention and Health Promotion (2016). *Determinants of Health*. Available at https://www.healthypeople.gov/2020/about/foundation-health-measures/Determinants-of-Health.

46. Centers for Disease Control and Prevention (2015). *Tobacco-Related Mortality*. Available at http://www.cdc.gov/tobacco/data_statistics/fact_sheets/health_effects/tobacco_related_mortality/.

47. Centers for Disease Control and Prevention (2016). *Current Cigarette Smoking among Adults in the United States*. Available at http://www.cdc.gov/tobacco/data_statistics/fact_sheets/adult_data/cig_smoking/index.htm.

48. Centers for Disease Control and Prevention (2016). *Chronic Disease Overview*. Available at http://www.cdc.gov/chronicdisease/overview/#ref10.

49. Office of Disease Prevention and Health Promotion (2016). *Physical Activity Guidelines*. Available at http://health.gov/paguidelines/.

50. Centers for Disease Control and Prevention (2015). *Overweight and Obesity*. Available at http://www.cdc.gov/obesity/index.html.

51. Zwald, M., J. Jernigan, G. Payne, and R. Farris (2013). "Developing Stories From the Field to Highlight Policy, Systems, and Environmental Approaches in Obesity Prevention." *Preventing Chronic Disease*, doi: http://dx.doi.org/10.5888/pcd10.120141.

52. National Institute on Alcohol Abuse and Alcoholism (2016). *Alcohol Facts and Statistics*. Available at http://www.niaaa.nih.gov/alcohol-health/overview-alcohol-consumption/alcohol-facts-and-statistics.

53. Substance Abuse and Mental Health Services Administration (2016). *Results from the 2014 National Survey on Drug Use and Health*. Available at http://www.samhsa.gov/data/sites/default/files/NSDUH-DetTabs2014/NSDUH-DetTabs2014.htm#toc.

54. March of Dimes (2016). *Alcohol During Pregnancy*. Available at http://www.marchofdimes.com/pregnancy/alcohol-during-pregnancy.aspx.

55. American Heart Association (2016). *High Blood Pressure*. Available at http://www.heart.org/HEARTORG/Conditions/HighBloodPressure/High-Blood-Pressure_UCM_002020_SubHomePage.jsp.

56. Centers for Disease Control and Prevention (2015). *High Blood Pressure Facts*. Available at http://www.cdc.gov/bloodpressure/facts.htm.

57. Centers for Disease Control and Prevention (2015). *Diabetes Report Card 2014*. Atlanta, GA: Author.

58. Centers for Disease Control and Prevention (2015). *Cholesterol*. Available at http://www.cdc.gov/cholesterol/index.htm.

59. U.S. Department of Agriculture and U.S. Department of Health and Human Services (2015). *2015–2020 Dietary Guidelines for Americans*, 8th ed. Available at http://health.gov/dietaryguidelines/.

60. Centers for Disease Control and Prevention (2015). *High Cholesterol Facts*. Available at http://www.cdc.gov/cholesterol/facts.htm.

61. Keener, D., K. Goodman, A. Lowry, S. Zaro, and L. Kettel Khan (2009). *Recommended Community Strategies and Measurements to Prevent Obesity in the United States: Implementation and Measurement Guide*. Atlanta, GA: U.S. Department of Health and Human Services, Centers for Disease Control and Prevention.

62. Ockene, J. K., E. A. Edgerton, S. M. Teutsch, L. N. Marion, T. Miller, J. L. Genevro, C. J. Loveland-Cherry, J. E. Fielding, and P. A. Briss (2007). "Integrating Evidence-Based Clinical and Community Strategies to Improve Health." *American Journal of Preventive Medicine*, 32: 244–252.

CHAPTER 9

Older Adults

Chapter Objectives

After studying this chapter, you will be able to:

1. Identify the characteristics of an aging population.
2. Define the following groups—*old, young old, middle old,* and *old old*.
3. Refute several commonly held myths about the older adult population.
4. Describe the factors that affect the size and age of a population.
5. Define fertility and mortality rates and explain how they affect life expectancy.
6. Explain the difference between dependency and labor-force ratios.
7. Describe older adults with regard to marital status, living arrangements, racial and ethnic background, education, economic status, and geographic location.

8. Discuss the effects of chronic conditions and physical impairments on older adults.
9. Explain how health behaviors can improve the quality of later life.
10. Briefly outline elder abuse and neglect in the United States.
11. Illustrate the six instrumental needs of older adults.
12. Explain the role of caregivers with older adults in the United States.
13. Describe different housing options available to older adults.
14. Briefly summarize the Older Americans Act of 1965.
15. List the commonly provided services for older adults in most communities.
16. Explain the difference between respite care and adult day care.

Scenario

Carl and Sarah have been retired for about 5 years. Carl retired in good health after 35 years as an insurance agent, and Sarah stopped working outside the home after their children were grown and had families of their own. Upon retirement, they sold their home and paid cash for a condominium that had about half the square footage of their home. This relocation forced them to pare down their belongings to fit into their new and smaller surroundings. As a consequence, though, they felt less tied down to possessions and felt more freedom to do the traveling they had anticipated for several years. Although they now live on a fixed income, the profit from their home has allowed them to live out the retirement they had dreamed about traveling and participating in community programs, and to visit or host their children and grandchildren over the holidays.

All is not completely rosy for Carl and Sarah, however. Though they enjoy their lives very much, they are faced with an increasing number of health problems. They have accepted this challenge and have begun to do brisk walking on a near daily basis. Also, Sarah has signed up for a yoga program. Carl joined a Tai Chi program at the senior center. They have also suffered the loss of good friends, several of whom have died, and their best friends and neighbors recently moved to be closer to their kids. Carl and Sarah are going to attend an orientation session at the local elementary school to help students read, in hopes of adding more meaning and purpose to their lives and to dwell less on their losses.

They look to the future with a mix of optimism and anxiety. The optimism is based on their consistent ability to meet the challenges of aging, even those losses that are very discouraging in the beginning. The anxiety is based on the unknown: What if their property taxes increase beyond what they can afford? What if their Medicare Part D provider continues to raise premiums, deductibles, and copayments? Many questions arise, with no definite answers. But Carl and Sarah feel up to the challenge and adventure of aging into the future and take satisfaction in looking back at lives well lived.

Introduction

The U.S. population is growing older. The number of older adults in America and their proportion of the total population increased dramatically during the twentieth and early twenty-first centuries. In 1950, there were 12 million people (8% of the population) aged 65 years, and by 2010, that number had increased to 40.2 million. This is 13.1% of the U.S. population, over one in every eight Americans.[1] For the first time in U.S. history, a significant number of Americans will achieve older adult status. We need only to look around us to see the change that is taking place (see **Figure 9.1**). The number of gray heads in restaurants, malls, and movie theaters is increasing. Senior centers, retirement villages, and assisted living facilities are being built in record numbers. And today, more than ever before, many people belong to multigenerational families, where there are opportunities to develop long-lasting relationships with parents, grandparents, and great-grandparents. There are now families in which members of three successive generations receive monthly Social Security checks. In the twenty-first century, the economic, social, and health issues associated with the growing proportion of people older than age 65 in the United States have become major political concerns. In this chapter, we will define terminology, describe the demographics, and discuss the special needs of and community service for the growing older adult population.

Definitions

How old is old? The ageless baseball pitcher Satchel Paige once said, "How old would you be if you didn't know how old you was [sic]?" Although his English might be found wanting, Paige's point is important (see **Figure 9.2**). A person's age might depend on who measures

FIGURE 9.1   The number of older adults in the United States is on the rise, and they are more energetic than previous cohorts.

© Lisa F. Young/Dreamstime.com.

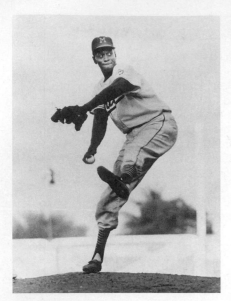

FIGURE 9.2 Some would say you are only as old as you think you are. (Satchel Paige remained active in professional baseball long after reaching the age at which others retired.)
© AP Photos.

it and how they define it. Children might see their 35-year-old teacher as old, whereas the 35-year-old teacher might regard her 61-year-old principal as old. Age is and always will be a relative concept.

In the United States and other developed countries, people are considered *old* once they reach the age of 65. But because there are a number of people who are very active and healthy at age 65 and will live a number of productive years after 65, researchers have subdivided old into the *young old* (65–74), the *middle old* (75–84), and the *old old* (85 and over). These distinctions can be important for community health programming. We can assume there are likely to be significant difference between a 65-year-old and a 95-year-old person, for example, just as there are between a 15-year-old and a 45-year-old person. Interestingly enough, it is the latter group, the old old, that makes up the fastest-growing segment of the older adult population.

Many terms have been used to describe individuals who are 65 years of age and older, including "seniors, senior citizens, golden agers, retired persons, mature adults, elderly, aged, and old people. There is no clear preference among older people for any of these terms."[2] We can also assume preferences will change with various generations.

Myths Surrounding Aging

Like other forms of prejudice and discrimination, **ageism** is the result of ignorance, misconceptions, and half-truths about aging and older adults. Because many people do not interact with older people on a daily basis, it is easy to create a stereotypical image of older adults based on the atypical actions of a few or negative images in the media.

When you think of older people, who comes to mind? Do you immediately think of a lonely man with a disheveled appearance sitting on a park bench or an older person lying in bed in a nursing home making incomprehensible noises? Or, do you think of Clint Eastwood and Sean Connery (each turned 85 years old in 2015) in an action-packed, high-suspense thriller?

Ferrini and Ferrini and Dychtwald and Flower have identified a number of commonly held myths about older adults.[2,3] They are presented here to remind us that older adults are not run-down, worn-out members of society but are for the most part independent, capable, and valuable resources for our communities. Do not forget that several U.S. presidents have been eligible for Social Security and Medicare while in office.

Here are the myths and the reasons why they are only myths:

1. Myth: "After age 65 life goes steadily downhill."

   Truth: Any chronological age that defines old age is arbitrary. Nonetheless, many gerontologists are substituting age 85 for age 65 as the new chronological definition of old age.

2. Myth: "Old people are all alike."

   Truth: There are more differences among elders than any other segment of the U.S. population.

3. Myth: "Old people are lonely and ignored by their families."

   Truth: Older adults are the least likely to be lonely of any age group; those who live alone are likely to be in close contact, either in person, by e-mail, or by telephone, with close friends and/or their family.

4. Myth: "Old age used to be better."

   Truth: It is only in the last half of the twentieth century that a large portion of the U.S. population lived to be 65 years old. If people did live to be old, they were not treated any better than they are today.

5. Myth: "Old people are senile."

   Truth: Cognitive impairments are the result of disease and are not a guaranteed part of older adulthood.

6. Myth: "Old people have the good life."

   Truth: Though elders do gain certain advantages when they retire and when their children leave home, they still face a number of concerns, such as loss of loved ones, loss of health, and loss of value in society.

7. Myth: "Most old people are sickly."

   Truth: Most older people do have at least one chronic health problem, but the majority of older adults live active lifestyles.

8. Myth: "Old people no longer have any sexual interest or ability."

   Truth: Sexual interest may or may not diminish with age, but there is an alteration in sexual response. Nonetheless, many older adults in reasonably good health have active and satisfying sex lives.

9. Myth: "Most old people end up in nursing homes."

   Truth: Only 3% to 4% of those above the age of 65 live in nursing homes. Only 1% of those aged 65 to 74 reside in such a place, though the percentage jumps to 19% for the oldest old (those 85 and older). However, this number is still well below half.

10. Myth: "Older people are unproductive."

    Truth: Older adults are more likely to be retired, but they are very likely to be productively engaged at home and in the community. The number of older adults engaged in professional employment is at an all-time high.

FIGURE 9.3   Many older adults are remaining active well after retirement age.
© Glenda M. Powers/ShutterStock, Inc.

Though a number of issues and concerns facing older adults are presented later in this chapter, the majority of older adults in the United States today are active and well (see **Figure 9.3**).

Demography of Aging

The demography of aging is typically defined as a study of those who are 65 years and older and of the variables that bring about change in their lives. In the following paragraphs, some of the demographic features of the elder population, including size, growth rate, and the factors that contribute to this growth are revealed. We also discuss other demographic characteristics of this population, such as living arrangements, racial and ethnic composition, geographic distribution, economic status, and housing.

Size and Growth of the Older Adult Population in the United States

The number of older adults and the proportion of the total population made up of older adults grew significantly during the twentieth and early twenty-first centuries. Demographers' projections suggest that populations will continue to age, not only in this country, but in most other countries as well. In 2011, the *baby boom* generation began to turn 65, and by 2030, it is projected that 72.7 million people (1 in 5) will be age 65 or older.[4] The population aged 85 and older is currently the fastest-growing segment of the older population. During this same

Median age the age at which half of the population is older and half is younger

time, it is expected that the percentage of people aged 18 and younger will decrease slightly to around 22%. **Figure 9.4** shows the difference in the population pyramid of 2000 and the projections for 2050.

As one might guess, the projected growth of the older adult population is expected to raise the **median age** of the U.S. population. In 2010, the median age was 37.2 years.[5] Projections put the median age at 39 years by 2035 where it will remain until 2050.[6]

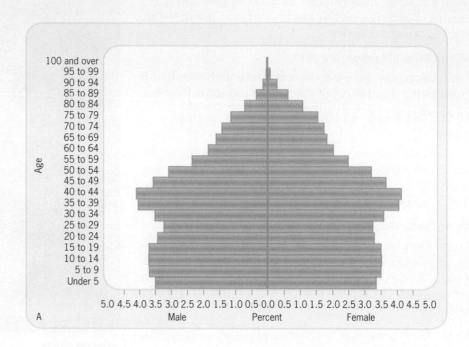

A. Male   Percent   Female

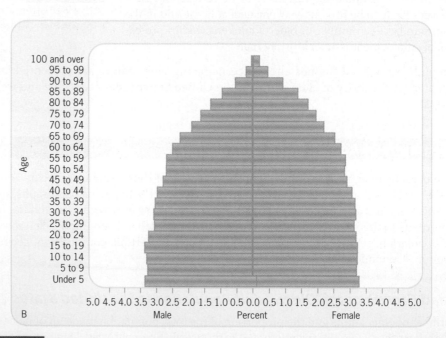

B. Male   Percent   Female

FIGURE 9.4   **A.** Projected resident population of the United States as of July 1, 2000, Middle Series. **B.** Projected resident population of the United States as of July 1, 2050, Middle Series.

Data from: A: U.S. Census Bureau, Population Division. *Interim State Population Projections.* https://www.census.gov/population/projections /files/natproj/pyramids/np_p2.pdf; **B:** U.S. Census Bureau, Population Division, *Interim State Population Projections.* https://www.census.gov /population/projections/files/natproj/pyramids/np_p4.pdf.

Factors That Affect Population Size and Age

Though one might assume that all populations will age with time, that is not necessarily true. Fertility rates and mortality rates both play a significant role in the "age" of any population.

Fertility Rates

The *fertility rate* is an expression of the number of births per 1,000 women of childbearing age (15–44) in the population during a specific time period. Fertility rates in the United States were at their highest at the beginning of the twentieth century. Those rates dipped during the Depression years but rebounded after World War II. The period of consistently high fertility rates immediately following World War II has become known as the "baby boom years," hence the name *baby boomers* for those born between 1946 and 1964. During those years, 76 million babies were born. As the baby boomers continue to age, a "human tidal wave" (bulge) will continue to move up the U.S. age pyramid. U.S. society has tried to adjust to the size and needs of the baby boom generation throughout the stages of the life cycle. Just as this generation had a dramatic impact on expanding obstetrics and pediatrics, creating split shifts for students in public schools, and disrupting government policy toward the Vietnam War, the baby boom cohorts will also place tremendous strain on programs and services (e.g., Social Security and Medicare) required by an elderly population.[7]

Mortality Rates

The *mortality* or *death rate* (usually expressed in deaths per 100,000 population) also has an impact on the aging population. The annual crude mortality rate in the United States in 1900 was 1,720 per 100,000. Recent data show that that figure has dropped by half to 810.[8] The decrease in the annual mortality rate achieved over the twentieth century was the result of triumphs in medical science and public health practice.

Another demographic variable that interacts with the mortality rate is life expectancy. Although the mortality rate in the United States has been fairly constant for 20+ years, life expectancy has continued to increase. In 1900, life expectancy at birth was 47.3 years; it was 77.9 years in 2007.[8] The life expectancy of men and black Americans has always trailed those of women and white Americans, respectively. Whereas the increase in life expectancy in the first half of the twentieth century could be attributed to the decrease in infant and early childhood deaths, the increase in life expectancy since 1970 can be traced to the postponement of death among the middle-aged and older adult population.

Dependency and Labor-Force Ratios

Other demographic signs of an aging population are changes in dependency and labor-force ratios. The **dependency ratio** is a comparison between those individuals whom society considers economically unproductive (the nonworking or dependent population) and those it considers economically productive (the working population). Traditionally, the productive and nonproductive populations have been defined by age; the productive population includes those who are 19 to 64. The unproductive population includes both youth (0–19 years old) and the old (65+ years). When the dependency ratio includes both youth and old, it is referred to as a **total dependency ratio**. When only the youth are compared to the productive group, the term used is **youth dependency ratio**; when only the old are compared, it is called **old-age dependency ratio**.

Changes in dependency ratios "provide an indirect broad indication of periods when we can expect the particular age distribution of the country to affect the need for distinct types of social services, housing, and consumer products."[9] Communities can refer to dependency ratio data as a guide for making the best social policy decisions and as a way to allocate resources. For example, leaders in a community with a relatively high youth dependency ratio compared to the old-age dependency ratio may want to concentrate community resources on programs such as education for the young, health promotion programs for children, special programs for working parents, and other youth-associated concerns. Communities with high old-age dependency ratios might increase programs for

Dependency ratio a ratio that compares the number of individuals whom society considers economically unproductive to the number it considers economically productive

Total dependency ratio the dependency ratio that includes both youth and old

Youth dependency ratio the dependency ratio that includes only youth

Old-age dependency ratio the dependency ratio that includes only the old

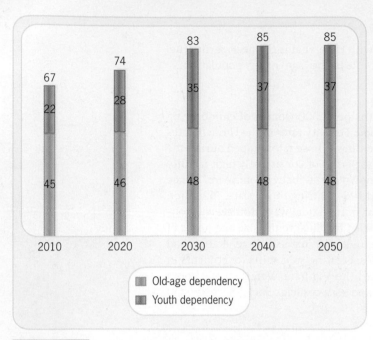

FIGURE 9.5 Dependency ratios for the United States: 2010 to 2050.

Notes: Total dependency = [(Population under age 20 + Population aged 65 years and over) / (Population aged 20 to 64 years)] × 100

Old-age dependency = (Population aged 65 years and over / Population aged 20 to 64 years) × 100
Youth dependency = (Population under age 20 / (Population aged 20 to 64 years) × 100.

Data from: U.S. Census Bureau (2010). "The Next Four Decades, The Older Population in the United States: 2010 to 2050, Current Population Reports." *Current Population Reports* (#P25–1138). Available at http://www.census.gov/newsroom/releases/archives/aging_population/cb10-72.html.

older adults including programs for caregivers and flexible employment opportunities.

The total dependency ratio (DR) is calculated by adding the number of youth and old, divided by the number of persons 20 to 64 years, times 100. In the twentieth century, the lowest DR (70.5) was recorded in 1900. The DR in 2010 was 67, but projections have it climbing to a peak of 85 in 2040 and staying steady through 2050[10] (see **Figure 9.5**). This increase over the next 30 to 40 years will be driven by the old-age dependency ratio and thus will guide future social policy.

Such an increase in the old-age dependency ratio provides an interesting political scenario because the costs to support youth and the old are not the same. Parents pay directly for most of the expenditures to support their children, with the primary exception being public education, which is paid for by taxes. In contrast, much of the support for elders comes from tax-supported programs such as Social Security, Medicare, and Medicaid. To meet the impending burden of the elderly, taxes will most certainly need to be raised or benefits reduced. Therefore, the two questions for the future are: Will the productive population be willing to pay increased taxes to support older adults? Will services to older adults be drastically reduced?

Although dependency ratio data clearly show one trend, they are merely an estimate and should not be the only accepted estimate. Actually, the dependency ratios presented in Figure 9.5 are based on the assumption that everyone of productive age supports all members of the nonproductive age group. Obviously, this is not the case. Many of those in the productive age group (for instance, homemakers, those who are unemployed, and those who are disabled) do not participate in the paid labor force. Conversely, many teenagers and older adults do. Thus, dependency ratios, in some situations, could provide misleading figures for decision makers.

Other experts believe that labor-force ratios also need to be considered. **Labor-force ratios** differ from dependency ratios in that they are based on the number of people who are actually working and those who are not, independent of their ages. When labor-force participation rates are used to calculate the labor-force ratios, it is projected that the burden of support for the labor force in the future will be somewhat lighter than that projected through dependency ratios. This is because of the fact that baby boomers plan to work longer than did members of the previous generations.[11] Nonetheless, under either method of calculation, the ratio of workers to dependents will be lower in the future than it is today.

Other Demographic Variables Affecting Older Adults

Other demographic variables that affect the community and public health programs of older Americans include marital status, living arrangements, racial and ethnic composition, geographic distribution, economic status, and housing.

Marital Status

Almost three-fourths of older men are married, whereas just under half of older women are married. In addition, over one-third of older women are widowed.[12] There are three primary reasons for these differences. First, men have shorter average life expectancies (76.4 years in

Labor-force ratio a ratio of the total number of those individuals who are not working to the number of those who are

2013)[13] than women (81.2 years in 2013)[13] and thus tend to precede their wives in death. Second, men tend to marry women who are younger than themselves. Finally, men who lose a spouse through death or divorce are more likely to remarry than women in the same situation. These statistics reveal that most older men have a spouse for assistance, especially when health fails, whereas most women do not. Widowed women tend to have a closer and wider network of social support, but generally suffer from a lowered financial status upon widowhood[2] (see **Figure 9.6**).

In 2014, the number of divorced elders was 14% of the older adult U.S. population.[12] As more baby boomers move into their older years, the number of divorced older adults will grow substantially. These divorced older adults represent a new type of need group—those who lack the retirement benefits, insurance, and net worth assets associated with being married.

FIGURE 9.6   Older women are three times more likely to be widowed than older men.
© rj lerich/ShutterStock, Inc.

Living Arrangements

"The living arrangements of America's older population are linked to income, health status, and the availability of caregivers."[7] In 2014, 57% of noninstitutionalized older adults lived with their spouse, and 28% lived alone.[12] Older women are more likely to live alone than older men. The proportion of those living alone is projected to remain about the same, but the numbers are expected to increase dramatically over the next 20 years.[4] Reasons for these increased numbers revolve around the aging of the baby boomers and the improved economic status of older adults, coupled with their strong desire to live as independently as possible.

Only a small percentage of the older adult population in the United States resides in nursing homes. About 1.5 million of those aged 65 years and older are in nursing homes, representing 3.4% of the older adult population.[12] This percentage is down from previous years in part as a result of the increase in other housing options and community services discussed later in this chapter. Of those who do live in nursing homes, older women at all ages have higher usage rates than men do. Approximately three-fourths of nursing home residents are women, and more than half of all nursing home residents are older than 85 years. As one might expect, the proportion of older adults living in a nursing home increases with age.[7]

Racial and Ethnic Composition

As the older adult population grows larger, it will also grow more diverse, reflecting the demographic changes in the U.S. population as a whole. In 2013, the older adult population was predominately white. Of the total older adult population in 2013, it was estimated that 78.8% were white, 8.6% were African American, 7.5% were of Hispanic origin, 3.9% were Asian, and Pacific Islanders, American Indians, and Alaska Natives were less than 1%.[12] It is expected that in the coming decades the percentage of older whites will decline and older Americans of Hispanic origin will become the largest older minority group in the United States.[2]

A number of health disparities exist among minority groups in the United States. Health professionals will have to work to achieve cultural competence in the services they provide to older adults of diverse backgrounds.[2]

Geographic Distribution

The proportion of older adults in the U.S. population varies greatly by state (see **Figure 9.7**). In 2013, 61% of persons age 65+ lived in 13 states: California (4.8 million); Florida (3.6 million); Texas (3.0 million); New York (2.8 million); Pennsylvania (2.1 million); and Ohio, Illinois,

Michigan, North Carolina, New Jersey, Georgia, Virginia, and Arizona each had well over one million.[12] Nineteen states have a proportion of their total 65+ population higher than the national average at over 15%.[12] About 81% of those age 65+ in the United States live in metropolitan areas.[12]

Economic Status

Significant improvements have occurred with the income and economic position of older adults in recent decades. In 1970, about 25% of elders lived in poverty,[7] but by 2013 the statistic had dropped to 9.5%.[12] Another 5.6% were classified as "near-poor" In 2013.[12]

"The major sources of income as reported by older persons in 2012 were Social Security (reported by 86% of older persons), income from assets (reported by 51%), private pensions (reported by 27%), government employee pensions (reported by 14%), and earnings (reported by 28%). In 2012, Social Security benefits accounted for 35% of the aggregate income of the older population. The bulk of the remainder consisted of earnings (34%), asset income (11%), and pensions (17%). Social Security constituted 90% or more of the income received by 36% of beneficiaries (22% of married couples and 47% of non-married beneficiaries)."[12] Because just more than one-fourth of older adult income comes from work earnings, they are economically more vulnerable to circumstances beyond their control, such as the loss of a spouse; deteriorating health and self-sufficiency; changes in Social Security, Medicare, and Medicaid legislation; and inflation.

Education

Older adults in the United States have completed fewer years of formal education than their younger counterparts. However, the education level has increased drastically in recent decades. The percentage of older adults who had completed high school rose from 28% in 1970 to 84% in 2014.[12] About one-fourth of older adults had a bachelor's degree or higher in 2014.[12]

Educational attainment of U.S. older adults differs by race and ethnic origin with more whites having completed high school than any of the minority groups. However, high school completion rate has increased in all racial and ethnic groups. Baby boomers are the most educated cohort in the history of the U.S., so it is expected that future older adults will have achieved higher educational attainment than today's older adults.[2]

Housing

In general, the majority of older Americans live in adequate, affordable housing.[7] "Of the 26.8 million households headed by older persons in 2013, 81% were owners and 19% were renters."[12] Older adults' homes tend to be older, of lower value, and in greater need of repairs than the homes of their younger counterparts.[14]

For 65% of older adults, housing represents an asset because they have no mortgage or rental payments,[12] or they can sell their home for a profit. But for others with low incomes, housing becomes a heavy burden. The cost of utilities, real estate taxes, insurance, repair, and maintenance have forced many to sell their property or live in a less-desirable residence.

A Health Profile of Older Adults

The health status of older adults has improved over the years, both in terms of living longer and remaining functional. The percentage of chronically disabled older persons—those with impairments for 3 months or longer that impede daily activities—has been slowly falling. However, the most consistent risk factor of illness and death across the total population is age; in general, the health status of older adults is not as good as their younger counterparts. In this section of the chapter, we examine some of the health concerns of aging, including mortality, morbidity, and health behaviors and lifestyle choices.

Mortality

In 2011, the top five causes of death for elders, in order of number of deaths, were heart disease, malignant neoplasms (cancer), chronic lower respiratory disease (CLRD), cerebrovascular disease (stroke), and Alzheimer's disease.[15] These five causes of death were responsible for almost two-thirds of the total deaths in older adults.[15] Over the past 50 years, the overall age-adjusted mortality rate for older adults has continued to fall. The primary reason for this has been the declining death rates for heart disease and stroke. Despite such drops, heart disease remains the leading cause of death in this age group, and it is responsible for one-fourth of the deaths.[15] Unlike the death rates for heart disease and stroke, the cancer death rate has stayed about the same in recent years. Diseases highly impacted by behaviors and modifiable risk factors continue to be a focus of community health efforts (see **Box 9.1**).

Morbidity

Among Medicare enrollees aged 65 and older, about one in five men and one in three women are unable to perform at least one of five physical activities (walking two to three blocks; writing; stooping or kneeling; reaching up overhead; lifting something as heavy as 10 pounds).[7] Activity limitations increase with age, and women are more likely than men to have physical limitations.[7] The causes of this reduced activity can be classified into two types—chronic conditions and impairments.

Chronic Conditions

Chronic conditions are systemic health problems that persist longer than 3 months, such as hypertension, arthritis, heart disease, diabetes, and emphysema. Most older adults have at least one chronic condition, and over three-fourths have at least two.[16] Chronic conditions may or may not be life threatening. Chronic conditions of older adults vary by gender

---

BOX 9.1   *Healthy People 2020*: Objectives

Diabetes

Goal: Reduce the disease and economic burden of diabetes mellitus (DM) and improve the quality of life for all persons who have, or are at risk for, DM.

Objective D-3: Reduce the diabetes death rate.

Target: 65.8 deaths per 100,000 population.

Baseline: 73.1 deaths per 100,000 population were related to diabetes in 2007 (age adjusted to the year 2000 standard population).

Target-setting method: 10% improvement.

Data source: National Vital Statistics System (NVSS), Centers for Disease Control and Prevention (CDC), National Centers for Health Statistics (NCHS).

Objective D-11: Increase the proportion of adults with diabetes who have a glycosylated hemoglobin (HbA1c) measurement at least twice a year.

Target: 71.1%.

Baseline: 64.6% of adults aged 18 years and older with diagnosed diabetes had a glycosylated hemoglobin measurement at least twice in the past 12 months, as reported in 2008 (age adjusted to the year 2000 standard population).

Target-setting method: 10% improvement.

Data source: Behavioral Risk Factor Surveillance System, CDC, National Center for Chronic Disease Prevention and Health Promotion (NCCDPHP).

For Further Thought

If you were given the responsibility of getting people with diabetes to get regular HbA1c measurements, what community health activities would you use?

Data from: U.S. Department of Health and Human Services, Office of Disease Prevention and Health Promotion (2016). *Healthy People 2020*. Washington, DC: U.S. Government Printing Office. Available at https://www.healthypeople.gov/2020/topics-objectives/topic/diabetes/objectives.

and race. The most common chronic conditions reported by those 65 and older in the United States are hypertension, arthritis, heart disease, cancer, and diabetes.[7] The actual number of chronic conditions increases with age; therefore, limitations from activities become increasingly prevalent with age. Furthermore, many chronic conditions can result in impairments, such as the loss of sight from diabetes. They create a burden on health and economic status, impede ability to engage with family and friends, and increase the demand for caregivers. At least 95% of health care costs for older adults in the United States is for chronic diseases.[17]

Impairments

Impairments are deficits in the functioning of one's sense organs or limitations in one's mobility or range of motion. Like chronic conditions, impairments are far more prevalent in older adults. The primary impairments that affect older adults are sensory impairments (i.e., vision, hearing, postural balance, or loss of feeling in the feet), physical limitations, and memory impairments[19] (see **Box 9.2**). Oral health problems and absence of natural teeth also create limitations for many elders.[7, 19] "Glasses, hearing aids, and regular dental care are not covered services under Medicare."[7]

Sensory impairments increase with age and the prevalence of them will increase as life expectancy increases. Currently, 5.3 million older adults have significant vision loss.[20] "Nearly 25% of those aged 65 to 74 and 50% of those who are 75 and older have disabling hearing loss."[21] Of adults over age 70 who could benefit from hearing aids, only about one-third have ever used them.[21] Falls are of great concern with older adults, particularly those with balance impairments. One in three older adults' falls each year, and one in five falls causes serious injury, with over 95% of hip fractures in older adults caused by falls.[22] The death rate from falls has been growing steadily in the United States over the past decade.[22] Balance impairment may be in part why so many older adults have physical limitations. *Physical limitations* refers to older adults having difficulty performing any of these eight physical activities: (1) walking a quarter of a mile—about 3 city blocks; (2) walking up 10 steps without resting; (3) standing or being on their feet for about 2 hours; (4) sitting for about 2 hours; (5) stooping, bending, or kneeling; (6) reaching over their head; (7) using their fingers to grasp or handle small objects; or (8) lifting or carrying something as heavy as 10 pounds, such as a full bag of groceries.[20] Like sensory impairments, physical limitations increase with age. Memory impairments are not a natural part of aging, but connected to diseases, illnesses, or conditions more commonly affecting older adults. Currently, Alzheimer's disease is the leading cause of memory loss in older adults. Like rates for chronic conditions, rates for impairments in older adults differ by gender and race.

BOX 9.2   *Healthy People 2020*: Objectives

Arthritis, Osteoporosis, and Chronic Back Conditions

Goal: Prevent illness and disability related to arthritis and other rheumatic conditions, osteoporosis, and chronic back conditions.

Objective AOCBC-10: Reduce the proportion of adults with osteoporosis.

Target: 5.3%.

Baseline: 5.9% of adults aged 50 years and older had osteoporosis in 2005–08 (age adjusted to the year 2000 standard population).

Target-setting method: 10% improvement.

Data source: National Health and Nutrition Examination Survey, CDC, NCHS.

For Further Thought

Have you seen any health care facilities in your community that have been advertising that they perform bone density testing? How is bone density measured? What are some community health activities that could be carried out in a community to reduce the proportion of adults with osteoporosis?

Data from: U.S. Department of Health and Human Services, Office of Disease Prevention and Health Promotion (2016). *Healthy People 2020*. Washington, DC: U.S. Government Printing Office. Available at https://www.healthypeople.gov/2020/topics-objectives/topic/Arthritis-Osteoporosis-and-Chronic-Back-Conditions /objectives.

Health Behaviors and Lifestyle Choices

Over 76% of people age 65 and older in the United States rate their health as excellent, very good, or good. Rates are similar among men and women, but as one ages, the ratings decrease in quality.[7,19] There is no question that health behavior and social factors play significant roles in helping older adults maintain health in later life. Some older adults believe that they are too old to gain any benefit from changing their health behaviors. This, of course, is not true; it is never too late to make a change for the better.

In interviews, older adults generally report more favorable health behaviors than their younger counterparts. They are less likely to (1) consume large amounts of alcohol, (2) smoke cigarettes, and (3) be overweight or obese. However, it should be noted that abusing alcoholic beverages, smoking cigarettes, and being overweight or obese decreases life expectancy, so the number of those over age 65 reporting these factors is likely to be decreased.

Even though older adults generally report better health behaviors than their younger counterparts, there is still room for improvement. The health behaviors that can most affect the health of older adults are healthy eating, exercise, and immunizations. These issues play a major role in preventing or delaying the onset of chronic diseases.

Physical Activity

Even among frail older adults balance, mobility, and daily functioning can be improved with regular physical activity.[7] Yet, older adults are the least physically active of any age group. All have experienced some loss of physical fitness due to the aging process, and many suffer from chronic conditions, which can complicate the ability to be active.[23] According to the *2008 Physical Activity Guidelines for Americans*, if older adults are fit and have no chronic conditions, their physical activity recommendations are basically the same as other aged adults.[23] They should focus on both aerobic conditioning and muscle strengthening. It is also advised that older adults focus on balance training because of their increased risk for, and complications from, falls.[23] About 11% of elders in the U.S. meet the physical activity guidelines.[7,24]

Nutrition

"Poor eating habits accelerate many age-related decrements and increase the likelihood of several chronic illnesses later in life."[2] Dietary quality and requirements for older adults vary greatly depending on life circumstances. Both obesity and malnutrition can pose challenges with the older adult population in the U.S. Although the types of nutrients needed are the same for people of all age groups, the amounts of each nutrient needed can vary as people age. Some dietary concerns for older adults include reduced sodium intake, reduced caloric needs, increased vegetable consumption, and increased water consumption.[7,25]

Obesity

As with all age groups, the number of obese people age 65 and over in the U.S. has increased in recent decades. In 2010, 38% of those age 65 and over were obese compared to 22% two decades earlier.[7] Only 26% of U.S. older adults are in a healthy weight range.[24]

Cigarette Smoking

Just over 9% of current older adults are cigarette smokers. This number decreased significantly over the past several decades, mostly due to the decreasing number of male smokers.[7,24] Of special concern are the number of older adults who are former smokers. Chronic lower respiratory diseases are the third leading cause of death among older adults, which indicates the cumulative effect of cigarette smoking over many years of life.[7]

Vaccinations

Immune systems tend to weaken over time, which increases the risk of infectious diseases. It is recommended that older adults receive vaccinations against influenza and pneumonia, illnesses that often create increased complications in the elderly population. An influenza vaccination is recommended every year and pneumococcal vaccination once in their lifetime.[7,26] In the 2014–2015 flu season, 66.7% of those 65 and over received a flu vaccination.[27] Only about 60% of older adults have ever received a pneumococcal vaccination.[13]

Although vaccination rates have improved over time, significant racial disparities occur. Black and Hispanic American older adults have lower vaccination rates than white older adults.[26]

Mistreatment of Older Adults

Reports of elder abuse and neglect have increased greatly in recent years. Perhaps a substantial part of the increase in these numbers was the result of all 50 states having passed some form of elder abuse prevention laws. Though the laws and definitions of terms vary from state to state, all states have reporting systems. Prior to the reporting systems, many incidences of abuse were never recorded. Even with reporting systems in place, it is difficult to determine the actual number of older adults experiencing some form of mistreatment.

Generally, the first line of contact in the reporting of elder abuse is with Adult Protective Services. Adult Protective Services (APS) are those services provided to insure the safety and well-being of elders and adults with disabilities who are in danger of being mistreated or neglected, are unable to take care of themselves or protect themselves from harm, and have no one to assist them. Interventions provided by Adult Protective Services include, but are not limited to, receiving reports of adult abuse, exploitation, or neglect, investigating these reports, case planning, monitoring, and evaluation. In addition to casework services, Adult Protection may provide or arrange for the provision of medical, social, economic, legal, housing, law enforcement, or other protective, emergency or supportive services."[28]

According to the first-ever National Elder Abuse Incidence Study, released in 1998, an estimated total of 551,000 elderly persons older than age 60 had experienced abuse (physical, emotional/psychological), neglect, or self-neglect in a domestic setting during the year of the study.[29] This study also revealed the following:

- Female elders are abused at a higher rate than are men.
- Elders 80 years and older are abused or neglected at two to three times the rate of their proportion of the elderly population.
- In almost 90% of all elder abuse and neglect incidents where a perpetrator is identified, the perpetrator is a family member, and two-thirds of the perpetrators are adult children or spouses.
- Victims of self-neglect are usually depressed, confused, or extremely frail.

Mistreatment is often the result of multiple factors, but older adults with dementia and cognitive impairment, a past experience with domestic violence, frailty, and experiencing social isolation appear to be at higher risk.[30]

Instrumental Needs of Older Adults

Six instrumental needs that determine lifestyles for people of all ages have been identified as income, housing, personal care, health care, transportation, and community facilities and services.[31] However, the aging process can alter these needs in unpredictable ways. Whereas those older adults in the young old group (65–74) usually do not experience appreciable changes in their lifestyles relative to these six needs, older adults in the middle old group (75–84) and the old old group (85 and older) eventually do. The rest of this chapter explores these six needs, discusses their implications, and describes community services for older adults.

Income

Though the need for income continues throughout one's life, achieving older adult status often reduces the income needs. Perhaps the major reduction occurs with one's retirement.

Retirees do not need to purchase job-related items such as special clothing or tools, pay union dues, or join professional associations. Expenses are further reduced because retirees no longer commute every day, buy as many meals away from home, or spend money on business travel. Reaching older adult status also usually means that children are grown and no longer dependent, and, as noted earlier, the home mortgage has often been retired. Taxes are usually lower because income is lower. In addition, many community services are offered at reduced prices for older adults.

However, aging usually means increased expenses for health care and for home maintenance and repairs that aging homeowners can no longer do themselves. Despite these increased costs, the overall need for income seems to decrease slightly for people after retirement.

As noted earlier in this chapter, the main sources of income for older adults are Social Security, pensions (e.g., government employee pensions, private pensions, or annuities), earnings from jobs, income from assets (e.g., savings accounts, stocks, bonds, real estate), and other miscellaneous sources (e.g., public assistance for poor older adults). Social Security benefits account for about 39% of income for older adults.[32] The average monthly Social Security benefit for a retired worker was about $1,335 in 2015.[32] This amounts to an average of $16,020 per year before Medicare deductions. About 90% of all people older than age 65 years receive Social Security benefits.[32] Of Social Security beneficiaries that are older adults, 53% of married couples and 74% of unmarried persons receive 50% or more of their income from Social Security, and 22% of married couples and 47% of unmarried persons depend on over 90% of their income from Social Security.[32] In recent years, the income of older adults has improved. When income and other assets are combined, the economic status of older adults and those younger than 65 is not that far apart. However, the fact remains that 9.5% of the older population lives in poverty. Certain subgroups of older adults have higher rates. Unmarried women and minorities have the highest poverty rates. Married persons have the lowest poverty rates.[7]

Housing

Housing, a basic necessity for all, is a central concern for older adults in terms of needs and costs. It is an important source of continuity for older adults. A home is more than just a place to live. It is a symbol of independence; a place for family gatherings; a source of pleasant memories; and a link to friends, the neighborhood, and the community.[31]

When housing for older adults is examined, the major needs are appropriateness, accessibility, adequacy, and affordability. These needs are not independent of each other; in fact, they are closely intertwined. Older adults may live in affordable housing, but the housing may not be appropriate for their special needs. Or, certain housing may be accessible, but it may not be affordable, or there may not be an adequate number available to meet demand.

Housing requirements may change more rapidly than housing consumption during the course of retirement years as a result of changes in household composition, decreasing mobility, and/or increasing morbidity. Thus, the single biggest change in the housing needs of older adults is the need for special modifications because of physical limitations. Such modifications can be very simple—such as handrails for support in bathrooms—or more complex—such as chair lifts for stairs. Sometimes there is need for live-in help, while at other times disabilities may force older adults to leave their homes and seek specialized housing.

The decision to remove older adults from their long-term residences is not easily made. Because of the psychological and social value of the home, changing an older adult's place of residence has negative effects for both the older adult and the family members who help make the arrangements for the move. Recognizing the importance of a home and independence, families often feel tremendous conflict and guilt in deciding to move an older relative. If the older adult does not adjust to the new situation, the guilt continues. Sometimes family members continue to question their decision even after the person dies. Though moving an older adult is very difficult, it is often best for all involved. For example, moving a frail person from a two-story to a one-story home makes good sense, and moving an older adult from a

Retirement communities
residential communities that have been specifically developed for individuals in their retirement years or of a certain age

very large home to a smaller home or an apartment is logical. A variety of housing options is available for older adults based on their needs and personal preferences. The following are general categories of housing options for older adults and their family members to explore.

Independent Living

Many older adults continue to live independently in their own home, condominium, or apartment. A variety of community services (discussed later in this chapter) are available in home to assist older adults in maintaining their independence. Some independent older adults choose to move from a long-term private residence into a group setting often referred to as independent living apartments, **retirement communities**, or senior housing (see **Figure 9.8**). Independent living settings are for older adults who require little to no assistance with daily activities. However, services are often provided for residents such as social activities, transportation, laundry, meals, and housekeeping.[33,34]

Assisted Living

Assisted living facilities offer housing options for individuals who need a wide range of support services to help them with activities of daily living such as medication management, bathing, dressing, and meals. Assisted living residents do not require the level of care that nursing home residents need. The level of care is assessed upon moving into the facility and reassessed whenever their condition changes, such as after a hospitalization.[33,34]

Assisted living residences can vary greatly from high-rise buildings, to multi-building campuses, to mansion-style homes. Most of them offer standard services including:[34]

- Three meals a day served in a common dining area
- Housekeeping services
- Transportation
- 24-hour security
- Exercise and wellness programs
- Personal laundry services
- Social and recreational activities
- Staff available to respond to both scheduled and unscheduled needs
- Assistance with eating, bathing, dressing, toileting, and walking
- Access to health and medical services, such as physical therapy and hospice
- Emergency call systems for each resident's apartment
- Medication management
- Care for residents with cognitive impairments

FIGURE 9.8   The number of planned retirement communities in the United States continues to rise.

© Brisbane/ShutterStock, Inc.

Costs for assisted living can vary dramatically according to the facility, location, and services needed. According to LongTermCare.gov, the average costs for a one-bedroom unit in an assisted living facility in the U.S. in 2010 was $3,293 per month.[35]

Continuing Care Retirement Communities

Continuing care retirement communities (CCRCs) offer a variety of levels of assistance in the same building, campus, or community. "There may be individual homes or apartments for residents who still live on their own, an assisted living facility for people who need some help with daily care, and a nursing home for those who require higher levels of care. Residents move from one level to another based on their individual needs, but usually stay within the CCRC."[36]

The focus of CCRCs is guaranteed lifelong residence and health care. They are typically paid for through long-term contracts/leases, large entry fees, and monthly fees. Additional services may require extra fees. Unfortunately, CCRCs are financially beyond the reach of many older adults.

Nursing Homes/Skilled Nursing Facilities

Nursing homes, also known as skilled nursing facilities or long-term care facilities, are generally the last housing option for individuals who can no longer live on their own and need 24-hour care or supervision.[34] Nursing homes may provide short-term care for those needing rehabilitation or who are convalescing from a hospitalization. They also provide long-term care for those who are not able to return to an independent state of living. In addition to providing assistance with activities of daily living, medical monitoring and treatment is provided by a registered nurse.

Paying for nursing home care is a major concern for individuals, families, and the government. According to LongTermCare.gov, the average costs for a semi-private room in a nursing home in the U.S. in 2010 was $6,235 per month and more for a private room.[35] Payment responsibility is dependent on many factors including type of care needed, type of insurance coverage one has, and financial status. Options for payment includes private payments, long-term care insurance, Medicare, and Medicaid. Generally, one privately pays for nursing home care until they are eligible for Medicaid. Medicare only covers stays in a nursing home for a limited period of time, and only if it is following a qualified hospital stay.[36] If an individual has a long-term care insurance policy, nursing home stays are generally covered as part of the policy.

Affordable Housing

Of all the housing problems that confront older adults, the availability of affordable housing is the biggest. Unfortunately, the older adults who are most in need of such housing are often frail and disabled, have low incomes, and live in rural areas. The U.S. Department of Housing and Urban Development (HUD) works to provide safe, decent, affordable housing for older adults and other groups. Eligibility and types of housing options are based on income and other criteria. Individuals can work with a HUD-approved housing counselor to determine qualifications.[37]

Personal Care

Although most older adults are able to care for themselves, there is a significant minority who require personal assistance for an optimal or even adequate existence. The size of this minority increases as the older adults attain middle old and old old status.

Four different levels of tasks have been identified with which older adults may need assistance:

1. Instrumental tasks—such as housekeeping, transportation, maintenance on the automobile or yard, and assistance with business affairs
2. Expressive tasks—including emotional support, socializing and inclusion in social gatherings, and trying to prevent feelings of loneliness and isolation

Continuing care retirement communities (CCRCs) planned communities for older adults that guarantee a lifelong residence and health care

3. Cognitive tasks—assistance that involves scheduling appointments, monitoring health conditions, reminding elders of the need to take medications, and in general acting as a backup memory

4. Tasks of daily living—such as eating, bathing, dressing, toileting, walking, getting in and out of bed or a chair, and getting outside

Note that this last group of tasks, in addition to being a part of this listing, has special significance. These items have been used to develop a scale, called **activities of daily living (ADLs)**, to measure **functional limitations**. *Functional limitation* refers to the difficulty in performing personal care and home management tasks. However, ADLs do not cover all aspects of disability and are not sufficient by themselves to estimate the need for long-term care. Some older adults have cognitive impairments that are not measured by ADLs. An additional, commonly used measure called **instrumental activities of daily living (IADLs)** measures more complex tasks such as handling personal finances, preparing meals, shopping, doing housework, traveling, using the telephone, and taking medications.[38]

Caregivers

When older adults begin to need help with one or more ADLs or IADLs, it is usually a spouse, adult children, or other family members who first provide the help, thus assuming the role of informal caregivers. An **informal caregiver** has been defined as one who provides unpaid care or assistance to one who has some physical, mental, emotional, or financial need that limits his or her independence. "There is wide latitude in the estimates of the number of informal caregivers in the United States, depending on the definitions and criteria used."[39] About 25% of adults in the U.S. report providing informal care in the past 30 days.[40] An informal caregiver can take on many roles. The **care provider** helps identify the needs of the individual as well as personally performs the caregiving service. The **care manager** helps to identify needs, but does not provide the service. The care manager makes arrangements for someone else (volunteer or paid) to provide the services.

With the aging of the population, it is now highly probable that many, if not most, adults can expect to have some responsibility as caregivers for their parents (see **Figure 9.9**). Caregivers for older adults face a number of health problems, including elevated levels of depression and anxiety, higher use of psychoactive medications, poorer physical health, compromised immune function, and increased risk of early death.[40] In addition to compromised health, caregivers also often experience less personal freedom and privacy, and are economically impacted due to their caregiving responsibilities. Even though caregiving can provide many challenges, caregivers may also experience positive feelings about their role. Caring for a loved one can provide fulfillment and feelings of "giving back." Additionally, caregivers may extend their personal networks to include others with similar experiences, and feel a sense of purpose and meaning in life.

The need for personal care and paying for long-term care services for older adults is projected to increase in the coming years. As noted elsewhere in this chapter, long-term care services can be very expensive for many Americans. Because of the financial burden, many opt to purchase long-term care insurance policies. These policies can be expensive if purchased late in life when need for long-term care services are the greatest. However, they often provide older adults with sufficient income protection against the depletion of assets. The high premiums and copayment costs of long-term care policies mean that many Americans cannot afford them unless they are willing to purchase them when they are younger and the costs are lower.[41,42]

To assist caregivers, federal legislation was passed called the Older Americans Act Amendments of 2000 (Public Law

FIGURE 9.9 Adult children are gaining greater responsibility as caregivers.
© Lisa F. Young/Fotolia.com.

106-501). This law established the National Family Caregiver Support Program (NFCSP), which has been administered by the Administration on Aging (AoA) of the U.S. Department of Health and Human Services. The program provides grants to states based on the percentage of their population age 70 and over. The funding is used to support services that assist families and informal caregivers to keep loved ones at home for as long as possible. "The NFCSP offers a range of services to support family caregivers. Under this program, states shall provide five types of services:"[43]

- Information to caregivers about available services
- Assistance to caregivers in gaining access to the services
- Individual counseling, organization of support groups, and caregiver training
- Respite care
- Supplemental services, on a limited basis

Eldercare support for working caregivers is a growing concern in the United States as more women are in the workplace and the percentage of the age 85+ population, those with the greatest needs, grows. A study of large U.S. companies found companies supporting employees caring for older adults offer employee programs that include paid time off and flexible scheduling to accommodate caregiver roles, access to geriatric care managers and consultations, employee wellness programs, and caregiver stress reduction and education programs.[44]

Health Care

Health care is a major issue for all segments of society, particularly for older adults. Although significant progress has been made in extending life expectancy, a longer life does not necessarily mean a healthier life. Health problems naturally increase with age. With these problems comes a need for increased health care services.

Older adults are the heaviest users of health care services. Approximately 20% of older adults have 10 or more visits a year to a physician, compared with 13% for all people in the United States.[45] They are also hospitalized more often and for longer stays. Although persons 65 years of age and older only represented approximately 13% of the total population in 2009, they accounted for almost 37% of the roughly 35 million patient discharges from nonfederal short-stay hospitals,[45] and they spend over twice as much per person on prescription drugs as those younger than 65 years of age. In addition, older adults have higher usage rates for professional dental care, vision aids, and medical equipment and supplies than people younger than age 65. Usage of health care services increases with age, and much of the money spent on health care is spent in the last year of life.

Whereas private sources, such as employer-paid insurance, are the major sources of health care payment for people younger than age 65, public funds are used to pay for the majority of the health care expenses for older adults. Medicare, which was enacted in 1965 and became effective July 1, 1966, provides almost universal health insurance coverage for older adults. Medicare coverage, however, is biased toward hospital care, while chronic care health needs such as eyeglasses (see **Figure 9.10**), hearing aids, and most long-term services are not covered.

In 2015, the Medicare program had 55 million enrollees[46] and expenditures of just over $597 billion.[47] With the increasing cost of health care and the aging population, these numbers will only grow. In addition, Medicaid, a federal-state program that was also approved in 1965, helps to cover the health care costs of poor older adults, primarily for nursing home care (continuing care), home health care, and prescription drugs. In 2012, over 8 million older adults were covered by Medicaid.[48]

Numerous changes have occurred to Medicare over the years, but the need for ongoing change remains inevitable as the first of the baby boomers turned 65 years old, and thus became eligible

FIGURE 9.10   Medicare provides almost universal health insurance for older adults.
© iStockphoto/Thinkstock.

for Medicare in 2011. Therefore, future legislators will be forced to choose from among the following alternatives: (1) raising taxes to pay for the care, (2) reallocating tax dollars from other programs to pay for care, (3) cutting back on coverage presently offered, (4) offering care to only those who truly cannot afford it otherwise (also known as *means testing*), or (5) completely revamping the present system under which the care is funded.

In the meantime, the importance of instilling in Americans the value of preventing the onset of chronic diseases through healthy living cannot be overstated. Although it is not possible to prevent all chronic health problems, encouraging healthy behaviors is a step in the right direction.

Transportation

In 2012, there were almost 36 million Americans over the age of 65 licensed to drive.[49] Transportation is of prime importance to older adults because it enables them to remain independent. "Housing, medical, financial and social services are useful only to the extent that transportation can make them accessible to those in need."[50] The two factors that have the greatest effect on the transportation needs of older adults are income and health status. Some older adults who have always driven their own automobiles eventually find that they are no longer able to do so. The ever-increasing costs of purchasing and maintaining an automobile sometimes become prohibitive on a fixed income. Also, with age come physical problems that restrict one's ability to operate an automobile safely. In addition, those with extreme disabilities may find that they will need a modified automobile (to accommodate their disability) or specialized transportation (e.g., a vehicle that can accommodate a wheel-chair) to be transported.

With regard to transportation needs, older adults can be categorized into three different groups: (1) those who can use the present forms of transportation, whether it be their own vehicle or public transportation, (2) those who could use public transportation if the barriers of cost and access (no service available) were removed, and (3) those who need special services beyond what is available through public transportation.[32]

The unavailability of transportation services has stimulated a number of private and public organizations that serve older adults (e.g., churches, community services, and local area agencies on aging) to provide these services. Some communities even subsidize the cost of public transportation by offering reduced rates for older adults. Although these services have been helpful to older adults, mobility is still more difficult for elders than for other adults. Try to imagine what it would be like if you had to depend constantly on someone else for all of your transportation needs.

To prepare professionals, family members, and concerned community members to have effective conversations about driver safety and community transportation issues with older adults, including alternatives to driving, the National Highway Traffic Safety Administration (NHTSA) has a variety of resources available.[51] For information visit www.nhtsa.gov.

The ideal solution to the transportation needs of older adults would include four components: (1) fare reductions or discounts for all public transportation, including that for interstate travel, (2) subsidies to ensure adequate scheduling and routing of present public transportation, (3) subsidized taxi fares for the disabled and infirm, and (4) funds for senior centers to purchase and equip vehicles to transport seniors properly, especially in rural areas.[32]

An innovative response to the challenge for older adults who give up driving is the Independent Transportation Network (ITN). Older adults who agree to stop driving trade in their cars, and the value is booked into an account from which they can draw to receive rides. A dollar amount is deducted for each car ride given by a paid driver, less when scheduling rides in advance or for sharing a ride.

The Independent Transportation Network program was started by Katherine Freund, whose son was hit by an elderly driver in Portland, Maine. For more information visit http://itnamerica.org.[52]

Community Facilities and Services

As has been mentioned previously, one of the most common occurrences of the aging process is loss of independence. Even some of the most basic activities of adults become major tasks for older adults because of low income, ill health, and lack of transportation. Because of the limitations of older adults and the barriers they must face, they have special needs in regard to community facilities and services. If these needs are met, the lifestyles of older adults are greatly enhanced. If not, they are confronted with anything from a slight inconvenience to a very poor quality of life.

With a view toward improving the lives of older adults, Congress enacted the **Older Americans Act of 1965 (OAA)** and has amended it several times. Among the programs created by key amendments are the national nutrition program for older adults, the State and Area Agencies on Aging, and other programs (e.g., the caregiver program discussed earlier) to increase the services and protect the rights of older Americans.

Though the initial act was important, the services and facilities available to older adults were greatly improved after the passage of the 1973 amendments, which established the State Departments on Aging and Area Agencies on Aging. These systems inform, guide, and link older persons to available, appropriate, and acceptable services to meet their needs. The amendments were written to provide the state and area agencies with the flexibility to develop plans that allow for local variations. "Most states are divided into planning and service areas (PSAs), so that programs can be tailored to meet the specific needs of older persons residing in those areas. Area Agencies on Aging are the agencies designated by the state to be the focal point for OAA programs within a PSA."[53]

With each part of the country—and for that matter each community—having its own peculiarities, the services available to older adults can vary greatly from one community to another. Even the names of the local agencies (few of which are called Area Agency on Aging) can vary a great deal. Individuals can find their local Area Agency on Aging by visiting www.eldercare.gov.

It is important to keep in mind, however, that the growth in our nation's older adult population, combined with this population's financial ability to pay for service, has created an entrepreneurial atmosphere surrounding adult care services. In some larger communities, or in those communities with a large number of older residents, the range of services can be astonishing. All of these services vary greatly in costs. In the following text, we provide brief descriptions of facilities and services available in many communities.

Meal Service

The 1972 amendments to the Older Americans Act outlined a national nutrition program for older adults and provided funds for communities to establish meal services. Today's meal services are provided through home-delivered meal and congregate meal programs. The concept of the home-delivered meal programs (often known as **Meals on Wheels**) is the regular delivery of meals—usually once a day, 5 days per week—to **homebound** individuals. These meals are prepared in a central location, sometimes in a hospital, school, or senior center, and are delivered by community volunteers.

Congregate meal programs are provided for individuals who can travel to a central site, often within senior centers or publicly funded housing units. Usually, it is the noon meal that is provided. Generally, these meals are funded by federal and state monies and make use of commodity food services. Congregate meal programs seem to be gaining favor over home-delivered meal programs because they also provide social interaction (see **Figure 9.11**) and the opportunity to

> **Older Americans Act of 1965 (OAA)** federal legislation to improve the lives of older adults
>
> **Meals on Wheels** a community-supported nutrition program in which prepared meals are delivered to individuals in their homes, usually by volunteers
>
> **Homebound** a person unable to leave home for normal activities
>
> **Congregate meal programs** community-sponsored nutrition programs that provide meals at a central site, such as a senior center

FIGURE 9.11 Congregate meal programs are not only valuable because of the enhanced nutrition but also because of the social interaction.

© Ken Hammond/USDA.

connect with other social services. However, there will always be a segment of the population requiring home-delivered meals because of their homebound status.

Both types of meal programs are strictly regulated by federal and state guidelines to ensure that the meals meet standard nutritional requirements. The cost of the meals varies by site and client income level. Older adults may pay full price, pay a portion of the cost, or just make a voluntary contribution.

Homemaker Service

For a number of older adults, periodic homemaker services can be the critical factor enabling them to remain in their own homes. For these individuals, physical impairment restricts their ability to carry out normal housekeeping activities such as house cleaning, laundry, and meal preparation. The availability of these services allows many older adults to live semi-independently and delays their moving in with relatives or into group housing.

Chore and Home Maintenance Service

Chore and home maintenance service includes such services as yard work, cleaning gutters and windows, installing screens and storm windows, making minor plumbing and electrical repairs, maintaining furnaces and air conditioners, and helping to adapt a home to any impairments older adults might have. This adaptation may include provisions for wheelchairs and installing ramps or special railings to assist older adults to move from one area to another.

Visitor Service

Social interaction and social contacts are an important need for every human being, regardless of age. **Visitor services** amount to one individual taking time to visit with another person who is homebound, or unable to leave his or her residence. This service is usually done on a voluntary basis, many times with older adults doing the visiting, and serves both the homebound and those who are institutionalized. It is not uncommon for church or social organizations to conduct a visitor program for homebound members.

Adult Day Care

Adult day care programs provide care during the daytime hours for older adults who are unable to be left alone. These services are modeled after child day care. Most programs offer meals, snacks, and social activities for the clients. Some either provide or make arrangements for the clients to receive therapy, counseling, health education, or other health services. Other day care programs are designed for older adults with special needs, such as Alzheimer clients, those who are blind, or veterans. Adult day care programs allow families to continue with daytime activities while still providing the primary care for a family member.

Respite Care

Respite care is planned, short-term care. Such care allows families who provide primary care for an older family member to leave them at home or alone in a supervised care setting for anywhere from a day to a few weeks. Respite services can provide full care, including sleeping quarters, meals, bathing facilities, social activities, and the monitoring of medications. This is the service most frequently requested by informal caregivers. Such a program allows primary caregivers to take a vacation, visit other relatives, or be otherwise relieved from their constant caregiving responsibilities.

Home Health Care

Home health care is "an important alternative to traditional institutional care. Services such as medical treatment, physical therapy, and homemaker services often allow patients to be cared for at lower cost than a nursing home or hospital and in familiar surroundings of their home."[54] These programs, run by official health agencies like the local health department, hospitals, or private companies, provide a full range of services, including preventive, primary, rehabilitative, and therapeutic services, in the client's home. The care is often provided by nurses, home health aides, and personal care workers (licensed health care workers). Some home health care expenditures are paid for by Medicare, but a significant portion may need to be paid for out of pocket. Other means of paying for this care could include long-term care insurance policies, Medicaid, or reimbursement by a supplemental insurance policy such as Medigap.

Senior Centers

The enactment of the Older Americans Act of 1965 provided funds to develop multipurpose senior centers, facilities where older adults can congregate for fellowship, meals, education, and recreation. More recently, a number of communities have built additional senior centers with local tax dollars. There are about 11,000 senior centers in the United States and they are the most common community facility aimed at serving seniors.[55] However, they are found much less commonly in rural areas.

In addition to the traditional services (meals, fellowship, and recreation) offered at senior centers, some communities use the centers to serve as a central location for offering a variety of other services, including legal assistance, income counseling, income tax return assistance, program referrals, employment services, and other appropriate services and information.

Other Services

There are many other services available to older adults in some communities. Usually, larger communities and those with more older adults provide a greater variety of services. The types of services provided in any one community are limited only by the creativity of those providing the service. In some communities, "service packages" are being offered. Such packages allow older adults to pick several services they need and to pay for them as if they were a single service.

Chapter Summary

- The median age of the U.S. population is at an all-time high and will continue to increase through the first third of this century.
- There are many myths about the older adult population.
- The increasing median age is affected by decreasing fertility rates and declining mortality rates.
- We are now at a point in history when a significant portion of Americans will assume some responsibility for the care of their aging parents.
- One of the most common occurrences of the aging process is the reduction in independence.
- An aging population presents the community with several concerns, which means legislators and taxpayers will be faced with decisions about how best to afford the costs (Social Security, government employee pensions, Medicare, etc.) of an ever-increasing old-age dependency ratio.

- Communities will need to deal with the special needs of income, housing, personal care, health care, transportation, and community facilities and services for older adults.
- All projections indicate that the incomes of older adults will remain lower than those of the general population, that the need for affordable and accessible housing will increase, that there will be increased needs for personal services and care, that health care needs and costs will increase, and that the demand for barrier-free transportation will increase for older adults.
- The growth in our nation's older population, combined with this population's financial ability to pay for service, has created an entrepreneurial atmosphere surrounding adult care services.

Scenario: Analysis and Response

1. Based on what you read in this chapter, how would you predict that Carl and Sarah's lives might progress over the next 20 years? Consider the six instrumental needs presented in the chapter.

2. What could Carl and Sarah have done when they were working to better plan for their retirement?

3. If you had to give Carl and Sarah two pieces of health care advice, what would they be?

Review Questions

1. What are some signs, visible to the average person, that the U.S. population is aging?

2. What years of life are defined by each of the following groups—old, young old, middle old, and old old?

3. Why is there a myth that old people are sickly?

4. How have life expectancy figures changed over the years in the United States? What were the major reasons for the change in the first half of the twentieth century? The second half?

5. Why are dependency and labor-force ratios so important and how are they calculated?

6. Are all older adults the same with regard to demographic variables?

7. Why is there a higher number of older married men than women?

8. How does the racial and ethnic composition of older Americans compare with the overall population?

9. How do the income needs of people change in later years of life?

10. What are the common physical limitations experienced by older adults?

11. What is the difference between a care provider and a care manager?

12. What are some of the major problems caregivers face?

13. Why are continuing care retirement communities attractive to older adults?

14. What is an assisted living residence?

15. What is the difference between activities of daily living and instrumental activities of daily living?

16. What are the most frequently occurring health problems of older adults?

17. From what financial sources do older adults normally pay for health care?

18. How do income and health status affect the transportation needs of older adults?

19. What is the ideal solution for the transportation needs of older adults?

20. What are Area Agencies on Aging?

21. Why is a visitor service so important for homebound and institutionalized persons?

22. What is the difference between adult day care programs and senior centers?

Activities

1. Make arrangements with a local long-term care facility to visit one of their residents. Make at least three 1-hour visits to a resident over a 6-week period of time. Upon completion of the visits, write a paper that answers the following questions:
   - What were your feelings when you first walked into the facility?
   - What were your feelings when you first met the resident?
   - What did you learn about older adults that you did not know before?
   - What did you learn about yourself because of this experience?
   - Did your feeling about the resident change during the course of your visits? If so, how?
   - If you had to live in a long-term care facility, would you be able to adjust to it? What would be most difficult for you in your adjustment? What character traits do you have that would help you adjust?

2. Interview a retired person over the age of 70. In your interview, include the following questions. Write a two-page paper about this interview.
   - What are your greatest needs as an older adult?
   - What are your greatest fears connected with aging?
   - What are your greatest joys at this stage in your life?
   - If you could have done anything differently when you were younger to affect your life now, what would it have been?
   - Have you had any problems getting health care with Medicare? If so, what were they?

- Do you have a Medigap policy? If so, has your Medigap policy been worth the cost?
- In what ways are you able to contribute to your community in retirement?
- Are there any barriers to seeking volunteer opportunities in your community? What do you think about paid part-time work in retirement?

3. Spend a half-day at a local senior center. Then, write a paper that (a) summarizes your experience, (b) identifies your reaction (personal feelings) to the experience, and (c) shares what you have learned from the experience.

4. Review a newspaper obituary column for 7 consecutive days. Using the information provided in the obituaries: (a) demographically describe those who died, (b) keep track of what community services are noted, and (c) consider what generalizations can be made from the group as a whole.

References

1. United States Census Bureau (2011). *The Older Population: 2010*. Available at http://www.census.gov/prod/cen2010/briefs/c2010br-09.pdf.
2. Ferrini, A. F., and R. L. Ferrini (2013). *Health in the Later Years*, 5th ed. Boston: McGraw-Hill Higher Education.
3. Dychtwald, K., and J. Flower (1989). *Age Wave: The Challenges and Opportunities of an Aging America*. Los Angeles: Jeremy P. Tarcher.
4. U.S. Census Bureau (2012). *Population Projections*. Available at http://www.census.gov/population/projections/data/national/2012/summarytables.html.
5. U.S. Census Bureau (2013). *Annual Estimates of the Resident Population for Selected Age Groups by Sex for the United States, States, Counties, and Puerto Rico Commonwealth and Municipios: April 1, 2010 to July 1, 2012*. Available at http://factfinder2.census.gov/bkmk/table/1.0/en/PEP/2012/PEPAGESEX.
6. U.S. Census Bureau (2012). *Statistical Abstract of the United States*. Available at http://www.census.gov/compendia/statab/2012/tables/12s0009.pdf.
7. Federal Interagency Forum on Aging-Related Statistics (2012). *Older Americans 2012: Key Indicators of Well-Being*. Available at http://www.agingstats.gov/agingstatsdotnet/Main_Site/Data/2012_Documents/Docs/EntireChartbook.pdf.
8. National Center for Health Statistics (2010). *Health, United States, 2009: With Special Feature on Medical Technology*. Hyattsville, MD: Author.
9. U.S. Bureau of the Census (1996). 65 in the United States (Current Population Reports P23-190). Washington, DC: U.S. Government Printing Office.
10. Vincent, G. K., and V. A. Velkoff (2010). *The Next Four Decades—The Older Population in the United States: 2010 to 2050* (Current Population Reports P25-1138). Washington, DC: U.S. Census Bureau.
11. Gordon, B., T. Mermin, Richard W. Johnson, Dan P. Murphy (2007), "Why Do Boomers Plan to Work Longer?" *Journal of Gerontology: Social Sciences*, 62B: S286–S294.
12. Administration on Aging (AoA). U.S. Department of Health and Human Services (2014). *A Profile of Older Americans: 2014*. Available at http://www.aoa.acl.gov/aging_statistics/Profile/2014/docs/2014-Profile.pdf.
13. U.S. Department of Health and Human Services (2015). *Health, United States, 2014*. Available at http://www.cdc.gov/nchs/data/hus/hus14.pdf#016.
14. U.S. Census Bureau (2011). *2011 American Housing Survey*. Available at http://www.census.gov/housing/ahs/.
15. Heron, M. (2016). "Deaths: Leading Causes for 2013." *National Vital Statistics Reports*, 65 (2). National Center for Health Statistics. Available at http://www.cdc.gov/nchs/data/nvsr/nvsr65/nvsr65_02.pdf.
16. National Council on Aging (2014). *Healthy Aging Fact Sheet*. Available at https://www.ncoa.org/wp-content/uploads/FactSheet_HealthyAging.pdf.
17. Centers for Disease Control and Prevention (2013). *The State of Aging and Health in America 2013*. Atlanta, GA: Centers for Disease Control and Prevention, U.S. Department of Health and Human Services.
18. Haber, D. (2010). *Health Promotion and Aging: Practical Applications for Health Professionals*, 5th ed. New York: Springer Publishing.
19. National Center for Health Statistics (2012). *Summary Health Statistics for U.S. Adults: National Health Interview Survey, 2011*. (Vital and Health Statistics, s10, n. 256). Available at www.cdc.gov/nchs/data/series/sr_10/sr10_256.pdf.
20. American Foundation for the Blind (2014). *Facts and Figures on Adults with Vision Loss*. Available at http://www.afb.org/info/blindness-statistics/adults/facts-and-figures/235.
21. National Institute on Deafness and Other Communication Disorders (2015). *Quick Statistics*. Available at http://www.nidcd.nih.gov/health/statistics/pages/quick.aspx#5.
22. Centers for Disease Control and Prevention (2015). Important Facts about Falls. Available at http://www.cdc.gov/homeandrecreational-safety/falls/adultfalls.html.
23. U.S. Department of Health and Human Services (2008). *2008 Physical Activity Guidelines for Americans*. Available at www.health.gov/paguidelines/pdf/paguide.pdf.
24. National Center for Health Statistics. (2013) *Health, United States, 2012: With Special Feature on Emergency Care*. Hyattsville, MD: Author. Available at http://www.cdc.gov/nchs/hus.htm.
25. U.S. Department of Agriculture (2011). *Dietary Guidelines for Americans 2010*. Available at www.health.gov/dietaryguidelines/2010.asp.
26. Centers for Disease Control and Prevention (2013). *Adult Vaccination*. Available at http://www.cdc.gov/vaccines/adults/rec-vac/older-adults.html.
27. Centers for Disease Control and Prevention (2015). *Flu Vaccination Coverage*. Available at http://www.cdc.gov/flu/pdf/fluvaxview/nfid-coverage-2014-15-final.pdf.
28. National Center on Elder Abuse (n.d.). *Adult Protective Services*. Available at: http://www.ncea.aoa.gov/Stop_Abuse/Partners/APS/index.aspx.
29. National Center on Elder Abuse, Administration on Aging (2005). *Fact Sheet: Elder Abuse Prevalence and Incidence*. Washington, DC: Author. Available at http://ncea.aoa.gov/AoARoot/AoA_Programs/Elder_Rights/Elder_Abuse/Index.aspx.
30. National Center on Elder Abuse (n.d.). *Frequently Asked Questions*. Available at: http://www.ncea.aoa.gov/faq/index.aspx.
31. Atchley, R. C. (1994). *Social Forces and Aging: An Introduction to Social Gerontology*, 7th ed. Belmont, CA: Wadsworth.

32. Social Security Administration (2015). *Social Security Basic Facts.* Available at https://www.ssa.gov/news/press/basicfact.html.

33. National Association of Area Agencies on Aging (n.d.). *Housing Options for Older Adults: A Guide for Making Housing Decisions.* Available at http://www.eldercare.gov/Eldercare.NET/Public/Resources/Brochures/docs/Housing_Options_Booklet.pdf.

34. Assisted Living Federation of America (2013). *Senior Living Options.* Available at http://www.alfa.org/alfa/Assisted_Living_Information.asp.

35. U.S. Department of Health and Human Services (2015). *LongTermCare.gov: Costs of Care.* Available at http://longtermcare.gov/costs-how-to-pay/costs-of-care/.

36. Centers for Medicare & Medicaid Services (2015). *Your Guide to Choosing a Nursing Home.* Available at http://www.medicare.gov/Pubs/pdf/02174.pdf.

37. U.S. Department of Housing and Urban Development (2013). *Information for Senior Citizens.* Available at http://portal.hud.gov/hudportal/HUD?src=/topics/information_for_senior_citizens.

38. Hooyman, N., and H. Kiyak (2008). *Social Gerontology: A Multidisciplinary Perspective*, 8th ed. Boston: Allyn and Bacon.

39. Family Caregiver Alliance (2010). *Selective Caregiver Statistics.* Available at http://www.caregiver.org/caregiver/jsp/content_node.jsp?nodeid=439.

40. Centers for Disease Control and Prevention. (2015). *Caregiving.* Available at http://www.cdc.gov/aging/caregiving/.

41. Feder, J., H. L. Komisar, R. B. Friedland (2007). *Long-Term Care Financing Project: Policy Options for the Future.* Georgetown University. Available at http://ltc.georgetown.edu/forum/ltcfinalpaper061107.pdf.

42. Stevenson, D. G, M. Cohen, E. Tell, and B. Burwell (2010). "The Complementarity of Public and Private Long-Term Care Coverage." *Health Affairs*, 29 (1): 96–101.

43. Administration on Aging (2015). National Family Caregiver Support Program (OAA Title IIIE). Available at http://www.aoa.acl.gov/AoA_Programs/HCLTC/Caregiver/.

44. National Alliance for Caregiving (March 2012). *Best Practices in Workplace Eldercare.* Available at http://www.caregiving.org/wp-content/uploads/2010/01/BestPractices-EldercareFinal1.pdf.

45. U.S. Census Bureau (2010). *The 2010 Statistical Abstract: The National Data Book—Population.* Available at http://www.census.gov/compendia/statab/.

46. Centers for Medicare & Medicaid Services (2016). On Its 50th Anniversary, More than 55 Million Americans Covered by Medicare. Available at https://www.cms.gov/Newsroom/MediaReleaseDatabase/Press-releases/2015-Press-releases-items/2015-07-28.html.

47. The Henry J. Kaiser Family Foundation (2015). *The Facts on Medicare Spending and Financing.* Available at http://kff.org/medicare/fact-sheet/medicare-spending-and-financing-fact-sheet/.

48. Centers for Medicare & Medicaid Services (2015). *Coverage By Population.* Available at http://www.medicaid.gov/Medicaid-CHIP-Program-Information/By-Population/By-Population.html.

49. Centers for Disease Control and Prevention (2015). *Older Adult Drivers.* Available at http://www.cdc.gov/motorvehiclesafety/older_adult_drivers/.

50. U.S. Administration on Aging (2007). *How to Find Help.* Available at http://www.aoa.gov/eldfam/How_To_Find/Agencies/Agencies.asp.

51. National Highway Traffic Safety Administration (2013). *Older Drivers.* Available at http://www.nhtsa.gov/Driving+Safety/Older+Drivers.

52. Independent Transportation Network (2013). Available at http://itnamerica.org/.

53. U.S. Administration on Aging (2013). *Eldercare Locator, State Units on Aging.* Available at http://www.eldercare.gov/ELDERCARE.NET/Public/About/Aging_Network/SUA.aspx.

54. Kramarow, E. H., H. Lentzner, R. Rooks, J. Weeks, and S. Saydah (1999). *Health and Aging Chartbook: Health United States, 1999* (HHS pub. no. PHS-99-123-1). Hyattsville, MD: National Center for Health Statistics.

55. National Council on Aging (2013). *National Institute of Senior Centers.* Available at http://www.ncoa.org/national-institute-of-senior-centers/.

CHAPTER 10

Community and Public Health and Racial/ Ethnic Populations

Chapter Outline

Chapter Objectives

After studying this chapter, you should be able to:

1. Explain the concept of diversity as it describes the American people.

2. Discuss the impact of a more diverse population in the United States as it relates to community and public health efforts.

3. Summarize the importance of the 1985 landmark report, *The Secretary's Task Force Report on Black and Minority Health*.

4. List the racial and ethnic categories currently used by the U.S. government in statistical activities and program administration reporting.

5. State some limitations related to collecting racial and ethnic health data.

6. Discuss selected sociodemographic characteristics of minority groups in the United States.

7. List and describe the six priority areas of the Race and Health Initiative.

8. Explain the role socioeconomic status plays in health disparities among racial and ethnic minority groups.

9. Define cultural and linguistic competence and the importance of each related to minority community and public health.

Scenario

Tom just returned from a cross-country business trip that took him from New York City to Miami, to San Antonio, to Los Angeles, and back to his Midwest hometown, Middletown, U.S.A. When his curious teenage children asked him to tell them about the people who live in the "big cities," he began by saying, "There seem to be more minorities and foreigners in the cities than before. I heard at least five or six different languages spoken. Signs in the hotels and in the storefronts are written in at least two, and sometimes three or four languages.

"Another thing that always amazes me is the number of ethnic restaurants. Here, we have just one Mexican, one Italian, and one Chinese restaurant, but in New York City and other big cities there are hundreds of restaurants serving foods from other cultures. I get the feeling that the United States is more culturally diverse than at anytime in its past, even when it was considered the 'melting pot' for the world's populations."

Majority those with characteristics that are found in more than 50% of a population

Minority group subgroup of the population that consists of fewer than 50% of the population

Introduction

The United States is a country proud of its global leadership, its rich heritage, and cultural profile that has evolved from centuries worth of immigrants who bring their traditions, language, culinary preferences, and myriad other customs. The rich cultural tapestry enjoyed by American residents today, however, is also the result of much debate that often has divided the nation.

The term *diversity* has different meanings to different people. Diversity refers to differences in gender, age groups, sexual orientation, socioeconomic status, language preference, religion, political views, and special needs as well as race and ethnicity.[1] To truly appreciate diversity would take a lifetime as it is not only multifaceted, but also dynamic. For many, diversity is synonymous with race and ethnicity and, while the focus of this chapter is in fact on the major racial and ethnic groups in the United States, it is important to remember that diversity is much more extensive than what we are able to present here.

According to the U.S. Census Bureau, the U.S. population reached 318 million in 2014.[2] In the same year, 62.2% of Americans, the **majority**, self identified as "white, non-Hispanic." The remaining 37.8 of the U.S. population are members of what are traditionally viewed as racial or ethnic **minority groups**. (see **Figure 10.1**).

Demographic changes pertaining to race and ethnicity, which started in the 1970s, are expected to continue in the next three decades. In fact, it is estimated that by 2060, over one-half of the U.S. population will be composed of racial minorities.[2-3] Increases in population by racial/ethnic minorities will be accomplished by corresponding decreases in the non-Hispanic white population, which is expected to represent 43.6% of the U.S. population by 2060 (see **Figure 10.2**).

While Hispanics* were considered the fastest growing ethnic group for the last two decades, the U.S. Census Bureau reported that Asians were the fastest growing population segment between 2010 and 2014. An examination of factors contributing to this growth reveals that most of the population gains experienced by Asian groups is the result of international migration.

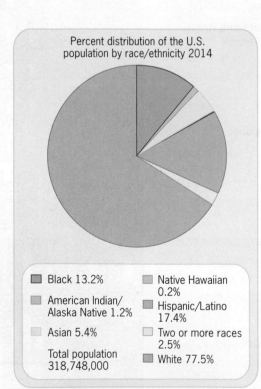

Percent distribution of the U.S. population by race/ethnicity 2014

- ■ Black 13.2%
- ■ American Indian/ Alaska Native 1.2%
- ■ Asian 5.4%
- Total population 318,748,000
- ■ Native Hawaiian 0.2%
- ■ Hispanic/Latino 17.4%
- Two or more races 2.5%
- ■ White 77.5%

FIGURE 10.1   Racial/ethnic distribution of the U.S. population, 2014.

Data from: Colby, S. L., and J. M. Ortman (2015). *Projections of the Size and Composition of the U.S. Population: 2014 to 2060.* Washington, DC: U.S. Department of Commerce, U.S. Census Bureau. Available at www.census.gov/content/dam/Census/library/publications/2015/demo/p25-1143.pdf.

* The term *Hispanic* is used in this chapter to reflect the definition provided by the U.S. Census Bureau.

Racial and Ethnic Classifications

It is standard practice for medical practitioners and public health professionals to describe participants and populations in terms of "race" or "ethnicity"; unfortunately these terms are often used interchangeably when in fact they are not. The term *race* refers to, "The categorization of parts of a population based on physical appearance due to particular historical social and political forces."[4] Despite this widely used classification, it should be noted that there are no scientifically established genotypes to delineate race, which leads to a subjective categorization into racial categories.

Ethnicity refers to a subcultural group within a multicultural society. Membership in an ethnic group is usually based on a common national or tribal heritage. Hutchinson and Smith[5] have proposed that the definition of an ethnic group includes six main features including:

1. A common proper name, to identify and express the "essence" of the community

2. A myth of common ancestry that includes the idea of common origin in time and place and that gives an ethnie a sense of fictive kinship

3. Shared historical memories, or better, shared memories of a common past or pasts, including heroes, events, and their commemoration

4. One or more elements of common culture, which need not be specified but normally include religion, customs, and language

5. A link with a homeland, not necessarily its physical occupation by the ethnie, only its symbolic attachment to the ancestral land, as with diaspora peoples

6. A sense of solidarity on the part of at least some sections of the ethnic's population

In the United States, racial and ethnic categories are used in statistical activities and program administration reporting, including the monitoring and enforcement of civil rights (see **Table 10.1**). In the 1980s, the regulations used for the statistical classification of racial

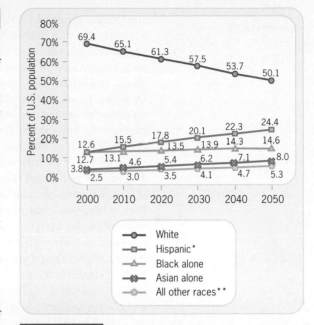

FIGURE 10.2   Projected U.S. population by race and Hispanic origin, selected years.

Note: Percentages for 2000 are actual.
* Hispanics can be of any race. Totals do not equal 100% for this reason.
** "All other races" includes American Indian and Alaska Native alone, Native Hawaiian and Other Pacific Islander alone, and two or more races.

Data from: U.S. Census Bureau, Population Division (2004). *U.S. Interim Projections by Age, Sex, Race, and Hispanic Origin.* Available at http://www.census.gov/ipc/www/usinterimproj/.

TABLE 10.1   Definitions for Racial and Ethnic Minority Populations

Race	Definition
Race	
Asian	People having origins in any of the original peoples of the Far East, Southeast Asia, or the Indian subcontinent
Black or African American	People having origins in any of the black racial groups of Africa
American Indian or Alaska Native	People having origins in any of the original peoples of North and South America (including Central America), and who maintain tribal affiliation or community attachment
Native Hawaiian or Other Pacific Islander	People having origins in any of the original peoples of Hawaii, Guam, Samoa, or other Pacific Islands
White	People having origins in any of the original peoples of Europe, the Middle East, or North Africa
Ethnicity	
Hispanic or Latino	A person of Cuban, Mexican, Puerto Rican, South or Central American, or other Spanish culture or origin, regardless of race

Data from: Centers for Disease Control and Prevention (CDC) (2014). *Definitions for Racial and Ethnic Minority Populations.* Available at http://wonder.cdc.gov/wonder/help/populations/bridged-race/Directive15.html.

Operationalize (operational definition) provide working definitions

and ethnic groups by federal agencies were based on the 1978 publication by the Office of Management and Budget (OMB) of Directive 15 titled, *Race and Ethnic Standards for Federal Statistics and Administrative Reporting.*[6] This directive presented brief rules for classifying persons into four racial categories (American Indian or Alaska Native, Asian or Pacific Islander, black, and white) and two ethnic categories (of Hispanic origin or not of Hispanic origin). Directive 15 was not intended to be scientific or anthropological in nature, but rather a way to **operationalize** race and ethnicity, and its guidelines provided the standards by which federal government agencies collected and classified racial and ethnic data in the 1980s and 1990s. The current definitions for racial and ethnic groups are presented in Table 10.1.[7]

As a result of criticism leveled against Directive 15, new standards were issued in 1997. The new classification standards expanded race from four to five categories by separating the "Asian or Pacific Islander" category into two categories: "Asian" and "Native Hawaiian or Other Pacific Islander." Additionally, the term "Hispanic" was changed to "Hispanic or Latino" and "Negro" can be used in addition to "black or African American." Finally, the reporting of more than one race for multiracial persons was strongly encouraged, along with specifying that the Hispanic origin question should precede the race question.[8] In October 1997, the U.S. Department of Health and Human Services (HHS) adopted a policy supporting the inclusion of the new revised federal standards for racial and ethnic data for employment in the HHS data systems and consequently in developing and measuring *Healthy People 2020* objectives.

The Affordable Care Act (ACA), enacted in 2010, reiterated the need to address race/ethnic racial data as well as the need to develop culturally appropriate efforts to reach diverse populations in an effort to improve the health status of all populations and to decrease health disparities (see **Table 10.2**). In 2011, the Office of Management and Budget updated Statistical Policy Directive 15 and suggested that data should preferably be collected both on race and ethnicity[9]

Of particular interest to community health professionals are the requirements to collect data for diverse populations at federally funded programs and the need to develop culturally and linguistically appropriate materials for providers and consumers.[10]

Health Data Sources and Their Limitations

The reporting of accurate and complete race and ethnicity data provides essential information to target and evaluate public health inventions aimed at under-represented populations. However, because of the diversity in race and ethnicity in the United States' population, community health

TABLE 10.2 Selected Culture-Related Components in the Affordable Care Act	
Component	Law Section
Culturally appropriate personal responsibility education.	2953
Culturally appropriate patient-decision aids.	3506
National oral health campaign, with emphasis on disparities.	4102
Require that population surveys collect and report data on race, ethnicity, and primary language.	4302
Collect/report disparities data in Medicaid and Children's Health Insurance Program.	4302
Monitor health disparities trends in federally funded programs.	4302
Develop and evaluate model cultural competence curricula.	5307
Disseminate cultural competence curricula through online clearinghouse.	5307
Provide cultural competence training for primary care providers.	5301
Transfer federal Office of Minority Health to Office of the Secretary.	10334

Data from: Dennis P. Andrulis, PhD, MPH, Nadia J. Siddiqui, MPH, Jonathan P. Purtle, MSc, and Lisa Duchon, PhD, MPA (2010, July). *Patient Protection and Affordable Care Act of 2010: Advancing Health Equity for Racially and Ethnically Diverse Populations*, Tables 1, 3, and 5. Reprinted by permission of the Joint Center for Political and Economic Studies.

professionals and researchers have long recognized many crucial issues in the way that racial and ethnic variables are assessed in the collection, analysis, and dissemination of health information.

Although race historically has been viewed as a biological construct, it is now known to be more accurately characterized as a social category that has changed over time and varies across societies and cultures.[11–13] Similarly, self-reported data regarding race and ethnicity may be unreliable because individuals of varied cultures and heritage and multiple races can have difficulty classifying their racial or ethnic identity on standardized forms. Likewise, many nonfederal health data systems do not collect self-reported race or ethnicity data, or in some cases, it may be uncertain who recorded the race and ethnicity data.

In addition to the issues identified above, there are many cases of biased analysis that occurs when two separate data reporting systems are used to obtain rates by race and Hispanic origin.[14]

One component of the ACA is the continued upgrading of data collection on race and ethnicity in public health surveys; therefore, the HHS continues to work with health data systems that do not collect self-reported race or ethnicity on individuals to do so. Increasing both the reliability and amount of data will assist in monitoring and assessing the outcomes related to meeting the proposed goal of *Healthy People 2020* to "achieve health equity, eliminate disparities, and improve the health of all groups."[15]

The next section provides a broad overview of selected characteristics as well as health and illness beliefs and practices among the larger racial and ethnic groups in the United States. However, caution is needed to avoid stereotyping because there is a considerable amount of heterogeneity within these groups. Making summary statements of cultural beliefs is difficult and can be questionable. Additionally, members of a cultural or ethnic group who are younger typically have higher levels of education and are more **acculturated** into mainstream U.S. society may not adhere to popular and traditional health beliefs.

Americans of Hispanic Origin Overview and Leading Causes of Death

The term *Hispanic* was introduced by the OMB in 1977, creating an ethnic category that included persons of Mexican, Puerto Rican, Cuban, Central American, South American, or some other Spanish origin regardless of race.[6] In 1997, the term Hispanic was changed to "Hispanic or Latino."[8] For the purposes of data collection, the only ethnic distinction that the U.S. government makes is "Hispanic" or "non-Hispanic" and, therefore, nearly all Americans of Hispanic origin are racially classified as Caucasians.

The Hispanic population is one of the most rapidly growing ethnic groups in the United States. In 2014, Americans of Hispanic origin constituted 17.4% of the total U.S. population, making them the largest minority group in the nation. A decreasing number of immigrants from this population group, however, have led the U.S. Census Bureau to scale back their population growth estimate for the next few decades.[16–18]

Data from the Census Bureau show that Arizona, California, Colorado, Florida, Illinois, New Jersey, New York, and Texas have a population of over 1 million Hispanics residing in the state (see **Figure 10.3**).

Hispanics are a heterogeneous group representing people living in vast geographic regions extending from Mexico to Tierra del Fuego in South America. People of Mexican origin are the largest Hispanic group in the United States followed by Puerto Ricans and Cubans. The remaining are of some other Central American, South American, or other Hispanic or Latino origins. **Table 10.3** shows the distribution of Hispanics by country of origin.[18]

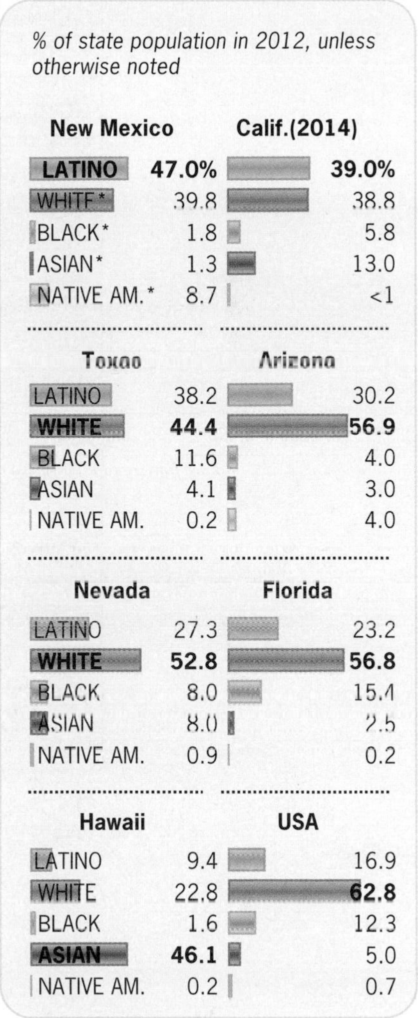

Acculturated cultural modification of an individual or group by adapting to or borrowing traits from another culture

% of state population in 2012, unless otherwise noted

New Mexico		Calif.(2014)
LATINO	47.0%	39.0%
WHITE*	39.8	38.8
BLACK*	1.8	5.8
ASIAN*	1.3	13.0
NATIVE AM.*	8.7	<1

Texas		Arizona
LATINO	38.2	30.2
WHITE	44.4	56.9
BLACK	11.6	4.0
ASIAN	4.1	3.0
NATIVE AM.	0.2	4.0

Nevada		Florida
LATINO	27.3	23.2
WHITE	52.8	56.8
BLACK	8.0	15.4
ASIAN	8.0	2.5
NATIVE AM.	0.9	0.2

Hawaii		USA
LATINO	9.4	16.9
WHITE	22.8	62.8
BLACK	1.6	12.3
ASIAN	46.1	5.0
NATIVE AM.	0.2	0.7

Source: IPUMS for all states except California. California estimate is from governor's 2014–15 budget summary. "*" indicates "non-Hispanic" population figures. Category labeled "Asian" includes Pacific Islanders.

FIGURE 10.3   Racial/ethnic population for selected states.

Data from: http://www.pewresearch.org/fact-tank/2014/01/24/in-2014-latinos-will-surpass-whites-as-largest-racialethnic-group-in-california/.

TABLE 10.3 Statistical Portrait of Hispanics in the United States, 2013

Detailed Hispanic Origin: 2013

Hispanic populations are listed in descending order of population size

Universe: 2013 Hispanic resident population

	Number	Percent
Mexican	34,582,182	64.1
Puerto Rican	5,121,921	9.5
Cuban	1,985,959	3.7
Dominican	1,788,050	3.3
All other Spanish/Hispanic/Latino	1,666,867	3.1
Guatemalan	1,304,378	2.4
Colombian	1,072, 946	2.0
Honduran	790,729	1.5
Spaniard	746,215	1.4
Ecuadorian	686,828	1.3
Peruvian	628,397	1.2
Nicaraguan	380,744	0.7
Venezuelan	247,830	0.5
Argentinean	243,354	0.5
Panamanian	176,828	0.3
Chilean	150,347	0.3
Costa Rican	137,809	0.3
Bolivian	122,083	0.2
Uruguayan	57,431	0.1
Other Central American	41,670	0.1
Other South American	32,759	0.1
Paraguayan	23,809	<0.05
Total	53,964,235	100.0

Note: Hispanic origin is based on self-described ancestry, lineage, heritage, nationality group or country of birth.

Data from: Pew Research Center (2016). *Statistical Portrait of Hispanics in the United States—Detailed Hispanic Origin: 2013.* Available at http://www.pewhispanic.org/2015/05/12/statistical-portrait-of-hispanics-in-the-united-states-1980-2013/ph_2015-03_statistical-portrait-of-hispanics-in-the-united-states-2013_current-04/.

An estimated 20% of U.S. youth between ages 10 and 19 was of Hispanic origin in 2012; however, that statistic is expected to increase to approximately 33% by 2040.[3] While high school graduation is considered an essential educational requirement to enter the labor force, the educational attainment level of Hispanic youth has been consistently lower when compared to their white counterparts (see **Figure 10.4**).[19]

Linked with education is earning power. The median income of Hispanic households was significantly lower in 2013 ($40,963) than that of Asian/Pacific Islanders ($67,065) and whites ($58,270; see **Figure 10.5**).[20] The poverty rate for persons of Hispanic origin was 23.5% in 2013, nearly three times the rate for white Americans. The poverty rate of foreign-born Hispanics was higher than for those who were born in the United States.

Curanderismo is a most common form of Hispanic folk medicine.[21] A *curandera's*, or healer's, ability includes a varied repertoire of religious belief systems (mainly Catholicism), herbal knowledge, witchcraft, and scientific medicine. There are several types of *curandero(as)*, which include *yerbero* (specialist in the use of herbs), *sobador* (who uses a type of deep tissue massage), and *espiritista* (or those who work in the spiritual realm). Traditionally, Hispanic Americans perceive good physical health as a matter of fortune, a balance between hot and cold forces, or reward from God for good behavior. Hispanic Americans' health beliefs are derived from a combination of Spanish traditions, native beliefs, religion. The leading causes of death for Hispanics are found in **Table 10.4**.

African Americans Overview and Leading Causes of Death

African Americans, or blacks, are people having origins in any of the black racial groups from Africa. In 2014, African Americans constituted 14.3% of the population, making them the second largest minority group in the nation. Even though African Americans live in all regions of the United States, more than one-half live in the southern states. An analysis of U.S. Census data show that all states have seen changes in their African American population in the last decade (see **Figure 10.6**).

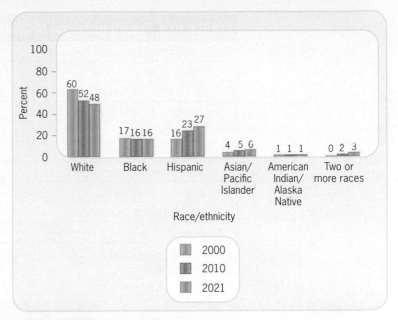

FIGURE 10.4   Percentage distribution of U.S. public school students enrolled in pre-kindergarten through 12th grade, by race/ethnicity: selected years, fall 2000–fall 2021.

Data from: U.S. Department of Education, National Center for Education Statistics. *Projections of Education Statistics to 2021*; and Common Core of Data (CCD). *State Nonfiscal Survey of Public Elementary and Secondary Education*, selected years, 2000–01 through 2010–11. See *Digest of Education Statistics* 2012, table 44.

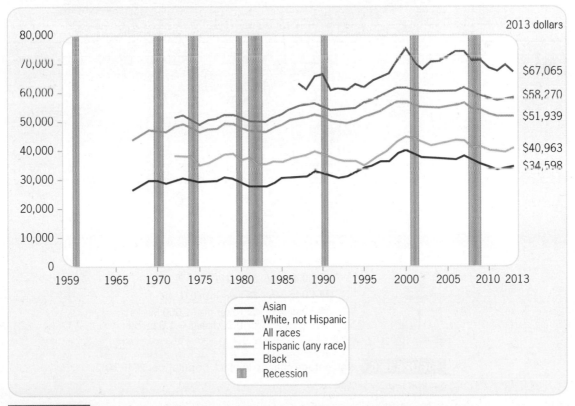

FIGURE 10.5   Real median household income by race and Hispanic origin: 1967 to 2013.

Data from: DeNavas-Walt, C. and B. D. Proctor. (2014). Income and Poverty in the United States: 2013 (Current Populations Reports, P60-249). Washington, DC: U.S. Census Bureau.

TABLE 10.4   Leading Causes of Death for Hispanics—2010
1. Malignant neoplasms (cancer)
2. Heart disease
3. Accidents (unintentional injuries)
4. Cerebrovascular diseases (stroke)
5. Diabetes mellitus
6. Chronic liver disease and cirrhosis
7. Chronic lower respiratory diseases
8. Alzheimer's disease
9. Influenza and pneumonia
10. Nephritis, nephrotic syndrome, and nephrosis

Heron, M. (2016). "Deaths: Leading Causes for 2013." National Vital Statistics Reports, Vol. 65, No. 2 Hyattsville, MD: National Center for Health Statistics.

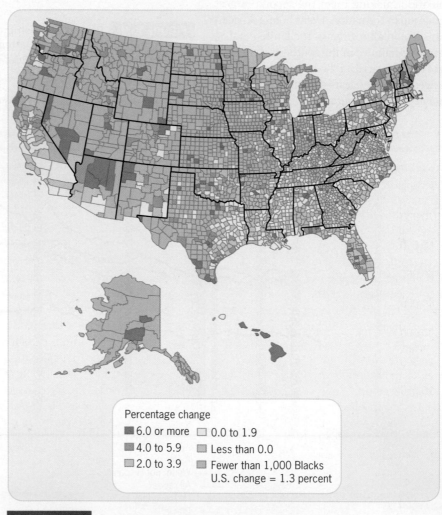

Percentage change
- 6.0 or more
- 4.0 to 5.9
- 2.0 to 3.9
- 0.0 to 1.9
- Less than 0.0
- Fewer than 1,000 Blacks
  U.S. change = 1.3 percent

FIGURE 10.6   Percentage change in black population: 2011–2012.

Data from: Jones-Puthoff, 2013.

TABLE 10.5   Leading Causes of Death for African Americans—2013

1. Heart disease
2. Cancer
3. Stroke
4. Unintentional Injuries
5. Diabetes
6. Chronic Lower respiratory disease
7. Nephritis, nephrotic syndrome, and nephrosis
8. Hominicide
9. Sepsis
10. 1. Alzheimer's disease

Data from: Centers for Disease Control and Prevention, National Center for Health Statistics, National Vital Statistics Reports. LCWK1. Deaths, percent of total deaths, and death rates for the 15 leading causes of death in 5-year age groups, by race and sex: United States, 2013, p 67. Available at http://www.cdc.gov/nchs/data/dvs/lcwk1_2013.pdf.

Data from the 2014 *American Community Survey* show that 84.4% of blacks age 25 and older obtained a high school diploma and 19.7% had a bachelor's degree or higher.[19] Despite improving educational attainments, African Americans continued to have lower high school graduation rates (67%) than the national average (79%) during school year 2010 to 2011. The same data, however, show that African-American students' high school graduation rates increased 3.7 percentage points compared to 2.6 percentage points for their white counterparts.[21]

The median income for African Americans has consistently ranked below all racial and ethnic groups[20–22] (see Figure 10.5) and in 2013 over one in four (27.2%) live in poverty, almost three times the rates for non-Hispanic whites. The Henry J. Kaiser Family Foundation has reported that over 40% of blacks in Minnesota, Mississippi, and Tennessee are classified as poor in those states.[23]

African-American health beliefs trace their roots to the African continent and to some Caribbean nations. Traditional views of physical health may perceive illness as being the result of conflicts in life, lack of harmony with nature, and/or punishment from God.

When discussing African-American culture, it is important to mention the effect of slavery in the health status of the population. Laws that forbade slaves from providing health care to each other—under the threat of death—led to an underground system of health care by mostly untrained providers because health care available through slave owners was often inadequate, assuming it was available at all.

After the Civil War, poverty, discrimination, and poor living conditions led to a high prevalence of disease, disability, and death among black Americans, a legacy that continues to this day.[24] Lacking access to more formalized health care, first by slavery and then by segregation and discrimination, many black Americans had to depend on traditional health methods.[25] These traditional methods include curing illnesses with roots, herbs, barks, and teas by an individual knowledgeable about their use. Many black Americans continue to use traditional health methods today because they are acceptable, available, and affordable. Finally, effects of social factors related to racism, discrimination, and the Tuskegee syphilis experiment continue to impact the health status of African Americans in the United States today. See **Table 10.5** for the leading causes of death for African Americans.[26]

Asian Americans Overview and Leading Causes of Death

In June 1999, President Clinton signed Executive Order (EO) 13125 to improve the quality of life of Asian Americans and Pacific Islanders through increased participation in federal programs where they may be underserved, and by collecting separate data on each group to decrease the concealment of substantial socioeconomic and health differences among the two groups.[27]

This EO attempted to address a significant concern regarding the reporting of data for these two different groups; however, even by 2001, most federal agencies were still collecting and reporting aggregate data for Asians and Pacific Islanders, citing methodological and funding constraints.[28] It would not be until the 2010 decennial census when data for these groups would be disaggregated.

The term *Asian American* refers to people of Asian descent who trace their roots to more than 20 different Asian countries, including Cambodia, China, India, Japan, Korea, Malaysia, Pakistan, the Philippine Islands, Thailand, and Vietnam.[29] In 2014, Asians accounted for 6.3% of the population and according to the U.S. Census Bureau, Asian Americans were the fastest growing population segment in 2012. Asian-American populations are generally concentrated in the western states, the Northeast, and parts of the South. Native Hawaiian and Other Pacific Islanders (NHOPIs) live throughout the United States, but their populations are most concentrated in the western mainland states and Hawaii[30] (see **Figure 10.7**).

Immigration is an integral part of Asian-American community growth, as many are seeking better economic and employment opportunities and/or are reuniting with family members.

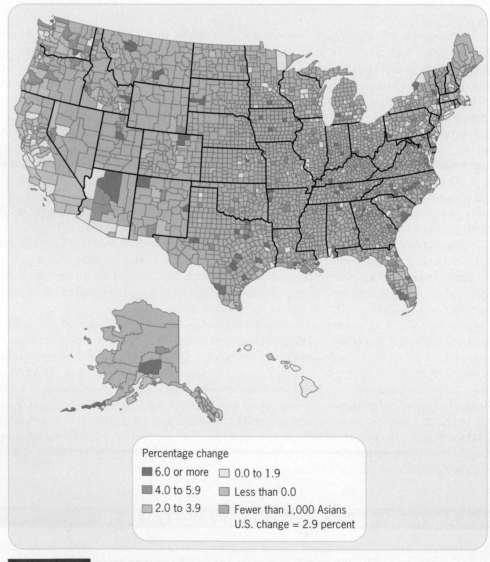

Percentage change

■ 6.0 or more   ☐ 0.0 to 1.9

■ 4.0 to 5.9   ▨ Less than 0.0

☐ 2.0 to 3.9   ▨ Fewer than 1,000 Asians

U.S. change = 2.9 percent

FIGURE 10.7   Percentage change in Asian population 2011–2012.

Data from: Jones-Puthoff, 2013.

Even among those who have come from the same country, immigration to the United States may have occurred at different times, and thus there are generational differences. For example, some families may have immigrated well over a hundred years ago as laborers, while those coming today carry with them professional degrees. These differences contribute to a substantial diversity in socioeconomic status among these groups.

High school graduation rates for Asian Americans conceal significant differences in their educational attainment. Approximately 86% of Asian Americans have a high school diploma, but the rates range from as high as 96% among Taiwanese Americans to as low as 61% in the Hmong community.[31] Unfortunately, these aggregated data mask the large variation within this population group.

Although variations among Asian Americans is the norm, many share similarities based on their religious background and the belief of equilibrium or balance. The concept of balance is related to health, and imbalance is related to disease. This balance or imbalance is highly related to diet, which influences people's daily activities of living within their environment. Therefore, to achieve health and avoid illness, people must adjust to the environment in a holistic manner. Traditional treatments reflect the diversity and heterogeneity of the Asian-American population. Traditional healing methods vary from the *Khout lom* in Laos to *Jup kchall* in Cambodia to offerings in Buddhist ceremonies in Thailand. The Hmong, native to the mountain regions in Laos, use shamans to intercede for their health status.[32-36]

As noted above, in 2010, the U.S. Census started separating information both Asians and for Native Hawaiian and Other Pacific Islanders (NHOPI). The term *NHOPI* includes peoples of Hawaii, Guam, Samoa, or other Pacific Islands and their descendants,[29] with the Native Hawaiian population forming the majority of PIs. In contrast to Asian Americans, there is no large-scale immigration of PIs into the continental United States. Two key health issues for Native Hawaiians include health care allocation and the question of reimbursement for medical care.[37]

Approximately 20% of Native Hawaiians live in rural Hawaii. However, the majority of the state's health care resources are fixed in the capital city of Honolulu. As a result of this imbalance of health care resource allocation, there is an inadequate number of health care professionals on the neighboring islands.[38] Transportation within and between the islands makes it difficult for the native population to access health care services. The second medical care issue deals with the Native Hawaiian health belief, which suggests that the healer cannot be reimbursed directly for his or her therapeutic work. According to Blaisdell,[39] such healer skill is not a question of learning but rather a question of righteousness. Therefore, it is not considered appropriate to be paid for doing what is right. The leading causes of death among Asian Americans or Pacific Islanders are found in **Table 10.6**.

TABLE 10.6   Leading Causes of Death for Asian Americans or Pacific Islanders—2013
1. Malignant neoplasms (cancer)
2. Diseases of the heart
3. Cerebrovascular diseases (stroke)
4. Accidents (unintentional injuries)
5. Diabetes mellitus
6. Influenza and pneumonia
7. Chronic lower respiratory diseases
8. Alzheimer's disease
9. Nephritis, nephrotic syndrome, and nephrosis (kidney disease)
10. Intentional self-harm (suicide)

Data from: Heron, M. (2016). "Deaths: Leading Causes for 2013." National Vital Statistics Reports, Vol. 65, No. 2. Hyattsville, MD: National Center for Health Statistics.

American Indians and Alaska Natives Overview and Leading Causes of Death

The American Indian and Alaska Native (AI/AN) population, the original inhabitants of the United States, accounted for 2% of the total population in 2014. Native Americans comprise many different American Indian tribal groups and Alaskan villages, according to the Bureau of Indian Affairs, there are some 566 federally recognized Indian tribes in the U.S. Each of these tribes/villages has distinct customs, language, and beliefs; however, the majority share similar cultural values including an emphasis on an individual's right to freedom, autonomy, and respect as well as respect for all living things, and an expectation that tribal/village members will bring honor and respect to their families, clans, and tribes.[40,41]

It has been estimated that prior to the arrival of European explorers, 12 million AI/ANs lived and flourished throughout what is now the United States. Exposure to diseases and ecological changes introduced by explorers and colonists decimated the AI/AN population. Although many of the descendants were assimilated by intermarriages or successfully adapted to the new culture, as a group the AI/ANs became economically and socially disadvantaged, and this status is reflected in their relatively poor health status today.[42,43] In 2013 the median household income for AI/ANs was $36,252, while their poverty rate for that same year was 29.2%,[44] which is the highest among all racial and ethnic groups. Similarly, their high school completion rate was among the lowest of any racial and ethnic group.

Central to Native American culture is that the people "strive for a close integration within the family, clan and tribe and live in harmony with their environment. This occurs simultaneously on physical, mental, and spiritual levels; thus, individual wellness is considered as harmony and balance among mind, body, spirit and the environment."[40,41] This concept is not always congruent with the medical model approach or public health; as a result, in many Native American communities there is conflict between the medical/public health approach and the approaches used by Native American healers. Providing appropriate health care for Native Americans usually involves resolving conflicts between the two approaches in such a way that they complement each other. The leading causes of death among this population group are listed in **Table 10.7**.

U.S. Government, Native Americans, and the Provision of Health Care

Though classified by definition and for statistical purposes as a minority group, Native Americans are unlike any other ethnic or racial group in the United States. Some tribes are sovereign nations, based in part on their treaties with the U.S. government. Tribal sovereignty, which came about when the tribes transferred virtually all the land in the United States to the federal government in return for the provision of certain services, creates a distinct and special relationship between various tribes and the U.S. government.

TABLE 10.7   Leading Causes of Death for American Indians/Alaska Natives—2013
1. Diseases of the heart
2. Maglignant neoplasms (cancer)
3. Accidents (unintentional injuries)
4. Diabetes mellitus
5. Chronic liver disease and cirrhosis
6. Chronic lower respiratory disease
7. Cerebrovascular diseases (stroke)
8. Intentional self-harm (suicide)
9. Influenza and pneunomia
10. Nephritis, nephrotic syndrome, and nephrosis

Data from: National Vital Statistics System (2014). LCWK1. Deaths, Percent of Total Deaths, and Death Rates for the 15 Leading Causes of Death by Race: United States, 2013; page 100.

Provisions of health services to Native Americans began in 1832.[42] The first medical efforts were carried out by Army physicians who vaccinated Native Americans against smallpox and applied sanitary procedures to curb other communicable diseases among tribes living in the vicinity of military posts. The health services provided for Native Americans after the signing of the early treaties were limited. It was not until 1921, when the Snyder Act created the Bureau of Indian Affairs (BIA) Health Division, that more emphasis was given to providing health services to Native Americans. In 1954 with the passage of Public Law 83-568, known as the Transfer Act, the responsibility of health care for Native Americans was transferred from the Department of Interior's BIA to the U.S. Public Health Service (PHS), which created the Indian Health Service (IHS) to carry out these responsibilities.

In keeping with the concept of tribal sovereignty, the Indian Self-Determination and Education Assistance Act (PL 93-63) of 1975 authorized the IHS to involve tribes in the administration and operation of all or certain programs under a special contract. It authorized the IHS to provide grants to tribes, on request, for planning, development, and operation of health programs.[42] Today, a number of programs are managed and operated under contract by individual tribes.[40,41,43]

> **Refugee** a person who flees one area or country to seek shelter or protection from danger in another

Indian Health Service

The IHS is responsible for providing federal health services to the 566 federally recognized Native Americans and Alaska Natives tribes.[43] This agency operates hospitals, clinics and health stations, and a variety of other programs. The goal of the IHS is to improve the health status of both urban and reservation American Indians and Alaska Natives to the highest possible level.[43] The IHS website (http://www.ihs.gov/) offers a wealth of information for both patients and the general public.

Immigrant and Refugee Health

According to the United Nations (UN) High Commissioner for Refugees there were some 19.5 million **refugees** around the world in 2014.[45] Most likely, refugees cannot return home because of a well-founded fear of persecution for reasons of race, religion, nationality, political opinion, or membership in a particular social group. War and ethnic, tribal, and religious violence are leading causes of refugees fleeing their countries. Refugees arriving in the United States may be seeking political asylum, refuge from war, or escape from famine or other environmental disaster. The majority of refugees to the United States come from developing countries or regions with unstable governments or affected by civil war (see **Figure 10.8**). Refugees should not be confused with returnees, stateless persons, or asylum seekers, as they have their own classification according to the UN Refugee Agency.

Region	2004	2005	2006	2007	2008	2009	2010	2011	2012	2013
Total	52,840	53,738	41,094	48,218	60,107	74,602	73,293	56,384	58,179	69,909
Africa	29,108	20,746	18,129	17,246	8,943	9,678	13,325	7,693	10,629	15,984
Asia	12,276	15,769	10,086	23,564	44,819	58,309	52,695	44,583	44,416	48,840
Europe	7,879	10,524	9,615	4,192	2,059	1,693	1,238	996	908	482
North America	2,998	6,368	3,145	2,922	4,177	4,800	4,856	2,930	1,948	4,206
Oceania	–	–	–	–	–	–	–	–	–	–
South America	579	331	119	54	100	57	126	46	130	233
Unknown	–	–	–	–	9	65	1,053	136	148	164

FIGURE 10.8   Refugee arrivals by region and year.
Data from: United States Department of Homeland Security (2014). *Yearbook of Immigration Statistics: 2013*. Washington, DC: Author.

Immigrant individuals who migrate from one country to another for the purpose of seeking permanent residence

The term **immigrants** describes individuals who migrate from another country for the purpose of seeking permanent residence and hopefully a better life. The United States has a checkered past in welcoming people from other countries that often is reflected in its immigration policies. These policies have provided the foundation for distinct waves of legal immigration to the United States from different countries (see **Figure 10.9**).

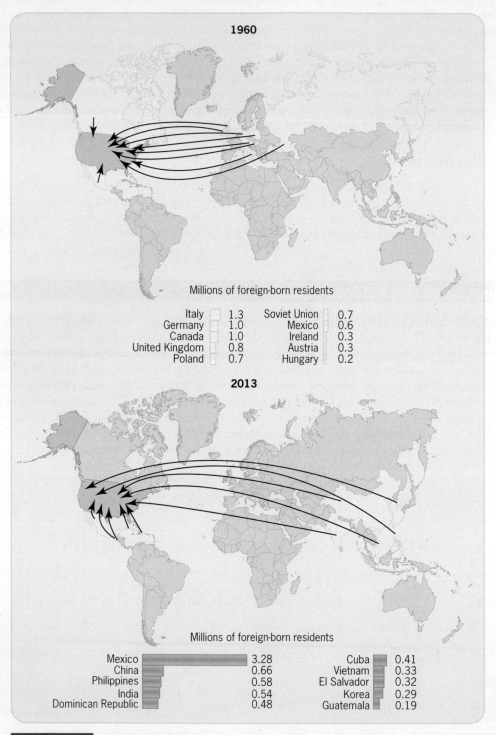

FIGURE 10.9 Top 10 countries of birth: 1960 and 2013.

Data from: Baker, B., and N. Rytina (2014). "Estimates of the Lawful Permanent Resident Population in the United States: January 2013." In *Population Estimates*. Washington, DC: U.S. Department of Homeland Security, Office of Immigration Statistics Policy Directorate.

Today's immigrants contribute to the diverse kaleidoscope that is American society. Their members, accounted for approximately 13% of the US population in 2013 [46] also contribute to the expansion of the U.S. population and have increased steadily since the 1970s (see **Figure 10.10**).

Aliens are defined as people born in and owing allegiance to a country other than the one in which they live. Thus, aliens are not citizens and are only allowed to stay in a foreign country for a specified period of time defined by law or policy. Sometimes, however, they violate this provision and find employment illegally. Last, **unauthorized immigrants** are those who enter this country without any permission whatsoever.[47,48]

Although all refugees and immigrants who enter the United States can be classified into one of the existing racial/ethnic categories used by our government, as a single group they present many special concerns not seen in minorities who are born and raised here. Most U.S. refugees arrive from developing countries, and many are poor, have low levels of formal education, and have few marketable work skills. Many arrive with serious health problems, including undernourishment or starvation, and physical and emotional injuries from hostile action or confinement in refugee camps, poor health care, and overcrowding.[49] A majority of the refugees are young, many of the women are of childbearing age, and most come from Latin American and Southeast Asian countries. Immigrants and refugees may also bring with them diseases for which the native population has no natural or acquired immunity.

The difficulties facing immigrants and refugees in the United States—including finding employment and obtaining access to education and appropriate human, health, and mental health services—represent significant barriers to the social integration of refugees into American society. Like most of the other minority groups in the United States, immigrants and refugees contribute to the enrichment of the U.S. culture.

Alien a person born in and owing allegiance to a country other than the one in which he/she lives

Unauthorized immigrant an individual who entered this country without permission

Minority health refers to the morbidity and mortality of American Indians/Alaska Natives, Americans of Hispanic origin, Asians and Pacific Islanders, and black Americans in the United States

Minority Health and Health Disparities

Minority health refers to the morbidity and mortality of American Indians/Alaska Natives, Asian Americans, Native Hawaiians and Other Pacific Islanders, black Americans, and Hispanics in the United States. The research literature suggests racial and ethnic minorities experience poorer health status, have lower levels of insurance coverage, and have inadequate access to

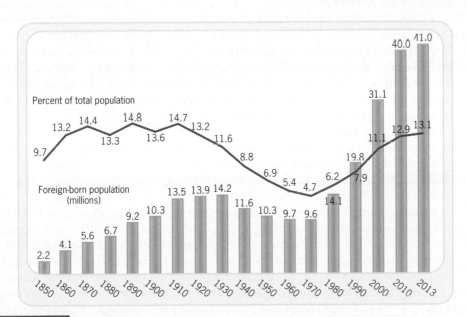

FIGURE 10.10   Foreign-born population as percentage of the total population.

Data from: U.S. Census Bureau (2011). *1850–2000 Decennial Census*; U.S. Census Bureau (2011). *2010 American Community Survey*, and U.S. Census Bureau. (2016). *Quick Facts, United States.* Available at https://www.census.gov/quickfacts/table/PST045215/00.

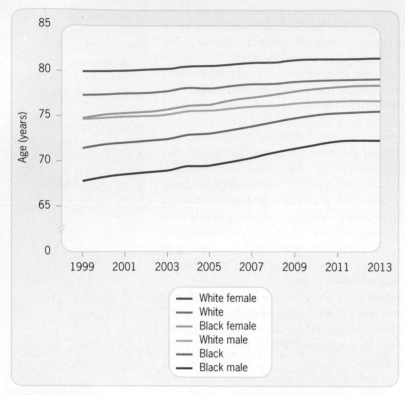

FIGURE 10.11 Life expectancy between white and black populations 1999 to 2013.

Data from: Kochanek, K. D., E. Arias, and R. N. Anderson (2015, November). *Leading Causes of Death Contributing to Decrease in Life Expectancy between Black and White Populations: United States, 1999–2013.* NCHS Data Brief No. 218. Available at http://www.cdc.gov/nchs/data/databriefs/db218.htm.

Health disparities differences in the incidence, prevalence, mortality, and burden of diseases and other adverse health conditions that exist among specific population groups

health care services. Given current and estimated demographic shifts in the U.S. population, decreasing health disparities is imperative to ensure the future health of all Americans.[60,61]

Health disparities refer to differences in the incidence, prevalence, mortality, and burden of diseases and other adverse health conditions that exist among specific population groups in the United States.[52] In the United States, health disparities are related to inequality in education, income, socioeconomic status, environmental disadvantages, and limited access to health care services. One example of health disparities can be seen in current life expectancies for non-Hispanic whites (79.1 years in 2013) compared to 75.5 years for blacks (See **Figure 10.11**) despite decreases in the leading causes of death among the African-American population.[53]

Efforts to eliminate health disparities are ongoing but, although progress has been made in advancing the health status of racial/ethnic minorities, we have a long way to go before these disparities are entirely eliminated.[43] The U.S. government along with professional and lay health organizations have devoted significant resources to the elimination of health disparities and these are now incorporated as a goal of the *Healthy People Initiative.* Concurrently, efforts to document and address health disparities in this country are being made and have been strengthened through provisions of the Affordable Care Act of 2010.

One of the most comprehensive reports dealing with racial/ethnic health disparities in the United States is the Institute of Medicine's report entitled, *Unequal Treatment: Confronting Racial and Disparities in Health Care.* In addition to identifying health disparities, the report proposed a blueprint for addressing them as a nation. Other noteworthy reports include the annual National Health Care Quality & Disparities Reports produced by the Agency for Health Care Research and Quality, which seek to quantify disparities and propose strategies to eliminate them. An advantage of these annual reports over similar efforts lies in the fact that they can track changes over a period of time.[54–56]

Other government efforts include the CDC's Racial and Ethnic Approaches to Community Health (REACH), which is designed to educate and empower people to seek and obtain needed health services; the Communities Putting Prevention to Work (CPPW); the U.S. Department of Health and Human Services (HHS) Strategic Action Plan to End the Tobacco Epidemic, and Efforts to Reduce Disparities in Influenza Vaccination. All these programs have the overarching goal of equalizing the health status of all population groups in the United States. The HHS has also developed an Action Plan to Reduce Racial and Ethnic Health Disparities[55] and in 2013 released its second Health Disparities & Inequalities Report, which seeks to "identify and address the factors that lead to health disparities among racial, ethnic, geographic, socioeconomic, and other groups so that barriers to health equity can be removed." An overall tool utilized by the federal government to achieve these goals is reflected in the *Healthy People 2020* and in funding priorities for research and health care services.

The genesis of these national efforts can be traced to the landmark 1985 *Secretary's Task Force Report on Black and Minority Health* report, which first documented the health status disparities of minority groups in the United States.[57] This report provided documentation about health disparities experienced by members of under-represented groups. Specifically, the report identified six causes of death that accounted for more than 80% of the excess mortality observed among black Americans and other groups. The *Secretary's Task Force Report on Black and Minority Health* contributed significantly to the development of a number of *Healthy People Initiative* objectives that resulted in some measurable decreases in age-adjusted death rates for seven specific causes of death by the year 2020.[15]

In 1997, then-President Clinton declared that the United States would continue to commit to a national goal of eliminating racial and ethnic health disparities by the year 2010,[58] and launched "One America in the 21st Century: The President's Initiative on Race." The purpose of this national effort was to enhance efforts in (1) preventing disease, (2) promoting health, and (3) delivering care to racial and ethnic minority communities. One of the primary aims of this initiative consists of consultation and collaboration among federal agencies; state, local, and tribal governments; and community professionals to research and address issues that affect health outcomes. It is not surprising that the *Race and Health Initiative* is a key component of the *Healthy People 2020*'s broad health goal to "achieve health equity, eliminate disparities, and improve the health of all groups."[15]

The *Race and Health Initiative* committed the nation to the ambitious goal of eliminating health disparities among racial and ethnic groups in six priority areas including (1) infant mortality, (2) cancer screening and management, (3) cardiovascular disease, (4) diabetes, (5) HIV/AIDS, and (6) adult and child immunization. The *Race and Health Initiative* reaffirms the government's extensive focus on minority health issues by emphasizing the six health issues that account for a substantial burden of disease that is highly modifiable if appropriate interventions are applied. Thus, the *Race and Health Initiative* is intertwined with *Healthy People 2020* and the goals of the nation for the next decade.

Infant Mortality

Infant mortality, defined as the death of an infant before his or her first birthday, is highly correlated to the general health and well-being of the nation. The United States made significant improvement in the twentieth century regarding infant health; however, whereas the vast majority of infants born in the U.S. today are healthy at birth, many are not. Additionally, infant mortality data within the United States are characterized by a long-standing and serious disparity among racial and ethnic minorities (see **Figure 10.12**). The greatest disparity exists for African Americans, whose infant death rate is more than two times that of white American infants.

There are many reasons associated with higher infant mortality rates among African Americans. Two of the more important explanations include lack of prenatal care and giving birth to low-birth-weight (LBW) babies. Women who receive early and continuous prenatal health care have better pregnancy outcomes than women who do not. African-American, Native American, and Hispanic women are less likely to receive early and comprehensive prenatal care.[59] In the same manner, African Americans and Native Americans are more likely to give birth to LBW babies.

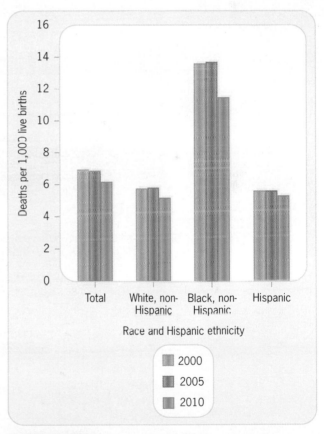

FIGURE 10.12   Infant mortality rates by race and Hispanic origin of mother: 2000, 2005, and 2010.

Source: Mathews, T. J., and M. F. MacDorman (2013). "Infant Mortality Statistics from the 2010 Period Linked Birth/Infant Death Data Set." *National Vital Statistics Report* 62(8). Centers for Disease Control and Prevention, National Center for Health Statistics. Available at http://www.cdc.gov/nchs/data/nvsr/nvsr62/nvsr62_08.pdf.

Cancer Screening and Management

Cancer is the second leading cause of death in the United States, accounting for more than 550,000 deaths and more than 1.6 million new cases of invasive cancer in 2015 alone [60] Cancer mortality is higher among African-American men (261.5 per 100,000) and lowest in Asian/Pacific Islander women (91.2 per 100,000).

More than half of all new cancer cases annually are cancers of the lung, colon and rectum, breast, and prostate. Cancer incidence rates per 100,000 population were highest among African Americans for lung, colon and rectum, and prostate cancers compared to white Americans, Asian/Pacific Islanders, American Indian/Alaska Natives, and Hispanics in 2010 (see **Figure 10.13**). During the same period of time, cancer death rates per 100,000 population were highest among African Americans for lung, colon and rectum, breast, and prostate cancers compared to white Americans, Asian/Pacific Islanders, American Indian/Alaska Natives, and Hispanics. Similar higher mortality rates are observed from lung cancer among Hispanics. A number of these disparities in cancer incidence and death rates among minorities are attributed to lifestyle factors, late diagnosis, and access to health care.[60-62]

Primary cancer prevention refers to preventing the occurrence of cancer.[61] Smoking is the most preventable cause of lung cancer death in our society. The death rate for lung cancer is

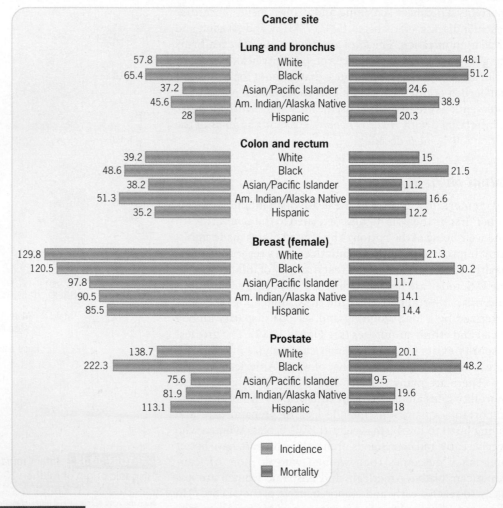

FIGURE 10.13   SEER cancer incidence and U.S. death rates, 2010, by cancer site and race.

Data from: Howlader, N., A. M. Noone, M. Krapcho, et al. (eds.) (2013). *SEER Cancer Statistics Review, 1975–2010*, based on November 2012 SEER data submission, posted to the SEER website. Bethesda, MD: Author.

20% higher in African Americans than in white Americans. Paralleling this death rate is the fact that African Americans have a higher incidence of smoking than white Americans.

Secondary cancer prevention refers to early detection of cancer through screening tests. The earlier a cancer is detected, the greater the chances the patient will survive. The racial/ethnic disparities in lower survival rates can partially be attributed to lower cancer screening rates among specific groups. Two cancers of significant interest are colorectal and breast. Colorectal cancer remains the second leading cause of cancer deaths in the United States and the leading cause of cancer deaths among nonsmokers. According to the CDC, 1,900 deaths could be prevented each year for every 10% increase in colonoscopy screening alone.

Breast cancer is the second leading cause of cancer death among women. Breast cancer survival rates are significantly increased if the cancer is detected early through monthly self-examination and/or periodic breast X-rays. Despite the importance of mammography, it is underutilized as an early detection procedure by many minority women (see **Box 10.1**). The goal of *Healthy People 2020* is to have at least 81% of women from all racial or ethnic groups aged 50 and older receiving a mammogram within the preceding 2 years.[15]

BOX 10.1   *Healthy People 2020*: Objective

Objective C.17:   Increase the proportion of women who receive a breast cancer screening based on the most recent guidelines.

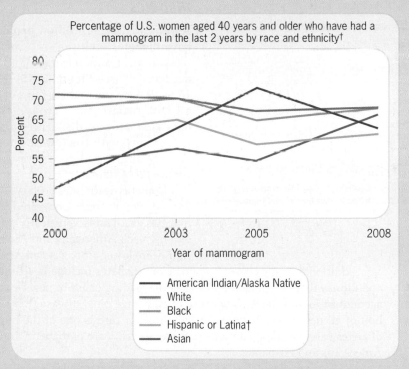

Percentage of U.S. women aged 40 years and older who have had a mammogram in the last 2 years by race and ethnicity†

Data from: National Center for Health Statistics (2010). *Health, United States, 2009 with Special Feature on Medical Technology* (DHHS pub. No. 2010-1232). Hyattsville, MD: Author. Available at http://www.cdc.gov/nchs/hus.htm.

For Further Thought

Research indicates that mortality resulting from breast cancer can be reduced through the use of mammography. Data for 2008 showed that 68% of white and black women received mammograms, whereas American Indian/Alaska Native, Asian/Pacific Islander, and Hispanic women were less likely to have had a mammogram. What type of program could be implemented to further increase the percentage of these minority women who participate in mammograms?

Source: U.S. Department of Health and Human Services, Office of Disease Prevention and Health Promotion (2010). *Healthy People 2020*. Available at http://www.healthypeople.gov/2020/default.aspx.

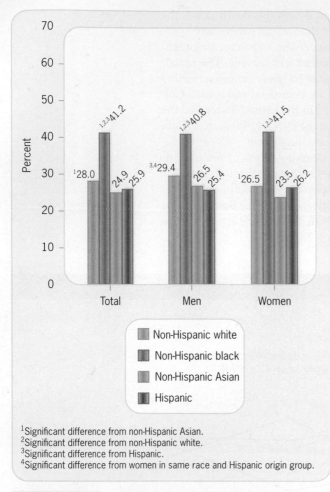

[1]Significant difference from non-Hispanic Asian.
[2]Significant difference from non-Hispanic white.
[3]Significant difference from Hispanic.
[4]Significant difference from women in same race and Hispanic origin group.

FIGURE 10.14   Hypertension by race/ethnic group.

Data from: Yoon, S. S., C. D. Fryar, and M. D. Carroll (2015). "Hypertension Prevalence and Control Among Adults: United States, 2011–2014." NCHS Data Brief, no. 220. Hyattsville, MD: National Center for Health Statistics. Available at http://www.cdc.gov/nchs/data/databriefs/db220.htm.

Cardiovascular Diseases

Cardiovascular disease (CVD), especially coronary heart disease and stroke, kills more Americans annually than any other disease. In fact, CVD claims more lives each year than the next five leading causes of death combined. Death rates from coronary heart disease and stroke vary widely among racial and ethnic groups.

One of the major modifiable risk factors for coronary artery disease and stroke is hypertension. One in three adult Americans suffers from hypertension. The prevalence of hypertension varies noticeably according to race/ethnicity, with the highest prevalence among African Americans[62–64] (see **Figure 10.14**). In addition, African Americans tend to develop hypertension earlier in life than whites. The reasons for this are unknown. In fact, the cause of 90% to 95% of the cases of hypertension in all races and ethnic groups is unknown. Therefore, secondary prevention or screening for hypertension is essential.

Diabetes

Approximately 24 million people in the United States have diabetes mellitus with increasing morbidity and mortality rates increasing for all groups in the last two decades[65–66] (see **Figure 10.15**). Native Americans aged 15 to 19 have the highest rates of diabetes type 2 among all U.S. racial/ethnic groups. A closer review of the data also denotes disparities among the different AI/AN groups, with the lowest rates found among Alaska Natives and the highest rates found among the Pima Indians in Arizona.[67]

Diabetes death rates do vary considerably among racial and ethnic groups.[68] Compared to white non-Hispanics, diabetes death rates were nearly two and a half times higher among black Americans and American Indians; however, rates were lower among Asian Americans.[65]

Additional serious complications from diabetes include heart disease, stroke, blindness, and kidney disease. In fact, diabetes is the leading cause of new cases of blindness in people aged 20 to 74 and the leading cause of end-stage renal disease (ESRD), accounting for nearly half of all new cases. Inpatient hospitalization care is one of the most expensive venues for diabetes care. Hospital admissions for long-term care of diabetes are highest among African Americans and Hispanics.

HIV Infection/AIDS

An HIV infection is a chronic condition that progressively damages the body's immune system, making an otherwise healthy person less able to resist a variety of infections and disorders resulting in a condition known as AIDS. Currently, there is no known cure for HIV infection or AIDS and no vaccine to prevent it. The CDC estimates that some 1.2 million persons in the United States were living with diagnosed or undiagnosed HIV by the end of 2012, with rates higher among African Americans than among other racial/ethnic groups[69–70] (see **Figure 10.16**).

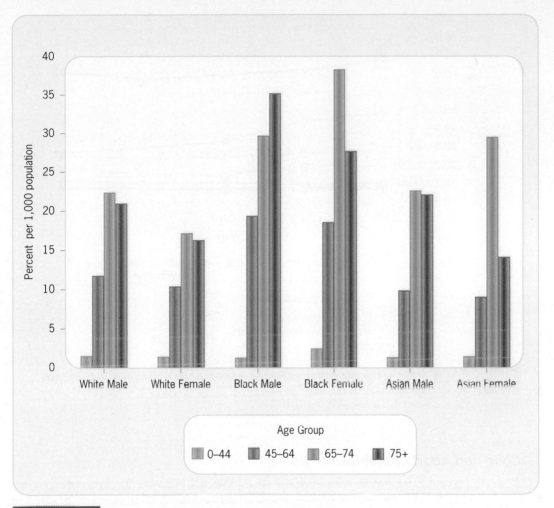

FIGURE 10.15   Age-specific rates of diagnosed diabetes per 100 civilian, non-institutionalized population, by race and sex, United States, 2014.

Data from: Centers for Disease Control and Prevention, National Center for Health Statistics (2015). *Age-Specific Rates of Diagnosed Diabetes per 100 Civilian, Non-Institutionalized Population, by Race and Sex, United States, 2014.* Available at http://www.cdc.gov/diabetes/statistics/prev/national/fig2004.htm.

AIDS has had a disproportionate impact on racial and ethnic minority groups in the United States since the disease was first recognized, with well over half of all identified cases since 1981 reported among racial and ethnic groups. The proportion of cases has increased among African Americans and Hispanics and decreased among whites. In 2012, African Americans and Hispanics, who represented less than half of the population, accounted for more than one-half of the estimated number of HIV/AIDS cases diagnosed. Consistent with the AIDS case rates are higher AIDS death rates for African Americans and Hispanics.[71]

Part of the reason for the disproportionate numbers of HIV and AIDS cases in African Americans and Americans of Hispanic origin has been attributed to a higher prevalence of unsafe or risky health behaviors (e.g., unprotected sexual intercourse and intravenous drug use), existing co-conditions (e.g., genital ulcer disease), and the lack of access to health care that would provide early diagnosis and treatment. A prevailing barrier to HIV/AIDS prevention may be that this condition is not being viewed as among the highest priorities in some minority communities when compared with other life survival problems.[72] With no cure for HIV/AIDS in sight, better health education to reduce and eliminate unsafe behaviors and increased access to medical resources for existing cases are essential to prevention.

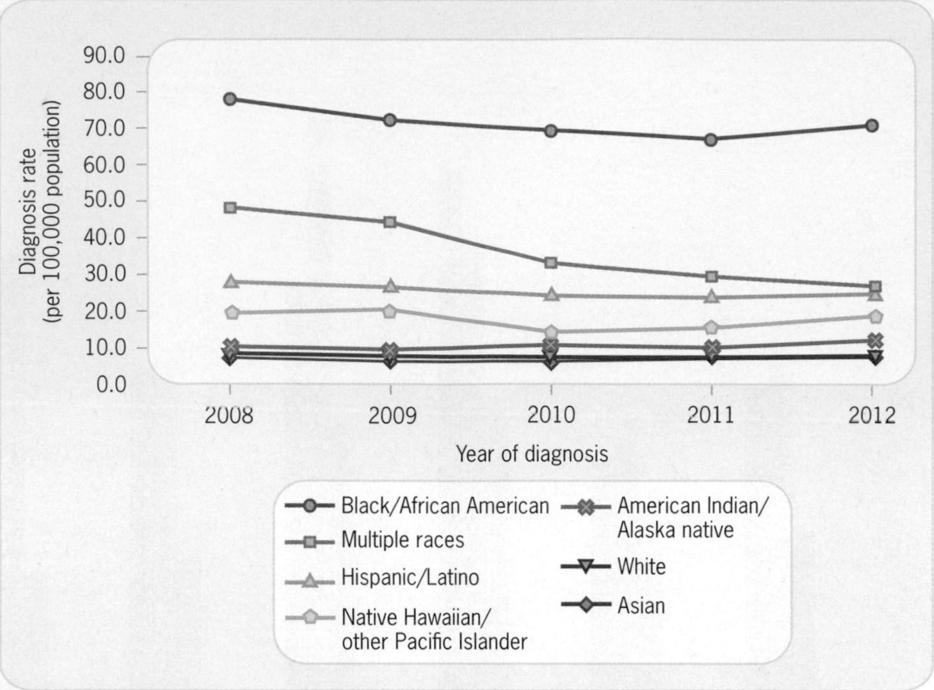

FIGURE 10.16   Rates of diagnosis of HIV infection among adults and adolescents by race/ethnicity: 2008–2012, United States.

Data from: Centers for Disease Control and Prevention, 2013, April.

Child and Adult Immunization Rates

As a result of widespread immunization practices, many infectious diseases that were once common have been significantly reduced. Childhood immunization rates provide one measure of the extent to which children are protected from dangerous vaccine-preventable illnesses. An important immunization rate for children aged 19 months to 35 months is the 4:3:1:3:3:1 vaccine series that includes DTP/DT/DTaP; poliovirus vaccine; measles, mumps, and rubella vaccine (MMR); *Haemophilus influenzae* type b vaccine; hepatitis B vaccine; and varicella vaccine. The overall rise must continue to achieve the *Healthy People 2020* target coverage for all recommended childhood immunizations in all populations.

It is important for adults, especially those 65 years and older, to become immunized against certain infectious diseases that can cause illness, disability, or death.[73] Two important adult immunizations included in the 2013 adult immunization schedule as well as among the infectious disease objectives stated in *Healthy People 2020*, are immunizations for influenza and pneumoccocal diseases (see **Figure 10.17**). The goal is to increase the number of noninstitutionalized adults 65 and older who are immunized annually against influenza and who have ever received an immunization against pneumoccocal disease to 90%. Immunization rates among non-minorities for influenza and pneumococcal infections are substantially lower than for white Americans.[74] Therefore, even though these two immunization rates among all adults have shown a significant increase since 1990, to reach the goal of 90% by 2020, increased efforts must be focused on minority populations.

Social Determinants of Health and Racial and Ethnic Disparities in Health

The World Health Organization has defined social determinants of health as the circumstances in which people are born, grow up, live, work, and age, and the systems put in place to deal with illness as well as life-enhancing resources, such as food supply, housing, economic and social relationships, transportation, education, and health care (see **Figure 10.18**).[75] In the U.S., *Healthy People*

Vaccine ▼ Age group ➤	19–21 yrs	22–26 yrs	27–49 yrs	50–59 yrs	60–64 yrs	≥65 yrs
Influenza[1],*	1 dose annually					
Tetanus, diphtheria, pertussis (Td/Tdap)[1],*	Substitute 1–time dose of Tdap for Td booster; then boost with Td every 10 years					
Varicella[1],*	2 doses					
Human papillomavirus (HPV), female[1],*	3 doses					
Human papillomavirus (HPV), male[1],*	3 doses					
Zoster[1]					1 dose	
Measles, mumps, rubella (MMR)[1],*	1 or 2 doses					
Pneumococcal poly-saccharide (PPSV23)[1]	1 or 2 doses					1 dose
Pneumococcal 13–valent conjugate (PCV13)[1],*	1 dose					
Meningococcal [1],*	1 or more doses					
Hepatitis A[1],*	2 doses					
Hepatitis B[1],*	3 doses					

*Covered by the Vaccine Injury Compensation Program.

Vaccine ▼ Indication ➤	Pregnancy	Immuno-compromising condition (excluding human immunodeficiency virus [HIV])[1]	HIV infection CD4+T lymphocyte count[1] <200 cells/μL / ≥200 cells/μL	Men who have sex with men (MSM)	Heart disease, chronic lung disease, chronic alcoholism	Asplenia (including elective splenectomy and persistent complement component deficiencies)[1]	Chronic liver disease	Kidney failure end-stage renal disease, receipt of hemodialysis	Diabetes	Health care personnel
Influenza[1],*	1 dose IIV annually		1 dose IIV or LAIV annually	1 dose IIV annually						1 dose IIV or LAIV annually
Tetanus, diphtheria, pertussis (Td/Tdap)[1],*	1 dose Tdap each pregnancy	Substitute 1–time dose of Tdap for Td booster; then boost with Td every 10 yrs								
Varicella[1],*	Contraindicated			2 doses						
Human papillomavirus (HPV), female[1],*		3 doses through age 26 yrs		3 doses through age 26 yrs						
Human papillomavirus (HPV), male[1],*		3 doses through age 26 yrs		3 doses through age 21 yrs						
Zoster[1]	Contraindicated			1 dose						
Measles, mumps, rubella (MMR)[1],*	Contraindicated			1 or 2 doses						
Pneumococcal poly-saccharide (PPSV23)[1]				1 or 2 doses						
Pneumococcal 13–valent conjugate (PCV13)[1],*				1 dose						
Meningococcal [1],*				1 or more doses						
Hepatitis A[1],*				2 doses						
Hepatitis B[1],*				3 doses						

*Covered by the Vaccine Injury Compensation Program.
1. For current recommendations visit the Centers for Disease Control and Prevention website at http://www.cdc.gov/vaccines/

☐ For all persons in this category who meet the age requirements and who lack documentation of vaccination or have no evidence of previous infection; zoster vaccine recommended regardless of prior episode of zoster

☐ Recommended if some other risk factor is present (e.g., on the basis of medical, occupational, lifestyle, or other indications)

☐ No recommendation

FIGURE 10.17   Recommended adult immunization schedule, United States, 2013, by age group and medical condition.

Data from: Centers for Disease Control and Prevention (2014). *Adult Immunization Schedule.* http://www.cdc.gov/vaccines/schedules/hcp/adult.html.

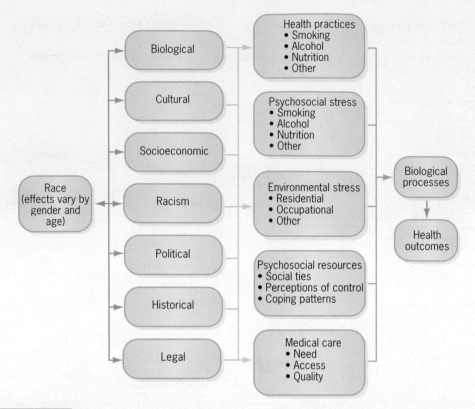

FIGURE 10.18   A framework for understanding the relationship between race and health.

Data from: Centers for Disease Control and Prevention (1993). "Use of Race and Ethnicity in Public Health Surveillance. Summary of CDC/ASTDR Workshop." *Morbidity and Mortality Weekly Report*, 42(RR-10).

2020 addresses the social determinants of health through its goal of creating social and physical environments that promote good health for all.[15] Given the critical role played by social determinants of health, it is important to examine at least two key social determinants of health among racial and ethnic groups in the United States: education and income[76] (see **Table 10.8**) since the literature suggests that they predict the greatest proportion of health status variance among individuals worldwide.

TABLE 10.8   Educational Attainment of the Population Aged 25 and Older and Real Household Median Income by Race and Hispanic Origin

Race/Ethnicity	High School Degree or GED	Bachelor's Degree	Median Income
African American	87.0%[1]	22.5%[1]	$34,598[3]
American Indian/ Alaska Native	82.2%[2]	17.6%[2]	$36,252[2]
Hispanic (any race)	66.7%[1]	15.5%[1]	$40,963[3]
Asians	89.1%[1]	53.9%[1]	$67,065[3]
Whites	88.8%[1]	32.8%[1]	$58,270[3]
General population	88.4%[1]	32.5%[1]	$51,939[3]

1= in 2015

2= in 2015

3= in 2013

Data from: Ryan, C. L. and K. Bauman (2016). "Educational Attainment in the United States: 2015." Current Population Reports: U.S. Census Bureau; U.S. Census Bureau (2015). Facts for Features: American Indian and Alaska Native Heritage, Mon: November 2014. Available at http://www.census.gov/newsroom/facts-for-features/2014/cb14-ff26.html.

Furthermore, many of these factors are not always direct in nature—they are what are referred to as indirect causal associations or intermediary factors. For example, poverty by itself may not cause disease and death; however, by precluding adequate nutrition, preventive medical care, and housing, it leads to increased morbidity and premature mortality.

As noted earlier, the categories of race are more of a social category than a biological one. In fact, biological differences between racial groups are small compared with biological differences within groups.[77] More than 90% of the differences in genetic makeup occur within racial and ethnic groups rather than between the groups. Such disparities in health status among minority groups are much better understood in terms of the groups' living circumstances. Public health research has long studied social determinants of health and explored its impact on the well-being of individuals. Many of these studies have shown that better health is associated with more years of education and having more income, a more prestigious job, and living in superior neighborhoods. Similarly, elevated levels of morbidity, disability, and mortality are associated with less education, lower income, poverty, unemployment, and poor housing. An extensive amount of research documents that social determinants of health play a significant role in the association of race and ethnicity with health and life expectancy. Furthermore, research in the last couple of decades indicates that the relationship between socioeconomic status (SES) and health occurs at every socioeconomic level and for a broad range of SES indicators including life expectancy.[76]

This relationship between SES and health can be described as a gradient. For example, research has documented that the more family income increases above the poverty threshold, the more health improves, and that the greater the gap in income, the greater the gap in health. Similarly, the percentage of individuals reporting good to excellent health increases based with higher income levels (see **Figure 10.19**).

This gradient effect between SES and health has important implications that are related to the gap between the privileged and nonprivileged, or the "haves and have-nots." In the United States, many inequalities still exist between all racial and ethnic groups related to level of education, income, and poverty (see Table 10.8). Minority groups often occupy the lowest socioeconomic rankings in the United States. These low rankings become a significant community health concern when one recognizes that progress toward the *Healthy People 2020* objectives was found to be greatest among higher SES groups and least among the lower SES groups.

Equity in Minority Health

One of the primary aims of the *Race and Health Initiative* consists of consultation and collaboration among federal agencies; state, local, and tribal governments; and community professionals to research and address issues of education, income, environment, and other socioeconomic factors that affect health outcomes. These health problems are inseparable from a variety of other social problems, making simple solutions unlikely. We also know that multiple resources are required to resolve these social and economic problems, and that solutions to these problems for one group may not work for another. Americans of Hispanic origin, Asian Americans, Native Hawaiians and Pacific Islanders, African Americans, and Native Americans each have unique cultural traditions that must be respected if the solutions are to be successful.

Cultural Competence

Cultural differences can and do present major obstacles to implementing effective community health programs and services. The demographic shifts in minority populations and the resulting diversity in health providers treating more patients have increased interest among health professionals to increase culturally appropriate services that lead to improved outcomes, efficiency, and satisfaction for their clients.[78–80] This increased interest is not only being found among

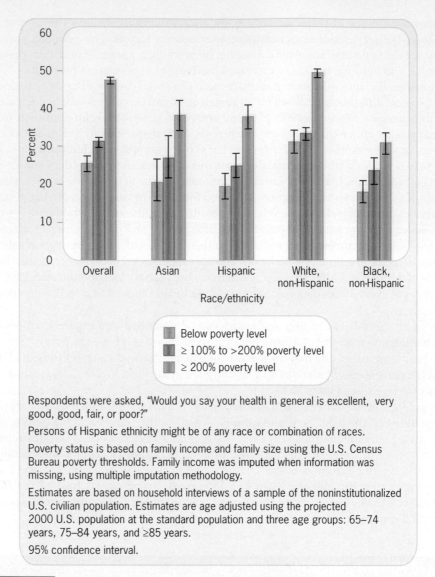

Respondents were asked, "Would you say your health in general is excellent, very good, good, fair, or poor?"

Persons of Hispanic ethnicity might be of any race or combination of races.

Poverty status is based on family income and family size using the U.S. Census Bureau poverty thresholds. Family income was imputed when information was missing, using multiple imputation methodology.

Estimates are based on household interviews of a sample of the noninstitutionalized U.S. civilian population. Estimates are age adjusted using the projected 2000 U.S. population at the standard population and three age groups: 65–74 years, 75–84 years, and ≥85 years.

95% confidence interval.

FIGURE 10.19   Health status by race, ethnicity, and income in 2012.

Data from: National Center for Health Statistics (2013). *Health, United States, 2012: With Special Feature on Emergency Care.* Hyattsville, MD: Author.

health care providers but also among patients, policymakers, educators, and accreditation and credentialing agencies.

The path to cultural competence is not as complicated as some might fear. In March 2001, the HHS and the Office of Minority Health and Health Disparities published standards for culturally and linguistically appropriate services (CLAS) in health care; the standards were revised and re-released in 2013 (see **Box 10.2**).[80,81] These criteria are the first comprehensive and nationally recognized standards of cultural and linguistic competence in health care service delivery that have been developed. In the past, national organizations and federal agencies independently developed their own standards and policies; the result was a wide spectrum of ideas about what constitutes culturally appropriate health services. The CLAS report went further and defined **cultural and linguistic competence** as

... a set of congruent behaviors, attitudes, and policies that come together in a system, agency, or among professionals that enables effective work in cross cultural situations. Culture refers to integrated patterns of human behavior that include language,

Cultural and linguistic competence a set of congruent behaviors, attitudes, and policies that come together in a system, agency, or among professionals, that enables effective work in cross-cultural situations

BOX 10.2 Culturally and Linguistically Appropriate Services (CLAS) Standards

Principal Standard

- Provide effective, equitable, understandable, and respectful quality care and services that are responsive to diverse cultural health beliefs and practices, preferred languages, health literacy, and other communication needs.

Governance, Leadership, and Workforce

- Advance and sustain organizational governance and leadership that promotes CLAS and health equity through policy, practices, and allocated resources.
- Recruit, promote, and support a culturally and linguistically diverse governance, leadership, and workforce that are responsive to the population in the service area.
- Educate and train governance, leadership, and workforce in culturally and linguistically appropriate policies and practices on an ongoing basis.

Communication and Language Assistance

- Offer language assistance to individuals who have limited English proficiency and/or other communication needs, at no cost to them, to facilitate timely access to all health care and services.
- Inform all individuals of the availability of language assistance services clearly and in their preferred language, verbally and in writing.
- Ensure the competence of individuals providing language assistance, recognizing that the use of untrained individuals and/or minors as interpreters should be avoided.

- Provide easy-to-understand print and multimedia materials and signage in the languages commonly used by the populations in the service area.

Engagement, Continuous Improvement, and Accountability

- Establish culturally and linguistically appropriate goals, policies, and management accountability, and infuse them throughout the organization's planning and operations.
- Conduct ongoing assessments of the organization's CLAS-related activities and integrate CLAS-related measures into measurement and continuous quality improvement activities.
- Collect and maintain accurate and reliable demographic data to monitor and evaluate the impact of CLAS on health equity and outcomes and to inform service delivery.
- Conduct regular assessments of community health assets and needs and use the results to plan and implement services that respond to the cultural and linguistic diversity of populations in the service area.
- Partner with the community to design, implement, and evaluate policies, practices, and services to ensure cultural and linguistic appropriateness.
- Create conflict and grievance resolution processes that are culturally and linguistically appropriate to identify, prevent, and resolve conflicts or complaints.
- Communicate the organization's progress in implementing and sustaining CLAS to all stakeholders, constituents, and the general public.

Data from: U.S. Department of Health and Human Services, Office of Minority Health. *What Are the National CLAS Standards?* Available at https://www.thinkculturalhealth.hhs.gov/Content/clas.asp.

---

thoughts, communications, actions, customs, beliefs, values, and institutions of racial, ethnic, religious or social groups. Competence implies having the capacity to function effectively as an individual and an organization within the context of the cultural beliefs, behaviors, and needs presented by consumers and their communities.[80]

Based on this definition, culture is a vital factor in both how community health professionals deliver services and how community members respond to community health programs and preventive interventions. In a society as culturally diverse as the United States, community health educators need to be able to communicate with different communities and understand how culture influences health behaviors.[82–83] It is important that community health promotion/disease prevention programs be understandable and acceptable within the cultural framework of the population to be reached.

For community health educators whose role is to educate groups and communities of diverse cultural backgrounds, cultural competence is critical.[83] Additionally, successful community health intervention and educational activities should be firmly grounded in an understanding and appreciation of the cultural characteristics of the target group. *Healthy*

People 2020 is firmly devoted to the principle that "every person in every community across the Nation deserves equal access to comprehensive, culturally competent, community-based health care systems that are committed to serving the needs of the individual and promoting community health."

Cultural competence among health educators can also be expanded by taking into account communication differences between different ethnic groups. Distinctions in language usage, term definition, respect denoted by terminology, and communication patterns among varied age groups can make a difference in their ability to reach target populations. Luquis (2014) suggests taking into account issues related to distance zone, nonverbal cues, prevailing gender roles, and dress code among factors that need to be considered when communicating with individuals of cultural backgrounds different from our own.[84]

Empowering the Self and the Community

A principle deeply etched in *Healthy People 2020* with respect to achieving equity is the ideal that the "greatest opportunities for reducing health disparities are in empowering individuals to make informed health care decisions and in promoting community-wide safety, education, and access to health care."[15] Given its importance in decreasing health disparities, it is not surprising that this principle is also found in the Sustainable Development Goals, which went into effect in 2015.[85]

A strategy to achieve the goals set forth in *Healthy People 2020* and the Sustainable Development Goals is to promote empowerment of marginalized groups. Friedman identifies three kinds of power associated with empowerment—social, political, and psychological.[86] An increase in social power brings with it access to "bases" of production such as information, knowledge and skills, participation in social organizations, and financial resources. Increased productivity enables greater influence on markets, which in turn can influence change.

Psychological power is best described as an individual sense of potency demonstrated in self-confident behavior. It is often the result of successful action in the social and political domains. With the investiture of all three types of power, empowerment can take place. Empowerment replaces hopelessness with a sense of being in control and a sense that one can make a difference. Once people are empowered, the power then needs to be transferred to the communities. When communities are empowered, they can cause change and solve problems. Under-represented groups have the potential to have a loud voice if united. Once united, they are in a position to influence decision makers at various governmental levels. In the specific case in which the goal is greater access to health care, this could mean getting the local health department to expand the types and numbers of available clinics, to increase education opportunities, to request culturally competent health services, and to be equal partners in addressing environmental issues among others.

A final strategy to improve the health status of diverse populations includes a focus on health literacy which is defined as " … the degree to which individuals have the capacity to obtain, process, and understand basic health information and services needed to make appropriate health decisions."[87] In dealing with diverse populations, health educators often focus on the primary language spoken by the individual; in so doing, they neglect to ascertain their ability to understand, retain, and apply the health information they receive. In order to achieve the health literacy goals embedded in *Healthy People 2020*, Perez [88]

The 1985 *Secretary's Task Force Report on Black and Minority Health* laid the foundation for the next three decades of *Healthy People* initiatives designed to decrease health disparities and to provide culturally competent health care services as well as health promotion and disease prevention programs. While progress has been made significant work remains to be done in achieving the goals embodied in *Healthy People 2020* and the UN Millennium Development Goals.

Chapter Summary

- One of the great strengths of the United States has been, and remains, the diversity of its people.
- The federal government has recently categorized the U.S. population into five racial groups (American Indian or Alaska Native, Asian, black or African American, Native Hawaiian or Other Pacific Islander, and white) and two ethnic groups (Hispanic or Latino and non-Hispanic or non-Latino).
- The reporting of accurate and complete race and ethnicity data provides essential information to target and evaluate public health inventions aimed at minority populations.
- All cultural and ethnic groups hold concepts related to health and illness and associated practices for maintaining well-being or providing treatment when it is indicated.
- The *Race and Health Initiative* includes six priority areas: (1) infant mortality, (2) cancer screening and management, (3) cardiovascular disease, (4) diabetes, (5) HIV/AIDS, and (6) adult and child immunization.

- These key areas are representative of the larger minority health picture and account for a substantial burden of disease that is highly modifiable if the appropriate interventions are applied.
- Socioeconomic status (SES) has been considered the most influential single contributor to premature morbidity and mortality by many public health researchers. Research in the last couple of decades indicates that the relationship between SES and health occurs at every socioeconomic level and for a broad range of SES indicators. This relationship between SES and health can be described as a gradient.
- Significant strides in the improvement of health in minority groups can be achieved if community and public health professionals become more culturally sensitive and competent.
- Minority groups must be empowered to solve their own problems through the processes of social, political, and psychological empowerment.

Scenario: Analysis and Response

1. Do you agree with Tom when he says the United States is more culturally diverse than at any time in the past? Why or why not? Do you see this as a strength or weakness for the country?
2. What signs are there in your community that the United States is becoming more internationalized and that minority groups are growing?

3. What strengths do you see as a result of an increasingly diverse population in the United States? What weaknesses?
4. Do you agree with the major health priorities as outlined in the *Race and Health Initiative* regarding the community you live in? Why or why not?

Review Questions

1. Why is it said that the United States was built on diversity?
2. What is the Office of Management and Budget's Directive 15?
3. Why is it important for community health workers to be aware of the significant health disparities among various minority groups in the United States?
4. What were the significant findings of the 1985 landmark report, *The Secretary's Task Force Report on Black and Minority Health*?

5. List and explain the six priority areas in the *Race and Health Initiative*.
6. What role does socioeconomic status play in health disparities among racial and ethnic minority groups?
7. Why is it important for community health professionals and workers to be culturally sensitive and competent?
8. List each of the three kinds of power associated with empowerment. What is the importance of each in empowering individuals and communities

Activities

1. Using the most recent U.S. Census report (available on the Internet), create a demographic profile of the state and county in which you live. Locate the following information—population; racial/ethnic composition; percentage of people represented by the different age groups, gender breakdown, and marital status; and percentage of people living in poverty.

2. Make an appointment with an employee of the health department in your hometown. Find out the differences in health status between the racial/ethnic groups in the community among the race/ethnicity–specific morbidity and mortality data. Discuss these differences with the health department employee, and then summarize your findings in a one-page paper.

3. In a two- to three-page paper, present the proposal you would recommend to the President of the United States for eliminating health disparities between the races and ethnic groups.

4. Identify a specific racial/ethnic minority group and select a health problem. Study the topic and present in a three-page paper the present status of the problem, the future outlook for the problem, and what could be done to reduce or eliminate the problem.

5. Write a two-page position paper on "Why racial/ethnic minority groups have a lower health status than the majority of white Americans."

References

1. Betancourt, J. R., A. R. Green, and E. J. Carillo (2002). *Cultural Competence in Health Care: Emerging Frameworks and Practical Approaches*. New York: The Commonwealth Fund.

2. Colby, S. L., and J. M. Ortman (2015, March). *Projections of the Size and Composition of the US Population: 2014 to 2060*. Washington, DC: U.S. Department of Commerce, U.S. Census Bureau. Available at www.census.gov/content/dam/Census/library/publications/2015/demo/p25-1143.pdf.

3. U.S. Census Bureau (2012). *Population Projections: 2012 National Population Projections*. Available at http://quickfacts.census.gov/qfd/states/00000.html.

4. Heurtin-Roberts, S. (2004). *Race and Ethnicity In Health and Vital Statistics*. Available at http://www.ncvhs.hhs.gov/040902p1.pdf.

5. Hutchinson, J., and A. Smith (1996). "Introduction." In J. Hutchison and A. Smith, eds., *Ethnicity*. Oxford, UK: Oxford University Press, 1–14.

6. United States Office of Management and Budget (1978). "Directive 15: Race and Ethnic Standards for Federal Statistics and Administrative Reporting." In U.S. Department of Commerce, Office of Federal Statistical Policy and Standards, *Statistical Policy Handbook*. Washington, DC: Author, 37–38.

7. Centers for Disease Control and Prevention (2014). *Definitions: Racial and Ethnic Minority Populations*. Available at http://www.cdc.gov/minorityhealth/populations/REMP/definitions.html.

8. United States Office of Management and Budget (1997). "Revisions to the Standards for the Classification of Federal Data on Race and Ethnicity." *Federal Register*. Washington, DC: Author.

9. Office of Management and Budget (n.d.). *Standards for the Classification of Federal Data on Race and Ethnicity*. Available at https://www.whitehouse.gov/omb/fedreg_race-ethnicity/.

10. Andrulis, D. P., N. J. Siddiqui, J. P. Purtle, and L. Duchon (2010). *Patient Protection and Affordable Care Act of 2010:Advancing Health Equity for Racially and Ethnically Diverse Populations*. Joint Center for Political and Economic Studies. Available at http://www.jointcenter.org.

11. Nelson, H., and R. Jurmain (1998). *Introduction to Physical Anthropology*, 4th ed. St. Paul, MN: West Publishing.

12. Williams, D. R., R. Lavizzo-Mourey, and R. C. Warren (1994). "The Concept of Race and Health Status in America." *Public Health Reports*, 109: 26–41.

13. Senior, P. A., and R. Bhopa (1994). "Ethnicity as a Variable in Epidemiological Research." *British Medical Journal*, 309: 327–330.

14. Centers for Disease Control and Prevention (1999). "Reporting Race and Ethnicity Data—National Electronic Telecommunications System for Surveillance, 1994–1997." *Morbidity and Mortality Weekly Report*, 48(15): 305–312.

15. U.S. Department of Health and Human Services, Office of Disease Prevention and Health Promotion (2010). *Healthy People 2020.* Washington, DC: U.S. Government Printing Office. Available at http://healthypeople.gov/2020/default.aspx.

16. Krogstad, J. M. (2014). *With Fewer New Arrivals, Census Lowers Hispanic Population Projections*. Pew Research Center. Available at http://www.pewresearch.org/fact-tank/2014/12/16/with-fewer-new-arrivals-census-lowers-hispanic-population-projections-2/.

17. Lopez, M. H. (2014, January). *In 2014, Latinos Will Surpass Whites as Largest Racial/Ethnic Group in California*. Pew Research Center. Available at http://www.pewresearch.org/fact-tank/2014/01/24/in-2014-latinos-will-surpass-whites-as-largest-racialethnic-group-in-california/.

18. Pew Research Center. (2016). *Detailed Hispanic Origin: 2013*. Available at http://www.pewhispanic.org/2015/05/12/statistical-portrait-of-hispanics-in-the-united-states-1980-2013/ph_2015-03_statistical-portrait-of-hispanics-in-the-united-states-2013_current-04/.

19. U.S. Department of Education, National Center for Education Statistics, Projections of Education Statistics to 2021; and Common Core of Data (CCD). "State Nonfiscal Survey of Public Elementary and Secondary Education," selected years, 2000–01 through 2010–11. See *Digest of Education Statistics* (2012), table 44.

20. DeNavas-Walt, C., and Proctor, B. D. (2015, September). "Income and Poverty in the United States: 2014." *Current Population Reports*. PGO 252.

21. Stetser, M. C., and Stillwell, R. (2014, April). *Public High School Four-Year On-Time Graduation Rates and Event Dropout Rates: School Years 2010–11 and 2011–12*. National Center for Education Statistics. U.S. Department of Education.

22. Office of Minority Health (2015). *Policy and Data*. Available at http://minorityhealth.hhs.gov/omh/browse.aspx?lvl=1&lvlid=4.

23. Henry J. Kaiser Family Foundation. (2016). *Poverty Rate by Race/Ethnicity*. Available at http://kff.org/other/state-indicator/poverty-rate-by-raceethnicity/.

24. Satcher, D., and D. J. Thomas (1990). "Dimensions of Minority Aging: Implications for Curriculum Development for Selected Health Professions." In M. S. Harper, ed., *Minority Aging: Essential Curricula Content for Selected Health and Allied Health Professions* (HHS pub. no. HRS-P-DV 90-4). Washington, DC:U.S. Government Printing Office, 23–32.

25. Airhihenbuwa, C. O., and I. E. Harrison (1993). "Traditional Medicine in Africa: Past, Present and Future." In P. Conrad and E. Gallagher, eds., *Healing and Health Care in Developing Countries*. Philadelphia: Temple University Press.

26. National Center for Health Statistics (2014, December). *Death, Percentage of Total Deaths, and Death Rates for the 15 Leading Causes of Death*. Available at http://www.cdc.gov/nchs/nvss/mortality/lcwk9.htm.

27. President's Advisory Commission on Asian Americans and Pacific Islanders (2003). *Asian Americans and Pacific Islanders Addressing Health Disparities: Opportunities for Building a Healthier America.* Available at http://www.aapi .gov/-Commission_Final_Health_Report.pdf.

28. Ghosh, C. (2003). "Healthy People 2010 and Asian Americans/ Pacific Islanders: Defining a Baseline of Information." *American Journal of Public Health*, 93: 2093–2098.

29. Humes, K., and J. McKinnon (2000). "The Asian and Pacific Islander Population in the United States." *U.S. Census Bureau, Current Population Reports* (Series P20-529). Washington, DC: U.S. Government Printing Office.

30. Pew Research Center (2012, June). *The Rise of Asian Americans.* Available at http://www.pewsocialtrends.org/2012/06/19 /the-rise-of-asian-americans/.

31. Centers for Disease Control and Prevention (2013). *Asian American Populations.* Available at http://www.cdc.gov/minorityhealth /populations/REMP/asian.html.

32. Mayeno, L., and S. M. Hirota (1994). "Access to Health Care." In N. W. S. Zane, D. T. Takeuchi, and K. N. J. Young, eds., *Confronting Critical Health Issues of Asian and Pacific Islander Americans.* Thousand Oaks, CA: Sage Publications.

33. Yoon, E., and E. Chien (1996). "Asian American and Pacific Islander Health: A Paradigm for Minority Health." *Journal of the American Medical Association*, 275: 736–737.

34. Kitano, H. H. L. (1990). "Values, Beliefs, and Practices of Asian American Elderly: Implications for Geriatric Education." In M. S. Harper, ed., *Minority Aging: Essential Curricula Content for Selected Health and Allied Health Professions* (HHS pub. no. HRS-P-DV 90-4). Washington, DC: U.S. Government Printing Office, 341–348.

35. Frye, B. A. (1995). "Use of Cultural Themes in Promoting Health among Southeast Asian Refugees." *American Journal of Health Promotion*, 9: 269–280.

36. Pinzon-Perez, H., N. Moua, and M. A. Pérez (2005). "Understanding Satisfaction with Shamanic Practices among the Hmong in Rural California." *The International Electronic -Journal of Health Education.* 8: 18–23.

37. Aiu, P. (2000). "Comparing Native Hawaiians' Health to the Nation." *Closing the Gap*, June/July: 8–9.

38. Hixon, A. L., and L. E. Buenconsejo-Lum (2010). "Developing the Rural Primary Care Workforce in Hawaii: A 10-Point Plan." *Hawaii Medical Journal*, 69(Supplement 3): 53–55.

39. Blaisdell, R. K. (1989). "Historical and Cultural Aspects of Native Hawaiian Health." In E. Wegner, ed., *Social Process in Hawai'i.* Honolulu: University of Hawai'i Press, 32.

40. Edwards, E. D., and M. Egbert-Edwards (1990). "Family Care and Native American Elderly." In M. S. Harper, ed., *Minority Aging: Essential Curricula Content for Selected Health and Allied Health Professions* (HHS pub. no. HRS-P-DV90-4). Washington, DC: U.S. Government Printing Office, 145–163.

41. Krenz, V. (2014). "Spirituality and Cultural Diversity." In M. A. Perez and R. Luquis, eds., *Cultural Competence in Health Education and Health Promotion.* San Francisco: Jossey-Bass, 119–144.

42. Garrett, J. T. (1990). "Indian Health: Values, Beliefs and Practices." In M. S. Harper, ed., *Minority Aging: Essential Curricula Content for Selected Health and Allied Health Professionals* (HHS pub. no. HRS-P-DV90-4). Washington, DC: U.S. Government Printing Office, 179–191.

43. U.S. Department of Health and Human Services, Indian Health Services, Program Statistics Team (2000). *Regional Differences in Indian Health 1998–99.* Available at http://www.ihs.gov/publicinfo /publications/trends98/region98.asp.

44. U.S. Census Bureau (2015). Facts for Features: American Indian and Alaska native Heritage Mon: November 2014. Available at http://www .census.gov/newsroom/facts-for-features/2014/cb14-ff26.html

45. United Nations High Commissioner for Refugees (n.d.) *Facts and Figures about Refugees.* Available at http://www.unhcr.org.uk /about-us/key-facts-and-figures.html.

46. United States Department of Homeland Security (2014). *Yearbook of Immigration Statistics: 2013.* Washington, DC: Author.

47. Hoffer, M., N. Rytina, and B. Baker (2010). "Estimates of the Unauthorized Immigrant Population Residing in the United States: January 2009." In *Population Estimates.* Washington, DC: Homeland Security, Office of Immigration Statistics. Retrieved from http ://www.dhs.gov/xlibrary/assets/-statistics/publications/ois_ill _pe_2009.pdf.

48. Baker, B., and N. Rytina (2014, September). *Estimates of the Lawful Permanent Resident Population in the United States: January 2013.* Office of Immigration Statistics Policy Directorate.

49. Uba, L. (1992). "Cultural Barriers to Health Care for Southeast Asian Refugees." *Public Health Reports*, 107(5): 544–548.

50. Centers for Disease Control and Prevention (1997). *Minority Health Is the Health of the Nation.* Washington, DC: U.S. Government Printing Office.

51. Truman, B. I., C. K. Smith, K. Roy, et al. (2011). "Rationale for Reporting on Health Disparities and Inequalities—United States." *Morbidity and Mortality Weekly Report.* 60 Supplement. Available at http ://www.cdc.gov/mmwr/preview/ind2011_su.html.

52. U.S. Department of Health and Human Services (2010, December). *Disparities.* Available at http://www.healthypeople.gov/2020/about /disparitiesAbout.aspx.

53. Kochanek, K., E. Arias, and R. Anderson (2015, November). *Leading Causes of Death Contributing to Decrease in Life Expectancy Gap between Black and White Populations: United States, 1999 to 2013.* Available http://www.cdc.gov/nchs/data/databriefs/db218.htm.

54. U.S. Department of Health and Human Services (2013, May). *National Health Care Quality Report 2012.* Agency for Health Care Research and Quality.

55. U.S. Department of Health and Human Services (n.d.). *HHS Action Plan to Reduce Racial and Ethnic Health Disparities: A Nation Free of Disparities in Heath and Health Care.* Available at http://minorityhealth .hhs.gov/npa/files/Plans/HHS/HHS_Plan_complete.pdf.

56. Centers for Disease Control and Prevention (n.d.). *CDC Health Disparities and Inequities Report.* Available at http://www.cdc.gov /minorityhealth/CHDIReport.html.

57. U.S. Department of Health and Human Services (1988). *Report of the Secretary's Task Force on Black and Minority Health.* Washington, DC: Author.

58. U.S. Department of Health and Human Services (2000). *Testimony of David Satcher, Assistant Secretary for Health and Surgeon General Before the House Commerce Committee, Subcommittee on Health and Environment.* Available at http://www.hhs.gov/asl/testify /t000511a.html.

59. National Center for Health Statistics (2010). *Percentage of Mothers Receiving Late or No Prenatal Care by Race and Hispanic Origin, 2006.* National Vital Statistics System. Available at http://www.cdc .gov/nchs/fastats/prenatal.htm.

60. National Cancer Institute. (n.d.). *Cancer Statistics.* Available at http://www.cancer.gov/about-cancer/what-is-cancer/statistics.

61. National Cancer Institute (2010). *SEER Cancer Incidence and US Death Rates, 2002–2006 by Cancer Site and Race.* Available at http ://seer.cancer.gov/csr/1975_2006/results_merged/topic_graph _rate_comparison.pdf.

62. Freeman, H. P. (2004). "Poverty, Culture, and Social Injustice: Determinants of Cancer Disparities." *CA: A Cancer Journal for Clinicians*, 54(2): 72–77.

63. Fryer, C. D., R. Hirsch, M. S. Eberhardt, S. S. Yoon, and J. D. Wright (2010). "Hypertension, High Serum Total Cholesterol, and Diabetes: Racial and Ethnic Prevalence Differences in U.S. Adults, 1999–2006" (*NCHS Data Brief*, no. 36). Hyattsville, MD: National Center for Health Statistics.

64. Yoon, S. S., C. D. Fryar, and M. Carroll (2015, November). "Hypertension Prevalence and Control among Adults: United States, 2011–2014" *(NCHS Data Brief*, no. 220). Hyattsville, MD: National Center for Health Statistics.

65. Centers for Disease Control and Prevention (2010). *National Diabetes Surveillance System.* Available at http://www.cdc.gov/diabetes/statistics/index.htm.

66. Centers for Disease Control and Prevention (2015, September). *Statistics Overview.* Available at http://www.cdc.gov/hiv/statistics/overview/index.html.

67. Agency for Health Care Research and Quality (2013, April). *AHRQ Research and Other Activities Relevant to American Indians and Alaska Natives.* AHRQ Pub. No. 13-P005-EF. Washington, DC: U.S. Department of Health and Human Services.

68. National Center for Health Statistics (2013). *Health, United States, 2012: With Special Feature on Emergency Care.* Hyattsville, MD: Author. Available at http://www.cdc.gov/nchs/hus.htm.

69. Centers for Disease Control and Prevention (2011). *HIV in the United States.* Atlanta, GA: Author. Available at http://www.cdc.gov/hiv/resources/factsheets/us.htm.

70. Centers for Disease Control and Prevention (2013, April). *Statistics Overview. Diagnosis of HIV Infection by Race/Ethnicity 2011.* Atlanta, GA: Author. Available at http://www. cdc.gov/hiv/statistics/basics.

71. Centers for Disease Control and Prevention (2015, September). *Diagnosis of HIV Infection, by Race/Ethnicity.* Available at http://www.cdc.gov/hiv/statistics/overview/index.html.

72. Barrow, R. Y., L. M. Newman, and J. M. Douglas, Jr. (2008). "Taking Positive Steps to Address STD Disparities for African-American Communities." *Sexually Transmitted Diseases*, 35(12 Suppl) S1–S3.

73. Centers for Disease Control and Prevention (2010). "Vaccination Coverage among Children Aged 19 to 35 Months—United States, 1994–2008." *National Immunization Program. NIS Data.* Atlanta, GA: Author. Available at http://www.cdc.gov/vaccines/stats-surv/imz-coverage.htm.

74. Centers for Disease Control and Prevention (2010). *Influenza and Pneumococcal Vaccination Levels among Persons Aged 65 Years and Older, United States, 2005–2006.* Atlanta, GA: Author. Available at http://www.cdc.gov/vaccines/stats-surv/imz-coverage.htm.

75. World Health Organization (2016). *Social Determinants of Health.* Geneva, Switzerland: Author. Available at http://www.who.int/social_determinants/en/.

76. Centers for Disease Control and Prevention (2013, May). "Quick Stats: Percentage of Adults Aged > 65 Who Report Excellent or Very Good Health, by Selected Race/Ethnicity and Poverty Status. National Health Interview Survey, 2009–2011." *Morbidity and Mortality Weekly Report*, 62 (21): 431–432.

77. Shiver, M. D. (1997). "Ethnic Variation as a Key to the Biology of Human Disease." *Annals of Internal Medicine*, 127: 401–403.

78. Luquis, R., and M. Perez. (2014). "Cultural Competency and Health Education: A Window of Opportunity." In M. A. Perez and R. Luquis, eds., *Cultural Competence in Health Education and Health Promotion.* San Francisco: Jossey-Bass, 293–310.

79. Pérez, M. A. (2008). "Strategies, Practices, and Models for Delivering Culturally Competent Health Education Programs." In M. A. Perez and R. R. Luquis, eds., *Cultural Competence in Health Education and Health Promotion.* San Francisco: Jossey Bass Publishers, 183–197.

80. Office of Minority Health (2001). *National Standards for Culturally and Linguistically Appropriate Services in Health Care—Final Report.* Available at http://minorityhealth.hhs.gov/assets/pdf/checked/finalreport.pdf.

81. Office of Minority Health (2013). *The National CLAS Standards.* Available at http://minorityhealth.hhs.gov/templates/browse.aspx?lvl=2&lvlID=15.

82. Loustaunau, M. (2000). "Becoming Culturally Sensitive: Preparing for Service as a Health Educator in a Multicultural World." In S. Smith, ed., *Community Health Perspectives.* Madison, WI: Coursewise Publishing, 33–37.

83. Luquis, R., and M. A. Pérez (2005). "Health Educators and Cultural Competence: Implications for the Profession." *American Journal of Health Studies*, 20(3): 156–163.

84. Luquis, R. (2014). "Culturally Appropriate Communication." In M. A. Perez and R. Luquis, eds., *Cultural Competence in Health Education and Health Promotion.* San Francisco: Jossey-Bass, 193–216.

85. United Nations (n.d.). Sustainable Development Goals: 17 Goals to Transform Our World. Available at http://www.un.org/sustainabledevelopment/sustainable-development-goals/.

86. Friedmann, J. (1992). *Empowerment: The Politics of Alternative Development.* Cambridge, MA: Blackwell Publishers.

87. U.S. Department of Health and Human Services (n.d.). *Quick Guide to Health Literacy.* Available at http://health.gov/communication/literacy/quickguide/factsbasic.htm.

88. Perez, M.A. (2014). "Foundations for Health Literacy and Culturally Appropriate Health Education Programs." In M. A. Perez and R. Luquis, eds., *Cultural Competence in Health Education and Health Promotion.* San Francisco: Jossey-Bass, 217–240.

CHAPTER 11

Community Mental Health

Chapter Objectives

After studying this chapter, you will be able to:

1. Define mental health and mental disorders, and explain the prevalence of mental disorders in the United States.

2. Explain what the *DSM-5* is, and give an example of its limitations.

3. Give an example of how cultural differences can impact the diagnosis of mental disorder.

4. Cite specific examples of the causes of mental disorders.

5. Define stress and explain its relationship to physical and mental health.

6. Briefly trace the history of mental health care in the United States,

highlighting the major changes both before and after World War II.

7. Define the term deinstitutionalization and list and discuss the forces that brought it about.

8. Describe community mental health centers as alternatives to state psychiatric hospitals.

9. Identify the major problems faced by people with mental illness who are homeless.

10. Illustrate some legal and practical issues affecting how society should deal with the problem of mental illness and violence.

11. Describe mental health courts, outpatient commitment, and the

use of "legal leverage" to compel treatment.

12. Discuss the challenges facing law enforcement personnel when dealing with community residents who are struggling with acute symptoms of severe mental illness.

13. Define primary, secondary, and tertiary prevention as they relate to mental disorders, and give an example of each.

14. List and briefly describe the basic approaches to treating mental disorders.

15. Define self-help groups, give examples, and explain how they are helpful to their members.

16. Describe what "recovery" means for people with mental illness in the U.S., and for those in less-developed countries such as India or Tanzania.

17. Discuss what is meant by psychiatric rehabilitation and list the kinds of services provided by effective programs.

18. Identify key clinical, multicultural, practical, and political challenges faced by the community mental health care system today.

19. Explain the federal government's role in supporting health care services to people with mental illness with respect to "parity" in insurance coverage, the Affordable Care Act, and integrative care.

Scenario

Maria Sanchez, her husband, and their three children had lived in their apartment building for about 2 years when they noticed a new person moving in on the floor below them. New families moved in from time to time, but this person didn't have a family and kept to herself. After asking around, Maria learned from a neighbor downstairs that the new person's name was Lynn and that she was not currently employed, but hoped to find work soon, perhaps as a cashier or a custodian. Maria is annoyed that Lynn keeps her television on late into the night. She has been meaning to say something about it, but so far Lynn keeps to herself and Maria hasn't found her very friendly—Lynn tends to look away without saying anything when Maria passes her in the hallway. Maria also learned that Lynn was recovering from a recent bout of mental illness

and that she was anxious about the demands of living independently once again. The neighbor added that Lynn meets monthly with a probation officer from the Department of Corrections.

Maria noticed that every few days a regular visitor arrived at the building in a van from the mental health center to spend an hour or so with Lynn in her apartment. Maria worries that people who see the mental health center van might think those in the van were visiting Maria's family. She knew that people with mental illness needed to live somewhere, but why did it have to be in her building? Would other recovering mental patients rent the next vacant apartment in her building? Would people begin loitering in front of the building or behaving strangely? Would Maria's children be safe? Would the reputation of their neighborhood begin to decline?

Introduction

Mental illness is one of the major health issues facing every community. It is the leading cause of disability in North America and Europe, and costs the United States more than half a trillion dollars per year in treatment and other expenses (see **Figure 11.1**).[1] Mental disorders are associated with smoking, reduced activity, poor diet, obesity, and hypertension, and also contribute to unintentional and intentional injury. Mental disorders reduce average life expectancy, in some cases (involving substance use disorders, anorexia nervosa, schizophrenia, and bipolar mood disorder) by the same amount as does smoking more than 20 cigarettes a day.[2] Clearly, there is "no health without mental health."[3]

Approximately 20% of American adults (about 45 million people) have diagnosable mental disorders during a given year, and about 5% of adults in the United States have serious mental illness, that is, illness that interferes with some aspect of social functioning. Only 38% of those diagnosed with a mental disorder receive treatment.[4] Some of these people require only minimal

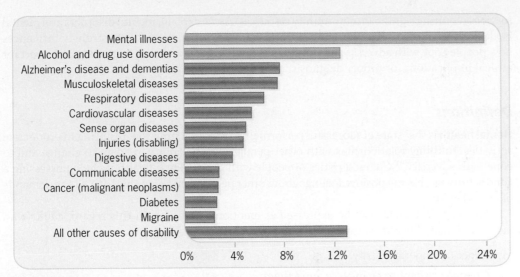

FIGURE 11.1   Causes of disability for all ages combined: United States, Canada, and Western Europe, 2000.

Note: Measures of disability are based on the number of years of "healthy" life lost with less than full health (i.e., YLD: years lost due to disability) for each incidence of disease, illness, or condition.

Data from: President's New Freedom Commission on Mental Health (2003). *Achieving the Promise: Transforming Mental Health Care in America.* Rockville, MD: Author, 20.

counseling, followed by regular attendance of supportive self-help group meetings to remain in recovery, while others suffer repeated episodes of disabling mental illness. These individuals require more frequent medical treatment and more significant community support. Finally, there are the most severely disturbed individuals, who require repeated hospitalization.

The tragic shootings at Virginia Tech and Northern Illinois Universities brought the issue of mental disorder in college students to national attention. Almost half of college students show a 12-month prevalence of some form of mental disorder (most often alcohol use disorder, at 20.37%), and less than 25% receive treatment (see **Table 11.1**).[5] In 2010, 2.9 million youths (12.2% of those aged 12 to 17) received treatment or counseling for problems with emotions or behavior in a specialty mental health setting (inpatient or outpatient care).[6]

Because the needs of people with mental illness are many and diverse, the services required to meet these needs are likewise diverse and include not only therapeutic services but social

TABLE 11.1 12-Month Prevalence of Mental Disorders in College Students and Non-College-Attending Peers, Ages 18–25		
Diagnostic Characteristic	**In College**	**Not in College**
Any psychiatric diagnosis	45.79	47.74
Any alcohol use disorder*	20.37	16.98
Any drug disorder*	5.08	6.85
Major depression	7.04	6.67
Bipolar disorder	3.24	4.62
Any anxiety disorder	11.94	12.66
Pathological gambling	0.35	0.23
Any personality disorder*	17.68	21.55

* Difference is statistically significant (p <.05).

Source: Modified from Blanco, C., O. Mayumi, C. Wright, et al. (2008). "Mental Health of College Students and Their Non-College-Attending Peers." *Archives of General Psychiatry,* 65(12), 1429–1437.

Mental health emotional and social well-being, including one's psychological resources for dealing with day-to-day problems of life

Mental illness a collective term for all diagnosable mental disorders

Mental disorders health conditions characterized by alterations in thinking, mood, or behavior (or some combination thereof) associated with distress and/or impaired functioning

services requiring significant community resources. As we explain, mental disorders and mental health care occur in a diverse social, cultural, and economic context that strongly influences how people cope with adversity, manifest emotional distress, and seek help, and has important ethical implications for proper diagnosis, treatment, and recovery.

Definitions

Mental health is the "state of successful performance of mental function, resulting in productive activities, fulfilling relationships with other people, and the ability to adapt to change and to cope with adversity."[7] Characteristics of people with good mental health include possessing a good self-image, having positive feelings about other people, and being able to meet the demands of everyday life.

Good mental health can be expressed as emotional maturity. In this regard, adults who have good mental health are able to do the following:

1. Function under adversity.
2. Change or adapt to changes around them.
3. Manage their tension and anxiety.
4. Find more satisfaction in giving than receiving.
5. Show consideration for others.
6. Curb hate and guilt.
7. Love others.

"**Mental illness** is a term that refers collectively to all diagnosable mental disorders. **Mental disorders** are health conditions that are characterized by alterations in thinking, mood, or behavior (or some combination thereof) associated with distress and/or impaired functioning."[7] People with mental illness have neurobiological disorders that prevent them from functioning effectively and happily in society. Many people with mental illness can be treated with medications and other forms of help, and are thus able to adapt successfully to community life.

Classification of Mental Disorders

The single most influential book in mental health is probably the *Diagnostic and Statistical Manual of Mental Disorders, Fifth Edition* (*DSM-5*), published by the American Psychiatric Association.[8] It identifies the various mental disorders, provides descriptive information and diagnostic instructions for each, and has significant implications for who merits a diagnosis, whether a treatment should be reimbursed by insurance, what school and social services a person is entitled to, the top priorities for mental health research, and what kinds of new therapeutic medications should be developed. (Furthermore, as a "living document" that can be updated online much more frequently than in the past, this latest edition should probably be regarded as *DSM-5.0*.) Disorders classified in *DSM-5* are listed in **Table 11.2**.

Like preceding editions, *DSM-5* places disorders in discrete categories on the basis of behavioral signs and symptoms rather than definitive tests or measurements of the brain or another body system. Not surprisingly, given the multiple purposes it serves, *DSM-5* has met with controversy. For example, one challenge in using a categorical system is to differentiate normal reactions to life (e.g., severe grief following the death of a loved one) from diagnosable disorder (e.g., **major depression**; see **Box 11.1**).[9] In addition, progress in genetic research has blurred both the boundaries between mental disorders and the boundaries between disorders and normal variations in behavior.[10] As a result, nearly half of people with mental illness (46.4%) are diagnosed with more than one disorder,[11] a problem known as comorbidity. Depression and anxiety are separate categories in *DSM-5*, for example, yet are found together in many individuals[12] and have similar genetic risk factors.[13]

Major depression an affective disorder characterized by a dysphoric mood, usually depression, and/or loss of interest or pleasure in almost all usual activities or pastimes

TABLE 11.2   Major Diagnostic Categories of Mental Disorders

Category	Examples
Neurodevelopmental Disorders	Autism Spectrum Disorder, Attention-Deficit/Hyper-activity Disorder
Schizophrenia Spectrum and Other Psychotic Disorders	Schizophrenia with Catatonia, Schizoaffective Disorder
Bipolar and Related Disorders	Bipolar Disorder, Cyclothymic Disorder
Depressive Disorders	Major Depressive Disorder, Premenstrual Dysphoric Disorder
Anxiety Disorders	Specific Phobia, Panic Disorder, Agoraphobia
Obsessive-Compulsive and Related Disorders	Obsessive-Compulsive Disorder, Body Dysmorphic Disorder, Hoarding Disorder
Trauma- and Stressor-Related Disorders	Posttraumatic Stress Disorder, Acute Stress Disorder
Dissociative Disorders	Dissociative Identity Disorder, Dissociative Amnesia
Somatic Symptom and Related Disorders	Somatic Symptom Disorder, Conversion Disorder
Feeding and Eating Disorders	Anorexia Nervosa, Bulimia Nervosa, Binge-Eating Disorder
Sexual Dysfunctions	Erectile Disorder, Female Sexual Interest/Arousal Disorder
Disruptive, Impulse-Control, and Conduct Disorders	Conduct Disorder, Pyromania
Substance-Related and Addictive Disorders	Alcohol Use Disorder, Cannabis Use Disorder, Gambling Disorder
Neurocognitive Disorders	Delirium, Alzheimer's Disease
Personality Disorders	Antisocial Personality Disorder, Paranoid Personality Disorder, Borderline Personality Disorder

BOX 11.1   Criteria for Major Depressive Episode

A. Five (or more) of the following symptoms have been present during the same 2-week period and represent a change from previous functioning; at least one of the symptoms is either (1) depressed mood or (2) loss of interest or pleasure.

Note: Do not include symptoms that are clearly attributable to another medical condition.

1. Depressed mood most of the day, nearly every day, as indicated by either subjective report (e.g., feels sad, empty, hopeless) or observation made by others (e.g., appears tearful). (*Note:* In children and adolescents, can be irritable mood.)
2. Markedly diminished interest or pleasure in all, or almost all, activities most of the day, nearly every day (as indicated by either subjective account or observation).
3. Significant weight loss when not dieting or weight gain (e.g., a change of more than 5% of body weight in a month), or decrease or increase in appetite nearly every day. (*Note:* In children, consider failure to make expected weight gain.)
4. Insomnia or hypersomnia nearly every day.
5. Psychomotor agitation or retardation nearly every day (observable by others, not merely subjective feelings of restlessness or being slowed down).
6. Fatigue or loss of energy nearly every day.
7. Feelings of worthlessness or excessive or inappropriate guilt (which may be delusional) nearly every day (not merely self-reproach or guilt about being sick).
8. Diminished ability to think or concentrate, or indecisiveness, nearly every day (either by subjective account or as observed by others).

(Continues)

BOX 11.1   Criteria for Major Depressive Episode (Continued)

9. Recurrent thoughts of death (not just fear of dying), recurrent suicidal ideation without a specific plan, or a suicide attempt or a specific plan for committing suicide.

B. The symptoms cause clinically significant distress or impairment in social, occupational, or other important areas of functioning.

C. The episode is not attributable to the physiological effects of a substance or to another medical condition.

Note: Criteria A–C represent a major depressive episode.

Note: Responses to a significant loss (e.g., bereavement, financial ruin, losses from a natural disaster, a serious medical illness or disability) may include feelings of intense sadness, rumination about the loss, insomnia, poor appetite, and weight loss noted in Criterion A, which may resemble a depressive episode. Although such symptoms may be understandable or considered appropriate

to the loss, the presence of a major depressive episode in addition to the normal response to a significant loss should also be carefully considered. This decision inevitably requires the exercise of clinical judgment based on the individual's history and the cultural norms for the expression of distress in the context of loss.

D. The occurrence of the major depressive episode is not better explained by schizoaffective disorder, schizophrenia, schizophreniform disorder, delusional disorder, or other specified and unspecified schizophrenia spectrum and other psychotic disorders.

E. There has never been a manic episode or a hypomanic episode.

Note: This exclusion does not apply if all of the manic-like or hypomanic-like episodes are substance-induced or are attributable to the physiological effects of another medical condition.

Data from: American Psychiatric Association (2013). *Diagnostic and Statistical Manual of Mental Disorders, Fifth Edition.* Arlington, VA: American Psychiatric Association.

Cultural competence service provider's degree of compatibility with the specific culture of the population served, for example, proficiency in language(s) other than English, familiarity with cultural idioms of distress or body language, folk beliefs, and expectations regarding treatment procedures (such as medication or psychotherapy) and likely outcomes

General Adaptation Syndrome (GAS) the complex physiological responses resulting from exposure to stressors

Differentiating people who are ill from those who are well based only on behavior inevitably ties diagnosis to culture rather than to precisely what is wrong with their brains. Given the same symptoms, for example, Hispanics are more likely to be diagnosed with major depression than are whites or African Americans,[14] while African Americans are more likely than other groups to be diagnosed with schizophrenia.[15] Lack of **cultural competence**[16] (language proficiency, familiarity with cultural idioms of distress or body language) may lead a diagnostician to misinterpret as depression what is simply a Hispanic patient's subdued and discouraged demeanor and reluctance to disclose symptoms. The social context also affects diagnosis. Worldwide, for example, women are diagnosed with mood disorders more often than are men, but this difference is smaller in countries that have less traditional gender-role differences in employment opportunities, educational attainment, and control of fertility.[17] A final concern is that diagnosis with a mental disorder can stigmatize a person by imposing negative stereotypes, prejudice, and discrimination that lead to mental distress, shame, avoidance of treatment, and fewer opportunities related to work and independent living. As a result, stigma may be the most debilitating aspect of a mental illness.[18] Despite these various problems, a reliable system for diagnosing mental disorders is essential for assessment, treatment, and research, and to guide the funding of all these activities. *DSM-5* remains the preferred tool for this purpose in the United States.

Causes of Mental Disorders

Symptoms of mental illness can arise from many causes, and the comorbidity that exists among disorders suggests they are not discrete conditions, each with a unique cause. Instead, a variety of mental disorders can result from genetic influences on complex brain functions that control a person's thoughts and emotions,[10] having an older father,[19] intrauterine infections,[20] preterm birth,[21] postnatal exposure to physical, chemical, and biological agents, including secondhand cigarette smoke,[22] head injury,[23] and diseases such as syphilis, cancer, or stroke.

The brain is very sensitive to stress and other environmental influences as it develops during childhood and adolescence (see **Figure 11.2**). In any given year up to one in five children experiences a mental disorder,[24] yet less than half of children and adolescents who need mental health services receive them.[25] Life-long mental disorders often have their onset in adolescence, when physical and hormonal changes intensify emotional reactivity, sensitivity to peer influence, impulsivity, and novelty-seeking, undermining the self-control and regulation needed for effective participation in society.[26]

Mental disorders reflect not just biological vulnerability but also stress, social support, coping, and motivation to recover, making social experience a direct determinant of who gets a mental illness and how the illness unfolds. Some children face considerable adversity, including poverty, abuse, loss, neglect, trauma, and parental psychiatric disorder.[27] Every year about 10% of children are physically or sexually abused. Early and cumulative adversity and maltreatment are believed to harm the development of the brain and affect later depression, post-traumatic stress disorder, suicide attempts, drug and alcohol misuse, and criminal behavior.[28] Bullying in childhood (as a victim, perpetrator, or both) is associated with anxiety and mood disorders in adolescence and young adulthood.[29] Social determinants of mental health, sometimes referred to as the "causes of the causes" of mental disorder, include inequality, discrimination and social exclusion, poor education, unemployment, poverty, housing instability, and poor access to care and to other resources.[30]

Clearly stress is a significant cause of mental illness (see **Box 11.2**). For example, people who survive disasters and soldiers returning from combat face increased risk. Twenty percent of Manhattan residents living near the World Trade Center at the time of the attacks of September 11, 2001 had symptoms consistent with posttraumatic stress disorder (PTSD) 5 to 8 weeks after

FIGURE 11.2   Severe adversity in childhood can increase a person's risk for later mental illness.
© Gerald Bernard/ShutterStock, Inc.

BOX 11.2   Stress: A Contemporary Mental Health Problem

Stress can be defined as one's psychologic and physiologic response to stressors—stimuli in the physical and social environment that produce feelings of tension and strain. Even Americans who believe they have good mental health carry out their everyday activities under considerable stress. Stressors can be subtle—such as having to wait in line, getting stuck in traffic, or having to keep an appointment[31]—or they can be major life events such as getting married or divorced or losing a loved one. Although some exposure to stressors is good, perhaps even essential to a satisfying life, over time stress upsets physical and psychological equilibrium in ways that can directly induce illness and also lead to addictive behaviors and risky sexual behaviors. Relevant stressful events include adverse childhood experiences (which include physical, emotional, and sexual abuse; neglect; parental separation or divorce; mental illness, substance use disorder, or incarceration of a household member; or domestic violence), poor and unequal education, food insecurity, poor housing quality and housing instability, unemployment and underemployment, limited access to health care, poverty, and discrimination.[32]

The process through which exposure to stressors results in health deficits has been described by Selye.[33] According

to Selye's model, which he called the **General Adaptation Syndrome (GAS)**, responding to a stressor occurs in three stages: (1) an alarm reaction, (2) a stage of resistance, and finally (3) exhaustion (see **Figure 11.3**). In the alarm reaction stage, various hormonal changes in the body increase the individual's heart rate, respiration, and blood pressure. This is the **fight-or-flight reaction**, a response that the body cannot maintain for very long. Continued challenge by the

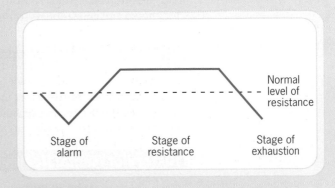

FIGURE 11.3   General Adaptation Syndrome.

(Continues)

BOX 11.2   Stress: A Contemporary Mental Health Problem (Continued)

stressor leads to resistance, where the body tries to adapt to the stressor. Physiologic arousal declines and the body begins to replenish the hormones released in the alarm reaction stage, but the ability to cope with new stressors is impaired. As a result, the person is vulnerable to certain health problems that are referred to as **diseases of adaptation**, including ulcers, high blood pressure, coronary heart disease, asthma, and impaired immune function. In the third stage of Selye's GAS, prolonged physiologic arousal produced by continual or repeated stress depletes energy stores to the point of exhaustion. During this stage, physiologic damage, physical diseases, mental health problems, and even death can occur.

Severe or prolonged stress is especially likely to raise the risk of psychiatric disorder in people with genetic predispositions, and when the stress occurs while the brain is still developing.[34] Stress affects health both directly, by way of physiologic changes in the body, and indirectly through changes in behavior. Stress-hormone levels that remain high for too long cause high blood pressure and suppress the immune system, which some authorities believe explains the association of stressful urban environments with disorders such as schizophrenia.[35] Hormones can produce fast or erratic beating of the heart, which can be fatal, and also increases in levels of blood lipids causing a buildup of plaque on the blood vessel walls and increasing the likelihood of hypertension, stroke, and heart attack. In terms of indirect effects, individuals under stress drink more alcohol and smoke more cigarettes,[36,37] behaviors that are associated with higher risks for heart disease and cancer, as well as injury and death from accidents.

Relationships and other social resources can mediate the effects of stress. People lacking support (in the form of marriage, church membership, social organization membership, and contacts with friends and relatives) face a greater risk than do others of experiencing mental illness, alcohol and drug abuse, suicide, illness, and mortality, independent of their overall health, socioeconomic status, smoking, drinking, obesity, and utilization of health care.[38] Effective time management, goal setting, and prioritizing tasks help reduce stress, as does being realistic about one's abilities and expectations. Experts recommend a combination of physical, social, environmental, and psychological approaches to managing stress.[39] Physical approaches to stress reduction include good nutrition and adequate sleep and aerobic exercise. Healthy social interaction and optimizing environmental factors such as noise, lighting, and living space can also reduce one's stress (see the American Institute of Stress website at www.stress.org).

Fight-or-flight reaction an alarm reaction that prepares one physiologically for sudden action

Diseases of adaptation diseases that result from chronic exposure to excess levels of stressors, which produce a General Adaptation Syndrome response

the attack, and nearly 10% suffered from depression, which occurred most often in those who had suffered losses as a result of the attack.[40] Ten years after Hurricane Katrina many survivors continued to experience mental health problems related to the storm.[41] Military service increases one's risk of experiencing posttraumatic stress disorder, depression, or other mental health problems[42] (see **Figure 11.4**), and from 2004 to 2009 suicides among U.S. soldiers more than doubled.[43]

Among middle-aged white Americans (especially those with a high school education or less) suicides and substance abuse led to an unexpected rise in death rates between 1999 and 2014.[44] One objective of *Healthy People 2020* aimed at improving the mental health status of Americans is to reduce the overall suicide rate. Community-wide education campaigns can improve public knowledge and attitudes regarding suicide, but the durability of such changes is not known and educational efforts have shown no effects on help-seeking or suicidal behavior.[45]

The prevalence of alcohol, tobacco, and other drug abuse in the U.S. is yet another indicator of the mental illness problem. For example, in 2002 40% of the college-aged young adults and 28% of high school seniors interviewed had drunk at least five or more drinks in a row in the previous 2 weeks, and 25% of twelfth graders reported using an illegal drug in the previous 30 days.[46] These figures, which will be discussed in more detail elsewhere, are further evidence that many young people lack the necessary psychological resources for coping with life's problems.

History of Mental Health Care in the United States

The response to mental illness in America has a history older than the country itself, and is marked by enthusiastic reform movements followed by periods of widespread ambivalence toward people with mental disorders. Cyclical periods of reform often began when existing approaches to caring for those with mental illness became intolerable for society, and ended when their economic burden became unbearable.

Mental Health Care before World War II

In Colonial America, when communities were sparsely populated, "distracted" persons or "lunatics," as they were called, were generally cared for by their families or private caretakers, and only as a last resort became the responsibility of the local community. Institutionalization did not begin until the eighteenth century when people with mental disorders were placed in undifferentiated poorhouses or almshouses alongside people with mental retardation, physical disabilities, and the otherwise deviant.[47]

By the early nineteenth century the situation in the poorhouses and almshouses worsened and the first efforts were made to separate people by their type of disability. In 1751 Thomas Bond opened Pennsylvania Hospital, the first institution in America specifically designed to care for those with mental illness.[48] Conditions in the hospital were harsh (see **Figure 11.5**), and treatments, which consisted of "blood letting, blistering, emetics, and warm and cold baths," were unpleasant.[49]

The Moral Treatment Era

Philippe Pinel of France developed a more humane approach that he called *traitement moral*, or in English, **moral treatment**, based upon the assumption that environmental changes could affect an individual's mind and thus alter behavior.[47] In the United States, William Tuke put moral treatment into practice beginning in 1792.

People with mental illness were removed from the everyday life stressors of their home environments and given "asylum" in a quiet country environment, where they received a regimen of rest, light food, exercise, fresh air, and amusements. Moral treatment was initially deemed successful and soon spread,[50] but with rising immigration and urbanization these asylums became overcrowded and indigent patients again ended up in poor houses. At this point noted reformer Dorothea Lynde Dix (1802–1897; see **Figure 11.6**) began a tireless campaign to establish public hospitals providing decent care to indigents with mental illness. When her lobbying for a federal law failed, Dix lobbied on a state-by-state basis. Her efforts were in most cases successful; all in all, Dix was personally involved in the founding of 32 public mental hospitals funded by individual states.[51]

The State Hospitals

The state mental hospitals were supposed to supply an environment in which therapeutic care was based on close personal relationships between patients and well-trained staff members, as prescribed in the methods of moral treatment (see **Figure 11.7**). Unfortunately, the chronic nature of mental illness made long-term or even lifetime hospital stays increasingly the norm.[51] "Maximum capacities" were quickly reached, exceeded, and repeatedly revised upward. Personalized care became impractical and physical restraints provided the most efficient way to manage patients on large wards.[48] States repeatedly cut funding for these institutions until all that remained was custodial care by an overworked staff that turned over frequently.

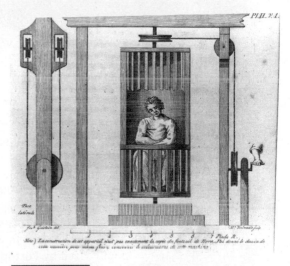

FIGURE 11.4   Military troops returning from duty in combat zones are heavy users of mental health services when these services are accessible.

Courtesy of Cpl. Brian Reimers/U.S. Marines.

FIGURE 11.5   Treatment for mental illness in the eighteenth and nineteenth centuries was often inhumane and unsuccessful.

© National Library of Medicine.

Moral treatment a nineteenth-century treatment in which people with mental illness were removed from the everyday life stressors of their home environments and given "asylum" in a rural setting, including rest, exercise, fresh air, and amusements

FIGURE 11.6 Dorothea Dix helped to establish public mental hospitals in many states.

© National Library of Medicine.

FIGURE 11.7 The state mental hospital was at one time viewed as the appropriate public response to the needs of those with mental illness.

Courtesy of Department of Social and Health Services, Washington State.

Electroconvulsive therapy (ECT) method of treatment for mental disorders involving the administration of electric current to the scalp to induce convulsions and unconsciousness

Lobotomy surgical severance of nerve fibers of the brain by incision

By 1940 the population in state mental institutions had grown to nearly one half million, and staff caseloads became so large that only subsistence care was possible. In response to this situation, dramatic new approaches to treatment were developed, including **electroconvulsive therapy (ECT)** and **lobotomy**. ECT (**Figure 11.8**) uses electric current to produce convulsions in patients with severe depression who have not responded to medication or who are at imminent risk of suicide or other acute clinical condition.[52]

The lobotomy, in which nerve fibers of the brain are severed by surgical incision, was popularized by Portuguese neuropsychiatrist Antônio Egas Moniz, and by U.S. neurologist Walter Freeman. Freeman streamlined the procedure with his invention of the so-called ice-pick lobotomy, enabling him and other physicians to perform tens of thousands of lobotomies between 1939 and 1967.[53] However, later research found that following this irreversible operation only one-third of patients showed stable improvement, while another one-third became worse off. The appearance of new antipsychotic and antidepressive drugs in the 1950s made the widespread use of lobotomies unnecessary.[53]

FIGURE 11.8 A team of doctors and nurses prepares to demonstrate the procedures involved in electroconvulsive therapy (shock treatment), 1942.

© AP Photos.

Mental Health Care after World War II

In the postwar 1940s, a number of factors brought about greater federal involvement in mental health care. New feelings of optimism in the country, together with testimony before the U.S. Congress by both military and civilian experts, soon resulted in the passage of the National Mental Health Act of 1946, which established the **National Institute of Mental Health (NIMH)**. Modeled after the National Cancer Institute, NIMH came under the umbrella of the National Institutes of Health. The purposes of NIMH were (1) to foster and aid research related to the cause, diagnosis, and treatment of neuropsychiatric disorders; (2) to provide training and award fellowships and grants for work in mental health; and (3) to aid the states in the prevention, diagnosis, and treatment of neuropsychiatric disorders.[51]

Deinstitutionalization

During the early 1950s, public distress about the conditions in state mental hospitals continued to grow until the necessity of finding a new approach to caring for those with mental illness was clear and inescapable.[49] The term **deinstitutionalization** has been used to describe the discharging of tens of thousands of patients from state-owned mental hospitals and the resettling and maintaining of these discharged persons in less restrictive community settings. To show the magnitude of deinstitutionalization, in 1955, 322 state psychiatric hospitals served 558,922 resident patients. By 1990 the number of patients had dropped to less than 120,000 (**Figure 11.9**), and by 2004 to under 30,000.[54,55]

Deinstitutionalization was not a preplanned policy. Rather, it was propelled by four forces that had been building up for more than half a century: (1) economics, (2) idealism, (3) legal considerations, and (4) the development and marketing of antipsychotic drugs.[49] Economically, the states needed to reduce expenditures for mental hospitals so that more money was available for the other three major state budgetary items—education, roads, and welfare. Meanwhile, Medicare and Medicaid legislation provided federal funds to reimburse the costs of outpatient and inpatient services for eligible people with mental illness who were not residing in a state institution. (For more information about Medicare and Medicaid, see Chapter 14.)

By the early 1960s questions arose about the legality of institutionalizing people against their will who had not been convicted of any crime, but simply because they had mental illness. The American Bar Association pointed out that people with mental disorders, even when institutionalized, had certain rights, including the right to treatment.[54] Over the ensuing decade, courts began to show more concern for the rights of individuals with mental illness—who were viewed as needing the courts' protection from inappropriate involuntary commitment—and less concern for society's right to be protected from these individuals.[49] Eventually, the test for involuntary civil commitment became one of whether these individuals could be considered dangerous to themselves or others.

Although economics, idealism, and legal considerations all helped to launch deinstitutionalization, new medications expedited it. One of the first was **chlorpromazine**, introduced

National Institute of Mental Health (NIMH) the nation's leading mental health research agency, housed in the National Institutes of Health

Deinstitutionalization the process of discharging, on a large scale, patients from state mental hospitals to less-restrictive community settings

Chlorpromazine (Thorazine) the first and most famous antipsychotic drug, introduced in 1954 under the brand name Thorazine

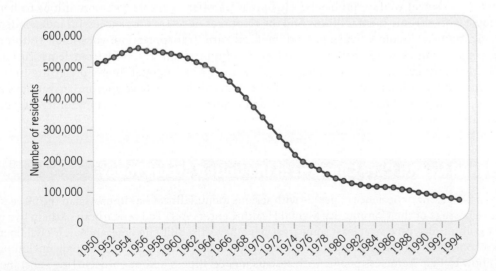

FIGURE 11.9 Number of resident patients in state and county mental hospitals at the end of the year, 1950–1994.

Data from: Frank, R. G., and S. A. Glied (2006). *Better But Not Well*. Baltimore: Johns Hopkins University Press, 55.

as **Thorazine** in 1954, and characterized as **neuroleptic drug** because it appeared to reduce nervous activity. Used first in hospitals, Thorazine and the other phenothiazines introduced later produced a remarkably calming effect in psychotic patients, and in many cases became the only form of treatment provided. In these situations, a **chemical straitjacket** was said to have been substituted for a physical one, and unfortunately some of the drugs' acute and chronic side effects were overlooked. Acute side effects (such as blurred vision, weight gain, and constipation) can cause compliance failures resulting in relapses or in attempts to self-medicate with other drugs, including drugs of abuse. Long-term use of chlorpromazine can impair the central nervous system and produce **tardive dyskinesia**, the irreversible, involuntary, and abnormal movements of the tongue, mouth, arms, and legs.[48] Despite these deleterious effects, phenothiazines are still used extensively to treat patients with severe disorders.

Thorazine (see chlorpromazine)

Neuroleptic drug drug that reduces nervous activity; another term for antipsychotic drugs

Chemical straitjacket a drug that subdues a psychiatric patient's behavior

Tardive dyskinesia irreversible condition of involuntary and abnormal movements of the tongue, mouth, arms, and legs, which can result from long-term use of certain antipsychotic drugs (such as chlorpromazine)

Mental Retardation Facilities and Community Mental Health Centers (CMHC) Act a law that made the federal government responsible for assisting in the funding of mental health facilities and services

Community mental health center (CMHC) a fully staffed center originally funded by the federal government that provides comprehensive mental health services to local populations

Transinstitutionalization transferring patients from one type of public institution to another, usually as a result of policy change

Community Mental Health Centers

In 1963 mental illness and its treatment gained national attention when President John F. Kennedy addressed Congress on the subject of mental health care.[47] The resulting **Mental Retardation Facilities and Community Mental Health Centers (CMHC) Act** promised funding to establish one fully staffed, full-time **community mental health center (CMHC)** in each of 1,499 designated catchment areas covering the entire United States (**Figure 11.10**). These centers were to provide five core services: (1) inpatient care, (2) outpatient services, (3) 24-hour-a-day emergency care, (4) day treatment or other partial hospitalization services, and (5) consultation and education.[56] Hundreds of CMHCs were established in the 1960s and 70s, but for a number of years after that they fell short of the lofty expectations outlined in Kennedy's speech. One problem was that many older patients with chronic mental illness never returned to the community and instead were simply **transinstitutionalized** to nursing homes. CMHCs also struggled to serve deinstitutionalized persons living in the community, since no effective services had been developed to supplement the use of medications with this population.

The federal government responded to the problems of deinstitutionalization and transinstitutionalization in 1977 by creating the Community Support Program, which was the first recognition that the problems of people with chronic mental illness are—first and foremost—social welfare problems. This program offered grants to communities to help people with chronic mental illness find the resources necessary for successful independent living, namely, income, housing, food, medical care, transportation, vocational training, and opportunities for recreation.[57] Despite the many problems resulting from deinstitutionalization, surveys indicate that most people with chronic mental illness prefer life in the community over life in an institution. Most communities now have appropriate services in place, and inpatient care is more effective and requires less time since community support is available following discharge.

Mental Health Care Concerns in the United States Today

On balance, the experience of people with serious mental illness has improved in the 50 years since passage of the Community Mental Health Centers Act. Today nearly all of them live in the community, receive at least some treatment, have disability income, and enjoy civil liberties; some of them also lead productive lives.[55] However, specific challenges remain, including: (1) how to help homeless people with serious mental illness and/or co-occurring substance use disorders, (2) what to do about the perception that mental illness is linked to extreme violence, and (3) resolving the problem of people with mental illness becoming involved with the criminal justice system and too often ending up in jail or prison.

Serious Mental Illness in People Who Are Homeless

More than 637,000 people are homeless during any given week in the United States, and 2.1 million adults experience homelessness over the course of a year.[58] An estimated 80% of these homeless individuals are temporarily homeless, 10% are episodically homeless, and 10% are chronically homeless (see **Figure 11.11**).

Homeless people are more exposed to environmental stresses and threats than people with homes, and about half of all adults who are homeless have substance use disorders, major depression, and other co-occurring mental illness.[59] They tend to remain homeless and (except for emergency rooms and the police) disengaged from services, and their rates of criminal behavior and victimization are higher than among housed adults with severe mental illness.[60]

While the problems of homeless people with mental illness are complex, their most pressing needs are for safe, affordable housing that they choose and actually want to live in, and services they need.[61] If available at all, services to people who are homeless are often fragmented, although integration of medical, mental health, substance abuse, and housing services is possible.[62]

FIGURE 11.11   As many as two-thirds of all people with serious mental illness have experienced homelessness or been at risk for homelessness at some point in their lives.

© Photos.com.

Mental Illness and Violence

Recent mass shootings at schools, theaters, places of worship, and other everyday settings by young men alleged to have mental illness drew extensive media coverage and reinforced an already widely held connection in Americans' minds between serious mental illness and violence.[63] It is misleading, however, to draw conclusions from individual cases in isolation. Mass shootings are a small percentage of all gun violence; the large majority of people with serious mental illnesses are never violent,[64] and histories of prior violence, substance use, and early trauma are more likely to contribute to subsequent violence than is mental illness per se.[65]

Furthermore, what we should do to prevent violence by people with mental illness is not clear in light of the individual rights granted all of us by the U.S. Constitution and the nature of serious mental illness. Legally, authorities can act to prevent potential violence only when someone voluntarily seeks assistance or has made frank threats. Relaxing these criteria so that more people believed to have a propensity for violence are detained could discourage individuals with mental illness from seeking help or being candid with their families and the authorities. Detaining larger numbers of people is also unlikely to prevent violence, since mental health experts do little better than chance in predicting who will be violent.

In addition, people with the most severe mental illnesses, especially if they are angry and alienated, do not often seek treatment voluntarily, and even those who do may not be fully engaged or cooperative. Many of those who perpetrated mass shootings received psychotherapy and other forms of treatment beforehand, but a lack of motivation to change and the fact that some psychiatric disorders are not particularly responsive to therapy make successful treatment difficult and very expensive.

People with serious mental illness are marginalized individuals who for the most part are unemployed, economically impoverished, live in disadvantaged neighborhoods, often misuse alcohol and illicit drugs, and are regularly victimized or even traumatized. Most violent behavior is due to factors like these rather than to mental illness, although psychiatric disorders such as depression are strongly implicated in suicide, which accounts for over half of U.S. firearms-related fatalities.[66]

Some public health authorities advocate restricting advertising and sales and increasing taxation on guns and ammunition, as well as mandatory licensing, locking devices, and safety inspections, citing the reduction of health problems related to poisoning, motor vehicle crashes, and tobacco use following the adoption of similar measures.[67] The difficulty facing society is

Bipolar disorder an affective disorder characterized by distinct periods of elevated mood alternating with periods of depression

Crisis Intervention Team specially trained police in direct collaboration with mental health authorities to remove barriers to mental health care for people with mental illness involved in the justice system

that, like mental illness itself, gun violence results from many causes, invokes deeply held values (public safety versus civil liberties), and in today's sociocultural context leaves policymakers with no easy options.

The New Asylums: Mental Health Care in Jails and Prisons

Cognitive and emotional deficits imposed by mental illness, coupled with homelessness and other intense stressors, increase the risk that people with serious mental illness will commit criminal acts. Before 1820 in the U.S., it was common to find people with mental illness in jails or prisons. Efforts by Dorothea Dix and others eventually convinced most state legislatures that people with mental illness belonged in hospitals rather than prisons, and by 1880 only 0.7% of U.S. prisoners had serious mental illness. Since that time, and largely out of public view, we have reversed this policy completely and in effect have recriminalized mental illness. Jails and prisons in the United States now hold an estimated 356,268 inmates with serious mental disorders, compared with just 35,000 individuals in state mental hospitals,[68] and rates of serious mental illness in U.S. correctional facilities are three to four times the rates in the general population[69] (**Figure 11.12**).

Inmates with mental illness must be closely monitored and may require medical treatment, yet the fundamental purpose of correctional facilities is to confine and punish, not treat. Harsh and socially isolating conditions in jail or prison can exacerbate mental illness, and courts have interpreted the U.S. Constitution as ensuring a right to treatment to protect prisoners who have medical and psychiatric needs against cruel and unusual punishment. However, U.S. prisons are seriously overcrowded, and effective treatment requires adequate space, a sufficient number of qualified treatment personnel, and timely access to services.[70] Some of the worst conditions are in juvenile justice centers, where adolescents from diverse cultural backgrounds and with a variety of disorders, criminal convictions, and family problems receive little or no treatment, and sometimes only multiple forms of medication.[71] Furthermore, even when treatment is available, severe mental illness (paranoid schizophrenia, **bipolar disorder**, or other serious mental disorder)[72] may hinder inmates' cooperation with their prescribed medication schedules, and without medication these inmates may be incapable of "good behavior," a prerequisite for parole or release.

In the community the police have become, by default, the authorities responsible for dealing with mentally ill people who are in crisis. Up to 10% of police calls nationally involve individuals with mental illness, and police officers write one-third of emergency mental health referrals.[73] Control and arrest techniques that are used routinely in other types of calls may inadvertently escalate a mental health crisis, leading to injuries to officers and subjects and the unnecessary arrest of persons whose only clear "crime," in some cases, is displaying symptoms of mental illness. Officers can learn alternative methods of policing, but managing serious mental illness in the community is beyond the scope of a police intervention alone and must become a community issue. Mental health services need to be better integrated with law enforcement to increase the availability of services and reduce the burden on the police of being the primary, and often sole, responders. One option, known as the **Crisis Intervention Team**, involves special training for police and direct collaboration with mental health authorities to remove barriers that interfere with immediate access to mental health services (for example, lack of beds and insurance processing delays).[74]

Individuals with criminal involvement and serious mental illness who do not receive treatment are more likely to commit another offense than are justice-involved people without mental disorders. While they constitute a small proportion of the people with mental illness, these individuals often resist participating in treatment and may pose a danger to himself or herself or the public, resulting in

FIGURE 11.12 Many prison inmates with mental illness remain in prison years beyond their original sentence because they are unable to conform to good conduct requirements of the prison system.

© Tim Harman/ShutterStock, Inc.

frequent psychiatric hospitalizations. In response, many communities have resorted to the use of mandatory "commitment" to outpatient treatment, "legal leverage" to compel cooperation, and special mental health courts.

Outpatient commitment refers to laws ordering an individual to obtain psychiatric treatment against his or her will or risk sanctions up to and including forced hospitalization. Outpatient commitment is intended to secure services for individuals who do not understand their illness and the risks of refusing treatment, protect the individual from imminent harm through suicide or self-neglect, and safeguard the public from acts of violence perpetrated by the individual.

Legal leverage to force the patient to accept treatment may involve service providers taking control of the patient's disability income and/or suspending the patient's eligibility for subsidized housing.[75] While controversial, legal leverage attempts to balance the values of civil rights and normalization with that of public safety.

Mental health courts use judges who have special training and nonadversarial procedures that mandate treatment and rehabilitation rather than incarceration if a defendant with mental illness is found guilty. In such cases the court will suspend the guilty person's sentence and work with local mental health professionals to develop treatment plans that the patient agrees to follow. If participants do not adhere to the agreement, the court can revoke the suspended sentence or charge the patient with violating the terms of probation. Hundreds of these courts now operate across the country, and evidence indicates that their use can help to lower recidivism, improve mental health outcomes,[76] and reduce the risk of violence by justice-involved persons with mental disorders.[77]

We should note that outpatient commitment, legal leverage, and mental health courts do not just commit patients to participate in treatment; they also involuntarily commit the community mental health system to provide it. All three of these policies are more successful when effective services targeting both psychiatric and criminogenic issues are available, and when the goals of treatment include meaningful recovery from mental illness or addiction and not just fewer days in jail.

Meeting the Needs of People with Mental Illness

The legal and moral obligation to provide cost-effective prevention, treatment, and rehabilitation services to people with mental illness is an important challenge facing every community today.[30]

Prevention

The concepts of primary, secondary, and tertiary prevention (see Chapter 4) are applicable to mental disorders. Primary prevention in community mental health reduces the incidence (rate of new cases) of mental illness and related problems. For example, in the 1990s a program known as "Moving to Opportunity" randomly identified more than 4,500 low-income and mostly female-headed families and gave them vouchers to move from public housing in extremely poor neighborhoods to lower-poverty neighborhoods in the same cities. Fifteen years later, families that had received the vouchers reported better mental health and higher subjective well-being (happiness) than did the control families.[78] Such findings are a useful reminder that mental health is determined not just by individual vulnerabilities but also social determinants such as neighborhood quality and other environmental and economic circumstances.[30]

Secondary prevention, although not reducing the incidence of mental illness, can reduce its prevalence by shortening the duration of episodes through prompt intervention. For example, soldiers exposed to high levels of combat who receive intensive cognitive skills training within a few days of returning home are significantly less likely to experience symptoms of PTSD and depression later on.[79] Other examples of secondary prevention include employee assistance programs, juvenile delinquency diversion programs, and crisis intervention, and can be provided by provided by licensed professionals in private clinics, CMHCs, hospital emergency rooms, and other social service agencies. Tertiary prevention, treatment, and rehabilitation ameliorate

Outpatient commitment laws mandating involuntary psychiatric treatment for individuals who do not understand their illness to protect the individual from harm and safeguard the public

Legal leverage service providers controlling the disability income or other benefits received by a person with mental illness to enforce participation in treatment in return for suspending a criminal sentence imposed by a court of law

Mental health court court where the judges have special training and use nonadversarial procedures that mandate treatment and rehabilitation rather than incarceration if a person with mental illness is found guilty of a crime

the symptoms of illness and prevent further problems for the individual and the community. Intensive community treatment programs, discussed later in connection with psychiatric rehabilitation, are examples of tertiary prevention.[80]

Treatment Approaches

Treatment goals for mental disorders are to (1) reduce symptoms, (2) improve personal and social functioning, (3) develop and strengthen coping skills, and (4) promote behaviors that make a person's life better. The basic approaches to treating mental disorders include psychopharmacology, psychotherapy, technology, self-help groups, and psychiatric rehabilitation.

Psychopharmacology

Psychopharmacological therapy involves treatment with medications. This approach to treatment regards mental disorders as medical illnesses just like hypothyroidism or diabetes, and as such treatable with drugs. Since the introduction of chlorpromazine in 1954 there has been enormous growth in the use of medications to treat mental disorders, and in recent years the sharpest increases in medication use have been to treat children and adolescents.[81] Conditions for which medications exist are schizophrenia, bipolar disorder, major depression, anxiety, panic disorder, and obsessive-compulsive disorder, although not everyone who has these disorders responds to medication,[82] which probably reflects both shortcomings of the diagnostic process and our limited understanding of the biological basis of mental disorders. Furthermore, because some of these drugs have serious side effects, and because of the nature of mental illness itself, almost half of patients may not cooperate fully in taking their medications.[83]

Another form of biomedical therapy is ECT, which was discussed earlier in this chapter. In ECT, alternating electric current passes through the brain to produce unconsciousness and a convulsive seizure. ECT is used for severe depression, selected cases of schizophrenia, or overwhelming suicide ideation, especially when the need for treatment is seen as urgent. Contemporary ECT methods use low doses of electric shock to the brain and general anesthetics to reduce the unpleasant side effects.[52]

Psychotherapy

Psychotherapy, or psychosocial therapy, involves treatment through verbal communication (see **Figure 11.13**). There are numerous approaches to psychotherapy, including interpersonal, couple, group, and family formats. Psychodynamic psychotherapy examines current problems as they relate to earlier experiences, even from childhood, while cognitive psychotherapy focuses on current thinking patterns that are faulty or distorted. **Cognitive-behavioral therapy** focuses on how maladaptive feelings and behaviors are the result of distorted thinking, and uses exercises, role playing, and other structured procedures to promote new thought patterns, and regular homework between sessions to practice more effective coping responses. In general, psychotherapy is most likely to be successful in less severe cases of emotional distress or when used in conjunction with other approaches (such as psychopharmacological therapy).[84]

Technology

As health care systems evolve to serve increasingly diverse racial, ethnic, and cultural groups, we need more ways to get effective interventions to the people who need them, when they need them, and where they want to access them. At present, language barriers can hinder direct verbal communication between therapists and clients, and psychotherapy resources are distributed unevenly across

FIGURE 11.13 Psychotherapy is usually only one of the services needed by persons who are suffering from mental illness.

© David Buffington/Photodisc/Getty Images.

geographic, socioeconomic, and cultural boundaries. However, technology in the form of telephone, video conferencing, Internet, email, and computer software can deliver flexible help directly to clients' living environments while also lowering its cost. For example, devices such as computers, tablets, smartphones, wearable and embedded sensors, and software (e.g., mobile health apps and Internet sites) allow people to easily and accurately monitor their own states and can be used to infer information relevant to behavioral and mental health, including levels of stress and quality and duration of sleep.[85] Patients can also use software to complete more traditional steps in psychotherapy (e.g., daily homework), contacting their therapists by telephone or email only when necessary. Moving the locus of treatment from therapists and their offices to settings more comfortable and familiar to clients increases privacy and may reduce the feelings of coerciveness that some clients experience. For certain individuals, who may have severe cognitive or language impairments or social anxiety, communicating with a therapist using a visual display of words on a screen can be more effective than face-to-face conversation.[86] Computer therapy and in-person therapy are about the same in overall effectiveness and, with greater convenience and more flexible use of client and therapist time, drop-out from computer treatments may occur less often than in face-to-face therapy.[87]

Self-Help Groups

Another aid to treatment and recovery is **self-help groups**, comprised of concerned members of the community who are united by a disability or predicament not shared by other members of the community. The shared characteristic is often stigmatizing or isolating and viewed as abnormal by the rest of the community.[80] Self-help groups meet regularly; members often share leadership responsibilities, and the roles of help-giver and help-receiver are entirely interchangeable. These groups replace the community that was "lost" through stigmatization or isolation. Self-help groups supply feedback and guidance to their members based on unique insights gained from their own recovery, and provide their members with adaptive attitudes and expectations about the future.[80] Examples of self-help groups are the **National Alliance on Mental Illness (NAMI)**, Recovery, Inc., and Alcoholics Anonymous (AA). For more information on NAMI, see **Box 11.3**.

Psychiatric Rehabilitation

One of the objectives of *Healthy People 2020* is to increase the proportion of adults with mental disorders who are receiving treatment (see **Box 11.4**). With financial considerations influencing most health care decisions today, the treatment of mental disorders is driven more and more by considerations of cost-effectiveness.

> **Self-help group** group of concerned members of the community who are united by a shared interest, concern, or deficit not shared by other members of the community (Alcoholics Anonymous, for example)
>
> **National Alliance on Mental Illness (NAMI)** a national self-help group that supports the belief that major mental disorders are brain diseases that are of genetic origin and biological in nature and are diagnosable and treatable with medications

---

BOX 11.3   National Alliance on Mental Illness

The National Alliance on Mental Illness (NAMI) "is the nation's largest grassroots mental health organization dedicated to improving the lives of persons living with serious mental illness and their families. Founded in 1979, NAMI has become the nation's voice on mental illness, a national organization including NAMI organizations in every state and in over 1,100 local communities across the country who join together to meet the NAMI mission through advocacy, research, support, and education."

According to its mission statement, "NAMI is dedicated to the eradication of mental illnesses and to the improvement of the quality of life of all whose lives are affected by these diseases." NAMI members, leaders, and friends share the agency's mission of "support, education, advocacy, and research for people living with mental illness through various activities" that include maintaining a website and toll-free help line, sponsoring a Mental Illness Awareness Week, and maintaining a public education speakers bureau.

NAMI also provides a cadre of educational programs and a network of support groups. NAMI "advocates on the federal level to ensure nondiscriminatory and equitable federal and private-sector policies are in place as well as a commitment to research for the treatment and cures for mental illness." As with other voluntary health organizations, NAMI is involved in fundraising, and does so with events such as NAMI Walks and an annual black-tie event, the Unmasking Mental Illness Science and Research Gala, held in Washington, DC.

More information about NAMI is available at their website: www.NAMI.org.

BOX 11.4 *Healthy People 2020*: Mental Health and Mental Disorder Objectives

Objective MHMD-9: Increase the proportion of adults with mental disorders who receive treatment.

Targets and baselines:

Objective	Demographic	2008 Baseline	2020 Target
MHMD-9.1	Adults aged 18 years and older with serious mental illness	58.7%	64.6%
MHMD-9.2	Adults aged 18 years and older with major depressive episode	71.1%	78.2%

Target-setting method: 10% improvement.

Data source: National Survey on Drug Use and Health (NSDUH), SAMHSA.

For Further Thought

Just over half of adults with serious mental illness received treatment in 2008. What reasons do you think contributed to this statistic? Do you think the Affordable Care Act of 2010 helped to increase the proportion of those who receive treatment so that the *Healthy People 2020* target (10% increase) can be met? One-third of adults with major depressive episodes do not receive treatment. How would reaching the *Healthy People 2020* target (10% increase in the proportion of adults with major depression who receive treatment) affect the overall adult suicide rate?

Data from: U.S. Department of Health and Human Services, Office of Disease Prevention and Health Promotion (2010). *Healthy People 2020.* Available at http://www.healthypeople.gov/2020/default.aspx. Accessed July 1, 2013.

We have seen that mental disorders are widely prevalent and can begin in adolescence, or even earlier. They entail not only neurobiological lesions that produce distortions in thinking and feeling but also deficits in coping skills that damage relationships, and stigma that interferes with social acceptance. Mental disorders can last a lifetime, and most who have them simply live with their symptoms (e.g., people with schizophrenia learn to tolerate voices in their head) just as people with chronic arthritis or diabetes live with their disabilities. Thus, today the primary objective is most often **recovery** rather than cure. Recovery from mental illness is social and economic as well as psychiatric. It means progress toward financial and residential independence, managing symptoms effectively, satisfaction with life, and basic "personhood"—that is, mental and physical well-being, supportive relationships, opportunities to spend time productively, and self-determination in exercising the adult rights and privileges that come with community life.[88]

Recovery requires change, such as community participation in the form of work, volunteer activities, the forming of new relationships, and sometimes parenthood. Change is difficult and brings added stress, making daily pursuit of recovery a challenge to persons with mental illness and the providers who work with them. The current recovery-oriented services are collectively known as **psychiatric rehabilitation**.[89] Psychiatric rehabilitation is modeled on rehabilitation practices for people with physical and developmental disabilities (e.g., independent living, gainful employment) and its services often carry the modifier support (as in supported employment, supported housing, supported education) in keeping with patient self-determination. Services include medication, therapy, and adaptive skills (e.g., helping a patient learn to use an Internet dating service) as needed, but also changing the environment through accommodations at work or school (e.g., extended time to complete tests and other assignments, use of aids such as tape recorders, and frequent breaks). In addition, practices are **evidence-based**, which means there is consistent evidence showing that they improve patient outcomes. The providers of psychiatric rehabilitation services typically represent diverse professional backgrounds (psychiatry, nursing, addictions, social work, and vocational services) and work collaboratively as an integrated team. Sometimes these team members are themselves recovering from mental illness, which brings a different perspective to the team's efforts.[90]

Recovery outcome sought by most people with mental illness; includes increased independence, effective coping, supportive relationships, community participation, and sometimes gainful employment

Psychiatric rehabilitation intensive, individualized services encompassing treatment, rehabilitation, and support delivered by a team of providers over an indefinite period to individuals with severe mental disorders to help them maintain stable lives in the community

Evidence-based way of delivering services to people using scientific evidence that shows that the services actually work

One of the best-known psychiatric rehabilitation services is **Assertive Community Treatment,** or ACT, which uses active outreach by a team of providers over an indefinite period of time to deliver intensive, individualized services (e.g., help finding a place to live, learning self-care skills needed for independence, using public transportation).[57] While ACT has been shown to reduce hospital use, it is expensive and critics have questioned its reliance on "legal leverage" and other coercive techniques that undermine privacy and autonomy of people in recovery.[91]

Another challenge of community life for people with serious mental illness is lack of employment, and over a third of them have annual incomes below $10,000.[92] Supported employment services help those wanting to work secure paid employment, and with it a higher quality of life and greater community integration. For example, **Individual Placement and Support** (IPS) is an evidence-based model that emphasizes real work opportunities matched to the individual's interests and values, integrated mental health and employment services, and individualized job supports. Even with such helpful resources, however, gainful employment for people with serious mental illness is usually part time and makes only a small difference in how much they earn and in their overall quality of life.[93] These modest recovery outcomes for adults with chronic histories of mental disorder have intensified the search for interventions to help younger people grappling with the earliest stages of mental illness. Besides medications and traditional treatment, these newer efforts offer help with jobs and school, as well as family counseling.[94]

Regardless of the effectiveness of formal services, recovery remains the overarching goal so that families and treatment providers do not underestimate what a person with mental illness can achieve in the world. Interestingly, recovery from disorders like schizophrenia tends to be better (with longer remissions and fewer relapses) in the developing world, including Africa, India, and Indonesia, than in developed countries such as the U.S.[95] Rather than being socially isolated, homeless, or in jail, for example, people in India who have schizophrenia are usually married and living with their families.[96] Non-western cultures use less stigmatizing explanations for mental illness and prescribe a recovery process that includes collaborative roles for everyone – patient, family, and community. In Tanzania, for example, supernatural spirits are believed to cause mental illness, which is seen as a stern test by God that a faithful person should accept with patience and grace. A person with mental illness is not a source of embarrassment needing coercion but a family member or neighbor whose odd behavior is dealt with gently and if possible without confrontation.[97] The lesson in recovery provided by these "less-developed" parts of the world is that mental disorders like schizophrenia are not just "broken brains" but also culturally determined social and moral phenomena that involve all of us.

Mental health care in the United States faces a number of serious challenges. Multiple services are needed by people with severe or comorbid disorders, and lack of some services (such as for addictions) limits the effectiveness of others (e.g., ACT). Staff turnover is relatively high in behavioral health care,[98] and successful psychosocial rehabilitation requires sustained commitment by staff to the principles of evidence-based practice and patient recovery.[99] People with serious mental illness still face high rates of poverty, social disadvantage, and stigma, and substantial recovery (e.g., stable, gainful employment) is achieved by relatively few of them.[55] Related to all these problems are the immediate and longer-term needs of family members of people with mental illness for information, financial help, coping with stigma, and sometimes therapeutic support for themselves.[100]

The mental health care system is very decentralized and fragmented, with many different kinds of providers.[55] General medical practitioners treat the largest number of people with mental disorders, with specialty mental health providers, human services, self-help groups, and various combinations serving the rest.[101] In 2006 there were about 350,000 licensed providers of mental health services (including psychiatrists, psychologists, social workers, psychiatric nurses, licensed counselors, and marital/family therapists) in the U.S., but relatively few of them served rural and low-income counties[102] (**Figure 11.14**). Patient sex, ethnicity, geography, immigration status, sexual orientation, and income are all related to the likelihood of receiving help. For example, racial-ethnic minorities are less engaged in therapy than are whites with

Assertive Community Treatment service that uses active outreach by a team of providers over an indefinite period of time to deliver intensive, individualized services

Individual Placement and Support an evidence-based model of employment services emphasizing real work opportunities, integrated mental health services, and individualized job supports

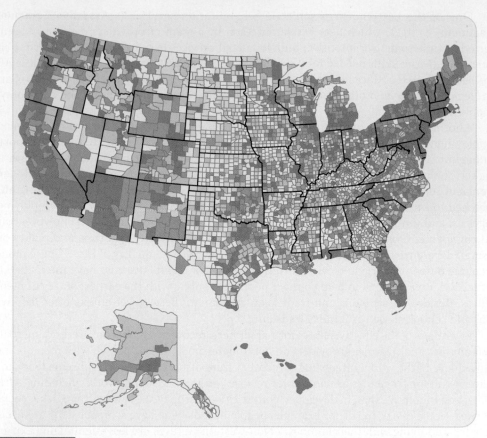

FIGURE 11.14   Number of mental health professionals, by county, for counties with mental health professionals (the darker the shading the higher the number of mental health professionals per 10,000 population).

Ellis, A., Konrad,T., Thomas, K., and Morrissey, J., (2009). "County-Level Estimates of Mental Health Professional Supply in the United States." Psychiatric Services, 60: 1315–1322. Reprinted with permission from Psychiatric Services (Copyright 2009). American Psychiatric Association.

respect to whether formal treatment is sought, the number of visits, retention in treatment, follow-up with aftercare, and adherence to medication.[103] The problem here may not be overt discrimination, but a lack of cultural competence on the part of providers regarding their multicultural patients' attitudes towards medications and medication side effects (such as weight gain), and patients' misguided expectations of treatment in the context of particular religious, spiritual, or folk beliefs.

Finally, in addition to their often pronounced deficits in thinking and coping, people with serious mental disorders tend to be among the poorest members of society and typically live in neighborhoods where crime, illicit drugs, victimization, homelessness, unemployment, and social disorganization are rampant.[104] It may be too much to expect that medications, psychotherapy, psychosocial rehabilitation, self-help, and other circumscribed supports and services are enough to overcome these systemic problems. From this vantage point, it is not the people with mental disorders who fail, but rather the communities and social systems they live in that have failed.

Government Policies and Mental Health Care

Until deinstitutionalization began in the 1950s, the state hospital system served as the de facto social insurance program for mental illness in the United States.[55] Following deinstitutionalization, the federal government's role in mental health funding and policy became substantial. For example, the federal Medicaid program now pays more than half of publicly funded mental health care, and its policies and regulations, which vary from state to state, impact what services are covered. Depending on individual state policies, Medicaid may pay for traditional services like inpatient hospitalization but not newer approaches such as psychiatric rehabilitation.

More recently the Mental Health Parity and Addiction Act of 2008 requires that if health care coverage includes mental health or substance abuse disorders there must be parity with physical disorders in any limitations or restrictions (i.e., any limits on the number of visits per year, annual or lifetime dollars spent, and deductibles or copayments must be the same for both mental and physical disorders). In combination with aggressive management of costs by provider organizations, **parity** has succeeded in removing previous insurance limitations that applied only to behavioral health care without unintended consequences such as eliminating behavioral health coverage.[105]

The Affordable Care Act

In 2010 Medicaid's important role in covering individuals with mental disorders grew even larger with the passage of the federal Patient Protection and **Affordable Care Act (ACA)**, the most ambitious expansion and regulatory overhaul of the U.S. health care system in 50 years. The ACA expands eligibility for public programs like Medicaid and increases the availability of private insurance, both of which must cover 10 essential benefits, including mental health and substance use disorder services. Millions of individuals have obtained coverage through Medicaid expansions, subsidies for private plans offered through state insurance exchanges, and the ACA provision requiring plans to cover children up to age 26 on their parents' policies.[106] Outcome studies to date have reported increased access to health care, reduced financial burden, and improvements in mental health, particularly depression.[107]

Historically, healing of mind and body was divided, with separate treatment and reimbursement systems. Parity and the ACA forged an opportunity to integrate mental health and general medical care by making it advantageous to deliver primary care and behavioral health services in the same conveniently located community settings. In this way recovery from mental illness becomes an integral part of physical well-being and overall wellness.

Integrative care is care a patient receives from a team of primary care and behavioral health clinicians, working together with patients and families, using shared, cost-effective care plans that incorporate patient goals.[108] Integrative care also increases opportunities for prevention through primary care practices such as behavioral health screening for depression, substance abuse, and domestic violence.[109]

Because individuals with mental disorders tend to have low incomes and are unlikely to be insured, they stand to be heavy consumers of care under the ACA, which could exacerbate the shortcomings of mental health services and the scarcity of professionals. In addition, the U.S. Supreme Court has allowed states to opt out of expanding Medicaid, giving state Medicaid policy makers considerable discretion in what coverages to provide and putting in doubt the status of costly services such as ACT and supported employment. By itself the ACA can do little to improve access to help if communities lack the necessary infrastructure to serve those in need, and thus the impact of the ACA on the overall rate of recovery from serious mental illness remains to be seen.[110]

These and other recent changes make it difficult to determine how the nation, states, and local communities will respond to the needs of those with mental illness in the future. The response will depend on economics, the degree to which taxpayers have been personally touched by mental illness, and the degree to which they are willing to tolerate the spectacle of homeless people with mental illness in their communities and in their jails and prisons. A key task facing communities is to find ways to unite formal services and informal supports to promote social inclusion and recovery by people who are coping with mental disorders.

Parity the concept of equality in health care coverage for people with mental illness and those with other medical illnesses or injuries

Affordable Care Act (ACA) federal legislation that expands eligibility for Medicaid and increases access to private insurance for low-income Americans not covered by employer-provided health insurance

Integrative care care a patient receives from a team of primary health care and behavioral health clinicians, working together with patients and families, using shared, cost-effective care plans that incorporate patient goals

Chapter Summary

- Mental illness constitutes a major community health concern because of its prevalence and chronicity, its effects on individual and community well-being, and the social, cultural, and economic attention and resources it demands from all of us.

- Americans are afflicted with a variety of mental disorders, caused by genetic factors, environmental factors, or a combination of both. These disorders, which can range from mild to severe, are often chronic and may limit the ability of some of those afflicted to live independently. The *Diagnostic and Statistical Manual of Mental Disorders, Fifth Edition (DSM-5)*, the most significant revision of the diagnostic system in almost 20 years, was published in 2013.

- Stress, resulting from social and environmental forces, can have a detrimental influence on both physical and mental health. Combat-zone military veterans and survivors of and responders to natural and human-made disasters are at especially high risk for developing mental disorders.

- Over the years, society's response to the needs of those with mental illness has been characterized by long periods of apathy interrupted by enthusiastic movements for new and enlightened approaches to care.

- Deinstitutionalization, in which hundreds of thousands of psychiatric patients housed in state and county hospitals were discharged and returned to their communities, was the most prominent movement of the twentieth century. The origins of many of the current problems in community mental health care, such as a large number of homeless people with mental illness, can be traced to this movement.

- Mass shootings have sometimes been linked to mental illness in media accounts and public perceptions, although most people with mental disorders are never violent and other factors (such as substance use and early trauma) also affect the likelihood of violence.

- Having serious mental illness can increase the risk that a person will become involved with the criminal justice system, raising a number of concerns about the use of incarceration and other traditional law enforcement practices in such cases.

- The basic concepts of prevention in community health (primary, secondary, and tertiary prevention) can be applied to reducing the incidence and prevalence of mental disorders.

- Among the most common approaches to treating mental disorders are psychopharmacology, which is based on the use of medications, and psychotherapy, including cognitive-behavioral therapy. Technology assumes an increasingly significant role in today's mental health services, and self-help groups provide additional support to people at risk for relapse.

- People with severe mental illness generally pursue recovery rather than cure. Recovery entails adaptive change, including increased independence, effective coping, supportive relationships, community participation, and sometimes gainful employment.

- Psychiatric rehabilitation programs for those with serious mental illness, such as Assertive Community Treatment and supported employment, represent the current "best practices" in support of recovery and community integration.

- The federal government now dominates overall mental health policy in the U.S. with its distribution of Medicaid funds and the enactment of the Affordable Care Act.

- Important issues face those concerned about people with mental disorders. The most daunting challenge is finding ways to provide a variety of easily accessible prevention and treatment services to people from culturally diverse backgrounds, who have multiple problems and few resources, in a climate where both the effectiveness of services and the cost of care are paramount concerns.

Scenario: Analysis and Response

1. Let's assume that Maria Sanchez is not alone in her concerns about Lynn, her new neighbor. Another neighbor, Paul, has called for a meeting of the residents to discuss this "new type" of resident. You are a resident too, and he is expecting you to attend. What is your response?

2. What worries might residents express regarding their new neighbor?

3. Would it make any difference to you whether Lynn found a job and was away at work during a good part of the day?

4. Do you suppose the landlord knew about Lynn's medical and criminal justice history when he or she rented the unit to her? Can landlords refuse to rent to someone like Lynn?

5. Are you aware of any federal laws, such as the Fair Housing Act or the Americans with Disabilities Act (ADA), which could bear on this matter?

6. If you were Maria, what would be your response? What would you do?

Resource: http://promoteacceptance.samhsa.gov/.

Review Questions

1. How prevalent is the problem of mental disorder in the United States?

2. How are mental disorders related to other chronic illnesses and overall life expectancy?

3. What is meant by the term mental health?

4. What are the characteristics of a mentally healthy person?

5. What is a mental disorder?

6. What is the *Diagnostic and Statistical Manual of Mental Disorders, Fifth Edition* (*DSM-5*)? How do issues of comorbidity and cultural competence affect the use of the *DSM-5*?

7. Give examples of the many different causes of mental disorders.

8. What is stress? Give some examples of stressors.

9. What is the relationship between stress and mental health?

10. How were people with mental illness cared for in Colonial America?

11. What was included in Tuke's therapy known as "moral treatment"?

12. What role did Dorothea Dix play in the care of indigent people with mental illness?

13. How would you characterize the treatment of those with mental illness in state hospitals prior to World War II?

14. What piece of legislation resulted in the establishment of the National Institute of Mental Health, and what were the purposes of the Institute?

15. Define the word deinstitutionalization. When did it start in the United States? What caused it?

16. What is a "chemical straitjacket"?

17. Why was there a movement to establish community mental health centers in the 1960s?

18. What services were originally provided by community mental health centers?

19. Why was the Community Support Program considered a novel approach to helping people with mental disorders?

20. Approximately what percentage of homeless people are living with mental illness?

21. What legal and practical concerns limit society's options for dealing with the potential for serious violence among people who have mental illness?

22. What number of state prison inmates are estimated to have mental health problems, and how does this compare with the prevalence of mental illness in the general U.S. population?

23. How are "outpatient commitment," "legal leverage," and "mental health courts" used to manage the risks that a person's mental illness will lead to self-harm and/or an adverse relationship with the criminal justice system?

24. Describe primary, secondary, and tertiary prevention of mental illness and give an example of a service for each level of prevention.

25. What is involved in psychotherapy for mental illness? In cognitive-behavioral therapy? In psychopharmacological therapy?

26. How is technology being used to improve the accessibility and flexibility of treatment services?

27. What are self-help groups? How do they supplement people's individual efforts to cope with long-term disorders?

28. What is meant by "recovery" from serious mental illness? How do psychiatric rehabilitation services like Assertive Community Treatment and supported employment promote recovery?

29. What kinds of clinical, multicultural, practical, and political challenges do mental health care efforts face early in the twenty-first century?

30. What role does federal government policy play in supporting care for people with mental illness in the United States?

Activities

1. Make a list of all the stressors you have experienced in the last 2 weeks. Select two of the items on the list and answer the following questions about them:
   - Did you realize the stressor was a stressor when you first confronted it? Explain.
   - What physiological responses did you notice that you had when confronted with the stressor?
   - Have you confronted the stressor before? Explain your answer.
   - What stress mediators (coping responses) do you have to deal with each of the stressors?
   - Do you feel you will some day fall victim to a disease of adaptation?

2. Using the Internet, identify the organizations in the community that you believe would provide mental health services. Then create a list of the agencies/organizations. Divide the list into three sections based upon the type of service (primary, secondary, tertiary prevention) offered. If you are not sure what type of services are offered, call the agency/organization to find out. After you have completed your list, write a paragraph or two about what you feel to be the status of mental health care in your community.

3. Make an appointment with someone in the counseling and psychological service center on your campus for an orientation to the services offered by the center. Most mental health services range from stress management to test anxiety to individual counseling. Find out what your school has to offer and write a one-page summary of available services.

4. Call agencies or service groups in your community to find out what services are needed for people who are homeless. Also find out how serious the homeless situation is in the community and what plans there are to deal with the problem. Summarize your findings in a two-page paper. Agencies or services to call include the American Red Cross, the local police department, the Salvation Army, the local soup kitchen, a community mental health center, local hospitals, local homeless shelters, and other shelters.

5. Look online or call the community information/crisis center to locate a mental health or substance abuse self-help group. Call the group's number and find out what kinds of open meetings or public education activities they have.

References

1. Eaton, W., S. Martins, G. Nestadt, O. Bienvenu, D. Clarke, and P. Alexandre (2008). "The Burden of Mental Disorders." *Epidemiologic Reviews*, 30: 1–14.

2. Chesney, E., E. Goodwin, and S. Fazel (2014). "Risks of All-Cause and Suicide Mortality in Mental Disorders: A Meta-Review." *World Psychiatry*, 13(2): 153–160.

3. Prince, M., V. Patel, S. Saxena, M. Maj, J. Maselko, and M. Phillips (2007). "Global Mental Health 1: No Health without Mental Health." *The Lancet*, 370(9590): 859–877.

4. Substance Abuse and Mental Health Services Administration (2012). *Mental Health, United States, 2010*. HHS Publication No. (SMA) 12-4681. Rockville, MD: Author.

5. Blanco, C., O. Mayumi, C. Wright, et al. (2008). "Mental Health of College Students and Their Non-College-Attending Peers." *Archives of General Psychiatry*, 65(12): 1429–1437.

6. Substance Abuse and Mental Health Services Administration (2012). *Results from the 2010 National Survey on Drug Use and Health: Mental Health Findings*. NSDUH Series H-42, HHS Publication No. (SMA) 11-4667. Rockville, MD: Author.

7. U.S. Department of Health and Human Services (1999). *Mental Health: A Report of the Surgeon General*. Rockville, MD: Substance Abuse and Mental Health Services Administration.

8. American Psychiatric Association (2013). *Diagnostic and Statistical Manual of Mental Disorders*, Fifth *Edition*. Arlington, VA: American Psychiatric Association.

9. Mojtabai, R. (2011). "Bereavement-Related Depressive Episodes." *Archives of General Psychiatry*. 68(9): 920–928.

10. Geschwind, D. H., and J. Flint (2015). "Genetics and Genomics of Psychiatric Disease." *Science*, 349(6255): 1489–1494.

11. Kessler, R. C., W. T. Chiu, O. Demler, and E. E. Walters (2005). "Prevalence, Severity, and Comorbidity of Twelve-Month DSM-IV Disorders in the National Comorbidity Survey Replication (NCS-R)." *Archives of General Psychiatry*, 62(6): 617–627.

12. Moffit, T., H. Harrington, A. Caspi, et al. (2007). "Depression and Generalized Anxiety Disorder." *Archives of General Psychiatry*, 64: 651–660.

13. Holden, C. (2010). "Experts Map the Terrain of Mood Disorders." *Science*, 327: 1068.

14. Gara, M., W. Vega, S. Arndt, M. Escamilla, D. Fleck, et al. (2012). "Influence of Patient Race and Ethnicity on Clinical Assessment in Patients with Affective Disorders." *Archives of General Psychiatry*. 69(6): 593–600.

15. Eack, S., A. Bahorik, C. Newhill, H. Neighbors, and L. Davis (2012). "Interviewer-Perceived Honesty as a Mediator of Racial Disparities in the Diagnosis of Schizophrenia." *Psychiatric Services*, 63: 875–880.

16. Hernandez, N., T. Nesman, D. Mowery, et al. (2009). "Cultural Competence: A Literature Review and Conceptual Model for Mental Health Services." *Psychiatric Services*, 60: 1046–1050.

17. Seedat, S., K. Scott, M. Angermeyer, et al. (2009). "Cross-National Associations between Gender and Mental Disorders in the World Health Organization World Mental Health Surveys." *Archives of General Psychiatry*, 66 (7), 785–795.

18. Corrigan, P. W. (2015). "Challenging the Stigma of Mental Illness: Different Agendas, Different Goals." *Psychiatric Services*, (66): 1347–1349.

19. D'Onofrio, B. M., M. Rickert, E. Frans, et al. (2014). "Paternal Age at Childbearing and Offspring Psychiatric and Academic Morbidity." *JAMA Psychiatry*, 71(4): 432–438.

20. Brown, A., and E. Derkits (2010). "Prenatal Infection and Schizophrenia: A Review of Epidemiologic and Translational Studies." *American Journal of Psychiatry*, 167: 261–280.

21. Nosarti, C. A. Reichenberg, R. Murray, et al. (2012). "Preterm Birth and Psychiatric Disorders in Young Adult Life." *Archives of General Psychiatry*. 69(6): 610–617.

22. Hamer, M., E. Stamatakis, and G. Batty (2010). "Objectively Assessed Secondhand Smoke Exposure and Mental Health in Adults." *Archives of General Psychiatry*, 67(8): 850–855.

23. Orlovska, S., M. Pedersen, M. Benros, P. Mortensen, E. Agerbo, and M. Nordentoft (2014). "Head Injury as Risk Factor for Psychiatric Disorders: A Nationwide Register-Based Follow-up Study of 113,906 Persons with Head Injury." *American Journal of Psychiatry*, 171: 463–469.

24. Centers for Disease Control and Prevention (2013). "Mental Health Surveillance Among Children — United States, 2005–2011." *Morbidity and Mortality Weekly Report*, 62(Suppl 2).

25. Costello, E. J., J-P. He, N. A. Sampson, R. C. Kessler, and K. R. Merikangas (2014). "Services for Adolescents with Psychiatric Disorders: 12-Month Data from the National Comorbidity Survey–Adolescent." *Psychiatric Services*, 65: 359–366.

26. Lee, F. S., H. Heimer, J. N. Giedd, et al. (2014). "Adolescent Mental Health—Opportunity and Obligation." *Science*, 346(6209): 547–549.

27. Brent, D., and M. Silverstein (2013). "Shedding Light on the Long Shadow of Childhood Adversity." *Journal of the American Medical Association*, 309(17): 1777–1778.

28. Gilbert, R., C. Widom, K. Browne, et al. (2009). "Burden and Consequences of Child Maltreatment in High-Income Countries." *Lancet*, 373(9657): 68–81.

29. Copeland, W., D. Wolke, A. Angold, and E. Costello (2013). "Adult Psychiatric Outcomes of Bullying and Being Bullied by Peers in Childhood and Adolescence." *JAMA Psychiatry*, 70(4): 419–426.

30. Compton, M.T., and R. C. Shim (2015). *The Social Determinants of Mental Health*. Washington, DC: American Psychiatric Association.

31. Charles, S. T., J. R. Piazza, J. Mogle, M. J. Sliwinski, and D. M. Almeida (2013). "The Wear and Tear of Daily Stressors on Mental Health." *Psychological Science*, 24(5): 733–741.

32. Sederer, L. I. (2016). "The Social Determinants of Mental Health." *Psychiatric Services*, 67: 234–235.

33. Selye, H. (1946). "The General Adaptation Syndrome and Disease of Adaptation." *Journal of Clinical Endocrinology and Metabolism*, 6: 117–130.

34. Abbott, A. (2012). "Urban Decay." *Nature*, 490: 162–164.

35. Lederbogen, F., P. Kirsch, L. Haddad, et al. (2011). "City Living and Urban Upbringing Affect Neural Social Stress Processing in Humans." *Nature*, 474: 498–501.

36. Baer, P. E., L. B. Garmezy, R. J. McLaughlin, A. D. Pokorny, and M. J. Wernick (1987). "Stress, Coping, Family Conflict, and Adolescent Alcohol Use." *Journal of Behavioral Medicine*, 10: 449–466.

37. Conway, T. L., R. R. Vickers, H. W. Ward, and R. H. Rahe (1981). "Occupational Stress and Variation in Cigarette, Coffee, and Alcohol Consumption." *Journal of Health and Social Behavior*, 22: 155–165.

38. House, J. S., Landis, K. R., and D. Umberson (1988). "Social Relationships and Health." *Science*, 241: 540–545.

39. Payne, W. A., D. B. Hahn, and E. B. Lucas (2006). *Understanding Your Health*, 9th ed. New York: McGraw-Hill Higher Education.

40. Galea, S., J. Ahern, H. Resnick, D. Kilpatrick, M. Bucuvalas, J. Gold, and D. Vlahov (2002). "Psychological Sequelae of the September 11 Terrorist Attacks in New York City." *New England Journal of Medicine*, 346(13): 982–1087.

41. Reardon, S. (2015). "Hurricane Katrina's Psychological Scars Revealed." *Nature*, 524: 395–396.

42. Kessler, R. C., S. G. Heeringa, M. B. Stein, et al. (2014). "Thirty-Day Prevalence of *DSM-IV* Mental Disorders among Nondeployed Soldiers in the US Army." *JAMA Psychiatry*, 71(5): 504–513.

43. Schoenbaum, M., R. C. Kessler, S. E. Gilman, et al. (2014). "Predictors of Suicide and Accident Death in the Army Study to Assess Risk and Resilience in Service Members (Army STARRS)." *JAMA Psychiatry*, 71(5): 493–503.

44. Case, A., and A. Deaton (2015). "Rising Morbidity and Mortality in Midlife among White Non-Hispanic Americans in the 21st Century." *Proceedings of the National Academy of Sciences*, 112(49): 15078–15083.

45. Dumesnil, H., and Verger, P. (2009). "Public Awareness Campaigns about Depression and Suicide: A Review." *Psychiatric Services*, 60(9): 1203–1213.

46. Johnston, L. D., P. M. O'Malley, J. G. Bachman, and J. E. Schulenbert (2006). *Monitoring the Future National Survey Results on Drug Use 1975–2005. Vol. I: Secondary School Students (NIH pub. no. 06-5883)*. Rockville, MD: National Institute on Drug Abuse. Available at http://www.monitoringthefuture.org/pubs/.

47. Grob, G. N. (1994). *The Mad among Us: A History of the Care of America's Mentally Ill*. New York: The Free Press.

48. Johnson, A. B. (1990). *Out of Bedlam: The Truth about Deinstitutionalization*. New York: Basic Books, 306.

49. Gerhart, U. C. (1990). *Caring for the Chronic Mentally Ill*. Itasca, IL: F. E. Peacock, 5.

50. Mosher, L. R., and L. Burti (1989). *Community Mental Health*. New York: W. W. Norton.

51. Foley, H. A., and S. S. Sharfstein (1983). *Madness and Government*. Washington, DC: American Psychiatric Press.

52. Kellner, C. H., R. M. Greenberg, J. W. Murrough, E. O. Bryson, M. C. Briggs, and R. M. Pasculli (2012). "ECT in Treatment-Resistant Depression." *American Journal of Psychiatry*, 169(12): 1238–1244.

53. El Hai, J. (2005). *The Lobotomist*. New York: Wiley.

54. Grob, G. N. (1991). *From Asylum to Community*. Princeton, NJ: Princeton University Press.

55. Frank, R. G., and S. A. Glied (2006). *Better but not Well*. Baltimore: Johns Hopkins University Press.

56. Bloom, B. (1984). *Community Mental Health*, 2nd ed. Belmont, CA: Wadsworth.

57. Levine, M., P. A. Toro, and D. V. Perkins (1993). "Social and Community Interventions." *Annual Review of Psychology*, 44: 525–558.

58. U.S. Department of Health and Human Services, Substance Abuse and Mental Health Services Administration (2003). Blueprint for Change: Ending Chronic Homelessness for Persons with Serious Mental Illnesses and/or Co-Occurring Substance Use Disorders (DHHS pub. no. SMA-04-3870). Rockville, MD: Author.

59. Schanzer, B., D. Boanerges, P. E. Shrout, and L. M. Caton (2007). "Homelessness, Health Status, and Health Care Use." *American Journal of Public Health*, 97(3): 464–469.

60. Roy, L., A. G. Crocker, T. L. Nicholls, E. A. Latimer, and A. R. Ayllon (2014). "Criminal Behavior and Victimization Among Homeless Individuals with Severe Mental Illness: A Systematic Review." *Psychiatric Services*, 65: 739–750.

61. Gulcur, L., S. Tsemberis, A. Stefancic, and R. M. Greenwood (2007). "Community Integration of Adults with Psychiatric Disabilities and Histories of Homelessness." *Community Mental Health Journal*, 43(3): 211–228.

62. Gilmer, T., A. Stefancic, S. Ettner, W. Manning, and S. Tsemberis (2010). "Effect of Full-Service Partnerships on Homelessness, Use and Costs of Mental Health Services, and Quality of Life among Adults with Serious Mental Illness." *Archives of General Psychiatry*, 67(6): 645–652.

63. McGinty E., D. Webster, and C. Barry (2013). "Effects of News Media Messages about Mass Shootings on Attitudes Toward Persons with Serious Mental Illness and Public Support for Gun Control Policies." *American Journal of Psychiatry*, 170: 494–501.

64. Metzl, J. M., and K. T. MacLeish (2015). "Mental Illness, Mass Shootings, and the Politics of American Firearms." *American Journal of Public Health*, 105: 240–249.

65. Steadman, H. J., J. Monahan, D. A. Pinals, R. Vesselinov, and P. C. Robbins (2015). "Gun Violence and Victimization of Strangers by Persons with a Mental Illness: Data From the MacArthur Violence Risk Assessment Study." *Psychiatric Services*, 66: 1238–1241.

66. Swanson, J. W., E. E. McGinty, S. Fazel, and V. M. Mays (2015). "Mental Illness and Reduction of Gun Violence and Suicide: Bringing Epidemiologic Research to Policy." *Annals of Epidemiology*, 25: 366–376.

67. Mozaffarian, D., D. Hemenway, and D. Ludwig (2013). "Curbing Gun Violence: Lessons from Public Health Successes." *Journal of the American Medical Association*, 309(6): 551–552.

68. Torrey, E. F., M. Zdanowicz, A. Kennard, et al. (2014). "The Treatment of Persons With Mental Illness in Prisons and Jails: A State Survey." Arlington, VA, Treatment Advocacy Center. Available at http://www.tacreports.org/storage/documents/treatment-behind-bars/treatment-behind-bars.pdf.

69. Steadman, H. J., F. C. Osher, P. C. Robbins, et al. (2009). "Prevalence of Serious Mental Illness among Jail Inmates." *Psychiatric Services*, 60: 761–765.

70. Metzner, J. L. (2012). "Treatment for Prisoners: A U.S. Perspective." *Psychiatric Services*, 63: 276.

71. Moore, S. (10 August 2009). "Mentally Ill Offenders Strain Juvenile System." *The New York Times*, A1.

72. Fovet, T., P. A. Geoffroy, G. Vaiva, et al. (2015). "Individuals with Bipolar Disorder and Their Relationship with the Criminal Justice System: A Critical Review." *Psychiatric Services*, 66: 348–353.

73. Compton, M. T., R. Bakeman, B. Broussard, et al. (2014). "The Police-Based Crisis Intervention Team (CIT) Model: I. Effects on Officers' Knowledge, Attitudes, and Skills. *Psychiatric Services*, 65(4): 517–522.

74. Cross, A. B., E. P. Mulvey, C. A. Schubert, et al. (2014). "An Agenda for Advancing Research on Crisis Intervention Teams for Mental Health Emergencies." *Psychiatric Services*, 65: 530–536.

75. Swanson, J., Van Dorn, R., Monahan, J., and Swartz, R. (2006). "Violence and Leveraged Treatment for Persons with Mental Disorders". *American Journal of Psychiatry*, 163: 1404–1411.

76. Scott, D. A., S. McGilloway, M. Dempster, F. Browne, and M. Donnelly (2013) "Effectiveness of Criminal Justice Liaison and Diversion Services for Offenders With Mental Disorders: A Review." *Psychiatric Services*, 64: 843–849.

77. McNiel, D. E., N. Sadeh, K. L. Delucchi, and R. L. Binder (2015). "Prospective Study of Violence Risk Reduction by a Mental Health Court." *Psychiatric Services*, 66: 598–603.

78. Ludwig, J., G. J. Duncan, L. A. Gennetian, et al. (2012). "Neighborhood Effects on the Long-Term Well-Being of Low-Income Adults." *Science*, 337(6101): 1505–1510.

79. Adler, A. B., R. D. Bliese, D. McGurk, S. W. Hoge, and C. A. Castro (2009). "Battlemind Debriefing and Battlemind Training as Early Interventions with Soldiers Returning from Iraq: Randomization by Platoon." *Journal of Consulting and Clinical Psychology*, 77: 928–940.

80. Levine, M., D. D. Perkins, and D. V. Perkins (2004). *Principles of Community Psychology: Perspectives and Applications*, 3rd ed. New York: Oxford University Press.

81. Olfson, M., C. Blanco, S.-M. Liu, S. Wang, and C. U. Correll (2012). "National Trends in the Office-Based Treatment of Children, Adolescents, and Adults with Antipsychotics." *Archives of General Psychiatry*, 69(12): 1247–1256.

82. Gaynes, B., D. Warden, M. Trivedi, et al. (2009). "What Did STAR*D Teach Us? Results from a Large-Scale, Practical, Clinical Trial for Patients with Depression." *Psychiatric Services*, 60: 1439–1445.

83. Sajatovic, M., M. Valenstein, F. Blow, D. Ganoczy, and R. Ignacio (2007). "Treatment Adherence with Lithium and Anticonvulsant Medications among Patients with Bipolar Disorder." *Psychiatric Services*, 58: 855–863.

84. Guidi, J., E. Tomba, and G. A. Fava (2016). "The Sequential Integration of Pharmacotherapy and Psychotherapy in the Treatment of Major Depressive Disorder: A Meta-Analysis of the Sequential Model and a Critical Review of the Literature." *American Journal of Psychiatry*, 173(2): 128–137.

85. Anthes, E. (2016). "Pocket Psychiatry." *Nature*, 532(7597): 20-23.

86. Rotondi, A. J., C. M. Anderson, G. L Haas, et al. (2010). "Web-Based Psychoeducational Intervention for Persons with Schizophrenia and Their Supporters: One-Year Outcomes." *Psychiatric Services*, 61: 1099–1105.

87. Andersson, G., P. Cuijpers, P. Carlbring, H. Riper, and E. Hedman (2014). "Guided Internet-Based vs. Face-to-Face Cognitive Behavior Therapy for Psychiatric and Somatic Disorders: A Systematic Review and Meta-Analysis." *World Psychiatry*, 13: 288–295.

88. Ware, N., K. Hopper, T. Tugenberg, et al. (2007). "Connectedness and Citizenship: Redefining Social Integration. *Psychiatric Services*, 58: 469–474.

89. Corrigan, P., Mueser, K., Bond, G., Drake, R., and Solomon, P. (2008). *Principles and Practice of Psychiatric Rehabilitation: An Empirical Approach*. New York: Guilford.

90. Austin, E., A. Ramakrishnan, and K. Hopper (2014). "Embodying Recovery: A Qualitative Study of Peer Work in a Consumer-Run Service Setting." *Community Mental Health Journal*, 50: 879–885.

91. Manuel, J. I., P. S. Appelbaum, S. M. Le Melle, et al. (2013). "Use of Intervention Strategies by Assertive Community Treatment Teams to Promote Patients' Engagement." *Psychiatric Services*, 64: 579–585.

92. Luciano, A., and E. Meara, (2014). "Employment Status of People with Mental Illness: National Survey Data From 2009 and 2010." *Psychiatric Services*, 65: 1201–1209.

93. Drake, R. E., W. Frey, G. R. Bond, et al. (2013). "Assisting Social Security Disability Insurance Beneficiaries with Schizophrenia, Bipolar Disorder, or Major Depression in Returning to Work." *American Journal of Psychiatry*, 170: 1433–1441.

94. Kane, J. M., D. G. Robinson, N. R. Schooler, et al. (2015 October 20). "Comprehensive versus Usual Community Care for First-Episode Psychosis: 2-Year Outcomes from the NIMH RAISE Early Treatment Program." *American Journal of Psychiatry* (Epub ahead of print)

95. Hopper, K. (2004). "Interrogating the Meaning of 'Culture' in the WHO International Studies of Schizophrenia." In J. Jenkins and R., Barrett (eds.), *Schizophrenia, Culture, and Subjectivity: The Edge of Experience*. Cambridge, UK: Cambridge University Press, 62–86.

96. Miller, G. (2006). "A Spoonful of Medicine—and a Steady Diet of Normality." *Science*, 311: 464–465.

97. McGruder, J. (2004). "Madness in Zanzibar: An Exploration of Lived Experience." In J. Jenkins and R. Barrett (eds.), *Schizophrenia, Culture, and Subjectivity: The Edge of Experience*. Cambridge, UK: Cambridge University Press, 255–281.

98. Woltmann, E. M., R. Whitley, G. J. McHugo, et al. (2008). "The Role of Staff Turnover in the Implementation of Evidence-Based Practices in Mental Health Care." *Psychiatric Services*, 59: 732–737.

99. Marshall, T., C. A. Rapp, D. R. Becker, and G. R. Bond (2008). "Key Factors for Implementing Supported Employment." *Psychiatric Services*, 59: 886–892.

100. Drapalski, A. L., T. Marshall, D. Seybolt, et al. (2008). "Unmet Needs of Families of Adults with Mental Illness and Preferences Regarding Family Services." *Psychiatric Services*, 59: 655–662.

101. Interian, A., R. Lewis-Fernández, and L. B. Dixon (2013). "Improving Treatment Engagement of Underserved U.S. Racial-Ethnic Groups: A Review of Recent Interventions." *Psychiatric Services*, 64: 212–222.

102. Thomas, K., A. Ellis, T. Konrad, et al. (2009). "County-Level Estimate of Mental Health Professional Shortage in the United States." *Psychiatric Services*, 60: 1323–1328.

103. Wang, P., O. Demler, M. Olfson, et al. (2006). "Changing Profiles of Service Sectors Used for Mental Health Care in the United States." *American Journal of Psychiatry*, 163: 1187–1198.

104. Byrne, T., J. P. Bettger, E. Brusilovskiy, Y-L. I. Wong, S. Metraux, and M. S. Salzer (2013). "Comparing Neighborhoods of Adults With Serious Mental Illness and of the General Population: Research Implications." *Psychiatric Services*, 64: 782–788.

105. Horgan, C. M., D. Hodgkin, M. T. Stewart, et al. (2016). "Health Plans' Early Response to Federal Parity Legislation for Mental Health and Addiction Services." *Psychiatric Services*, 67(2): 162–168.

106. Beronio, K., S. Glied, and R. Frank (2014) "How the Affordable Care Act and Mental Health Parity and Addiction Equity Act Greatly Expand Coverage of Behavioral Health Care." *Journal of Behavioral Health Services and Research*, 41: 410–428.

107. Baicker, K., S. L. Taubman, H. L. Allen, et al. (2013). "The Oregon Experiment —Effects of Medicaid on Clinical Outcomes." *New England Journal of Medicine*, 368: 1713–22.

108. Raney, L. E. (2015). "Integrating Primary Care and Behavioral Health: The Role of the Psychiatrist in the Collaborative Care Model." *American Journal of Psychiatry*, 172: 8, 721–728.

109. Shim, R. S., C. Koplan, F. J. P. Langheim, et al. (2012). "Health Care Reform and Integrated Care: A Golden Opportunity for Preventive Psychiatry." *Psychiatric Services*, 63: 1231–1233.

110. Roll, J. M., J. Kennedy, M. Tran, and D. Howell (2013). "Disparities in Unmet Need for Mental Health Services in the United States, 1997–2010." *Psychiatric Services*, 64: 80–82.

CHAPTER 12

Alcohol, Tobacco, and Other Drugs: A Community Concern

Chapter Outline

Scenario
Introduction
  Scope of the Current Drug Problem in the United States
  Definitions
Factors that Contribute to Alcohol, Tobacco, and Other Drug Abuse
  Inherited Risk Factors
  Environmental Risk Factors
Types of Drugs Abused and Resulting Problems
  Legal Drugs
  Controlled Substances and Illicit (Illegal) Drugs

Prevention and Control of Drug Abuse
  Levels of Prevention
  Elements of Prevention
  Governmental Drug Prevention and Control Agencies and Programs
  Nongovernmental Drug Prevention and Control Agencies and Programs
Chapter Summary
Scenario: Analysis and Response
Review Questions
Activities
References

Chapter Objectives

After studying this chapter, you will be able to:

1. Identify personal and community consequences of alcohol and other drug abuse.
2. Describe the trends of alcohol and other drug use by high school students.
3. Define drug use, misuse, and abuse.
4. Define drug dependence.
5. List and discuss the risk factors for the abuse of alcohol and other drugs.
6. Explain why alcohol is considered the number one drug abuse problem in the United States.
7. Describe the health risks of cigarette smoking.

8. Define the terms over-the-counter and prescription drugs and explain the purposes of these drugs and how they are regulated.
9. Define the terms controlled substances and illicit (illegal) drugs and provide examples.
10. Characterize recent trends in the prevalence of drug use among American high school seniors.
11. List and explain four elements of drug abuse prevention and control.
12. Give an example of primary, secondary, and tertiary prevention activities in drug abuse prevention and control programs.

13. Summarize the federal government's drug abuse control efforts.

14. List and describe an effective community and an effective school drug abuse prevention program.

15. List the five facets of a typical workplace substance abuse prevention program.

16. Name some voluntary health agencies and self-help support groups involved in the prevention, control, and treatment of alcohol, tobacco, and other drug abuse.

Scenario

Andy is 36 years old. He lives in the suburbs with his wife, Sara, and their twin boys. Andy and Sara have been married for 10 years. Andy works fulltime as a sales consultant for a mid-size company, where he has been employed since he graduated with his MBA 8 years ago. He also leads the local chamber of commerce. Andy plays soccer in a local adult co-ed league, and he coaches his boys' soccer team on the weekends. He and Sara are very social and spend a lot of time out in the community with friends.

Last year, Andy hurt his knee playing soccer. He had reconstructive knee surgery to repair a torn ligament. His doctor prescribed an opioid pain reliever to help with pain management following surgery. Andy was given a 2-week supply. The medication helped, and Andy looked forward to starting physical therapy the week after surgery. The first physical therapy appointment went well, but Andy was in a lot of pain. The pain was so bad that he thought of little else, had trouble sleeping, and was very discouraged. The physical therapist recommended an over-the-counter pain reliever, rest, elevation, and ice. Andy followed this regimen and continued to take the opioid pain reliever as prescribed. He ran out of his medication after 2 weeks, 2 days before his 2-week, post-operative checkup with his surgeon. During those 2 days, Andy took over-the-counter pain relievers, but he felt he could not get a handle on his pain. He also felt down and repeatedly thought, "If only I had the opioid medication, I would be fine."

At Andy's checkup with his surgeon, he talked about his high level of pain, how well the opioid pain reliever was working, and how much progress he was able to make in physical therapy when he was taking it. He also told the surgeon that he tried over-the-counter pain relievers but they did not help. He asked for a refill of the opioid pain reliever, and the surgeon agreed to prescribe another 2-week supply. They would reevaluate things in 2 weeks at the next appointment. At first, Andy took the opioid pain reliever as prescribed. As he continued with physical therapy, though, he realized that he needed to take more of the medication to get the same effect. This led to him taking the medication more times a day than prescribed. After a week, Andy ran out of the medication. He quickly noticed a change

in how he was feeling—when he was on the medication, he felt great about himself and had little pain, but when he was off the medication, he felt awful. He knew he could not tell his doctor that he ran out, and so he turned to over-the-counter medications, taking and misusing a combination of ibuprofen, acetaminophen, and naproxen as soon as he felt any twinge of pain. However, he could not recapture the sense of well-being he felt when he was taking the opioid pain reliever.

At his next checkup, Andy asked the surgeon for another refill. At first, the surgeon said no and recommended over-the-counter pain relievers from that point on. After Andy stated his case, however, the surgeon relented, giving him another 2-week supply. The surgeon made it clear that this would be the last opioid pain reliever prescription he would receive.

Andy finished the prescription in less than a week and was consumed with dread for how he would feel without it. Andy had a friend at work who recently had back surgery and who had been prescribed the same opioid pain reliever. The friend did not respond well to the medication and never finished the prescription. Andy asked him if he could have his extra pills, and the friend gave them to him.

Over the next 6 months, Andy became addicted to opioid pain relievers, needing more and more to achieve the same sense of well-being. Andy desperately sought more pills through legal and illegal channels. He intermittently took money out of the joint savings account that he and Sara shared, hoping that Sara would not notice, to pay for his expensive addiction. She knew something was wrong but when she asked him about it, he yelled at her, lied that everything was fine, and started pushing her away. Andy stopped showing up to his boys' soccer games and started dropping out of social obligations. His work was affected too as he became unreliable, especially if he ran out of pills and experienced withdrawal. He met someone who told him that heroin had the same effect as opioid pain relievers but was a much cheaper option. Andy agreed to try it one time. He overdosed but did not die. The paramedics who found him administered naloxone, which saved his life. He is now in a drug rehabilitation program and on long-term disability from his job.

Introduction

The use, misuse, and abuse of mind-altering substances undoubtedly predates our recorded history. Early civilizations may have used drugs as a vehicle to communicate with spirits. Even today, drugs are used for this purpose in some cultures.

For many Americans, drug-taking is experimental or social, a temporary departure from a natural, nondrugged physical and mental state. For many others, it is a misguided attempt to self-medicate or to cope with personal problems such as depression, loneliness, guilt, or low self-esteem. For a small but significant segment of the population, drug-taking ceases to be a matter of conscious choice; these people have become chronic drug abusers or drug dependent. In most cultures, chronic alcohol or other drug abuse or dependence is regarded as destructive behavior, both to oneself and to the surrounding community. Community members whose lives center around drug acquisition and use usually provide little benefit to their communities and often detract from their communities.

Scope of the Current Drug Problem in the United States

More deaths, illnesses, and disabilities can be attributed to the abuse of alcohol, tobacco, and other drugs than to any other preventable health condition.[1] About one-fourth of the approximately 2.5 million deaths each year are due to alcohol, tobacco, or illicit drug use (see **Table 12.1**). In 2011, 2.4 million emergency department visits were due to drug use and misuse.[2] The estimated economic cost of substance abuse in the United States is more than $700 billion per year.[3-5] These estimates include direct costs (such as health care expenditures, premature death, and impaired productivity) and indirect costs, which include the costs of crime and law enforcement, courts, jails, and social work. Of the $742 billion annual drug bill, the cost of alcohol abuse and alcoholism is estimated at $249 billion, drug abuse at $193 billion, and smoking at $300 billion (see Table 12.1).[3-5] Another study estimates that federal, state, and local governments spend $467.7 billion as a result of substance abuse and addiction: $238.2 billion by federal, $135.8 by state, and $93.8 billion by local governments.

TABLE 12.1   The Annual Cost in Lives and Dollars Attributable to Alcohol, Tobacco, and Illicit Drug Abuse in the United States

Type of Drug	Estimated Number of Deaths Each Year	Economic Cost to Society (in Billions)
Alcohol	87,798	$249
Tobacco	480,000	$300
Illicit drugs	47,055	$193
TOTAL	614,853	$742

Data from: Horgan, C., K. C. Skwara, and G. Strickler (2001). *Substance Abuse: The Nation's Number One Health Problem*. Princeton, NJ: Robert Wood Johnson Foundation; Centers for Disease Control and Prevention (2008). "Smoking-Attributable Mortality, Years of Potential Life Lost, and Productivity Losses—United States, 2000–2004." *Morbidity and Mortality Weekly Report*, 57(45): 1226–1228; Centers for Disease Control and Prevention (2016). *Data on Drug-Poisoning Deaths*. National Center for Health Statistics. Available at http://www.cdc.gov/nchs/data/factsheets/factsheet_drug_poisoning.htm; Centers for Disease Control and Prevention (2013). Alcohol-Related Disease Impact (ARDI) application. Available at www.cdc.gov/ARDI; Sacks, J. J., K. R. Gonzales, E. E. Bouchery, L. E. Tomedi, and R. D. Brewer (2015). "2010 National and State Costs of Excessive Alcohol Consumption." *American Journal of Preventive Medicine*, 49(5): e73–e79.; Xu, X., E. E. Bishop, S. M. Kennedy, S. A. Simpson, and T. F. Pechacek (2014). "Annual Health care Spending Attributable to Cigarette Smoking: An Update." *American Journal of Preventive Medicine*, 48(3): 326–33; National Institute on Drug Abuse (2014). *Trends and Statistics*. Available at https://www.drugabuse.gov/related-topics/trends-statistics#costs; and U.S. Department of Health and Human Services (2014). *The Health Consequences of Smoking—50 Years of Progress: A Report of the Surgeon General*. Atlanta, GA: U.S. Department of Health and Human Services, Centers for Disease Control and Prevention, National Center for Chronic Disease Prevention and Health Promotion, Office on Smoking and Health. Available at http://www.cdc.gov/tobacco/data_statistics/sgr/50th-anniversary/index.htm.

This spending amounted to 10.7% of their entire $4.4 trillion budgets.[6] Clearly, the abuse of alcohol and other drugs is one of the United States' most expensive community and public health problems.

Those abusing alcohol and other drugs represent serious health threats to themselves, their families, and their communities. They are a threat to themselves and their families because they put themselves and their families at risk for physical, mental, and financial ruin. The habitual drug user may develop a psychological and/or **physical dependence** on the drug and thus experience great difficulty in discontinuing use, even in the face of deteriorating physical and mental health and erosion of financial resources. If the drug is an illegal one, its use constitutes criminal activity and may carry with it the added risks of arrest and incarceration.

Abusers of alcohol and other drugs represent a serious threat to the community because they have greater health care needs, suffer more injuries, and are less productive than those who do not. Community consequences range from loss of economic opportunity and productivity to social and economic destruction (see **Table 12.2**). Additionally, those who abuse drugs may perpetrate more violent acts that result in economic loss, injury, and death. The violence associated with the abuse of alcohol and other drugs is depicted in **Figure 12.1**.

The *Monitoring the Future* surveys on drug use among high school and college students have been carried out annually since 1975.[7] Survey results for the year 1992 were remarkable because use of almost all drugs reached their lowest level since the first survey.[7] Since 1992, use levels for any illicit drug have fluctuated. Among those in grades 8, 10, and 12, annual prevalence of any illicit drug use peaked in 1999 at 55%, and steadily declined to 47% in 2009.[7] Since 2009, use has remained steady between 47% and 50%.[7] In recent years, overall use levels have stabilized.[7] Marijuana use accounts for more than half of that figure.[7]

Physical dependence a physiological state in which discontinued drug use results in clinical illness

TABLE 12.2 Personal and Community Consequences of Drug Abuse

Personal Consequences	Community Consequences
Absenteeism from school or work	Loss of productivity and revenue
Underachievement at school or work	Lower than average SAT scores
Scholastic failure/interruption of education	Loss of economic opportunity
Loss of employment	Increase in public welfare load
Marital instability/family problems	Increase in number of broken homes
Risk of infectious diseases	Epidemics of sexually transmitted diseases
Risk of chronic or degenerative diseases	Unnecessary burden on health care system
Increased risk of accidents	Unnecessary deaths and economic losses
Financial problems	Defaults on mortgages, loans/bankruptcies
Criminal activity	Increased cost of insurance and security
Arrest and incarceration	Increased cost for police/courts/prisons
Risk of adulterated drugs	Increased burden on medical care system
Adverse drug reactions or "bad trips"	Greater need for emergency medical services
Drug-induced psychoses	Unnecessary drain on mental health services
Drug overdose	Unnecessary demand for medical services
Injury to fetus or newborn baby	Unnecessary use of expensive neonatal care
Loss of self-esteem	Increase in mental illness, underachievement
Suicide and death	Damaged and destroyed families

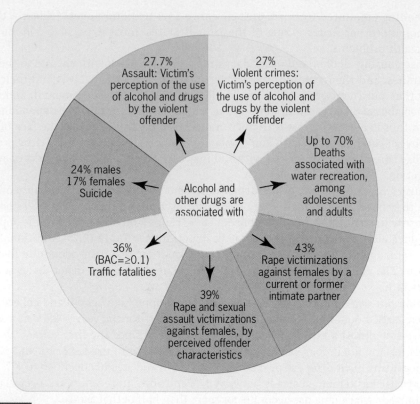

FIGURE 12.1   Violence associated with the use of alcohol and other drugs.

Data from: Fatality Analysis Reporting System, U.S. Department of Transportation (2013). *Persons Killed, by Highest Driver Blood Alcohol Concentration (BAC) in the Crash, 1994–2011–State: USA*. Available at http://www-fars.nhtsa.dot.gov/Trends/TrendsAlcohol.aspx; Black, M. C., K. C. Basile, M. J. Breiding, et al. (2011). *The National Intimate Partner and Sexual Violence Survey (NISVS): 2010 Summary Report*. Atlanta, GA: National Center for Injury Prevention and Control, Centers for Disease Control and Prevention.

Use levels for specific drugs have fluctuated since 1992. For most drugs, use levels peaked in the mid-to-late 1990s and early 2000s. Some drugs, such as cocaine, are currently at their lowest reported levels. The annual prevalence of cocaine use among those in grades 8, 10, and 12 peaked in 1999 at 4.5%, and steadily declined to 1.6% in 2015.[7] For other drugs, such as marijuana and Ecstasy (3,4-methelenedioxymethamphetamine or MDMA), use remains below peak levels, but it is still well above the lowest levels reported during the past decade. For example, the annual prevalence of marijuana use among those in grades 8, 10, and 12 peaked in 1997 at 30.1%, hit its lowest level of 21.4% in 2007, and increased to 23.7% in 2015.[7] The 30-day prevalence of marijuana use for grades 8, 10, and 12 peaked in 1997 at 17.9%, hit its lowest level of 12.4% in 2007, and increased to 14% in 2015.[7] It is interesting to note that college students report lower levels of usage of virtually all illicit drugs than high school seniors (see **Table 12.3**), suggesting that drug-using high school seniors are less likely to attend college than their non-drug-using classmates.[7]

When the words *drug abuse* are mentioned, most people think of illicit drugs, such as heroin, LSD, cocaine, and other illegal substances. Although the abuse of illicit drugs is certainly a major problem in the United States, abuse of alcohol and tobacco products are, perhaps, more serious challenges to American's health. Although the rate of cigarette smoking and alcohol consumption has declined among those in grades 8, 10, and 12 since 1992, use levels remain high (see **Figure 12.2**). In 2015, 20.6% of high school seniors reported having been drunk during the past 30 days, while 35.3% of high school seniors reported any alcohol use during the past 30 days.[7] For grades 8, 10, and 12 combined, the 30-day prevalence for any alcohol use in 2015 was 21.8%.[7] In that same year, the 30-day prevalence for cigarette use among those in grades 8, 10, and 12 was about 7%, while 11.4% of high school seniors reported cigarette use during the past 30 days.[7]

TABLE 12.3   Percentage of High School Seniors Who Have Used Drugs

Drug	Class of 1992,%			Class of 2015,%		
	Ever Used	Past Month	Daily Use	Ever Used	Past Month	Daily Use
Alcohol	87.5	51.3	3.4	64.0	35.3	1.9
Cigarettes	61.8	27.8	17.2	31.1	11.4	5.5
Marijuana	32.6	11.9	1.9	44.7	21.3	6.0
Amphetamines	13.9	2.8	—	10.8	3.2	—
Methamphetamine	—	—	—	1.0	0.4	—
Inhalants	16.6	2.3	—	5.7	0.7	—
Cocaine	6.1	1.3	—	4.0	1.1	—
Tranquilizers	6.0	1.0	—	6.9	2.0	—
LSD	8.6	2.0	—	4.3	1.1	—
MDMA	—	—	—	5.9	1.1	—
Crack	2.6	0.6	—	1.7	0.6	—
PCP	2.4	0.6	—	—	*	—
Heroin	1.2	0.3	—	0.8	0.3	—
E-cigarettes	—	—	—	—	16.2	

Data from: Johnston, L. D., O'Malley, P. M., Miech, R. A., Bachman, J. G., & Schulenberg, J. E. (2016). Monitoring the Future national survey results on drug use, 1975–2015: Overview, key findings on adolescent drug use. Ann Arbor: Institute for Social Research, The University of Michigan. Available at http://www.monitoringthefuture.org/pubs/monographs/mtf-overview2015.pdf.

The United States has been trying to solve the problem of drug abuse for decades. Most adults who abuse drugs eventually "mature out" of the behavior, but there is a constant supply of potential drug users among U.S. children. This "generational forgetting" means that drug prevention education is never finished. Instead, drug prevention efforts must become a permanent part of our culture. That is, we must teach our children about the dangers of experimental drug use in the same way we teach them to look both ways before they cross the street.

Definitions

We begin a discussion of alcohol, tobacco, and other drugs as a community health problem by defining some terms. A **drug** is a substance, other than food or vitamins, that upon entering the body in small amounts alters one's physical, mental, or emotional state. **Psychoactive drugs** are drugs that alter sensory perceptions, mood, thought processes, or behavior.

In this chapter, the term **drug use** is a nonevaluative term referring to drug-taking behavior in general, regardless of whether the behavior is appropriate. **Drug misuse** refers primarily to the inappropriate use of legally purchased prescription or nonprescription drugs. For example, drug misuse occurs when one discontinues the use of a prescribed antibiotic before the entire prescribed dose is completed or when one takes four aspirin rather than two as specified on the label. **Drug abuse** can be defined in several ways depending upon the drug and the situation. Drug abuse occurs when one takes a prescription or nonprescription drug for a purpose other than that for which it is medically approved. For example, drug abuse occurs when one takes a prescription diet pill for its mood-altering effects (stimulation). The abuse of legal drugs such as nicotine or alcohol is said to occur when one is aware that continued use is detrimental to

FIGURE 12.2   The prevalence of alcohol use among American high school seniors in the middle and late 1990s remained high, while cigarette smoking rose dramatically.
© Monkey Business/Fotolia.com.

Drug a substance other than food that when taken in small quantities alters one's physical, mental, or emotional state

Psychoactive drugs drugs that alter sensory perceptions, mood, thought processes, or behavior

Drug use a nonevaluative term referring to drug-taking behavior in general; any drug-taking behavior

Drug misuse inappropriate use of prescription or nonprescription drugs

Drug abuse use of a drug when it is detrimental to one's health or well-being

Drug (chemical) dependence a psychological and sometimes physical state characterized by a craving for a drug

Psychological dependence a psychological state characterized by an overwhelming desire to continue use of a drug

one's health. Because illicit drugs have no approved medical uses, any illicit drug use is considered drug abuse. Likewise, the use of alcohol and nicotine by those under the legal age is considered drug abuse.

Drug (chemical) dependence occurs when a user feels that a particular drug is necessary for normal functioning. It may be **psychological dependence**, in which case the user experiences a strong emotional or psychological desire to continue use of the drug even though clinical signs of physical illness may not appear; or it can be physical, in which discontinuation of drug use results in clinical illness. Usually, both psychological and physical dependence are present at the same time, making the discontinuation of drug use very difficult. Such is frequently the case with cigarette smoking.

Factors that Contribute to Alcohol, Tobacco, and Other Drug Abuse

The factors that contribute to the abuse of alcohol, tobacco, and other drugs are many, and the decision to use drugs lies ultimately with the individual; it's a matter of choice. However, studies have determined that individuals are differentially at risk for engaging in drug-taking behavior.[9] Factors that increase the probability of drug use are called *risk factors*; those that lower the probability of drug use are called *protective factors*. People with a high number of risk factors are said to be vulnerable to drug abuse or dependence, while those who have few risk factors and more protective factors are said to be resistant to drug abuse.

Risk and protective factors can be either genetic (inherited) or environmental. Numerous studies have concluded that inherited traits can increase one's risk of developing dependence on alcohol, and it is logical to assume that susceptibility to other drugs might also be inherited. Environmental risk factors, such as one's home and family life, school and peer groups, and society and culture, have also been identified.

Inherited Risk Factors

The vast majority of the data supporting the notion that the risk of drug dependence can be inherited comes from studies on alcoholism. Evidence for the heritability of risk for alcoholism is provided by numerous studies,[8–12] which have been reviewed by Tabakoff and Hoffman[13] and in the *Tenth Special Report to the U.S. Congress on Alcohol and Health*, from the Secretary of Health and Human Services.[14] Studies of alcoholics' families have found that there are at least two types of inherited alcoholism,[10] now referred to as Type I (or milieu-limited), and Type II (or male-limited) alcoholism.[14] These observational studies of alcoholics' families are supported by research using genetic and biological markers in animal models. Some of these markers predispose an individual biochemically to increased susceptibility to developing alcohol-related problems, while others may actually be protective in nature. For example, genes that code for enzymes that inhibit the normal metabolism of alcohol could cause one to respond positively to the effects of alcohol and thus to drink more, or respond negatively to alcohol and thus drink less or not at all.[13] Studies provided evidence in support of the idea that genes also influence cigarette smoking.[15–17] The heritability of susceptibility to other drugs is still under investigation.

Environmental Risk Factors

There are a great many environmental factors, both psychological and social, that influence the use and abuse of alcohol and other drugs. Included are personal factors such as the influences of home and family life, school and peer groups, and other components of the social and cultural environment.

Personal Factors

Personal factors include personality traits, such as impulsiveness, depressive mood, susceptibility to stress, or possibly personality disturbances. Some of these factors have been reviewed by Needle and colleagues.[18] Although models that involve personal factors provide frameworks for research and theorizing about the etiology of alcohol and drug abuse, they have their limitations. It is difficult to determine the degree to which these factors are inherited or are simply the product of the family environment. For example, one's choice to use alcohol or drugs in response to a stressful situation (and the outcome of that decision) could be the result of either inherited characteristics or learned behavior, or a combination of these factors.

Home and Family Life

The importance of home and family life on alcohol and drug abuse has been the subject of numerous studies, some of which have been reviewed by Meller[19] and by Needle and colleagues.[18] Research demonstrates that not all family-associated risk is genetic in origin. Family structure, family dynamics, quality of parenting, and family problems can all contribute to drug experimentation by children and adolescents (see **Figure 12.3**). Family turmoil (deaths and divorces) have been associated with the initiation of alcohol and other drug use.[18,20] In this sense, alcohol and drug use is a symptom of personal and/or family problems, not a cause.[21]

The development of interpersonal skills, such as communication skills, independent living skills, and learning to get along with others, is nurtured in the home. The failure of parents to provide an environment conducive to the development of these skills can result in the loss of self-esteem and increase in delinquency, nonconformity, and sociopathic behavior, all personal risk factors for alcohol and drug abuse.[22]

Finally, family attitudes toward alcohol and drug use influence adolescents' beliefs and expectations about the effects of drugs. These expectations have been shown to be important factors in adolescents' choices to initiate and continue alcohol use.[22] The age of first use of alcohol, tobacco, and illicit drugs is correlated to later development of alcohol and drug problems, especially if use begins before age 15.[23]

School and Peer Groups

Perceived and actual drug use by peers influences attitudes and choices by adolescents (see **Figure 12.4**). Some studies have shown that perceived support of drinking by peers is the single most important factor in an adolescent's choice to drink.[22] Peers can also influence expectations for a drug. Alcohol may be perceived as "a 'magic elixir' that can enhance social and physical pleasure, sexual performance and responsiveness, power and aggression and social competence."[22] It is interesting to note that these are precisely the mythical qualities about alcohol portrayed in advertisements for beer and other alcoholic beverages.

Sociocultural Environment

The notion of environmental risk includes the effects of sociocultural and physical settings on drug-taking behavior. The study of the effects of the physical and social environment upon the individual is termed *social ecology*.[24] Environmental risk for drug-taking can stem from one's immediate neighborhood or from society at large. For example, living in an inner city—in which citizens are exposed to crime, the city's physical decay, and threats to personal safety—could set into motion a variety of changes in values and behaviors, including some related to alcohol or drug use.

Opportunities for community interventions exist, though. For example, federal, state, and local drug-prevention education programs, law enforcement successes, and treatment availability can improve the social environment and reduce the prevalence of drug abuse. Also, increasing taxes on tobacco products and alcoholic beverages and developing zoning ordinances that limit the number of bars and liquor stores in certain neighborhoods can be effective in reducing the alcohol, tobacco, and other drug problems in a community.

Types of Drugs Abused and Resulting Problems

Almost any psychoactive drug available is subject to abuse by at least some segment of the population. Classification systems of drugs of abuse are many, but none of them is perfect. Problems of classification arise because all drugs have multiple effects and because the legal status of a drug can depend upon its formulation and strength and, in some cases, upon the age of the user. In this chapter, our classification system includes legal drugs and illegal drugs. Legal (licit) drugs include alcohol, nicotine, and nonprescription and prescription drugs. Illegal (illicit) drugs can be classified further on the basis of physiological effects as stimulants, depressants, narcotics, hallucinogens, marijuana, and other drugs.

Legal Drugs

Legal drugs are drugs that can be legally bought and sold in the marketplace, including those that are closely regulated, like morphine; those that are lightly regulated, like alcohol and tobacco; and still others that are not regulated at all, like caffeine.

Alcohol

Alcohol is the number one problem drug in the U.S. by almost any standard of measurement—the number of those who abuse it, the number of injuries and injury deaths it causes, the amount of money spent on it, and its social and economic costs to society through broken homes and lost wages. Alcohol is consumed in a variety of forms, including beer, wine, fortified wines and brandies, and distilled spirits. Although many people view distilled spirits as the most dangerous form of alcohol, it is now recognized that the form of alcohol involved in most heavy-episodic drinking is beer. Much of this beer is drunk by high school and college students, and much of this drinking is **binge drinking** (consuming five or more drinks on a single occasion for males and four or more drinks for females).

A major community health concern is underage drinking, that is, drinking by those younger than 21 years. Underage drinkers, many of them children and teenagers, can destroy their own lives and the lives of others through reckless driving, risky sexual behavior that can lead to disease transmission and unintentional pregnancies, and the commission of other violent and injurious acts. At issue is the fact that an estimated $22.5 billion, or 17.5% of all money spent on alcohol, can be accounted for by underage drinking.[25,26] The alcohol industry would take a huge hit if underage drinking were to stop. The industry relies on underage drinkers for two reasons: the amount of alcohol consumed by them and the fact that many pathological underage drinkers will become pathological adult drinkers, a group that accounts for $25.8 billion, or 20.1%, of the consumer expenditures for alcohol.[25,26]

Drinking by high school and college students continues to be very widespread despite the fact that it is illegal for virtually all high school students and for most college students to purchase these beverages. In 2015, 64% of high school seniors reported having drunk alcohol (more than a few sips) at least once in their lifetime, with 58.2% in the past year, and 35.3% in the past 30 days.[7] In that same year, 20.6% of high school seniors reported having been drunk during the past 30 days.[7] One study revealed that 7.1% of high school students meet clinical criteria for alcohol abuse or dependence.[27] Another analysis showed that nearly 26% of all underage drinkers meet clinical criteria for alcohol abuse or dependence, compared with 9.6% of adult drinkers.[25,26] College students reported an even higher prevalence of drinking. During the past 30 days, 57.2%

Binge drinking consuming five or more drinks in a row for males and four or more drinks in a row for females

of undergraduate college students consumed any alcohol; 30.4% reported binge drinking in the past 2 weeks.[28] The rate of binge drinking among all college students has fluctuated over the past 5 years, from 31.4% in 2011, to 30.3% in 2013, to 33.7% in 2014, to 30.4% in 2015.[29–32]

Most of those who experiment with alcohol begin their use in a social context and become light or moderate drinkers. Alcohol use is reinforcing in two ways: It lowers anxieties and produces a mild euphoria. For many people, alcohol use does not become a significant problem, but for about 7% of those who drink, it does.[27] Some of these people become **problem drinkers**; that is, they begin to experience personal, interpersonal, legal, or financial problems because of their alcohol consumption. Still others lose control of their drinking and develop a dependence upon alcohol. Physical dependence on alcohol and the loss of control over one's drinking are two important characteristics of **alcoholism**. According to the National Council on Alcoholism and Drug Dependence and the American Society of Addiction Medicine,

> Alcoholism is a primary, chronic disease with genetic, psychosocial, and environmental factors influencing its development and manifestations. The disease is often progressive and fatal. It is characterized by impaired control over drinking, preoccupation with the drug alcohol, use of alcohol despite adverse consequences, and distortions in thinking, most notably denial. Each of these symptoms may be continuous or periodic.[33]

The cost of alcohol abuse and alcoholism in the United States is estimated to be $249 billion.[4] That is $774.69 for every U.S. citizen.[34] Binge drinking accounts for three-quarters of that total.[4] More than 72% of the cost is due to lost productivity, 11% is due to health care costs, and 9.4% is from criminal justice costs.[04] Health care costs for alcoholics are about twice those for nonalcoholics.[1]

Alcohol and other drugs are contributing factors to a variety of unintentional injuries and injury deaths. The risk of a motor vehicle crash increases progressively with alcohol consumption and **blood alcohol concentration (BAC)** (see **Figure 12.5**).

> The risk of a single-vehicle fatal crash for male drivers, aged 21 to 34, with BACs between 0.02 and 0.049 is estimated to be 2.75 times higher than that of male drivers, aged 21 to 34, who have not consumed alcohol; for those with BACs between 0.05 and 0.079, it is estimated to be 6.53 times higher; for those with BACs between 0.08 and 0.099, it is estimated to be 13.43 times higher; for those with BACs between 0.1 and 0.149, it is estimated to be 36.89 times higher; and for those with BACs at or above 0.15 percent, the risk is estimated to be 572.55 times higher.[35]

Young drivers are particularly at risk because they are inexperienced drivers and inexperienced drinkers. This combination can be deadly. One study found that 19% of drivers aged 16 to 20 years old who were involved in fatal motor vehicle crashes had alcohol in their blood.[36]

Despite these grim statistics, some progress has been made in reducing the overall rate of alcohol-related vehicle deaths. In 1994, 38% of all persons killed in traffic fatalities had a BAC of 0.01 or greater. That figure decreased to 36% in 2014.[37] The *Healthy People 2020* objective is to decrease the rate of alcohol-impaired driving (0.08 or greater blood-alcohol concentration) fatalities from 0.4 to 0.38 per 100 million miles traveled (see **Box 12.1**). Past success and the promise of future achievement of the target came through public policy changes—raising the minimum legal drinking age, strengthening and enforcing state license revocation laws, and lowering the BAC tolerance levels from 0.10% to 0.08% in some states—stricter law enforcement, and better education for those cited for driving while intoxicated.[38] In October 2000, President Clinton signed a bill that made 0.08% BAC the national standard. States that refused to impose the standard by October 2004 would lose millions of dollars of federal highway construction money.[39] By the end of 2004, all 50 states, Puerto Rico, and the District

Problem drinker one for whom alcohol consumption results in a medical, social, or other type of problem

Alcoholism a disease characterized by impaired control over drinking, preoccupation with drinking, and continued use of alcohol despite adverse consequences

Blood alcohol concentration (BAC) the percentage of concentration of alcohol in the blood

FIGURE 12.5   The risk of a motor vehicle crash increases progressively with alcohol consumption.
© Mark Humphrey/AP Photos.

BOX 12.1 *Healthy People 2020*: Objectives

Objective SA-17: Decrease the rate of alcohol-impaired driving fatalities.

Target-setting method: Maintain consistency with national programs, regulations, policies, and laws.

Data source: Fatality Analysis Reporting System (FARS), U.S. Department of Transportation.

Target and baseline:

Objective		2008 Baseline	2020 Target
		Per 100 million vehicle miles traveled	
SA-17	Decrease the rate of alcohol-impaired driving from 0.40 to 0.38 (0.08 or greater blood alcohol content) fatalities.	0.40	0.38

For Further Thought

The reduction of alcohol-related vehicle deaths is one of the greatest success stories of public health during the twentieth century. What are some factors that have contributed to decreasing alcohol-related vehicle deaths? Similar success has not been achieved for substance abuse–related deaths or drug abuse–related emergency department visits overall. What explanation can you offer for this difference?

Data from: U.S. Department of Health and Human Services, Office of Disease Prevention and Health Promotion (2016). *Healthy People 2020*. Available at http://www.healthypeople.gov/2020/default.aspx.

---

of Columbia had adopted the 0.08% standard. In May 2013, the National Transportation Safety Board released new recommendations to states to reduce the legal BAC limit from 0.08 to 0.05.[40]

Alcohol has also been found to increase one's risk for other types of unintentional injuries, such as drowning, falls, fires, and burns. Associations between unintentional injuries and the abuse of other drugs are less well documented, but given knowledge of the effects of such drugs, one can assume that they increase neither the alertness nor the coordination of users.

Alcohol also contributes to intentional violence in the community. For example, alcohol consumption is associated with child abuse, rape and other sexual assault, homicide, assault, suicide, and spouse and partner abuse (see **Figure 12.1**). Among college students aged 18 to 24, alcohol has been associated with sexual assault, assault, suicide, vandalism, and property damage.[41–43] Approximately 97,000 (or 2%) of college students aged 18 to 24 have experienced a sexual assault by another college student who was drinking.[42] In 2006, Wisconsin became the 50th state to enact a law designed to protect women at risk of sexual assault by acquaintances at social gatherings where alcohol is served. A person convicted under the law can be fined up to $100,000 and sentenced up to 25 years in prison.[43]

Another community health problem resulting from drinking is **fetal alcohol spectrum disorder (FASD)**. FASDs are caused by drinking during pregnancy and include diagnoses such as fetal alcohol syndrome (FAS), alcohol-related birth defects (ARBD), and alcohol-related neurodevelopmental disorders (ARND). Prevalence of FASD in the United States is difficult to determine because there is no universal method for tracking individual cases. Estimates vary greatly, from 0.3 cases of FASD per 1,000 live births to 9.0 cases per 1,000 live births.[44,45] FASD costs society thousands of dollars over a diagnosed person's lifetime. Costs can be attributable to medical treatment for pre- and postnatal growth defects requiring surgery; services for developmentally disabled children; home health care, special education, social services, training and supervision, and institutional care for affected individuals; and lost productivity. It is estimated that the lifetime cost for one individual with FASD is $2 million.[46] For FAS cases alone, the annual cost to the U.S. is estimated at over $4 billion.[46]

Fetal alcohol spectrum disorder (FASD) a range of disorders caused by prenatal exposure to alcohol. FASD refers to conditions such as fetal alcohol syndrome (FAS), fetal alcohol effects (FAE), alcohol-related neurodevelopmental disorder (ARND), and alcohol-related birth defects (ARBD)

Nicotine

Nicotine is the psychoactive and addictive drug present in tobacco products such as cigarettes, e-cigarettes, cigars, smokeless or "spit" tobacco (chewing tobacco and snuff), and pipe tobacco. An estimated 66 million Americans ages 12 or older, or 25.2% of persons in that age group, used a tobacco product in the past 30 days.[47] Approximately 16% of adults ages 18 and over are current cigarette smokers.[48] Among youth, tobacco use is prevalent but has steadily declined since 1997.[49] In 2015, 10.8% of high school students were current smokers compared to 36.4% in 1997.[49] In 2015, past 30-day cigarette use among those in grades 8, 10, and 12 combined was 7%, the lowest reported level since 1996 and 1997 when use was at 28.3%.[7] Among high school seniors, past 30-day use fell from 18.7% in 2011 to 11.4% in 2015.[7] This decline is significant because tobacco use primarily begins in adolescence. About 88% of adult smokers begin smoking by age 18, and 99% begin smoking by age 26.[50]

The use of electronic cigarettes, or e-cigarettes, is emerging as a concern. E-cigarettes are categorized as electronic nicotine delivery systems (ENDS). Through the use of ENDS, a liquid that contains nicotine and other ingredients is heated into an aerosol that is then inhaled by the user.[51] Among adults, 12.6% had ever tried an e-cigarette and 3.7% were regular users in 2014.[52] E-cigarettes have the highest use of all tobacco products among high school students.[7] In 2015, the 30-day prevalence among high school seniors and 10th grade students was 16.2% and 14%, respectively.[7] In the same year, 11.4% of 12th graders and 6.3% of 10th graders used cigarettes in the past month.[7] Between 2011 and 2015, the prevalence of high school students who used e-cigarettes rose from 1.5% to 16%.[51] One factor that has affected this increase is perceived risk. In 2015, only 17% of 10th grade students viewed regular e-cigarette use as risky, compared to 52.9% of 10th grade students who perceived smoking one to five cigarettes a day as risky.[7] Product appeal is another factor that has affected the increase. Between 2013 and 2014, four in five youth who were current e-cigarette users cited the availability of appealing flavors as the main reason for trying e-cigarettes.[51] Associated with the spike in use among high school students, advertising for e-cigarettes has increased significantly in recent years. The tobacco industry tripled its expenditures on e-cigarette advertising from $6.4 million to $18.3 million between 2011 and 2012.[53]

The consequences of tobacco use on individuals and communities are devastating. Tobacco use is the single most preventable cause of disease, disability, and death in the United States. The health consequences of tobacco use are familiar to all (see **Box 12.2**). They include increased risks for heart disease, lung cancer, chronic obstructive lung disease, stroke, emphysema, and other conditions. Each year in the United States, smoking results in approximately 480,000 premature deaths and 5.1 million years of potential life lost.[54–56] Worldwide, tobacco use results in approximately 6 million premature deaths each year; by 2030, this number is expected to rise to 8 million per year.[57] The economic cost of tobacco smoking in the United States is estimated at more than $300 billion per year.[3] More than half of this total, $156 billion, is due to lost productivity; the remainder is due to health care costs.[3] A significant portion of the health care costs attributed to smoking (43%) are paid with government funds, including Medicaid and Medicare.[1] Inasmuch as tobacco use and nicotine addiction increase the cost of these programs, they clearly add to the economic burden on society.

Well-established research findings have demonstrated that one does not have to use tobacco products to be adversely affected. The 1986 U.S. Surgeon General's report on the effects of **environmental tobacco smoke (ETS)** or **secondhand smoke** indicated that adults and children who inhale the tobacco smoke of others (passive smoking) are also at increased risk for cardiac and respiratory illnesses.[58,59] These findings resulted in new smoking regulations in many public indoor environments. Then, in December 1992, the U.S. Environmental Protection Agency (EPA) released the report entitled, *Respiratory Health Effects of Passive Smoking: Lung Cancer and Other Disorders*.[60] This report stated that ETS is a human class A carcinogen (the same class that contains asbestos) and that it is responsible for 42,000 deaths annually among nonsmoking Americans.[55] Further, it stated that ETS exposure is causally associated with as many as 150,000 to 300,000 cases of lower respiratory infections (such as bronchitis and pneumonia) in infants and young children up to 18 months of age. The EPA study also found that ETS aggravates

Environmental tobacco smoke (ETS; secondhand smoke) tobacco smoke in the ambient air

BOX 12.2   Ten Great Public Health Achievements, 2000–2010: Tobacco Control

Less Smoke, More Prevention

During the last century, smoking went from being an accepted norm to being recognized as the number one preventable cause of death and disability in the United States. The first decade of the twenty-first century saw an increase in the adoption of policies at the federal, state, and local levels designed to prevent and reduce tobacco use. Major achievements include:

- Adoption of the Family Smoking Prevention and Tobacco Control Act (Tobacco Control Act) in 2009, which gives the U.S. Food and Drug Administration (FDA) the authority to regulate tobacco
- Adoption of comprehensive smoke-free laws by 25 states and the District of Columbia by 2010 and 30 states by 2012

- The largest federal cigarette tax increase in history
- Increased restrictions on advertising and marketing of tobacco products to youth

Although substantial progress has been made and millions of lives have been saved, increased prevention efforts are needed to reduce the impact of tobacco use on public health. Each year, smoking still kills more people than all of the following health hazards combined:

- HIV
- Alcohol abuse
- Drug abuse
- Motor vehicle crash injuries
- Murders
- Suicides

Data from: U.S. Food and Drug Administration (2013). *Overview of the Family Smoking Prevention and Tobacco Control Act: Consumer Fact Sheet.* Available at http://www.fda.gov/downloads/TobaccoProducts/GuidanceComplianceRegulatoryInformation/UCM336940.pdf; Centers for Disease Control and Prevention (2011). "Ten Great Public Health Achievements—United States, 2001–2010." *Morbidity and Mortality Weekly Report*, 60(19);619–623. Available at http://www.cdc.gov/mmwr/preview/mmwrhtml/mm6019a5.htm; and Murphy S. L., J. Q. Xu, and K. D. Kochanek (2013). "Deaths: Final Data for 2010." *National Vital Statistics Reports*, 61(4). Hyattsville, MD: National Center for Health Statistics. Available at http://www.cdc.gov/nchs/data/nvsr/nvsr61/nvsr61_04.pdf.

asthma in children and is a risk factor for new cases of childhood asthma. During 2007 to 2008, approximately 88 million nonsmokers 3 years old or older were exposed to secondhand smoke.[61]

For many years the enforcement of state laws prohibiting the sale of cigarettes and other tobacco products to minors was varied and inconsistent. In other cases, cigarettes could easily be purchased by youth from vending machines. The problem of uneven state tobacco laws regarding sales to minors and the lack of enforcement of these laws was remedied in 1992 by the **Synar Amendment**, a federal law that requires all states to adopt legislation that prohibits the sale and distribution of tobacco products to people under age 18. States that do not comply with this regulation lose federal dollars for alcohol, tobacco, and other drug prevention and treatment programs.[62] States may choose to adopt stricter regulations regarding the sale of tobacco products to minors. For example, in late 2013, New York state passed a law that raised the legal age to purchase tobacco products from 18 to 21. In 2016, California became the second state to enact such legislation.

In a past effort to market cigarettes to children and adolescents, R. J. Reynolds Tobacco Company began selling candy-, fruit-, and liquor-flavored cigarettes. In 2006, an agreement was reached between R. J. Reynolds Tobacco Company and the Attorneys General of 40 states to end the sale of these items.[63]

On June 22, 2009, President Obama signed the Family Smoking Prevention and Tobacco Control Act into law, giving the U.S. Food and Drug Administration oversight over tobacco products.[64] The law also banned deceptive marketing practices by the tobacco industry, specifically the use of the words "light," "low," or "mild" on cigarette packaging. It remains to be seen how effective this new law will be in lowering smoking rates among young Americans. The tobacco industry spends billions of dollars each year on advertising and promotions to sell its products. In 2011, this amounted to $8.37 billion.[65] Another proven way to reduce smoking rates is to increase taxes on cigarettes, thereby increasing the financial cost of smoking. Cigarettes are taxed at the federal level, state level, and, in some jurisdictions, at the county or city level. In 2009, the federal tax increased to $1.01 per pack. In 2016, the average state tax was $1.61 per pack.[66] In 2016, Chicago had the highest combined state and local tax at $6.16 per pack.[66] In the same year, New York City had the second highest state and local cigarette tax at $5.85 per

Synar Amendment a federal law that requires states to set the minimum legal age for purchasing tobacco products at 18 years and requires states to enforce this law

pack.[66] The state of Missouri had the lowest state cigarette tax at $0.17 per pack.[67] Virginia had the second lowest state cigarette tax at $0.30 per pack.[67] By April 2016, the average retail cost for a pack of cigarettes in the state of New York was the highest in the nation at $10.45.[67] Perhaps raising the cost of cigarettes in this manner will reduce smoking rates among young people.

More recently, in May 2016, the U.S. Food and Drug Administration extended its authority to regulate tobacco products to ENDS, including e-cigarettes, in response to the significant rise in e-cigarette use.[56] Prior to this date, retailers could sell e-cigarettes to people under the age of 18.[56]

Over-the-Counter Drugs

Over-the-counter (OTC) drugs are those legal drugs, with the exception of tobacco and alcohol, which can be purchased without a physician's prescription. Included in this category are internal analgesics such as aspirin, acetaminophen (Tylenol), and ibuprofen (Advil); cough and cold remedies (Robitussin); emetics; laxatives; mouthwashes; vitamins; and many others. Thousands of different OTC products are sold by pharmacies, supermarkets, convenience stores, and in vending machines. These products are manufactured and sold to those who self-diagnose and self-medicate their own illnesses.

Over-the-counter drugs are carefully regulated by the **U.S. Food and Drug Administration (FDA)**, an agency of the U.S. Department of Health and Human Services. The FDA ensures the safety and effectiveness of these products when they are used according to their label directions. There is no person or agency that supervises the actual sale or use of these substances.

Naturally, some of these substances are misused and abused. Examples of misuse are not following the dosage directions or using the drugs after their expiration date. A specific example of OTC drug abuse is the taking of laxatives or emetics to lose weight or to avoid gaining weight. Other OTC drugs that are often abused are appetite suppressants (Dexatrim), stimulants (NoDoz), and nasal sprays (Neo-Synephrine). Recently, common cold OTC products that contain pseudoephedrine have been the target of thieves whose intent is to manufacture methamphetamine. This has led to tighter regulation by the FDA. In 2006, the Combat Methamphetamine Epidemic Act of 2005 was signed into law. The law requires, among other things, that retailers limit the sale of pseudoephedrine products and place pseudoephedrine products where customers do not have direct access to such products before a sale is made, such as behind the pharmacy counter.[68]

Most OTC drugs provide only symptomatic relief and do not provide a cure. For example, cough and cold remedies relieve the discomfort that accompanies a cold but do not in any way rid a person of the cold virus that is causing these symptoms. Therefore, a real danger of OTC drug misuse and abuse is that symptoms that should be brought to the attention of a physician remain unreported. Another danger is that those who abuse these drugs may become dependent, thus unable to live normally without them. Last, abuse of OTC drugs may establish a pattern of dependency that predisposes the abuser to developing dependent relationships with prescription drugs or illicit drugs.

Prescription Drugs

Because all prescription drugs have serious side effects for some people, they can be purchased only with a physician's (or dentist's) written instructions (prescription). Like OTC drugs, prescription drugs are carefully regulated by the FDA. The written prescription connotes that the prescribed drugs are being taken by the patient under the prescribing physician's supervision. Each prescription includes the patient's name, the amount to be dispensed, and the dosage. The percent of people in the United States using at least one prescription drug during the past month is estimated at 47.4.[69] Nonetheless, prescription drugs are also subject to misuse and abuse. Types of misuse include those previously cited for the OTC drugs and also the giving of one person's prescription drug to another. Furthermore, certain prescription drugs such as stimulants (amphetamines), depressants (Valium), and prescription opioid pain relievers (fentanyl, morphine, codeine) have a higher potential for abuse than others. Because prescription drugs are usually stronger or more concentrated than OTC drugs, there is a greater risk of

Over-the-counter (OTC) drugs (nonprescription drugs) drugs (except tobacco and alcohol) that can be legally purchased without a physician's prescription

U.S. Food and Drug Administration (FDA) a federal agency in the U.S. Department of Health and Human Services charged with ensuring the safety and efficacy of all prescription and nonprescription drugs

Controlled substances
drugs regulated by the Comprehensive Drug Abuse Control Act of 1970, including all illegal drugs and prescription drugs that are subject to abuse and can produce dependence

Controlled Substances Act of 1970 (Comprehensive Drug Abuse Control Act of 1970) the central piece of federal drug legislation that regulates illegal drugs and legal drugs that have a high potential for abuse

Illicit (illegal) drugs drugs that cannot be legally manufactured, distributed, or sold, and that usually lack recognized medicinal value. Drugs that have been placed under Schedule I of the Controlled Substances Act of 1970

developing dependence or taking an overdose from these drugs. Those who develop dependence may try to obtain duplicate prescriptions from other physicians or steal the drugs from hospital dispensaries or pharmacies.

In recent years, the number of deaths from unintentional drug overdoses has risen to unprecedented levels. The abuse and misuse of opioid pain relievers, in particular, has risen to epidemic proportions. Between 2000 and 2014, the rate of overdose deaths in the United States involving opioids, including heroin and prescription opioid pain relievers, increased 200%.[68] During that time period, more than 165,000 overdose deaths involving prescription opioids occurred, and overdose deaths involving prescription opioids quadrupled.[69–71] In 2014, the leading cause of death in the United States for ages 1 to 44 was unintentional injuries.[72] For ages 25 to 64, unintentional poisoning was the leading cause of unintentional injury death.[73]

The increase in overdoses involving prescription opioids is influenced by several factors. First, prescription opioids are potent pain relievers, with similar effects to heroin.[74] Their potency makes them highly addictive. Second, when mixed with illicit drugs, such as cocaine and heroin, they can be lethal. Third, they have been increasingly available. The primary factor contributing to overdoses is an increase in prescriptions for opioid pain relievers.[75] Prescription opioid misuse and abuse can lead to dependency. Use of prescription opioids is a risk factor for heroin use; some prescription opioid users may progress to heroin.[74]

Prescription drug misuse and abuse leads to other serious consequences. Prescription drug abuse puts an additional strain on our already overburdened emergency departments (EDs). Between 2004 and 2011, emergency department visits involving the misuse or abuse of prescription drugs increased from 626,470 to 1,428,145 visits.[76] This represents approximately a 128% increase and accounts for 28% of all drug-related emergency department visits for 2011.[76] Prescription drug abuse can also lead to the development of drug-resistant strains of pathogens. When patients fail to complete the entire antibiotic treatment (i.e., 3 days of a 10-day prescription), some of the bacteria survive and multiply, reinfecting the body with drug-resistant organisms. Thus, succeeding treatments are less effective. When this strain of the disease is transmitted to another, the antibiotic treatment fails. New drugs are then needed to treat these patients. As drug misuse continues to occur, bacteria become resistant to multiple drugs. Multidrug-resistant tuberculosis (MDR-TB) is an example. Another example is the growing number of reports of community-associated methicillin-resistant *Staphylococcus aureus* (CA-MRSA) infections. These are bacterial infections of the skin or other organs that are resistant to some antibiotics. The prevalence of MDR-TB and the increase in the incidence of CA-MRSA point both to the dangers of drug misuse and the need to continue to develop new antibiotics for the treatment of bacterial infections.

FIGURE 12.6   Marijuana is the nation's most popular illicit drug.
© Tiburon Studios/ShutterStock, Inc.

Controlled Substances and Illicit (Illegal) Drugs

Controlled substances are those regulated by the **Controlled Substances Act of 1970 (CSA)**, officially called the **Comprehensive Drug Abuse Control Act of 1970**. Many of the drugs discussed next belong to Schedule I under this Act because they have a high potential for abuse and have no accepted medical uses and, hence, no acceptable standards of safe use. These are considered **illicit (illegal) drugs**. They cannot be cultivated, manufactured, bought, sold, or used within the confines of the law. Well over 150 drugs are listed in this category, including heroin, methaqualone, marijuana (see **Figure 12.6**), LSD, psilocybin, mescaline, and MDMA.[75]

Other drugs, which do have medical uses, are placed in Schedules II to V of the Act, depending upon their potential for abuse and risk of causing dependence. Included in Schedule II is a variety of very powerful compounds that have specific medical uses but have a high risk for potential abuse. Included in this category are many opium derivatives, such as morphine, fentanyl, oxycodone, and methadone. Also included in Schedule II are the stimulants amphetamine and methamphetamine, certain depressants such as amobarbital, pentobarbital, secobarbital, and phencyclidine, and several other drugs. Schedule III drugs have medical uses and exhibit a lower risk of potential abuse than Schedule II drugs. Included are less concentrated forms of certain Schedule II drugs and also many of the anabolic steroids. Schedule IV drugs exhibit even less potential for abuse than Schedule III drugs. Included are many milder stimulants and depressants. Schedule V drugs are primarily very dilute concentrations of opium or opiates used in such medicines as cough syrups.[77]

The **Drug Enforcement Administration (DEA)**, under the U.S. Department of Justice, has the primary responsibility of enforcing the provisions of the Controlled Substances Act. Once a drug is placed in Schedule I of the CSA, it becomes the primary responsibility of the DEA to interdict the trafficking (manufacturing, distribution, and sales) of the substance. The only sources of these drugs are illegal growers and manufacturers. Schedule II to V substances often reach the street illegally, either by illegal production (in clandestine labs) or by diversion of legally manufactured prescription drugs.

Marijuana

Marijuana is the most abused illicit drug in the United States. "Pot" and the related products, hashish and hash oil, are derived from the hemp plant, *Cannabis sativa*. The products are most commonly used by smoking but can also be ingested. Although marijuana abuse has declined, it remains a concern for several reasons. First, it is illegal, and therefore brings the user into contact with those involved in illegal activities. Second, the act of smoking is detrimental to one's health. Third, marijuana smoking often occurs in conjunction with the drinking of alcohol or the use of other drugs. The effects of **polydrug use** (the use of more than one drug at a time) may be more serious than those of single-drug use. Last, as is true of all drugs, the adolescent who uses marijuana is delaying the accomplishment of developmental tasks such as attaining an adult self-identity, achieving independence, and developing the interpersonal skills necessary for successful independent living.

In a 2015 survey, the percentage of high school seniors who reported having smoked marijuana at least once in their lives was 44.7%.[7] Also, 21.3% reported having smoked marijuana in the past 30 days.[7] As with many of the other drugs, the prevalence of marijuana use has waxed and waned over the past 30 years. The perceived risk of use is one of the factors that seems to contribute to the level of use. In 1992, when 76.5% of high school seniors felt there was great risk associated with regular marijuana use, the 30-day use prevalence was 11.9%. In 2015, when 31.9% of seniors felt there was great risk associated with regular marijuana use, the 30-day use prevalence was 21.3.[7] Another measurement of students' attitudes is disapproval rates. Over the past 5 years among high school seniors, disapproval rates for trying marijuana once or twice, smoking marijuana occasionally, or regularly using marijuana have steadily declined.[7] One of the objectives of *Healthy People 2020* is to increase the proportion of adolescents (8th, 10th, and 12th graders) who disapprove of trying marijuana or hashish once or twice. The target is set at 10% improvement (see **Box 12.3**).

The acute health effects of marijuana use include reduced concentration, slowed reaction time, impaired short-term memory, and impaired judgment. Naturally, these effects can have serious consequences for someone operating a motor vehicle or other machinery or can even result in a medical emergency. Marijuana use in combination with other drugs can be especially dangerous because drugs in combination may affect the brain differently. In 2011, marijuana, used alone or with one or more other drugs, was involved in an estimated 455,668 emergency department visits.[76]

The chronic effects of smoking marijuana include damage to the respiratory system by the smoke itself and, for some, the development of a controversial condition known as **amotivational syndrome**. Amotivational syndrome has been described as a chronic apathy toward maturation and the achievement of the developmental tasks listed previously (e.g., developing skills for independent living, setting and achieving goals, and developing an adult self-identity).

Drug Enforcement Administration (DEA) the federal government's lead agency with the primary responsibility for enforcing the nation's drug laws, including the Controlled Substances Act of 1970

Marijuana dried plant parts of the hemp plant, *Cannabis sativa*

Polydrug use concurrent use of multiple drugs

Amotivational syndrome a pattern of behavior characterized by apathy, loss of effectiveness, and a more passive, introverted personality

BOX 12.3 *Healthy People 2020*: **Objectives**

Objectives SA-3.4, SA-3.5, and SA-3.6: Increase the proportion of adolescents who disapprove of trying marijuana or hashish once or twice—eighth graders, tenth graders, and twelfth graders.

Target-setting method: 10% improvement.

Data source: *Monitoring the Future Study*, National Institutes of Health (NIH), National Institute of Drug Abuse (NIDA).

Targets and baselines:

Objective	2009 Baseline	2020 Target
	Percentage	
SA-3.4 Eighth graders	75.3	82.8
SA-3.5 Tenth graders	60.1	66.1
SA-3.6 Twelfth graders	54.8	60.3

For Further Thought

Attitudes and beliefs are often key factors influencing drug-taking behavior among adolescents. Studies have shown that when there is a high level of disapproval of marijuana use by adolescents, the prevalence of marijuana use declines.

Conversely, an increase in marijuana use occurs when there is an apparent decline in those expressing strong disapproval of use. How strong are prevailing feelings of disapproval of marijuana use in your community? Do adolescents in your community feel that it is "OK" to try marijuana once or twice?

Data from: U.S. Department of Health and Human Services, Office of Disease Prevention and Health Promotion (2016). *Healthy People 2020*. Available at http://www.healthypeople.gov/2020/default.aspx.

There is also evidence now that long-term marijuana users experience physiological and psychological withdrawal symptoms. Although these "unpleasant behavioral symptoms are less obvious than those for heroin or alcohol, they are significant and do perhaps contribute to continued drug use."[78] Further evidence of the dependence-producing nature of marijuana is the number of persons seeking admission to treatment programs. Between 2003 and 2013, admissions to treatment programs for marijuana abuse averaged at around 326,000 per year.[79] Admissions due to marijuana was only second to admissions due to opiates and alcohol. In 2013, marijuana was reported as the primary drug of abuse for approximately 17% of those ages 12 and older who entered drug treatment programs in the United States.[79] Finally, one of the chief concerns with marijuana is that those who smoke marijuana are more likely to use other, more addictive drugs. For example, 89% of those who use cocaine first used cigarettes, alcohol, and marijuana.[80]

Synthetic Marijuana

Another cause for concern is the manufacture, distribution, and use of synthetic marijuana or synthetic cannabinoids. Synthetic marijuana is a category of drugs that are chemically produced and have properties similar to THC, the psychoactive ingredient found in marijuana.[81] These drugs are typically sold in the form of small packets of plant material that are laced with synthetic THC-like compounds.[81] They may be labeled as incense or potpourri and have been sold at convenience stores, gas stations, and online. Street names include K2 or "Spice." Synthetic marijuana has been deceptively marketed as a "safe," legal alternative to marijuana.[81] Among 8th, 10th, and 12th grade students, use of synthetic marijuana steadily declined from 8% in 2012 to 4.2% in 2015.[7] However, attitudes about the perceived harmfulness of synthetic marijuana pose a risk. Less than one-third of 10th graders perceived occasional use as harmful.[7]

Despite safety claims by sellers, synthetic marijuana poses a serious threat to public health. It has the potential for abuse and other adverse health effects, and its long-term effects are still unknown. Some users have reported immediate effects similar to those of marijuana, while others have reported symptoms such as rapid heart rate, increased blood pressure, hallucinations, agitation, and vomiting.[81] Since 2011, over 27,000 calls related to synthetic marijuana use have been placed to poison control centers across the country.[82] In 2010, an estimated 11,406 emergency department visits involved synthetic marijuana.[82]

To protect the public against these harms, in March 2011, five chemicals used to produce synthetic marijuana were temporarily placed into Schedule I of the Controlled Substances Act, in accordance with the CSA's emergency scheduling provision.[84] In July 2012, President Obama signed the Synthetic Drug Abuse Prevention Act of 2012 (SDAPA). The SDAPA permanently places specific known classes of cannabimimetic agents, the chemicals used to produce synthetic marijuana, into Schedule I of the CSA.[85] It also expands the list of temporarily scheduled chemicals. States also have taken steps to ban synthetic drugs. Since 2011, all 50 states have banned synthetic marijuana.[86] In 2012, the DEA initiated "Project Synergy," a collaborative international effort to target and take down synthetic drug traffickers. In June 2013, it was announced that the effort resulted in more than 227 arrests and the seizure of 1,252 kilograms of synthetic marijuana.[87]

Despite these efforts, synthetic marijuana laws are difficult to enforce. One challenge lies in identifying synthetic marijuana. Products are labeled as incense or potpourri, or as legal, not as synthetic marijuana. They must be tested in a lab to determine whether they contain any banned cannabimimetic agents. Another challenge is that manufacturers are discovering and utilizing new classes of cannabimimetic agents that are not already banned by federal or state laws, thus finding ways to get around the law to produce synthetic marijuana.

Narcotics: Opium, Morphine, Heroin, and Others

Opium and its derivatives, morphine and heroin, come from the oriental poppy plant, *Papavor somniforum*. These **narcotics** numb the senses and reduce pain. As such, they have a high potential for abuse. The narcotic that is most widely abused is heroin, a derivative of morphine. In 2014, 914,000 (0.3%) reported use in the past year.[47] In 2011, 620,000 reported use in the past year.[49] The sharp increase has been fueled, in part, by the prescription opioid epidemic. Heroin is a less expensive alternative to prescription opioids, while users experience a similar effect. Users who become dependent on prescription opioids may seek out heroin because it is a less expensive option. Use among high school seniors has not increased. In 2015, 0.5% of 12th grade students reported using heroin in the past year. This is the lowest the level has been since 1993.[7]

Opium poppies do not grow in the continental United States. Heroin arrives in the United States from four geographic areas: Southwest Asia, Southeast Asia, Mexico, and South America. Most of the heroin available in the United States now enters across our southwestern border. Although significant amounts of heroin reaching the United States originate in South America, the proportion of heroin seizures in which the heroin originated in Mexico has grown. Mexican heroin production has increased in recent years, and the influence of Mexican drug trafficking organizations is expanding.[88]

Heroin remains the number one illicit narcotic of abuse and the third leading cause of drug-related emergency department visits after cocaine and marijuana.[76] Historically, heroin has been the leading cause of unintentional narcotic-induced drug deaths. Now, however, heroin has been overtaken by other synthetic opioids, including methadone, as the leading cause of narcotic-induced overdose drug deaths. Together, these substances accounted for more than 28,000 overdose deaths in the United States in 2014.[70]

Narcotics produce euphoria, analgesia, and drowsiness. They reduce anxiety and pain without affecting motor activity the way alcohol and barbiturates do. If use continues, the body makes physiological adjustments to the presence of the drug. This **tolerance** means that larger and larger doses are required to achieve the same euphoria and numbing as the initial dose. Whereas tolerance develops rapidly to the euphoric effects, the depressing effects on respiration may continue to increase with dose level, increasing the risk of a fatal overdose. As the cost of the drug habit becomes higher, the abuser usually attempts to quit. This results in withdrawal symptoms because the body has become physically dependent upon the drug. Heroin addicts have a difficult time changing their lifestyle for several reasons. First, there is the addiction itself, both physical and psychological. Often, there are underlying psychosocial problems as well, such as poor self-image, lack of job skills, and absence of supporting family and friends.

Narcotics drugs derived from or chemically related to opium that reduce pain and induce stupor, such as morphine

Tolerance physiological and enzymatic adjustments that occur in response to the chronic presence of drugs, which are reflected in the need for ever-increasing doses

Addicts usually mistrust official programs set up to help them. They are usually in poor health mentally and physically. Because the duration of action of heroin is only 4 to 5 hours, the addict is usually too concerned with finding the next dose or recovering from the previous one to be productive in the community.

The community is affected by more than just the loss of productivity. The addict must obtain money to purchase heroin, and the price of the habit can be very high—as much as $200 per day. The money is usually obtained illegally through burglaries, thefts, robberies, muggings, prostitution (male and female), and selling drugs. The result is not only a deteriorating community but also epidemics of sexually transmitted diseases, such as gonorrhea, syphilis, chlamydia, herpes, and AIDS. Because most heroin addicts inject the drug, there are also epidemics of bloodborne diseases, such as those caused by HIV and hepatitis viruses. In 2015, a rural county in Indiana experienced an outbreak of HIV that was associated with the use of heroin that was taken intravenously.[89]

In this way, drug abuse increases the burden on community and public health resources. Addicts who turn to dealing drugs to support their habit do even more damage because they increase the availability of the drug and may introduce it to first-time users. There is an additional burden on the criminal justice system when these addicts are arrested, prosecuted, incarcerated, and rehabilitated.

Cocaine and Crack Cocaine

Cocaine is the psychoactive ingredient in the leaves of the coca plant, *Erythoxolyn coca*, which grows in the Andes Mountains of South America. Cocaine is a **stimulant**; that is, it increases the activity of the central nervous system. For centuries, natives of the Andes Mountains have chewed the leaves to improve stamina during work and long treks. In its more purified forms, as a salt (white powder) or dried paste (crack), cocaine is a powerful euphoriant/stimulant and very addictive.

Cocaine use among high school seniors peaked in 1985, when 13.1% reported use within the past year. By 1992 the annual prevalence dropped to only 3.1%, but by 1999 the figure had doubled to 6.2%.[7] In 2015, the annual prevalence was at its lowest reported level of 2.5%.[7] In 2014, 4.5 million Americans ages 12 and older used cocaine.[47] An estimated 1.5 million used cocaine in the past month.[47] Therefore, cocaine remains a serious drug problem in the United States.

Hallucinogens

Hallucinogens are drugs that produce illusions, hallucinations, and other changes in one's perceptions of the environment. These effects are due to the phenomenon known as **synesthesia**, a mixing of the senses. Hallucinogens include both naturally derived drugs such as mescaline, from the peyote cactus, and psilocybin and psilocin, from the *Psilocybe* mushroom; and synthetic drugs, such as lysergic acid diethylamide (LSD). Although physical dependence has not been demonstrated with the hallucinogens, tolerance does occur. Though overdose deaths are rare, "bad trips" (unpleasant experiences) do occur, and a few people have experienced permanent visual disturbances. Because there are no legal sources for these drugs, users are always at risk for taking fake, impure, or adulterated drugs.

Stimulants

As previously mentioned, stimulants are drugs that increase the activity level of the central nervous system. Examples include the amphetamines, such as amphetamine itself (bennies), dextroamphetamine (dexies), methamphetamine (meth), dextromethamphetamine (ice); methylphenidate (Ritalin); and methcathinone (cat). These drugs cause the release of high levels of the neurotransmitter dopamine, which stimulates brain cells. Tolerance builds quickly, so abusers must escalate their doses rapidly. Chronic abusers can develop tremors and confusion, aggressiveness, and paranoia. The long-term effects include memory loss and permanent brain damage.[90]

Amphetamines are Schedule II prescription drugs that have been widely abused for many years. Increased regulatory efforts in the 1970s probably contributed to the rise in the cocaine trade in the

Cocaine the psychoactive ingredient in the leaves of the coca plant, *Erythoxolyn coca*, which, when refined, is a powerful stimulant/euphoriant

Stimulant a drug that increases the activity of the central nervous system

Hallucinogens drugs that produce profound distortions of the senses

Synesthesia impairment of mind characterized by a sensation that senses are mixed

Amphetamines a group of synthetic drugs that act as stimulants

1980s. When cocaine abuse declined in the late 1980s, there was a resurgence of amphetamine abuse, primarily **methamphetamine**, also known as "crystal," "crank," "speed," "go fast," or just "meth." At first, the clandestine labs that produced methamphetamine, and those abusing the substance, were concentrated primarily in the southwestern states. However, by 1995 production and abuse had spread to the Midwest, and by 1999 methamphetamine abuse had become the fastest growing drug threat in the United States. The popularity of amphetamines has been in decline. In 2015, 6.2% of those in grades 8, 10, and 12 reported any amphetamine use in the past year.[7] Annual prevalence of methamphetamine use among those in grades 8, 10, and 12 declined from 4.1% in 1999 to 0.6%, the lowest reported level, in 2015.[7] In 2014, 0.5% of those ages 12 and older, or 1.4 million, were current users of methamphetamine.[47] This is a decline from the time period of 2002 to 2006. In 2014, the DEA seized 2,946 kilograms of methamphetamine and recorded 9,338 clandestine lab incidents, including labs, dumpsters, chemicals and glassware, and equipment (see **Figures 12.7** and **12.8**).[91,92]

Methylphenidate (Ritalin) is a Schedule II drug used to treat attention deficit hyperactivity disorder. Though not produced in clandestine labs, the drug is often diverted from its intended use and abused by those for whom it was not prescribed.

Depressants

Barbiturates, **benzodiazapines**, **methaqualone**, and other **depressants** slow down the central nervous system. They are attractive to some people because, like alcohol, among the first effects of taking these drugs are the

FIGURE 12.7 Dismantling a clandestine methamphetamine lab is hazardous work.
© Kyle Carter/The Meridian Star/AP Photos.

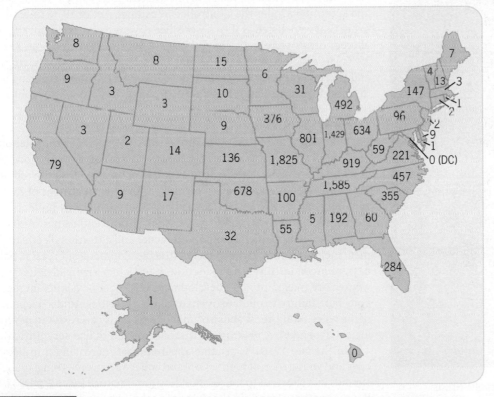

FIGURE 12.8 Total of all clandestine laboratory incidents involving methamphetamine (including labs, dump sites, and chemicals, glassware, or equipment), calendar year 2014.
Data from: El Paso Intelligence Center (EPIC/National Secure System NSS).

Methamphetamine the amphetamine most widely abused

Barbiturates depressant drugs based on the structure of barbituric acid

Benzodiazapines nonbarbiturate depressant drugs

Methaqualone an illicit depressant drug

Depressants drugs that slow central nervous system activity, for example, alcohol, barbiturates, and benzodiazapines

Club drugs a general term for those illicit drugs, primarily synthetic, that are most commonly encountered at night clubs and "raves" (examples include MDMA, GHB, GBL, LSD, PCP, ketamine, Rohypnol, and methamphetamine)

Rohypnol (flunitrazepam) a powerful depressant in the benzodiazapine group that has achieved notoriety as a date-rape drug because its toxic and sedative affects when combined with alcohol can last up to 8 hours

Designer drug drug synthesized illegally that is similar to, but structurally different from, known controlled substances

Anabolic drug compound, structurally similar to the male hormone testosterone, that increases protein synthesis and thus muscle building

lowering of anxiety and the loss of inhibitions. These effects produce the feeling of a "high," even though these drugs depress the central nervous system. As one continues to use these drugs, tolerance develops, and the user experiences the need for greater and greater doses to feel the same effects that the previous dose provided. Strong physical dependence develops so that abstinence results in severe clinical illness; thus, abusers of these substances must often rely on medical assistance during detoxification and recovery.

Club Drugs and Designer Drugs

Club drugs is a term for a number of illicit drugs, primarily synthetic, that are most commonly encountered at nightclubs, bars, and parties. These drugs include MDMA, ketamine, GHB, GBL, Rohypnol, LSD, PCP, methamphetamine, and others. They are often taken in combination with alcohol or other drugs. Because these drugs are illegal, there is no guarantee of their safety or even their identity. Long-term effects of club drugs are still under evaluation, but there is evidence that these drugs may cause brain damage.[90,93] MDMA, also known as "Ecstasy" or "Molly," is the most popular of the club drugs. MDMA was initially popular among teens and young adults at raves (all-night dance parties). In recent years, use has spread to other a broader audience beyond the nightclub scene.[93] Annual use of MDMA among those in grades 8, 10, and 12 peaked at 6% in 2001. In 2015, levels declined to 2.4%.[7]

Rohypnol (flunitrazepam) is another club drug that is also known as a "date-rape" or "predatory" drug. This drug, which exhibits all of the characteristics of a depressant, is a legal prescription drug in more than 50 countries. In the United States, the drug is regarded as more dangerous, and thus less medically useful than other sedatives. Thus, it is an illegal (Schedule I) drug.

Designer drugs is a term coined in the 1980s to describe drugs synthesized by amateur chemists in secret laboratories. By constantly changing the design of their drugs, these chemists hoped to stay one step ahead of law enforcement. Examples of designer drugs included MDMA (3,4-methylenedioxy-methamphetamine), synthetic narcotics, and dissociative anesthetics such as PCP (angel dust) and ketamine. Under the Controlled Substance Act of 1970, only those drugs that were listed as illegal were illegal, whereas similar, but slightly altered, drugs were not. The Controlled Substances Analogue Act of 1986 was enacted to reduce the flow of designer drugs into the market and make it easier to prosecute those involved in manufacturing and distributing these drugs. Designer and club drugs are still a problem.

FIGURE 12.9 Abuse of anabolic drugs carries the risk of serious acute and chronic health problems.
© Netea Mircea Valentin/ShutterStock, Inc.

Anabolic Drugs

Anabolic drugs are protein-building drugs. Included are the anabolic/androgenic steroids (AS), testosterone, and human growth hormone (HGH). These drugs have legitimate medical uses, such as the rebuilding of muscles after starvation or disease and the treatment of dwarfism. But they are sometimes abused by athletes and body builders as a shortcut to increasing muscle mass, strength, and endurance. Abuse of steroids is accompanied by numerous acute and chronic side effects for men, including acne, gynecomastia (the development of breasts), baldness, reduced fertility, and reduction in testicular size. Side effects for women are masculinizing: development of a male physique, increased body hair, failure to ovulate (menstrual irregularities), and a deepening of the voice. Long-term abuse of anabolic steroids can result in psychological dependence, making the discontinuation of use very difficult.[94]

In the late 1980s, it became apparent that increasing numbers of boys and young men of high school and college age were taking anabolic steroids as a shortcut to muscle building or to maturity (see **Figure 12.9**). Because of these trends in the abuse of anabolic steroids, the drugs were placed in Schedule III of the Controlled Substance Act in 1990. Abuse of steroids increased during the 1990s but has leveled off recently. As with other drugs discussed earlier, "steroids" sold on the Internet may not be authentic. Purchasing such substances online is certainly an example of the phrase "Buyer, beware."

Inhalants breathable substances that produce mind-altering effects

Inhalants

Inhalants are a collection of psychoactive, breathable chemicals. They include paint solvents, motor fuels, cleaners, glues, aerosol sprays, cosmetics, and other types of vapor. Because of their easy availability and low cost, they are often the drug of choice for the young. The primary effect of most of the inhalants is depression. As with alcohol, the user may at first experience a reduction of anxieties and inhibitions, making the user feel high. Continued use may result in hallucinations and loss of consciousness. Many of these chemicals are extremely toxic to the kidneys, liver, and nervous system. The use of inhalants by youth results from boredom and perhaps peer pressure and represents a maladaptation to these conditions.

Prevention and Control of Drug Abuse

The prevention and control of alcohol and other drug abuse require a knowledge of the causes of drug-taking behavior, sources of illicit drugs, drug laws, and treatment programs. Also required are community organizing skills, persistence, and cooperation among a vast array of concerned individuals and official and unofficial agencies.

From a community health standpoint, drug abuse tends to be a chronic condition. Thus, the activities of drug abuse and prevention agencies and organizations can be viewed as chronic disease-prevention activities. This approach, involving three different levels of prevention, is discussed next in relation to drug abuse prevention and control.

Levels of Prevention

Drug abuse prevention activities can be viewed as primary, secondary, or tertiary depending upon the point of intervention. *Primary prevention* programs are aimed at those who have never used drugs, and their goal is to prevent or forestall the initiation of drug use. Drug education programs that stress primary prevention of drug and alcohol use are most appropriate and successful for children at the elementary school age. In a broader sense, almost any activity that would reduce the likelihood of primary drug use could be considered primary prevention. For example, raising the price of alcohol, increasing cigarette taxes, arresting a neighborhood drug pusher, or destroying a cocaine crop in Bolivia could be considered primary prevention if it forestalled primary drug use in at least some individuals.

Secondary prevention programs are aimed at those who have begun alcohol or other drug use but who have not become chronic abusers and have not suffered significant physical or mental impairment from their drug or alcohol abuse. Alcohol and other drug abuse education programs that stress secondary prevention are often appropriate for people of high school or college age. They can be presented in educational, workplace, or community settings.

Tertiary prevention programs are designed to provide drug abuse treatment and aftercare, including relapse prevention programs. As such, they are usually designed for adults. Tertiary programs for teenagers are far too uncommon. Tertiary prevention programs may receive clients who "turn themselves in" for treatment voluntarily, but more often than not their clients are referred by the courts.

Elements of Prevention

Four basic elements play a role in drug abuse prevention and control. These are (1) education, (2) treatment, (3) public policy, and (4) enforcement. The goals of education and treatment are the same: to reduce the demand for drugs. Likewise, setting effective public policy and law enforcement share the same goal: to reduce the supply and availability of drugs in the community.

Education

The purpose of **drug abuse education** is to limit the demand for drugs by providing information about drugs and the dangers of drug abuse, changing attitudes and beliefs about drugs, providing the skills necessary to abstain from drugs, and ultimately changing drug abuse behavior. Education, principally a primary prevention activity, can be school based or community based. Examples of school-based drug abuse prevention programs are Project ALERT, LifeSkills Training (LST), and Class Action.[95] For these programs and other school-based programs to be successful, community members such as parents, teachers, local business people, and others must visibly support the program. Examples of community-based programs are the American Cancer Society's Great American Smokeout; Race Against Drugs (RAD), a nationwide program that links drug abuse prevention with motor sports; and the Reality Check Campaign, a program to boost awareness of the harmful effects of marijuana smoking among youth.

Treatment

The goal of **treatment** is to remove the physical, emotional, and environmental conditions that have contributed to drug dependency. Like education, treatment aims to reduce demand for drugs. It also aims to save money. Consider the money saved on law enforcement, medical costs, and lost productivity when treatment is successful. It is estimated that for every $1 spent on treatment, between $4 and $7 are saved in criminal justice-related costs.[96] Treatment for drug abuse occurs in a variety of settings and involves a variety of approaches. Treatment may be residential (inpatient) or nonresidential (outpatient). Under managed care, "behavioral health care" guidelines usually limit inpatient care to 28 days, after which the care may continue on an outpatient basis. In drug abuse treatment, what happens after the initial treatment phase is critical. **Aftercare**, the continuing care provided to the recovering former drug abuser, often involves peer group or self-help support group meetings, such as those provided by Alcoholics Anonymous (AA) or Narcotics Anonymous (NA). Despite frequent relapses, treatment for drug dependence is viewed as an important component of a community's comprehensive drug abuse prevention and control strategy.

Beginning January 1, 2010, The Paul Wellstone and Pete Domenici Mental Health Parity and Addiction Equity Act of 2008 (MHPAEA) took effect. This law "requires health insurers and group health plans to provide the same level of benefits for mental and/or substance use treatment and services that they do for medical/surgical care."[97] In 2010, the Patient Protection and Affordable Care Act (Affordable Care Act) was signed into law. The Affordable Care Act bars insurance companies from establishing eligibility rules based on pre-existing conditions, including history of addiction and substance abuse treatment. It also defines essential health benefits that must be covered, which include services and treatment for substance use disorders. Implementation of the provisions of these laws should improve substance abuse treatment options for many people.

Public Policy

Public policy embodies the guiding principles and courses of action pursued by governments to solve practical problems affecting society. Examples include passing drunk-driving laws or zoning ordinances that limit the number of bars in a neighborhood and enacting ordinances that regulate the type and amount of advertising for such legal drugs as alcohol and tobacco. Public policy should guide the budget discussions that ultimately determine how much a community spends for education, treatment, and law enforcement. Further examples of public policy decisions are restrictions of smoking in public buildings, the setting of 0.08% blood alcohol concentration as the point at which driving becomes illegal, and zero tolerance laws for BACs for minors. Setting the level of state excise taxes on alcohol and tobacco is also a public policy decision.

Law Enforcement

Law enforcement in drug abuse prevention and control is the application of federal, state, and local laws to arrest, jail, bring to trial, and sentence those who break drug laws or break laws because of drug use. The primary roles of law enforcement in a drug abuse prevention and control program are to (1) control drug use; (2) to control crime, especially crime related to drug use and drug trafficking—the buying, selling, manufacturing, or transporting of illegal drugs; (3) to prevent the establishment of crime organizations; and (4) to protect neighborhoods. Law enforcement is concerned with limiting the supply of drugs in the community by interrupting the source, transit, and distribution of drugs. There are law enforcement agencies at all levels of government. The principal agencies are discussed next.

> **Office of National Drug Control Policy (ONDCP)** the headquarters of the United States' drug control effort, located in the executive branch of the U.S. government, headed by a director appointed by the president

Governmental Drug Prevention and Control Agencies and Programs

Governmental agencies involved in drug abuse prevention, control, and treatment include a multitude of federal, state, and local agencies. At each of these levels of government, numerous offices and programs aim to reduce either the supply of or the demand for drugs.

Federal Agencies and Program

Our nation's anti-drug efforts are headed up by the White House **Office of National Drug Control Policy (ONDCP)**, which annually publishes a report detailing the nation's drug control strategy and budget. The 2015 National Drug Control Strategy focuses on seven priority areas:[98]

- Preventing drug use in our communities
- Seeking early intervention opportunities in health care
- Integrating treatment for substance use disorders into health care and supporting recovery
- Breaking the cycle of drug use, crime, and incarceration
- Disrupting domestic drug trafficking and production
- Strengthening international partnerships
- Improving information systems to better address drug use and its consequences

The National Drug Control Strategy Goals to be attained by 2015:

Goal 1: Curtail illicit drug consumption in the United States.

   1a. Decrease the 30-day prevalence of drug use among 12-to-17-year-olds by 15%.

   1b. Decrease the lifetime prevalence of eighth graders who have used drugs, alcohol, or tobacco by 15%.

   1c. Decrease the 30-day prevalence of drug use among young adults aged 18–25 by 10%.

   1d. Reduce the number of chronic drug users by 15%.

Goal 2: Improve the public health and public safety of the American people by reducing the consequences of drug abuse.

   2a. Reduce drug-induced deaths by 15%.

   2b. Reduce drug-related morbidity by 15%.

   2c. Reduce the prevalence of drugged driving by 10%.

For the 2015 fiscal year, 56.1% of the National Drug Control budget was aimed at reducing the supply of drugs; 43.9% was aimed at reducing the demand for drugs (see **Figure 12.10**).[99] Domestic law enforcement received about 35% of the budget, treatment received about 39%, about 14% was spent on interdiction, 6% on international support, and about 5% on prevention (**Figure 12.11**).[99]

The National Drug Control Strategy budget request for the fiscal year (FY) 2016 was about $27.6 billion. For the 2015 fiscal year, the request was about $26 billion.[98] The department scheduled to receive the largest portion of funds in FY 2016 is the U.S. Department of Health and Human Services (the National Institute on Drug Abuse and the Substance Abuse and Mental Health Services Administration). This is followed by the U.S. Department of Justice. The U.S. Department of Homeland Security is slated for the third-largest portion. The remainder of the

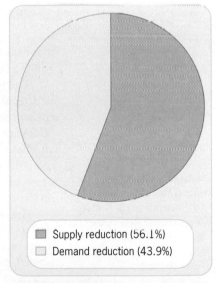

- Supply reduction (56.1%)
- Demand reduction (43.9%)

FIGURE 12.10   Federal drug control spending by function for fiscal year 2015; supply reduction vs. demand reduction.

Data from: Office of National Drug Control Policy, The White House (2015). FY16 Budget Summary. Available at https://www.whitehouse.gov//sites/default/files /ondcp/policy-and-research/fy_2016_budget _summary.pdf.

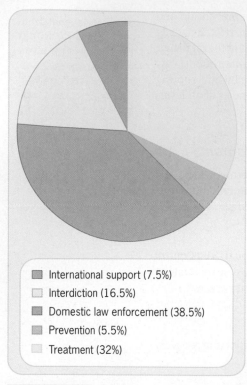

International support (7.5%)

Interdiction (16.5%)

Domestic law enforcement (38.5%)

Prevention (5.5%)

Treatment (32%)

FIGURE 12.11   Federal drug control spending by function for fiscal years 2012–2014.

Data from: Office of the National Drug Control Policy, The White House (2013). *National Drug Control Budget FY 2014 Funding Highlights*. Washington, DC: The White House. Available at http ://www.whitehouse.gov/sites/default/files/ondcp/policy-and -research/fy_2014_drug_control_budget_highlights_3.pdf.

Substance Abuse and Mental Health Services Administration (SAMHSA) the agency within the U.S. Department of Health and Human Services that provides leadership in drug abuse prevention and treatment. It houses the Center for Substance Abuse Prevention and the Center for Substance Abuse Treatment

National Institute on Drug Abuse (NIDA) the federal government's lead agency for drug abuse research, one of the National Institutes of Health

funding is spread over the U.S. Departments of Defense, State, Education, Veterans Affairs, Treasury, Labor, Transportation, Interior, Agriculture, and the Office of National Drug Control Policy.

U.S. Department of Health and Human Services

The United States Department of Health and Human Services (HHS) receives the largest portion of the federal drug budget, more than $9.5 billion in FY 2015.[99] This money is spent on drug prevention education, treatment programs, and research into the causes and physiology of drug abuse. The preponderance of these funds is spent to reduce the demand for drugs. The approach of HHS to the drug problem is broad and includes research, treatment, and educational activities.

The misuse and abuse of tobacco, alcohol, and other drugs are addressed primarily as lifestyle problems, that is, as health promotion issues—like physical fitness and nutrition. As such, HHS recognizes that the problems of drug misuse and abuse are complex—involving inherited, environmental, social, and economic causes. Therefore, the solutions are also viewed as being complex. The typical approach involves the application of the three levels of prevention—primary, secondary, and tertiary. It also recognizes the importance of incorporating the three primary prevention strategies of education, regulation, and automatic protection.

The HHS has published health status, risk reduction, and service and protection objectives on the use of tobacco, alcohol, and other drugs in *Healthy People 2020* (see Boxes 12.1 and 12.3). These objectives are but two examples of objectives that set the direction and standards for success of all of our national drug control efforts.

The lead agency within HHS is the **Substance Abuse and Mental Health Services Administration (SAMHSA)**. Within SAMHSA, there are four centers: the Center for Substance Abuse Prevention (CSAP), the Center for Substance Abuse Treatment (CSAT), the Center for Mental Health Services (CMHS), and the Center for Behavioral Health Statistics and Quality (CBHSQ). In addition to SAMHSA, there are two other important agencies that deal with the problems of alcohol and other drugs: the National Institute on Drug Abuse and the Food and Drug Administration.

The **National Institute on Drug Abuse (NIDA)** is the largest institution in the world devoted to drug abuse research. At NIDA, research efforts are aimed at understanding the causes and consequences of drug abuse and at evaluating prevention and treatment programs. Within NIDA are several important divisions and centers, such as the Division of Clinical Neuroscience and Behavioral Research; Division of Basic Neuroscience and Behavioral Research; Division of Epidemiology, Services, and Prevention Research; and Division of Pharmacotherapies and Medical Consequences of Drug Abuse. These agencies conduct research and publish articles on the causes, prevention, and treatment of tobacco, alcohol, and other drug abuse.

Another important agency in HHS is the U.S. Food and Drug Administration (FDA). As stated earlier, the FDA is charged with ensuring the safety and efficacy of all prescription and nonprescription drugs. The FDA dictates which drugs reach the market and how they must be labeled, packaged, and sold. The FDA is more concerned with drug misuse than abuse.

U.S. Department of Justice

The second-largest portion of federal spending for drug control, $7.5 billion in FY 2015, goes to the U.S. Department of Justice (DOJ).[99] The DOJ addresses the supply side of the drug trade most directly by identifying, arresting, and prosecuting those who break drug laws. It tries to protect the welfare of society by incarcerating the most serious offenders, deterring others from becoming involved in drug trade, and providing a clear picture to all of the cost of drug trade and abuse. Regarding the latter, the DOJ indirectly contributes to reducing the demand for drugs.

The DOJ's budget is large because, in addition to its enforcement responsibilities, the department maintains prisons and prisoners. The DOJ employs not only those who manage the penal system, but also many marshals, attorneys, and judges. The single largest portion of the DOJ's budget goes to the Bureau of Prisons. The DOJ also operates treatment, education, and rehabilitation programs in these prisons.

Within the DOJ are several important drug-fighting agencies. The lead agency in this respect is the Drug Enforcement Agency (DEA), which investigates and assists in the prosecution of drug traffickers and their accomplices in the United States and abroad and seizes the drugs as well as the assets on which they depend. The DEA employs more than 5,000 special agents and support personnel.

Three other important agencies in the DOJ that are involved in the prevention and control of drug abuse are the Federal Bureau of Investigation (FBI), the Office of Justice Programs (OJP), and the **Bureau of Alcohol, Tobacco, Firearms, and Explosives (ATF)**. The FBI investigates multinational organized crime networks that control the illegal drug market. The OJP provides leadership to federal, state, local, and tribal justice systems by disseminating knowledge and practices and providing grants for the implementation of these crime-fighting strategies. The OJP does not directly carry out law enforcement and justice activities, but it works with the justice community to identify crime-related challenges and to provide information, training, coordination, and innovative strategies and approaches for addressing these challenges.[90] The ATF has a wide range of responsibilities. One of its responsibilities is to protect our communities from the illegal diversion of alcohol and tobacco products. ATF partners with communities, industries, law enforcement, and public safety agencies to safeguard the public through information sharing, training, research, and use of technology.[100]

> **Bureau of Alcohol, Tobacco, Firearms, and Explosives (ATF)** the federal agency in the U.S. Department of Justice that regulates alcohol and tobacco

U.S. Department of Homeland Security

Shortly following the terrorist attacks on the World Trade Center and the Pentagon on September 11, 2001, President George W. Bush authorized the establishment of the U.S. Department of Homeland Security (DHS). Subsequently, a number of federal agencies involved in drug control activities were transferred into this new department, which received the third-largest portion of funding from the National Drug Control Budget ($4.1 billion).[99] Those agencies receiving funds are Immigration and Customs Enforcement, Customs and Border Protection, Counternarcotics Enforcement, and the United States Coast Guard. In the current environment, in which protection from terrorist acts is DHS's primary concern, the prevention and control of drug trafficking seem somewhat less urgent by comparison. Nonetheless, it is part of the mission of these agencies. For example, Immigration and Customs Enforcement works to prevent the immigration to this country of criminals, including those involved in drug trafficking. Customs and Border Protection works with Immigration and Customs Enforcement to protect our borders from external threats, including illegal drugs (see **Figure 12.12**). The United States Coast Guard helps to interdict illegal drug trafficking in our coastal waters.

Other Federal Agencies

Other federal agencies involved in drug abuse prevention and control are the U.S. Departments of State, Defense, Veterans Affairs, and Education. The U.S. State Department, through various diplomatic efforts, including "drug summits," attempts to achieve a reduction in the production and shipment of illicit drugs into this country. The U.S. Defense Department assists foreign allies to control the cultivation of illegal drug crops and the production of illegal drugs. Funding slated for the U.S. Department of Veteran Affairs is aimed primarily at the treatment of drug-related health problems of veterans.

The U.S. Department of Education (DOE) launched a program to support drug-free schools and communities in the late 1980s. The effort was aimed at encouraging schools to adopt

FIGURE 12.12   Customs agents assist in the arrest and prosecution of those involved in drug trafficking.
Courtesy of Gerald L. Nino/U.S. Customs and Border Protection.

clear "no drug use" policies and to provide a message that both communities and schools do not condone or approve of alcohol or drug use by minors. A handbook titled, *What Works: Schools Without Drugs*, was prepared and distributed to schools and communities.[101] The U.S. Department of Education continues to participate in the federal drug prevention effort. The National Drug Control budget for the U.S. Department of Education for fiscal year 2015 is $50.2 million.[99]

State and Local Agencies and Programs

Whereas considerable economic resources can be brought to bear on the drug problem at the federal level, it is becoming increasingly clear that to achieve success, the drug war in the United States must be fought at the local level—in homes, neighborhoods, and schools. State support usually comes in the form of law enforcement expertise in education and mental health, the coordination of local and regional programs, and sometimes funding initiatives. It is usually up to local citizens to put these state initiatives into action or to begin initiatives of their own.

State Agencies

State agencies that address drug abuse prevention and control issues include the offices of the governor, as well as state departments of health, education, mental health, justice, and law enforcement. Sometimes there is an umbrella agency that coordinates the activities of these various offices and departments; other times there is not. To review agencies involved in the prevention and control of drug abuse and drug dependence problems in your state, visit your state government's homepage and search using the terms "drug abuse prevention agencies" or "drug abuse prevention programs" (You can usually find your state government's homepage by typing "www.nameofyourstate.gov," or "www.postalcodeforyourstate.gov." For example, www.texas.gov will take you to the Texas government's homepage; www.in.gov will take you to the homepage of the Indiana state government.). Searching these sites in this way will reveal the agencies involved in drug abuse prevention at the state level.

The role of these state-level agencies is evident from their titles. Some state agencies provide actual services; others provide statistics or other information. Still others provide expertise or serve as a conduit for federal funding aimed at local (city or county) governments.

The role of state government is to promote, protect, and maintain the health and welfare of its citizens. Thus, each state has its own laws regulating the sale of tobacco, alcohol, and prescription drugs. States issue licenses to doctors, dentists, pharmacists, liquor stores, and taverns. Each state also passes laws and sets the penalties for the manufacture, sale, and possession of illicit drugs such as marijuana. For example, in California, possession of 28.5 grams (1 ounce) of marijuana or less is a civil infraction but not an arrestable offense; it carries a $100 fine. Possession of more than 28.5 grams is a misdemeanor, punishable by 6 months in jail and a $500 fine.[102]

In some cases, states have passed laws that conflict with federal laws. For example, some states have decriminalized marijuana cultivation and possession for medical or recreational use. Almost half of all U.S. states have legalized marijuana for medical purposes.[103] As of 2016, the possession and recreational use of small amounts of marijuana for recreational purposes is legal in Colorado, Washington, Oregon, Alaska, and the District of Columbia. The use of marijuana for medical purposes also has been legalized in almost half of all U.S. states and the District of Columbia. States that have legalized marijuana, either for recreational or medical purposes, maintain laws that regulate its use.[103] These people could still be arrested by the DEA and prosecuted under federal law. In 2013, the U.S. Department of Justice announced a revision to its marijuana enforcement policy. While marijuana use still violates federal law, the U.S. Department of Justice announced that it would rely heavily on states to enforce their own marijuana laws.[104]

Local Agencies

Agencies of local governments that are involved in drug abuse prevention and control include mayors' offices, police and sheriffs' departments, school corporations, health departments, family services offices, mental health services, prosecutors' offices, the juvenile justice system, judges and courts, drug task forces, and so on. In some communities, there is a community drug task force or coordinating council that includes both government officials and representatives of nongovernmental agencies. Such task forces or councils might include local religious leaders, representatives from local industry (both labor and management), health care providers, and members from local voluntary agencies. The task of these organizations is usually to prioritize problems faced by the community and decide on approaches to solving them. The goal is to develop a coordinated and effective effort to resolve the issue. Sometimes a solution might involve selecting an approach that has been used with success in another community or school system.

Nongovernmental Drug Prevention and Control Agencies and Programs

Many nongovernmental programs and agencies make valuable contributions to the prevention and control of drug abuse in the U.S. Among these are community- and school-based programs, workplace programs, and voluntary agencies.

Community-Based Drug Education Programs

Community-based drug education can occur in a variety of settings, such as child care facilities, public housing, religious institutions, businesses, and health care facilities. Information about the abuse of alcohol, tobacco, and other drugs can be disseminated through television and radio programs, movies, newspapers, and magazines.

Community-based drug education programs are most likely to be successful when they include six key features:[105]

1. A comprehensive strategy
2. An indirect approach to drug abuse prevention
3. The goal of empowering youth
4. A participatory approach
5. A culturally sensitive orientation
6. Highly structured activities

Community-based drug education programs that address broader issues (e.g., coping and learning skills) are most effective, as are those embedded in other existing community activities (see **Figure 12.13**). Participation can be increased by planning drug education programs around sporting or cultural events. Culturally sensitive programs are crucial for reaching minorities in the community. Use of the appropriate language, reading level, and spokespersons can mean the difference between success or failure of a program.

In the past 30 years, a great many drug abuse prevention education programs have been conceived and tested. Some of these have been scientifically proven to be effective. The Substance Abuse and Mental Health Services Administration in the U.S. Department of Health and Human Services has a searchable database of successful programs linked to its website.[95]

An example of a community-based program with a record of success is Across Ages. Across Ages is a school- and community-based drug prevention program for youth age 9 to 13 years that seeks to strengthen the bonds between adults and youth and provide opportunities for positive community involvement. The unique and highly effective feature of Across Ages is the pairing of older adult mentors (age 55 and above) with young adolescents, specifically youth making the transition to middle school. The program employs mentoring, community service, social competence training, and family activities to build youths' sense of personal responsibility for self and community.[95]

FIGURE 12.13 Use of appropriate language can be the difference between success and failure of a community drug prevention program.
© Lisa C. McDonald/ShutterStock, Inc.

FIGURE 12.14 Drug Abuse Resistance Education (DARE) programs involve police in school drug education.

Courtesy of D.A.R.E. America

Across Ages has been able to demonstrate success in the following areas: decreased substance use, decrease in tobacco and alcohol use, increased problem-solving ability, increased school attendance, decreased suspensions from school, improved attitude toward adults, and improved attitude toward school and the future.[95]

School-Based Drug Education Programs

Most health educators believe that a strong, comprehensive school health education program—one that occupies a permanent and prominent place in the school curriculum—is the best defense against all health problems, including drug abuse. However, many schools lack these strong programs and, in their absence, substitute drug education programs developed specifically for school use.

One such program is the Drug Abuse Resistance Education (DARE) program, which began in Los Angeles. In the DARE program, local police enter the classroom to teach grade-school children about drugs (see **Figure 12.14**). While imparting some knowledge, the program's primary approach is to change attitudes and beliefs about drugs. It is also successful in improving children's images of the police themselves. Unfortunately, although very popular in many communities, DARE programs have been unable to demonstrate any real success in reducing actual drug use.[106]

An example of a program that has been scientifically proven to be effective is Project ALERT. Project ALERT reduced students' current marijuana use by 60%, reduced the likelihood of alcohol use by 24%, and substantially reduced students' pro-drug-use attitudes and beliefs.[107]

Student assistance programs (SAPs) are school-based programs modeled after employee assistance programs in the workplace. They are aimed at identifying and intervening in cases of drug problems. **Peer counseling programs** are also present in some schools. In these programs, students talk about mutual problems and receive support and perhaps learn coping skills from peers who have been trained in this intervention activity and do not use drugs.

Workplace-Based Drug Education Programs

In September 1986, concern about widespread drug use in the workplace led then President Ronald Reagan to sign Executive Order 12564, proclaiming a Drug-Free Federal Workplace.[108] The rationale for the order signed in September 1986 was cited in the document itself: the desire and need for the well-being of employees, the loss of productivity caused by drug use, the illegal profits of organized crime, the illegality of the behavior itself, the undermining of public confidence, and the role of the federal government as the largest employer in the nation to set a standard for other employers to follow in these matters. It had also become apparent to all that drug abuse is not just a personal health problem and a law enforcement problem, but that it also is a behavior that affects the safety and productivity of others, especially at work. Studies have shown that substance abusers (1) are less productive, (2) miss more work days, (3) are more likely to injure themselves, and (4) file more workers' compensation claims than their non-substance-abusing counterparts.

The Drug-Free Federal Workplace order required federal employees to refrain from using illegal drugs, and it required agency heads to develop plans for achieving drug-free workplaces for employees in their agencies. The order further required the setting up of drug-testing programs and procedures and employee assistance programs that would include provisions for rehabilitation.[108] Similar workplace substance abuse programs, which include drug testing, soon spread to the private sector so that by the mid-1990s, such programs were in place in more than 80% of American companies.[109]

Student assistance programs (SAPs) school-based drug education programs to assist students who have alcohol or other drug problems

Peer counseling programs school-based programs in which students discuss alcohol and other drug-related problems with peers

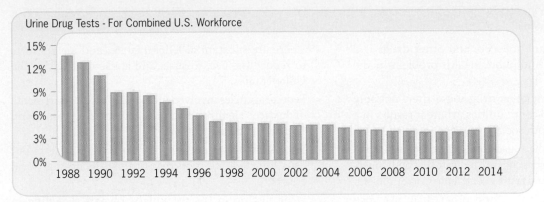

FIGURE 12.15   Drug positivity rates for combined U.S. workforce, 1988 through 2014.

Data from: Quest Diagnostics Incorporated (2015). The Quest Diagnostics Drug Testing Index®. Available at http://www.questdiagnostics.com /home/physicians/health-trends/drug-testing/table1.html. Reprinted with permission.

A typical workplace substance abuse prevention program has five facets.[110] The first is a formal written substance abuse policy that reflects the employer's commitment to a drug-free workplace. The second is an employee drug education and awareness program. Third is the supervisor training program. Fourth is the **employee assistance program (EAP)** to help those who need counseling and rehabilitation. The last component is a drug-testing program. Large companies are more likely than small companies to have the major components of a drug-free workplace program.

Although a substantial part of the problem can be attributed to alcohol consumption, illicit drug use remains a problem in many workplaces. Fortunately, the prevalence of workplace drug use has declined significantly, in part because of the proliferation of workplace drug abuse and prevention programs that include drug testing. In 1987, the first year of workplace drug testing, 18.1% of all tests were positive;[111] by 1998, this statistic had dropped below 5%, where it has remained. In 2014, only 4.7% of all workplace drug tests were positive (see **Figure 12.15**).[112]

Voluntary Health Agencies

Drug prevention and control programs are carried out at the local level with the cooperation and effort of many community members. Some of these programs are of local origin, whereas others have received national recognition and even endorsement. The people who actually deliver drug abuse prevention programs include teachers, community health educators, social workers, law enforcement officers, and volunteers.

The programs presented vary greatly in their message and approach. Some programs seek to educate or provide knowledge, others seek to change beliefs or attitudes about alcohol or other drug use, while still others seek to alter behavior by providing new behavior skills. Studies have shown that programs incorporating all these approaches are most successful.

A large number of voluntary health agencies have been founded to prevent or control the social and personal consequences of alcohol, tobacco, and other drug abuse. Among these are such agencies as Mothers Against Drunk Driving (MADD), Students Against Destructive Decisions (SADD), Alcoholics Anonymous (AA), Narcotics Anonymous (NA), the American Cancer Society (ACS), and many others. Each of these organizations is active locally, statewide, and nationally.

An important function of community leaders is to encourage parents, school officials, members of law enforcement, businesses, social groups, community health workers, and the media to work together in an effort to reduce the abuse of alcohol, tobacco, and other drugs. Every approach should be used, including seeking favorable-legislation and judicial appointments, fairness in advertising, school and community education and treatment, and law enforcement. Only through citizen support and vigilance can there be a reduction in the threat that alcohol and other drugs pose to our community.

Employee assistance program (EAP) a workplace drug program designed to assist employees whose work performance is suffering because of a personal problem such as alcohol or other drug problems

Chapter Summary

- The abuse of alcohol, tobacco, and other drugs is a major community and public health problem in the United States.

- Alcohol, tobacco, and other drug abuse affect not only individuals but also communities, where it results in a substantial drain both socially and economically.

- Investigations into the causes of drug experimentation, drug abuse, and drug dependence indicate that both inherited and environmental factors contribute to the problem.

- Rates of tobacco, alcohol, and other drug use rose during the 1990s. After peaking in 1999, use of these drugs began to level off and decline, and they have remained steady in recent years.

- Chronic alcohol and tobacco use results in the loss of billions of dollars and thousands of lives in the United States each year.

- The misuse and abuse of prescription and nonprescription drugs remain a problem of concern.

- There are four principal elements of drug abuse prevention and control—education, treatment, public policy, and law enforcement.

- Prevention activities can be categorized as primary, secondary, and tertiary prevention.

- There are substantial federal, state, and local efforts to reduce the use, misuse, and abuse of drugs in the United States.

- Federal agencies involved include the U.S. Departments of Justice, Health and Human Services, Homeland Security, and many others.

- Efforts at the state level vary from state to state but usually include attempts to coordinate federal and local efforts.

- Drug testing in the workplace reveals a decline in illicit drug use in the workplace since testing began in 1987.

- Alcohol, tobacco, and other drug abuse continue to cause injuries and lost productivity in the American workplace.

- A typical workplace substance abuse prevention program has five components: a written policy, a drug education program, a supervisor training program, an employee assistance program, and a drug testing program.

- A large number of voluntary health agencies are involved in drug abuse prevention and control activities.

Scenario: Analysis and Response

Please reread the scenario at the beginning of this chapter. How would you respond to the following questions?

1. Re-examine Table 12.2. Which of the personal consequences of drug use were evident in Andy's story?

2. Which of the factors discussed in this chapter that contribute to drug abuse could have contributed to Andy's drug dependence?

3. The use of opioid pain relievers and heroin has become a nationwide problem. Is the use of opioid pain relievers and heroin a widespread problem in your state? What have you heard about opioid or heroin use in your community?

4. What is the current mortality rate for opioid pain reliever use and heroin use in your state? Where could you find this information?

5. Which state or local agencies are available to help Andy get into and stay in recovery?

Review Questions

1. What are some personal consequences resulting from the abuse of alcohol and other drugs?

2. What are some community consequences resulting from the abuse of alcohol and other drugs?

3. What are the recent trends in drug use by high school seniors?

4. What do you believe is our most serious drug problem? Why?

5. Explain the differences among drug use, misuse, and abuse.

6. How are physical and psychological dependence different?

7. What are the two sources of risk factors that contribute to substance abuse?

8. Name the four categories of environmental risk factors that contribute to substance abuse and give an example of each.

9. What are the two major types of abused drugs? Give examples of each.

10. Why is alcohol considered the number one problem drug in the United States?

11. In what forms do Americans consume nicotine, and in what groups of people do we see the heaviest users?

12. What agency regulates over-the-counter and prescription drugs? What two characteristics must a drug have to be approved for sale?

13. How can misuse of prescription drugs become a risk to your health?

14. What is the most commonly abused illicit drug? Why is this drug a concern?

15. What are controlled substances? Give some examples.

16. What are the side effects for both men and women that result from the use of anabolic drugs?

17. What are the four elements of drug prevention and control?

18. What are primary, secondary, and tertiary prevention strategies for the drug problem?

19. Describe the roles of each of the following federal departments in controlling drug abuse: Health and Human Services, Homeland Security, and Justice.

20. What role do state governments play in preventing and controlling drug abuse? Local governments?

21. What is Across Ages? What does it do? What is Project ALERT? What does it do?

22. How would you respond to the statement "Most drug abusers are unemployed"?

23. What are the names of four voluntary agencies and self-help groups involved in the prevention, control, and treatment of alcohol, tobacco, and other drug abuse?

Activities

1. Schedule an appointment with the Vice President of Student Affairs, the Dean of Students, or the alcohol and drug abuse prevention educator on your campus to find out more about drug (including alcohol) problems. Find out what the greatest concerns are and how the administration is trying to deal with the issues.

2. Make an appointment with the health educator or another employee in your local health department to find out more about the existing alcohol, tobacco, and other drug problems in the community. Collect the same information as noted in the first activity, except find information for the community, not the campus.

3. Find six articles that appeared in your local newspaper during the past 2 weeks that deal with drugs. Find two that related to problems at the national or international

level, two at the state level, and two at the local level. Summarize each and present your reaction to these articles in a written paper.

4. Conduct a survey of at least 100 students on your campus. Try to get a random sample of people. Interview these people and find out what they think are the major drug problems on your campus and how they might be solved. Feel free to include other questions on your survey. Summarize the results in a two-page paper.

5. Attend a meeting of a community group that is involved in the prevention and control of drug abuse (e.g., local drug task force, AA, a smoking cessation group, MADD, or SADD). In a two-page paper, summarize the meeting and share your reaction to it.

References

1. Horgan, C., K. C. Skwara, and G. Strickler (2001). *Substance Abuse: The Nation's Number One Health Problem.* Princeton, NJ: Robert Wood Johnson Foundation.

2. Substance Abuse and Mental Health Services Administration (2011). *Drug Abuse Warning Network, 2011: National Estimates of Drug-Related Emergency Department Visits, 2004–2011 — All Misuse and Abuse.* Available at http://www.samhsa.gov/data/dawn/nations/Nation_2011_AllMA.xls.

3. Xu, X., E. E. Bishop, S. M. Kennedy, S. A. Simpson, and T. F. Pechacek (2014). "Annual Health care Spending Attributable to Cigarette Smoking: An Update." *American Journal of Preventive Medicine,* 48(3): 326–33.

4. Sacks, J. J., K. R. Gonzales, E. E. Bouchery, L. E. Tomedi, and R. D. Brewer (2015). "2010 National and State Costs of Excessive Alcohol

Consumption." *American Journal of Preventive Medicine,* 49(5): e73–e79.

5. National Institute on Drug Abuse (2014). *Trends and Statistics.* Available at https://www.drugabuse.gov/related-topics/trends-statistics#costs.

6. National Center on Addiction and Substance Abuse at Columbia University (2009). *Shoveling Up II: The Impact of Substance Abuse on Federal, State and Local Budgets.* Available at http://www.centeronaddiction.org/addiction-research/reports/shoveling-ii-impact-substance-abuse-federal-state-and-local-budgets.

7. Johnston, L. D., P. M. O'Malley, R. A. Miech, J. G. Bachman, and J. E. Schulenberg (2016). *Monitoring the Future National Survey Results on Drug Use, 1975–2015: Overview, Key Findings on Adolescent Drug Use.* Ann Arbor: Institute for Social Research, The University of

Michigan. Available at http://www.monitoringthefuture.org/pubs/monographs/mtf-overview2015.pdf.

8. Glantz, M., and R. Pickens (1992). "Vulnerability to Drug Abuse: Introduction and Overview." In M. Glantz and R. Pickens, eds., *Vulnerability to Drug Abuse*. Washington, DC: American Psychological Association.

9. Cotton, N. S. (1979). "The Familial Incidence of Alcoholism: A Review." *Journal of Studies on Alcohol*, 40: 89–116.

10. Cloninger, C. R., M. Bohman, and S. Sigvardsson (1981). "Inheritance of Alcohol Abuse." *Archives of General Psychiatry*, 38: 861–868.

11. Schuckit, M. A., S. C. Risch, and E. O. Gold (1988). "Alcohol Consumption, ACTH Level, and Family History of Alcoholism." *American Journal of Psychiatry*, 145(11): 1391–1395.

12. U.S. Department of Health and Human Services (2012). "Update on the Genetics of Alcoholism." *Alcohol Research: Current Reviews*, 34(3). Available at http://pubs.niaaa.nih.gov/publications/arcr343/toc34_3.htm.

13. Tabakoff, B., and P. L. Hoffman (1988). "Genetics and Biological Markers of Risk for Alcoholism." *Public Health Report*, 103(6): 690–698.

14. U.S. Department of Health and Human Services (2000). *Tenth Special Report to the U.S. Congress*. Washington, DC: U.S. Government Printing Office. Available at http://pubs.niaaa.nih.gov/publications/10report/intro.pdf.

15. Zickler, P. (2000). "Evidence Builds that Genes Influence Cigarette Smoking. *NIDA Notes*, 15(2): 1–2.

16. Goldman D., G. Oroszi, and F. Ducci (2005). "The Genetics of Addictions: Uncovering the Genes." *Nature Reviews Genetics*, 6(7): 521–532.

17. Lessov-Schlaggar C. N., M. L. Pergadia, T. V. Khroyan, and G. E. Swan (2008). "Genetics of Nicotine Dependence and Pharmacotherapy." *Biochemical Pharmacology*, 75:178–195.

18. Needle, R., Y. Lavee, S. Su, et al. (1988). "Familial, Interpersonal, and Intrapersonal Correlates of Drug Use: A Longitudinal Comparison of Adolescents in Treatment, Drug-Using Adolescents Not in Treatment, and Non-Drug-Using Adolescents." *International Journal of Addictions*, 239(12): 1211–1240.

19. Meller, W. H., R. Rinehart, R. J. Cadoret, and E. Troughton (1988). "Specific Familial Transmission in Substance Abuse." *International Journal of Addictions*, 23(10): 1029–1039.

20. Thompson R. G., Jr., D. Lizardi, K. M. Keye, and D. S. Hasin (2008). "Childhood or Adolescent Parental Divorce/Separation, Parental History of Alcohol Problems, and Offspring Lifetime Alcohol Dependence." *Drug and Alcohol Dependence*, 98(3): 264–269.

21. Shedler, J., and J. Block (1990). "Adolescent Drug Use and Psychological Health: A Longitudinal Inquiry." *American Psychologist*, 45(5): 612–630.

22. U.S. Department of Health and Human Services (1990). *Seventh Special Report to the U.S. Congress* (DHHS pub. no. ADM-90-1656). Washington, DC: U.S. Government Printing Office.

23. Horgan, C., K. C. Skwara, and G. Strickler, (2001). *Substance Abuse: The Nation's Number One Health Problem*. Princeton, NJ: Robert Wood Johnson Foundation, 30.

24. Dembo, R., W. R. Blount, J. Schmeidler, and W. Burgos (1986). "Perceived Environmental Drug Use Risk and the Correlates of Early Drug Use or Nonuse among Inner-City Youths: The Motivated Actor." *International Journal of Addictions*, 21(9–10): 977–1000.

25. National Center on Addiction and Substance Abuse at Columbia University (2006). *The Commercial Value of Underage and Pathological Drinking to the Alcohol Industry*. New York: CASAColumbia.

26. Foster, S. E., R. D. Vaughan, W. H. Foster, and J. A. Califano, Jr. (2006). "Estimate of the Commercial Value of Underage Drinking and Adult Abusive and Dependent Drinking to the Alcohol Industry." *Archives of Pediatrics and Adolescent Medicine*, 160(5): 473–478.

27. National Institute on Alcohol Abuse and Alcoholism (2016). *Alcohol Facts and Statistics*. Available at http://www.niaaa.nih.gov/alcohol-health/overview-alcohol-consumption/alcohol-facts-and-statistics.

28. American College Health Association (2016). *American College Health Association National College Health Assessment II: Undergraduate Students Reference Group Data Report Fall 2015*. Hanover, MD: Author. Available at http://www.acha-ncha.org/docs/NCHA-II%20FALL_2015_UNDERGRADUATE_REFERENCE_GROUP_DATA_REPORT.pdf.

29. American College Health Association (2012). *National College Health Assessment II: Reference Group Data Report Fall 2011*. Hanover, MD: Author. Available at http://www.acha-ncha.org/docs/ACHA-NCHA-II_ReferenceGroup_DataReport_Fall2011.pdf

30. American College Health Association (2014). *American College Health Association National College Health Assessment II: Reference Group Data Report Fall 2013*. Hanover, MD: Author. Available at http://www.acha-ncha.org/docs/ACHA-NCHA-II_ReferenceGroup_DataReport_Fall2013.pdf.

31. American College Health Association (2015). *American College Health Association National College Health Assessment II: Reference Group Data Report Fall 2014*. Hanover, MD: Author. Available at http://www.acha-ncha.org/docs/NCHA-II_FALL_2014_REFERENCE_GROUP_DATA_REPORT.pdf.

32. American College Health Association (2016). *American College Health Association National College Health Assessment II: Reference Group Data Report Fall 2015*. Hanover, MD: Author. Available at http://www.acha-ncha.org/docs/NCHA-II%20FALL%202015%20REFERENCE%20GROUP%20DATA%20REPORT.pdf.

33. Morse, R. M., and D. K. Flavin (1992). "The Definition of Alcoholism." *Journal of the American Medical Association*, 268(8): 1012–1014.

34. United States Census (2016). *U.S.A. Quick Facts*. Available at http://www.census.gov/quickfacts/table/PST045215/00.

35. U.S. Department of Transportation (2000). *Relative Risk of Fatal Crash Involvement by BAC, Age, and Gender*. Springfield, VA: National Technical Information Service.

36. U.S. Department of Transportation (2009). *Traffic Safety Facts: Alcohol-Impaired Driving*. Available at http://www.nrd.nhtsa.dot.gov/Pubs/811385.pdf.

37. U.S. Department of Transportation, Fatality Analysis Reporting System (n.d.). *Persons Killed, by Highest Driver Blood Alcohol Concentration (BAC) in the Crash, 1994–2014—State: USA*. Available at http://www.fars.nhtsa.dot.gov/Trends/TrendsAlcohol.aspx.

38. U.S. Department of Health and Human Services, Public Health Service (2000). *Healthy People 2010: Understanding and Improving Health*. Washington, DC: U.S. Government Printing Office.

39. U.S. Department of Transportation (2001). *Legislative History of .08 Per Se Laws Final Report*. Available at http://icsw.nhtsa.gov/people/injury/research/pub/alcohol-laws/08History/.

40. National Transportation Safety Board (NTSB) (2013). *NTSB Unveils Interventions to Reach Zero Alcohol-Impaired Crashes*. Available at http://www.ntsb.gov/news/2013/130514.html.

41. National Institute on Alcohol Abuse and Alcoholism (2013). *A Snapshot of Annual High-Risk College Drinking Consequences*. Available at http://www.collegedrinkingprevention.gov/StatsSummaries/snapshot.aspx.

42. Hingson R.W., W. Zha, and E. R. Weitzman (2009). "Magnitude of and Trends in Alcohol-Related Mortality and Morbidity among U.S. College Students Ages 18–24, 1998–2005." *Journal of Studies on Alcohol and Drugs*, July(Suppl 16): 12–20.

43. Cole, T. B. (2006). "Rape at U.S. Colleges Often Fueled by Alcohol." *Journal of the American Medical Association*, 296(5): 504–505.

44. Centers for Disease Control and Prevention (2016). *Fetal Alcohol Spectrum Disorders (FASD), Data and Statistics.* Available at http://www.cdc.gov/ncbddd/fasd/data.html.

45. May P.A., J. P. Gossage, W. O. Kalberg, L. K. Robinson, D. Buckley, M. Manning, and H. E. Hoyme (2009). "Prevalence and Epidemiologic Characteristics of FASD from Various Research Methods with an Emphasis on Recent In-School Studies." *Developmental Disabilities Research Reviews*, 15(3): 176–192.

46. Centers for Disease Control and Prevention (2016). *Fetal Alcohol Spectrum Disorders (FASD), Data & Statistics.* Available at http://www.cdc.gov/ncbddd/fasd/data.html.

47. Substance Abuse and Mental Health Services Administration (2015). *Results from the 2014 National Survey on Drug Use and Health: Detailed Tables.* Available at http://www.samhsa.gov/data/sites/default/files/NSDUH-DetTabs2014/NSDUH-DetTabs2014.htm.

48. Centers for Disease Control and Prevention, Behavioral Risk Factor Surveillance System (2014). *Nationwide (States, DC, and Territories)—2014 Tobacco Use, Adults Who Are Current Smokers.* Available at http://www.cdc.gov/brfss/brfssprevalence/index.html.

49. Centers for Disease Control and Prevention, Youth Risk Behavior Surveillance System (n.d.). *Trends in Prevalence of Tobacco Use, National YRBS—1997–2015.* Available at http://www.cdc.gov/healthyyouth/data/yrbs/pdf/trends/2015_tobacco_trend_yrbs.pdf.

50. U.S. Department of Health and Human Services (2012). *Preventing Tobacco Use among Youth and Young Adults: A Report of the Surgeon General.* Atlanta, GA: U.S. Department of Health and Human Services, Centers for Disease Control and Prevention, Office on Smoking and Health.

51. U.S. Food and Drug Administration (2016). *Vaporizers, E-Cigs, and Other Electronic Nicotine Delivery Systems (ENDS).* Available at http://www.fda.gov/TobaccoProducts/Labeling/ProductsIngredientsComponents/ucm456610.htm.

52. Schoenborn, C.A., and Gindi, R.M. (2015). *Electronic Cigarette Use among Adults: United States, 2014 (NCHS data brief, no. 217).* Hyattsville, MD: National Center for Health Statistics. Available at http://www.cdc.gov/nchs/data/databriefs/db217.pdf

53. Kim, A. E., K. Y. Arnold, and O. Makarenko (2014). "E-Cigarette Advertising Expenditures in the U.S., 2011–2012." *American Journal of Preventive Medicine*, 46(4): 409–12.

54. Centers for Disease Control and Prevention (2008). "Smoking-Attributable Mortality, Years of Potential Life Lost, and Productivity Losses—United States, 2000–2004." *Morbidity and Mortality Weekly Report*, 57(45): 1226–1228.

55. U.S. Department of Health and Human Services (2014). *The Health Consequences of Smoking—50 Years of Progress: A Report of the Surgeon General.* Atlanta, GA. U.S. Department of Health and Human Services, Centers for Disease Control and Prevention, National Center for Chronic Disease Prevention and Health Promotion, Office on Smoking and Health. Available at http://www.cdc.gov/tobacco/data_statistics/sgr/50th-anniversary/index.htm.

56. U.S. Food and Drug Administration (2016). Press Announcement – *FDA Takes Significant Steps to Protect Americans from Dangers of Tobacco through New Regulation.* Available at http://www.fda.gov/NewsEvents/Newsroom/PressAnnouncements/ucm499234.htm.

57. World Health Organization (2011). *WHO Report on the Global Tobacco Epidemic, 2011: The MPOWER Package.* Geneva, Switzerland: Author.

58. U.S. Department of Health and Human Services, Public Health Service, Centers for Disease Control (1986). *The Health Consequence of Involuntary Smoking.* A Report of the Surgeon General (DHHS pub. no. CDC-87-8398). Washington, DC: U.S. Government Printing Office.

59. Byrd, J. C., R. S. Shapiro, and D. L. Schiedermayer (1989). "Passive Smoking: A Review of Medical and Legal Issues." *American Journal of Public Health*, 79(2): 209–215.

60. Environmental Protection Agency (1991). *Respiratory Health Effects of Passive Smoking: Lung Cancer and Other Disorders (EPA/600/6-90/006F).* Washington, DC: Indoor Air Quality Clearinghouse.

61. Centers for Disease Control and Prevention (2010). "Vital Signs: Nonsmokers' Exposure to Secondhand Smoke—United States, 1999–2008." *Morbidity and Mortality Weekly Report*, 59(35): 1141–1146. Available at http://www.cdc.gov/mmwr/preview/mmwrhtml/mm5935a4.htm?s_cid=mm5935a4_w.

62. Substance Abuse and Mental Health Services Administration (n.d.). *FFY 2013 Annual Synar Reports, Tobacco Sales to Youth.* Available at http://www.samhsa.gov/sites/default/files/synar-annual-report-2013.pdf.

63. Office of Maryland Attorney General J. Joseph Current (11 October 2006). *Curran and R. J. Reynolds Reach Historic Settlement to End the Sale of Flavored Cigarettes* [Press Release]. Available at http://www.oag.state.md.us/Press/2006/101106.htm.

64. U.S. Food and Drug Administration (2013). *Overview of the Family Smoking Prevention and Tobacco Control Act: Consumer Fact Sheet.* Available at http://www.fda.gov/tobaccoproducts/guidancecomplianceregulatoryinformation/ucm246129.htm.

65. U.S. Federal Trade Commission (2013). *Federal Trade Commission Cigarette Report for 2011.* Available at http://www.ftc.gov/os/2013/05/130521cigarettereport.pdf.

66. Campaign for Tobacco-Free Kids (2016). *Top Combined State-Local Cigarette Tax Rates* (As of January 6, 2016). Available at http://www.tobaccofreekids.org/research/factsheets/pdf/0267.pdf.

67. Campaign for Tobacco-Free Kids (2016). *State Excise and Sales Taxes per Pack of Cigarettes, Total Amounts & State Rankings.* Available at http://www.tobaccofreekids.org/research/factsheets/pdf/0202.pdf.

68. U.S. Drug Enforcement Administration (2006). *General Information Regarding The Combat Methamphetamine Epidemic Act of 2005* [Title VII of Public Law 109-177]. Available at http://www.deadiversion.usdoj.gov/meth/cma2005_general_info.pdf.

69. National Center for Health Statistics (2013). *Health, United States 2013: With Special Feature on Prescription Drugs.* Available at http://www.cdc.gov/nchs/data/hus/hus13.pdf.

70. Rudd, R. A., N. Aleshire, J. E. Zibbel, and N. Gladden (2016). "Increases in Drug and Opioid Overdose Deaths—United States, 2000–2014." *Morbidity and Mortality Weekly Report*, 64(50): 1378s82.

71. Centers for Disease Control and Prevention (2016). *Injury Prevention and Control: Opioid Overdose.* Available at http://www.cdc.gov/drugoverdose/data/overdose.html.

72. Centers for Disease Control and Prevention (n.d.). *Ten Leading Causes of Death by Age Group, United States – 2014.* Available at http://www.cdc.gov/injury/images/lc-charts/leading_causes_of_death_age_group_2014_1050w760h.gif.

73. Centers for Disease Control and Prevention (n.d.). *Ten Leading Causes of Death by Age Group Highlighting Unintentional Injury Deaths, United States – 2014.* Available at http://www.cdc.gov/injury/images/lc-charts/leading_causes_of_injury_deaths_unintentional_injury_2014_1040w740h.gif.

74. National Institute on Drug Abuse (2015). *Prescription Opioids and Heroin.* Available at https://www.drugabuse.gov/publications/research-reports/relationship-between-prescription-drug-abuse-heroin-use/.

75. Centers for Disease Control and Prevention (2014). *Vital Signs, Opioid Painkiller Prescribing.* Available at http://www.cdc.gov/vitalsigns/opioid-prescribing/.

76. Substance Abuse and Mental Health Services Administration (2013). *Drug Abuse Warning Network (DAWN), National Estimates of Drug-Related Emergency Department Visits 2011.* Available at http://www.samhsa.gov/data/2k13/DAWN2k11ED/DAWN2k11ED.pdf.

77. U.S. Department of Justice, Drug Enforcement Agency, Office of Diversion Control (n.d.) *Schedules of Controlled Substances.* Federal Register,

Code of Federal Regulations, Food and Drugs, Part 1308. Available at http://www.deadiversion.usdoj.gov/21cfr/cfr/2108cfrt.htm.

78. Zickler, P. (2000). "Evidence Accumulates that Long-Term Marijuana Users Experience Withdrawal." *NIDA Notes*, 15(1).

79. Substance Abuse and Mental Health Services Administration (2013). *Treatment Episode Data Set (TEDS): 2003–2013: National Admissions to Substance Abuse Treatment Services.* Available at http://www.samhsa.gov/data/sites/default/files/2013_Treatment_Episode_Data_Set_National/2013_Treatment_Episode_Data_Set_National_Tables.html.

80. National Center for Addiction and Substance Abuse at Columbia University (1994). *Cigarettes, Alcohol, Marijuana: Gateways to Illicit Drug Use.* New York: CASAColumbia.

81. National Institute on Drug Abuse (2015). *DrugFacts: Synthetic Cannabinoids.* Available at https://www.drugabuse.gov/publications/drugfacts/synthetic-cannabinoids.

82. American Association of Poison Control Centers (2016 April 30). *Synthetic Cannabinoid Data.* Available at https://aapcc.s3.amazonaws.com/files/library/Syn_Marijuana_Web_Data_through_4.30.16_ohgf4Dr.pdf.

83. Substance Abuse and Mental Health Services Administration (2012). *Drug Abuse Warning Network: Drug-Related Emergency Department Visits Involving Synthetic Cannabinoids.* Available at http://www.samhsa.gov/data/2k12/DAWN105/SR105-synthetic-marijuana.htm.

84. U.S. Drug Enforcement Administration (2011). "January 2011 Scheduling Update." *Microgram Bulletin.* Washington, DC: U.S. Department of Justice. Available at http://www.justice.gov/dea/pr/micrograms/2011/mg0111.pdf.

85. U.S. Food and Drug Administration (2012). *Safety and Innovation Act.* S.3187.ENR. Washington, DC: U.S. Government Printing Office. Available at http://www.gpo.gov/fdsys/pkg/BILLS-112s3187enr/pdf/BILLS-112s3187enr.pdf.

86. National Conference of State Legislatures (2015). *Synthetic Drug Threats.* Available at http://www.ncsl.org/research/civil-and-criminal-justice/synthetic-drug-threats.aspx.

87. U.S. Drug Enforcement Administration (2013). *Updated Results From DEA's Largest-Ever Global Synthetic Drug Takedown Yesterday* [Press Release]. Available at http://www.justice.gov/dea/divisions/hq/2013/hq062613.shtml.

88. U.S. Department of Justice (2015). *National Drug Threat Assessment 2015.* Available at http://www.dea.gov/docs/2015%20NDTA%20Report.pdf.

89. Centers for Disease Control and Prevention (2015). "Community Outbreak of HIV Infection Linked to Injection Drug Use of Oxymorphone — Indiana, 2015." *Morbidity and Mortality Weekly Report*, 64(16): 443–444. Available at http://www.cdc.gov/mmwr/preview/mmwrhtml/mm6416a4.htm.

90. National Institute on Drug Abuse (2016). *Commonly Abused Drug Charts.* Available at https://www.drugabuse.gov/drugs-abuse/commonly-abused-drugs-charts.

91. U.S. Drug Enforcement Administration (2014). *DEA Domestic Drug Seizures.* Available at http://www.justice.gov/dea/resource-center/statistics.shtml#seizures.

92. U.S. Drug Enforcement Administration (2014). *Methamphetamine Lab Incidents, 2004–2014.* Available at http://www.dea.gov/resource-center/meth-lab-maps.shtml.

93. National Institute on Drug Abuse (2016). "DrugFacts: MDMA (Ecstasy/Molly)." *NIDA DrugFacts.* Washington, DC: National Institutes of Health. Available at https://www.drugabuse.gov/publications/drugfacts/mdma-ecstasymolly.

94. National Institute on Drug Abuse (2016). "DrugFacts: Anabolic Steroids." *NIDA DrugFacts.* Available at https://www.drugabuse.gov/publications/drugfacts/anabolic-steroids.

95. Substance Abuse and Mental Health Services Administration (n.d.). *National Registry of Evidence-Based Programs and Practices.* Available at http://nrepp.samhsa.gov.

96. National Institute on Drug Abuse (2016). *Understanding Drug Abuse and Addiction: What Science Says.* Available at https://www.drugabuse.gov/understanding-drug-abuse-addiction-what-science-says.

97. Substance Abuse and Mental Health Services Administration (2016). *Implementation of the Mental Health Parity and Addiction Equity Act (MHPAEA).* Available at http://www.samhsa.gov/health-financing/implementation-mental-health-parity-addiction-equity-act.

98. Office of National Drug Control Policy, The White House (2015). *National Drug Control Strategy 2015.* Washington, DC: The White House. Available at https://www.whitehouse.gov/ondcp/national-drug-control-strategy.

99. Office of National Drug Control Policy, The White House (2015). *FY16 Budget Summary.* Available at https://www.whitehouse.gov//sites/default/files/ondcp/policy-and-research/fy_2016_budget_summary.pdf.

100. U.S. Department of Justice, Bureau of Alcohol, Tobacco, Firearms, and Explosives (n.d.). *Who We Are.* Available at https://www.atf.gov/about/who-we-are.

101. U.S. Department of Education (1987). *What Works: Schools without Drugs.* Washington, DC: U.S. Government Printing Office.

102. California Legislative Information (n.d.). *Health and Safety Code - HSC, Division 10. Uniform Controlled Substances Act [11000 – 11651].* Available at http://leginfo.legislature.ca.gov/faces/codes.xhtml.

103. National Conference of State Legislatures (2016). *State Medical Marijuana Laws.* Available at http://www.ncsl.org/research/health/state-medical-marijuana-laws.aspx.

104. U.S. Department of Justice (2013). *Justice Department Announces Update to Marijuana Enforcement Policy.* Available at https://www.justice.gov/opa/pr/justice-department-announces-update-marijuana-enforcement-policy.

105. Brown, M. E. (1993). "Successful Components of Community and School Prevention Programs." *National Prevention Evaluation Report: Research Collection*, 1(1): 4–5.

106. Lynam, D. R., R. Milich, R. Zimmerman, et al. (1999). "Project DARE: No Effects at 10-Year Follow-Up." *Journal of Consulting and Clinical Psychology*, 67(4): 590–593.

107. Project ALERT (n.d.). *Project ALERT at a Glance.* Available at http://legacy.nreppadmin.net/ViewIntervention.aspx?id=62.

108. Drug-Free Federal Workplace (Executive Order 12564) (17 September 1986). *Federal Register*, 51 (180). Available at http://www.archives.gov/federal-register/codification/executive-order/12564.html.

109. American Management Associates (1996). *AMA Survey: Workplace Drug Testing and Drug Abuse Policy.* New York: Author.

110. U.S. Department of Labor (1991). *What Works: Workplaces without Alcohol or Other Drugs* (Pub. no. 282-148/54629). Washington, DC: U.S. Government Printing Office.

111. SmithKline Beecham Clinical Laboratories (29 February 1996). *Drug Detection in the Workplace in 1995 Declines for the Eighth Straight Year* [Press Release]. Collegeville, PA: Author.

112. Quest Diagnostics Incorporated (2015). *The Quest Diagnostics Drug Testing Index*. Available at http://www.questdiagnostics.com/home/physicians/health-trends/drug-testing.html.

CHAPTER 13

Health Care Delivery in the United States

Chapter Outline

Chapter Objectives

After studying this chapter, you will be able to:

1. Define the term *health care system*.
2. Trace the history of health care delivery in the United States from colonial times to the present.
3. Discuss and explain the concept of the spectrum of health care delivery.
4. Distinguish between the different kinds of health care, including population-based public health practice, medical practice, long-term practice, and end-of-life practice.
5. List and describe the different levels of medical practice.
6. Name and characterize the various groups of health care providers.
7. Explain the differences among allopathic, osteopathic, and nonallopathic providers.
8. Define complementary and alternative medicine.
9. Explain why there is a need for health care providers.
10. Prepare a list of the different types of facilities in which health care is delivered.
11. Explain the differences among private, public, and voluntary hospitals.
12. Explain the difference between inpatient and outpatient care facilities.
13. Briefly discuss the options for long-term care.
14. Explain what The Joint Commission does.
15. Identify the major concerns with the health care system in the United States.
16. Discuss the various means of reimbursing health care providers.
17. Briefly describe the purpose and concept of insurance.
18. Define the term *insurance policy*.

19. Explain the insurance policy terms *deductible, co-insurance, copayment, fixed indemnity, exclusion,* and *pre-existing condition.*

20. Explain what is meant when a company or business is said to be self-insured.

21. List the different types of medical care usually covered in a health insurance policy.

22. Briefly describe Medicare, Medicaid, and Medigap insurance.

23. Briefly summarize the Children's Health Insurance Program (CHIP).

24. Briefly explain long-term care health insurance.

25. Define managed care.

26. Define the terms *health maintenance organization* (HMO), *preferred provider organization* (PPO), and *point-of-service option.*

27. Identify the advantages and disadvantages of managed care.

28. Define consumer-directed health plans and give several examples.

29. Provide a brief overview of the Affordable Care Act passed in 2010.

30. Summarize the four cases that have been heard by the U.S. Supreme Court that have had an impact on the Affordable Care Act.

Scenario

Chad had adapted well and was enjoying his first year in college. He liked his classes and professors, had made friends quickly, and enjoyed the freedom that came with living in a resident hall on a college campus. What he missed was being a part of a formal athletic team because while in high school he was a three-sport letterman. However, he was enjoying participation in the campus intramural program and found the competition to be reasonably good. He played on a flag football team in the fall and was now member of a pretty good basketball team.

Chad was an aggressive player and didn't mind trying to drive to the basket when the odds were against him or scrambling for a loose ball on the floor. It was during the seventh game of the year, when his team was playing the other undefeated team in the league, that his aggressive play got the best of him. He was under the basket going after a rebound against a much taller player. He got the ball, but when he came down his foot landed on top of his opponent's and he "rolled" his ankle. He also heard a strange sound when it happened—like something popped in his ankle. The intramural staff responded quickly with some first aid and information on the Recreational Sports Department's protocol for injuries. The intramural supervisor told Chad that the campus health center was closed but that he would be happy to call 911 for him. Chad wasn't sure if emergency medical technicians (EMTs) were necessary. He thought that he would just go to his dorm room, "ice it down," take some aspirin, and see how things were in the morning. He could then decide whether he would go to the campus health center, the hospital emergency room, the local orthopedic walk-in clinic, the "doc-in-the-box" emergi-center, or just make an appointment with his own family doctor back home.

Introduction

The process by which health care is delivered in the United States is unlike the processes used in other countries of the world. Other developed countries have national health insurance run or organized by the government and paid for, in large part, by general taxes. Also, in these countries almost all citizens are entitled to receive health care services, including routine and basic health care.[1] Even with the changes that were made to the U.S health care system in 2010 to improve the access to health insurance for many Americans, the health care delivery system is still uniquely American.[2] Health care is still delivered by an array of **providers**, in a variety of settings, under the watchful eye of regulators, and paid for in a variety of ways. Because of this process, many question the notion that the United States has a health care

Providers health care facilities or health professionals that provide health care services

delivery system (see **Figure 13.1**). That is, "[a]lthough these various individuals and organizations are generally referred to collectively as 'the health care delivery system,' the phrase suggests order, integration, and accountability that do not exist. Communication, collaboration, or systems planning among these various entities is limited and is almost incidental to their operations."[3] Whether or not health care delivery in the United States should be called a "system," there is a process in place in which health care professionals, located in a variety of facilities, provide services to deal with disease and injury for the purpose of promoting, maintaining, and restoring health to the citizens. In this chapter, we provide a brief history of health care delivery in the United States, examine the structure of health care, and describe how our unique system functions. And finally, we discuss health care reform in the United States.

FIGURE 13.1   Do we really have a health care system?

© Brian Snyder/Reuters/Landov.

A Brief History of Health Care Delivery in the United States

For as long as humankind has been concerned with disease, injury, and health, there has always been a category of health care in which people have tried to help or treat themselves. This category of care is referred to as *self-care* or *self-treatment*. For example, in most American homes, there are usually provisions to deal with minor emergencies, nursing care, and the relief of minor pains or ailments. This type of care continues today. The following discussion of the history of health care delivery in the United States does not include self-care because it is assumed that most people would engage in some type of self-care prior to seeking professional help. Instead, we review the development of professional care provided by those trained to do so.

As might be assumed with the birth of a new country, from colonial times through the latter portion of the nineteenth century, health care and medical education in the United States lagged far behind their counterparts in Great Britain and Europe. During this period of time anyone, trained or untrained, could practice medicine. Much of the early health care was provided by family members and neighbors and consisted of home and folk remedies that had been handed down from one generation to another. When a person did receive training as a physician, it was nothing like the rigorous training that a physician goes through today. The early medical education in the colonies was not grounded in science. Prior to 1870, medical education was provided primarily through an apprenticeship with a practicing physician who may have been trained in the same way.[4] Consequently, medical care was primitive and considered to be more a trade than a profession.[1] In addition, most of the health care was provided in the patient's home and not in an office or clinic.

There were some hospitals during these early years, but they were located primarily in large cities and seaports such as New York, Philadelphia, and New Orleans. However, the hospitals were much different from the hospitals of today and served more in a social welfare function than as places to receive health care. They were not very clean, and unhygienic practices prevailed. The forerunner of today's hospital and nursing home was the *almshouse* (also called a *poorhouse*).[1] Almshouses were run by the local government primarily to provide food, shelter, and basic nursing care for indigent people (i.e., the elderly, homeless, orphans, the ill, and the disabled) who could not be cared for by their own families.[1] In addition to almshouses, local government also operated *pesthouses*, which served as a place to isolate people who had contracted an infectious disease such as cholera, smallpox, or typhoid.[1]

In the late nineteenth century, formal health care gradually moved from the patient's home to the physician's office and into the hospital. The primary reason for this change was the building and staffing of many new hospitals. It was felt that patients could receive better care in a setting designed for patient care, staffed with trained people, and equipped with the latest medical supplies and instruments. In addition, physicians could treat more patients in a central location because of the reduced travel time.

It was also during the latter portion of the nineteenth century that the scientific method began to play a more important role in medical education and health care. Medical procedures backed by scientific findings began to replace "rational hunches," "good ideas," and "home remedies" as the standards for medical care. With the acceptance of the germ theory of disease and the identification of infectious disease agents, there was real hope for the control of communicable diseases, which were the leading health problems of that period.

At the beginning of the twentieth century, although communicable diseases were still the leading causes of death, mortality rates were beginning to decline. Most of the decline can be attributed to improved public health measures. Yet, at the end of World War I, mortality rates spiked not only in the United States but also worldwide because of the 1918–1919 influenza pandemic. This deadliest pandemic in history killed as many as 100 million people. Shortly after the pandemic in the early 1920s, a major shift took place in the United States as chronic diseases moved past communicable diseases as the leading causes of death.

At the same time that chronic diseases were pushing to the top of the list of causes of death, much change was taking place in health care. New medical procedures such as X-ray therapy, specialized surgical procedures, and chemotherapy were developed, group medical practices were started, and new medical equipment and instruments (such as the electrocardiograph to measure heart function) were invented. The training of doctors and nurses also improved and became more specialized. By 1929, the United States was spending about 3.9% of its gross domestic product (GDP) on health care, which means that 3.9% of all goods and services produced by the nation that year were associated with health care.

Even with some of these "new" advances in the practice of medicine, U.S. medicine was still limited pretty much to two parties—patients and physicians. "Diagnosis, treatment, and fees for services were considered confidential between patients and physicians. Medical practice was relatively simple and usually involved long-standing relationships with patients and, often, several generations of families. Physicians set and often adjusted their charges to their estimates of patients' ability to pay and collected the payments. This was the intimate physician–patient relationship the profession held sacred."[5]

By the early 1940s, the United States was again at war. World War II affected health care in the United States in a variety of ways. One consequence of the war that would have a lasting impact on health care was employers' use of health insurance to lure workers to their companies. Because of the large number of men and women in the armed services, there was a shortage of workers to fill the jobs back home. Also, because of the need for resources for the war effort, the U.S. government put restrictions on the wages that companies could pay their employees. However, there were no restrictions on the health care insurance that employers could provide for their employees. Thus, companies began using health insurance to recruit and retain workers, and as a result employer-provided health insurance took a foothold at this time.

Also as a result of World War II, huge technical strides were made in the late 1940s and 1950s as medical procedures and processes developed during the war found applications in civilian medicine. However, adequate health facilities to treat long-term diseases were lacking in many areas of the country. The **Hospital Survey and Construction Act of 1946**, better known as the **Hill-Burton Act** (after the authors of the legislation), provided substantial funds for hospital construction. The infusion of federal funds helped to remedy the serious hospital shortage caused by the lack of construction during the Depression and World War II. The Hill-Burton Act was primarily a federal–state partnership. State agencies were given grants to determine the need for hospitals and then were provided with seed money to begin construction of the facilities.[6] However, the major portion of construction dollars came from state and local sources.[7] Through the years, the Hill-Burton Act has been amended several times to help meet health care needs in the United States. Funds have been made available for additional construction, modernization, and replacement of other health care facilities, and for comprehensive health planning.

Hospital Survey and Construction Act of 1946 (Hill-Burton Act) federal legislation that provided substantial funds for hospital construction

With improved procedures, equipment, and facilities and the increase in noncommunicable diseases, the cost of health care began to rise. As the cost of health care rose, it became too expensive for some people. Concerns were expressed about who should receive health care and who should pay for it. The debate over whether health care is a basic right or a privilege in the United States began in earnest. By the end of the 1950s, there remained an overall shortage of quality health care in the United States. There was also a maldistribution of health care services—metropolitan areas were being better served than the less-developed rural areas.

In the 1960s, there was an increased interest in health insurance, and it became common practice for workers and their bargaining agents to negotiate for better health benefits (see **Figure 13.2**). Undoubtedly, some employers preferred to increase benefits rather than to raise wages. Few then could foresee the escalation in health care costs for Americans. Thus, the **third-party payment system** for health care became solidified as the standard method of payment for health care costs in the United States. The third-party payment system gets its name from the fact that the insurer—government, private insurance company, or a self-insured organization (third party)—reimburses (pays the bills) to the provider (second party) for the health care given to the patient (first party).[8] (A detailed explanation of the third-party payment system is presented later in this chapter.) More recently, when some speak of the third-party payment system, they add a fourth party—the purchaser of the insurance, often an employer. It should be noted that the government and private insurers pay the medical bills with tax dollars and collected premiums, respectively—not with their own funds.

With the growth of the third-party system of paying for health care, the cost of health care rose even more rapidly than before because patients enjoyed increased access to care without or with little out-of-pocket expenses. However, those without insurance found it increasingly difficult to afford care. When the Democrats regained the White House in the 1960s, they led a federal policy change to increase citizen access to health care, which culminated in 1965 with the authorization of Medicare and Medicaid by Titles XVIII and XIX, respectively, of the Social Security Act. (These programs, which were enacted to help provide care for the elderly, the disabled, and the poor, are also discussed later in this chapter.) Also in the 1960s, the federal government increased funding for medical research and technology to support transplants and life extension.

By the late 1960s and early 1970s, it had become apparent that the Hill-Burton Act had stimulated not only the growth of health care facilities, but also the demand for health care services. With this growth came a continuing rise in health care costs and a need for better planning in health care delivery.

Among the early attempts at planning were the 1964 amendments to the Hill-Burton Act. The amendments called for comprehensive planning on a regional level. Their purpose was to make more efficient use of federal funds by preventing the duplication of facilities. However, they depended on good faith efforts and could not be enforced. It soon became evident that more powerful legislation was needed to control costs and to coordinate and control rapid growth in health care facilities.

Another attempt was made to encourage better planning 2 years later. The Comprehensive Health Planning and Public Service Amendments of 1966 authorized funds for state- and area-wide Comprehensive Health Planning Agencies. These too failed because they had no teeth. Then, in 1974, Public Law 93-641 was passed. This law, known as the National Health Planning and Resources Development Act of 1974, combined several pieces of previous legislation to put teeth into comprehensive planning efforts. There were high hopes and expectations that these pieces of legislation would provide reason and order to the development and modification of health care services.[9] This legislation led to the formation of health systems agencies throughout the entire country. Their purpose was to cut costs by preventing the building of "unnecessary"

FIGURE 13.2   Health benefits have become an important part of the total compensation package for workers.

© David McNew/Getty Images/Thinkstock.

Third-party payment system a health insurance term indicating that bills from a health care provider for services rendered to a patient are paid by the insurer

facilities or the purchase of unnecessary equipment. Although some money may have been saved, the health systems agencies were viewed by some as yet another unnecessary government bureaucracy, and when the late President Reagan took office in 1980, he, along with Congress, eliminated this program.

Before leaving our health care discussion of the 1970s, it should be noted that another piece of legislation was passed that did not seem all that important at the time but that would have a profound impact on the way health care was delivered later. This legislation was the Health Maintenance Organization (HMO) Act of 1973. This act "provided both loans and grants for the planning, development, and implementation of combined insurance and health care delivery organizations and required that a minimum prescribed array of services be included in the HMO arrangement."[5]

The 1980s brought many changes to the health care industry, the most notable of which was probably the deregulation of health care delivery. In 1981, with Ronald Reagan in the White House, it was announced that the administration would let the competitive market, not governmental regulation, shape health care delivery.[10] Open competition is a philosophy of allowing consumers to regulate delivery by making choices about where and from whom they receive their care. In theory, those who provide good care will get more patients and in turn be able to offer the care at a lower price. In other words, the resulting competition would help squeeze out costly waste and ineffective care.[11]

Some economists, however, do not believe that the health care system behaves like a normal market. For example, it is not likely that an ill patient seeking medical care will shop for a less expensive physician. Physicians do not advertise the cost of their services. Also, it is the physician who tells the patient which hospital to go to and when to check in and out, due to the admitting privileges that physicians have. In addition, providers tend to offer more and more services to entice the market to "shop with us," which in effect drives up health care spending. For these reasons, the competitive market approach is of questionable value in lowering health care costs.

The 1980s also saw a proliferation of new medical technology (e.g., magnetic resonance images [MRIs] and ultrasound). Along with this new technology have come new health care issues such as medical ethics (e.g., prolonging life, ending life, and gene therapy) and more elaborate health insurance programs (e.g., policies that cover specific diseases such as cancer and AIDS, home care, and rehabilitation).

Many of the concerns of the 1980s continued into the 1990s. The 1992 presidential campaign again brought attention to the United States' problems with health care delivery. Bill Clinton, then governor of Arkansas, based his election campaign strategy on being a new kind of Democrat—one who could take on the nation's domestic ills. He saw health care as one of those ills because the present system failed to cover everyone, and its spiraling costs threatened to bankrupt the government and cripple American industry.

Shortly after being elected president, Mr. Clinton appointed the first lady, Hillary Rodham Clinton, to head a committee to develop a plan to overcome the shortcomings of the health care system. By the fall of 1993, the committee had completed a plan that the president then presented to a joint session of the U.S. Congress in front of a national television audience. This detailed plan, referred to informally as the president's Health Security Plan and formally as the **American Health Security Act of 1993**, was over 1,500 pages in length. The focal point of the plan was to provide universal coverage. President Clinton's health care plan was much discussed in Congress in 1994; however, opposition kept it from ever reaching the floor for a vote before Congress adjourned. This was the sixth time in U.S. history that the concept of universal coverage was defeated. (The other attempts at universal coverage are discussed later in this chapter.) Although the plan was never approved, the pressures generated by the plan transformed the private health care system in the United States.

In the mid- to late 1990s, rapid changes occurred in the organization and financing of health care. These changes can be summed up in two words—managed care. **Managed care** "is a system of health care delivery that (1) seeks to achieve efficiency by integrating the four functions of health care delivery, (2) employs mechanisms to control (manage) utilization of medical services, and (3) determines the price at which the services are purchased, and consequently, how much the providers get paid."[12]

American Health Security Act of 1993 the comprehensive health care reform introduced by then President Clinton, but never enacted

Managed care a system that integrates the functions of financing, insurance, delivery, and payment and uses mechanisms to control costs and utilization of services

With the advent of managed care, the increase of health care costs slowed in the mid-1990s; in fact, the actual growth for several years was almost flat. Even so, both the percentage of the GDP and the dollars spent on health care continued to inch up. Health care is the one segment of the U.S. economy that continues to grow consistently faster than the cost of inflation (see **Table 13.1**). Ever-newer technology, ever-increasing demands for the best care, growing medical liability, new diagnostic procedures, the lengthening of life spans, the development of new drugs, and newly identified diseases put great demands on the system.

By the mid- to late 1990s, managed care had become the dominant form of health care financing and delivery, but it became apparent that support for it, with some exceptions, was not deep.[13] In addition, it was obvious that the slowdown in health care costs, which was attributed to managed care, would be just a one-time savings if other measures were not taken. President Clinton saw this as an opportunity to again seek health care reform. This time President Clinton treaded carefully, offering small but politically popular programs. The most notable of which was the State Children's Health Insurance Program (SCHIP), health care coverage for uninsured children (*Note:* SCHIP is now known as CHIP; see the discussion of CHIP later in this chapter).

The most notable change to U.S. health care during the presidency of George W. Bush was the passage of the Medicare Prescription Drug, Improvement, and Modernization Act of 2003 (MMA). The most visible components of the MMA have been the voluntary outpatient prescription drug benefit for people on Medicare, known as Part D (see the discussion of Medicare Part D later in the chapter), and health savings accounts (HSAs). HSAs are tax-free savings accounts that can be used to pay for near-term medical expenses incurred by individuals, spouses, and dependents and to save for future longer-term costs. (HSAs are also discussed in greater detail later in the chapter.)

Throughout the early part of the twenty-first century, both consumers and health care providers agreed that health care delivery in the United States needed to be changed. The Institute on Medicine (IOM) claimed "health care today harms too frequently and routinely fails to deliver its potential benefits."[14] Further, the health care system suffered from lack of coordinated, comprehensive services, resulting in both the wasteful duplication of efforts and unaccountable gaps in care.[14] In its reports, the IOM outlined a number of recommendations for changing health care delivery in the United States. These recommendations, combined with the release of the World Health Organization's report *The World Health Report 2000—Health Systems: Improving Performance*, in which the U.S. health system was ranked thirty-seventh out of 191 countries,[15] provided some direction for changing the way health care was delivered.

Because of the great concern for health care reform, much attention was given to the topic during the presidential debates in 2008. In fact, all major candidates outlined plans for change if elected. As it is now known, when President Obama took office one of the top issues on his agenda for change was health care reform. However, one of the first pieces of legislation signed into law by President Obama was the Children's Health Insurance Program (CHIP)

TABLE 13.1   Consumer Price Index and Average Annual Percentage of Change for All Items and Selected Items: United States, Selected Years 1960–2015

Year	All Items	Medical Care	Food	Apparel	Housing	Energy
1960	29.6	22.3	30.0	45.7	—	22.4
1980	82.4	74.9	86.8	90.0	81.1	86.0
2000	172.2	260.8	167.8	129.6	169.6	124.6
2010	218.0	388.4	219.6	119.5	216.3	192.9
2015	236.5	451.1	247.5	122.8	239.5	186.4

Notes: Data are based on reporting by samples of providers and other retail outlets; —, data not available; 1982–1984 = 100.

Data from: U.S. Department of Labor, Bureau of Labor Statistics (2016). *Consumer Price Index.* Available at http://www.bls.gov/cpi/.

Reauthorization Act of 2009 (*Note*: CHIP was formerly known as SCHIP). This law expanded CHIP to approximately 4.1 million uninsured children and was funded by a 62¢ increase in the federal tax on cigarettes.

It took another year before more comprehensive health care reform was passed. In 2010, President Obama signed into law two bills—the Patient Protection and Affordable Care Act (Public Law 111-148) and the Health Care and Education Reconciliation Act of 2010 (Public Law 111-152). These two acts were consolidated with other approved legislation and are now referred to as the Affordable Care Act (or ACA, nicknamed ObamaCare). Portions of this act went into effect in 2010, and the last portion is scheduled to go into effect in 2020. The road for ACA implementation has not been smooth. As of the writing of this text the start dates for some portions of the ACA have been pushed back, a number of technical difficulties were encountered with the health insurance exchange website, the U.S. Congress has voted to repeal the ACA 62 times,[16] and on four occasions parts of the ACA have been litigated in the U.S. Supreme Court. A more complete presentation of the act comes in the last part of this chapter.

Health Care System: Structure

The structure of the health care system of the United States is unique in the world. In the sections that follow, we examine the *spectrum of health care delivery* and describe the various types of health care providers and the facilities in which health care is delivered.

The Spectrum of Health Care Delivery

Because health care in the United States is delivered by an array of providers in a variety of settings, reference is sometimes made to the spectrum of health care delivery (see **Table 13.2**). The spectrum of health care delivery refers to the various types of care. Within this spectrum, four levels of practice have emerged: population-based public health practice, medical practice, long-term practice, and end-of-life practice.

Public Health Practice

Public health practice incorporates "the development and application of preventive strategies and interventions to promote and protect the health of populations."[17] A primary component of public health practice is education. If people are going to behave in a way that will promote their health and the health of their community, they first must know how to do so. Health education not only provides such information but also attempts to empower and motivate people to put this information to use by discontinuing unhealthy behaviors and adopting healthy ones. Though much of public health practice takes place in governmental health agencies, it also takes place in a variety of other settings (such as voluntary health agencies, social service agencies, schools, businesses and industry, and even in some traditional medical care settings).[17]

Medical Practice

Medical practice means "those services usually provided by or under the supervision of a physician or other traditional health care provider."[17] Such services are offered at several different levels. You may remember from elsewhere in the text that we used the terms *primary, secondary*, and *tertiary* as they related to levels of prevention. These terms have a similar meaning here, but they are now applied to health care delivery rather than prevention.

Primary Medical Care

Primary care is "front-line" or "first-contact" care. "The unique characteristic of primary care is the role it plays as a regular or usual source of care for patients and their families."[3] Formally, **primary care** has been defined as "clinical preventive services, first-contact treatment services,

Public health practice incorporates the development and application of preventive strategies and interventions to promote and protect the health of populations

Primary care clinical preventive services, first-contact treatment services, and ongoing care for commonly encountered medical conditions

TABLE 13.2 The Spectrum of Health Care Delivery

Level of Practice	Description	Examples of Delivery Settings
Public health practice	Practice aimed at the development and application of preventive interventions to promote and protect the health of populations	Community and school health programs; public health clinics
Medical practice		
Primary care	Clinical preventive services, first-contact treatment services, and ongoing care for commonly encountered medical conditions; emphasizes prevention, early detection, and routine care	Primary care provider offices; public clinics; managed care organizations; community mental health centers
Secondary care	Specialized attention and ongoing management for common and less frequently encountered medical conditions, including support services for people with special challenges due to chronic or long-term conditions	
Acute care	Short-term, intense medical care that may require hospitalization	Emergency rooms; urgent/emergency care centers; outpatient/inpatient surgical centers; hospitals
Subacute care	Convalescence after acute care, need for more nursing intervention	Special subacute units in hospitals (e.g., transitional care units); skilled nursing facilities; home health care
Tertiary care	Subspecialty referral care requiring highly specialized personnel and facilities	Specialty hospitals (e.g., psychiatric, chronic disease) and general hospitals with highly specialized facilities
Long-term practice		
Restorative care	Intermediate follow-up care such as surgical post-operative care	Home health; progressive and extended care facilities; rehabilitation facilities that specialize in therapeutic services; halfway houses
Long-term care or chronic care	Care for chronic conditions; personal care	Nursing homes; facilities for the mentally retarded or emotionally disturbed; geriatric day care centers
End-of-life practice	Care provided to those who have less than 6 months to live	Hospice services provided in a variety of settings

Data from: Cambridge Research Institute (1976). *Trends Affecting the U.S. Health Care System.* Washington, DC: U.S. Government Printing Office; U.S. Public Health Service (1994). *For a Healthy Nation: Return on Investments in Public Health.* Washington, DC: Author; Pratt, J. R. (2016). *Long-Term Care: Managing Across the Continuum,* 4th ed. Burlington, MA: Jones & Bartlett Learning, Turnock, D. J. (2016). *Public Health: What It Is and How It Works,* 6th ed. Burlington, MA: Jones & Bartlett Learning; Shi, L., and D. A. Singh (2017). *Essentials of the U.S. Health Care System,* 4th ed. Burlington, MA: Jones & Bartlett Learning.

and ongoing care for commonly encountered medical conditions."[17] Eighty percent of necessary medical care is provided by primary care.[17] Primary care includes routine medical care to treat common illnesses or to detect health problems in their early stages, and thus includes such things as semiannual dental checkups; annual physical exams; health screenings for hypertension, high blood cholesterol, and breast or testicular cancer; and sore throat cultures. Physicians, nurse practitioners, physician assistants, and an array of other individuals on the primary care team usually provide primary care in practitioners' offices, clinics, and other outpatient facilities. Primary care is the most difficult for the poor and uninsured to obtain (see **Box 13.1**).

Secondary Medical Care

Secondary medical care is "specialized attention and ongoing management for common and less frequently encountered medical conditions, including support services for people with special

Secondary medical care specialized attention and ongoing management for common and less frequently encountered medical conditions, including support services for people with special challenges due to chronic or long-term conditions

FIGURE 13.3 Restorative care can follow either secondary or tertiary care.

© Jason Reed/Reuters/Landov.

Tertiary medical care specialized and technologically sophisticated medical and surgical care for those with unusual or complex conditions

Restorative care care that is provided after successful treatment or when the progress of an incurable disease has been arrested

challenges due to chronic or long-term conditions."[17] This type of care is usually provided by physicians, ideally upon referral from a primary care provider.[17]

Tertiary Medical Care

Tertiary medical care "is even more highly specialized and technologically sophisticated medical and surgical care for those with unusual or complex conditions (generally no more than a few percent of the need in any service category)."[17] This care is not usually performed in smaller hospitals; however, it is provided in specialty hospitals, academic health centers, or on specialized floors of general hospitals. Such facilities are equipped and staffed to provide advanced care for people with illnesses such as cancer and heart disease, and procedures such as heart bypass surgery.

Long-Term Practice

Long-term practice can be divided into two subcategories—restorative care and long-term care.

Restorative Care

Restorative care is the health care provided to patients after surgery or other successful treatment, during remission in cases of an oncogenic (cancerous) disease, or when the progression of an incurable disease has been arrested. This level of care includes follow-up to secondary and tertiary care, rehabilitative care, therapy, and home care (see **Figure 13.3**). Typical settings for this type of care include inpatient and outpatient rehabilitation units, nursing homes, assisted-living facilities, halfway houses, and private homes.

Long-Term Care

Long-term care includes the different kinds of help that people with chronic illnesses, disabilities, or other conditions that limit them physically or mentally need. In some situations time-intensive skilled nursing care is needed, while some people just need help with basic daily tasks like bathing, dressing, and preparing meals. Long-term services and supports (LTSS) assist people in maintaining or improving an optimal level of functioning and quality of life and can include help from other people, special equipment, and assistive devices.[18] LTSS "should (1) fit the needs of different individuals, (2) address their changing needs over time, and (3) suit their personal preferences."[12] This type of care is provided in various settings such as nursing homes, facilities for the mentally and emotionally disturbed, assisted-living facilities, and adult and senior day care centers, but often long-term care is used to help people live at home rather than in institutions.

End-of-Life Practice

The final level of practice in the health care delivery is end-of-life practice. **End-of-life practice** is usually thought of as those health care services provided to individuals shortly before death. The primary form of end-of-life practice is hospice care. **Hospice care** is "a cluster of special services for the dying, which blends medical, spiritual, legal, financial, and family support services. The venue can vary from a specialized facility to a nursing home to the patient's own home."[12] The most common criterion for admission to hospice care is being terminally ill with a life expectancy of less than 6 months. The first hospice program in the United States was established in 1974,[19] while in 2012 there were 3,700 Medicare-certified providers and suppliers of hospice services in the United States.[18]

Types of Health Care Providers

To offer comprehensive health care that includes services at each of the levels just mentioned, a great number of health care workers are needed. In 2014, the number of civilians employed in the health service industry was 12.4 million. These 12.4 million represented approximately 1 of every 12 (8.2%) employed civilians in the United States.[20]

Despite the large number of health care workers, the demand for more is expected to continue to grow. Health Care workers are projected to be the fastest growing occupational group during the 2014 to 2024 projections decade. This group is expected to contribute 2.3 million new jobs representing about one in four of all new jobs during that 10-year period.[20] Due to the continuing geographic maldistribution of health care workers, the need will be greater in some settings than in others. The settings of greatest need will continue to be the rural and inner-city areas.

About two-fifths (39%) of all health care employees work in hospitals, more than one-fourth (26%) work in offices of health practitioners (i.e., offices and clinics), one-fifth (20%) work in nursing and residential care facilities, and 8% each work in home health services and outpatient, laboratory, and other ambulatory care services.[21] As changes have come to the way health care is offered, the proportions of health care workers by setting have also changed, with fewer persons working in hospitals (in 1970, 63% worked in hospitals), and more employed in nursing homes and ambulatory care settings (such as surgical and emergency centers). This trend is expected to continue in the future, with special needs in the area of long-term care workers to meet the needs of the aging baby boom generation.

There are well over 200 different careers in the health care industry. To help simplify the discussion of the different types of health care workers, they have been categorized into six different groups—independent providers, limited care providers, nurses, nonphysician practitioners, allied health care professionals, and public health professionals.

Independent Providers

Independent providers are those health care workers who have the specialized education and legal authority to treat any health problem or disease that an individual has. This group of workers can be further divided into allopathic, osteopathic, and nonallopathic providers.

Long-term care different kinds of help that people with chronic illnesses, disabilities, or other conditions that limit them physically or mentally need

End-of-life practice health care services provided to individuals shortly before death

Hospice care a cluster of special services for the dying that blends medical, spiritual, legal, financial, and family support services

Independent provider health care professional with the education and legal authority to treat any health problem

Allopathic provider independent provider whose remedies for illnesses produce effects different from those of the disease

Osteopathic provider independent health care provider whose remedies emphasize the interrelationships of the body's systems in prevention, diagnosis, and treatment

Intern a first-year resident

Resident a physician who is training in a specialty

Nonallopathic providers independent providers who provide nontraditional forms of health care

Allopathic and Osteopathic Providers

Allopathic providers are those who use a system of medical practice in which specific remedies for illnesses, often in the form of drugs or medication, are used to produce effects different from those of diseases. The practitioners who fall into this category are those who are referred to as Doctors of Medicine (MDs). The usual method of practice for MDs includes the taking of a health history, a physical examination—perhaps with special attention to one area of the complaint—and the provision of specific treatment, such as antibiotics for a bacterial infection or a tetanus injection and sutures for a laceration.

Another group of physicians that provides services similar to those of MDs are **osteopathic providers**—Doctors of Osteopathic Medicine (DOs). At one time, MDs and DOs would not have been grouped together because of differences in their formal education, methods, and philosophy of care. While the educational requirements and methods of treatment used by MDs have remained essentially consistent over the years, those of DOs have not. The practice of osteopathy was started in 1874 by Andrew Taylor Still, MD, DO, who was dissatisfied with the effectiveness of nineteenth-century medicine.[22] The distinctive feature of osteopathic medicine is the recognition of the reciprocal interrelationship between the structure and function of the body. The actual work of DOs and MDs is very similar today. Both types of physicians use all available scientific modalities, including drugs and surgery, in providing care to their patients. Both can also serve as primary care physicians (approximately 30% of MDs,[23] while 56% of DOs are primary care physicians)[24] or as board-certified specialists. Their differences are most notably the DOs' greater tendency to use more manipulation in treating health problems and the DOs' perception of themselves as being more holistically oriented than MDs. DOs constitute 7% of all physicians today.[25] Few patients today would be able to tell the difference between the care given by a DO and an MD.

The educational requirements for MD and DO degrees are very similar. Both complete a bachelor's degree, 4 years of medical education, and 3 years (such as in family medicine) to 7 years (such as neurosurgery) of medical specialty training known as a *residency*. The first year of a residency is referred to as the *internship year*, and the physicians are referred to as **interns** or first-year **residents**. During this year, the interns can only practice medicine under the guidance of a licensed physician. Upon successful completion of the internship year, the interns are then eligible to sit for the third part of the licensing examination (the first two parts are taken during medical school). If they pass the exam, they are then entitled to practice medicine without the supervision of another licensed physician. At this point, almost all interns will complete the remaining years of residency (and are referred to generically as residents) to be eligible to sit for the board specialty examinations. Passing this examination will make them "board certified" in their specialty.

The American Medical Association (AMA) Physician Masterfile lists more than 200 specialty categories.[26] With so many specialties and subspecialties, even though primary care specialties (which includes family medicine/general practice, internal medicine, internal medicine/pediatrics, and pediatrics) make up the largest percentage of physicians, health care experts are worried that not enough primary care physicians will be trained. This became an even bigger concern in 2010 with the passage of the Affordable Care Act (ACA) because of the emphasis the ACA placed on prevention and primary care.

Nonallopathic Providers

Nonallopathic providers are identified by their nontraditional means of providing health care. Some have referred to much of the care provided by these providers as complementary/alternative medicine (CAM) or complementary/integrative medicine. Included in this group of providers are chiropractors, acupuncturists (see **Figure 13.4**), naturopaths (those who use natural therapies), herbalists (those who use herbal brews for treating illness), and homeopaths (those who use small doses of herbs, minerals, and even poisons for therapy).

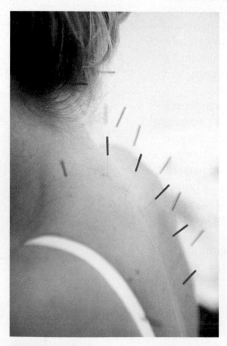

FIGURE 13.4 Many people seek out nontraditional means of health care, such as acupuncture.

© Stuart Pearce/Pixtal/age fotostock.

The best-known and most often used nonallopathic providers in the United States are **chiropractors**. The underlying premise of the care provided by chiropractors is that all health problems are caused by misalignments of the vertebrae in the spinal column. The chiropractic (done by hand) approach to the treatment is (1) the identification of the misalignment through X-rays, and (2) the realignment of the bones through a series of treatments called "adjustments."

Chiropractors are educated in 4-year chiropractic colleges. The Council on Chiropractic Education accredits colleges of chiropractic medicine in the United States. As with allopathic and osteopathic programs, students usually enter chiropractic programs after earning a bachelor's degree. Those who graduate from chiropractic colleges earn a Doctor of Chiropractic (DC) degree. Chiropractors are licensed in all 50 states and must pass either a state licensing examination or an examination given by the National Board of Chiropractic Examiners. There are approximately 42,500 chiropractors in the United States today.[27]

As noted earlier, much of the care provided by nonallopathic providers is often referred to as **complementary/alternative medicine (CAM)** or *complementary/integrative medicine.* CAM has been defined as "a group of diverse medical and health care systems, practices, and products that are not presently considered to be a part of conventional medicine."[28] When using a non-mainstream approach together with conventional medicine, it is identified as *complementary.*[28] An example of a complementary medicine is using acupuncture in addition to conventional medicine to help lessen pain. When using a non-mainstream approach in place of conventional medicine, it is labeled as *alternative.*[28] An example of alternative is using a special diet to treat cancer instead of undergoing surgery, radiation, or chemotherapy that has been recommended by a conventional doctor. When mainstream medical therapies are combined with CAM therapies for which there is some high-quality scientific evidence of safety and effectiveness, it is referred to as *integrative medicine.*[29] CAM is one of the fastest growing areas of health care today. Data indicate that approximately 33.2% of adults and 11.6% of children in the United States reported using CAM in 2012,[30] although the percentage changes depending on what is considered CAM. While natural products (i.e., dietary supplements other than vitamins and minerals) was the most commonly used complementary approach, pain was the condition for which most use a complementary approach.[30] The percentage of use is highest when the definition of CAM includes prayer specifically for health reasons. Even with its popularity, Americans paid for most CAM out of pocket. A nationwide government survey showed that U.S. adults spent $33.9 billion out of pocket in 1 year on CAM.[31] Nearly two-thirds of that total was spent for self-care purchases of CAM products, classes, and materials, while the remaining portion was spent on practitioner visits. Despite this emphasis on self-care therapies, adults made more than 354 million visits to CAM practioners.[31] "Insurance coverage of complementary health approaches is complex and confusing—so much so that it's almost impossible to make any general statements about it. Coverage may vary greatly depending on state laws, regulations, and differences among specific insurance plans. If you would like to use a complementary approach and you're wondering whether your health insurance will cover it, it's a good idea to do some investigating. Contacting your health insurance provider is a good way to start."[32]

There are literally hundreds of systems, approaches, and techniques that fall within the CAM rubric. CAM practices are often grouped into broad categories, such as natural products (e.g., herbal medicines also known as botanicals), mind-body medicine (e.g., meditation, yoga, acupuncture, hypnotherapy, tai chi), manipulative and body-based practices (e.g., spinal manipulation and massage therapy), and other CAM practices (movement therapies [e.g., Pilates, Rolfing], traditional healers, manipulation of energy fields [i.e., magnet therapy], and whole medical systems [e.g., Ayurvedic medicine, homeopathy, naturopathy]).[28]

Limited (or Restricted) Care Providers

Much health care is provided by **limited (or restricted) care providers** who have advanced training, usually a doctoral degree, in a health care specialty. Their specialty enables them to provide care for a specific part of the body. This group of providers includes but is not limited to dentists (teeth and oral cavity), optometrists (eyes, specifically refractory errors), podiatrists (feet and ankles), audiologists (hearing), and psychologists (mental health).

Chiropractor a nonallopathic, independent health care provider who treats health problems by adjusting the spinal column

Complementary/alternative medicine (CAM) a group of diverse medical and health care systems, practices, and products that are not presently considered to be a part of conventional medicine

Limited (restricted) care providers health care providers who provide care for a specific part of the body

FIGURE 13.5   There is still a need for more nurses.

© Rob Marmion/ShutterStock, Inc.

Nurses

We have categorized nurses into a group of their own because of their unique degree programs, the long-standing tradition of nursing as a profession, and their overall importance in the health care industry. It has been estimated that there are a between 4 and 5 million individuals who work in the nursing profession. These include registered nurses, licensed practical nurses, and ancillary nursing personnel such as nurse's aides.[33–35] Nurses outnumber physicians, dentists, and every other single group of health care workers in the United States. Even with such numbers, the need for nurses will continue[33–35] (see **Figure 13.5**).

Training and Education of Nurses

Nurses can be divided into subcategories based on their level of education and type of preparation. The first are those who are prepared as licensed practical nurses. Once they complete their 1 to 2 years of education in a vocational, hospital, or associate degree program and pass a licensure examination, these nurses are referred to as **licensed practical nurses (LPNs)**, or licensed vocational nurses (LVNs) in some states. LPNs care for people who are sick, injured, convalescent, or disabled under the supervision of physicians or registered nurses.[36] "The nature of the direction and supervision required varies by state and job setting."[36] Not too many years ago it was thought that LPNs would be phased out and replaced with more qualified nurses. In 2014, there were 719,900 LPNs or LVNs working in the United States, and that number was projected to grow by 16% to 837,200 by 2024.[33]

A second group of nurses is *registered nurses*. **Registered nurses (RNs)** are those who have successfully completed an accredited academic program and a state licensing (registration) examination. The three typical educational paths to registered nursing are a bachelor's degree (BSN), an associate degree (ADN), and a diploma from an approved nursing program.[34] ADN programs take about 2 to 3 years to complete and are typically offered by community or junior colleges. Diploma programs are offered by hospitals and last about 3 years. RNs holding BSN degrees are considered to have been more thoroughly prepared for additional activities involving independent judgment. Of the employed registered nurses, 61% worked in hospitals, about 7% in offices of physicians, 7% in nursing and residential care facilities, 6% in home health care services, and 6% in government.[34] In 2014, there were 2.75 million RNs working in the United States, and that number was projected to grow by 16% to 3.2 million by 2024.[34]

Advanced Practice Registered Nurses

With advances in technology and the development of new areas of medical specialization, there is a growing need for specialty-prepared advanced practice registered nurses (APRNs). Many professional nurses continue their education and earn master's and doctoral degrees in nursing. The master's degree programs are aimed primarily at specialties such as nurse practitioners (NPs; e.g., pediatric nurse practitioners and school nurse practitioners), clinical nurse specialists (CNSs), certified registered nurse anesthetists (CRNAs), and certified nurse midwives (CNMs). The largest portion of APRNs is nurse practitioners (NPs). NPs "assess patients, order and interpret diagnostic tests, make diagnoses, and initiate and manage treatment plans—including prescribing medications."[37] Not only do they provide high-quality care in a cost-effective manner, but they are also considered primary care providers in chronically medically underserved inner-city and rural areas. Close to 90% of all NPs are prepared in primary care.[37] The authors of the Affordable Care Act (ACA) saw the value of NPs to the U.S. health care system and as such included funding to increase both the number of those trained as NPs and number of clinics in which NPs practice.

Even though there is evidence to show value of NPs, regulatory barriers prevent many NPs from practicing to their full potential. Currently, NPs in 20 states and the District of

Licensed practical nurse (LPN) one who is prepared in 1- to 2-year programs to provide nontechnical bedside nursing care under the supervision of physicians or registered nurses

Registered nurse (RN) one who has successfully completed an accredited academic program and a state licensing examination

Columbia have full practice authority.[38] "Nineteen states require NPs to have a formal, written collaborative agreement with a physician in order to provide care, and these states restrict NP practice in at least one domain (e.g., treatment, prescribing). In the remaining 12 states, NP practice is even more restricted. These states require physician supervision or delegation for NPs to provide care."[38]

Like other nurses, the demand for NPs is also expected to increase, especially as a greater portion of the population gains access to health care and more of the population becomes enrolled in managed care. In 2014, there were 205,000 NPs licensed in the United States, and that number was projected to grow to 244,000 by 2025.[37]

The relatively few nurses who hold doctorate degrees in nursing are highly sought after as university faculty. Nurses with doctorates teach, conduct research, and otherwise prepare other nurses or hold administrative (leadership) positions in health care institutions.

Physician Assistants

Physician assistants (PAs) are health care professionals who practice medicine with physician supervision.[39] They are considered midlevel providers with training and skills beyond those of RNs and less than those of physicians.[36] Physician assistant programs began in response to the shortage of primary care physicians. Most PAs have a bachelor's degree then complete a 2-year accredited educational program for PAs that typically leads to a master's degree.[33] After completion of the program or degree, PAs must pass a national certifying examination. PAs always work under the direct supervision of a licensed physician (thus the name *physician extenders*). They carry out many of the same duties that are thought of as the responsibilities of physicians, such as taking medical histories, examining patients, ordering and interpreting laboratory tests and X-rays, counseling patients, making preliminary diagnoses, treating minor injuries, and, in most states, prescribing medications.[36] PAs' specific duties would depend on (1) the setting in which they work, (2) their level o experience, (3) their specialty, and (4) the laws in the state where they practice.[40] In 2014, there were 94,400 PAs working in the United States, and that number was projected to grow by 30% to 123,100 between from 2010 to 2024.[41]

Allied Health Care Professionals

Allied health describes a large group of health-related professions that fulfill necessary roles in the health care delivery system. These **allied health care professionals**, which constitute approximately 60% of the health care workforce, assist, facilitate, and complement the work of physicians, dentists, and other health care specialists. These health care workers provide a variety of services that are essential to patient care. Often they are responsible for highly technical services and procedures. Allied health care professionals can be categorized into several groups. They include (1) laboratory technologists and technicians (e.g., medical technologists, emergency medical technicians, nuclear medicine technicians, operating room technicians, dental technicians and hygienists, and radiographers [X-ray technicians]); (2) therapeutic science practitioners (e.g., occupational, physical, radiation, and respiratory therapists and speech pathologists); (3) behavioral scientists (e.g., health education specialists, social workers, and rehabilitation counselors); and (4) support services (e.g., medical record keepers and medical secretaries). The educational backgrounds of allied health workers range from vocational training to clinical doctoral degrees. Many of these professionals also must pass a state or national licensing examination before they can practice.

The demand for allied health care workers in all of the areas previously noted is expected to continue. The primary reasons for this are the growth of the entire health care industry and the continuing arrival of the baby boomers as senior citizens.

Public Health Professionals

A discussion about health care providers would be incomplete without the mention of a group of health workers who provide unique health care services to the community—**public health professionals**. They support the delivery of health care by such hands-on

Physician assistant health care professionals who practice medicine with physician supervision

Allied health care professional health care worker who provides services that assist, facilitate, and complement the work of physicians and other health care specialists

Public health professional a health care worker who works in a public health organization

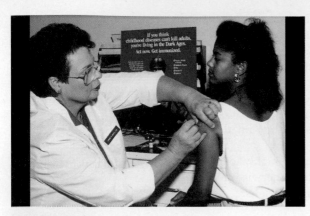

FIGURE 13.6 Public health professionals, such as this public health nurse, make up a key component of the health care system.

Courtesy of Barbara Rice/CDC.

providers as public health physicians, dentists, nurses, and dieticians who work in public health clinics sponsored by federal, state, local, and voluntary health agencies (see **Figure 13.6**). Examples of other public health professionals are environmental health workers, public health administrators, epidemiologists, health education specialists, public health nurses and physicians, biostatisticians, the U.S. Surgeon General, and the research scientists at the Centers for Disease Control and Prevention. Public health professionals often make possible the care that is practiced in immunization clinics, nutritional programs for women, infants, and children (WIC), dental health clinics, and sexually transmitted infection clinics. School nurses are also considered public health professionals. Public health services are usually financed by tax dollars and, although available to most taxpayers, serve primarily the economically disadvantaged.

Health Care Facilities and Their Accreditation

Health care is provided in a variety of settings in the United States. The major settings and the accreditation of these facilities are discussed in the sections that follow.

Health Care Facilities

Health care facilities are the physical settings in which health care is actually provided. They include a wide variety of settings but can be divided into two large categories of inpatient and outpatient care facilities. *Inpatient care facilities* include any in which a patient stays overnight, such as a hospital. *Outpatient care facilities* refer to any facility in which the patient receives care and does not stay overnight.

FIGURE 13.7 Hospitals are often categorized by ownership.

© James F. McKenzie

Inpatient Care Facilities

The primary inpatient care facilities are hospitals, nursing homes, and assisted-living facilities. Because nursing home and assisted-living facilities are discussed elsewhere, we discuss only hospitals here. In 2013, there were 5,686 hospitals in the United States[23] and they varied in size, mission, and organizational structure. The major purpose of hospitals is to provide a place for secondary and tertiary care.

Hospitals can be categorized in several different ways; one way is by hospital ownership (see **Figure 13.7** and **Table 13.3**). A **private (proprietary or investor-owned) hospital** is one that is owned as a business for the purpose of making a profit. "Most for-profit hospitals belong to one of the large hospital management companies that dominate the for-profit hospital network."[5] A subset of the private hospitals is **specialty hospitals**. These hospitals are stand-alone, single-specialty (e.g., women's health, surgery, cardiac, or orthopedic) facilities not within the walls of a full-service hospital.[42] Most are owned, at least in part, by the physicians who practice in them.[5] When this is the case such hospitals have been referred to as physician-owned hospitals (POHs). A lot of controversy surrounds these hospitals. Larger general hospitals, which are losing patients and revenue to the specialty hospitals, say that these specialty hospitals are just a "grab for money" by the physicians who own them. Physicians say specialty hospitals allow them to practice medicine the way it should be practiced, without answering to a hospital administrator who is trying to cut corners to make a profit. Because of the controversy surrounding POHs, a section of the Affordable Care Act (ACA) placed a ban on building new or expanding POHs. However, a recent study concluded that "[a]lthough

TABLE 13.3   Number of Beds and Hospitals According to Ownership: United States, 2013

Type	Number	Beds
All hospitals	5,686	914,513
Federal	213	38,747
Nonfederal community hospitals	5,473	875,766
Private or proprietary or investor-owned (for-profit)	1,060	134,643
Public (state or local)	1,010	117,031
Voluntary (not-for-profit)	2,904	543,929

Data from: National Center for Health Statistics (2015). *Health, United States, 2014: With Special Feature on Adults Aged 55–64.* Hyattsville, MD: Author.

Private (proprietary or investor-owned) hospital a for-profit hospital

Specialty hospital a stand-alone, single-specialty (e.g., women's health, surgery, cardiac, or orthopedic) facility not within the walls of a full-service hospital

Public hospital a hospital that is supported and managed by governmental jurisdictions

Voluntary hospital a nonprofit hospital administered by a not-for-profit corporation or charitable community organization

Full-service hospital a hospital that offers services in all or most of the levels of care defined by the spectrum of health care delivery

Limited-service hospital a hospital that offers only the specific services needed by the population served

POHs may treat slightly healthier patients, they do not seem to systematically select more profitable or less disadvantaged patients, or to provide lower value care."[43] In addition, ratings of POHs by the Centers for Medicare and Medicaid Services (CMS) and the U.S. Department of Health and Human Services have shown POHs have fared well in comparison to general hospitals in quality, costs, and consumer satisfaction.[44] Because of these data several attempts have been made amend the ACA to lift the ban but to no avail, in part because of the controversy in the U.S. Congress on the best way to offer health care.

A second type is a **public hospital**. These hospitals are supported and managed by governmental jurisdictions and are usually found in larger cities. Public hospitals can be operated by agencies at all levels of government. Hospitals operated by the federal government include military hospitals (e.g., Walter Reed National Medical Center in Bethesda, Maryland) and the many hospitals run by the Veterans Administration and Indian Health Service. There are also hospitals that are owned or partially financed by states and local governments. Examples include university hospitals, state mental hospitals, and local city and county hospitals.

Voluntary hospitals make up the third category of hospitals. These are nonprofit hospitals administered by not-for-profit corporations or religious, fraternal, and other charitable community organizations. These hospitals make up about one-half of all hospitals in the United States. Examples of this latter group are the Southern Baptist hospitals, the Shriners' hospitals, and many community hospitals. In recent years, voluntary hospitals have been expanding their scope of services and many now include wellness centers, stress management centers, chemical dependency programs, and a variety of satellite centers.

A second way of classifying hospitals is by dividing them into *teaching* and *nonteaching* hospitals. Teaching hospitals have, as a part of their mission, the responsibility to prepare new health care providers. These hospitals are typically aligned with medical schools, universities, and medical residency programs. However, a number of hospitals not affiliated with medical schools provide medical residency programs, clinical education for nurses, allied health personnel, and a wide variety of technical specialties.

A third means of categorizing hospitals is by the services offered. **Full-service hospitals**, or general hospitals, are those that offer care at all or most of the levels of care discussed earlier in the chapter. These are the most expensive hospitals to run and are usually found in metropolitan areas. **Limited-service hospitals** offer the specific services needed by the population served, such as emergency, maternity, general surgery, and so on, but they lack much of the sophisticated technology available at full-service hospitals. This type of hospital is more common in rural areas. Many limited-service hospitals were once full-service hospitals but have become limited-service hospitals because of the low volume of patients, a shortage of health care personnel, and financial distress.

Outpatient Care Facilities

An *outpatient care facility* is one where a patient receives ambulatory care (i.e., patients voluntarily leave their home to seek care) without being admitted as an inpatient.[1,45] Because of the variety of outpatient care services offered throughout the United States and the variety of arrangements for ownership of the services (e.g., hospitals, hospital systems, physician groups, and for-profit or not-for-profit chains), it is difficult to identify all possible outpatient care facilities. "For example, agencies providing home health services can be freestanding, hospital based, or nursing home based. In many instances, physician group practices are merging with hospitals, and hospitals and freestanding surgical centers often compete against each other for various types of surgical procedures."[1]

What is known is that today, care and procedures that once were performed only on an inpatient basis are increasingly being performed in a variety of outpatient settings.[19] In fact, today the majority of all surgical procedures are performed on an outpatient basis.[5] The growth and movement of services to outpatient care facilities have resulted from a combination of new medical and diagnostic procedures, technological advances, consumer demand for user-friendly environments, the reimbursement process, and financial mandates from insurance companies and government.[5] The types of outpatient care facilities found in communities are health care practitioners' offices, clinics, primary care centers, retail clinics, urgent/emergent care centers, ambulatory surgery centers, and freestanding service facilities.

Probably the outpatient care facilities with which people have the most familiarity are health care practitioners' offices that house private practices. In 2012, there were more than one billion patient visits to physician offices in the United States[46] with the average person having a little over three visits a year.[46]

Because it is very expensive to set up a private practice, it is increasingly common to see more than one practitioner sharing both an office and staff. These practices are often referred to as *group practices* to distinguish them from *solo* (single practitioner) *practices*. Also, when two or more physicians practice as a group, the facility in which they provide medical services is called a *clinic*. Some clinics are small, with just a few providers, while others are very large with many providers, such as the Mayo Clinic in Rochester, Minnesota, or the Cleveland Clinic in Cleveland, Ohio. Some clinics provide care only for individuals with special health needs such as treatment of cancer or diabetes or assistance in family planning; others accept patients with a wide range of problems. A misconception held by many is that clinics are not much different from hospitals. One big difference is that clinics do not have inpatient beds, and hospitals do. Some clinics do have an administrative relationship with inpatient facilities so that if a person needs to be admitted to a hospital, it is a relatively simple process; other clinics may be free-standing, or independent of all other facilities.

Although many of the clinics are run as either for-profit or not-for-profit facilities, some are also funded by tax dollars. These clinics have been created primarily to meet the needs of the **medically indigent**—those lacking the financial ability to pay for their own medical care. Most of these clinics are located in large urban areas or rural areas that are underserved by the private sector. Two examples of this type of clinic are *public health clinics* and *community health centers* (CHCs). The former are usually a part of a local health department (LHD). The scope of health care services offered by LHDs varies greatly. These services can range from prevention-oriented programs, such as immunizations and well-baby care, to complete personal health services such as those offered at private-sector clinics. CHCs have been around since the late 1960s, known initially as *neighborhood health centers*. Those CHCs that receive funding under Section 330 of the Public Health Service (PHS) Act are known as **Federally Qualified Health Centers (FQHCs)**. FQHCs operate under the auspices of the Bureau of Primary Health Care, which is part of the U.S. Department of Health and Human Services.[47] Today, there are over 1,200 FQHCs that are located in every state and territory.[47] The importance of FQHCs to the primary health care needs of the underserved populations in the United States is huge.[5] In 2013, FQHCs served almost 22 million patients nationally, many being from racial and ethnic minority groups. Of those patients, 72% had family incomes at or below the poverty level, 35% were uninsured, and another 41% depended on Medicaid.[47] The importance of FQHCs was reinforced when additional funding for them was included in the Affordable Care Act.[48]

Medically indigent those lacking the financial ability to pay for their own medical care

Federally Qualified Health Center (FQHC) community health center that receives funding under Section 330 of the Public Health Service (PHS) Act

Some of the most recent additions to outpatient care facilities are retail clinics found in pharmacies (e.g., CVS and Walgreens), supermarkets (e.g., Kroger), and retail stores (e.g., Walmart and Target). The concept was born in 2000 when the first retail clinic opened in a grocery store in Minnesota.[49] In 2014 the number was approximately 1,800[50] and it was projected that there would be 3,000 such clinics by 2016.[49] The services offered are limited, but they "represent an entrepreneurial response to consumer demand for fast, affordable treatment of easy-to-diagnose, acute conditions."[5] The facilities are often operated by an outside company, maybe even a hospital, and are generally staffed by nurses, nurse practitioners, and physician assistants. Initially, payment at these clinics was out of the pocket of the consumer, but the concept has caught the eye of insurers as a lower cost way of providing acute care, and thus many insurers now have contracts with the clinics allowing patients to pay only copays.[5] Employers like the idea too and waive the copay when employees use them,[5] and some employers have even set up similar "Quick Clinics" within their own facility. Response to these clinics has been good from the insurers and consumers, but some in the medical community question the quality of care received.

Urgent/emergent care centers have been around in the United States since the early 1970s. They "fill gaps in the delivery system created by the rigidity of private physician appointment and unavailability during nonbusiness hours. The centers also can provide a much more convenient and user friendly alternative to a hospital emergency department during hours when private physicians are not available."[5] Urgent/emergent care centers often provide quicker service with less paperwork, particularly for those with cash or credit cards. These facilities (often not much larger than a fast-food restaurant) have sometimes been referred to as "Docs in a Box"! These facilities are not appropriate for all emergency cases. A majority of patients with life-threatening conditions are still taken to hospital emergency rooms, where top-of-the-line, advanced life support equipment and emergency physicians are on staff. Although emergency rooms are expensive for hospitals to maintain, they obviously perform a needed service (see **Figure 13.8**).

Ambulatory surgery centers do not perform major surgery, such as heart transplants, but perform same-day surgeries where a hospital stay following the surgery is not needed. As noted earlier, today the majority of all surgical procedures are performed in these types of facilities.[5] The factors that have promoted the increase in ambulatory surgical procedures as alternatives to inpatient surgery include the development of new, safe, and faster-acting general anesthetics; advances in surgical equipment and materials; development of noninvasive or minimally invasive surgical and nonsurgical procedures; and reduced coverage by insurance companies for hospital stays.

One area of tremendous growth in outpatient care facilities in recent years has been in the development of freestanding, non-hospital-based, specialty facilities. Often, these facilities offer a single service, such as dialysis for individuals with kidney failure, or several similar services, such as those found in a diagnostic imaging center. In this latter example, the services often included are simple radiograph technology (X-rays) and computed tomography (CT) and magnetic resonance imaging (MRI), which are used for viewing the body's anatomical structures in several planes. These technologies are ideal for outpatient facilities because of their noninvasive nature and profitability.

Even though convenience and cost are often the reasons for the development of new outpatient care facilities, the establishment of a new outpatient care facility in a community is not always received with enthusiasm. In previously underserved communities, fast-growing communities, or communities with many temporary residents such as resort communities, they have been well received. However, in stable or shrinking communities where an adequate number of health providers exists, the arrival of a new

FIGURE 13.8   Many outpatient care facilities provide medical services safely and efficiently without the overhead of a hospital.

© James F. McKenzie

freestanding ambulatory care facility is sometimes viewed as unfriendly competition. In some of these cases the "unfriendly competition" has come from outside for-profit health care companies, but a more recent trend has been physicians breaking away from voluntary (independent or not-for-profit) hospitals where they once performed the procedures in the hospital's outpatient facility to create their own facilities in which to perform the procedures. The primary reasons for this trend are physicians wishing to have control over how the facility is run (e.g., the times and days procedures are scheduled, who is hired to work in the facilities) and to receive a greater share of the profits.

Rehabilitation Centers

Rehabilitation centers are health care facilities in which patients work with health care providers to restore functions lost because of injury, disease, or surgery. These centers are sometimes part of a clinic or hospital but may also be freestanding facilities. Rehabilitation centers may operate on both an outpatient and an inpatient basis. Those providers who commonly work in a rehabilitation center include physical, occupational, and respiratory therapists as well as exercise physiologists.

Long-Term Care Options

Not too many years ago, when the topic of long-term care was mentioned, most people thought of nursing homes and state hospitals for the mentally ill and emotionally disabled. Today, however, the term *long-term care* includes not only the traditional institutional residential care, but also special units within these residential facilities (such as for Alzheimer patients), halfway houses, group homes, assisted-living facilities, transitional (step-down) care in a hospital, day care facilities for patients of all ages with health problems that require special care, and personal home health care. Elders are the biggest users of long-term care, but other users include those with disabilities or chronic conditions, and those with acute and subacute conditions who are unable to care for themselves.

One area of long-term care that has received special attention in recent years is home health care. The demand for home health care has been driven by the restructuring of the health care delivery system, technological advances that enable people to be treated outside a hospital and to recover more quickly, and the cost containment pressures that have shortened hospital stays. **Home health care** involves providing health care via health personnel and medical equipment to individuals and families in their places of residence, for the purpose of promoting, maintaining, or restoring health or to maximize the level of independence while minimizing the effects of disability and illness, including terminal disease. Home health care can be either long term, to help a chronically ill patient avoid institutionalization, or it can be short term to assist a patient following an acute illness and hospitalization until the patient is able to return to independent functioning. Home health care can be provided either through a formal system of paid professional health caregivers (e.g., home health care agency) or through an informal system where the care is provided by family, friends, and neighbors.[5] Medicare is the largest single payer for home health care, accounting for about one-third of the total annual expenditures.[5]

The need for professional health caregivers will continue into the future because of the "increase in the number of older persons and their expressed desire to remain in their homes for care whenever possible."[5] In 2013, there were 11,062 Medicare-certified home health agencies in the United States. That number is almost four times as many as existed in 1980.[18] During 2013 these agencies submitted over 6 million claims and Medicare paid approximately $18 billion towards those claims.[51] Even though Medicare and Medicaid are the largest payers for home health care services, the amounts spent are relatively small in comparison to the total dollars spent on the Medicare and Medicaid programs.[23]

Accreditation of Health Care Facilities

One way of determining the quality of a health care facility is to find out if it is accredited by a reputable group. **Accreditation** is the process by which an agency or organization evaluates and recognizes an institution as meeting certain predetermined standards. The predominant organization responsible for accrediting health care facilities is **The Joint Commission**, formerly known as the Joint Commission on Accreditation of Health care Organizations (JCAHO). The

---

Rehabilitation center a facility in which restorative care is provided following injury, disease, or surgery

Home health care care that is provided in the patient's residence for the purpose of promoting, maintaining, or restoring health

Accreditation the process by which an agency or organization evaluates and recognizes an institution as meeting certain predetermined standards

The Joint Commission the predominant organization responsible for accrediting health care facilities

Joint Commission is an independent, not-for-profit organization that accredits and certifies more than 21,000 health care organizations and programs in the United States. The health care facilities/organizations that can be accredited by The Joint Commission include ambulatory health care centers, behavioral health care organizations, independent or freestanding laboratories, home care agencies/organizations, hospitals (e.g., general, children's, psychiatric, rehabilitation, and critical access), and long-term care facilities (e.g., nursing homes and rehabilitation centers). To earn and maintain The Joint Commission accreditation, a facility or organization must complete an application and undergo an on-site survey (visit) by a Joint Commission survey team. The Joint Commission surveyors conduct an unannounced visit to accredited health care organizations a minimum of once every 39 months (2 years for laboratories) to evaluate standards compliance.[52] Only those organizations that are in compliance with all standards at the time of the on-site survey are accredited. The Joint Commission feels that compliance with its standards is not an every 3-year process but rather an ongoing process.

> The Joint Commission accreditation does not begin and end with the on-site survey. It is a continuous process. Every time a nurse double checks a patient's identification before administering a medication, every time a surgical team calls a "time out" to verify they agree they're about to perform the correct procedure, at the correct site, on the correct patient, they live and breathe the accreditation process. Every 3 months, hospitals submit data to The Joint Commission on how they treat conditions such as heart attack care and pneumonia—data that is [sic] available to the public and updated quarterly on qualitycheck.org. Every year, organizations evaluate their ongoing standards compliance through a periodic performance review. The Joint Commission accreditation is woven into the fabric of a health care organization's operations.[52]

Health Care System: Function

Like the structure of the health care system, the function of the health care system of the United States is also unique compared to the health care systems of other developed countries of the world. The Affordable Care Act (ACA) is most notable for the transformations it made "to health insurance—both access to it and its contents—rather than for structural reforms made to the delivery system."[2] The purpose of the ACA was to (1) expand health insurance coverage, (2) hold insurance companies accountable, (3) lower health care costs, (3) guarantee more choice, and (5) enhance the quality of care for all Americans.[53] Some parts of the ACA went into effect shortly after the legislation was signed (e.g., Patient Bill of Rights), some of its biggest parts (e.g., individual mandate for health insurance) were rolled out in 2014, implementation of other parts have been postponed or delayed (e.g., employer responsibility provision). Some parts have been repealed (e.g., the unsustainable Community Living Assistance Services and Supports [CLASS] program of government-subsidized long-term care insurance),[54] and the final portions will be implemented in 2020. The remainder of the chapter includes some of the structure from the past that led to the new law and what can be expected in terms of the change in structure as the new law continues to be implemented.

Understanding the Structure of the Health Care System

To begin, it must be understood that the health care system of the United States is big and complicated. It is big from the standpoint of cost—it is very expensive (see **Figure 13.9**)—and

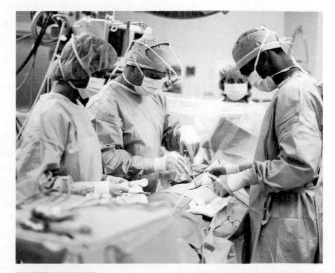

FIGURE 13.9   Health care services offered by U.S. providers are perhaps the best in the world, but at what cost?

© Photos.com.

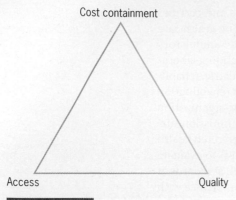

FIGURE 13.10 The cost containment, access, and quality triangle of health care.

Data from: Kissick, W.L. (1994). *Medicine's Dilemmas: Infinite Needs versus Finite Resources*. Yale University Press. © 1994. Reprinted by permission of Yale University Press.

because of the many stakeholders that include but are not limited to health care consumers, health care providers, health care administrators, politicians, policymakers, government regulators, insurance companies, and professional and trade associations. It is complicated because health care policy is intertwined with other policies (e.g., the U.S. tax code, where credits for employers who provide health insurance for employees and health care consumers who get deductions on their income taxes if their health care spending reaches certain levels in a year), and because of the politics and ideological viewpoints of the decision makers.

The major issues of the health care system in the United States can be represented by the cost containment, access, and quality triangle noted by Kissick[55] (see **Figure 13.10**). In Kissick's equilateral triangle, the equal 60-degree angles represent equal priorities. That is, access is just as important as quality and cost containment and vice versa. However, an expansion of any one of the angles compromises one or both of the other two. For example, if we were interested in increasing the quality of our already good services, it would also increase the costs and decrease access. Or, some feel, if we increase access, costs will go up, and the quality will decrease. Or, if we concentrate on containing costs, both quality of care and access will decrease. With such dilemmas, the United States continues to struggle to find the right combination of policy and accountability to deal with these shortcomings. Concerns associated with each of the three sides of the cost containment, access, and quality triangle are discussed later in this chapter.

Access to Health Care

Even with several different means of gaining access to health care services, access has been and continues to be a major health policy issue in the United States. Health insurance coverage and the generosity of coverage are major determinants of access to health care.[56] Decreasing the number of uninsured Americans was a key goal of the ACA. Since the major coverage provisions of the ACA went into effect in January 2014 the number of uninsured has declined.[57] In 2015, 28.8 million persons of all ages (9.1%) were uninsured—16.0 million fewer persons than in 2013 and 17.5 million fewer than in 2011.[58] Stated another way, almost 91% of Americans now have health insurance. This number represents a historic increase in the number of Americans insured. However, 28.8 million uninsured is still too many. Most uninsured people are adults in low-income working families, with minorities being at higher risk of being uninsured than non-Hispanic whites[57] (see **Box 13.2**). The uninsured numbers are greatest in states that did not expand Medicaid eligibility under the ACA.[57] Based on the current components of the ACA, the Congressional Budget Office has projected that the percentage of the nonelderly (< 65 years of age) population with health insurance will remain steady, at around 90% through 2025.[59] If unauthorized immigrants are removed from the data, the projections rise to 92%.[59]

Interestingly enough, the uninsured do not lack emergency or urgent care because no one needing such care and willing to go to a hospital emergency room will be turned away. However, studies repeatedly demonstrate that the uninsured are less likely than those with insurance to receive preventive care (i.e., checkups, screenings, and prenatal care) and services for major health conditions and chronic diseases[57] (see Box 13.1). Without adequate primary care, many patients eventually find themselves in need of more costly and often less effective medical treatment.

A brief summary of the most notable steps of Affordable Care Act to increase the number of Americans with health insurance are presented in **Box 13.3**. Among these steps, the one that has made the biggest impact on allowing the uninsured to gain access to insurance, and in turn access to care, is the *Health Insurance Marketplace*. **Health Insurance Marketplaces** (or exchanges) are organizations that were set up to create more organized and competitive markets for buying health insurance.[60] A Marketplace simplifies the search for health coverage by gathering the options available for consumers in one place. The Marketplaces, which can be run by a state or the federal government, were created primarily for two groups: individuals buying insurance on their own and small businesses with up to 50 employees (*Note:* Some

Health Insurance Marketplace organization established to create more organized and competitive markets for purchasing health insurance

BOX 13.2 *Healthy People 2020:* **Objectives**

Access to Health Services

Goal: Improve access to comprehensive, quality health care services.

Objective: AHS-1, Increase the proportion of persons with health insurance.

Objective: AHS-1.1, Medical insurance.

Target: 100%.

Baseline: 83.2% of persons had medical insurance in 2008.

Target-setting method: Total coverage.

Data source: National Health Interview Survey (NHIS), CDC/NCHS.

Objective: AHS-1.2 (Developmental). Increase the proportion of persons with dental insurance.

Target: TBD

Baseline: TBD

Target-setting method: TBD

Potential data source: National Health Interview Survey (NHIS), CDC/NCHS.

Objective: AHS-1.3 (Developmental). Increase the proportion of persons with prescription drug insurance.

Target: TBD

Baseline: TBD

Target-setting method: TBD

Potential data source: NHIS, CDC/NCHS.

Objective: AHS-2 (Developmental). Increase the proportion of insured persons with coverage for clinical preventive services.

Target: TBD

Baseline: TBD

Target-setting method: TBD

Potential data source: CMS; AGing Integrated Database (AGID), Administration on Aging (AoA); Medicare Current Beneficiary Survey (MCBS), CMS.

    Note: TBD = To be determined.

For Further Thought

Do you think the Affordable Care Act was the best way to go about reaching these objectives? Defend your response. Do you think the United States should adopt a national health insurance plan like the other developed countries of the world to make sure all persons have health insurance? Why or why not?

Data from: U.S. Department of Health and Human Services, Office of Disease Prevention and Health Promotion (2016). *Healthy People 2020*. Washington, DC: U.S. Government Printing Office. Available at http://www.healthypeople.gov/2020/topics-objectives/topic/Access-to-Health-Services/objectives.

BOX 13.3 **Components of the Affordable Care Act to Increase Access to Care**

1. *Individual mandate.* In 2014, all individuals were required to have health insurance or pay a fee. The fee was phased in from 2014–2016. The fee for 2016 was the higher of 2.5% of household income or $695 per adult ($347.50 per child), up to a maximum of $2,085. The fee is paid through the federal income tax return. There are some exceptions to this requirement that include financial hardship, religious objections, incarcerated individuals, and for American Indians.

2. *Expansion of public programs.* Medicaid expanded to cover non-Medicaid eligible individuals under the age of 65 up to 133% (*Note:* Because of the way it is calculated, it turns out to be 138%) of the federal poverty level based on modified adjusted gross income (as under current law undocumented immigrants are not eligible for Medicaid). In 2016, the federal poverty level for a family of four was $24,300, making the 133% level $36,450. This expansion created a national uniform eligibility standard across states if states accepted the expansion.* The federal government pays for most of the expansion.

3. *Health Insurance Marketplace* (i.e., exchanges). For people who do not receive employer-sponsored insurance and who make more than 133% of the federal poverty level, health insurance is available through new exchanges created by states." (*Note.* States that did not create exchanges could have either partnered with the federal government to operate an exchange, or used a federally facilitated exchange.) Plans in the exchanges must provide benefits that meet a minimum set of standards. Insurers offer four levels of coverage (bronze, silver, gold, and platinum) that vary based on premiums, out-of-pocket costs, and benefits beyond the minimum required plus a catastrophic coverage plan (*Note:* A catastrophic plan is available to those up to age 30 and people of any age with a hardship exemption from mandate to purchase coverage). The silver plan has become the most popular. Various premium credits and cost-sharing subsidies are available to those with incomes between 100% and 400% of the federal poverty level.

4. *Changes to private insurance.* New health insurance regulations changed the way insurers must operate. Insurers: (1) cannot deny coverage to people because of health status (i.e., pre-existing condition); (2) cannot charge people more because of health status or gender; (3) with all new health plans, have to provide comprehensive coverage that includes a minimum

(Continues)

BOX 13.3   (Continued)

set of services, caps out-of-pocket spending, does not impose cost-sharing for preventive services, and does not impose annual or lifetime limits on coverage; (4) have to allow young adults to remain on their parents' health insurance up until age 26; and (5) have to limit waiting periods to no longer than 90 days on employer-sponsored plans.

5. *Employer responsibility provision.* Employers with 50 or more full-time employees, or full-time equivalents, must offer health insurance that is affordable (i.e., ≤ 9.66% of an employee's W-2 wages in 2016) and pro vides minimum value (i.e., 60%+ of the costs of covered services) to their full-time employees and their children up to age 26 or be subject to a penalty. Employers who failed to offer health insurance were assessed a fee of $2,160 per full-time employee (in excess of 30 employees) in 2016 if they had at least one full-time

employee who received a premium tax credit (i.e., subsidy) through a Marketplace. Employers who did provide insurance but did not offer health insurance that was affordable and provided a minimum value and had at least one employee who received a premium tax credit from Marketplace coverage were required to pay the lesser of $3,240 per employee in 2016 who received a premium tax credit or $2,160 per employee (in excess of 30 employees). If employees offer coverage and have workers who do not sign up for the plan or do not opt out of a plan, the employer must automatically enroll employees in the lowest cost premium plan. The employer provision penalty for employers with 100 or more employees went into effect in January 2015; for employers with 50 to 99 employees it went into effect in January 2016.

*As of July 2016, 33 states (including the District of Columbus) had expanded Medicaid, 2 other states were in discussion about expansion, and the remaining 16 had not adopted expansion.

**As of January 2016, 13 states had state-based Marketplaces, 4 states had federally supported marketplaces, 7 had a state-partnership Marketplace, and 27 used federally facilitated marketplaces.

Data from: Families USA (2016). *Federal Poverty Guidelines.* Author: Washington, DC. Available at http://familiesusa.org/product/federal-poverty-guidelines; The Henry J. Kaiser Family Foundation (2013). *Summary of the Affordable Care Act.* Available at http://kff.org/health-reform/fact-sheet/summary-of-new-health-reform-law/; The Henry J. Kaiser Family Foundation (2016). *State Health Facts.* Available at http://kff.org/statedata/.

states may use different employee maximums to define small businesses). The marketplace for small businesses is called the Small Business Health Options Program (SHOP) Marketplace.[61]

By using the Marketplaces consumers can compare plans based on price, benefits, quality, and other features important to them before making a choice. Consumers can also get help online, by phone, by chat, or in person.[61] The insurance plans in Marketplaces are offered by private companies and must meet the same set of benefits called the essential health benefits[61] (see **Box 13.4**). Marketplaces became available to consumers via the federal website (Health Care. gov) or a state website, if a state had its own state-based Marketplace on October 1, 2013, with health insurance policies purchased before December 15, 2013 going into effect on January 1, 2014. The initial roll out of the Heathcare.gov website was not without its problems. Most, but not all of the problems dealt with technical glitches. Now that the website has been up and running for several years online enrollment has run much more smoothly.

Quality of Health Care

All people are entitled to and should receive quality health care. Yet several different reports, including one that compared U.S. health care to that of Australia, Canada, France, Germany, the Netherlands, New Zealand, Norway, Sweden, Switzerland, and the United Kingdom,[62] indicate that the U. S. health care system underperforms relative to other countries on most dimensions of performance and people in the United States could be receiving better care. *Quality health care* has been defined as, "the degree to which health services for individuals and populations increase the likelihood of desired health outcomes and are consistent with current professional knowledge."[63] The Institute of Medicine (IOM) has further delineated that quality health care should be:[64]

- *Effective.* Delivering health care based on scientific evidence to all who could benefit based on need
- *Safe.* Delivering health care to patients that avoids injuries to patients from the care that is intended to help them

BOX 13.4 Essential Health Benefits Included in Health Insurance Available through the Marketplaces

The essential health benefits that all private health insurance plans must offer include:

- Ambulatory patient services (outpatient care you get without being admitted to a hospital)
- Emergency services
- Hospitalization
- Maternity and newborn care (care before and after your baby is born)
- Mental health and substance use disorder services, including behavioral health treatment, counseling, and psychotherapy

- Prescription drugs
- Rehabilitative and habilitative services and devices (services and devices to help people with injuries, disabilities, or chronic conditions gain or recover mental and physical skills)
- Laboratory services (i.e., lab tests)
- Preventive and wellness services including counseling, screenings, and vaccinations, and chronic disease management
- Pediatric services

Note: Plans may offer more than benefits listed above. Specific health care benefits may vary by state. Even within the same state, there can be small differences among health insurance plans.

Data from: Centers for Medicare & Medicaid Services (2013). *10 Health Care Benefits Covered in the Health Insurance Marketplace.* Available at https://www.healthcare.gov/blog/10-health-care-benefits-covered-in-the-health-insurance-marketplace/.

- *Timely.* Delivering health care in a way that reduces waits and sometimes harmful delays
- *Patient-centered.* Providing health care that is respectful of and responsive to individual patient preferences, needs, and values
- *Equitable.* Delivering health care that does not vary in quality because of personal characteristics of patients
- *Efficient.* Delivering health care that maximizes resources and avoids waste

Though the definitions of quality health care are easily understood, operationalizing quality health care is not as easy, yet a number of groups have created measures for health care quality. Since 2003, the Agency for Health care Research and Quality (AHRQ), together with the U.S. Department of Health and Human Services (HHS) and some private sector partners, has annually reported on progress and opportunities for improving health care quality as mandated by the U.S. Congress by publishing the National Health care Quality Report (NHQR) and the National Health care Disparities Report (NHDR). Beginning in 2014, the findings on health care quality and health care disparities was integrated into a single document—*National Health care Quality and Disparities Report* (QDR).[65] Both the NHQR and the NHDR are built on, for the most part, the same dimensions. The QDR "is based on 250 measures of quality and disparities covering a broad array of health care services and settings."[65]

Another group that measures health care quality is the National Committee for Quality Assurance (NCQA).[66] The NCQA is a private, not-for-profit organization that has been assessing and accrediting health care plans since 1990. It assesses how well a health plan manages and delivers health care in four different ways: (1) through accreditation (a rigorous on-site review of key clinical and administrative processes); (2) through certification (a rigorous review of certain functions—for example, credentialing or utilization management—that health plans or employers have delegated to another organization); (3) through the Health care Effectiveness Data and Information Set (HEDIS—a tool that consists of 81 measures across five domains that is used to measure performance in key areas such as immunization and mammography screening rates) and members' satisfaction with their care in areas such as claims processing, customer service, and getting needed care quickly;[67] and (4) through physician recognition programs that identify physicians who provide quality care in areas such as diabetes, back pain, and heart/stroke care. Although participation with NCQA is voluntary, the NCQA accredited health plans cover 109 million or 70.5% of all Americans enrolled in health plans.[66] The data from NCQA's assessments are available at its website. Employers, consultants, and consumers use HEDIS data, along with the accreditation, certification, and recognition information to help them select the best-managed care programs for their needs.[67]

Regardless of what method is used to measure the quality of health care delivered in the United States, the results have been similar. The general consensus is that the quality of health care has been getting better at a modest pace but is not as good as it could or should be.

Dealing with the problem of "less than desirable quality in health care" is not easy because it runs through every aspect of care. That is why there are not just a few items in the Affordable Care Act that deal with quality—there are many. Examples include (1) requiring health care plans to offer preventive services (e.g., screenings and vaccinations) without charging a copay, co-insurance, or deductible, (2) providing information about the quality of nursing homes and making it easier to file complaints about the quality of care in nursing homes, (3) linking payments to physicians and hospitals based on the quality of care provided, and (4) incentivizing health care providers to use electronic medical records. Other activities aimed at improving quality of health that have gained much attention are the National Quality Strategy, accountable care organizations (ACOs), and the patient-centered medical home program. Each of these is discussed below.

National Quality Strategy

The National Quality Strategy (NQS)[68] was mandated by the ACA to serve as a catalyst and compass for a nationwide focus on quality improvement efforts and measuring quality. The NQS was developed by a broad-based group of more than 300 organizations and individuals representing all sectors of the health care industry. In addition, the general public was given an opportunity to provide comments on it. The NQS is guided by a set of three overarching aims to provide better, more affordable care for individuals and the community. The aims are also used to assess the efforts to improve the quality of care. To achieve the three aims, the NQS applies six priorities that address the most common health concerns that affect most Americans. "Achievement of the National Quality Strategy can only occur if individuals, family members, payers, providers, employers, and communities work together."[69] To assist these stakeholders with their work for improving quality, the NQS includes nine levers that can be used by the stakeholders to align their work to the NQS (see **Box 13.5**). The NQS is the basis for the annual report to Congress on the quality improvement in health care.[70]

Accountable Care Organizations

Accountable care organizations (ACOs) are groups of doctors, hospitals, and other health care providers who come together voluntarily as a legal entity to give coordinated high quality care to Medicare patients. "The goal of coordinated care is to ensure that patients, especially the chronically ill, get the right care at the right time, while avoiding unnecessary duplication of services and preventing medical errors"[71] and therefore reduce costs for care. ACOs were not created by the ACA, they have been around since 2006,[72] but provisions for ACOs were included in the ACA. The ACA authorized Medicare to contract with ACOs in a Medicare Shared Savings Program.[73] The incentive for providers to form an ACO is financial. "The ACA enables ACOs to share in savings to the federal government based on ACO performance in improving quality and reducing health care costs."[5]

Patient-Centered Medical Home

Like ACOs, the concept of the *patient-centered medical home* (PCMH) is not new; early forms of it can be traced back to the 1960s in a response to try and improve the way care was offered. And, like ACOs, the PCMH is a model of care that reorganizes the way care is offered. The **patient-centered medical home**, which applies to patients of all ages, has been defined as "a care delivery model whereby patient treatment is coordinated through their primary care physician to ensure they receive the necessary care when and where they need it, in a manner they can understand."[74] The PCMH is responsible for providing all of the patient's health care needs (i.e., preventive services, treatment of acute care and chronic illnesses, and assistance with the end-of-life issues) or appropriately arranging a patient's care with other qualified providers.[5] The Agency for Health care Research and Quality has identified five functions and attributes of a medical home: (1) comprehensive care, (2) patient-centered care, (3) coordinated care, (4) accessible services, and (5) quality and safety.[75] The PCMH has gained momentum in the

Accountable care organization (ACO) a group of doctors, hospitals, and other health care providers who come together voluntarily as a legal entity to give coordinated high-quality care to Medicare patients

Patient-centered medical home a care delivery model whereby patient treatment is coordinated through their primary care physician to ensure they receive the necessary care when and where they need it, in a manner they can understand

---

BOX 13.5 National Quality Strategy Aims, Priorities, and Levers

Aims

The National Quality Strategy pursues three broad aims. These aims will be used to guide and assess local, state, and national efforts to improve health and the quality of health care.

- Better care: Improve the overall quality by making health care more patient-centered, reliable, accessible, and safe.
- Healthy People/Healthy Communities: Improve the health of the U.S. population by supporting proven interventions to address behavioral, social, and environmental determinants of health in addition to delivering higher quality care.
- Affordable care: Reduce the cost of quality health care for individuals, families, employers, and government.

Priorities

- Make care safer by reducing harm caused in the delivery of care.
- Ensure that each person and family is engaged as partners in their care.
- Promote effective communication and coordination of care.
- Promote the most effective prevention and treatment practices for the leading causes of mortality, starting with cardiovascular disease.
- Work with communities to promote wide use of best practices to enable healthy living.

- Make quality care more affordable for individuals, families, employers, and governments by developing and spreading new health care delivery models.

Levers

- Measurement and feedback: Provide performance feedback to plans and providers to improve care.
- Public reporting: Compare treatment results, costs, and patient experience for consumers.
- Learning and technical assistance: Foster learning environments that offer training, resources, tools, and guidance to help organizations achieve quality improvement goals.
- Certification, accreditation, and regulation: Adopt or adhere to approaches to meet safety and quality standards.
- Consumer incentives and benefit designs: Help consumers adopt healthy behaviors and make informed decisions.
- Payment: Reward and incentivize providers to deliver high-quality, patient-centered care.
- Health information technology: Improve communication, transparency, and efficiency for better coordinated health and health care.
- Innovation and diffusion: Foster innovation in health care quality improvement, and facilitate rapid adoption within and across organizations and communities.
- Workforce development: Invest in people to prepare the next generation of health care professionals and support lifelong learning for providers.

Data from: U.S. Department of Health and Human Services, Agency for Health care Research and Quality (2015). *About the National Quality Strategy (NQS)*. Available at http://www.ahrq.gov/workingforquality/about.htm.

---

medical community in recent years, and in 2006 the Patient-Centered Primary Care Collaborative (PCPCC), a not-for-profit organization, was created. The PCPCC "is dedicated to advancing an effective and efficient health system built on a strong foundation of primary care and the patient-centered medical home."[76] The ACA supports provisions for the continuing development of the PCMH model as it relates to Medicaid expansion, payment rates for primary care, primary care provider shortages, and the Center for Medicare and Medicaid Innovation to test various service delivery and payment models. For the PCMH to be fully accepted there will need to be some changes in the way physicians are reimbursed in order to compensate them for the time in organizing the patents' care.

The Cost of and Paying for Health Care

The cost of health care and paying for health care continue to be burdens on both individuals and the U.S. population as a whole. In 2014, health expenditures grew 5.3% to $3.0 trillion and consumed 17.5% of the gross domestic product (GDP). That amounted to $9,523 per person. It is estimated that health care spending will continue to grow at 5.8% per year through the next decade. With such growth, spending is expected to reach $5.4 trillion and 19.6% of the GDP by 2024.[77] These figures make the United States' health care system the most costly in the world.[62] In fact, the United States spends "more on health care than the next 10 biggest spenders combined: Japan, Germany, France, China, United Kingdom, Italy, Canada, Brazil, Spain, and Australia."[78] Under the U.S. system, the actual cost of the service, for the most part, is usually not known until after the service has been provided, unless the consumer is bold enough to inquire ahead of time. However, starting in 2013, and continuing each year since, in an effort to make the U.S. health care system more affordable and accountable, the Centers for Medicare and Medicaid Service has released data and information comparing the charges for the 100 most common inpatient services, 30 common outpatient services, all physician and other supplier procedures and services, and all Part D prescriptions for Medicare patients. The data showed that there were significant variations across the country and within communities in what providers charged for common services.[79] Many journalists picked up on this information and confronted providers, making providers respond to why their charges may be different than in other parts of the country. Such transparency is needed if health care is to become a true market system.

Even with more transparency, the cost of health care continues to go up and is growing at an unsustainable rate.[78] There are several reasons[80–82] for this growth. They include, but are not limited to, (1) major coverage expansions of Medicaid and private health insurance under the Affordable Care Act; (2) paying providers and hospitals in ways that reward doing more, rather than being efficient; (3) an aging U.S. population with many chronic health conditions; (4) the demand for medical advances in the form of new drugs, technologies, services, and procedures; (5) relatively price-insensitive patients who have limited out-of-pocket costs; (6) the lack of evidence to make decisions on which medical care is best; (7) hospital and providers that are increasingly gaining market share and are better able to demand higher prices; (8) supply and demand issues (e.g., restricting the practices of nurse practitioners and physician assistants when there is a need for more primary care), and (9) legal issues (e.g., malpractice premiums) that complicate efforts to slow spending.

So who pays the health care bill? Payments for the U.S. health care bill come from four sources. The first is the consumers themselves. In 2014, these direct or out-of-pocket payments represented approximately one-tenth (10.9%) of all payments. The remaining portion of health care payments, nine-tenths (89.1%), comes almost entirely from indirect, or third-party, payments. The first source of third-party payments is private insurance companies. Private insurance companies paid about one-third (32.7%) of the health care bill in 2014. These payments were made from premiums paid to the insurance company by the employees and/or their employers. The second source of third-party payments is governmental insurance programs (e.g., Medicare, Medicaid, Veterans Administration, Children's Health Insurance Program, or military). These government programs are funded by a combination of federal and state taxes and premiums (as in the case of Part B Medicare coverage). In 2014, about two-fifths (40.9%) of the health care bill was paid for by governmental insurance programs. The remainder (15.5%) of the health care bill was paid by other third-party payers[77] (see **Figure 13.11**).

It is clear that the cost of health care is going to continue to rise. One of the major selling points of the Affordable Care Act was to try to slow down the cost of health care, thus the title "Affordable Care." The Congressional Budget Office (CBO) and the Joint Committee on Taxation (JCT) estimated that the ACA's coverage provisions will result in a net cost to the federal government of $41 billion in 2014 and $1,487 billion over the period from 2015 to 2024."[83] These costs are financed through a combination of savings from Medicare and Medicaid and new taxes and fees. The savings from Medicare and Medicaid come mostly from how the government pays providers. Examples of new taxes include taxes on high-cost health insurance and tanning bed use, while examples of new fees include those that have to be paid by those individuals who chose not to purchase health insurance. Many believe that in addition to the cost savings from Medicare and Medicaid, health care costs have the potential to be lower because millions of people who were uninsured before the law will now be paying premiums, and many of them are young and healthy and will not use a lot of health care.

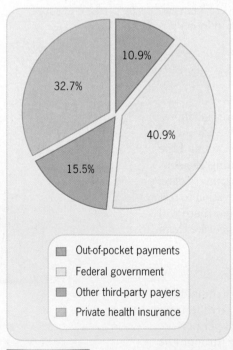

10.9%

32.7%

40.9%

15.5%

- ■ Out-of-pocket payments
- □ Federal government
- ■ Other third-party payers
- ▨ Private health insurance

FIGURE 13.11 Health expenditures by source of funds, United States, 2014.

Data from: Centers for Medicare & Medicaid Services (2014). *National Health Expenditure Data.* Available at https://www. cms.gov/Research-Statistics-Data-and-Systems/Statistics-Trends-and-Reports/NationalHealthExpendData/index.html.

The monetary value that health care providers and facilities receive for providing services to patients is referred to as **reimbursement**.[84] As noted earlier, *third-party payers* (i.e., insurance companies and government entities) provide most of the reimbursement for health services. The process for receiving reimbursement from a third-party payment usually begins when a health care provider or his or her staff requests information about the patient's health insurance plan. They normally request the name of the insuring company (e.g., Aetna, Blue Cross/Blue Shield, Cigna), the policy number, and a personal identification number (PIN). The insurer usually provides this information to the insured on a wallet-sized card. The provider may then ask the patient to sign an insurance claim form in two places. The first signature indicates that the service has been provided and authorizes the provider to submit patient information with the claim for payment. The second signature instructs the insurance company to make the payment directly to the provider. Upon receiving and reviewing the completed and signed form, the insurance company then issues payments to the provider for services based on the provisions of the insurance policy. Depending on the level of reimbursement for the claim, the provider will either consider the bill paid in full or will request payment from the patient in the amount of the difference between the provider's full fee and the portion paid by the insurance company.

In recent years, the methods by which the amount of the reimbursement has been determined have changed. Traditionally, providers have favored the **fee-for-service** method, but it is not used much any more because of the cost escalation.[1] The fee-for-service is based on the assumption that services are provided in a set of identifiable and individually distinct units such as a doctor's office visit or a specific medical procedure.[1] Under the fee-for-service format, consumers select a provider, receive care (service) from the provider, and incur expenses (a fee) for the care. The provider is then reimbursed for covered services in part by the insurer and in part by the consumer, who is responsible for the balance unpaid by the insurer. Initially, the providers set the fees and insurers would pay the claim. But because of increased costs, insurers started to limit the amount they would pay for "usual, customary, and reasonable charges." The biggest drawback of the fee-for-service format is that providers have a greater incentive to provide services, some of which may not be essential.

Under the fee-for-service format, consumers are obligated to pay their fee at the time the service is rendered. In the past, before health insurance was common, some physicians provided care when needed and worried about payment later. Others often accepted "in kind" payment, such as farm produce or other products or services, as payment in full for a medical service rendered. Today, for patients to receive care via fee-for-service, they are often required to demonstrate the ability to pay (to assume financial responsibility for the fee) before the service is rendered. A provider's receptionist may ask, "How do you plan to settle your bill?" In other cases, providers have signs placed around the waiting room that state, "Payment is expected when service is rendered, unless other arrangements have been made prior to the appointment."

The more recent methods of reimbursement for health services have included *packaged pricing, resource-based relative value scale, capitation, prospective reimbursement*, and *pay-for-performance*. In **packaged pricing**, also referred to as *bundled charges*, several related services are included in one price. For example, optometrists will bundle the cost for an eye exam, frames, and lenses into a single charge.[1]

Resource-based relative value scale (RBRVS) was created for Medicare as part of the Omnibus Budget Reconciliation Act of 1989 to reimburse physicians according to the *relative value* of the service provided. The relative values units (RVUs) are derived through a complex formula based on time, skill, and intensity to provide the service. Also, included in the RVU is an overhead charge to run a practice.[12] Each year, Medicare publishes the Medicare Physician Fee Schedule, adjusted for geographic parts of the country, which provides the reimbursement amount for services and procedures under the Current Procedural Terminology (CPT) code.[1]

Managed care organizations (MCOs; see information about managed care later in this chapter) use several different approaches for reimbursement. Preferred provider organizations (PPOs) use a variation of the fee-for-service method. The variation is that the PPOs "establish

Reimbursement the monetary value that health care providers and facilities receive for providing services to patients

Fee-for-service a method of paying for health care in which after the service is rendered, a fee is paid

Packaged pricing several related health services are included in one price

Resource-based relative value scale (RBRVS) reimbursement to physicians according to the relative value of the service provided

Capitation a method of paying for covered health care services on a per-person premium basis for a specific time period prior to the service being rendered

Prospective reimbursement uses pre-established criteria to determine in advance the amount of reimbursement

Pay-for-performance (P4P) a payment system that offer financial rewards to providers and facilities for meeting, improving, or exceeding quality measures or other performance goals

fee schedules based on discounts negotiated with providers participating in its network."[1] Health maintenance organizations (HMOs), depending on their structure, have either paid providers a salary if they are employed by the HMO or have reimbursed using a mechanism called *capitation.*

Under **capitation**, insurers make arrangements with health care providers to provide agreed-upon covered health care services to a given population of consumers for a (usually discounted) set price—the per-person premium fee—over a particular time period. Often the arrangements are set up on a per-member, per-month (PMPM) rate called a *capitated fee.* The provider receives the capitated fee per enrollee regardless of whether the enrollee uses health care services and regardless of the quality of services provided. The provider is responsible for providing all needed services determined to be medically necessary and covered under the plan. In addition to the capitated fee, consumers may pay additional fees (copayments) for office visits and other services used. The insurer organizes the delivery of care by building an infrastructure of providers and implementing the systems to monitor and influence the cost and quality of care.

Prospective reimbursement has been around since 1983 when it was first used in the form of diagnosis-related groups (DRGs) for hospital stays under Medicare Part A (see discussion of Medicare and DRGs later in the chapter). It replaced *retrospective reimbursement* that was based on the length of stay and services provided. Thus, providers were rewarded for longer stays and more services, which increased costs. **Prospective reimbursement**, referred to as the prospective pricing system (PPS), "uses certain pre-established criteria to determine in advance, the amount of reimbursement."[1] Because of the success of DRGs, the Balanced Budget Act of 1997 mandated implementation of a Medicare PPS for hospital outpatient services and post-acute providers such as skilled nursing facilities, home health agencies, and inpatient rehabilitation facilities.[12] Thus, the four primary prospective reimbursement methods used today are DRGs (used for Medicare Part A), ambulatory payment classifications (APCs; used for payment to hospital outpatient departments), resource utilization groups (RUGs; used for payment to skilled nursing facilities), and home health resource groups (HHRGs; used for payment of home health care).[1]

Pay-for-performance (P4P) or "value-based purchasing" is a payment system that offers financial rewards to providers and facilities for meeting, improving, or exceeding quality measures (i.e., process, outcome, patience experience, and structure) or other performance goals.[84,85] Thus its purpose is to improve the quality, efficiency, and overall value of health care.[86] For example, providers can receive incentives for achieving a quality measure goal such as the reduction in hemoglobin A1c in patients with diabetes.[84] In addition to incentives, P4P payment systems can also include disincentives or penalties for not providing quality care. An example of a penalty that is part of the ACA is Medicare's Hospital Readmissions Reduction Program, which took effect 2012. With this program Medicare "can reduce payments by 1% to hospitals that have excessively high rates of avoidable readmissions for patients experiencing heart attacks, heart failure, or pneumonia."[85] Further, accountable care organizations (ACOs), which we noted earlier are mandated in the ACA, are the best-known P4P programs. To date, P4P programs have received mixed reviews about their effectiveness.[85] Time will tell if this type of payment system can be improved and in turn improve the quality of care.

Health Insurance

Health insurance, like all other types of insurance, is a risk- and cost-spreading process. That is, the cost of one person's injury or illness is shared by all in the group. Each person in the group has a different chance (or risk) of having a problem and thus needing health care. Some members of the group, for example, those who suffer from chronic and/or congenital health problems, will probably need more care while others in the group will need less. The concept of insurance has everyone in the group, no matter what their individual risk, helping to pay for the collective risk of the group. The risk of costly ill health is spread in a reasonably equitable fashion among all persons purchasing insurance, and everyone is protected from having to pay an insurmountable bill for a catastrophic injury or illness.

There are some exceptions to the "equitable fashion." If someone in the group knowingly engages in a behavior that increases his or her risk, such as smoking cigarettes or driving in a reckless manner, that person may have to pay more for the increased risk. In short, the greater the risk (or probability of using the insurance), the more the individual or group has to pay for insurance.

The concept of health insurance is not a new one in this country. Group health and life insurance are considered American inventions of the early twentieth century. In 1911, Montgomery Ward and Company sold health insurance policies based on the principles still used today in the business. Currently, hundreds of companies in the United States sell health and life insurance policies.

The Health Insurance Policy

A **health insurance policy** is a contract between an insurer (i.e., private insurance company or the government) and an individual (known as the insured or policyholder) that outlines in exact terms what health care services are covered, how the insured will be compensated, the cost of the policy to the insured (i.e., **premium**), and any associated information, for example the mode of premium payment or *deductibles*. The insurance company benefits in that it anticipates collecting more money in premiums than it has to pay out for services; hence, it anticipates a profit. The insured benefits by not being faced with medical bills he or she cannot pay, because the insurance company is obligated to pay them according to the terms of the contract. The added benefit for those insured as a group is that group premiums are less expensive than premiums for individuals.

The expectations of both insurers and insured are not always met. An insurer occasionally has to pay out more than it collects in premiums. Alternatively, the insured often purchases insurance that is never used.

Although the language of health insurance policies can be confusing, everyone needs to understand several key terms. One of the most important is **deductible**. The deductible is the amount of money that the beneficiary (insured) must incur (pay out of pocket) generally up to an annual limit before the insurance company begins to pay for covered services. A common yearly deductible level is $500 per individual policyholder, or a maximum of $1,000 per family. This means that the insured must pay the first $500/$1,000 of medical costs before the insurance company begins paying. The higher the deductible of a policy, the lower the premiums will be.

Usually, but not always, after the deductible has been met, most insurance companies pay a percentage of what they consider the "usual, customary, and reasonable" charge for covered services. The insurer generally pays 80% of the usual, customary, and reasonable costs, and the insured is responsible for paying the remaining 20%. This 20% is referred to as **co-insurance**. If the health care provider charges more than the usual, customary, and reasonable rates, the insured will have to pay both the co-insurance and the difference. A form of co-insurance, often associated with managed care programs, is **copayment** (or *copay* for short). A copayment is a negotiated set amount a patient pays for certain services—for example, $20 for an office visit and $15 for a prescription. Some insurance policies may have both co-insurance and copayments included. The greater the proportion of co-insurance paid by the insured, the lower the premiums.

A fourth key term, **fixed indemnity**, refers to the maximum amount an insurer will pay for a certain service. For example, a policy may state that the maximum amount of money paid for orthodontia is $2,000. Depending on the language of a policy, the fixed indemnity benefit may or may not be subject to the provisions of the deductible or co-insurance clause. Costs above the fixed indemnity amount are the responsibility of the insured.

Another key term related to health insurance is **exclusion**. When an exclusion is written into a policy, it means that a specified health condition is excluded from coverage. That is, the policy does not pay for service to treat the condition. Common exclusions include a pregnancy that began before the health insurance policy went into effect or a chronic disease or condition such as diabetes or hypertension that has been classified as a pre-existing condition. A **pre-existing condition** is a medical condition that had been diagnosed or treated usually

---

Health insurance policy a contract between an insurer and the insured that outlines what health services are covered and they will be paid for

Premium a regular periodic payment for an insurance policy

Deductible the amount of expenses that the beneficiary must incur before the insurance company begins to pay for covered services

Co-insurance the portion of the insurance company's approved amounts for covered services that a beneficiary is responsible for paying

Copayment a negotiated set amount that a patient pays for certain services

Fixed indemnity the maximum amount an insurer will pay for a certain service

Exclusion a health condition written into the health insurance policy indicating what is not covered by the policy

Pre-existing condition a medical condition that had been diagnosed or treated usually within the 6 months before the date a health insurance policy goes into effect

within the 6 months before the date the health insurance policy went into effect. Prior to the mid-1990s, because of such exclusions, people who had a serious condition or disease were often unable to get health insurance coverage for the condition/disease or in general. Some health insurance policies also excluded a condition/disease for a specified period of time, such as 9 months for pregnancy or 1 year for all other exclusions.

The rule that a pre-existing condition could be an exclusion "trapped" many people in jobs, because the employees were afraid of losing their health insurance for the condition if they changed employers. To deal with this issue, Congress passed the Health Insurance Portability and Accountability Act of 1996 (Public Law 104-102, known as HIPAA). This law was created, in part, to ensure that people would not have to wait for health insurance to go into effect when changing jobs. More specifically, a pre-existing condition had to be covered without a waiting period when a person joined a new plan if the person had been insured for the previous 12 months. If a person had a pre-existing condition and it had not been covered the previous 12 months before joining a new plan, the longest that person had to wait before being covered for that condition is 12 months.

Even with HIPAA many people, mostly older Americans, were unable to get health insurance because of pre-existing conditions. Thus, pre-existing conditions were addressed in the Affordable Care Act. Beginning in 2014, insurance companies were required to cover all individuals regardless of health status and charge the same premium regardless of pre-existing conditions.[87]

Types of Health Insurance Coverage

As has been noted in the previous discussions, there are a number of different types of services that health insurance policies cover. The more common types of coverage are hospitalization, surgical, regular medical, major medical, dental, and disability. **Table 13.4** presents a short overview of each of these coverage types.

Though the types of health insurance coverage remain constant, several trends associated with health insurance plans and the products they offer are emerging. The trends that characterize health insurance plans today are (1) the plans are becoming more complex and are concentrated in a fewer number of companies; (2) there is an increase in the diversity of products, so consumers have many more options in the type of plan they select, especially with the passage of the Affordable Care Act; (3) there is an increased focus on delivering care through a network of providers rather than independent providers; (4) there is a movement of shifting to financial structures and incentives among purchasers, health plans, and providers;

TABLE 13.4   Types of Health Insurance Coverage

Insurance	Coverage
Dental	Dental procedures.
Disability (income protection)	Income when insured is unable to work because of a health problem.
Hospitalization	Inpatient hospital expenses including room, patient care, supplies, and medications.
Long-term care	An umbrella term for an array of supportive services to help people function in their daily lives. Services may include but are not limited to nursing care, home health care, personal care, rehabilitation, adult day care, case management, social services, assistive technology, and assisted-living services. Services may be provided at home or in another place of residence like a nursing home.
Major medical	Large medical expenses usually not covered by regular medical or dental coverage.
Optical (vision)	Nonsurgical procedures to improve vision.
Regular medical	Nonsurgical service provided by health care providers. Often has set amounts (fixed indemnity for certain procedures).
Surgical	Surgeons' fees (for inpatient or outpatient surgery).

and (5) more health insurance plans are developing clinical infrastructures to manage utilization and to improve the quality of care. Such trends will make understanding health insurance plans more challenging for consumers. These trends will require a greater investment in education and information to help consumers understand how insurance products differ, how best to navigate managed care systems, and what differences exist in structure or performance across the plans.

The Cost of Health Insurance

Over the years, the cost of health insurance has pretty much mirrored the cost of health care. From the early 1970s through the early 1990s, health care costs and the costs of health care insurance were growing in the neighborhood of 10% to 12% per year.[77] Since that time, there have been some years when the cost of premiums slowed. One example was when there was a shift in the health insurance marketplace away from traditional fee-for-service indemnity insurance to managed care in the mid- to late-1990s. The rate of growth of premiums slowed again in the early years after the passage of the ACA. Even with the slower growth, the cost of health insurance continues to outpace the cost of inflation and growth in salaries. In the period between 2002 and 2012 premiums increased 97%.[88] The burden of the cost of health insurance for those who are working falls primarily on the employer and, to a lesser but a growing extent, on the employee. In 2014, 56% of Americans younger than 65 years of age received their health insurance through their employer or the employer of their parent or spouse/partner.[89] In 2014 the cost of the average yearly health insurance premium for an individual was $5,832; employers contributed $4,598 of that amount and the employee contributed $1,234.[90] The average yearly health insurance premium for a family in that same year was $16,655; employers contributed $12,137 of that amount and the employee contributed $4,518.[90] Because of the increasing costs of health insurance and its impact on the "bottom line" of companies, employers are shifting more of the cost onto their employees by (1) increasing the workers' share of the premium, (2) raising the deductibles that workers must pay, (3) increasing the copayments for prescription drugs, and (4) increasing the number of items on the exclusion list. A vivid example of the cost of health insurance comes from coffee store giant Starbucks. This company spends more money on health insurance than it does on coffee beans.[91]

The cost of health insurance for those who purchase it through a marketplace created by the ACA varies greatly depending on a number of factors including (1) the state in which you live, (2) where within the state, (3) your age, (4) the yearly family income, (5) whether you smoke or not, (6) whether health insurance coverage is available via your employer or a spouse's employer, (7) the number of people in your family, (8) the breakdown of the number of adults and children, and (9) the type of plan (i.e., bronze, silver, gold, or platinum) purchased. Based upon this information, it will be determined if the person applying would qualify for either a *premium tax credit* or a *cost-sharing subsidy*. Premium tax credits are available to people with family incomes between 100% (in 2016 for a family of four it was $24,300) and 400% (in 2016 for a family of four it was $97,200) of the poverty level who buy coverage through the marketplace.[92] "These individuals and families will have to pay no more than 2.03% to 9.66% of their incomes for a mid-level plan ("silver") premium. Anything above that is paid by the government."[92] Cost-sharing subsidies help people with their costs when they use health services like when seeing a physician or having a hospital stay.[92] Cost-sharing subsidies are only available to people purchasing their own insurance and who make between 100% and 250% of the poverty level. These subsidies also are available to some Native Americans.[92]

In the end, the actual cost of a policy is determined by two major factors—the risk of those in the group and the amount of coverage provided. An increase in either risk or coverage will result in an increase in the cost of the policy.

Self-Funded Insurance Programs

With the high cost of health care, since the 1970s some employers (or other group, such as a union or trade association)[5] that provide health insurance for their employees have decided to cut their costs by becoming self-insured. With such an arrangement, a **self-funded insurance program** pays the health care costs of its employees with the premiums collected from the employees and the contributions made by the employer instead of using a commercial carrier.[5] Self-funded insurance programs "often use the services of an actuarial firm to set premium rates and a third-party administrator to administer benefits, pay claims, and collect data on utilization. Many third-party administrators also provide case management services for potentially extraordinarily expensive cases to help coordinate care and control employee risk of catastrophic expenses."[5]

There are several benefits to being self-funded. First, the organization gets to set most of the parameters of the policy—deductibles, co-insurance, fixed indemnities, and exclusions. If the organization wants to exclude some services and include others, it can. For example, if the organization has an older workforce, it may wish to delete obstetrics from the policy but include a number of preventive health services. Second, the organization holds on to the cash reserves in the benefits account instead of sending them to a commercial carrier, and thus gets to accrue interest on them. Third, the self-funded organizations have been exempt from the *Employee Retirement and Income Security Act of 1974* (ERISA), which mandates minimum benefits under state law.[5] However, self-insured employer plans do need to meet the 10 essential health benefits required in the Affordable Care Act (ACA).[93] And fourth, generally the administrative costs of self-funded organizations have been less than those of traditional commercial carriers and, in general, health insurance costs to these groups have risen at a slower rate.[5] Other than the need to meet the ACA 10 essential benefits requirement, the four points presented above have not been affected by the ACA; however, the law did include language that indicates that the Secretary of the U.S. Department of Labor is required to provide an annual report about self-funded insurance programs to the appropriate committees of Congress so that they can study their workings. In addition, the law requires the Secretary of the U.S. Department of Health and Human Services to conduct a study of self-funded insurance programs to determine if there are any adverse effects on the components of health care reform.[94]

For self-funded insurance to work, there must be a sizable group of employees over which to spread the risk. Larger organizations usually find it more useful than smaller ones. However, if a small workforce is composed primarily of low-health-risk employees, say, for example, younger employees, then self-funded programs make sense.

Health Insurance Provided by the Government

Although there are some in the United States who would like to see all health insurance provided by the government—a national health insurance plan—at the present time government health insurance plans are only available to select groups in the United States. The only government health insurance plans—those funded by governments at federal, state, and local levels—that exist today are Medicare, Medicaid, the Children's Health Insurance Program (CHIP), Veterans Administration (VA) benefits (see **Figure 13.12**), Indian Health Service, and health care benefits for the uniformed services (military and U.S. Public Health Service or TRICARE), federal employees (Federal Employees Health Benefits Program), and prisoners. Our discussion here is limited to Medicare, Medicaid, and CHIP. Medicare and Medicaid were created in 1965 by amendments to the Social Security Act and were implemented for the first time in 1966. CHIP was created in 1997 and codified as Title XXI of the Social Security Act.

FIGURE 13.12 Insurance provided for veterans is one of several insurance plans paid for by the U.S. government.
© James F. McKenzie

Medicare

Medicare, which currently covers more than 55.2 million people,[95] is a federal health insurance program for people 65 years of age or older, people of any age with permanent kidney failure, and certain disabled people under 65. It is administered by the Centers for Medicare and Medicaid Services (CMS) of the U.S. Department of Health and Human Services (HHS). The Social Security Administration provides information about the program and handles enrollment. Medicare is considered a contributory program, in that employers and employees are required to contribute a percentage of each employee's wages/salaries through Social Security (FICA) tax to the Medicare fund. Medicare has four parts: hospital insurance (Part A), medical insurance (Part B), Medicare Advantage plans (Part C), and prescription drug plans (Part D).

The Medicare hospital insurance (Part A) portion is mandatory and is provided for those eligible without further cost. Some seniors who are not eligible for premium-free Part A because they or their spouses did not pay into Social Security at all, or paid only a limited amount, may be able to purchase Part A coverage. In 2016, those premiums were $411 per month.[96] Although Medicare Part A has deductible ($1,288 in 2016) and co-insurance provisions, it helps pay for inpatient care in a hospital and in a skilled nursing facility after a hospital stay, hospice care, and some home health care.[97]

Those who are enrolled in Part A of Medicare are automatically enrolled in Part B unless they decline. In 2016, the premium for Part B was $104.90 per month.[96] Most Part A enrollees are also enrolled in Part B and have their premium deducted directly from their Social Security check. Part B of Medicare helps cover physicians' and other health care providers' services, outpatient care, durable medical equipment, home health care, and some preventive services. Part B also has a deductible ($166 per year in 2016) and co-insurance (80/20 coverage). Whereas most Medicare beneficiaries pay the standard premium rate, a small percentage pay a higher rate based on their income. In 2016, the higher rates ranged from $121.80 to $389.80 per month depending on the extent to which an individual beneficiary's income exceeded $85,000 (or $170,000 for those filing a joint tax return), with the highest rates paid by those whose incomes were more than $214,000 (or $428,000 for those filing a joint tax return).[96]

Part C of Medicare is formally called Medicare Advantage (MA plans) and was added to Medicare as part of the Balanced Budget Act (BBA) of 1997. It was introduced primarily as a means to try to reduce costs compared with the original fee-for-service Medicare plan. Medicare Advantage plans provide all of the coverage provided in Parts A and B and must cover medically necessary services except for hospice care. They generally offer extra benefits; thus, there is no need to purchase a separate supplemental Medigap policy (see the discussion of Medigap later in this chapter), and many include Part D prescription drug coverage. Part C plans are offered by private insurance companies and are not available in all parts of the country. Because private companies offer them, the specifics of the plans are not consistent from plan to plan. Some are set up on a fee-for-service arrangement while others are offered as managed care plans (i.e., PPOs, HMOs, and medical savings accounts). Most have an annual deductible and require a monthly premium in addition to premiums paid for Part B.[97] In 2015, there were 16.5 million enrolled in Part C plans.[95] To participate in Part C, a beneficiary must first be enrolled in both Part A and Part B. The beneficiary must pay Part B premiums to Medicare and an additional premium to the managed care organization, although some plans with high deductibles have no premium.[1]

Medicare Part D, which currently covers more than 39.4 million people,[95] is the prescription drug program. Part D is optional and run by insurance companies and other private companies approved by Medicare. To use it, those eligible must sign up for it and pay a monthly premium (most range from $20 to $60 per month). The premium varies based on the plan selected (most states offer approximately 50 different plans). Like Part B, there is an additional fee for those with higher incomes. A special provision in Part D—"Extra Help"—offers drug coverage at low cost for qualified people with limited incomes and resources. Although Part D has provided welcome help with the cost of prescription drugs to those who are eligible, the process of using Part D has been hard for many seniors to understand. It is complicated for several reasons. The first is the large number of plans available. The plans vary in drugs covered and costs. For example, one drug may be on the list of drugs covered (called the formulary) by one plan but not another. Many plans cover only generic drugs, whereas others cover both generic and brand-name drugs. Most plans have copayments or co-insurance. And then there is the coverage gap, or what has become known as the donut hole. In 2016, all plans (with the exception of the Extra Help plan) had a $360 deductible. Once the deductible was met, the plans covered the cost of drugs (minus copayment/co-insurance) between $361 and $3,310. Then, at $3,311 the enrollees had to pay out of pocket 45% of the plan's cost for covered brand-name prescription drugs and 42% of the price for generic drugs until they had spent $4,850. (This includes yearly deductible, copayment/co-insurance, and all costs while in the coverage gap. This does not include the plan's premium.) Once enrollees reached the plan's out-of-pocket limit, the donut hole closed and the enrollees had catastrophic coverage. This means that those covered paid a small co-insurance amount or a copayment for the rest of the calendar year.[96] Some of the complexity of Part D will be resolved with the Affordable Care Act. As part of that legislation, the confusing donut hole (i.e., coverage gap) is to be gradually reduced, and by 2020 it will be eliminated.[94]

It should be noted that when health care providers take assignment (are willing to accept Medicare patients) on a Medicare claim, they agree to accept the Medicare-approved amount as payment in full. These providers are paid directly by the Medicare carrier, except for the deductible and co-insurance amounts, which are the patient's responsibility.

Finally, Medicare, like private health insurance programs, is affected by the high costs of health care and, therefore, the government is always looking for ways of cutting the costs of the programs. As noted earlier in the chapter, Medicare has used several types of prospective reimbursement to help cut costs. The oldest of these, diagnosis-related groups (DRGs), has been around since 1983. When patients with Medicare coverage are admitted to a hospital they are assigned a DRG and the hospital is reimbursed the predetermined amount of money for the DRG as opposed to the actual cost to render care. "The correct DRG for each patient is decided by considering the patient's major or principal diagnosis; any complications or other problems that might arise; any surgery performed during the hospital stay; and other factors."[98] The amount of money assigned to each DRG is not the same for each hospital. The figure is based on a formula that takes into account the type of service, the type of hospital, the location of the hospital, and the sex and age of the patient. Using this prospective pricing system, hospitals are encouraged to provide services at or below the DRG rate. If the hospital delivers the service below the DRG rate, the hospital can retain the difference. If it is delivered above the DRG rate, the hospital incurs the extra expenses. "However, when a Medicare patient's condition requires an unusually long hospital stay or exceptionally costly care, Medicare makes additional payment to the hospital."[98] Because of DRGs, some have believed that hospitals are quicker to discharge Medicare patients to keep their expenses down. This phenomenon has resulted in an increase in the need for skilled nursing care in homes, in adult day care facilities, and in nursing homes.

In recent years, much discussion has centered around whether there are sufficient funds in Medicare (i.e., Trust Fund solvency) to pay for the health care costs of the 76 million baby boomers when they started to become eligible in 2011. Most projections about the Medicare program indicate that there is enough money to begin to cover the baby boomers, but as they age Medicare will run out of money unless changes are made. Specifically, steps need to be taken to slow the rate of spending and increase the revenue needed to fund Medicare. To deal in part with this problem, the Affordable Care Act included a number of provisions that will help extend the life of Medicare by as slowing the amount of "reimbursement for Medicare Advantage, hospital costs, home health services, hospices, and skilled nursing services."[99] In addition, steps have been taken to increase revenue. Beginning in 2013 the dedicated payroll tax paid by employees and their employers that goes into the Hospital Insurance (HI) trust fund that covers 88% of the cost of Part A of Medicare was raised from 1.45% to 2.35% for higher -income taxpayers.[100] Also in 2013 the premiums, which fund the majority of the costs for both Parts B and D of Medicare, were increased for higher income beneficiaries.[100] Based upon these changes, in 2014 the Medicare Trustees projected that the Part A trust fund, which is the common way of measuring Medicare's financial status, will be depleted in 2030, 4 years later than was projected in the 2013 report and 6 years later than was projected in the 2012 report.[100] This is good news, but additional steps will need to be taken to ensure Medicare lasts past 2030.

Medicaid

A second type of government health insurance is **Medicaid**, a health insurance program for low-income Americans. The option to combine the Medicaid program with the Children's Health Insurance Program (CHIP; see discussion that follows) is available to states and several have chosen to do so to provide better health care for low-income Americans. Currently, approximately 68.8 million people are covered by Medicaid.[95] Prior to the passage of the Affordable Care Act (ACA), eligibility for enrollment in Medicaid was determined by each state in consultation with the federal government. Under health reform, eligibility is based solely on income and is extended to more low-income people, including both parents and adults without dependent children. As a result of these changes, nearly everyone under the age of 65 years with income below 133% of the poverty level (in 2016 for a family of four it was $24,300) could qualify for Medicaid, significantly reducing the number of uninsured and state variation in coverage. In the previous sentence we use the phrase "could qualify." The reason for this deals with the 2012 Supreme Court ruling that allowed states to opt out of this Medicaid provision. As a part of that ruling the court limited, but did not invalidate the provision. Prior to the ruling states had to expand Medicaid or risk losing all Medicaid funding—an option no state could afford. The Supreme Court ruled that the federal government could not force this significant change to an already existing program on the states.[101] Thus, states could opt out of covering up to 133% of the poverty level. As noted earlier in this chapter in Box 13.3, as of July 2016, 33 states (including the District of Columbus) had expanded Medicaid, two other states were in discussion about expansion, and the remaining 16 had decided not to adopted expansion. "Some health care experts said it was unthinkable that state leaders would really opt out, because the vast majority of the cost is covered by the federal government—taxes their citizens will pay, regardless of whether the state opts in or out. For the first two years, the federal government pays for 100% of the expansion. Starting in 2017, the states start chipping in, but they will never contribute more than 10% of the cost."[101]

Children's Health Insurance Program

The **Children's Health Insurance Program (CHIP)** was created as part of the Balanced Budget Act of 1997 and funded for 10 years. It was enacted to provide coverage to eligible low-income, uninsured children who do not qualify for Medicaid. "Uninsured children pay a heavy price: Study after study shows that they are more likely to report poor health, to see doctors less often (even when they are sick), to go without preventive care, and to turn to emergency rooms when in need of treatment. The result is needless illness, learning problems, disabilities, and sometimes even death."[102]

Like Medicaid, CHIP is a joint state–federal funded program. Currently, there are approximately 8.1 million children covered by CHIP.[103] In 2009, President Obama extended CHIP through 2013 by signing the 2009 Children's Health Insurance Program Reauthorization Act (CHIPRA; Public Law 111-3).[103] To help offset the cost of the reauthorization, the law included an increase in the federal excise tax rate on tobacco products. The Affordable Care Act maintains the CHIP eligibility standards in place as of enactment through 2019 and has provisions in it to increase enrollment and extend funding until 2015.[103] In 2015, President Obama signed into law H.R. 2, the Medicare Access and CHIP Reauthorization Act of 2015, that extended the funding through 2017.[104]

Problems with Medicare and Medicaid

In theory, both the Medicare and Medicaid programs seem to be sound programs that help provide health care to two segments of the society who would otherwise find it difficult or impossible to obtain health insurance. In practice, there are two recurrent problems with these programs. One problem is that some physicians and hospitals do not accept Medicare and Medicaid patients because of the tedious and time-consuming paperwork, lengthy delays in reimbursement, and insufficient reimbursement. As a result, it is difficult if not impossible for some of those eligible for Medicare and Medicaid to receive health care. The second problem occurs when physicians and hospitals file Medicare and Medicaid claims for care or services not rendered or rendered incompletely. This is known as *Medicare/Medicaid fraud*.

These problems were known to Congress, so when the Affordable Care Act passed it included provisions to both increase payment to physicians and hospitals and crack down on fraud.

Medicaid a jointly funded federal–state health insurance program for low-income Americans

Children's Health Insurance Program (CHIP) a title insurance program under the Social Security Act that provides health insurance to uninsured children

Medigap private health insurance that supplements Medicare benefits

Supplemental Health Insurance

Medigap

As noted earlier, Parts A and B of Medicare have deductibles and co-insurance stipulations. To help cover these out-of-pocket costs and some other services not covered by Medicare, people can purchase supplemental policies from private insurance companies. These policies have come to be known as **Medigap** (also called "Medicare Supplement Insurance") policies because they cover the "gaps" not covered by Medicare (see **Figure 13.13**). Federal and state laws mandate national standardization of Medigap policies. Since their inception, 14 different standardized Medigap plans (titled A through N) have been used. Currently, there are only 10 plans (A–D, F–G, K–N) available[105] (see **Box 13.6**). All plans are required to have a core set of benefits referred to as basic benefits; however, some of the basic benefits of plans K through N are offered at a reduced level. By law, the letters and benefits of the individual plans cannot be changed by the insurance companies. However, they may add names or titles to the letter designations. Companies are not required to offer all the plans. "Cost is usually the only difference between Medigap policies with the same letter sold by different insurance companies."[105] "Insurance companies selling Medigap policies are required to make Plan A available. If they offer any other Medigap plan, they must also offer either Medigap Plan C or Plan F."[105] Three states—Minnesota, Massachusetts, and Wisconsin—have exceptions to the 10-plan setup because they had alternative Medigap standardization programs in effect before the federal legislation was enacted. Individuals should contact the state insurance office in these states if interested in these plans.

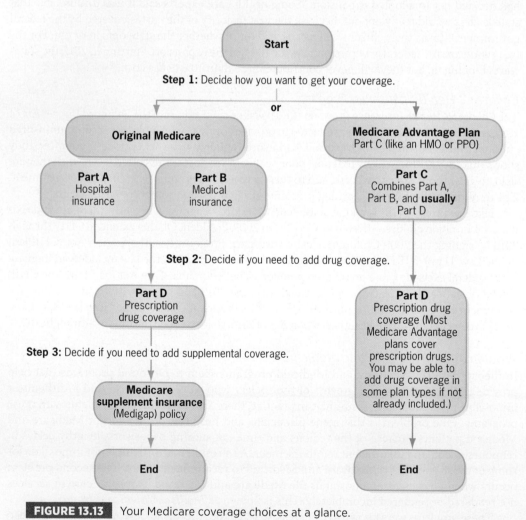

FIGURE 13.13   Your Medicare coverage choices at a glance.

Data from: Centers for Medicare & Medicaid Services (2015). *Choosing a Medigap Policy: A Guide to Health Insurance for People with Medicare*, 7. Available at https://www.medicare.gov/Pubs/pdf/02110.pdf.

BOX 13.6　Medigap Plans

How to Read the Chart

The chart below shows basic information about the different benefits that Medigap policies cover. If a percentage appears, the Medigap plan covers that percentage of the benefit. If a row is blank, the policy doesn't cover that benefit.

Benefits	Medicare Supplement Insurance (Medigap) Plans									
	A	B	C	D	F*	G	K**	L**	M	N***
Medicare Part A coinsurance and hospital costs (up to an additional 365 days after Medicare benefits are used)	100%	100%	100%	100%	100%	100%	100%	100%	100%	100%
Medicare Part B coinsurance or copayment	100%	100%	100%	100%	100%	100%	50%	75%	100%	100%***
Blood (first 3 pints)	100%	100%	100%	100%	100%	100%	50%	75%	100%	100%
Part A hospice care coinsurance or copayment	100%	100%	100%	100%	100%	100%	50%	75%	100%	100%
Skilled nursing facility care coinsurance			100%	100%	100%	100%	50%	75%	100%	100%
Part A deductible		100%	100%	100%	100%	100%	50%	75%	50%	100%
Part B deductible			100%		100%					
Part B excess charges					100%	100%				
Foreign travel emergency (up to plan limits)			80%	80%	80%	80%			80%	80%
							Out-of-pocket limit in 2016**			
							$4,960	$2,480		

*Plan F also offered as a high-deductible plan by some insurance companies in some states. If you choose this option, this means you must pay for Medicare-covered costs (coinsurance, copayments, deductibles) up to the deductible amount of $2,180 in 2016 before your policy pays anything.

** For Plans K and L, after you meet your out-of-pocket yearly limit and your yearly Part B deductible ($166 in 2016), the Medigap plan pays 100% of covered services for the rest of the calendar year.

*** Plan N pays 100% of the Part B coinsurance, except for a copayment of up to $20 for some office visits and up to a $50 copayment for emergency room visits that don't result in an inpatient admission.

Data from: Centers for Medicare & Medicaid Services (2016). *Choosing a Medigap Policy: A Guide to Health Insurance for People with Medicare*, 11. Available at https://www.medicare.gov/Pubs/pdf/02110-Medicare-Medigap.guide.pdf

Two other variances to these Medigap rules should be noted. The first deals with those individuals enrolled in the Medicare Advantage program. Because Medicare Advantage is more comprehensive in coverage than is the traditional Medicare program, Medigap policies are not needed. In fact, it is illegal for insurance companies to sell a Medigap policy if they know a person is enrolled in Medicare Advantage.[105] Another variance in Medigap policy deals with Medicare SELECT. Medicare SELECT is a type of Medigap policy that is available in some states. This type of policy still provides one of the standardized Medigap plans (A–D, F–G, K–N), but requires policy holders to use specific hospitals and, in some cases, doctors (except in emergencies) to receive full Medigap benefits.[105]

Other Supplemental Insurance

Medigap is a supplemental insurance program specifically designed for those on Medicare. However, a number of supplemental insurance policies exist for people regardless of their age. Included are specific-disease insurance, hospital indemnity insurance, and long-term care insurance. Specific-disease insurance, though not available in some states, provides benefits for only a single disease (such as cancer) or a group of specific diseases. Many policies are written as fixed-indemnity policies. Hospital indemnity coverage is insurance that pays a fixed amount for each day a person receives inpatient hospital services, and it pays up to a designated number of days. Long-term care insurance, which pays cash amounts for each day of covered nursing home or at-home care, is of great concern to many people, and it is presented next.

Long-Term Care Insurance

With people living longer and the cost of health care on the rise, more and more individuals are considering the purchase of long-term care insurance. It has been estimated that "70 percent of people over age 65 can expect to use some form of long-term care during their lives."[106] About 35% will need care in a nursing home.[106] And, contrary to what many people believe, Medicare and private health insurance programs do not pay for the majority of long-term care services that most people need—such as help with bathing, or for supervision often called custodial care.[106] Women, who on average live 5 years longer than men, are more likely to live at home alone when they are older, and will have a need for care for longer than do men (3.7 vs. 2.2 years).[106] Whereas one-third of today's 65-year-olds may never need long-term care services, 20% of them will need care for more than 5 years.[106] Most—about 80%—of long-term care will be provided in the home by unpaid caregivers,[106] usually family and friends.

Planning for long-term care requires people to think about possible future health care needs and how they will pay for them. Obviously, the cost of long-term care varies based on the level of care, the length of time the care is provided, and where the care is provided. The most costly long-term care is nursing home care. Recent figures show that the median cost of residing in a nursing home was $220 per day (range $90 to $1,255) or $6,710 per month or $80,300 per year for a semi private room, $250 per day (range $101 to $1,255) or $7,625 per month or $91,250 per year for a private room, while assisted-living facilities were $3,600 per month or $43,200 per year for care in a one-bedroom unit.[107] The costs vary by parts of the country, but such costs for long-term care have many people worried about their financial future. This cost is something that can quickly deplete a lifetime of savings. Medicare and other health insurance do not include most long-term care services. If people have fairly low income and savings, they may qualify for Medicaid, which is the primary payer for institutional and community-based long-term services and supports (see **Figure 13.14**). There is a good chance that individuals will have to pay for all or some of theses services out of pocket; therefore it may be important to consider long-term care insurance.[106]

Though long-term care is expensive, not everyone needs to buy long-term care insurance. Those who do not need it are those with low incomes and few

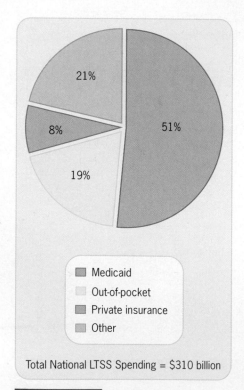

21%

8%

19%

51%

- ■ Medicaid
- □ Out-of-pocket
- ■ Private insurance
- ▨ Other

Total National LTSS Spending = $310 billion

FIGURE 13.14 Who pays for long-term services and supports?

Data from: The Henry J. Kaiser Family Foundation (2015). *Medicaid and Long-Term Services and Supports: A Primer*. Available at http://kff.org/medicaid/report/medicaid-and-long-term-services-and-supports-a-primer/.

assets who could be covered by Medicaid and the very wealthy who are able to pay the cost of the care out of pocket. Those who are most likely to benefit from long-term care insurance are those in between the poor and wealthy, especially older women. However, there are several reasons why all people should consider purchasing long-term insurance. They include the following:

- To preserve financial assets
- To prevent the need for family members or friends to provide the care
- To enable people to stay independent in their homes longer
- To make it easier to get into the nursing home or assisted-living home of their choice

Managed Care

As noted earlier in this chapter, the failed attempt to adopt universal health care in the United States during the first term of President Bill Clinton led to the movement of managed care. Managed care is "a system that integrates the functions of financing, insurance, delivery, and payment and uses mechanisms to control costs and utilization of services."[12] The transition to managed care in the United States was largely driven by a desire of employers, insurance companies, and the public to control soaring health care costs. Although the exact number of individuals enrolled in managed care programs is constantly changing, in 2014 69.1% of Americans were enrolled in some form of a managed care plan. In that same year, over 99% of employees covered by an employers' health plan was in some form of a managed care plan.[108]

Managed health care plans are offered by managed care organizations (MCOs). MCOs function like insurance organizations. They offer policies, collect premiums, and bear financial risk. That is, MCOs take on the financial responsibility if the costs of the services exceed the revenue from the premiums. These organizations have agreements with certain doctors, hospitals, and other health care providers to give a range of services to plan members at reduced cost. MCOs have been structured in a variety of ways and are similar to the other health care organizations with which we are familiar (such as hospitals). Some are structured as nonprofit organizations, while others are for-profit and owned by a group of investors. "Regardless of their structure, their goals, however, are similar: to control costs through improved efficiency and coordination, to reduce unnecessary or inappropriate utilization, to increase access to preventive care, and to maintain or improve quality of care."[109]

The managed health care plans offered by these organizations vary and are always evolving as managed care practices mature and new processes are developed to improve quality and contain costs. The plans also differ, both in cost and ease of receiving needed services. Although no plan pays for all the costs associated with medical care, some plans cover more than others. Common features in managed care arrangements include: (1) provider panels often referred to as the network—specific physicians and other providers are selected to care for plan members; (2) limited choice—members must use the providers affiliated with the plan or pay an additional amount for providers outside the network; (3) gatekeeping—members must obtain a referral from a case manager for specialty care or inpatient services; (4) risk sharing—providers bear some of the health plan's financial risk through capitation and withholds; and (5) **quality management and utilization review**—the plan monitors provider practice patterns and medical outcomes to identify deviations from quality and efficiency standards. The utilization review can take the form of *prospective utilization review* (as precertification), *concurrent utilization review* (i.e., during the course of health care utilization), or *retrospective utilization review* (completed by reviewing medical records after the care has been provided).[1] This latter type of review may involve "analysis of data to examine patterns of excessive utilization or underutilization. *Underutilization* occurs when medically necessary care is not delivered. *Overutilization* occurs when medical services that are not necessary are delivered."[1]

Types of Managed Care

As noted earlier, there are several different types of managed care arrangements. Prior to 1990, the various types of MCOs were quite distinct. Since then, the differences between traditional forms of health insurance and managed care have narrowed considerably. The following are the most commonly available arrangements.

Quality management and utilization review the analysis of provided health care for its appropriateness by someone other than the patient and provider

Preferred Provider Organizations

The **preferred provider organization (PPO)** is a form of managed care closest to a fee-for-service plan. A PPO differs from the traditional fee-for-service plan in that the fee has been fixed (at a discounted rate) through a negotiation process between a health care provider (e.g., physicians, dentists, hospitals) and the PPO, and the provider agrees to accept this discounted rate as payment in full. It works in the following manner: A PPO approaches a provider, such as a group dental practice, and contracts with the dentists to provide dental services to all those covered by the PPO's insurance plan at a fixed (discount) rate. To the extent that the PPO succeeds in obtaining favorable prices, it can offer lower premiums, co-insurance, and copayments, and hence can attract more patients to enroll in its insurance plan. In addition to using the PPO network of providers, plan members can also use out-of-network providers. However, if they do choose to go outside the network, they will have to meet the deductible and pay higher co-insurance. In addition, they may have to pay the difference between what the provider charges and what the plan pays. "The additional out-of-pocket expenses largely act as a deterrent to going outside the network for care."[1] PPOs also control costs by requiring (1) preauthorization for hospital admissions (excluding emergencies) and expensive procedures, and (2) second opinions for major procedures such as surgery.[5] Advantages for the providers are that they (1) do not share in any financial risk as a condition of participation,[5] (2) are reimbursed on a fee-for-service basis (but at a discounted rate) to which they are accustomed,[5] (3) are assured a certain volume of patients, and (4) are assured that the patients will pay promptly (via the PPO). Of the various types of managed care plans, PPOs enroll the largest number of Americans.[108] In 2014, it was about 152.8 million people.[108] Much of the increase in enrollment in PPOs was the result of people leaving HMOs (see the discussion of HMOs later in this chapter) because of increased costs and the restrictions in the choice of providers.

Health Maintenance Organizations

Health maintenance organizations (HMOs) are the oldest form of managed care. Behind PPOs, HMOs enroll the second largest number of Americans.[108] Enrollment in HMOs peaked in 1999 at about 80 million and has dropped every year since then.[108] In 2014, the number of enrollees was about 74.7 million.[108] As noted earlier, many of those leaving HMOs switched to PPOs. In an HMO, the insurance coverage and the delivery of medical care are combined into a single organization. The organization hires (through salaries or contracts) an individual doctor or groups of doctors to provide care and either builds its own hospital or contracts for the services of a hospital within the community. The organization then enrolls members, usually, but not always, through the workplace. Members (or their employers or the government [in the case of HMOs for Medicare and Medicaid]) make regular payments in advance on a fixed contract fee to the HMO. This contract may also include a deductible and copayment when service is provided. In return, the HMO is contractually obligated to provide the members with a comprehensive range of outpatient and inpatient services that are spelled out in the contract for a specific time period.

When members enroll in an HMO, they are given a list (network) of specific physicians/providers from which to select their primary care doctor (usually a family physician, internist, or pediatrician) and other health care providers. The primary care doctor (which some have referred to as the gatekeeper) serves as the member's regular doctor and coordinates the member's care, which means the member must contact his or her primary care doctor to be referred to a specialist. In many plans, care by a specialist is only paid for if the member is referred by the primary care doctor, thus the term *gatekeeper*. Also, if patients receive care outside the network, they must pay for all the costs, except in cases of emergency when physically not near a member of the network.

How do HMOs make a profit? An HMO's focus of care is different from that of a traditional fee-for-service provider. In an HMO, ill and injured patients become a "cost." An HMO does not make money on the ill but on keeping people healthy. The less the providers of an HMO see a patient, the lower the costs and the more profitable the organization. Therefore, most HMOs emphasize health promotion activities and primary and secondary care. "As an incentive to the enrollees to seek wellness care, HMO plans typically do not have annual deductibles, and they also have lower copayments than do other types of plans."[1]

There are two broad organizational models of HMOs—*closed-panel plans* and *open-panel plans*. A **closed-panel HMO** is one "that contracts with physicians on an exclusive basis for services and does not allow those physicians to see patients for another managed care organization."[110] Examples of closed-panel HMOs include the *staff* and *group models*. An **open-panel HMO** is one "that contracts (either directly or indirectly) with private physicians to deliver care in their own offices."[110] Examples of the open-panel HMOs include *independent practice associations (IPAs)* and *network model HMOs*. Each of the types of HMOs noted here has spawned several hybrids. These hybrids are referred to **mixed model HMOs**. Due to space available we have limited our discussion to staff and IPA HMOs. The other models are defined in the glossary of the book.

Staff Model

In **staff model HMOs**, the health care providers are employed (usually salaried) by the HMO and practice in common facilities paid for by the HMO. Staff model HMOs employ providers in all common specialties to provide services to their members. Special contracts are established with subspecialties for infrequently needed services. These providers are expected to follow the practice and procedures determined by the HMO. With the exception of the special contracts, the providers work only for the HMO, and thus do not have their own private practices. In most instances, the HMO contracts with a hospital for inpatient services. Nationwide, the number of staff model HMOs has been declining.

Independent Practice Association Model

Independent practice associations (IPAs) are the most common type of HMO today. IPAs are legal entities separate from the HMO[110] that are physician organizations composed of community-based independent physicians in solo or group practices who provide services to HMO members.[5] Instead of establishing contracts with individual physicians or groups, the HMO contracts with the IPA for physician services. Physicians do not have contracts with the HMO, but with the IPA.[1] Thus, the IPA acts as an intermediary and is paid a capitation amount by the HMO.[1]

Other Items Related to HMOs

Point-of-Service Option

One of the major objections to HMOs is that the patients cannot freely select their provider. They are restricted to those with whom the HMO has contracted. Some HMOs have solved this problem with the **point-of-service (POS) option**, which allows for a more liberal policy of enabling patients to select providers but still retain the benefits of tight utilization management.[1] With this option, members may choose a provider from within or outside the HMO network. Patients who obtain services outside the network generally must pay a higher deductible and co-insurance. Initially POSs were a good selling point for HMOs, but after reaching their peak enrollments, the numbers have gradually declined mainly because of high out-of-pocket expenses with them.[1] In 2014, the number of Americans enrolled in HMOs that had the POS option was 7.1 million.[108]

Medicare Advantage

As noted earlier, in some parts of the country Medicare recipients may have HMO or PPO options available to them through the Medicare Advantage plan. In such plans, the Medicare recipient receives all Medicare-covered services and often services not covered by Medicare from the HMO or PPO. Some of these plans may also include prescription drug coverage (Part D). If this is the case, Medigap coverage cannot be purchased. The HMO or PPO may charge the beneficiary a premium (in addition to the Medicare Part B premium) to cover co-insurance and deductibles of Medicare, but some plans that have high deductibles may have no premium.[1] In 2015, approximately 64% of the people enrolled in Medicare Advantage received their care through an HMO and another 31% received their care from a PPO.[111]

Closed-panel HMO an organization in which private physicians are contracted on an exclusive basis for services at a health maintenance organization

Open-panel HMO an organization in which private practice physicians are contracted by a health maintenance organization to deliver care in their own offices

Mixed model HMO a hybrid form of health maintenance organization

Staff model HMO a health maintenance organization that hires its own staff of health care providers

Independent practice association (IPA) legal entity separate from the HMO that is a physician organization composed of community-based independent physicians in a solo or group practice who provide services to HMO members

Point-of-service (POS) option an option of an HMO plan that enables enrollees to be at least partially reimbursed for selecting a health care provider outside the plan

Medicaid and Managed Care

As has been noted throughout this chapter, managed care plans are also available for those covered by Medicaid. The rationale for offering such plans is to improve access to care by the establishment of contracted provider networks, as well as by promoting greater accountability for quality and costs. Each state in the United States offers such a plan, and depending on the state requirements, enrollment may or may not be voluntary. If it is mandatory, then the state is required to offer a choice of managed care plans and make efforts to inform beneficiaries about their choices.[4] In 2015, more than half of the people covered by Medicaid were enrolled in managed care plans.[112]

Before leaving our discussion on managed care, we want to remind the reader that, like other aspects of the health care system, there have been efforts to measure the quality of managed care too. Please see our discussion of quality of health care earlier in the chapter where we present information on the National Committee on Quality Assurance (NCQA).

Other Arrangements for Delivering Health Care

Because the majority of people in the United States receive their health care through a managed care plan or a fee-for-service plan, the majority of this chapter focused on those plans. However, there are other ways of delivering health care. A few of the more highly visible arrangements are discussed next.

National Health Insurance

National health insurance, or national health care, suggests a system in which the federal government assumes the responsibility for the health care costs of the entire population. In such a system, the costs are primarily paid for with tax dollars. Presently among all the developed countries of the world, there is only one that does not have a national health care plan for its citizens: the United States.

The national health care systems of the developed countries of the world fall into two basic models. The first is a *national health service* model with universal coverage and general tax-financed government ownership of the facilities and doctors as public employees. Countries using this model include the United Kingdom, Spain, Italy, Greece, and Portugal. The second is a *social insurance model* that provides universal coverage under social security, financed by various ways including taxes or contributions paid by employers and employees. In Canada, contributions are made to a government entity. In France and Germany, contributions go to nonprofit funds with national negotiation on fees. Japan also has a compulsory system that relies heavily on employer-based coverage.

When one considers the level of satisfaction with health care, the better access to health care services, the lower health care costs, and the superior health status indicators in these other countries, one must ask why the United States has not adopted such a program (see **Figure 13.15**). It is not because the United States has not considered such a plan—in fact, there have been seven failed attempts at addressing the issue over the past 70+ years. The first came when President Roosevelt tried to include it as part of the New Deal. President Harry Truman presented a proposal to Congress on two different occasions, only to have it defeated twice. Other unsuccessful attempts at national health care legislation were made during the Kennedy, Nixon, and Clinton administrations. There was also talk about a national health insurance program in the United States during the presidential campaign and debates of 2008. During that campaign, all of the front-running candidates pledged to work toward a national program, though all had different plans for getting there. As history has shown us, President Obama was unsuccessful in getting a national health insurance program, but he was successful in getting major health care reform via the Affordable Care Act. At the time this edition of this book was written, the candidates vying for the Democrat nomination identified a national health insurance program as a priority, while most of the Republican candidates indicated they wanted to repeal the Affordable Care Act and build a different health care delivery system.

Country Rankings

Top 2*
Middle
Bottom 2*

	AUS	CAN	FRA	GER	NETH	NZ	NOR	SWE	SWIZ	UK	US
Overall Ranking (2013)	4	10	9	5	5	7	7	3	2	1	11
Quality Care	2	9	8	7	5	4	11	10	3	1	5
Effective Care	4	7	9	6	5	2	11	10	8	1	3
Safe Care	3	10	2	6	7	9	11	5	4	1	7
Coordinated Care	4	8	9	10	5	2	7	11	3	1	6
Patient-Centered Care	5	8	10	7	3	6	11	9	2	1	4
Access	8	9	11	2	4	7	6	4	2	1	9
Cost-Related Problem	9	5	10	4	8	6	3	1	7	1	11
Timeliness of Care	6	11	10	4	2	7	8	9	1	3	5
Efficiency	4	10	8	9	7	3	4	2	6	1	11
Equity	5	9	7	4	8	10	6	1	2	2	11
Healthy Lives	4	8	1	7	5	9	6	2	3	10	11
Health Expenditures/ Capita, 2011**	$3,800	$4,522	$4,118	$4,495	$5,099	$3,182	$5,669	$3,925	$5,643	$3,405	$8,508

Notes: *Includes ties. ** Expenditures shown in $US PPP (purchasing power parity); Australian $ data are from 2010.

FIGURE 13.15   Comparison of health systems: overall ranking.

Data from: Davis, K., K. Stremikis, C. Schoen, and D. Squires (2014). *Mirror, Mirror on the Wall, 2014 Update: How the U.S. Health Care System Compares Internationally.* New York: Commonwealth Fund, 7. Available at http://www.commonwealthfund.org/publications/fund-reports/2014/jun/mirror-mirror.

Health Care Reform in the United States

Prior to the passage of the Affordable Care Act (ACA), the health care reform that has taken place in the United States in recent times has been with specific smaller, but not insignificant, portions of the health care system—for example, President Clinton's creation of the Children's Health Insurance Program (CHIP) in 1997 and the reauthorization of the program by President Obama in 2009. During President George W. Bush's term in office, the reform came in the form of the Medicare Prescription Drug Improvement and Modernization Act (MMA) of 2003 (Public Law 108-173). The portion of MMA that gained the greatest publicity—that dealing with prescription drugs via Medicare Part D—was discussed earlier in the chapter. However another significant component of the MMA was health savings accounts (HSAs), sometimes referred to as the savings option (SO). HSAs are one of several different forms of consumer-directed health plans (CDHPs). In the sections that follow, we discuss CDHPs, high deductible health plans (HDHPs), and the Affordable Care Act.

Consumer-Directed Health Plans

Consumer-directed health plans (CDH/CDHPs; also called consumer-driven health plans, consumer-directed health arrangements [CDHAs], consumer choice, and self-directed health plans [SDHPs])[113] are health care plans that combine a high-deductible health plan (HDHP) with a pretax payment account to pay for out-of-pocket medical expenses. In theory such plans should create more consumer responsibility for health care decisions. CDHPs have sought "to marshal the power of consumers making cost-conscious choices to constrain rising U.S. health care spending."[114] A critical part of CDHPs is providing those enrolled in such plans with comparative information to increase their knowledge about health care choices and associated

Consumer-directed health plan (CDHP) health care plan that combines a high-deductible health plan (HDHP) with a pretax payment account to pay for out-of-pocket medical expenses

costs.[5] The central idea behind CDHPs is that consumers will still have catastrophic health insurance, but because they are required to use more of their own money to pay for health care they will be more careful about their use of services than they would be under a traditional health plan that provides greater coverage of their initial health care costs.[110] The options of pretax payment accounts available for CDHPs include health savings accounts (HSAs), health reimbursement arrangements (HRAs), and flexible spending accounts (FSAs).

The most visible option of a pretax payment account for the CDHPs is the health savings account (HSA). An HSA is a type of medical savings account that allows people to save money to pay for current and future medical expenses on a tax-free basis. To be eligible for an HSA, people must be covered by a high-deductible health plan (in 2016, the deductible was $1,300 for individuals and $2,600 for families),[115] not have any other health insurance (including Medicare), and not be claimed as a dependent on someone else's tax return. Those with HSAs can use this account to pay for qualified health expenses, including expenses that the plan ordinarily does not cover, such as hearing aids.[110] By law, there is a maximum amount that people with HSAs would have to pay out of pocket for health expenses in a year. The amount is adjusted for inflation each year, but in 2016 the amount was $6,550 for individuals and $13,000 for families.[115]

During the year, those with HSAs can make voluntary contributions to the account using before-tax dollars. In 2016, the maximum amount that could be set aside was $3,350 for an individual, $6,750 for families,[115] or the amount of the deductible of the health insurance policy, whichever was lower. People aged 55 and older can make additional "catch-up" contributions (in 2016, $1,000)[115] until they enroll in Medicare. These contributions are 100% tax deductible from gross income—thus the "pretax" tag. In some cases, employers may set up and help fund HSAs for their employees, but they are not required to do so. An HSA earns interest. If there is a balance in a person's HSA at the end of the year, it will roll over, allowing the person to build up a cushion against future health expenses. In addition, HSAs allow people to accumulate funds and retain them when they change plans or retire.[110] Money can be withdrawn from the account without penalty to pay for care before the deductible is met and for things not covered under the health insurance policy after the deductible is met. Money can be withdrawn and pay for anything (including nonhealth expenses) after 65 years of age, but the person must pay income tax on it. The advantages of such a plan are reduced premiums and, it is hoped, more prudent use of health care dollars—which should be good for both employers and employees. In addition, HSAs are portable from one employer to another. The major disadvantage for consumers is that they might have to pay more out of pocket for health care, and therefore might skip needed care. At the present, HSAs seem best suited for the healthy and wealthy.

As noted throughout this chapter the Affordable Care Act has made a number of changes to health care but it only made two changes to HSAs that both went into effect in 2011. They included (1) HSAs could no longer be used tax free for over-the-counter medications unless the medications were prescribed by a doctor; and (2) if people use their HSA funds for nonmedical expenses, they must pay a 20% penalty instead of the former 10% penalty.[116]

Although HSAs must be combined with high-deductible health plans (HDHPs), HDHPs do not have to be combined with HSAs. In fact, HDHPs continue to grow in popularity because of their lower premium costs. When these plans are used they are often accompanied by health promotion and wellness, disease management, case management, and health coaching programs to help participants improve and maintain health and keep medical conditions under control. One concern that has arisen with the HDHPs is that "as deductibles have grown in recent years, a surprising percentage of people with private insurance, and especially those with lower and moderate incomes, simply do not have the resources to pay their deductibles and will either have to put off care or incur medical debt."[117]

Another type of pretax payment account for a CDHP is health reimbursement arrangements (HRAs). HRAs are not as flexible as HSAs. Only employers are allowed to set up HRAs for employees, and only employers can contribute to (i.e., fund) them. The employer decides how much money to put in a health reimbursement arrangement, and the employee can withdraw funds from the account to cover allowed expenses. The Affordable Care Act (ACA) did put into place some changes to the use of HRAs. In the past HRAs were often established in conjunction with an

HDHP, but they could be paired with any type of health plan. Since January 2014, HRAs can only be paired with ACA-compliant plans.[118] In addition, federal law continues to allow employers to determine whether employees can carry over all or a portion of unspent funds from year to year. But again beginning in January 2014, employers can no longer decide whether account balances will be forfeited if an employee leaves the job or changes health plans; now such accounts are forfeited upon termination of employment.[118] Also, employees must have the option to opt out of an HRA so that they can obtain health coverage via the marketplace and be eligible for premium tax credits.[118] And finally like HSAs, as of January 2011, HRA funds can no longer be used tax free for over-the-counter medications unless the medications were prescribed by a doctor.[53]

A third pretax payment account CDHP option is flexible spending accounts (FSAs). FSAs are set up by employers to allow employees to set aside pretax money to pay for qualified medical expenses during the year. Only employers may set up an account, and employers may or may not contribute to the account, but usually FSAs are 100% employee funded.[119] There is a limit on the amount that employers can contribute to a health flexible spending arrangement. In 2016, that amount was $2,550. Like other CDHP options, the Affordable Care Act also made changes to FSAs. First, just like HSAs and HRAs, as of January 2011, the ACA no longer allowed FSA funds to be used tax free for over-the-counter medications unless the medications were prescribed by a doctor.[53] Second, FSAs can now only be offered in conjunction with an employer ACA-compliant health insurance plan, and no longer can they be offered on a standalone basis. Third, there is now a limit on the amount employers can contribute to a FSA. Employers can contribute no more than $500 or, if more, a match of up to $1 for every dollar contributed by the employee.[120] Fourth, in the past, FSAs were subject to a use-it-or-lose-it rule within the year of contributions with a 2.5-month grace period at the end of the plan year to use up funds in the account. Employers are now allowed to offer the grace period or a $500 rollover provision to the next year, though not both.[120] The tricky part of having an FSA is trying to determine how much money to place in the account in a year to avoid losing any money at year's end. In 2014, 14 million families used FSAs.[119]

Enrollment in CDHPs has been rising in recent years for three major reasons: (1) employers trying to cut health care costs, (2) consumers trying to reduce the cost of health insurance premiums, and (3) the tax advantages of most of the plans. Data from the 2007 National Health Interview Study (NHIS) showed that those more likely to be enrolled in a CDHP were those (1) who directly purchased private health plans, (2) with more education, and (3) with higher incomes.[121] More recent data from the 2015 NHIS show that "36.0% of persons under age 65 with private health insurance were enrolled in an HDHP, including 13.3% who were enrolled in a CDHP [an HDHP with a health savings account (HSA)] and 22.7% who were enrolled in an HDHP without an HSA"[122] (see **Figure 13.16**). In terms of numbers, American Association of Preferred Provider Organizations estimated that 45 million people were enrolled in CDHPs in 2013, up from 39 million in 2012—an increase of more than 15%.[123]

It should be noted that CDHPs are not without critics. There are three major concerns about CDHPs. One, will consumers become educated enough to make good decisions? Health insurance and health care are very complicated; will consumers take the time to become well educated? Two, is the health care field transparent enough to get enough information to make a good decision? When was the last time that a patient received a health care service and knew in advance what the cost would be? Also, how do consumers know when they are receiving quality care? Who is the best physician in the community? Who is the worst? And three, will consumers seek health care in a timely manner because with CDHPs they have to use more of their own money? For example, on a traditional plan maybe pneumonia vaccination was covered with a zero deductible, but with a CDHP that has a high deductible it now costs consumers $50 out of pocket. Will they still get the vaccine or will they try to save the $50 and forgo the vaccine?

Health Care Reform in the U.S: How Did It Happen, Where Is It Headed?

After many failed attempts to provide health care reform in the United States, the signing by President Obama in 2010 of the Affordable Care Act (ACA) was most significant in expanding access to health insurance and thus health care to many who did not have health insurance previously.

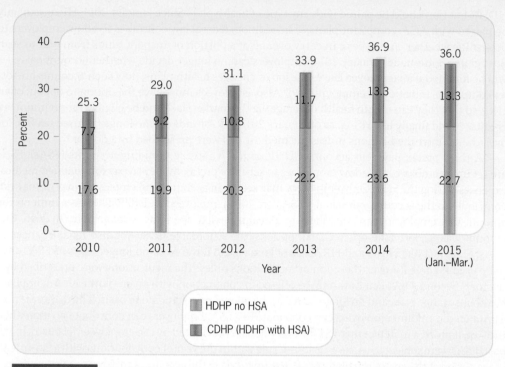

FIGURE 13.16   Percentage of persons under age 65 enrolled in HDHPs without a HSA or in a CDHP, among those with private health insurance coverage: United States—2010 to March 2015.

Data from: Cohen, R. A., and M. E. Martinez (2015). *Health Insurance Coverage: Early Release of Estimates from the National Health Interview Survey, January–March 2015*. Available at http://www.cdc.gov/nchs/data/nhis/earlyrelease/insur201508.pdf.

As has been noted, the process to get the ACA passed was not easy. In addition to the many failed attempts before it, it took much discussion, and much political wrangling by both Democrats and Republicans. Some called the wrangling an "ideological split." However, "[p]assage of the ACA was a historic political achievement, breaking the logjam that long stymied national progress toward equitable, quality, universal, affordable health care in the United States."[124] In the end, the Democrat members of the U.S. Senate and House of Representatives were more pleased with the results than were the Republican members. Not only was its initial passage difficult, but it has survived a number of challenges including many votes (62 as of February 2016)[16] in the U.S. Congress to repeal or dismantle it; on four occasions parts of the ACA have been litigated in U.S. Supreme Court.[2]

As the ACA was written, implementation of the law was spread over multiple years beginning in 2010, with the final portions scheduled for implementation in 2020. Also, with any new piece of legislation that contains so many components there are bound to be parts that prove to be less than useful and other parts that are found too complicated to implement as passed. Therefore, as of February 2016 a number of changes have been made to the original passed legislation. According to the Galen Institute, more than 70 significant changes have been made to the ACA. At least 43 changes have been made unilaterally by the Obama administration, another 24 have been made by the U.S Congress and signed by the president, and another four have resulted from cases heard before the U.S. Supreme Court.[54] It was the three cases before the U.S. Supreme Court that worried many of the ACA proponents because two of the four cases dealt with major components of the law that could have derailed its implementation.

The first challenge to the ACA heard by the U.S. Supreme Court came in the case of the *National Federation of Independent Businesses et al. versus Sebelius, Secretary of Health and Human Services, et al.*[125] In this case the U.S. Supreme Court was asked to decide "(1) whether Congress had the power under the federal Constitution to enact the individual insurance coverage requirement, and (2) whether it was constitutionally coercive for Congress, through the ACA, to threaten to take away existing Medicaid funding from states that did not want to implement the Medicaid expansion."[2] In the former issue the court ruled, "violating the law's mandate that Americans must purchase government-approved health insurance would not produce a 'penalty,' as stated in the legislation, but rather would result in individuals' paying a 'tax.' Paying a tax would make it, legally speaking, optional for people to comply and therefore would not violate the U.S. Constitution."[54] On latter issue the court ruled "that it was voluntary, rather than mandatory, for states to expand Medicaid eligibility to people with incomes up to 138% of poverty. The court rewrote the statute to say the federal government could not block funds for existing state Medicaid programs if states choose not to expand the program."[54]

The second challenge to the ACA heard by the U.S. Supreme Court came in the case of the *Burwell, Secretary of Health and Human Services, et al. versus Hobby Lobby Stores, Inc., et al.*[126] At question in this case was the portion of the ACA referred to as the contraceptive (or birth control) mandate that requires that health care plans must include coverage for the FDA-approved contraceptive methods and counseling for all women, as prescribed by a health care provider.[127] The plaintiffs in the case were two private for-profit companies owned by members of single family. The companies were the Hobby Lobby Stores, owned by a family who were Evangelical Christians, and Conestoga Wood Specialists, owned by a family who were members of the Mennonite faith. In this case the court was asked to decide, under a federal statute called the Religious Freedom Restoration Act (RFRA) of 1993, if a closely held private for-profit corporation (i.e., one with a limited number of shareholders) had the legal right to refuse to comply with provisions of the ACA that required them to provide certain contraceptive coverage (in this case the plaintiffs objected only to the abortive Plan B drug) to which the employees would otherwise be entitled.[2] The court ruled in favor of Hobby Lobby Stores, et al. in stating that closely held private for-profit corporations cannot be forced to pay for insurance coverage for contraception for employees over their religious objections. Some think that this ruling might cause other closely held corporations to refuse all FDA-approved contraceptives for their employees,[2] while others believe this ruling opened the door to many more challenges from corporations over laws that they claim violate their religious liberty.[128]

The third challenge to the ACA heard by the U.S. Supreme Court came in the case of the *King et al. versus Burwell, Secretary of Health and Human Services, et al.*[129] This challenge to the ACA focused on whether or not the subsidies provided by the ACA were intended to be available to all who qualified for them and purchased their insurance through the marketplace regardless of who created the marketplace (i.e., the state or federal government). "In essence, the court case boiled down to the meaning of the four words "established by the State" or were the federal subsidies reserved only for individuals in states that established their own state-run exchange?"[2] The "court overruled the plain meaning of the ACA limiting subsidies to people living in states that created their own exchanges and instead allowed tax credits for insurance purchased through federally facilitated exchanges as well."[54]

The fourth and most recent challenge to the ACA was heard by the Supreme Court in March 2016 in the case of *Zubik et al. versus Burwell, Secretary of Health and Human Services, et al.* The challenge was brought by an order of Nuns called the Little Sisters of the Poor, and consisted of seven consolidated cases brought by other nonprofit religiously affiliated groups who lost in the lower courts. Their concern was with the ACA's requirement that group health plans provide a full range of contraceptive coverage to women at no cost because it violates a federal law meant to protect religious freedom. They were seeking an exemption to this part of the ACA that the Obama administration provided houses of worship. "In an unanimous opinion, the Supreme Court 'vacated,' meaning erased, all the lower court cases and required them to reconsider the claims brought by the Little Sisters of the Poor and others that the regulations promulgated pursuant to Obamacare violate their religious exercise in light of the government's admission that it could indeed provide contraceptive coverage without the Little Sisters' collaboration.'[130] This opinion included specific instructions that government find a compromise by tweaking the contraceptive mandate so it does not include religious concerns."[130]

As noted throughout this chapter, the ACA is not a simple piece of legislation. It was almost 2,000 pages long and had many items in it that changed the way health insurance is provided in the United States. Some of the changes are very obvious and easy to understand, while others could be skipped over by one not reading closely. Others are complicated and will take many people much time to completely understand and implement properly. In addition, the enormity of ACC causes it to impact more than just health care. The ACA also has implications for the economy like with productivity and wages, the labor market, mergers in the health care sector (e.g., insurance companies, pharmacies, wellness companies, pharmaceutical companies),[131] commercial liability insurance,[132] and U.S. tax code to name some. As we move forward with the ACA, there is no indication that the rough road the ACC has experienced to date will get much smoother. As noted earlier, the law will not be fully implemented until 2020 and there are still details that need to be worked out. In addition, there is still much hostility that many (mostly Republican) federal legislators, state governors and legislators, and citizens have for the ACA.[2] Many Americans are confused about what the law does for them.[2] Depending on the outcome of the 2016 Presidential election there may be attempts to repeal parts or all of the ACA.[133] Even if the outcome of the 2016 presidential election does not impact the ACA, there are still other lingering questions such as: (1) Will the United States continue working towards universal health care? Will it ever reach it? (2) Will the ACA be able to control the cost of health insurance and thus the cost of health care?[2] (3) Will the 19 states that have not expanded Medicaid do so in the future? (4) Will any of the 32 states and the District of Columbia who expanded Medicaid regress to some other plan? (5) Will the functionality of the Health Care.gov website continue to improve? (6) Will the marketplaces set up by the federal and state governments actually perform well over time? [2] (7) How many more lawsuits may there be challenging the legality of the ACA or some of its components? (8) Will higher taxes be needed to sustain the provisions of the ACA? (9) What impact will the ACA have on medical research? All of these questions need answers and only time will tell if how they will be answered.

Back in 2009 prior to the passage of the ACA, President Obama stated to a joint session of Congress, "I am not the first president to take up the cause [i.e., health care reform], but I intend to be the last."[134] Although that was his intention, it will probably not come true. Data show that the cost of health care in the United States is too high, there are still too many Americans without health insurance, and compared to the other developed countries of the world there is still room to improve the quality of care. The United States health care system will continue to be reformed in the future.

Chapter Summary

- The concept of a health care system has been and continues to be questioned in the United States. Is it really a system or is treatment provided in an informal, cooperative manner?

- Health care in the United States has evolved from home and folk remedies to the modest services of the independent country doctor who often visited the sick in their homes to a highly complex almost $3 trillion plus industry.

- The spectrum of health care includes four domains of practice—public health practice, medical practice, long-term practice, and end-of-life practice.

- Within the medical practice domain of health care are the following types of health care providers: independent providers (allopathic, osteopathic, and non-allopathic), limited (restricted) care providers, nurses, nonphysician practitioners, allied health care professionals, and public health professionals.

- Complementary and alternative medicine (CAM) is "a group of diverse medical and health care systems, practices, and products that are not presently considered to be a part of conventional medicine."[28]

- Health care providers perform services in both inpatient and outpatient care facilities.

- Inpatient care facilities include hospitals, nursing homes, and assisted-living facilities.

- The types of outpatient care facilities found in communities are health care practitioners' offices, clinics, primary care centers, retail clinics, urgent/emergent care centers, ambulatory surgery centers, and freestanding service facilities.

- Long-term care options include traditional institutional residential care as well as special units within these residential facilities, halfway houses, group homes, assisted-living facilities, transitional (step-down) care in a hospital, day care facilities for patients, and personal home health care.

- The predominant organization responsible for accrediting health care facilities is The Joint Commission.

- The major issues of concern with the health care system in the United States can be summed up by the cost containment, access, and quality triangle.

- Some of the barriers to access to health care in the United States have been the lack of health insurance, inadequate insurance, and poverty.

- There are a number of different methods by which the amount of reimbursement to health care providers is determined. They include fee-for-service, packaged pricing, resource-based relative value scale, prepaid health care, capitation, and prospective reimbursement.

- Most health care in the United States is paid for via third-party payment.

- Key health insurance terms include *deductible, co-insurance, copayment, fixed indemnity, exclusion,* and *pre-existing condition.*

- The two largest government administered health insurance programs in the United States are Medicare and Medicaid.

- The government's Children's Health Insurance Program (CHIP) is for many children who were previously uninsured.

- Two major supplemental insurance programs in the United States are Medigap and long-term care insurance.

- Most Americans today are covered by some form of managed care.

- The more common forms of managed care include health maintenance organizations (HMOs), preferred provider organizations (PPOs), and point-of-service (POS) options.

- The United States is the only developed country in the world without national health insurance.

- Consumer-directed health plans, including health savings accounts (HSAs), high-deductible health plans (HDHPs), health reimbursement arrangements (HRAs), and flexible spending accounts (FSAs) are becoming more popular health plan options.

- Health care reform in the United States has not come easily, but the Affordable Care Act (ACA) has significantly increased the number of Americans who have health insurance.

- Health care access, costs, and quality are not as they could be in the United States, therefore additional health care reform will be needed.

Scenario: Analysis and Response

1. Have you ever experienced a situation similar to the one described in the scenario? If so, briefly describe it.

2. If we truly had a "health care system" in this country, how would this scenario be different?

3. Do you think Chad did the right thing?

4. If you were Chad, what would you have done? If you had zero-deductible health insurance, would it make a difference in what you would do?

5. Which of the options available to Chad do you think was the most expensive? Least expensive? Why?

Review Questions

1. Why have some questioned whether the United States really has a health care system?

2. Describe some of the major changes that have taken place in health care delivery over the years.

3. What is meant by *third-party payment*?

4. Why has the cost of health care in the United States continued to grow faster than the cost of inflation?

5. What is meant by a *spectrum of health care*?

6. What are the domains of practice noted in the spectrum of health care?

7. Is there a demand for health care workers in the United States today? If so, why?

8. In what type of facility are most health care workers employed?

9. What is the difference between independent and limited (restricted) care providers?

10. What are the differences between allopathic and non-allopathic health care providers?

11. What is the difference between *complementary* and *alternative medicine*? Give a few examples of each.

12. What kind of education do limited (restricted) care providers have?

13. What is the difference between LPNs and RNs?

14. What are advanced practice registered nurses (APRNs)?

15. What is a physician assistant?

16. What role do public health professionals play in health care delivery?

17. What are the advantages of outpatient care facilities?

18. What is meant by a long-term care facility? Give two examples.

19. Why has the number of home health care agencies increased in recent years?

20. What is The Joint Commission? What does it do?

21. What are three major problems facing the health care system in the United States?

22. How is the quality of health care services measured?

23. Explain how each of the following types of reimbursement works: fee-for-service, packaged pricing, resource-based relative value scale, prepaid health care, capitation, and prospective reimbursement.

24. On what basic concept is insurance based?

25. Explain the following insurance policy provisions: (a) a $500 deductible, (b) 20/80 co-insurance, (c) a $4,500 fixed indemnity for a basic surgical procedure, (d) an exclusion of the pre-existing condition of lung cancer, and (e) a $10 copayment.

26. What is the difference between Medicare and Medicaid?

27. What is covered in each of the four parts of Medicare—Parts A, B, C, and D?

28. What relationship does Medigap insurance have to Medicare?

29. What is the Children's Health Insurance Program (CHIP)?

30. Briefly explain the differences among health maintenance organizations (HMOs), preferred provider organizations (PPOs), and a point-of-service (POS) option.

31. What are the advantages and disadvantages of managed care?

32. What is meant by the term *consumer-directed health plans*? Give some examples.

33. What is the major result of the Affordable Care Act passed in 2010?

34. Summarize the four cases about the Affordable Care Act that have been heard by the U.S. Supreme Court.

Activities

1. Using Table 13.2, identify two different health care facilities in your community for each of the levels of care. Briefly describe each facility and determine whether each one is private, public, or voluntary.

2. Make an appointment to interview three health care workers in your community who have different types of jobs. Ask them what they like and dislike about their work, what kind of education they needed, whether they are happy with their work, and whether they would recommend that others seek this line of work. Summarize your findings in a written paper.

3. Get online and look at a copy of a local newspaper (the Sunday edition is best) and look through the classified section for health care worker jobs. In a one-page paper, briefly describe what you have found and summarize the status of health care position openings in your community.

4. Create a list of all the health care providers from whom your family has sought help in the past 5 years. Group the individuals into the six provider groups outlined in the chapter. When appropriate, identify the providers' specialties and whether they were allopathic, osteopathic, or nonallopathic providers.

5. Make an appointment to interview an administrator in the local (city or county) health department. In the interview, find out what kind of people, by profession, work in the department. Also find out what type(s) of health care services and clinics are offered by the department. Summarize your findings in a two-page paper.

6. Obtain a copy of the student health insurance policy available at your school. After reading the policy, summarize in writing what you have read. In your summary, indicate what type of reimbursement system is used to pay providers, list specifics about the premium costs, deductible, co-insurance, copayment, fixed indemnity, and any exclusions.

7. Visit the Health care.gov website and find the answers to the following: (a) When is the open enrollment period each year? (b) Who can enroll for health insurance outside of the open enrollment period during the special enrollment period? (c) What is meant by minimum essential coverage? (d) What are the special arrangements for people under the age of 30 years? and (e) What does the ACA say about same-sex spouses?

References

1. Shi, L., and D. A. Singh (2017). *Essentials of the U.S. Health Care System*, 4th ed. Burlington, MA: Jones & Bartlett Learning.

2. Wilensky, S. E., and J. B. Teitelbaum (2017). *2016 Annual Health Reform Update*. Burlington, MA: Jones & Bartlett Learning.

3. Institute of Medicine (2003). *The Future of the Public's Health in the 21st Century*. Washington, DC: National Academies Press.

4. Rothstein, W. G. (1972). *American Physicians in the Nineteenth Century: From Sect to Science*. Baltimore: Johns Hopkins University Press.

5. Sultz, H. A., and K. M. Young (2014). *Health Care USA: Understanding Its Organization and Delivery*, 8th ed. Burlington, MA: Jones & Bartlett Learning.

6. Cambridge Research Institute (1976). *Trends Affecting the U.S. Health Care System* (DHEW pub. no. HRA 75-14503). Washington, DC: U.S. Government Printing Office, 261.

7. U.S. Department of Health, Education, and Welfare, Health Resources Administration (1974, September). *Fact Sheet: The Hill-Burton Program*. Washington, DC: U.S. Government Printing Office.

8. Lokkeberg, A. R. (1988). "The Health Care System." In E. T. Anderson and J. M. McFarlane, eds., *Community as Client: Application of the Nursing Process*. Philadelphia: Lippincott, 3–14.

9. Koff, S. Z. (1987). *Health Systems Agencies: A Comprehensive Examination of Planning and Process*. New York: Human Services Press.

10. Stockman, D. A. (1981). "Premises for a Medical Marketplace: A Neoconservative's Vision of How to Transform the Health System." *Health Affairs*, 1(1): 5–18.

11. Wessel, D. (2006, September 7). "In Health Care, Consumer Theory Falls Flat." *Wall Street Journal*, A2.

12. Shi, L., and D. A. Singh (2015). *Delivering Health Care in America: A Systems Approach*, 6th ed. Burlington, MA: Jones & Bartlett Learning.

13. Zatkin, S. (1997). "A Health Plan's View of Government Regulation." *Health Affairs*, 16(6): 33–35.

14. Institute of Medicine (2001). *Crossing the Quality Chasm: A New Health System for the 21st Century*. Washington, DC: National Academies Press.

15. World Health Organization (2000). *World Health Organization Assesses the World's Health Systems*. Available at: http://www.who.int/whr/2000/media_centre/press_release/en/.

16. Steinhauer, J. (2016, January 6). "House Votes to Send Bill to Repeal Health Law to Obama's Desk." *The New York Times*. Available at: http://www.nytimes.com/2016/01/07/us/politics/house-votes-to-send-bill-to-repeal-health-law-to-obamas-desk.html.

17. Turnock, B. J. (2016). *Public Health: What It Is and How It Works*, 6th ed. Burlington, MA: Jones & Bartlett Learning.

18. Harris-Kojetin, L., M. Sengupta, E. Park-Lee, and R. Valverde (2013). "Long-Term Care Services in the United States: 2013 Overview." *Vital and Health Statistics*, 3(37). Hyattsville, MD: National Center for Health Statistics.

19. Bernstein, A. B., E. Hing, A. J. Moss, K. F. Allen, A. B. Siller, and R. B. Tiggle (2004). *Health Care in America: Trends in Utilization*. Hyattsville, MD: National Center for Health Statistics.

20. U.S. Department of Labor, Bureau of Labor Statistics (2015, December 8). *Employment Projections—2014–24* [News Release]. Available at http://www.bls.gov/news.release/pdf/ecopro.pdf.

21. U.S. Department of Labor, Bureau of Labor Statistics (2014, Spring). "Health care: Millions of Jobs Now and in the Future." *Occupational Outlook Quarterly*. Available at http://www.bls.gov/careeroutlook/2014/spring/art03.pdf.

22. American Association of Colleges of Osteopathic Medicine (2016). *A Brief History of Osteopathic Medicine*. Available at http://www.aacom.org/become-a-doctor/about-om/history.

23. National Center for Health Statistics (2016). *Health, United States, 2015: With Special Feature on Racial and Ethnic Disparities*. Hyattsville, MD: Author.

24. American Osteopathic Association (2016). *OMP Report: Strength in Primary Care*. Available at https://www.osteopathic.org/inside-aoa/about/aoa-annual-statistics/Pages/strength-in-primary-care.aspx.

25. American Association of Colleges of Osteopathic Medicine (2016). *What Is Osteopathic Medicine?* Available at http://www.aacom.org/become-a-doctor/about-om#aboutom.

26. Association of American Medical Colleges (2014). *2014 Physician Specialty Data Book*. Washington, DC: Author. Available at https://members.aamc.org/eweb/upload/Physician%20Specialty%20Databook%202014.pdf.

27. U.S. Department of Labor, Bureau of Labor Statistics (2015). *Chiropractors*. Available at http://www.bls.gov/ooh/healthcare/chiropractors.htm.

28. National Institutes of Health, National Center for Complementary and Alternative Medicine (2012). *CAM Basics: What Is Complementary and Alternative Medicine?* Available at https://nccih.nih.gov/sites/nccam.nih.gov/files/D347_05-25-2012.pdf.

29. National Institutes of Health, National Center for Complementary and Alternative Medicine (2015). *What Is Complementary, Alternative, or Integrative Health?* Available at https://nccih.nih.gov/health/integrative-health.

30. National Institutes of Health, National Center for Complementary and Alternative Medicine (2015). *Uses of Complementary Health Approaches in the U.S.: National Health Interview Survey*. Available at https://nccih.nih.gov/research/statistics/NHIS/2012/key-findings.

31. Nahin, R. L., P. M. Barnes, B. J. Stussman, and B. Bloom (2009). "Costs of Complementary and Alternative Medicine (CAM) and Frequency of Visits to CAM Practitioners: United States, 2007." *National Health Statistics Reports*, no. 18. Hyattsville, MD: National Center for Health Statistics. Available at https://nccih.nih.gov/research/statistics/costs.

32. National Institutes of Health, National Center for Complementary and Alternative Medicine (2015). *Paying for Complementary Health Approaches*. Available at https://nccih.nih.gov/health/financial.

33. U.S. Department of Labor, Bureau of Labor Statistics (2015). "Licensed Practical and Licensed Vocational Nurses." *Occupational Outlook Handbook*. Available at http://www.bls.gov/ooh/healthcare/licensed-practical-and-licensed-vocational-nurses.htm.

34. U.S. Department of Labor, Bureau of Labor Statistics (2015). "Registered Nurses." *Occupational Outlook Handbook*. Available at http://www.bls.gov/ooh/healthcare/registered-nurses.htm.

35. U.S. Department of Labor, Bureau of Labor Statistics (2015). "Nursing Assistants and Orderlies," *Occupational Outlook Handbook*. Available at http://www.bls.gov/ooh/healthcare/nursing-assistants.htm.

36. Stanfield, P. S., N. Cross, and Y. H. Hui (2012). Introduction to the Health Professions, 6th ed. Burlington, MA: Jones & Bartlett Learning.

37. American Association of Nurse Practitioners (2015). *NP Fact Sheet*. Available at https://www.aanp.org/all-about-nps/np-fact-sheet.

38. The Henry J. Kaiser Family Foundation (2016). *Tapping Nurse Practitioners to Meet Rising Demand for Primary Care*. Available

at http://kff.org/medicaid/issue-brief/tapping-nurse-practitioners-to-meet-rising-demand-for-primary-care/.

39. Woolsey, C. V. (n.d). "What Is a Physician Assistant?" *A Patient's Guide to The Physician Assistant*. Available at http://www.pg2pa.org/index.html.

40. American Academy of Physician Assistants (n.d.). *What Is a PA?* Available at https://www.aapa.org/what-is-a-pa/?utm_source=aapa.org&utm_medium=blue_buttons&utm_content=what&utm_campaign=homepage.

41. U.S. Department of Labor, Bureau of Labor Statistics (2015). "Physician Assistants." *Occupational Outlook Handbook*. Available at http://www.bls.gov/ooh/healthcare/physician-assistants.htm.

42. American College of Emergency Physicians (2014). *Specialty Hospitals*. Available at https://www.acep.org/Clinical---Practice-Management/Specialty-Hospitals/.

43. Blumenthal, D. M., E. J. Orav, A. B. Jena, D. M. Dudzinski, S. T. Le, and A. K. Jha (2015). "Access, Quality, and Costs of Care at Physician Owned Hospitals in the United States: Observational Study." *BMJ*, 2(351): h4466.

44. Turner, G-M. (2015, November 6). "Lift the Ban On Physician-Owned Hospitals." *Forbes* online. Available at http://www.forbes.com/sites/gracemarieturner/2015/11/06/lift-the-ban-on-physician-owned-hospitals/#23f664044b00.

45. Griffin, D. J. (2012). Hospitals: What They Are and How They Work, 4th ed. Sudbury, MA: Jones & Bartlett Learning.

46. Centers for Disease Control and Prevention (2014). *Ambulatory Care Use and Physician Office Visits*. Available at http://www.cdc.gov/nchs/fastats/physician-visits.htm.

47. National Association of Community Health Centers (2014). *America's Health Centers*. Available at http://www.nachc.com/client/documents/Americas_CHCs1014.pdf.

48. The Henry J. Kaiser Family Foundation (2013). *Summary of the Affordable Care Act (#8061-02)*. Available at http://kff.org/health-reform/fact-sheet/summary-of-the-affordable-care-act/.

49. Robert Wood Johnson Foundation (2015). *Growing Retail Clinic Industry Employs, Empowers Nurse Practitioners*. Available at http://www.rwjf.org/en/library/articles-and-news/2015/02/growing-retail-clinic-industry-employs--empowers-nurse-practitio.html.

50. Robert Wood Johnson Foundation (2015). *Building a Culture of Health: The Value Proposition of Retail Clinic*. Available at http://www.rwjf.org/content/dam/farm/reports/issue_briefs/2015/rwjf419415.

51. Centers for Medicare & Medicaid Services (2015). *Medicare Home Health Agency (HHA) Transparency Data (CY2013)*. Available at https://www.cms.gov/Newsroom/MediaReleaseDatabase/Fact-sheets/2015-Fact-sheets-items/2015-12-18.html.

52. The Joint Commission (2016). *Joint Commission FAQ Page*. Available at http://www.jointcommission.org/about/jointcommissionfaqs.aspx?CategoryId=10.

53. Centers for Medicare & Medicaid Services (2015). *Affordable Care Act*. Available at https://www.medicaid.gov/affordablecareact/affordable-care-act.html.

54. Turner, G-M. (2016, January 28). *70 Changes to ObamaCare ... So Far*. Alexandria, VA: Galen Institute. Available at http://galen.org/newsletters/changes-to-obamacare-so-far/.

55. Kissick, W. L. (1994). *Medicine's Dilemmas: Infinite Needs versus Finite Resources*. New Haven, CT: Yale University Press.

56. Institute of Medicine (2004). *Insuring America's Health: Principles and Recommendations*. Available at http://www.iom.edu/Reports/2004/Insuring-Americas-Health-Principles-and-Recommendations.aspx.

57. The Henry J. Kaiser Family Foundation (2015). *Key Facts about the Uninsured Population*. Available at http://kff.org/uninsured/fact-sheet/key-facts-about-the-uninsured-population/.

58. Martinez, M. E., R. A. Cohen, and E. P. Zammitti (2016). *Health Insurance Coverage: Early Release of Estimates from the National Health Interview Survey, January–September 2015*. Atlanta, GA: Centers for Disease Control and Prevention, National Center for Health Statistics. Available at http://www.cdc.gov/nchs/data/nhis/earlyrelease/insur201602.pdf.

59. Congressional Budget Office (2015). *Insurance Coverage Provisions of the Affordable Care Act––CBO's January 2015 Baseline*. Available at https://www.cbo.gov/sites/default/files/cbofiles/attachments/43900-2015-01-ACAtables.pdf.

60. The Henry J Kaiser Family Foundation (2016). *Health Reform FAQs*. Available at http://kff.org/health-reform/faq/health-reform-frequently-asked-questions/.

61. Centers for Medicare & Medicaid Services (2016). *Overview of the SHOP Marketplace*. Available at https://www.healthcare.gov/small-businesses/provide-shop-coverage/.

62. Davis, K., K. Stremikis, C. Schoen, and D. Squires (2014). *Mirror, Mirror on the Wall, 2014 Update: How the U.S. Health Care System Compares Internationally*. New York: Commonwealth Fund. Available at http://www.commonwealthfund.org/publications/fund-reports/2014/jun/mirror-mirror.

63. Institute of Medicine (2001). *Crossing the Quality Chasm: A New Health Care System for the 21st Century*. Washington, DC: Author. Available at http://www.iom.edu/Reports/2001/Crossing-the-Quality-Chasm-A-New-Health-Care-System-for-the-21st-Century.aspx.

64. Institute of Medicine (1999). *To Err Is Human: Building a Safer Health System*. Washington, DC: Author. Available at http://www.iom.edu/Reports/1999/To-Err-is-Human--Building-A-Safer-Health-System.aspx.

65. U.S. Department of Health and Human Services, Agency for Health care Research and Quality (2015). *2014 National Health care Quality and Disparities Report* (AHRQ pub. no. 15-0007). Rockville, MD: Author: Available at http://www.ahrq.gov/sites/default/files/wysiwyg/research/findings/nhqrdr/nhqdr14/2014nhqdr.pdf.

66. National Committee for Quality Assurance (2016). *About NCQA*. Available at http://www.ncqa.org/AboutNCQA.aspx.

67. National Committee for Quality Assurance (2016). *HEDIS® and Quality Compass®* Available at http://www.ncqa.org/HEDISQualityMeasurement/WhatisHEDIS.aspx.

68. U.S. Department of Health and Human Services, Agency for Health care Research and Quality (2015). *About the National Quality Strategy (NQS)*. Available at http://www.ahrq.gov/workingforquality/about.htm.

69. U.S. Department of Health and Human Services, Agency for Health care Research and Quality (2015). *The National Quality Strategy (NQS)*. Available at http://www.ahrq.gov/workingforquality/index.html.

70. U.S. Department of Health and Human Services, Agency for Health care Research and Quality (2015). *2015 Annual Progress Report to Congress: National Strategy for Quality Improvement in Health Care*. Available at http://www.ahrq.gov/workingforquality/reports/annual-reports/nqs2015annlrpt.htm.

71. Centers for Medicare & Medicaid Services (2015). *Accountable Care Organizations (ACO)*. Available at https://www.cms.gov/Medicare/Medicare-Fee-for-Service-Payment/ACO/index.html?redirect=/ACO/.

72. Physicians for a National Health Program. (2010). *The History and Definition of the "Accountable Care Organization."* Available at http://pnhpcalifornia.org/2010/10/the-history-and-definition-of-the-%E2%80%9Caccountable-care-organization%E2%80%9D/.

73. The Henry J Kaiser Family Foundation (2016). *Accountable Care Organizations: A New Paradigm for Health Care Delivery?* Available at http://kff.org/health-costs/event/accountable-care-organizations-a-new-paradigm-for/.

74. American College of Physicians (2016). *What Is the Patient-Centered Medical Home?* Available at https://www.acponline.org

/running_practice/delivery_and_payment_models/pcmh /understanding/what.htm.

75. Agency for Health care Research and Quality (n.d.). *Defining the PCMH*. Available at https://www.pcmh.ahrq.gov/page /defining-pcmh.

76. Patient-Centered Primary Care Collaborative (2016). *About Us*. Available at https://www.pcpcc.org/about.

77. Centers for Medicare & Medicaid Services (2014). *National Health Expenditure Data*. Available at https://www.cms.gov/Research -Statistics-Data-and-Systems/Statistics-Trends-and-Reports /NationalHealthExpendData/index.html.

78. Brill, S. (2014, March 4). "Bitter Pill." *Time*, 16–55. Available at http://www.ncpssm.org/EntitledtoKnow/entryid/1978/-Bitter -Pill-A-Time-Magazine-Article-Every-Senior-in--Medicare -Should-Read.

79. Centers for Medicare & Medicaid Services (2015). *Medicare Provider Utilization and Payment Data*. Available at https://www.cms.gov /research-statistics-data-and-systems/statistics-trends-and-reports /medicare-provider-charge-data/.

80. Farell, D., E. Jensen, B. Kocher, N. Lovegrove, F. Melhem, L. Mendonca, and B. Parish (2008, December). "Accounting for the Cost of US Health Care: A New Look at Why Americans Spend More." *McKinsey Global Institute Report*. Available at http ://www.mckinsey.com/insights/health_systems_and_services /accounting_for_the_cost_of_us_health_care.

81. Bipartisan Policy Center (2012). *What Is Driving U.S. Health Care Spending: America's Unsustainable Health Care Cost Growth*. Available at https://kaiserhealthnews.files.wordpress.com/2012/10/bpc _health_care_cost_drivers_brief_sept_2012.pdf.

82. Martin, A. B., M. Hartman, J. Benson, A. Catlin, and The National Health Expenditure Accounts Team (2015). "National Health Spending in 2014: Faster Growth Driven by Coverage Expansion and Prescription Drug Spending." *Health Affairs*, 35(1): 150–160 (epub before print), doi:10.1377/hlthaff.2015.1194.

83. Congressional Budget Office (2014). *Updated Estimates of the Insurance Coverage Provisions of the Affordable Care Act*. Available at https://www.cbo.gov/publication/45159.

84. Harrington, M. K. (2016). *Health Care Finance and the Mechanics of Insurance and Reimbursement*. Burlington, MA: Jones & Bartlett Learning.

85. James, J. (2012, October 11). Health Policy Brief: Pay-for-Performance. *Health Affairs*. Available at http://www.healthaffairs.org /healthpolicybriefs/brief.php?brief_id=78.

86. Health Care Incentives Improvement Institute (2015). *Pay for Performance – Models*. Available at http://www.hci3.org /thought-leadership/why-incentives-matter/pay-performance /pay-performance-models.

87. U.S. Department of Health and Human Services (2014). *Pre-Existing Conditions*. Available at http://www.hhs.gov/healthcare/about-the -law/pre-existing-conditions/index.html.

88. The Commonwealth Fund (2012). *Slower Growth in Health Insurance Premiums is Found––but the Mystery Is Why*. Available at http://www.commonwealthfund.org/search#/q=growth%20of%20 health%20insurance%20premiums&sort=relevancy.

89. Zane Benefits (2016). *Do the Majority of Americans Still Get Health Insurance Through Work?* Available at http://www.zanebenefits. com/blog/do-the-majority-of-americans-still-get-health-insurance -through-work.

90. The Henry J Kaiser Family Foundation (2016). *Health Insurance Premiums*. Available at http://kff.org/search/?s=health±insurance ±premiums&tab=data&facets[post_type][]=state-indicator.

91. Jennings, P. (2005, December 15). "Peter Jennings Reporting: Breakdown—America's Health Insurance Crisis." As cited in J. P. Rooney and D. Perrin (2008). *America's Health Care Crisis Solved*. Hoboken, NJ: John Wiley & Sons.

92. The Henry J Kaiser Family Foundation (2016). *Health Insurance Premiums Marketplace Calculator*. Available at http://kff .org/interactive/subsidy-calculator/#state=pa&zip=17022&locale =Lancaster&income-type=dollars&income=50%2C000&employer -coverage=0&people=2&alternate-plan-family=individual &adult-count=2&adults[0][age]=36&adults[0][tobacco]=0&adults[1] [age]=38&adults[1][tobacco]=0&child-count=0&child-tobacco=0.

93. Cigna (2013 September 23). *Informed on Reform*. Available at http://www.cigna.com/assets/docs/about-cigna/Webinar%20PPTs /Cigna_IoR_Sept-Web-Mtg-FAQs_10-01-13.pdf.

94. U.S. Congress (2010, March 23). *The Patient Protection and Affordable Care Act* (Public Law Numbers 111-148 and 111-152, Consolidated Print). Available at http://www.gpo.gov/fdsys/pkg /PLAW-111publ148/pdf/PLAW-111publ148.pdf.

95. U.S. Department of Health and Human Services, Centers for Medicare & Medicaid Services (2016). *CMS Fast Facts*. Available at https://www.cms.gov/fastfacts/.

96. U.S. Department of Health and Human Services, Centers for Medicare & Medicaid Services (2016). *Medicare Costs at a Glance*. Available at https://www.medicare.gov/your-medicare-costs/costs -at-a-glance/costs-at-glance.html.

97. U.S. Department of Health and Human Services, Centers for Medicare & Medicaid Services (2016). *Medicare and You 2016*. Available at https://www.medicare.gov/Pubs/pdf/10050.pdf.

98. U.S. Department of Health and Human Services (1989). *Your Hospital Stay Under Medicare's Prospective Payment System* (DHHS pub. no. HCFA 02163). Washington, DC: U.S. Government Printing Office.

99. AARP (2014). *Is Your Medicare Safe?* Available at http://www.aarp.org /health/medicare-insurance/info-12-2013/medicare-and-affordable -care-act.html.

100. The Henry J Kaiser Family Foundation (2016). *How Is Medicare Financed and What Are Medicare's Future Financing Challenges?* Available at http://kff.org/report-section/a-primer-on-medicare -how-is-medicare-financed-and-what-are-medicares-future -financing-challenges/.

101. Condon, S. (2012, July 2). "States Opting Out of Medicaid Expansion Could Leave Many Uninsured." *CBS News Political Hotsheet*. Available from http://www.cbsnews.com/8301-503544_162-57465110-503544 /states-opting-out-of-medicaid-expansion-could-leave-many -uninsured/?tag=cbsnewsMainColumnArea.

102. Dorn, S., M. Teitelbaum, and C. Cortez (1998). *An Advocate's Tool Kit for the State Children's Health Insurance Program*. Washington, DC: Children's Defense Fund.

103. U.S. Department of Health and Human Services, Centers for Medicare & Medicaid Services (2010). *Children's Health Insurance Program (CHIP)*. Available at https://www.medicaid.gov/chip /chip-program-information.html.

104. National Conference of State Legislatures (2015). *Children's Health Insurance Program Overview*. Available at http://www.ncsl.org /research/health/childrens-health-insurance-program-overview .aspx.

105. Centers for Medicare & Medicaid Services (2015). *Choosing a Medigap Policy: A Guide to Health Insurance for People with Medicare*. Available at https://www.medicare.gov/Pubs /pdf/02110.pdf.

106. U.S. Department of Health and Human Services, Administration on Aging (n.d.). *Find Your Path Forward*. Available at http ://longtermcare.gov.

107. Genworth Life Insurance Company (2015). *Cost of Care Survey 2015: National Data*. Available at https://www.genworth .com/dam/Americas/US/PDFs/Consumer/corporate/cost-of -care/118928USA_040115_gnw.pdf.

108. MCOL (2016). *Managed Care Fact Sheets*. Available at http://www .mcol.com/factsheetindex.

109. Institute of Medicine (1997). *Managing Managed Care: Quality Improvement in Behavioral Health*. Washington, DC: National Academies Press.

110. Kongstvedt, P. R. (2013). Essentials of Managed Health Care, 6th ed. Burlington, MA: Jones & Bartlett Learning.

111. The Henry J Kaiser Family Foundation (2016). *Medicare Advantage 2015 Spotlight: Enrollment Market Update*. Available at http://kff.org/medicare/issue-brief/medicare-advantage-2015-spotlight-enrollment-market-update/.

112. The Henry J Kaiser Family Foundation (2016). *Medicaid Managed Care Market Tracker*. Available at http://kff.org/data-collection/medicaid-managed-care-market-tracker/.

113. Slee, D. A., V. N. Slee, and H. J. Schmidt (2008). Slee's Health Care Terms, 5th ed. Burlington, MA: Jones & Bartlett Learning.

114. Alliance for Health Reform (November 2006). *HSAs and High Deductible Health Plans: A Primer*. Washington, DC: Author.

115. U.S. Department of the Treasury (2015). *Health Savings Accounts (HSA)*. Available at https://www.treasury.gov/resource-center/faqs/Taxes/Pages/Health-Savings-Accounts.aspx.

116. United Health Care Services, Inc. (2015). *Health Savings Accounts (HAS) and Health Care Reform*. HSACenter. Available at http://www.hsacenter.com/Health-Savings-Accounts-and-Health-Care-Reform.html.

117. Altman, D. (2015, March 11). "Health-Care Deductibles Climbing Out of Reach." *The Wall Street Journal* online. Available at http://blogs.wsj.com/washwire/2015/03/11/health-care-deductibles-climbing-out-of-reach/.

118. LeTourneau, J. (2013, December). "ACA Changes for Health Reimbursement Arrangements." *Broker World Magazine* online. Available at https://www.wageworks.com/media/184548/WW-BW-ACA-CHANGES-FOR-HRAs.pdf.

119. Zane Benefits (2016). *Flexible Spending Accounts (FSAs) – New 'Use It or Lose It' Rules*. Available at http://www.zanebenefits.com/blog/bid/323382/Flexible-Spending-Accounts-FSAs-New-Use-It-Or-Lose-It-Rules.

120. LeTourneau, J. (2013, November). "ACA Changes for Flexible Spending Accounts." *Broker World Magazine* online. Available at https://www.wageworks.com/media/184521/ACA-Changes-LeTourneau_1113.pdf.

121. Cohen, R. A., and M. E. Martinez (2009). *Consumer-Directed Health Care for Persons under 65 Years of Age with Private Health Insurance: United States, 2007* (NCHS Data Brief, no. 15). Hyattsville, MD: National Center for Health Statistics.

122. Cohen, R. A., and M. E. Martinez (2015). *Health Insurance Coverage: Early Release of Estimates from the National Health Interview Survey, January–March 2015*. Available at http://www.cdc.gov/nchs/data/nhis/earlyrelease/insur201508.pdf.

123. American Association of Preferred Provider Organizations (2015). *Large Employers Add CDHPs in 2013*. Available at http://aappo.interactivemedialab.com/Portals/0/Documents/CDHP_2014.pdf.

124. Shaffer, E. R. (2013). "The Affordable Care Act: The Value of Systemic Disruption." *American Journal of Public Health*, 103(6), 969–972.

125. U.S. Supreme Court of the United States (2012). *National Federation of Independent Businesses et al. versus Sebelius, Secretary of Health and Human Services, et al.* Available at http://www.supremecourt.gov/opinions/11pdf/11-393c3a2.pdf.

126. U.S. Supreme Court of the United States (2013). *Burwell, Secretary of Health and Human Services, et al. versus Hobby Lobby Stores, Inc. et al.* Available at http://www.supremecourt.gov/opinions/13pdf/13-354_olp1.pdf.

127. U.S. Department of Health and Human Services (2016). *Birth Control Benefits*. Available at https://www.healthcare.gov/coverage/birth-control-benefits/.

128. Liptak, A. (2014, June 30). "Supreme Court Rejects Contraceptives Mandate for Some Corporations." *The New York Times* online. Available at http://www.nytimes.com/2014/07/01/us/hobby-lobby-case-supreme-court-contraception.html

129. Supreme Court of the United States (2014). *King et al. versus Burwell, Secretary of Health and Human Services, et al.* Available at http://www.supremecourt.gov/opinions/14pdf/14-114_qol1.pdf.

130. de Vogue, A. (2016, March 23). *Supreme Court Hears Challenge to Obamacare Contraceptive mandate*. CNN Politics online. Available at http://www.cnn.com/2016/03/23/politics/supreme-court-obamacare-contraceptive-mandate/

131. Rosenthal, P. (2015, October 28). Obama ACA Side Effects Include Mergers Like Walgreens Boots, Rite Aid. *Chicago Tribune* online. Available at http://www.chicagotribune.com/business/ct-rosenthal-walgreens-rite-aid-1029-biz-20151028-column.html.

132. Benet, L. (2014, May 21). *ACA Side Effects: 5 Ways It May Impact Commercial Liability Insurance*. General Re. Available at http://www.genre.com/knowledge/blog/aca-side-effects-5-ways-it-may-impact-commercial-liability-insurance-.html.

133. McDonough, J., and Fletcher, M. (2015, September 18). "What Would Republicans Do Instead of the Affordable Care Act?" *Health Affairs Blog*. Available at http://healthaffairs.org/blog/2015/09/18/what-would-republicans-do-instead-of-the-affordable-care-act/.

134. Petty, P. (2009, September 9). "President Barack Obama Gives Health Care Reform Speech to Congress." *The Express-Times*. Available at http://www.lehighvalleylive.com/elections/index.ssf/2009/09/president_barack_obama_gives_h.html.

UNIT THREE

Environmental Health and Safety

CHAPTER 14

Community and Public Health and the Environment

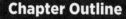

Chapter Outline

Chapter Objectives

After studying this chapter, you will be able to:

1. List the sources and types of air pollutants, including the criteria pollutants, and explain the difference between primary and secondary pollutants.

2. Describe the role of the Environmental Protection Agency in protecting the environment.

3. Outline the provisions of the Clean Air Act, and explain the purposes of the National Ambient Air Quality Standards and the Air Quality Index.

4. Recall the major types of indoor air pollutants, including radon, and describe ways to reduce exposure to them.

5. Explain the difference between point source and nonpoint source pollution.

6. Discuss the various types of pollutants that threaten the safety of our drinking water and give examples of each type.

7. Define what is meant by the term *waterborne disease outbreak* and list some of the causative agents.

8. Illustrate the measures communities take to ensure the quality of drinking water and the measures communities take to manage wastewater.

9. Explain the purposes of the Clean Water Act and Safe Drinking Water Act.

10. Define the term *foodborne disease outbreak*, name some of the agents that cause these outbreaks, and describe some of the practices that increase the risk of a foodborne disease outbreak.

11. Name some of the agencies that help protect the safety of our food, and describe how they accomplish this task.

12. Define pest, pesticides, target organism, and nontarget organism. Explain some of the safety and health concerns with pesticide use.

13. Describe the composition of our municipal solid waste (MSW) and outline acceptable MSW management strategies.

14. Define hazardous waste and give some examples.

15. Explain the purposes of the Resource Conservation and Recovery Act and the Comprehensive Environmental Response, Compensation, and Liability Act.

16. Discuss the health hazards associated with exposure to lead in our environment.

17. Define the terms *vector* and *vectorborne disease* and explain why these are community concerns.

18. Define ionizing radiation and describe the health hazards associated with it.

19. List examples of natural hazards and complex disasters and the ways they can affect the health of a community.

20. Interpret the relationships among population growth, the environment, and human health.

21. Explain the roles of the Federal Emergency Management Agency and the American Red Cross in preparing for and providing assistance to people and communities after a disaster.

Scenario

Juan and Maria had been trying to have a baby for 2 years. Their first child, Elaina, conceived before they moved to their current home and born without a problem, was now 4 1/2 years old. But yesterday, Maria experienced her third miscarriage in the past 14 months. Before they moved into their current home, about 3 years ago, Juan and Maria had taken a sample of the well water and had it tested. At that time, the water was determined to be safe to drink. Six months after that, however, a large-scale, rural hog farm had been built less than one-half mile away and began operations shortly afterward. At first, the smell wasn't noticeable, but now the stench from the huge waste lagoon was evident most days. State inspectors had made several visits to the operation in the past year. Juan wondered whether the water in their well was still safe to drink. He decided to have their well water tested again.

Introduction

Our health is affected by the quality of our environment, including the air we breathe, the water we drink, the food we eat, and the communities in which we live. The activities of our growing population and our demand for ever-increasing amounts of energy endanger the quality of our air, the purity of our water, the safety of our food, and the health of our planet. Having recognized the implications of environmental degradation on our health and the health of our communities, we have enacted regulatory measures to address some of the most egregious environmental assaults and accept our responsibility for the stewardship of our planet.

Environmental health the study and management of environmental conditions that affect the health and well-being of humans

Environmental hazards factors or conditions in the environment that increase the risk of human injury, disease, or death

Air pollution contamination of the air that interferes with the comfort, safety, and health of living organisms

Primary pollutant air pollutant emanating directly from transportation, power and industrial plants, and refineries

Secondary pollutant air pollutant formed when primary air pollutants react with sunlight and other atmospheric components to form new harmful compounds

Photochemical smog haze or fog formed when air pollutants interact with sunlight

Industrial smog haze or fog formed primarily by sulfur dioxide and suspended particles from the burning of coal, also known as gray smog

Ozone (O_3) an inorganic molecule considered to be a pollutant in the atmosphere because it harms human tissue, but considered beneficial in the stratosphere because it screens out UV radiation

Environmental health is the study and management of environmental conditions that affect our health and well-being. **Environmental hazards** are those factors or conditions in the environment that increase the risk of human injury, disease, or death. The aim of this chapter is to examine common environmental hazards and describe community efforts to protect our health. We begin with a discussion of environmental concerns surrounding our air, water, and food resources. Then, we discuss how communities manage solid and hazardous waste. We conclude with a discussion of natural, human-made, and environmental hazards.

The Air We Breathe

Nothing has been more important to the development of life on earth than the composition of the air we breathe. Yet many of our everyday activities alter the quality of this essential environmental component. By polluting the air, we endanger our health and risk leaving a deteriorating environment to future generations. In some cases, we further endanger our health with unhealthy indoor air.

Outdoor Air Pollution

Air pollution is the contamination of the air by substances—gases, liquids, or solids—in amounts great enough to harm humans, the environment, or that alter climate. These contaminants or pollutants originate from natural or human sources. Natural sources include dust storms, forest fires, and volcanic eruptions. Human sources can be divided into mobile sources, such as motor vehicles, and stationary sources, such as power plants and factories.

In the United States, major sources are (1) transportation, including privately owned motor vehicles; (2) electric power plants fueled by oil and coal; and (3) industry, primarily mills and refineries. In addition to these major sources, there are many smaller sources, such as wood- and coal-burning stoves, fireplaces, dry-cleaning facilities, and waste incinerators.

Pollutants are generally divided further into primary and secondary pollutants. **Primary pollutants** include those emanating directly from the sources listed previously. They include carbon monoxide, carbon dioxide, sulfur dioxide, nitrogen oxides, hydrocarbons, and suspended particulates. **Secondary pollutants** are formed when primary pollutants react with one another or with other atmospheric components to form new harmful chemicals. Secondary pollutants include nitrogen dioxide, nitric acid, nitrate salts, sulfur trioxide, sulfate salts, sulfuric acid, peroxyacyl nitrates, and ozone.[1] Because sunlight promotes the formation of these secondary pollutants, the resulting smog is referred to as **photochemical smog** (brown smog). This term is used to contrast photochemical smog with **industrial smog** (gray smog) formed primarily by sulfur dioxide and suspended particulates.

Living in communities where air pollution reaches harmful levels can result in both acute and chronic health problems. Acute effects include burning eyes, shortness of breath, and increased incidences of colds, coughs, nose irritation, and other respiratory illness. In severe pollution episodes, deaths have been reported.[2] Chronic effects include chronic bronchitis, emphysema, and increased incidence of bronchial asthma attacks. There is even evidence of increased risk of lung cancer from air pollution (see **Figure 14.1**).[2]

Ozone (O_3), perhaps, represents the single most dangerous air pollutant. Breathing ozone can result in a variety of health problems even at low levels, including chest pain, coughing, throat irritation, congestion, bronchitis, emphysema, asthma, and reduced lung function. Repeated exposure to ground-level ozone may permanently scar lung tissue. Even healthy people can experience breathing problems if exposed to ozone at high enough levels. In many urban and suburban areas throughout the U.S. concentrations of ground-level ozone exceed air quality standards.[3]

FIGURE 14.1 Air pollution from heavy traffic.

One cause of excessive levels of ground-level ozone is a phenomenon referred to as a **thermal inversion**. This occurs when a layer of warm air settles above cooler air close to the Earth's surface, preventing the cooler air from rising. Ozone and other air pollutants then accumulate in the cooler air, the air we breathe. The longer a thermal inversion continues, the more likely it is that pollutants will reach dangerously high levels (see **Figure 14.2**).[2]

Regulation of Outdoor Air Quality

Steady deterioration of air quality in the 1950s and 1960s led to the nation's first serious attempt to regulate air pollution, the **Clean Air Act (CAA)** of 1963. The CAA, which provided the federal government with the authority to address interstate air pollution problems, was amended several times in the late 1960s, but much of the regulation was based on voluntary compliance.

The 1970 amendments to the CAA provided the first comprehensive approach to dealing with air pollution nationwide. Three significant components of these amendments were emission standards for automobiles, emission standards for new industries, and ambient air quality standards for urban areas.[2] The latter are known as the **National Ambient Air Quality Standards (NAAQSs)**.

Thermal inversion a condition that occurs when warm air traps cooler air at the surface of the Earth

Clean Air Act (CAA) the federal law that provides the government with authority to address interstate air pollution

National Ambient Air Quality Standards (NAAQSs) standards created by the EPA for allowable concentration levels of outdoor air pollutants

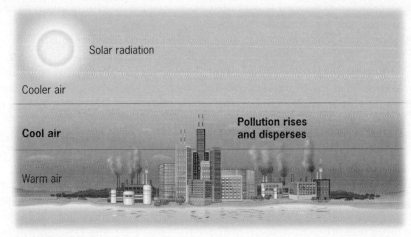

A. Normal pattern.

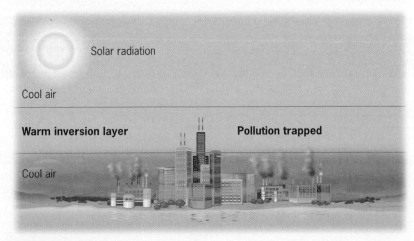

B. Thermal inversion.

FIGURE 14.2   A thermal inversion.

Source: Chiras, D. D. (2010). *Environmental Science*. 8th ed. Burlington, MA: Jones & Bartlett Learning.

The U.S. **Environmental Protection Agency (EPA)** is the federal agency primarily responsible for setting, maintaining, and enforcing environmental standards. The legislation allows states to adopt and implement programs with equivalent or more stringent standards in lieu of the EPA. As such, states are empowered to regulate air quality and are authorized to levy fines against those who violate the standards. The EPA oversees these state programs or enforces standards in states where no state program exists or is inadequate.[4] The EPA sets limits on how much of a pollutant can be in the air anywhere in the U.S.. The air pollutants of greatest concern in the U.S. are called **criteria pollutants**. These are sulfur dioxide, carbon monoxide, nitrogen oxides, ground-level ozone, respirable particulate matter, and lead (see **Table 14.1**). The levels of each of these six pollutants is monitored in the ambient (outdoor) air to determine if and when they exceed the NAAQSs. Between 1990 and 2014, the U.S. substantially reduced the ambient air concentrations of all six of the criteria pollutants namely, lead by 97%, particulate matter by 36%, ozone by 23%, sulfur dioxide by 76%, carbon monoxide by 77%, and nitrogen oxides by 45%.[5] Nonetheless, in 2014, approximately 57 million people in the U.S. lived in counties with pollution levels above the NAAQSs.[5] However, this reflects a positive trend in that 54% fewer people were living in counties exceeding the NAAQSs than in 2010. To make it easier for all of us to understand daily air quality and what it means for your health, the EPA calculates the **Air Quality Index (AQI)** for five criteria air pollutants regulated by the Clean Air Act. The index tells you how clean or polluted your air is, and what associated health effects might be of concern for you or sensitive people in your community.

The value of the AQI on a particular day can range from 0 (good air quality) to 500 (hazardous air quality). AQI values below 100 are generally thought of as satisfactory, whereas values above 100 are considered to be unhealthy. Those most sensitive to air pollutants will be the first to be affected as the AQI rises above 100. Weather channels and websites might use a color-coded AQI for easier understanding (see **Figure 14.3**).[6] The AQI can be obtained for any area of the U.S. at http://airnow.gov.

The 1990 amendments to the CAA set deadlines for establishing emission standards for 190 toxic chemicals that had not been previously addressed, established a tax on toxic chemical emissions, and tightened emission standards for automobiles.[4]

Auto industry lobbyists have successfully influenced Congress not to increase corporate average fuel efficiency (CAFE) standards. But finally, market competition, primarily from other countries, and higher fuel prices have forced American automakers to begin to produce more fuel-efficient models. Still, for the most part, the U.S. "continues to rely mostly on pollution cleanup rather than prevention."[2] Carpooling, increased reliance on

TABLE 14.1   Criteria Pollutants

Pollutants (Designation)	Form(s)	Major Sources (in order of percentage of contribution)
Carbon monoxide (CO)	Gas	Transportation, industrial processes, other solid waste, stationary fuel combustion
Lead (Pb)	Metal or aerosol	Transportation, industrial processes, stationary fuel combustion, solid waste
Nitrogen dioxide (NO_2)	Gas	Stationary fuel combustion, transportation, industrial processes, solid waste
Ground-level ozone (O_3)	Gas	Transportation, industrial processes, solid waste, stationary fuel combustion
Particulate matter	Solid or liquid	Industrial processes, stationary fuel combustion, transportation, solid waste
Sulfur dioxide (SO_2)	Gas	Stationary fuel combustion, industrial processes, transportation, other wastes

Air quality index levels of health concern	Numerical value	Meaning
Good (green)	0–50	Air quality is considered satisfactory, and air pollution poses little or no risk.
Moderate (yellow)	51–100	Air quality is acceptable; however, for some pollutants there may be a moderate health concern for a very small number of people who are unusually sensitive to air pollution.
Unhealthy for sensitive groups (orange)	101–150	Members of sensitive groups may experience health effects. The general public is not likely to be affected.
Unhealthy (red)	151–200	Everyone may begin to experience health effects; members of sensitive groups may experience more serious health effects.
Very unhealthy (purple)	201–300	Health alert: everyone may experience more serious health effects.
Hazardous (maroon)	> 300	Health warnings of emergency conditions. The entire population is more likely to be affected.

FIGURE 14.3   Color codes for various Air Quality Indices.

Data from: U.S. Environmental Protection Agency (2015). *Air Quality Index (AQI): A Guide to Air Quality and Your Health.* Washington, DC: Author. Available at http://airnow.gov/index.cfm?action=aqibasics.aqi. Accessed January 9, 2016.

mass transit systems, and further development of hybrid, electric, and solar-powered motor vehicles will all help to reduce air pollution.

Coal-fired power plants provide 37% of the nation's electric power, but also produce significant pollution. Three-quarters of these plants have exceeded their 30-year lifespan, and 17% have operated more than 50 years. Many of these plants lack essential modern pollution controls and discharge excess sulfur, mercury, and other harmful chemicals into the air and waterways. The toxic soot and ash constitute hazards to both human health and the environment. These plants are the nation's leading source of heat-trapping carbon dioxide (CO_2). As of December 2013, 150 coal-fired generating units were scheduled for retirement; but there are 329 additional coal-fired electric power plants that are "ripe for retirement."[7] Replacing these units with cleaner and more efficient technology could reduce air pollution and reduce CO_2 emissions from 9.8% to 16.4%.[8]

Although our primary focus has been on the health benefits of air quality regulation, some mention should be made of the role of air pollution on climate change. In this regard, it should be noted that reducing the level of **greenhouse gases**, such as CO_2, chlorofluorocarbons, ozone, methane, water vapor, and nitrous oxide, will reduce heat retention in the atmosphere and slow global climate change.

Indoor Air Pollutants

Sources of indoor air pollution include building and insulation materials, biogenic pollutants, combustion by-products, home furnishings and cleaning agents, radon gas, and tobacco smoke. These pollutants can arise from a number of sources (see **Figure 14.4**). **Asbestos** is a naturally occurring mineral fiber that was commonly used as insulation and fireproofing material. It was often used in older buildings to insulate pipes, walls, and ceilings; as a component of floor and ceiling tiles; and was sprayed in structures for fireproofing. It is harmless if intact and left alone, but, when disturbed, inhaled airborne fibers can cause serious health problems. **Biogenic pollutants** are airborne materials of biological origin such as living and nonliving fungi and their toxins, bacteria, viruses, molds, pollens, insect parts, and animal dander. They normally enter the human body by being inhaled. These contaminants can trigger allergic reactions, including asthma; cause infectious illnesses, such as influenza and measles; or release disease-producing toxins. Symptoms of health problems include sneezing, watery eyes, coughing, and shortness of breath, dizziness,

Greenhouse gases atmospheric gases, principally carbon dioxide, chlorofluorocarbons, ozone, methane, water vapor, and nitrous oxide, that are transparent to visible light but absorb infrared radiation

Asbestos a naturally occurring mineral fiber identified as a Class A carcinogen by the EPA

Biogenic pollutants airborne biological organisms or their particles or gases or other toxic materials that can produce illness

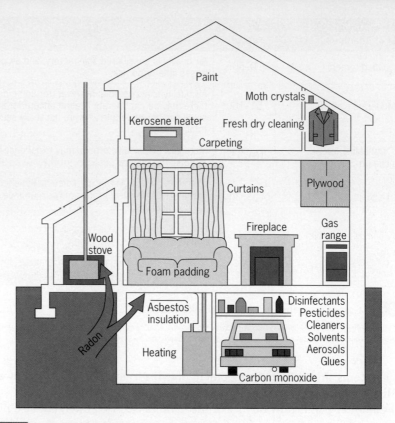

FIGURE 14.4   Air pollution sources in the home.

Data from: U.S. Environmental Protection Agency (1988). *The Inside Story: A Guide to Indoor Air Quality.* Washington, DC.

lethargy, fever, and even digestive problems. Children, elderly people, and people with breathing problems, allergies, or lung diseases are particularly susceptible to airborne biogenic pollutants. People can minimize exposure to these pollutants by controlling the relative humidity level in a home or office; a relative humidity of 30% to 50% is generally recommended for homes. To reduce airborne biogenic pollutants in their homes, people should remove standing water, and any wet or water-damaged materials from around the home, and, if they suspect a problem, have the home inspected by someone knowledgeable about indoor air pollution problems.

Combustion by-products include gases (e.g., CO, NO_2, and SO_2) and particulates (e.g., ash and soot). The major sources of these items are fireplaces, wood stoves, kerosene heaters, candles, incense, secondhand tobacco smoke, and improperly maintained gas stoves and furnaces. Prolonged exposure to these substances can cause serious illness and possibly death.

Volatile organic compounds (VOCs) are compounds that exist as vapors over the normal range of air pressures and temperatures. The health effects of these chemicals vary with their concentration and one's length of exposure. Acute symptoms include irritation of the eyes and respiratory tract, headaches, dizziness, and memory impairment. Some of these chemicals are known or suspected carcinogens. In any one building, one might find hundreds of different VOCs. Sources of VOCs include construction materials (e.g., insulation and paint), structural components (e.g., vinyl tile and sheet rock), furnishings (e.g., drapes and upholstery fabric), cleansers and solvents (e.g., liquid detergent and furniture polish), personal care products (e.g., deodorant and eyeliner pencils), insecticides/pesticides, electrical equipment (e.g., computers), and combustion of wood and kerosene.[9] **Formaldehyde**, a pungent water-soluble gas, is one of the most ubiquitous VOCs. It is a widely used chemical that can be found in hundreds of products. Exposure occurs when it evaporates from wood products such as plywood and particle board, in which it is a component of the glue that binds these products together. Formaldehyde can also be found in products such as grocery bags, wallpaper, carpet, insulation, wall paneling, and

Combustion by-products gases and particulates generated by burning

Volatile organic compound (VOC) compound that exists as vapor over the normal range of air pressures and temperatures

Formaldehyde (CH_2O) a water-soluble gas used in aqueous solutions in hundreds of consumer products

wallboard.[9] Exposure to formaldehyde can cause watery eyes, burning in the eyes and throat, and difficulty in breathing. It can precipitate asthma attacks in susceptible people. Formaldehyde may also be a **carcinogen**. So, how can people protect their families and themselves? When building or renovating a residence, use exterior-grade products that emit less formaldehyde. Increase ventilation in the home, use a dehumidifier and air conditioning to control humidity, and keep temperature at moderate levels in the home to reduce formaldehyde emissions.

Radon is the number one cause of lung cancer among nonsmokers and the second leading cause of lung cancer overall. This radioactive gas, which cannot be seen, smelled, or tasted, is responsible for about 21,000 lung cancer deaths every year.[10,11] It is a naturally occurring gas that seeps into a home from surrounding soil, rocks, and water and through openings such as cracks, drains, and sump pumps. However, exposure to radon is preventable, and homeowners can do something about it. Every home and office building should be tested for radon, and homeowners can administer this inexpensive and easy test. More homes with operating radon mitigation systems is one of the *Healthy People 2020* objectives (see **Box 14.1**).

Mold is another indoor air pollutant, which can be associated with allergic reactions and respiratory difficulties, such as asthma. While eliminating mold in the indoor environment removing damp or wet furnishing or building materials, preventing condensation, and maintaining indoor humidity between 30% to 60% can reduce mold growth significantly. Venting damp air out of the home, using air conditioners, dehumidifiers, and bathroom exhaust fans are ideal ways to control moisture in homes.[12]

Environmental tobacco smoke (ETS), also known as **secondhand smoke**, includes both **mainstream smoke** (the smoke inhaled and exhaled by the smoker) and **sidestream tobacco smoke** (the smoke that comes off the end of a burning tobacco product). The involuntary inhalation of ETS by nonsmokers is referred to as **passive smoking**. Hundreds of toxic agents and more than 40 carcinogens are in secondhand smoke. A few of these harmful agents are CO, NO_2, CO_2, hydrogen cyanide, formaldehyde, nicotine, and suspended particles.[13]

Approximately 18% (42 million) of adult Americans 12 years of age or older were active cigarette smokers in 2014.[13] As a result, many nonsmokers are exposed to environmental tobacco smoke. ETS is classified as a known human (group A) carcinogen and causes approximately 3,000 lung cancer deaths annually in U.S. nonsmokers.[13]

In 2014, the U.S. Public Health Service released *The Health Consequences of Smoking — 50 Years of Progress: A Report of the Surgeon General*. This reports discusses the progress made, efforts that have resulted in the reduction of tobacco use, and evidence of the continued burden tobacco use imposes on the U.S. It is expected that 5.6 million minors that are alive in 2014 will

Carcinogen agent, usually chemical, which causes cancer

Radon a naturally occurring colorless, tasteless, odorless, radioactive gas formed during the radioactive decay of uranium-238

Mold fungi that spread and reproduce by making spores; grow best in warm, damp, and humid conditions; and can cause respiratory difficulties for sensitive people

Environmental tobacco smoke (ETS), also known as **secondhand smoke**, tobacco smoke in the environment that is a mixture of mainstream and sidestream smoke that can be inhaled by nearby or transient nonsmokers

Mainstream smoke tobacco smoke inhaled and exhaled by the smoker

Sidestream smoke tobacco smoke that comes off the end of burning tobacco products

Passive smoking the inhalation of ETS by nonsmokers

BOX 14.1   *Healthy People 2020*: Objectives

Objective EH-14: Increase the number of homes with an operating radon mitigation system for persons in homes at risk for radon exposure.

Target-setting method: Consistency with national programs/regulations/policies/laws.

Data sources: Annual report to EPA by radon vent fan manufacturers, EPA, Indoor Environments Division.

Target and baseline:

Objective	2007 Baseline	2020 Target
EH-14 Increase the number of homes at risk (radon level of 4 picocuries per liter of air (pCi/L or more) with an operating radon mitigation system.	788,000 of 7.7 million homes (10.2%)	3.1 million of 9.2 million homes (30%)

For Further Thought

Have you tested your house for radon? What was the reading? What is the potential radon level in your area? Go to the EPA map of radon zones and search for the map of your state, where you can identify the potential by county.

Data from: U.S. Department of Health and Human Services, Office of Disease Prevention and Health Promotion (2010). *Healthy People 2020*. Washington, DC: U.S. Government Printing Office. Available at http://www.healthypeople.gov/2020/default.aspx.

Sick building syndrome a situation in which the air quality in a building produces generalized signs and symptoms of ill health in the building's occupants

die prematurely due to smoking.[13] The report discusses the evidence that links ETS and adverse health effects, such as cancer, heart disease, and stroke. Additionally, such exposure has been shown to increase the risk of adverse prenatal consequences and postnatal health conditions in infants. Specifically, this exposure has been associated with intrauterine growth retardation, low birth weight, preterm delivery, orofacial clefts, respiratory tract infections, and behavioral and cognitive abnormalities.[13] Furthermore, young children are especially susceptible to secondhand smoke and are likely to suffer from coughing, wheezing, breathlessness, an increased risk of developing asthma, and disruptive behavioral disorders.[13]

Protecting Indoor Air

Because we spend 50% to 90% of our time indoors,[1,2] we need to take measures to protect the quality of our indoor air. The energy crisis of the 1970s led to a conservation movement that included reducing the ventilation rate in buildings. The accepted rate was reduced from 20 cubic feet per minute to 5 cubic feet per minute as a cost savings and energy savings measure. This reduced ventilation resulted in the creation of "tight buildings," which came to be known as "sick buildings," as reports of illness traced to such buildings increased.[14] **Sick building syndrome** refers to a situation in which the air quality in a building produces nonspecific signs and symptoms of ill health in the building occupants. Electronic controls and more efficient filtration, heating, and cooling systems have enabled the ventilation rate of 20 cubic feet per minute to be reinstated.

Even though indoor air pollution may be more harmful to human health than outdoor air pollution, measures to monitor and correct indoor air pollution have been limited. The U.S. government has not yet established a framework for the development of indoor air policies as it has for outdoor air. It has, however, usually supported voluntary industry standards. For example, there are safety codes for kerosene space heaters, an "action guideline" for radon, and smoking restrictions for commercial airlines and an increasing number of public buildings. There also has been federal guidance on the handling of asbestos in schools, including demolition and disposal, and a prohibition on new uses of asbestos.

In the absence of federal indoor clean air legislation, some states, counties, and municipalities have developed their own. In an attempt to protect workers and citizens from heart disease, cancer, and respiratory illness and to reduce forced inhalation through passive smoking, many U.S. counties and states as well as countries around the world, have banned or are in the process of outlawing smoking in workplaces and public areas, such as restaurants. In some areas, even outdoor smoking has been banned within a certain distance of entrances, exits, and air intakes of public and state-owned buildings. As of September 2015, 28 states and the District of Columbia have met the American Lung Association's "Smokefree Challenge" to pass comprehensive legislation prohibiting smoking in all public places and workplaces. However, only 24 states earned an A grade for smoke-free air laws that protect the public from ETS.[15] The website of the American Lung Association includes a summary of prevention and control efforts in each state.

Some states still have preemptive laws that impede the passage and enforcement of stronger local tobacco control laws. One of the *Healthy People 2010* objectives was to eliminate state laws that preempt stronger local legislation. During the period of 2005 to 2009, preemptive smoking legislation was rescinded by legislation, ballot initiative, or court ruling in 7 more states, leaving 12 states ("the dirty dozen") with preemptive smoking legislation (see **Figure 14.5**).[16]

FIGURE 14.5   Nonsmokers' rights advocates sometimes take their campaign to their statehouse.
© Mike Wintroath/AP Photos.

The Water We Use

Clean, uncontaminated water is essential for life and health. In many regions of the world, such as parts of Asia and Africa, the scarcity of potable water limits development and challenges health. Furthermore, lack of basic sanitation, including the inability to properly treat wastewater, has immediate and dire health consequences. Consumption of polluted water can result in outbreaks of such waterborne diseases as cholera, typhoid fever, dysentery, and other gastrointestinal diseases. Worldwide, such diseases are responsible for 1.5 million deaths every year. Most of those affected are children in developing countries. In 2010, more than one-third of the world's population (2.5 billion people) lived without proper sanitation and 11% of the world's population (783 million people) had no access to clean drinking water.[17]

Here in the U.S., virtually 100% of the population has access to a clean water supply and the **sanitation** rate, the establishment and maintenance of healthy or hygienic conditions in the environment, is among the highest reported rate for any world region. Nonetheless, nearly 100 waterborne disease outbreaks (WBDOs) linked to drinking or recreational use water occur annually. A major source of drinking water contamination is waste produced by humans through their daily activities. Thus, both the prevention of water pollution and the treatment of polluted water are essential community activities.

Sources of Water

We acquire water for our domestic, industrial, and agricultural needs from either surface water or groundwater. Water in streams, rivers, lakes, and reservoirs is called **surface water**. The water that infiltrates into the soil is referred to as subsurface water or **groundwater**. Groundwater that is not absorbed by the roots of vegetation moves slowly downward until it reaches the zone of soil completely saturated with water, referred to as an *aquifer*. **Aquifers** are porous, water-saturated layers of underground bedrock, sand, and gravel that can yield economically significant amounts of water.[1]

The Earth's supply of freshwater available for our use is limited. Only 0.003% of the Earth's water is available for use by humans, and much of this is hard to reach and too costly to be of practical value.[2] Thus, the continual contamination of our groundwater through the improper disposal of human waste, trash, and solid and hazardous waste should be of paramount concern to everyone.

Sources of Water Pollution

Water pollution includes any physical or chemical change in water that can harm living organisms or make it unfit for other uses, such as drinking, domestic use, recreation, fishing, industry, agriculture, or transportation. The sources of water pollution fall into two categories—point sources and nonpoint sources (see **Figure 14.6**).[1] **Point source pollution** refers to a single identifiable source that discharges pollutants into the water, such as a pipe, ditch, or culvert. Examples of such pollutants might include release of pollutants from a factory or sewage treatment plant. Point sources of pollution are relatively easy to identify, control, and treat.

Nonpoint source pollution includes all pollution that occurs through the runoff, seepage, or falling of pollutants into the water. Examples include the runoff of water from cities, highways, and farms resulting from rain events (called stormwater runoff), seepage of leachates from landfills, and acid rain. Nonpoint source pollution is a greater problem than point source pollution is because it is often difficult to track the actual source of pollution and, therefore, to control it. Although many sanitary districts across the U.S. are implementing new plans to capture and treat urban stormwater runoff from their streets, it is not yet a common practice. Because of increased urbanization and the growing proportion of land that is covered by impervious concrete, rainwater cannot infiltrate the land surface and is therefore collected by storm and sewer lines and often dumped into rivers without any treatment.

Sanitation the practice of establishing and maintaining healthy or hygienic conditions in the environment

Surface water precipitation that does not infiltrate the ground or return to the atmosphere by evaporation; the water in streams, rivers, and lakes

Groundwater water located under the surface of the ground

Aquifer porous, water-saturated layers of underground bedrock, sand, and gravel that can yield economically significant amounts of water

Water pollution any physical or chemical change in water that can harm living organisms or make the water unfit for other uses

Point source pollution pollution that can be traced to a single identifiable source

Nonpoint source pollution all pollution that occurs through the runoff, seepage, or falling of pollutants into the water where the source is difficult or impossible to identify

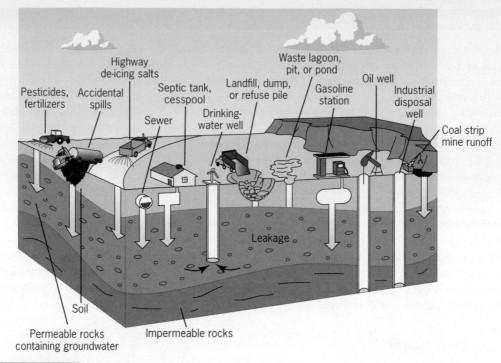

FIGURE 14.6 Sources of groundwater contamination.

Reproduced from: U.S. Environmental Protection Agency.

Types of Water Pollutants

Water pollutants can be classified as biological or nonbiological. Biological pollutants include pathogens or undesirable living organisms; nonbiological pollutants are nonliving hazardous materials, such as chemicals.

Biological Pollutants of Water

Biological pollutants are living organisms or their products that make water unsafe for human consumption. Examples include pathogens such as parasites, bacteria, viruses, and other undesirable living microorganisms. Waterborne viral agents and the diseases they cause include poliomyelitis virus (polio) and hepatitis A virus (hepatitis). Waterborne bacteria and the diseases they cause include *Escherichia coli* (gastroenteritis), *Legionella* spp. (legionellosis), *Salmonella typhi* (typhoid fever), *Shigella* spp. (shigellosis or bacillary dysentery), and *Vibrio cholerae* (cholera). Waterborne parasites include *Entamoeba histolytica* (amebiasis or amebic dysentery), *Giardia lamblia* (giardiasis), and *Cryptosporidium parvum* (cryptosporidiosis; see **Table 14.2**). Each of these diseases can be serious, and two in particular—typhoid fever and cholera—have killed thousands of people in single epidemics.

These pathogens enter the water mainly through human and other animal wastes that were disposed of improperly or without being treated before their disposal. Sources of such contamination include **runoff** from animal farms that contain manure; failed septic systems that leach untreated or only partially treated human fecal waste to groundwater and surface water; combined sewer overflow that discharges a mix of untreated stormwater and human sewage to rivers or streams; and stormwater runoff from our cities, highways, and towns, which carries animal and human fecal waste left on land surfaces. These biological wastes spread viruses, bacteria, and parasites into rivers, lakes, reservoirs, and drinking water supplies, where they can cause human illness. For example, people can become ill by drinking water from a groundwater well contaminated with fecal waste from a septic system or from ingesting water while swimming in a lake or reservoir contaminated by runoff from surrounding cities or farms.

Runoff water that flows over land surfaces (including paved surfaces), typically from precipitation

TABLE 14.2   Leading Causes of Waterborne Disease Outbreaks—United States, 2011–2012

Predominant Cause of Illness	No. of Outbreaks (%)	No. of Cases (%)
Bacteria	**45 (37)**	**352 (16)**
Legionella spp.	30	144
Shigella spp.	4	61
Pseudomonas aeruginosa	2	16
Escherichia coli	8	119
Campylobacter spp.	0	0
Salmonella spp.	0	0
Other	1	12
Parasites	**43 (35)**	**10,016 (46)**
Cryptosporidium spp.	37	890
Giardia intestinalis	5	83
Cyclospora cayetanensis	0	0
Avian schistosomes	1	43
Cryptosporidium/Giardia spp.	0	0
Viruses	**7 (6)**	**345 (16)**
Norovirus	6	313
Hepatitis A virus	0	0
Chemicals/Toxins	**5 (4)**	**91 (4)**
Multiple	**3 (2)**	**91 (4)**
Suspected/Unidentified	**19 (16)**	**188 (8)**
Total	**122 (100)**	**2,219 (100)**

Data from: Centers for Disease Control and Prevention (2015). "Surveillance for Waterborne Disease and Outbreaks and Other Health Events Associated with Recreational Water Use—United States, 2011–2012." *Morbidity and Mortality Weekly Report*, 64(24): 668–672; and "2011–2012 Drinking Water-Associated Outbreak Surveillance Report: Supplemental Tables." *Morbidity and Mortality Weekly Report*, 64(31): 842–848.

Nonbiological Pollutants of Water

Nonbiological pollutants include heat; inorganic chemicals such as lead, copper, and arsenic; organic chemicals; and radioactive contaminants. Among the organic chemicals are industrial solvents such as trichloroethylene (TCE); pesticides such as dichlorodiphenyltrichloroethane (DDT); herbicides such at atrazine; and the specialty chemicals, such as the polychlorinated biphenyls (PCBs), and dioxin (TCDD), a by-product of improper incineration of paper products and chlorinated plastics.

Historically, governmental regulation of chemical pollutants has targeted those chemicals discharged by industries and municipal sewage treatment facilities. These pollutants, present in high concentrations and known to be detrimental to human health, are relatively easy to identify. Since 2002, however, two types of pollutants have been detected in our waterways and are raising health concerns. These are **endocrine-disrupting chemicals (EDCs)** and **pharmaceuticals and personal care products (PPCPs)**.

Endocrine disruptors include pesticides, commercial chemicals, and environmental contaminants that can disrupt, imitate, or block the body's normal hormonal activity, causing developmental or reproductive problems. Evidence for this has been found in certain wildlife species. Thus far, the relationship between EDCs and human disease is a complex issue, however, there is evidence of adverse reproductive outcomes, and effects on the thyroid and

Endocrine-disrupting chemical (EDC) a chemical that interferes in some way with the body's endocrine (hormone) system

Pharmaceuticals and personal care products (PPCPs) synthetic chemicals found in everyday consumer health care products and cosmetics

brain.[18] The EPA has developed a two-tier process to screen and evaluate chemicals and has published a list of 109 chemicals for Tier 1 screening.[19] EPA has completed Tier 1 screening for 52 chemicals with 34 indicating no evidence for interaction with the endocrine system and 18 with potential to interact.[20]

PPCPs are synthetic chemicals found in everyday consumer health care products and cosmetics. These products include prescription and over-the-counter drugs; cosmetics, including soaps and shampoos; fragrances; sunscreens; diagnostic agents; biopharmaceuticals; and many others. PPCPs have been detected in water supplies around the world, and their effects on human health are the subject of scientific investigations. How do PPCPs get into our water sources? They are flushed down our toilets and washed down our drains and transported to our wastewater treatment plants, where they are discharged, mostly unchanged, into our rivers and streams. There have been a few studies conducted that have studied the effects of exposure to low-concentrations of PPCPs on humans. Screening methodologies suggest that exposure to the low concentrations measured when compared to a "minimum therapeutic dose" provides a margin of safety for humans.[21] However, such an approach is unlikely to be appropriate for aquatic life and does not account for bioaccumulation through the food chain.

While the EPA and other researchers are working to assess the effects of EDCs and PPCPs, there are no governmental regulations or guidance for the disposal of pharmaceuticals meant for personal use. Because it is important to take some personal action to reduce their presence in our environment, we should dispose of unused or unwanted medication in an environmentally sound manner. Disposal into the domestic sewage system is the least desirable option. Contact the local pharmacy, hospital, or law enforcement for disposal locations and times for expired or unwanted medicines. If this option in not available, disposal in household trash is a better than disposal in the sewage system.[22]

A **waterborne disease outbreak (WBDO)** is a water exposure in which at least two persons have been epidemiologically linked to recreational or drinking water by location, time, and illness. In the case of a recreational exposure, two or more persons must experience a similar illness after ingestion of drinking water or after exposure to water used for recreational purposes and epidemiological evidence must implicate water as the probable source of the illness.[23,24] In recent years, while the number of WBDOs associated with drinking water has declined, the number of those associated with recreational exposure has increased (see **Figure 14.7**). The Centers for Disease Control and Prevention (CDC) issues biennial surveillance summaries based on WBDOs reported to the Waterborne Disease and Outbreak Surveillance System. In the most recent reports, 171 WBDOs associated with recreational water were reported from at least 28 states and Puerto Rico. These resulted in 3,114 cases of illness. Seventy-three percent of these outbreaks were traced to exposure to treated water venues (swimming pools, wading pools, spas, etc.). In 60% of the outbreaks, the illnesses were described as acute gastroenteritis illnesses, 19% as skin disorders, and 12% as acute respiratory illnesses. The leading cause of WBDOs associated with recreational water was parasites (67%), followed by bacteria (13%), viruses (7%), and chemicals/toxins, or the cause was unidentified (13%).[23,24]

Sixty-five WBDOs associated with drinking water were reported from at least 14 states and Puerto Rico. Of these, 36 were associated with drinking water, 8 were associated with water not intended for drinking, and 4 were associated with water of unknown intent. The 36 WBDOs associated with water intended for drinking caused illness in at least 1,471 people and resulted in 23 deaths. About 83% of the outbreaks resulted in acute gastrointestinal illness and 12% in acute respiratory illness. In those outbreaks where the etiological agent was determined, the leading cause was bacteria (76%), followed by viruses (13%), parasites (7%), chemicals (2%), mixed (2%), and unidentified (1%).[25,26] The leading cause of WBDOs associated with drinking water is the bacterium *Legionella*.

Waterborne disease outbreaks can usually be traced to a source either within or outside of the jurisdiction of a water utility. During 2009 to 2012, 77% of WBDOs were associated with community water supplies, while 23% were associated with non-community water, bottled water, or individual supplies.[25,26] Outbreaks associated with municipal water systems can

Waterborne disease outbreak (WBDO) a disease in which at least two persons experience a similar illness after the ingestion of drinking water or after exposure to water used for recreational purposes and epidemiological evidence implicates water as the probable source of the illness

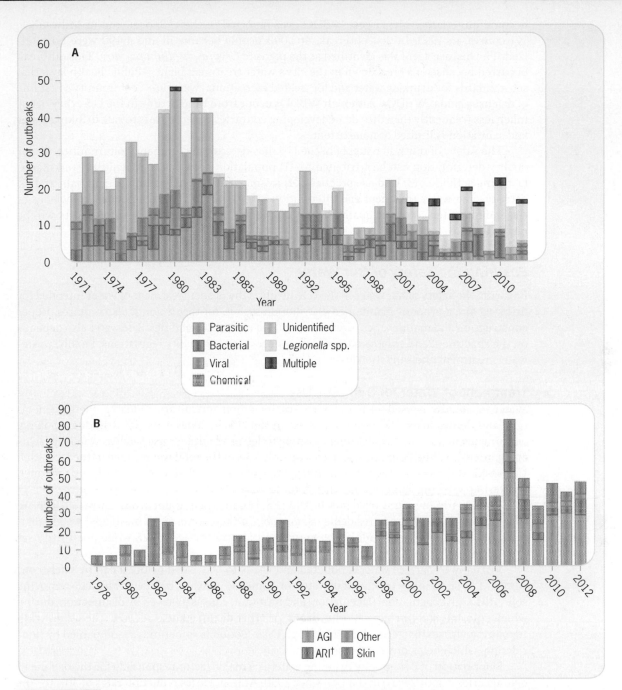

FIGURE 14.7   A. Number of waterborne disease outbreaks associated with drinking water (n = 883)* by year and etiology—Waterborne Disease and Outbreak Surveillance System, United States, 1978–2012. B. Number of waterborne disease outbreaks associated with recreational water (n = 879)*, by predominant illness and year—Waterborne Disease and Outbreak Surveillance System, United States, 1978–2012.

† All outbreaks of legionellosis (i.e., Legionnaires' disease and Pontiac fever) are classified as ARI.

AGI: acute gastrointestinal illness; Skin: illness, condition, or symptom related to skin; ARI: acute respiratory illness; Other: includes keratitis, conjunctivitis, otitis, bronchitis, meningitis, meningoencephalitis, hepatitis, leptospirosis, and combined illnesses.

Data from: Centers for Disease Control and Prevention (2013, September 6). "Surveillance for Waterborne Disease Outbreaks Associated with Drinking Water and Other Non-Recreational Water—United States, 2009–2010." *Morbidity and Mortality Weekly Report*, 62(35): 714–720 (Table 1). Available at http://www.cdc.gov/mmwr/preview/mmwrhtml/mm6235a3.htm?s_cid=mm6235a3_w#tab1; Centers for Disease Control and Prevention (2015 August 14). "Surveillance for Waterborne Disease Outbreaks Associated with Drinking Water—United States, 2011–2012." *Morbidity and Mortality Weekly Report*, 64(31): 842–848 (Table 1). Available at http://www.cdc.gov/mmwr/preview/mmwrhtml/mm6431a2.htm#Tab1; Centers for Disease Control and Prevention (2014, January 10). "Recreational Water-Associated Disease Outbreaks—United States, 2009–2010." *Morbidity and Mortality Weekly Report*, 63(01): 6–10. Available at http://www.cdc.gov/mmwr/preview/mmwrhtml/mm6301a2.htm?s_cid=mm6301a2_w; Centers for Disease Control and Prevention (2015, June 26). "Outbreaks of Illness Associated with Recreational Water—United States, 2011–2012." *Morbidity and Mortality Weekly Report*, 64(24): 668–672. Available at http://www.cdc.gov/mmwr/preview/mmwrhtml/mm6424a4.htm?s_cid=mm6424a4_w.

become quite large. The largest WBDO ever reported in the U.S. occurred in Milwaukee, Wisconsin, in 1993. In that outbreak, 403,000 people became ill and 4,400 were hospitalized. The disease agent was identified as the parasite *Cryptosporidium parvum.* This outbreak occurred because of a breakdown in the city's water treatment plant.[27] Public health laws that set standards for drinking water and for treated recreational water are a community's first line of defense against WBDOs. Although WBDOs occur from time to time in the U.S., they occur much less frequently than they do in developing countries, where access to safe drinking water and sanitation is limited or nonexistent.

The safety of our water supply in the U.S. has deteriorated in many communities. Water quality deterioration can be attributed to: (1) population growth, (2) agricultural and manufacturing activities, (3) land use practices, (4) mismanagement of hazardous materials, and (5) deteriorating water treatment and distribution infrastructure.[28] As the public's knowledge of the endangerment of water quality in the U.S. grows, it is hoped that greater efforts will be made to protect our water.

Ensuring the Safety of Our Water

Ensuring the safety of our water in the U.S. involves the proper treatment of water intended for drinking and a properly maintained distribution system for that water. It also requires proper construction and maintenance of water-associated recreation facilities. Safe water also depends on the enactment and enforcement of well-conceived water quality regulations. Finally, wastewater treatment and sanitation are required.

Treatment of Water for Domestic Use

Water in the U.S. is used for many purposes, including agriculture, industry, energy generation, and domestic use. Domestic water use in the U.S. includes water for drinking, cooking, washing dishes and laundry, bathing, flushing toilets, and outdoor use (such as watering lawns and gardens). While domestic use makes up only 13% of the total water usage in the U.S., each U.S. resident uses an average of 80 to 100 gallons of water each day, just by flushing the toilet, showering, washing laundry, and other domestic uses.[29,30]

Whereas many rural residents in the U.S. obtain their water from untreated private wells (groundwater), urban residents usually obtain their water from municipal water treatment plants. About two-thirds of the municipalities use surface water, while one-third uses groundwater.

Virtually all surface water is polluted and needs to be treated before it can be safely consumed. The steps in the treatment of water for domestic use vary, but usually include removing solids through coagulation, flocculation, and filtration. This is followed by disinfection, during which chlorine, sodium hypochlorite, ozone, or other disinfectant is added to the water to kill remaining viruses, bacteria, algae, and fungi. Disinfection is sometimes accompanied by fluoridation, which helps prevent dental decay.

Fluoridation of community drinking water is a major factor responsible for the decline in dental caries (tooth decay) in the U.S. since 1950. At first, caries reduction rates of 50% to 70% were reported. More recently, the reduction among adolescents has averaged 25%. Because fluoride has appeared in other products, such as toothpaste and mouthwashes, the difference in rates of caries between those who receive fluoridated water and those who do not has declined. By 1992, 144 million people were receiving fluoridated water, at an average cost of 31¢ per person per year. The savings from prevention of dental caries attributable to fluoridation was estimated for the period 1979 to 1989 at $39 billion (1990 dollars), a savings per person that in some communities reached $53 per person per year.[31]

The responsibility of municipal water treatment plants is to provide water that is chemically and bacteriologically safe for human consumption. It is also desirable that the water be aesthetically pleasing in regard to taste, odor, color, and clarity. Above all, the municipal water supply must be reliable. Reliability in regard to both quantity and quality has always been regarded as nonnegotiable in operating a treatment facility.

Wastewater Treatment

Wastewater is the substance that remains after humans have used water for domestic or commercial purposes. Such water, also referred to as liquid waste or sewage, consists of about 99.9% water and 0.1% suspended and dissolved solids. The solids consist of human feces, soap, paper, garbage grindings (food parts), and a variety of other items that are put into wastewater systems from homes, schools, commercial buildings, hotels/motels, hospitals, industrial plants, and other facilities connected to the sanitary sewer system. The primary purpose of **wastewater treatment** is to improve the quality of wastewater to the point that it might be released into a body of water without seriously disrupting the aquatic environment, causing health problems in humans in the form of waterborne disease, or causing nuisance conditions. Most municipalities and many large companies have wastewater treatment plants that incorporate at least primary and secondary treatment processes (see **Figure 14.8**).

FIGURE 14.8   A wastewater treatment facility.
© Robert Malota/Dreamstime.com.

Primary Wastewater Treatment

Primary wastewater treatment occurs in a sedimentation tank, also called a *clarifier*, where wastewater remains in a quiescent condition for about 2 to 4 hours. Here, heavier solid particles settle to the bottom, forming a layer referred to as **sludge**. Sludge is a gooey, semi-solid mixture that includes bacteria, viruses, organic matter, toxic metals, synthetic organic chemicals, and solids.[1,2] Above the sludge remains most of the wastewater, including many bacteria and chemicals. On top of this aqueous layer is a layer of oils and fats, also called scum. The layers of sludge and scum are removed, and the clarified wastewater enters the secondary stage of treatment.

Secondary Wastewater Treatment

During secondary treatment, aerobic bacteria are added and mixed with clarified wastewater to break down the organic waste; this mixture then flows to aeration tanks. Here, oxygen is continuously added to support aerobic decomposition of organic waste into carbon dioxide, water, and minerals. When this biological process is completed (after about 6 to 10 hours), the wastewater is sent to sedimentation tanks, where solids and flocks of bacteria are separated from the treated liquid portion of wastewater in quiescent conditions. After this process, many treatment plants disinfect and discharge the treated wastewater to surface water bodies while other wastewater plants perform tertiary treatment.

Tertiary Wastewater Treatment

Tertiary wastewater treatment involves filtration through sand and carbon filters. During this process, many remaining dissolved pollutants are removed. The treated water is finally disinfected and discharged. The least expensive way of disinfecting wastewater is to chlorinate it. After chlorination is completed, chlorine is removed from the water through a process called dechlorination to prevent poisoning of aquatic life in streams or rivers downstream of the discharge point. Discharges of treated wastewater are regulated by the EPA.

Septic Systems

Those who live in unsewered areas (25% of Americans) dispose of their wastewater using a septic system. A septic system consists of two major components—a septic tank and a buried sand filter or absorption field (see **Figure 14.9**). The **septic tank**, which is a watertight concrete or fiberglass tank, is buried in the ground some distance from the house and is connected to it by a pipe. Sewage leaves the home via the toilets or drains and goes through the pipe to the septic tank. The wastewater is retained in quiescent conditions for 1 to 2 days, during which

Wastewater the aqueous mixture that remains after water has been used or contaminated by humans

Wastewater treatment the process of improving the quality of wastewater (sewage) to the point that it can be released into a body of water without seriously disrupting the aquatic environment, causing health problems in humans, or causing nuisance conditions

Sludge a semiliquid mixture of solid waste that includes bacteria, viruses, organic matter, toxic metals, synthetic organic chemicals, and solid chemicals

Septic tank a watertight concrete or fiberglass tank that holds sewage; one of two main parts of a septic system

Absorption field the element of a septic system in which the liquid portion of waste is distributed

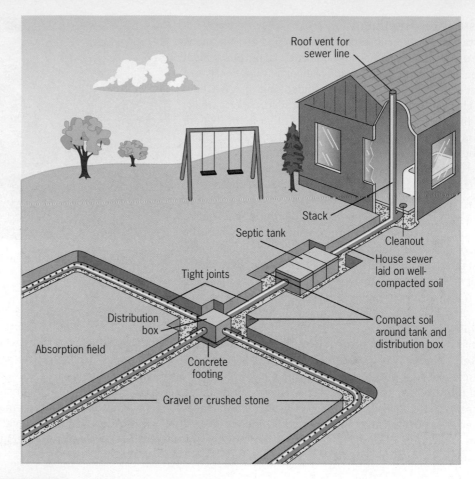

FIGURE 14.9   A septic system consists of a septic tank and an absorption field. This system is commonly used to treat domestic wastewater in suburban and rural areas.

separation of heavier solids and lighter scum from liquid wastewater occurs in the process called sedimentation. The liquid portion of wastewater is then carried by a pipe to an **absorption field**, a system of trenches (dugout channels) where perforated pipes are surrounded by gravel. As wastewater trickles through the gravel, films of aerobic microorganisms develop and feed on this liquid wastewater, causing decomposition of organic waste. This treated wastewater then infiltrates through the soil profile into the groundwater.

FIGURE 14.10   The northern house mosquito (*Culex pipiens*) is the most important vector of St. Louis encephalitis and West Nile virus in the eastern U.S.
Courtesy of United States Geological Survey.

Clearly, proper installation and regular maintenance of the septic system are absolutely crucial for its optimal performance. Septic systems cannot be legally installed in most communities without a permit. Local health departments are responsible for issuing permits, inspecting the systems, and enforcing state and local regulations regarding them. The system must be (1) located in appropriate soil, (2) properly constructed and inspected prior to being buried, and (3) maintained regularly. Septic tanks need to be pumped out every 3 to 5 years to remove sludge and thus prevent overflow, sewage backup to the house, or failure of the absorption field. Failure to properly maintain the system can result in fecal contamination of both land and water sources. Improperly functioning or overflowing septic systems also provide optimal breeding sites for disease-transmitting mosquitoes such as the northern house mosquito, *Culex pipiens*, the vector of West Nile virus (see **Figure 14.10**).

Regulating Water Quality

Surface water and drinking water are regulated by two important laws, the Clean Water Act and the Safe Drinking Water Act. Growing public concern over the pollution of surface water sources, such as rivers, lakes, estuaries, coastal waters, and wetlands, led to enactment of the Federal Water Pollution Control Act Amendments of 1972 and 1977, when this law became commonly known as the **Clean Water Act (CWA)**. The goal of the CWA is to restore and maintain the chemical, physical, and biological integrity of the waters in the U.S. so that they can support "the protection and propagation of fish, shellfish, and wildlife and recreation in and on the water."[32] In other words, the goal is to return the quality of surface waters to swimmable and fishable status. To achieve this goal, the EPA employs various regulatory and nonregulatory programs to reduce direct pollutant discharges into waterways by industrial and wastewater treatment facilities. In addition, the agency attempts to manage polluted runoff by implementing nonregulatory programs.

In the early years of the CWA's implementation, the agency's efforts focused on regulating discharges from traditional point source facilities, such as municipal sewage plants and industrial facilities. The CWA made it unlawful for any person to discharge any pollutant from a point source into navigable waters without a permit. Since the late 1980s, however, the EPA has significantly increased its efforts to address polluted nonpoint source from urban, agricultural, and stormwater runoff, and implemented either voluntary or regulatory programs to curb this problem. In its efforts to reduce water pollution, the EPA considers land use and sources of pollution within the entire **watershed** rather than controlling and regulating only individual pollution sources or contaminants. The watershed approach emphasizes protecting healthy waters and restoring impaired ones to protect not only human but also environmental health.

The quality of drinking water is regulated by the **Safe Drinking Water Act (SDWA)** and its amendments. The SDWA implements many actions to protect drinking water and its sources (rivers, lakes, reservoirs, springs, and groundwater). Under the SDWA, the EPA sets national standards to limit the levels of contaminants in drinking water and oversees the states, localities, and water suppliers who implement those standards.[33] The national standard for each contaminant is set at the level allowed in drinking water to protect public health; this standard is known as the maximum contaminant level (MCL). Currently, 87 MCLs are implemented and enforced. The list of contaminants includes organic and inorganic chemicals, microorganisms, disinfectants and disinfectant by-products, and radionuclides.[34] The SDWA requires the EPA to go through a long and intensive process to identify new contaminants that may require regulation in the future. The EPA must periodically release a list of unregulated contaminants—the Contaminant Candidate List—to prioritize research and data collection that would help determine whether it should regulate a specific contaminant. The most recent list included 104 chemicals and 12 microbiological agents.[34]

Environmentalists and others would like to see the provisions of the SDWA strengthened and more vigorously enforced, but others point to the high administrative and enforcement costs of this Act and the cost burden it places on municipal and privately owned water supply systems as reasons not to strengthen the provisions. Meanwhile, the quality and safety of our drinking water remain the envy of the world (see **Figure 14.11**).

Clean Water Act (CWA) the federal law aimed at ensuring that all rivers are swimmable and fishable and that limits the discharge of pollutants in U.S. waters to zero

Watershed the area of land from which all of the water that is under it or drains from it goes into the same place and drains in one point; for example, the Mississippi River watershed drains and collects all the water from the land extending from east of the Rocky Mountains to the Appalachian Mountains and from the upper Midwest all the way south to the Gulf of Mexico

Safe Drinking Water Act (SDWA) the federal law that regulates the safety of public drinking water

FIGURE 14.11   In the United States, virtually 100% of the population has access to clean, safe drinking water.

© Jaimie Duplass/ShutterStock, Inc.

The Food We Eat

One way in which humans interact with their environment is by ingesting bits of it, which we call *food*. In a worldwide comparison, the U.S. food supply probably ranks as one of the safest. The safety of our food supply is a result of public health efforts and regulatory actions during the past century. In fact, safer and healthier foods in the U.S. have been designated one of the 10 greatest achievements in public health in the twentieth century.[35]

Unfortunately, additional progress must be made before we completely eliminate foodborne disease. "More than 200 known diseases are transmitted through food. In these cases, food is the vehicle; and the agents can be viruses, bacteria, parasites, toxins, metals, and prions."[35] Foodborne diseases cause an estimated 47.8 million cases of illness, 127,839 hospitalizations, and 3,037 deaths per year in the U.S.[36–38] A majority of these cases are never reported to the CDC. The annual economic cost of foodborne illness in the U.S. has been estimated at $78 billion.[39] Healthy food can become contaminated at several points between farm or factory and the consumer. This can result in an outbreak of foodborne disease.

Foodborne Disease Outbreaks

The CDC defines a **foodborne disease outbreak (FBDO)** as the occurrence of two or more cases of a similar illness resulting from the ingestion of a common food.[40,41] During the most recent years for which data are available (2011–2012), 1,632 FBDOs (801 in 2011 and 831 in 2012) were reported, resulting in 29,112 cases of illness, 1,930 hospitalizations, and 68 deaths. Among the 1,081 outbreaks with a single laboratory-confirmed cause, norovirus was the most commonly reported agent, accounting for 31% of the outbreaks, followed by *Salmonella* (14% of outbreaks). The leading causes of foodborne illness, including the number of outbreaks and cases, appear in **Table 14.3**. Common food vehicles most often implicated were poultry (4%), fish (4%), dairy (3%), fruits (2%), and vegetable row crops (2%).[40,41]

Leading factors that contributed to FBDOs were inadequate cooking temperatures or improper holding temperatures for foods (especially for bacterial outbreaks); unsanitary conditions or practices at the point of service, such as failure to wash hands (norovirus outbreaks); or drinking raw (nonpasteurized) milk (bacterial outbreaks).[40,41] State laws permitting the sale of nonpasteurized dairy products vary, but 75% of the FBDOs involving nonpasteurized dairy products were reported in states that permit their sale.[42] Other factors that often contribute to FBDOs are contaminated equipment or obtaining food from an unsafe source (such as shellfish from polluted waters).

To protect the public from foodborne diseases requires the coordinated efforts of federal, state, and local health agencies. At the federal level, the CDC, under its Emerging Infections Program, has established the Foodborne Diseases Active Surveillance Network (FoodNet) to provide better data on foodborne diseases. FoodNet tracks diseases caused by enteric pathogens transmitted through foods. The CDC coordinates these surveillance activities with officials from the U.S. Department of Agriculture's Food Safety and Inspection Service, the U.S. Food and Drug Administration's Center for Food Safety and Applied Nutrition, and respective state epidemiologists. Data were collected from a combined surveillance population of approximately 15% of the U.S. population (48 million people) in 10 states.[43] One set of the *Healthy People 2020* objectives aims to reduce the number of outbreak-associated infections due to foodborne disease agents (see **Box 14.2**).

Growing, Processing, and Distributing Our Food Safely

Despite the surveillance efforts described earlier, much remains to be done to ensure the safety of our food supply. Greater efforts need to be made to make sure our plants and animals are free from harmful biological and chemical agents during growing, harvesting, and processing of food products before they reach retail outlets and food service establishments.

TABLE 14.3   Leading Causes of Reported Foodborne Disease Outbreaks—United States, 2011–2012

Predominant Cause of Illness	N Outbreaks (%)	N Cases (%)
Bacteria	**483 (30)**	**10,780 (37)**
Salmonella sp.	227	6,441
Clostridium perfingens	45	1,729
Escherichia coli, Shiga toxin-producing (STEC)	52	737
Campylobacter	67	767
Bacillus	11	124
Shigella	6	58
Other bacteria	75	924
Chemical	**73 (4)**	**266 (1)**
Scombroid toxin/histamine	29	82
Ciguatoxin	23	82
Mushroom toxins	8	25
Pesticides	0	0
Other chemicals	13	77
Parasites	**9 (1)**	**144 (<1)**
Cyclospora	2	111
Giardia	2	7
Other parasites	5	26
Viruses	**516 (32)**	**11,238 (39)**
Calicivirus (Norovirus)	510	11,144
Hepatitis A	1	7
Other viruses	5	26
Unknown	**532 (33)**	**6,295 (22)**
Multiple causes	**19 (1)**	**389 (1)**
Total	**1,632**	**29,112**

Data from: Centers for Disease Control and Prevention (2014). *Surveillance for Foodborne Disease Outbreaks United States, 2011, Annual Report*. Atlanta, GA: U.S. Department of Health and Human Services. Available at http://www.cdc.gov /foodsafety/pdfs/foodborne-disease outbreaks-annual-report-2011-508c.pdf; and Centers for Disease Control and Prevention (2014). *Surveillance for Foodborne Disease Outbreaks United States, 2012, Annual Report*. Atlanta, GA: U.S. Department of Health and Human Services. Available at http://www.cdc.gov/foodsafety/pdfs/foodborne-disease-outbreaks-annual-report-2012-508c.pdf.

Historically, our food was supplied by independent farmers whose field crops or livestock reached the marketplace relatively free from modern chemicals. Over the past century, farming has increasingly become "big business" with more and more farmland owned by large corporations. Modern agriculture in the U.S. has been characterized as the process of converting petroleum into food. Although this seems like an extreme statement, it contains elements of truth. On the modern industrial farm, significant amounts of fuel are required to run the tractors, combines, and other equipment. Tractors are used to apply petroleum-based chemical fertilizers, herbicides, and insecticides, usually from plastic tanks made from petroleum. It is hard to imagine a modern farm operation without these petroleum-based materials.

BOX 14.2 *Healthy People 2020:* **Objectives**

Objective FS-2: Reduce the number of outbreak-associated infections due to Shiga toxin-producing *E. coli* O157, or *Campylobacter, Listeria,* or *Salmonella* species associated with food commodity groups.

Target-setting method: 10% improvement.

Data sources: National Outbreak Reporting System (NORS), CDC, and states.

Target and baseline:

Objective	2006–2008 Baseline	2020 Target
FS-2.1 Beef	200	180
FS-2.2 Dairy	786	707
FS-2.3 Fruits and nuts	311	280
FS-2.4 Leafy vegetables	205	185
FS-2.5 Poultry	258	232

For Further Thought

Are you aware of any foodborne outbreaks in your area? Outbreaks of *E. coli* O157:H7 have been associated with undercooked beef. How do you make sure that you are protecting yourself and your guests when you cook hamburgers at home? How do you make sure you do not contaminate fresh leafy vegetables with raw meat or poultry?

Data from: U.S. Department of Health and Human Services, Office of Disease Prevention and Health Promotion (2010). *Healthy People 2020.* Washington, DC: U.S. Government Printing Office. Available at http://www.healthypeople.gov/2020/default.aspx.

Two health concerns with the ubiquitous nature of agricultural chemicals, especially pesticides, are (1) the risk of unintentional poisonings where these chemicals are stored and used, and (2) the residues reaching food workers and consumers.

Pesticides

The term **pest** refers to any organism (plant, animal, or microbe) that has an adverse effect on human interests. Some common examples are weeds in the vegetable garden, termites in the house, and mold on the shower curtain. **Pesticides** are natural or synthetic chemicals that have been developed and manufactured for the purpose of killing pests. As of March 2013, 18,810 products containing a total of 1,118 active ingredients held current EPA registrations. These products, produced by 1,723 companies, were being distributed by 12,777 vendors, who had arranged with the producers to sell these products under private labels.[44] Many of these pesticides are used in agriculture, where it is estimated that pests destroy about 37% of the food crop before it reaches the marketplace, an estimated loss of $122 billion to consumers and producers.[1,2] Without the use of agricultural chemicals, farm production would be greatly decreased. Because of this, it seems certain that pesticides will be present in our environment for the foreseeable future.

Although chemical companies market pesticides to control a particular pest, most of them in fact kill a wide range of organisms; that is, they are broad-spectrum pesticides. The pest organism against which the pesticide is applied is referred to as the target pest or **target organism** (see **Table 14.4**). All other organisms in the environment that may also be affected are called **nontarget organisms**. For example, most weed killers will not only kill the weeds but also (nontarget) flowers and ornamental plants. Similarly, it is not uncommon for domestic animals to be poisoned and killed by rodenticides (rat poison).

The two most widely used types of pesticides are *herbicides* (pesticides that kill plants) and *insecticides* (pesticides that kill insects). These account for 46% and 10% of the pesticides applied for agriculture, respectively.[2] It is also from these two types of pesticides that most human pesticide poisonings occur. The two groups at highest risk for pesticide poisoning

Pest any organism—a multi-celled animal or plant, or a microbe—that has an adverse effect on human interests

Pesticide synthetic chemical developed and manufactured for the purpose of killing pests

Target organism (target pest) the organism (or pest) for which a pesticide is applied

Nontarget organisms all other susceptible organisms in the environment, for which a pesticide was not intended

TABLE 14.4 Types of Pesticides	
Type of Agent	**Target Pest to Be Destroyed**
Acaricides/miticides	Ticks/mites
Bactericides	Bacteria
Fungicides	Fungi, molds
Herbicides	Weeds, plants
Insecticides	Insects
Larvicides/grubicides	Insect larvae
Molluscicides	Snails, slugs
Nematocides	Worms
Rodenticides	Rats, mice

are young children and the workers who apply the pesticides. Many of these persons live on farms or are engaged in farm work. Poisonings occur when the pesticides are consumed orally, inhaled, or when they come in contact with the skin. The majority of children poisoned by pesticides consume them orally when the pesticides are left within their reach. Most adult poisonings occur because of careless practice. Examples include eating food without washing hands after handling pesticides, mouth-siphoning to transfer pesticides from one container to another, applying pesticides while one's skin is exposed, or spilling the pesticide on one's body. In agricultural settings, poisonings often occur when agricultural workers fail to follow directions on the pesticide label. For example, workers (who may not be able to read English) may enter sprayed fields too soon after a pesticide application, even a field with posted warning signs, or employers may even tell farm workers to enter the field too soon after a pesticide application. If the workers' children are with them, the children would be at higher risk of becoming poisoned. In addition to occupational exposure of farm workers, consumers may be exposed to low concentrations of pesticides daily through their handling and ingestion of food.

The effects of exposure to pesticides depend on the pesticide type, dose, route, and duration of exposure, and the characteristics of the person exposed. Exposures may be acute (single, high-level exposure) or chronic (repeated exposure over an extended period of time). Some signals of poisoning are headaches, weakness, rashes, fatigue, and dizziness. More serious effects include respiratory problems, convulsions, coma, and death. Chronic effects can include cancer, mutations, and birth defects.

Regulating Food Safety

Because of the poisonous nature of pesticides, their unregulated manufacture and sale and indiscriminant use are unthinkable. Therefore, they are regulated by a combination of federal and state authorities. The EPA regulates the registration and labeling of pesticides. Individual state agencies license those who can buy, sell, or apply pesticides within their state. The safety of our food supply at the national level is further insured by the U.S. Department of Agriculture (USDA), which inspects meat and dairy products, and the U.S. Food and Drug Administration (FDA), charged with ensuring the safety of the remainder of our foods (see **Figure 14.12**). In recent years, several instances have occurred that call into question the quality of food processing and its inspection process. These include scares associated with fresh spinach, tomatoes, and peanut butter products.

The task of enforcing state regulations at the local level falls on **registered environmental health specialists (REHSs)**, also known as **sanitarians**. Hired by local health departments, REHSs inspect restaurants and other food-serving establishments (such as hospitals, nursing homes,

Registered environmental health specialist (REHS) (sanitarian) environmental worker responsible for the inspection of restaurants, retail food outlets, public housing, and other sites to ensure compliance with public health codes

FIGURE 14.12 The U.S. Food and Drug Administration (FDA) is charged with ensuring the safety of our foods, except for meat and dairy products.
Courtesy of U.S. Food and Drug Administration.

churches, and schools), retail food outlets (grocery stores and supermarkets), temporary and seasonal points of food service (such as those at fairs and festivals), and food vending machines to ensure that environmental conditions favorable to the growth and development of pathogens do not exist. When unsafe or unhealthy conditions are found, establishments are cited or, in cases of eminent danger to the public, closed. By enforcing food safety laws, public health officials protect the health of the community by reducing the incidence of FBDOs.

Finally, it is important to recognize that consumers, themselves, can further reduce their risk for foodborne illness by following safe food-handling practices and by avoiding consumption of certain unsafe foods. Examples of foods that are often unsafe include unpasteurized milk and milk products and raw or undercooked oysters, eggs, ground beef, pork, fish, or poultry. Guidelines for preventing foodborne disease transmission at home are simple and straightforward (see **Box 14.3**).

BOX 14.3 Guidelines for Preventing Foodborne Illnesses

To prevent foodborne illness, use the following strategies:

Clean: Wash Hands and Surfaces Often

- Wash your hands with warm water and soap for at least 20 seconds before and after handling food and after using the bathroom, changing diapers, and handling pets.
- Wash your cutting boards, dishes, utensils, and countertops with hot soapy water after preparing each food item and before you go on to the next food.
- Use paper towels to clean up kitchen surfaces. If you use cloth towels, wash them often in the hot cycle of your washing machine.
- Rinse fresh fruits and vegetables under running tap water, including those with skins and rinds that are not eaten.
- Rub firm-skin fruits and vegetables under running tap water or scrub with a clean vegetable brush while rinsing with running tap water.

Separate: Don't Cross-Contaminate!

- Separate raw meat, poultry, seafood, and eggs from other foods in your grocery shopping cart, grocery bags, and in your refrigerator.
- Use one cutting board for fresh produce and a separate one for raw meat, poultry, and seafood.
- Never place cooked food on a plate that previously held raw meat, poultry, seafood, or eggs.

Cook to Proper Temperature

- Use a food thermometer to measure the internal temperature and make sure that the food is cooked to a safe internal temperature (e.g., roasts and steaks to a minimum

of 145°F, poultry to a minimum of 165°F in the innermost part of the thigh and wing and the thickest part of the breast). Cook ground meat to at least 160°F.
- Cook eggs until the yolk and white are firm, not runny. Don't use recipes in which eggs remain raw or only partially cooked.
- Cook fish to 145°F or until the flesh is opaque and separates easily with a fork.
- When cooking in a microwave oven, make sure there are no cold spots in food where bacteria can survive. For best results, cover food, stir, and rotate for even cooking.
- Bring sauces, soups, and gravy to a boil when re-heating. Heat leftovers thoroughly to 165°F.

Chill: Refrigerate Promptly

- Refrigerate foods quickly and as soon as you get them home from the store because cold temperatures slow the growth of harmful bacteria. Keeping a constant refrigerator temperature of 40°F or below is one of the most effective ways to reduce the risk of foodborne illness.
- Never let raw meat, poultry, eggs, cooked food, or cut fresh fruits or vegetables sit at room temperature more than 2 hours before putting them in the refrigerator or freezer.
- Never defrost food at room temperature. Food must be kept at a safe temperature during thawing, which you can achieve by defrosting your food in the refrigerator, in cold water, and in the microwave.
- Always marinate food in the refrigerator.
- Divide large amounts of leftovers into shallow containers for quicker cooling in the refrigerator.
- Use or discard refrigerated food on a regular basis.

Data from: Partnership for Food Safety Education (2015). *The Core Four Practices*. Available at http://www.fightbac.org/food-safety-basics/the-core-four-practices/.

The Place We Live

Environmental hazards occur where we live because of our household and land management practices, including the production and mismanagement of our solid waste. The result can be environmental degradation, increased exposure to unsanitary and hazardous materials, and the amplification and transmission of vectorborne diseases.

Solid and Hazardous Waste

Solid waste is garbage, refuse, sludge, and other discarded solid materials. Most solid waste, 95% to 98%, can be traced to agriculture, mining and gas and oil production, and industry. The remaining 2% to 5%, termed **municipal solid waste (MSW)**, comprises the waste generated by households, businesses, and institutions (e.g., schools) located within municipalities. In 2013, we produced a daily average of 4.40 pounds of MSW per person, up from the 2.6 pounds of waste produced per person in 1960, but down slightly from the 4.74 pounds per person we generated in 2000 (see **Figure 14.13**). There are nine major categories—paper, yard waste, food scraps, rubber and textiles, wood, metals, glass, plastics, and other. Paper makes up the largest percentage (27%), followed by food scraps (14.6%), yard trimmings (13.5%), and plastics (12.8%) (see **Figure 14.14**).[45]

Hazardous waste is solid waste with properties that make it dangerous or potentially harmful to human health or the environment and, therefore, requires special management and disposal. A waste is hazardous if it is ignitable, corrosive, reactive, or toxic, or if it is otherwise designated hazardous by the EPA. Designated hazardous wastes can be found among the by-products of manufacturing and industrial processes (e.g., solvents and cleaning fluids), and the by-products of petroleum refining operations and pesticide manufacturing. Also, certain wastes, including batteries, mercury-containing instruments, and fluorescent light bulbs, fall into the category of universal (hazardous) wastes. The total amount of hazardous waste created each year in the U.S. is difficult to estimate but, according to the EPA's 2013 Toxic Release Inventory, 25.63 billion pounds of production-related waste were managed in 2013.[46] This statistic does not include any wastes that were discarded improperly or illegally.

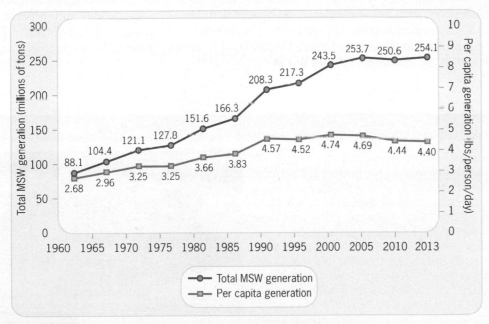

FIGURE 14.13 Municipal solid waste generation rates, 1960–2013.

Data from: U.S. Environmental Protection Agency (2015). *Advancing Sustainable Materials Management 2013 Fact Sheet*. Available at http://www2.epa.gov/sites/production/files/2015-09/documents/2013_advncng_smm_fs.pdf.

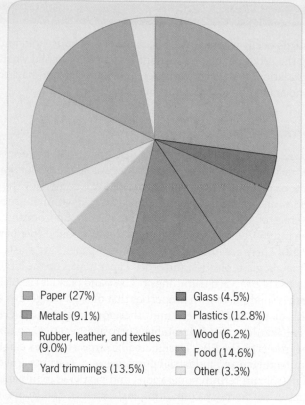

Paper (27%)

Glass (4.5%)

Metals (9.1%)

Plastics (12.8%)

Rubber, leather, and textiles (9.0%)

Wood (6.2%)

Food (14.6%)

Yard trimmings (13.5%)

Other (3.3%)

FIGURE 14.14 Total municipal solid waste generation by material.

Data from: U.S. Environmental Protection Agency (2015). *Advancing Sustainable Materials Management 2013 Fact Sheet.* Available at http://www2.epa.gov/sites/production/files/2015-09/documents/2013_advncng_smm_fs.pdf.

Electronic waste (*e-waste*), not included in the preceding total, often contains hazardous components, such as polyvinylchloride, brominated flame retardants, lead, and mercury. In 2013, it was estimated that 3.14 million tons of electronics, including personal computers, displays, printers, keyboards and mice, TVs, and mobile devices (phones) were discarded (ready for end-of-life management)[47] (see **Box 14.4**).

BOX 14.4 Electronic Waste

As we become more dependent on electronic products to make our lives more convenient, we also generate a vast amount of electronic waste (e-waste) as we dispose of used and obsolete products. In 2009, over 462 million computers, 422 million computer displays, and 262 million hard-copy devices were at end-of-life. TVs and monitors with cathode ray tubes (CRTs) comprised nearly half of the 2.37 short tons of the obsoleted electronics by weight; mobile devices, such as cell phones, was the most common end-of-life product making up more than half the total. Only 25% of these end-of-life products were collected for recycling. Electronic waste makes up about 1% to 2% of total municipal solid waste production. Growth in electronic and electrical equipment waste is driven by sales of new electronics, which have doubled from 1997. Mobile device sales have increased ninefold.

FIGURE B14.1 Electronic waste.

© michael ledray/ShutterStock, Inc.

BOX 14.4 Electronic Waste (Continued)

Why Is e-Waste Hazardous?

Older computer monitors and televisions have CRTs that contain, on average, 4 pounds of lead, as well as other toxic heavy metals, such as chromium, cadmium, mercury, beryllium, nickel, and zinc, and brominated flame retardants. These toxic substances require special handling at the end of their lives. When electronics are not properly disposed of or recycled, these toxic materials can be released into the environment through landfill leachate or incinerator ash—both potential pathways to pollution that can negatively affect the health of nearby communities.

Can I Find Environmentally Friendly Products?

Buying green involves purchasing new equipment that has been designed with environmentally preferable attributes. Look for electronics that:

- Contain fewer toxic constituents.
- Use recycled materials in the new product.
- Are energy efficient (look for the Energy Star label).
- Are designed for easy upgrading or disassembly.
- Use minimal packaging.
- Offer leasing or take-back options.
- Have been recognized by independent certification groups (such as TCO or Blue Angel) as environmentally preferable.

What Should I Do with Used and Obsolete Electronic Products?

If products cannot be upgraded, individual users should check with the local municipal solid waste facility to dispose of computer monitors and televisions properly. Local facilities may recycle these products, thus promoting the safe management of hazardous components and supporting the recovery and reuse of recyclable materials. Another option is recycling used electronic products by donating them for reuse by others. This extends the life of the products, keeps them out of the waste stream for a longer period of time, and prevents unnecessary e-waste pollution. For example, recycling 1 million laptops saves the energy equivalent to the electricity used by more than 3,500 U.S. homes in a year. Also, for every million cell phones recycled, 35 thousand pounds of copper, 772 pounds of silver, 75 pounds of gold, and 33 pounds of palladium can be recovered.

Where Can I Donate Electronic Products?

Donating or recycling consumer electronics can benefit schools, nonprofit organizations, and lower-income families who would otherwise be unable to obtain such equipment.

- Your MSW disposal facility may have information.
- Nonprofit organizations such as:
  - Reuse Development Organization: www.redo.org
  - Students Recycling Used Technology: www.strut.org
  - Goodwill Industries: www.goodwill.org

Where Can I Recycle Electronic Products?

- Information on your nearest electronic recycling location can be found at Electronic Industries Alliance: www.ecyclingcentral.com/.
- International Association of Electronic Recyclers: www.iaer.org.
- Also, manufacturers and retailers offer several options to donate or recycle electronics. To learn about these, visit: www.epa.gov/recycle/electronics-donation-and-recycling.

Source: U.S. Environmental Protection Agency (2015). *Electronics Donation and Recycling.* Available at http://www.epa.gov/recycle/electronics-donation-and-recycling.

Managing Our Solid Waste

Imagine what would happen if our local garbage and other refuse were not removed for just 2 or 3 weeks. The resulting accumulation of solid waste would produce undesirable odors and attract vermin such as rats, flies, and other disease reservoirs and vectors; it would constitute a community-wide environmental health hazard. Although the necessity of the timely removal of municipal solid waste (MSW) from community neighborhoods is evident to all, its heterogeneous makeup precludes its efficient disposal.

FIGURE 14.15   Recycling involves collecting, sorting, and processing materials to manufacture new products that prevent waste, pollution, and use of virgin natural resources.

© auremar/Shutterstock, Inc.

Resource Conservation and Recovery Act of 1976 (RCRA) the federal law that sets forth guidelines for the proper handling and disposal of hazardous wastes

Solid waste management (integrated waste management) the collection, transportation, and disposal of solid waste

Source reduction a waste management approach involving the reduction or elimination of the use of materials that produce an accumulation of solid waste

Recycling the collecting, sorting, and processing of materials that would otherwise be considered waste into raw materials for manufacturing new products, and the subsequent use of those new products

Composting the natural, aerobic biodegradation of organic plant and animal matter to compost

Sanitary landfill waste disposal site on land suited for this purpose and on which waste is spread in thin layers, compacted, and covered with a fresh layer of clay or plastic foam each day

Leachates liquids created when water mixes with wastes and removes soluble constituents from them by percolation

Combustion (incineration) the burning of solid wastes

The **Resource Conservation and Recovery Act of 1976 (RCRA)** was an amendment to the Solid Waste Disposal Act of 1965 intended to comprehensively address the management of nonhazardous and hazardous wastes. **Solid waste management** (integrated waste management) encompasses all approaches to managing the constantly accumulating solid waste, including collection, source reduction, product reuse and recycling, treatment, and disposal. Of these approaches, the most desirable is **source reduction**. Examples of waste source reduction include not buying or using such throwaway products as paper towels and disposable diapers and minimizing packaging associated with groceries and carryout foods. The second best approach to waste management is to reuse or recycle the waste. **Recycling** is the collecting, sorting, and processing of materials that would otherwise be considered waste into raw materials that can be used to manufacture new products (see **Figure 14.15**). Recycling diverts items, such as paper, glass, plastic, and metals, from the waste stream and conserves sanitary landfill space. The U.S. currently recycles about 34% of its MSW.[45] Although progress has been made, the recycling rate in the U.S. is far below the rates of some European countries. Austria, for example, recycles or composts 60% of its household solid waste.[48] **Composting** is a form of recycling that can be done easily at home because it doesn't require special knowledge or equipment. In composting, yard waste and food wastes are recycled through a natural process of aerobic biodegradation during which microorganisms convert organic plant and animal matter into compost that can be used as a mulch or fertilizer. Composting conserves precious landfill space.

Once created, MSW that cannot be reused or recycled must be disposed. The currently acceptable methods of disposal are sanitary landfills or combustion (incineration). Currently, 53.8% of municipal solid waste is placed in **sanitary landfills**, sites issued operating permits that are judged suitable for in-ground disposal of solid waste.[49] At the end of 2012, there were 1,908 permitted landfills.[49] These must be located and constructed so that **leachates**, that is, liquids that drain from wastes to the bottom of a landfill, do not contaminate the underlying groundwater (see **Figure 14.16**). Despite these precautions, according to the EPA, all landfills will eventually leak.

Another concern with landfills is the accumulation of dangerous amounts of methane gas (a greenhouse gas) created by the anaerobic decomposition of refuse. In some cases, explosions have occurred when the methane gas was ignited. Although some communities have systems in place to harness the methane gas and use it as an energy source, only a small minority of landfills operating today collect gases. It has been estimated that landfills are responsible for 18.2% of all methane emissions in the U.S.[50]

Nobody wants to live next to a sanitary landfill, even a properly operating one. For this reason, it is exceedingly difficult to establish new landfills in areas where they are needed most. As existing landfill space becomes more restricted, demand will drive up the cost of MSW disposal. This has led to an increased interest in combustion as an alternative to MSW waste disposal.

Combustion (incineration), or the burning of wastes, is the second major method of refuse disposal. The passage of the Clean Air Act of 1970 severely restricted the rights of individuals and municipalities to burn refuse because most could not comply with the strict emission standards. About 12% of all municipal waste is combusted.[49] Eighty-six of these incinerators are waste-to-energy incinerators or energy recovery plants; that is, they are able to convert some of the heat generated from the incineration process into steam and electricity.[49] Combustion reduces the weight of solid waste by 75% and the volume of solid waste by as much as 90%. The resulting waste, if nontoxic, will take up less sanitary landfill space, and because an incinerator can be located closer to the source of the solid waste, transportation costs may be less than for landfills. But there are disadvantages: (1) startup costs are high because large commercial incinerators are expensive; (2) nitrogen oxides, sulfur dioxide, and other toxic air pollutants are produced; and (3) the ash may be too toxic to place in a sanitary landfill. Regular testing is required to ensure that residual ash is nonhazardous before it is placed in a landfill.

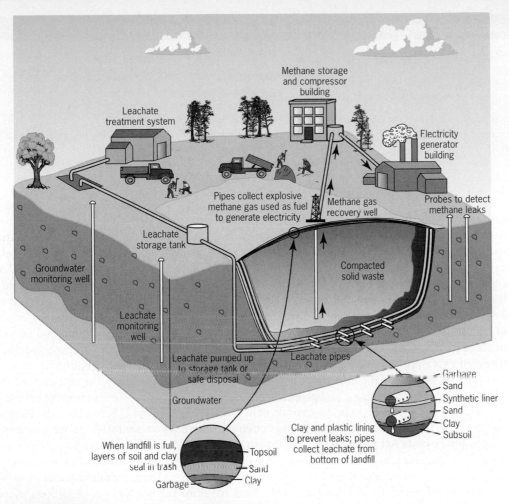

Methane storage
and compressor
building

Leachate
treatment system

Electricity
generator
building

Pipes collect explosive
methane gas used as fuel
to generate electricity

Methane gas
recovery well

Probes to detect
methane leaks

Leachate
storage tank

Compacted
solid waste

Groundwater
monitoring well

Leachate
monitoring
well

Leachate pumped up
to storage tank or
safe disposal

Leachate pipes

Groundwater

Garbage
Sand
Synthetic liner
Sand
Clay
Subsoil

Clay and plastic lining
to prevent leaks; pipes
collect leachate from
bottom of landfill

When landfill is full,
layers of soil and clay
seal in trash

Topsoil

Sand
Clay

Garbage

FIGURE 14.16   A state-of-the-art sanitary landfill.

Data from: Adapted from Miller, G. T. (2008). *Living in the Environment: Principles, Connections, and Solutions*, 16th ed. Pacific Grove, CA: Brooks /Cole; and Solid Waste Authority of Central Ohio. SWACO Sanitary Landfill Poster. Available http://www.swaco.org/smartKids/Presentations.aspx.

Managing Our Hazardous Waste

RCRA established a system for controlling hazardous waste from the time it is generated until its disposal (called cradle-to-grave regulation) and mandated strict controls over the treatment, storage, and disposal of hazardous waste. More than 400 substances are listed on the EPA's hazardous waste list. The EPA list includes neither radioactive wastes, which are controlled by the Nuclear Regulatory Commission, nor biomedical wastes, which are regulated by the individual states. The EPA Office of Solid Waste has the responsibility to oversee the management of hazardous waste, including its treatment, storage, and disposal. More than 34.3 million tons of hazardous waste were generated in U.S. in 2011.[51] There are about 15 methods of hazardous waste management overseen and regulated by the EPA. The most commonly used method is deep well or underground injection, which is used for disposal of about 59% of hazardous waste.[51] Most of these wells are found in the states of Texas and Florida. The remaining 41% of hazardous waste is managed by various methods, such as special landfills, impoundment, recycling, and incineration.

Managing present and future hazardous wastes is one issue; dealing with the inappropriate past disposal of hazardous wastes is another. Leaking underground storage tanks, abandoned mine lands, and abandoned hazardous chemical waste sites all present serious threats to human health and the environment (see **Box 14.5**). An underground storage tank (UST) system includes

BOX 14.5 Brownfields, Superfund Sites, and Underground Storage Tanks in Your Area

Search the EPA website (www.epa.gov/emefdata/em4ef.home) for brownfields, Superfund sites, USTs, and abandoned mine lands and find the following maps:

- EnviroMapper for Superfund
- EnviroMapper for brownfields
- Abandoned mine lands
- Underground storage tanks

Based on the maps you found, answer the following questions:

1. What types of sites and how many have you found in your area of residence?
2. What specific contaminants of concern are at these sites?
3. Have they been cleaned up?
4. Reflect on your findings and evaluate what this means for the health of your community.

the tank, underground connected piping, and any containment system that stores either petroleum or certain hazardous substances. Gasoline leaking from service stations is one of the most common sources of groundwater pollution. Just 1.5 cups of leaking hazardous chemicals can contaminate more than 1 million gallons of groundwater. Because nearly 90 million U.S. residents get their water from a community water system derived at least in part from groundwater, and 13 million more U.S. residents drink from private wells, groundwater pollution is a serious concern.[52] Many municipal and private wells have had to be shut down as a result of contamination. Additionally, fumes and vapors can travel beneath the ground and collect in areas such as basements, utility vaults, and parking garages, where they can pose a serious threat of explosion, fire, asphyxiation, or other adverse health effects. Remediating hazardous substance released into the subsurface is difficult and expensive; therefore, the best prevention of groundwater contamination is appropriate management and maintenance to prevent releases.

The primary participant in the cleanup of hazardous waste in the U.S. has been the federal government. In 1980, Congress passed the **Comprehensive Environmental Response, Compensation, and Liability Act (CERCLA)** in response to the public's demand to clean up leaking dump sites. This law, also known as the *Superfund*, created a tax on the chemical and petrochemical industries to clean up abandoned hazardous waste sites that might endanger human health and the environment. CERCLA established a National Priority List (NPL) of hazardous waste sites and provided funds for remediation. Whenever possible, the responsible parties pay for those cleanups instead of using the Superfund. These sites were placed on the list after an assessment in order of priority based on the threat posed to public health or the environment. Once on the NPL, sites were eligible for Superfund dollars if no private party was identified that could be used for remediation and for the temporary or permanent relocation of residents affected by the contaminated sites. The Superfund does not provide compensation to victims for health-related problems.

Since the inception of this program, more than 47,929 contaminated sites have been placed in the database from which the individual states and the U.S. EPA select the sites for cleanup. Of the 12,595 active, selected sites, 1,706 were listed on the NPL for cleanup. Through the end of 2014, construction of the remedy was complete at 1,164 of the 1,706 sites on the NPL.[53] The Superfund is now more than 35 years old and has provided billions of dollars for the assessment and cleanup of the NPL sites. Unfortunately, thousands of hazardous waste sites remain to be cleaned up. By one estimate, the cost to do this may be as high as $750 billion.[2]

Comprehensive Environmental Response, Compensation, and Liability Act (CERCLA) the federal law (known as the Superfund) created to clean up abandoned hazardous waste sites

Brownfields property where reuse is complicated by the presence of hazardous substances from prior use

Brownfields

Another problem is the more than 450,000 abandoned industrial plants, factories, commercial worksites, junkyards, and gas stations. These so-called **brownfields** are contaminated properties where expansion, redevelopment, or reuse may be complicated by the presence or potential presence of a hazardous substance, pollutant, or contaminant that can pose a threat to human health.[1] Cleaning up and reinvesting in these properties take development pressures off undeveloped open land, increase local tax bases, facilitate job growth, and improve and protect both the environment and human health.

Lead and Other Heavy Metals

Among the more ubiquitous and harmful environmental hazards are heavy metals, such as lead, mercury, cadmium, chromium, and arsenic. They often contaminate well water and are ingested by unsuspecting people. Heavy metals occur naturally throughout the environment and many are also used in industrial processes or products. For example, **lead** is used in batteries, pipe, solder, paint and plastic pigments, and, until 1986, in gasoline. EPA regulates disposal of heavy metals by industry or businesses under RCRA.

Because of its past widespread use, lead can be found in soil, household dust, air, paint, old painted toys and furniture, water pipes made of lead or soldered with lead, foods and liquids stored in lead crystal or lead-based porcelain, or contaminated private wells. In 2013, it was estimated that there were approximately 24 million housing units in the U.S. that still contain dangerous levels of lead-based paint, and that more than 4 million of these dwellings are homes to children.[54] Families living in older homes with children should have their homes tested for lead paint. Most local health departments provide this service.

The EPA has estimated that about 40 million Americans who live in homes built before 1930 (when copper began to replace lead in water pipes) are drinking water containing more than the legally permissible level of lead (15 parts per billion). Those who are at greatest risk of lead poisoning are young children, who may inadvertently ingest lead paint, but adults can be poisoned too. It is estimated that as much as 50% of the lead ingested by young children is absorbed, compared with only 10% in adults. Absorption by the fetus in pregnant women is expected to be equivalent to the blood lead levels (BLLs) in the mother.[55]

The health problems from exposure to lead include anemia, birth defects, bone damage, depression of neurological and psychological functions, kidney damage, learning disabilities, miscarriages, and sterility.[2] Since 1976, BLLs in children greater than 10 µg/dL has decreased from 88% to less than 1% in 2010.[56] Between 1997 and 2009 the percentage of children under 6 years of age with elevated blood lead levels declined from 7.61% to 0.52% of those tested.[57] Unfortunately, disparities remain among racial and ethnic groups. The children with the highest blood lead levels are non-Hispanic African American children.[54] The major source of lead exposure for these children is dust and chips of lead paint in their homes (see **Figure 14.17**). However, increased attention is being given to exposure to high lead levels in household water due to older infrastructure or inadequate water treatment (See **Box 14.6**). Unlike children, the major source of lead intake for adults is occupational exposure through inhalation.

The solution to preventing lead poisoning includes education, regulation, and prudent behavior. Educational efforts to inform people of the dangers of lead in paint have been in effect for a number of years, and for the most part they seem to have been well received, although significant effort is required to reach the *Healthy People 2020* objective to reduce BLLs in all children.[56] Between 2007 and 2012, 87,601 children < 5 years of age had blood lead levels greater than 10 µg/dL.[56] In 2016, CDC estimated that 500,000 children ages 1 to 5 have BLLs greater than the action level of 5 µg/dL.[58]

Controlling Vectorborne Diseases

Standing water, including runoff water from overflowing septic systems or overloaded sewer systems, and improperly handled solid waste are more than unsavory sights. They provide a habitat for, and support the proliferation of, disease vectors. As discussed elsewhere in the text, a

Lead a naturally occurring mineral element found throughout the environment and used in large quantities for industrial products, including batteries, pipes, solder, paints, and pigments

FIGURE 14.17   Lead poisoning from paint dust continues to be a problem in the United States.
© Aurora Photos/Alamy.

BOX 14.6 Lead in Flint, Michigan Drinking Water

Lead piping that was installed in the early twentieth century can pose a health threat due to mismanagement of water supplies by municipal governments that may result in harmful consequences not only in terms of lead exposure to children but to the infrastructure that provides drinking water to a community.

In 2014, the water supply for Flint, Michigan was changed from Lake Huron to a less expensive option; the Flint River. This change would likely not have been noticeable except for the fact that a corrosion inhibitor, which cost $80 to $100 per day to operate, was not added to the Flint River water as part of the required treatment to ensure the water is safe to distribute to the community. This oversight resulted in water that was corrosive to the iron and lead pipes that make up the distribution system. As a result, household water in Flint was discolored, foul-smelling, and distasteful, and contained high levels of lead. Unbelievably, local and state officials reassured the public often that the water was safe to drink.

In 2015, a preliminary study concluded that BLLs in Flint increased approximately 2% for all children, but in one area, where lead levels exceeded 13,000 ppb in some homes, BLLs increased approximately 6.6%. During the same period, children outside Flint showed no significant increase. The water supply no longer comes from the Flint River; however, the damage to the piping will continue to contaminate the water, even properly treated water, until it is replaced. In this case, the lead exposure and damage to infrastructure was entirely preventable.

Data from: Hanna-Attisha, M., J. LaChance, R. C. Sadler, and A.C. Schnepp (2016). "Elevated Blood Lead Levels in Children Associated with the Flint Drinking Water Crisis: A Spatial Analysis of Risk and Public Health Response." *American Journal of Public Health*, 106(2): 283–290. doi: 10.2105/AJPH.2015.303003; and Sanburn, J. (2016, February 1) "The Toxic Tap: How a Disastrous Chain of Events Corroded Flint's Water System—And the Public Trust." *Time*, 14 (online).

vector is a living organism, usually an insect or other arthropod, which transmits microscopic disease agents to susceptible hosts. Examples of vectors and the diseases they transmit include mosquitoes, fleas, lice, and ticks (see **Table 14.5**).

Mosquito larvae require standing water in which to complete their development. The improper handling of wastewater or inadequate drainage of rainwater provides an ideal habitat for mosquitoes and increases the risk for a **vectorborne disease outbreak**. Of particular concern in this regard is the northern house mosquito, *Culex pipiens* (see Figure 14.10). *Culex pipiens* is the most important vector of St. Louis encephalitis (SLE) in the eastern U.S. In California, SLE virus is transmitted by another mosquito species, *Culex tarsalis*, which proliferates in mismanaged irrigation water. SLE is a disease to which the elderly are particularly susceptible. Those at greatest risk live in unscreened houses without air conditioning.

Vector a living organism, usually an insect or other arthropod that can transmit a communicable disease agent to a susceptible host (e.g., a mosquito or tick)

Vectorborne disease outbreak (VBDO) an occurrence of an unexpectedly large number of cases of disease caused by an agent transmitted by insects or other arthropods

TABLE 14.5 Vectorborne Biological Hazards

Hazard	Agent	Vector	Disease
Virus	SLE virus	Mosquito	St. Louis encephalitis
	LaCrosse	Mosquito	LaCrosse encephalitis
	Chikungunya virus	Mosquito	Chikungunya virus
	West Nile virus	Mosquito	West Nile fever, encephalitis, or meningitis
	Zika virus	Mosquito	Zika virus
Rickettsiae	*Rickettsia typhi*	Flea	Murine typhus
	Rickettsia rickettsii	Tick	Rocky Mountain spotted fever
	Ehrlichia chaffeensis	Tick	Ehrlichiosis
Bacteria	*Yersinia pestis*	Flea	Bubonic plague
	Borrelia burgdorferi	Tick	Lyme disease
Protozoa	*Plasmodium* spp.	Mosquito	Malaria

Data from: Heymann, D. L., ed. (2015). *Control of Communicable Diseases Manual*, 20th ed. Washington, DC: American Public Health Association.

Culex pipiens also transmits West Nile virus (WNV), which causes West Nile fever, West Nile encephalitis, and West Nile meningitis. The latter two are severe forms of the disease that affect the nervous system. *Encephalitis* refers to an inflammation of the brain; *meningitis* is an inflammation of the membrane surrounding the brain and spinal cord. WNV first appeared in New York in 1999, where it caused 62 human cases of disease, including 7 deaths.[59] The virus quickly spread westward until it became established throughout the country. The occurrence of West Nile cases varies from year to year. Since 2002, an average number of 3,201 cases and 134 deaths have occurred annually.[60] The lowest incident of cases and deaths occurred in 2000 with 21 and 2 respectively. However, the highest incidences occurred in different years with 9,862 cases in 2003 and with 286 deaths in 2012.[60]

Another species of mosquito that thrives on environmental mismanagement in the north-central and eastern U.S. is the eastern tree-hole mosquito, *Aedes triseriatus*. Whereas the natural habitat for this mosquito is tree holes, it flourishes in water held in discarded automobile and truck tires. It is estimated that there are 2 billion used tires discarded in various places in the U.S. today, and 2 million more discarded tires are added to the environment each year. In the eastern U.S., *A. triseriatus* transmits LaCrosse encephalitis, an arbovirus that produces a serious and sometimes fatal disease in children.

C. pipiens and *A. triseriatus* are only two of several hundred species of mosquitoes that occur in the U.S. Because we have become a global economy, new exotic pest species are constantly being introduced into our country. Two of these are the Asian tiger mosquito, *Aedes albopictus*, first discovered in Texas in 1985,[61] and *Aedes japonicus*, first detected in 1998.[62] Although no human cases of disease have been traced directly to either of these vectors in the U.S., laboratory studies indicate that both of them can transmit pathogenic viruses.

Aedes aegypti and *Aedes albopictus* are commonly involved in the transmission of the Chikungunya virus and Zika virus. Chikungunya infections were initially identified in the U.S. in 2006. Between 2006 and 2013, an average of 28 persons per year were identified as infected.[63] There has been a sharp increase in the incidence of the disease as 7,521 cases were reported from U.S. states and territories in 2014.[63] These statistics may be under-reported as Chikungunya virus is not a nationally notifiable disease.[63] The Zika virus, a nationally notifiable disease, typically results in mild symptoms. However, reports from South America in 2016 potentially linked the virus to incidents of Guillain-Barre syndrome and birth defects in babies born to women that contracted the disease while pregnant.[64]

Federal, state, and local governments all have units whose primary responsibility is the prevention and control of vectorborne diseases. At the federal level, the lead agency is CDC's Division of Vector-Borne Diseases (DVBD), a unit of the National Center for Emerging and Zoonotic Infectious Diseases (NCEZID). The DVBD, located in Ft. Collins, Colorado, conducts and funds research on vectorborne diseases, maintains surveillance of vectorborne diseases, assists states in investigating vectorborne disease outbreaks, and, in some cases, assists other countries with vectorborne problems. Most state departments of health also have offices or labs that maintain vectorborne disease surveillance programs and provide expertise to local health departments, which have the primary task of reducing mosquito populations and preventing disease transmission. Most of us have seen county or district mosquito abatement workers inspecting or treating standing water or driving through our neighborhood with a mosquito sprayer or fogger. Although most of us appreciate these efforts to protect our health and our comfort, it is discouraging to think that despite the millions of dollars spent on mosquito control in communities across the country, many cases of mosquito-borne diseases are reported annually. Proper land, solid waste, and wastewater management, mosquito control efforts, the promotion of personal protection against mosquito bites, and active surveillance for vectorborne diseases are all important defenses against mosquito-borne disease outbreaks.

The number one vectorborne disease in the U.S. is not a mosquito-borne disease, but a tick-borne disease, Lyme disease. In 2014, more than 33,000 confirmed and probable cases of Lyme disease were reported to the CDC (see **Figure 14.18**).[65] Lyme disease is transmitted by the blacklegged tick, *Ixodes scapularis*, a species of tick that flourishes when deer are abundant. During the latter half of the twentieth century, deer populations rapidly increased in the U.S.

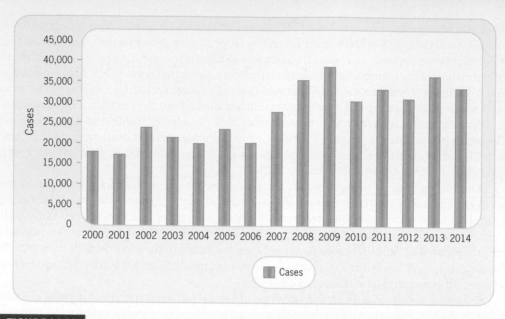

FIGURE 14.18   Number of reported cases of Lyme disease in the United States from 1994 to 2014.

Data from: Centers for Disease Control and Prevention, Division of Vector-Borne Diseases (2015). *Lyme Disease Data and Statistics*. Available at http://www.cdc.gov/lyme/stats/index.html.

through conservation efforts. This resulted in an explosion of populations of the blacklegged tick, sometimes called "the deer tick." The tick transmits the bacterial spirochete *Borrelia burgdorferi*, the cause of Lyme disease. It is important to note that Lyme disease is a bigger problem in some regions of the country. For example, of the 10 states reporting the highest incidences of Lyme disease in 2014, 8 were in the east. Listed in order beginning with the highest incidence the 10 states were: Pennsylvania, Massachusetts, New York, New Jersey, Connecticut, Minnesota, Maine, Maryland, Wisconsin, and Virginia.[65]

Because there is no vaccine for Lyme disease, and community tick control is virtually non-existent, personal protection is the best defense. Health departments often remind citizens to take the following precautions: (1) avoid entering tick-infested areas when possible; these are usually wooded and bushy areas with high grass and a lot of leaf litter; (2) if entering an area possibly infested with ticks, dress appropriately—wear long pants and tuck them into your socks and wear a long-sleeved shirt; (3) apply a tick repellent; (4) examine oneself and family members for ticks after leaving the area; and (5) carefully remove any ticks found with a pair of tweezers. Tick control efforts include using landscaping techniques that discourage ticks—reduce leaf litter and tall grass, and establish a litter-free (and tick-free) border around the perimeter of the yard. Keep the lawn short and, if using acaricides, do so in accordance with instructions on the label.

Improper management of waste—such as occurs at open dumps, ill-managed landfills, and urban slums—fosters the expansion of rat and mouse populations. These rodents are hosts for fleas that transmit murine typhus, a rickettsial disease characterized by headache, fever, and rash. The closing of most of the open dumps has relegated murine typhus to the status of an uncommon disease in the U.S., but improper MSW management could provide an environment conducive to murine typhus transmission.

Natural Hazards

Natural hazard a naturally occurring phenomenon or event that produces or releases energy in amounts that exceed human endurance, causing injury, disease, or death (such as radiation, earthquakes, tsunamis, volcanic eruptions, hurricanes, tornados, and floods)

Natural disaster a natural hazard that results in substantial loss of life or property

Natural hazards are naturally occurring phenomena or events that produce/release energy in amounts that exceed human endurance, causing injury, disease, or death. Examples include naturally occurring radiation, geologic activity (earthquakes and volcanoes), and severe weather-driven events (tornados, hurricanes, and floods). When natural hazards involve human injuries and deaths, they are often termed **natural disasters**.

Radiation

Radiation is the process in which energy is emitted as particles or waves. Heat, sound, and visible light are examples of long-wavelength, low-energy radiation. High-energy (ionizing) radiation is radiation with shorter wavelengths, such as ultraviolet light, X-rays, and gamma rays, or particles, such as alpha or beta particles (see **Box 14.7**). High-energy **ionizing radiation** is released when atoms are split or naturally decay from a less stable to a more stable form. This type of radiation has enough energy to knock electrons out of orbit and break chemical bonds among molecules in living cells and tissues. Mild tissue damage may be able to be repaired, but if the damage is too severe or widespread, it cannot be repaired and is manifested as radiation burns, radiation sickness, or both. Radiation sickness includes nausea, weakness, hair loss, skin burns, diminished organ function, premature aging, cancer, or even death. The amount of radiation and the duration of exposure affect the severity of the injury or illness.

> **Radiation** a process in which energy is emitted as particles or waves
>
> **Ionizing radiation** high-energy radiation that can knock an electron out of orbit, creating an ion, and can thereby damage living cells and tissues (UV radiation, gamma rays, X-rays, alpha and beta particles)
>
> **Ultraviolet (UV) radiation** radiant energy with wavelengths of 0 to 400 nanometers

Radiation from Natural Sources

Radiation arises from both natural and human-made sources. Sources of natural radiation are extraterrestrial (outer space and the Sun) or terrestrial (radioactive minerals emanating from the Earth). The radiation we receive from the Sun is considerable. Sunshine comprises energy in many wavelengths, including visible light, heat, and **ultraviolet (UV) radiation**. UV radiation includes energy at wavelengths between 0 and 400 nanometers (nm). UV radiation between 290 and 330 nanometers, called UV-B, causes most of the harm to humans.

Much of the UV radiation emanating from the Sun is screened out by the layer of ozone in the stratosphere. In recent years, with the erosion of the ozone layer, the quantity of UV-B radiation reaching the Earth has been increasing.[1,2] Each year, more than one million new cases of skin cancer are reported in the U.S., and, in recent years, the incidence rate of skin cancer has been increasing about 3% per year.[66] The vast majority of these cases are the highly curable basal cell and squamous cell carcinomas, the most common forms of cancer. The most serious and least common skin cancer is malignant melanoma. The American Cancer Society estimated

---

BOX 14.7   About the Electromagnetic Spectrum

Electromagnetic radiation emitted from different sources has characteristic wavelengths. Taken together, these types of radiation make up the electromagnetic spectrum, which ranges from the very-long-wavelength radiation of power lines (thousands of meters) to the very-short-wavelength cosmic radiation that originates in outer space (less than one-trillionth of a meter).

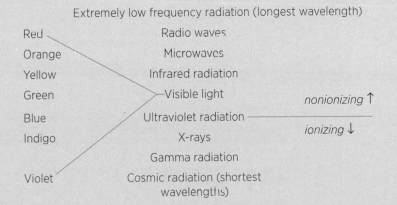

In the middle of the electromagnetic spectrum, infrared and ultraviolet radiation bracket the familiar spectrum of visible light. Sunlight is made up of infrared radiation, visible light, and ultraviolet radiation. Infrared radiation is simply heat; any object that is warmer than its surroundings gives off infrared radiation.

that more than 73,000 new cases of melanoma would be diagnosed and about 9,940 patients would die from this disease in 2015. This type of skin cancer is the most dangerous because of its ability to grow and spread quickly. However, like the other skin cancers, melanoma is curable if discovered and treated early.[66]

Skin cancer morbidity and mortality rates can be lowered by reducing one's exposure to UV radiation and by early detection and treatment. One can reduce the risk of exposure by staying out of the Sun or by covering the skin with clothing or commercial sunscreens. Sunscreens work by absorbing, reflecting, or scattering ultraviolet light, thereby reducing the amount that reaches the skin. To reduce exposure to UV radiation, individuals can also find out the UV index for a specific day through the weather forecast on the Internet, or visit EPA's Sun Safety website.[67] The UV index is reported on a scale of 1 (low danger) to 11 (extreme danger; see **Figure 14.19**). The EPA also issues UV Alerts, which are warnings when the level of solar radiation in a particular area is predicted to be unusually high. Obtaining information about the strength of UV radiation is the most important step people can take in protecting their health.

The second way people can protect their health is through early diagnosis and prompt treatment. The key to discovering whether treatment is warranted is to practice monthly skin self-examination. Basal and squamous cell carcinomas often appear as a pale, waxlike, peely

11+	A UV Index reading of 11 or more means extreme risk of harm from unprotected sun exposure. Take all precautions because unprotected skin and eyes can burn in minutes. • Try to avoid sun exposure between 10 a.m. and 4 p.m. • If outdoors, seek shade and wear protective clothing, a wide-brimmed hat, and UV-blocking sunglasses. • Generously apply broad spectrum SPF 30+ sunscreen every 2 hours, even on cloudy days, and after swimming or sweating. • Watch out for bright surfaces, like sand, water and snow, which reflect UV and increase exposure.
10 **9** **8**	A UV Index reading of 8 to 10 means very high risk of harm from unprotected sun exposure. Take extra precautions because unprotected skin and eyes will be damaged and can burn quickly. • Minimize sun exposure between 10 a.m. and 4 p.m. • If outdoors, seek shade and wear protective clothing, a wide-brimmed hat, and UV-blocking sunglasses. • Generously apply broad spectrum SPF 30+ sunscreen every 2 hours, even on cloudy days, and after swimming or sweating. • Watch out for bright surfaces, like sand, water and snow, which reflect UV and increase exposure.
7 **6**	6 to 7 means high risk of harm from unprotected sun exposure. Protection against skin and eye damage is needed. • Reduce time in the sun between 10 a.m. and 4 p.m. • If outdoors, seek shade and wear protective clothing, a wide-brimmed hat, and UV-blocking sunglasses. • Generously apply broad spectrum SPF 30+ sunscreen every 2 hours, even on cloudy days, and after swimming or sweating. • Watch out for bright surfaces, like sand, water and snow, which reflect UV and increase exposure.
5 **4** **3**	3 to 5 means moderate risk of harm from unprotected sun exposure. • Stay in shade near midday when the sun is strongest. • If outdoors, wear protective clothing, a wide-brimmed hat, and UV-blocking sunglasses. • Generously apply broad spectrum SPF 30+ sunscreen every 2 hours, even on cloudy days, and after swimming or sweating. • Watch out for bright surfaces, like sand, water and snow, which reflect UV and increase exposure.
<2	0 to 2 means low danger from the sun's UV rays for the average person. • Wear sunglasses on bright days. • If you burn easily, cover up and use broad spectrum SPF 30+ sunscreen. • Watch out for bright surfaces, like sand, water and snow, which reflect UV and increase exposure

FIGURE 14.19 UV index scale.

Data from: U.S. Environmental Protection Agency (2015). *UV Index Scale.* Available at http://www.epa.gov/sunsafety/uv-index-scale-1.

nodule or a red, scaly, sharply outlined patch. A physician should check either of these abnormalities or the sudden change in a mole's appearance. Melanomas often appear first as small mole-like growths. The simple ABCD rule from the American Cancer Society outlines warning signs of melanoma.[66]

A is for asymmetry (half of the mole does not match the other half).
B is for border irregularity (the edges are ragged, notched, or blurred).
C is for color (the pigmentation is not uniform).
D is for diameter greater than 6 millimeters (any sudden or progressive change in size should be of concern).

Fortunately, most of us can reduce our exposure to solar radiation through wise behavioral choices. These include avoiding excess direct Sun exposure and tanning beds. Communities can support healthy behavior by passing and enforcing legislation that prohibits youths from tanning facilities.

Natural Environmental Events

Natural environmental events include geologic activity such as volcanic eruptions and earthquakes (and resulting tsunamis) and weather-driven events such as tornados, cyclones, hurricanes, and floods. These events can result in serious physical and psychological health consequences for humans. Examples of recent natural disasters include the geologic activity resulting in the 2004 tsunami that struck Southeast Asia including Thailand and Indonesia, and the earthquakes that stuck Haiti and Chile in 2010; and the weather-driven events such as tornados like the one that struck Joplin, Missouri in 2012 and hurricanes, such as Hurricane Katrina (2005) and Hurricane Sandy (2012; see **Figure 14.20**).

In each of these natural disasters, health concerns included not only the immediate loss of life and destruction of homes and businesses, but also the unavailability of clean water, food, and sanitation. Also, the loss of loved ones left many survivors feeling sad, depressed, and in need of social services.

Longer-term consequences from such events usually continue for days or months after these natural events. For example, homes flooded because of Hurricane Katrina were contaminated with high levels of mold that led to respiratory problems. Similarly, volcanic eruptions that release large quantities of ash into the atmosphere are responsible for the acute respiratory symptoms commonly reported by people during and after ash falls, including nasal irritation and discharge (runny noses), throat irritation and sore throat, coughing, and uncomfortable breathing. People with pre-existing conditions can develop severe bronchitis, shortness of breath, wheezing, and coughing. Flooding from hurricanes or other causes can produce prodigious numbers of mosquitoes, resulting in outbreaks of vector-borne diseases, including encephalitis and malaria.

After a natural disaster, because of the remaining physical, biological, sociological, and psychological conditions, a variety of needs may exist, including clean water, food, shelter, health care, and clothing. Failure of a community, state, or nation to provide for these needs in an efficient and effective manner can exacerbate the extent of human suffering.

Complex Disasters

A **complex disaster** can result when a natural disaster further escalates an ongoing crisis, such as a civil war, or causes a technological disaster. A complex disaster can

FIGURE 14.20   Natural disasters, such as earthquakes, tsunamis, hurricanes, tornadoes, and floods, can result in substantial loss of life and property.

© Anton Oparin/ShutterStock.com.

Complex disaster a natural disaster that further escalates an ongoing crisis or causes a technological disaster resulting in communities being affected by the consequences of a combination of natural and human-made hazards

Carrying capacity the maximum population of a particular species that a given habitat can support over a given period of time

result from several different hazards and include a combination of natural and human-made causes.[68] An example of a complex disaster was the Tohoku earthquake in 2011 causing the tsunami that resulted in the destruction of the Fukushima Daiichi Nuclear Power Plant. The damage to the Fukushima Daiichi facility resulted in widespread radioactive contamination. Hazardous materials, such as radioactive substances, not only cause physical damage and add to the needs resulting from the natural disaster, but psychological, sociological, and economic consequences that are not easily overcome.

Radiation from Human-Made Sources

Sources of human-made radiation are those associated with medical and dental procedures, such as X-rays, nuclear medicine diagnoses, and radiation therapy; consumer products, such as smoke detectors, television and computer screens; and nuclear energy and weaponry. Most would agree that most of radiation used for medical and dental purposes is beneficially justifiable.

However, there is less agreement about the cost–benefit question in the case of nuclear power plants. The advantages and disadvantages of nuclear power are often discussed. The 103 operating nuclear power stations currently generate about 20% of our nation's total electricity and fit comfortably into the nation's electricity grid.[2] They do this while producing very little air pollution. However, these facilities produce large volumes of radioactive waste, pose significant environmental and human health risks should failure occur, and are costly to build, operate, and decommission. The contamination of the environment caused by a release of nuclear materials due to an accident is long lasting because the half-life of uranium is measured in the billions of years and necessitates expensive remediation or abandonment of the contaminated areas.

The health effects that have resulted from the 1986 meltdown of the nuclear facility at Chernobyl, in the Ukraine, are staggering. Hundreds of thousands of people, including many children, were exposed to high levels of radiation. A large increase in the incidence of thyroid cancer has occurred among people who were young children or adolescents at the time of the disaster. The incidence of leukemia has doubled in those who experienced high doses of radiation, and there have been an estimated 4,000 additional cancer deaths in the highest exposed groups. Other concerns are cataracts, cardiovascular disease, mental health effects, and reproductive and hereditary effects.[69] In 2011, an earthquake and tsunami led to a release of radioactive material from the Fukushima Daiichi nuclear power station. Preliminary studies suggest citizens in Fukushima Prefecture have been exposed to 10 to 200 times the normal level of radiation to which other Japanese citizens are exposed.[70] It will take many years to establish the totality of health issues that result from this exposure.

Psychological and Sociological Hazards

Living around other people exposes us to psychological and sociological hazards that can affect our health. Among these are overpopulation and crowding, hate crimes, wars, and acts of terrorism. Many of these hazards can be related directly or indirectly to population growth.

Population Growth

Population growth can be attributed to three factors—birth rate, death rate, and migration. In considering world population growth, migration is not a factor so that when the birth rate and death rate are equal, population growth is zero. When the birth rate exceeds the death rate, the population size increases. Increases in population size and per capita consumption result in an ever-increasing environmental impact. The maximum impact that can be supported by available resources (air, water, shelter, etc.) is referred to as the **carrying capacity** of the environment.[71]

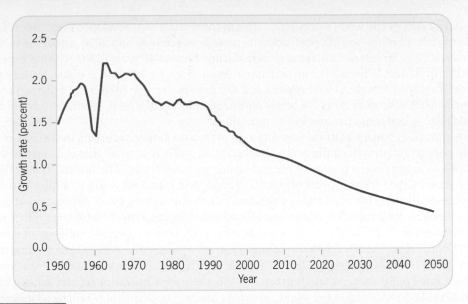

FIGURE 14.21   World population growth rate between 1950 and 2050.

Data from: U.S. Census Bureau (2015). *International Data Base, July 2015 Update*. Available at https://www.census.gov/population/
international/data/idb/worldgrgraph.php.

The world's population now exceeds 7 billion. During the past three decades, the rate of world population growth has begun to decline (see **Figure 14.21**). Although the population growth rate is projected to continue to decline, the world population is forecast to grow to 11 billion by the end of the twenty-first century[72] (see **Figure 14.22**).

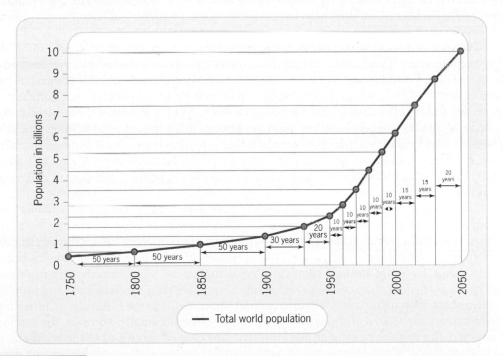

FIGURE 14.22   World population growth in historical perspective between 1800 and 2050, a typical J-shaped curve.

Data from: United Nations, Department of Economic and Social Affairs, Population Division. "The World at Six Billion". Available at http://www
.un.org/esa/population/publications/sixbillion/sixbillion.htm; United Nations, Department of Economic and Social Affairs, Population Division.
"World Population Prospects, the 2015 Revision. Total population (both sexes combined) by major area, region and country, annually for
1950–2100 (thousands)." Available at https://esa.un.org/unpd/wpp/Download/Standard/Population/.

About 80% of the world's population lives in the world's less-developed countries (LDCs), and virtually all of the world's population increase between now and 2050 will occur in these countries.[73] The largest percentage of growth during the next 40 years (2010–2050) is expected to occur in Africa. Whereas the growth rate remains high for LDCs as a whole, fertility rates are decreasing in less-developed regions and the growth rate for MDCs has fallen quite low. In many MDCs, fertility rates are below replacement levels (the level at which children born would just replace those persons lost to mortality).[73]

Although exponential world population growth is no longer occurring in absolute terms, world population growth continues to be substantial, and it is at a rate that is unsustainable if we wish to maintain the quality of life and health we enjoy today. The ramifications of overpopulation include the prospects of climate change, acid rain, vast waste landfills, increasing crime rates, increasing vulnerability to epidemics and pandemics, smog, exhaustion of usable water supplies, contamination of soils and groundwater, degradation of arable land, and growing international tensions, and complex emergencies. Each year we degrade millions of acres of arable land.[74] Also, there will be a dwindling of natural resources for energy, housing, and living space. Since 1950, the urban population has more than tripled. It is estimated that three-fourths of the current population growth is urban. In 1975, there were only 5 megacities (cities of more than 10 million residents) in the world; now there are 28.[75] By 2030, there will be 43 megacities accounting for 9% of the global urban population or more than 400 million persons.[75] Such rapid growth and large density of humans in one area results in pollution and degradation that negatively affects the health of everyone.

Most experts agree that the world population is approaching the maximum sustainable limit. However, no one knows what the ultimate population size will be, what the ultimate carrying capacity of the Earth is, and how many people it can support. There are some encouraging signs. The world population growth rate was over 2% just 30 years ago; it is now just 1.2%.[73] Although there are still great concerns with the population growth rates in parts of the Middle East and Africa, some developing countries have succeeded in slowing growth. For example, the average number of children born to a Mexican woman has plunged from 7 to just 2.5 in the past 30 years.[76]

The so-called humane means of limiting population growth include (1) various methods of conception control such as the oral contraceptive pill, physical or chemical barrier methods, or sterilization (tubal ligation and vasectomy); (2) birth control methods such as intrauterine devices, legalized abortion, and morning-after pills; and (3) social policies such as financial incentives and societal disincentives for having children. Although some of these methods are unacceptable to certain people, all are proactive solutions to the mounting population problem. The alternative is to allow exponential population growth to continue until it declines naturally, by way of famine, epidemic diseases, and perhaps warfare. Nature's way will require a good deal more environmental deterioration, social disintegration, poverty, and human suffering. The choice is still ours.

The world is more of a global community than ever. The terms *global economy* and *global health* illustrate the notion that we are "all in it together," that we are one big community. Yet ethnic, racial, tribal, and religious differences remain. Whereas some celebrate this diversity, others are unable to shed their prejudices, suspicions, and hatred of peoples unlike themselves. **Bias and hate crimes** are crimes that occur "when offenders choose a victim because of some characteristic—for example, race, ethnicity, or religion—and provide evidence that the hate prompted them to commit the crime."[77] In the U.S., race is the leading characteristic associated with bias and hate crimes. Internationally, however, the leading characteristics seem to be religion and ethnicity. One only needs to look to the Middle East to find examples. When these acts are committed not against individuals but against populations or with the intention of influencing government or policy, they fall into the realm of terrorism.[78] Terrorism is a sociological hazard because it affects entire societies, but it is also a psychological hazard because it produces fear, stress, and hysteria and endangers mental health.

Bias or hate crime is a criminal offense against a person or property motivated in whole or in part by an offender's bias against a race, religion, disability, sexual orientation, ethnicity, gender, or gender identity

Preparedness and Response

Whether to a terrorist attack, human-made crisis, or a natural disaster, a community must be prepared to respond to minimize the loss of lives, help the injured, and perhaps prevent further disruption or catastrophe. The **Federal Emergency Management Agency (FEMA)** has the mission to "support our citizens and first responders to ensure that as a nation we work together to build, sustain, and improve our capability to prepare for, protect against, respond to, recover from, and mitigate all hazards."[79] FEMA takes a whole community approach in providing resources for preparing for, responding to, and recovery from all hazards that threaten the stability and sustainability of communities. As an agency within the U.S. Department of Homeland Security, FEMA provides programs, grants, and resources, both written and personnel, to achieve its mission and manages federal response and recovery efforts following any national incident, such as hurricanes or terrorism (see **Figure 14.23**). For example, the response to and recovery of the communities affected by Hurricane Sandy was led or supported by more than 7,500 FEMA deployed personnel, and approximately 10,000 additional deployed federal personnel, and has provided nearly $3.5 billion in assistance to victims, flood insurance payments, and restoration and mitigation efforts.[80,81]

FIGURE 14.23   The Federal Emergency Management Agency (FEMA) helps communities prepare for disasters and manages federal response and recovery efforts following a national incident.

Courtesy of Patsy Lynch/FEMA.

The FEMA website (www.fema.gov) provides links to a vast array of information, reports, and publications that can help individuals and communities prepare for emergencies. FEMA works in partnership with other organizations that are part of the nation's emergency management system, including state and local emergency management agencies, other federal agencies, and numerous nongovernmental organizations, such as the **American Red Cross**.

Natural disasters can occur at any place and at any time. Although a variety of federal and state agencies and other organizations have as all or part of their mission to respond to such disasters, recent experiences should have taught us that local communities, especially those located in high-risk areas, need to prepare too. Only through careful planning and preparation can communities hope to minimize loss of human health and life if a disaster should occur.

Federal Emergency Management Agency (FEMA) the nation's official emergency response agency

American Red Cross a nonprofit, humanitarian organization led by volunteers and guided by its Congressional Charter that provides relief to victims of disasters

Chapter Summary

- Environmental health is the study and management of environmental conditions that affect our health and well-being. Environmental hazards increase our risk of injury, disease, or death.
- Air pollution is contamination of the air by gases, liquids, or solids in amounts that harm humans, other living organisms, or the ecosystem, or that change the climate. Sources of primary air pollutants are stationary or mobile. Secondary air pollutants arise from the interaction of primary air pollutants and sunlight.
- Efforts to regulate air quality include the Clean Air Act of 1963 and its amendments, which resulted in the

establishment of the National Ambient Air Quality Standards. The U.S. Environmental Protection Agency calculates the Air Quality Index to help people relate air quality to their health.

- Indoor air pollutants include asbestos, biogenic materials, combustion by-products, and volatile organic compounds. Radon gas and environmental tobacco smoke pose additional indoor air threats to our health.
- The United States has the safest water in the world. Nonetheless, point source and increasingly nonpoint source pollution threaten the safety of our water supply.

- Waterborne disease outbreaks caused by biological and nonbiological pollutants are reported each year, with an increasing proportion of outbreaks being associated with recreational water use.

- Population growth, chemical manufacturing, and reckless land use practices contribute to the deterioration of our water quality.

- Municipal water treatment plants provide water for domestic use, and wastewater treatment plants remove much of the waste before used water is returned to the environment.

- Water quality is regulated by two important laws: the Clean Water Act and the Safe Drinking Water Act.

- More than 200 known diseases are transmitted through the food we eat. Foodborne disease outbreaks occur each year and are reported to the Centers for Disease Control and Prevention.

- The U.S. Department of Agriculture and the U.S. Food and Drug Administration inspect food-processing plants and enforce health and safety standards. Registered environmental health specialists inspect local restaurants and retail food outlets to enforce food preparation and food-handling laws, thereby protecting consumers.

- The Resource Conservation and Recovery Act (RCRA) governs the management of both municipal solid waste and hazardous solid waste, and the Comprehensive Environmental Response, Compensation, and Liability Act (CERCLA) governs the cleanup of existing hazardous waste sites.

- Of special concern are the many toxic chemicals and heavy metals, such as lead, that can leach into sources of our drinking water.

- Vectorborne diseases such as West Nile fever, St. Louis encephalitis, LaCrosse encephalitis, Lyme disease, murine typhus, and Zika virus represent another group of environmental health concerns. These diseases affect thousands of people each year and are difficult to predict or control.

- Natural hazards include high-energy radiation and natural environmental events such as earthquakes, tsunamis, volcanic eruptions, and weather-driven events such as tornados, hurricanes, and floods. Natural disasters occur when these events involve human injuries and/or deaths.

- Avoiding exposure to ionizing radiation can reduce one's risk for skin cancer and other health problems.

- Complex disasters result when a natural disaster further escalates an ongoing crisis, such as a civil war, or causes a technological disaster.

- Uncontrolled population growth can contribute to psychological and sociological hazards.

- The Federal Emergency Management Agency (FEMA) and the American Red Cross are two agencies that prepare for and respond to natural disasters.

Scenario: Analysis and Response

Please take a moment to reread the scenario at the beginning of this chapter. Then, reflect on the questions that follow.

1. Many people like Juan and Maria live where industrial poultry or livestock operations have become established. What additional precautions could Juan and Maria have taken before moving into their current home to protect their health?

2. Suppose the well water is found to contain high levels of nitrates. Assuming that Juan and Maria cannot move, what steps could they take to improve their chances of a successful pregnancy? What might they do to restore the safety of their well water? What local, state, or federal agencies might be able to help them? Environmental injustice is a term used to describe situations in which undesirable industries or waste disposal sites are preferentially located in minority areas. Is there anything about this situation that might suggest that this is a case of environmental injustice?

3. Are industrial hog farms a problem in the county or state where you live? What about cattle feedlots? What are your state's regulations regarding the establishment of huge factory farms?

Review Questions

1. What are the major sources of air pollutants? What are criteria pollutants? What is the difference between primary and secondary pollutants?

2. What role does the Environmental Protection Agency (EPA) play in protecting the environment?

3. What is the Clean Air Act? What are the National Ambient Air Quality Standards? What is the Air Quality Index?

4. What are some major kinds of indoor air pollutants? How can we reduce our exposure to them? What is radon and why is it dangerous?

5. What is the difference between point source and non-point source pollution? Which is the bigger problem? Why?

6. What types of pollutants threaten our water supply? Give an example of each type.

7. What are waterborne disease outbreaks? Name some waterborne disease agents.

8. What are endocrine disruptors and why are they an environmental concern? What are pharmaceuticals and personal care products and why should we be concerned with them?

9. How do communities ensure the quality of drinking water, and what steps do communities take to reduce the likelihood that their wastewater harms the environment?

10. What are the purposes of the Clean Water Act and the Safe Drinking Water Act?

11. What is a foodborne disease outbreak? What factors contribute to foodborne disease outbreaks? Name some common foodborne disease causative agents.

12. What are some of the local, state, and federal agencies that help protect our food? How do they accomplish this task?

13. What is a pest? What is a pesticide? Explain the difference between target organisms and nontarget organisms and give examples. Explain some safety and health concerns associated with our use of pesticides.

14. What types of refuse make up our municipal solid waste (MSW)? How much MSW do we generate per person per year? What options do communities have for managing MSW?

15. What is hazardous waste? Can you give some examples?

16. What are the purposes of the Resource Conservation and Recovery Act (RCRA) and the Comprehensive Environmental Response, Compensation, and Liability Act (CERCLA)?

17. How do excessive amounts of lead get into our environment? How is lead detrimental to our health? Which segment of our population is at highest risk for lead poisoning?

18. What is a vector? What is a vectorborne disease? Give some examples of each.

19. What is ionizing radiation? Why is it a health hazard? How can individuals lower their health risk?

20. What is a natural disaster and what is a complex disaster? How do disasters affect the health of a community? What planning activities can a community engage in to minimize the potential for and impact of disasters?

21. How would you interpret the relationships among population growth, the environment, and human health?

22. What role does the Federal Emergency Management Agency (FEMA) play in preparing for and responding to catastrophic events?

Activities

1. For 2 weeks, watch a television weather program that mentions the Air Quality Index (AQI). During that 2 week period, chart the AQI in a graph form and identify the major pollutant for each day.

2. During the next week, create a list of at least 10 things you could have done to conserve the water you use.

3. Write a one-page paper describing either your support for or opposition to (a) nuclear power plants or (b) strengthening the Safe Drinking Water Act.

4. In a one-page paper, identify what you believe to be the number one waste or pollution problem faced by the U.S., and then detail your rationale for thinking this way.

5. Call your local health department and find out what kind of efforts have been made to eliminate lead poisoning. Ask about education programs and possible state or local laws. Also, find out if the health department will test for lead in the water and paint. If they will, ask about the procedures they use to do so. Write the results of your findings in a two-page paper.

6. For all of us to be better stewards of our environment, we need to be aware of how our community handles various important environmental issues. Find the answers to the following questions about your community and state:

    a. How does your community dispose of solid waste?

    b. How far do you live from a secured landfill? What is the closest community to it?

    c. Where does your community get its water? If you personally get your water from a well, when was the last time the water was evaluated?

    d. Where is the closest nuclear power plant to your home? What are you supposed to do in case of an accident?

    e. Does your state have legislation to protect communities and individuals from factory farm operations that might pollute aquifers or surface water?

7. Make arrangements to interview a director of environmental health in a local health department. Find answers to the following questions and summarize these answers in a two-page paper.
   a. What are all the tasks this division of the health department carries out?
   b. What is the primary environmental health problem of your community? Why is it a problem? How is it being dealt with?
   c. If they inspect restaurants, which ones have the best sanitation practices?
   d. What is an average day like for a health department sanitarian?

8. Monitor the Internet or reporting service, such as www.ubalert.com, for 2 weeks and record in a table the number, type, and location of disasters reported. How many are due to natural hazards? How many are complex disasters or human made? What are the possible health consequences?

References

1. Wright, R. T., and D. F.Boorse (2014). *Environmental Science: Toward a Sustainable Future*, 12th ed. Upper Saddle River, NJ: Pearson Education, Inc.

2. Chiras, D. D. (2013). *Environmental Science*, 9th ed. Burlington, MA: Jones & Bartlett Learning.

3. U.S. Environmental Protection Agency (2015). *Ground-Level Ozone: Health Effects*. Available at http://www3.epa.gov/ozonepollution/health.html.

4. U.S. Environmental Protection Agency (2015). *Clean Air Act Overview: 1990 Clean Air Act Amendment Summary*. Available at http://www.epa.gov/airprogm/oar/caa/caaa_overview.html.

5. U.S. Environmental Protection Agency (2015). *Air Quality Trends*. Available at http://www3.epa.gov/airtrends/aqtrends.html#comparison.

6. U.S. Environmental Protection Agency (2009). *Air Trends: Basic Information*. Washington, DC: U.S. Government Printing Office. Available at http://www.epa.gov/airtrends/2011/report/highlights.pdf; U.S. Environmental Protection Agency (2009). *AirNow: Local Air Quality Conditions and Forecasts*. Available at http://airnow.gov/.

7. Fleischman, L., R.Cleetus, J.Deyette, S.Clemmer, and S.Frenkel (2013). "Ripe for Retirement: An Economic Analysis of the U.S. Coal Fleet." *The Electricity Journal*, 26(10): 51–63. Available at: http://dx.doi.org/10.1016/j.tej.2013.11.005.

8. Union of Concerned Scientists (2012). *Ripe for Retirement: The Case for Closing America's Costliest Coal Plants* (Executive Summary). Available at http://www.ucsusa.org/assets/documents/clean_energy/Ripe-for-Retirement-Full-Report.pdf.

9. U.S. Environmental Protection Agency (2015). *Indoor Air: In Introduction to Indoor Air Quality*. Available at http://www.epa.gov/indoor-air-quality-iaq/inside-story-guide-indoor-air-quality.

10. Lantz, P. M., D.Mendez, and M. A.Philbert (2013). "Radon, Smoking, and Lung Cancer: The Need to Refocus Radon Control Policy." *American Journal of Public Health*, 103(3): 443–447.

11. U.S. Environmental Protection Agency (2012). *Radon: Health Risks*. Available at http://www.epa.gov/radon/healthrisks.html.

12. U.S. Environmental Protection Agency (2015, October 15). *Mold*. Available at http://www2.epa.gov/mold.

13. U.S. Department of Health and Human Services (2014). *The Health Consequences of Smoking – 50 Years of Progress: A Report of the Surgeon General*. Atlanta, GA: Author. Available at: http://www.surgeongeneral.gov/library/reports/50-years-of-progress/full-report.pdf.

14. Moeller, D. W. (1997). *Environmental Health*. Cambridge, MA: Harvard University Press, 93.

15. American Lung Association (2015). *State of Tobacco Control: 2015*. Available at http://www.stateoftobaccocontrol.org/.

16. Centers for Disease Control and Prevention (2010). "State Preemption of Local Smoke-Free Laws in Government Worksites, Private Worksites, and Restaurants—United States, 2005–2009." *Morbidity and Mortality Weekly Report*, 59(4): 105–108.

17. United Nations Children's Fund (2013). *Millennium Development Goal Target of Clean Drinking Water Met*. Available at: http://www.unicefusa.org/news/releases/millennium-development-goal-clean-drinking-water.html.

18. United Nations, Environment Programme, and the World Health Organization (2013). *State of the Science of Endocrine Disrupting Chemicals 2012: Summary for Decision-Makers*. Geneva: World Health Organization Press. Available at http://apps.who.int/iris/bitstream/10665/78102/1/WHO_HSE_PHE_IHE_2013.1_eng.pdf?ua=1.

19. U.S. Environmental Protection Agency (2013). "Endocrine Disruptor Screening Program; Final Second List of Chemicals and Substances for Tier 1 Screening." *Federal Register*, 78(115): 35922–35928. Available at http://www.gpo.gov/fdsys/pkg/FR-2013-06-14/pdf/2013-14232.pdf.

20. U.S. Environmental Protection Agency (2015). *Endocrine Disruptor Screening Program Tier 1 Assessments*. Available at http://www2.epa.gov/ingredients-used-pesticide-products/endocrine-disruptor-screening-program-tier-1-assessments.

21. World Health Organization (2012). *Pharmaceuticals in Drinking Water*. Geneva: World Health Organization Press. Available at http://apps.who.int/iris/bitstream/10665/44630/1/9789241502085_eng.pdf?ua=1.

22. U.S. Food and Drug Administration (2014). *How to Dispose of Unused Medicines*. Available at http://www.fda.gov/ForConsumers/ConsumerUpdates/ucm101653.htm.

23. Centers for Disease Control and Prevention (2014, January 10). "Recreational Water-Associated Disease Outbreaks—United States, 2009–2010." *Morbidity and Mortality Weekly Report*, 63(01): 6–10. Available at http://www.cdc.gov/mmwr/preview/mmwrhtml/mm6301a2.htm?s_cid=mm6301a2_w.

24. Centers for Disease Control and Prevention (2015, June 26). "Outbreaks of Illness Associated with Recreational Water—United States, 2011–2012." *Morbidity and Mortality Weekly Report*, 64(24): 668–672. Available at http://www.cdc.gov/mmwr/preview/mmwrhtml/mm6424a4.htm?s_cid=mm6424a4_w.

25. Centers for Disease Control and Prevention (2013). "Surveillance for Waterborne Disease Outbreaks Associated with Drinking Water and Other Non-Recreational Water—United States, 2009–2010." *Morbidity and Mortality Weekly Report*, 62(35): 714–720 (Table 1). Available at http://www.cdc.gov/mmwr/preview/mmwrhtml/mm6235a3.htm?s_cid=mm6235a3_w#tab1.

26. Centers for Disease Control and Prevention (2015). "Surveillance for Waterborne Disease Outbreaks Associated with Drinking Water—United States 2011–2012." *Morbidity and Mortality Weekly Report*, 64(31): 842–848 (Table 1). Available at http://www.cdc.gov/mmwr/preview/mmwrhtml/mm6431a2.htm#Tab1.

27. Centers for Disease Control and Prevention (1996). "Surveillance for Waterborne Disease Outbreaks—United States, 1993–1994." *Morbidity and Mortality Weekly Report*, 45(SS-1): 1–33.

28. United Nations, Environmental Programme (2010). *Clearing the Waters: A Focus on Water Quality Solutions*. Nairobi: United Nations at Nairobi. Available at http://www.unep.org/PDF/Clearing_the_Waters.pdf.

29. Barber, N. L. (2014). *Summary of Estimated Water Use in the United States in 2010*. U.S. Geological Survey Fact Sheet 2014-3109. Available at: http://pubs.usgs.gov/fs/2014/3109/pdf/fs2014-3109.pdf.

30. U.S. Geological Survey (2015). *Water Questions & Answers: How Much Water Does the Average Person Use at Home per Day*. Available at http://water.usgs.gov/edu/qa-home-percapita.html.

31. Centers for Disease Control and Prevention (1999). "Achievements in Public Health, 1900–1999: Fluoridation of Drinking Water to Prevent Dental Caries." *Morbidity and Mortality Weekly Report*, 48(41): 933–940.

32. U.S. Senate Committee on Environment and Public Works (2002). *Federal Water Pollution Control Act (33 U.S.C. 1251 ed seq.) [as amended through P.L. 107–303, November 27, 2002]*. Available at http://epw.senate.gov/water.pdf.

33. U.S. Environmental Protection Agency (2015). *Safe Drinking Water Act (SWDA)*. Available at: http://water.epa.gov/lawsregs/rulesregs/sdwa/index.cfm.

34. U.S. Environmental Protection Agency (2012). *Water: Contaminant Candidate List—CCL and Regulatory Determinations Home*. Available at http://water.epa.gov/scitech/drinkingwater/dws/ccl/index.cfm.

35. Centers for Disease Control and Prevention (1999). "Achievements in Public Health, 1900–1999: Safer and Healthier Foods." *Morbidity and Mortality Weekly Report*, 48(4): 905–913.

36. Morris, Jr., J. G. (2012). "How Safe Is Our Food?" *Emerging Infectious Diseases*, 17(1): 126–127.

37. Scallan, E., R. M.Hoekstra, F. J.Angulo, et al. (2012). "Foodborne Illness Acquired in the United States—Major Pathogens." *Emerging Infectious Diseases*, 17(1): 7–15.

38. Scallan, E., P. M.Griffin, F. J.Angulo, R. V.Tauxe, M. A.Widdowson, and R. M.Hoekstra (2012). "Foodborne Illness Acquired in the United States—Unspecified Agents." *Emerging Infectious Diseases*, 17(1): 16–22.

39. Scharff, R. L. (2012). "Economic Burden from Health Losses Due to Foodborne Illness in the United States." *Journal of Food Protection*, 75(1):123–131. doi: 10.4315/0362-028X.JFP-11-058.

40. Centers for Disease Control and Prevention (2014). *Surveillance for Foodborne Disease Outbreaks United States, 2011, Annual Report*. Atlanta, GA: U.S. Department of Health and Human Services. Available at http://www.cdc.gov/foodsafety/pdfs/foodborne-disease-outbreaks-annual-report-2011-508c.pdf.

41. Centers for Disease Control and Prevention (2014). *Surveillance for Foodborne Disease Outbreaks United States, 2012, Annual Report*. Atlanta, Georgia: US Department of Health and Human Services. Available at http://www.cdc.gov/foodsafety/pdfs/foodborne-disease-outbreaks-annual-report-2012-508c.pdf.

42. Langer, A. J., T.Ayers, J.Grass, M.Lynch, F. J.Angulo, and B. E.Mahon (2012). "Nonpasteurized Dairy Products, Disease Outbreaks, and State Laws: United States, 1993–2006." *Emerging Infectious Diseases*, 18(3): 385–391.

43. Henao, O. L., T. F.Jones, D. J.Vugia, and P. S.Griffin. (2015). "Foodborne Diseases Active Surveillance Network – 2 Decades of Achievements, 1996–2015." *Emerging Infectious Diseases*, 21(9): 1529–1536.

44. National Pesticide Information Retrieval Systems (n.d.). *PPIS*. Purdue University. Available at http://ppis.ceris.purdue.edu/.

45. U.S. Environmental Protection Agency (2011). *Advancing Sustainable Materials Management 2013 Fact Sheet*. Available at http://www2.epa.gov/sites/production/files/2015-09/documents/2013_advncng_smm_fs.pdf.

46. U.S. Environmental Protection Agency (2015). *TRI National Analysis 2013*. Available at http://www2.epa.gov/sites/production/files/2015-06/documents/2013-tri-national-analysis-complete_1_0.pdf.

47. U.S. Environmental Protection Agency, Office of Resource Conservation and Recovery (2011). "Electronics Waste Management in the United States through 2009." EPA 530-R-11-002. Available at http://www.epa.gov/epawaste/conserve/materials/ecycling/docs/fullbaselinereport2011.pdf.

48. BBC News (2005, June 25). *Recycling around the World*. Available at http://news.bbc.co.uk/2/hi/europe/4620041.stm.

49. U.S. Environmental Protection Agency, Office of Resource Conservation and Recovery (2014). *Municipal Solid Waste Generation, Recycling, and Disposal in the United States Detailed Tables and Figures for 2012*. Available at http://www3.epa.gov/epawaste/nonhaz/municipal/pubs/2012_msw_dat_tbls.pdf.

50. U.S. Environmental Protection Agency (2015). *Landfill Methane Outreach Program*. Available at http://www3.epa.gov/lmop/basic-info/index.html.

51. U.S. Environmental Protection Agency (2011) *National Analysis: The National Biennial RCRA Hazardous Waste Report (Based on 2011 Data)*. Washington, DC: U.S. Government Printing Office. Available at http://www.epa.gov/epawaste/inforesources/data/br11/national11.pdf.

52. Centers for Disease Control and Prevention (2015). *Ground Water Awareness Week—March 8–14, 2015*. Available at http://www.cdc.gov/Features/GroundWaterAwareness/.

53. U.S. Environmental Protection Agency (2015). *Superfund Remedial Annual Accomplishments*. Available at http://www.epa.gov/superfund/superfund-remedial-annual-accomplishments.

54. Centers for Disease Control and Prevention, National Center for Environmental Health (2013). *Childhood Lead Poisoning*. Available at http://www.cdc.gov/nceh/lead/factsheets/Lead_fact_sheet.pdf.

55. World Health Organization (2010). *Childhood Lead Poisoning*. Geneva: WHO Document Production Services. Available at http://www.who.int/ceh/publications/leadguidance.pdf.

56. Centers for Disease Control and Prevention. "Blood Lead Levels in Children Aged 1–5 Years—United States 1999–2010." *Morbidity and Mortality Weekly Report*. 62(13): 245–248.

57. Centers for Disease Control and Prevention, National Center for Environmental Health (2015). *Number of Children Tested and Confirmed BLLs ≥10 μg/dL by State, Year and BLL Group, Children < 72 Months Old*. Available at http://www.cdc.gov/nceh/lead/data/Website_StateConfirmedByYear_1997_2014_12092015.htm.

58. Centers for Disease Control and Prevention (2016). *Lead*. Available at http://www.cdc.gov/nceh/lead/.

59. Centers for Disease Control and Prevention (1999). "Outbreak of West Nile–Like Viral Encephalitis—New York, 1999." *Morbidity and Mortality Weekly Report*, 48(38): 845–849.

60. Centers for Disease Control and Prevention, Division of Vector-Borne Infectious Diseases (2015). *West Nile Virus Disease Cases and Deaths Reported to CDC by Year and Clinical Presentation, 1999–2014*. Available at http://www.cdc.gov/westnile/resources/pdfs/data/1-wnv-disease-cases-by-year_1999-2014_06042015.pdf.

61. Centers for Disease Control and Prevention, Division of Vector-Borne Infectious Diseases (2005). *Information on Aedes*

albopictus. Available at http://www.cdc.gov/ncidod/dvbid/arbor/albopic_new.htm.

62. Centers for Disease Control and Prevention, Division of Vector-Borne Infectious Diseases (2005). *Information on Aedes japonicus*. Available at http://www.cdc.gov/ncidod/dvbid/arbor/japonicus.htm.

63. Centers for Disease Control and Prevention, Division of Vector-Borne Infectious Diseases (2015). *Chikungunya Virus in the United States*. Available at http://www.cdc.gov/chikungunya/geo/united-states.html.

64. Centers for Disease Control and Prevention (2016). *Zika Virus*. Available at www.cdc.gov/zika/.

65. Center for Disease Control and Prevention, Division of Vector-Borne Diseases (2015). *Lyme Disease Data and Statistics*. Available at http://www.cdc.gov/lyme/stats/index.html.

66. American Cancer Society (2015). *Cancer Facts & Figures 2015*. Atlanta, GA: Author. Available at http://www.cancer.org/acs/groups/content/@editorial/documents/document/acspc-044552.pdf.

67. U.S. Environmental Protection Agency (2015). *UV Index Scale*. Available at http://www.epa.gov/sunsafety/uv-index-scale-1.

68. International Federation of Red Cross and Red Crescent Societies (n.d.). *Complex/Manmade Hazards: Complex Emergencies*. Available at http://www.ifrc.org/en/what-we-do/disaster-management/about-disasters/definition-of-hazard/complex-emergencies/.

69. World Health Organization (2005). *Chernobyl: the True Scale of the Accident*. Available at http://www.who.int/mediacentre/news/releases/2005/pr38/en/index.html.

70. World Health Organization (2012). *Preliminary Dose Estimate from the Nuclear Accident after the 2011 Great East Japan Earthquake and Tsunami*. Geneva, Switzerland: Author. Available at http://apps.who.int/iris/bitstream/10665/44877/1/9789241503662_eng.pdf.

71. Maxwell, N. I. (2014). *Understanding Environmental Health: How We Live in the World*, 2nd ed. Burlington, MA: Jones & Bartlett Learning.

72. United Nations, Department of Economic and Social Affairs, Population Division (2015). *World Population Prospects, the 2015 Revision: Data*. New York: Author. Available at http://esa.un.org/unpd/wpp/DataQuery/.

73. United Nations, Economic and Social Affairs. Population Division (2013). *World Population Prospects: the 2012 Revision, Highlights and Advance Tables*. Working Paper ESA/P/WP.228. Available at http://esa.un.org/unpd/wpp/publications/Files/WPP2012_HIGHLIGHTS.pdf.

74. Hinrichsen, D., and B.Robey (Fall 2000). *Population and the Environment: The Global Challenge* (Population Reports, Series M, no. 15). Baltimore, MD: Johns Hopkins University School of Public Health, Population Information Program.

75. United Nations, Department of Economic and Social Affairs, Population Division (2014). *World Urbanization Prospects: Highlights* (ST/ESA/SER.A/352). New York: Author. Available at http://esa.un.org/unpd/wup/highlights/wup2014-highlights.pdf.

76. Kluger, J. (2000). "The Big Crunch." *Time* (Special Edition), Earth Day 2000: 44–47.

77. Harlow, C. S. (2005). "Hate Crimes Reported by Victims and Police." In *Bureau of Justice Special Report, National Criminal Victimization Survey and Uniform Crime Reporting*. U.S. Department of Justice, Office of Justice Programs, NCH 209911.

78. U.S. Department of Justice, Federal Bureau of Investigation (2015). *Terrorism*. Available at https://www.fbi.gov/about-us/investigate/terrorism/terrorism-definition.

79. Federal Emergency Management Agency (2015). *About the Agency*. Available at http://www.fema.gov/about-agency.

80. Federal Emergency Management Agency (2013). *Hurricane Sandy FEMA After-Action Report*. Available at https://www.fema.gov/media-library-data/20130726-1923-25045-7442/sandy_fema_aar.pdf.

81. Federal Emergency Management Agency (2015). *Sandy Anniversary Infographic*. Available at http://www.fema.gov/media-library-data/1446042082195-179d93a1d9f3ca512de588ebf4091336/Sandy_anniv3_by_the_numbers.pdf.

CHAPTER 15

Injuries as a Community and Public Health Problem

Chapter Outline

Chapter Objectives

After studying this chapter, you will be able to:

1. Describe the importance of injuries as a community and public health problem.

2. Explain why the terms *accidents* and *safety* have been replaced by the currently more acceptable terms *unintentional injuries, injury prevention,* and *injury control* when dealing with such occurrences.

3. Briefly discuss the difference between intentional and unintentional injuries and provide examples of each.

4. List the four elements usually included in the definition of the term *unintentional injury*.

5. Summarize the epidemiology of unintentional injuries, that is, when, where, and to whom do injuries occur.

6. List strategies for the prevention and control of unintentional injuries.

7. Explain how education, regulation, automatic protection, and litigation can reduce the number and seriousness of unintentional injuries.

8. Define the term *intentional injuries* and provide examples of behavior that results in intentional injuries.

9. Describe the significance of intentional injuries as a community and public health problem in the United States.

10. Name the victims and perpetrators of domestic violence. Discuss the types of injuries that result from domestic violence.

11. List some contributing factors to domestic violence and some strategies for reducing it.

12. Define the term *youth gang* and explain how youth gangs finance themselves. Explain why some young people join these gangs.

13. Give examples of ways communities can reduce youth gang activity.

14. Discuss local, state, and national resources available to communities for reducing the number and severity of intentional injuries resulting from violence in the community.

Scenario

Home from college on her fall break, Alyssa had offered to pick up her younger brother from soccer practice. As she drove to the soccer field, she listened to music and took a sip of her diet cola. When her cell phone rang, she placed the cola in the cup holder and turned the music down, then felt for her phone on the passenger's seat. Although she had intended to keep her eyes on the road the entire time, her attention was distracted just long enough that she failed to notice that the car immediately in front of her had stopped for a pedestrian. Alyssa glanced up just in time to realize that she would crash into it. As she belatedly applied the brakes, she felt the impact of the crash and heard the sound of the impact and glass breaking. If she hadn't been wearing her safety belt, her head might have hit the steering wheel. But damage to both cars was substantial, and as the driver got out of the car in front of her, he was rubbing the back of his neck. Alyssa felt ashamed as she called her mother to let her know that she wouldn't be able to pick up her brother after all. When she had more time to think, she realized that the money she was saving for spring break would not even cover the insurance deductible to repair her car.

Introduction

This chapter first defines and then examines the scope, causes, and significance of both unintentional and intentional injuries in community and public health. It also reviews approaches to the prevention and control of injuries and injury deaths.

Definitions

The word **injury** is derived from the Latin word for "not right."[1] Injuries result from "acute exposure to physical agents such as mechanical energy, heat, electricity, chemicals, and ionizing radiation interacting with the body in amounts or at rates that exceed the threshold of human tolerance."[2] In this chapter we discuss both **unintentional injuries**, injuries judged to have occurred without anyone intending that harm be done (such as those that result from car crashes, falls, drowning, and fires), and **intentional injuries**, injuries judged to have been purposely inflicted, either by another or oneself (such as assaults, intentional shootings and stabbings, and suicides).

Cost of Injuries to Society

Injuries are costly to society in terms of both human suffering and economic loss. Injuries are a leading cause of death and disability in the world. Globally, more than 5 million people die from injuries each year, more than 14,000 per day. This exceeds the number of people dying of malaria, tuberculosis, and HIV/AIDS combined.[3]

    Each year in the United States, nearly 200,000 people die from **fatal injuries**, making this the fourth leading cause of death in this country. Specifically, in 2014, there were 199,756 injury deaths,[4] which accounted for 7.6% of all deaths among residents of the United States.[5] Injuries, from all causes—unintentional and intentional—account for 59% of all deaths among people aged 1 to 44 years in the United States.[6] Of all injury deaths, 136,053 (68%) were classified as unintentional injury deaths, 42,773 (21%) as suicides, and 15,809 (8%) as homicides. Of the

Injury physical damage to the body resulting from mechanical, chemical, thermal, or other environmental energy

Unintentional injury an injury that occurs without anyone intending that harm be done

Intentional injury an injury that is purposely inflicted, either by the victim or by another

Fatal injury an injury that results in one or more deaths

remaining deaths, 4,592 (2%) were of undetermined intent and 515 (less than 1%) were the result of legal intervention (see **Figure 15.1**).[4]

Deaths are only a small part of the total cost of injuries. Worldwide, 10.9% of the human burden of disease can be attributed to injuries.[7] In the United States, each year, there are approximately 39.1 million medically consulted injuries or poisonings.[8] Many of these are considered **disabling injuries** (person was disabled beyond the day of the injury), including more than 3 million people who are hospitalized (see **Figure 15.2**). Another 31 million visit emergency departments because of injuries.[8] Injuries place a special burden on our emergency departments because they are the leading cause of such visits, making up 29% of all emergency department visits. Included in this total were visits for injury, poisoning, or adverse effects of medical treatment.[9] In addition to the physical and emotional harm caused by these injuries and poisonings, there are significant associated economic costs. For example, in 2013 these costs were estimated at $671 billion in the United States, including $214 billion for fatal injuries and $457 for nonfatal injuries.[6] Other estimates are higher, for example the National Safety Council puts the estimate at $853 billion, including $432 billion in wage and productivity losses, $173 billion in medical expenses, $143 billion in administrative costs, $70 billion in motor vehicle damage, $23 billion in employer uninsured costs, and $12 billion in fire losses.[9] This amounted to more than $2,600 per person in the United States. The true economic burden of injuries is much greater than this estimate because it does not include value of life lost to premature mortality, loss of patient and caregiver time, and nonmedical expenditures such as insurance costs, property damage, litigation, decreased quality of life, and disability. This figure was estimated to be $4,198.9 billion for 2014.[9]

Injuries are a major contributor to premature deaths (deaths that occur before reaching the age of one's life expectancy) in the United States. Leading causes of years of potential life lost before 75 years of age (YPLL-75) and number of deaths for selected causes of death are shown in **Table 15.1**.[10,11] Unintentional

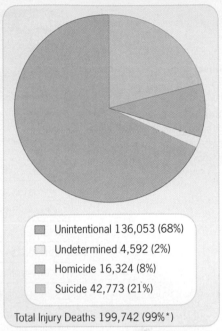

- ▦ Unintentional 136,053 (68%)
- ▢ Undetermined 4,592 (2%)
- ▩ Homicide 16,324 (8%)
- ▦ Suicide 42,773 (21%)

Total Injury Deaths 199,742 (99%*)

*Percentage do not equal 100% because of rounding.

FIGURE 15.1   Injury deaths: United States, 2014.

Data from: Centers for Disease Control and Prevention (2015). *Fatal Injury Reports*. Injury Prevention & Control: Data & Statistics (WISQARS™). Available at http://www.cdc.gov/injury/wisqars/fatal_injury_reports.html.

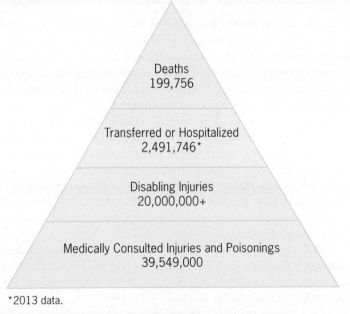

Deaths
199,756

Transferred or Hospitalized
2,491,746*

Disabling Injuries
20,000,000+

Medically Consulted Injuries and Poisonings
39,549,000

*2013 data.

FIGURE 15.2   Burden of injury, United States, 2014.

Data from: Centers for Disease Control and Prevention (2015). *Fatal Injury Reports*. Injury Prevention & Control: Data & Statistics (WISQARS™). Available at http://www.cdc.gov/injury/wisqars/fatal_injury_reports.html; Centers for Disease Control and Prevention, National Centers for Health Statistics (2015). *Summary Health Statistics for the U.S. Population: National Health Interview Survey, 2014*. Available at http://ftp.cdc.gov/pub/Health_Statistics/NCHS/NHIS/SHS/2014_SHS_Table_P-8.pdf; and Centers for Disease Control and Prevention (2014). National Safety Council (2016). *Injury Facts, 2016 Edition*. Itasca, IL: Author.

Disabling injury an injury causing any restriction of normal activity beyond the day of the injury's occurrence

Injury prevention (control) an organized effort to prevent injuries or to minimize their severity

Unsafe act any behavior that would increase the probability of an injury occurring

Unsafe condition any environmental factor or set of factors (physical or social) that would increase the probability of an injury occurring

TABLE 15.1   Years of Potential Life Lost (YPLL) and Number of Deaths for Selected Causes of Death: United States, 2013

Disease or Condition	Age-Adjusted YPLL Before Age 75 (per 100,000 population)	Number of Deaths
Cancer	1,328.6	584,881
Injury	1,051.2	192,945
Heart disease	952.3	796,494
Stroke	158.1	128,978
Diabetes mellitus	168,.3	75,578
Chronic lower respiratory diseases	176.6	149,205
Human immunodeficiency virus	82.3	6,955
Influenza and pneumonia	82.3	56,979
Kidney diseases	65.7	47,112
Chronic liver diseases	176.9	36,427

Data from: Centers for Disease Control and Prevention, National Center for Health Statistics (2016). *Deaths: Final Data for 2013.* Available at http://www.cdc.gov/nchs/data/nvsr/nvsr64/nvsr64_02.pdf; and Centers for Disease Control and Prevention, National Center for Health Statistics (2014). *Health, United States, 2014: With Special Feature on Adults Aged 55–64.* Hyattsville, MD: Author.

injuries are the second leading cause of YPLL-75 after cancer. However, if one were to consider all injuries, both intentional and unintentional, then injuries would be the leading cause of YPLL-75.

Unintentional Injuries

Unintentional injuries are the cause of nearly two-thirds of all injury-related deaths in the United States and ranked as the fourth leading cause of death in 2014.[5] There were 136,053 unintentional injury deaths in 2014.[4] Accounting for those deaths were unintentional poisonings 42,032 (31%), followed by motor vehicle crashes, 35,398 (26%), and falls 31,959 (23%), along with other causes.[4] In addition to the human death toll were the economic costs, mentioned earlier. Clearly, unintentional injuries constitute one of the United States' major public health problems.

The term *accident* has fallen into disfavor and disuse with many public health officials whose goal it is to reduce the number and seriousness of all injuries. The very word accident suggests a chance occurrence or an unpreventable mishap. Yet, we know that many, if not most, accidents are preventable. The term *unintentional injury* is now used in its place. Similarly, the rather vague term *safety* has largely been replaced by **injury prevention** or **injury control**. These terms are inclusive of all measures to prevent injuries, both unintentional and intentional, or to minimize their severity.

Four significant features characterize unintentional injuries: (1) They are unplanned events. (2) They usually are preceded by an unsafe act or condition (hazard). (3) They often are accompanied by economic loss. (4) They interrupt the efficient completion of a task.

An **unsafe act** is any behavior that would increase the probability of an unintentional injury. For example, driving an automobile while being impaired by alcohol or operating a power saw without eye protection is an unsafe act (see **Figure 15.3**). An **unsafe condition** is any environmental factor (physical or social) that would increase the probability of an unintentional injury. Icy streets

FIGURE 15.3 An unsafe act is a behavior that increases the probability of an injury.

© EduardSV/iStock/Thinkstock.

are an example of an unsafe condition. Unsafe acts and unsafe conditions are **hazards**. Whereas hazards do not actually cause unintentional injuries (an alcohol-impaired person may reach home uninjured, even over icy streets), they do increase the probability that an unintentional injury will occur.

Hazard an unsafe act or condition

Types of Unintentional Injuries

There are many types of unintentional injuries. The majority occur as a result of unintentional poisonings, motor vehicle crashes, falls, drowning, suffocation, fires and burns, and firearms. These are discussed briefly here.

Poisonings

Poisonings were the leading cause of unintentional deaths in 2014, when unintentional poisoning deaths numbered 42,032.[4] These deaths resulted from unintentional ingestion of fatal doses of medicines and drugs, consumption of toxic foods such as mushrooms and shellfish, and from exposure to toxic substances in the workplace or elsewhere. Eighty-five percent of these poisonings occurred in homes, where poisonings cause more than half of all injury deaths.[9] Contributing to poisoning death totals is the current epidemic of opioid pain reliever–related deaths. More information on this epidemic is available elsewhere in this text.

Motor Vehicle Crashes

Road traffic crash victims can be found throughout the world. Worldwide, 1.25 million people were killed (3,400 each day) and 20 to 50 million are injured in road traffic crashes annually. Teenagers and young adults (15 to 44 years of age) account for 59% of global traffic deaths.[12] An estimated 91% of deaths occurred in middle- or low-income countries as compared with just 9% in developed countries. Motor vehicle–related deaths are the leading cause of fatalities in the 15-to 29-year age group and 59% of all deaths among those 15 to 44 years of age. Seventy-seven percent of these deaths are among males.[12]

In the United States, motor vehicle related deaths were the second leading cause of unintentional injury deaths in 2014; 35,398 people were killed.[4] Of these, 32,675 people died in motor vehicle traffic crashes and an additional 2.3 million people were injured.[13] A majority of those killed were drivers (50.3%), followed by passengers (17.6%), motorcycle riders (14%), pedestrians (14.9%), and pedalcyclists (2.2%).[13]

Because of its public health importance, motor vehicle fatality rates were included in the *Healthy People 2020 (HP2020)* set of objectives. Targets were set to focus the nation's attention on lowering the rate of fatal injuries per 100 million vehicle miles traveled (VMT). The good news is that the fatal injury rate per 100 million VMT, which had declined almost every year since 1995, reached a record low of 1.08 in 2014, while the fatality rate per 100,000 population fell to 10.25. Both of these rates exceeded the nation's *Healthy People 2020* objectives, which were to reduce the number of motor vehicle deaths per 100,000 population from 12.4, the number of motor vehicle deaths per 100 million vehicle miles traveled, to 1.2 by 2020 (See **Box 15.1**).[14] Success in reducing deaths from motor vehicle crashes during 2001 to 2010 ranks as one of the ten significant public health achievements in the United States during that period.[15]

Falls

The third leading cause of unintentional fatal injuries is falls, which resulted in 31,959 deaths in 2014.[10] Falls were the leading cause of injury-related, medically consulted injury in 2012, with 13.4 million visits.[8] Falls can occur from one surface level to another—stairs or ladders, for example—or on the same level. About 64% of all fall-related deaths occur at home, where falls account for 29% all unintentional injuries deaths.[9]

Falls disproportionately affect elders, with more than one-third of older adults falling each year in the United States.[16] Falls are the leading cause of both nonfatal and fatal injury among

BOX 15.1   *Healthy People 2020:* **Objectives**

Objective IVP-13:   Reduce motor vehicle crash-related deaths.

Target-setting method: 10% improvement.

Data sources: National Vital Statistics System–Mortality (NVSS–M), Centers for Disease Control and Prevention, National Center for Health Statistics (CDC, NCHS), Fatality Analysis Reporting System (FARS), U.S. Department of Transportation (DOT), National Highway Transportation Safety Administration (NHTSA).

Target and baseline:

Objective	2007 Baseline	2014 Status	2020 Target
IVP-13.1 Reduce deaths per 100,000 population.	13.8	10.25	12.4

Objective	2008 Baseline	2014 Status	2020 Target
IVP-13.2 Reduce deaths per 100 million vehicle miles traveled.	1.3	1.08	1.2

For Further Thought

Note that the *HP2020* targets for reducing the rates of motor vehicle crash–related deaths had already been achieved by 2014. What reasons can you give to explain this success? Also, in 2011, drivers between 16 and 20 years of age experienced the highest rates of involvement in crashes resulting in fatal injuries (35 per 100,000 licensed drivers). By 2014, this rate had fallen to 32.64 per 100,000 licensed drivers, nearly equal to the rate for licensed drivers aged 21 to 24 (32.41). This was still far higher than the fatal injury involvement rate for all drivers (21 per 100,000 licensed drivers). Do you think that the practice of issuing graduated driver's licenses to new drivers in some states is responsible for this reduction in the rate of fatal injuries among 16-to-20-year-old drivers? If not, then how would you explain the rate drop?

Data from: U.S. Department of Health and Human Services, Office of Disease Prevention and Health Promotion (2010). *Healthy People 2020.* Washington, DC: U.S. Government Printing Office. Available at http://www.healthypeople.gov/2020/default.aspx; and U.S. Department of Transportation, National Highway Traffic Safety Administration (2013). *Traffic Safety Facts 2011: A Compilation of Motor Vehicle Crash Data from the Fatality Analysis Reporting System and the General Estimates System* (DOT HS 811 754). Washington, DC: U.S. DOT.

elders, and the number one reason for ED visits among this population. Fifty-eight percent of all nonfatal-injury ED visits by elders in 2011 were attributed to falls.[8]

Other Types of Unintentional Injuries

Other leading causes of unintentional injury deaths in 2014 were drowning (3,406), fires and burns (2,772), and other transportation-related injuries (1,797). All other types of unintentional injury deaths numbered 18,689.[4]

Epidemiology of Unintentional Injuries

Unintentional injuries are a major community health concern because they account for a disproportionately large number of early deaths in our society. However, deaths are only a part of the human toll; incapacitation is another significant aspect of the problem. One in six hospital days can be attributed to unintentional injuries. As mentioned earlier, medical costs from unintentional injuries run into the billions of dollars annually. Many of these injuries, such as head and spinal cord injuries, result in long-term or permanent disabilities that can affect individuals and their families for years.

Some of the factors that describe where, when, and to whom unintentional injuries occur are discussed in the following sections. In addition to describing the occurrence of injuries by person, place, and time, we include a discussion of alcohol and other drugs as risk factors in unintentional injuries.

Person

Unintentional injuries resulting in death and disability occur in all age groups, genders, races, and socioeconomic groupings. However, certain groups are at greater risk for injury than others.

Age

After the first year of life, unintentional injuries become the leading cause of death in children. They are the leading cause of death in all age groups: 1–44 years. They are the third leading cause of death in the 45-to-54- and the 55-to-64-year age groups (after cancer and heart disease). Unintentional injuries account for 40% of the deaths in the 15-to-19-year age group and 41% of the deaths in the 20-to-24-year age group; in this latter age group, the percentage is higher for males (42.2%) than for females (38.5%).[17]

Drowning is the leading cause of injury deaths for children ages 1–4 years, and the second leading cause of injury deaths for children ages 5–9 years. Motor vehicle crashes are the leading cause of injury death for ages 5–9, 10–14, and 15–24 years. Unintentional poisoning is the leading cause of injury deaths in all age groups 25–64 years.[4]

Teenagers are most likely to experience nonfatal injuries at a higher than average rate. The highest rate of medically consulted injury and poisoning episodes (183 visits per 100,000 population) is by 15-to-24-year olds (see **Figure 15.4**).[18] Note also that rates injury-related ED visits are high among those 75 years of age and older.

Teenagers and young adults (ages 15 to 24 years) are at a higher than average risk of dying as a result of unintentional firearm injury and are at the highest risk of suffering a nonfatal firearm injury (see **Figure 15.5**).[18] Nationwide, 8.7% of high school males carried a gun at least once in the 30 days prior to the 2015 survey.[19] Some people believe that childhood firearm deaths are

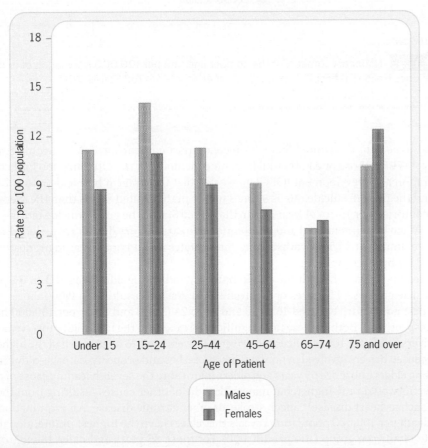

FIGURE 15.4   Rates of medically consulted injuries by age and sex, 2013.

Data from: Centers for Disease Control and Prevention (2015). *Nonfatal Injury Reports*. Injury Prevention & Control: Data & Statistics (WISQARS™). Available at http://www.cdc.gov/injury/wisqars/nonfatal.html.

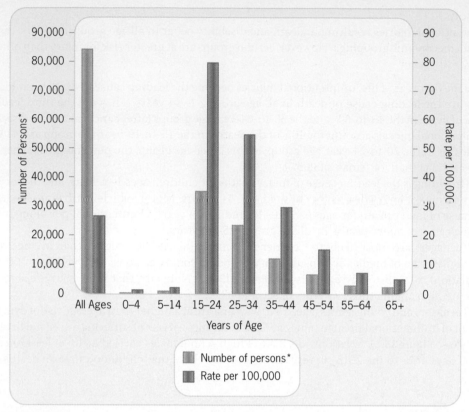

*In thousands

FIGURE 15.5   National estimates of the number and rate per 100,000 population of nonfatal firearm injuries treated in hospital emergency departments, United States, 2013.

Data from: Centers for Disease Control and Prevention (2015). *Nonfatal Injury Reports.* Injury Prevention & Control: Data & Statistics (WISQARS™). Available at: http://www.cdc.gov/injury/wisqars/nonfatal.html.

a national tragedy in the United States. A recent report comparing violent death rates in the United States with those of 23 other high-income members of the Organization for Economic Co-Operation and Development (OECD) revealed that the firearm homicide rate is 25 times higher and the firearm suicide rate is 8 times higher in the United States than the average rate of these countries. For 15-to-24-year olds in the United States, the gun homicide rate is 49 times higher.[20] When both intentional and unintentional firearm-injury deaths are included, firearm injuries accounted for 33,599 deaths in the United States in 2014,[4] nearly as many deaths as are accounted for by motor vehicles.

The leading cause of death for children, teens, and young adults (aged 5 to 34 years) is motor vehicle crashes.[4] The rates of involvement in crashes resulting in fatal injuries in 2014 were highest among drivers aged 16 to 20 and 21 to 24 (32.64 and 32.41 per 100,000 licensed drivers, respectively). Both of these rates significantly exceeded the fatal injury involvement rate for all drivers (21.01 per 100,000 licensed drivers). Drivers aged 16 to 20 also had the highest rate among licensed drivers involved in nonfatal injury crashes and property-damage-only crashes.[13]

Among elders (those age 65 years and older), injuries are the seventh leading cause of death.[17] Injury deaths would rank higher, but many elders die of other causes resulting from the aging process, such as heart disease, cancer, stroke, or other chronic disease. An examination of the rates of death per 100,000 population reveals that elders have the highest unintentional injury death rate of any age group (104 per 100,000). For those 85 years and older, the injury death rate climbs to 337 per 100,000.[18] Elders are less likely to survive an injury than younger persons.

Falls disproportionately affect elders 75 years of age and older, who are at nearly three times the average risk of experiencing a medically attended fall-injury episode (see **Figure 15.6**).[8,21]

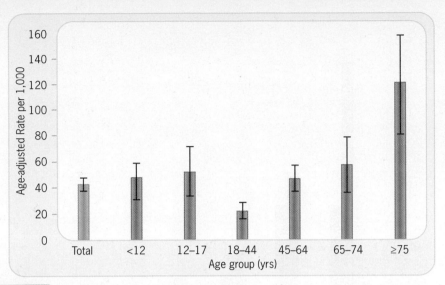

FIGURE 15.6   Rate of medically consulted fall injuries by age group—National Health Interview Survey, United States, 2012.

Data from: Centers for Disease Control and Prevention (2014). "Rate of Nonfatal Fall Injuries Receiving Medical Attention, by Age Group—National Health Interview Survey, United States, 2012." *Morbidity and Mortality Weekly Report*, 63(29): 641; and Adams, P. F., W. K Kirzinger, and M.E. Martinez (2013). "Summary Health Statistics for the U.S. Population: National Health Interview Survey, 2012." National Center for Health Statistics *Vital and Health Statistics*, 10(259).

Elders represent the fastest-growing segment of drivers; one-fourth of all drivers will be over 65 years of age by 2025. Elders are at age-increased risk of dying in car crashes because they are the most fragile drivers on the road; as many as 95% use medications that could affect their driving.[22] Elders have a higher death rate per mile driven than any other age group.[23] The overall fatality rate for those aged 75 and over (15 per 100,000 population) is higher than that of the 16-to-20-year age group.[13] A report published by the AAA Foundation revealed that drivers 65 years and over are almost twice as likely to die in car crashes as drivers aged 55 to 64. Drivers 75 years of age and older were two and one-half times as likely to die, and drivers 85 years of age and older were almost four times as likely to die in car crashes compared with drivers aged 55 to 64.[24] Elders also experience high rates of nonfatal injuries. In 2013, elders made nearly 4 million injury-related visits to emergency departments.[18] Elders are three times more likely to be hospitalized following an injury than are those younger than 65.[18]

Gender

At every age level, males are much more likely to become involved in a fatal unintentional injury than are females. Overall, the ratio of male injury deaths to female injury deaths is 2:1. In the 20-to-24-year age group, males die from unintentional injuries at greater than three times the rate of their female counterparts.[17] Although differences in unintentional injury death rates between the sexes decline with age, men retain a marginally higher rate even in the over-75-year age group. Death rates from unintentional injury among adults 65 years of age and older for five causes of death are illustrated in **Figure 15.7**.

Minority Status

In 2012, unintentional injuries and adverse effects were the leading cause of death for all ages through the 25-to-34-year age group in all racial and ethnic groups except for blacks and Asian and Pacific Islanders. Assault (homicide) replaced unintentional injuries as the leading cause of death for the 15-to-19-year, 20-to-24-year, and 25-to-34-year old black males and non-Hispanic black males.[17] Malignant neoplasms (cancer) were the leading cause of death among 10-to-14-year old Asians and Pacific Islanders. Age-adjusted death rates for unintentional injuries in 2012 were highest for the non-Hispanic white population (49.5 per 100,000) and lowest for the Asian and Pacific Islander population (13.1 per 100,000). The white population had a rate of 44.6, while

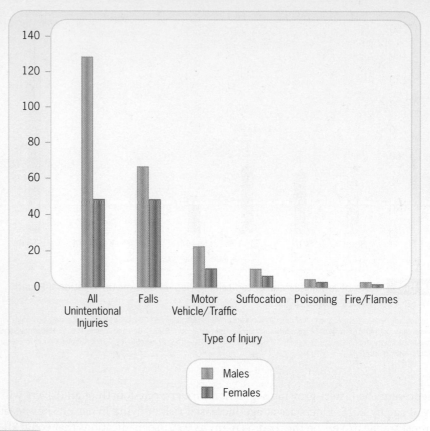

the Hispanic population had a lower rate of 21.6 per 100,000 population.[17] One explanation for these figures is that a higher percentage of the white population owns and operates motor vehicles than do other populations.

Place

Unintentional injuries occur wherever people are—at home, at work, or on the road. More injuries (fatal and nonfatal) occur in and around the home than anywhere else.

Home

People spend more time at home than any other place, so it is not surprising that nearly half (48.5%) of all medically consulted injury and poisoning episodes reported in the 2012 National Health Interview Survey occurred in or around the home (see **Figure 15.8**).[8] Unintentional injuries at home result from poisonings, falls, choking, burns, mechanical suffocation, drowning, firearms, and other causes. Within the home, some areas are more dangerous than others. The presence of electric appliances and sharp knives in the kitchen makes this room one of the more dangerous in the house. Another location where many unintentional injuries occur, particularly to the very young and old, is on stairways. For children, the bathroom, garage, and basement are hazardous areas because of the drugs, cleaning agents, and other poisonous materials that are often stored in these areas, and swimming and wading pools.

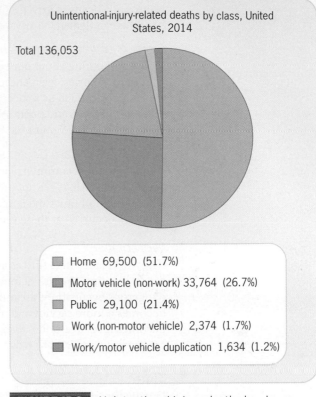

Unintentional-injury-related deaths by class, United States, 2014

Total 136,053

- Home 69,500 (51.7%)
- Motor vehicle (non-work) 33,764 (26.7%)
- Public 29,100 (21.4%)
- Work (non-motor vehicle) 2,374 (1.7%)
- Work/motor vehicle duplication 1,634 (1.2%)

FIGURE 15.9 Unintentional injury deaths by class, United States, 2014.

Note: Deaths for sections of chart add to more than total because some deaths are included in more than one section.

Data from: National Safety Council (2016). *Injury Facts, 2016 Edition,* Itasca, IL. Author.

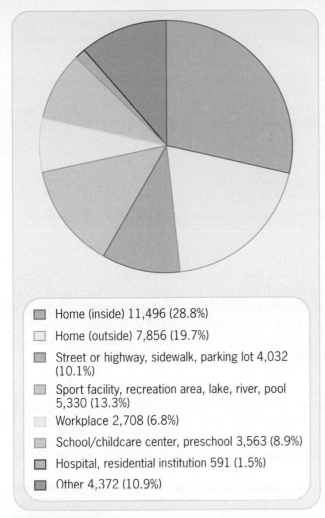

- Home (inside) 11,496 (28.8%)
- Home (outside) 7,856 (19.7%)
- Street or highway, sidewalk, parking lot 4,032 (10.1%)
- Sport facility, recreation area, lake, river, pool 5,330 (13.3%)
- Workplace 2,708 (6.8%)
- School/childcare center, preschool 3,563 (8.9%)
- Hospital, residential institution 591 (1.5%)
- Other 4,372 (10.9%)

FIGURE 15.8 Number (in thousands) and percentage of medically consulted injury episodes by place of occurrence, United States, 2014.

Data from: Centers for Disease Control and Prevention, National Centers for Health Statistics (2015). *Summary Health Statistics for the U.S. Population: National Health Interview Survey, 2014.* Available at http://ftp.cdc.gov/pub/Health_Statistics/NCHS /NHIS/SHS/2014_SHS_Table_P-8.pdf.

The home is also the leading place for fatal, unintentional injuries (**Figure 15.9**). In the home, many people die in bedrooms, where they may be sleeping during a fire, or may have lain down with a fatal drug overdose.

Highway

The second most likely place where a medically consulted injury might occur is streets, highways, sidewalks, and parking lots. According to the 2012 National Health Interview Survey of the U.S. population, 12.6% of all medically attended injuries were sustained on streets, highways, and in parking lots.[8] However, with regard to unintentional fatal injuries, 26% were sustained at these venues.

While significant progress has been made to make our streets and highways safer, concerns remain. One of these concerns is the number of unlicensed or improperly licensed drivers on the highways. A 5-year study revealed that 20% of all fatal crashes—one in five—involve at least one improperly licensed driver. These are drivers with a license that is suspended, revoked, expired, cancelled, or denied. Nearly 4% of drivers involved in fatal crashes had no known license at all.[24]

Recreation and Sports Venues

It says something about our society and culture that recreation or sports areas are important venues for injuries, even ahead of schools and the workplace. This category includes not only sport facilities such as a soccer fields, baseball diamonds, or basketball courts, but also lakes, reservoirs, rivers, and pools. About 12.0% of medically consulted injury or poisoning episodes occurred in these venues.[8]

School, Child Care Center, or Preschool

The fourth most common place for injuries to occur is in a school, preschool, or child care setting. These settings are not unusually hazardous places, but outside the home, these are places where much of our time is spent. Nine percent of medically consulted injury and poisoning episodes occurred at these venues.[8]

Workplace

The workplace ranks fifth as a location where unintentional injuries frequently occur.[8] As one might imagine, the risk of injury varies widely among different occupations. Among the most dangerous occupations are mining, farming (including logging), and construction. As the U.S. becomes a more service and information-based economy, the typical workplace environment becomes less hazardous. Also, significant efforts have been made by workers, employers, and government agencies to reduce the frequency and seriousness of workplace injuries.

Time

During the twentieth century, there were declines for some types of unintentional injuries and increases for others. For example, motor vehicle traffic deaths fell from 51,091 in 1980 to 32,675 in 2014. This reduction occurred despite the fact that Americans drove twice as many miles in 2014 as they did in 1980. The fatality rate per 100 million VMT declined from 3.35 to 1.08 during that 32-year period.[13]

Since 1975, unintentional deaths from drowning, fires, and burns have declined by more than half, and from firearms by two-thirds. However, deaths from falls, which declined significantly from 1975 to 1986, have begun to increase in the past few years, as the U.S. population ages. Deaths from unintentional poisonings have also increased and now rank as the leading cause of unintentional injury deaths.[10] In 1980 the death rate per 100,000 population was 4.8; in 2014 it was 12.1.[10,25]

There are seasonal variations in the incidence of some types of unintentional injuries, but these depend on the types of injury. For example, 58% of all drowning occur in four months—May, June, July, and August—when more people take part in water sports. Conversely, 61% of all deaths due to fires and burns are recorded during the 6 months from November through April, when furnaces, fireplaces, wood-burning stoves, and electric and kerosene space heaters are most often in use.[9]

Motor vehicle crash rates per 100 million VMT in 2014 were highest during October through February. During weekdays (Monday through Thursday), the fatal crash rate peak coincided with the peak of evening rush hour, 3:00 to 6:00 p.m. Fatal crash rates were higher on weekend nights than weekday nights. The hours between 9 p.m. and midnight on Fridays and Saturdays, and between midnight and 3 a.m. Saturdays and Sundays, are the most dangerous periods to travel by car (see **Figure 15.10**).[13]

Much publicity surrounds the number of motor vehicle deaths that occur during the following six major holiday periods: Memorial Day, Fourth of July, Labor Day, Thanksgiving, Christmas, and New Year. However, it has been shown that the number of crash-related deaths for these periods is not significantly different from the number occurring during nonholiday periods. Even so, the proportion of fatal crashes in which the driver is alcohol impaired is

FIGURE 15.10   Motor vehicle crash rates are higher in winter, during nights, and on weekends.

© Jack Dagley Photography/ShutterStock, Inc.

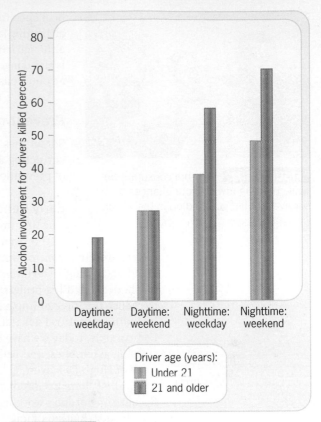

higher during holiday periods (about 53% for New Year's Day, 36% for Memorial Day, 41% for the Fourth of July, 40% for Labor Day; 35% for Thanksgiving, and 34% for Christmas) than the year overall (about 31% in 2014).[13]

Alcohol and Other Drugs as Risk Factors

An examination of the factors that contribute to intentional and unintentional injuries reveals that alcohol may be the single most important factor. This is certainly the case with fatal motor vehicle crashes, in which 31% of persons killed in traffic crashes in 2014 died in alcohol-related crashes. Although 31% represents a significant decline from the 55% reported in 1982, it is still too high. There has also been a decline in the percentage of those killed in crashes who were intoxicated—that is, who had blood alcohol concentrations (BACs) that exceeded 0.08% (BAC ≥ 0.08%)—from 48% in 1982 to 21% in 2014.[13]

The percentage of drivers in fatal crashes whose BAC exceeded the legal limit (BAC ≥ 0.08%) was 21% in 2014, but this percentage was nearly four times higher at night than during the day. On weekend nights, alcohol was involved in 67% of the single-car crashes in which a 21-year old or older driver or motorcycle operator was killed, and 41% of the single car crashes in which a driver under 21 years of age was killed (see **Figure 15.11**). The percentage of drivers or motorcycle operators involved in fatal crashes whose BAC was equal to or exceeded 0.08% was significantly higher for males (23%) than for females (15%).[13] Thirty-eight percent of drivers and motorcycle operators involved in fatal crashes had a previous record of crashes, license suspension or revocation, driving while intoxicated (DWI) conviction, speeding conviction, or other harmful moving violation conviction.[13]

Tragically, drivers are not the only persons killed in alcohol-related motor vehicle crashes. Motor vehicle crashes are the leading cause of death among children aged 1 year and older in the United States.[4,10] A recent study has revealed that one-third of children who died in 2011 were unrestrained.[26] Both drivers and their child passengers are more likely to be unrestrained if the driver is alcohol impaired.[27]

Passage of primary enforcement safety belt laws (laws that allow police to stop and ticket a driver solely because an occupant is unbelted) existed in only 33 states, the District of Columbia, and Puerto Rico in 2014.[13] Child restraint laws exist in all 50 states but vary from state to state. Passage of primary enforcement safety belt laws in the remaining states, and stricter enforcement of both laws in all states, could reduce passenger deaths among both adults and children.

Excessive drinking can also increase a pedestrian's or pedalcylist's chances of being killed by a motor vehicle. In 2014, 696 pedestrians (14% of the total) killed by motor vehicles were intoxicated. Ninety-eight (13.5%) pedalcyclists who died in motor vehicle–related deaths were alcohol or other drug impaired.[13]

Alcohol has also been determined to be an important factor in other types of unintentional injuries and deaths, including aquatic-related deaths. Nearly half of adults who drown have evidence of alcohol in their blood. Alcohol was the primary contributing factor in fatal boating accidents; it was listed as the primary contributing factor in 108 of 610 deaths and 17.7% of fatal boating deaths in 2014.[28] Alcohol consumption lowers a person's chance of survival should that person end up in the water. Of the 610 deaths mentioned above, 418 drowned; 80% of those who drowned were not wearing life jackets. A U.S. Coast Guard study estimates that boat operators with a BAC above 0.10% are more than 10 times as likely to be killed in a boating accident than are

FIGURE 15.11   Alcohol Impairment (BAC ≥ 0.08%) for drivers or motorcycle operators killed in single vehicle crashes, by driver age, time of day, and day of week, in 2013.

Data from: U.S. Department of Transportation, National Highway Traffic Safety Administration (2015). *Traffic Safety Facts 2013: A Compilation of Motor Vehicle Crash Data from the Fatality Analysis Reporting System and the General Estimates System* (DOT HS 812 139). Washington, DC: U.S. DOT.

FIGURE 15.12 Alcohol consumption while boating lowers your chances of survival should you end up in the water.

© Ingram Publishing/Index Stock Imagery, Inc.

boat operators with zero BACs.[29] In another study, it was found that nearly half of all boating fatalities occurred when vessels were not under way. This implies that although it is dangerous when the person who is operating the boat is drinking, it is also dangerous when passengers have been drinking (see **Figure 15.12**). Clearly, alcohol consumption and aquatic recreation are a dangerous combination.

Prevention through Epidemiology

Sometimes it has been society's nature to wait until after a tragedy before correcting an existing hazard or dangerous situation. Most implementation of prevention activities related to injuries occurs only after costly disasters.

Early Contributors to Injury Prevention and Control

The first important efforts toward injury prevention and control began early in the twentieth century. Four of the most important contributors to early efforts at injury control were Hugh DeHaven, John E. Gordon, James Gibson, and William Haddon, Jr. Hugh DeHaven was a World War I combat pilot, who, after surviving a plane crash, dedicated his professional life to studying victims of falls in an effort to design ways to reduce the force of impact on a body. Many of his ideas have led to better design concepts, including structural adaptations to protect drivers and other occupants of moving vehicles. For example, today we have at our disposal the protection of safety belts, air bags, collapsible steering assemblies, and padded dashboards. Many of these safety devices built on the early work of Hugh DeHaven.[30]

In 1949, John E. Gordon proposed that the tools of epidemiology be used to analyze injuries. Because of Gordon's work, a great deal was learned about risk factors, susceptible populations, and the distribution of injuries in populations.

In 1961, James Gibson proposed the idea that injury harm was caused by "energy interchange." Although this definition didn't fit well with certain injury deaths such as drowning and freezing, William Haddon, Jr., realized that in these cases, injury occurred because of the lack of necessary energy elements. Thus, the definition of injury supported by the National Center for Injury Prevention and Control (NCIPC) is "any intentional or unintentional damage to the body resulting from acute exposure to thermal, mechanical, electrical, or chemical energy or from the absence of such essentials as heat or oxygen."[30]

William Haddon, Jr. was both an engineer and a physician and is often considered the founding father of modern injury prevention research.[30] He was an unrelenting proponent of the epidemiological approach to injury control and insisted that the results of this work be used in the development of public policy. He was the foremost expert on highway safety in the 1960s and developed many successful countermeasures to reduce the number of unintentional highway injuries.

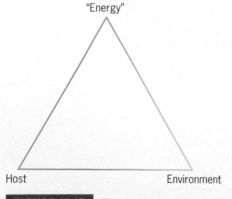

"Energy"

Host   Environment

FIGURE 15.13 The public health model for unintentional injuries.

Model for unintentional injuries the public health triangle (host, agent, and environment) modified to indicate energy as the causative agent of injuries

A Model for Unintentional Injuries

Until the 1950s, little progress occurred in the reduction of unintentional injuries and deaths. One reason for this was the failure to identify the causative agent associated with unintentional injuries. The public health model that describes communicable diseases in terms of the host, agent, and environment, arranged in a triangle, was discussed elsewhere in the text. A similar **model for unintentional injuries** has been proposed. In this model, the injury-producing agent is energy (see **Figure 15.13**).

Examples of injury-producing energy are plentiful. A moving car, a falling object (or person), and a speeding bullet all have kinetic energy. When one of these moving objects strikes another object, energy is released, often resulting in injury or trauma. Similarly, a hot stove or pan contains energy in the form of heat. Contact with one of these objects results in the rapid transfer of heat. If the skin is unprotected, tissue damage (a burn) occurs. Electrical energy is all around us and represents a potential source of unintentional injuries. Even accidental poisonings fit nicely into the model that incorporates energy as the causative agent of injury. Cleansers, drugs, and medicines represent stored chemical energy which, when released inappropriately, can cause serious injury or death.

Prevention and Control Tactics Based on the Model

Based on the epidemiological model just described, four types of actions can be taken to prevent or reduce the number and seriousness of unintentional injuries and deaths.[30] These four tactics are modified from those of Haddon. The first is to prevent the accumulation of the injury-producing agent, energy. Examples of implementing this principle include reducing speed limits to decrease motor vehicle injuries, lowering the height of children's high chairs and of diving boards to reduce fall injuries, and lowering the settings on hot water heaters to reduce the number and seriousness of burns. In our electrical example, circuit breakers in the home prevent the accumulation of excess electrical energy.

The second type of action is to prevent the inappropriate release of excess energy or to modify its release in some way. Flame-retardant fabric that will not ignite is an example of this type of prevention. Currently, there is a law that requires that such a fabric be used in the manufacture of children's pajamas. The use of automobile safety belts is another example. In this case, excess energy (movement of a human body) is released into the safety belt instead of into the car's windshield (see **Figure 15.14**). In the prevention of fall injuries, hand rails, walkers, and nonslip surfaces in bathtubs prevent the inappropriate release of kinetic energy resulting from falls.

The third tactic involves placing a barrier between the host and agent. The insulation around electrical wires and the use of potholders and non-heat–transferring handles on cookware are examples of this preventive strategy. The use of sunscreen lotion and the wearing of a hat in the summer place a barrier between the Sun's energy and a person's skin. Another example is the cable barriers now visible between opposing traffic lanes on many interstate highways. These installations not only serve as a barrier to protect oncoming traffic but also modify the release of energy and provide drivers and occupants with a relatively soft landing.

Finally, it is sometimes necessary or useful to completely separate the host from potentially dangerous sources of energy. Examples include the locked gates and high fences around electrical substations and swimming pools. At home, locking up guns and poisons provides protection against the likelihood of unintentional injury of young children.

Other Tactics

By viewing energy as the cause of unintentional injuries and deaths, it is possible to take positive steps in their prevention and control. There are still other actions that a community can take. First, injury-control education in the schools and in other public forums can be helpful. Second, improvements in the community's ability to respond to emergencies, such as encouraging the public to enroll in first aid and cardiopulmonary resuscitation (CPR) classes and expanding 911 telephone services, can limit disability and save lives. Third, communities can ensure that they have superior emergency and paramedic personnel by instituting the best possible training programs. The result will be improved emergency medical care and rehabilitation for the injured. Finally, communities can strengthen ordinances against high-risk behaviors, such as driving while impaired by alcohol, and then support their enforcement.

Community Approaches to the Prevention of Unintentional Injuries

It has been estimated that 39% of unintentional injury deaths could be prevented by correcting the following hazards: lack of vehicle restraint use, lack of motorcycle helmet use, unsafe consumer products, and drug and alcohol use (including prescription drug misuse, exposure to

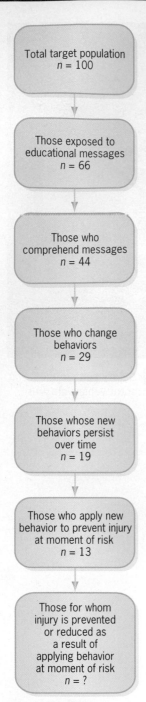

FIGURE 15.15

Attenuation of the effect of a public health education program.

Data from McLoughlin, E., C.J. Vince, A.M. Lee, et al. (1982). "Project Burn Prevention: Outcome and Implications." *American Journal of Public Health*, 72(3): 241–247. As presented in U.S. Congress, Office of Technology Assessment (February 1988). *Healthy Children: Investing in the Future* (pub no. OTA-H-345). Washington, DC: U.S. Government Printing Office.

occupational hazards, and unsafe home and community environments).[31] There are four broad strategies for preventing unintentional injuries—education, regulation, automatic protection, and litigation.

Education

Injury prevention education is the process of changing people's health-directed behavior in such a way as to reduce unintentional injuries. Education certainly has a place in injury prevention. Many of us remember the school fire drill, lessons on bicycle safety, and the school crossing guard. Undoubtedly, millions of injuries were prevented in these ways. However, injury prevention education has its limitations. **Figure 15.15** illustrates both the inefficiency of public education and the difficulties of measuring a successful outcome.

Regulation

The former 55-mile-per-hour national speed limit is an example of the power of **regulation**—the enactment and enforcement of laws to control conduct—as a means of reducing the number and seriousness of unintentional injuries. For years, motorists were advised to drive more responsibly. Public service announcements in the 1960s and 1970s informed audiences that "speed kills," and advised motorists not to "drink and drive." However, the highway death toll continued to mount until 1974, when then President Gerald Ford issued the national 55-mile-per-hour speed limit. Although the primary purpose of the slower speed limit was to conserve gasoline during the oil embargo by the Organization of the Petroleum Exporting Countries (OPEC), more than 9,000 lives were saved as the number of motor vehicle deaths dropped from 55,511 in 1973 to 46,200 in 1974 because of the slower speeds.

State laws requiring child safety seats and safety belt use are another example of regulation to reduce injuries. Beginning in the 1980s, automobile child restraint and safety belt legislation spread across the United States. All states now have occupant restraint requirements (seatbelt laws) for children, and all states except for New Hampshire have occupant restraint laws for adults.[13] State laws vary with regard to enforcement, level of fines, seats of the vehicle covered (front seat or all seats), and type of vehicle covered. Passage and vigorous enforcement of safety belt regulations is one reason why motor vehicle fatalities have declined in recent years. Enforcement laws can be primary (allowing police to stop drivers and issue citations solely because occupants were unbelted) or secondary (allowing police to issue a seatbelt citation after stopping the motorist for another reason). A recent study found that the rate of seatbelt use was 9% higher (89% to 80%) in states with primary enforcement laws.[32] Regulation is often aimed not at the consumer, but at the industry. For example, beginning with the 1990 models, car makers were required to equip all passenger cars with safety belts or air bags.

Another regulatory change that has helped reduce motor vehicle–related injuries is the lowering of the blood alcohol concentration at which a person is legally intoxicated to 0.08%. In 2004, Delaware became the final state to adopt this standard, which has now been adopted by all 50 states, Puerto Rico, and the District of Columbia. A systematic review of the effectiveness of such laws has revealed that they decrease fatal alcohol-related motor vehicle crashes an average of 7%. This saves an estimated 400 to 600 lives per year nationally and significantly decreases the number and seriousness of injuries.[33]

Distracted driving is now recognized as a major roadway hazard for everyone. Motorists have indicated that distracted driving is the single most common reason for feeling unsafe on the road.[34] "In 2014, distracted driving was reported in crashes that killed 3,179 people (10% of all fatalities),"[35] although many instances may go unreported. Since the first workshop on distracted driving research was held by the National Highway Traffic Safety Administration (NHTSA) in 2000, the number of personal electronic devices in use has increased dramatically. Examples are cell phones, Blackberries, personal digital assistants (PDAs), laptops, electronic notebooks, iPods, iPads, and global positioning devices (GPSs). Furthermore, beyond texting, a variety of social media available on these devices—Snapchat, Instagram, Twitter, Facebook, and a variety of music applications—vie for the driver's attention. In addition, availability of in-car entertainment devices, such as DVD players and gaming devices, is more widespread than in the past. It has been estimated that drivers' use of mobile phones up to 10 minutes before a crash is associated with a fourfold increased likelihood of a crash.[36] It has also been revealed that high school students who text while driving (nearly half of all U.S. high school students who drive) are more likely to engage in additional risky motor vehicle behaviors, such as not always wearing seatbelts, riding with a driver who had been drinking alcohol, and drinking alcohol and driving.[37]

Use of electronic devices is only part of the problem. Drivers also become distracted when eating or drinking, putting on makeup, tending to children, talking to a passenger, looking for something in the car or in a purse, fidgeting with controls, singing along with music, and reading a map. But add to these all of the technological devices now in widespread use, and the impact of distracted driving on highway safety becomes significant. In 2013, an estimated 3,154 people were killed and 424,000 injured in motor vehicle crashes that were recorded as distracted-related traffic fatalities. Drivers younger than 20 years of age had the highest proportion of fatal crashes in which the driver was reported as being distracted at the time of the crash (16%).[38]

"Currently, 46 states, the District of Columbia, Puerto Rico, Guam, and the U.S. Virgin Islands ban text messaging for all drivers. All but five have primary enforcement. Of the four states without an all-driver texting ban, two prohibit text messaging by novice drivers, and one restricts school bus drivers from texting. Fourteen states, the District of Columbia, Puerto Rico, Guam, and the U.S. Virgin Islands prohibit drivers of all ages from using handheld cell phones while driving."[38]

Forty-three states and the District of Columbia have reported that the emphasis on distracted driving has increased since 2010; only seven states indicated that that has remained unchanged. In 2013, 47 states and the District of Columbia collected data specifically related to distracted driving.[39]

States are taking a comprehensive approach to reducing text messaging and e-mailing while driving, including education, legislation, and enforcement. Forty-one states indicate that they have initiated public education/information campaigns on this topic using either traditional methods or new media/social networking, and eight states indicate that they have begun efforts to educate judges on the issue of distracted driving. Text messaging has been banned for all drivers in 39 states, the District of Columbia, Puerto Rico, Guam, and the U. S. Virgin Islands. An additional six states prohibit text messaging for novice drivers. Efforts to regulate cell phone usage and texting are ongoing; to see the laws in a particular state, visit Distraction.gov.[40]

In a "free society," such as the one in which Americans live, there is a limit to how much can be accomplished through legislation. For example, it has been very difficult to reduce the number of firearm injuries in the United States through legislation because the National Rifle Association (NRA), gun and ammunitions manufacturers, and other interests have been able to lobby successfully against restrictions on gun ownership.

Another example of the difficulty of achieving a balance between personal freedoms and society's legitimate health interests is motorcycle helmet legislation. Studies show that helmet laws are associated with a 29% to 33% decrease in annual per capita motorcycle fatalities.[41] In 1975, all but two states required motorcyclists to use helmets. Beginning in 1976, states began to repeal these laws. By the end of 2014, only 19 states, Puerto Rico, and the District of Columbia required a helmet for all motorcyclists.[13].

The strategy of prevention through regulation can be difficult to implement. The idea of regulating health behavior grates against the individual freedom that Americans have come to expect. Why should someone be required to wear a safety belt? The answer to that is: for the good of the total public, to protect the resources, including human life, of the greater public. Others say, "It's my life, and if I choose to take the risk of dying by not wearing a safety belt, who should care?" That response is all well and good; but when life is lost, it affects many others, such as family members, friends, and coworkers, not just the deceased. This scenario would become worse if the person not wearing a safety belt does not die but becomes a paraplegic and a ward of the state. Many public resources then would have to be used.

Injury prevention education the process of changing people's health-directed behavior to reduce unintentional injuries

Regulation the enactment and enforcement of laws to control conduct

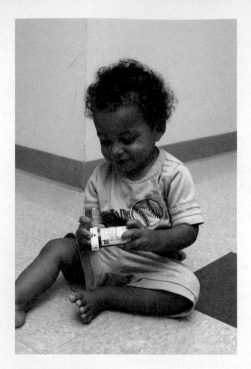

FIGURE 15.16 Child safety caps are an example of automatic or passive protection.

© Jones & Bartlett Learning. Courtesy of MIEMSS.

At what point is some legislation enough? It is known that safety belts and air bags are good and effective, but so are helmets—at least they think so at the Indianapolis 500. So, should people now work to pass a law that requires all automobile and truck drivers to wear helmets? How much legislated health behavior is enough?

Automatic Protection

When engineered changes are combined with regulatory efforts, remarkable results can sometimes be achieved. The technique of improving product or environmental design to reduce unintentional injuries is termed **automatic (passive) protection**.[30] A good example is childproof safety caps (see **Figure 15.16**). Childproof safety caps on aspirin and other medicine were introduced in 1972. By 1977, deaths attributed to ingestion of analgesics and antipyretics had decreased 41%.[42] We are all familiar with automatic protection devices. Common examples include automatic shut-off mechanisms on power tools (such as lawn mowers), safety caps on toxic products, and the warning lights and sounds that remind us to buckle our safety belts, warn us that a nearby vehicle is backing up, or, in some newer cars, let us know if we are too close to another vehicle. Recently, the National Highway Traffic Safety Administration released a new rule requiring that as of 2018, new cars under 10,000 pounds will be equipped with rear visibility technology.[43]

Litigation

When other methods fail, behavioral changes can sometimes come about through the courts. **Litigation**—lawsuits filed on behalf of injured victims or their families—has been successful in removing dangerous products from store shelves or otherwise influencing changes in dangerous behavior. Litigation against a manufacturer of unsafe automobile tires, for example, might result in safer tires. Sometimes these lawsuits can be very large. General Motors (GM) has settled lawsuits caused by ignition switch problem that affected millions of vehicles. In these cases, when the vehicle suddenly shut off, the airbags may have also been shut off, causing them to fail to deploy as needed. More than 100 people died. The GM settlement is expected to run into the millions of dollars. Furthermore, the National Highway Traffic Safety Administration fined GM a record $35 million over their handling of the recall.[44] In these ways, litigation can encourage companies to provide safer products.

Lawsuits against bartenders and bar owners for serving alcohol to alcohol-impaired customers, who have then injured other people, have produced more responsible server behavior at public bars. Alcohol-related deaths and injuries on college campuses have caused insurance companies to re-examine their liability insurance policies with fraternities and sororities. This has forced some of these organizations and the universities themselves to restrict the way alcohol is used. The outcome may be a drop in unintentional injuries on these campuses.

Intentional Injuries

Automatic (passive) protection the modification of a product or environment to reduce unintentional injuries

Litigation the process of seeking justice for injury through courts

Intentional injuries, the outcome of self-directed and interpersonal violence, are a staggering community health problem in the United States. More than 50,000 people die, and millions of others receive nonfatal injuries, each year as a result of self-directed or interpersonal violence.[10] In 2013, an estimated 2.2 million persons were treated for nonfatal physical assault–related injuries and 371,566 were hospitalized.[18] Although the physical assault rate is higher for males than for females, the rate of ED visits for sexual assault–related injuries can be five times higher for females. The highest injury rates for both males and females that resulted in ED visits were for the 15-to-24-year age group.[45] In 2013, the violence-related nonfatal injury rate for black males of all ages was about 2.8 times higher than the rate for non-Hispanic white males.[18]

Types of Intentional Injuries

The spectrum of violence includes assaults, rapes, suicides, and homicides. These acts of violence can be perpetrated against family members (children, elders, and intimate partners), community members, or complete strangers. In 2013, residents of the United States 12 years of age or older reported being victims of an estimated 5.4 million violent victimizations and 15.3 million property crimes. Between 1993 and 2014, the rate of violent victimizations has fallen from 79.8 to 20.1 per 1,000 persons.[46]

Interpersonal violence is a costly community and public health problem, not only because of the loss of life and productivity but also because of the economic cost. Consider the community, state, and national resources expended because of interpersonal violence. There are those of the police, the legal system, the penal system, emergency health care services, medical services, social workers, and many others. Clearly, this is a problem for which prevention is the most economic approach.

Epidemiology of Intentional Injuries

To better understand the problem of intentional injuries, it is instructive to look more closely at both the victims and the perpetrators of violence. Interpersonal violence disproportionately affects those who are frustrated and hopeless, those who are jobless and live in poverty, and those with low self-esteem. More violent acts, whether self-directed or directed at others, are committed by males. Firearms are increasingly involved in violent acts, with ever-increasing fatal consequences. Abuse of drugs, especially alcohol, also contributes to the number of intentional injuries. Additionally, perpetrators of violent acts are more likely to have been abused or neglected as children or exposed to violence and aggression earlier in their lives.

Homicide, Assault, Rape, and Property Crimes

In 2014, 14,249 murders and non-negligent manslaughters were reported to the Federal Bureau of Investigation (FBI).[47] Although the U.S. homicide rate has declined from 9.3 per 100,000 inhabitants in 1992 to 4.5 in 2014, it remains higher than the rates of most other industrialized nations.[48] Homicide and legal intervention were not ranked among the 15 leading cause of death for the overall population in the United States in 2013, although they were among the top 15 leading causes of death in some states.[49] In the 15-to-24-year age group, homicide ranked as the second leading cause of death in 2012.[17] Firearms accounted for 70% of all homicides reported in the United States in 2011. Between 70% and 80% of firearm homicides and 90% of nonfatal firearm victimizations were committed with a handgun from 1993 to 2011.[50]

Males, blacks, and young people (ages 12 to 17 and 18 to 24 years of age) experience the highest rates of violent victimization, although in 2014, these rates had declined and were comparable to those ages 25 to 34 years. Married and widowed people and those living in the suburbs experience lower than average violent victimization rates. In 2014, males experienced violent victimization at a rate of 21 per 1,000 population as compared with 19 per 1,000 for females. In comparison, victimization rates per 1,000 were 20.3 for blacks, 22.5 for whites, 16.2 for Hispanics, and 23.0 for those of other races. Overall, it is estimated that only 46% of all violent crimes committed in 2014 were reported to police. In the case of rapes or sexual assaults, even fewer (34%) were reported to police.[46] This makes the acquisition of accurate statistics on rape and attempted rape difficult. If the perpetrator is a stranger, the incident is more likely to be reported to the police. However, during 2005 to 2010, 78% of sexual violence involved an offender who was a family member, intimate partner, friend, or acquaintance.[51]

Suicide and Attempted Suicide

As previously indicated, more than 40,000 suicides are reported each year in the United States, accounting for one-fifth of all injury mortality. In 2014, 42,773 suicide deaths were reported, making this the 10th leading cause of deaths.[4] The age-adjusted suicide rate for men (20.3 per 100,000) was nearly four times that for women (5.5 per 100,000) in 2013.[4] The rates of suicide in young people (15 to 24 years of age) edged up from 2009 to 2013 from 10.0 to 11.1 per 100,000, the highest rate in more than a decade. Those for the elderly have remained fairly constant over the past decade at about 15 per 100,000 for those 65 to 74 years of age, and slightly higher for 75 to 84 and 85+ year age groups.[10] But suicide rate in men 65 years of age and older is the highest for any population subgroup (31 per 100,000), six times higher than the rate for elder women (5.04 per 100,000).[4]

Firearm Injuries and Injury Deaths

Statistics on fatal and nonfatal firearm injuries include data covering both intentional and unintentional incidents. When one considers all firearm deaths—those that result from both intentional and unintentional acts—firearms were the third leading cause of injury deaths after poisoning and motor vehicles in 2013 (see **Figure 15.17**).[10] In 2013, there were 33,636 firearm injury deaths. Of these, 21,175 (63%) were classified as suicides, 11,208 (33%) as homicides, 976 (3%) as unintentional, 467 (1%) as resulting from legal intervention, and 281 (<1%) were of undetermined intent.[10] In 2014, as in most years, males were six times more likely to die or be treated in an emergency department for a gunshot wound than were females.[4,18]

At highest risk for homicide and suicide involving firearms are teenage boys and young men, aged 15 to 24 years. As previously stated, a national survey reported that in 2013, nearly 9.4% of high school males had carried a gun on at least one occasion during the 30 days before the survey.[19] Also, nationwide, 5.2% of students had carried a weapon (e.g., a gun, knife, or club) on school property at least one day in the 30 days prior to the survey. Gun-carrying behavior increases the risk of deadly violence against others as well as oneself; nearly 17% of high school students indicated that they had seriously considered suicide at least once in the 12 months before the survey.[19]

The gun-toting behavior continues even in college. In a random sample of 10,000 undergraduate students, 4.3% reported that they had a working firearm at college, and 1.6% said they had been threatened with a gun while at college.[52] When this study was conducted a majority

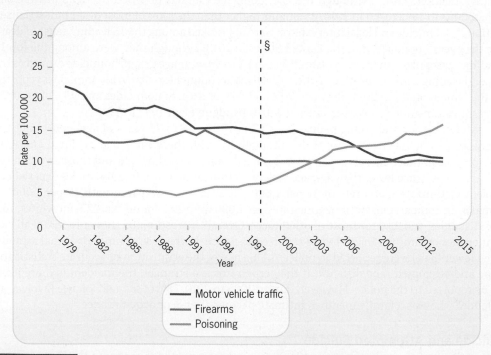

FIGURE 15.17   Leading causes of injury deaths, 1979 to 2014. By 2008 poisonings had superseded motor-vehicle crashes as the leading cause of injury death in the United States.

Data from: Centers for Disease Control and Prevention (2015). *Fatal Injury Reports.* Injury Prevention & Control: Data & Statistics (WISQARS™). Available at http://www.cdc.gov/injury/wisqars/fatal_injury_reports.html.

of American colleges and universities prohibited the carrying of firearms on their campuses. This prohibition has contributed to the relative safe nature of campuses of higher education. Although there have been heinous and well-publicized violent crimes on campuses (Virginia Tech, 2007; Northern Illinois University, 2008; Oikos University (CA), 2012; Umpqua Community College (OR), 2015; and others), statistics reveal that college and university campuses are much safer than other busy venues. The average homicide rate on American campuses is one homicide per one million students. By comparison, in some years, the homicide rate in New York City is 70 times greater.[53]

This situation is now changing, as the national gun lobby, backed by the National Rifle Association and the American Legislative Exchange Council, has encouraged state legislatures to introduce bills that would force colleges and universities to allow guns on campuses, where historically they were banned.[54] The banning of firearms on college and university campuses was successfully challenged in Utah where, in 2006, the Utah Supreme Court ruled that the University of Utah cannot bar guns from campus.[54] As of July 2015, 18 states prohibited carrying concealed weapons on college campuses, and in 24 other states, the decision to permit or ban concealed weapons on campus is left to each college or university campus. Six states require colleges to allow guns on campus in some circumstances; only two states force colleges to allow all concealed carry permit holders to carry guns everywhere on campus.[54]

These decisions have raised concern among students, faculty, college presidents, and police chiefs in institutions of higher education, where campus safety is an ever-present concern.[55-58] It is not difficult to understand their concern. About 40% of college students binge drink regularly and 85% of campus arrests involve alcohol.[53] Allowing students to possess/carry guns would virtually guarantee that violence on college campuses would become more deadly. Also, college students are under considerable stress, often citing stress, anxiety, relationship problems, financial matters, or academic or career concerns. The reported suicide ideation rate among college students is estimated at about 10%. More than 50% of suicides involve firearms. Firearms on campus would probably increase the suicide completion rate among college students. One other concern with allowing firearms on campuses is the increase in security and insurance costs, which would further burden the budgets of many colleges and universities.

One barrier to preventing firearm injuries and deaths is the absence of a detailed, federally supported reporting system. Unlike the highly developed reporting system for motor vehicle crashes and crash injuries, there is no such system for firearm-related injuries. At the bequest of the national gun lobby, the United States Congress has prevented such a system from being put in place and has cut funding for research on firearm injuries;[59] it also failed to pass legislation to close loopholes in background checks for gun buyers. In the absence of federal leadership, some states have used a public health approach to curb gun violence, by denying firearms from those who have prior convictions for violent misdemeanors from owning or possessing firearms and requiring background checks for all transfers of firearms.[60] A recent study has revealed that a higher number of firearm laws in a state, the lower the rate of firearm fatalities overall and for suicides and homicides individually.[61]

Violence in Our Society and Resources for Prevention

A sixth-grade student brings a gun to school to shoot a bully, a mother is run off the road and injured by an aggressive driver, and a child dies from physical punishment for breaking a rule at home. These newspaper reports are signs of unnecessary but common acts of violence in our communities. Over the past few years, it seems as if violence in the U.S. has been increasing. Many young people do not have the interest or skills to resolve a conflict through verbal negotiation, and they resort to physical violence to resolve it. Some of these confrontations are gang related, while others are simply individual actions. In the next sections, we discuss individual, family, and gang violence.

Individuals and Violence

A significant number of violent acts committed in the United States each year are committed by individuals who lack basic communication and problem-solving skills. Many of these

Family violence the use of physical force by one family member against another, with the intent to hurt, injure, or cause death

Child maltreatment an act or failure to act by a parent, caretaker, or other person as defined under state law that results in physical abuse, neglect, medical neglect, sexual abuse, emotional abuse, or an act or failure to act that presents an imminent risk of serious harm to a child

Child abuse the intentional physical, emotional, verbal, or sexual mistreatment of a minor

Child neglect the failure of a parent or guardian to care for or otherwise provide the necessary subsistence for a child

people are not interested in resolving an argument through discussion, compromise, and understanding. Instead, they are intent on "winning" their argument, by physical force if necessary. (After all, isn't that the way arguments are won on television, in computer games, and in the movies?)

The availability and proliferation of firearms makes this approach particularly deadly. In 2012, homicide and legal intervention were the number one cause of death for black Americans in the 15-to-24 and 25-to-34 age groups, and the third leading cause of death for entire American population in those age groups.[17] Because of the level of violence, many schools and community organizations offer conflict resolution programs that teach youths alternative ways to resolve disagreements. These programs are designed for various grade levels and teach about the nature of conflicts, the harmful effects of violence, alternatives to violent behavior, and how to make safe decisions. Some of these programs can be found by searching the Violence Prevention website of Centers for Disease Control and Prevention, where programs are listed by social setting (youth, intimate partner, elder). An example of one such program is *STRYVE: Striving to Reduce Youth Violence Everywhere.*[62]

Family Violence and Abuse

One in every six homicides is the result of family violence. **Family violence** includes the maltreatment of children, intimate partner violence, sibling violence, and violence directed toward elder family members. Because children are our most important resources, and because being abused or neglected as a child increases one's risk for violent behavior as an adult, it is of paramount importance that society increase its efforts to intervene in cases of family violence. In recent years there has been increased attention paid to family violence, including violence against children and intimate partners. Between 1993 and 2014, the victimization rates for intimate partners and children declined.[63] Some of this decline has resulted from improved efforts by those social service agencies tasked with intervening and preventing family violence. But some can be attributed to economic conditions—lower unemployment rates means less domestic violence. Beginning in 2001, as the economy weakened, the decline in intimate partner violence rate slowed while the overall violent crime rate continued to decline.

FIGURE 15.18 Child neglect is the failure to provide care or other necessary subsistence for a child.

© Pixel Memoirs/ShutterStock, Inc.

Child Maltreatment

Child maltreatment is an act or failure to act by a parent, caretaker, or other person as defined under state law that results in physical abuse, neglect, medical neglect, sexual abuse, emotional abuse, or an act or failure to act that presents an imminent risk of serious harm to a child. Also included are other forms of child maltreatment, such as child abandonment and congenital drug addiction. **Child abuse** can be physical, emotional, verbal, or sexual. Physical abuse is the intentional (nonaccidental) inflicting of injury on another person by shaking, throwing, beating, burning, or other means. Emotional abuse can take many forms, including showing no emotion and the failure to provide warmth, attention, supervision, or normal living experiences. Verbal abuse is the demeaning or teasing of another verbally. Sexual abuse includes the physical acts of fondling or intercourse, nonphysical acts such as indecent exposure or obscene phone calls, or violent physical acts such as rape and battery. **Child neglect** is a type of maltreatment that refers to the failure by the parent or legal caretaker to provide necessary, age-appropriate care when financially able to do so, or when offered financial or other means to do so. Neglect may be physical, such as the failure to provide food, clothing, medical care, shelter, or cleanliness. It also may be emotional, such as the failure to provide attention, supervision, or other support necessary for a child's well-being (see **Figure 15.18**). Or, it may be educational, such as the failure to ensure that a child attends school regularly. Educational neglect is one of the most common categories of neglect, followed by physical, and then emotional neglect.

In 2014, 702,000 children under the age of 18 years were victims of abuse or neglect nationwide at a rate of 9.4 per 1,000 children. Eighty-one percent of the perpetrators were parents.[64] There has been a steady decline from the rate of reported child maltreatment since 1993, when the rate was 15.3 per 1,000 children (see **Figure 15.19**). Of the 676,569 children who were maltreated in 2014, 75% suffered neglect and 17% suffered physical abuse and 8.3% were sexually abused. Many children suffered more than one kind of maltreatment, including psychological maltreatment (6%), medical neglect (2.2%), or abandonment, threats of harm, or congenital drug addiction.[64] Seventy-eight percent of perpetrators of abuse were the children's parents. The highest victimization rates were for infants (24.4 maltreatments per 1,000 children) and children between 1 and 2 years of age (12.3 per 1,000 children), and these rates decline with age (see **Figure 15.20**). Rates of many types

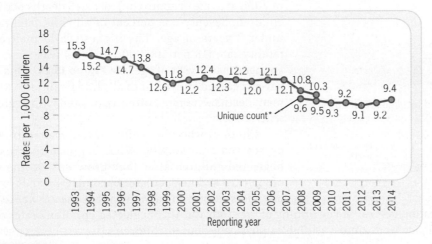

FIGURE 15.19 Child maltreatment rates steadily declined between 1993 and 2009, but have remained essentially unchanged since then.

Data from: U.S. Department of Health and Human Services, Administration for Children & Families, Administration on Children, Youth and Families, Children's Bureau (2016). *Child Maltreatment 2014*. Available at http://www.acf.hhs.gov/programs/cb/research-data-technology/statistics-research/child-maltreatment.

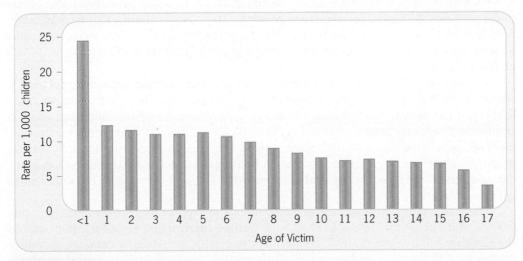

FIGURE 15.20 Victimization rates per 1,000 children by age, 2014.

Data from: U.S. Department of Health and Human Services, Administration for Children & Families, Administration on Children, Youth and Families, Children's Bureau (2016). *Child Maltreatment 2014*. Available at http://www.acf.hhs.gov/programs/cb/research-data-technology/statistics-research/child-maltreatment.

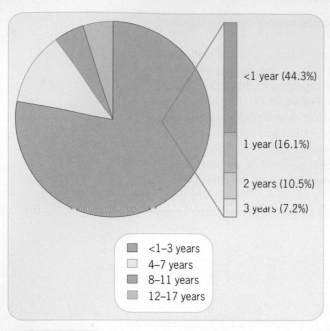

<1 year (44.3%)

1 year (16.1%)

2 years (10.5%)

3 years (7.2%)

- ▩ <1–3 years
- ▢ 4–7 years
- ▨ 8–11 years
- ▩ 12–17 years

FIGURE 15.21 Percentage of child fatalities resulting from maltreatment by age, 2014.

Data from: U.S. Department of Health and Human Services, Administration for Children & Families, Administration on Children, Youth and Families, Children's Bureau (2016). *Child Maltreatment 2014*. Available at http://www.acf.hhs.gov/programs/cb/research-data-technology/statistics-research/child-maltreatment.

of maltreatment are slightly higher until 5 years of age, after which they are slightly higher for females. Victimization rates vary by race and ethnicity. In 2014, the lowest rates were for Asian children (1.7 children per 1,000), and the highest rates were for black children (15.3 children per 1,000), followed by children of American Indian or Alaska Natives (13.4 per 100,000), and Hispanics (8.8 per 100,000), Pacific Islanders (8.6 per 100,000), and whites (8.4 per 100,000) Multiple race children experienced abuse at a rate of 10.6 per 100,000. Although recurrence of child maltreatment does occur, data reveal that in about 95% of cases, no recurrence occurs in the first 6 months after initial occurrence.[64]

An estimated 1,580 children died of abuse or neglect in 2014, at a rate of approximately 2.13 deaths per 100,000 children. Seventy-one percent of all child fatalities were under 3 years of age. The highest child maltreatment fatality rate (18 per 100,000 children) was among those younger than 1 year of age (see **Figure 15.21**). One or both parents caused four-fifths of all child fatalities.[64] Maltreatment deaths were more often associated with neglect than with abuse.

Children who physically survive maltreatment may be scarred emotionally. What happens to abused and neglected children after they grow up? Do the victims of violence and neglect later become criminals or violent offenders? Research has shown that the answer to the latter question is "Yes." A key finding of the study was that neglected children's rates of arrest for violence were almost as high as physically abused children's.[65]

Prevention of Child Maltreatment

One of the keys to protecting children from maltreatment is a system of timely reporting and referral to one of the many state and local child protective service (CPS) agencies. Anyone may make such a report (e.g., relative, neighbor, or teacher). In 2014, 63% of child abuse and neglect reports were received from professionals, including law enforcement personnel (18%), educational personnel (18%), and social services personnel (11%). Nonprofessionals—friends, neighbors, and relatives—were responsible for 19% of reports.[64] Signs of neglect include extremes in behavior, an uncared-for appearance, evidence of a lack of supervision at home, or the lack of medical care.

CPS agencies provide services to prevent future instances of child abuse or neglect and to remedy harm that has occurred as a result of child maltreatment. These services are designed to increase the parents' child-rearing competence and knowledge of developmental stages of childhood. There may be an assessment of the family's strengths and weaknesses, the development of a plan based on the family's needs, and post-investigative follow-up services. Services might include respite care, parenting education, housing assistance, substance abuse treatment, day care, home visits, counseling, and other services. The goal is to ensure the safety of the child or children.[64]

There are many useful sources of information and support for those interested in preventing child abuse and neglect. The Child Welfare Information Gateway, sponsored by the Children's Bureau of the U.S. Department of Health and Human Services' Administration for Children & Families provides information, products, and technical assistance services to help professionals locate information related to child abuse and neglect and related child welfare issues (available at www.childwelfare.gov/). Another source of information is the Committee for Children. Its mission is to promote the safety, well-being, and social development of children (available at www.cfchildren.org). The Centers for Disease Control and Prevention, Injury Prevention & Control's Division of Violence Prevention has valuable information on child maltreatment prevention (www.cdc.gov/violence prevention/childmaltreatment/index.html).

Elder Maltreatment

The maltreatment of elders (persons 65 years of age and older) is a problem worldwide, where it is estimated that 1 in 10 older people experience abuse every month.[66] Globally, maltreatment of elders is expected to increase as populations age; the number of those 60 years of age and older is predicted to double from 900 million in 2015 to 2 billion in 2050. In the U.S. population the proportion of the population made up of elders is growing. Elders living in the United States numbered 43.1 million in 2012, but is expected to nearly double to 83.7 million by 2050.[67] Although elders experience violent crime at a lower rate than people of other age groups (3 per 1,000 population vs. 11 per 1,000 for the population as a whole in 2014),[46] about 7.6% to 10% of elders experienced maltreatment within the past year.[68] Women over the age of 75 are particularly vulnerable, and elders over 80 are three times more likely to be abused as are younger elders.[69] The vast majority (90%) of abusers are family members, either adult children, spouses, partners, or other relatives.[70]

Abuse can be physical, sexual, psychological or emotional, or financial, or may involve abandonment, neglect, or self-neglect. Elders may be kicked, hit, denied food and medical care, or have their Social Security checks or other financial resources stolen or otherwise misappropriated. Most cases of elder abuse are not reported or only become apparent following other legal or medical proceedings; thus, accurate statistics on the incidence of elder abuse are unavailable. As the American population ages, elder maltreatment is likely to become a community health problem of increasing importance.

Prevention of Elder Maltreatment

Prevention of elder maltreatment begins with learning the signs of elder abuse, listening to elders and their caregivers, learning how to report maltreatment, and reporting maltreatment to Adult Protective Services.[71] One could also learn the risk and protective factors for perpetration. Perpetrators of elder abuse and neglect may have mental illness or a substance abuse problem, or they may have high levels of hostility or inadequate coping skills, or may have been mistreated as a child. Also, the perpetrator may not have adequate preparation and training for caregiving.[71] Finally, one may wish to seek assistance by calling the elder abuse hotline at 1-800-677-1116. More information is available from the National Center on Elder Abuse (www.ncea.aoa.gov).

Intimate Partner Violence

According to the CDC, the term **intimate partner violence (IPV)** "describes physical violence, sexual violence, stalking, or psychological aggression (including coercive acts) by a current or former intimate partner." The term intimate partner includes current and former spouses, boyfriends or girlfriends, dating partners, or sexual partners (hetero- or homosexual) and does not require sexual intimacy.[72] Each year countless women and men are victimized by their intimate partners. About 634,600 persons age 12 or older experienced nonfatal violent victimization by an intimate partner in 2014.[46] This is equivalent to a rate of 2.4 victimizations per 1,000, a 37% decline from 2005, when the intimate partner victimization rate was 3.3 per 1,000. Women were more likely to be victims of physical violence or severe physical violence than men. For women, 31.5% and 22.3% experience intimate partner violence and severe intimate partner violence respectively in their lifetimes.[73] For men these figures were 27.5% and 14.0%. However, 8.8% of women versus only 0.5% of men reported being raped by an intimate partner in their lifetime. Sometimes intimate partner violence is deadly. In 2014, 953 women and 250 men were murdered by an intimate partner.[47] During 2005 to 2010, 78% of rapes and sexual assaults against females were committed by an offender whom they knew, 34% by an intimate partner.[48] Injuries to women from intimate partner physical violence are underreported, but

Intimate partner violence (IPV) describes physical violence, sexual violence, stalking, or psychological aggression (including coercive acts) by a current or former intimate partner, including current and former spouses, boyfriends or girlfriends, dating partners, or sexual partners (hetero- or homosexual) and does not require sexual intimacy

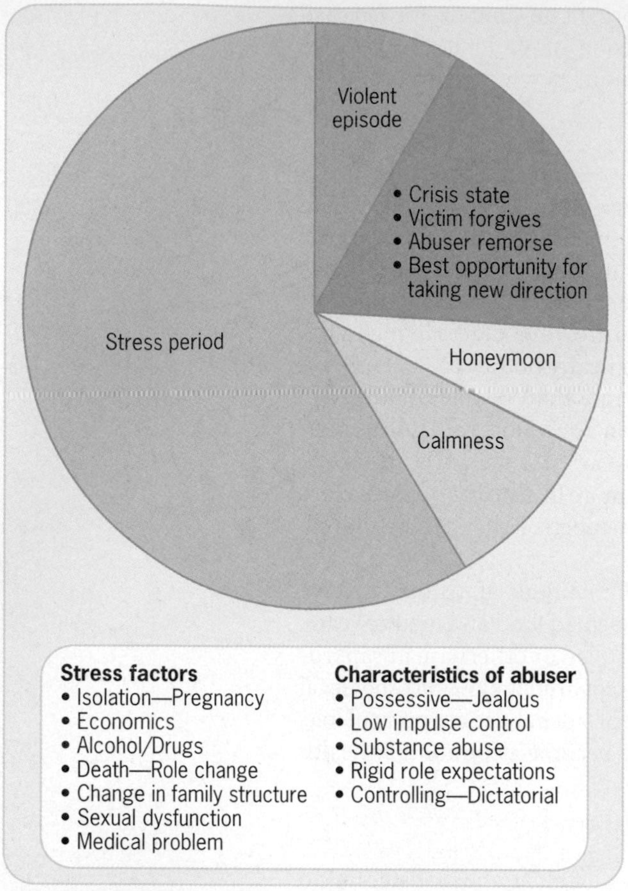

Stress factors
- Isolation—Pregnancy
- Economics
- Alcohol/Drugs
- Death—Role change
- Change in family structure
- Sexual dysfunction
- Medical problem

Characteristics of abuser
- Possessive—Jealous
- Low impulse control
- Substance abuse
- Rigid role expectations
- Controlling—Dictatorial

FIGURE 15.22   Cycle of violence.

Data from: Domestic Abuse Intervention Project in Duluth, Minnesota, as reported in the *AHEC News*, a publication of the Area Health Education Centers of Oklahoma (February 1994). *AHEX News*, 2(1): 9. Used with permission.

more than 500,000 women injured as a result of IPV require medical treatment each year. Women spend more days in bed, miss more work, and suffer more from stress and depression than men. The health care and time away from work costs of intimate partner rape, physical assault, and stalking exceed $8.3 billion each year.[74]

Three in 10 women residing in the United States has been physically assaulted, raped, or stalked by an intimate partner; one of 10 men has reported such an experience.[74] Each year, thousands of American children witness IPV within their families. Witnessing such violence is a risk factor for developing long-term physical and mental health problems, including alcohol and substance abuse, becoming a victim of abuse, and perpetrating IPV.[74]

Risk factors for women who are likely to experience IPV include having a family income below $25,000, being young (18–34 years of age), living alone in a house with children, and living with an intimate partner who uses alcohol or other drugs. Another risk factor is a previous episode of abuse. In a dysfunctional relationship, the male intimate partner may seek to exert power and control over his female intimate partner, resulting in a cycle in which violence recurs (see **Figure 15.22**). The cycle of violence depicts the progression of steps leading up to an attack or episode of violence and the restoration of calm. A violent episode may result from the loss of a job, a divorce, illness, death of a family member, or misbehavior (actual or perceived) of children or an intimate partner. The likelihood that abuse will occur is greatly increased if alcohol has been consumed. While selected interventions aimed at one factor (for example, the abuser) might mitigate against family violence, community efforts to reduce violence should be both comprehensive, involving a variety of approaches, and coordinated among all agencies involved in order to be effective.

Prevention of Intimate Partner Violence

Prevention of IPV involves improvements in identifying and documenting cases of IPV and increasing access to services for victims and perpetrators of IPV and their children. Coordinating community initiatives strengthens the safety networks for high-risk individuals and families. Some communities have established a "Violence Coordinating Council" that holds monthly meetings to set an agenda and action plans for the community and to determine and clarify the roles and responsibilities of agencies and individuals. It is important for communities to develop and implement a coordinated response with strong advocates from criminal justice, victim services, children's services, and allied professions. Health care providers make up a particularly important group in this regard. Educational materials and programs on IPV and sexual assault are available at the National Center for Injury Prevention & Control website (www.cdc.gov/injury/).

Violence in Schools

Although schools are one of the safest places for children to spend their time (see **Figure 15.23**), even rare acts of violence in schools strike terror into parents, teachers, and the children themselves. Highly publicized incidents of fatal shootings on school grounds have focused the nation's attention on the question of just how safe (or unsafe) our nation's schools are.

Our nation's schools should be safe havens for teaching and learning, free of crime and violence. Any instance of crime or violence at school not only affects the individuals involved but also may disrupt the educational process and affect bystanders, the school itself, and the surrounding community.[75]

The National Center for Educational Statistics (NCES), in the U.S. Department of Education (DoE), and the Bureau of Justice Statistics (BJS) in the U.S. Department of Justice jointly collect and publish data annually on the frequency, seriousness, and incidence of violence in elementary and secondary schools.[76] During the 2011 to 2012 school year, 45 student, staff, and nonstudent, school-associated violent deaths were recorded, including 26 homicides, 14 suicides and 5 legal interventions. Of these, there were 15 homicides, 5 suicides, and 0 legal intervention deaths of school-age youth (ages 5 to 18). The percentage of homicides of youths at school has remained well below 2% of all youth homicides, and the percentage of youth suicides has remained less than 1% of all youth suicides occurring nationwide. This amounts to about one homicide or suicide per 2.1 million students enrolled during the 2011 to 2012 school year. In 2013, among students aged 12 to 18 years, there were about 1,420,900 nonfatal victimizations at school, including 454,900 thefts and 966,000 violent victimization (simple assault and serious violent crime). In 2013, the rate of violent victimization in school (37 per 1,000 students) was higher than the rate away from school (15 per 1,000). The total crime victimization rate at school was greater for students ages 12 to 14 (67 per 1,000 students compared with students ages 15 to 18 (44 per 1,000 students). During 2009 to 2010, 85% of public schools recorded that one or more incidents of crime had occurred at their school, and 74% reported one or more violent incidents of violent crime.[76]

FIGURE 15.23 Despite several highly publicized tragic events, schools are one of the safest places for students to spend time.
© Blend Images/Alamy Images.

There has been an overall decline in victimization rates at school for students aged 12 to 18 years, but most of that decline occurred before 2004; victimization rates have remained steady during the past 3 years at about 3% of students. Theft was reported by 2%, violent victimization by 1%, and serious violent victimization by less than 0.5%. Although student victimization rates remained unchanged in 2004 to 2013, an increase has been noticed in teachers reporting being threatened. During the 2011 to 2012 school year, the percentage of teachers who reported being threatened varied by type of school—10% in public schools vs. 3% in private schools, or being attacked 6% in public schools vs. 3% in private schools.[76]

Fighting and weapon carrying are also concerns. In 2015, nearly one-fourth (22.6%) of students in grades 9 to 12 reported they had been in a fight during the previous year, 7.8% on school property. Sixteen percent reported having carried a weapon in the past 30 days. Three times as many males reported carrying a weapon as did females. As stated earlier, 8.7% of males in grades 9 to 12 reported carrying a gun in the past 30 days in 2015. Nationwide, 4.1% or students had carried a weapon (for example, a gun, knife, or club) on school property on at least one day in the 30 days prior to the survey.[19]

Most schools try to deal with violence problems by instituting zero tolerance policies toward serious student offenses. These policies, defined as school or district policy mandating predetermined consequences for various student offenses, have recently come under fire because administering such policies sometimes leads to somewhat extreme outcomes. In 2013, almost all schools utilized some type of security measure, such as a student code of conduct (96%), and requiring visitor sign-ins (96%), security staff (90%), security cameras (77%), and locked entrance and exit doors during the day (76%). More schools are also requiring faculty to wear badges or picture IDs and providing telephones in most classrooms. Some schools have established electronic notification systems for school-wide emergencies, and/or implemented structured anonymous threats systems. In 2011 to 2012, 19% of schools required students to wear uniforms.[76] Bullying and being bullied at school are increasingly being recognized as associated with violence-related behavior (such as carrying a weapon to school, fighting, or becoming injured in a fight).

Bullying includes being made fun of; being made the subject of rumors; being threatened with harm; being pushed, shoved, tripped, or spat on; being pressured to do something one does not want to do; being excluded, or having one's property destroyed. In 2013, 22% of 12-to

18-year olds reported having been bullied at school during the school year and 7% reported having been cyberbullied. One-third of students who reported being bullied at school and one-fourth or those who reported being cyberbullied indicated they were bullied once or twice a month during the school year.[76]

Safe Schools/Healthy Students Initiative

The *Safe Schools/Healthy Students Initiative* is a unique grant program jointly administered by the U.S. Departments of Education, Health and Human Services (Mental Health Services), and Justice. The program promotes a comprehensive, integrated problem-solving process for use by communities in addressing school violence. "Since 1999, more than 240 urban, rural, suburban, and tribal school districts—in collaboration with local mental health and juvenile justice providers—have received grants using a single application process."[77] Steps in the process are as follows:

1. Establishing school–community partnerships
2. Identifying and measuring the problem
3. Setting measurable goals and objectives
4. Identifying appropriate research-based programs and strategies
5. Implementing programs and strategies in an integrated fashion
6. Evaluating the outcomes of programs and strategies
7. Revising the plan on the basis of evaluation information

The initiative requires comprehensive, integrated community-wide plans to address at least the following six elements:[77]

1. A safe school environment
2. Alcohol and other drugs and violence prevention and early intervention programs
3. School and community mental health preventive and treatment intervention services
4. Early childhood psychosocial and emotional development services
5. Supporting and connecting schools and communities (2004–present grantees); education reform (1999–2012 grantees)
6. Safe school policies

Youth Violence after School

Although violence in schools has grabbed the headlines, the real problem area is violence committed after school. Fewer and fewer children have a parent waiting for them at home after school. Whereas many youths are able to supervise themselves and their younger siblings responsibly after school or are engaged in sports or other after-school activities, some are not. Statistics show that serious violent crime committed by juveniles peaks in the hours immediately after school (see **Figure 15.24**). Also, during these after-school hours, juveniles are most likely to become victims of crime, including violent crimes such as robberies and aggravated assaults. This is because at this unsupervised time, youth are more vulnerable to exploitation, injuries, and even death.[78]

For individuals and communities that want to engage in youth violence prevention, a variety of federal and state government agencies and private organizations offering leadership and support can be found by searching the Internet. The Centers for Disease Control and Prevention has an excellent website that lists information and resources for youth violence and youth violence prevention.[79]

Violence in Our Communities

Youth gangs and gang violence contribute to the overall level of violence in the community and are a drain on community resources.

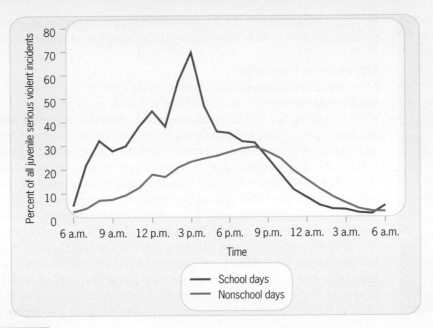

FIGURE 15.24   Serious violent crime committed by juveniles peaks in the hours immediately after school.

Data from: U.S. Department of Justice, Office of Juvenile Justice and Delinquency Prevention (1999). *Violence After School* (1999 National Report Series). Washington, DC: Author.

Youth Gang Violence

Whereas most young women and men in the United States grow up subscribing to such American ideals as democracy, individualism, equality, and education, others do not. Many of those who do not are economically disadvantaged and have lost faith in society's capacity to work on their behalf. Some of these seek refuge and reward in organized subculture groups of youngsters who feel similarly disenfranchised.

One popular subculture structure is the **youth gang**, a self-formed association of peers bound together by mutual interests, with identifiable leadership and well-defined lines of authority. Youth gangs act in concert to achieve a specific purpose, and their acts generally include illegal activities and the control over a particular territory or enterprise. Types of illegal activities in which gang members participate include larceny/theft, aggravated assault, burglary/breaking and entering, and street drug sales.

A recent survey of a representative sample of 2,199 law enforcement agencies revealed youth gang activity in 30% of the districts under their jurisdiction. This is a significant decline since 1996, when 53% of jurisdictions reported youth gang activity. An estimated 30,700 gangs were active in the United States in 2012. Gang activity is more prevalent in cities with a population of 250,000 or greater. There were more than 850,000 active gang members in 2012.[80] While youth gang activity has decline in recent years in many jurisdictions of the country, it remains attractive to some disenfranchised and unemployed youths.

Costs to the Community

Youth gangs and youth gang–related violence present an enormous drain on the law enforcement resources of a community beyond the injuries and injury deaths that result from their activities. Pressured to "do something," field officers may be pulled from other duties and not replaced. If additional police are hired, it can cost the community $75,000 per year per officer. Next, there is the additional need to strengthen the prosecutor's office if the operation is to be effective. In short, the suppression of gangs by law enforcement is costly for communities, often depleting resources for other needed community improvements. Another problem is vandalism and the defacing of public and private buildings

Youth gang an association of peers, bound by mutual interests and identifiable lines of authority, whose acts generally include illegal activity and control over a territory or an enterprise

by gang-related graffiti. This money spent repairing damage and erasing graffiti could be used to hire teachers or to support educational activities.

Community Response

Many communities have responded effectively to the increased violence resulting from gang-related activity. Perhaps the best approach is a multifaceted effort involving law enforcement, education, diversion activities, and social services support. Suppression of gang activity by law enforcement is justified because many gang-related activities—such as selling illicit drugs, carrying and discharging weapons, and defacing property—are illegal. Education of children, teachers, parents, and community leaders is another facet of gang-related violence prevention. Just as there are drug abuse prevention curricula in schools, there are now anti-gang awareness programs in some schools. Diversion activities, including job opportunities and after-school activities such as enrichment programs, sports, and recreation, can reduce the attractiveness of less wholesome uses of free time. Sports and recreational activities have long been touted as a healthy outlet for pent-up physical energy. It seems logical to assume that young persons who participate in such activities would be less likely to become involved in destructive, violent behavior (see **Figure 15.25**).

FIGURE 15.25 Adequate recreational opportunities for youth can reduce violence in a community.
© Charlie Hutton/ShutterStock, Inc.

State Response

Most, if not all, states have agencies with programs aimed at preventing or reducing the level of injuries caused by intentional violence. By searching the Internet using the words "injury prevention" or "violence prevention" and "state," one can find many of these state-funded agencies and programs. Many of the agencies or programs are concerned with both unintentional and intentional injury prevention. For example, one agency might include programs for child occupant safety, older driver safety, residential fire prevention, domestic violence, or violence against women programs, youth violence prevention, suicide prevention, and so on, with links to other injury prevention and control agency websites. Funding sources for these programs are variable. Some are funded as line items on state budgets; other programs are grant driven.

Federal Response

Several federal agencies house programs aimed at preventing or reducing the number and seriousness of intentional and unintentional injuries. The Center for Injury Prevention & Control of the Centers for Disease Control and Prevention, in the U.S. Department of Health and Human Services, has a website that provides links to a vast array of programs specifically aimed at preventing both unintentional injuries and those that result from violence (www.cdc.gov/injury/). Programs and topics are wide ranging, from child abuse/maltreatment, to dog bites, to falls among older adults, to youth violence, just to name a few.

The Office of Justice Programs (www.ojp.usdoj.gov/) is another federal agency whose mission includes improving public safety by supporting law enforcement and the justice system. The agency monitors crime and victimization, gang-related activity, substance abuse and crime, juvenile justice, and the corrections system. Their Crime Solutions website (www.crimesolutions.gov/default.aspx) lists many community-based programs under topics ranging from A–Z. These programs are briefly described and rated as their effectiveness. Another site, the Center for Faith Based & Neighborhood Partnerships (www.ojp.usdoj.gov/fbnp/), offers a variety of programs including prisoner reentry, violence prevention, and promoting reasonable fatherhood programs. Injuries, including intentional injuries, are a worldwide problem, but here in the United States, firearm availability is much greater than in most other countries. Legislative attempts aimed at making it more difficult for certain persons to acquire handguns and/or automatic weapons have failed to reduce the level of firearm injuries and deaths. Some local governments have banned guns in their jurisdictions in an effort to reduce the frequency of firearm injuries.

However, many of these bans are now in jeopardy. In June 2010, the U.S. Supreme Court ruled 5–4 that the Second Amendment applies to states and city governments in regard to gun laws and ended a nearly 30-year handgun ban in the city of Chicago.

In conclusion, intentional injuries resulting from interpersonal violence remain a national as well as a community concern. Significant resources are available at the federal level (from the U.S. Departments of Health and Human Services and Justice) to help states and local communities reduce the number and seriousness of violence-related injuries. It is up to each concerned citizen to make sure that his or her own community is taking advantage of these resources.

Chapter Summary

- Injuries are the fourth leading cause of death in the United States and the second leading cause of premature deaths, years of potential life lost (YPLL).

- Unintentional and intentional injuries represent a major community and public health problem, not only because of the loss of life but also because of lost productivity, medical costs, and the increase in the number of disabled Americans.

- Unintentional injuries are unplanned events that are usually preceded by an unsafe act or condition. They are often accompanied by economic loss, and they interrupt the efficient completion of a task.

- More fatal and nonfatal unintentional injuries occur in the home than at any other location.

- Unintentional injuries occur across all age groups; however, they are the leading cause of death for younger Americans, ages 1 to 44 years.

- Poisonings are the leading cause of unintentional injury deaths, followed by motor vehicle crashes, falls, drowning, fires and burns, and other causes.

- Males and certain minority groups suffer proportionately more unintentional injuries.

- Measures to prevent or reduce the number and severity of unintentional injuries and injury fatalities can be successful when based on a familiar public health model in which energy is the causative agent for injuries.

- There are also four broad strategies that can prevent unintentional injuries—education, regulation, automatic protection, and litigation. Together, these strategies may be used to reduce the numbers and seriousness of unintentional injuries in the community.

- Intentional injuries are the outcome of self-directed or interpersonal violence.

- The spectrum of violence includes suicides, assaults, rapes, robberies, and homicides in our communities, and the maltreatment of children, elders, and intimate partners in our homes.

- Minorities and young adults are at highest risk for injury or death from an intentional violent act.

- Family violence, including child and elder maltreatment and intimate partner violence, is a serious and pervasive community and public health problem.

- Widely publicized fatal shootings in schools have once again focused national attention on violence in our schools. However, schools remain a relatively safe place for the nation's youth.

- Youth gang activity has declined in recent years in many jurisdictions of the country, but remains attractive to some disenfranchised and unemployed youths.

- Significant resources are available at the state and federal levels (from the U.S. Departments of Health and Human Services and Justice) to assist local communities in reducing the number and seriousness of violence-related injuries

Scenario: Analysis and Response

Please take a moment to reread the scenario at the beginning of this chapter. Then, reflect on the questions that follow.

1. In what ways does the incident described in the scenario fit the definition on unintentional injury provided early in the chapter? Can you identify each element of the definition as it pertains to the incident described in the scenario?

2. Think about the four approaches to the prevention of unintentional injuries (education, regulation, automatic protection, and litigation). Provide an example of how each of these four approaches could prevent or reduce the seriousness of another, similar injury from occurring.

Review Questions

1. List the ways in which injuries are costly to society and quantify the costs in terms of the United States.

2. Identify the leading types of unintentional injury deaths and the risk factors associated with each type of death.

3. Why have the terms *accident* and *safety* lost favor with injury prevention professionals?

4. What is a hazard? Do hazards cause accidents? Explain your answer.

5. What types of injuries are most likely to occur in the home, and in which rooms are they most likely to occur?

6. Characterize injuries from the following activities by time—motor vehicle driving, swimming, and heating the home. How does alcohol consumption contribute to unintentional injuries?

7. Summarize the contributions of Hugh DeHaven, John E. Gordon, and William Haddon, Jr. to injury prevention and control.

8. Describe the epidemiological model for injuries and provide three examples of how energy causes injuries.

9. For each of your examples from Question 8, explain how the injury could have been prevented using prevention and control tactics.

10. List four broad strategies for the reduction of unintentional injuries and give an example of each.

11. Identify the different types of violent behavior that result in intentional injuries.

12. Describe the cost of intentional injuries to society.

13. Define family violence and give some examples.

14. Explain the difference between child abuse and child neglect. List some contributing factors to these phenomena.

15. What is intimate partner violence? List the types of behaviors included in the definition.

16. How safe are our schools for children? For teachers and staff? How are schools responding to safety concerns?

17. What is a youth gang? Why are gangs attractive to some youths? How can communities compete for youths' attention?

18. Describe the best ways in which communities can respond to youth gang violence.

19. What resources are available at the state and federal levels to help communities reduce the number and seriousness of injuries resulting from violence?

Activities

1. Obtain a copy of a local newspaper and find three stories dealing with unintentional injuries. Provide a two- or three-sentence summary of each article and then provide your best guess of (a) what the unsafe act or condition that preceded the event was, (b) what the resulting economic loss or injury was, and (c) what task was not completed.

2. Make an appointment and interview the director of safety on your campus. Find out what the most prevalent unintentional injuries are on campus, what strategies have been used to deal with them, and what could be done to eliminate them.

3. With guidance from your course instructor, conduct a random survey of safety belt use at your campus. Collect the data in such a manner that you can compare the results between school employees and students. Then, analyze your results and draw some conclusions.

4. Survey your home, apartment, or residence hall and create a room-by-room list of the unsafe conditions that may exist. Then, create a strategy for changing each condition.

5. Using a local newspaper, locate three articles that deal with violence. For each article, (a) provide a two-sentence summary, (b) identify and describe the victim and the perpetrator, (c) identify what you feel was the underlying cause of the violence, and (d) offer a suggestion as to how the violence could have been avoided or prevented.

6. Make an appointment with an officer of the local police department to interview him or her about violent crime in your hometown. Write a two-page summary of your interview and include answers to the following questions: (a) What is the number one violent crime? (b) What is the law enforcement department doing to control violent crime? (c) Does the city have a comprehensive program against crime? (d) What can the typical citizen do to help reduce violence?

7. Write a two-page paper on what the typical citizen can do about violence.

8. Think about the public health triangle model of disease (agent, host, and environment) and gang violence. Describe in writing who or what represents each of these factors. What steps can be taken to reduce gang-related violence using this public health model? List the steps explaining each one.

References

1. Baker, S. P. (1989). "Injury Science Comes of Age." *Journal of the American Medical Association*, 262(16): 2284–2285.
2. Miniño, A. M., and R. N. Anderson (2006). "Deaths: Injuries, 2002." *National Vital Statistics Reports*, 54(10): 1–128.
3. World Health Organization (2014). *Injuries and Violence: The Facts, 2014*. Geneva, Switzerland: Author. Available at: http://www.who.int/violence_injury_prevention/media/news/2015/Injury_violence_facts_2014/en/.
4. Centers for Disease Control and Prevention (2015). *Fatal Injury Reports*. Injury Prevention & Control: Data & Statistics (WISQARS™). Available at http://www.cdc.gov/injury/wisqars/fatal_injury_reports.html.
5. Murphy, S. L., K. D. Kochanek, J. Q. Xu, and E. Arias (2015). *Mortality in the United States, 2014*. NCHS data brief, no. 229. Hyattsville, MD, National Center for Health Statistics. Available at: http://www.cdc.gov/nchs/data/DataBriefs/db229.htm.
6. Centers for Disease Control and Prevention (2015). *Cost of Injuries and Violence in the United States*. Injury Prevention & Control: Data & Statistics (WISQARS™). Available at http://www.cdc.gov/injury/wisqars/overview/cost_of_injury.html.
7. Lopez, A. D., C. D. Mathers, M. Ezzati, D. T. Jamison, and C. Murray (2006). *Global Burden of Disease and Risk Factors*. New York: World Bank and Oxford University Press.
8. Centers for Disease Control and Prevention, National Centers for Health Statistics (2015). *Summary Health Statistics for the U.S. Population: National Health Interview Survey, 2014*. Available at http://ftp.cdc.gov/pub/Health_Statistics/NCHS/NHIS/SHS/2014_SHS_Table_P-8.pdf.
9. National Safety Council (2016). *Injury Facts*, 2016 Edition. Itasca, IL: Author.
10. Centers for Disease Control and Prevention, National Center for Health Statistics (2016). *Deaths: Final Data for 2013*. Available at: http://www.cdc.gov/nchs/data/nvsr/nvsr64/nvsr64_02.pdf.
11. Centers for Disease Control and Prevention, National Center for Health Statistics (2014). *Health, United States, 2014: With Special Feature on Adults Aged 55–64*. Hyattsville, MD: Author.
12. World Health Organization (2013). *Violence and Injury Prevention: Global Status Report on Road Safety 2013*. Geneva, Switzerland: Author. Available at http://www.who.int/violence_injury_prevention/road_safety_status/2013/en/index.html.
13. U.S. Department of Transportation, National Highway Traffic Safety Administration (2016). *Traffic Safety Facts 2014: A Compilation of Motor Vehicle Crash Data from the Fatality Analysis Reporting System and the General Estimates System* (DOT HS 812 261). Washington, DC: U.S. Department of Transportation. Available at https://crashstats.nhtsa.dot.gov/Api/Public/ViewPublication/812261
14. U.S. Department of Health and Human Services (2016). *Healthy People 2020 Topics & Objectives*. Available at http://www.healthypeople.gov/2020/topicsobjectives2020/default.aspx.
15. Centers for Disease Control and Prevention (2013). "Ten Significant Public Health Achievements—United States, 2001–2010: Motor Vehicle Safety." Available at http://www.cdc.gov/Motorvehicle-safety/mmwr_achievements.html.
16. Centers for Disease Control and Prevention (2014). "Falls and Fall Injuries among Adults with Arthritis—United States, 2012." *Morbidity and Mortality Weekly Report*, 63(17): 379–385. Available at http://www.cdc.gov/mmwr/preview/mmwrhtml/mm6317a3.htm?s_cid=mm6317a3_w.
17. Heron, M. (2015). "Deaths: Leading Causes for 2012." *National Vital Statistics Reports*, 64(10): 1–93.
18. Centers for Disease Control and Prevention (2015). *Nonfatal Injury Data*. Injury Prevention & Control: Data & Statistics (WISQARS™). Available at http://www.cdc.gov/injury/wisqars/nonfatal.html.
19. Centers for Disease Control and Prevention (2016). "Youth Risk Behavior Surveillance—United States, 2015." *Morbidity and Mortality Weekly Report*, 65(SS-6): 1–174. Available at http://www.cdc.gov/healthyyouth/data/yrbs/pdf/2015/ss6506_updated.pdf.
20. Grinshteyn, E., and D. Hemenway (2016, March). "Violent Death Rates: The US Compared with Other High-Income OECD Countries, 2010. *The American Journal of Medicine*, 129(3): 266–73.
21. Centers for Disease Control and Prevention (2014). "Rate of Nonfatal Fall Injuries Receiving Medical Attention, by Age Group—National Health Interview Survey, United States, 2012." *Morbidity Mortality Weekly Report*, 63(29): 641. Available at http://www.cdc.gov/mmwr/preview/mmwrhtml/mm6329a8.htm?s_cid=mm6329a8_w.
22. AAA Foundation for Traffic Safety (n.d.). *Senior Drivers*. Available at: https://www.aaafoundation.org/senior-drivers.
23. Griffin III, L. I. (2004). *Older Driver Involvement in Injury Crashes in Texas, 1975–1999*. Washington, DC: AAA Foundation for Traffic Safety. Available at http://www.aaafoundation.org/e-news/issue7/seniorcrashes.cfm.
24. Griffin III, L. I., and S. DeLaZerda (2000). *Unlicensed to Kill*. Washington, DC: AAA Foundation for Traffic Safety. Available at www.aaafoundation.org/pdf/unlicensed2kill.pdf.
25. Warner, M. L., H. Chen, D. M. Makuc, R. N. Anderson, and A. M. Miniño (2011). *Drug Poisoning Deaths in the United States, 1980–2008*. National Center for Health Statistics Data Brief No. 81. Available at http://www.cdc.gov/nchs/data/databriefs/db81.htm.
26. Centers for Disease Control and Prevention (2014). "Vital Signs: Restraint Use and Motor Vehicle Occupant Death Rates Among Children Aged 0–12 Years—United States, 2002–2011. *Morbidity and Mortality Weekly Report*, 63(5): 113–118. Available at http://www.cdc.gov/mmwr/pdf/wk/mm6305.pdf.
27. Centers for Disease Control and Prevention (2004). "Child Passenger Deaths Involving Drinking Drivers—United States, 1997–2002." *Morbidity and Mortality Weekly Report*, 53(4): 77–79. Available at http://www.cdc.gov/mmwr/PDF/wk/mm5304.pdf.
28. U.S. Department of Homeland Security, U.S. Coast Guard (2015). *Recreational Boating Statistics 2014* (COMDTPUB P16754.28). Available at http://www.uscgboating.org/library/accident-statistics/Recreational-Boating-Statistics-2014.pdf.
29. U.S. Department of Homeland Security, U.S. Coast Guard (2000). *Boating Statistics—1999* (COMDTPUB P16754.16). Available at http://www.uscgboating.org/assets/1/-Publications/Boating_Statistics_1999.pdf.
30. Christoffel, T., and S. S. Gallagher (2006). *Injury Prevention and Public Health: Practical Knowledge, Skills, and Strategies*, 2nd ed. Burlington, MA: Jones & Bartlett Learning.
31. Centers for Disease Control and Prevention (2014). "Potentially Preventable Deaths from the Five Leading Causes of Death—United States, 2008–2010." *Morbidity and Mortality Weekly Report* 63(17): 369–374. Available at http://www.cdc.gov/mmwr/pdf/wk/mm6317.pdf.
32. Shults, R. A., and L. F. Beck (2012). "Self-Reported Seatbelt Use, United States, 2002–2010: Does Prevalence Vary by State and Type of Seatbelt Law?" *Journal of Safety Research*, 43(2012): 417–420.
33. Centers for Disease Control and Prevention (2010). "Reducing Alcohol-Impaired Driving: 0.08% Blood Alcohol Concentration (BAC) Laws." *The Community Guide: The Guide to Community Preventive Services*. Available at http://www.thecommunityguide.org/mvoi/AID/BAC-laws.html.
34. Hamilton, B. C., L. S. Arnold, and B. C. Tefft (2013). "*Distracted and Risk-Prone Drives: Select Findings from the 2012 Traffic Safety*

Culture Index." Washington, DC: AAA Foundation for Traffic Safety. Available at https://www.aaafoundation.org/sites/default/files/Distracted%20and%20Risk%20Prone%20Drivers%20FINAL.pdf.

35. National Highway Traffic Safety Administraton (2015). *2014 Crash Data Key Findings.* Traffic Safety Facts Crash Stats, DOT HS 812 219. Available at http://www-nrd.nhtsa.dot.gov/Pubs/812219.pdf.

36. McEvoy, S. P., M. R. Stevenson, A. T. McCartt, M. Woodward, C. Haworth, P. Palmara, and R. Cercarelli (2005). "Role of Mobile Phones in Motor Vehicle Crashes Resulting in Hospital Attendance: A Case-Crossover Study." *British Medical Journal,* 331(7514): 428–430.

37. Olsen, E. O., R. A. Shults, and D. K. Eaton (2013). "Texting While Driving and Other Risky Motor Vehicle Behaviors Among U. S. High School Students." *Pediatrics,* 131(6): e1798–1715. Available at: http://pediatrics.aappublications.org/content/early/2013/05/08/peds.2012-3462.

38. National Highway Traffic Safety Administration (2015). *Distracted Driving: Facts and Statistics.* Available at http://www.distraction.gov/stats-research-laws/facts-and-statistics.html.

39. Governors Highway Safety Association (2013) *2013 Distracted Driving: Survey of the States.* Available at http://www.ghsa.org/html/publications/survey/distraction2013.html.

40. National Highway Traffic Safety Administration, U.S. Department of Transportation (2015). *Key Facts and Statistics.* Distraction. Gov: The Official U.S. Government Website for Distracted Driving. Available at http://www.distraction.gov/stats-research-laws/state-laws.html.

41. Waller, P. F. (2002). "Challenges in Motor Vehicle Safety." *Annual Review of Public Health,* 23: 93–113.

42. Centers for Disease Control and Prevention (1982). "Unintentional and Intentional Injuries—United States." *Morbidity and Mortality Weekly Report,* 31(18): 240–248.

43. National Highway Traffic Safety Administration (2014). *NHTSA Announces Final Rule Requiring Rear Visibility Technology.* Press Release. Available at http://www.nhtsa.gov/About+NHTSA/Press+Releases/2014/NHTSA+Announces+Final+Rule+Requiring+Rear+Visibility+Technology.

44. Jackson, I. (2014). *GM Settlements to be Paid for Accidents Where Airbags Did Not Deploy.* Available at http://www.aboutlawsuits.com/gm-settlement-fund-67181/.

45. Centers for Disease Control and Prevention, National Center for Health Statistics (2013). *National Hospital Ambulatory Care Survey: 2010 Emergency Department Summary Tables.* Available at http://www.cdc.gov/nchs/data/ahcd/nhamcs_emergency/2010_ed_web_tables.pdf.

46. Truman, J. L., and L. Langton (2015). *Criminal Victimization, 2014.* (NCJ 248973) Washington, DC: U.S. Department of Justice, Bureau of Justice Statistics. Available at http://www.bjs.gov/content/pub/pdf/cv14.pdf.

47. Federal Bureau of Investigation (2015). "Crime in the United States 2014." *Uniform Crime Reports.* Available at https://www.fbi.gov/about-us/cjis/ucr/crime-in-the-u.s/2014/crime-in-the-u.s.-2014.

48. United Nations Office on Drugs and Crime (2012). *UNODC Homicide Statistics.* Available at http://www.unodc.org/unodc/en/data-and-analysis/homicide.html.

49. Centers for Disease Control and Prevention, National Center for Health Statistics (2015). *Deaths, Percent of Total Deaths, and Death Rates for the 15 Leading Causes of Death: United States and Each State, 2013.* Available at http://www.cdc.gov/nchs/data/dvs/LCWK9_2013.pdf.

50. Planty, M., and J. L. Truman (2013). *Firearm Violence, 1993–2011.* Washington, DC: U.S. Department of Justice, Office of Justice Programs, Bureau of Justice Statistics. NCJ 241730. Available at http://www.bjs.gov/content/pub/pdf/fv9311.pdf.

51. Planty, M., L. Langton, C. Krebs, M. Berzofsky, and H. Smiley-McDonald (2013). *Female Victims of Sexual Violence, 1994–2010.* Washington, DC: U. S. Department of Justice, Office of Justice Programs, Bureau of Justice Statistics, NCJ 240655. Available at http://www.bjs.gov/content/pub/pdf/fvsv9410.pdf.

52. Miller, M., D. Hemenway, and H. Wechsler (2002). "Guns and Gun Threats at College." *Journal of American College Health,* 51(2): 57–65.

53. Schwartz, V., J. Kay, and P. Appelbaum (2010, May 12). "Keep Guns off College Campuses." *Huffington Post.* Available at http://www.huffingtonpost.com/victor-schwartz/keep-guns-off-college-cam_b_573634.htmlL.

54. Everytown for Gun Safety (2015). *Guns on Campus.* Available at http://everytownresearch.org/fact-sheet-guns-on-campus/.

55. Thompson, A., J. H. Price, J. A. Drake, et al. (2013). "Student Perceptions and Practices Regarding Carrying Concealed Handguns on University Campuses." *Journal of American College Health,* 61(5): 243–253.

56. Thompson, A., J. H. Price, J. A. Drake, and K. Teeple (2013). "Faculty Perceptions and Practices Regarding Carrying Concealed Handguns on University Campuses." *Journal of Community Health,* 38(2): 366–373.

57. Price, J. H., A. Thompson, J. Khubchandani, J. A. Drake, E. Payton, and K. Teeple (2014). "University Presidents' Perceptions and Practice Regarding the Carrying of Concealed Handguns on College Campuses." *Journal of American College Health,* 62(7): 461–469.

58. Thompson, A., J. H. Price, A. J. Mrdjenovich, and J. Khubchandani (2009). "Reducing Firearm-Related Violence on College Campuses—Police Chiefs' Perceptions and Practices." *Journal of American College Health,* 58(3): 247–254.

59. Wadman, M. (2013). "The Gunfighter." *Nature,* 496: 412–414.

60. Kuehn. B. M. (2013). "States Take a Public Health Approach to Curb Gun Violence." *Journal of the American Medical Association,* 310(5): 468–469.

61. Fleegler, E. W., L. K. Lee, M. C. Monuteaux, D. Hemenway, and R. Mannix (2013). "Firearm Legislation and Firearm-Related Fatalities in the United States." *Journal of the American Medical Association Internal Medicine,* 173(9): 732–740.

62. Centers for Disease Control and Prevention (2015). *STRIVE: Striving to Reduce Your Violence Everywhere.* Injury Prevention & Control: Division of Violence Prevention. Available at http://www.cdc.gov/violenceprevention/stryve/index.html.

63. Catalano, S. (2012). *Intimate Partner Violence, 1993–2010. Special Report.* Washington, DC: U.S. Department of Justice, Office of Justice Programs, Bureau of Justice Statistics, NCJ 239203. Available at http://www.bjs.gov/index.cfm?ty=pbdetail&iid=4536.

64. U.S. Department of Health and Human Services, Administration for Children & Families, Administration on Children, Youth and Families, Children's Bureau (2016). *Child Maltreatment 2014.* Available from http://www.acf.hhs.gov/programs/cb/research-data-technology/statistics-research/child-maltreatment.

65. National Institute of Justice (1996). *The Cycle of Violence Revisited.* Washington, DC: U.S. Department of Justice.

66. World Health Organization (2015). *Elder Abuse: Fact Sheet.* Geneva, Switzerland: Author. Available at http://www.who.int/mediacentre/factsheets/fs357/en/.

67. U.S. Census Bureau (2014). *An Aging Nation: The Older Population in the United States.* Available at https://www.census.gov/prod/2014pubs/p25-1140.pdf.

68. National Center on Elder Abuse, Administration on Aging, Department of Health and Human Services (2015). *Elder Abuse: Research/Data.* Available at http://www.ncea.aoa.gov/Library/Data/index.aspx#problem.

69. Bonnie, R. J., and R. B. Wallace (2003). *National Research Council. Elder Mistreatment: Abuse, Neglect, and Exploitation in an Aging America.* Washington, DC: National Academies Press.

70. Centers for Disease Control and Prevention (2016). *Understanding Elder Abuse: Fact Sheet 2016.* Available at http://www.cdc.gov /violenceprevention/pdf/em-factsheet-a.pdf.

71. Centers for Disease Control and Prevention, Injury Prevention & Control, Division of Violence Prevention (2014). *Elder Abuse: Risk and Protective Factors.* Available at http://www.cdc.gov/violence prevention/elderabuse/riskprotectivefactors.html.

72. Centers for Disease Control and Prevention (2016). *Intimate Partner Violence: Definitions.* Available at http://www.cdc.gov/violence prevention/intimatepartnerviolence/definitions.html.

73. Centers for Disease Control and Prevention (2014). "Prevalence and Characteristics of Sexual Violence, Stalking and Intimate Partner Violence Victimization—National Intimate Partener and Sexual Violence Survey, United States, 2011." *Morbidity and Mortality Weekly Report, Surveillance Summaries,* 63(8): 1–18. Available at http://www.cdc.gov/mmwr/preview/mmwrhtml/ss6308a1 .htm?s_cid=ss6308a1_w.

74. Centers for Disease Control and Prevention, National Center for Injury Control & Prevention (2009). *Understanding Intimate Partner Violence. Fact Sheet.* Available at http://www.cdc.gov/violence prevention/pdf/IPV_factsheet-a.pdf.

75. Henry, S. (2000). "What Is School Violence? An Integrated Definition." *Annals of the American Academy of Political and Social Science, 567: 16–29.* As cited in Indicators of School Crime and Safety: 2006 (NCES 2007-003).

76. Robers, S., J. Zhang, R. E. Morgan, and L. Musu-Gillette (2015). *Indicators of School Crime and Safety: 2014* (NCES2015-072/NCJ 248036). Washington, DC: National Center for Education Statistics, U.S. Department of Education, and Bureau of Justice Statistics, Office of Justice Programs, U.S. Department of Justice. Available at http://nces.ed.gov/pubs2015/2015072.pdf.

77. National Center for Mental Health Promotion and Youth Violence Prevention (2012). *Safe Schools/Healthy Students: Promotion and Prevention.* Available at http://sshs.promoteprevent.org/.

78. U.S. Department of Justice, Office of Juvenile Justice and Delinquency Prevention (1999). *Violence After School* (1999 National Report Series). Washington, DC: Author.

79. Centers for Disease Control and Prevention, National Center for Injury Prevention & Control (2011). *Youth Violence: Prevention Strategies.* Available at http://nces.ed.gov/pubs2015/2015072.pdf.

80. Egley, Jr., A., and J. C. Howell (2014). "Highlights of the 2012 National Youth Gang Survey." *OJJDP Fact Sheet,* NCJ 248025. U.S. Department of Justice, Office of Justice Programs, Office of Juvenile Justice and Delinquency Prevention. Available at http://www.ojjdp.gov /pubs/248025.pdf.

CHAPTER 16

Safety and Health in the Workplace

Chapter Objectives

After studying this chapter, you will be able to:

1. Describe the scope of the occupational safety and health problem in the United States and its importance to the community.

2. Identify some pioneers in the prevention of occupational injuries and disease.

3. Provide a short history of state and federal legislation on occupational safety and health.

4. Explain the difference between occupational injuries and occupational diseases and give several examples of each.

5. Discuss the types of injuries that frequently occur in the workplace and describe their occurrence with regard to person, place, and time.

6. Briefly describe broad strategies for preventing injuries in the workplace.

7. Outline the causes of, and risk factors for, violence in the workplace and describe prevention strategies.

8. Name the different types of occupational illnesses and disorders and list some of the causative agents.

9. Outline some general strategies for preventing and controlling these disorders and illnesses.

10. List several occupational safety and health professions and describe what the professionals in each of these do.

11. List and describe several kinds of workplace safety and health programs.

12. Explain the purpose of worksite health and wellness promotion programs and describe some of their features.

13. Discuss the concept behind Total Worker Health.

Scenario

Nguyen Thi Linh, "Lynn" to her friends, had been working at her new summer job in a nail salon business for 6 weeks now. With the money she earned as a manicurist, Linh planned to eventually continue her college education. Linh worked quickly and accurately, and enjoyed her work. Now, though, she had begun to worry about the safety of the chemicals in the various nail products used in the salon—products such as polishes, strengtheners, removers, and artificial nail liquids. Sometimes, after a long day in the salon, Linh would experience headaches. Once, when she was there alone, she read the list of contents of some of the products: acetone, acetonitrile, butyle acetate, dibutyl phthalate,

ethyl acetate, ethyl methacrylate, formaldehyde, isopropyl acetate, methacrilic acid, methyl methacrylate, quaternary ammonium compounds, toluene... Linh wrote down the names of some of the chemicals. When she returned home, she searched the Internet to learn whether any of them could be responsible for her headaches. She learned that some of these chemicals irritate the skin and nose and cause asthma. Others cause headaches, dizziness, and irritated eyes, nose, and throat; still others can damage liver and kidneys, and can even harm to unborn children. Linh began to wonder whether she should continue to work as a nail technician.

Introduction

The global workforce exceeds 3.3 billion workers and is continuously growing. Approximately 85% of these workers are in less developed countries, where working conditions are more hazardous than in more developed countries. Each year as many as 317 million workers experience nonfatal occupational injuries and 321,000 workers are fatally injured. This amounts to nearly 1 million workplace injuries and 1 thousand injury deaths every day. Also, each year diseases acquired in the workplace sicken 160 million and kill an estimated 2.02 million workers.[1] Therefore, nearly 440,000 people are sickened and 5,500 workers die each day from a workplace exposure. It is estimated that the equivalent of $1.25 trillion are lost annually from the global gross domestic product by direct and indirect costs of occupational injuries and diseases.[2]

The number of civilian Americans employed in the labor force, as of January 2016, was approximately 158 million.[3] After home, Americans spend the next largest portion of their time at work; thus, safe and healthy workplaces are essential if the United States is to reach its future health objectives. It is not always easy to distinguish between the terms *occupational injury* and *occupational illness* or *disease*. However, it is generally accepted that an **occupational disease** is any abnormal condition or disorder, other than one resulting from an occupational injury, caused by factors associated with employment. It includes acute or chronic illnesses or disease that may be caused by inhalation, absorption, ingestion, or direct contact. An **occupational injury** is any injury, such as a cut, fracture, sprain, or amputation, which results from a work-related event or from a single, instantaneous exposure in the work environment.[4]

Scope of the Problem

Each day in the United States, on average, fewer than 11 workers die from an injury sustained at work. Although even one worker death is one too many, it is instructive to note that the work-related fatality rates in the U.S. have declined significantly over the past 85 years. In 1928, an estimated 19,000 work-related unintentional injury deaths occurred, a death rate of 16 per 100,000 workers.[5] In 2014, there were 4,679 such deaths, and the death rate for occupational injury deaths had fallen to 3.3 per 100,000 workers.[6]

Nearly 3 million nonfatal injuries and illnesses were reported in private industry workplaces during 2014, resulting in a rate of 3.2 cases per 100 equivalent full-time workers. More than one-half of these injuries and illnesses in private industry required recuperation away from work beyond the day of the incident or transfer or restriction in 2014. The vast majority of these events, 95.1%, were classified as injuries; 4.9% were classified as illnesses.[7]

Occupational disease an abnormal condition, other than an occupational injury, caused by an exposure to environmental factors associated with employment

Occupational injury an injury that results from exposure to a single incident in the work environment

Even though more workplace injuries are reported than workplace illnesses, the estimated number of deaths is higher for workplace illnesses. For example, in the United Kingdom, where these data are carefully maintained, 2,535 people died from mesothelioma alone in 2012, compared with 133 workers who died from fatal workplace injuries; 23.5 million working days were lost because of work-related illness compared with 4.3 million due to workplace injury.[8] Worldwide, it is estimated that fewer than one in five work-related deaths is the result of an injury.[2]

Occupational injuries and illnesses are an economic issue, too. It has been estimated that workplace injuries and illnesses and resulting deaths cost $140 billion annually, including $45.7 billion in lost wages and productivity, $31 billion in medical costs, and $44 billion in administrative costs. It also includes employers' uninsured costs of lost time of workers other than those with disabling injuries ($11 billion), investigation costs, vehicle damage losses and fire losses[5] Thus, each worker in the U.S. must produce $1,000 in goods and services just to offset the cost of work-related injuries and illnesses.

Importance of Occupational Safety and Health to the Community

Because of the grim statistics previously stated, it is important to recognize how occupational and community health problems are linked. The population of those working in industry is a subset of the population of the larger community in which the industry is located. Workers, usually the healthiest people in the community, are exposed in the course of their jobs to specific hazardous materials at the highest concentrations. It is in the factory that the most accurate exposure and health data are available for extrapolation to the general community. Most pollutants for which safe exposure levels have been adopted are workplace materials for which occupational exposures were studied first.

Hazardous agents in the workplace affect not only workers but also those outside the worksite. This can occur through soil and groundwater contamination with solids and liquids or air pollution with industrial gases and dusts. It can also occur through clothing and vehicle contamination, as in the case of asbestos workers whose wives and children became exposed to asbestos from these sources or, more recently, electronic waste recyclers who unknowingly exposed their families to lead dust from their workplace. It is important to note that the general population, which includes children, the elderly, and pregnant women, is more sensitive to exposure to pollutants than the workforce.

Another way that industries and their communities share health problems is in the instance of an industrial disaster. Examples include the Three Mile Island (Pennsylvania) nuclear reactor near-meltdown in the United States in 1979, the Bhopal tragedy in India in 1984, and the Chernobyl nuclear catastrophe in the Ukraine in 1986. In these cases, the risk of exposure to a chemical or nuclear energy source, which was originally limited to the workplace, became a community-wide risk.

Finally, it is important to recognize the workers themselves as a community, with common social problems and environmental risks. The failure to recognize the community nature of occupational groups and to monitor chronic conditions such as dermatitis, headaches, blood pressure, or blood chemistries has been a major weakness in our conventional approach to occupational health problems.

History of Occupational Safety and Health Problems

Occupational risks undoubtedly occurred even in prehistoric times, not only during hunting and warfare, but also in more peaceful activities such as the preparation of flint by knapping. The discovery of flint heaps suggests that even these earliest of workers may have been at risk for silicosis (dust in the lungs).

An extensive historical review of occupational safety and health problems from early Egyptian times to late in the twentieth century has been published.[9] Among the early milestones was George Agricola's treatise on mining in 1561, *De Re Metallica*, which emphasized the need for ventilation of mines. In 1567, the work of Philippus Aureolus Theophrastus Bombastus von Hohenheim, also known as Paracelsus, was published under the title, *On the Miners' Sickness and Other Miners' Diseases*. These were the first significant works describing specific occupational diseases. The first work on occupational diseases in general was Ramazzini's *Discourse on the Diseases of Workers*, which appeared in 1700.[10,11] In this chapter, we concentrate only on recent events in the United States and make only brief references to earlier milestones.

Occupational Safety and Health in the United States Before 1970

The Industrial Revolution, which began in Britain in the eighteenth century, soon spread to continental Europe and then to the United States. Factors creating and driving the Industrial Revolution were the substitution of steam and coal for animal power, the substitution of machines for human skills, and other advances in industrial technology. These changes resulted in the rise of mass manufacturing, the organization of large work units such as mills and factories, and eventually the exposure of masses of workers to new hazards. Although mining remained the most dangerous form of work, there were soon other unsafe occupations, such as iron smelting and working in cotton mills and textile factories (see **Figure 16.1**).

FIGURE 16.1 Cotton mills in the late nineteenth century offered little protection from injuries.

Courtesy of Library of Congress, Prints & Photographs Division, National Child Labor Committee Collection [reproduction number LC-DIG-nclc-01640].

The recognition of the need to reduce workplace injuries began long before any attention was paid to workplace diseases. The earliest efforts of those responsible for inspecting workplaces were aimed primarily at the sanitation and cleanliness of workplaces. They soon became concerned with equipment safeguards and tending to those who had become injured or ill at work.[11] These efforts, while much needed and appreciated, did little to improve the overall health of the workforce.

State Legislation

The first official responses to new hazards in the workplace did not occur until 1835, when Massachusetts passed the first Child Labor Law, and later in 1867, when it created a Department of Factory Inspection to enforce it (see **Figure 16.2**). Under this law, factories were prohibited from hiring children younger than 10 years of age.[12] At this time the federal government was concerned only with working conditions of federal employees. In 1877, Massachusetts passed the first worker safety law, aimed at protecting textile workers from hazardous spinning machinery.[13]

In 1902, Maryland became the first state to pass any kind of workers' compensation legislation. In 1908, the U.S. Congress, at the insistence of President Theodore Roosevelt, finally enacted the first of several **workers' compensation laws**; this first law covered certain federal employees. Over the next 40 years, all states and territories eventually enacted some type of workers' compensation legislation, beginning with New York in 1910 and ending with Mississippi in 1948.[9] So ended the first wave of reform in occupational safety and health. With the exception of several other legislative efforts, little progress was achieved during the first half of the twentieth century in protecting workers from injuries in the workplace, and almost nothing was done about occupational illnesses.

FIGURE 16.2 Before child labor laws were passed, many children worked long hours at dangerous jobs such as mining.

Courtesy of Library of Congress, Prints & Photographs Division, National Child Labor Committee Collection [reproduction number LC-DIG-nclc-01137].

FIGURE 16.3 Alice Hamilton (1869–1970) was a pioneer in occupational safety and health in the United States.
© National Library of Medicine.

Workers' compensation laws a set of federal laws designed to compensate those workers and their families who suffer injuries, disease, or death from workplace exposure

Occupational Safety and Health Act of 1970 (OSH Act) comprehensive federal legislation aimed at ensuring safe and healthful working conditions for working men and women

Occupational Safety and Health Administration (OSHA) the federal agency located within the U.S. Department of Labor and created by the OSH Act, which is charged with the responsibility of administering the provisions of the OSH Act

National Institute for Occupational Safety and Health (NIOSH) a research body within the U.S. Department of Health and Human Services, which is responsible for developing and recommending occupational safety and health standards

There was one exception. Alice Hamilton (1869–1970) was a strong proponent of occupational health and a true pioneer in this field (see **Figure 16.3**). Over her 40-year career in occupational health, she led crusades to reduce poisonings from heavy metals such as lead and mercury. She investigated silicosis in Arizona copper mines, carbon disulfide poisoning in the viscose rayon industry, and many other industrial health problems.[12]

In spite of Hamilton's efforts, progress in occupational health legislation was slow in the first half of the twentieth century. Occupational diseases were by and large ignored. There was some safety legislation, such as the Coal Mine Safety Act of 1952. Beginning in the 1960s, some people began to take a closer look at the various state workers' safety and workers' compensation laws. It then was discovered that in most states, legislation was a fragmentary patchwork of laws; some states had good laws, but many had inadequate legislation. Many of the laws had failed to keep up with new technology or with inflation. Some groups of workers, including agricultural workers, were not covered at all by legislation. Other problems were the division of authority among various departments within state governments, fragmented record keeping, and inadequate administrative personnel.[14]

Federal Legislation

In 1884, the federal government created a Bureau of Labor, in 1910 the Federal Bureau of Mines, and in 1914 the Office of Industrial Hygiene and Sanitation in the Public Health Service. In 1916, Congress passed the Federal Employees' Compensation Act, which provided federal employees compensation if injured while on the job.[13] Quite a few important laws were passed between 1908 and 1970 (see **Table 16.1**), but the two most comprehensive laws were the Coal Mine Health and Safety Act of 1969 and the **Occupational Safety and Health Act of 1970 (OSH Act)**, also known as the Williams-Steiger Act in honor of Senator Harrison A. Williams, Jr., and Congressman William A. Steiger, who worked for passage of the Act. At the time the act was passed, 14,000 workers died each year on the job. Since its passage, the Act has served to raise the consciousness of both management and labor to the problems of health and safety in the workplace.

Occupational Safety and Health Act of 1970

The purpose of the Occupational Safety and Health Act of 1970 is to ensure that employers in the private sector furnish each employee "employment and a place of employment which are free from recognized hazards that are causing or likely to cause death or serious physical harm."[13] Furthermore, employers were henceforth required to comply with all occupational safety and health standards promulgated and enforced under the Act by the **Occupational Safety and Health Administration (OSHA)**, which was established by the legislation.

Also established by the OSH Act was the **National Institute for Occupational Safety and Health (NIOSH)**, a research body now located in the Centers for Disease Control and Prevention of the U.S. Department of Health and Human Services. NIOSH is responsible for recommending occupational safety and health standards to OSHA, which is located in the U.S. Department of Labor (DOL).

The OSH Act contains several noteworthy provisions. Perhaps the most important is the employee's right to request an OSHA inspection. Under this right, any employee or any employee representative may notify OSHA of violations of standards or of the general duty obligation (to provide a safe and healthy workplace) by the employer. Under the Act, the employee's name must be withheld if desired, and the employee or a representative may accompany the OSHA inspectors in their inspection. By another provision of the OSH Act, individual states can regain

TABLE 16.1   Highlights of Federal Occupational Safety and Health Legislation

Year	Legislation
1908	Federal Workmen's Compensation Act—limited coverage
1916	Federal Highway Aid Act
1926	Federal Workmen's Compensation Act—amended to include all workers
1927	Federal Longshoremen's and Harbor Workers' Compensation Act
1936	Walsh-Healey Public Contracts Act
1952	Coal Mine Safety Act
1958	Federal Longshoremen's and Harbor Workers' Compensation Act—amended to include rigid safety precautions
1959	Radiation Standards Act
1960	Federal Hazardous Substances Labeling Act
1966	National Traffic and Motor Vehicle Safety Act
1966	Child Protection Act—banned hazardous household substances
1967	National Commission on Product Safety created
1968	Natural Gas Pipeline Safety Act
1969	Construction Safety Act
1969	Child Protection Act—amended to broaden the coverage
1969	**Coal Mine Health and Safety Act**
1970	**Occupational Safety and Health Act**

Source: U.S. Department of Labor, Bureau of Labor Statistics (2015). *"2014 Survey of Occupational Injuries & Illness Summary Estimates Charts Package."* Available at http://www.bls.gov/iif/oshwc/osh/os/osch0054.pdf

local authority over occupational health and safety by submitting state laws that are and will continue to be as effective as the federal programs.[13]

Prevalence of Occupational Injuries, Diseases, and Deaths

In this section, a brief overview of current trends in workplace injuries and illness is followed by a discussion of the occurrence and prevalence of work-related injuries and work-related diseases.

Overview of Recent Trends in Workplace Injuries and Illnesses

Since 1992, there has been a decline in the number of workplace injuries and illnesses reported in private industry. There were nearly 3 million injuries and illnesses reported in 2014, resulting in a rate of 3.3 cases per 100 equivalent full-time workers per year.[7] Approximately 1.16 million of these injuries and illnesses were cases with days away from work.[15] About 147,000 new, nonfatal cases of occupational illnesses were reported in private industry in 2014. This statistic does not include long-term latent illnesses, which are often difficult to relate to the workplace and therefore are underreported.[7]

In the private sector in 2014, the goods-producing industries had a higher rate of nonfatal injuries and illnesses per 100 full-time workers (3.8) than the service-providing industries (3.0). Within the goods-producing industries, agriculture, forestry, fishing, and hunting had the highest rate of nonfatal injuries and illnesses (5.5 per 100 full-time workers), followed by manufacturing (4.0), construction (3.6), and mining (2.0). Within the service-providing industries, health care and social assistance had the highest nonfatal injury rate (4.5), followed by art,

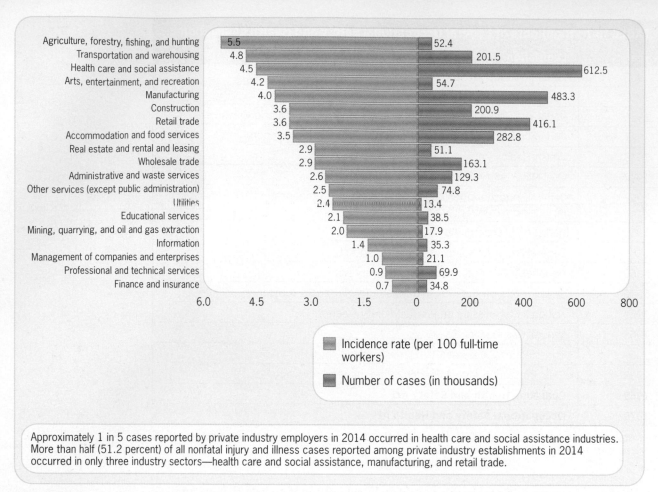

Approximately 1 in 5 cases reported by private industry employers in 2014 occurred in health care and social assistance industries. More than half (51.2 percent) of all nonfatal injury and illness cases reported among private industry establishments in 2014 occurred in only three industry sectors—health care and social assistance, manufacturing, and retail trade.

FIGURE 16.4   Incidence rates and numbers of nonfatal occupational injuries and illnesses by private industry sector, 2014.

Data from: U.S. Department of Labor, Bureau of Labor Statistics (2015). *2014 Survey of Occupational Injuries & Illness: Summary Estimates Charts Package.* Available at http://www .bls.gov/iif/oshwc/osh/os/osch0054.pdf.

entertainment, and recreation (4.2), and retail trade. Management of companies and enterprises (1.0), professional and technical services (0.9), and finance and insurance (0.7) had the lowest rates (see **Figure 16.4**).[7]

Specific industries within industry groups had higher nonfatal injury and illness rates. For example, the animal production industry had a rate of 7.1 per 100 full-time workers, transportation and warehousing had 4.8, hospitals had 6.2, and nursing homes and residential facilities workers had a nonfatal injury and illness rate of 7.1 per 100 full-time workers.[7] In one recent report it was revealed that in 2011, U.S. health care personnel experienced seven times the national rate of musculoskeletal disorders compared with all other private sector workers.[16] Nonfatal occupational injury and illness incidence rates have declined steadily since 2003, although little change was noted from 2013 to 2014 (see **Figure 16.5**).[7,15]

Unintentional Injuries in the Workplace

Unintentional injuries in the workplace include minor injuries (such as bruises, cuts, abrasions, and minor burns), and major injuries (such as amputations, fractures, severe lacerations, eye losses, acute poisonings, and severe burns). Statistics on injuries and injury deaths are available from several sources, including the National Center for Health Statistics (NCHS), the National

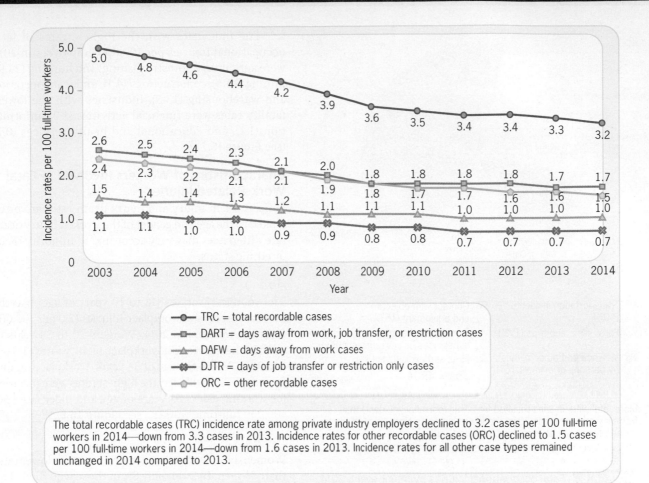

The total recordable cases (TRC) incidence rate among private industry employers declined to 3.2 cases per 100 full-time workers in 2014—down from 3.3 cases in 2013. Incidence rates for other recordable cases (ORC) declined to 1.5 cases per 100 full-time workers in 2014—down from 1.6 cases in 2013. Incidence rates for all other case types remained unchanged in 2014 compared to 2013.

FIGURE 16.5   Nonfatal occupational injury and illness incidence rates by case type, private industry, 2003–2014.

Data from: U.S. Department of Labor, Bureau of Labor Statistics (2015). *2014 Survey of Occupational Injuries & Illness: Summary Estimates Charts Package.* Available at http://www.bls.gov/iif/oshwc/osh/os/osch0054.pdf.

Safety Council (NSC), the Bureau of Labor Statistics (BLS), and NIOSH. For this reason, estimates of the number of occupational injuries and injury deaths vary. However, beginning in 1992, the NSC adopted the figures published by BLS reports, including its Census of Fatal Occupational Injuries (CFOI) and its annual report on workplace injuries and illnesses. The BLS reports are the source of figures used in this text.[6,7,15,17]

Fatal Work-Related Injuries

In 2014, there were 4,679 fatal work-related injuries, or about 12.8 per day. The fatal occupational injury rate for 2014 was 3.3 per 100,000 full-time equivalent workers.[6,17] Overall, the 2014 total of fatal occupational injuries based on preliminary data was higher than the revised counts for 2013, although the fatality rate remained the same. It is assumed that when the revisions for 2014 are made, additional fatalities will be reported. A recovering economy may be the reason that the overall number of workplace fatalities increased in 2014.

Transportation incidents (1,891) accounted for two out of every five fatal workplace injuries. Roadway incidents continued to lead the way, with 1,075 deaths (23% of the total); followed by violence with 749 deaths (16%), being struck by an object or equipment with 708 (15%), falls with 793 deaths (17%), exposure to harmful substances or environments with 390 deaths (8%), and fire and explosions with 137 deaths (3%) (**Figure 16.6**).[6,17]

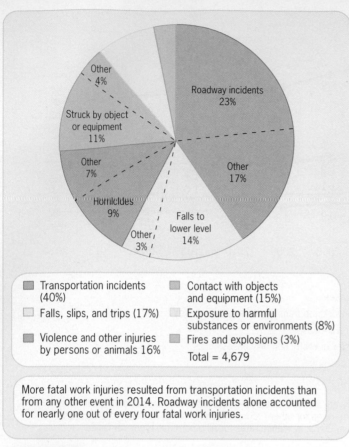

Transportation incidents (40%)

Falls, slips, and trips (17%)

Violence and other injuries by persons or animals 16%

Contact with objects and equipment (15%)

Exposure to harmful substances or environments (8%)

Fires and explosions (3%)

Total = 4,679

More fatal work injuries resulted from transportation incidents than from any other event in 2014. Roadway incidents alone accounted for nearly one out of every four fatal work injuries.

FIGURE 16.6   Fatal occupational injuries by major event, 2014.

Data from: U.S. Department of Labor, Bureau of Labor Statistics (2015). *Census of Fatal Occupational Injuries, 2014 (Chart Package)*. Available at http://www.bls.gov/iif/oshwc/cfoi/cfch0013.pdf.

The industries with the highest rates of fatal occupational injuries per 100,000 employees in 2014 were agriculture, forestry, fishing, and hunting (24.9), mining (13.5), construction (14.1), and transportation and warehousing (13.5). Industries with the lowest fatality rates were financial activities (1.2), information (1.1), and educational and health services (0.7) (see **Figure 16.7**).[6,17]

Characteristics of Workers Involved in Fatal Work-Related Injuries

Differences in injury and injury death rates are often related to the age and gender of the worker. Injury death rate differences may vary according to minority racial or ethnic status.

Age

The youngest workers (18 to 19 years of age) had the lowest rates of fatal workplace injuries (2.0 per 100,000 full-time workers) in 2014. Workers 20 to 34 years of age had the next lowest workplace fatality rates (2.3 per 100,000). Above the age of 34 years, workplace fatality rates increased with age; the highest rates were recorded for working elders 65 years of age and older (10.2 per 100,000 full-time workers; see **Figure 16.8**).[6,17]

Gender

Women die of work-related injuries at much lower rates than do men. In 2014, only 8% of those who died of an injury in the workplace were women even though they worked 43% of all the hours worked (see **Figure 16.9**).[17] When statistics are adjusted for the numbers of each sex in the workforce, the overall occupational death rate for men is nine times higher than for women (5.4 deaths per 100,000 for men, compared with 0.6 per 100,000 workers for women).[6] A significant portion of the difference results from men being employed in more dangerous jobs. Industries with the highest fatality rates are the same for both men and women—mining, agriculture, construction, and transportation. Although the number of homicides is higher among men, proportionally homicides are greater for women, accounting for nearly one in five of women's job-related fatalities.[17]

Minority Status

Fatality rates for Hispanic or Latino workers were lower in 2014 than in 2013, but still the highest among worker groups (3.6 fatalities per 100,000 full-time workers). Only slightly lower were workplace fatality rates for white (non-Hispanic) workers (3.4) and black or African-American (non-Hispanic) workers (3.0). Asian (non-Hispanic) workers had the lowest workplace fatality rates (1.7 fatalities per 100,000 full-time workers).[6]

Nonfatal Work-Related Injuries

Nonfatal work-related injuries diminish productivity and jeopardize both employee wages and employer profits. In 2014, nearly 3 million injuries and illnesses were reported in private industry and 722,300 injuries and illnesses were reported in state and local government workers. Approximately 2.8 million work-related injuries were treated in emergency departments and 140,000 workers were hospitalized in 2013, the most recent year for which data are available.[18] The economic burden of worker injuries and illnesses for 2010 was estimated at $263 billion.[19]

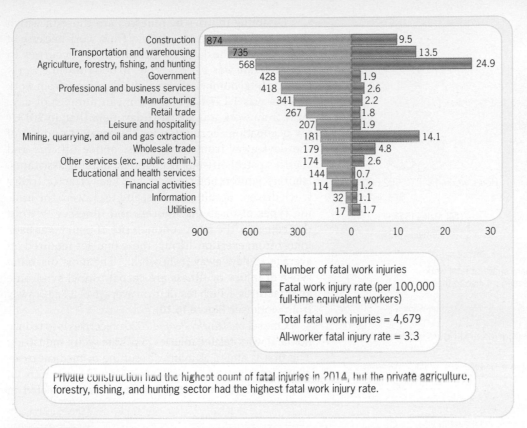

Private construction had the highest count of fatal injuries in 2014, but the private agriculture, forestry, fishing, and hunting sector had the highest fatal work injury rate.

FIGURE 16.7 Number and rate of fatal occupational injuries, by industry sector, 2014.

Data from: U.S. Department of Labor, Bureau of Labor Statistics (2015). *Census of Fatal Occupational Injuries, 2014 (Chart Package).* Available at http://www.bls.gov/iif/oshwc/cfoi/cfch0013.pdf.

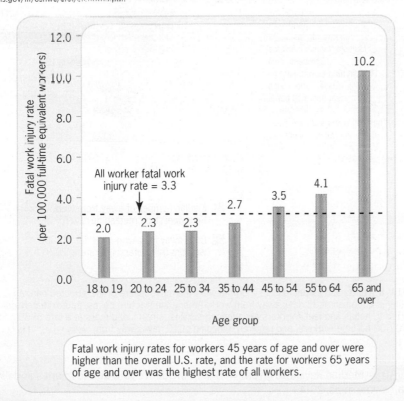

Fatal work injury rates for workers 45 years of age and over were higher than the overall U.S. rate, and the rate for workers 65 years of age and over was the highest rate of all workers.

FIGURE 16.8 Fatal work injury rates, by age group, 2014.

Data from: U.S. Department of Labor, Bureau of Labor Statistics (2015). *Census of Fatal Occupational Injuries, 2014 (Chart Package).* Available at http://www.bls.gov/iif/oshwc/cfoi/cfch0013.pdf.

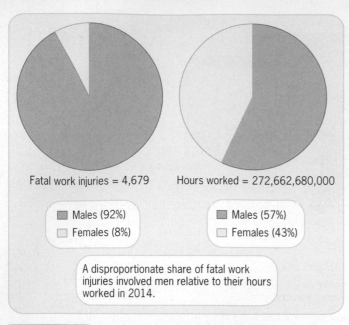

Fatal work injuries = 4,679

Hours worked = 272,662,680,000

- ■ Males (92%)
- □ Females (8%)

- ■ Males (57%)
- □ Females (43%)

A disproportionate share of fatal work injuries involved men relative to their hours worked in 2014.

FIGURE 16.9   Fatal work injuries and hours worked by gender of worker, 2014.

Data from: U.S. Department of Labor, Bureau of Labor Statistics (2015). *Census of Fatal Occupational Injuries, 2014 (Chart Package)*. Available at http://www.bls.gov/iif/oshwc/cfoi /cfch0013.pdf.

Disabling injuries or illnesses are those in which the injured worker remains away from work because of injury beyond the day on which the injury occurred. In 2014, the rate was 107 cases per 10,000 full-time workers. The total number of cases with days away from work in 2014 was 1,157,410 and the mean number of days away from work was 9 days, 1 day more than in 2013.[15] Six occupations accounted for the greatest number of the days-away-from-work cases: police officers and sheriff's patrol officers, firefighters, nursing assistants, laborers, janitors and cleaners, and heavy tractor-trailer truck drivers. Sprains, strains, and tears were the leading types of disabling injuries and illnesses. Within this category, the most common site of injury was back injury from exertion/lifting; these injuries required on average 13 days away from work.[15] The most disabling types of injury or illness are carpal tunnel syndrome and fractures, which result in an average of 32 days away from work (see **Figure 16.10**).[15]

One set of *Healthy People 2020* objectives is to reduce nonfatal work-related injuries in private sector industries. The first is aimed at injuries resulting in medical treatment, lost time from work, or restricted work activity; a second objective targets nonfatal injuries treated in

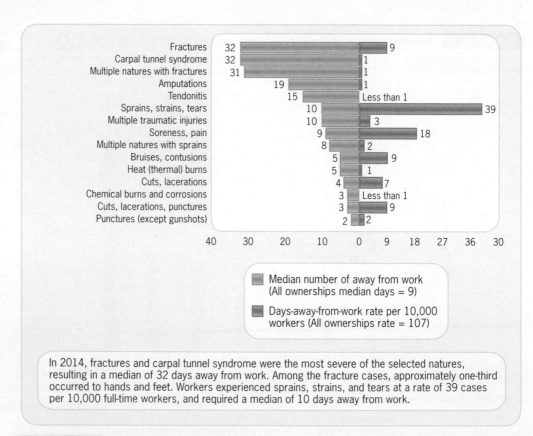

In 2014, fractures and carpal tunnel syndrome were the most severe of the selected natures, resulting in a median of 32 days away from work. Among the fracture cases, approximately one-third occurred to hands and feet. Workers experienced sprains, strains, and tears at a rate of 39 cases per 10,000 full-time workers, and required a median of 10 days away from work.

FIGURE 16.10   Median days away from work and incidence rate due to injuries and illnesses by nature, all ownerships, 2014.

Data from: U.S. Department of Labor, Bureau of Labor Statistics (2015). *2014 Nonfatal Occupational Injuries and Illnesses: Cases with Days Away from Work: Cases and Demographics*. Available at http://stats.bls.gov/iif/oshwc/osh/case/osch0055.pdf.

emergency departments. A third objective aims at reducing nonfatal injuries among adolescent workers. According to available data, the target rates for each of these objectives had been surpassed by 2012 (see **Box 16.1**).[20]

Characteristics of Workers Involved in Work-Related Injuries

Age

Workers aged 45 to 54 years had the highest incidence of workplace injuries and illnesses (117.2 cases per 10,000 full-time workers). Workers aged 55 to 64 had nearly as high a rate (116.3 cases per 10,000 full-time workers).[15] Younger workers typically experience a lower rate of fatal workplace injuries, but a higher rate of nonfatal injuries than workers 25 years of age and older.[21] Younger workers typically spend fewer days away from work for each disabling injury. In 2014, young workers spent the lowest median number of days away from work (4 days) for each disabling injury or illness of any age group. The fewer days away from work per disabling injury or illness and the lower fatality rates being experienced by younger workers may reflect the types of employment today's young people find—fewer are finding manufacturing jobs and more are finding employment in service-providing industries. The median number of days spent away from work for a disabling injury in 2014 was 9 days. Days away from work for each disabling injury increase with age; 55-to-64-year olds average 12 days away from work, while workers 65 years and older required a median of 17 days away from work for each disabling injury or illness.[15]

One group of workers that is of special concern is children. An estimated 70% to 80% of teens have worked for pay at some time during their high school years; 50% of employed youths work more than 15 hours during the school week. One in six works more than 25 hours during the school week. Although some level of employment may be desirable, studies show that teens

---

BOX 16.1   *Healthy People 2020*: Objectives

OSH-2.1:   Reduce nonfatal work-related injuries in private sector industries.

Target-setting method: 10% improvement.

Data sources: Survey of Occupational Injuries and Illnesses (SOII), DOL, BLS; National Electronic Injury Surveillance System-Work Supplement (NEISS-Work), CDC, NIOSH; Current Population Survey, U.S. Bureau of the Census.

Target and baseline:

Objective	2008 Baseline	Status (year)	2020 Target
	Injuries per 100 full-time equivalent workers		
OSH-2.1 Reduce nonfatal work-related injuries resulting in medical treatment, lost time from work, or restricted work activity, as reported by employers.	4.2	3.3 (2013)	3.8
OSH-2.2 Reduce nonfatal work-related injuries treated in emergency departments.	2.4	2.0 (2012)	2.2
OSH-2.3 Reduce nonfatal work-related injuries among adolescent workers aged 15 to 19 years.	5.5	4.5 (2012)	4.9

For Further Thought

The target for each of these reductions in nonfatal work-related injuries is 10% reduction in injury rates. In retrospect that target seems modest. According to the available data (middle column of figures), the announced targets had been surpassed by 2012. What do you think the effect of a stronger or weaker economy would have on meeting the target level? How does the shift to a "service economy" from a "manufacturing economy" affect the rate of nonfatal injuries in the workplace?

who work more than 20 hours a week do worse academically and are more likely to abuse drugs and alcohol. There are other dangers, too. Every 9 minutes, a teenaged worker is injured in the workplace and, in a typical year, every 14 days a child worker dies. The five most dangerous jobs for teens in 2015 were (1) tobacco harvesting, (2) harvesting crops and using machinery, (3) traveling youth sales crews, (4) construction and height work, and (5) landscaping, grounds keeping, and lawn service.[22] Agriculture is usually ranked as the most dangerous industry by the National Safety Council.[5]

At particular risk are those youth who are employed in violation of child labor laws. An estimated 148,000 youth are illegally employed during an average week in the United States. This figure does not include the roughly 300,000 to 500,000 youth aged 6 to 17 years who are working as migrant and seasonal farmworkers.[23] Violations of child labor regulations are all too common and not always rigorously enforced. In 2011, three states—Missouri, Maine, and Wisconsin—have actually rolled back protections or removed limits on the number of hours children can work during a school week.[22] Youth employment peaks during summers, when an estimated 5.5 million youths find jobs. Young workers are at particular risk for injury because (1) they may not be trained to perform the assigned task, (2) they may not be adequately supervised, (3) they lack experience and maturity needed to perform assigned tasks and to recognize hazards, and (4) they may be unaware of child labor laws aimed at protecting them. **Box 16.2** provides recommendations for protecting the safety and health of young workers.[24]

BOX 16.2   Hazardous Work for Adolescents and Practical Steps for Protecting Their Safety and Health

Work Too Hazardous for Adolescents

- Working in or around motor vehicles
- Operating tractors and other heavy equipment
- Working in retail and service industries where there is a risk of robbery-related homicide
- Working on ladders, scaffolds, roofs, or construction sites
- Continuous manual lifting or lifting of heavy objects

Recommendations

Young Workers

Young workers should take the following steps to protect themselves:

1. *Know about and follow safe work practices.*
   - Recognize the potential for injury at work.
   - Follow safe work practices.
   - Seek information about safe work practices from employers, school counselors, parents, state labor departments, and the Department of Labor (DOL). Visit www.youthrules.dol.gov, or call 1-866-4-USWAGE.

2. *Ask about training:* Participate in training programs offered by your employer, or request training if none is offered.

3. *Ask about hazards:* Don't be afraid to ask questions if you are not sure about the task you are asked to do. Discuss your concerns with your supervisor or employer first.

4. *Know your rights:* Be aware that you have the right to work in a safe and healthful work environment free of recognized hazards. Visit www.osha.gov/sltc /teenworkers/index.html.
   - You have the right to refuse unsafe work tasks and conditions.
   - You have the right to file complaints with DOL when you feel your rights have been violated or your safety has been jeopardized.
   - You are entitled to workers' compensation for a work-related injury or illness.

5. *Know the laws:* Before you start work, learn what jobs young workers are prohibited from doing. State child labor laws may be more restrictive than federal laws, and they vary considerably from state to state. Visit www.youthrules.dol.gov or call 1-866-4-USWAGE.

Employers

Employers should take the following steps to protect young workers:

1. *Recognize the hazards.*
   - Reduce the potential for injury or illness in young workers by assessing and eliminating hazards in the workplace.
   - Make sure equipment used by young workers is safe and legal. Visit www.dol.gov/dol/topic/youthlabor /hazardousjobs.htm or call 1-866-4-USADOL.

(Continues)

BOX 16.2   Hazardous Work for Adolescents and Practical Steps for Protecting Their Safety and Health (Continued)

2. *Supervise young workers.*
   - Make sure that young workers are appropriately supervised.
   - Make sure that supervisors and adult coworkers are aware of tasks young workers may or may not perform.
   - Label equipment that young workers cannot use, or color-code uniforms of young workers so that others will know they cannot perform certain jobs.
3. *Provide training.*
   - Provide training in hazard recognition and safe work practices.
   - Have young workers demonstrate that they can perform assigned tasks safely and correctly.
   - Ask young workers for feedback about the training.
4. *Know and comply with the laws:* Know and comply with child labor laws and occupational safety and health regulations that apply to your business. State laws may be more restrictive than federal laws, and they vary considerably from state to state. Post these regulations for workers to read. For information about federal child labor laws, visit www .dol.gov/dol/topic/youthlabor/index.htm or call 1-866-4 USADOL. Links to state labor offices are available at www.youthrules.dol/gov/states.htm (1-866-4-USWAGE). Information about OSHA regulations that apply to workers of all ages is available at www.osha.gov.
5. *Develop an injury and illness prevention program:* Involve supervisors and experienced workers in developing a comprehensive safety program that includes an injury and illness prevention program and a process for identifying and solving safety and health problems. OSHA consultation programs are available in every state to help employers identify hazards and improve their safety and health management programs.

Educators

Educators should take the following steps to protect young workers:

1. *Talk to students about work:* Talk to students about safety and health hazards in the workplace and students' rights and responsibilities as workers.
2. *Ensure the safety of school-based work experience programs:* Ensure that vocational education programs, school-to-work, or Workforce Investment Act partnerships offer students work that is allowed by law and is in safe and healthful environments free of recognized hazards. All such programs should include safety and health training.
3. *Include worker safety and health in the school curriculum:* Incorporate occupational safety and health topics into high school and junior high curricula (e.g., safety and health regulations, how to recognize hazards, how to communicate safety concerns, where to go for help). Information is available from NIOSH at 1-800-35-NIOSH.
4. *Know the laws:* If you are responsible for signing work permits or certificates, know the child labor laws. State laws may be more restrictive than federal laws, and they vary considerably from state to state. Visit www .dol.gov/gol/topic/youthlabor/ResourcesforEducators .htm (or call 1-866-USADOL), or www. youthrules.dol .gov (or call 1-866-4-USWAGE).

Parents

Parents should take the following steps to protect young workers:

1. *Take an active role in your child's employment.*
   - Know the name of your child's employer and your child's work address and phone number.
   - Ask your child about the types of work involved, work tasks, and equipment he or she uses at work.
   - Ask your child about training and supervision provided by the employer.
   - Be alert for signs of fatigue or stress as your child tries to balance demands of work, school, home, and extracurricular activities.
2. *Know the laws:* Be familiar with child labor laws. State laws may be more restrictive than federal laws, and they vary considerably from state to state. Don't assume that your child's employer knows about these laws. Visit www.dol.gov/dol/topic/youthlabor /ParentsofYoung.htm (or call 1-866-4-USADOL) or www.youthrules.dol.gov (or call 1-866-4-USWAGE).
3. *Be aware of young workers' rights:* Report unsafe working conditions or employment in violation of child labor laws to DOL. Young workers are eligible for workers' compensation benefits if injured on the job.
4. *Share information with other parents:* Studies have shown that most young workers and parents are not aware of the laws and rights of young workers.

Data from: U.S. Department of Health and Human Services, Centers for Disease Control and Prevention, National Institute for Occupational Safety and Health (2003). *NIOSH Alert: Preventing Deaths, Injuries, and Illnesses of Young Workers* (DHHS [NIOSH] pub. no. 2003-128). Available at http://www.cdc.gov/niosh /docs/2003-128/pdfs/2003128.pdf.

Gender

Nearly 73 million women are part of the American labor force.[3] Since 1950, the labor force participation rate of women has nearly doubled, so that today more than half of all adult women work. In 2015, females made up 47% of the American workforce.[3] Although males made up 53% of the workforce, they worked 57% of all the hours worked. Because they work more hours and because there are still some dangerous jobs filled predominantly by males, males accounted for nearly two-thirds (60%) of all the injury and illness cases involving days away from work; they also required more days (10 days) away from work for each disabling injury compared with females (7 days).[15,17] One group of disorders in which women make up a higher proportion of cases with days away from work is anxiety, stress, and neurotic disorders.[25]

Working women are more likely than nonworking women to receive certain health benefits such as workplace prenatal education, weight control programs, and cancer education. Women in the workforce are more likely to be covered by health insurance than nonworking women and are more likely to have a preventive health tests.

Poverty and Minority Status

Nonfatal injury and illness rates for those of minority status and income levels are not available from the Bureau of Labor Statistics because the numbers of workers within these characteristics is not known. We know that 38% of cases with days away from work were taken by white workers in 2014 (unchanged from 2013); Hispanic or Latino workers accounted for 12% of the injuries and illnesses in 2014 (unchanged from 2012), and that the number of illnesses and injuries among Asian workers and among Native Hawaiian and Pacific Islander workers also increased from previous years.[15] But race and ethnicity were unreported in 40% of all cases, so incidence rates are unavailable.

Geographic Differences in Workplace Injuries

For 2014, occupational injury and illness rates were highest in the following states: Maine, Montana, Vermont, Washington, Wisconsin, Iowa, Indiana, and Alaska.[26] In all, 19 states reported private injury and illness rates above the national average of 3.3 cases per 100 full-time workers, while 14 states and the District of Columbia reported rates below the average. Eight states were not significantly different from the national average. Nine states did not report a rate (see **Figure 16.11**).[26]

Temporal Variations in Workplace Injuries

As mentioned previously, between 1928 and 2014 injury death rates among workers have declined 79% (from 16 per 100,000 workers to 3.3 per 100,000). During this period, the workforce in the U.S. has quadrupled in size, and the amount of goods and services produced has increased ninefold.[5] These improvements in workplace safety have been considered one of the 10 greatest achievements in public health during the past century.[27]

There is a seasonality to work-related deaths. Injury death rates from machinery, falling objects, electric current, and explosions are highest in the summer, when farming and construction work increase. Deaths from these causes are also more often reported during weekdays than on weekends, when, in general, more injury deaths occur.

Workplace Injuries by Industry and Occupation

Fatal and nonfatal occupational injury rates vary according to type of industry and type of occupation.

Fatal Occupational Injuries by Industry

Some jobs are more dangerous than others. Injury death rates are one indication of the risk associated with employment in an industry or in a particular job within an industry. Although the total number of deaths is highest in the construction industry, workers in agriculture, forestry,

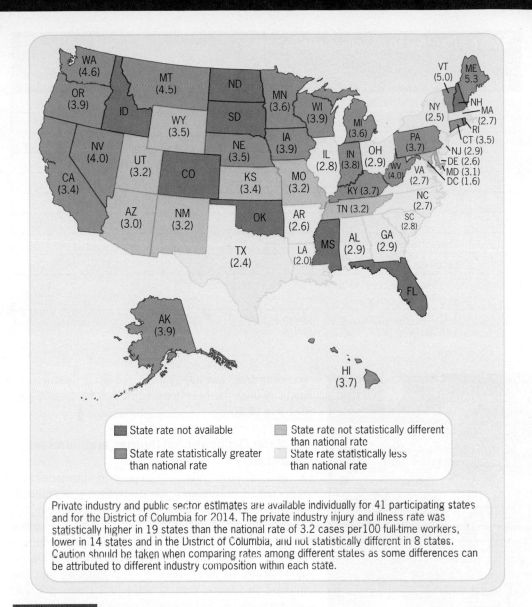

State rate not available

State rate statistically greater than national rate

State rate not statistically different than national rate

State rate statistically less than national rate

Private industry and public sector estimates are available individually for 41 participating states and for the District of Columbia for 2014. The private industry injury and illness rate was statistically higher in 19 states than the national rate of 3.2 cases per 100 full-time workers, lower in 14 states and in the District of Columbia, and not statistically different in 8 states. Caution should be taken when comparing rates among different states as some differences can be attributed to different industry composition within each state.

FIGURE 16.11 State nonfatal occupational injury and illness incidence rates compared to the national rate, private industry, 2014.*

*Total recordable cases (TRC) incidence rate per 100 full-time workers.

Data from: U.S. Department of Labor, Bureau of Labor Statistics (2015). *2014 Survey of Occupational Injuries & Illness: Summary Estimates Charts Package*. Available at http://www.bls.gov/iif/oshwc/osh/os/osch0054.pdf.

fishing, and hunting have the highest workplace fatality rates (24.9 deaths per 100,000 full-time workers; see Figure 16.7).[17] Within this industry category, logging and commercial fishing were the most dangerous occupations in 2014, with death rates of 109.5 and 80.8 deaths per 100,000 workers respectively. (Remember the overall fatality rate for American workers is less than 4 deaths per 100,000 workers.) Aircraft pilots and flight engineers have the third highest fatality rates (63.2 deaths per 100,000 workers; see **Table 16.2**).

The industries with the second highest workplace fatality rate are mining, quarrying, and oil and gas extraction (14.1 deaths per 100,000 workers in 2014). On April 6, 2010, an explosion at the Upper Big Branch mine in West Virginia killed 29 miners. This was the country's worst disaster in four decades,[28] and an unneeded reminder of the hazardous nature of coal mining (see **Figure 16.12**). One set of *Healthy People 2020* objectives is to reduce deaths from work-related injuries in private sector industries. Mining, construction, transportation and

Rank	Occupation	Death Rate/ 100,000	Total Deaths
TABLE 16.2 Top 10 Deadliest Jobs in 2014			
1	Logging workers	109.5	77
2	Fishers and related fishing workers	80.8	22
3	Aircraft pilots and flight engineers	63.2	81
4	Roofers	46.2	81
5	Refuse and recyclable material collectors	35.8	27
6	Farmers, ranchers, and other agricultural managers	26.0	263
7	Structural iron and steel workers	25.2	15
8	Driver/sales workers and truck drivers	23.4	835
9	Electrical power-line installers and repairers	19.2	25
10	First-line supervisors of construction trades and extraction workers	17.9	130

Data from: U.S. Department of Labor, Bureau of Labor Statistics (2015). *Census of Fatal Occupational Injuries Summary, 2014.* Available at http://www.bls.gov/news.release/pdf/cfoi.pdf.

FIGURE 16.12 President Barack Obama attended the memorial service for miners killed in the Upper Big Branch mine disaster in West Virginia in April, 2010.
© Steve Helber/AP Photos.

warehousing, and agriculture, forestry, fishing, and hunting offer the best opportunities for improvement (see **Box 16.3**).

Nonfatal Occupational Injuries and Illnesses by Industry

A total of 3.67 million injuries and illnesses were reported in public and private industry workplaces during 2014, resulting in a rate of 3.4 cases per 100 equivalent full-time workers.[7] Goods-producing industries had higher rates than service-producing industries. Among goods-producing industries, agriculture, forestry, fishing, and hunting had the highest incidence rate in 2014 (5.5 cases per 100 full-time workers). In the service-producing industries, transportation and warehousing had the highest incidence rate (4.6), followed by education and health services (4.2 cases per 100 full-time workers; see Figure 16.4). All 2014 incidence rates showed declines from 2003 levels.[7]

Agricultural Safety and Health

One particularly hazardous occupation is farming. Those working on farms are at considerable risk not just for injuries, but for lung diseases, noise-induced hearing loss, skin diseases, and certain cancers associated with chemical use and sun exposure. In 2012, there were approximately 2.2 million farms in the United States, with about 1,854,000 full-time workers involved in production agriculture. In addition, 1.4 to 2.1 million seasonal crop workers are hired annually.[29] More than 955,400 youth lived on farms in 2012 and nearly half worked on their farm. Also, more than 250,000 youth were hired in agriculture that year. Every day about 38 children are injured, and about every 3 days a child dies in an agriculture-related incident.[30] In 2014, 263 farm-related deaths were reported,[6] and farming and ranching alone ranked sixth among the top 10 most dangerous jobs in 2014 (see Table 16.2).

BOX 16.3   *Healthy People 2020:* **Objectives**

Objective OSH-1: Reduce deaths from work-related injuries.

Target-setting method: 10% improvement.

Data sources: Census of Fatal Occupational Injuries (CFOI), DOL, BLS; Current Population Survey (CPS), U.S. Bureau of the Census.

Target and baseline:

Objective	Industry	2007 Baseline	Progress (2012)	2020 Target
		Deaths per 100,000 full-time equivalent workers		
OSH-1.1	All industry	4.0	3.4	3.6
OSH-1.2	Mining	21.4	15.4	19.3
OSH-1.3	Construction	10.8	9.7	9.7
OSH-1.4	Transportation and warehousing	16.5	12.5	14.8
OSH-1.5	Agriculture, forestry, fishing, and hunting	27.0	22.6	24.3

For Further Thought

Targets call for reducing deaths from work-related injuries by 10%. Data available for 2012 indicate that the target for all industry has been exceeded; the death rate per 100,000 full-time workers was calculated at 3.4. Targets for mining, transportation and warehousing, and agriculture, forestry, fishing, and hunting have also been exceeded. In your opinion, which of these industries has the best chance of sustaining its safety achievements? Why? Why do you think the construction industry met but did not exceed its target?

A major contribution to farm-related fatalities is farm machinery, particularly farm tractors. For more than two out of five farm worker deaths, the source of the fatal injury was a tractor, and more than half of these deaths resulted from tractor rollovers. Rollover incidents are those in which the tractor tips sideways or backward (especially when the tractor is improperly hitched), crushing the operator (see **Figure 16.13**). While all tractors manufactured since 1985 are fitted with seat belts and **rollover protective structures (ROPS)**, many tractors in use in the United States lack this equipment.

The effectiveness of ROPS in protecting the tractor operator was demonstrated by statistics collected in Nebraska, where only 1 (2%) of 61 persons operating ROPS-equipped tractors that rolled over died. These data compare favorably with a 40% death rate for the 250 persons

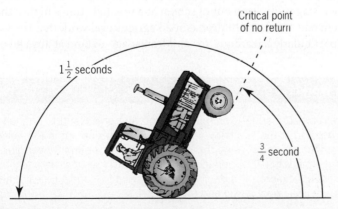

FIGURE 16.13   The timing of events during rear rollovers of farm tractors.

Rollover protective structure (ROPS) factory-installed or retrofitted reinforced framework on a cab to protect the operator of a tractor in case of a rollover

FIGURE 16.14   It is not unusual for farm children under the age of 12 to be seen driving tractors.

© David R. Photolibrary, Inc./Alamy Images.

involved in unprotected tractor rollover incidents. The single fatality in the ROPS-equipped tractor was not wearing a seat belt and was ejected from the ROPS-protected area.[31]

Although today's tractors are the safest ever, they are still a leading cause of farm injuries and deaths.[32] The OSHA standard requiring ROPS be installed on all tractors is not actively enforced on farms with fewer than 11 employees, and family farms without other employees are exempt from OSHA regulations. NIOSH promotes the installation of ROPS systems but has no authority to require them. Recently, NIOSH has developed cost-effective rollover protective structure (CROPS) designs and installation instructions to the public for older tractors for which ROPS are otherwise not available. As of 2012, 59% of all tractors used on farms were equipped with ROPS.[32]

Farming is one of the few industries in which the families of workers are also exposed to many of the same risks. In the past, it was not unusual for farm boys under the age of 12 to be seen driving tractors (see **Figure 16.14**). Perhaps this practice is less common today. Certainly, childhood agricultural injury rates declined between 1998 (16.6 injuries per 1,000 farms) and 2012 (6.4 injuries per 1,000 farms).[30]

Another group of workers being exposed to health and safety risks in agricultural settings are members of the migrant workforce, where children as young as 12, 10, 8, and even 4 years of age can be found working in the fields. Testimony before the U.S. Senate Committee on Labor and Human Resources by Fernando Cuevas, Jr., paints a grim picture of migrant children (see **Box 16.4**).[33]

Of our 50 states, 48 rely heavily on migrant workers during the peak harvest season. These migrant workers have poor access to health care facilities; infant mortality is about 50 per 1,000 compared with the national average of about 6 per 1,000. In many cases, working conditions are hazardous, and water shortages require workers to drink water from irrigation ditches. Not only is such water unpurified, it is usually laden with agricultural chemicals and biological wastes. Migrant workers are also exposed to long hours in the sun, other unsanitary conditions, and numerous harmful pesticides from crop-dusting airplanes.

It is an unfortunate fact that virtually no progress has been made in addressing the plight of migrant farm workers. In 2000, Human Rights Watch (HRW) documented the exploitive and dangerous conditions under which these workers and their children labor in a report titled, *Fingers to the Bone: United States Failure to Protect Child Farmworkers*. Nearly 10 years later, when HRW reexamined the situation, they discovered that conditions for child farmworkers were essentially unchanged.[34] Children often work 10 or more hours a day and, during peak harvest times, may work dawn to dusk (see **Figure 16.15**). They typically earn less than the minimum wage and are often forced to spend their own money on tools, gloves, and even drinking water. They may be exposed to agricultural chemicals that make them sick. Because of missed days at school, farm-working youth drop out of school at a rate four times higher than the national average. "Under current U.S. law, children can do agricultural work that the U.S. Department of Labor deems 'particularly hazardous' for children at age 16 (and at any age on farms owned

BOX 16.4   Comments of a Young Farm Worker

"When I was younger it was all a game to me. But as I started getting older it became a job, and at the age of about 7 and 8, I was competing with my parents and my older sisters. . . . I was able to get out of the fields permanently at the age of 15 to try and get a decent education. I also became an organizer for the Farm Labor Organizing Committee at the age of 16, and I continue to see many, many young children working out in the fields at the same age that I was—4-, 5-, 6-, 7-, and 8-year olds. They are still working out in the fields. I see it every year, up in Ohio, I see it down in Texas, I see it in Florida, I see it anywhere that we go and organize."

Data from: Committee on Labor and Human Resources (1991, March 19). "Prepared Statement of Fernando Cuevas, Jr." *Childhood Labor Amendments of 1991* (S. HRG. 102-201, S. 600). Washington, DC: U.S. Government Printing Office.

or operated by their parents). In non-agricultural sectors, no one under age 18 can do such jobs."[34]

Even these lax labor laws are not enforced diligently. Between 2001 and 2009, enforcement of child labor laws overall by the U.S. Department of Agriculture declined dramatically. Despite the hazardous conditions and frequent injuries and illnesses suffered by farmworkers, relatively few complain for fear of being fired or even deported. Even though many of the children may be U.S. citizens, the entire family may fear being deported. One such hazardous job is tobacco farming. Sixteen-year-old Elena G., who has worked in the tobacco fields every summer since she was 12 years old, told Human Rights Watch,

FIGURE 16.15   Children of migrant farm workers often work 10 or more hours a day and tend to drop out of school at a rate four times the national average.
© Pat Sullivan/AP Images.

> "I don't feel any different in the fields than when I was 12," she told Human Rights Watch. "I [still] get headaches and. . . my stomach hurts. And like I feel nauseous. . . . I just feel like my stomach is like rumbling around. I feel like I'm gonna throw up."[35]

"The United States spent more than $26 million in 2009 to eliminate child labor around the world, yet the country's law and practice concerning child farmworkers are in violation of or are inconsistent with international conventions on the rights of children."[34] Legislation aimed at eliminating the double standard in child labor laws is introduced during each session of Congress. So far, none of these bills has reached a vote.

Prevention and Control of Unintentional Injuries in the Workplace

Reducing the number and seriousness of injuries and illnesses in the workplace involves four fundamental tasks: anticipation, recognition, evaluation, and control.[36] Anticipation involves the foresight to envision future adverse events and take action to prevent them. A hazard inventory should be conducted to detect and record physical, ergonomic, chemical, biological, and psychological hazards in the workplace. Recognition involves surveillance and monitoring of the workforce for injuries and illnesses, including near misses. It includes inspections of the workplace for hazards, monitoring it for toxins, recording injuries, and conducting employee health screenings.

All of the aforementioned activities include data collection. Evaluation is the assessment of the data that were collected during the recognition and monitoring activities. This includes toxicological, exposure, and clinical assessment as well as risk assessment. Epidemiology is part of the evaluation process. Risk assessment enables the translation of scientific information about hazards into decisions and policies that can improve workplace safety and health. Upon establishing the need for intervention, a decision concerning control can be made. The control may involve changes in the production process to make it safer, changes in the work environment to make it safer, or improvements in the use of personal protective equipment or apparel to protect individual workers. Finally, the education and training of workers can help to reduce workplace injuries and illnesses.[36]

National leadership in reducing the number and seriousness of workplace injuries and illnesses resides with OHSA and NIOSH. In an effort to chart the future course for research on workplace safety and health problems, NIOSH has developed a partnership with more than 500 public and private outside organizations and individuals, the National Occupational Research Agenda (NORA) in 1996. Partners include stakeholders from universities, large and small businesses, professional societies, government agencies, and worker organizations. Partners work together to develop research goals and objectives for resolving the most critical workplace issues based upon (1) the numbers of workers at risk, (2) the seriousness of the hazard, and (3) the probability that new information and approaches will make a difference. The various councils within NORA are based upon sectors in the North American Industry Classification System (NAICS). Examples include the following: Agriculture, Forestry, and Fishing; Construction; Manufacturing; Mining; and so on.[37] Some of the successful projects coming out of NORA include the development of CROPS discussed above, projects on commercial fishing, pesticide safety training among farmworkers, and the evaluation of safety in nighttime highway work zones.[38]

Workplace Violence: Intentional Workplace Injuries

Although only a small number of the incidents of workplace interpersonal violence that occur each day make the news, 1.7 million Americans are victims of workplace violence each year.[39] Between 1992 and 2010, 13,827 workplace homicide victims were reported.[40] In 2014, 403 homicides occurred in the workplace, making homicide the fourth leading cause of workplace fatalities behind roadway incidents, contact with objects and equipment, and falls.[17] In some years, homicide is the second leading cause of workplace deaths among women.[25]

In addition to the fatalities mentioned above, thousands of nonfatal workplace injuries and illnesses are a direct or indirect result of workplace violence. In 2009 it was estimated that more than 137,000 workers were treated in emergency departments for nonfatal assaults.[40]

There are many reasons for workplace homicides and violence. Researchers have divided workplace violence into four categories:[39]

Criminal intent (Type I): The perpetrator has no legitimate relationship to the business or its employees and is usually committing a crime, such as robbery, shoplifting, and trespassing. This category makes up 85% of the work-related homicides.

Customer/client (Type II): The perpetrator has a legitimate relationship with the business and becomes violent while being served. This category includes customers, clients, patients, students, and inmates. This category represents 3% of the work-related homicides.

Worker-on-worker (Type III): The perpetrator is an employee or past employee of the business who attacks or threatens another employee or past employee of the workplace. Worker-on-worker violence accounts for 7% of workplace homicides.

Personal relationship (Type IV): The perpetrator usually does not have a relationship with the business but has a personal relationship with the intended victim. This category, which includes victims of domestic violence assaulted or threatened at work, makes up just 2% of workplace homicides.

During 2003 through 2010, more than half of the workplace homicides occurred within three occupation classifications: sales and related occupations (28%), protective service occupations (17%), and transportation and material moving occupations (13%).[40] Data on nonfatal workplace violence are more difficult to obtain than data on workplace homicides. Assaults occur almost equally among men and women. Most of these assaults occur in service settings such as hospitals, nursing homes, and social service agencies. Forty-eight percent of nonfatal assaults in the workplace are committed by health care patients.[39]

Risk Factors

Risk factors for encountering violence at work are listed in **Box 16.5**. They include working with the public, working around money or valuables, working alone, and working late at night. Additionally, certain industries and occupations put workers at particular risk. For workplace homicides, the taxicab industry has the highest risk at 41.4 cases per 100,000, nearly 60 times the national average rate of 0.70 per 100,000. Other jobs that carry a higher than average risk for homicide are jobs in liquor stores (7.5), detective and protective services (7.0), gas service stations (4.8), and jewelry stores (4.7). The workplaces that have the highest risk of nonfatal assault (and the highest percentage of all assaults that occurred) are nursing homes (27%), social services (13%), hospitals (11%), grocery stores (6%), and restaurants or bars (5%).[39]

BOX 16.5   Factors That Increase a Worker's Risk for Workplace Assault

- Contact with the public
- Exchange of money
- Delivery of passengers, goods, or services
- Having a mobile workplace such as a taxicab or police cruiser
- Working with unstable or volatile persons in health care, social services, or criminal justice settings

- Working alone or in small numbers
- Working late at night or during early morning hours
- Working in high-crime areas
- Guarding valuable property or possessions
- Working in community-based settings

Data from: Centers for Disease Control and Prevention, National Institute for Occupational Safety and Health (2004). *Violence on the Job* (NIOSH pub. no. 2004–100d). Available at http://www.cdc.gov/niosh/docs/video/violence.html.

Prevention Strategies

Prevention strategies for workplace violence can be grouped into three categories—environmental designs, administrative controls, and behavior strategies. Before these strategies can be implemented, a workplace violence prevention policy should be in place. Such a policy should clearly indicate a zero tolerance of violence at work. Just as workplaces have mechanisms for reporting and dealing with sexual harassment, they must also have a policy in place to deal with violence. Such a policy must spell out how such incidents are to be reported, to whom, and how they are to be addressed.

Environmental designs to limit the risk of workplace violence might include implementing safer cash handling procedures, physically separating workers from customers, improving lighting, and installing better security systems at entrances and exits. Administrative controls include staffing policies (having more staff is generally safer than having fewer staff), procedures for opening and closing the workplace, and reviewing employee duties (such as handling money) that may be especially risky. Behavior strategies include training employees in nonviolent response and conflict resolution and educating employees about risks associated with specific duties and about the importance of reporting incidents and adhering to administrative controls. Training should also include instruction on the appropriate use and maintenance of any protective equipment that may be provided.[39]

Occupational Illnesses and Disorders

Precise data on the number of cases of occupational illnesses are more difficult to acquire than data on injuries. It is more difficult to link illnesses to occupational exposure. Some illnesses that can result from occupational exposure (e.g., tuberculosis, cancer, and asthma) appear no different from those that result from exposure elsewhere. Also, there is usually a lengthy period of time between exposure and the appearance of disease, unlike injuries, which are usually evident immediately. Reported cases of illnesses in the workplace in 2014 accounted for only 4.9% of the nearly 3 million injury and illness cases. In private industry, 189,400 new cases of occupational illness were reported, a rate of 17.5 cases per 10,000 full-time workers in all employment settings. Skin diseases and disorders had the highest incidence, 2.6 cases per 10,000 full-time workers, followed by hearing loss, 1.9 cases per 10,000 full-time workers, and respiratory conditions, 1.6 cases per 10,000 full-time workers.[7] The illnesses reported in the statistics are only the cases reported during 2014. Some conditions, such as various cancers, are slow to develop and are difficult to associate with the workplace. These diseases and conditions are often unrecognized and underreported in annual reports of injuries and illnesses.[7]

Types of Occupational Illnesses

Occupational diseases can be categorized by cause and by the organ or organ system affected. For example, repeated trauma is the cause, and the musculoskeletal system is the affected organ system. Exposure to asbestos is a cause of illness; the respiratory system, especially the lung, is the system affected.

Pneumoconiosis a fibrotic lung disease caused by the inhalation of dusts, especially mineral dusts

Coal workers' pneumoconiosis (CWP) an acute and chronic lung disease caused by the inhalation of coal dust (black lung disease)

Musculoskeletal Disorders

Musculoskeletal disorders are the most frequently reported occupational disorders. They include both acute and chronic injury to muscles, tendons, ligaments, nerves, joints, bones, and supporting vasculature. The leading type of musculoskeletal disorder was repeated trauma disorders, which can make up 65% of all cases of nonfatal occupational illness in a given year.[25] Included in this category are carpal tunnel syndrome and noise-induced hearing loss. These disorders are sometimes referred to as repeated trauma disorders.

Skin Diseases and Disorders

Reported skin disorders included allergic and irritant dermatitis, eczema, rash, oil acne, chrome ulcers, and chemical burns. The highest incidences of occupational skin disorders were reported in agriculture, forestry, and fishing.[25] The skin may serve as the target organ for disease, or it may be the route through which toxic chemicals enter the worker's body.

Noise-Induced Hearing Loss

Noise-induced hearing loss is another form of repeated trauma. Approximately 30 million Americans are exposed to hazardous noise on the job, and an additional 9 million are at risk for hearing loss from other agents such as solvents and metals. Cases include workers with a permanent noise-induced hearing loss or with a standard threshold shift. Most of the cases were reported within manufacturing; within the manufacturing sector, 51% of the cases were associated with manufacturing.[25]

Respiratory Disorders

Occupational respiratory disorders are the result of the inhalation of toxic substances present in the workplace. The lungs, like the skin, can be both the target organ of disease and a portal of entry for toxic substances. Characteristic of occupational lung diseases are their chronic nature and the difficulty in early recognition (the latent period for such diseases may be 15 to 30 years). Also, there is the problem of multiple or mixed exposures in the home and the workplace.

Work-related asthma (WRA) is the most commonly reported occupational respiratory disease, even though estimates suggest that most cases are not recognized or reported as being work related. There is no estimate on how many cases of WRA occur nationwide. The highest percentage of cases occurs among operators, fabricators, and laborers.[25] Approximately 10% to 16% or adult-onset asthma cases are attributable to worksite factors. It is important for physicians and other health care providers to ask adult-onset asthma patients about work-related exposure. Unfortunately, sometimes complete exposure cessation is the only intervention for a worker who has become sensitized to the agent or agents causing asthma.[41]

One of the most important categories of lung diseases is **pneumoconiosis**, a fibrotic lung disease caused by the inhalation of dusts, especially mineral dusts. During the period 1979 to 2014, pneumoconiosis was either the underlying or contributing cause in 107,509 deaths in U.S. workers.[42]

Types of pneumoconiosis include coal workers' pneumoconiosis, asbestosis, silicosis, and byssinosis. The largest number of pneumoconiosis deaths was from coal workers' pneumoconiosis (CWP). **Coal workers' pneumoconiosis** (also called black lung disease) is an acute or chronic lung disease that is caused by inhaling coal dust (see **Figure 16.16**).

Historically, deaths from CWP clearly outnumber all other types of pneumoconiosis deaths. During the period from 1968 to 2014, there were 77,996 deaths attributed to CWP, making up more than 50% of all reported pneumoconiosis deaths for that period. However, deaths from CWP have declined during the last 40 years, from a high of 2,910 in 1972 to 363 in 2014.[42] The human cost of CWP can be measured another way, through analysis of years of potential life lost (YPLL). During the period 1968 to 2014, a total of 915,196

FIGURE 16.16 Mining is a dangerous occupation because of exposure to injuries and to coal dust, which can cause chronic lung disease.

© Rubberball Productions/Creatas.

YPLL were attributed to CWP, an average of 11.7 years per fatality.[42] This means that workers who developed CWP during this period died, on average, 11.7 years sooner than expected. Most troubling is the finding that, after a period of decline, the number of YPLL has been increasing, from a low of 9.9 years in 2002 to 13.6 years in 2014.[42]

NIOSH has been monitoring trends in CWP, including progressive massive fibrosis (PMF), an advanced debilitating, and lethal form of CWP. The incidence of PMF, which results solely from the inhalation of coal dust, has increased dramatically among miners in the Appalachian states (see **Figure 16.17**).[43] This increase could be caused by the changing nature of the coal dust inhaled, to inadequate enforcement of standards and unrepresentative dust sample measurements, or to miners working longer hours. With the widest coal seams already mined, modern day miners must work narrower seams surrounded in some cases by rock containing silica. Also, machinery used now creates finer dust particles. So miners inhale both coal dust and silica dust.[44] Finally, miners worked an average of 25.6% more hours underground during 2003 to 2007 than they did during 1978 to 1982, thereby increasing their exposure to coal dust.[45] A recent study found that surface coal miners are also susceptible to pneumoconiosis and advanced occupational lung disease.[46] No effective medical treatment is available for pneumoconiosis; therefore, primary prevention is essential.

Asbestos workers suffer from diseases that include **asbestosis** (an acute or chronic lung disease), lung cancer, and malignant mesothelioma (cancer of the epithelial linings of the heart and other internal organs). In contrast to CWP, asbestosis deaths increased from 78 in 1968 to 1,221 in 2014. During the same period (1968 to 2014), the years of potential life lost (YPLL) for each death for which asbestosis was either the underlying cause or a contributing case was 11.3 years. During the period 1999 to 2014, 42,662 mesothelioma deaths were reported. A total of 2,785 mesothelioma deaths were reported in 2014.[42] The average number of YPLL for these deaths was 13.5 years.[42] The number of deaths from lung cancer to which asbestosis may have contributed has not been determined.

Workers in mines, stone quarries, sand and gravel operations, foundries, abrasive blasting operations, and glass manufacturing run the risk of **silicosis** (sometimes referred to as dust on the lungs) that is caused from inhaling crystalline silica. Mortality from silicosis has significantly declined in recent years from 1,065 in 1968 to 84 in 2014. The average number of YPLL for these deaths was 12.8 years.[42]

Asbestosis an acute or chronic lung disease caused by the deposition of asbestos fibers on lungs

Silicosis an acute or chronic lung disease caused by the inhalation of free crystalline silica

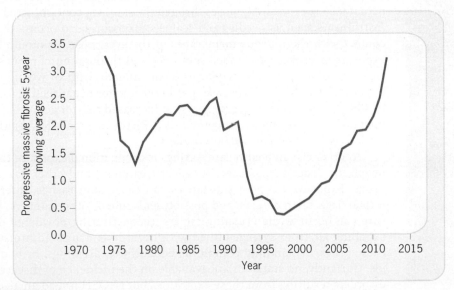

FIGURE 16.17   Prevalence of progressive massive fibrosis among working underground coal miners with 25 or more years of underground mining tenure (1974–2012) in Kentucky, West Virginia, and Virginia.

Data from: Blackley, D. J., C. N. Halldin, and A. S. Laney (2014). "Resurgence of a Debilitating and Entirely Preventable Respiratory Disease among Working Coal Miners." *American Journal of Respiratory and Critical Care Medicine*, 190(6): 708-709.

Byssinosis an acute or chronic lung disease caused by the inhalation of cotton, flax, or hemp dusts (brown lung disease)

Textile factory workers who inhale dusts from cotton, flax, or hemp often acquire **byssinosis** (sometimes called brown lung disease), an acute or chronic lung disease. In comparison with the other types of pneumoconiosis, byssinosis deaths are uncommon—10 or fewer cases were reported annually between 1996 and 2006, and 5 or fewer between 2007 and 2014. During 1979 through 2014, 341 deaths were attributed to byssinosis. Byssinosis has the highest YPLL of any of the types of pneumoconiosis discussed here, 15.1 years.[42] One reason for the decreasing number of byssinosis deaths in the United States might be that much of the textile manufacturing takes place in other countries.

Other agents that can affect the lungs include metallic dusts, gases and fumes, and aerosols of biological agents (viruses, bacteria, and fungi). Health conditions that can result from exposure to these agents include occupational asthma, asphyxiation, pulmonary edema, histoplasmosis, and lung cancer.

Other Work-Related Diseases and Disorders

Other types of work-related illnesses and disorders are those that arise from poisonings and infections. Poisoning agents include heavy metals (including lead), toxic gases, organic solvents, pesticides, and other substances. Pesticides, when used properly, offer benefits to society, increasing crop production, preserving produce, and combating insect infestations. However, pesticides do represent a health risk, especially for agricultural workers. Approximately 1.1 billion pounds of pesticide active ingredients are used annually in the United States, where 20,000 separate pesticide products are marketed. Each year, 10,000 to 20,000 physician-diagnosed pesticide poisonings occur among the approximately 2 million agricultural workers.[47] During 1998 through 2005, 3,271 cases of acute pesticide-related occupational illness were identified in the United States.[48] The vast majority of these cases (71%) occurred in farm workers. Insecticides are responsible for the highest percentage of occupational poisoning cases (49%).[25]

In 2014, 11.8 million people were employed by hospitals or in the health care industry in the United States, making up nearly 8% of the employed workforce.[3] More than 8 million of these workers are exposed to a variety of hazardous conditions, including infectious disease agents (see **Figure 16.18**). Among the agents of concern are hepatitis B virus and human immunodeficiency virus (HIV). Health care workers are at risk if they become exposed to the blood or bodily fluids of patients or coworkers. The major route of exposure to these agents (82% of the cases) is percutaneous exposure (injuries through the skin) via contaminated sharp instruments such as needles and scalpels. Exposure also occurs through contact with the mucous membranes of the eyes, nose, or mouth (14%), exposure to broken or abraded skin (3%), and through human bites (1%). Up to 800,000 percutaneous injuries occur annually, with an average risk of infection for HIV of 0.3% (3 cases per 1,000) and for hepatitis B of from 6% to 30%.[25] Health care workers are also at increased risk for acquiring other infectious diseases such as tuberculosis (TB); the incidence for health care workers is 3.7 cases per 100,000 workers.[25]

Another risk in health care settings is occupational exposure to antineoplastic drugs (drugs used in cancer treatment) and other hazardous drugs. Exposure to these substances can cause skin rashes, infertility, miscarriage, birth defects, and possibly leukemia or other cancers. Exposure can occur while crushing tablets, reconstituting powdered drugs, expelling air from syringes filled with hazardous drugs, administering these drugs, or handling contaminated clothing, dressings, or body fluids. Currently, no statistics are available on the incidence of diseases and disorders resulting from these exposures, but NIOSH issued an alert and guidelines for preventing exposure in 2004.[49] In 2012, NIOSH published a list of about 167 drugs used in health care settings that should be handled as hazardous.[50] This list is updated periodically; updates are available at the NIOSH website.

FIGURE 16.18   Health care workers are exposed to a variety of workplace hazards, including infectious diseases.
© Photos.com.

In the past decade and a half, the field of nanotechnology has experienced rapid growth. One nanometer equals one billionth of an inch. Nanoscale materials, systems, and devices exhibit unique properties that affect their behavior. As this field becomes commercialized, concerns have arisen concerning the safety and health of those working with these materials. Recently, NIOSH issued a recommendation for a level of exposure to airborne concentrations of certain nanomaterials.[51] Certainly, there will be more news to come regarding this new workplace setting.

As stated previously, many of our most prevalent chronic health problems may arise from multiple exposures, both within the workplace and at home. Among these are cardiovascular diseases, cancers, and reproductive disorders. Perhaps a million or more workers are exposed to agents that can produce cancer, for example. However, there are no reliable estimates on the actual number of cancer deaths that can be traced directly to occupational exposure. Thus, we have discussed here only conditions generally accepted to be solely or predominantly related to work.

Prevention and Control of Occupational Diseases and Disorders

Preventing and controlling occupational diseases requires the vigilance of employer and employee alike and the assistance of governmental agencies. The agent-host-environment disease model discussed earlier in this book is applicable to preventive strategies outlined here. Specific activities that should be employed to control occupational diseases include identification and evaluation of agents, standard setting for the handling of and exposure to causative agents, elimination or substitution of causative factors, engineering controls to provide for a safer work area, environmental monitoring, medical screenings, personal protective devices, health promotion, disease surveillance, therapeutic medical care and rehabilitation, and compliance activities. In this regard, prevention and control of occupational diseases and disorders is similar to the prevention of occupational injuries.[36] Coordinated programs to monitor and reduce occupational hazards require professionally trained personnel who work with employers and employees to reduce the number and seriousness of workplace injuries and illnesses.

Resources for Preventing Workplace Injuries and Illnesses

Prevention of workplace injuries and illnesses requires professional expertise as well as effective prevention and intervention programs.

Occupational Safety and Health Protection Professionals

The need for safety and health protection professionals in the workplace is substantial. Among those with specialized training in their fields are safety engineers and certified safety professionals, health physicists, industrial hygienists, occupational physicians, and occupational health nurses.

Safety Engineers and Certified Safety Professionals

Approximately 400 academic institutions offer accredited programs that train occupational safety professionals. Many of these professionals will join the professional organization called the American Society of Safety Engineers (ASSE). "Founded in 1911, ASSE is the oldest and largest professional safety organization."[52] It has about 36,000 members who are involved in safety, health, and environmental issues in industry, insurance, government, and education. In spite of the name of this society, not all members are engineers. In fact, the background of the group is varied and includes a number of health educators.

Another recognizable group of trained professionals in this field is the Board of Certified Safety Professionals (BCSP). This group, founded in 1969, is slightly smaller; there are about 27,000 certified safety professionals (CSPs). "The Board of Certified Safety Professionals (BCSP) was organized as a peer certification board with the purpose of certifying practitioners in

Safety engineer a safety professional employed by a company for the purpose of reducing unintentional injuries in the workplace

Certified safety professional (CSP) a health and safety professional, trained in industrial and workplace safety, who has met specific requirements for board certification

Health physicist safety professional with responsibility for developing plans for coping with radiation accidents

Industrial hygienist health professional concerned with health hazards in the workplace and with recommending plans for improving the healthiness of workplace environments

Occupational physician (OP) or occupational medical practitioner (OMP) a practitioner (physician) whose primary concern is preventive medicine in the workplace

Occupational health nurse (OHN) a registered nurse (RN) whose primary responsibilities include prevention of illness and promotion of health in the workplace

the safety profession."[53] Certification usually requires a bachelor's degree in engineering or in another scientific curriculum and the passing of two examinations.

Safety engineers and **certified safety professionals (CSPs)** design safety education programs, detect hazards in the workplace, and try to correct them (see **Figure 16.19**). Increased federal regulations have made the workload heavier for these occupational health professionals.

Health Physicists

Health physicists are concerned with radiation safety in the workplace. They monitor radiation within the work environment and develop plans for decontamination and coping with accidents involving radiation. It is estimated that there are approximately 11,000 health physicists in the United States, certified by the American Academy of Health Physics. Many of these belong to the Health Physics Society, a 5,000-member, international scientific organization of professionals that traces its beginning to 1956. Health physicists are dedicated to promoting the practice of radiation safety.[54,55]

Industrial Hygienists

Whereas the safety engineer or certified safety professional is primarily concerned with hazards in the workplace and injury control, the **industrial hygienist** is concerned with environmental factors that might cause illness. Examples of such factors might include poor ventilation, excessive noise, poor lighting, and the presence of hazardous substances.

It is estimated that there are 7,600 industrial hygienists practicing in the United States. Perhaps a third of them hold the title of certified industrial hygienist (CIH), and many belong to the American Industrial Hygiene Association. To be certified requires a two-part written examination; the first part is given following 1 year of post-baccalaureate experience. The second is given after 5 years of professional activity. Many industrial hygienists belong to the American Conference of Governmental Industrial Hygienists (ACGIH), founded in 1938. This 5,000-member organization advances worker health and safety through education and the development and dissemination of scientific and technical knowledge through their publications.[56]

Occupational Physicians

The **occupational physician (OP)** or **occupational medical practitioner (OMP)** is a medical practitioner whose primary concern is preventive medicine in the workplace. Many OPs or OMPs belong to the American College of Occupational and Environmental Medicine (ACOEM), which represents more than 4,500 physicians and other health care professionals specializing in the field of occupational and environmental medicine (OEM). "The American Board of Preventive Medicine (ABPM) recognizes and certifies qualified physicians in the medical specialty of occupational medicine. Approximately 2,200 physicians have been 'board certified' in occupational medicine within the United States."[57]

Because physicians are highly skilled and highly salaried occupational health professionals, only the largest companies maintain full-time OPs. Smaller companies may hire OPs on a part-time basis or as consultants.

Occupational Health Nurses

The role of the **occupational health nurse (OHN)** has changed over the years from running the company's medical department and first aid station to one of greater emphasis on health promotion and illness prevention. Because the OHN may be the only health professional employed in smaller plants, it is clear that if injury prevention and health promotion programs are to be offered, the job will fall to this individual.

FIGURE 16.19   Safety engineers prevent workplace injuries by detecting hazards.
© Blaj Gabriel/ShutterStock, Inc.

The OHN must be a registered nurse (RN) in the state in which he or she practices. It is unlikely that these persons will have had much formal training in occupational health nursing prior to receiving their baccalaureate degrees because most nursing curricula do not provide much training in this area. However, the American Board of Occupational Health Nurses, Inc. (ABOHN), established in 1972, now offers certifications. Requirements include many hours of continuing-education credits and 5 years of experience in the field of occupational health nursing. ABOHN is the only certifying body for occupational health nurses in the United States. More than 12,000 active, certified occupational health nurses are working today.[58] Many OHNs belong to the American Association of Occupational Health Nurses (AAOHN), which was founded in 1942 and includes about 5,000 members.[59]

Worksite Safety and Health and Wellness Promotion Programs

A number of programs can be put in place in occupational settings to reduce injuries and diseases. These include preplacement examinations, health maintenance programs, safety awareness programs, health promotion programs, investigation of accidents, stress management programs, employee assistance programs, and rehabilitation programs.

Preplacement Examinations

The purpose of **preplacement examinations** is to make sure that the worker fits the job. By selecting the employee who is the best physically and mentally qualified for a specific job, probabilities of job-related injuries or illnesses are minimized. Periodic evaluations are necessary to ensure that the selected individual continues to be physically and mentally qualified to carry out the job assignment. Examinations are also recommended for transferred and return-to-work employees. Sometimes a phasing in of these employees is desirable.

Occupational Disease Prevention Programs and Safety Programs

Occupational health services that facilitate preventive activities in the workplace include disease prevention programs and safety programs.

Disease Prevention Programs

Originally, occupational disease programs focused on controlling occupational diseases that one might succumb to from exposure in the work environment. Agents of concern were chemicals, radiation, and perhaps even psychological and social factors that could lead to sickness or disability. Gradually, these disease prevention efforts broadened into health maintenance programs and included the early detection and treatment of such diseases as hypertension, diabetes, obesity, and heart disease to keep employees healthier and on the job longer.

Safety Programs

Safety programs are those portions of the workplace health and safety program aimed at reducing the number and seriousness of unintentional injuries on the job. Each company needs to have a policy statement, safe operating procedures, a disaster plan, policies for hazard control, and policies for the investigation of injuries in the workplace. Provisions must be made for regular safety inspections of the workplace and for the maintenance of accurate records for each injury and for analysis of such records. Each safety program should include safety orientation and training programs and programs on first aid and cardiopulmonary resuscitation.

Worksite Health and Wellness Promotion Programs

Worksite health and wellness promotion (WHWP) programs are workplace-based programs aimed at improving the health and wellness of employees through changes in behavior and lifestyle. The goals for the employer include reduction of absenteeism, lowering health insurance premiums, increasing productivity, and improving employee morale. Other reasons why

Preplacement examination a physical examination of a newly hired or transferred worker to determine medical suitability for placement in a specific position

Safety programs those parts of the workplace safety and health program aimed at reducing unintentional injuries on the job

Worksite health and wellness promotion (WHWP) programs workplace-based programs aimed at improving the health and wellness of employees by identifying and acting on existing health conditions and by encouraging employees to optimize their health by improving health behaviors and lifestyle choices

employers might support WHWP programs include reducing workers' compensation costs, increasing employee retention, and enhancing the company's image.[60]

In the United States, historically, health care insurance has come through one's employment. In 1965, the employers' share of the nation's health care bill was 18%; in 2006, it was 40%. In some companies the cost of providing health care for employees is equal to about 50% of the companies' profits.[60] Obviously, this upward trend in the cost of health care for employers cannot continue much longer. Until this system changes, however, employers are making serious efforts to reduce health care costs, and one effective way to do this is worksite health and wellness promotion.

Worksite health and wellness promotion programs go by various names such as, "Working Well," "Worksite Health and Family Services," "Work-Life Balance," or "Wellness and Work/Life." Generally, the objectives of these programs are to facilitate changes in behavior or lifestyle to prevent disease and to promote employee health and wellness. WHWP programs range in size from modest programs that might include only a "wellness assessment, and, perhaps, hypertension screening, to more comprehensive programs that offer cancer risk screening, nutrition and weight management, fitness classes, smoking cessation, stress management programs, telephone health coaching to help manage chronic conditions, and medication therapy management. Physical activity is an important component of any wellness program and linkages to or agreements with recreation facilities is essential. But the goals of these programs have evolved from simply improving the physical health of employees to improving the quality of life, especially as it relates to work/life balance. Many include inducements, such as a free FitBit Flex®, or even monetary rewards, for participation by employees.

All indications are that WHWP programs will continue to grow. Corporations, colleges, and universities not only see them as a means to control health care costs and show a concern for the employees, but also as a means by which to retain current employees and recruit new ones. Undergraduate and graduate programs now exist to specifically train people to staff these programs; these professionals go by such titles as worksite wellness coordinator, worksite wellness manager, or wellness instructor.

The National Institute of Safety and Health located in the Centers for Disease Control and Prevention supports and promotes worksite wellness programs through its initiative, **Total Worker Health (TWH)**. Total Worker Health is defined as policies, programs, and practices that integrate protection from work-related safety and health hazards with promotion of injury and illness prevention efforts to advance worker well-being.[61] The TWH approach advocates for a holistic understanding of the factors that contribute to worker well-being. Scientific evidence now supports what many safety and health professionals, as well as workers themselves, have long suspected—that risk factors in the workplace can contribute to health problems previously considered unrelated to work. The TWH website provides resources for those wishing to start or enhance existing "workplace programs and policies for improving worker health and well-being."[61]

Employee Assistance Programs

Employee assistance programs (EAPs) are programs that assist employees who have substance abuse, domestic, psychological, or social problems that interfere with their work performance. These programs, which arrived at many workplaces before WHWP programs, originally arose in response to occupational alcohol problems. EAPs provide help to employees with a variety of problems that affect their work performance. EAPs may be administered separately from WHWP programs or even through a contract with a third party. The goal of EAPs is intervention when an employee has a behavioral or other problem that interferes with his or her work before such problems become costly for both the employer and employee. During the intervention EAP personnel, together with the employee, try to identify resolve the problem so that the employee's work performance can return to normal.

Chapter Summary

- After time spent at home, Americans spend the next largest portion of their time at work; thus, safe and healthy workplaces are essential if the U.S. is to reach its health potential.

- Every day approximately 11 people die from work-related injuries and many more people die of work-related diseases.

- Occupational health issues affect the quality of life economically as well as medically in communities in which workers live. Although occupational injuries and illnesses have been a long-standing concern of workers in the U.S., rapid progress in reducing the number and seriousness of workplace injuries and illnesses became possible only after the passage of the Occupational Safety and Health Act (OSH Act) of 1970.

- The OSH Act established the Occupational Safety and Health Administration (OSHA) and the National Institute of Occupational Safety and Health (NIOSH) and required private industry to provide safe jobs and workplaces.

- The number and type of workplace injuries vary by person, place, time, and type of industry. Roadway injuries are the leading cause of fatal work-related injuries. Violence, being struck by an object or equipment, and falls are the second, third, and fourth leading causes of unintentional workplace deaths.

- Nonfatal work-related injuries diminish productivity and jeopardize both employee wages and employer profits.

- Workplace violence affects 1.7 million workers in the United States each year, and homicide is the fourth leading cause of workplace fatalities.

- Work-related injuries can be controlled by applying a variety of injury prevention strategies, including eliminating a dangerous job, improving the work environment, using safer machinery, and improving the selection and training of workers.

- Work-related illnesses and disorders kill thousands of workers and former workers each year.

- The types of illnesses and disorders that can be attributed to workplace exposure are many, including musculoskeletal conditions, dermatological conditions, lung diseases, and cancers, among many others.

- Repeated trauma is the leading cause of work-related nonfatal illnesses.

- There are numerous resources to aid in the prevention of occupational injuries and diseases, including occupational health professionals, workplace injury and illness prevention programs, and worksite health promotion programs.

- Worksite health and wellness promotion (WHWP) programs are workplace-based programs aimed at improving the health and wellness of employees through changes in behavior and lifestyle.

- Total Worker Health is defined as policies, programs, and practices that integrate protection from work-related safety and health hazards with promotion of injury and illness prevention efforts to advance worker well-being.

Scenario: Analysis and Response

Please take a moment to reread the scenario at the beginning of this chapter. Here is some additional information on the nail salon industry from the CDC/NIOSH website:

Approximately 350,000 people are employed in nail salons and other personal care services in the United States according to industry estimates (*Nails Magazine*, 2008–2009). These estimates indicate the workforce is largely female (96%) with the industry employing a large number of minority workers (63%). Nail salon employees are potentially exposed to dozens of chemicals including acrylates, solvents, and biocides as dusts or vapors.

Then, reflect on the questions that follow.

1. If you were Linh, what would you do?

2. What federal agencies, mentioned in this chapter (or elsewhere in the text), provide information, advice, or assistance? Does your state regulate nail salon operations in a way that protects nail technicians?

3. This scenario raises concerns about workplace exposure to environmental hazards nail salons, but environmental hazards can occur anywhere. What types of environmental hazards might be present where you work?

4. Suppose you suspected that you were being exposed to a toxic agent where you worked. What would you do? Who would you contact? How could OSHA be of assistance?

Review Questions

1. Provide definitions of the terms occupational injury and occupational disease and give three examples of each.

2. In what ways are health problems in the workplace related to health problems in the general community?

3. How did the Industrial Revolution contribute to an increase in occupational health problems?

4. Who was Alice Hamilton? What did she do?

5. What were the deficiencies in state occupational safety and health laws in the early 1960s?

6. Briefly discuss the purpose of the Occupational Safety and Health Act of 1970 and outline its major provisions.

7. What is OSHA and what does it do? What is NIOSH and what does it do?

8. What are some of the most frequently reported workplace injuries? Which are the leading causes of workplace injury deaths?

9. Which age group and gender of workers suffer the most occupational injuries? Which have the most fatal injuries?

10. Why is farming a particularly hazardous occupation? What are ROPS and how do they prevent deaths? Describe some of the workplace hazards experienced by migrant farmworkers and their children.

11. What are the risk factors for encountering violence in the workplace? Which occupation is at greatest risk for workplace homicides?

12. Outline some general control strategies that can reduce the number and seriousness of workplace injuries.

13. What is the most frequently reported occupational disorder?

14. What determines whether a musculoskeletal condition or skin condition should be considered an injury or a disease?

15. List four well-documented lung conditions that are related to occupational exposure. Name the occupations whose workers are at high risk for each of these conditions.

16. Why is it often difficult to prove that a disease or condition resulted from workplace exposure?

17. Outline some features of a workplace program to prevent or control occupational diseases. For each activity, indicate whether it is aimed at the agent, host, or environment aspect of the disease model.

18. List five health occupations that deal with worker safety and health. Describe their training and job assignments.

19. Name and describe four occupational safety and health programs.

20. What are some of the benefits of worksite health and wellness promotion programs for employers and employees?

Activities

1. Examine your local newspaper every day for a week for articles dealing with occupational injury or illness. Find three articles and, after reading them, provide the following: a brief summary, the resulting injury or disease, the cause of the injury or disease, and a brief plan for how the organization could eliminate the cause.

2. Interview someone who works in the profession you wish to enter after graduation. Ask about prevalent injuries and illnesses connected with his or her job. Also ask about specific preservice and in-service education the interviewee has had to protect against these problems. Finally, ask him or her to propose measures to prevent future injuries or illnesses. Summarize your interview on paper in a two-page report.

3. If you have ever become injured or ill as a result of a job, explain what happened to you. In a two-page paper, identify the causative agent, how the injury could have been prevented, and what kind of training you had to prepare you for a safe working environment.

4. Go to the school library and research the injuries and diseases connected with your future profession. In a two-page paper, identify the major problems and what employers and employees should do about them and express concerns that you have about working in the profession because of these problems.

5. Visit any job site related to your future profession. At that site, find 10 things that employers and employees are doing to make it a safe work environment. List these 10 things briefly and explain the benefit of each one.

References

1. International Labour Organization (2013). *ILO Calls for Urgent Global Action to Fight Occupational Diseases.* Available at http://www.ilo.org/global/about-the-ilo/media-centre/press-releases/WCMS_211627/lang--en/index.htm.

2. International Labour Organization (2009). *World Day for Safety and Health at Work 2009: Facts on Safety and Health at Work.* Geneva, Switzerland: Author. Available at http://www.ilo.org/wcmsp5/groups/public/dgreports/dcomm/documents/publication/wcms_105146.pdf.

3. U.S. Department of Labor, Bureau of Labor Statistics (2016). *Economic News Release: Table A-1. Employment Status of the Civilian Population and Age.* Available at http://www.bls.gov/news.release/empsit.t01.htm.

4. U.S. Department of Labor, Bureau of Labor Statistics (2008). *BLS Glossary.* Available at http://www.bls.gov/bls/glossary.htm.

5. National Safety Council (2016). Injury Facts 2016 Edition. Itasca, IL. Author. 210 p.

6. U.S. Department of Labor, Bureau of Labor Statistics (2015). *Census of Fatal Occupational Injuries Summary, 2014.* Available at http://www.bls.gov/news.release/pdf/cfoi.pdf.

7. U.S. Department of Labor, Bureau of Labor Statistics (2015). *Employer-Reported Workplace Injuries and Illness—2014.* Available at http://www.bls.gov/news.release/pdf/osh.pdf.

8. Health and Safety Executive (United Kingdom) (2014). *Health and Safety Statistics: Annual Report for Great Britain 2013/14.* Available at http://www.hse.gov.uk/statistics/overall/hssh1314.pdf.

9. Felton, J. S. (1986). "History of Occupational Health and Safety." In J. LaDou, ed., *Introduction to Occupational Health and Safety.* Itasca, IL: National Safety Council.

10. Rosen, G. (1993). *A History of Public Health.* New York: Johns Hopkins University Press.

11. LaDou, J., J. Olishifski, and C. Zenz (1986). "Occupational Health and Safety Today." In J. LaDou, ed., *Introduction to Occupational Health and Safety.* Itasca, IL: National Safety Council.

12. Schilling, R. S. F. (1989). "Developments in Occupational Health." In H. A. Waldron, ed., *Occupational Health Practice.* Boston: Butterworth-Heinemann.

13. Ashford, N. A. (1976). *Crisis in the Workplace: Occupational Disease and Injury—A Report to the Ford Foundation.* Cambridge, MA: MIT Press.

14. Page, J. A., and M. W. O'Brien (1973). *Bitter Wages.* New York: Grossman Publishers.

15. U.S. Department of Labor, Bureau of Labor Statistics (2012). *Nonfatal Occupational Injuries and Illnesses Requiring Days Away from Work, 2014.* Available at http://www.bls.gov/news.release/osh2.nr0.htm.

16. Centers for Disease Control and Prevention (2015). "Occupational Traumatic Injuries among Workers in Health Care Facilities—United States, 2012–2014." *Morbidity and Mortality Weekly Report,* 64(15): 405–410. Available at http://www.cdc.gov/mmwr/pdf/wk/mm6415.pdf.

17. U.S. Department of Labor, Bureau of Labor Statistics (2015). *Census of Fatal Occupational Injuries, 2014 (Chart Package).* Available at http://www.bls.gov/iif/oshwc/cfoi/cfch0013.pdf.

18. Centers for Disease Control and Prevention (2015). "Workers' Memorial Day—April 28, 2015." *Morbidity and Mortality Weekly Report,* 64(15): 405.

19. Centers for Disease Control and Prevention, National Institute of Occupational Safety and Health Programs (n.d.). *Economics, Inputs: Occupational Safety and Health Risks.* Available at http://www.cdc.gov/niosh/programs/econ/risks.html.

20. U.S. Department of Health and Human Services, Office of Disease Prevention and Health Promotion (2010). "Occupational Safety and Health." *Healthy People 2020 Topics & Objectives.* Washington, DC: U.S. Government Printing Office. Available at http://www.healthypeople.gov/2020/topicsobjectives2020/objectiveslist.aspx?topicId=30.

21. Centers for Disease Control and Prevention (2010). "Occupational Injuries and Deaths among Younger Workers—United States, 1998–2007." *Morbidity and Mortality Weekly Report,* 59(15): 449–455. Available at http://www.cdc.gov/mmwr/pdf/wk/mm5915.pdf.

22. National Consumers League (2015). *Teens: Avoid This Year's Most Dangerous Summer Work.* Available at http://www.nclnet.org/worst_teen_jobs.

23. Child Labor Coalition (2013). *The CLC's Open Letter to President Obama on His Next Secretary of Labor.* Available at http://stopchildlabor.org/?p=3381.

24. U.S. Department of Health and Human Services, Centers for Disease Control and Prevention, National Institute for Occupational Safety and Health (2003). *NIOSH Alert: Preventing Deaths, Injuries, and Illnesses of Young Workers* (DHHS [NIOSH] pub. no. 2003-128). Cincinnati, OH: NIOSH Publications. Available at http://www.cdc.gov/niosh/topics/youth/.

25. U.S. Department of Health and Human Services, Centers for Disease Control and Prevention, National Institute for Occupational Safety and Health (2004). *Worker Health Chartbook, 2004* (DHHS [NIOSH] pub. no. 2004-146). Available at http://www.cdc.gov/niosh/docs/2004-146.

26. U.S. Department of Labor, Bureau of Labor Statistics (2015). *State Nonfatal Occupational Injury and Illness Rates Compared to the National Rate, Private Industry, 2014.* Available at http://stats.bls.gov/iif/oshwc/osh/os/osch0054.pdf.

27. Centers for Disease Control and Prevention (1999). "Achievements in Public Health, 1900–1999: Improvements in Workplace Safety—United States, 1900–1999." *Morbidity and Mortality Weekly Report,* 48(22): 461–469. Available at http://www.cdc.gov/mmwr/PDF/wk/mm4822.pdf.

28. Urbina, I. (2010, April 9). "No Survivors Found After West Virginia Mine Disaster." *The New York Times.* Available at http://www.nytimes.com/2010/04/10/us/10westvirginia.html.

29. Centers for Disease Control and Prevention, National Institute for Occupational Safety and Health, Division of Safety Research (2014). *Agricultural Safety.* Available at http://www.cdc.gov/niosh/topics/aginjury/.

30. National Children's Center for Rural and Agricultural Health and Safety (2013). *2014 Fact Sheet: Childhood Agricultural Injures in the U.S.* Available at https://www3.marshfieldclinic.org/proxy/MCRF-Centers-NFMC-NCCRAHS-2014_Child_Ag_Injury_FactSheet.1.pdf.

31. Ayers, P. D. (2005). *Safety: General Tractor Safety* (Farm and Ranch Series, no. 5.016). Ft. Collins: Colorado State University Extension. Available at http://www.ext.colostate.edu/pubs/farmmgt/05016.pdf.

32. Centers for Disease Control and Prevention, National Institute for Occupational Safety and Health (2012). *Agricultural Safety: Cost-Effective Rollover Protective Structures (CROPS).* Available at http://www.cdc.gov/niosh/topics/aginjury/crops/.

33. Committee on Labor and Human Resources (19 March 1991). "Prepared Statement of Fernando Cuevas, Jr." *Childhood Labor Amendments of 1991* (S. HRG. 102-201. S 600). Washington, DC: U.S. Government Printing Office.

34. Human Rights Watch (2010). *Fields of Peril: Child Labor in U.S. Agriculture.* New York: Author. Available at http://www.hrw.org/node/90126.

35. Human Rights Watch (2015). *Teens of the Tobacco Fields: Child Labor in United States Tobacco Farming.* New York: Author. Available at https://www.hrw.org/world-report/2016/photo-essay-tobacco-fields-united-states.

36. Weeks, J. L., G. R. Wagner, K. M. Rest, and B. S. Levy (2005). "A Public Health Approach to Preventing Occupational Diseases and Injuries." In B. S. Levy, G. R. Wagner, K. M. Rest, and J. L. Weeks, eds., *Preventing Occupational Disease and Injury*, 2nd ed. Washington, DC: American Public Health Association.

37. Centers for Disease Control and Prevention, National Institute of Occupational Safety and Health (2006). *The National Occupational Research Agenda (NORA).* Available at http://www.cdc.gov/niosh/nora/default.html.

38. Centers for Disease Control and Prevention, National Institute of Occupational Safety and Health (2011) *NORA: Symposium 2011. Achieving Impact through Research and Partnerships.* Available at http://www.cdc.gov/niosh/nora/symp11/NORA-Symposuim-2011--ProgramBook.pdf.

39. Centers for Disease Control and Prevention, National Institute for Occupational Safety and Health (2004). *Violence on the Job* (NIOSH pub. no. 2004-100d). Available at http://www.cdc.gov/niosh/docs/video/violence.html.

40. Centers for Disease Control and Prevention, National Institute for Occupational Safety and Health (2014). *Occupational Violence.* Available at http://www.cdc.gov/niosh/topics/violence/.

41. Casey, M., M. L. Stanton, K. J. Cummings, et al. (2015). "Work-Related Asthma Cluster at a Synthetic Foam Manufacturing Factory—Massachusetts 2008–2013." *Morbidity and Mortality Weekly Report*, 64(15): 411–414.

42. Centers for Disease Control and Prevention (2016). *Occupational Respiratory Disease Surveillance.* NORMS National Database. Available at http://webappa.cdc.gov/ords/norms-national.html 43.

43. Blackley, D.J., C. N. Halldin, and A. S. Laney (2014). "Resurgence of a Debilitating and Entirely Preventable Respiratory Disease among Working Coal Miners." *American Journal of Respiratory and Critical Care Medicine*, 190(6): 708–709.

44. Arnold, C. (2016). "A Scourge Returns: Black Lung in Appalachia." *Environmental Health Perspectives*, 124(1): A13–A18.

45. Centers for Disease Control and Prevention (2009). "Coal Worker's Pneumoconiosis-Related Years of Potential Life Lost Before Age 65 Years—United States, 1968–2006." *Morbidity and Mortality Weekly Report*, 58(50): 1412–1416. Available at http://www.cdc.gov/mmwr/PDF/wk/mm5850.pdf.

46. Centers for Disease Control and Prevention (2012). "Pneumoconiosis and Advanced Occupational Lung Diseases among Surface Coal Miners—16 States, 2010–2011." *Morbidity and Mortality Weekly Report*, 61(23): 431–434. Available at http://www.cdc.gov/mmwr/pdf/wk/mm6123.pdf.

47. U.S. Department of Health and Human Services, Centers for Disease Control and Prevention, National Institute for Occupational Safety and Health (2012). *NIOSH Pesticide Poisoning Monitoring Program Protects Farmworkers* (DHHS [NIOSH] Publication Number 2012-108). Cincinnati, OH: Author. Available at http://www.cdc.gov/niosh/docs/2012-108/.

48. Calvert, G. M., J. Karnik, L. Meler, et al. (2008). "Acute Pesticide Poisoning among Agricultural Workers in the United States, 1998–2005." *American Journal of Industrial Medicine*, 51: 883–898. Available at http://www.cdc.gov/niosh/topics/pesticides/ajim2008.html.

49. U.S. Department of Health and Human Services, Centers for Disease Control and Prevention, National Institute for Occupational Safety and Health (2004). *NIOSH Alert: Preventing Occupational Exposures to Antineoplastic and Other Hazardous Drugs in Health care Settings* (DHHS [NIOSH] pub. no. 2004-165). Cincinnati, OH: Author.

50. U.S. Department of Health and Human Services, Centers for Disease Control and Prevention, National Institute for Occupational Safety and Health (2012). *NIOSH List of Antineoplastic and Other Hazardous Drugs in Health care Settings 2012* (DHHS [NIOSH] Publication Number 2012-150). Available at http://www.cdc.gov/niosh/docs/2012-150/pdfs/2012-150.pdf.

51. U.S. Department of Health and Human Services, Centers for Disease Control and Prevention, National Institute for Occupational Safety and Health (2013). *Current Intelligence Bulletin 65: Occupational Exposure to Carbon Nanotubes and Nanofibers* (DHHS [NIOSH] Publication Number 2013-145). Available at http://www.cdc.gov/niosh/docs/2013-145/.

52. American Society of Safety Engineers (2016). Website. Available at http://www.asse.org.

53. Board of Certified Safety Professionals (2013). Website. Available at http://www.bcsp.org.

54. Health Physics Society (2013). *About the Health Physics Society.* Available at http://hps.org/aboutthesociety/.

55. American Academy of Health Physics (2013). *Welcome to the Home Page of the AAHP.* Available at http://hps1.org/aahp/.

56. American Conference of Governmental Industrial Hygienists (2013). Website. Available at http://www.acgih.org.

57. American College of Occupational and Environmental Medicine (2015). Website. Available at http://www.acoem.org/.

58. American Board for Occupational Health Nurses, Inc. (2015). *Who We Are and What We Do.* Available at http://www.abohn.org.

59. American Association of Occupational Health Nurses, Inc. (2015). Website. Available at http://www.aaohn.org.

60. Chenoweth, D. H. (2007). *Worksite Health Promotion*, 2nd ed. Champaign, IL: Human Kinetics.

61. Centers for Disease Control and Prevention (2015). *Total Worker Health*. Available at http://www.cdc.gov/niosh/TWH/default.html.

GLOSSARY

absorption field   The element of a septic system in which the liquid portion of waste is distributed.

accreditation   The process by which an agency or organization evaluates and recognizes an institution as meeting certain predetermined standards.

acculturated   The cultural modification of an individual or group by adapting to or borrowing traits from another culture.

accountable care organization (ACO)   Group of doctors, hospitals, and other health care providers, who come together voluntarily as a legal entity to give coordinated high-quality care to their Medicare patients.

active immunity   Occurs when exposure to a disease-causing organism prompts the immune system to develop antibodies against that disease.

activities of daily living (ADLs)   Tasks such as eating, toileting, dressing, bathing, walking, getting in and out of a bed or chair, and getting outside.

acute disease   A disease that lasts 3 months or less.

Administration on Aging   An operating division of the U.S. Department of Health and Human Services designated to carry out the provisions of the Older Americans Act of 1965.

Administration for Children and Families   An operating division of the U.S. Department of Health and Human Services that coordinates programs that promote the economic and social well-being of families, children, individuals, and communities.

adolescents and young adults   Those people who fall into the 10-to-24-year-old age range.

adult day care programs   Daytime care provided to older adults who are unable to be left alone.

Affordable Care Act   A law passed in 2010 with goals of lowering both the number of uninsured and the cost of health care, and increasing the quality by expanding both public and private health insurance. It includes a mandate that individuals have health insurance.

aftercare   The continuing care provided to the recovering former drug abuser.

age pyramid   A conceptual model that illustrates the age distribution of a population.

age-adjusted rates   Rates used to make comparisons across groups and over time when groups differ by age structure.

ageism   Prejudice and discrimination against the aged.

Agency for Health care Research and Quality (AHRQ)   An operating division of the U.S. Department of Health and Human Services that has the responsibility of overseeing health care research.

Agency for Toxic Substances and Disease Registry (ATSDR)   An operating division of the U.S. Department of Health and Human Services created by Superfund legislation to prevent or mitigate adverse health effects and diminished quality of life resulting from exposure to hazardous substances in the environment.

agent (pathogenic agent)   The cause of the disease or health problem.

air pollution   Contamination of the air that interferes with the comfort, safety, and health of living organisms.

Air Quality Index (AQI)   An index that indicates the level of pollution in the air and associated health risk.

airborne disease   A communicable disease that is transmitted through the air (e.g., influenza).

Alcoholics Anonymous (AA)   A fellowship of recovering alcoholics who offer support to anyone who desires to stop drinking.

alcoholism   A disease characterized by impaired control over drinking, preoccupation with drinking, and continued use of alcohol despite adverse consequences.

alien   A person born in and owing allegiance to a country other than the one in which he or she lives.

allied health care professional   Health care worker who provides services that assist, facilitate, and complement the work of physicians and other health care specialists.

allopathic provider   Independent provider whose remedies for illnesses produce effects different from those of the disease.

American Cancer Society   A voluntary health agency dedicated to fighting cancer and educating the public about cancer.

American Health Security Act of 1993   The comprehensive health care reform introduced by then President Bill Clinton, but never enacted.

American Red Cross   A nonprofit, humanitarian organization led by volunteers and guided by its Congressional Charter that provides relief to victims of disasters.

amotivational syndrome   A pattern of behavior characterized by apathy, loss of effectiveness, and a more passive, introverted personality.

amphetamines   A group of synthetic drugs that act as stimulants.

anabolic drugs   Compounds, structurally similar to the male hormone testosterone, that increase protein synthesis and thus muscle building.

analytic study   An epidemiological study aimed at testing hypotheses.

anthroponosis   A disease that infects only humans.

aquifers   Porous, water saturated layers of underground bedrock, sand, and gravel that can yield economically significant amounts of water.

asbestos   A naturally occurring mineral fiber that has been identified as a class A carcinogen by the Environmental Protection Agency.

asbestosis   Acute or chronic lung disease caused by the deposit of asbestos fibers on lungs.

assertive community treatment   Service that uses active outreach by a team of providers over an indefinite period of time to deliver intensive, individualized services.

assisted-living facility   "A system of housing and limited care that is designed for senior citizens who need some assistance with daily activities but do not require care in a nursing home." (Merriam-Webster Online Dictionary (n.d.). *Assisted Living.* Available at http://www.merriam-webster.com/dictionary/assisted%20living.)

attack rate   An incidence rate calculated for a particular population for a single disease outbreak and expressed as a percentage.

automatic (passive) protection   The modification of a product or the environment in such a way as to reduce unintentional injuries.

bacteriological period of public health   The period of 1875 to 1900, during which the causes of many bacterial diseases were discovered.

barbiturates   Depressant drugs based on the structure of barbituric acid.

behavioral health care services   The managed care term for mental health and substance abuse/dependence care services.

benzodiazapines   Nonbarbiturate depressant drugs.

best experience   Intervention strategies used in prior or existing programs that have not gone through the critical research and evaluation studies and thus fall short of best practice criteria.

best practices   "Recommendations for interventions based on critical review of multiple research and evaluation studies that substantiate the efficacy of the intervention." (Green, L. W., and M. W. Kreuter (2005). *Health Program Planning: An Educational and Ecological Approach*, 4th ed. Boston: McGraw-Hill.)

best processes   Original intervention strategies that the planners create based on their knowledge and skills of good planning processes including the involvement of those in the priority population and the theories and models.

bias and hate crimes   A criminal offense against a person or property motivated in whole or in part by an offender's bias against a race, religion, disability, sexual orientation, ethnicity, gender, or gender identity.

binge drinking   Consuming five or more alcoholic drinks in a row for males, four or more for females.

biogenic pollutants   Airborne biological organisms or their particles or gases or other toxic materials that can produce illness.

biological hazards   Living organisms (and viruses), or their products, that increase the risk of disease or death in humans.

bioterrorism   The threatened or intentional release of biological agents for the purpose of influencing the conduct of government or intimidating or coercing a civilian population to further political or social objectives.

bipolar disorder   An affective disorder characterized by distinct periods of elevated mood alternating with periods of depression.

birth rate   See *natality (birth) rate*.

blood alcohol concentration (BAC)   The percentage of concentration of alcohol in the blood.

Bloodborne Pathogen Standard   A set of regulations promulgated by OSHA that sets forth the responsibilities of employers and employees with regard to precautions to be taken concerning bloodborne pathogens in the workplace.

bloodborne pathogens   Disease agents, such as HIV, that are transmissible in blood and other body fluids.

body mass index (BMI)   The ratio of weight (in kilograms) to height (in meters, squared).

bottom-up community organization   Organization efforts that begin with those who live within the community affected.

brownfield   Property where reuse is complicated by the presence of hazardous substances from prior use.

built environment   "The design, construction, management, and land use of human-made surroundings as an interrelated whole, as well as their relationship to human activities over time." (Coupland, K., S. Rikhy, K. Hill, and D. McNeil (2011). *State of Evidence: The Built Environment and Health 2011–2015*. Alberta, Canada; Public Health Innovation and Decision Support, Population, & Public Health, Alberta Health Services.)

Bureau of Alcohol, Tobacco, Firearms, and Explosives (ATF)   The federal agency in the U.S. Department of Justice that regulates alcohol, tobacco, firearms, and explosives.

Bureau of Indian Affairs (BIA)   The original federal government agency charged with the responsibility for the welfare of American Indians.

byssinosis   Acute or chronic lung disease caused by the inhalation of cotton, flax, or hemp dusts; those affected include workers in cotton textile plants (sometimes called brown lung disease).

capitation   A method of paying for covered health care services on a per-person premium basis for a specific time period prior to the service being rendered.

carcinogen   Agent, usually chemical, that causes cancer.

care manager   One who helps identify the health care needs of an individual but does not actually provide the health care services.

care provider   One who helps identify the health care needs of an individual and also personally performs the caregiving service.

carrier   A person or animal that harbors a specific communicable agent in the absence of discernible clinical disease and serves as a potential source of infection to others.

carrying capacity   The maximum population of a particular species that a given habitat can support over a given period of time.

case   A person who is sick with a disease.

categorical programs   Programs available only to people who can be categorized into a group based on specific variables.

census   The enumeration of the population of the United States that is conducted every 10 years; begun in 1790.

Center for Mental Health Services (CMHS)   The federal agency, housed within the U.S. Department of Health and Human Service's Substance Abuse and Mental Health Services Administration, whose mission it is to conduct research on the causes and treatments for mental disorders.

Centers for Disease Control and Prevention (CDC)   One of the operating divisions of the U.S. Public Health Service;

charged with the responsibility for surveillance and control of diseases and other health problems in the United States.

Centers for Medicare & Medicaid Services (CMS) The federal agency responsible for overseeing Medicare, Medicaid, and the related quality assurance activities.

cerebrovascular disease (stroke) A chronic disease characterized by damage to blood vessels of the brain, resulting in disruption of circulation to the brain.

certified safety professional (CSP) A health and safety professional, trained in industrial and workplace safety, who has met specific requirements for board certification.

chain of infection A model to conceptualize the transmission of a communicable disease from its source to a susceptible host.

chemical hazard Hazard caused by the mismanagement of chemicals.

chemical straitjacket A drug that subdues a mental patient's behavior.

child abuse The intentional physical, emotional, verbal, or sexual mistreatment of a minor.

child maltreatment The act or failure to act by a parent, caretaker, or other person as defined under state law that results in physical abuse, neglect, medical neglect, sexual abuse, or emotional abuse, or an act or failure to act that presents an imminent risk of serious harm to the child.

child neglect The failure of a parent or guardian to care for or otherwise provide the necessary subsistence for a child.

childhood diseases Infectious diseases that normally affect people in their childhood (e.g., measles, mumps, rubella, and pertussis).

children Persons between 1 and 9 years of age.

Children's Health Insurance Program (CHIP) A title insurance program under the Social Security Act that provides health insurance to uninsured children.

chiropractor A nonallopathic, independent health care provider who treats health problems by adjusting the spinal column.

chlorpromazine The first and most famous antipsychotic drug, introduced in 1954 under the brand name Thorazine.

chronic disease A disease or health condition that lasts longer than 3 months.

citizen-initiated community organization See *bottom-up community organization.*

Clean Air Act (CAA) The federal law that provides the government with authority to address interstate air pollution.

Clean Water Act (CWA) The federal law aimed at ensuring that all rivers are swimmable and fishable and that limits the discharge of pollutants in U.S. waters to zero.

closed panel HMO An organization in which private physicians are contracted on an exclusive basis for services at a health maintenance organization.

club drugs A general term for those illicit drugs, primarily synthetic, that are most commonly encountered at night clubs and "raves." Examples include MDMA, LSD, GHB, GBL, PCP, ketamine, Rohypnol, and methamphetamines.

coal workers' pneumoconiosis (CWP) Acute and chronic lung disease caused by the inhalation of coal dust (sometimes called black lung disease).

coalition "A formal alliance of organizations that come together to work for a common goal." (Butterfoss, F. D. (2007). *Coalitions and Partnerships in Community Health.* San Francisco, CA: Jossey-Bass.)

cocaine The psychoactive ingredient in the leaves of the coca plant, *Erythoxolyn coca*, which, when refined, is a powerful stimulant/euphoriant.

cognitive-behavioral therapy Treatment based on learning new thought patterns and adaptive skills, with regular practice between therapy sessions.

co-insurance The portion of insurance company's approved amounts for covered services that the beneficiary is responsible for paying.

combustion (incineration) The burning of solid wastes.

common source epidemic curve A graphic display of a disease where each case can be traced to a single source of exposure.

combustion by-products Gases and other particulates generated by burning.

communicable (infectious) disease An illness caused by some specific biological agent or its toxic products that can be transmitted from an infected person, animal, or inanimate reservoir to a susceptible host.

communicable disease model The minimal requirements for the occurrence and spread of communicable diseases in a population—agent, host, and environment.

community A collective body of individuals identified by common characteristics such as geography, interests, experiences, concerns, or values.

community analysis A process by which community needs are identified.

community building "An orientation to practice focused on community, rather than a strategic framework or approach, and on building capacities, not fixing problems." (Minkler, M., (2012). "Introduction to Community Organizing and Community Building." In M. Minkler, ed., *Community Organizing and Community Building for Health and Welfare*, 3rd ed. New Brunswick, NJ: Rutgers University Press, 5–26.)

community capacity "The characteristics of communities that affect their ability to identify, mobilize, and address social and public health problems." (Minkler, M., and N. Wallerstein (2012). "Improving Health through Community Organization and Community Building: Perspectives from Health Education and Social Work." In M. Minkler, ed., *Community Organizing and Community Building for Health and Welfare*, 3rd ed. New Brunswick, NJ: Rutgers University Press, 37–58.)

community diagnosis See *community analysis.*

community health The health status of a defined group of people and the actions and conditions to promote, protect, and preserve their health.

community mental health center (CMHC) A fully staffed center originally funded by the federal government that provides comprehensive mental health services to local populations.

community organizing   "The process by which community groups are helped to identify common problems or change targets, mobilize resources, and develop and implement strategies for reaching their collective goals." (Minkler, M., and N. Wallerstein (2012). "Improving Health through Community Organization and Community Building: Perspectives from Health Education and Social Work." In M. Minkler, ed., *Community Organizing and Community Building for Health and Welfare*, 3rd ed. New Brunswick, NJ: Rutgers University Press, 37–58.)

Community Support Program   A federal program that offers financial incentives to communities to develop a social support system for the mentally ill.

complementary/alternative medicine (CAM)   "A group of diverse medical and health care systems, practices, and products that are not presently considered to be a part of conventional medicine. " (National Institutes of Health, National Center for Complementary and Alternative Medicine (2012). *CAM Basics: What is Complementary and Alternative Medicine?* Available at https://nccih.nih.gov/sites/nccam.nih.gov/files/D347_05-25-2012.pdf.)

complex disaster   A natural disaster that further escalates an ongoing crisis or causes a technological disaster resulting in communities being affected by the consequences of a combination of natural and human-made hazards.

composting   The natural, aerobic biodegradation of organic plant and animal matter to compost.

Comprehensive Environmental Response, Compensation, and Liability Act (CERCLA)   The federal law (known as the Superfund) created to clean up abandoned hazardous waste sites.

congregate meal programs   Community-sponsored nutrition programs that provide meals at a central site, such as a senior center.

consumer-directed health plan (CDH/CDHP)   Health care plan that combines a pretax payment account to pay for out-of-pocket medical expenses with a high-deductible health plan (HDHP).

continuing care   Long-term care for chronic health problems, usually including personal care.

continuing care retirement communities (CCRCs)   Planned communities for older adults that guarantee a lifelong residence and health care.

continuous source epidemic   A type of epidemic where cases are exposed to a common source over time.

controlled substances   Drugs regulated by the Comprehensive Drug Abuse Control Act of 1970, including all illegal drugs and prescription drugs that are subject to abuse and can produce dependence.

Controlled Substances Act of 1970 (Comprehensive Drug Abuse Control Act of 1970)   The central piece of federal drug legislation that regulates illegal drugs and legal drugs that have a high potential for abuse.

coordinated school health (CSH)   An organized set of policies, procedures, and activities designed to protect, promote, and improve the health and well-being of pre-K through 12th grade students and staff, thus improving a student's ability to learn. It includes, but is not limited to, health education; school health services; a healthy school environment; school counseling, psychological, and social services; physical education; school nutrition services; family and community involvement in school health; and school-site health promotion for staff.

copayment   A negotiated set amount a patient pays for certain services.

core functions of public health   Health assessment, policy development, and health assurance.

coronary heart disease (CHD)   A chronic disease characterized by damage to the coronary arteries in the heart.

Crisis Intervention Team   Specially trained police in direct collaboration with mental health authorities to remove barriers to mental health care for people with mental illness involved in the justice system.

criteria of causation   Aspects of the association between two variables that should be considered before deciding that the association is one of causation.

criteria pollutants   The most pervasive air pollutants and those of greatest concern in the United States.

cross-sectional study   An observational study where information about exposure and disease are collected at the same time.

crude rate   A rate in which the denominator includes the total population.

cultural competence   Service provider's degree of compatibility with the specific culture of the population served, for example, proficiency in language(s) other than English, familiarity with cultural idioms of distress or body language, folk beliefs, and expectations regarding treatment procedures (such as medication or psychotherapy) and likely outcomes.

cultural and linguistic competence   A set of congruent behaviors, attitudes, and policies that come together in a system, agency, or among professionals that enables effective work in cross-cultural situations.

culturally sensitive   Having respect for cultures other than one's own.

curriculum   A written plan for instruction.

cycles per second (cps)   A measure of sound frequency.

death rate   See *mortality (fatality) rate*.

deductible   The amount of expense that the beneficiary must incur before the insurance company begins to pay for covered services.

deinstitutionalization   The process of discharging, on a large scale, patients from state mental hospitals to less restrictive community settings.

demography   The study of a population and those variables bringing about change in that population.

Department of Health and Human Services (HHS)   The largest federal department in the United States government, formed in 1980 and headed by a secretary who is a member of the president's cabinet.

dependency ratio A ratio that compares the number of individuals whom society considers economically productive to the number of those it considers economically unproductive.

depressant A psychoactive drug that slows down the central nervous system.

descriptive study An epidemiological study that describes a disease with respect to person, place, and time.

designer drugs Drugs synthesized illegally that are similar to, but structurally different from, known controlled substances.

diagnosis-related groups (DRGs) A procedure used to classify the health problems of all Medicare patients when they are admitted to a hospital.

direct transmission The immediate transfer of an infectious agent by direct contact between infected and susceptible individuals.

disability-adjusted life years (DALYs) A measure for the burden of disease that takes into account premature death and loss of healthy life resulting from disability.

disabling injury An injury causing any restriction of normal activity beyond the day of the injury's occurrence.

diseases of adaptation Diseases resulting from chronic exposure to excess levels of stressors that produce a General Adaptation Syndrome response.

disinfection The killing of communicable disease agents outside the host, on countertops, for example.

dose The number of program units delivered as part of the intervention.

drug A substance other than food or vitamins that, when taken in small quantities, alters one's physical, mental, or emotional state.

drug abuse Use of a drug when it is detrimental to one's health or well-being.

drug abuse education Provides information about drugs and the dangers of drug abuse, changing attitudes and beliefs about drugs, and provides skills necessary to abstain from drugs, ultimately changing drug abuse behavior.

drug (chemical) dependence A psychological and sometimes physical state characterized by a craving for a drug.

Drug Enforcement Administration (DEA) The federal government's lead agency with the primary responsibility for enforcing the nation's drug laws, including the Controlled Substances Act of 1970.

drug misuse Inappropriate use of prescription or nonprescription drugs.

drug use A non-evaluative term referring to drug-taking behavior in general; any drug-taking behavior.

Earth Day Annual public observance for concerns about the environment; the first was held April 22, 1970.

electroconvulsive therapy (ECT) A method of treatment for mental disorders involving the administration of electric current to the scalp to induce convulsions and unconsciousness.

employee assistance program (EAP) Workplace-based program that assists employees who have substance abuse, domestic, psychological, or social problems that interfere with their work performance.

empowerment "Social action process for people to gain mastery over their lives and the lives of their communities." (Minkler, M., and N. Wallerstein (2012). "Improving Health through Community Organization and Community Building: Perspectives from Health Education and Social Work." In M. Minkler, ed., *Community Organizing and Community Building for Health and Welfare*, 3rd ed. New Brunswick, NJ: Rutgers University Press, 37–58.)

endocrine-disrupting chemical (EDC) A chemical that interferes in some way with the body's endocrine (hormone) system.

end-of-life practice Health care services provided to individuals shortly before death.

endemic disease A disease that occurs regularly in a population as a matter of course.

environmental hazard Factor or condition in the environment that increases the risk of human injury, disease, or death.

environmental health The study and management of environmental conditions that affect the health and well-being of humans.

Environmental Protection Agency (EPA) The federal agency primarily responsible for setting, maintaining, and enforcing environmental standards.

environmental sanitation The practice of establishing and maintaining healthy or hygienic conditions in the environment.

environmental tobacco smoke (ETS) Also known as **secondhand smoke**, tobacco smoke in the environment that is a mixture of mainstream and sidestream smoke that can be inhaled by nearby or transient nonsmokers.

epidemic An unexpectedly large number of cases of an illness, specific health-related behavior, or other health-related event in a particular population.

epidemic curve A graphic display of the cases of disease according to the time or date of onset of symptoms.

epidemiologist One who practices epidemiology.

epidemiology The study of the distribution and determinants of health-related states or events in specific populations, and the application of this study to control health problems.

eradication The complete elimination or uprooting of a disease (e.g., smallpox eradication).

etiology The cause of a disease.

evaluation Determining the value or worth of the objective of interest.

evidence The body of data that can be used to make decisions.

evidence-based practice Systematically finding, appraising, and using evidence as the basis for decision making.

exclusion A health condition written into a health insurance policy indicating what is not covered by the policy.

experimental (interventional) study An analytic study in which investigators allocate exposure or intervention and follow development of disease.

Family and Medical Leave Act (FMLA)   Federal law that provides up to a 12-week unpaid leave to men and women after the birth of a child, an adoption, or an event of illness in the immediate family.

family planning   Determining the preferred number and spacing of children and choosing the appropriate means to accomplish it.

family violence   The use of physical force by one family member against another, with the intent to hurt, injure, or cause death.

fatal injury   An injury that results in one or more deaths.

fatality rate   See *mortality (fatality) rate.*

Federal Emergency Management Agency (FEMA)   The nation's official emergency response agency.

Federal Water Pollution Control Act Amendments   See *Clean Water Act (CWA).*

Federally Qualified Health Centers (FQHCs)   Those community health centers that receive funding under Section 330 of the Public Health Service (PHS) Act.

fee-for-service pricing   A method of paying for health care in which after the service is rendered, a fee is paid.

fertility rate   The number of live births per 1,000 women of childbearing age (15–44 years).

fetal alcohol spectrum disorder (FASD)   A range of disorders caused by prenatal exposure to alcohol. FASD refers to conditions such as fetal alcohol syndrome (FAS), fetal alcohol effects (FAE), alcohol-related neuro-developmental disorder (ARND), and alcohol-related birth defects (ARBD).

fetal alcohol syndrome (FAS)   A group of abnormalities that may include growth retardation, abnormal appearance of face and head, and deficits of central nervous system function, including mental retardation in babies born to mothers who have consumed heavy amounts of alcohol during their pregnancies.

fetal death   Death in utero with a gestational age of at least 20 weeks.

fight-or-flight reaction   An alarm reaction that prepares one physiologically for sudden action.

fixed indemnity   The maximum amount an insurer will pay for a certain service.

flunitrazepam   See *Rohypnol.*

Food and Drug Administration (FDA)   A federal agency in the U.S. Department of Health and Human Services charged with ensuring the safety and efficacy of all prescription and nonprescription drugs.

foodborne disease   A disease transmitted through the contamination of food.

foodborne disease outbreak (FBDO)   The occurrence of two or more cases of a similar illness resulting from the ingestion of food.

formaldehyde (CH_2O)   A water-soluble gas used in aqueous solutions in hundreds of consumer products.

formative evaluation   The evaluation that is conducted during the planning and implementing processes to improve or refine a program.

full-service hospital   A hospital that offers services in all or most of the levels of care defined by the spectrum of health care delivery.

functional limitation   Difficulty in performing personal care and home management tasks.

gag rule   Regulations that barred physicians and nurses in clinics receiving federal funds from counseling clients about abortions.

gatekeeper   One who controls, both formally and informally, the political climate of the community.

General Adaptation Syndrome (GAS)   The complex physiological responses resulting from exposure to stressors.

global health   Describes health problems, issues, and concerns that transcend national boundaries, may be influenced by circumstances or experiences in other countries, and are best addressed by cooperative actions and solutions.

government hospital   A hospital that is supported and managed by governmental jurisdictions.

governmental health agency   Health agency that is part of the governmental structure (federal, state, or local) and that is funded primarily by tax dollars.

grassroots   A process that begins with those affected by the problem/concern.

grassroots participation   "Bottom-up efforts of people taking collective actions on their own behalf; they involve the use of a sophisticated blend of confrontation and cooperation in order to achieve their ends." (Perlman J. (1978). "Grassroots Participation from Neighborhood to Nation." In S. Langton, *Citizen Participation in America.* Lexington, MA: Lexington Books, 65–79.)

greenhouse gases   Atmosphere gases, principally carbon dioxide, chlorofluorocarbons, ozone, methane, water vapor, and nitrous oxide, that are transparent to visible light but absorb infrared radiation.

groundwater   Water located under the surface of the ground.

group model HMO   An HMO that contracts with a multispecialty group practice.

hallucinogen   Drug that produces profound distortions of the senses.

hard-to-reach population   Those in a priority population that are not easily reached by normal programming efforts.

hate crimes   See *bias and hate crimes.*

hazard   An unsafe act or condition.

hazardous waste   A solid waste or combination of solid wastes that is dangerous to human health or the environment.

health   A dynamic state or condition of the human organism that is multidimensional in nature, a resource for living, and results from a person's interactions with and adaptations to his or her environment; therefore, it can exist in varying degrees and is specific to each individual and his or her situation.

health disparities   The differences in the incidence, prevalence, mortality, and burden of diseases, and other adverse health conditions that exist among specific population groups.

health education "Any combination of planned learning experiences using evidence-based practices and/or sound theories that provide the opportunity to acquire knowledge, attitudes, and skills needed to adopt and maintain health behaviors." (Joint Committee on Health Education and Promotion Terminology (2012). *Report of the 2011 Joint Committee on Health Education and Promotion Terminology.* Reston, VA: American Association of Health Education.)

health insurance marketplaces Organizations established to create more organized and competitive markets for purchasing health insurance.

health insurance policy A contract between an insurer and the insured that outlines what health services are covered and how they will be paid for.

health maintenance organization (HMO) Group that supplies prepaid comprehensive health care with an emphasis on prevention.

health physicist A safety professional with responsibility for monitoring radiation within a plant environment, developing instrumentation for that purpose, and developing plans for coping with radiation accidents.

health promotion "Any planned combination of educational, political, environmental, regulatory, or organizational mechanisms that support actions and conditions of living conducive to the health of individuals, groups, and communities." (Joint Committee on Health Education and Promotion Terminology (2012). *Report of the 2011 Joint Committee on Health Education and Promotion Terminology.* Reston, VA: American Association of Health Education.)

health resources development period The years 1900 to 1960; a time of great growth in health care facilities and providers.

Health Resources and Services Administration (HRSA) An operating division of the U.S. Department of Health and Human Services established in 1982 to improve the nation's health resources and services and their distribution to underserved populations.

health-adjusted life expectancy (HALE) The number of years of healthy life expected, on average, in a given population.

Healthy People 2020 The fourth set of health goals and objectives for the U.S. that defines the nation's health agenda and guides its health policy.

healthy school environment The promotion, maintenance, and utilization of safe and wholesome surroundings in a school.

herbicide A pesticide designed specifically to kill plants.

herd immunity The resistance of a population to the spread of an infectious agent based on the immunity of a high portion of individuals.

home health care Care that is provided in the patient's residence for the purpose of promoting, maintaining, or restoring health.

home health care services Health care services provided in the patient's place of residence.

homebound A person unable to leave home for normal activities.

hospice care "A cluster of special services for the dying that blends medical, spiritual, legal, financial, and family support services." (Shi, L., and D. A. Singh (2015). *Delivering Health Care in America: A Systems Approach*, 6th ed. Burlington, MA: Jones & Bartlett Learning.)

Hospital Survey and Construction Act of 1946 (Hill-Burton Act) Federal legislation that provided substantial funds for hospital construction.

host A person or other living organism that affords subsistence or lodgment to a communicable agent under natural conditions.

hypercholesterolemia High levels of cholesterol in the blood.

hypertension Systolic pressure equal to or greater than 140 mm of mercury (Hg) and/or diastolic pressure equal to or greater than 90 mm Hg for extended periods of time.

illicit (illegal) drugs Drugs that cannot be legally manufactured, distributed, bought, or sold and that usually lack recognized medical value. Drugs that have been placed under Schedule I of the Controlled Substances Act of 1970.

immigrant Individuals who migrate from one country to another for the purpose of seeking permanent residence.

impact evaluation The evaluation that focuses on immediate observable effects of a program.

impairments Defects in the functioning of one's sense organs or limitations in one's mobility or range of motion.

implementation Putting a planned program into action.

incidence rate The number of new health-related events or cases of a disease divided by the total number in the population at risk.

incubation period The period of time between exposure to a disease and the onset of symptoms.

independent practice association (IPA) Legal entity separate from the HMO that is a physician organization composed of community-based independent physicians in solo or group practices that provide services to HMO members.

independent provider Health care professional with the education and legal authority to treat any health problem.

Indian Health Service (IHS) An operating division of the U.S. Department of Health and Human Services whose goal is to raise the health status of the American Indian and Alaska Native to the highest possible level by providing a comprehensive health services delivery system.

indirect transmission Communicable disease transmission involving an intermediate step.

Individual Placement and Support An evidence-based model of employment services emphasizing real work opportunities, integrated mental health services, and individualized job supports.

industrial hygienist Health professional concerned with health hazards in the workplace and with recommending plans for improving the healthiness of workplace environments.

industrial smog Haze or fog formed primarily by sulfur dioxide and suspended particles from the burning of coal, also known as gray smog.

infant death (infant mortality) Death of a child under 1 year of age.

infant mortality rate The number of deaths of children under 1 year of age per 1,000 live births.

infection The lodgment and growth of a virus or microorganism in a host organism.

infectious disease See *communicable disease*.

infectivity The ability of a biological agent to enter and grow in a host.

informal caregiver One who provides unpaid care or assistance to one who has some physical, mental, emotional, or financial need that limits his or her independence.

inhalant Breathable substance that produces mind altering effects.

injury Physical harm or damage to the body resulting from an exchange of mechanical, chemical, thermal, or other environmental energy.

injury prevention (control) An organized effort to prevent injuries or to minimize their severity.

injury prevention education The process of changing people's health-directed behavior in such a way as to reduce unintentional injuries.

inpatient care facilities Any in which a patient stays overnight, such as a hospital.

insecticide Pesticide designed specifically to kill insects.

instrumental activities of daily living (IADLs) More complex tasks such as handling personal finances, preparing meals, shopping, doing house work, traveling, using the telephone, and taking medications.

integrative care Care a patient receives from a team of primary healthcare and behavioral health clinicians, working together with patients and families, using shared, cost-effective care plans that incorporate patient goals.

intensity Cardiovascular workload measured by heart rate.

intentional injury An injury that is purposely inflicted, either by the victim or another.

intern A first-year resident.

intervention (1) Efforts to control a disease in progress. (2) An activity or activities designed to create change in people.

intimate partner violence (IPV) Describes physical violence, sexual violence, stalking, or psychological aggression (including coercive acts) by a current or former intimate partner, including current and former spouses, boyfriends or girlfriends, dating partners, or sexual partners (hetero- or homosexual) and does not require sexual intimacy.

ionizing radiation High-energy radiation (e.g., UV radiation, gamma rays, X-rays, alpha and beta particles) that can knock an electron out of orbit creating an ion and can thereby damage living cells and tissues.

isolation The separation of infected persons from those who are susceptible.

labor-force ratio A ratio of the total number of those individuals who are not working (regardless of age) to the number of those who are.

law enforcement The application of federal, state, and local laws to arrest, jail, bring to trial, and sentence those who break drug laws or break laws because of drug use.

leachate Liquid created when water mixes with wastes and removes soluble constituents from them by percolation.

lead A naturally occurring mineral element found throughout the environment and used in large quantities for industrial products, including batteries, pipes, solder, paints, and pigments.

legal leverage Service providers controlling the disability income or other benefits received by a person with mental illness to enforce participation in treatment in return for suspending a criminal sentence imposed by a court of law.

licensed practical nurse (LPN) Those prepared in 1- to 2-year programs to provide nontechnical bedside nursing care under the supervision of physicians or registered nurses.

life expectancy The average number of years a person from a specific cohort is projected to live from a given point in time.

limited (restricted) care provider Health care provider who provides care for a specific part of the body.

limited-service hospital A hospital that offers only the specific services needed by the population served.

litigation The process of seeking justice for injury through courts.

lobotomy Surgical severance of nerve fibers of the brain by incision.

long-term care Different kinds of help that people with chronic illnesses, disabilities, or other conditions that limit them physically or mentally need.

low birth weight infant One that weighs less than 2,500 grams, or 5.5 pounds, at birth.

Lyme disease A systematic, bacterial, tickborne disease with symptoms that include dermatologic, arthritic, neurologic, and cardiac abnormalities.

macro practice The methods of professional change that deal with issues beyond the individual, family, and small group level.

mainstream smoke Tobacco smoke inhaled and exhaled by the smoker.

major depression An affective disorder characterized by a dysphoric mood, usually depression, or loss of interest or pleasure in almost all usual activities or pastimes.

majority Those with characteristics that are found in more than 50% of a population.

malignant neoplasm Uncontrolled new tissue growth resulting from cells that have lost control over their growth and division.

managed care "A system that integrates the functions of financing, insurance, delivery, and payment and uses mechanisms to control costs and utilization of services." (Shi, L., and D. A. Singh (2015). *Delivering Health Care in America: A Systems Approach*, 6th ed. Burlington, MA: Jones & Bartlett Learning.)

mapping community capacity A process of identifying community assets.

marijuana Dried plant parts of the hemp plant, *Cannabis sativa.*

maternal, infant, and child health The health of women of childbearing age and that of the child up to adolescence.

maternal mortality The death of a woman while pregnant or within 42 days of termination of pregnancy, irrespective of the duration and the site of the pregnancy, from any cause related to or aggravated by the pregnancy or its management but not from accidental or incidental causes.

maternal mortality rate Number of mothers dying per 100,000 live births in a given year.

Meals on Wheels program A community-supported nutrition program in which prepared meals are delivered to individuals in their homes, usually by volunteers.

median age The age at which half of the population is older and half is younger.

Medicaid A jointly funded federal–state health insurance program for low-income Americans.

medical preparedness "The ability of the health care system to prevent, protect against, quickly respond to, and recover from health emergencies, particularly those whose scale, timing, or unpredictability threatens to overwhelm routine capabilities." (Centers for Disease Control and Prevention (2014). *The Community Guide: Emergency Preparedness and Response*. Available at http://www.thecommunityguide.org/emergencypreparedness/index.html.)

medically indigent Those lacking the financial ability to pay for their own medical care.

Medicare A national health insurance program for people 65 years of age and older, certain younger disabled people, and people with permanent kidney failure.

Medigap Private health insurance that supplements Medicare benefits.

mental disorders Health conditions characterized by alterations in thinking, mood, or behavior (or some combination thereof) associated with distress and/or impaired functioning.

mental health Emotional and social well-being, including one's psychological resources for dealing with the day-to-day problems of life.

mental health court Court where the judges have special training and use nonadversarial procedures that mandate treatment and rehabilitation rather than incarceration if a person with mental illness is found guilty of a crime.

mental illness A collective term for all diagnosable mental disorders.

Mental Retardation Facilities and Community Mental Health Centers (CMHC) Act A law that made the federal government responsible for assisting in the funding of mental health facilities and services.

metastasis The spread of cancer cells to distant parts of the body by the circulatory or lymphatic system.

methamphetamine The amphetamine drug most widely abused.

methaqualone An illicit depressant drug.

methcathinone (cat) An illicit, synthetic drug, similar to the amphetamines, that first appeared in the United States in 1991.

middle old Those 75 to 84 years of age.

migration Movement of people from one country to another.

minority groups Subgroups of the population that consist of less than 50% of the population.

minority health Refers to the morbidity and mortality of American Indians/Alaska Natives, Asian Americans and Pacific Islanders, black Americans, and Americans of Hispanic origin in the United States.

mixed model HMO A hybrid form of a health maintenance organization.

model for unintentional injuries The public health triangle (host, agent, and environment) modified to indicate energy as the causative agent of injuries.

modern era of public health The era public health that began in 1850 and continues today.

modifiable risk factor Contributor of a noncommunicable disease that can be altered by modifying one's behavior or environment.

mold Fungi that spread and reproduce by making spores; grow best in warm, damp, and humid conditions; and can cause respiratory difficulties for sensitive people.

moral treatment A nineteenth century treatment in which people with mental illness were removed from the everyday life stressors of their home environments and given "asylum" in a rural setting, including rest, exercise, fresh air, and amusements.

morbidity rate The number of people who are sick divided by the total population at risk.

mortality (fatality) rate The number of deaths in a population divided by the total population.

multicausation disease model A visual representation of the host, together with various internal and external factors that promote and protect against disease.

multiplicity The number of components or activities that make up the intervention.

municipal solid waste (MSW) Waste generated by individual households, businesses, and institutions located within municipalities.

narcotic Drug derived from or chemically related to opium that reduces pain and induces stupor, such as morphine.

natality (birth) rate The number of live births divided by the total population.

National Alliance on Mental Illness (NAMI) A national self-help group that supports the belief that major mental disorders are brain diseases that are of genetic origin and biological in nature and are diagnosable and treatable with medications.

National Ambient Air Quality Standards (NAAQSs) Standards created by the EPA for allowable concentration levels of outdoor air pollutants.

National Electronic Telecommunications System (NETS) The electronic reporting system used by state health departments and the CDC.

National Institute of Mental Health (NIMH)   The nation's leading mental health research agency, housed in the National Institutes of Health.

National Institute for Occupational Safety and Health (NIOSH)   A research body within the Centers for Disease Control and Prevention, U.S. Department of Health and Human Services, that is responsible for developing and recommending occupational safety and health standards.

National Institute on Drug Abuse (NIDA)   The federal government's lead agency for drug abuse research; part of the National Institutes of Health.

National Institutes of Health (NIH)   The research division of the U.S. Department of Health and Human Services. It is part of the U.S. Public Health Service.

National Mental Health Association (NMHA)   A national voluntary health association that advocates for mental health and for those with mental illnesses; it has 600 affiliates in 43 states.

natural disaster   A natural hazard that results in substantial loss of life or property.

natural hazard   A naturally occurring phenomenon or event that produces or releases energy in amounts that exceed human endurance, causing injury, disease, or death (such as radiation, earthquakes, tsunamis, volcanic eruptions, hurricanes, tornados, and floods).

needs assessment   "The process of identifying, analyzing, and prioritizing the needs of a priority population." (McKenzie, J. F., B. L. Neiger, and R. Thackeray (2017). *Planning, Implementing, and Evaluating Health Promotion Programs: A Primer*, 7th ed. Boston: Pearson Education, Inc.)

neonatal death (neonatal mortality)   Death occurring during the first 28 days after birth.

neonatologist   A medical doctor who specializes in the care of newborns from birth to 2 months of age.

network model HMO   A type of HMO that contracts with more than one medical group practice.

neuroleptic drug   Drug that reduces nervous activity; another term for antipsychotic drug.

nonallopathic provider   Independent provider who provides nontraditional forms of health care.

noncommunicable (noninfectious) disease   A disease that cannot be transmitted from infected host to susceptible host.

nonpoint source pollution   All pollution that occurs through the runoff, seepage, or falling of pollutants into the water where the source is difficult or impossible to identify.

nontarget organisms   All other susceptible organisms in the environment, for which a pesticide was not intended.

notifiable diseases   Diseases for which health officials request or require reporting for public health reasons.

observational study   An analytic, epidemiological study in which an investigator observes the natural course of events, noting exposed and unexposed subjects and disease development.

occupational disease   An abnormal condition or disorder, other than one resulting from an occupational injury, caused by an exposure to environmental factors associated with employment.

occupational health nurse (OHN)   A registered nurse (RN) whose primary responsibilities include prevention of illness and promotion of health in the workplace.

occupational injury   An injury that results from exposure to a single incident in the work environment.

occupational physician (OP) or **occupational medical practitioner (OMP)**   A medical practitioner (physician) whose primary concern is preventive medicine in the workplace.

Occupational Safety and Health Act of 1970 (OSH Act)   Comprehensive federal legislation aimed at assuring safe and healthful working conditions for working men and women.

Occupational Safety and Health Administration (OSHA)   The federal agency located within the U.S. Department of Labor and created by the OSH Act that is charged with the responsibility of administering the provisions of the OSH Act.

Office of National Drug Control Policy (ONDCP)   The headquarters of the United States' drug control effort, located in the executive branch of the federal government, and headed by a director appointed by the president.

official health agency   See *governmental health agency*.

old   Those 65 years of age and older.

old-age dependency ratio   The dependency ratio that includes only the old.

old old   Those 85 years of age and older.

Older Americans Act of 1965 (OAA)   Federal legislation to improve the lives of older adults.

open panel HMO   An organization in which private practice physicians are contracted by a health maintenance organization to deliver care in their own offices.

Operationalize (operational definition)   To provide working definitions.

osteopathic provider   Independent health care provider whose remedies emphasize the interrelationships of the body's systems in prevention, diagnosis, and treatment.

outcome evaluation   The evaluation that focuses on the end result of the program.

outpatient care facilities   Any facility in which the patient receives care and does not stay overnight.

outpatient commitment   Laws mandating involuntary psychiatric treatment for individuals who do not understand their illness to protect the individual from harm and safeguard the public.

over-the-counter (OTC) drug (nonprescription drug)   Drug (except tobacco and alcohol) that can be legally purchased without a physician's prescription.

ownership   A feeling that one has a stake in or "owns" the object of interest.

ozone (O_3)   An inorganic molecule considered to be a pollutant in the atmosphere because it harms human tissue, but considered beneficial in the stratosphere because it screens out UV radiation.

packaged pricing Several related health services are included in one price.

pandemic An outbreak of disease over a wide geographical area, such as a continent or multiple continents.

parity The concept of equality in health care coverage for people with mental illness and those with other medical illnesses or injuries.

participation and relevance "Community organizing should 'start where the people are' and engage community members as equals." (Minkler, M., and N. Wallerstein (2012). "Improving Health through Community Organization and Community Building: Perspectives from Health Education and Social Work." In M. Minkler, ed., *Community Organizing and Community Building for Health and Welfare*, 3rd ed. New Brunswick, NJ: Rutgers University Press, 37–58.)

passive immunity Occurs when a person receives antibodies against a disease rather than their immune system producing them.

passive smoking The inhalation of environmental tobacco smoke by nonsmokers.

patient-centered medical home "A care delivery model whereby patient treatment is coordinated through their primary care physician to ensure they receive the necessary care when and where they need it, in a manner they can understand" (applies to patients of all ages.) (American College of Physicians (2016). *What Is the Patient-Centered Medical Home?* Available at https://www.acponline.org/running_practice/delivery_and_payment_models/pcmh/understanding/what.htm.)

pathogenicity The capability of a communicable disease agent to cause disease in a susceptible host.

pay-for-performance (P4P) purchasing A payment system that offers financial rewards to providers and facilities for meeting, improving, or exceeding quality measures or other performance goals.

peer counseling program School-based program in which students discuss alcohol and other drug-related problems with peers.

pest Any organism—multicelled animal or plant, or microbe—that has an adverse effect on human interests.

pesticide Synthetic chemical developed and manufactured for the purpose of killing pests.

pharmaceuticals and personal care products (PPCPs) Synthetic chemicals found in everyday consumer health care products and cosmetics.

phasing in Implementation of an intervention with small groups instead of the entire population.

philanthropic foundation An endowed institution that donates money for the good of humankind.

photochemical smog Haze or fog formed when air pollutants interact with sunlight.

physical dependence A physical state in which discontinued drug use results in clinical illness.

physician assistant (PA) Healthcare professionals who practice medicine with physician supervision. (Woolsey, C. V. (n.d.) "What Is a Physician Assistant." A *Patient's Guide to The Physician Assistant*. Available at http://www.pg?pa.org/index.html_

pilot test A trial run of an intervention.

placebo A blank treatment.

pneumoconiosis Fibrotic lung disease caused by the inhalation of dusts, especially mineral dusts.

point-of-service (POS) option An option of a health maintenance organization plan that allows enrollees to be at least partially reimbursed for selecting a health care provider outside the plan.

point source epidemic A type of epidemic where all cases were exposed at the same point in time.

point source pollution Pollution that can be traced to a single identifiable source.

polydrug use Concurrent use of multiple drugs.

population at risk Those in the population who are susceptible to a particular disease or condition.

population health "The health outcomes of a group of individuals, including the distribution of such outcomes within the group." (Kindig, D., and G. Stoddart (2003). "What Is Population Health?" *American Journal of Public Health*, 93(3): 380–383.)

population-based public health practice Incorporates interventions aimed at disease prevention and health promotion, specific protection, and case findings.

postneonatal death (postneonatal mortality) Death that occurs between 28 days and 365 days after birth.

preconception health care Medical care provided to a women of reproductive age to promote health prior to conception.

pre-existing condition A medical condition that had been diagnosed or treated usually within 6 months before the date a health insurance policy goes into effect.

preferred provider organization (PPO) An organization that buys fixed-rate health services from providers and sells them to consumers.

premature infant One born following a gestation period of 38 weeks or less, or one born at a low birth weight.

premium A regular periodic payment for an insurance policy.

prenatal health care Medical care provided to a pregnant woman from the time of conception until the birth process occurs.

prepaid health care A method of paying for covered health care services on a per-person premium basis for a specific period of time prior to service being rendered. Also referred to as *capitation*.

preplacement examination A physical examination of a newly hired or transferred worker to determine medical suitability for placement in a specific position.

prevalence rate The number of new and old cases of a disease in a population in a given period of time, divided by the total number of that population.

prevention The planning for and taking of action to forestall the onset of a disease or other health problem.

preventive care Care given to healthy people to keep them healthy.

primary care　Clinical preventive services, first-contact treatment services, and ongoing care for commonly encountered medical conditions.

primary data　Original data collected by planners.

primary pollutants　Air pollutants emanating directly from transportation, power and industrial plants, and refineries.

primary prevention　Preventive measures that forestall the onset of illness or injury during the prepathogenesis period.

priority population (audience)　Those whom a program is intended to serve.

private (proprietary) or investor-owned hospital　A for-profit hospital.

pro-choice　A medical/ethical position that holds that women have a right to reproductive freedom.

pro-life　A medical/ethical position that holds that performing an abortion is an act of murder.

problem drinker　One for whom alcohol consumption results in a medical, social, or other type of problem.

program planning　A process by which an intervention is planned to help meet the needs of a priority population.

propagated epidemic curve　An epidemic curve depicting a distribution of cases traceable to multiple sources of exposure.

prospective reimbursement　"Uses pre-established criteria to determine in advance the amount of reimbursement." (Shi, L., and D. A. Singh (2017). *Essentials of the U.S. Health Care System*, 4th ed. Burlington, MA: Jones & Bartlett Learning.)

prospective study　An epidemiological study that begins in the present and continues into the future for the purpose of observing the development of disease (e.g., cohort study).

protective factor　Factors that increase an individual's ability to avoid risks or hazards, and promote social and emotional competence to thrive in all aspects of life.

provider　Health care facility or health professional that provides health care services.

psychiatric rehabilitation　Intensive, individualized services encompassing treatment, rehabilitation, and support delivered by a team of providers over an indefinite period to individuals with severe mental disorder to help them maintain stable lives in the community.

psychoactive drug　Drug that alters sensory perceptions, mood, thought processes, or behavior.

psychological dependence　A psychological state characterized by an overwhelming desire to continue use of a drug.

psychopharmacological therapy　Treatment for mental illness that involves medications.

psychotherapy　A treatment that involves verbal communication between the patient and a trained clinician.

public health　Actions that society takes collectively to ensure that the conditions in which people can be healthy can occur.

public health practice　Incorporates "the development and application of preventive strategies and interventions to promote and protect the health of populations." (Turnock, B. J. (2016). *Public Health: What It Is and How It Works*, 6th ed. Burlington, MA: Jones & Bartlett Learning.)

public health preparedness　"The ability of the public health system, community, and individuals to prevent, protect against, quickly respond to, and recover from health emergencies, particularly those in which scale, timing, or unpredictability threatens to overwhelm routine capabilities." (Centers for Disease Control and Prevention (2014). *The Community Guide: Emergency Preparedness and Response*. Available at http://www.thecommunityguide.org/emergency preparedness/index.html.)

public health professional　A health care worker who works in a public health organization.

Public Health Service (PHS)　An agency in the U.S. Department of Health and Human Services (HHS) that comprises 8 of the 11 operating divisions of HHS.

public health system　The organizational mechanism of those activities undertaken within the formal structure of government and the associated efforts of private and voluntary organizations and individuals.

public hospital　A hospital that is supported and managed by governmental jurisdictions.

public policy　The guiding principles and courses of action pursued by governments to solve practical problems affecting society.

quality management and utilization review　The analysis of provided health care for its appropriateness by someone other than the patient and provider.

quarantine　Limitation of freedom of movement of those who have been exposed to a disease and may be incubating it.

quasi-governmental health organizations　Organizations that have some responsibilities assigned by the government but operate more like voluntary agencies.

radiation　A process in which energy is emitted as particles or waves.

radon　A naturally occurring, colorless, tasteless, odorless, radioactive gas formed during the radioactive decay of uranium-238.

rate　The number of events that occur in a given population in a given period of time.

recovery　Outcome sought by most people with mental illness; includes increased independence, effective coping, supportive relationships, community participation, and sometimes gainful employment.

recycling　The collecting, sorting, and processing of materials that would otherwise be considered waste into raw materials for manufacturing new products, and the subsequent use of those new products.

reform phase of public health　The years 1900 to 1920, characterized by social movements to improve health conditions in cities and in the workplace.

refugee　A person who flees one area or country to seek shelter or protection from danger in another.

registered environmental health specialist (REHS) (sanitarian)　Environmental worker responsible for the inspection of restaurants, retail food outlets, public housing, and other sites to ensure compliance with public health codes.

registered nurse (RN)   One who has successfully completed an accredited academic program and a state licensing examination.

regulation   The enactment and enforcement of laws to control conduct.

rehabilitation center   A facility in which restorative care is provided following injury, disease, or surgery.

reimbursement   The monetary value that health care providers and facilities receive for providing services to patients.

resident   A physician who is training in a specialty.

resource-based relative value scale (RBRVS)   Reimbursement to physicians according to the relative value of the service provided.

Resource Conservation and Recovery Act of 1976 (RCRA)   The federal law that sets forth guidelines for the proper handling and disposal of solid and hazardous wastes.

respite care   Planned short-term care, usually for the purpose of relieving a full-time informal caregiver.

restorative care   That which is provided after successful treatment or when the progress of a incurable disease has been arrested.

retirement communities   Residential communities that have been specifically developed for individuals in their retirement years or of a certain age.

retrospective study   An epidemiological study that looks into the past for clues to explain the present distribution of disease.

risk factor   Factor that increases the probability of disease, injury, or death.

Roe v. Wade   1973 Supreme Court decision that made it unconstitutional for state laws to prohibit abortions in the first trimester for any reason and placed restrictions on the conditions under which states could regulate them in the second and third trimesters.

Rohypnol (flunitrazepam)   A powerful depressant in the benzodiazepine group that has achieved notoriety as a date rape drug because its toxic and sedative affects when combined with alcohol can last up to 8 hours.

rollover protective structure (ROPS)   Factory installed or retrofitted reinforced framework on a cab to protect the operator of a tractor in case of a rollover.

runoff   Water that flows over land surfaces (including paved surfaces), typically from precipitation.

Safe Drinking Water Act (SDWA)   The federal law that regulates the safety of public drinking water.

safety engineer   A health and safety professional, sometimes with an engineering background, employed by a company for the purpose of reducing unintentional injuries in the workplace.

safety programs   Those parts of the workplace health and safety program aimed at reducing unintentional injuries on the job.

sanitary landfill   Waste disposal site on land suited for this purpose and on which waste is spread in thin layers, compacted, and covered with a fresh layer of clay or plastic foam each day.

sanitation   The practice of establishing and maintaining healthy or hygienic conditions in the environment.

school health coordinator   A trained professional at the state, district, or school level who is responsible for managing, coordinating, planning, implementing, and evaluating school health policies, programs, and resources.

school health advisory council   An advisory group composed of school, health, and community representatives who act collectively to advise the school district or school on aspects of coordinated school health, also known as school wellness council.

school health education   The development, delivery, and evaluation of a planned curriculum, kindergarten through grade 12.

school health policies   Written statements that describe the nature and procedures of a school health program.

school health services   Health services provided by school health workers to appraise, protect, and promote the health of students.

scope   Part of the curriculum that outlines what will be taught.

secondary data   Those that have been collected by someone else and are available for use by the planners.

secondary medical care   "Specialized attention and ongoing management for common and less frequently encountered medical conditions, including support services for people with special challenges due to chronic or long-term conditions." (Turnock, B. J. (2016). *Public Health: What It Is and How It Works*, 6th ed. Burlington, MA: Jones & Bartlett Learning.)

secondary pollutants   Air pollutants formed when primary air pollutants react with sunlight and other atmospheric components to form new harmful compounds.

secondary prevention   Preventive measures that lead to early diagnosis and prompt treatment of a disease or injury to limit disability and prevent more severe pathogenesis.

secondhand smoke   See *environmental tobacco smoke*.

self-funded insurance program   One that pays the health care costs of its employees with the premiums collected from the employees and the contributions made by the employer.

self-help group   Group of concerned members of the community who are united by a shared interest, concern, or deficit not shared by other members of the community (e.g., Alcoholics Anonymous).

senior center   Facility where elders can congregate for fellowship, meals, education, and recreation.

septic tank   A watertight concrete or fiberglass tank that holds sewage; one of two main parts of a septic system.

sequence   Part of the curriculum that states in what order the content will be taught.

sick building syndrome   A term to describe a situation in which the air quality in a building produces generalized signs and symptoms of ill health in the building's occupants.

sidestream tobacco smoke   The smoke that comes off the end of burning tobacco products.

silicosis   Acute or chronic lung disease caused by the inhalation of free crystalline silica.

sliding scale   The scale used to determine the fee for services based on ability to pay.

sludge   A semiliquid mixture of solid waste that includes bacteria, viruses, organic matter, toxic metals, synthetic organic chemicals, and solid chemicals.

SMART objectives   Those that are specific, measurable, achievable, realistic, and time-phased.

smokeless tobacco (or spit tobacco)   Includes oral snuff, loose leaf chewing tobacco, plug chewing tobacco, and nasal snuff.

social capital   "Processes and conditions among people and organizations that lead to their accomplishing a goal of mutual social benefit, usually characterized by interrelated constructs of trust, cooperation, civic engagement, and reciprocity, reinforced by networking." (Last, J. M., ed. (2007). *A Dictionary of Public Health*. New York: Oxford University Press.)

Social Security Administration (SSA)   An independent federal agency that administers programs that provide financial support to special groups of Americans.

socioeconomic status   Relating to a combination of social and economic factors.

socio-ecological approach (or ecological perspective)   Individuals influence and are influenced by their families, social networks, the organizations in which they participate (workplaces, schools, religious organizations), the communities of which they are a part, and the society in which they live.

solid waste   Solid refuse from households, agriculture, mining, and businesses.

solid waste management (integrated waste management)   The collection, transportation, and disposal of solid waste.

sound-level meter   Instrument used to measure sound.

source reduction   A waste management approach involving the reduction or elimination of use of materials that produce an accumulation of solid waste.

Special Supplemental Food Program for Women, Infants and Children   See *WIC*.

specialty hospital   A standalone, single-specialty (e.g., women's health, surgery, cardiac, or orthopedic) facility not within the walls of a full-service hospital.

spectrum of health care delivery   The array of types of care—from preventive to continuing, or long-term, care. It comprises four levels of care.

spiritual era of public health   A time during the Middle Ages when the causation of communicable disease was linked to spiritual forces.

staff model HMO   A health maintenance organization that hires its own staff of health care providers.

standard of acceptability   A comparative mandate, value, norm, or group.

stimulant   A drug that increases the activity of the central nervous system.

student assistance program (SAP)   School-based drug education program to assist students who have alcohol or other drug problems.

Substance Abuse and Mental Health Services Administration (SAMHSA)   The agency within the U.S. Department of Health and Human Services that provides leadership in drug abuse prevention and treatment. It houses the Center for Substance Abuse Prevention and the Center for Substance Abuse Treatment.

sudden infant death syndrome (SIDS)   Sudden unanticipated death of an infant in whom, after examination, there is no recognized cause of death.

summative evaluation   The evaluation that determines the effect of a program on the priority population.

Superfund legislation   See *Comprehensive Environmental Response Compensation an Liability Act (CERCLA)*.

Supplemental Security   Program of the Social Security Administration that provides cash benefits to elderly, blind, and disabled Americans with minimal resources.

surface water   Precipitation that does not infiltrate the ground or return to the atmosphere by evaporation; the water in streams, rivers, and lakes.

Sustainable Development Goals (SDGs)   A set of goals created by the World Health Organization to build on the work accomplished via the Millennium Development Goals (MDGs).

Synar Amendment   A federal law that requires states to set the minimum legal age for purchasing tobacco products at 18 years and that requires states to enforce this law.

synesthesia   Impairment of mind (by hallucinogens) characterized by a sensation that senses are mixed (e.g., seeing sounds and hearing images).

tardive dyskinesia   Irreversible condition of involuntary and abnormal movements of the tongue, mouth, arms, and legs, which can result from long-term use of certain antipsychotic drugs (such as chlorpromazine).

target organism (target pest)   The organism (or pest) for which a pesticide is applied.

task force   A temporary group that is brought together for dealing with a specific problem.

terrorism   Calculated use of violence (or threat of violence) against civilians to attain goals that are political or religious in nature.

tertiary medical care   Specialized and technologically sophisticated medical and surgical care for those with unusual or complex conditions.

tertiary prevention   Measures aimed at rehabilitation following significant pathogenesis.

The Joint Commission   The predominant organization responsible for accrediting health care facilities.

thermal inversion   A condition that occurs when warm air traps cooler air at the surface of the Earth.

third-party payment system   A health insurance term indicating that bills from a health care provider for services rendered to a patient are paid by the insurer.

Thorazine See *chlorpromazine*.

Title X A portion of the Public Health Service Act of 1970 that provides funds for family planning services for low-income people.

tolerance Physiological and enzymatic adjustments that occur in response to the chronic presence of drugs, which are reflected in the need for ever-increasing doses.

top-down funding A method of funding in which funds are transmitted from the federal or state government to the local level.

total dependency ratio The dependency ratio that includes both youth and old.

Total Worker Health® "Policies, programs, and practices that integrate protection from work-related safety and health hazards with promotion of injury and illness prevention efforts to advance worker well-being." (Centers for Disease Control and Prevention, National Institute for Occupational Safety and Health (2016). *Total Worker Health®*. Available at http://www.cdc.gov/niosh/twh/.)

transinstitutionalization Transferring patients from one type of public institution to another, usually as a result of policy change.

treatment (for drug abuse and dependence) Care that removes the physical, emotional, and environmental conditions that have contributed to drug abuse and/or dependence.

ultraviolet (UV) radiation Radiation energy with wavelengths of 0 to 400 nanometers.

unauthorized immigrant An individual who entered this country without permission.

unintentional injury An injury judged to have occurred without anyone intending that harm be done.

unmodifiable risk factor Factor contributing to the development of a noncommunicable disease that cannot be altered by modifying one's behavior or environment.

unsafe act Any behavior that would increase the probability of an injury occurring.

unsafe condition Any environmental factor or set of factors (physical or social) that would increase the probability of an injury occurring.

U.S. Census The enumeration of the population of the United States that is conducted every 10 years; begun in 1790.

vector A living organism, usually an insect or other arthropod (e.g., mosquitoes, ticks, lice, fleas), that can transmit a communicable disease agent to a susceptible host.

vectorborne disease A communicable disease transmitted by insects or other arthropods; for example, St. Louis encephalitis.

vectorborne disease outbreak (VBDO) An occurrence of an unexpectedly large number of cases of disease caused by an agent transmitted by insects or other arthropods.

vehicle An inanimate material or object that can serve as a source of infection.

vehicleborne disease A communicable disease transmitted by nonliving objects; for example, typhoid fever can be transmitted by water.

visitor services One individual taking time to visit with another who is unable to leave his or her residence.

vital statistics Statistical summaries of vital records of major life events, such as births, deaths, marriages, divorces, and infant deaths.

volatile organic compounds (VOCs) Compounds that exist as vapors over the normal range of air pressures and temperatures.

voluntary health agency A nonprofit organization created by concerned citizens to deal with health needs not met by governmental health agencies.

voluntary hospital A nonprofit hospital administered by a not-for-profit corporation or other charitable community organization.

wastewater The aqueous mixture that remains after water has been used or contaminated by humans.

wastewater treatment The process of improving the quality of wastewater (sewage) to the point that it can be released into a body of water without seriously disrupting the aquatic environment, causing health problems in humans, or causing nuisance conditions.

water pollution Any physical or chemical change in water that can harm living organisms or make the water unfit for other uses.

waterborne disease A disease that is transmitted through contamination of water.

waterborne disease outbreak (WBDO) A disease in which at least two persons experience a similar illness after the ingestion of drinking water or after exposure to water used for recreational purposes and epidemiological evidence implicates water as the probable source of the illness.

watershed The area of land from which all of the water that is under it or drains from it goes into the same place and drains in one point; for example, the Mississippi River watershed drains and collects all the water from the land extending from east of the Rocky Mountains to the Appalachian Mountains and from the upper Midwest all the way south to the Gulf of Mexico.

Whole School, Whole Community, Whole Child (WSCC) model One that focuses on addressing the educational and health needs of children within the context of the school setting, which is a critical component of the local community.

Women, Infants and Children (WIC) A special supplemental food program for women, infants, and children, sponsored by the U.S. Department of Agriculture.

workers' compensation laws A set of federal laws designed to compensate those workers and their families who suffer injuries, disease, or death from workplace exposure.

worksite health and wellness promotion (WHP) programs Workplace-based programs aimed at improving the health and wellness of employees by identifying and acting on existing health conditions and by encouraging employees to optimize their health by improving health behavior and lifestyle choices.

World Health Assembly   A body of delegates of the member nations of the World Health Organization.

World Health Organization (WHO)   The most widely recognized international governmental health organization.

years of potential life lost (YPLL)   The number of years lost when death occurs before the age of 65 or 75.

young old   Those 65 to 74 years of age.

youth dependency ratio   The dependency ratio that includes only youth.

youth gang   An association of peers, bound by mutual interests and identifiable lines of authority, whose acts generally include illegal activity and control over a territory or an enterprise.

zoonosis   A communicable disease transmissible under natural conditions from vertebrate animals to humans.

INDEX